STUDENTS...

Want to get **better grades**? *(Who doesn't?)*

Prefer to do your **homework online**? *(After all, you are online anyway...)*

Need **a better way** to **study** before the big test?
(A little peace of mind is a good thing...)

With **McGraw-Hill's *Connect® Plus Economics*,**

STUDENTS GET:

- **Easy online access** to homework, tests, and quizzes assigned by your instructor.
- **Immediate feedback** on how you're doing. (No more wishing you could call your instructor at 1 a.m.)
- **Quick access** to lectures, practice materials, e-book, and more. (All the material you need to be successful is right at your fingertips.)
- **LearnSmart**--intelligent flash cards that adapt to your specific needs and provide you with customized learning content based on your strengths and weaknesses.

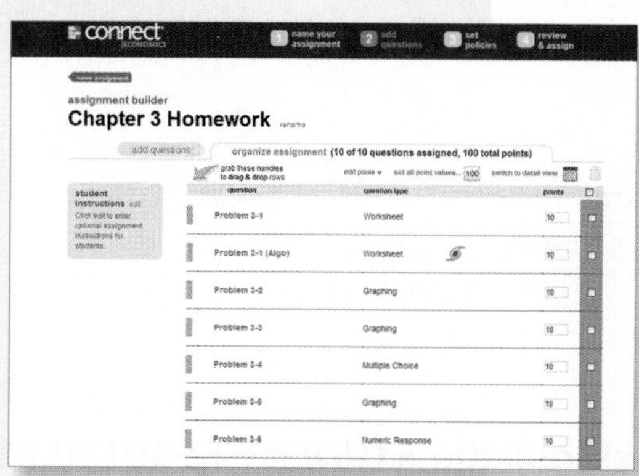

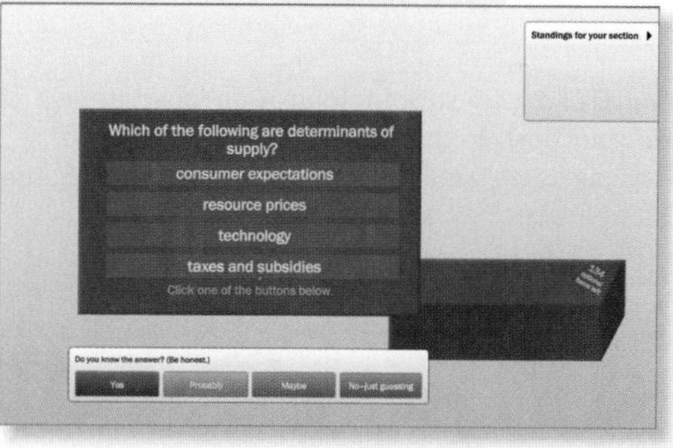

Want an online, **searchable version** of your textbook?

Wish your textbook could be **available online** while you're doing your assignments?

Connect® *Plus Economics* e-book

If you choose to use *Connect*® *Plus Economics*, you have an affordable and searchable online version of your book integrated with your other online tools.

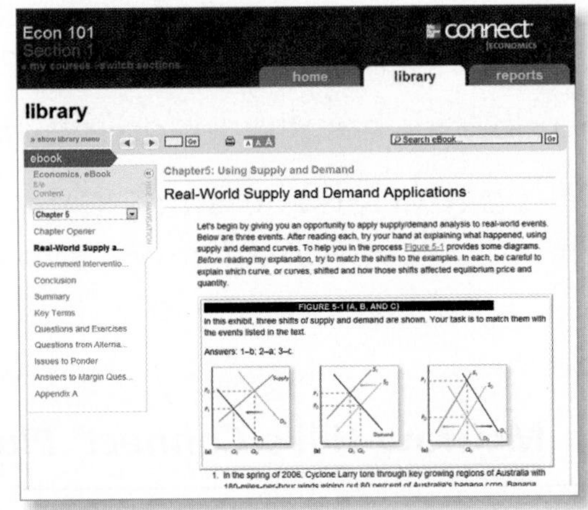

Connect® *Plus Economics* e-book offers features like:

- Topic search
- Direct links from assignments
- Adjustable text size
- Jump to page number
- Print by section

Want to get more **value** from your textbook purchase?

Think learning economics should be a bit more **interesting**?

Check out the STUDENT RESOURCES section under the *Connect*® Library tab.

Here you'll find a wealth of resources designed to help you achieve your goals in the course. Every student has different needs, so explore the STUDENT RESOURCES to find the materials best suited to you.

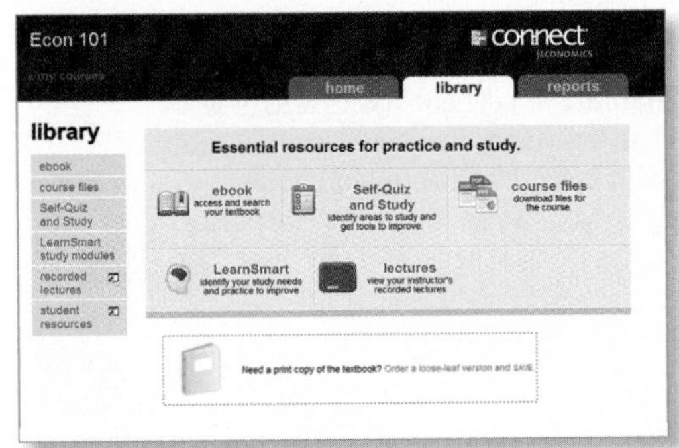

Macroeconomics

The McGraw-Hill Series in Economics

Essentials of Economics

Brue, McConnell, and Flynn
Essentials of Economics
Second Edition

Mandel
Economics: The Basics
Second Edition

Schiller
Essentials of Economics
Eighth Edition

Principles of Economics

Colander
Economics, Microeconomics, and Macroeconomics
Ninth Edition

Frank and Bernanke
Principles of Economics, Principles of Microeconomics, Principles of Macroeconomics
Fifth Edition

Frank and Bernanke
Brief Editions: Principles of Economics, Principles of Microeconomics, Principles of Macroeconomics
Second Edition

McConnell, Brue, and Flynn
Economics, Microeconomics, and Macroeconomics
Nineteenth Edition

McConnell, Brue, and Flynn
Brief Editions: Microeconomics and Macroeconomics
Second Edition

Miller
Principles of Microeconomics
First Edition

Samuelson and Nordhaus
Economics, Microeconomics, and Macroeconomics
Nineteenth Edition

Schiller
The Economy Today, The Micro Economy Today, and The Macro Economy Today
Thirteenth Edition

Slavin
Economics, Microeconomics, and Macroeconomics
Tenth Edition

Economics of Social Issues

Guell
Issues in Economics Today
Sixth Edition

Sharp, Register, and Grimes
Economics of Social Issues
Twentieth Edition

Econometrics

Gujarati and Porter
Basic Econometrics
Fifth Edition

Gujarati and Porter
Essentials of Econometrics
Fourth Edition

Managerial Economics

Baye
Managerial Economics and Business Strategy
Seventh Edition

Brickley, Smith, and Zimmerman
Managerial Economics and Organizational Architecture
Fifth Edition

Thomas and Maurice
Managerial Economics
Eleventh Edition

Intermediate Economics

Bernheim and Whinston
Microeconomics
First Edition

Dornbusch, Fischer, and Startz
Macroeconomics
Twelfth Edition

Frank
Microeconomics and Behavior
Eighth Edition

Advanced Economics

Romer
Advanced Macroeconomics
Fourth Edition

Money and Banking

Cecchetti and Schoenholtz
Money, Banking, and Financial Markets
Third Edition

Urban Economics

O'Sullivan
Urban Economics
Eighth Edition

Labor Economics

Borjas
Labor Economics
Sixth Edition

McConnell, Brue, and Macpherson
Contemporary Labor Economics
Tenth Edition

Public Finance

Rosen and Gayer
Public Finance
Ninth Edition

Seidman
Public Finance
First Edition

Environmental Economics

Field and Field
Environmental Economics: An Introduction
Sixth Edition

International Economics

Appleyard and Field
International Economics
Seventh Edition

King and King
International Economics, Globalization, and Policy: A Reader
Fifth Edition

Pugel
International Economics
Fifteenth Edition

Macroeconomics

NINTH EDITION

David C. Colander

Middlebury College

Dedicated to the memory of
Helen Reiff (1928–2012),
my personal editor and long-time friend.

The McGraw-Hill Companies

McGraw-Hill Irwin

MACROECONOMICS, NINTH EDITION

Published by McGraw-Hill/Irwin, a business unit of The McGraw-Hill Companies, Inc., 1221 Avenue of the Americas, New York, NY, 10020.

This book is printed on acid-free paper.

3 4 5 6 7 8 9 0 DOW/DOW 1 0 9 8 7 6 5

ISBN 978-0-07-750186-0
MHID 0-07-750186-1

Senior Vice President, Products & Markets: *Kurt L. Strand*
Vice President, General Manager, Products & Markets: *Brent Gordon*
Vice President, Content Production & Technology Services: *Kimberly Meriwether David*
Managing Director: *Douglas Reiner*
Brand Manager: *Scott Smith*
Executive Director of Development: *Ann Torbert*
Managing Development Editor: *Christina Kouvelis*
Development Editor: *Alyssa Lincoln*
Director of Digital Content: *Doug Ruby*
Digital Development Editor: *Kevin Shanahan*
Marketing Manager: *Katie White*
Director, Content Production: *Sesha Bolisetty*
Content Project Manager: *Bruce Gin*
Senior Buyer: *Carol A. Bielski*
Cover/Interior Designer: *Pam Verros*
Cover Image: *©Getty Images/Southern Stock*
Content Licensing Specialist: *Joanne Mennemeier*
Photo Researcher: *Michelle Buhr*
Typeface: *10.5/12 Times*
Compositor: *Aptara®, Inc.*
Printer: *R. R. Donnelley*

All credits appearing on page or at the end of the book are considered to be an extension of the copyright page.

Library of Congress Cataloging-in-Publication Data

Colander, David C.
Macroeconomics / David C. Colander. — 9th ed.
p. cm.
Includes index.
ISBN-13: 978-0-07-750186-0 (alk. paper)
ISBN-10: 0-07-750186-1 (alk. paper)
1. Macroeconomics. I. Title.
HB172.5.C638 2013
339—dc23

2012034265

www.mhhe.com

About the Author

David Colander is the Christian A. Johnson Distinguished Professor of Economics at Middlebury College. He has authored, coauthored, or edited over 40 books and over 150 articles on a wide range of economic topics.

He earned his B.A. at Columbia College and his M.Phil. and Ph.D. at Columbia University. He also studied at the University of Birmingham in England and at Wilhelmsburg Gymnasium in Germany. Professor Colander has taught at Columbia University, Vassar College, the University of Miami, and Princeton University as the Kelley Professor of Distinguished Teaching. He has also been a consultant to Time-Life Films, a consultant to Congress, a Brookings Policy Fellow, and Visiting Scholar at Nuffield College, Oxford.

He has been president of both the History of Economic Thought Society and the Eastern Economics Association. He has also served on the editorial boards of the *Journal of Economic Perspectives, The Journal of Economic Education, The Journal of Economic Methodology, The Journal of the History of Economic Thought, The Journal of Socio-Economics,* and *The Eastern Economic Journal.* He has been chair of the AEA Committee on Electronic Publishing, a member of the AEA Committee on Economic Education, and is currently the associate editor for content of the *Journal of Economic Education.*

He is married to a pediatrician, Patrice. In their spare time, the Colanders designed and built an oak post-and-beam house on a ridge overlooking the Green Mountains to the east and the Adirondacks to the west. The house is located on the site of a former drive-in movie theater. (They replaced the speaker poles with fruit trees and used the I-beams from the screen as support for the second story of the carriage house and the garage.) They now live in both Florida and Vermont.

Preface for the Instructor

"Imagine . . . a textbook that students enjoy!" That comment, from an instructor who taught at Purdue, was e-mailed to me as I was struggling to write the preface to an earlier edition. That comment still captures what I believe to be the most distinctive feature of the core of this edition. It speaks to students.

An Entire Learning Platform

That comment continues to guide this edition. But because students today learn differently than they did twenty years ago, it does so in new ways. Students today grew up with the Internet and social media that provide them with access to a broad range of digital resources and instant feedback. That changes the way they learn, and if we are to reach them, we have to present material to them in ways that fit their learning style. They want to be able to bring their course with them—to access it anywhere, anytime—at a coffee shop in the afternoon, in their dorm room late at night, or at lunch hour at work. They still want material that speaks to them, but it has to speak to them in their language at the time they want to listen. Modern learning is blended learning in which online presentations, review and testing of material, and feedback are seamlessly blended with the narrative of the text.

The strengths of previous editions translate well in this new environment. Students don't want an automaton. They want a person who speaks to them, even if it is online. They don't differentiate a "virtual" world from a "real" world. Both are real and students seek the same thing in both—the presentation of material that engages them. And that's what I do. I tell stories. I use colloquial language, and I offer material that they read about in the newspaper—today's economic issues. The material speaks to them in ways that they can hear and enjoy.

A guiding principle of this edition has been to reach out to students in the digital language of online communication. To teach modern students effectively, we've got to get their attention and hold it, and digital tools give us that opportunity. That's why I've worked hard in this revision to provide the material that students can engage in a single, seamless, and fully digital product.

Embracing the digital environment has led to some significant pedagogical improvements. All of the content, including end-of-chapter questions, lines up directly with learning objectives. These learning objectives serve as the organizational structure for the material. As a result, within McGraw Hill's online Connect Plus platform, students can learn the core building blocks online with instant feedback; instructors can assess student learning data and know what their students understand, and what they don't. With that information, they can devote class time to those issues with which students are having problems.

The end-of-chapter material has been revised for optimal online delivery: All of the standard questions and problems are auto-gradable and integrated with the eBook experience. Such integration allows students to move seamlessly between homework problems and portions of the narrative to get the information they need, when they need it. This is a significant advance in pedagogy. Now, even professors in large lecture classes can assign questions and exercises at the end of chapters and provide feedback to students at the point of need.

In addition to the standard questions and exercises at the end of every chapter I also provide a set of Issues of Ponder and Alternative Perspective Questions that have no "correct" answer, but instead are designed to get the students to think. In a blended learning environment, these are the questions that can form the basis for rich classroom discussions that engage the students with broad issues as much as the online material engages them with the building blocks. Classes become discussion and thinking time, not regurgitation and repetition time.

I am confident that the combination of the digital tools via Connect Plus, the modern material presented, and the colloquial style I have worked so hard to perfect will engage students in the ninth edition like never before. (Additional information about Connect is presented on p. xv.)

Modern, Not Outdated 1950s Economics

You can have the best online platform and presentation in the world, but if the content isn't relevant or engaging, it serves little purpose. My goal is to present students with the best economics I can. That means that I want to teach *modern economics,* not neoclassical economics (or whatever else the collection of models that developed in the 1950s is called). That doesn't mean that I don't teach the traditional models; it just means that I integrate modern interpretations and insights with them. That approach makes the tone and format somewhat different from the 1950s' tone and format of many competitors that make it seem as if economics hasn't changed in 60 years.

Why haven't competitors changed? Because it is really, really hard to deviate from the standard template developed in the 1950s. I fully recognize the difficulty. (After all I'm the one who coined the "15 percent rule" for revising textbooks.) I know and accept that if we are going to teach modern economics, it has to involve an evolutionary, not revolutionary, template. But recognizing the importance of the existing template is not a call for laziness and complacency in what we teach; it is a call for creativity. Economics has changed from what it was, and that means the content of the texts has to change as well. Texts that don't embrace that change are becoming more and more out-of-date.

If we are to consider ourselves serious teachers of economics, we can and should be doing whatever we can to teach students modern economics, not some vestige from the past. Over the past decade I have been working on ways to introduce modern economics into the principles course—trying different ideas on my students and colleagues and discovering what works and what doesn't. In the last edition I started to integrate modern economics into the standard principles template, and I continue that integration in this edition after getting useful comments from many of my users about the best way to do it.

One of the biggest problems that many people have pointed out with presenting students with the subtleties of modern economics is that many of their students are, shall we say, less-than-perfect students. I am not unaware of the nature of students—in fact I was one of those far-less-than-perfect students. I am no utopian; I am a realist who recognizes that many, perhaps most, students could care less about how economists think. They are taking the course because it is required, because their parents told them they had to, or because it was what fit in their schedule. That is the reality, and they are the students I'm writing for.

Why do I take this approach? Because I figure that if I can excite these marginal students about economics, I will likely also excite those more perfect, self-motivated students who professors dream of having in class. So my target student is a non-economics major who doesn't especially care about the content they are learning; he or she is much more likely to be concerned with what is going to be on the exam (and sometimes they don't even care about that). I regard this fact as liberating, not confining. It makes it even more important that we teach them modern economics, not a set of models from an outdated template. I want students to know TANSTAAFL, to know the strengths of markets, the weaknesses of markets, the importance of incentives, and why economic policy is so complicated and messy.

How does a teacher excite students who are less than excited about economics? My answer to that question is that you challenge them, you talk to them, you speak a language that they can understand, and you recognize their pain. That's what I try to do. I will fail with many of them, but if I don't try, then I don't deserve to be called a teacher, which in my view is the highest calling an economist can have.

A Student-Friendly Colloquial Style

To reach these less-than-perfect students, I convey ideas in a highly colloquial manner; I don't lecture students, or talk to them in textbookese; I talk to them in conversational English. I strongly believe that most students have the ability to understand economic concepts even though on exams it often appears as if they have serious problems. In my opinion, many of their problems in exams are not conceptual; rather, they are problems of motivation, reading, and math. The economics found in principles courses is not the student's highest priority; it certainly wasn't mine when I was 18. I'm continuously amazed at how many supposedly not-so-good students are conceptually bright. The reality is that most principles books bore this Internet generation. To teach them effectively, we've got to get their attention and hold it.

My colloquial style helps get their attention. It makes them feel that they are getting an additional tutor to back up the professor. This secondary tutor, while a bit of a pain in the ass at times, is at least human. That colloquial style helps with one of the biggest problems in the course—getting students involved with the material.

I get lots of e-mails from students—some ask me if I have sons who share my perverse sense of humor because they'd like to marry them; others tell me that I goofed somewhere in the book. Others complain about their professor—to which I answer the professor is always right. My point is not the content of the e-mails; my point is that students feel comfortable e-mailing and even phoning me. Students hear my voice in the book. It is the only economics textbook that establishes a connection with the student. To toot my own horn (what else are prefaces for?), let me share an e-mail that the publisher received from a friend of theirs (an insider to the publishing business) and that they forwarded to me. It said:

> Dear X, My son is a freshman at The University of X. Like many kids he has grown to be less-and-less a reader until fairly recently. He is in the business school at college and he is wandering in search of an eventual major, like so many. He took the Principles Micro in the Fall and "hated" economics. On Monday he told me that his favorite course is Macro. His instructor is "not so helpful" but he is reading the

> book and making straight A's because the book is "so much fun to read" and he is "learning a ton of stuff." He has registered for the WSJ online and reads it every day. He is thinking of pursuing Econ as a major. It is actually the most positive review by an "end user" of a text-book that I've heard in a long time and, although it took me three days to find out the author and publisher (he didn't know; he just liked reading the book), the book is the latest edition of Colander. So: Thanks!

One of the reasons I keep working on this book is that I get a number of letters and e-mails like this one, and it boosts my admittedly already big ego, but what is life if not a big ego trip? (Yes, I recognize that that last statement is not standard textbookese, but I include it here to give you a sense of what I mean by my colloquial style, and to explain to you how I keep the students' attention as I am pounding into them the need to equate marginal cost and marginal benefits.)

Numerous students tell me that they actually break a smile when they read my book, and a few tell me they crack up. Just about everyone tells me that they recognize that the person writing this book is very human—all too human in some people's view. My colloquial style allows me greater flexibility in the material I present to students than most textbook authors have. Because I'm having a conversation with the students, I can explain to them what material is new and is to be read casually rather than to be memorized. Then, elsewhere where I am presenting material that will likely be on their exam, I can tell them that it is time to buckle down and memorize. So my colloquial style allows me to vary the presentation and I take full advantage of it in explaining to students what modern economics is.

Modern Critical Thinking Economics

Modern economics can mean different things to different people, and my interpretation of it centers around critical thinking. Modern economics is economics that is based on the traditional models, but that subjects them to critical thinking, and does not apply the models where they don't fit empirically. It focuses on the real world, rather than on abstract models.

To maintain that critical thinking approach, two principles stand out: (1) institutions and history are important in policy discussions and (2) good economics is open to dealing with all ideas. The mantra of modern critical thinking economics is, "Tell me something I don't already know, using whatever method works." Let me discuss each of these principles briefly.

Institutions and History Are Important to Understand Policy

If one opens up Adam Smith's *Wealth of Nations,* John Stuart Mill's *Principles of Political Economy,* or Alfred Marshall's *Principles of Economics,* one will see economic analysis placed in historical and institutional context. The modern textbook template moved away from that, and in previous editions, I tried to return the principles of economics toward that broader template, presenting models in a historical and institutional context. This edition continues that emphasis on institutions and history. Modern work in game theory and strategic decision making is making it clear that the implications of economic reasoning depend on the institutional setting. To understand economics requires an understanding of existing institutions and the historical development of those institutions. In a principles course we don't have time to present much about history and institutions, but that does not preclude us from letting students know that we know that these issues are important. And that's what I try to do.

When I say that institutions and history are important, I am talking about economic policy. As I stated above, this text and accompanying package is *not* designed for future economics majors. Most principles students aren't going to go on in economics. I write for students who will probably take only one or two economics courses in their lifetime. These students are interested in policy, and what I try to present to them are the basics of modern economic reasoning as they relate to policy questions.

Because I think policy is so important in explaining how to apply economic reasoning, I utilize a distinction made by J.N. Keynes (John Maynard Keynes' father) and Classical economists generally. That distinction is between *theorems*—the deductive conclusions of models—and *precepts*—the considered judgments of economists about the policy implications of the models. I make it clear to students that models do not tell us what to do about policy—they give us theorems. Only when we combine the model's results with our understanding of institutions, our understanding of the social context, and the normative goals one wants to achieve, can we arrive at policy conclusions, which are embodied in precepts.

Openness to Various Views

While I present modern economics, I present it in such a way that it is open to many different points of view. I don't present the material as "the truth" but simply as the conventional wisdom, the learning of which is a useful hurdle for all students to jump over. To encourage students to question conventional wisdom, the end of each chapter includes a set of questions—Questions from Alternative Perspectives—written by economists from a variety of different perspectives. These include Post-Keynesian, feminist, Austrian, Radical, Institutionalist, and religious questions. The Radical questions come from the Dollars and Sense Collective, a group with whom I've worked to coordinate their readers (www.dollarsandsense.org/bookstore.html) with this text. I also often integrate Austrian ideas into my class; I find that *The Free Market* (www.mises.org) is a provocative resource.

I often pair an article in *The Free Market* with one in *Dollars and Sense* in my assignments to students for supplementary reading. Having students read both radical and Austrian views, and then integrate those views into their own, generally middle-of-the-road, views is, for me, a perfect way of teaching the principles course. (If I have radicals and libertarians in the class, I argue in favor of middle-of-the-road views.) If you like to teach the course emphasizing alternative views, you might want to assign the brief survey of different approaches to economics in the "Preface for the Student" close to the beginning of the course, and then have the students discuss the alternative perspective questions at the end of each chapter.

There are many other ways to teach this open view approach, and for shorter classes, I have students read the various chapters on their own, and then do a presentation or have a discussion in class of how they really feel about various policies. The idea is to engage students about policy and policy debates as part of the course.

Teaching both Models and Critical Thinking

The goal in most principles courses is to teach students economic insights by presenting them a collection of models. Models are central to modern economics. Robert Solow nicely captured its importance when he said that, for better or worse, economics is a modeling science. This means that an important aspect of teaching students modern economics involves introducing them to the modeling approach to understanding the world. But teaching models, in my view, should be along the lines of Alfred Marshall, not Mas-Colell, Whinston, and Green. Marshall emphasized that economics was an approach to problems, not a body of confirmed truths.

In my view, *the modeling method, not the models,* is the most important to an economics class. In my presentation of models, I carefully try to guide students in the modeling method, rather than having them memorize truths from models. I carefully emphasize the limitations of the models and the assumptions that underlie them, and am constantly urging students to think beyond the models. This approach pushes the students a bit harder than the alternative, but it is, in my view, the best pedagogical approach; it is the critical thinking approach.

Changes in This Edition

I strongly believe that content has to be both up to date and relevant. Economic understanding and the economy in which we live are continually evolving. This means that course materials have to continually evolve as well so that they are teaching modern economics. For that reason, you will see many more changes in the text's organization and presentation than you will see in other long-standing principles texts. This is not a "change a few words here and there" revision. This is a substantial revision. They are changes that will keep your teaching fresh and engaging. The first change is obvious: All data, institutional detail and policy discussion had to be brought up to date. But that was only the beginning.

The changes in macro are more substantial. The reason is that the United States is facing economic changes not seen for 80 years. It's been in a significant and sustained macroeconomic slump. Students know this because the labor market is tough out there; many cannot find jobs, at least not the jobs they want. As a profession we just can't keep teaching models designed to discuss problems of a previous era and do justice to our students. When the world and the U.S. economy is teetering of the edge of a depression, policy is not a matter of tweaking a smooth running macroeconomy as the previous models made it seem. Policy involves preventing the economy from taking a significant nose-dive while making the needed long-term structural changes. To make the discussion relevant to these difficult times meant adding some new chapters, reorganizing some of the content and changing the ordering of some existing chapters.

Specifically, I added a chapter on a structural stagnation interpretation of the economic slump, and contrasted that with the more standard models. Since international issues are central to the current problems, I moved discussions of globalization, exchange rates, and trade deficits earlier so that they can be incorporated into the discussion. I also significantly increased the discussion of the financial sector's role in the crisis, explaining how the bursting of the financial bubble in 2007 has contributed to an ongoing slump, and the difficulties with using monetary policy and fiscal policy in pulling the economy back to a sustainable expansion.

In revising, I use my students as sounding boards, and one of them reported back to me that "these chapters were a sudden jolt of reality; they were addictive; I couldn't put them down until I had finished them." He had multiple questions, as I suspect most readers will. So, if you want to teach students about the problems currently facing the economy—problems that students read on the Internet and in the newspapers—then this text is for you.

In-Depth Chapter-by-Chapter Discussion of Changes

Major changes include:

Chapter 1, Economics and Economic Reasoning

Deleted the discussion of induction, deduction, and abduction to simplify the presentation.

Chapter 2, The Production Possibility Model, Trade, and Globalization

The discussion of opportunity costs and its relationship to tradeoffs has been clarified. The "combined PPC with trade" diagram has been removed to simplify the discussion. The presentation now includes two simple graphs, each showing the production possibility curve for one country. The discussion allows the identification of a new level of possible consumption based on trade for each country separately.

I changed the discussion of outsourcing so it fits better with the broader term, "globalization." The issues go beyond U.S. companies moving production abroad and include the impact of global competition for U.S. firms, including shutting down U.S. production as well as retooling into more competitive sectors. This sets the stage for an expanded discussion of globalization throughout the text.

Chapter 3, Economic Institutions

I simplified the discussion of evolving economic systems by cutting the discussion of feudalism, mercantilism, and the Industrial Revolution. These topics are covered in the chapter's appendix. I added a discussion of for-benefit corporations, a rising form of business that includes social goods along with profit in their charters. I added a new box, "Who Are the 1 Percent" to include recent conversations in the Occupy Movement.

Chapter 4, Supply and Demand

I focused the discussion of the shift factors of supply on technology, while continuing to list the same four from the eighth edition.

Chapter 5, Using Supply and Demand

I replaced the example of the effect of Cyclone Larry with the more recent example of Hurricane Irene. I moved the discussion of the determination of exchange rates to Chapter 8, "Comparative Advantage, Exchange Rates, and Globalization."

Macroeconomics

Chapter 6, Economic Growth, Business Cycles, and Structural Stagnation

This chapter draws from the eighth edition Chapters 7 and 10. It begins with the historical development of macro and its more recent development into modern models of the economy, and discusses the problems that the economy is presenting to macroeconomic policy makers. The chapter retains Chapter 7's focus on growth and business cycles and adds a new distinction for structural stagnation. The technical material on inflation is moved to Chapter 18, devoted entirely to inflation.

Chapter 7, Measuring the Aggregate Economy

This is the eighth edition Chapter 8 with an expanded section on the global dimensions of production and the problems that it can raise. I added an introductory discussion of exchange rates and of trade deficits and balance of payments issues. I moved the discussion of real and nominal concepts and deflators from Chapter 7 of the eighth edition here.

Chapter 8, Comparative Advantage, Exchange Rates, and Globalization

This chapter is based on the first part of Chapter 19 in the eighth edition and incorporates material about exchange rates from eighth edition Chapter 20. Much of the institutional and data discussion about government policy is moved to Chapter 19 in this new edition. I added a number of new concepts to the chapter, including exchange rate determination and the distributional effects of international trade. It discusses how international adjustment are "supposed" to work in theory, but it also discusses how reality often does not quickly adjust, causing complications for economies when trade flows are unequal. It introduces the concept of import-led stagnation as the mirror image of export-led growth.

Chapter 9, The Short-Run Keynesian Policy Model: Demand-Side Policies

This is the eighth edition Chapter 10 with a simplified discussion of feedback effects in the AS/AD model to make the chapter easier. I moved the discussion of the history of macroeconomics to an earlier chapter. The eight edition Chapter 28 "The Multiplier Model" is now web Chapter 9W.

Chapter 10, The Classical Long-Run Policy Model: Growth and Supply-Side Policies

This is eighth edition Chapter 9. The major change is that it is simplified into a verbal discussion of economic growth and technological change rather than a graphical presentation. The eighth edition Chapter 29 "Thinking Like a Modern Macroeconomist" is now web Chapter 10W.

Chapter 11, The Structural Stagnation Policy Dilemma

This is a new chapter that relates the AS/AD model to the current problems facing the U.S. economy. The structural stagnation hypothesis is presented, and an explanation is provided for how globalization without international exchange rate adjustment can lead to sustained trade deficits and import-led stagnation. It provides a possible explanation of how the financial bubble occurred and how the bursting of that financial bubble left the U.S. economy in a weakened state.

Chapter 12, The Financial Sector and the Economy

This is based on the eighth edition Chapter 13, modified to better relate to the problems the economy is currently facing. It provides a discussion of how consumer credit expanded tremendously between 1990 and 2007 and how that could have made the economy seem in better shape than it actually was. The more complicated money multiplier discussion with people holding cash is removed to simplify the analysis. The chapter ends with a short section on risk premiums on loans and the problems facing Greece and other European economies.

Chapter 13, Monetary Policy

This is based on the eighth edition Chapter 14. It explains how asset inflation presents significant problems for the conduct of monetary policy, and how the huge rise in excess reserves held by banks starting in 2008 limited the Fed's effectiveness in using conventional monetary policy tools.

Chapter 14, Financial Crises, Panics, and Unconventional Monetary Policy

This chapter is based on eighth edition Chapter 15, but the focus is changed so that it is less on the lender of last resort function of monetary policy in a financial crisis, and more on post-crisis monetary policy where conventional monetary policy is ineffective. It presents the new policy tools that the Fed has introduced recently and includes a discussion of the need for, and problems of, financial regulation.

Chapter 15, Deficits and the Debt

This is eighth edition Chapter 17 updated. It includes a new discussion of the financial risks of continued high deficits and the debate about how large government debt can be before it causes serious problems for the economy. The appendix on Social Security and Medicare has been cut to save space.

Chapter 16, The Fiscal Policy Dilemma

This is eighth edition Chapter 18, updated to take account of recent events. It presents the debate about whether the U.S. debt will soon reach a tipping point that will undermine the sustainability of the U.S. economy.

Chapter 17, Jobs and Unemployment

This new chapter is designed to relate the models presented in earlier chapters to the current problem of a jobless recovery that faces the U.S. economy. It incorporates some of the material from Chapter 7 in the eighth edition. The chapter presents the debate about whether unemployment is an individual or social responsibility along with a provocative proposal to provide a guaranteed job for every person who wants one.

Chapter 18, Inflation, Deflation, and Macro Policy

This is eighth edition Chapter 16 along with introductory material from Chapter 7, modified to fit the current problems the economy is facing. The chapter distinguishes asset price inflation and goods price inflation and relates the discussion to financial bubbles and bursting of those bubbles. The discussion of the Phillips curve is shortened.

Chapter 19, International Trade Policy

This chapter looks more closely at trade and trade policy, and is based on portions of the eighth edition Chapter 19 with much of the comparative advantage and globalization material moving into Chapter 8.

Chapter 20, International Financial Policy

This is a modification of the eighth edition Chapter 20. The discussion of the determination of exchange rates was moved to Chapter 8, so this chapter reviews the earlier presentation of exchange rate determination. The discussion of the advantages and disadvantages of a common currency is modified to account for recent problems in the European Union.

Chapter 21, Macro Policy in a Global Setting

The chapter is updated from the eighth edition but remains largely intact.

Chapter 22, Macro Policy in Developing Countries

Much of the chapter remains similar to the eighth edition Chapter 22.

Key Pedagogical Features

Learning Objectives

Four or five learning objectives are presented at the beginning of each chapter and are referenced again in the summary and end-of-chapter review questions and exercises to which they relate. The learning objectives (LO) serve as a quick introduction to the material and concepts to be mastered before moving to the next chapter. All of the assignable content within Connect is also organized around learning objectives to make it easier to plan, track, and analyze student performance across learning outcomes.

Margin Comments

Located throughout the text in the margin, these key takeaways underscore and summarize the importance of the material, at the same time helping students focus on the most relevant topics critical to their understanding.

Margin Questions

These self-test questions are presented in the margin of the chapter to enable students to determine whether the preceding material has been understood and to reinforce understanding before students read further. Answers to Margin Questions are found at the end of each chapter.

WWW Web Note

Web Notes

Jenifer Gamber has updated the Web Notes; this feature extends the text discussion onto the web. Web Notes are denoted in the margin and are housed on the Online Learning Center at **www.mhhe.com/colander9e** and within Connect Plus.

Podcasts

Written and recorded by Robert Guell of Indiana State University, more than 50 three- to five-minute audio clips delve deeper into the concepts. The audio clips (and summaries) occur throughout the text wherever you see the iPod icon in the margin. The podcasts are also housed on the Online Learning Center at **www.mhhe.com/colander9e** and within Connect Plus.

Supplements

McGraw-Hill has established a strong history of top-rate supplements to accompany this text, and this ninth edition strives to carry on the tradition of excellence.

For the Instructor

The following ancillaries are available for quick download and convenient access via the Online Learning Center at **www.mhhe.com/colander9e** and within Connect Plus. Both are password protected for security.

Instructor's Manual

This text boasts one of the strongest Instructor's Manuals on the market. Paul Fisher of Henry Ford Community College worked incredibly hard to maintain the high standard set in previous editions. Elements include:

- *Learning Objectives:* Lists the learning objectives for each chapter for a quick review.
- *Teaching Objectives:* Alerts new professors to common student difficulties with the material and provides help for addressing them.
- *For Professors New to Colander:* Notes some of the names, notations, definitions, and symbols that Colander uses as compared to other products to help professors transition into this product.
- *Problem Sets with Solutions:* Additional questions for each chapter are included here. They are designed to be photocopied and distributed for student use.

Solutions Manual

Prepared by Jenifer Gamber and me, this manual provides answers to all end-of-chapter questions—the Questions and Exercises, Questions from Alternative Perspectives, and Issues to Ponder.

Test Banks

The test bank contains more than thousands of quality questions for instructors to draw from in their classrooms. Brian Lynch of Lakeland Community College and Timothy Terrell of Wofford College worked diligently to make sure that this revised version is clear and useful. Each question is categorized by learning objective, level of difficulty, economic concept, AACSB learning categories, and Bloom's Taxonomy objectives. Questions were reviewed by professors and students alike to ensure that each one was effective for classroom use. All of the test bank content is available for assigning within Connect.

Computerized Test Banks

McGraw-Hill's EZ Test is a flexible and easy-to-use electronic testing program. The program allows you to create tests from text-specific items. It accommodates a wide range of question types and you can add your own questions.

Multiple versions of the test can be created and any test can be exported for use with course management systems such as WebCT, BlackBoard, or Page Out. EZ Test Online is a service that gives you a place to easily administer your EZ Test-created exams and quizzes online. The program is available for Windows and Macintosh environmnents.

PowerPoint Presentations

Shannon Aucoin of the University of Louisiana at Lafayette and Edward Gullason of Dowling College worked tirelessly to revise the PowerPoint slide program, animating graphs and emphasizing important concepts. Each chapter has been scrutinized to ensure an accurate, direct connection to the text.

For the Student

Online Learning Center

www.mhhe.com/colander9e

This Online Learning Center provides a number of useful study tools including practice quizzes, a set of study PowerPoints, Web Notes, and web chapters. Premium content is also available for purchase. The premium content contains podcasts and Paul Solman videos, which are downloadable to MP3 devices.

Study Guide

The study guide—written by Jenifer Gamber and me—provides a review of the concepts from each chapter. It gives students options to match a variety of learning styles: short-answer questions, matching terms with definitions, problems and applications, multiple-choice questions, and potential essay questions. To make the guide a true study tool, each answer includes an explanation of why it is correct.

Digital Solutions

McGraw-Hill *Connect Economics*

Less Managing. More Teaching. Greater Learning.

Connect Economics is an online assignment and assessment solution that offers a number of powerful tools and features that make managing assignments easier so faculty can spend more time teaching. With *Connect Economics,* students can engage with their coursework anytime and anywhere, making the learning process more accessible and efficient.

Simple Assignment Management

With *Connect Economics,* creating assignments is easier than ever, so you can spend more time teaching and less time managing. The assignment management function enables you to:

- Create and deliver assignments easily with selectable end-of-chapter questions and test bank items.
- Streamline lesson planning, student progress reporting, and assignment grading to make classroom management more efficient than ever.
- Go paperless with the eBook and online submission and grading of student assignments.

Smart Grading

Connect Economics helps students learn more efficiently by providing feedback and practice material when they need it, where they need it. The grading function in *Connect Economics* also enables instructors to:

- Score assignments automatically, giving students immediate feedback on their work and side-by-side comparisons with correct answers.
- Access and review each response; manually change grades or leave comments for students to review.
- Reinforce classroom concepts with practice tests and instant quizzes.

Instructor Library

The *Connect Economics* Instructor Library is your repository for additional resources to improve student engagement in and out of class. You can select and use any asset that enhances your lecture.

Student Study Center

The *Connect Economics* Student Study Center is the place for students to access additional resources. The Student Study Center:

- Offers students quick access to lectures, practice materials, eBooks, and more.
- Provides instant practice material and study questions, easily accessible on the go.

Diagnostic and Adaptive Learning of Concepts: LearnSmart

The LearnSmart adaptive self-study technology within *Connect Economics* provides students with a seamless combination of practice, assessment, and remediation for major concepts in the course. LearnSmart's intelligent software adapts to every student response and automatically delivers concepts that advance the student's understanding while reducing time devoted to the concepts already mastered. LearnSmart:

- Applies an intelligent concept engine to identify the relationships between concepts and to serve new concepts to each student only when he or she is ready.
- Adapts automatically to each student, so students spend less time on the topics they understand and more on those they have yet to master.
- Provides continual reinforcement and remediation, but gives only as much guidance as students need.
- Enables you to assess which concepts students have efficiently learned on their own, thus freeing class time for more applications and discussion.

Student Progress Tracking

Connect Economics keeps instructors informed about how each student, section, and class is performing, allowing for more productive use of lecture and office hours. The progress-tracking function enables you to:

- View scored work immediately and track individual or group performance with assignment and grade reports.
- Access an instant view of student or class performance relative to learning objectives.
- Collect data and generate reports required by many accreditation organizations like AACSB.

McGraw-Hill *Connect Plus Economics*

McGraw-Hill reinvents the textbook learning experience for the modern student with *Connect Plus Economics.* A seamless integration of an eBook and *Connect Economics, Connect Plus Economics* provides all of the *Connect Economics* features plus the following:

- An integrated eBook, allowing for anytime, anywhere access to the text.
- Dynamic links between the problems or questions you assign to your students and the location in the eBook where that problem or question is covered.
- A powerful search function to pinpoint and connect key concepts in a snap.

In short, *Connect Economics* offers you and your students powerful tools and features that optimize your time and energies, enabling you to focus on course content, teaching, and student learning. *Connect Economics* also offers a wealth of content resources for both instructors and students. This state-of-the-art, thoroughly tested system supports you in preparing students for the world that awaits.

For more information about Connect, go to **www.mcgrawhillconnect.com** or contact your local McGraw-Hill sales representative.

Tegrity Campus is a service that makes class time available 24/7 by automatically capturing every lecture in a searchable format for students to review when they study and complete assignments. With a simple one-click start-and-stop process, you capture all computer screens and corresponding audio. Students can replay any part of any class with easy-to-use browser-based viewing on a PC or Mac.

Educators know that the more students can see, hear, and experience class resources, the better they learn. In fact, studies prove it. With Tegrity Campus, students quickly recall key moments by using Tegrity Campus's unique search feature. This search helps students efficiently find what they need, when they need it, across an entire semester of class recordings. Help turn all your students' study time into learning moments immediately supported by your lecture.

To learn more about Tegrity watch a two-minute Flash demo at **http://tegritycampus.mhhe.com.**

Assurance of Learning Ready

Many educational institutions today are focused on the notion of *assurance of learning,* an important element of some accreditation standards. *Macroeconomics, 9e* is designed specifically to support your assurance of learning initiatives with a simple yet powerful solution.

Each test bank question for *Macroeconomics, 9e* maps to a specific chapter learning outcome/objective listed in the text. You can use our test bank software, EZ Test and EZ Test Online, or *Connect Economics* to easily query for learning outcomes/objectives that directly relate to the learning objectives for your course. You can then use the reporting features of EZ Test to aggregate student results in similar fashion, making the collection and presentation of assurance of learning data simple and easy.

AACSB Statement

The McGraw-Hill Companies is a proud corporate member of AACSB International. Understanding the importance and value of AACSB accreditation, the author of *Macroeconomics, 9e* recognizes the curricula guidelines detailed in the AACSB standards for business accreditation by connecting questions in the test bank and end-of-chapter material to the general knowledge and skill guidelines found in the AACSB standards.

The statements contained in *Macroeconomics, 9e* are provided only as a guide for the users of this textbook. The AACSB leaves content coverage and assessment within the purview of individual schools, the mission of the school, and the faculty. While *Macroeconomics, 9e* and the teaching package make no claim of any specific AACSB qualification or evaluation, we have within *Macroeconomics, 9e* labeled selected questions according to the general knowledge and skills areas.

McGraw-Hill Customer Care Contact Information

At McGraw-Hill, we understand that getting the most from new technology can be challenging. That's why our services don't stop after you purchase our products. You can e-mail our Product Specialists 24 hours a day to get product-training online. Or you can search our knowledge bank of Frequently Asked Questions on our support website. For Customer Support, call **800-331-5094** or visit **www.mhhe.com/support.** One of our Technical Support Analysts will be able to assist you in a timely fashion.

CourseSmart

CourseSmart is a new way for faculty to find and review eTextbooks. It's also a great option for students who are interested in accessing their course materials digitally. CourseSmart offers thousands of the most commonly adopted textbooks across hundreds of courses from a wide variety of higher education publishers. It is the only place for faculty to review and compare the full text of a textbook online. At CourseSmart, students can save up to 50% off the cost of a print book, reduce their impact on the environment, and gain access to powerful web tools for learning including full text search, notes and highlighting, and e-mail tools for sharing notes between classmates. Complete tech support is also included with each title.

Finding your eBook is easy. Visit **www.CourseSmart.com** and search by title, author, or ISBN.

Dollars and Sense Readers

While not directly an ancillary to the book, the *Dollars and Sense* readers are annotated to fit with chapters of this book for professors who want to supplement the text with a radical perspective. Contact your McGraw-Hill representative for more information.

Package Pricing

To help lower costs of using ancillaries, McGraw-Hill has developed a variety of separate packages in which the book can be bought together with the ancillaries for a price that is close to the price of the book alone. Each of these packages has a separate ISBN number. For information on these packages, contact your McGraw-Hill sales representative.

People to Thank

Let me conclude this preface by thanking the hundreds of people who have offered suggestions, comments, kudos, and criticism on this project since its inception. This book would not be what it is without their input. So many people have contributed to this text in so many ways that I cannot thank everyone. So, to all the people who helped—many, many thanks. I specifically want to thank the ninth edition reviewers, whose insightful comments kept me on track. Reviewers include:

John Abell
Randolph College

Rose-Marie Avin
University of Wisconsin, Eau Claire

John Beck
Gonzaga University

Anthony Becker
St. Olaf College

Susan Bell
Seminole State College of Florida

Randall Bennett
Gonzaga University

Tami Bertelsen
Arapahoe Community College

Gerald Bialka
University of North Florida

John Blair
Wright State University

John Boschen
College of William & Mary

Taggert Brooks
University of Wisconsin–La Crosse

Keith Brouhle
Grinnell College

Neil Browne
Bowling Green State University

Joan Buccino
Florida Southern College

Douglas Bunn
Blackburn College

Eric Burns
Herbert W. Armstrong College

Colleen Callahan
American University

Kaycea Campbell
West Los Angeles Community College

Regina Cassady
Valencia County College

Suparna Chakraborty
Baruch College

Darian Chin
California State University–Los Angeles

Lisa Citron
Cascadia Community College

Jennifer Clark
Roosevelt University

George Darko
Tusculum College

Dennis Edwards
Coastal Carolina University

Gregory DeFreitas
Hofstra University

Diana Denison
Red Rocks Community College

Liang Ding
Macalester College

Justin Dubas
Texas Lutheran University

Sarah Estelle
Rhodes College

Doug Fain
Regis University

Christine Farrell
University of the Ozarks

Lucia Farriss
Saint Leo University Center for Online Learning

Fadi Fawaz
Texas Tech University

Shelby Frost
Georgia State University

Julie Gallaway
Missouri State University

Karen Gebhardt
Colorado State University

Scott Gilbert
Southern Illinois University–Carbondale

Robert Gitter
Ohio Wesleyan University

Nicholas Gomersall
Luther College

Michael Goode
Central Piedmont Community College

Mehdi Haririan
Bloomsburg University

Kevin Henrickson
Gonzaga University

Kermelle Hensley
Columbus Technical College

Elizabeth Hickman
Oakland City University–Bedford

Jannett Highfill
Bradley University

Reza Hossain
Mount Saint Mary College

Jack Hou
California State University–Long Beach

Chris Inama
Golden Gate University

Miren Ivankovic
Anderson University

Donna Rue Jenkins
National University

Paul Jones
National University

Lillian Kamal
University of Hartford

Jonathan Kaplan
California State Sacramento

Michele Kegley
Southern State Community College

Logan Kelly
Bryant University

Farida Khan
University of Wisconsin, Parkside

Chong-Uk Kim
Sonoma State University

Judy Klein
Mary Baldwin College

Rachel Kreier
Deanza College

Paul Kubik
DePaul University

Anil Lal
Pittsburgh State University

Simon Yuexing Lan
Auburn University–Montgomery

Gary Langer
Roosevelt University

Anthony Laramie
Merrimack College

Mark Lautzenheiser
Earlham College

Samuel Liu
West Valley College

Christine Lloyd
Western Illinois University

John Marcis
Coastal Carolina University

Ann Mari May
University of Nebraska–Lincoln

Warren Mazek
U.S. Merchant Marine Academy

Chris McNamara
Finger Lakes Community College

Lewis Metcalf
Parkland College

Peter Mikek
Wabash College

Garrett Milam
University of Puget Sound

William Milberg
The New School for Social Research

Frannie Miller
Texas A&M University–Commerce

Daniel Mizak
Frostburg State University

Karla Morgan
Whitworth College

Wayne Morra
Arcadia University

Muhammad Mustafa
South Carolina State University

Ronald Nate
Brigham Young University–Idaho

Nasrin Nazemzadeh
Lone Star College–Tomball

Brendan O'Flaherty
Columbia University

Ozgur Orhangazi
Roosevelt University

Peter Paluch
State University of New York–Delhi

Jodi Pelkowski
Wichita State University

Nathan Perry
University of Utah–Salt Lake

Liz Peterson
Eastern Washington University

Chiara Piovani
University of Utah

Brennan Platt
Brigham Young University–Provo

Roxanna Postolache
Capital University–Columbus

Ayman Reda
Grand Valley State University

Robert Rogers
Ashland University

Jonathan Sandy
University of San Diego

Richard Schatz
Whitworth University

Carol Schwartz
New York Institute of Technology

Robert Shoffner
Central Piedmont Community College

Jeffrey Silman
Paul Smith's College

Kevin Simmons
Austin College

John Somers
Portland Community College–Sylvania

Robert Sonora
Fort Lewis College

Robin Sturik
Cuyahoga Community College, Western Campus

Della Sue
Marist College

Thom Swanke
Morningside College

John Swinton
Georgia College & State

Richard Tarmey
Colorado Mountain College

Eric Taylor
Central Piedmont Community College

Zdravka Todorova
Wright State University

Dossee Toulaboe
Fort Hays State University

Stephen Tubene
University of Maryland–East Shore

Don-Joseph Uy-Barreta
Deanza College

Ramya Vijaya
Richard Stockton College of New Jersey

Randy Wade
Rogue Community College

Lynn Wallis
Clackamas Community College

Bruce Webb
Gordon College

Katherine Whitman
Mount St. Mary's College–Doheny

Van Wigginton
San Jacinto College–Pasadena

Andrew Williams
Delaware Tech Community College–Dover

Dmitry Yarushkin
Grand View University

In addition to the comments of the formal reviewers listed above, I have received helpful suggestions, encouragement, and assistance from innumerable individuals via e-mails, letters, symposia, and focus groups. Their help made this edition even stronger than its predecessor. They include James Wetzel, Virginia Commonwealth University; Dmitry Shishkin, Georgia State University; Amy Cramer, Pima Community College–West; Andrea Terzi, Franklin College; Shelby Frost, Georgia State University; Doris Geide-Stevenson, Weber State University; James Chasey, Advanced Placement Economics Teaching Consultant and Homewood-Flossmoor High School (ret.); David Tufte, Southern Utah University; Eric Sarpong, Georgia State University; Jim Ciecka, DePaul University; Fran Bradley, George School; Ron Olive, University of Massachusetts–Lowell; and Rachel Kreier, Hofstra University.

I want to give a special thank-you to the supplements authors including Shannon Aucoin, the University of Louisiana at Lafayette; Edward Gullason, Dowling College; Timothy Terrell, Wofford College; Brian Lynch, Lakeland Community College; and Paul Aaron Fisher, Henry Ford Community College. They all did an outstanding job.

I'd also like to thank the economists who wrote the alternative perspective questions. These include Ann Mari May of the University of Nebraska–Lincoln, John Miller of Wheaton College, Dan Underwood of Peninsula College, Ric Holt of Southern Oregon University, and Bridget Butkevich of George Mason University. I enjoyed working with each of them, and while their views often differed substantially, they were all united in wanting questions that showed economics as a pluralist field that encourages students to question the text from all perspectives.

I have hired numerous students to check aspects of the book, to read over my questions and answers to questions, and to help proofread. These include Kelly Liss, Anne Sexton Powers, Taran Jondaro, Alexander Veerman, Andrew Vollmer, Elena Zhang, Emily Duh, Olivia Lau, William Gamber, and Samatha Gluck. I thank them all.

A special thank-you for this edition goes to two people. The first is Jenifer Gamber, whose role in the book cannot be overestimated. She helped me clarify its vision by providing research, critiquing expositions and often improving them, and being a good friend. She has an amazing set of skills, and I thank her for using them to improve the book. The second is Christina Kouvelis, who came into this project and with her hard work, dedication, and superb ability made it possible to get the book done on time, even during a period of turmoil. She and Jenifer are two amazing women.

Next, I want to thank the entire McGraw-Hill team, including Douglas Reiner, managing director; Scott Smith, the brand manager; Alyssa Lincoln, the development editor; Bruce Gin, the content project manager; Pam Verros, the designer; Carol Bielski, the senior buyer; and Katie White, the marketing manager. All of them have done a superb job, for which I thank them sincerely.

Finally, I want to thank Pat, my wife, and my sons, Kasey and Zach, for helping me keep my work in perspective, and for providing a loving environment in which to work.

Preface for the Student: Alternative Perspectives

This text is written for you, the student. It's meant to give you a sense of what economics is, how economists think, and how they approach policy problems. There's only so much that an introductory course can cover, which means that much is left out. That includes much of the subtlety of economic thinking. So if you have a problem swallowing some of the ideas, and you believe that there's more to the issue than is presented here, rest assured; generally you're right. Hard choices have to be made for pedagogical purposes—issues have to be simplified and presentations curtailed. Otherwise this would be a 1,600-page book and much too heavy to carry around in a backpack.

Economics as a Method of Reasoning, Not the Truth

The approach I use is what would be called mainstream (it presents the conventional wisdom of economists) both because I'm mainstream and because most economists are as well. But pedagogically, I also believe that students learn by questioning—to say, no, that's not right, that's not the way I see things, and then to compare their way of thinking with the conventional way. Despite my being mainstream, I'm by nature also a skeptic, and in terms of pedagogy often find myself in sympathy with Joan Robinson, a famous economist, who argued that "the purpose of studying economics is not to acquire a set of ready-made answers to economic questions, but to learn how to avoid being deceived by economists." So, to encourage questioning everything, I don't present models and insights of economists as the truth (the field of economics is far too complicated to have arrived at a single truth) but as a set of technical hurdles, reasoning processes, and arguments that students should know, and that will help prepare them to deal with economic issues. Economics primarily teaches you how to approach problems; it does not provide definitive answers about what is right and what is wrong. It is a method, not a set of truths.

Alternative Perspectives in Economics

One of the pedagogical choices I made was to concentrate almost exclusively on the mainstream view. I strongly believe that focusing on that view is the best way to teach the course. However, I also believe that students should be aware of the diversity in economics and know that the mainstream view is not the only view out there. In fact, there are probably as many views out there as there are economists. Still, for a majority of economists, the concepts presented are an acceptable pedagogical simplification of the myriad views held by economists.

Some economists, however, might see this presentation as misleading, or as diverting the discussion away from other, more relevant, issues. These economists are generally called nonmainstream or heterodox economists. A heterodox economist is *one who doesn't accept the basic underlying model used by a majority of economists as the most useful model for analyzing the economy.*

In this preface, I will briefly introduce six heterodox economic approaches to give you a sense of how their analyses differ from the mainstream analyses presented. The six heterodox approaches are Austrian, Post-Keynesian, Institutionalist, Radical, feminist, and religious. Below are brief descriptions of each group, written with the help of the team of alternative-perspective economists.

Austrian Economists

Austrian economists believe in methodological individualism, by which they mean that social goals are best met through voluntary, mutually beneficial interactions. Lack of information and unsolvable incentive problems undermine the ability of government to plan, making the market the best method for coordinating economic activity. Austrian economists oppose state intrusion into private property and private activities. They are not economists from Austria; rather, they are economists from anywhere who follow the ideas of Ludwig von Mises and Friedrich Hayek, two economists who were from Austria.

Austrian economists are sometimes classified as conservative, but they are more appropriately classified as libertarians, who believe in liberty of individuals first and in other social goals second. Consistent with their views, they are often willing to support what are sometimes considered radical ideas, such as legalizing addictive drugs or eliminating our current monetary system—ideas that most mainstream economists would oppose. Austrian economists emphasize the uncertainty in the economy and the inability of a government controlled by self-interested politicians to undertake socially beneficial policy.

One proposal of Austrian economists will give you a flavor of their approach. That proposal is to eliminate the Federal Reserve System and to establish a free market in money—a policy that would leave people free to use any money they want and that would significantly reduce banking regulation. In a sense, their proposal carries the Classical argument in favor of laissez-faire to its logical conclusions. Why should the government have a monopoly of the money supply? Why shouldn't people be free to use whatever money they desire, denominated in whatever unit they want? Why don't we rely upon competition to prevent inflation? Why don't we have a free market in money? Well-known Austrian economists include Peter Boettke, Veronique de Rugy, Mario Rizzo, David Gordon, Israel Kirzner, Peter Leeson, Chris Coyne, Steve Horwitz, Roger Garrison, and Roger Koppl.

Institutionalist Economists

Institutionalist economists argue that any economic analysis must involve specific considerations of institutions. The lineage of Institutionalist economics begins with the pioneering work of Thorstein Veblen, John R. Commons, and Wesley C. Mitchell. Veblen employed evolutionary analysis to explore the role of institutions in directing and retarding the economic process. He saw human behavior driven by cultural norms and conveyed the way in which they were with sardonic wit and penetrating insight, leaving us with enduring metaphors such as the leisure class and conspicuous consumption. Commons argued that institutions are social constructs that could improve general welfare. Accordingly, he established cooperative investigative programs to support pragmatic changes in the legal structure of government. Mitchell was a leader in developing economics as an empirical study; he was a keen observer of the business cycle and argued that theory must be informed by systematic attention to empirical data, or it was useless.

Contemporary Institutionalists employ the founders' "trilogy"—empirically informed evolutionary analysis directed toward pragmatic alteration of institutions shaping economic outcomes—in their policy approach. Examples include indicative planning—a macroeconomic policy in which the government sets up an overall plan for various industries and selectively directs credit to certain industries; and income support programs, including those assuring employment for all willing. Well-known Institutionalists include Greg Hayden, Geoff Hodgson, Anne Mayhew, James Peach, and Ronnie Phillips.

Radical Economists

Radical economists believe substantial equality-preferring institutional changes should be implemented in our economic system. Radical economists evolved out of Marxian economics. In their analysis, they focus on the lack of equity in our current economic system and on institutional changes that might bring about a more equitable system. Specifically, they see the current economic system as one in which a few people—capitalists and high-level managers—benefit enormously at the expense of many people who struggle to make ends meet in jobs that are unfulfilling or who even go without work at times. They see the fundamental instability and irrationality of the capitalist system at the root of a wide array of social ills that range from pervasive inequality to alienation, racism, sexism, and imperialism. Radical economists often use a class-oriented analysis to address these issues and are much more willing to talk about social conflict and tensions in our society than are mainstream economists.

A policy favored by many Radicals is the establishment of worker cooperatives to replace the corporation. Radicals argue that such worker cooperatives would see that the income of the firm is more equitably allocated. Likewise, Radical theorists endorse policies such as universal health care insurance that conform to the ethic of "putting people before profits."

There are a number of centers of Radical thought, including The Political Economy Research Institute, The New School for Social Research, and some campuses of the University of Massachusetts. A good place to find Radical views is the *Dollars and Sense* magazine. Well-known Radical economists include Lourdes Beneria, Sam Bowles, Arthur MacEwan, Robert Pollin, Gerald Epstein, Anwar Shaikh, Michael Reich, Richard Wolff, and Stephen Resnick, as well as a number of feminist economists who would be considered both Radicals and feminists.

Feminist Economists

Feminist economics offers a substantive challenge to the content, scope, and methodology of mainstream economics. Feminist economists question the boundaries of what we consider economics to be and examine social arrangements surrounding provisioning. Feminist economists have many different views, but all believe that in some way traditional economic analysis misses many important issues pertaining to women.

Feminist economists study issues such as how the institutional structure tends to direct women into certain types of jobs (generally low-paying jobs) and away from other types of jobs (generally high-paying jobs). They draw our attention to the unpaid labor performed by women throughout the world and ask, "What would GDP look like if women's work were given a value and included?" They argue for an expansion in the content of economics to include women as practitioners and as worthy of study and for the elimination of the masculine bias in mainstream economics. Is there such a bias? To see it, simply compare the relative number of women in your economics class to the relative number of women at your school. It is highly likely that your class has relatively more men. Feminist economists want you to ask why that is, and whether anything should be done about it.

The historical roots of feminist economics can be found in the work of such authors as Mary Wollstonecraft, John Stuart Mill, Harriet Taylor Mill, and Charlotte Perkins Gilman. Feminist economics has expanded significantly in the past 25 years and has emerged as an influential body of thought. Well-known feminist economists include Myra Strober, Diana Strassmann, Barbara Bergmann, Julie Nelson, Jane Humphries, Marianne Ferber, Randy Albelda, Nancy Folbre, and Heidi Hartmann.

Religious Economists

Religion is the oldest and, arguably, the most influential institution in the world—be it Christianity, Islam, Judaism, Buddhism, Hinduism, or any of the many other religions in the world. Modern science, of which economics is a part, emphasizes the rational elements of thought. It attempts to separate faith and normative issues from rational analysis in ways that some religiously oriented economists find questionable. The line between a religious and non-religious economist is not hard and fast; all economists bring elements of their ethical considerations into their analysis. But those we call "religious economists" integrate the ethical and normative issues into economic analysis in more complex ways than the ways presented in the text.

Religiously oriented economists have a diversity of views; some believe that their views can be integrated reasonably well into standard economics, while others see the need for the development of a distinctive faith-based methodology that focuses on a particular group of normative concerns centered on issues such as human dignity and caring for the poor.

One religious perspective that is represented by a defined group in the U.S. economics profession is Christianity, and a number of Christian economists have joined together in the Association of Christian Economists (ACE). Its stated goal is "to encourage Christian scholars to explore and communicate the relationship between their faith and the discipline of economics, and to promote interaction and communication among Christian economists." Centers of ACE are Pepperdine University, Calvin College, and Gordon College. Leading Christian economists include Kurt Schaefer, Andrew Yuengert, and Stephen Smith.

Many of the religious alternative perspective questions that we provide in the text are from the Judeo-Christian perspective, the perspective most familiar to U.S. students. However, we intersperse some questions from other religious perspectives, both to show the similarity of views and to encourage students to think in a multicultural framework.

Post-Keynesian Economists

Post-Keynesian economists believe that uncertainty is a central issue in economics. They follow J. M. Keynes' approach more so than do mainstream economists in emphasizing institutional imperfections in the economy and the importance of fundamental uncertainty that rationality cannot deal with. They agree with Institutionalists that the study of economics must emphasize and incorporate the importance of social and political structure in determining market outcomes.

While their view about the importance of uncertainty is similar to the Austrian view, their policy response to that uncertainty is quite different. They do not see uncertainty as eliminating much of government's role in the economy; instead, they see it leading to policies in which government takes a larger role in guiding the economy.

One of their policy proposals that gives you a flavor of their approach is tax-based income policies—policies in which the government tries to directly affect the nominal wage- and price-setting institutions. Under a tax-based income policy, any firm raising its wage or price would be subject to a tax, and any firm lowering its wage or price would get a subsidy. Such a plan, they argue, would reduce the upward pressure on the nominal price level and reduce the rate of unemployment necessary to hold down inflation. Well-known Post-Keynesian economists include Paul Davidson, Jamie Galbraith, Barkley Rosser, John Cornwall, Shelia Dow, Malcolm Sawyer, Philip Arestis, Victoria Chick, Jan Kregel, and Geoff Harcourt.

Consistency of the Various Approaches

A characteristic of almost all heterodox economists of all types is that their analyses tend to be less formal than mainstream analysis. *Less formal* doesn't mean better or worse. There are advantages and disadvantages to formality, but *less formal* does mean that there's more potential for ambiguity in interpretation. It's easy to say whether the logic in a formal model is right or wrong. It's much harder to say whether the logic in an informal model is right or wrong because it's often hard to see precisely what the logic is. The advantage of an informal model is that it can include many more variables and can be made more realistic, so you can discuss real-world problems more easily with that model. Nonmainstream economists often want to talk about the real world, which is why they use informal models.

Often, after I discuss the mainstream and heterodox approaches, some student asks which is right. I respond with a story told by a former colleague of mine, Abba Lerner:

> "But look," the rabbi's wife remonstrated, "when one party to the dispute presented their case to you, you said, 'You are quite right,' and then when the other party presented their case you again said, 'You are quite right.' Surely they cannot both be right?" To which the Rabbi answered, "My dear, you are quite right!"

The moral of the story is that there's nothing necessarily inconsistent among mainstream and heterodox economists' approaches. Their approaches are simply different ways of looking at the same event. Which approach is most useful depends on what issues and events you are analyzing. The class analysis used by radicals is often more appropriate to developing countries than it is to the United States, and, in analyzing developing countries, many mainstream economists also include class fights in their approach. Similarly, Austrian analysis provides more insight into the role of the entrepreneur and individual in the economy than does mainstream analysis, while Post-Keynesian and Institutionalist analyses are useful when considering major institutional changes.

The distinctions between heterodox and mainstream economists can be overdone. One economist may well fall into two or three different groupings and use a combination of various analyses.

I follow the work of heterodox economists carefully. Their writing is often more interesting than mainstream writing, which can often get rather technical and boring. But in this book, I present primarily mainstream views. I do that because that's what I see as the job of the principles of economics course. My goal, however, is to present those views to you, not to indoctrinate you with those views, and throughout the text I include some challenges to the standard views. At the end of each chapter, I also include some questions that challenge the view presented in the chapter. These questions are written by representatives of different heterodox groups. I also encourage you to look for these other views in your outside reading. The *Dollars and Sense* companion to the book has radical critiques and *Free Market,* an Austrian newsletter found at www.mises.org, has Austrian critiques. There are many other sources and websites for heterodox groups. Exploring these sites and learning about the many different views that are competing in the marketplace for ideas make your economics course more interesting.

A Concluding Thought

There are many ways to explore economics, and in your exploration, this text and accompanying package is only a map. You and your professor determine what you discuss and learn and what path you will take. Ultimately, that's the way it has to be. Most of you are in this course for the grade—college is a way of progressing up the ladder. That's how it was for me. But the process also can be transforming; it can change how you look at issues, how you think, and who you are. The economics courses I took were especially important in determining who I have become.

Much of the principles course is what I call hurdle jumping—calisthenics of the mind. It is a set of mind-strengthening exercises. Separately, each is not especially relevant, but combined, they help turn your weak cranial muscle into a strong muscle better able to handle the problems that life throws at you. So, do the work, even if it seems boring; follow your professor's reasoning, even if you don't agree with what he or she is arguing; and keep thinking. Take advantage of this product's digital tools, even if they aren't required. Read newspapers and try to apply the lessons, deciding when they apply and when they don't. But, in the process, be happy—enjoy the moment because that moment will never be again.

Brief Contents

Contents

PART I

INTRODUCTION: THINKING LIKE AN ECONOMIST

PART I

Introduction: Thinking Like an Economist

Part I is an introduction, and an introduction to an introduction seems a little funny. But other sections have introductions, so it seemed a little funny not to have an introduction to Part I; and besides, as you will see, I'm a little funny myself (which, in turn, has two interpretations; I'm sure you will decide which of the two is appropriate). It will, however, be a very brief introduction, consisting of questions you may have had and some answers to those questions.

Some Questions and Answers

Why study economics?

Because it's neat and interesting and helps provide insight into events that are constantly going on around you.

Why is this book so big?

Because there's a lot of important information in it and because the book is designed so your teacher can pick and choose. You'll likely not be required to read all of it, especially if you're on the quarter system. But once you start it, you'll probably read it all anyhow. (Would you believe?)

Why does this book cost so much?

To answer this question, you'll have to read the book.

Will this book make me rich?

No.

Will this book make me happy?

It depends.

This book doesn't seem to be written in a normal textbook style. Is this book really written by a professor?

Yes, but he is different. He misspent his youth working on cars; he married his high school sweetheart after they met again at their 20th high school reunion, they remain happily married today, still totally in love. Twenty-five years after graduating from high school, his wife went back to medical school and got her MD because she was tired of being treated poorly by doctors. Their five kids make sure he doesn't get carried away in the professorial cloud.

Will the entire book be like this?

No, the introduction is just trying to rope you in. Much of the book will be hard going. Learning happens to be a difficult process: no pain, no gain. But the author isn't a sadist; he tries to make learning as pleasantly painful as possible.

What do the author's students think of him?

Weird, definitely weird—and hard. But fair, interesting, and sincerely interested in getting us to learn. (Answer written by his students.)

So there you have it. Answers to the questions that you might never have thought of if they hadn't been put in front of you. I hope they give you a sense of me and the approach I'll use in the book. There are some neat ideas in it. Let's now briefly consider what's in the first five chapters.

A Survey of the First Five Chapters

This first section is really an introduction to the rest of the book. It gives you the background necessary so that the later chapters make sense. Chapter 1 gives you an overview of the entire field of economics as well as an introduction to my style. Chapter 2 focuses on the production possibility curve, comparative advantage, and trade. It explains how trade increases production possibilities but also why, in the real world, free trade and no government regulation may not be the best policy. Chapter 3 gives you some history of economic systems and introduces you to the institutions of the U.S. economy. Chapters 4 and 5 introduce you to supply and demand, and show you not only the power of those two concepts but also the limitations.

Now let's get on with the show.

chapter 1

Economics and Economic Reasoning

> *In my vacations, I visited the poorest quarters of several cities and walked through one street after another, looking at the faces of the poorest people. Next I resolved to make as thorough a study as I could of Political Economy.*
>
> —Alfred Marshall

When an artist looks at the world, he sees color. When a musician looks at the world, she hears music. When an economist looks at the world, she sees a symphony of costs and benefits. The economist's world might not be as colorful or as melodic as the others' worlds, but it's more practical. If you want to understand what's going on in the world that's really out there, you need to know economics.

I hardly have to convince you of this fact if you keep up with the news. You will be bombarded with stories of unemployment, interest rates, how commodity prices are changing, and how businesses are doing. The list is endless. So let's say you grant me that economics is important. That still doesn't mean that it's worth studying. The real question then is: How much will you learn? Most of what you learn depends on you, but part depends on the teacher and another part depends on the textbook. On both these counts, you're in luck; since your teacher chose this book for your course, you must have a super teacher.[1]

After reading this chapter, you should be able to:

- **LO1-1** Define economics and identify its components.
- **LO1-2** Discuss various ways in which economists use economic reasoning.
- **LO1-3** Explain real-world events in terms of economic forces, social forces, and political forces.
- **LO1-4** Explain how economic insights are developed and used.
- **LO1-5** Distinguish among positive economics, normative economics, and the art of economics.

What Economics Is

Economics is *the study of how human beings coordinate their wants and desires, given the decision-making mechanisms, social customs, and political realities of the society*. One of the key words in the definition of the term "economics" is *coordination*. Coordination can mean many things. In the study of economics,

[1]This book is written by a person, not a machine. That means that I have my quirks, my odd sense of humor, and my biases. All textbook writers do. Most textbooks have the quirks and eccentricities edited out so that all the books read and sound alike—professional but dull. I choose to sound like me—sometimes professional, sometimes playful, and sometimes stubborn. In my view, that makes the book more human and less dull. So forgive me my quirks—don't always take me too seriously—and I'll try to keep you awake when you're reading this book at 3 a.m. the day of the exam. If you think it's a killer to read a book this long, you ought to try writing one.

coordination refers to how the three central problems facing any economy are solved. These central problems are:

1. What, and how much, to produce.
2. How to produce it.
3. For whom to produce it.

Three central coordination problems any economy must solve are what to produce, how to produce it, and for whom to produce it.

How hard is it to make the three decisions? Imagine for a moment the problem of living in a family: the fights, arguments, and questions that come up. "Do I have to do the dishes?" "Why can't I have piano lessons?" "Bobby got a new sweater. How come I didn't?" "Mom likes you best." Now multiply the size of the family by millions. The same fights, the same arguments, the same questions—only for society the questions are millions of times more complicated. In answering these questions, economies find that inevitably individuals want more than is available, given how much they're willing to work. That means that in our economy there is a problem of **scarcity**—*the goods available are too few to satisfy individuals' desires.*

The coordination questions faced by society are complicated.

Scarcity

Scarcity has two elements: our wants and our means of fulfilling those wants. These can be interrelated since wants are changeable and partially determined by society. The way we fulfill wants can affect those wants. For example, if you work on Wall Street, you will probably want upscale and trendy clothes. In Vermont, I am quite happy wearing Levi's and flannel.

The degree of scarcity is constantly changing. The quantity of goods, services, and usable resources depends on technology and human action, which underlie production. Individuals' imagination, innovativeness, and willingness to do what needs to be done can greatly increase available goods and resources. Who knows what technologies are in our future—nannites or micromachines that change atoms into whatever we want could conceivably eliminate scarcity of goods we currently consume. But they would not eliminate scarcity entirely since new wants are constantly developing.

The quantity of goods, services, and usable resources depends on technology and human action.

So, how does an economy deal with scarcity? The answer is coercion. In all known economies, coordination has involved some type of coercion—limiting people's wants and increasing the amount of work individuals are willing to do to fulfill those wants. The reality is that many people would rather play than help solve society's problems. So the basic economic problem involves inspiring people to do things that other people want them to do, and not to do things that other people don't want them to do. Thus, an alternative definition of economics is: the study of how to get people to do things they're not wild about doing (such as studying) and not to do things they are wild about doing (such as eating all the lobster they like), so that the things some people want to do are consistent with the things other people want to do.

Microeconomics and Macroeconomics

Economic theory is divided into two parts: microeconomic theory and macroeconomic theory. Microeconomic theory considers economic reasoning from the viewpoint of individuals and firms and builds up to an analysis of the whole economy. **Microeconomics** is *the study of individual choice, and how that choice is influenced by economic forces.* Microeconomics studies such things as the pricing policies of firms, households' decisions on what to buy, and how markets allocate resources among alternative ends.

Microeconomics is the study of how individual choice is influenced by economic forces.

As we build up from microeconomic analysis to an analysis of the entire economy, everything gets rather complicated. Many economists try to uncomplicate matters by taking a different approach—a macroeconomic approach—first looking at the aggregate, or whole, and then breaking it down into components. **Macroeconomics** is *the study of the*

Macroeconomics is the study of the economy as a whole. It considers the problems of inflation, unemployment, business cycles, and growth.

economy as a whole. It considers the problems of inflation, unemployment, business cycles, and growth. Macroeconomics focuses on aggregate relationships such as how household consumption is related to income and how government policies can affect growth.

Consider an analogy to the human body. A micro approach analyzes a person by looking first at each individual cell and then builds up. A macro approach starts with the person and then goes on to his or her components—arms, legs, fingernails, feelings, and so on. Put simply, microeconomics analyzes from the parts to the whole; macroeconomics analyzes from the whole to the parts.

Q-1 Classify the following topics as primarily macroeconomic or microeconomic:

1. The impact of a tax increase on aggregate output.
2. The relationship between two competing firms' pricing behavior.
3. A farmer's decision to plant soy or wheat.
4. The effect of trade on economic growth.

Microeconomics and macroeconomics are very much interrelated. What happens in the economy as a whole is based on individual decisions, but individual decisions are made within an economy and can be understood only within its macro context. For example, whether a firm decides to expand production capacity will depend on what the owners expect will happen to the demand for their products. Those expectations are determined by macroeconomic conditions. Because microeconomics focuses on individuals and macroeconomics focuses on the whole economy, traditionally microeconomics and macroeconomics are taught separately, even though they are interrelated.

A Guide to Economic Reasoning

People trained in economics think in a certain way. They analyze everything critically; they compare the costs and the benefits of every issue and make decisions based on those costs and benefits. For example, say you're trying to decide whether a policy to eliminate terrorist attacks on airlines is a good idea. Economists are trained to put their emotions aside and ask: What are the costs of the policy, and what are the benefits? Thus, they are open to the argument that security measures, such as conducting body searches of every passenger or scanning all baggage with bomb-detecting machinery, might not be the appropriate policy because the costs might exceed the benefits. To think like an economist involves addressing almost all issues using a cost/benefit approach. Economic reasoning also involves abstracting from the "unimportant" elements of a question and focusing on the "important" ones by creating a simple model that captures the essence of the issue or problem. How do you know whether the model has captured the important elements? By collecting empirical evidence and "testing" the model—matching the predictions of the model with the empirical evidence—to see if it fits. Economic reasoning—how to think like a modern economist, making decisions on the basis of costs and benefits—is the most important lesson you'll learn from this book.

Economic reasoning is making decisions on the basis of costs and benefits.

The book *Freakonomics* gives examples of the economist's approach. It describes a number of studies by University of Chicago economist Steve Levitt that unlock seemingly mysterious observations with basic economic reasoning. For example, Levitt asks the question: Why do drug dealers on the street tend to live with their mothers? The answer he arrives at is that it is because they can't afford to live on their own; most earn less than $5 an hour. Why, then, are they dealing drugs and not working a legal job that, even for a minimum-wage job, pays over $7.00 an hour? The answer to that is determined through cost/benefit analysis. While their current income is low, their potential income as a drug dealer is much higher since, given their background and current U.S. institutions, they are more likely to move up to a high position in the local drug business (and *Freakonomics* describes how it is a business) and earn a six-figure income than they are to move up from working as a Taco Bell technician to an executive earning a six-figure income in corporate America. Levitt's model is a very simple one—people do what is in their best interest financially—and it assumes that people rely on a cost/benefit analysis to make decisions. Finally, he supports his argument through careful empirical work, collecting and organizing the data to see if they fit the model. His work is a good example of "thinking like a modern economist" in action.

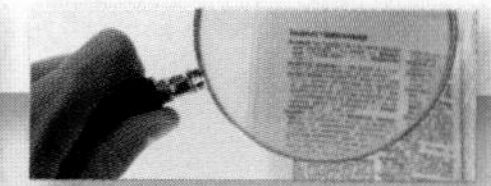

ADDED DIMENSION

Economic Knowledge in One Sentence: TANSTAAFL

Once upon a time, Tanstaafl was made king of all the lands. His first act was to call his economic advisers and tell them to write up all the economic knowledge the society possessed. After years of work, they presented their monumental effort: 25 volumes, each about 400 pages long. But in the interim, King Tanstaafl had become a very busy man, what with running a kingdom of all the lands and all. Looking at the lengthy volumes, he told his advisers to summarize their findings in one volume.

Despondently, the economists returned to their desks, wondering how they could summarize what they'd been so careful to spell out. After many more years of rewriting, they were finally satisfied with their one-volume effort, and tried to make an appointment to see the king. Unfortunately, affairs of state had become even more pressing than before, and the king couldn't take the time to see them. Instead he sent word to them that he couldn't be bothered with a whole volume, and ordered them, under threat of death (for he had become a tyrant), to reduce the work to one sentence.

The economists returned to their desks, shivering in their sandals and pondering their impossible task. Thinking about their fate if they were not successful, they decided to send out for one last meal. Unfortunately, when they were collecting money to pay for the meal, they discovered they were broke. The disgusted delivery man took the last meal back to the restaurant, and the economists started down the path to the beheading station. On the way, the delivery man's parting words echoed in their ears. They looked at each other and suddenly they realized the truth. "We're saved!" they screamed. "That's it! That's economic knowledge in one sentence!" They wrote the sentence down and presented it to the king, who thereafter fully understood all economic problems. (He also gave them a good meal.) The sentence?

There **A**in't **N**o **S**uch **T**hing **A**s **A** **F**ree **L**unch—**TANSTAAFL**

Economic reasoning, once learned, is infectious. If you're susceptible, being exposed to it will change your life. It will influence your analysis of everything, including issues normally considered outside the scope of economics. For example, you will likely use economic reasoning to decide the possibility of getting a date for Saturday night, and who will pay for dinner. You will likely use it to decide whether to read this book, whether to attend class, whom to marry, and what kind of work to go into after you graduate. This is not to say that economic reasoning will provide all the answers. As you will see throughout this book, real-world questions are inevitably complicated, and economic reasoning simply provides a framework within which to approach a question. In the economic way of thinking, every choice has costs and benefits, and decisions are made by comparing them.

Marginal Costs and Marginal Benefits

The relevant costs and relevant benefits to economic reasoning are the expected *incremental,* or additional, costs incurred and the expected *incremental* benefits that result from a decision. Economists use the term *marginal* when referring to additional or incremental. Marginal costs and marginal benefits are key concepts.

A **marginal cost** is *the additional cost to you over and above the costs you have already incurred.* That means not counting **sunk costs**—*costs that have already been incurred and cannot be recovered*—in the relevant costs when making a decision. Consider, for example, attending class. You've already paid your tuition; it is a sunk cost. So the marginal (or additional) cost of going to class does not include tuition.

WWW Web Note 1.1
Costs and Benefits

Similarly with marginal benefit. A **marginal benefit** is *the additional benefit above what you've already derived.* The marginal benefit of reading this chapter is the *additional* knowledge you get from reading it. If you already knew everything in this chapter before you picked up the book, the marginal benefit of reading it now is zero.

Marginal Cost and Marginal Benefit

The Economic Decision Rule

Comparing marginal (additional) costs with marginal (additional) benefits will often tell you how you should adjust your activities to be as well off as possible. Just follow the **economic decision rule:**

If the marginal benefits of doing something exceed the marginal costs, do it. If the marginal costs of doing something exceed the marginal benefits, don't do it.

If the marginal benefits of doing something exceed the marginal costs, do it.

If the marginal costs of doing something exceed the marginal benefits, don't do it.

As an example, let's consider a discussion I might have with a student who tells me that she is too busy to attend my classes. I respond, "Think about the tuition you've spent for this class—it works out to about $60 a lecture." She answers that the book she reads for class is a book that I wrote, and that I wrote it so clearly she fully understands everything. She goes on:

> I've already paid the tuition and whether I go to class or not, I can't get any of the tuition back, so the tuition is a sunk cost and doesn't enter into my decision. The marginal cost to me is what I could be doing with the hour instead of spending it in class. I value my time at $75 an hour [people who understand everything value their time highly], and even though I've heard that your lectures are super, I estimate that the marginal benefit of attending your class is only $50. The marginal cost, $75, exceeds the marginal benefit, $50, so I don't attend class.

Q-2 Say you bought a share of Oracle for $100 and a share of Cisco for $10. The price of each is currently $15. Assuming taxes are not an issue, which would you sell if you need $15?

I congratulate her on her diplomacy and her economic reasoning, but tell her that I give a quiz every week, that students who miss a quiz fail the quiz, that those who fail all the quizzes fail the course, and that those who fail the course do not graduate. In short, she is underestimating the marginal benefits of attending my classes. Correctly estimated, the marginal benefits of attending my class exceed the marginal costs. So she should attend my class.

Economics and Passion

WWW Web Note 1.2 Blogonomics

Recognizing that everything has a cost is reasonable, but it's a reasonableness that many people don't like. It takes some of the passion out of life. It leads you to consider possibilities like these:

- Saving some people's lives with liver transplants might not be worth the additional cost. The money might be better spent on nutritional programs that would save 20 lives for every 2 lives you might save with transplants.
- Maybe we shouldn't try to eliminate all pollution because the additional cost of doing so may be too high. To eliminate all pollution might be to forgo too much of some other worthwhile activity.
- Providing a guaranteed job for every person who wants one might not be a worthwhile policy goal if it means that doing so will reduce the ability of an economy to adapt to new technologies.
- It might make sense for the automobile industry to save $12 per car by not installing a safety device, even though without the safety device some people will be killed.

Economic reasoning is based on the premise that everything has a cost.

You get the idea. This kind of reasonableness is often criticized for being cold-hearted. But, not surprisingly, economists disagree; they argue that their reasoning leads to a better society for the majority of people.

Q-3 Can you think of a reason why a cost/benefit approach to a problem might be inappropriate? Can you give an example?

Economists' reasonableness isn't universally appreciated. Businesses love the result; others aren't so sure, as I discovered some years back when my then-girlfriend told me she was leaving me. "Why?" I asked. "Because," she responded, "you're so, so . . . reasonable." It took me many years after she left to learn what she already knew: There are many types of reasonableness, and not everyone thinks an economist's reasonableness is a virtue. I'll discuss such issues later; for now, let me simply warn you that, for better or worse, studying economics will lead you to view questions in a cost/benefit framework.

Opportunity costs have always made choice difficult, as we see in the early-19th-century engraving *One or the Other.*

Opportunity Cost

Putting economists' cost/benefit rules into practice isn't easy. To do so, you have to be able to choose and measure the costs and benefits correctly. Economists have devised the concept of opportunity cost to help you do that. **Opportunity cost** is *the benefit that you might have gained from choosing the next-best alternative*. To obtain the benefit of something, you must give up (forgo) something else—namely, the next-best alternative. The opportunity cost is the value of that next-best alternative; it is a cost because in choosing one thing, you are precluding an alternative choice. The TANSTAAFL story in the box on page 7 embodies the opportunity cost concept because it tells us that there is a cost to everything; that cost is the next-best forgone alternative.

Opportunity cost is the basis of cost/benefit economic reasoning; it is the benefit that you might have gained from choosing the next-best alternative.

Let's consider some examples. The opportunity cost of going out once with Natalie (or Nathaniel), the most beautiful woman (attractive man) in the world, is the benefit you'd get from going out with your solid steady, Margo (Mike). The opportunity cost of cleaning up the environment might be a reduction in the money available to assist low-income individuals. The opportunity cost of having a child might be two boats, three cars, and a two-week vacation each year for five years, which are what you could have had if you hadn't had the child. (Kids really are this expensive.)

Opportunity Cost

Examples are endless, but let's consider two that are particularly relevant to you: what courses to take and how much to study. Let's say you're a full-time student and at the beginning of the term you had to choose five courses. Taking one precludes taking some other, and the opportunity cost of taking an economics course may well be not taking a course on theater. Similarly with studying: You have a limited amount of time to spend studying economics, studying some other subject, sleeping, or partying. The more time you spend on one activity, the less time you have for another. That's opportunity cost.

Notice how neatly the opportunity cost concept takes into account costs and benefits of all other options, and converts these alternative benefits into costs of the decision you're now making.

WWW Web Note 1.3 Opportunity Cost

The relevance of opportunity cost isn't limited to your individual decisions. Opportunity costs are also relevant to government's decisions, which affect everyone in society. A common example is what is called the guns-versus-butter debate. The resources that a society has are limited; therefore, its decision to use those resources to have more guns (more weapons) means that it will have less butter (fewer consumer goods). Thus, when society decides to spend $50 billion more on an improved health care system, the opportunity cost of that decision is $50 billion not spent on helping the homeless, paying off some of the national debt, or providing for national defense.

ADDED DIMENSION

Economics in Perspective

All too often, students study economics out of context. They're presented with sterile analysis and boring facts to memorize, and are never shown how economics fits into the larger scheme of things. That's bad; it makes economics seem boring—but economics is not boring. Every so often throughout this book, sometimes in the appendixes and sometimes in these boxes, I'll step back and put the analysis in perspective, giving you an idea from whence the analysis sprang and its historical context. In educational jargon, this is called *enrichment.*

I begin here with economics itself.

First, its history: In the 1500s there were few universities. Those that existed taught religion, Latin, Greek, philosophy, history, and mathematics. No economics. Then came the *Enlightenment* (about 1700), in which reasoning replaced God as the explanation of why things were the way they were. Pre-Enlightenment thinkers would answer the question "Why am I poor?" with "Because God wills it." Enlightenment scholars looked for a different explanation. "Because of the nature of land ownership" is one answer they found.

Such reasoned explanations required more knowledge of the way things were, and the amount of information expanded so rapidly that it had to be divided or categorized for an individual to have hope of knowing a subject. Soon philosophy was subdivided into science and philosophy. In the 1700s, the sciences were split into natural sciences and social sciences. The amount of knowledge kept increasing, and in the late 1800s and early 1900s social science itself split into subdivisions: economics, political science, history, geography, sociology, anthropology, and psychology. Many of the insights about how the economic system worked were codified in Adam Smith's *The Wealth of Nations,* written in 1776. Notice that this is before economics as a subdiscipline developed, and Adam Smith could also be classified as an anthropologist, a sociologist, a political scientist, and a social philosopher.

Throughout the 18th and 19th centuries, economists such as Adam Smith, Thomas Malthus, John Stuart Mill, David Ricardo, and Karl Marx were more than economists; they were social philosophers who covered all aspects of social science. These writers were subsequently called *classical economists.* Alfred Marshall continued in that classical tradition, and his book, *Principles of Economics,* published in the late 1800s, was written with the other social sciences much in evidence. But Marshall also changed the questions economists ask; he focused on those questions that could be asked in a graphical supply/demand framework.

This book falls solidly in the Marshallian tradition. It presents economics as a way of thinking—as an engine of analysis used to understand real-world phenomena. But it goes beyond Marshall, and introduces you to a wider variety of models and thinking than the supply and demand models that Marshall used.

Marshallian economics is primarily about policy, not theory. It sees institutions as well as political and social dimensions of reality as important, and it shows you how economics ties in to those dimensions.

Q-4 John, your study partner, has just said that the opportunity cost of studying this chapter is about 1/38 the price you paid for this book, since the chapter is about 1/38 of the book. Is he right? Why or why not?

The opportunity cost concept has endless implications. It can even be turned upon itself. For instance, thinking about alternatives takes time; that means that there's a cost to being reasonable, so it's only reasonable to be somewhat unreasonable. If you followed that argument, you've caught the economic bug. If you didn't, don't worry. Just remember the opportunity cost concept for now; I'll infect you with economic thinking in the rest of the book.

Economic Forces, Social Forces, and Political Forces

Q-5 Ali, your study partner, states that rationing health care is immoral—that health care should be freely available to all individuals in society. How would you respond?

The opportunity cost concept applies to all aspects of life and is fundamental to understanding how society reacts to scarcity. When goods are scarce, those goods must be rationed. That is, a mechanism must be chosen to determine who gets what.

Let's consider some specific real-world rationing mechanisms. Dormitory rooms are often rationed by lottery, and permission to register in popular classes is often rationed by a first-come, first-registered rule. Food in the United States, however, is generally rationed by price. If price did not ration food, there wouldn't be enough food to go around. All scarce goods must be rationed in some fashion. These rationing mechanisms are examples of **economic forces,** *the necessary reactions to scarcity.*

One of the important choices that a society must make is whether to allow these economic forces to operate freely and openly or to try to rein them in. A **market force** is *an economic force that is given relatively free rein by society to work through the market.* Market forces ration by changing prices. When there's a shortage, the price goes up. When there's a surplus, the price goes down. Much of this book will be devoted to analyzing how the market works like an invisible hand, guiding economic forces to coordinate individual actions and allocate scarce resources. The **invisible hand** is *the price mechanism, the rise and fall of prices that guides our actions in a market.*

When an economic force operates through the market, it becomes a market force.

Economic reality is controlled by three forces:

1. Economic forces (the invisible hand).
2. Social and cultural forces.
3. Political and legal forces.

Societies can't choose whether or not to allow economic forces to operate—economic forces are always operating. However, societies can choose whether to allow market forces to predominate. Social, cultural, and political forces play a major role in deciding whether to let market forces operate. Economic reality is determined by a contest among these various forces.

Social, cultural, and political forces can play a significant role in the economy.

Let's consider an example in which social forces prevent an economic force from becoming a market force: the problem of getting a date for Saturday night. If a school (or a society) has significantly more heterosexual people of one gender than the other (let's say more men than women), some men may well find themselves without a date—that is, men will be in excess supply—and will have to find something else to do, say study or go to a movie by themselves. An "excess supply" person could solve the problem by paying someone to go out with him or her, but that would probably change the nature of the date in unacceptable ways. It would be revolting to the person who offered payment and to the person who was offered payment. That unacceptability is an example of the complex social and cultural norms that guide and limit our activities. People don't try to buy dates because social forces prevent them from doing so.

Q-6 Your study partner, Joan, states that market forces are always operative. Is she right? Why or why not?

Now let's consider another example in which political and legal influences stop economic forces from becoming market forces. Say you decide that you can make some money delivering mail in your neighborhood. You try to establish a small business, but suddenly you are confronted with the law. The U.S. Postal Service has a legal exclusive right to deliver regular mail, so you'll be prohibited from delivering regular mail in competition with the post office. Economic forces—the desire to make money—led you to want to enter the business, but in this case political forces squash the invisible hand.

Often political and social forces work together against the invisible hand. For example, in the United States there aren't enough babies to satisfy all the couples who desire them. Babies born to particular sets of parents are rationed—by luck. Consider a group of parents, all of whom want babies. Those who can, have a baby; those who can't have one, but want one, try to adopt. Adoption agencies ration the available babies. Who gets a baby depends on whom people know at the adoption agency and on the desires of the birth mother, who can often specify the socioeconomic background (and many other characteristics) of the family in which she wants her baby to grow up. That's the economic force in action; it gives more power to the supplier of something that's in short supply.

If our society allowed individuals to buy and sell babies, that economic force would be translated into a market force. The invisible hand would see to it that the quantity of babies supplied would equal the quantity of babies demanded at some price. The market, not the adoption agencies, would do the rationing.[2]

Most people, including me, find the idea of selling babies repugnant. But why? It's the strength of social forces reinforced by political forces. One can think of hundreds of examples of such social and political forces overriding economic forces.

What is and isn't allowable differs from one society to another. For example, in Cuba and North Korea, many private businesses are against the law, so not many people start their own businesses. In the United States, until the 1970s, it was against the law to hold gold except in jewelry and for certain limited uses such as dental supplies, so most people refrained from holding gold. Ultimately a country's laws and social norms determine whether the invisible hand will be allowed to work.

WWW Web Note 1.4
Hip Hop Economics

Social and political forces are active in all parts of your life. You don't practice medicine without a license; you don't sell body parts or certain addictive drugs. These actions are against the law. But many people do sell alcohol; that's not against the law if you have a permit. You don't charge your friends interest to borrow money (you'd lose friends); you don't charge your children for their food (parents are supposed to feed their children); many sports and media stars don't sell their autographs (some do, but many consider the practice tacky); you don't lower the wage you'll accept in order to take a job from someone else (you're no scab). The list is long. You cannot understand economics without understanding the limitations that political and social forces place on economic actions.

What happens in society can be seen as a reaction to, and interaction of, economic forces with other forces.

In summary, what happens in a society can be seen as the reaction to, and interaction of three sets of forces: (1) economic forces, (2) political and legal forces, and (3) social and historical forces. Economics has a role to play in sociology, history, and politics, just as sociology, history, and politics have roles to play in economics.

Using Economic Insights

Economic insights are based on generalizations, called theories, about the workings of an abstract economy as well as on contextual knowledge about the institutional structure of the economy. In this book I will introduce you to economic theories and models. Theories and models tie together economists' terminology and knowledge about economic institutions. Theories are inevitably too abstract to apply in specific cases, and thus a theory is often embodied in an **economic model**—*a framework that places the generalized insights of the theory in a more specific contextual setting*—or in an **economic principle**—*a commonly held economic insight stated as a law or principle.* To see the importance of principles, think back to when you learned to add. You didn't memorize the sum of 147 and 138; instead, you learned a principle of addition. The principle says that when adding 147 and 138, you first add 7 + 8, which you memorized was 15. You write down the 5 and carry the 1, which you add to 4 + 3 to get 8. Then add 1 + 1 = 2. So the answer is 285. When you know just one principle, you know how to add millions of combinations of numbers.

Theories, models, and principles are continually "brought to the data" to see if the predictions of the model match the data. Increases in computing power and new statistical

[2]Even though it's against the law, some babies are nonetheless "sold" on a semilegal market, also called a gray market. At the turn of the century, the "market price" for a healthy baby was about $30,000. If selling babies were legal (and if people didn't find it morally repugnant to have babies in order to sell them), the price would be much lower because there would be a larger supply of babies. (It was not against the law to sell human eggs in the early 2000s, and one human egg was sold for $50,000. The average price was much lower; it varied with donor characteristics such as SAT scores and athletic accomplishments.)

techniques have given modern economists a far more rigorous set of procedures to determine how well the predictions fit the data than was the case for earlier economists. This has led to a stronger reliance on quantitative empirical methods in modern economics than in earlier economics.

Modern empirical work takes a variety of forms. In certain instances, economists study questions by running controlled laboratory experiments. That branch of economics is called **experimental economics**—*a branch of economics that studies the economy through controlled laboratory experiments.* Where laboratory experiments are not possible, economists carefully observe the economy and try to figure out what is affecting what. To do so they look for **natural experiments**—*naturally occurring events that approximate a controlled experiment where something has changed in one place but has not changed somewhere else.* Economists can then compare the results in the two cases. An example of a natural experiment was when New Jersey raised its minimum wage and neighboring state Pennsylvania did not. Economists Alan Kruger and David Card compared the effects on unemployment in both states and found that increases in the minimum wage in New Jersey did not significantly affect employment. This led to a debate about what the empirical evidence was telling us. The reason is that in such natural experiments, it is impossible to hold "other things constant," as is done in laboratory experiments, and thus the empirical results in economics are often subject to dispute.

While economic models are less general than theories, they are still usually too general to apply in specific cases. Models lead to **theorems** (*propositions that are logically true based on the assumptions in a model*). To arrive at policy **precepts** (*policy rules that conclude that a particular course of action is preferable*), theorems must be combined with knowledge of real-world economic institutions and value judgments determining the goals for which one is striving. In discussing policy implications of theories and models, it is important to distinguish precepts from theorems.

Theories, models, and principles must be combined with a knowledge of real-world economic institutions to arrive at specific policy recommendations.

The Invisible Hand Theorem

Knowing a theory gives you insight into a wide variety of economic phenomena even though you don't know the particulars of each phenomenon. For example, much of economic theory deals with the *pricing mechanism* and how the market operates to coordinate *individuals' decisions*. Economists have come to the following theorems:

> *When the quantity supplied is greater than the quantity demanded, price has a tendency to fall.*
>
> *When the quantity demanded is greater than the quantity supplied, price has a tendency to rise.*

Q-7 There has been a superb growing season and the quantity of tomatoes supplied exceeds the quantity demanded. What is likely to happen to the price of tomatoes?

Using these generalized theorems, economists have developed a theory of markets that leads to the further theorem that, under certain conditions, markets are efficient. That is, the market will coordinate individuals' decisions, allocating scarce resources efficiently. **Efficiency** means *achieving a goal as cheaply as possible.* Economists call this theorem the **invisible hand theorem**—*a market economy, through the price mechanism, will tend to allocate resources efficiently.*

Theories, and the models used to represent them, are enormously efficient methods of conveying information, but they're also necessarily abstract. They rely on simplifying assumptions, and *if you don't know the assumptions, you don't know the theory.* The result of forgetting assumptions could be similar to what happens if you forget

REAL-WORLD APPLICATION

Winston Churchill and Lady Astor

There are many stories about Nancy Astor, the first woman elected to Britain's Parliament. A vivacious, fearless American woman, she married into the English aristocracy and, during the 1930s and 1940s, became a bright light on the English social and political scenes, which were already quite bright.

One story told about Lady Astor is that she and Winston Churchill, the unorthodox genius who had a long and distinguished political career and who was Britain's prime minister during World War II, were sitting in a pub having a theoretical discussion about morality. Churchill suggested that as a thought experiment Lady Astor ponder the following question: If a man were to promise her a huge amount of money—say a million pounds—for the privilege, would she sleep with him? Lady Astor did ponder the question for a while and finally answered, yes, she would, if the money were guaranteed. Churchill then asked her if she would sleep with him for five pounds. Her response was sharp: "Of course not. What do you think I am—a prostitute?" Churchill responded, "We have already established that fact; we are now simply negotiating about price."

Lady Astor

One moral that economists might draw from this story is that economic incentives, if high enough, can have a powerful influence on behavior. But an equally important moral of the story is that noneconomic incentives also can be very strong. Why do most people feel it's wrong to sell sex for money, even if they might be willing to do so if the price were high enough? Keeping this second moral in mind will significantly increase your economic understanding of real-world events.

that you're supposed to add numbers in columns. Forgetting that, yet remembering all the steps, can lead to a wildly incorrect answer. For example,

$$\begin{array}{r} 147 \\ +138 \\ \hline 1{,}608 \end{array} \text{ is wrong.}$$

Knowing the assumptions of theories and models allows you to progress beyond gut reaction and better understand the strengths and weaknesses of various economic theories and models. Let's consider a central economic assumption: the assumption that individuals behave rationally—that what they choose reflects what makes them happiest, given the constraints. If that assumption doesn't hold, the invisible hand theorem doesn't hold.

I find it useful to distinguish two types of modern economists: modern traditional economists and modern behavioral economists. Modern traditional economists use models that focus on traditional assumptions of rationality and self-interest; modern behavioral economists modify these assumptions, and are working on models that incorporate some predictably irrational behavior. Yet another group of modern economists deemphasizes deductive models almost completely and develops empirical models that are primarily based on statistical patterns they discover in data.

Presenting the invisible hand theorem in its full beauty is an important part of any economics course. Presenting the assumptions on which it is based and the limitations of the invisible hand is likewise an important part of the course. I'll do both throughout the book.

Economic Theory and Stories

Theory is a shorthand way of telling a story.

Economic theory, and the models in which that theory is presented, often developed as a shorthand way of telling a story. These stories are important; they make the theory come alive and convey the insights that give economic theory its power. In this book I present plenty of theories and models, but they're accompanied by stories that provide the context that makes them relevant.

At times, because there are many new terms, discussing theories takes up much of the presentation time and becomes a bit oppressive. That's the nature of the beast. As Albert Einstein said, "Theories should be as simple as possible, but not more so." When a theory becomes oppressive, pause and think about the underlying story that the theory is meant to convey. That story should make sense and be concrete. If you can't translate the theory into a story, you don't understand the theory.

Economic Institutions

To know whether you can apply economic theory to reality, you must know about economic institutions—laws, common practices, and organizations in a society that affect the economy. Corporations, governments, and cultural norms are all examples of economic institutions. Many economic institutions have social, political, and religious dimensions. For example, your job often influences your social standing. In addition, many social institutions, such as the family, have economic functions. I include any institution that significantly affects economic decisions as an economic institution because you must understand that institution if you are to understand how the economy functions.

To apply economic theory to reality, you've got to have a sense of economic institutions.

Economic institutions differ significantly among countries. For example, in Germany banks are allowed to own companies; in the United States they cannot. This helps explain why investment decisions are made differently in Germany as compared to the United States. Alternatively, in the Netherlands workers are highly unionized, while in the United States they are not. Unions in the Netherlands therefore have the power to agree to keep wages lower in exchange for more jobs. This means that government policies to control inflation might differ in these two countries.

Economic institutions sometimes seem to operate in ways quite different than economic theory predicts. For example, economic theory says that prices are determined by supply and demand. However, businesses say that they set prices by rules of thumb—often by what are called cost-plus-markup rules. That is, a firm determines what its costs are, multiplies by 1.4 or 1.5, and the result is the price it sets. Economic theory says that supply and demand determine who's hired; experience suggests that hiring is often done on the basis of whom you know, not by market forces.

These apparent contradictions have two complementary explanations. First, economic theory abstracts from many issues. These issues may account for the differences. Second, there's no contradiction; economic principles often affect decisions from behind the scenes. For instance, supply and demand pressures determine what the price markup over cost will be. In all cases, however, to apply economic theory to reality—to gain the full value of economic insights—you've got to have a sense of economic institutions.

Economic Policy Options

Economic policies are *actions (or inaction) taken by government to influence economic actions.* The final goal of the course is to present the economic policy options facing our society today. For example, should the government restrict mergers between firms? Should it run a budget deficit? Should it do something about the international trade deficit? Should it decrease taxes?

I saved this discussion for last because there's no sense talking about policy options unless you know some economic terminology, some economic theory, and something about economic institutions. Once you know something about them, you're in a position

REAL-WORLD APPLICATION

Economists and Market Solutions

Economic reasoning is playing an increasing role in government policy. Consider the regulation of pollution. Pollution became a policy concern in the 1960s as books such as Rachel Carson's *Silent Spring* were published. In 1970, in response to concerns about the environment, the Clean Air Act was passed. It capped the amount of pollutants (such as sulfur dioxide, carbon monoxide, nitrogen dioxides, lead, and hydrocarbons) that firms could emit. This was a "command-and-control" approach to regulation, which brought about a reduction in pollution, but also brought about lots of complaints by firms that either found the limits costly to meet or couldn't afford to meet them and were forced to close.

Enter economists. They proposed an alternative approach, called cap-and-trade, that achieved the same overall reduction in pollution but at a lower overall cost. In the plan they proposed, government still set a pollution cap that firms had to meet, but it gave individual firms some flexibility. Firms that reduced emissions by less than the required limit could buy pollution permits from other firms that reduced their emissions by more than their limit. The price of the permits would be determined in an "emissions permit market." Thus, firms that had a low cost of reducing pollution would have a strong incentive to reduce pollution by more than their limit in order to sell these permits, or rights to pollute, to firms that had a high cost of reducing pollution and therefore could reduce their pollution by less than what was required. The net reduction was the same, but the reduction was achieved at a lower cost.

In 1990 Congress adopted economists' proposal and the Clean Air Act was amended to include tradable emissions permits. An active market in emissions permits developed and it is estimated that the tradable permit program has lowered the cost of reducing sulfur dioxide emissions by $1 billion a year while at the same time, reducing emissions by more than half, to levels significantly below the cap. Economists used this same argument to promote an incentive-based solution to world pollution in an agreement among some countries known as the Kyoto Protocol. In this plan countries would agree to caps with emissions permits traded on a global market. You can read more about the current state of tradable emissions at www.epa.gov/airmarkets.

to consider the policy options available for dealing with the economic problems our society faces.

To carry out economic policy effectively, one must understand how institutions might change as a result of the economic policy.

Policies operate within institutions, but policies also can influence the institutions within which they operate. Let's consider an example: welfare policy and the institution of the two-parent family. In the 1960s, the United States developed a variety of policy initiatives designed to eliminate poverty. These initiatives provided income to single parents with children, and assumed that family structure would be unchanged by these policies. But family structure changed substantially, and, very likely, these policies played a role in increasing the number of single-parent families. The result was the programs failed to eliminate poverty. Now this is not to say that we should not have programs to eliminate poverty, nor that two-parent families are always preferable to one-parent families; it is only to say that we must build into our policies their effect on institutions.

Q-8 True or false? Economists should focus their policy analysis on institutional changes because such policies offer the largest gains.

Objective Policy Analysis

Good economic policy analysis is objective; that is, it keeps the analyst's value judgments separate from the analysis. Objective analysis does not say, "This is the way things should be," reflecting a goal established by the analyst. That would be subjective analysis because it would reflect the analyst's view of how things should be. Instead, objective analysis says, "This is the way the economy works, and if society (or the individual or firm for whom you're doing the analysis) wants to achieve a particular goal, this is how it might go about doing so." Objective analysis keeps, or at least tries to keep, subjective views—value judgments—separate.

To make clear the distinction between objective and subjective analysis, economists have divided economics into three categories: *positive economics, normative economics,* and the *art of economics.* **Positive economics** is *the study of what is, and how the economy works.* It explores the pure theory of economics, and it discovers agreed-upon empirical regularities. These empirical regularities are often called empirical facts—for example, large price fluctuations in financial markets tend to be followed by additional large price fluctuations. Economic theorists then relate their theories to those facts. Positive economics asks such questions as: How does the market for hog bellies work? How do price restrictions affect market forces? These questions fall under the heading of economic theory.

Positive economics is the study of what is, and how the economy works.

As I stated above, economic theory does not provide definitive policy recommendations. It is too abstract and makes too many assumptions that don't match observed behavior. In positive economic theory, one looks for empirical facts and develops *theorems*—propositions that logically follow from the assumptions of one's model. Theorems and agreed-upon empirical facts are almost by definition beyond dispute and serve as the foundation for economic science. But these theorems don't tell us what policies should be followed.

Q-9 John, your study partner, is a free market advocate. He argues that the invisible hand theorem tells us that the government should not interfere with the economy. Do you agree? Why or why not?

Policies are built on two other branches of economics: normative economics and political economy, or the art of economics. **Normative economics** is *the study of what the goals of the economy should be.* Normative economics asks such questions as: What should the distribution of income be? What should tax policy be designed to achieve? In discussing such questions, economists must carefully delineate whose goals they are discussing. One cannot simply assume that one's own goals for society are society's goals. For example, let's consider a debate that is currently ongoing in economics. Some economists are worried about global warming; they believe that high consumption in rich societies is causing global warming and that the high consumption is a result of interdependent wants—people want something only because other people have it—but having it isn't necessarily making people happier. These economists argue that society's normative goal should include a much greater focus on the implications of economic activities for global warming, and the distribution of income, than is currently the case. Discussion of these goals falls under the category of normative economics.

Normative economics is the study of what the goals of the economy should be.

The **art of economics,** also called political economy, is *the application of the knowledge learned in positive economics to achieve the goals one has determined in normative economics.* It looks at such questions as: To achieve the goals that society wants to achieve, how would you go about it, given the way the economy works?[3] Most policy discussions fall under the art of economics. The art of economics branch is specifically about policy; it is designed to arrive at *precepts,* or guides for policy. Precepts are based on theorems and empirical facts developed in positive economics and goals developed in normative economics. The art of economics requires economists to assess the appropriateness of theorems to achieving the normative goals in the real world. Whereas once the assumptions are agreed upon, theorems derived from models are not debatable, precepts are debatable, and economists that use the same theorems can hold

The art of economics is the application of the knowledge learned in positive economics to achieve the goals determined in normative economics.

[3]This three-part distinction was made back in 1891 by a famous economist, John Neville Keynes, father of John Maynard Keynes, the economist who developed macroeconomics. This distinction was instilled into modern economics by Milton Friedman and Richard Lipsey in the 1950s. They, however, downplayed the art of economics, which J. N. Keynes had seen as central to understanding the economist's role in policy. In his discussion of the scope and method of economics, Lionel Robbins used the term "political economy" rather than Keynes' term "the art of economics."

REAL-WORLD APPLICATION

Economics and Global Warming

A good example of the central role that economics plays in policy debates is the debate about global warming. Almost all scientists are now convinced that global warming is occurring and that human activity such as the burning of fossil fuel is one of the causes. The policy question is what to do about it. To answer that question, most governments have turned to economists. The first part of the question that economists have considered is whether it is worth doing anything, and in a well-publicized report commissioned by the British government, economist Nicholas Stern argued that, based upon his cost/benefit analysis, yes it is worth doing something. The reason: Because the costs of not doing anything would likely reduce output by 20 percent in the future, and that those costs (appropriately weighted for when they occur) are less than the benefits of policies that can be implemented.

The second part of the question is: What policies to implement? The policies he recommended were policies that changed incentives—specifically, policies that raised the costs of emitting greenhouse gases and decreased the cost of other forms of production. Those recommended policies reflected the economist's opportunity cost framework in action: if you want to change the result, change the incentives that individuals face.

There is considerable debate about Stern's analysis—both with the way he conducted the cost/benefit analysis and with his policy recommendations. Such debates are inevitable when the data are incomplete and numerous judgments need to be made. I suspect that these debates will continue over the coming years with economists on various sides of the debate. Economists are generally not united in their views about complicated policy issues since they differ in their normative views and in their assessment of the problem and of what politically can be achieved; that's because policy is part of the art of economics, not part of positive economics. But the framework of the policy debate about global warming is the economic framework. Thus, even though political forces will ultimately choose what policy is followed, you must understand the economic framework to take part in the debate.

Q-10 Tell whether the following five statements belong in positive economics, normative economics, or the art of economics.

1. We should support the market because it is efficient.
2. Given certain conditions, the market achieves efficient results.
3. Based on past experience and our understanding of markets, if one wants a reasonably efficient result, markets should probably be relied on.
4. The distribution of income should be left to markets.
5. Markets allocate income according to contributions of factors of production.

Web Note 1.5
The Art of Economics

different precepts. For example, a model may tell us that rent controls will cause a shortage of housing. That does not mean that rent controls are necessarily bad policies since rent controls may also have some desirable effects. The precept that rent controls are bad policy is based upon a judgment about the importance of those other effects, and one's normative judgments about the benefits and costs of the policy. In this book, when I say that economists tend to favor a policy, I am talking about precepts, which means that alternative perspectives are possible even among economists.

In each of these three branches of economics, economists separate their own value judgments from their objective analysis as much as possible. The qualifier "as much as possible" is important, since some value judgments inevitably sneak in. We are products of our environment, and the questions we ask, the framework we use, and the way we interpret the evidence all involve value judgments and reflect our backgrounds.

Maintaining objectivity is easiest in positive economics, where you are working with abstract models to understand how the economy works. Maintaining objectivity is harder in normative economics. You must always be objective about whose normative values you are using. It's easy to assume that all of society shares your values, but that assumption is often wrong.

Maintaining objectivity is hardest in the art of economics because it can suffer from the problems of both positive and normative economics. Because noneconomic forces affect policy, to practice the art of economics we must make judgments about how these noneconomic forces work. These judgments are likely to reflect our own value judgments. So we must be exceedingly careful to be as objective as possible in practicing the art of economics.

Policy and Social and Political Forces

When you think about the policy options facing society, you'll quickly discover that the choice of policy options depends on much more than economic theory. Politicians, not economists, determine economic policy. To understand what policies are chosen, you must take into account historical precedent plus social, cultural, and political forces. In an economics course, I don't have time to analyze these forces in as much depth as I'd like. That's one reason there are separate history, political science, sociology, and anthropology courses.

While it is true that these other forces play significant roles in policy decisions, specialization is necessary. In economics, we focus the analysis on the invisible hand, and much of economic theory is devoted to considering how the economy would operate if the invisible hand were the only force operating. But as soon as we apply theory to reality and policy, we must take into account political and social forces as well.

An example will make my point more concrete. Most economists agree that holding down or eliminating tariffs (taxes on imports) and quotas (numerical limitations on imports) makes good economic sense. They strongly advise governments to follow a policy of free trade. Do governments follow free trade policies? Almost invariably they do not. Politics leads society in a different direction. If you're advising a policy maker, you need to point out that these other forces must be taken into account, and how other forces should (if they should) and can (if they can) be integrated with your recommendations.

Conclusion

Tons more could be said to introduce you to economics, but an introduction must remain an introduction. As it is, this chapter should have:

1. Introduced you to economic reasoning.
2. Surveyed what we're going to cover in this book.
3. Given you an idea of my writing style and approach.

We'll be spending long hours together over the coming term, and before entering into such a commitment it's best to know your partner. While I won't know you, by the end of this book you'll know me. Maybe you won't love me as my mother does, but you'll know me.

This introduction was my opening line. I hope it also conveyed the importance and relevance of economics. If it did, it has served its intended purpose. Economics is tough, but tough can be fun.

Summary

- The three coordination problems any economy must solve are what to produce, how to produce it, and for whom to produce it. In solving these problems, societies have found that there is a problem of scarcity. *(LO1-1)*
- Economics can be divided into microeconomics and macroeconomics. Microeconomics is the study of individual choice and how that choice is influenced by economic forces. Macroeconomics is the study of the economy as a whole. It considers problems such as inflation, unemployment, business cycles, and growth. *(LO1-1)*
- Economic reasoning structures all questions in a cost/benefit framework: If the marginal benefits of doing something exceed the marginal costs, do it. If the

marginal costs exceed the marginal benefits, don't do it. *(LO1-2)*

- Sunk costs are not relevant in the economic decision rule. *(LO1-2)*
- The opportunity cost of undertaking an activity is the benefit you might have gained from choosing the next-best alternative. *(LO1-2)*
- "There ain't no such thing as a free lunch" (TANSTAAFL) embodies the opportunity cost concept. *(LO1-2)*
- Economic forces, the forces of scarcity, are always working. Market forces, which ration by changing prices, are not always allowed to work. *(LO1-3)*
- Economic reality is controlled and directed by three types of forces: economic forces, political forces, and social forces. *(LO1-3)*
- Under certain conditions, the market, through its price mechanism, will allocate scarce resources efficiently. *(LO1-4)*
- Theorems are propositions that follow from the assumptions of a model; precepts are the guides for policies based on theorems, normative judgments, and empirical observations about how the real world differs from the model. *(LO1-4)*
- Economics can be subdivided into positive economics, normative economics, and the art of economics. Positive economics is the study of what is, normative economics is the study of what should be, and the art of economics relates positive to normative economics. *(LO1-5)*

Key Terms

art of economics *(17)*
economic decision rule *(8)*
economic force *(11)*
economic model *(12)*
economic policy *(15)*
economic principle *(12)*
economics *(4)*
efficiency *(13)*
experimental economics *(13)*
invisible hand *(11)*
invisible hand theorem *(13)*
macroeconomics *(5)*
marginal benefit *(7)*
marginal cost *(7)*
market force *(11)*
microeconomics *(5)*
natural experiment *(13)*
normative economics *(17)*
opportunity cost *(9)*
positive economics *(17)*
precept *(13)*
scarcity *(5)*
sunk cost *(7)*
theorem *(13)*

Questions and Exercises

1. Why does the textbook author focus on coordination rather than on scarcity when defining economics? *(LO1-1)*
2. State whether the following are primarily microeconomic or macroeconomic policy issues: *(LO1-1)*
   a. Should U.S. interest rates be lowered to decrease the amount of unemployment?
   b. Will the fact that more and more doctors are selling their practices to managed care networks increase the efficiency of medical providers?
   c. Should the current federal income tax be lowered to reduce unemployment?
   d. Should the federal minimum wage be raised?
   e. Should Sprint and Verizon both be allowed to build local phone networks?
   f. Should commercial banks be required to provide loans in all areas of the territory from which they accept deposits?
3. List two microeconomic and two macroeconomic problems. *(LO1-1)*
4. Calculate, using the best estimates you can: *(LO1-2)*
   a. Your opportunity cost of attending college.
   b. Your opportunity cost of taking this course.
   c. Your opportunity cost of attending yesterday's lecture in this course.
5. List one recent choice you made and explain why you made the choice in terms of marginal benefits and marginal costs. *(LO1-2)*
6. You rent a car for $29.95. The first 150 miles are free, but each mile thereafter costs 15 cents. You plan to drive it 200 miles. What is the marginal cost of driving the car? *(LO1-2)*
7. Economists Henry Saffer of Kean University, Frank J. Chaloupka of the University of Illinois at Chicago, and Dhaval Dave of Bentley College estimated that the

government must spend $4,170 on drug control to deter one person from using drugs and the cost that one drug user imposes on society is $897. Based on this information alone, should the government spend the money on drug control? (*LO1-2*)

8. What is the opportunity cost of buying a $20,000 car? (*LO1-2*)
9. Suppose you currently earn $30,000 a year. You are considering a job that will increase your lifetime earnings by $300,000 but that requires an MBA. The job will mean also attending business school for two years at an annual cost of $25,000. You already have a bachelor's degree, for which you spent $80,000 in tuition and books. Which of the above information is relevant to your decision whether to take the job? (*LO1-2*)
10. Suppose your college has been given $5 million. You have been asked to decide how to spend it to improve your college. Explain how you would use the economic decision rule and the concept of opportunity costs to decide how to spend it. (*LO1-2*)
11. Give two examples of social forces and explain how they keep economic forces from becoming market forces. (*LO1-3*)
12. Give two examples of political or legal forces and explain how they might interact with economic forces. (*LO1-3*)
13. Individuals have two kidneys, but most of us need only one. People who have lost both kidneys through accident or disease must be hooked up to a dialysis machine, which cleanses waste from their bodies. Say a person who has two good kidneys offers to sell one of them to someone whose kidney function has been totally destroyed. The seller asks $30,000 for the kidney, and the person who has lost both kidneys accepts the offer. (*LO1-3*)
    a. Who benefits from the deal?
    b. Who is hurt?
    c. Should a society allow such market transactions? Why?
14. What is an economic model? What besides a model do economists need to make policy recommendations? (*LO1-4*)
15. Does economic theory prove that the free market system is best? Why? (Difficult) (*LO1-4*)
16. Distinguish between theorems and precepts. Is it possible for two economists to agree about theorems but disagree about precepts? Why or why not? (*LO1-4*)
17. What is the difference between normative and positive statements? (*LO1-5*)
18. State whether the following statements belong in positive economics, normative economics, or the art of economics. (*LO1-5*)
    a. In a market, when quantity supplied exceeds quantity demanded, price tends to fall.
    b. When determining tax rates, the government should take into account the income needs of individuals.
    c. When deciding which rationing mechanism is best (lottery, price, first-come/first-served), one must take into account the goals of society.
    d. California currently rations water to farmers at subsidized prices. Once California allows the trading of water rights, it will allow economic forces to be a market force.

Questions from Alternative Perspectives

1. Is it possible to use objective economic analysis as a basis for government planning? (Austrian)
2. In "Rational Choice with Passion: Virtue in a Model of Rational Addiction," Andrew M. Yuengert of Pepperdine University argues that there is a conflict between reason and passion.
    a. What might that conflict be?
    b. What implications does it have for applying the economic model? (Religious)
3. Economic institutions are "habits of thought" that organize society.
    a. In what way might patriarchy be an *institution* and how might it influence the labor market?
    b. Does the free market or patriarchy better explain why 98 percent of secretaries are women and 98 percent of automobile mechanics are men? (Feminist)
4. In October of 2004, the supply of flu vaccine fell by over 50 percent. The result was that the vaccine had to be rationed, with a priority schedule established: young children, people with weakened immunity, those over 65, etc., taking priority.
    a. Compare and contrast this allocation outcome with a free market outcome.
    b. Which alternative is more just? (Institutionalist)
5. The textbook model assumes that individuals have enough knowledge to follow the economic decision rule.
    a. How did you decide what college you would attend?
    b. Did you have enough knowledge to follow the economic decision rule?
    c. For what type of decisions do you not use the economic decision rule?
    d. What are the implications for economic analysis if most people don't follow the economic decision rule in many aspects of their decisions? (Post-Keynesian)

6. Radical economists believe that all of economics, like all theorizing or storytelling, is value-laden. Theories and stories reflect the values of those who compose them and tell them. For instance, radicals offer a different analysis than most economists of how capitalism works and what ought to be done about its most plaguing problems: inequality, periodic economic crises with large-scale unemployment, and the alienation of the workers.
   a. What does the radical position imply about the distinction between positive economics and normative economics that the text makes?
   b. Is economics value-laden or objective and is the distinction between positive and normative economics tenable or untenable? (Radical)

Issues to Ponder

1. At times we all regret decisions. Does this necessarily mean we did not use the economic decision rule when making the decision?
2. Economist Steven Landsburg argues that if one believes in the death penalty for murderers because of its deterrent effect, using cost/benefit analysis we should execute computer hackers—the creators of worms and viruses—because the deterrent effect in cost saving would be greater than the deterrent effect in saving lives. Estimates are that each execution deters eight murders, which, if one valued each life at about $7 million, saves about $56 million; he estimates that executing hackers would save more than that per execution, and thus would be the economic thing to do.
   a. Do you agree or disagree with Landsburg's argument? Why?
   b. Can you extend cost/benefit analysis to other areas?
3. Adam Smith, who wrote *The Wealth of Nations,* and who is seen as the father of modern economics, also wrote *The Theory of Moral Sentiments*. In it he argued that society would be better off if people weren't so selfish and were more considerate of others. How does this view fit with the discussion of economic reasoning presented in the chapter?
4. A *Wall Street Journal* article asked readers the following questions. What's your answer?
   a. An accident has caused deadly fumes to enter the school ventilation system where it will kill five children. You can stop it by throwing a switch, but doing so will kill one child in another room. Do you throw the switch?
   b. Say that a doctor can save five patients with an organ transplant that would end the life of a patient who is sick, but not yet dead. Does she do it?
   c. What is the difference between the two situations described in *a* and *b*?
   d. How important are opportunity costs in your decisions?
5. Economics is about strategic thinking, and the strategies can get very complicated. Suppose you kiss someone and ask whether the person liked it. You'd like the person to answer "yes" and you'd like that answer to be truthful. But they know that, and if they like you, they may well say that they liked the kiss even if they didn't. But you know that, and thus might not really believe that they liked the kiss; they're just saying "yes" because that's what you want to hear. But they know that you know that, so sometimes they have to convey a sense that they didn't like it, so that you will believe them when they say that they did like it. But you know that . . . You get the picture.
   a. Should you always be honest, even when it hurts someone?
   b. What strategies can you figure out to avoid the problem of not believing the other person?
6. Go to two stores: a supermarket and a convenience store.
   a. Write down the cost of a gallon of milk in each.
   b. The prices are most likely different. Using the terminology used in this chapter, explain why that is the case and why anyone would buy milk in the store with the higher price.
   c. Do the same exercise with shirts or dresses in Walmart (or its equivalent) and Saks (or its equivalent).
7. About 100,000 individuals in the United States are waiting for organ transplants, and at an appropriate price many individuals would be willing to supply organs. Given those facts, should human organs be allowed to be bought and sold?
8. Name an economic institution and explain how it affects economic decision making or how its actions reflect economic principles.
9. Tyler Cowen, an economist at George Mason University, presents an interesting case that pits the market against legal and social forces. The case involves payola—the payment of money to disk jockeys for playing a songwriter's songs. He reports that Chuck Berry was having a hard time getting his music played because of racism. To counter this, he offered a well-known disk jockey, Alan Freed, partial songwriting credits, along with partial royalties, on any Chuck Berry song of his choice. He chose *Maybellene,*

which he played and promoted. It went on to be a hit, Chuck Berry went on to be a star, and Freed's estate continues to receive royalties.

a. Should such payments be allowed? Why?
b. How did Freed's incentives from the royalty payment differ from Freed's incentives if Chuck Berry had just offered him a flat payment?
c. Name two other examples of similar activities—one that is legal and one that is not.

10. Name three ways a limited number of dormitory rooms could be rationed. How would economic forces determine individual behavior in each? How would social or legal forces determine whether those economic forces become market forces?
11. Prospect theory suggests that people are hurt more by losses than they are uplifted by gains of a corresponding size. If that is true, what implications would it have for economic policy?
12. Is a good economist always objective? Explain your answer.

Answers to Margin Questions

1. (1) Macroeconomics; (2) Microeconomics; (3) Microeconomics; (4) Macroeconomics. (*p. 6; LO1-1*)
2. Since the price of both stocks is now $15, it doesn't matter which one you sell (assuming no differential capital gains taxation). The price you bought them for doesn't matter; it's a sunk cost. Marginal analysis refers to the future gain, so what you expect to happen to future prices of the stocks—not past prices—should determine which stock you decide to sell. (*p. 8; LO1-2*)
3. A cost/benefit analysis requires that you put a value on a good, and placing a value on a good can be seen as demeaning it. Consider love. Try telling an acquaintance that you'd like to buy his or her spiritual love, and see what response you get. (*p. 8; LO1-2*)
4. John is wrong. The opportunity cost of reading the chapter is primarily the time you spend reading it. Reading the book prevents you from doing other things. Assuming that you already paid for the book, the original price is no longer part of the opportunity cost; it is a sunk cost. Bygones are bygones. (*p. 10; LO1-2*)
5. Whenever there is scarcity, the scarce good must be rationed by some means. Free health care has an opportunity cost in other resources. So if health care is not rationed, to get the resources to supply that care, other goods would have to be more tightly rationed than they currently are. It is likely that the opportunity cost of supplying free health care would be larger than most societies would be willing to pay. (*p. 10; LO1-3*)
6. Joan is wrong. Economic forces are always operative; market forces are not. (*p. 11; LO1-3*)
7. According to the invisible hand theorem, the price of tomatoes will likely fall. (*p. 13; LO1-4*)
8. False. While such changes have the largest gain, they also may have the largest cost. The policies economists should focus on are those that offer the largest net gain—benefits minus costs—to society. (*p. 16; LO1-5*)
9. He is wrong. The invisible hand theorem is a positive theorem and does not tell us anything about policy. To do so would be to violate Hume's dictum that a "should" cannot be derived from an "is." This is not to say that government should or should not interfere; whether government should interfere is a very difficult question. (*p. 17; LO1-5*)
10. (1) Normative; (2) Positive; (3) Art; (4) Normative; (5) Positive. (*p. 18; LO1-5*)

chapter 2

The Production Possibility Model, Trade, and Globalization

> *No one ever saw a dog make a fair and deliberate exchange of one bone for another with another dog.*
>
> —Adam Smith

After reading this chapter, you should be able to:

- **LO2-1** Demonstrate trade-offs with a production possibility curve.
- **LO2-2** Relate the concepts of comparative advantage and efficiency to the production possibility curve.
- **LO2-3** State how, through comparative advantage and trade, countries can consume beyond their individual production possibilities.
- **LO2-4** Explain how globalization is guided by the law of one price.

Every economy must solve three main coordination problems:

1. What, and how much, to produce.
2. How to produce it.
3. For whom to produce it.

In Chapter 1, I suggested that you can boil down all economic knowledge into the single phrase "There ain't no such thing as a free lunch." There's obviously more to economics than that, but it's not a bad summary of the core of economic reasoning—it's relevant for an individual, for nonprofit organizations, for governments, and for nations. Oh, it's true that once in a while you can snitch a sandwich, but what economics tells you is that if you're offered something that approaches free-lunch status, you should also be on the lookout for some hidden cost.

Economists have a model, the production possibility model, that conveys the trade-offs society faces. This model is important for understanding not only the trade-offs society faces but also why people specialize in what they do and trade for the goods they need. Through specialization and trade, individuals, firms, and countries can achieve greater levels of output than they could otherwise achieve.

The Production Possibilities Model

The production possibilities model can be presented both in a table and in a graph. (Appendix A has a discussion of graphs in economics.) I'll start with the table and then move from that to the graph. A **production possibility table** is *a table that lists the trade-offs between two choices.*

A Production Possibility Curve for an Individual

Let's consider a study-time/grades example. Say you have exactly 20 hours a week to devote to two courses: economics and history. (So maybe I'm a bit optimistic.) Grades are given numerically and you know that the following relationships exist: If you study 20 hours in economics, you'll get a grade of 100; 18 hours, 94; and so forth.[1]

Let's say that the best you can do in history is a 98 with 20 hours of study a week; 19 hours of study guarantees a 96, and so on. The production possibility table in Figure 2-1(a) shows the highest combination of grades you can get with various allocations of the 20 hours available for studying the two subjects. One possibility is getting 70 in economics and 78 in history.

Q-1 In the graph below, what is the opportunity cost of producing an extra unit of good *X* in terms of good *Y*?

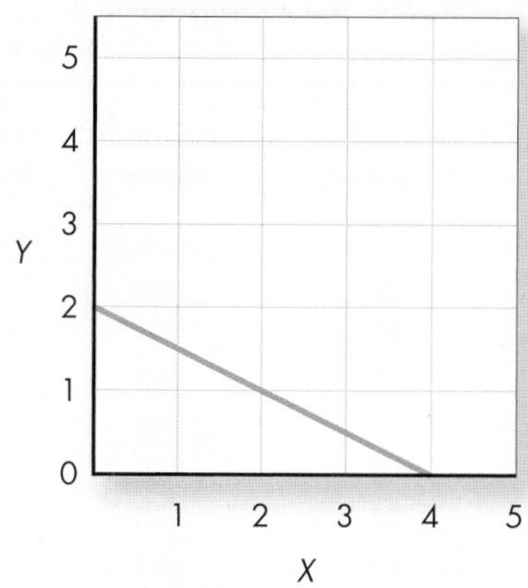

Notice that the opportunity cost of studying one subject rather than the other is embodied in the production possibility table. The information in the table comes from experience: We are assuming that you've discovered that if you transfer an hour of study from economics to history, you'll lose 3 points on your grade in economics and gain 2 points in history. Assuming studying economics is your next best alternative, the opportunity cost of a 2-point rise in your history grade is a 3-point decrease in your economics grade.

The information in the production possibility table also can be presented graphically in a diagram called a production possibility curve. A **production possibility curve (PPC)** is *a curve measuring the maximum combination of outputs that can be obtained from a given number of inputs.* It gives you a visual picture of the tradeoff embodied in a decision.

The production possibility curve is a curve measuring the maximum combination of outputs that can be obtained from a given number of inputs.

A production possibility curve is created from a production possibility table by mapping the table in a two-dimensional graph. I've taken the information from the table in Figure 2-1(a) and mapped it into Figure 2-1(b). The history grade is mapped, or plotted, on the horizontal axis; the economics grade is on the vertical axis.

As you can see from the bottom row of Figure 2-1(a), if you study economics for all 20 hours and study history for 0 hours, you'll get grades of 100 in economics and 58 in history. Point *A* in Figure 2-1(b) represents that choice. If you study history for all 20 hours and study economics for 0 hours, you'll get a 98 in history and a 40 in economics. Point *E* represents that choice. Points *B, C,* and *D* represent three possible choices between these two extremes.

Notice that the production possibility curve slopes downward from left to right. That means that there is an inverse relationship (a trade-off) between grades in economics and grades in history. The better the grade in economics, the worse the grade in history, and vice versa.

The slope of the production possibility curve tells you the trade-off between the cost of one good in terms of another.

To summarize, the production possibility curve demonstrates that:

1. There is a limit to what you can achieve, given the existing institutions, resources, and technology.
2. Every choice you make has an opportunity cost. You can get more of something only by giving up something else.

Increasing Opportunity Costs of the Trade-off

In the study-time/grade example, the cost of one grade in terms of the other remained constant; you could always trade two points on your history grade for three points on your economics grade. This assumption of an unchanging trade-off made the production possibility curve a straight line. Although this made the example easier, is it realistic? Probably not, especially if we are using the PPC to describe the choices that a

Production Possibilities Curve

[1]Throughout the book I'll be presenting numerical examples to help you understand the concepts. The numbers I choose are often arbitrary. After all, you have to choose something. As an exercise, you might choose different numbers than I did, numbers that apply to your own life, and work out the argument using those numbers.

FIGURE 2-1 (A AND B) A Production Possibility Table and Curve for Grades in Economics and History

The production possibility table (**a**) shows the highest combination of grades you can get with only 20 hours available for studying economics and history. The information in the production possibility table in (**a**) can be plotted on a graph, as is done in (**b**). The grade received in economics is on the vertical axis, and the grade received in history is on the horizontal axis.

Hours of Study in History	Grade in History	Hours of Study in Economics	Grade in Economics
20	98	0	40
19	96	1	43
18	94	2	46
17	92	3	49
16	90	4	52
15	88	5	55
14	86	6	58
13	84	7	61
12	82	8	64
11	80	9	67
10	78	10	70
9	76	11	73
8	74	12	76
7	72	13	79
6	70	14	82
5	68	15	85
4	66	16	88
3	64	17	91
2	62	18	94
1	60	19	97
0	58	20	100

(a) Production Possibility Table

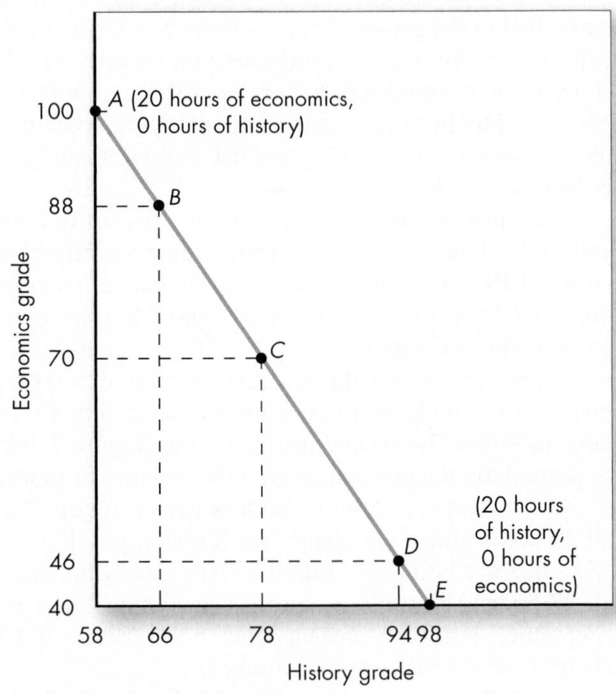

(b) Production Possibility Curve

society makes. For many of the choices society must make the perceived opportunity costs of society's next best alternative tend to increase as we choose more and more of an item. This principle can be summarized as follows:

> *In order to get more of something, generally one must give up ever-increasing quantities of something else.*

The principle of increasing marginal opportunity cost tells us that opportunity costs increase the more you concentrate on the activity.

In other words, initially the opportunity costs of an activity are low, but they increase the more we concentrate on that activity. A production possibility curve that exhibits increasing opportunity costs of a trade-off is bowed outward, as in Figure 2-2(b).

Why are production possibility curves typically bowed outward? Because some resources are better suited for the production of certain kinds of goods than other kinds of goods. To understand what that means, let's talk about the graph in Figure 2-2(b), which is derived from the table in Figure 2-2(a). This curve represents society's choice between defense spending (guns) and spending on domestic needs (butter).

Suppose society is producing only butter (point *A*). Giving up a little butter (1 pound) initially gains us a lot of guns (4), moving us to point *B*. The next 2 pounds of butter we give up gain us slightly fewer guns (point *C*). If we continue to trade butter for guns, we find that at point *D* we gain very few guns from giving up a pound of butter. The opportunity cost of choosing guns in terms of butter increases as we increase the production of guns.

FIGURE 2-2 (A AND B) A Production Possibility Table and Curve

The table in (**a**) contains information on the trade-off between the production of guns and butter. This information has been plotted on the graph in (**b**). Notice in (**b**) that as we move along the production possibility curve from *A* to *F*, trading butter for guns, we get fewer and fewer guns for each pound of butter given up. That is, the opportunity cost of choosing guns over butter increases as we increase the production of guns. The phenomenon occurs because some resources are better suited for the production of butter than for the production of guns, and we use the better ones first.

% of Resources Devoted to Production of Guns	Number of Guns	% of Resources Devoted to Production of Butter	Pounds of Butter	Row
0	0	100	15	*A*
20	4	80	14	*B*
40	7	60	12	*C*
60	9	40	9	*D*
80	11	20	5	*E*
100	12	0	0	*F*

(a) Production Possibility Table

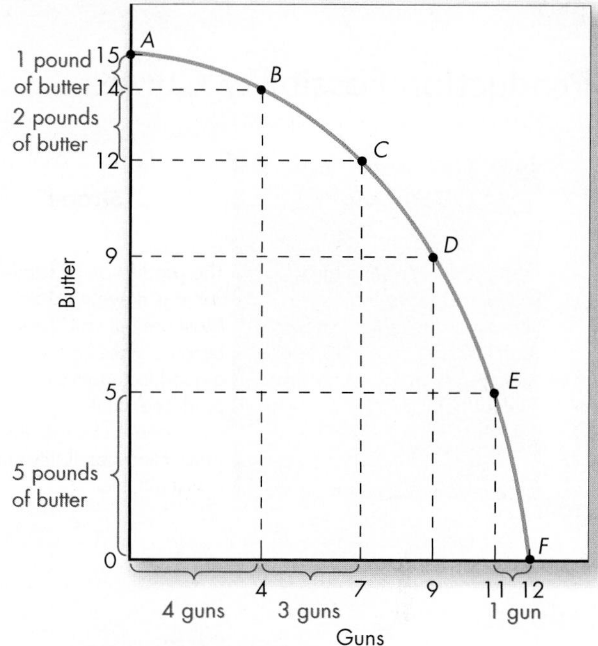

(b) Production Possibility Curve

Comparative Advantage

The reason we must give up more and more butter as we produce more guns is that some resources are relatively better suited to producing guns, while others are relatively better suited to producing butter. Put in economists' terminology, some resources have a **comparative advantage**—*better suited to the production of one good than to the production of another good.* In this example, some resources have a comparative advantage over other resources in the production of butter, while other resources have a comparative advantage in the production of guns.

Q-2 If no resource had a comparative advantage in the production of any good, what would the shape of the production possibility curve be? Why?

Comparative Advantage

When making small amounts of guns and large amounts of butter, we primarily use those resources whose comparative advantage is in the production of guns to produce guns. All other resources are devoted to producing butter. Because the resources used in producing guns aren't good at producing butter, we're not giving up much butter to get those guns. As we produce more and more of a good, we must use resources whose comparative advantage is in the production of the other good—in this case, more suitable for producing butter than for producing guns. As we continue to remove resources from the production of butter to get the same additional amount of guns, we must give up increasing amounts of butter. Guns' costs in terms of butter increase because we're using resources to produce guns that have a comparative advantage in producing butter.

Let's consider two more examples. Say the United States suddenly decides it needs more wheat. To get additional wheat, we must devote additional land to growing it. This land is less fertile than the land we're already using, so our additional output of wheat per acre of land devoted to wheat will be less. Alternatively, consider the use of relief pitchers in a baseball game. If only one relief pitcher is needed, the manager sends in the best; if he must send in a second one, then a third, and even a fourth, the likelihood of winning the game decreases.

A REMINDER 

Production Possibility Curves

Definition	Shape	Shifts	Points In, Out, and On
The production possibility curve is a curve that measures the maximum combination of outputs that can be obtained with a given number of inputs.	The production possibility curve is downward sloping. Most are outward bowed because of the cost of producing a good increases as more is produced. If the opportunity cost doesn't change, the production possibility curve is a straight line.	Increases in inputs or increases in the productivity of inputs shift the production possibility curve out. Decreases have the opposite effect; the production possibility curve shifts along the axis whose input is changing.	Points inside the production possibility curve are points of inefficiency; points on the production possibility curve are points of efficiency; points outside the production possibility curve are not obtainable.

Efficiency

Q-3 Identify the point(s) of inefficiency and efficiency. What point(s) are unattainable?

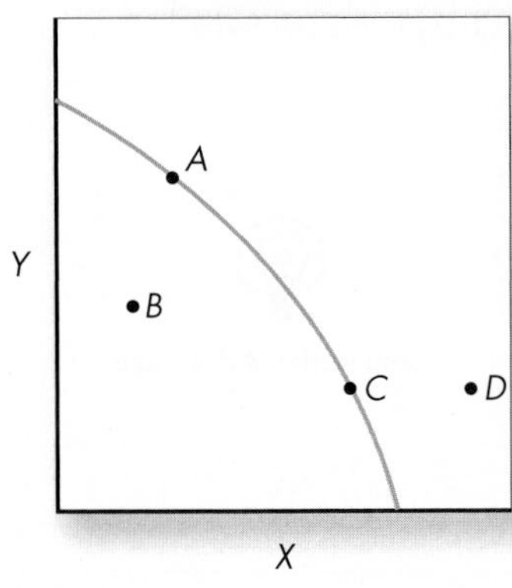

Efficiency

We would like, if possible, to get as much output as possible from a given amount of inputs or resources. That's **productive efficiency**—*achieving as much output as possible from a given amount of inputs or resources*. We would like to be efficient. The production possibility curve helps us see what is meant by productive efficiency. Consider point *A* in Figure 2-3(a), which is inside the production possibility curve. If we are producing at point *A*, we are using all our resources to produce 6 guns and 4 pounds of butter. Point *A* in Figure 2-3(a) represents **inefficiency**—*getting less output from inputs that, if devoted to some other activity, would produce more output*. That's because with the same inputs we could be getting either 8 guns and 4 pounds of butter (point *B*) or 6 pounds of butter and 6 guns (point *C*). As long as we prefer more to less, both points *B* and *C* represent **efficiency**—*achieving a goal using as few inputs as possible*. We always want to move our production out to a point on the production possibility curve.

Why not move out farther, to point *D?* If we could, we would, but by definition the production possibility curve represents the most output we can get from a certain combination of inputs. So point *D* is unattainable, given our resources and technology.

When technology improves, when more resources are discovered, or when the economic institutions get better at fulfilling our wants, we can get more output with the same inputs. What this means is that when technology or an economic institution improves, the entire production possibility curve shifts outward from *AB* to *CD* in Figure 2-3(b). How the production possibility curve shifts outward depends on how the technology improves. For example, say we become more efficient at producing butter, but not more efficient at producing guns. Then the production possibility curve shifts outward to *AC* in Figure 2-3(c).

Distribution and Productive Efficiency

In discussing the production possibility curve for a society, I avoided questions of distribution: Who gets what? But such questions cannot be ignored in real-world situations. Specifically, if the method of production is tied to a particular income

ADDED DIMENSION

Choices in Context: Decision Trees

The production possibility curve presents choices without regard to time and therefore makes trade-offs clear-cut; there are two choices, one with a higher cost and one with a lower cost. The reality is that most choices are dependent on other choices; they are made sequentially. With sequential choices, you cannot simply reverse your decision. Once you have started on a path, to take another path you have to return to the beginning. Thus, following one path often lowers the costs of options along that path, but it raises the costs of options along another path.

Such sequential decisions can best be seen within the framework of a decision tree—a visual description of sequential choices. A decision tree is shown in the accompanying figure.

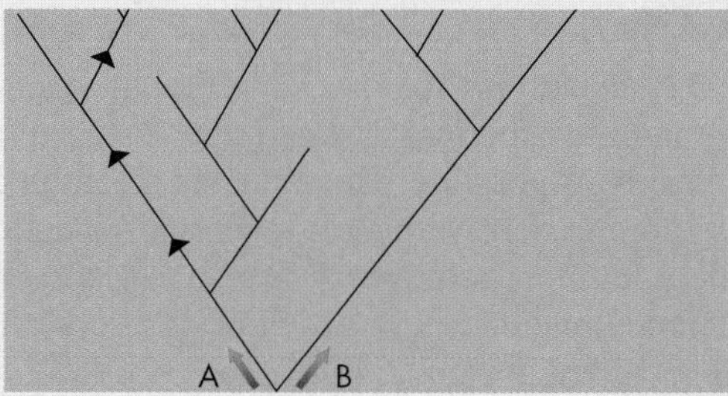

Once you make the initial decision to go on path A, the costs of path B options become higher; they include the costs of retracing your path and starting over. The decision trees of life have thousands of branches; each decision you make rules out other paths, or at least increases their costs significantly. (Remember that day you decided to blow off your homework? That decision may have changed your future life.)

Another way of putting this same point is that *all decisions are made in context:* What makes sense in one context may not make sense in another. For example, say you're answering the question "Would society be better off if students were taught literature or if they were taught agriculture?" The answer depends on the institutional context. In a developing country whose goal is large increases in material output, teaching agriculture may make sense. In a developed country, where growth in material output is less important, teaching literature may make sense.

Recognizing the contextual nature of decisions is important when interpreting the production possibility curve. Because decisions are contextual, what the production possibility curve for a particular decision looks like depends on the existing institutions, and the analysis can be applied only in institutional and historical context. The production possibility curve is not a purely technical phenomenon. The curve is an engine of analysis to make contextual choices, not a definitive tool to decide what one should do in all cases.

FIGURE 2-3 (A, B, AND C) Efficiency, Inefficiency, and Technological Change

The production possibility curve helps us see what is meant by efficiency. At point *A*, in (**a**), all inputs are used to make 4 pounds of butter and 6 guns. This is inefficient since there is a way to obtain more of one without giving up any of the other, that is, to obtain 6 pounds of butter and 6 guns (point *C*) or 8 guns and 4 pounds of butter (point *B*). All points inside the production possibility curve are inefficient. With existing inputs and technology, we cannot go beyond the production possibility curve. For example, point *D* is unattainable.

A technological change that improves production techniques will shift the production possibility curve outward, as shown in both (**b**) and (**c**). How the curve shifts outward depends on how technology improves. For example, if we become more efficient in the production of both guns and butter, the curve will shift out as in (**b**). If we become more efficient in producing butter, but not in producing guns, then the curve will shift as in (**c**).

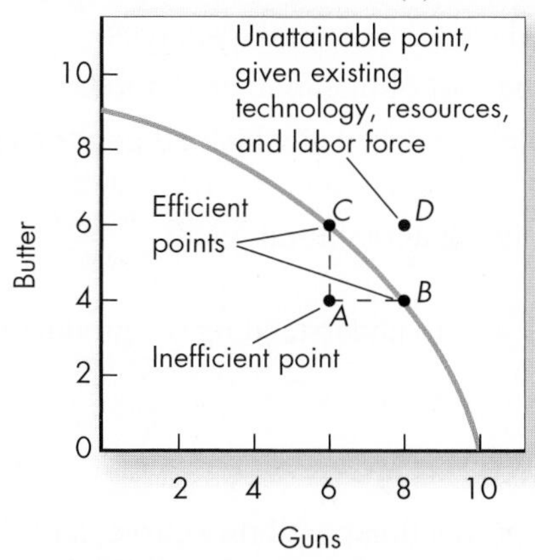

(a) Efficiency and Inefficiency

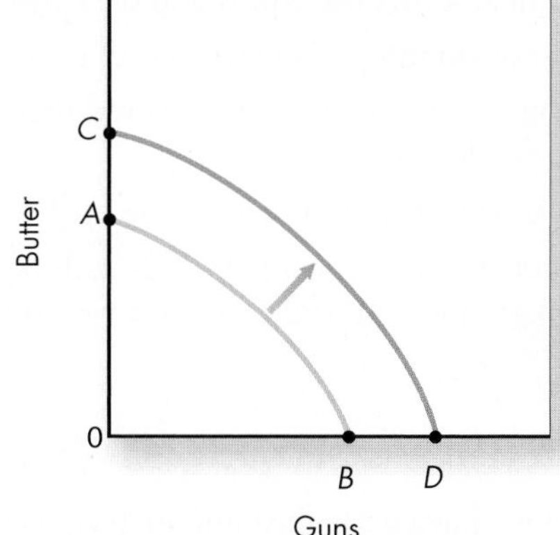

(b) Neutral Technological Change

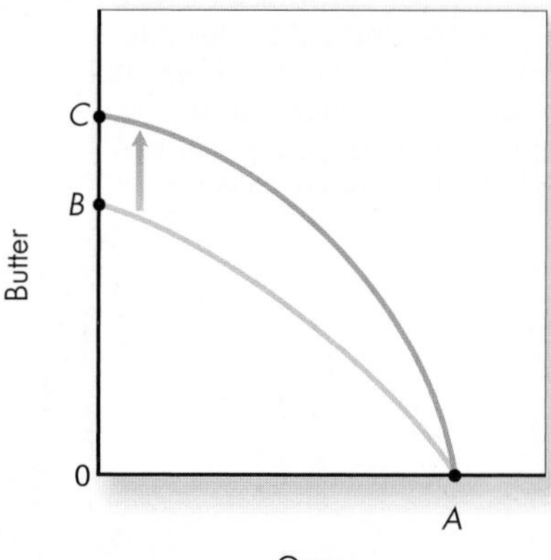

(c) Biased Technological Change

FIGURE 2-4 (A, B, C, AND D) Examples of Shifts in Production Possibility Curves

Each of these curves reflects a different type of shift. (The axes are left unlabeled on purpose. Manufactured and agricultural goods may be placed on either axis.) Your assignment is to match these shifts with the situations given in the text.

(a)

(b)

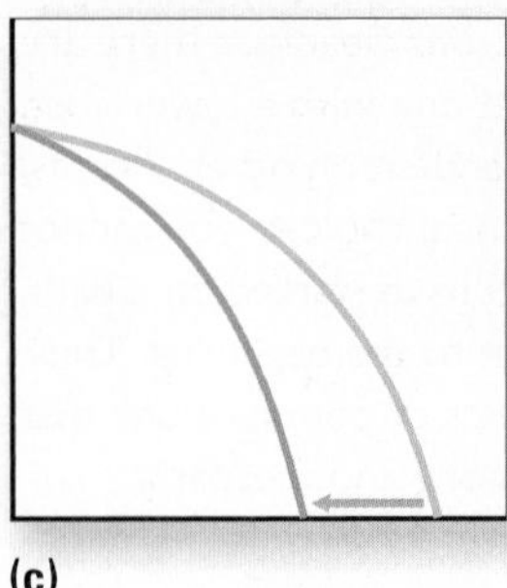

(c)

(d)

Q-4 Your firm is establishing a trucking business in Saudi Arabia. The managers have noticed that women are generally paid much less than men in Saudi Arabia, and they suggest that hiring women would be more efficient than hiring men. How should you respond?

distribution and choosing one method will help some people but hurt others, we can't say that one method of production is efficient and the other inefficient, even if one method produces more total output than the other. As I stated above, the term *efficiency* involves achieving a goal as cheaply as possible. The term has meaning only in regard to a specified goal. Say, for example, that we have a society of ascetics who believe that consumption above some minimum is immoral. For such a society, producing more for less (productive efficiency) would not be efficient since consumption is not its goal. Or say that we have a society that cares that what is produced is fairly distributed. An increase in output that goes to only one person and not to anyone else would not necessarily be efficient.

In our society, however, most people prefer more to less, and many policies have relatively small distributional consequences. On the basis of the assumption that more is better than less, economists use their own kind of shorthand for such policies and talk about efficiency as identical to productive efficiency—increasing total output. But it's important to remember the assumptions under which that shorthand is used: The distributional effects of the policy are deemed acceptable, and we, as a society, prefer more output.

Examples of Shifts in the PPC

To see whether you understand the production possibility curve, let us now consider some situations that can be shown with it. Below, I list four situations. To test your understanding of the curve, match each situation to one of the curves in Figure 2-4.

Q-5 When a natural disaster hits the midwestern United States, where most of the U.S. butter is produced, what happens to the U.S. production possibility curve for guns and butter?

1. A meteor hits the world and destroys half the earth's natural resources.
2. Nanotechnology is perfected that lowers the cost of manufactured goods.
3. A new technology is discovered that doubles the speed at which all goods can be produced.
4. Global warming increases the cost of producing agricultural goods.

The correct answers are: 1–d; 2–a; 3–b; 4–c.

If you got them all right, you are well on your way to understanding the production possibility curve.

Trade and Comparative Advantage

WWW Web Note 2.1 Wine and Cloth

Now that we have gone through the basics of the production possibility curve, let's dig a little deeper. From the above discussion, you know that production possibility curves are generally bowed outward and that the reason for this is comparative advantage. To

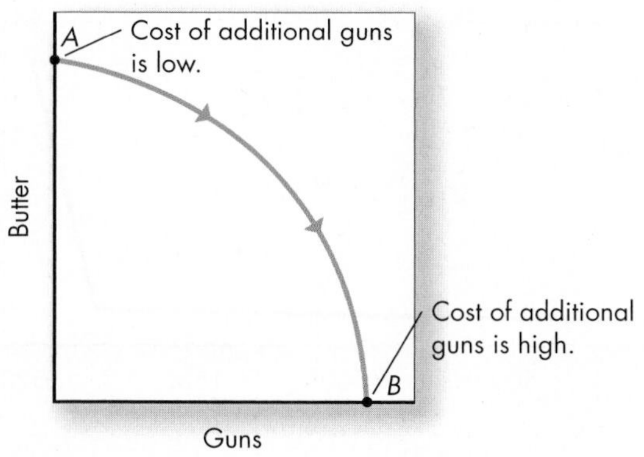

FIGURE 2-5 Comparative Advantage and the Production Possibility Curve

As we move down along the production possibility curve from point *A* to point *B,* the cost of producing guns is increasing since we are using resources less suited for gun production.

remind you of the argument, consider Figure 2-5, which is the guns and butter production possibility example I presented earlier.

At point *A,* all resources are being used to produce butter. As more guns are produced, we take resources away from producing butter that had a comparative advantage in producing guns, so we gain a lot of guns for little butter (the opportunity cost of additional guns is low). As we continue down the curve, the comparative advantage of the resources we use changes, and as we approach *B,* we use almost all resources to produce guns, so we are using resources that aren't very good at producing guns. Thus, around point *B* we gain few guns for a lot of butter (the opportunity cost of additional guns is high).

A society wants to be on the frontier of its production possibility curve. This requires that individuals produce those goods for which they have a comparative advantage. The question for society, then, is how to direct individuals toward those activities. For a firm, the answer is easy. A manager can allocate the firm's resources to their best use. For example, he or she can assign an employee with good people skills to the human resources department and another with good research skills to research and development. But our economy has millions of individuals, and no manager directing everyone what to do. How do we know that these individuals will be directed to do those things for which they have a comparative advantage? It was this question that was central to the British moral philosopher Adam Smith when he wrote his most famous book, *The Wealth of Nations* (1776). In it he argued that it was humankind's proclivity to trade that leads to individuals using their comparative advantage. He writes:

> This division of labour, from which so many advantages are derived, is not originally the effect of any human wisdom, which foresees and intends that general opulence to which it gives occasion. It is the necessary, though very slow and gradual consequence of a certain propensity in human nature which has in view no such extensive utility; the propensity to truck, barter, and exchange one thing for another . . . [This propensity] is common to all men, and to be found in no other race of animals, which seem to know neither this nor any other species of contracts . . . Nobody ever saw a dog make a fair and deliberate exchange of one bone for another with another dog. Nobody ever saw one animal by its gestures and natural cries signify to another, this is mine, that yours; I am willing to give this for that.

Adam Smith argued that it is humankind's proclivity to trade that leads to individuals using their comparative advantage.

As long as people trade, Smith argues, the market will guide people, like an invisible hand, to gravitate toward those activities for which they have a comparative advantage.

FIGURE 2-6 Growth in the Past Two Millennia

For 1,700 years the world economy grew very slowly. Then, since the end of the 18th century with the introduction of markets and the spread of democracy, the world economy has grown at increasing rates.

Source: Angus Maddison, *Monitoring the World Economy,* OECD, 1995; Angus Maddison, "Poor until 1820," *The Wall Street Journal,* January 11, 1999; and author extrapolations.

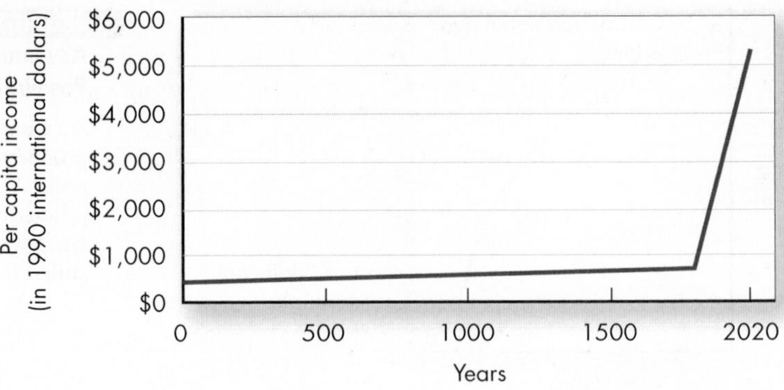

Markets, Specialization, and Growth

We can see the effect of trade on our well-being empirically by considering the growth of economies. As you can see from Figure 2-6, for 1,700 years the world economy grew very slowly. Then, at the end of the 18th century, the world economy started to grow, and it has grown at a high rate since then.

What changed? The introduction of markets that facilitate trade and the spread of democracy. There's something about markets that leads to economic growth. Markets allow specialization and encourage trade. The bowing out of the production possibilities from trade is part of the story, but a minor part. As individuals compete and specialize, they learn by doing, becoming even better at what they do. Markets also foster competition, which pushes individuals to find better ways of doing things. They devise new technologies that further the growth process.

Markets can be very simple or very complicated.

The new millennium is offering new ways for individuals to specialize and compete. More and more businesses are trading on the Internet. For example, colleges such as the University of Phoenix are providing online competition for traditional colleges. Similarly, online stores are proliferating. As Internet technology becomes built into our economy, we can expect more specialization, more division of labor, and the economic growth that follows.

The Benefits of Trade

WWW Web Note 2.2 Gains from Trade

The reasons why markets can direct people to use their comparative advantages follow from a very simple argument: When people freely enter into a trade, both parties can be expected to benefit from the trade; otherwise, why would they have traded in the first place? So when the butcher sells you meat, he's better off with the money you give him, and you're better off with the meat he gives you.

When there is competition in trading, such that individuals are able to pick the best trades available to them, each individual drives the best bargain he or she can. The end result is that both individuals in the trade benefit as much as they possibly can, given what others are willing to trade. This argument for the benefits from trade underlies the general policy of **laissez-faire**—*an economic policy of leaving coordination of individuals' actions to the market.* (*Laissez-faire,* a French term, means "Let events take their course; leave things alone.") Laissez-faire is not a theorem in economics; it is a precept because it extends the implications of a model to reality and draws conclusions about the real world. It is based on normative judgments, judgments about the relevance of the model, and assumptions upon which the model is based.

Q-6 What argument underlies the general laissez-faire policy argument?

Let's consider a numerical example of the gains that accrue to two countries when they trade. I use an international trade example so that you can see that the argument

FIGURE 2-7 (A AND B) The Gains from Trade

Trade makes those involved in the trade better off. If each country specializes and takes advantage of its comparative advantage, each can consume a combinations of goods beyond its production possibilities curve. In the example shown, Pakistan can consume at point *B* and Belgium at point *E*.

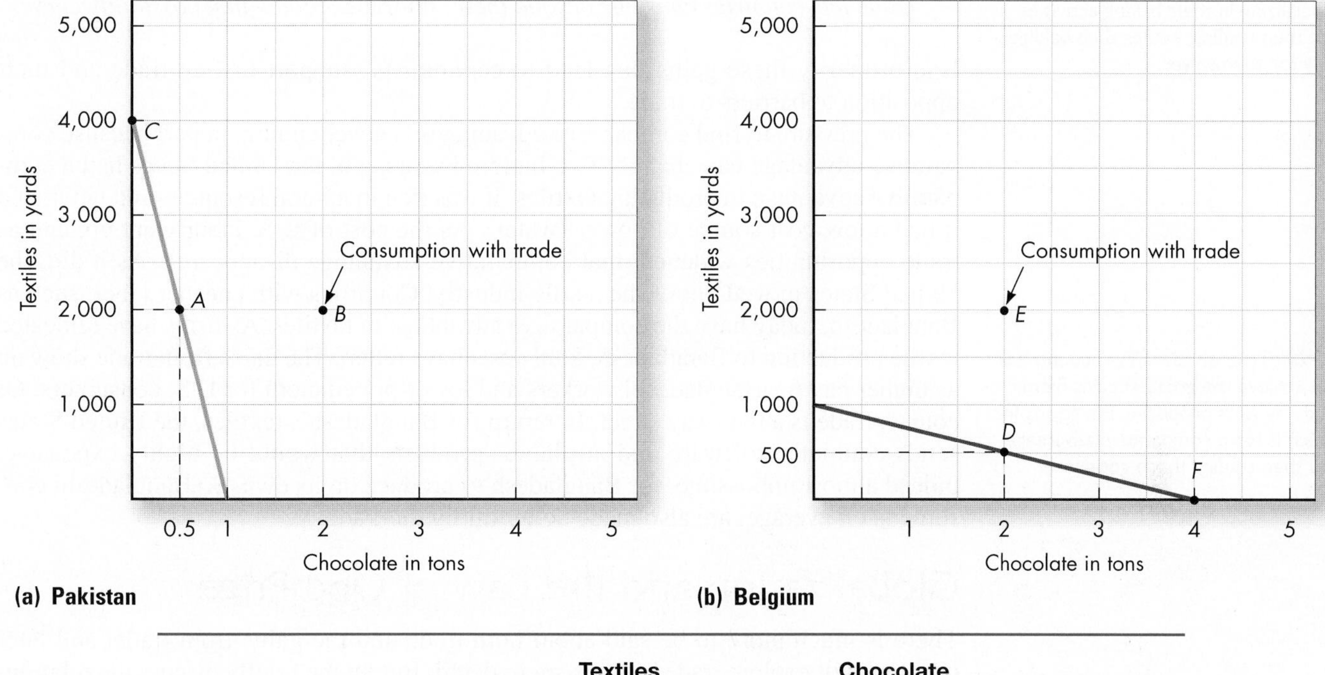

	Textiles	Chocolate
Pakistan	2,000 yards	0.5 ton
Belgium	500 yards	2 tons

holds for international trade as well as domestic trade. Let's say that the two countries are Pakistan and Belgium, and that Pakistan has a comparative advantage in producing textiles, while Belgium has a comparative advantage in producing chocolate. Specifically, Pakistan can produce 4,000 yards of textiles a day or 1 ton of chocolate a day, or any proportional combination in between. Pakistan's production possibility curve is shown in Figure 2-7(a). Similarly, in a given day, Belgium can produce either 1,000 yards of textiles or 4 tons of chocolate, or any proportion in between. Its production possibility curve is shown in Figure 2-7(b).

In the absence of trade, the most each country can consume is some combination along its production possibility curve. Say Pakistan has chosen to produce and consume 2,000 yards of textiles and 0.5 ton of chocolate (point *A* in Figure 2-7(a)), while Belgium has chosen to produce and consume 500 yards of textiles and 2 tons of chocolate (point *D* in Figure 2-7(b)).

Let's now consider what would happen if each specialized, doing what it does best, and then traded with the other for the goods it wants. This separates the production and consumption decisions. Because Pakistan can produce textiles at a lower cost in terms of chocolate, it makes sense for Pakistan to specialize in textiles, producing 4,000 yards (point *C* in Figure 2-7(a)). Similarly, it makes sense for Belgium to specialize in chocolate, producing 4 tons (point *F* in Figure 2-7(b)). By specializing, the countries together produce 4 tons of chocolate and 4,000 yards of textiles. If the countries divide

Specialization and trade create gains that make all better off.

Q-7 Steve can bake either 4 loaves of bread or 8 dozen cookies a day. Sarah can bake either 4 loaves of bread or 4 dozen cookies a day. Show, using production possibility curves, that Steve and Sarah would be better off specializing in their baking activities and then trading, rather than baking only for themselves.

Q-8 True or false? Two countries can achieve the greatest gains from trade by each producing the goods for which it has a comparative advantage and then trading those goods.

The global economy increases the number of competitors for the firm.

production so that each country gets 2,000 yards of fabric and 2 tons of chocolate, Pakistan can consume at point *B* and Belgium at point *E*. Both are consuming beyond their production possibility curves without trade. This tells us an important principle about trade:

Trade lets countries consume beyond their "no-trade" *production possibility curve.*

It is primarily these gains that lead to economists' support of free trade and their opposition to barriers to trade.

The pressure to find comparative advantages is never ending, in part because comparative advantage can change. Two hundred years ago, the United States had a comparative advantage in producing textiles. It was rich in natural resources and labor, and it had a low-cost source of power (water). As the cost of U.S. labor went up, and as trade opportunities widened, that comparative advantage disappeared. As it did, the United States moved out of the textile industry. Countries with cheaper labor, such as Bangladesh, today have the comparative advantage in textiles. As firms have relocated textile production to Bangladesh, total costs have fallen. The gains from trade show up as higher pay for Bangladeshi workers and lower-priced cloth for U.S. consumers. Of course, trade is a two-way street. In return for Bangladesh's textiles, the United States sends computer software and airplanes, products that would be highly expensive, indeed almost impossible, for Bangladesh to produce on its own. So Bangladeshi consumers, on average, are also made better off by the trade.

Globalization and the Law of One Price

There is much more to be said about both trade and the gains from trade, and later chapters will explore trade in much more detail. But let me briefly discuss the relationship of the theory of comparative advantage to globalization.

Globalization

Globalization *is the increasing integration of economies, cultures, and institutions across the world.* In a globalized economy, firms think of production and sales at a global level. They produce where costs are lowest, and sell across the world at the highest price they can get. A globalized world is a world in which economies of the world are highly integrated. Globalization has two effects on firms. The first is positive; because the world economy is so much larger than the domestic economy, the rewards for winning globally are much larger than the rewards for winning domestically. The second effect is negative; it is much harder to win, or even to stay in business, competing in a global market. A company may be the low-cost producer in a particular country yet may face foreign competitors that can undersell it. The global economy increases the number of competitors for the firm. Consider the automobile industry. Three companies are headquartered in the United States, but more than 40 automobile companies operate worldwide. U.S. automakers face stiff competition from foreign automakers; unless they meet that competition, they will not survive.

These two effects are, of course, related. When you compete in a larger market, you have to be better to survive, but if you do survive the rewards are greater.

Globalization increases competition by allowing greater specialization and division of labor, which, as Adam Smith first observed in *The Wealth of Nations,* increases growth and improves the standard of living for everyone. Thus, in many ways globalization is simply another name for increased specialization. Globalization allows (indeed, forces) companies to move operations to countries with a comparative advantage.

REAL-WORLD APPLICATION

Made in China?

Barbie and her companion Ken are as American as apple pie, and considering their origins gives us some insight into the modern U.S. economy and its interconnection with other countries. Barbie and Ken are not produced in the United States; they never were. When Barbie first came out in 1959, she was produced in Japan. Today, it is unclear where Barbie and Ken are produced. If you look at the box they come in, it says "Made in China," but looking deeper we find that Barbie and Ken are actually made in five different countries, each focusing on an aspect of production that reflects its comparative advantage. Japan produces the nylon hair. China provides much of what is normally considered manufacturing—factory spaces, labor, and energy for assembly—but it imports many of the components. The oil for the plastic comes from Saudi Arabia. That oil is refined into plastic pellets in Taiwan. The United States even provides some of the raw materials that go into the manufacturing process—it provides the cardboard, packing, paint pigments, and the mold.

The diversification of parts that go into the manufacturing of Barbie and Ken is typical of many goods today. As the world economy has become more integrated, the process of supplying components of manufacturing has become more and more spread out, as firms have divided up the manufacturing process in search of the least-cost location for each component.

But the global diversity in manufacturing and supply of components is only half the story of modern production. The other half is the shrinking of the relative importance of that manufacturing, and it is this other half that explains how the United States maintains its position in the world when so much of the manufacturing takes place elsewhere. It does so by maintaining its control over the distribution and marketing of the goods. In fact, of the $15 retail cost of a Barbie or Ken, $12 can be accounted for by activities not associated with manufacturing—design, transportation, merchandising, and advertising. And, luckily for the United States, many of these activities are still done in the United States, allowing the country to maintain its high living standard even as manufacturing spreads around the globe.

As they do so, they lower costs of production. Globalization leads to companies specializing in smaller portions of the production process because the potential market is not just one country but the world. Such specialization can lead to increased productivity as firms get better and better at producing through practice, what economists call *learning by doing*.

Q-9 How does globalization reduce the costs of production?

In a globalized economy production will shift to the lowest-cost producer. Globalization scares many people in the United States because, with wages so much lower in many developing countries than in the United States, they wonder whether all jobs will move offshore: Will the United States be left producing anything? Economists' answer is: Of course it will. Comparative advantage, by definition, means that if one country has a comparative advantage in producing one set of goods, the other country has to have a comparative advantage in the other set of goods. The real questions are: In what goods will the United States have comparative advantages? and: How will those comparative advantages come about?

Q-10 Is it likely that all U.S. jobs one day will have moved abroad? Why or Why not?

One reason people have a hard time thinking of goods in which the United States has a comparative advantage is that they are thinking in terms of labor costs. They ask: Since wages are lower in China, isn't it cheaper to produce all goods in China? The answer is no; production requires many more inputs than just labor. Technology, institutional structure, specialized types of knowledge, and entrepreneurial know-how are also needed to produce goods, and the United States has significant advantages in these other factors. It is these advantages that result in higher U.S. wages compared to other countries.

WWW Web Note 2.3 Trade and Wages

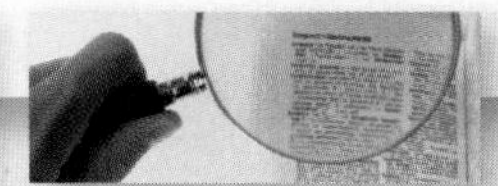

ADDED DIMENSION

The Developing Country's Perspective on Globalization

This book is written from a U.S. point of view. From that perspective, the relevant question is: Can the United States maintain its high wages relative to the low wages in China, India, and other developing countries? I suspect that most U.S. readers hope that it can. From a developing country's perspective, I suspect that the hope is that it cannot; their hope is that their wage rates catch up with U.S. wage rates. Judged from a developing country's perspective, the question is: Is it fair that U.S. workers don't work as hard as we do but earn much more?

The market does not directly take fairness into account. The market is interested only in who can produce a good or service at the lowest cost. This means that in a competitive economy, the United States can maintain its high wages only to the degree that it can produce sufficient goods and services cheaper than low-wage countries can at the market exchange rate. It must keep the trade balance roughly equal.

Developing countries recognize that, in the past, the United States has had a comparative advantage in creativity and innovation, and they are doing everything they can to compete on these levels as well as on basic production levels. They are actively trying to develop such skills in their population and to compete with the United States not only in manufacturing and low-tech jobs but also in research, development, finance, organizational activities, artistic activities, and high-tech jobs. Right now companies in China and India are working to challenge U.S. dominance in all high-tech and creativity fields. (For example, they too are working on nanotechnology.) To do this, they are trying to entice top scientists and engineers to stay in their country, or to return home if they have been studying or working in the United States. Since more than 50 percent of all PhD's given in science, engineering, and economics go to non-U.S. citizens (in economics, it is more than 70 percent), many observers believe that the United States cannot assume its past dominance in the innovative and high-tech fields will continue forever. The competitive front that will determine whether the United States can maintain much higher wages than developing countries is not the competition in current industries, but competition in industries of the future.

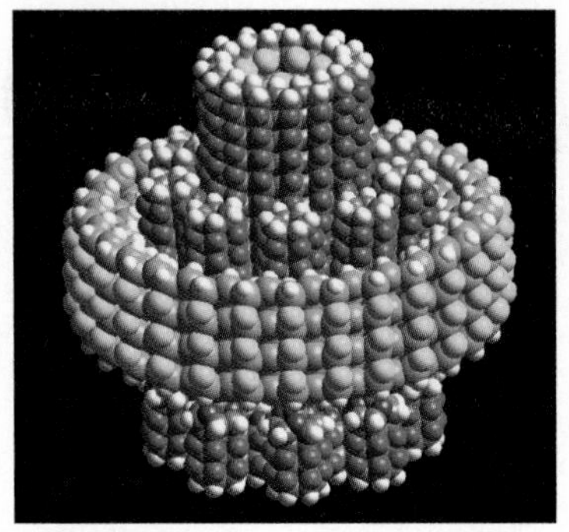
Nanotechnology—dynamic industry of the future?

The United States has excelled particularly in goods that require creativity and innovation. The United States has remained the leader of the world economy and has kept a comparative advantage in many goods even with its high relative wages, in part because of continual innovation. For example, the Internet started in the United States, which is why the United States is the location of so many information technology firms. The United States also has led the way in biotechnology innovation. Similarly, the creative industries, such as film, art, and advertising, have flourished in the United States. These industries are dynamic, high-profit, high-wage industries. (One of the reasons insourcing occurs is that the United States has such a great comparative advantage in these other aspects of production.) As long as U.S. production maintains a comparative advantage in innovation, the United States will be able to specialize in goods that allow firms to pay higher wages.

Exchange Rates and Comparative Advantage

There is, however, reason to be concerned. If innovation and creativity don't develop new industries in which the United States has a comparative advantage fast enough, as the current dynamic industries mature and move to low-wage areas, at current exchange rates (the value of a currency relative to the value of foreign currencies), the United States will not maintain comparative advantages in sufficient industries to warrant the relative wage differentials that exist today. In that case, U.S. demand for foreign goods and services will be higher than foreign demand for U.S. goods and services. For the last 20 years that has been the case. To bring them into equilibrium, the U.S. wage premium will have to decline to regain our comparative advantages. Since nominal wages (the wages that you see in your paycheck) in the United States are unlikely to fall, this will most likely occur through a decline in the U.S. exchange rate, large increases in foreign wages, or both. Either of these will make foreign products imported into the United States more expensive and U.S. products cheaper for foreigners, and eventually will balance the comparative advantages and trade flows.

The Law of One Price

Many Americans do not like the "exchange rate answer," but in terms of policy, it is probably the best the United States can hope for. If the United States tries to prevent production from moving to other countries with trade restrictions, U.S.-based companies will find that they can no longer compete internationally, and the United States will be in worse shape than if it had allowed outsourcing. The reality is that competition, combined with transferable technology and similar institutions, drives wages and prices of similar factors and goods toward equality. This reality often goes by the name of the **law of one price**—*the wages of workers in one country will not differ significantly from the wages of (equal) workers in another institutionally similar country.* As we will discuss in a later chapter, the debate is about what an "equal" worker is and what an equivalent institutional structure is.

The law of one price states that wages of workers in one country will not differ significantly from the wages of (equal) workers in another institutionally similar country.

Because of a variety of historical circumstances, the United States has been able to avoid the law of one price in wages since World War I. One factor has been the desire of foreigners to increase their holding of U.S. financial assets by trillions of dollars, which has let the United States consume more goods than it produces. Another is that the United States' institutional structure, technology, entrepreneurial labor force, and nonlabor inputs have given the United States sufficiently strong comparative advantages to offset the higher U.S. wage rates. The passage of time and modern technological changes have been eroding the United States' comparative advantages based on institutional structure and technology. To the degree that this continues to happen, to maintain a balance in the comparative advantages of various countries, the wages of workers in other countries such as India and China will have to move closer to the wages of U.S. workers.

Globalization and the Timing of Benefits of Trade

One final comment about globalization and the U.S. economy is in order. None of the above discussion contradicts the proposition that trade makes both countries better off. Thus, the discussion does not support the position taken by some opponents to trade and globalization that foreign competition is hurting the United States and that the United States can be made better off by imposing trade restrictions. Instead, the discussion is about the timing of the benefits of trade. Many of the benefits of trade already have been consumed by the United States during the years that the United States has been running trade deficits (importing more than it is exporting). The reality is that the United States has been living better than it could have otherwise precisely because of trade. It also has been living much better than it otherwise could because it is paying for some of its imports with IOUs promising payment in the future instead of with exports. But there is no free lunch, and when these IOUs are presented for payment, the United States will have to pay for some of the benefits that it already has consumed.

The reality is that the United States has been living better than it could have otherwise precisely because of trade and outsourcing.

Conclusion

While the production possibility curve model does not give unambiguous answers as to what government's role should be in regulating trade, it does serve a very important purpose. It is a geometric tool that summarizes a number of ideas in economics: trade-offs, opportunity costs, comparative advantage, efficiency, and how trade leads to

The production possibility curve represents the tough choices society must make.

efficiency. These ideas are all essential to economists' conversations. They provide the framework within which those conversations take place. Thinking of the production possibility curve (and picturing the economy as being on it) directs you to think of the trade-offs involved in every decision.

Look at questions such as: Should we save the spotted owl or should we allow logging in the western forests? Should we expand the government health care system or should we strengthen our national defense system? Should we emphasize policies that allow more consumption now or should we emphasize policies that allow more consumption in the future? Such choices involve difficult trade-offs that can be pictured by the production possibility curve.

Not everyone recognizes these trade-offs. For example, politicians often talk as if the production possibility curve were nonexistent. They promise voters the world, telling them, "If you elect me, you can have more of everything." When they say that, they obscure the hard choices and increase their probability of getting elected.

Economists continually point out that seemingly free lunches often involve significant hidden costs.

Economists do the opposite. They promise little except that life is tough, and they continually point out that seemingly free lunches often involve significant hidden costs. Alas, political candidates who exhibit such reasonableness seldom get elected. Economists' reasonableness has earned economics the nickname *the dismal science*.

Summary

- The production possibility curve measures the maximum combination of outputs that can be obtained from a given number of inputs. *(LO2-1)*
- In general, in order to get more and more of something, we must give up ever-increasing quantities of something else. *(LO2-1)*
- Trade allows people to use their comparative advantage and shift out society's production possibility curve. *(LO2-2)*
- The rise of markets coincided with significant increases in output. Specialization, trade, and competition have all contributed to the increase. *(LO2-2)*
- Points inside the production possibility curve are inefficient, points along the production possibility curve are efficient, and points outside are unattainable. *(LO2-2)*
- By specializing in producing those goods for which one has a comparative advantage (lowest opportunity cost), one can produce the greatest amount of goods with which to trade. Doing so, countries can increase consumption. *(LO2-3)*
- Globalization is the increasing integration of economies, cultures, and institutions across the world. *(LO2-4)*
- Because many goods are cheaper to produce in countries such as China and India, production that formerly took place in the United States is now taking place in foreign countries. *(LO2-4)*
- If the United States can maintain its strong comparative advantage in goods using new technologies and innovation, the jobs lost by production moving outside the United States can be replaced with other high-paying jobs. If it does not, then some adjustments in relative wage rates or exchange rates must occur. *(LO2-4)*
- Business's tendency to shift production to countries where it is cheapest to produce is guided by the law of one price. *(LO2-4)*

Key Terms

comparative advantage *(27)*
efficiency *(28)*
globalization *(34)*
inefficiency *(28)*
laissez-faire *(32)*
law of one price *(37)*
production possibility curve (PPC) *(25)*
production possibility table *(24)*
productive efficiency *(28)*

Questions and Exercises 

1. Show how a production possibility curve would shift if a society became more productive in its output of widgets but less productive in its output of wadgets. *(LO2-1)*
2. Show how a production possibility curve would shift if a society became more productive in the output of both widgets and wadgets. *(LO2-1)*
3. Design a grade production possibility table and curve that demonstrates a rising trade-off as the grade in each subject rises. *(LO2-1)*
4. In two hours JustBorn Candies can produce 30,000 Peeps or 90,000 Mike and Ikes or any combination in between. *(LO2-2)*
   a. What is the trade-off between Peeps and Mike and Ikes?
   b. Draw a production possibility curve that reflects this trade-off.
   c. Identify and label three points: efficient production, inefficient production, impossible.
   d. Illustrate what would happen if JustBorn candies developed a technology that increased productivity equally for both products.
5. How does the theory of comparative advantage relate to production possibility curves? *(LO2-2)*
6. A country has the following production possibility table: *(LO2-2)*

Resources Devoted to Clothing	Output of Clothing	Resources Devoted to Food	Output of Food
100%	20	0%	0
80	16	20	5
60	12	40	9
40	8	60	12
20	4	80	14
0	0	100	15

   a. Draw the country's production possibility curve.
   b. What's happening to the trade-off between food and clothing?
   c. Say the country gets better at the production of food. What will happen to the production possibility curve?
   d. Say the country gets equally better at producing both food and clothing. What will happen to the production possibility curve?
7. If neither of two countries has a comparative advantage in either of two goods, what are the gains from trade? *(LO2-3)*
8. Does the fact that the production possibilities model tells us that trade is good mean that in the real world free trade is necessarily the best policy? Explain. *(LO2-3)*
9. Suppose the United States and Japan have the following production possibility tables: *(LO2-3)*

Japan		United States	
Bolts of Cloth	Tons of Wheat	Bolts of Cloth	Tons of Wheat
1,000	0	500	0
800	100	400	200
600	200	300	400
400	300	200	600
200	400	100	800
0	500	0	1,000

   a. Draw each country's production possibility curve.
   b. In what good does the United States have a comparative advantage?
   c. Is there a possible trade that benefits both countries?
   d. Demonstrate your answer graphically.
10. What effect has globalization had on the ability of firms to specialize? How has this affected the competitive process? *(LO2-4)*
11. If workers in China and India become as productive as U.S. workers, what adjustments will allow the United States to regain its competitiveness? *(LO2-4)*
12. State the law of one price. How is it related to the movement of production out of the United States? *(LO2-4)*

Questions from Alternative Perspectives

1. Why might government be less capable than the market to do good? (Austrian)
2. The text makes it look as if maximizing output is the goal of society.
   a. Is maximizing output the goal of society?
   b. If the country is a Christian country, should it be?
   c. If not, what should it be? (Religious)
3. It has been said that "capitalism robs us of our sexuality and sells it back to us."
   a. Does sex sell?

b. Is sex used to sell goods from Land Rovers to tissue paper?
c. Who, if anyone, is exploited in the use of sex to sell commodities?
d. Are both men and women exploited in the same ways? (Feminist)

4. Thorstein Veblen wrote that *vested interests* are those seeking "something for nothing." In this chapter, you learned how technology shapes the economy's production possibilities over time so that a country becomes increasingly good at producing a subset of goods.
   a. In what ways have vested interests used their influence to bias the U.S. economy toward the production of military goods at the expense of consumer goods?
   b. What are the short-term and long-term consequences of that bias for human welfare, in the United States and abroad? (Institutionalist)
5. Writing in 1776, Adam Smith was concerned not only with the profound effects of the division of labor on productivity (as your textbook notes) but also its stultifying effect on the human capacity. In *The Wealth of Nations,* Smith warned that performing a few simple operations over and over again could render any worker, no matter his or her native intelligence, "stupid and ignorant."
   a. Does the division of labor in today's economy continue to have both these effects?
   b. What are the policy implications? (Radical)

Issues to Ponder

1. When all people use economic reasoning, inefficiency is impossible because if the benefit of reducing that inefficiency were greater than the cost, the inefficiency would be eliminated. Thus, if people use economic reasoning, it's impossible to be on the interior of a production possibility curve. Is this statement true or false? Why?
2. If income distribution is tied to a particular production technique, how might that change one's view of alternative production techniques?
3. Research shows that after-school jobs are highly correlated with decreases in grade point averages. Those who work 1 to 10 hours get a 3.0 GPA and those who work 21 hours or more have a 2.7 GPA. Higher GPAs are, however, highly correlated with higher lifetime earnings. Assume that a person earns $8,000 per year for working part-time in college, and that the return to a 0.1 increase in GPA gives one a 10 percent increase in one's lifetime earnings with a present value of $80,000.
   a. What would be the argument for working rather than studying harder?
   b. Is the assumption that there is a trade-off between working and grades reasonable?
4. Lawns produce no crops but occupy more land (25 million acres) in the United States than any single crop, such as corn. This means that the United States is operating inefficiently and hence is at a point inside the production possibility curve. Right? If not, what does it mean?
5. Groucho Marx is reported to have said "The secret of success is honesty and fair dealing. If you can fake those, you've got it made." What would likely happen to society's production possibility curve if everyone could fake honesty? Why? (Hint: Remember that society's production possibility curve reflects more than just technical relationships.)
6. Say that the hourly cost to employers per German industrial worker was $44. The hourly cost to employers per U.S. industrial worker was $34, while the average cost per Taiwanese industrial worker was $8.
   a. Give three reasons why firms produce in Germany rather than in a lower-wage country.
   b. Germany has an agreement with other EU countries that allows people in any EU country, including Greece and Italy, which have lower wage rates, to travel and work in any EU country, including high-wage countries. Would you expect a significant movement of workers from Greece and Italy to Germany right away? Why or why not?
   c. Workers in Thailand are paid significantly less than workers in Taiwan. If you were a company CEO, what other information would you want before you decided where to establish a new production facility?

Answers to Margin Questions

1. You must give up 2 units of good *Y* to produce 4 units of good *X*, so the opportunity cost of *X* is ½ *Y*. (*p. 25; LO2-1*)
2. If no resource had a comparative advantage, the production possibility curve would be a straight line connecting the points of maximum production of each product as in the graph below.

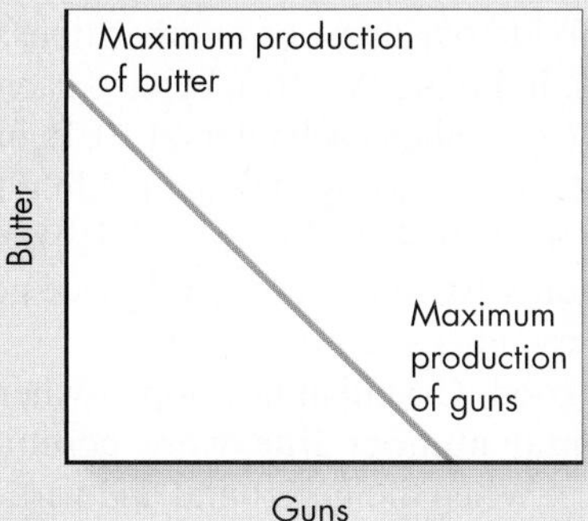

At all points along this curve, the trade-off between producing guns and butter is equal. (*p. 27; LO2-2*)

3. Points *A* and *C* are along the production possibility curve, so they are points of efficiency. Point *B* is inside the production possibility curve, so it is a point of inefficiency. Point *D* is to the right of the production possibility curve, so it is unattainable. (*p. 28; LO2-2*)
4. Remind them of the importance of cultural forces. In Saudi Arabia, women are not allowed to drive. (*p. 30; LO2-2*)
5. The production possibility curve shifts in along the butter axis as in the graph below. (*p. 30; LO2-2*)

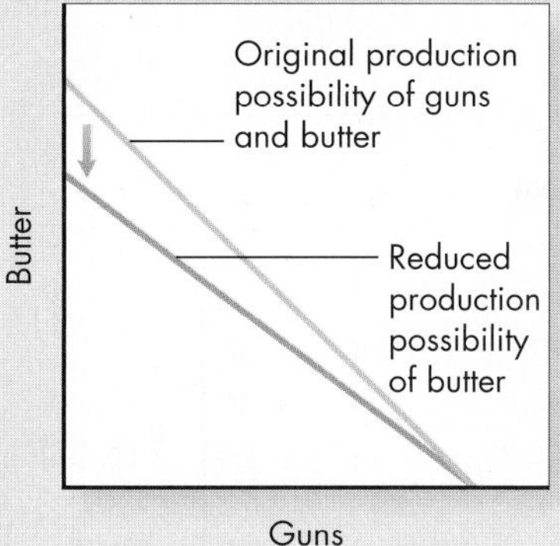

6. The argument that underlies the general laissez-faire policy argument is that when there is competition in trade, individuals are able to pick the best trades available to them and the end result is that both parties to the trade benefit as much as they possibly can. (*p. 32; LO2-3*)
7. Steve's and Sarah's production possibility curves are shown in the figure below. If they specialize, they can, combined, produce 4 loaves of bread and 8 dozen cookies, which they can split up. Say that Steve gets 2 loaves of bread and 5 dozen cookies (point *A*). This puts him beyond his original production possibility curve, and thus is an improvement for him. That leaves 2 loaves of bread and 3 dozen cookies for Sarah (point *B*), which is beyond her original production possibility curve, which is an improvement for her. Both are better off than they would have been without trade. (*p. 34; LO2-3*)

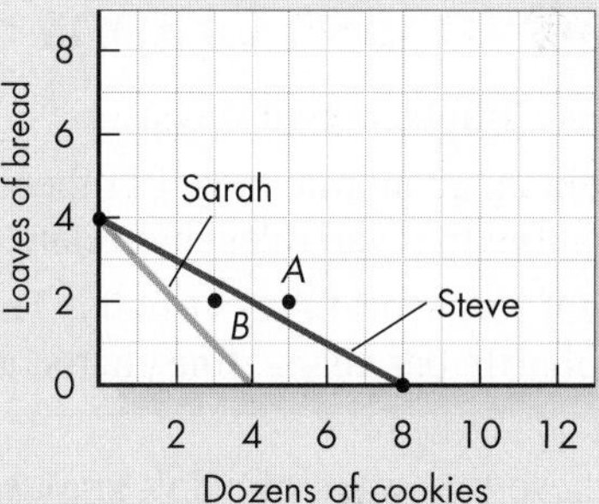

8. True. By producing the good for which it has a comparative advantage, a country will have the greatest amount of goods with which to trade and will reap the greatest gains from trade. (*p. 34; LO2-3*)
9. Globalization allows more trade and specialization. That specialization lowers costs of production since it allows the lowest-cost producer to produce each good. (*p. 35; LO2-4*)
10. No. By definition, if one country has a comparative advantage in producing one set of goods, the other country has a comparative advantage in the production in the other set. Jobs will be needed to support this production. Additionally, many jobs cannot be moved abroad effectively because they require physical proximity to the point of sale. (*p. 35; LO2-4*)

Graphish: The Language of Graphs

A picture is worth 1,000 words. Economists, being efficient, like to present ideas in **graphs,** *pictures of points in a coordinate system in which points denote relationships between numbers.* But a graph is worth 1,000 words only if the person looking at the graph knows the graphical language: *Graphish,* we'll call it. (It's a bit like English.) Graphish is usually written on graph paper. If the person doesn't know Graphish, the picture isn't worth any words and Graphish can be babble.

I have enormous sympathy for students who don't understand Graphish. A number of my students get thrown for a loop by graphs. They understand the idea, but Graphish confuses them. This appendix is for them, and for those of you like them. It's a primer in Graphish.

Two Ways to Use Graphs

In this book I use graphs in two ways:

1. To present an economic model or theory visually, showing how two variables interrelate.
2. To present real-world data visually. To do this, I use primarily bar charts, line charts, and pie charts.

Actually, these two ways of using graphs are related. They are both ways of presenting visually the *relationship* between two things.

Graphs are built around a number line, or axis, like the one in Figure A2-1(a). The numbers are generally placed in order, equal distances from one another. That number line allows us to represent a number at an appropriate point on the line. For example, point *A* represents the number 4.

The number line in Figure A2-1(a) is drawn horizontally, but it doesn't have to be; it also can be drawn vertically, as in Figure A2-1(b).

How we divide our axes, or number lines, into intervals is up to us. In Figure A2-1(a), I called each interval 1; in Figure A2-1(b), I called each interval 10. Point *A* appears after 4 intervals of 1 (starting at 0 and reading from left to right), so it represents 4. In Figure A2-1(b), where each interval represents 10, to represent 5, I place point *B* halfway in the interval between 0 and 10.

So far, so good. Graphish developed when a vertical and a horizontal number line were combined, as in Figure A2-1(c). When the horizontal and vertical number lines are put together, they're called *axes.* (Each line is an axis. *Axes* is the plural of *axis.*) I now have a **coordinate system**—*a two-dimensional space in which one point represents two numbers.* For example, point *A* in Figure A2-1(c) represents the numbers (4, 5)—4 on the horizontal number line and 5 on the vertical number line. Point *B* represents the numbers (1, 20). (By convention, the horizontal numbers are written first.)

Being able to represent two numbers with one point is neat because it allows the relationships between two numbers to be presented visually instead of having to be expressed verbally, which is often cumbersome. For example, say the cost of producing 6 units of something is \$4 per unit and the cost of producing 10 units is \$3 per

FIGURE A2-1 (A, B, AND C) **Horizontal and Vertical Number Lines and a Coordinate System**

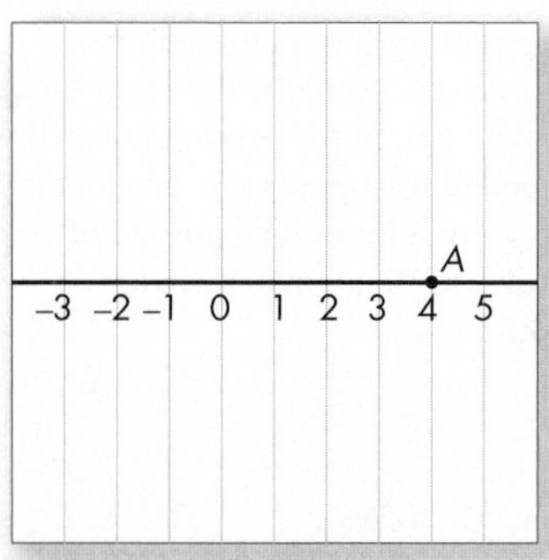

(a) Horizontal Number Line

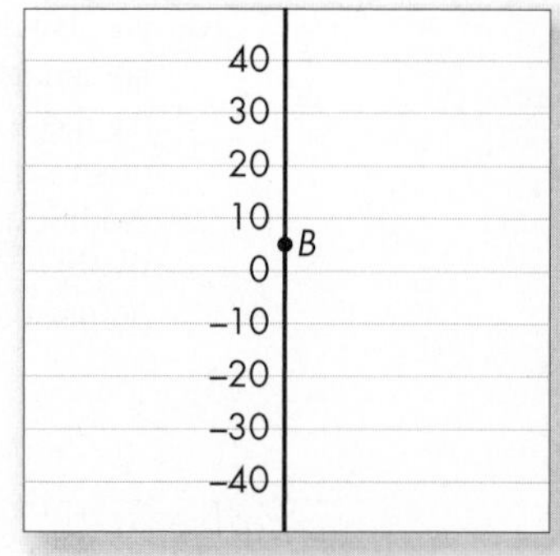

(b) Vertical Number Line

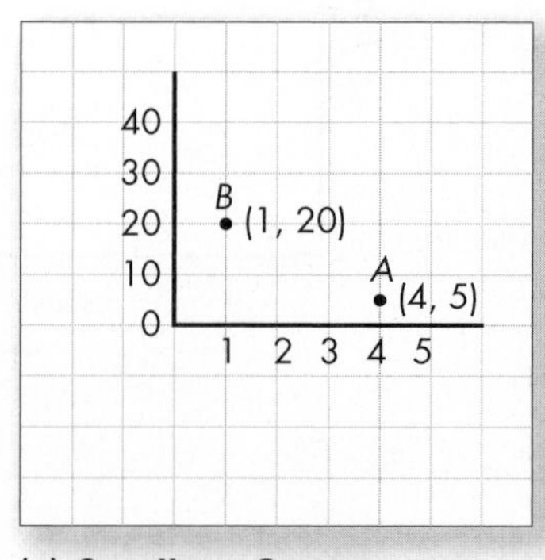

(c) Coordinate System

FIGURE A2-2 (A, B, C, AND D) A Table and Graphs Showing the Relationships between Price and Quantity

	Price per Pen	Quantity of Pens Bought per Day
A	$3.00	4
B	2.50	5
C	2.00	6
D	1.50	7
E	1.00	8

(a) Price Quantity Table

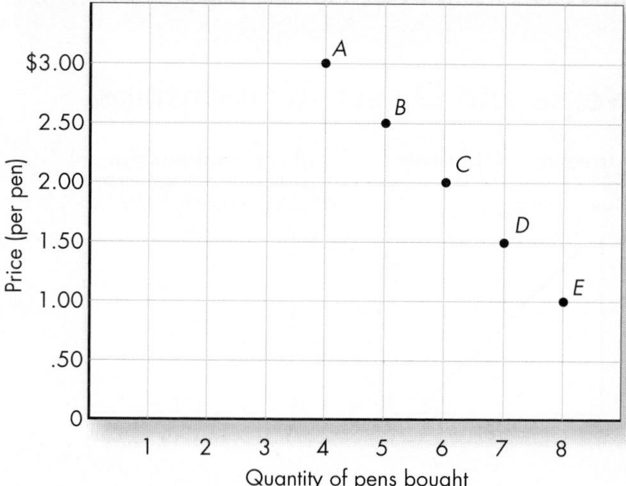

(b) From a Table to a Graph (1)

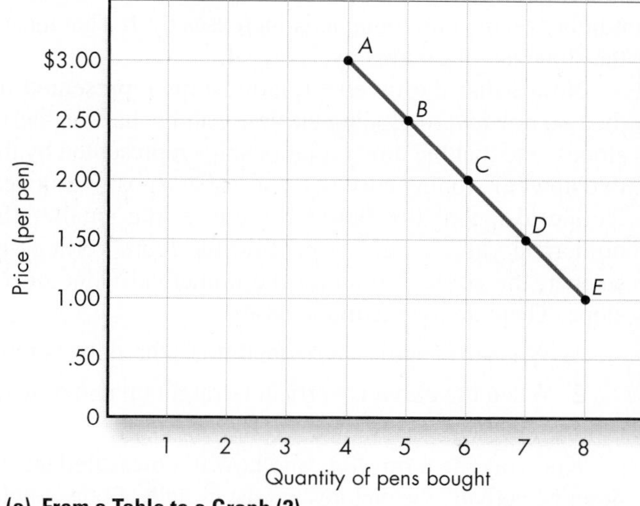

(c) From a Table to a Graph (2)

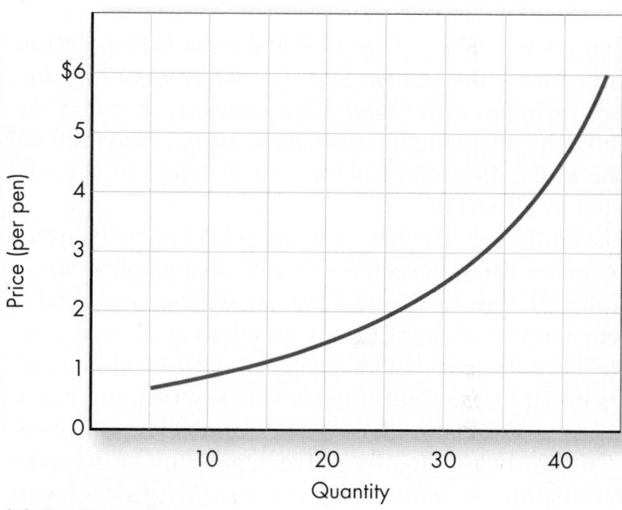

(d) Nonlinear Curve

unit. By putting both these points on a graph, we can visually see that producing 10 costs less per unit than does producing 6.

Another way to use graphs to present real-world data visually is to use the horizontal line to represent time. Say that we let each horizontal interval equal a year, and each vertical interval equal $100 in income. By graphing your income each year, you can obtain a visual representation of how your income has changed over time.

Using Graphs in Economic Modeling

I use graphs throughout the book as I present economic models, or simplifications of reality. A few terms are often used in describing these graphs, and we'll now go over them. Consider Figure A2-2(a), which lists the number of pens bought per day (column 2) at various prices (column 1).

We can present the table's information in a graph by combining the pairs of numbers in the two columns of the table and representing, or plotting, them on two axes. I do that in Figure A2-2(b).

By convention, when graphing a relationship between price and quantity, economists place price on the vertical axis and quantity on the horizontal axis.

I can now connect the points, producing a line like the one in Figure A2-2(c). With this line, I interpolate the numbers between the points (which makes for a nice

A REMINDER 

Inverse and Direct Relationships

Inverse relationship:
When *X* goes up, *Y* goes down.
When *X* goes down, *Y* goes up.

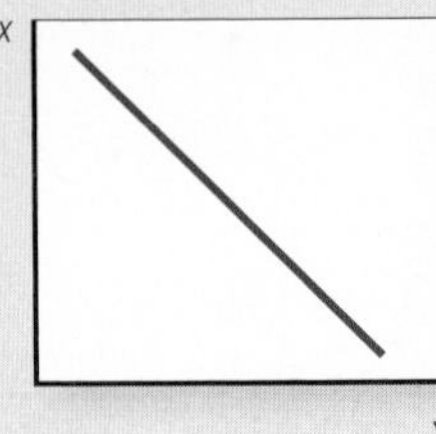

Direct relationship:
When *X* goes up, *Y* goes up.
When *X* goes down, *Y* goes down.

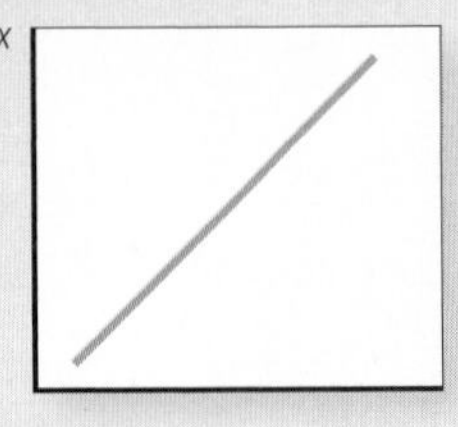

visual presentation). That is, I make the **interpolation assumption**—*the assumption that the relationship between variables is the same between points as it is at the points.* The interpolation assumption allows us to think of a line as a collection of points and therefore to connect the points into a line.

Even though the line in Figure A2-2(c) is straight, economists call any such line drawn on a graph a *curve.* Because it's straight, the curve in A2-2(c) is called a **linear curve**—*a curve that is drawn as a straight line.* Notice that this curve starts high on the left-hand side and goes down to the right. Economists say that any curve that looks like that is *downward-sloping.* They also say that a downward-sloping curve represents an **inverse relationship**—*a relationship between two variables in which when one goes up, the other goes down.* In this example, the line demonstrates an inverse relationship between price and quantity—that is, when the price of pens goes up, the quantity bought goes down.

Figure A2-2(d) presents a **nonlinear curve**—*a curve that is drawn as a curved line.* This curve, which really is curved, starts low on the left-hand side and goes up to the right. Economists say any curve that goes up to the right is *upward-sloping.* An upward-sloping curve represents a **direct relationship**—*a relationship in which when one variable goes up, the other goes up too.* The direct relationship I'm talking about here is the one between the two variables (what's measured on the horizontal and vertical lines). *Downward-sloping* and *upward-sloping* are terms you need to memorize if you want to read, write, and speak Graphish, keeping graphically in your mind the image of the relationships they represent.

Slope

One can, of course, be far more explicit about how much the curve is sloping upward or downward by defining it in terms of **slope**—*the change in the value on the vertical axis divided by the change in the value on the horizontal axis.* Sometimes the slope is presented as "rise over run":

$$\text{Slope} = \frac{\text{Rise}}{\text{Run}} = \frac{\text{Change in value on vertical axis}}{\text{Change in value on horizontal axis}}$$

Slopes of Linear Curves

In Figure A2-3, I present five linear curves and measures of their slopes. Let's go through an example to show how we can measure slope. To do so, we must pick two points. Let's use points *A* (6, 8) and *B* (7, 4) on curve *a.* Looking at these points, we see that as we move from 6 to 7 on the horizontal axis, we move from 8 to 4 on the vertical axis. So when the number on the vertical axis falls by 4, the number on the horizontal axis increases by 1. That means the slope is −4 divided by 1, or −4.

Notice that the inverse relationships represented by the two downward-sloping curves, *a* and *b,* have negative slopes, and that the direct relationships represented by the two upward-sloping curves, *c* and *d,* have positive slopes. Notice also that the flatter the curve, the smaller the numerical value of the slope; and the more vertical, or steeper, the curve, the larger the numerical value of the slope. There are two extreme cases:

1. When the curve is horizontal (flat), the slope is zero.
2. When the curve is vertical (straight up and down), the slope is infinite (larger than large).

Knowing the term *slope* and how it's measured lets us describe verbally the pictures we see visually. For example, if I say a curve has a slope of zero, you should picture in your mind a flat line; if I say "a curve with a slope of minus one," you should picture a falling line that makes a 45° angle with the horizontal and vertical axes. (It's the hypotenuse of an isosceles right triangle with the axes as the other two sides.)

Slopes of Nonlinear Curves

The preceding examples were of *linear* (*straight*) *curves.* With *nonlinear curves*—the ones that really do curve—the slope of the curve is constantly changing. As a result, we must talk about the slope of the curve at a particular point, rather than the slope of the whole curve. How can a point have a slope? Well, it can't really, but it can almost, and if that's good enough for mathematicians, it's good enough for us.

FIGURE A2-3 Slopes of Curves

The slope of a curve is determined by rise over run. The slope of curve *a* is shown in the graph. The rest are shown below:

	Rise	÷	Run	=	Slope
b	−1		+2		−.5
c	1		1		1
d	4		1		4
e	1		1		1

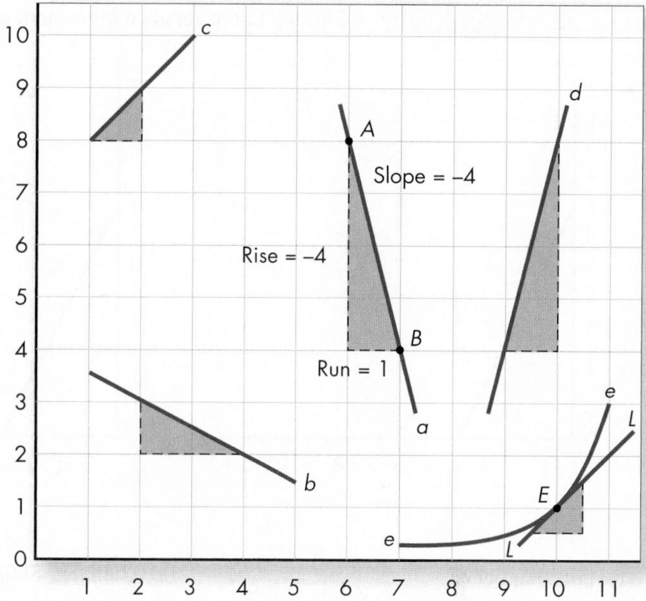

Defining the slope of a nonlinear curve is a bit more difficult. The slope at a given point on a nonlinear curve is determined by the slope of a linear (or straight) line that's tangent to that curve. (A line that's tangent to a curve is a line that just touches the curve, and touches it only at one point in the immediate vicinity of the given point.) In Figure A2-3, the line *LL* is tangent to the curve *ee* at point *E*. The slope of that line, and hence the slope of the curve at the one point where the line touches the curve, is +1.

Maximum and Minimum Points

Two points on a nonlinear curve deserve special mention. These points are the ones for which the slope of the curve is zero. I demonstrate those in Figure A2-4(a) and (b). At point *A* we're at the top of the curve, so it's at a maximum point; at point *B* we're at the bottom of the curve, so it's at a minimum point. These maximum and minimum points are often referred to by economists, and it's important to realize that the value of the slope of the curve at each of these points is zero.

There are, of course, many other types of curves, and much more can be said about the curves I've talked about. I won't do so because, for purposes of this course, we won't need to get into those refinements. I've presented as much Graphish as you need to know for this book.

FIGURE A2-4 (A AND B) A Maximum and a Minimum Point

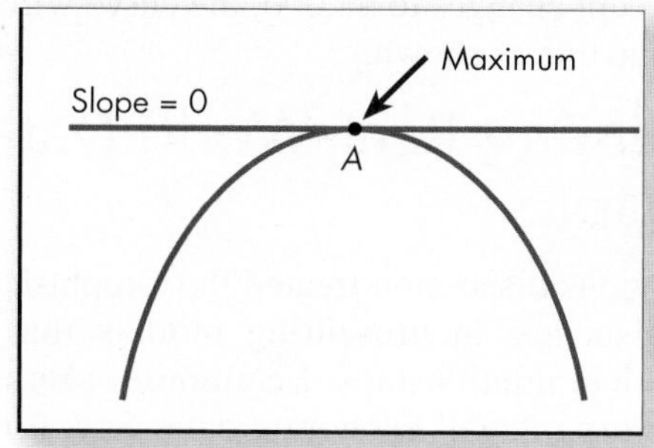

(a) Maximum Point

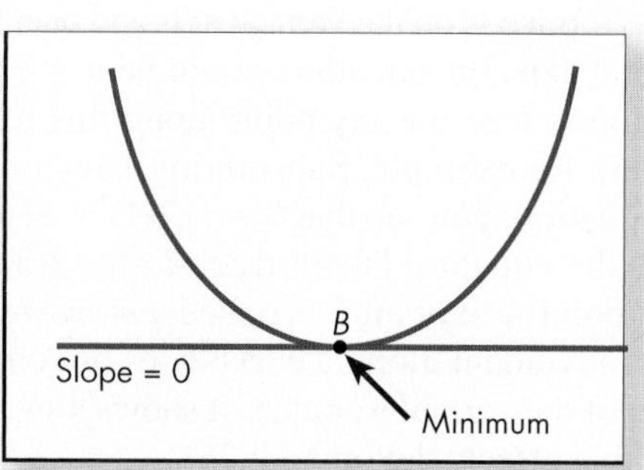

(b) Minimum Point

FIGURE A2-5 (A, B, AND C) **A Shifting Curve versus a Movement along a Curve**

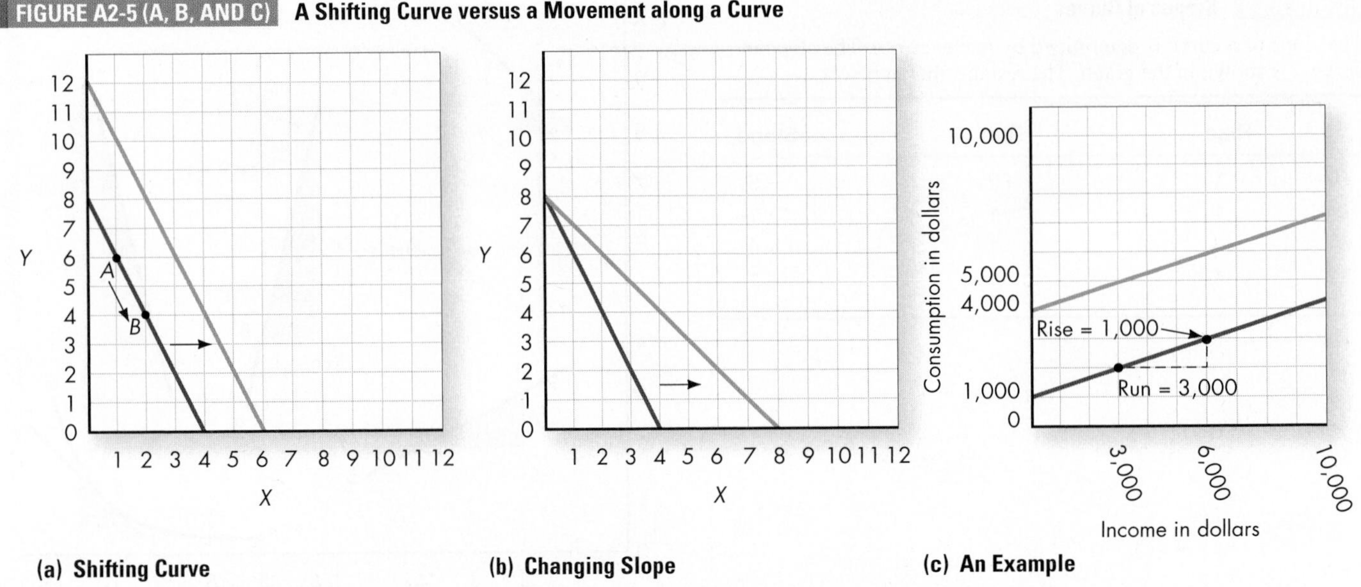

Equations and Graphs

Sometimes economists depict the relationships shown in graphs using equations. Since I present material algebraically in the appendixes to a few chapters, let me briefly discuss how to translate a linear curve into an equation. Linear curves are relatively easy to translate because all linear curves follow a particular mathematical form: $y = mx + b$, where y is the variable on the vertical axis, x is the variable on the horizontal axis, m is the slope of the line, and b is the vertical-axis intercept. To write the equation of a curve, look at that curve, plug in the values for the slope and vertical-axis intercept, and you've got the equation.

For example, consider the blue curve in Figure A2-5(a). The slope (rise over run) is -2 and the number where the curve intercepts the vertical axis is 8, so the equation that depicts this curve is $y = -2x + 8$. It's best to choose variables that correspond to what you're measuring on each axis, so if price is on the vertical axis and quantity is on the horizontal axis, the equation would be $p = -2q + 8$. This equation is true for any point along this line. Take point A (1, 6), for example. Substituting 1 for x and 6 for y into the equation, you see that $6 = -2(1) + 8$, or $6 = 6$. At point B, the equation is still true: $4 = -2(2) + 8$. A move from point A to point B is called a *movement along a curve*. A movement along a curve does not change the relationship of the variables; rather, it shows how a change in one variable affects the other.

Sometimes the relationship between variables will change. The curve will shift, change slope, or both shift and change slope. These changes are reflected in changes to the m and b variables in the equation. Suppose the vertical-axis intercept rises from 8 to 12, while the slope remains the same. The equation becomes $y = -2x + 12$; for every value of y, x has increased by 4. Plotting the new equation, we can see that the curve has *shifted* to the right, as shown by the orange line in Figure A2-5(a). If instead the slope changes from -2 to -1, while the vertical-axis intercept remains at 8, the equation becomes $y = -x + 8$. Figure A2-5(b) shows this change graphically. The original blue line stays anchored at 8 and rotates out along the horizontal axis to the new orange line.

Here's an example for you to try. The lines in Figure A2-5(c) show two relationships between consumption and income. Write the equation for the blue line.

The answer is $C = \frac{1}{3}Y + \$1,000$. Remember, to write the equation you need to know two things: the vertical-axis intercept ($1,000) and the slope (⅓). If the intercept changes to $4,000, the curve will shift up to the orange line as shown.

Presenting Real-World Data in Graphs

The previous discussion treated the Graphish terms that economists use in presenting models that focus on hypothetical relationships. Economists also use graphs in presenting actual economic data. Say, for example, that you want to show how exports have changed over time. Then you would place years on the horizontal axis

FIGURE A2-6 (A, B, AND C) **Presenting Information Visually**

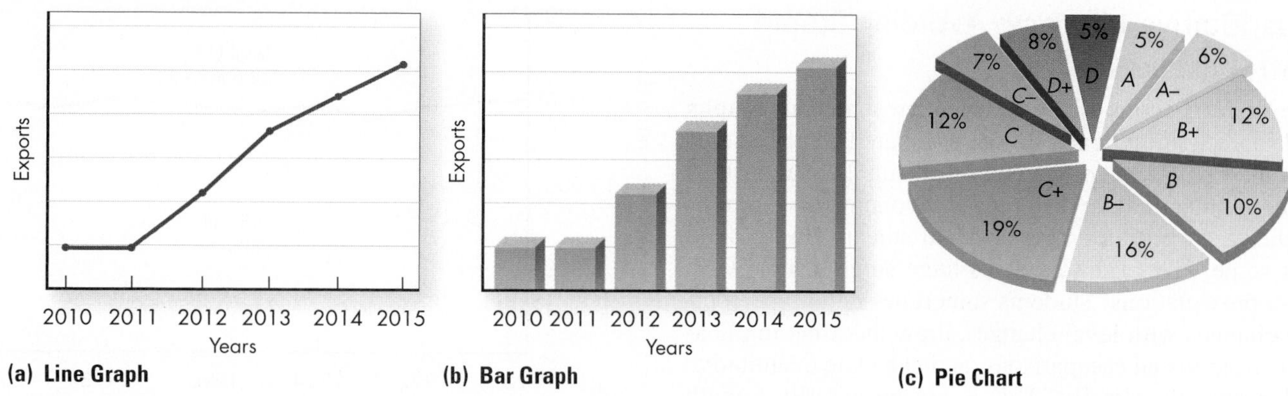

(a) Line Graph **(b) Bar Graph** **(c) Pie Chart**

(by convention) and exports on the vertical axis, as in Figure A2-6(a) and (b). Having done so, you have a couple of choices: you can draw a **line graph**—*a graph where the data are connected by a continuous line;* or you can make a **bar graph**—*a graph where the area under each point is filled in to look like a bar.* Figure A2-6(a) shows a line graph and Figure A2-6(b) shows a bar graph.

Another type of graph is a **pie chart**—*a circle divided into "pie pieces," where the undivided pie represents the total amount and the pie pieces reflect the percentage of the whole pie that the various components make up.* This type of graph is useful in visually presenting how a total amount is divided. Figure A2-6(c) shows a pie chart, which happens to represent the division of grades on a test I gave. Notice that 5 percent of the students got As.

There are other types of graphs, but they're all variations on line and bar graphs and pie charts. Once you understand these three basic types of graphs, you shouldn't have any trouble understanding the other types.

Interpreting Graphs about the Real World

Understanding Graphish is important because, if you don't, you can easily misinterpret the meaning of graphs. For example, consider the two graphs in Figure A2-7(a) and (b). Which graph demonstrates the larger rise in income? If you said (a), you're wrong. The intervals in the vertical axes differ, and if you look carefully you'll see that the curves in both graphs represent the same combination of points. So when considering graphs,

FIGURE A2-7 (A AND B) **The Importance of Scales**

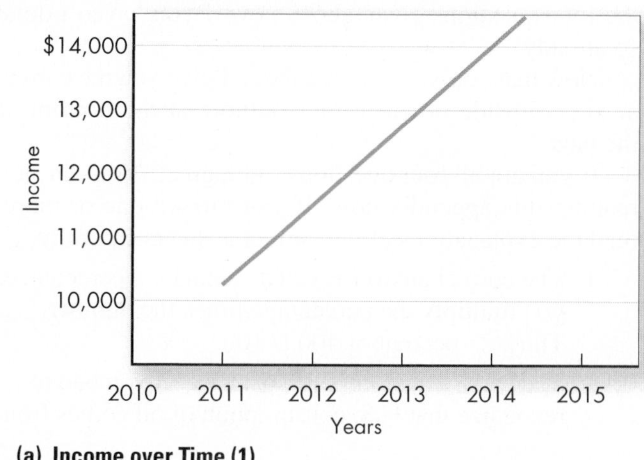

(a) Income over Time (1)

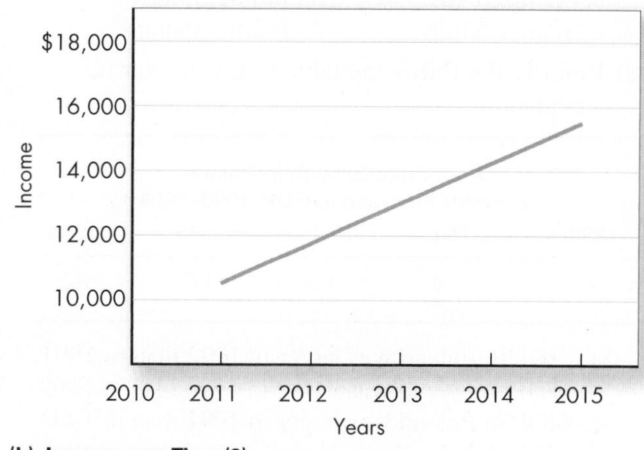

(b) Income over Time (2)

always make sure you understand the markings on the axes. Only then can you interpret the graph.

Quantitative Literacy: Avoiding Stupid Math Mistakes

The data of economics are often presented in graphs and tables. Numerical data are compared by the use of percentages, visual comparisons, and simple relationships based on quantitative differences. Economists who have studied the learning process of their students have found that some very bright students have some trouble with these presentations. Students sometimes mix up percentage changes with level changes, draw incorrect implications from visual comparisons, and calculate quantitative differences incorrectly. This is not necessarily a math problem—at least in the sense that most economists think of math. The mistakes are in relatively simple stuff—the kind of stuff learned in fifth, sixth, and seventh grades. Specifically, as reported in "Student Quantitative Literacy: Is the Glass Half-full or Half-empty?" (Robert Burns, Kim Marie McGoldrick, Jerry L. Petr, and Peter Schuhmann, 2002 University of North Carolina at Wilmington Working Paper), when the professors gave a test to students at a variety of schools, they found that a majority of students missed the following questions.

1. What is 25 percent of 400?
   a. 25 b. 50 c. 100
   d. 400 e. none of the above
2. Consider Figure A2-8, where U.S. oil consumption and U.S. oil imports are plotted for 1990–2000. Fill in the blanks to construct a true statement: U.S. domestic oil consumption has been steady while imports have been ______________; therefore U.S. domestic oil production has been ______________.
   a. rising; rising b. falling; falling
   c. rising; falling d. falling; rising
3. Refer to the following table to select the true statement.

Economic Growth in Poland
Percent Increase in GDP, 1990–1994

1990	1991	1992	1993	1994
−11.7	−7.8	−1.5	4.0	3.5

   a. GDP in Poland was larger in 1992 than in 1991.
   b. GDP in Poland was larger in 1994 than in 1993.
   c. GDP in Poland was larger in 1991 than in 1992.
   d. GDP in Poland was larger in 1993 than in 1994.
   e. Both b and c are true.

FIGURE A2-8

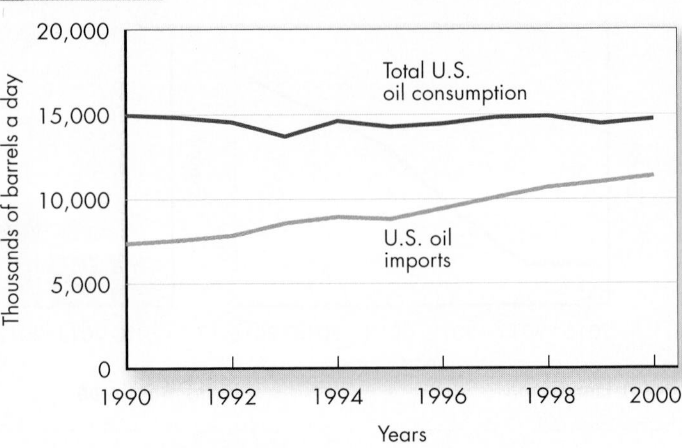

4. If U.S. production of corn was 60 million bushels in 2002 and 100 million bushels in 2003, what was the percentage change in corn production from 2002 to 2003?
   a. 40 b. 60 c. 66.67
   d. 100 e. 200

The reason students got these questions wrong is unknown. Many of them had had higher-level math courses, including calculus, so it is not that they weren't trained in math. I suspect that many students missed the questions because of carelessness: the students didn't think about the question carefully before they wrote down the answer.

Throughout this book we will be discussing issues assuming a quantitative literacy sufficient to answer these questions. Moreover, questions using similar reasoning will be on exams. So it is useful for you to see whether or not you fall in the majority. So please answer the four questions given above now if you haven't done so already.

Now that you've answered them, I give you the correct answers upside-down in the footnote at the bottom of the page.[1]

If you got all four questions right, great! You can stop reading this appendix now. If you missed one or more, read the explanations of the correct answers carefully.

1. The correct answer is c. To calculate a percentage, you multiply the percentage times the number. Thus, 25 percent of 400 is 100.
2. The correct answer is c. To answer it you had to recognize that U.S. consumption of oil comes from

[1] 1-c; 2-c; 3-e; 4-c.

U.S. imports and U.S. production. Thus, the distance between the two lines represents U.S. production, which is clearly getting smaller from 1990 to 2000.

3. The correct answer is e. The numbers given to you are percentage changes, and the question is about levels. If the percentage change is positive, as it is in 1993 and 1994, the level is increasing. Thus, 1994 is greater (by 3.5 percent) than 1993, even though the percentage change is smaller than in 1993. If the percentage change is negative, as it is in 1992, the level is falling. Because income fell in 1992, the level of income in 1991 is greater than the level of income in 1992.
4. The correct answer is c. To calculate percentage change, you first need to calculate the change, which in this case is 100 − 60, or 40. So corn production started at a base of 60 and rose by 40. To calculate the percentage change that this represents, you divide the amount of the rise, 40, by the base, 60. Doing so gives us $40/60 = 2/3 = .6667$, which is 66.67 percent.

Now that I've given you the answers, I suspect that most of you will recognize that they are the right answers. If, after reading the explanations, you still don't follow the reasoning, you should look into getting some extra help in the course either from your teacher, from your TA, or from some program the college has. If, after reading the explanations, you follow them and believe that if you had really thought about them you would have gotten them right, then the next time you see a chart or a table of numbers being compared *really think about them.* Be a bit slower in drawing inferences since they are the building blocks of economic discussions. If you want to do well on exams, it probably makes sense to practice some similar questions to make sure that you have concepts down.

A Review

Let's now review what we've covered.

- A graph is a picture of points on a coordinate system in which the points denote relationships between numbers.
- A downward-sloping line represents an inverse relationship or a negative slope.
- An upward-sloping line represents a direct relationship or a positive slope.
- Slope is measured by rise over run, or a change of y (the number measured on the vertical axis) over a change in x (the number measured on the horizontal axis).
- The slope of a point on a nonlinear curve is measured by the rise over the run of a line tangent to that point.
- At the maximum and minimum points of a nonlinear curve, the value of the slope is zero.
- A linear curve has the form $y = mx + b$.
- A shift in a linear curve is reflected by a change in the b variable in the equation $y = mx + b$.
- A change in the slope of a linear curve is reflected by a change in the m variable in the equation $y = mx + b$.
- In reading graphs, one must be careful to understand what's being measured on the vertical and horizontal axes.

Key Terms

bar graph *(47)*
coordinate system *(42)*
direct relationship *(44)*
graph *(42)*
interpolation assumption *(44)*
inverse relationship *(44)*
line graph *(47)*
linear curve *(44)*
nonlinear curve *(44)*
pie chart *(47)*
slope *(44)*

Questions and Exercises

1. Create a coordinate space on graph paper and label the following points:
   a. (0, 5)
   b. (−5, −5)
   c. (2, −3)
   d. (−1, 1)

2. Graph the following costs per unit, and answer the questions that follow.

Horizontal Axis: Output	Vertical Axis: Cost per Unit
1	$30
2	20
3	12
4	6
5	2
6	6
7	12
8	20
9	30

   a. Is the relationship between cost per unit and output linear or nonlinear? Why?
   b. In what range in output is the relationship inverse? In what range in output is the relationship direct?
   c. In what range in output is the slope negative? In what range in output is the slope positive?
   d. What is the slope between 1 and 2 units?

3. Within a coordinate space, draw a line with
   a. Zero slope.
   b. Infinite slope.
   c. Positive slope.
   d. Negative slope.

4. Calculate the slope of lines *a* through *e* in the following coordinate system.

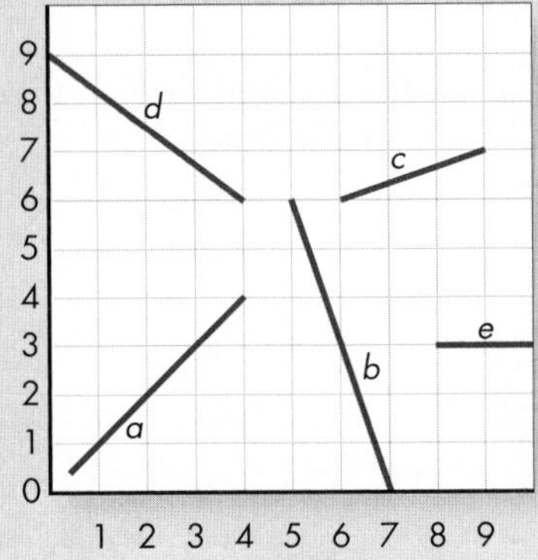

5. Given the following nonlinear curve, answer the following questions:

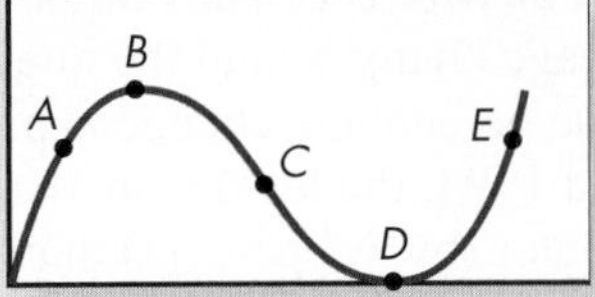

   a. At what point(s) is the slope negative?
   b. At what point(s) is the slope positive?
   c. At what point(s) is the slope zero?
   d. What point is the maximum? What point is the minimum?

6. Draw the graphs that correspond to the following equations:
   a. $y = 3x - 8$
   b. $y = 12 - x$
   c. $y = 4x + 2$

7. Using the equation $y = 3x + 1{,}000$, demonstrate the following:
   a. The slope of the curve changes to 5.
   b. The curve shifts up by 500.

8. State what type of graph or chart you might use to show the following real-world data:
   a. Interest rates from 1929 to 2013.
   b. Median income levels of various ethnic groups in the United States.
   c. Total federal expenditures by selected categories.
   d. Total costs of producing between 100 and 800 shoes.

Economic Institutions

> *Nobody can be a great economist who is only an economist—and I am even tempted to add that the economist who is only an economist is likely to become a nuisance if not a positive danger.*
>
> —Friedrich Hayek

The powerful U.S. economy generates a high standard of living and sense of economic well-being (compared to most other countries) for almost all those living in the United States. The reason why is often attributed to its use of markets, and to the wonders of a market economy. To some degree, that's true, but simply saying markets are the reason for the strength of the U.S. economy obscures as much information as it conveys. First, it misses the point that other countries have markets too, but many of those have much lower standards of living. Second, it conveys a sense that markets exist independently of social and cultural institutions, and that's just not correct. Markets are highly developed social constructs that are part of a country's social and economic institutions. Markets are based on **institutions,** which Nobel Prize–winning economist Douglass North defines as "*the formal and informal rules that constrain human economic behavior.*" Institutions include laws that protect ownership of property and the legal system to enforce and interpret laws. They also include political institutions that develop those laws, the cultural traits of society that guide people's tastes and behaviors, and the many organizational structures such as corporations, banks, and nonprofit organizations that make up our economy. To understand markets, you need to understand institutions. In a principles course, we don't have time to develop a full analysis of institutions, but what we can do is to provide an overview of U.S. economic institutions and a brief discussion of why they are important. That's what we do in this chapter.

We begin by looking at the U.S. economic system in historical perspective, considering how it evolved and how it relates to other historical economic systems. Then we consider some of the central institutions of the modern U.S. economy and how they influence the way in which the economy works.

After reading this chapter, you should be able to:

LO3-1 Define *market economy* and compare and contrast socialism with capitalism.

LO3-2 Describe the role of businesses and households in a market economy.

LO3-3 List and discuss the various roles of government.

LO3-4 Explain why global policy issues differ from national policy issues.

Economic Systems

A market economy is an economic system based on private property and the market. It gives private property rights to individuals and relies on market forces to coordinate economic activity.

The U.S. economy is a **market economy**—*an economic system based on private property and the market in which, in principle, individuals decide how, what, and for whom to produce.* In a market economy, individuals follow their own self-interest, while market forces of supply and demand are relied on to coordinate those individual pursuits. Businesses, guided by prices in the market, produce goods and services that they believe people want and that will earn a profit for the business. Prices in the market guide businesses in deciding what to produce. Distribution of goods is to each individual according to his or her ability, effort, inherited property, and luck.

Reliance on market forces doesn't mean that political, social, and historical forces play no role in coordinating economic decisions. These other forces do influence how the market works. For example, for a market to exist, government must allocate and defend **private property rights**—*the control a private individual or firm has over an asset.* The concept of private ownership must exist and must be accepted by individuals in society. When you say "This car is mine," you mean that it is unlawful for someone else to take it without your permission. If someone takes it without your permission, he or she is subject to punishment through the legal system.

Q-1 John, your study partner, is telling you that the best way to allocate property rights is through the market. How do you respond?

How Markets Work

Markets work through a system of rewards and payments. If you do something, you get paid for doing that something; if you take something, you pay for that something. How much you get is determined by how much you give. This relationship seems fair to most people. But there are instances when it doesn't seem fair. Say someone is unable to work. Should that person get nothing? How about Joe down the street, who was given $10 million by his parents? Is it fair that he gets lots of toys, like Corvettes and skiing trips to Aspen, and doesn't have to work, while the rest of us have to work 40 hours a week and maybe go to school at night?

I'll put those questions about fairness off at this point—they are very difficult questions. For now, all I want to present is the concept of fairness that underlies a market economy: "Them that works, gets; them that don't, starve."[1] In a market economy, individuals are encouraged to follow their own self-interest.

In market economies, individuals are free to do whatever they want as long as it's legal. The market is relied on to see that what people want to get, and want to do, is consistent with what's available. Price is the mechanism through which people's desires are coordinated and goods are rationed. If there's not enough of something to go around, its price goes up; if more of something needs to get done, the price given to individuals willing to do it goes up. If something isn't wanted or doesn't need to be done, its price goes down. In a market economy, fluctuations in prices play a central role in coordinating individuals' wants.

Fluctuations in prices play a central role in coordinating individuals' wants in a market economy.

---

[1]How come the professor gets to use rotten grammar but screams when he sees rotten grammar in your papers? Well, that's fairness for you. Actually, I should say a bit more about writing style. All writers are expected to know correct grammar; if they don't, they don't deserve to be called writers. Once you know grammar, you can individualize your writing style, breaking the rules of grammar where the meter and flow of the writing require it. In college you're still proving that you know grammar, so in papers handed in to your teacher, you shouldn't break the rules of grammar until you've proved to the teacher that you know them. Me, I've done lots of books, so my editors give me a bit more leeway than your teachers will give you.

What's Good about the Market?

WWW Web Note 3.1
What Are Markets?

Is the market a good way to coordinate individuals' activities? Much of this book will be devoted to answering that question. The answer that I, and most U.S. economists, come to is: Yes, it is a reasonable way. True, it has problems; the market can be unfair, mean, and arbitrary, and sometimes it is downright awful. Why then do economists support it? For the same reason that Oliver Wendell Holmes supported democracy—it is a lousy system, but, based on experience with alternatives, it is better than all the others we've thought of.

The primary debate among economists is not about using markets; it is about how markets should be structured, and whether they should be modified and adjusted by government regulation. Those are much harder questions, and on these questions, opinions differ enormously.

The primary debate among economists is not about using markets but about how markets are structured.

Capitalism and Socialism

The view that markets are a reasonable way to organize society has not always been shared by all economists. Throughout history strong philosophical and practical arguments have been made against markets. The philosophical argument against the market is that it brings out the worst in people—it glorifies greed. It encourages people to beat out others rather than to be cooperative. As an alternative some economists have supported socialism. In theory, **socialism** is *an economic system based on individuals' goodwill toward others, not on their own self-interest, and in which, in principle, society decides what, how, and for whom to produce.* The concept of socialism developed in the 1800s as a description of a hypothetical economic system to be contrasted with the predominant market-based economic system of the time, which was called capitalism. **Capitalism** is defined as *an economic system based on the market in which the ownership of the means of production resides with a small group of individuals called capitalists.*

Q-2 Which would be more likely to attempt to foster individualism: socialism or capitalism?

You can best understand the idea behind theoretical socialism by thinking about how decisions are made in a family. In most families, benevolent parents decide who gets what, based on the needs of each member of the family. When Sabin gets a new coat and his sister Sally doesn't, it's because Sabin needs a coat while Sally already has two coats that fit her and are in good condition. Victor may be slow as molasses, but from his family he still gets as much as his superefficient brother Jerry gets. In fact, Victor may get more than Jerry because he needs extra help.

Q-3 Are there any activities in a family that you believe should be allocated by a market? What characteristics do those activities have?

Markets have little role in most families. In my family, when food is placed on the table, we don't bid on what we want, with the highest bidder getting the food. In my family, every person can eat all he or she wants, although if one child eats more than a fair share, that child gets a lecture from me on the importance of sharing. "Be thoughtful; be considerate. Think of others first" are lessons that many families try to teach.

In theory, socialism was an economic system that tried to organize society in the same way as most families are organized, trying to see that individuals get what they need. Socialism tried to take other people's needs into account and adjust people's own wants in accordance with what's available. In socialist economies, individuals were urged to look out for the other person; if individuals' inherent goodness does not make them consider the general good, government would make them. In contrast, a capitalist economy expected people to be selfish; it relied on markets and competition to direct that selfishness to the general good.[2]

Socialism is, in theory, an economic system that tries to organize society in the same way as most families are organized—all people contribute what they can and get what they need.

[2]As you probably surmised, the above distinction is too sharp. Even capitalist societies wanted people to be selfless, but not too selfless. Children in capitalist societies were generally taught to be selfless at least in dealing with friends and family. The difficulty parents and societies face is finding a balance between the two positions: selfless but not too selfless; selfish but not too selfish.

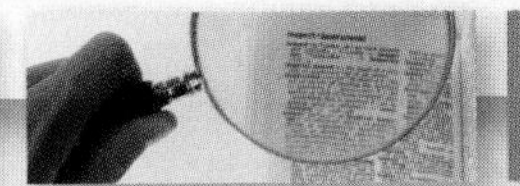

ADDED DIMENSION

Tradition and Today's Economy

In a tradition-based society, the social and cultural forces create an inertia (a tendency to resist change) that predominates over economic and political forces.

"Why did you do it that way?"

"Because that's the way we've always done it."

Tradition-based societies had markets, but they were peripheral, not central, to economic life. In feudal times, what was produced, how it was produced, and for whom it was produced were primarily decided by tradition.

In today's U.S. economy, the market plays the central role in economic decisions. But that doesn't mean that tradition is dead. As I said in Chapter 1, tradition still plays a significant role in today's society, and, in many aspects of society, tradition still overwhelms the invisible hand. Consider the following:

1. The persistent view that women should be homemakers rather than factory workers, consumers rather than producers.
2. The raised eyebrows when a man is introduced as a nurse, secretary, homemaker, or member of any other profession conventionally identified as women's work.
3. Society's unwillingness to permit the sale of individuals or body organs.
4. Parents' willingness to care for their children without financial compensation.

Each of these tendencies reflects tradition's influence in Western society. Some are so deeply rooted that we see them as self-evident. Some of tradition's effects we like; others we don't—but we often take them for granted. Economic forces may work against these traditions, but the fact that they're still around indicates the continued strength of tradition in our market economy.

As I stated above, the term *socialism* originally developed as a description of a hypothetical, not an actual, economic system. Actual socialist economies came into being only in the early 1900s, and when they developed they differed enormously from the hypothetical socialist economies that writers had described earlier.

Q-4 What is the difference between socialism in theory and socialism in practice?

In practice socialist governments had to take a strong role in guiding the economy. Socialism became known as an economic system based on government ownership of the means of production, with economic activity governed by central planning. In a centrally planned socialist economy, sometimes called a command economy, government planning boards set society's goals and then directed individuals and firms as to how to achieve those goals.

For example, if government planning boards decided that whole-wheat bread was good for people, they directed firms to produce large quantities and priced it exceptionally low. Planners, not prices, coordinated people's actions. The results were often not quite what the planners desired. Bread prices were so low that pig farmers fed bread to their pigs even though pig feed would have been better for the pigs and bread was more costly to produce. At the low price, the quantity of bread demanded was so high that there were bread shortages; consumers had to stand in long lines to buy bread for their families.

As is often the case, over time the meaning of the word *socialism* expanded and evolved further. It was used to describe the market economies of Western Europe, which by the 1960s had evolved into economies that had major welfare support systems and governments that were very much involved in their market economies. For example, Sweden, even though it relied on markets as its central coordinating institution, was called a socialist economy because its taxes were high and it provided a cradle-to-grave welfare system.

When the Union of Soviet Socialist Republics (USSR) broke apart, Russia and the countries that evolved out of the USSR adopted a market economy as their organizing framework. China, which is ruled by the Communist Party, also adopted many market institutions. As they did, the terms *capitalism* and *socialism* fell out of favor. People today talk little about the differences in economic systems such as capitalism and socialism; instead they talk about the differences in institutions. Most economies today are differentiated primarily by the degree to which their economies rely on markets, not whether they are a market, capitalist, or socialist economy.

People today talk little about differences in economic systems; instead they talk about differences in institutions.

The term *socialism,* however, still shows up in the news. China, for example, continues to call itself a socialist country, even though it is relying more and more heavily on markets to organize production, and is sometimes seen as more capitalistic than many Western economies. Another example of the interest in socialism can be found in the rhetoric of Venezuelan President Hugo Chávez, who is attempting to transform Venezuela into what he calls "21st century socialism." He defines 21st century socialism as government ownership, or at least control, of major resources, and an economy dominated by business cooperatives owned and operated by workers supported by government loans and contracts. President Chávez argues that this "21st century socialism" will serve as a new economic model of egalitarianism for the entire world. Most observers are doubtful. But what is likely is that economic systems and the institutions that make them up are constantly evolving, and will likely continue to evolve.[3]

Revolutionary shifts that give rise to new economic systems are not the only way economic systems change. Systems also evolve internally, as I discussed above. For example, the U.S. economy is and has always been a market economy, but it has changed over the years, evolving with changes in social customs, political forces, and the strength of markets. In the 1930s, during the Great Depression, the U.S. economy integrated a number of what might be called socialist institutions into its existing institutions. Distribution of goods was no longer, even in theory, only according to ability; need also played a role. Governments began to play a larger role in the economy, taking control over some of the *how, what,* and *for whom* decisions. From the 1980s until recently the process has been reversed. The United States became even more market oriented and the government tried to pull back its involvement in the market in favor of private enterprise. That movement slowed, and possibly ended, with the financial crisis of 2007. Which direction the future will take remains to be seen, but we can expect institutions to continue to change.

Economic Institutions in a Market Economy

Now that we have put the U.S. economic system in historical perspective, let's consider some of its main components. The U.S. economy can be divided into three sectors: businesses, households, and government, as Figure 3-1 shows. Households supply labor and other factors of production to businesses and are paid by businesses for doing so. The market where this interaction takes place is called a *factor market.* Businesses produce goods and services and sell them to households and government. The market where this interaction takes place is called the *goods market.*

Q-5 Into what three sectors are market economies generally broken up?

Each of the three sectors is interconnected; moreover, the entire U.S. economy is interconnected with the world economy. Notice also the arrows going out to and coming in from both business and households. Those arrows represent the connection of an

[3]The appendix to this chapter traces the development of economic systems.

FIGURE 3-1 Diagrammatic Representation of a Market Economy

This circular-flow diagram of the economy is a good way to organize your thinking about the aggregate economy. As you can see, the three sectors—households, government, and business—interact in a variety of ways.

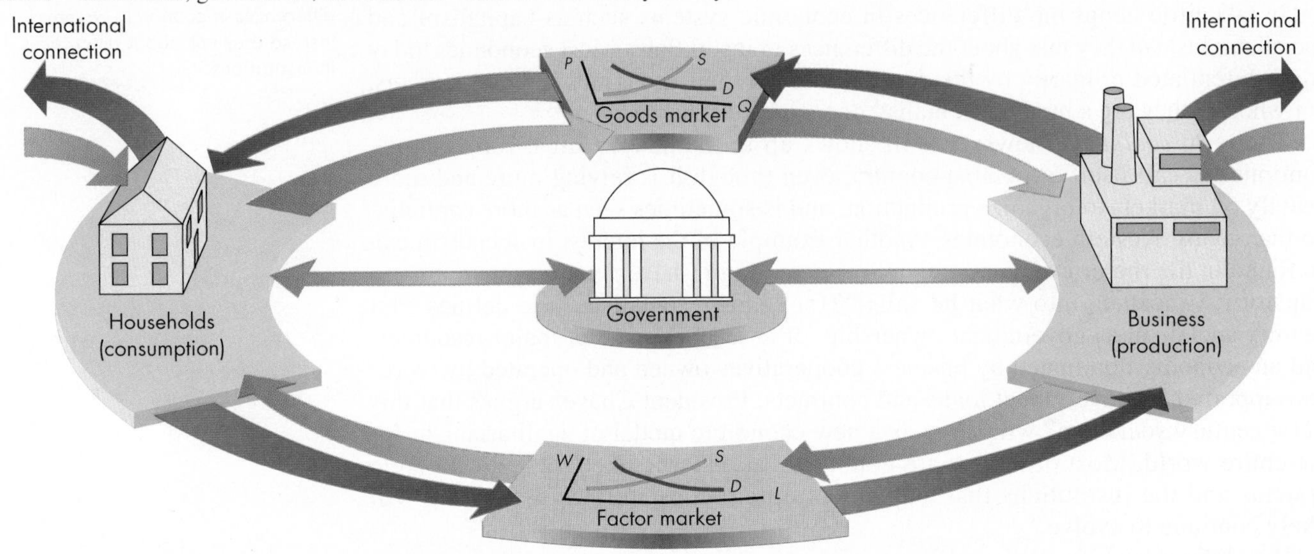

economy to the world economy. It consists of interrelated flows of goods (exports and imports) and money (capital flows). Finally, consider the arrows connecting government with households and business. Government taxes business and households. It buys goods and services from business and buys labor services from households. Then, with some of its tax revenue, it provides services (for example, roads, education) to both business and households and gives some of its tax revenue directly back to individuals. In doing so, it redistributes income. But government also serves a second function. It oversees the interaction of business and households in the goods and factor markets. Government, of course, is not independent. The United States, for instance, is a democracy, so households vote to determine who shall govern. Similarly, governments are limited not only by what voters want but also by their relationships with other countries. They are part of an international community of countries, and they must keep up relations with other countries in the world. For example, the United States is a member of many international organizations and has signed international treaties in which it has agreed to limit its domestic actions, such as its ability to tax imports.

Now let's look briefly at the individual components.

Business

WWW Web Note 3.2 Starting a Business

President Calvin Coolidge once said "The business of America is business." That's a bit of an overstatement, but business is responsible for over 80 percent of U.S. production. (Government is responsible for the other 20 percent.) In fact, anytime a household decides to produce something, it becomes a business. **Business** is simply the name given to *private producing units in our society*.

Businesses in the United States decide *what* to produce, *how* much to produce, and *for whom* to produce it.

Businesses in the United States decide *what* to produce, *how* much to produce, and *for whom* to produce it. They make these central economic decisions on the basis of their own self-interest, which is influenced by market incentives. Anyone who wants to can start a business, provided he or she can come up with the required cash and meet the necessary regulatory requirements. Each year, about 600,000 businesses are started.

Don't think of business as something other than people. Businesses are ultimately made up of a group of people organized together to accomplish some end. Although corporations account for about 80 percent of all sales, in terms of numbers of businesses, most are one- or two-person operations. Home-based businesses are easy to start. All you have to do is say you're in business, and you are. However, some businesses require licenses, permits, and approvals from various government agencies. That's one reason why **entrepreneurship** (*the ability to organize and get something done*) is an important part of business.

Entrepreneurship is an important part of business.

What Do U.S. Firms Produce? Producing physical goods is only one of society's economic tasks. Another task is to provide services (activities done for others). Services do not involve producing a physical good. When you get your hair cut, you buy a service, not a good. Much of the cost of the physical goods we buy actually is not a cost of producing the good, but is a cost of one of the most important services: distribution, which includes payments associated with having the good where you want it when you want it. After a good is produced, it has to be transported to consumers, either indirectly through retailers or directly to consumers. If the good isn't at the right place at the right time, it can often be useless.

Let's consider an example: hot dogs at a baseball game. How many of us have been irked that a hot dog that costs 40 cents to fix at home costs $5.00 at a baseball game? The reason why the price can differ so much is that a hot dog at home isn't the same as a hot dog at a game and you are willing to pay the extra $4.60 to have the hot dog when and where you want it. *Distribution*—getting goods where you want them when you want them—is as important as production and is a central component of a service economy.

The importance of the service economy can be seen in modern technology companies. They provide information and methods of handling information, not physical goods. Google and Facebook produce no physical product but they provide central services to our lives. As the U.S. economy has evolved, the relative importance of services has increased. Today, services make up approximately 80 percent of the U.S. economy, compared to 20 percent in 1947, and services are likely to continue to rise in importance in the future.

Consumer Sovereignty and Business To say that businesses decide what to produce isn't to say that **consumer sovereignty** (*the consumer's wishes determine what's produced*) doesn't reign in the United States. Businesses decide what to produce based on what they believe will sell. A key question a person in the United States generally asks about starting a business is: Can I make a profit from it? **Profit** is *what's left over from total revenues after all the appropriate costs have been subtracted.* Businesses that guess correctly what the consumer wants generally make a profit. Businesses that guess wrong generally operate at a loss.

Although businesses decide what to produce, they are guided by consumer sovereignty.

People are free to start businesses for whatever purposes they want. No one asks them: "What's the social value of your term paper assistance business, your Twinkies business, your pornography business, or your textbook publishing business?" In the United States we rely on the market to channel individuals' desire to make a profit into the general good of society. That's the invisible hand at work. As long as the business violates no law and conforms to regulations, people

Q-6 True or false? In the United States, the invisible hand ensures that only socially valuable businesses are started. Why?

FIGURE 3-2 (A AND B) Forms of Business

The charts divide firms by the type of ownership. Approximately 72 percent of businesses in the United States are sole proprietorships (**a**). In terms of annual receipts, however, corporations surpass all other forms (**b**).

Source: *Statistics of Income,* IRS, Summer 2011 (www.irs.ustreas.gov/taxstats).

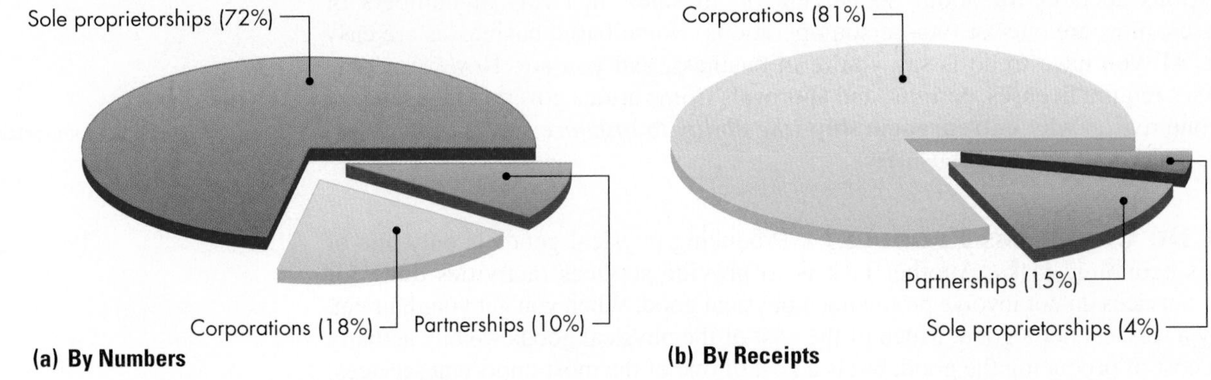

in the United States are free to start whatever business they want, if they can get the money to finance it.

Q-7 Are most businesses in the United States corporations? If not, what are most businesses?

Forms of Business The three primary forms of business are sole proprietorships, partnerships, and corporations. **Sole proprietorships**—*businesses that have only one owner*—are the easiest to start and have the fewest bureaucratic hassles. **Partnerships**—*businesses with two or more owners*—create possibilities for sharing the burden, but they also create unlimited liability for each of the partners. **Corporations**—*businesses that are treated as a person, and are legally owned by their stockholders, who are not liable for the actions of the corporate "person"*—are the largest form of business when measured in terms of receipts. In corporations, ownership is separated from control of the firm. Of the 35 million businesses in the United States, approximately 72 percent are sole proprietorships, 10 percent are partnerships, and 18 percent are corporations, as we see in Figure 3-2(a). In terms of total receipts, however, we get a quite different picture, with corporations far surpassing all other business forms, as Figure 3-2(b) shows.[4]

A corporation provides the owner with limited liability.

In the past few years a number of companies—what might be *called flexible-purpose corporations or benefit corporations (B-corporations)*—have arisen that explicitly take social mission in addition to profit into consideration when making decisions. An example is Maine's Own Organic Milk Company (MOO Milk Co), which has both selling milk and educating the public about the value of local family farming as explicit goals. Some states have established a new form of corporation—the L3C, which allows companies, such as MOO Milk Co, to blend social and private goals. Unlike for-profit companies, L3Cs can receive grants and endowments otherwise reserved for nonprofits. Other companies, such as Google, are retaining their for-profit corporate status but are explicitly including social welfare in their charters.

[4]As laws have evolved, the sharp distinctions among forms of businesses have blurred. Today there are many types of corporations and types of partnerships that have varying degrees of limited liabilities.

The advantages and disadvantages of each form of business are summarized in the following table:

Advantages and Disadvantages of Various Forms of For-Profit Businesses

	Sole Proprietorship	Partnership	Corporation
Advantages	1. Minimum bureaucratic hassle 2. Direct control by owner	1. Ability to share work and risks 2. Relatively easy to form	1. No personal liability 2. Increasing ability to get funds 3. Ability to avoid personal income taxes
Disadvantages	1. Limited ability to get funds 2. Unlimited personal liability	1. Unlimited personal liability (even for partner's blunder) 2. Limited ability to get funds	1. Legal hassle to organize 2. Possible double taxation of income 3. Monitoring problems

Finance and Business Much of what you hear in the news about business concerns financial assets—assets that acquire value from an obligation of someone else to pay. Stocks are one example of a financial asset; bonds are another. Financial assets are traded in markets such as the New York Stock Exchange. Trading in financial markets can make people rich (or poor) quickly. Stocks and bonds also can provide a means through which corporations can finance expansions and new investments.

Trading in financial markets can make people rich (or poor) quickly.

An important tool investors use to decide where to invest is the accounting statements firms provide. From these, individuals judge how profitable firms are, and how profitable they are likely to be in the future. In the early 2000s, investors' trust in firms was shattered by a series of accounting frauds, which led government to increase the regulatory control of business accounting practices.

Households

The second classification we'll consider in this overview of U.S. economic institutions is households. **Households** (*groups of individuals living together and making joint decisions*) are the most powerful economic institution. They ultimately control government and business, the other two economic institutions. Households' votes in the political arena determine government policy; their decisions about supplying labor and capital determine what businesses will have available to work with; and their spending decisions or expenditures (the "votes" they cast with their dollars) determine what business will be able to sell.

In the economy, households vote with their dollars.

The Power of Households While the ultimate power does in principle reside with the people and households, we, the people, have assigned much of that power to representatives. As I discussed above, corporations are only partially responsive to owners of their stocks, and much of that ownership is once-removed from individuals. Ownership of 1,000 shares in a company with a total of 2 million shares isn't going to get you any influence over the corporation's activities. As a stockholder, you simply accept what the corporation does.

REAL-WORLD APPLICATION

Who Are the 1%?

The differences between the very rich and everyone else has come to the fore with the Occupy movement. The slogan "We are the 99%" pits most people against the 1%. Who are the 1%?

When presidential candidate Mitt Romney was asked about his income in 2012, he declined to answer, but he did note that in 2011 he got speakers' fees from time to time, but that they were "not very much." Elsewhere he had listed those "not very much" speaker fees—they totaled $375,000. When you can say that $375,000 is not very much, you are definitely part of the 1%. In fact, that "not very much" alone would have almost put him in the top 1%, since a household's income needs to be at least $383,000 to be in the top 1%. That's approximately eight times the median income. $188,000 puts you in the top 5% while $90,000 put you in the top 25%.

Those numbers are an average for the country as a whole. The threshold differs a lot by state. In Flint, Michigan, $180,000 would put you in the top 1% but in the New York City area that's only the top 10%. In Stamford, Connecticut, you'd have to earn about $900,000 to be in the top 1%.

This top 1% earns about 20% of total pretax income in the United States and pays about 25% of all federal taxes. Forty percent of them inherited money as well as earning it, and they are twice as likely to be married, in part because that gives them two incomes, and in part because they are good "marriage material." They don't have more cars than middle-class, but they do tend to drive ritzier cars—you see lots of Lexus's and Mercedes's in Naples, Florida. You see a lot more clunkers in Flint.

When thinking about the 1%, it is important to realize that one can consume only so much "stuff." Capitalism may create inequalities but it also can improve the life of the poor. As economist, Joseph Schumpeter pointed out: "Electric lighting is no great boon to anyone who has money enough to buy a sufficient number of candles and to pay servants to attend them. It is the cheap cloth, the cheap cotton and rayon fabric, boots, motorcars and so on that are the typical achievements of capitalist production, and not as a rule improvements that would mean much to a rich man. Queen Elizabeth owned silk stockings. The capitalist achievement does not typically consist in providing more silk stockings for queens but in bringing them within the reach of factory girls in return for steadily decreasing amounts of effort."

Consumer sovereignty reigns, but it works indirectly by influencing businesses.

A major decision that corporations make independently of their stockholders concerns what to produce. True, ultimately we, the people, decide whether we will buy what business produces, but business spends a lot of money telling us what services we want, what products make us "with it," what books we want to read, and the like. Most economists believe that consumer sovereignty reigns—that we are not fooled or controlled by advertising. Still, it is an open question in some economists' minds whether we, the people, control business or whether the business representatives control the people.

Because of this assignment of power to other institutions, in many spheres of the economy households are not active producers of output but merely passive recipients of income, primarily in their role as suppliers of labor.

Suppliers of Labor The largest source of household income is wages and salaries (the income households get from labor). Households supply the labor with which businesses produce and government governs. The total U.S. labor force is about 155 million people, about 8 percent of whom were unemployed in 2012. The average U.S. workweek is about 41 hours for males and about 36 hours for females. The median pay in the United States was $850 per week for males and $700 for females. The median hourly wage for all workers is about $16.50. Of course, that average represents enormous variability and depends on the occupation and region of the country where one is employed. For example, lawyers often earn $100,000 per year; physicians earn about $190,000 per year; and CEOs of large corporations often make $2 million per year or more. A beginning McDonald's employee generally makes about $13,000 per year.

The Roles of Government

The third major U.S. economic institution I'll consider is government. Government plays two general roles in the economy. It's both a referee (setting the rules that determine relations between business and households) and an actor (collecting money in taxes and spending that money on projects such as defense and education). Let's first consider government's role as an actor.

Government as an Actor

The United States has a federal government system, which means we have various levels of government (federal, state, and local), each with its own powers. Together they consume about 20 percent of the country's total output and employ about 22 million individuals. The various levels of government also have a number of programs that redistribute income through taxation and social welfare and assistance programs designed to help specific groups.

WWW Web Note 3.3
Government Websites

State and local governments employ over 19 million people and spend about $2.1 trillion a year. As you can see in Figure 3-3(a), state and local governments get much of their income from taxes: property taxes, sales taxes, and state and local income taxes. They spend their tax revenues on public welfare, administration, education (education through high school is available free in U.S. public schools), and transportation, as Figure 3-3(b) shows.

Probably the best way to get an initial feel for the federal government and its size is to look at the various categories of its tax revenues and expenditures in Figure 3-4(a). Notice income taxes make up about 42 percent of the federal government's revenue, and Social Security taxes make up about 35 percent. That's about 80 percent of the federal government's revenues, most of which show up as a deduction from your paycheck. In Figure 3-4(b), notice that the federal government's two largest categories of spending are income security and health and education, with expenditures on national defense close behind.

Q-8 The largest percentage of federal expenditures is in what general category?

FIGURE 3-3 (A AND B) **Income and Expenditures of State and Local Governments**

The charts give you a sense of the importance of state and local governments—where they get (**a**) and where they spend (**b**) their revenues.

Source: *State and Local Government Finance Estimates*, Bureau of the Census (www.census.gov).

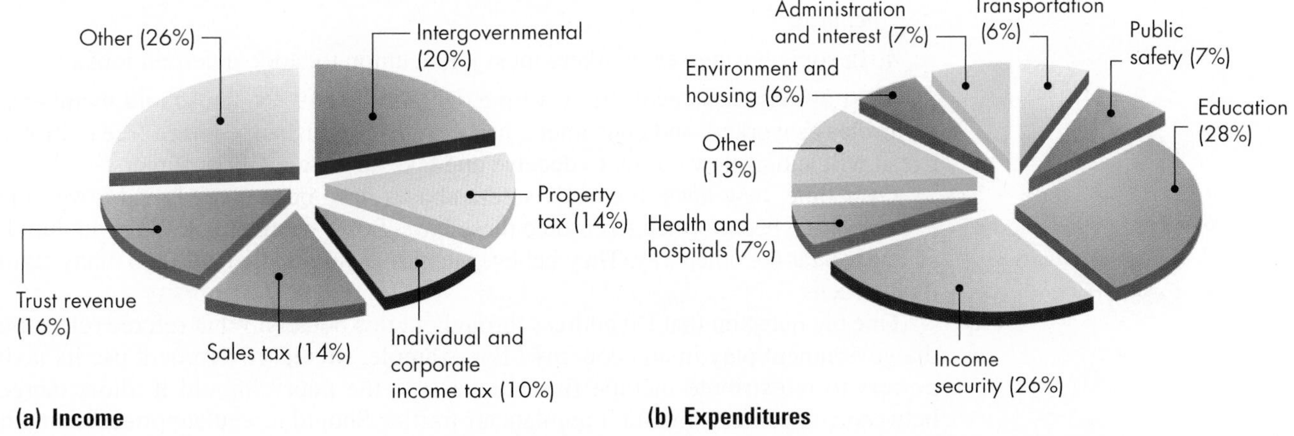

FIGURE 3-4 (A AND B) Income and Expenditures of the Federal Government

The pie charts show the sources and uses of federal government revenue. It is important to note that, when the government runs a deficit, expenditures exceed income and the difference is made up by borrowing, so the size of the income and expenditure pies may not be equal. In recent years expenditures have significantly exceeded income.

Source: *Survey of Current Business,* Bureau of Economic Analysis (www.bea.doc.gov).

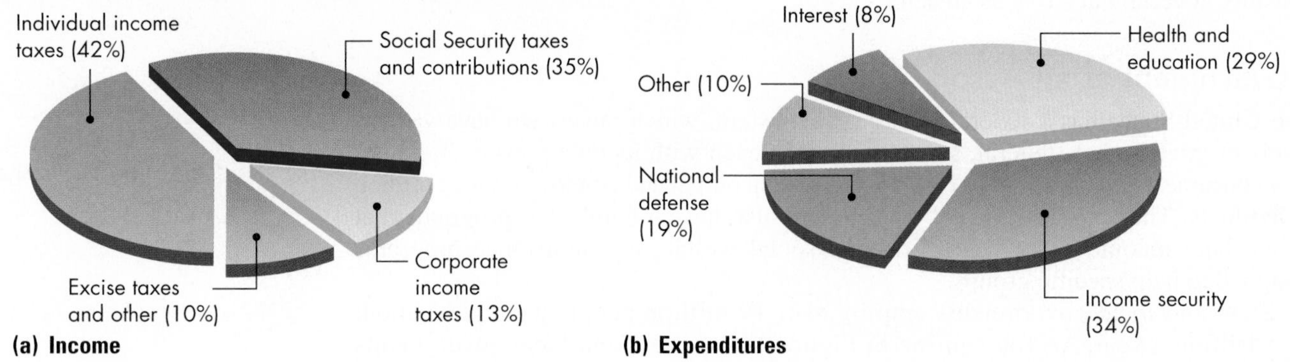

Government as a Referee

Even if government spending made up only a small proportion of total expenditures, government would still be central to the study of economics. The reason is that, in a market economy, government sets the rules of interaction between households and businesses, and acts as a referee, enforcing the rules and changing them when it sees fit. Government decides whether economic forces will be allowed to operate freely.

Some examples of U.S. laws regulating the interaction between households and businesses today are:

1. Businesses are not free to hire and fire whomever they want. They must comply with equal opportunity and labor laws. Even closing a plant requires 60 days' notice for many kinds of firms.
2. Many working conditions are subject to government regulation: safety rules, wage rules, overtime rules, hours-of-work rules, and the like.
3. Businesses cannot meet with other businesses to agree on prices they will charge.
4. In some businesses, workers must join a union to work at certain jobs.

Most of these laws evolved over time. Up until the 1930s, household members, in their roles as workers and consumers, had few rights. Businesses were free to hire and fire at will and, if they chose, to deceive and take advantage of consumers.

Over time, new laws to curb business abuses have been passed, and government agencies have been formed to enforce these laws. Some people think the pendulum has swung too far the other way. They believe businesses are saddled with too many regulatory burdens.

One big question that I'll address throughout this book is: What referee role should the government play in an economy? For example, should government use its taxing powers to redistribute income from the rich to the poor? Should it allow mergers between companies? Should it regulate air traffic? Should it regulate prices? Should it attempt to stabilize fluctuations of aggregate income?

Specific Roles for Government

In its role as both an actor and a referee, government plays a variety of specific roles in the economy. These include:

1. Providing a stable set of institutions and rules.
2. Promoting effective and workable competition.
3. Correcting for externalities.
4. Ensuring economic stability and growth.
5. Providing public goods.
6. Adjusting for undesirable market results.

PROVIDE A STABLE SET OF INSTITUTIONS AND RULES A basic role of government is to provide a stable institutional framework that includes the set of laws specifying what can and cannot be done as well as a mechanism to enforce those laws. For example, if someone doesn't pay you, you can't go take what you are owed; you have to go through the government court system. Where governments don't provide a stable institutional framework, as often happens in developing and transitional countries, economic activity is difficult; usually such economies are stagnant. Somalia in the early 2000s is an example. As various groups fought for political control, the Somalian economy stagnated.

PROMOTE EFFECTIVE AND WORKABLE COMPETITION In a market economy, the pressure to monopolize—for one firm to try to control the market—and competition are always in conflict; the government must decide what role it is to play in protecting or promoting competition. Thus, when Microsoft gained monopolistic control of the computer operating system market with Windows, the U.S. government took the company to court and challenged that monopoly.

What makes this a difficult function for government is that most individuals and firms believe that competition is far better for the other guy than it is for themselves, that their own monopolies are necessary monopolies, and that competition facing them is unfair competition. For example, most farmers support competition, but these same farmers also support government farm subsidies (payments by government to producers based on production levels) and import restrictions. Likewise, most firms support competition, but these same firms also support tariffs, which protect them from foreign competition. Most professionals, such as architects and engineers, support competition, but they also support professional licensing, which limits the number of competitors who can enter their field. As you will see when reading the newspapers, there are always arguments for limiting entry into fields. The job of the government is to determine whether these arguments are strong enough to overcome the negative effects those limitations have on competition.

The government may be able to help correct for externalities.

CORRECT FOR EXTERNALITIES When two people freely enter into a trade or agreement, they both believe that they will benefit from the trade. But unless they're required to do so, traders are unlikely to take into account any effect that an action may have on a third party. Economists call *the effect of a decision on a third party not taken into account by the decision maker* an **externality.** An externality can be positive (in which case society as a whole benefits from the trade between the two parties) or negative (in which case society as a whole is harmed by the trade between the two parties).

An example of a positive externality is education. When someone educates herself or himself, all society benefits, since better-educated people usually make better citizens and are better equipped to figure out new approaches to solving problems—approaches that benefit society as a whole. An example of a negative externality involves the burning of coal, which puts sulfur dioxide, carbon dioxide, and fine particulates into the air. Sulfur dioxide contributes to acid rain, carbon dioxide contributes to global warming, and fine particulates damage people's lungs. This means that burning coal has an externality associated with it—an effect of an action that is not taken into account by market participants.

When there are externalities, there is a potential role for government to adjust the market result through taxes, subsidies, or regulation. Throughout this book we will be considering the advantages and disadvantages of each.

Ensure Economic Stability and Growth In addition to providing general stability, government has the potential role of providing economic stability. Most people would agree that if it's possible, government should prevent large fluctuations in the level of economic activity, maintain a relatively constant price level, and provide an economic environment conducive to economic growth. These aims, which became the goals of the U.S. government in 1946 when the Employment Act was passed, are generally considered macroeconomic goals. They're justified as appropriate aims for government to pursue because they involve **macroeconomic externalities** (*externalities that affect the levels of unemployment, inflation, or growth in the economy as a whole*).

A macroeconomic externality is the effect of an individual decision that affects the levels of unemployment, inflation, or growth in an economy as a whole but is not taken into account by the individual decision maker.

Here's how a macro externality could occur. When individuals decide how much to spend, they don't take into account the effects of their decision on others; thus, there may be too much or too little spending. Too little spending often leads to unemployment. But in making their spending decision, people don't take into account the fact that spending less might create unemployment. So their spending decisions can involve a macro externality. Similarly, when people raise their price and don't consider the effect on inflation, they too might be creating a macro externality.

Provide Public Goods Another role for government is to supply public goods. A **public good** is *a good that if supplied to one person must be supplied to all and whose consumption by one individual does not prevent its consumption by another individual.* In contrast, a **private good** is *a good that, when consumed by one individual, cannot be consumed by another individual.* An example of a private good is an apple; once I eat that apple, no one else can consume it. An example of a public good is national defense, which, if supplied to one, will also protect others. In order to supply defense, governments must require people to pay for it with taxes, rather than leaving it to the market to supply it.

Adjust for Undesirable Market Results A controversial role for government is to adjust the results of the market when those market results are seen as socially undesirable. Government redistributes income, taking it away from some individuals and giving it to others whom it sees as more deserving or more in need. In doing so, it attempts to see that the outcomes of trades are fair. Determining what's fair is a difficult philosophical question that economists can't answer. That question is for the people, through the government, to decide.

An example of this role involves having government decide what's best for people, independently of their desires. The market allows individuals to decide. But what if people don't know what's best for themselves? Or what if they do know but don't act on that knowledge? For example, people might know that addictive drugs are bad for them, but because of peer pressure, or because they just don't care, they may take drugs anyway. Government action prohibiting such activities through laws or high taxes may then be warranted. *Goods or activities that government believes are bad for*

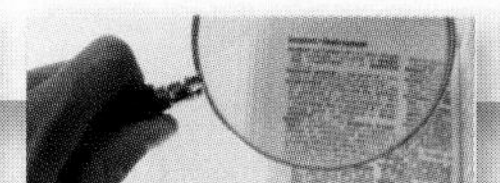

ADDED DIMENSION

Our International Competitors

The world economy is often divided into three main areas or trading blocs: the Americas, Europe and Africa, and East Asia. These trading blocs are shown in the map below.

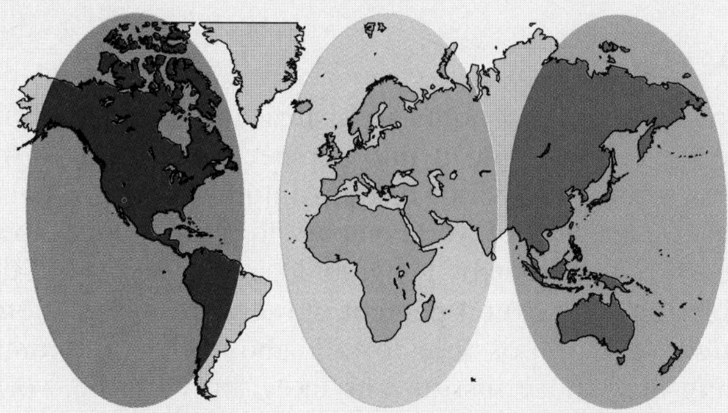

Each area has a major currency. In the Americas, it is the dollar; in Europe, it is the euro; and in East Asia, it is the Japanese yen. These areas are continually changing; the EU recently expanded to 28 countries, incorporating many of the countries of eastern Europe. China's economy has been growing fast and, given the size of its population, is likely to overtake Japan as the key Asian economy in the coming decades.

The accompanying table gives you a sense of the similarities and differences in the economies of the United States, China, and the European Union.

	United States	China	European Union
Area (square miles)	3,537,438	3,705,407	1,691,588
Population	314 million	1.3 billion	507 million
GDP*	$15.6 trillion	$13 trillion	$15.7 trillion
Percentage of world output	19%	14%	19%
GDP per capita	$50,000	$10,000	$31,000
Natural resources	Coal, copper, lead, and others	Coal, iron ore	Coal, iron ore, natural gas, fish, and others
Exports as a percentage of GDP	14%	17%	11%
Imports as a percentage of GDP	18%	15%	13%
Currency Value (as of July 2012)	Dollar ($1 = $1)	Yuan (¥6.36 = $1)	Euro (€0.82 = $1)

*Calculated using purchasing power parity.

Source: *CIA World Factbook 2012* (www.cia.gov) and current exchange rate tables. Currency changes can affect GDP figures. GDP updated by the author.

people even though they choose to use the goods or engage in the activities are called **demerit goods or activities.** Illegal drugs are a demerit good and using addictive drugs is a demerit activity.

Alternatively, there are some activities that government believes are good for people, even if people may not choose to engage in them. For example, government may believe that going to the opera or contributing to charity is a good activity. But in the United States only a small percentage of people go to the opera, and not everyone in the United States contributes to charity. Similarly, government may believe that whole-wheat bread is more nutritious than white bread. But many consumers prefer white bread. Goods like whole-wheat bread and activities like contributing to charity are known as **merit goods or activities**—*goods and activities that government believes are good for you even though you may not choose to engage in the activities or to consume the goods.* Government sometimes provides support for them through subsidies or tax benefits.

With merit and demerit goods, individuals are assumed to be doing what is not in their self-interest.

Market Failures and Government Failures

The reasons for government intervention are often summed up in the phrase *market failure*. **Market failures** are *situations in which the market does not lead to a desired*

Q-9 If there is an externality, does that mean that the government should intervene in the market to adjust for that externality?

result. In the real world, market failures are pervasive—the market is always failing in one way or another. But the fact that there are market failures does not mean that government intervention will improve the situation. There are also **government failures**—*situations in which the government intervenes and makes things worse.* Government failures are pervasive in the government—the government is always failing in one way or another. So real-world policy makers usually end up choosing which failure—market failure or government failure—will be least problematic.

Global Institutions

So far in this chapter we've put the U.S. economy in historical and institutional perspective. In this last section, we briefly put it into perspective relative to the world economy. By doing so, we gain a number of insights into the U.S. economy. The U.S. economy makes up about 20 percent of world output and consumption, a percentage that is much larger than its relative size by geographic area (6 percent of the world's land mass) or by population (just over 4 percent of the world population). It is becoming more integrated; it is impossible to talk about U.S. economic institutions without considering how those institutions integrate with the world economy.

Global Corporations

Global corporations are corporations with substantial operations on both the production and sales sides in more than one country.

Consider corporations. Most large corporations today are not U.S., German, or Japanese corporations; they are **global corporations** (*corporations with substantial operations on both the production and sales sides in more than one country*). Just because a car has a Japanese or German name doesn't mean that it was produced abroad. Many Japanese and German companies now have manufacturing plants in the United States, and many U.S. firms have manufacturing plants abroad. When goods are produced by global corporations, corporate names don't always tell much about where a good is produced. As global corporations' importance has grown, most manufacturing decisions are made in reference to the international market, not the U.S. domestic market. This means that the consumer sovereignty that guides decisions of firms is becoming less and less U.S. consumer sovereignty, and more and more global consumer sovereignty.

Web Note 3.4
Global 500

Global corporations offer enormous benefits for countries. They create jobs; they bring new ideas and new technologies to a country; and they provide competition for domestic companies, keeping them on their toes. But global corporations also pose a number of problems for governments. One is their implication for domestic and international policy. A domestic corporation exists within a country and can be dealt with using policy measures within that country. A global corporation exists within many countries and there is no global government to regulate or control it. If it doesn't like the policies in one country—say taxes are too high or regulations too tight—it can shift its operations to other countries.

Coordinating Global Issues

Global economic issues differ from national economic issues because national economies have governments to referee disputes among players in the economy; global economies do not; no international government exists. Some argue that we need a global government to oversee global businesses. But no such government exists. The closest institution there is to a world government is the United Nations (UN), which, according to critics, is simply a debating society. It has no ability to tax and no ability to impose its will separate from the political and military power of its members. When the United States opposes a UN mandate, it can, and often does, ignore it. Hence, international problems must be dealt with through negotiation, consensus, bullying, and concessions.

Governments, however, have developed a variety of international institutions to promote negotiations and coordinate economic relations among countries. Besides the United Nations, these include the World Bank, the World Court, and the International Monetary Fund (IMF). These organizations have a variety of goals. For example, the World Bank, a multinational, international financial institution, works with developing countries to secure low-interest loans, channeling such loans to them to foster economic growth. The International Monetary Fund (IMF), a multinational, international financial institution, is concerned primarily with monetary issues. It deals with international financial arrangements. When developing countries encountered financial problems in the 1980s and had large international debts that they could not pay, the IMF helped work on repayment plans.

Governments have developed international institutions to promote negotiations and coordinate economic relations among countries. Some are: the UN; the World Bank; the World Court; and the International Monetary Fund.

Countries also have developed global and regional organizations whose job it is to coordinate trade among countries and reduce trade barriers. On the international level, the World Trade Organization (WTO) works to reduce trade barriers among countries. On the regional level, there are the European Union (EU), which is an organization of European countries that developed out of a trade association devoted to reducing trade barriers among member countries; the North American Free Trade Agreement (NAFTA), an organization devoted to reducing trade barriers between the United States, Mexico, and Canada; and Mercosur, an organization devoted to reducing trade barriers among North, Central, and South American countries.

Countries have developed global and regional organizations to coordinate trade and reduce trade barriers. Some are: the WTO; the EU; and NAFTA.

In addition to these formal institutions, there are informal meetings of various countries. These include the Group of Eight, which meets to promote negotiations and to coordinate economic relations among countries. The eight are Japan, Germany, Britain, France, United States, Canada, Italy, and Russia.

Since governmental membership in international organizations is voluntary, their power is limited. When the United States doesn't like a World Court ruling, it simply states that it isn't going to follow the ruling. When the United States is unhappy with what the United Nations is doing, it withholds some of its dues. Other countries do the same from time to time. Other member countries complain but can do little to force compliance. It doesn't work that way domestically. If you decide you don't like U.S. policy and refuse to pay your taxes, you'll wind up in jail.

Since governmental membership in international organizations is voluntary, their power is limited.

What keeps nations somewhat in line when it comes to international rules is a moral tradition: Countries want to (or at least want to look as if they want to) do what's "right." Countries will sometimes follow international rules to keep international opinion favorable to them. But perceived national self-interest often overrides international scruples.

Q-10 If the United States chooses not to follow a World Court decision, what are the consequences?

Conclusion

This has been a whirlwind introduction to economic institutions and their role in the economy. Each of them—business, households, and government—is important, and to understand what happens in the economy, one must have a sense of how these institutions work and the role they play. In the remainder of the book we won't discuss institutions much as we concentrate on presenting economic analysis. I rely upon you to integrate the analysis with institutions, as you apply the economic analysis and reasoning that you learn to the real world.

Summary

- A market economy is an economic system based on private property and the market. It gives private property rights to individuals and relies on market forces to solve the *what, how,* and *for whom* problems. *(LO3-1)*
- In a market economy, price is the mechanism through which people's desires are coordinated and goods are rationed. The U.S. economy today is a market economy. *(LO3-1)*
- The predominant market-based system during the early 1900s was capitalism, an economic system based on the market in which the ownership of production resided with a small group of individuals called capitalists. *(LO3-1)*
- In principle, under socialism society solves the *what, how,* and *for whom* problems in the best interest of the individuals in society. It is based on individuals' goodwill toward one another. *(LO3-1)*
- In practice, socialism is an economic system based on government ownership of the means of production, with economic activity governed by central planning. Socialism in practice is sometimes called a command economy. *(LO3-1)*
- A diagram of the U.S. market economy shows the connections among businesses, households, and government. It also shows the U.S. economic connection to other countries. *(LO3-2)*
- In the United States, businesses make the *what, how,* and *for whom* decisions. *(LO3-2)*
- Although businesses decide what to produce, they succeed or fail depending on their ability to meet consumers' desires. That's consumer sovereignty. *(LO3-2)*
- The three main forms of business are corporations, sole proprietorships, and partnerships. Each has its advantages and disadvantages. *(LO3-2)*
- Although households are the most powerful economic institution, they have assigned much of their power to government and business. Economics focuses on households' role as the supplier of labor. *(LO3-2)*
- Government plays two general roles in the economy: (1) as a referee and (2) as an actor. *(LO3-3)*
- Six roles of government are to (1) provide a stable set of institutions and rules, (2) promote effective and workable competition, (3) correct for externalities, (4) ensure economic stability and growth, (5) provide public goods, and (6) adjust for undesirable market results. *(LO3-3)*
- To understand the U.S. economy, one must understand its role in the world economy. *(LO3-4)*
- Global corporations are corporations with significant operations in more than one country. They are increasing in importance. *(LO3-4)*
- Global economic issues differ from national economic issues because national economies have governments. The global economy does not. *(LO3-4)*

Key Terms

business *(56)*
capitalism *(53)*
consumer sovereignty *(57)*
corporation *(58)*
demerit good or activity *(65)*
entrepreneurship *(57)*
externality *(63)*
global corporation *(66)*
government failure *(66)*
households *(59)*
institutions *(51)*
macroeconomic externality *(64)*
market economy *(52)*
market failure *(65)*
merit good or activity *(65)*
partnership *(58)*
private good *(64)*
private property right *(52)*
profit *(57)*
public good *(64)*
socialism *(53)*
sole proprietorship *(58)*

Questions and Exercises 

1. In a market economy, what is the central coordinating mechanism? *(LO3-1)*
2. In a centrally planned socialist economy, what is the central coordinating mechanism? *(LO3-1)*
3. How does a market economy solve the what, how, and for whom to produce problems? *(LO3-1)*
4. How does a centrally planned socialist economy solve the what, how, and for whom to produce problems? *(LO3-1)*
5. Is capitalism or socialism the better economic system? Why? *(LO3-1)*
6. Why does an economy's strength ultimately reside in its people? *(LO3-2)*
7. Why is entrepreneurship a central part of any business? *(LO3-2)*
8. List the three major forms of business. *(LO3-2)*
   a. What form is most common?
   b. What form accounts for the largest proportion of sales?
9. You're starting a software company in which you plan to sell software to your fellow students. What form of business organization would you choose? Why? *(LO3-2)*
10. What are the two largest categories of federal government expenditures? *(LO3-3)*
11. What are the six roles of government listed in the text? *(LO3-3)*
12. Say the government establishes rights to pollute so that without a pollution permit you aren't allowed to emit pollutants into the air, water, or soil. Firms are allowed to buy and sell these rights. In what way will this correct for an externality? *(LO3-3)*
13. Give an example of a merit good, a demerit good, a public good, and a good that involves an externality. *(LO3-3)*
14. Name two international organizations that countries have developed to coordinate economic actions. *(LO3-4)*
15. What are two organizations that countries can use to coordinate economic relations and reduce trade barriers? *(LO3-4)*
16. Why are international organizations limited in their effectiveness? *(LO3-4)*

Questions from Alternative Perspectives

1. Friedrich Hayek, the man quoted at the start of the chapter, is an Austrian economist who won a Nobel Prize in economics. He argued that government intervention is difficult to contain. Suppose central planners have decided to financially support all children with food vouchers, free day care, and public school.
   a. What problems might this create?
   b. How might this lead to further interference by central planners into family choices? (Austrian)
2. In his *The Social Contract,* Jean-Jacques Rousseau argued that "no State has ever been founded without a religious basis [but] the law of Christianity at bottom does more harm by weakening than good by strengthening the constitution of the State." What does he mean by that, and is he correct? (Religious)
3. In economics, a household is defined as a group of individuals making joint decisions as though acting as one person.
   a. How do you think decisions are actually made about things like consumption and allocation of time within the household?
   b. Does bargaining take place?
   c. If so, what gives an individual power to bargain effectively for his or her preferences?
   d. Do individuals act cooperatively within the family and competitively everywhere else?
   e. Does this make sense? (Feminist)
4. This chapter emphasized the importance of the relationship between how the economic system is organized and value systems. Knowing that how I raise my child will greatly shape how he or she will ultimately fit into the social and economic process, should I raise my child to be selfless, compassionate, and dedicated to advancing the well-being of others, knowing she will probably be poor; or shall I raise her to be self-centered, uncaring, and greedy to increase her chances to acquire personal fortune? Which decision is just and why? (Institutionalist)
5. The text discusses consumer sovereignty and suggests that it guides the market choices.
   a. Is consumer sovereignty a myth or reality in today's consumer culture?
   b. Do consumers "direct" the economy as suggested by the text, or has invention become the mother of necessity, as Thorstein Veblen once quipped?
   c. If the consumer is not sovereign, then who is and what does that imply for economics? (Radical)

Issues to Ponder

1. What arguments can you give for supporting a socialist organization of a family and a market-based organization of the economy?
2. Economists Edward Lazear and Robert Michael calculated that the average family spends two and a half times as much on each adult as they do on each child.
   a. Does this mean that children are deprived and that the distribution is unfair?
   b. Do you think these percentages change with family income? If so, how?
   c. Do you think that the allocation would be different in a family in a command economy than in a capitalist economy? Why?
3. One of the specific problems socialist economies had was keeping up with capitalist countries technologically.
   a. Can you think of any reason inherent in a centrally planned economy that would make innovation difficult?
   b. Can you think of any reason inherent in a capitalist economy that would foster innovation?
   c. Joseph Schumpeter, a famous Harvard economist of the 1930s, predicted that as firms in capitalist societies grew in size, they would innovate less. Can you suggest what his argument might have been?
   d. Schumpeter's prediction did not come true. Modern capitalist economies have had enormous innovations. Can you provide explanations as to why?
4. Tom Rollins heads a company called Teaching Co. He has taped lectures at the top universities, packaged the lectures on DVD and sells them for between $20 and $230 per series.
   a. Discuss whether such an idea could be expanded to include college courses that one could take at home.
   b. What are the technical, social, and economic issues involved?
   c. If it is technically possible and cost-effective, will the new venture be a success?
5. Go to a store in your community.
   a. Ask what limitations the owners faced in starting their business.
   b. Were these limitations necessary?
   c. Should there have been more or fewer limitations?
   d. Under what heading of reasons for government intervention would you put each of the limitations?
   e. Ask what kinds of taxes the business pays and what benefits it believes it gets for those taxes.
   f. Is it satisfied with the existing situation? Why? What would it change?
6. A market system is often said to be based on consumer sovereignty—the consumer determines what's to be produced. Yet business decides what's to be produced. Can these two views be reconciled? How? If not, why?
7. How might individuals disagree about the government's role in intervening in the market for merit, demerit, and public goods?
8. Discuss the concepts of market failure and government failure in relation to operas.
9. You've set up the rules for a game and started the game but now realize that the rules are unfair. Should you change the rules?
10. In trade talks with Australia, the United States proposed that Australia cannot regulate the amount of foreign content on new media without first consulting the United States. Actress Bridie Carter of *McLeod's Daughters* argued against adopting the trade agreement, arguing the agreement trades away Australia's cultural identity. This highlights one of the effects of globalization: the loss of variety based on cultural differences. How important should such cultural identity issues be in trade negotiations?

Answers to Margin Questions

1. He is wrong. Property rights are required for a market to operate. Once property rights are allocated, the market will allocate goods, but the market cannot distribute the property rights that are required for the market to operate. (*p. 52; LO3-1*)
2. Capitalism places much more emphasis on fostering individualism. Socialism tries to develop a system in which the individual's needs are placed second to society's needs. (*p. 53; LO3-1*)
3. Most families allocate basic needs through control and command. The parents do (or try to do) the controlling and commanding. Generally parents are well-intentioned, trying to meet their perception of their children's needs. However, some family activities that are not basic needs might be allocated through the market. For example, if one child wants a go-cart and is willing to do extra work at home in order to get it, go-carts might be allocated through the market, with the child earning chits that can be used for such nonessentials. (*p. 53; LO3-1*)

4. In theory, socialism is an economic system based upon individuals' goodwill. In practice, socialism involved central planning and government ownership of the primary means of production. (*p. 54; LO3-1*)
5. Market economies are generally broken up into businesses, households, and government. (*p. 55; LO3-2*)
6. False. In the United States, individuals are free to start any type of business they want, provided it doesn't violate the law. The invisible hand sees to it that only those businesses that customers want earn a profit. The others lose money and eventually go out of business, so in that sense only businesses that customers want stay in business. (*p. 57; LO3-2*)
7. As can be seen in Figure 3-2, most businesses in the United States are sole proprietorships, not corporations. Corporations, however, generate the most revenue. (*p. 58; LO3-2*)
8. The largest percentage of federal expenditures is for income security. (*p. 61; LO3-3*)
9. Not necessarily. The existence of an externality creates the possibility that government intervention might help. But there are also government failures in which the government intervenes and makes things worse. (*p. 66; LO3-3*)
10. The World Court has no enforcement mechanism. Thus, when a country refuses to follow the court's decisions, the country cannot be directly punished except through indirect international pressures. (*p. 67; LO3-4*)

APPENDIX A

The History of Economic Systems

In Chapter 1, I made the distinction between market and economic forces: Economic forces have always existed—they operate in all aspects of our lives—but market forces have not always existed. Markets are social creations societies use to coordinate individuals' actions. Markets developed, sometimes spontaneously, sometimes by design, because they offered a better life for at least some—and usually a large majority of—individuals in a society.

To understand why markets developed, it is helpful to look briefly at the history of the economic systems from which our own system descended.

Feudal Society: Rule of Tradition

Let's go back in time to the year 1000 when Europe had no nation-states as we now know them. (Ideally, we would have gone back further and explained other economic systems, but, given the limited space, I had to draw the line somewhere—an example of a trade-off.) The predominant economic system at that time was feudalism. There was no coordinated central government, no unified system of law, no national patriotism, no national defense, although a strong religious institution simply called the Church fulfilled some of these roles. There were few towns; most individuals lived in walled manors, or "estates." These manors "belonged to" the "lord of the manor." (Occasionally the "lord" was a lady, but not often.) I say "belonged to" rather than "were owned by" because most of the empires or federations at that time were not formal nation-states that could organize, administer, and regulate ownership. No documents or deeds gave ownership of the land to an individual. Instead, tradition ruled, and in normal times nobody questioned the lord's right to the land. The land "belonged to" the lord because the land "belonged to" him—that's the way it was.

Without a central nation-state, the manor served many functions a nation-state would have served had it existed. The lord provided protection, often within a walled area surrounding the manor house or, if the manor was large enough, a castle. He provided administration and decided disputes. He also decided *what* would be done, *how* it would be done, and *who* would get what, but these decisions were limited. In the same way that the land belonged to the lord because that's the way it always had been, what people did and how they did it were determined by what they always had done. Tradition ruled the manor more than the lord did.

Problems of a Tradition-Based Society

Feudalism developed about the 8th and 9th centuries and lasted until about the 15th century, though in isolated countries such as Russia it continued well into the 19th century, and in all European countries its influence lingered for hundreds of years (as late as about 150 years ago in some parts of Germany). Such a long-lived system must have done some things right, and feudalism did: It solved the *what, how,* and *for whom* problems in an acceptable way.

But a tradition-based society has problems. In a traditional society, because someone's father was a baker, the son also must be a baker, and because a woman was a homemaker, she wouldn't be allowed to be anything but a homemaker. But what if Joe Blacksmith Jr., the son of Joe Blacksmith Sr., is a lousy blacksmith and longs to knead dough, while Joe Baker Jr. would be a superb blacksmith but hates making pastry? Tough. Tradition dictated who did what. In fact, tradition probably arranged things so that we will never know whether Joe Blacksmith Jr. would have made a superb baker.

As long as a society doesn't change too much, tradition operates reasonably well, although not especially efficiently, in holding the society together. However, when a society must undergo change, tradition does not work. Change means that the things that were done before no longer need to be done, while new things do need to get done. But if no one has traditionally done these new things, then they don't get done. If the change is important but a society can't figure out some way for the new things to get done, the society falls apart. That's what happened to feudal society. It didn't change when change was required.

The life of individuals living on the land, called *serfs,* was difficult, and feudalism was designed to benefit the lord. Some individuals in feudal society just couldn't take life on the manor, and they set off on their own. Because there was no organized police force, they were unlikely to be caught and forced to return to the manor. Going hungry, being killed, or both, however, were frequent fates of an escaped serf. One place to which serfs could safely escape, though, was a town or city—the remains of what in Roman times had been thriving and active cities. These cities, which had been decimated by plagues, plundering bands, and starvation in the preceding centuries, nevertheless remained an escape hatch for runaway serfs because they relied far less on tradition than did manors. City dwellers had to live by their wits; many became merchants who lived predominantly by trading. They were middlemen; they would buy from one group and sell to another.

Trading in towns was an alternative to the traditional feudal order because trading allowed people to have an income independent of the traditional social structure. Markets broke down tradition. Initially merchants traded using barter (exchange of one kind of good for another): silk and spices from the Orient for wheat, flour, and artisan products in Europe. But soon a generalized purchasing power (money) developed as a medium of exchange. Money greatly expanded the possibilities of trading because its use meant that goods no longer needed to be bartered. They could be sold for money, which could then be spent to buy other goods.

In the beginning, land was not traded, but soon the feudal lord who just had to have a silk robe but had no money was saying, "Why not? I'll sell you a small piece of land so I can buy a shipment of silk." Once land became tradable, the traditional base of the feudal society was undermined. Tradition that can be bought and sold is no longer tradition—it's just another commodity.

From Feudalism to Mercantilism

Toward the end of the Middle Ages (mid-15th century), markets went from being a sideshow, a fair that spiced up people's lives, to being the main event. Over time, some traders and merchants started to amass fortunes that dwarfed those of the feudal lords. Rich traders settled down; existing towns and cities expanded and new towns were formed. As towns grew and as fortunes shifted from feudal lords to merchants, power in society shifted to the towns. And with that shift came a change in society's political and economic structure.

As these traders became stronger politically and economically, they threw their support behind a king (the strongest lord) in the hope that the king would expand their ability to trade. In doing so, they made the king even stronger. Eventually, the king became so powerful that his will prevailed over the will of the other lords and even over the will of the Church. As the king consolidated his power, nation-states as we know them today evolved. *The government became an active influence on economic decision making.*

As markets grew, feudalism evolved into mercantilism. The evolution of feudal systems into mercantilism occurred in the following way: As cities and their markets grew in size and power relative to the feudal manors and the traditional economy, a whole new variety of possible economic activities developed. It was only natural that individuals began to look to a king to establish a new tradition that would determine who would do what. Individuals in particular occupations organized into groups called *guilds,* which were similar to strong labor unions today. These guilds, many of which had financed and supported the king, now expected the king and his government to protect their interests.

As new economic activities, such as trading companies, developed, individuals involved in these activities similarly depended on the king for the right to trade and for help in financing and organizing their activities. For example, in 1492, when Christopher Columbus had the wild idea that by sailing west he could get to the East Indies and trade for their riches, he went to Spain's Queen Isabella and King Ferdinand for financial support.

Since many traders had played and continued to play important roles in financing, establishing, and supporting the king, the king was usually happy to protect their interests. The government doled out the rights to undertake a variety of economic activities. By the late 1400s, western Europe had evolved from a feudal to a mercantilist economy.

The mercantilist period was marked by the increased role of government, which could be classified in two ways: by the way it encouraged growth and by the way it limited growth. Government legitimized and financed a variety of activities, thus encouraging growth. But government also limited economic activity in order to protect the monopolies of those it favored, thus limiting growth. So mercantilism allowed the market to operate, but it kept the market under its control. The market was not allowed to respond freely to the laws of supply and demand.

From Mercantilism to Capitalism

Mercantilism provided the source for major growth in western Europe, but mercantilism also unleashed new tensions within society. Like feudalism, mercantilism limited entry into economic activities. It used a different form of limitation—politics rather than social and cultural tradition—but individuals who were excluded still felt unfairly treated.

The most significant source of tension was the different roles played by craft guilds and owners of new businesses, who were called industrialists or capitalists (businesspeople who have acquired large amounts of money and use it to invest in businesses). Craft guild members were artists in their own crafts: pottery, shoemaking, and the like. New business owners destroyed the art of production by devising machines to replace hand production. Machines produced goods cheaper and faster than craftsmen.[1] The result was an increase in supply and a downward pressure on the price, which was set by the government. Craftsmen didn't want to be replaced by machines. They argued that machine-manufactured goods didn't have the same quality as hand-crafted goods, and that the new machines would disrupt the economic and social life of the community.

Industrialists were the outsiders with a vested interest in changing the existing system. They wanted the freedom to conduct business as they saw fit. Because of the enormous cost advantage of manufactured goods over crafted goods, a few industrialists overcame government opposition and succeeded within the mercantilist system. They earned their fortunes and became an independent political power.

Once again, the economic power base shifted, and two groups competed with each other for power—this time, the guilds and the industrialists. The government had to decide whether to support the industrialists (who wanted government to loosen its power over the country's economic affairs) or the craftsmen and guilds (who argued for strong government limitations and for maintaining traditional values of workmanship). This struggle raged in the 1700s and 1800s. But during this time, governments themselves were changing. This was the Age of Revolutions, and the kings' powers were being limited by democratic reform movements—revolutions supported and financed in large part by the industrialists.

The Need for Coordination in an Economy

Craftsmen argued that coordination of the economy was necessary, and the government had to be involved. If government wasn't going to coordinate economic activity, who would? To answer that question, a British moral philosopher named Adam Smith developed the concept of the invisible hand, in his famous book *The Wealth of Nations* (1776), and used it to explain how markets could coordinate the economy without the active involvement of government.

As stated in Chapter 2, Smith argued that the market's invisible hand would guide suppliers' actions toward the general good. No government coordination was necessary.

With the help of economists such as Adam Smith, the industrialists' view won out. Government pulled back from its role in guiding the economy and adopted a laissez-faire policy.

[1]Throughout this section I use *men* to emphasize that these societies were strongly male-dominated. There were almost no businesswomen. In fact, a woman had to turn over her property to a man upon her marriage, and the marriage contract was written as if she were owned by her husband!

The Industrial Revolution

The invisible hand worked; capitalism thrived. Beginning about 1750 and continuing through the late 1800s, machine production increased enormously, almost totally replacing hand production. This phenomenon has been given a name, the Industrial Revolution. The economy grew faster than ever before. Society was forever transformed. New inventions changed all aspects of life. James Watt's steam engine (1769) made manufacturing and travel easier. Eli Whitney's cotton gin (1793) changed the way cotton was processed. James Kay's flying shuttle (1733),[2] James Hargreaves' spinning jenny (1765), and Richard Arkwright's power loom (1769), combined with the steam engine, changed the way cloth was processed and the clothes people wore.

The need to mine vast amounts of coal to provide power to run the machines changed the economic and physical landscapes. The repeating rifle changed the nature of warfare. Modern economic institutions replaced guilds. Stock markets, insurance companies, and corporations all became important. Trading was no longer financed by government; it was privately financed (although government policies, such as colonial policies giving certain companies monopoly trading rights with a country's colonies, helped in that trading). The Industrial Revolution, democracy, and capitalism all arose in the middle and late 1700s. By the 1800s, they were part of the institutional landscape of Western society. Capitalism had arrived.

From Capitalism to ~~Socialism~~ *Welfare Capitalism*

Capitalism was marked by significant economic growth in the Western world. But it was also marked by human abuses—18-hour workdays; low wages; children as young as five years old slaving long hours in dirty, dangerous factories and mines—to produce enormous wealth for an elite few. Such conditions and inequalities led to criticism of the capitalist or market economic system.

[2]The invention of the flying shuttle frustrated the textile industry because it enabled workers to weave so much cloth that the spinners of thread from which the cloth was woven couldn't keep up. This challenge to the textile industry was met by offering a prize to anyone who could invent something to increase the thread spinners' productivity. The prize was won when the spinning jenny was invented.

Marx's Analysis

The best-known critic of this system was Karl Marx, a German philosopher, economist, and sociologist who wrote in the 1800s and who developed an analysis of the dynamics of change in economic systems. Marx argued that economic systems are in a constant state of change, and that capitalism would not last. Workers would revolt, and capitalism would be replaced by a socialist economic system.

Marx saw an economy marked by tensions among economic classes. He saw capitalism as an economic system controlled by the capitalist class (businessmen). His class analysis was that capitalist society is divided into capitalist and worker classes. He said constant tension between these economic classes causes changes in the system. The capitalist class made large profits by exploiting the proletariat class—the working class—and extracting what he called surplus value from workers who, according to Marx's labor theory of value, produced all the value inherent in goods. Surplus value was the additional profit, rent, or interest that, according to Marx's normative views, capitalists added to the price of goods. What standard economic analysis sees as recognizing a need that society has and fulfilling it, Marx saw as exploitation.

Marx argued that this exploitation would increase as production facilities became larger and larger and as competition among capitalists decreased. At some point, he believed, exploitation would lead to a revolt by the proletariat, who would overthrow their capitalist exploiters.

By the late 1800s, some of what Marx predicted had occurred, although not in the way that he thought it would. Production moved from small to large factories. Corporations developed, and classes became more distinct from one another. Workers were significantly differentiated from owners. Small firms merged and were organized into monopolies and trusts (large combinations of firms). The trusts developed ways to prevent competition among themselves and ways to limit entry of new competitors into the market. Marx was right in his predictions about these developments, but he was wrong in his prediction about society's response to them.

The Revolution That Did Not Occur

Western society's response to the problems of capitalism was not a revolt by the workers. Instead, governments stepped in to stop the worst abuses of capitalism. The hard edges of capitalism were softened.

Evolution, not revolution, was capitalism's destiny. The democratic state did not act, as Marx argued it would, as a mere representative of the capitalist class. Competing pressure groups developed; workers gained political power that offset the economic power of businesses.

In the late 1930s and the 1940s, workers dominated the political agenda. During this time, capitalist economies developed an economic safety net that included government-funded programs, such as public welfare and unemployment insurance, and established an extensive set of regulations affecting all aspects of the economy. Today, depressions are met with direct government policy. Antitrust laws, regulatory agencies, and social programs of government softened the hard edges of capitalism. Laws were passed prohibiting child labor, mandating a certain minimum wage, and limiting the hours of work. Capitalism became what is sometimes called welfare capitalism.

Due to these developments, government spending now accounts for about a fifth of all spending in the United States, and for more than half in some European countries. Were an economist from the late 1800s to return from the grave, he'd probably say socialism, not capitalism, exists in Western societies. Most modern-day economists wouldn't go that far, but they would agree that our economy today is better described as a welfare capitalist economy than as a capitalist, or even a market, economy. Because of these changes, the U.S. and Western European economies are a far cry from the competitive "capitalist" economy that Karl Marx criticized. Markets operate, but they are constrained by the government.

The concept *capitalism* developed to denote a market system controlled by one group in society, the capitalists. Looking at Western societies today, we see that domination by one group no longer characterizes Western economies. Although in theory capitalists control corporations through their ownership of shares of stock, in practice corporations are controlled in large part by managers. There remains an elite group who control business, but *capitalist* is not a good term to describe them. Managers, not capitalists, exercise primary control over business, and even their control is limited by laws or the fear of laws being passed by governments.

Governments, in turn, are controlled by a variety of pressure groups. Sometimes one group is in control; at other times, another. Government policies similarly fluctuate. Sometimes they are proworker, sometimes proindustrialist, sometimes progovernment, and sometimes prosociety.

From Feudalism to Socialism

You probably noticed that I crossed out *Socialism* in the previous section's heading and replaced it with *Welfare Capitalism.* That's because capitalism did not evolve to socialism as Karl Marx predicted it would. Instead, Marx's socialist ideas took root in feudalist Russia, a society that the Industrial Revolution had in large part bypassed. Since socialism arrived at a different place and a different time than Marx predicted it would, you shouldn't be surprised to read that socialism arrived in a different way than Marx predicted. The proletariat did not revolt to establish socialism. Instead, World War I, which the Russians were losing, crippled Russia's feudal economy and government. A small group of socialists overthrew the czar (Russia's king) and took over the government in 1917. They quickly pulled Russia out of the war, and then set out to organize a socialist society and economy.

Russian socialists tried to adhere to Marx's ideas, but they found that Marx had concentrated on how capitalist economies operate, not on how a socialist economy should be run. Thus, Russian socialists faced a huge task with little guidance. Their most immediate problem was how to increase production so that the economy could emerge from feudalism into the modern industrial world. In Marx's analysis, capitalism was a necessary stage in the evolution toward the ideal state for a very practical reason. The capitalists exploit the workers, but in doing so capitalists extract the necessary surplus—an amount of production in excess of what is consumed. That surplus had to be extracted in order to provide the factories and machinery upon which a socialist economic system would be built. But since capitalism did not exist in *Russia,* a true socialist state could not be established immediately. Instead, the socialists created *state socialism*—an economic system in which government sees to it that people work for the common good until they can be relied upon to do that on their own.

Socialists saw state socialism as a transition stage to pure socialism. This transition stage still exploited the workers; when Joseph Stalin took power in Russia in the late 1920s, he took the peasants' and small farmers' land and turned it into collective farms. The government then paid farmers low prices for their produce. When farmers balked at the low prices, millions of them were killed.

Simultaneously, Stalin created central planning agencies that directed individuals what to produce and how to produce it, and determined for whom things would be produced. During this period, *socialism* became synonymous with *central economic planning,* and Soviet-style socialism became the model of socialism in practice.

Also during this time, Russia took control of a number of neighboring states and established the Union of Soviet Socialist Republics (USSR), the formal name of the Soviet Union. The Soviet Union also installed Soviet-dominated governments in a number of eastern European countries. In 1949 most of China, under the rule of Mao Zedong, adopted Soviet-style socialist principles.

Since the late 1980s, the Soviet socialist economic and political structure has fallen apart. The Soviet Union as a political state broke up, and its former republics became autonomous. Eastern European countries were released from Soviet control. Now they faced a new problem: transition from socialism to a market economy. Why did the Soviet socialist economy fall apart? Because workers lacked incentives to work; production was inefficient; consumer goods were either unavailable or of poor quality; and high Soviet officials were exploiting their positions, keeping the best jobs for themselves and moving themselves up in the waiting lists for consumer goods. In short, the parents of the socialist family (the Communist party) were no longer acting benevolently; they were taking many of the benefits for themselves.

These political and economic upheavals in eastern Europe and the former Soviet Union suggest the kind of socialism these societies tried did not work. However, that failure does not mean that socialist goals are bad; nor does it mean that no type of socialism can ever work. The point is that all systems have problems, and it is likely that the political winds of change will lead to new forms of economic organization being tried as the problems of the existing system lead to political demands for change. Venezuela's recent attempt to establish a new form of socialism is an example. Given past experience with socialist systems, however, most economists believe that any future workable "new socialist" system will include important elements of market institutions.

chapter 4

Supply and Demand

> *Teach a parrot the terms supply and demand and you've got an economist.*
>
> —Thomas Carlyle

Supply and demand. Supply and demand. Roll the phrase around in your mouth; savor it like a good wine. *Supply* and *demand* are the most-used words in economics. And for good reason. They provide a good off-the-cuff answer for any economic question. Try it.

> Why are bacon and oranges so expensive this winter? *Supply and demand.*
>
> Why are interest rates falling? *Supply and demand.*
>
> Why can't I find decent wool socks anymore? *Supply and demand.*

The importance of the interplay of supply and demand makes it only natural that, early in any economics course, you must learn about supply and demand. Let's start with demand.

After reading this chapter, you should be able to:

- **LO4-1** State the law of demand and distinguish shifts in demand from movements along a demand curve.
- **LO4-2** State the law of supply and distinguish shifts in supply from movements along a supply curve.
- **LO4-3** Explain how the law of demand and the law of supply interact to bring about equilibrium.
- **LO4-4** Discuss the limitations of demand and supply analysis.

Demand

People want lots of things; they "demand" much less than they want because demand means a willingness and ability to pay. Unless you are willing and able to pay for it, you may *want* it, but you don't *demand* it. For example, I want to own a Ferrari. But, I must admit, I'm not willing to do what's necessary to own one. If I really wanted one, I'd mortgage everything I own, increase my income by doubling the number of hours I work, not buy anything else, and get that car. But I don't do any of those things, so at the going price, $650,000, I do not demand a Ferrari. Sure, I'd buy one if it cost $30,000, but from my actions it's clear that, at $650,000, I don't demand it. This points to an important aspect of demand: The quantity you demand at a low price differs from the quantity you demand at a high price. Specifically, the quantity you demand varies inversely—in the opposite direction—with price.

Prices are the tool by which the market coordinates individuals' desires and limits how much people demand. When goods become scarce, the market reduces the quantity people demand; as their prices go up, people buy fewer goods. As goods become abundant, their prices go down, and people buy more of them. The invisible hand—the price mechanism—sees to it that what people demand (do what's necessary to get) matches what's available.

The Law of Demand

The law of demand states that the quantity of a good demanded is inversely related to the good's price.

The ideas expressed above are the foundation of the **law of demand:**

Quantity demanded rises as price falls, other things constant.

Or alternatively:

Quantity demanded falls as price rises, other things constant.

This law is fundamental to the invisible hand's ability to coordinate individuals' desires; as prices change, people change how much they're willing to buy.

Web Note 4.1
Markets without Money

What accounts for the law of demand? If the price of something goes up, people will tend to buy less of it and buy something else instead. They will *substitute* other goods for goods whose relative price has gone up. If the price of MP3 files from the Internet rises, but the price of CDs stays the same, you're more likely to buy that new Coldplay recording on CD than to download it from the Internet.

To see that the law of demand makes intuitive sense, just think of something you'd really like but can't afford. If the price is cut in half, you—and other consumers—become more likely to buy it. Quantity demanded goes up as price goes down.

When price goes up, quantity demanded goes down. When price goes down, quantity demanded goes up.

Just to be sure you've got it, let's consider a real-world example: demand for vanity—specifically, vanity license plates. When the North Carolina state legislature increased the vanity plates' price from $30 to $40, the quantity demanded fell from 60,334 to 31,122. Assuming other things remained constant, that is the law of demand in action.

The Demand Curve

Q-1 Why does the demand curve slope downward?

A **demand curve** is *the graphic representation of the relationship between price and quantity demanded.* Figure 4-1 shows a demand curve.

As you can see, the demand curve slopes downward. That's because of the law of demand: As the price goes up, the quantity demanded goes down, other things constant. In other words, price and quantity demanded are inversely related.

FIGURE 4-1 A Sample Demand Curve

The law of demand states that the quantity demanded of a good is inversely related to the price of that good, other things constant. As the price of a good goes up, the quantity demanded goes down, so the demand curve is downward-sloping.

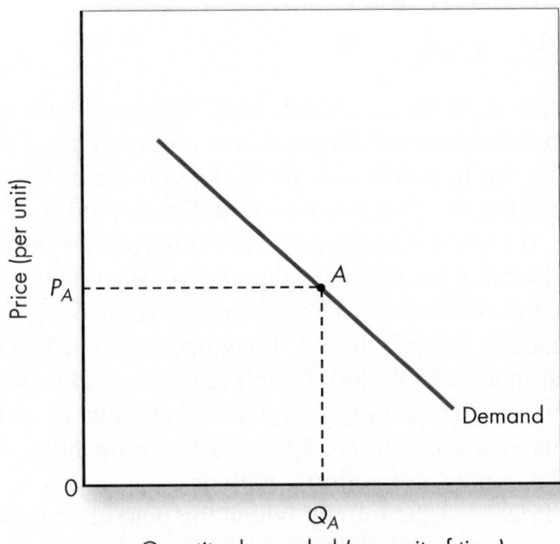

Notice that in stating the law of demand, I put in the qualification "other things constant." That's three extra words, and unless they were important I wouldn't have included them. But what does "other things constant" mean? Say that over two years, both the price of cars and the number of cars purchased rise. That seems to violate the law of demand, since the number of cars purchased should have fallen in response to the rise in price. Looking at the data more closely, however, we see that individuals' income has also increased. Other things didn't remain the same.

"Other things constant" places a limitation on the application of the law of demand.

The increase in price works as the law of demand states—it decreases the number of cars bought. But the rise in income increases the quantity demanded at every price. That increase in demand outweighs the decrease in quantity demanded that results from a rise in price, so ultimately more cars are sold. If you want to study the effect of price alone—which is what the law of demand refers to—you must make adjustments to hold income constant. Because other things besides price affect demand, the qualifying phrase "other things constant" is an important part of the law of demand.

The other things that are held constant include individuals' tastes, prices of other goods, and even the weather. Those other factors must remain constant if you're to make a valid study of the effect of an increase in the price of a good on the quantity demanded. In practice, it's impossible to keep all other things constant, so you have to be careful when you say that when price goes up, quantity demanded goes down. It's likely to go down, but it's always possible that something besides price has changed.

Shifts in Demand versus Movements along a Demand Curve

Shifts in Demand versus Movements along a Demand Curve

To distinguish between the effects of price and the effects of other factors on how much of a good is demanded, economists have developed the following precise terminology—terminology that inevitably shows up on exams. The first distinction is between demand and quantity demanded.

- **Demand** refers to *a schedule of quantities of a good that will be bought per unit of time at various prices, other things constant.*
- **Quantity demanded** refers to *a specific amount that will be demanded per unit of time at a specific price, other things constant.*

In graphical terms, the term *demand* refers to the entire demand curve. *Demand* tells us how much will be bought *at various prices. Quantity demanded* tells us how much will be bought at a specific price; it refers to a point on a demand curve, such as point *A* in Figure 4-1. This terminology allows us to distinguish between *changes in quantity demanded* and *shifts in demand.* A change in price changes the quantity demanded. It refers to a **movement along a demand curve**—*the graphical representation of the effect of a change in price on the quantity demanded.* A change in anything other than price that affects demand changes the entire demand curve. A shift factor of demand causes a **shift in demand,** *the graphical representation of the effect of anything other than price on demand.*

Q-2 The uncertainty caused by the terrorist attacks of September 11, 2001, made consumers reluctant to spend on luxury items. This reduced ________. Should the missing words be *demand for luxury goods* or *quantity of luxury goods demanded?*

To make sure you understand the difference between a movement along a demand curve and a shift in demand, let's consider an example. Singapore has one of the world's highest number of cars per mile of road. This means that congestion is considerable. Singapore adopted two policies to reduce road use: It increased the fee charged to use roads and it provided an expanded public transportation system. Both policies reduced congestion. Figure 4-2(a) shows that increasing the toll charged to use roads from \$1 to \$2 per 50 miles of road reduces quantity demanded from 200 to 100 cars per mile

Change in price causes a movement along a demand curve; a change in a shift factor causes a shift in demand.

FIGURE 4-2 (A AND B) Shift in Demand versus a Change in Quantity Demanded

A rise in a good's price results in a reduction in quantity demanded and is shown by a movement up along a demand curve from point *A* to point *B* in (**a**). A change in any other factor besides price that affects demand leads to a shift in the entire demand curve, as shown in (**b**).

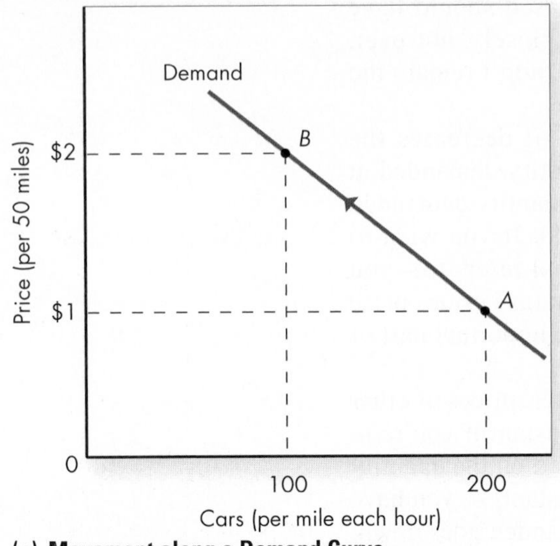

(a) Movement along a Demand Curve

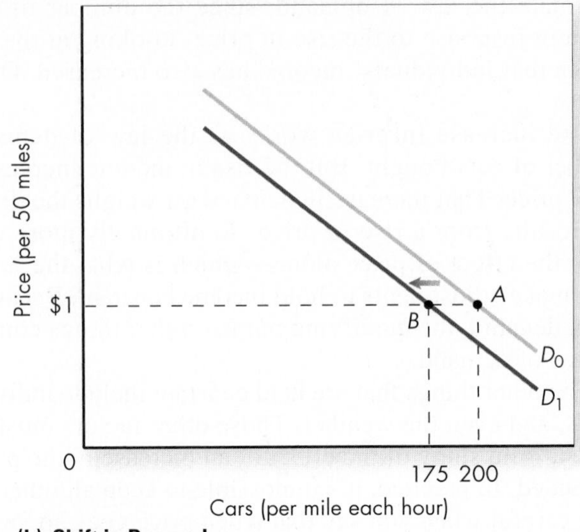

(b) Shift in Demand

every hour (a movement along the demand curve). Figure 4-2(b) shows that providing alternative methods of transportation such as buses and subways shifts the demand curve for roads in to the left so that at every price, demand drops by 25 cars per mile every hour.

Some Shift Factors of Demand

Important shift factors of demand include:

1. Society's income.
2. The prices of other goods.
3. Tastes.
4. Expectations.
5. Taxes and subsidies.

Web Note 4.2
Influencing Demand

Let's consider a couple of them. First, income. From our example above of the "other things constant" qualification, we saw that a rise in income increases the demand for goods. For most goods this is true. As individuals' income rises, they can afford more of the goods they want, such as steaks, computers, or clothing. These are normal goods. For other goods, called inferior goods, an increase in income reduces demand. An example is urban mass transit. A person whose income has risen tends to stop riding the bus to work because she can afford to buy a car and rent a parking space.

Next, let's consider the price of other goods. Because people make their buying decisions based on the price of related goods, demand will be affected by the prices of other goods. Suppose the price of jeans rises from $25 to $35, but the price of khakis remains at $25. Next time you need pants, you're apt to try khakis instead of jeans. They are substitutes. When the price of a substitute rises, demand for the good whose price has remained the same will rise. Or consider another example. Suppose the price of movie tickets falls. What will happen to the demand for popcorn? You're likely to increase the number of times you go to the movies, so you'll also likely increase the amount of popcorn you purchase. The lower cost of a movie ticket increases the demand for popcorn because popcorn and movies are complements. When the price of a good declines, the demand for its complement rises.

Let's consider taxes and subsidies as examples of shift factors. Taxes levied on consumers increase the cost of goods to consumers and therefore reduce demand for those goods. Subsidies to consumers have the opposite effect. When states host tax-free weeks during August's back-to-school shopping season, consumers load up on products to avoid sales taxes. Demand for retail goods rises during the tax holiday.

There are many other shift factors in addition to the ones I've listed. In fact anything—except the price of the good itself—that affects demand (and many things do) is a shift factor. While economists agree these shift factors are important, they believe that no shift factor influences how much of a good people buy as consistently as its price. That's why economists make the law of demand central to their analysis.

Before we move on let's test your understanding: What happens to your demand curve for CDs in the following examples: First, let's say you buy an iPod. Next, let's say that the price of CDs falls. Finally, say that you won $1 million in a lottery. What happens to the demand for CDs in each case? If you answered: It shifts in to the left; it remains unchanged; and it shifts out to the right—you've got it.

Q-3 Explain the effect of each of the following on the demand for new computers:

1. The price of computers falls by 30 percent.
2. Total income in the economy rises.

WWW Web Note 4.3 Shifting Demand

The Demand Table

As I emphasized in Chapter 2, introductory economics depends heavily on graphs and graphical analysis—translating ideas into graphs and back into words. So let's graph the demand curve.

Figure 4-3(a), a demand table, describes Alice's demand for online movies. For example, at a price of $4, Alice will rent (buy the use of) six movies per week, and at a price of $1 she will rent nine.

Four points about the relationship between the number of movies Alice rents and the price of renting them are worth mentioning. First, the relationship follows the law of demand: As the rental price rises, quantity demanded decreases. Second, quantity demanded has a specific *time dimension* to it. In this example, demand refers to the number of movie rentals per week. Without the time dimension, the table wouldn't provide us with any useful information. Nine movie rentals per year is quite different from nine movie rentals per week. Third, the analysis assumes that Alice's movie rentals are interchangeable—the ninth movie rental doesn't significantly differ from the first, third, or any other movie rental. The fourth point is already familiar to you: The analysis assumes that everything else is held constant.

From a Demand Table to a Demand Curve

Figure 4-3(b) translates the demand table in Figure 4-3(a) into a demand curve. Point *A* (quantity = 9, price = $1.00) is graphed first at the (9, $1.00) coordinates. Next we plot points *B, C, D,* and *E* in the same manner and connect the resulting dots with a solid line. The result is the demand curve, which graphically conveys the same information that's in the demand table. Notice that the demand curve is downward sloping, indicating that the law of demand holds.

FIGURE 4-3 (A AND B) From a Demand Table to a Demand Curve

The demand table in (**a**) is translated into a demand curve in (**b**). Each combination of price and quantity in the table corresponds to a point on the curve. For example, point *A* on the graph represents row *A* in the table: Alice demands nine movie rentals at a price of 50 cents. A demand curve is constructed by plotting all points from the demand table and connecting the points with a line.

	Price per Movie	Movie Rentals Demanded per Week
A	$1.00	9
B	2.00	8
C	4.00	6
D	6.00	4
E	8.00	2

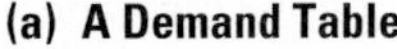

(a) A Demand Table

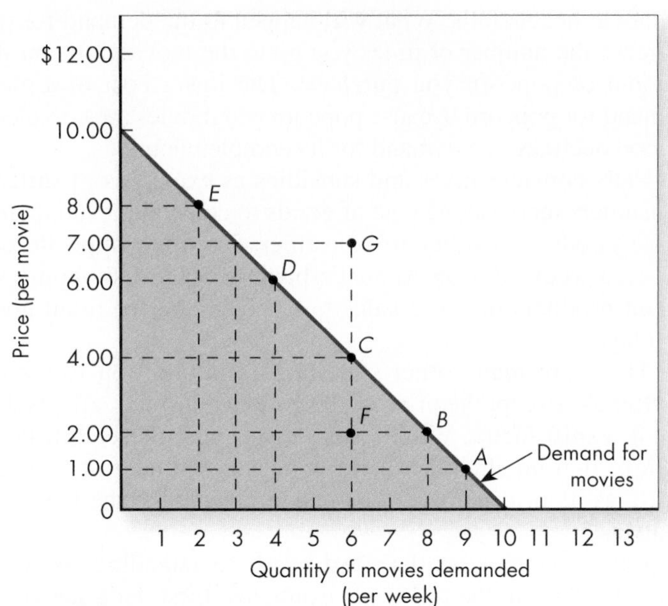

(b) A Demand Curve

The demand curve represents the maximum price that an individual will pay.

The demand curve represents the *maximum price* that an individual will pay for various quantities of a good; the individual will happily pay less. For example, say iTunes offers Alice six movie rentals at a price of $2 each (point *F* of Figure 4-3(b)). Will she accept? Sure; she'll pay any price within the shaded area to the left of the demand curve. But if iTunes offers her six rentals at $7 each (point *G*), she won't accept. At a price of $7 apiece, she's willing to rent only three movies.

Individual and Market Demand Curves

Q-4 Derive a market demand curve from the following two individual demand curves:

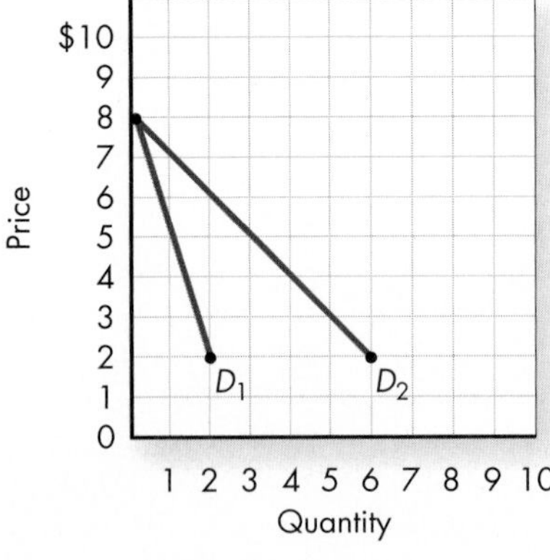

Normally, economists talk about market demand curves rather than individual demand curves. A **market demand curve** is *the horizontal sum of all individual demand curves*. Firms don't care whether individual A or individual B buys their goods; they only care that *someone* buys their goods.

Adding individual demand curves together to create a market demand curve is a good graphical exercise. I do that in Figure 4-4. In it I assume that the market consists of three buyers, Alice, Bruce, and Carmen, whose demand tables are given in Figure 4-4(a). Alice and Bruce have demand tables similar to the demand tables discussed previously. At a price of $6 each, Alice rents four movies; at a price of $4, she rents six. Carmen is an all-or-nothing individual. She rents one movie as long as the price is equal to or less than $2; otherwise she rents nothing. If you plot Carmen's demand curve, it's a vertical line. However, the law of demand still holds: As price increases, quantity demanded decreases.

The quantity demanded by each consumer is listed in columns 2, 3, and 4 of Figure 4-4(a). Column 5 shows total market demand; each entry is the horizontal sum of the entries in columns 2, 3, and 4. For example, at a price of $6 apiece (row *F*), Alice demands four movie rentals, Bruce demands one, and Carmen demands zero, for a total market demand of five movie rentals.

FIGURE 4-4 (A AND B) **From Individual Demands to a Market Demand Curve**

The table (**a**) shows the demand schedules for Alice, Bruce, and Carmen. Together they make up the market for movie rentals. Their total quantity demanded (market demand) for movie rentals at each price is given in column 5. As you can see in (**b**), Alice's, Bruce's, and Carmen's demand curves can be added together to get the total market demand curve. For example, at a price of \$4, Carmen demands 0, Bruce demands 3, and Alice demands 6, for a market demand of 9 (point *D*).

	(1) Price (per Movie)	(2) Alice's Demand	(3) Bruce's Demand	(4) Carmen's Demand	(5) Market Demand
A	\$1.00	9	6	1	16
B	2.00	8	5	1	14
C	3.00	7	4	0	11
D	4.00	6	3	0	9
E	5.00	5	2	0	7
F	6.00	4	1	0	5
G	7.00	3	0	0	3
H	8.00	2	0	0	2

(a) A Demand Table

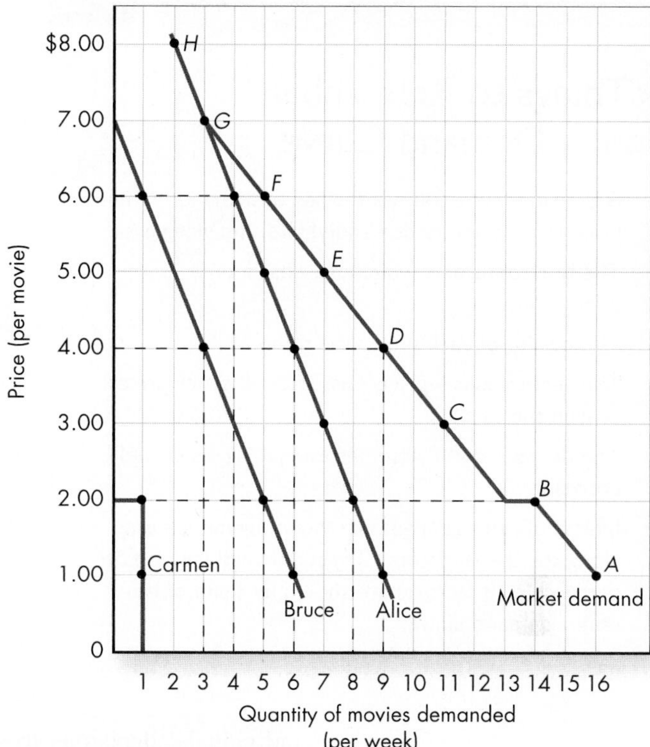

(b) Adding Demand Curves

Figure 4-4(b) shows three demand curves: one each for Alice, Bruce, and Carmen. The market, or total, demand curve is the horizontal sum of the individual demand curves. To see that this is the case, notice that if we take the quantity demanded at \$2 by Alice (8), Bruce (5), and Carmen (1), they sum to 14, which is point *B* (14, \$2) on the market demand curve. We can do that for each price. Alternatively, we can simply add the individual quantities demanded, given in the demand tables, prior to graphing (which we do in column 5 of Figure 4-4(a)), and graph that total in relation to price. Not surprisingly, we get the same total market demand curve.

Individual and Market Demand Curves

In practice, of course, firms don't measure individual demand curves, so they don't sum them up in this fashion. Instead, they statistically estimate market demand. Still, summing up individual demand curves is a useful exercise because it shows you how the market demand curve is the sum (the horizontal sum, graphically speaking) of the individual demand curves, and it gives you a good sense of where market demand curves come from. It also shows you that, even if individuals don't respond to small changes in price, the market demand curve can still be smooth and downward sloping. That's because, for the market, the law of demand is based on two phenomena:

1. At lower prices, existing demanders buy more.
2. At lower prices, new demanders (some all-or-nothing demanders like Carmen) enter the market.

For the market, the law of demand is based on two phenomena:

1. At lower prices, existing demanders buy more.
2. At lower prices, new demanders enter the market.

A REMINDER 

Six Things to Remember about a Demand Curve

- A demand curve follows the law of demand: When price rises, quantity demanded falls, and vice versa.
- The horizontal axis—quantity—has a time dimension.
- The quality of each unit is the same.
- The vertical axis—price—assumes all other prices remain the same.
- The demand curve assumes everything else is held constant.
- Effects of price changes are shown by movements along the demand curve. Effects of anything else on demand (shift factors) are shown by shifts of the entire demand curve.

Supply

In one sense, supply is the mirror image of demand. Individuals control the factors of production—inputs, or resources, necessary to produce goods. Individuals' supply of these factors to the market mirrors other individuals' demand for those factors. For example, say you decide you want to rest rather than weed your garden. You hire someone to do the weeding; you demand labor. Someone else decides she would prefer more income instead of more rest; she supplies labor to you. You trade money for labor; she trades labor for money. Her supply is the mirror image of your demand.

For a large number of goods and services, however, the supply process is more complicated than demand. For many goods there's an intermediate step: Individuals supply factors of production to firms.

Let's consider a simple example. Say you're a taco technician. You supply your labor to the factor market. The taco company demands your labor (hires you). The taco company combines your labor with other inputs such as meat, cheese, beans, and tables, and produces tacos (production), which it supplies to customers in the goods market. For produced goods, supply depends not only on individuals' decisions to supply factors of production but also on firms' ability to transform those factors of production into usable goods.

Supply of produced goods involves a much more complicated process than demand and is divided into analysis of factors of production and the transformation of those factors into goods.

The supply process of produced goods is generally complicated. Often there are many layers of firms—production firms, wholesale firms, distribution firms, and retailing firms—each of which passes on in-process goods to the next layer of firms. Real-world production and supply of produced goods is a multistage process.

The supply of nonproduced goods is more direct. Individuals supply their labor in the form of services directly to the goods market. For example, an independent contractor may repair your washing machine. That contractor supplies his labor directly to you.

Thus, the analysis of the supply of produced goods has two parts: an analysis of the supply of factors of production to households and to firms and an analysis of the process by which firms transform those factors of production into usable goods and services.

The Law of Supply

There's a law of supply that corresponds to the law of demand. The **law of supply** states:

Quantity supplied rises as price rises, other things constant.

Or alternatively:

Quantity supplied falls as price falls, other things constant.

Price determines quantity supplied just as it determines quantity demanded. Like the law of demand, the law of supply is fundamental to the invisible hand's (the market's) ability to coordinate individuals' actions.

The law of supply is based on substitution and the expectation of profits.

The law of supply is based on a firm's ability to switch from producing one good to another, that is, to substitute. When the price of a good a person or firm supplies rises, individuals and firms can rearrange their activities in order to supply more of that good to the market. They want to supply more because the opportunity cost of *not*

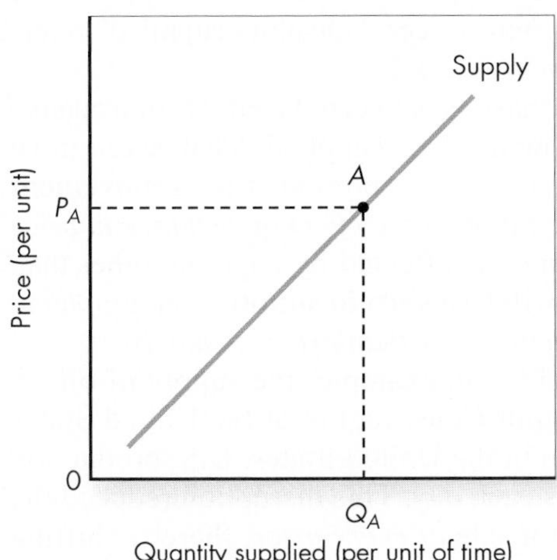

FIGURE 4-5 A Sample Supply Curve

The supply curve demonstrates graphically the law of supply, which states that the quantity supplied of a good is directly related to that good's price, other things constant. As the price of a good goes up, the quantity supplied also goes up, so the supply curve is upward sloping.

supplying the good rises as its price rises. For example, if the price of corn rises and the price of soybeans has not changed, farmers will grow less soybeans and more corn, other things constant.

With firms, there's a second explanation of the law of supply. Assuming firms' costs are constant, a higher price means higher profits (the difference between a firm's revenues and its costs). The expectation of those higher profits leads it to increase output as price rises, which is what the law of supply states.

The Supply Curve

A **supply curve** is *the graphical representation of the relationship between price and quantity supplied.* A supply curve is shown in Figure 4-5.

Notice how the supply curve slopes upward to the right. That upward slope captures the law of supply. It tells us that the quantity supplied varies *directly*—in the same direction—with the price.

As with the law of demand, the law of supply assumes other things are held constant. If the price of soybeans rises and quantity supplied falls, you'll look for something else that changed—for example, a drought might have caused a drop in supply. Your explanation would go as follows: Had there been no drought, the quantity supplied would have increased in response to the rise in price, but because there was a drought, the supply decreased, which caused prices to rise.

Shifts in Supply versus Movements along a Supply Curve

As with the law of demand, the law of supply represents economists' off-the-cuff response to the question "What happens to quantity supplied if price rises?" If the law seems to be violated, economists search for some other variable that has changed. As was the case with demand, these other variables that might change are called shift factors.

Shifts in Supply versus Movements along a Supply Curve

The same distinctions in terms made for demand apply to supply.

Supply refers to *a schedule of quantities a seller is willing to sell per unit of time at various prices, other things constant.*

Quantity supplied refers to *a specific amount that will be supplied at a specific price.*

Q-5 Assume that the price of gasoline rises, causing the demand for hybrid cars to rise. As a result, the price of hybrid cars rises. This makes _______ rise. Should the missing words be *the supply* or *the quantity supplied?*

In graphical terms, supply refers to the entire supply curve because a supply curve tells us how much will be offered for sale at various prices. "Quantity supplied" refers to a point on a supply curve, such as point *A* in Figure 4-5.

The second distinction that is important to make is between the effects of a change in price and the effects of shift factors on how much is supplied. Changes in price cause changes in quantity supplied; such changes are represented by a **movement along a supply curve**—*the graphical representation of the effect of a change in price on the quantity supplied.* If the amount supplied is affected by anything other than price, that is, by a shift factor of supply, there will be a **shift in supply**—*the graphical representation of the effect of a change in a factor other than price on supply.*

To make that distinction clear, let's consider an example: the supply of oil. In September 2005, Hurricane Katrina hit the Gulf Coast region of the United States and disrupted oil supply lines and production in the United States. U.S. production of oil declined from 4.6 to 4.1 million barrels each day. This disruption reduced the amount of oil U.S. producers were offering for sale *at every price,* thereby shifting the supply of U.S. oil to the left from S_0 to S_1, and the quantity of oil that would be supplied at the $50 price fell from point *A* to point *B* in Figure 4-6. But the price did not stay at $50. It rose to $80. In response to the higher price, other areas in the United States increased their quantity supplied (from point *B* to point *C* in Figure 4-6). That increase *due to the higher price* is called a movement along the supply curve. So if a change in quantity supplied occurs because of a higher price, it is called a *movement along the supply curve;* if a change in supply occurs because of one of the shift factors (i.e., for any reason other than a change in price), it is called a *shift in supply.*

Shift Factors of Supply

Shift factors of supply are similar to those for demand. Examples include:

1. Price of inputs.
2. Technology.
3. Expectations.
4. Taxes and subsidies.

Other factors besides price that affect how much will be supplied include the price of inputs used in production, technology, expectations, and taxes and subsidies. The analysis of how these affect supply parallels the analysis of the law of demand, so we will only consider technology, leaving the analysis of other shift factors to you.

FIGURE 4-6 Shifts in Supply versus Movement along a Supply Curve

A *shift in supply* results when the shift is due to any cause other than a change in price. It is a shift in the entire supply curve (see the arrow from *A* to *B*). A *movement along a supply curve* is due to a change in price only (see the arrow from *B* to *C*). To differentiate the two, movements caused by changes in price are called *changes in the quantity supplied,* not changes in supply.

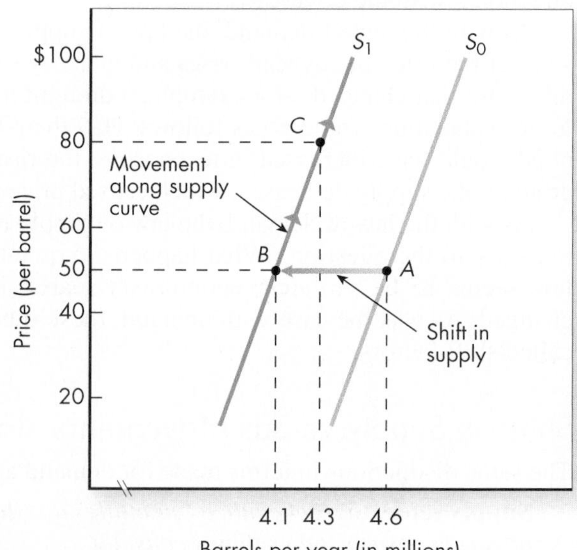

Advances in technology change the production process, reducing the number of inputs needed to produce a good, and thereby reducing its cost of production. A reduction in the cost of production increases profits and leads suppliers to increase production. Advances in technology increase supply.

Remember, as was the case with demand, a shift factor of supply is anything other than its price that affects supply. It shifts the entire supply curve. A change in price causes a movement along the supply curve.

To be sure you understand shifts in supply, explain what is likely to happen to your supply curve for labor in the following cases: (1) You suddenly decide that you absolutely need a new car. (2) You win a million dollars in the lottery. And finally, (3) the wage you earn doubles. If you came up with the answers: Shift out to the right, shift in to the left, and no change—you've got it down. If not, it's time for a review.

Do we see such shifts in the supply curve often? Yes. A good example is computers. For the past 30 years, technological changes have continually shifted the supply curve for computers out to the right.

Q-6 Explain the effect of each of the following on the supply of romance novels:

1. The price of paper rises by 20 percent.
2. Government provides a 10 percent subsidy to book producers.

The Supply Table

Remember Figure 4-4(a)'s demand table for movie rentals? In Figure 4-7(a), we follow the same reasoning to construct a supply table for three hypothetical movie suppliers. Each supplier follows the law of supply: When price rises, each supplies more, or at least as much as each did at a lower price.

From a Supply Table to a Supply Curve

Figure 4-7(b) takes the information in Figure 4-7(a)'s supply table and translates it into a graph of each supplier's supply curve. For instance, point C_A on Ann's supply curve corresponds to the information in columns 1 and 2, row *C*. Point C_A is at a price of \$2 per movie and a quantity of two movies per week. Notice that Ann's supply curve is upward sloping, meaning that price is positively related to quantity. Charlie's and Barry's supply curves are similarly derived.

The supply curve represents the set of *minimum* prices an individual seller will accept for various quantities of a good. The market's invisible hand stops suppliers from charging more than the market price. If suppliers could escape the market's invisible hand and charge a higher price, they would gladly do so. Unfortunately for them, and fortunately for consumers, a higher price encourages other suppliers to begin selling movies. Competing suppliers' entry into the market sets a limit on the price any supplier can charge.

Individual and Market Supply Curves

The market supply curve is derived from individual supply curves in precisely the same way that the market demand curve was. To emphasize the symmetry, I've made the three suppliers quite similar to the three demanders. Ann (column 2) will supply two at \$2; if price goes up to \$4, she increases her supply to four. Barry (column 3) begins supplying at \$2, and at \$6 supplies five, the most he'll supply regardless of how high price rises. Charlie (column 4) has only two units to supply. At a price of \$7 he'll supply that quantity, but higher prices won't get him to supply any more.

The **market supply curve** is *the horizontal sum of all individual supply curves.* In Figure 4-7(a) (column 5), we add together Ann's, Barry's, and Charlie's supplies to arrive at the market supply curve, which is graphed in Figure 4-7(b). Notice that each

Individual and Market Supply Curves

FIGURE 4-7 (A AND B) From Individual Supplies to a Market Supply

As with market demand, market supply is determined by adding all quantities supplied at a given price. Three suppliers—Ann, Barry, and Charlie—make up the market of movie suppliers. The total market supply is the sum of their individual supplies at each price, shown in column 5 of (**a**).

Each of the individual supply curves and the market supply curve have been plotted in (**b**). Notice how the market supply curve is the horizontal sum of the individual supply curves.

Quantities Supplied	(1) Price (per Movie)	(2) Ann's Supply	(3) Barry's Supply	(4) Charlie's Supply	(5) Market Supply
A	$0.00	0	0	0	0
B	1.00	1	0	0	1
C	2.00	2	1	0	3
D	3.00	3	2	0	5
E	4.00	4	3	0	7
F	5.00	5	4	0	9
G	6.00	6	5	0	11
H	7.00	7	5	2	14
I	8.00	8	5	2	15

(a) A Supply Table

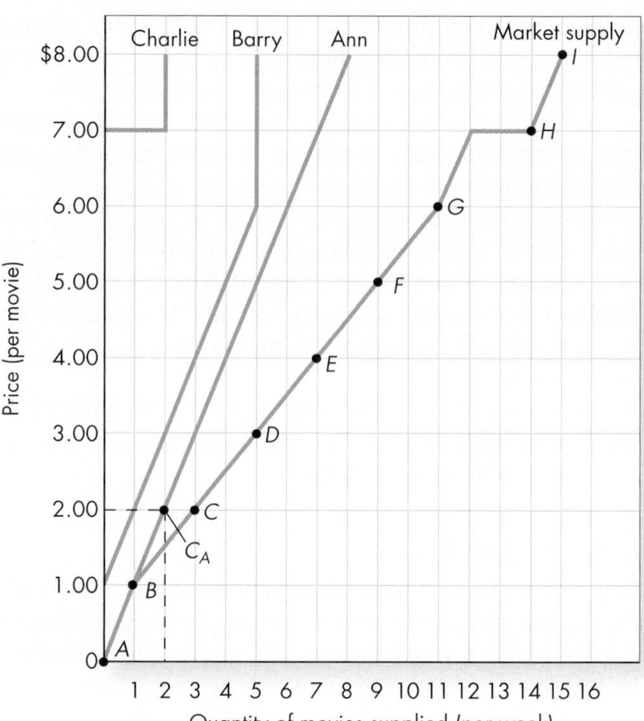

(b) Adding Supply Curves

The law of supply is based on two phenomena:

1. At higher prices, existing suppliers supply more.
2. At higher prices, new suppliers enter the market.

point corresponds to the information in columns 1 and 5 for each row. For example, point *H* corresponds to a price of $7 and a quantity of 14.

The market supply curve's upward slope is determined by two different sources: As price rises, existing suppliers supply more and new suppliers enter the market. Sometimes existing suppliers may not be willing to increase their quantity supplied in response to an increase in prices, but a rise in price often brings brand-new suppliers into the market. For example, a rise in teachers' salaries will have little effect on the number of hours current teachers teach, but it will increase the number of people choosing to be teachers.

The Interaction of Supply and Demand

Thomas Carlyle, the English historian who dubbed economics "the dismal science," also wrote this chapter's introductory tidbit. "Teach a parrot the terms *supply* and *demand* and you've got an economist." In earlier chapters, I tried to convince you that economics is *not* dismal. In the rest of this chapter, I hope to convince you that, while supply and demand are important to economics, parrots don't make good economists. If students think that when they've learned the terms *supply* and *demand* they've learned economics, they're mistaken. Those terms are just labels for the ideas behind supply and demand, and it's the ideas that are important. What matters about supply and demand isn't the labels but how the concepts interact. For instance, what happens if a freeze kills the blossoms on the orange trees? If price doesn't change, the quantity of oranges supplied isn't expected to equal the quantity demanded. But in the real world, prices do change, often before the frost hits, as expectations of the frost lead people to adjust. It's in understanding the interaction of supply and demand that economics becomes interesting and relevant.

Six Things to Remember about a Supply Curve

- A supply curve follows the law of supply. When price rises, quantity supplied increases, and vice versa.
- The horizontal axis—quantity—has a time dimension.
- The quality of each unit is the same.
- The vertical axis—price—assumes all other prices remain constant.
- The supply curve assumes everything else is constant.
- Effects of price changes are shown by movements along the supply curve. Effects of nonprice determinants of supply are shown by shifts of the entire supply curve.

Equilibrium

When you have a market in which neither suppliers nor consumers collude and in which prices are free to move up and down, the forces of supply and demand interact to arrive at an equilibrium. The concept of equilibrium comes from physics—classical mechanics. **Equilibrium** is *a concept in which opposing dynamic forces cancel each other out.* For example, a hot-air balloon is in equilibrium when the upward force exerted by the hot air in the balloon equals the downward pressure exerted on the balloon by gravity. In supply/demand analysis, equilibrium means that the upward pressure on price is exactly offset by the downward pressure on price. **Equilibrium quantity** is *the amount bought and sold at the equilibrium price.* **Equilibrium price** is *the price toward which the invisible hand drives the market.* At the equilibrium price, quantity demanded equals quantity supplied.

What happens if the market is not in equilibrium—if quantity supplied doesn't equal quantity demanded? You get either excess supply or excess demand, and a tendency for prices to change.

Excess Supply If there is **excess supply** (a surplus), *quantity supplied is greater than quantity demanded,* and some suppliers won't be able to sell all their goods. Each supplier will think: "Gee, if I offer to sell it for a bit less, I'll be the lucky one who sells my goods; someone else will be stuck with goods they can't sell." But because all suppliers with excess goods will be thinking the same thing, the price in the market will fall. As that happens, consumers will increase their quantity demanded. So the movement toward equilibrium caused by excess supply is on both the supply and demand sides.

Bargain hunters can get a deal when there is excess supply.

Excess Demand The reverse is also true. Say that instead of excess supply, there's **excess demand** (a shortage)—*quantity demanded is greater than quantity supplied.* There are more consumers who want the good than there are suppliers selling the good. Let's consider what's likely to go through demanders' minds. They'll likely call long-lost friends who just happen to be sellers of that good and tell them it's good to talk to them and, by the way, don't they want to sell that . . . ? Suppliers will be rather pleased that so many of their old friends have remembered them, but they'll also likely see the connection between excess demand and their friends' thoughtfulness. To stop their phones from ringing all the time, they'll likely raise their price. The reverse is true for excess supply. It's amazing how friendly suppliers become to potential consumers when there's excess supply.

Price Adjusts This tendency for prices to rise when the quantity demanded exceeds the quantity supplied and for prices to fall when the quantity supplied exceeds the quantity demanded is a central element to understanding supply and demand. So remember:

Prices tend to rise when there is excess demand and fall when there is excess supply.

When quantity demanded is greater than quantity supplied, prices tend to rise.

When quantity supplied is greater than quantity demanded, prices tend to fall.

Two other things to note about supply and demand are (1) the greater the difference between quantity supplied and quantity demanded, the more pressure there is for prices to rise or fall, and (2) when quantity demanded equals quantity supplied, the market is in equilibrium.

Price Adjustment and Equilibrium

People's tendencies to change prices exist as long as quantity supplied and quantity demanded differ. But the change in price brings the laws of supply and demand into play. As price falls, quantity supplied decreases as some suppliers leave the business (the law of supply). And as some people who originally weren't really interested in buying the good think, "Well, at this low price, maybe I do want to buy," quantity demanded increases (the law of demand). Similarly, when price rises, quantity supplied will increase (the law of supply) and quantity demanded will decrease (the law of demand).

Whenever quantity supplied and quantity demanded are unequal, price tends to change. If, however, quantity supplied and quantity demanded are equal, price will stay the same because no one will have an incentive to change.

The Graphical Interaction of Supply and Demand

Figure 4-8 shows supply and demand curves for movie rentals and demonstrates the force of the invisible hand. Let's consider what will happen to the price of movies in three cases:

1. When the price is $7 each.
2. When the price is $3 each.
3. When the price is $5 each.

1. When price is $7, quantity supplied is seven and quantity demanded is only three. Excess supply is four. Individual consumers can get all they want, but most suppliers can't sell all they wish; they'll be stuck with movies that they'd like to rent. Suppliers will tend to offer their goods at a lower price and demanders, who see plenty of suppliers out there, will bargain harder for an even lower price. Both these forces will push the price as indicated by the down arrows in Figure 4-8.

Now let's start from the other side.

2. Say price is $3. The situation is now reversed. Quantity supplied is three and quantity demanded is seven. Excess demand is four. Now it's consumers who can't get what they want and suppliers who are in the strong bargaining position. The pressures will be on price to rise in the direction of the up arrows in Figure 4-8.
3. At $5, price is at its equilibrium: Quantity supplied equals quantity demanded. Suppliers offer to sell five and consumers want to buy five, so there's no pressure on price to rise or fall. Price will tend to remain where it is (point *E* in Figure 4-8). Notice that the equilibrium price is where the supply and demand curves intersect.

What Equilibrium Isn't

It is important to remember two points about equilibrium. First, equilibrium isn't a state of the world. It's a characteristic of the model—the framework you use to look at the world. The same situation could be seen as an equilibrium in one framework and as

FIGURE 4-8 The Interaction of Supply and Demand

Combining Ann's supply from Figure 4-7 and Alice's demand from Figure 4-4, let's see the force of the invisible hand. When there is excess demand, there is upward pressure on price. When there is excess supply, there is downward pressure on price. Understanding these pressures is essential to understanding how to apply economics to reality.

Price (per Movie)	Quantity Supplied	Quantity Demanded	Surplus (+)/ Shortage (−)
$7.00	7	3	+4
$5.00	5	5	0
$3.00	3	7	−4

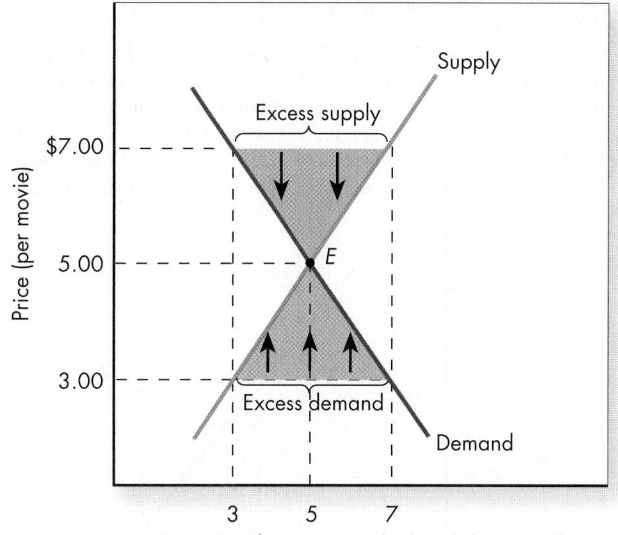

a disequilibrium in another. Say you're describing a car that's speeding along at 100 miles an hour. That car is changing position relative to objects on the ground. Its movement could be, and generally is, described as if it were in disequilibrium. However, if you consider this car relative to another car going 100 miles an hour, the cars could be modeled as being in equilibrium because their positions relative to each other aren't changing.

Second, equilibrium isn't inherently good or bad. It's simply a state in which dynamic pressures offset each other. Some equilibria are good—a market in competitive equilibrium is one in which people can buy the goods they really want at the best possible price. Other equilibria are awful. Say two countries are engaged in a nuclear war against each other and both sides are blown away. An equilibrium will have been reached, but there's nothing good about it.

Equilibrium is not inherently good or bad.

Political and Social Forces and Equilibrium

Understanding that equilibrium is a characteristic of the model, not of the real world, is important in applying economic models to reality. For example, in the preceding description, I said equilibrium occurs where quantity supplied equals quantity demanded. In a model where economic forces were the only forces operating, that's true. In the real world, however, other forces—political and social forces—are operating. These will likely push price away from that supply/demand equilibrium. Were we to consider a model that included all these forces—political, social, and economic—equilibrium would be likely to exist where quantity supplied isn't equal to quantity demanded. For example:

- Farmers use political pressure to obtain prices that are higher than supply/demand equilibrium prices.
- Social pressures often offset economic pressures and prevent unemployed individuals from accepting work at lower wages than currently employed workers receive.

FIGURE 4-9 (A AND B) Shifts in Supply and Demand

If demand increases from D_0 to D_1, as shown in (**a**), the quantity of movie rentals that was demanded at a price of $4.50, 8, increases to 10, but the quantity supplied remains at 8. This excess demand tends to cause prices to rise. Eventually, a new equilibrium is reached at the price of $5, where the quantity supplied and the quantity demanded are 9 (point *B*).

If supply of movie rentals decreases, then the entire supply curve shifts inward to the left, as shown in (**b**), from S_0 to S_1. At the price of $4.50, the quantity supplied has now decreased to 6 movies, but the quantity demanded has remained at 8 movies. The excess demand tends to force the price upward. Eventually, an equilibrium is reached at the price of $5 and quantity 7 (point *C*).

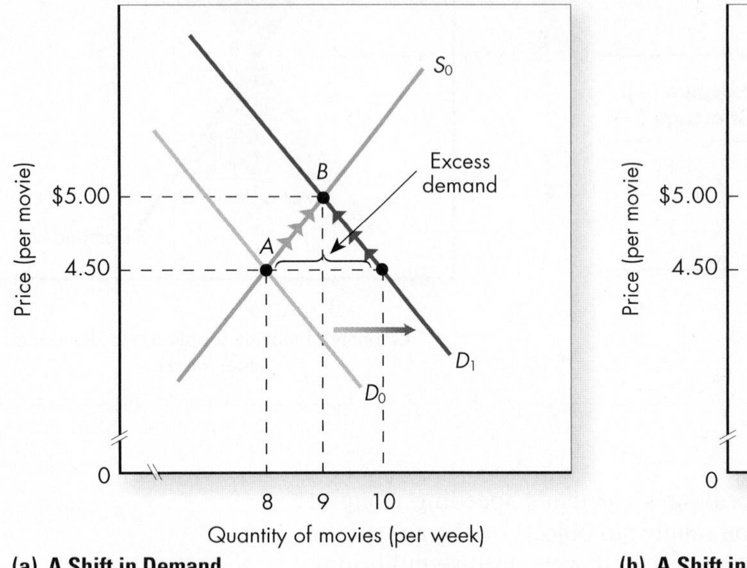

(a) A Shift in Demand

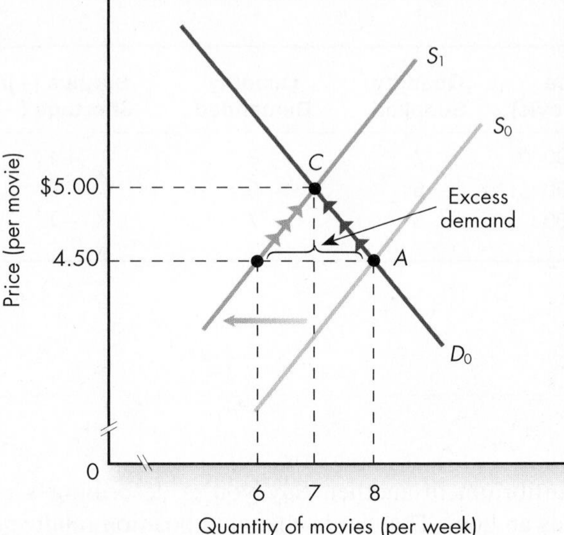

(b) A Shift in Supply

- Existing firms conspire to limit new competition by lobbying Congress to pass restrictive regulations and by devising pricing strategies to scare off new entrants.
- Renters often organize to pressure local government to set caps on the rental price of apartments.

If social and political forces were included in the analysis, they'd provide a counter–pressure to the dynamic forces of supply and demand. The result would be an equilibrium with continual excess supply or excess demand if the market were considered only in reference to economic forces. Economic forces pushing toward a supply/demand equilibrium would be thwarted by social and political forces pushing in the other direction.

Shifts in Supply and Demand

Supply and demand are most useful when trying to figure out what will happen to equilibrium price and quantity if either supply or demand shifts. Figure 4-9(a) deals with an increase in demand. Figure 4-9(b) deals with a decrease in supply.

Q-7 Demonstrate graphically the effect of a heavy frost in Florida on the equilibrium quantity and price of oranges.

Let's consider again the supply and demand for movie rentals. In Figure 4-9(a), the supply is S_0 and initial demand is D_0. They meet at an equilibrium price of $4.50 per movie and an equilibrium quantity of 8 movies per week (point *A*). Now say that the demand for movie rentals increases from D_0 to D_1. At a price of $4.50, the quantity of movie rentals supplied will be 8 and the quantity demanded will be 10; excess demand of 2 exists.

ADDED DIMENSION

The Supply and Demand for Children

In Chapter 1, I distinguished between an economic force and a market force. Economic forces are operative in all aspects of our lives; market forces are economic forces that are allowed to be expressed through a market. My examples in this chapter are of market forces—of goods sold in a market—but supply and demand also can be used to analyze situations in which economic, but not market, forces operate. An economist who is adept at this is Gary Becker of the University of Chicago. He has applied supply and demand analysis to a wide range of issues, even the supply and demand for children.

Becker doesn't argue that children should be bought and sold. But he does argue that economic considerations play a large role in people's decisions on how many children to have. In farming communities, children can be productive early in life; by age six or seven, they can work on a farm. In an advanced industrial community, children provide pleasure but generally don't contribute productively to family income. Even getting them to help around the house can be difficult.

Becker argues that since the price of having children is lower for a farming society than for an industrial society, farming societies will have more children per family. Quantity of children demanded will be larger. And that's what we find. Developing countries that rely primarily on farming often have three, four, or more children per family. Industrial societies average fewer than two children per family.

The excess demand pushes prices upward in the direction of the small arrows, decreasing the quantity demanded and increasing the quantity supplied. As it does so, movement takes place along both the supply curve and the demand curve.

WWW Web Note 4.4
Changes in Equilibrium

The upward push on price decreases the gap between the quantity supplied and the quantity demanded. As the gap decreases, the upward pressure decreases, but as long as that gap exists at all, price will be pushed upward until the new equilibrium price ($5) and new quantity (9) are reached (point *B*). At point *B*, quantity supplied equals quantity demanded. So the market is in equilibrium. Notice that the adjustment is twofold: The higher price brings about equilibrium by both increasing the quantity supplied (from 8 to 9) and decreasing the quantity demanded (from 10 to 9).

Figure 4-9(b) begins with the same situation that we started with in Figure 4-9(a); the initial equilibrium quantity and price are eight movies per week and $4.50 per movie (point *A*). In this example, however, instead of demand increasing, let's assume supply decreases—say because some suppliers change what they like to do and decide they will no longer supply movies. That means that the entire supply curve shifts inward to the left (from S_0 to S_1). At the initial equilibrium price of $4.50, the quantity demanded is greater than the quantity supplied. Two more movies are demanded than are supplied. (Excess demand = 2.)

This excess demand exerts upward pressure on price. Price is pushed in the direction of the small arrows. As the price rises, the upward pressure on price is reduced but will still exist until the new equilibrium price, $5, and new quantity, seven, are reached. At $5, the quantity supplied equals the quantity demanded. The adjustment has involved a movement along the demand curve and the new supply curve. As price rises, quantity supplied is adjusted upward and quantity demanded is adjusted downward until quantity supplied equals quantity demanded where the new supply curve intersects the demand curve at point *C*, an equilibrium of seven and $5.

Q-8 Demonstrate graphically the likely effect of an increase in the price of gas on the equilibrium quantity and price of hybrid cars.

Here is an exercise for you to try. Demonstrate graphically how the price of computers could have fallen dramatically in the past 10 years, even as demand increased. (Hint: Supply has increased even more, so even at lower prices, far more computers have been supplied than were being supplied 10 years ago.)

A Limitation of Supply/Demand Analysis

Supply and demand are tools, and, like most tools, they help us enormously when used appropriately. Used inappropriately, however, they can be misleading. Throughout the book I'll introduce you to the limitations of the tools, but let me discuss an important one here.

In supply/demand analysis, other things are assumed constant. If other things change, then one cannot directly apply supply/demand analysis. Sometimes supply and demand are interconnected, making it impossible to hold other things constant. Let's take an example. Say we are considering the effect of a fall in the wage rate on unemployment. In supply/demand analysis, you would look at the effect that fall would have on workers' decisions to supply labor, and on business's decision to hire workers. But there are also other effects. For instance, the fall in the wage lowers people's income and thereby reduces demand for goods. That reduction in demand for goods may feed back to firms and reduce the firms' demand for workers which might further reduce the demand for goods. If these ripple effects do occur, and are important enough to affect the result, they have to be added for the analysis to be complete. A complete analysis always includes the relevant feedback effects.

Q-9 When determining the effect of a shift factor on price and quantity, in which of the following markets could you likely assume that other things will remain constant?

1. Market for eggs.
2. Labor market.
3. World oil market.
4. Market for luxury boats.

There is no single answer to the question of which ripples must be included. There is much debate among economists about which ripple effects to include, but there are some general rules. Supply/demand analysis, used without adjustment, is most appropriate for questions where the goods are a small percentage of the entire economy. That is when the other-things-constant assumption will most likely hold. As soon as one starts analyzing goods that are a large percentage of the entire economy, the other-things-constant assumption is likely not to hold true. The reason is found in the **fallacy of composition**—*the false assumption that what is true for a part will also be true for the whole.*

The fallacy of composition is the false assumption that what is true for a part will also be true for the whole.

Consider a lone supplier who lowers the price of his or her good. People will substitute that good for other goods, and the quantity of the good demanded will increase. But what if all suppliers lower their prices? Since all prices have gone down, why should consumers switch? The substitution story can't be used in the aggregate. There are many such examples.

An understanding of the fallacy of composition is of central relevance to macroeconomics. In the aggregate, whenever firms produce (whenever they supply), they create income (demand for their goods). So in macro, when supply changes, demand changes. This interdependence is one of the primary reasons we have a separate macroeconomics. In macroeconomics, the other-things-constant assumption central to microeconomic supply/demand analysis often does not hold.

Q-10 Why is the fallacy of composition relevant for macroeconomic issues?

It is to account for these interdependencies that we separate macro analysis from micro analysis. In macro we use curves whose underlying foundations are much more complicated than the supply and demand curves we use in micro and in modern economics there is an active debate about how more complex structural models can extend our understanding of how markets operate.

It is to account for interdependency between aggregate supply decisions and aggregate demand decisions that we have a separate micro analysis and a separate macro analysis.

One final comment: The fact that supply and demand may be interdependent does not mean that you can't use supply/demand analysis; it simply means that you must modify its results with the interdependency that, if you've done the analysis correctly, you've kept in the back of your head. Using supply and demand analysis is generally a step in any good economic analysis, but you must remember that it may be only a step.

Conclusion

Throughout the book, I'll be presenting examples of supply and demand. So I'll end this chapter here because its intended purposes have been served. What were those intended purposes? First, I exposed you to enough economic terminology and economic thinking to allow you to proceed to my more complicated examples. Second, I have set your mind to work putting the events around you into a supply/demand framework. Doing that will give you new insights into the events that shape all our lives. Once you incorporate the supply/demand framework into your way of looking at the world, you will have made an important step toward thinking like an economist.

Summary

- The law of demand states that quantity demanded rises as price falls, other things constant. (*LO4-1*)
- The law of supply states that quantity supplied rises as price rises, other things constant. (*LO4-2*)
- Factors that affect supply and demand other than price are called shift factors. Shift factors of demand include income, prices of other goods, tastes, expectations, and taxes on and subsidies to consumers. Shift factors of supply include the price of inputs, technology, expectations, and taxes on and subsidies to producers. (*LO4-1, LO4-2*)
- A change in quantity demanded (supplied) is a movement along the demand (supply) curve. A change in demand (supply) is a shift of the entire demand (supply) curve. (*LO4-1, LO4-2*)
- The laws of supply and demand hold true because individuals can substitute. (*LO4-1, LO4-2*)
- A market demand (supply) curve is the horizontal sum of all individual demand (supply) curves. (*LO4-1, LO4-2*)
- When quantity supplied equals quantity demanded, prices have no tendency to change. This is equilibrium. (*LO4-3*)
- When quantity demanded is greater than quantity supplied, prices tend to rise. When quantity supplied is greater than quantity demanded, prices tend to fall. (*LO4-3*)
- When the demand curve shifts to the right (left), equilibrium price rises (declines) and equilibrium quantity rises (falls). (*LO4-3*)
- When the supply curve shifts to the right (left), equilibrium price declines (rises) and equilibrium quantity rises (falls). (*LO4-3*)
- In the real world, you must add political and social forces to the supply/demand model. When you do, equilibrium is likely not going to be where quantity demanded equals quantity supplied. (*LO4-4*)
- In macro, small side effects that can be assumed away in micro are multiplied enormously and can significantly change the results. To ignore them is to fall into the fallacy of composition. (*LO4-4*)

Key Terms

demand *(79)*
demand curve *(78)*
equilibrium *(89)*
equilibrium price *(89)*
equilibrium quantity *(89)*
excess demand *(89)*
excess supply *(89)*
fallacy of composition *(94)*
law of demand *(78)*
law of supply *(84)*
market demand curve *(82)*
market supply curve *(87)*
movement along a demand curve *(79)*
movement along a supply curve *(86)*
quantity demanded *(79)*
quantity supplied *(85)*
shift in demand *(79)*
shift in supply *(86)*
supply *(85)*
supply curve *(85)*

Questions and Exercises

1. State the law of demand. Why is price inversely related to quantity demanded? *(LO4-1)*
2. You're given the following individual demand tables for comic books. *(LO4-1)*

Price	John	Liz	Alex
$ 2	4	36	24
4	4	32	20
6	0	28	16
8	0	24	12
10	0	20	8
12	0	16	4
14	0	12	0
16	0	8	0

   a. Determine the market demand table.
   b. Graph the individual and market demand curves.
   c. If the current market price is $4, what's total market demand? What happens to total market demand if price rises to $8?
   d. Say that an advertising campaign increases demand by 50 percent. What will happen to the individual and market demand curves?
3. List four shift factors of demand and explain how each affects demand. *(LO4-1)*
4. Distinguish the effect of a shift factor of demand on the demand curve from the effect of a change in price on the demand curve. *(LO4-1)*
5. State the law of supply. Why is price directly related to quantity supplied? *(LO4-2)*
6. Mary has just stated that normally, as price rises, supply will increase. Her teacher grimaces. Why? *(LO4-2)*
7. List four shift factors of supply and explain how each affects supply. *(LO4-2)*
8. Derive the market supply curve from the following two individual supply curves. *(LO4-2)*

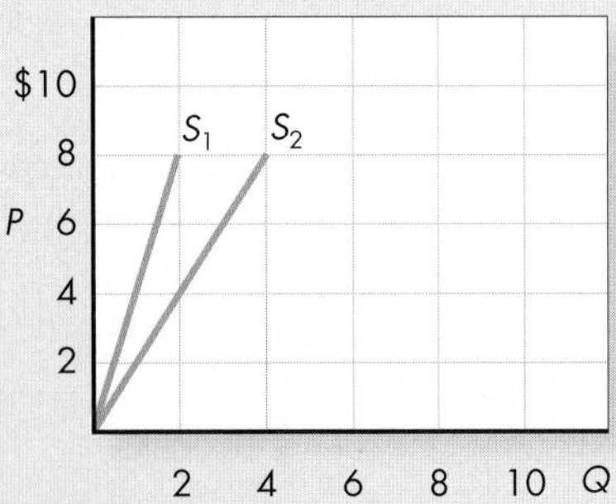

9. You're given the following demand and supply tables: *(LO4-3)*

P	Demand D_1	D_2	D_3
$30	20	5	10
40	15	3	7
50	10	0	5
60	5	0	0

P	Supply S_1	S_2	S_3
$30	0	4	11
40	0	8	17
50	10	12	18
60	10	15	20

   a. Draw the market demand and market supply curves.
   b. What is excess supply/demand at price $30? Price $60?
   c. Label equilibrium price and quantity.
10. It has just been reported that eating red meat is bad for your health. Using supply and demand curves, demonstrate the report's likely effect on the equilibrium price and quantity of steak sold in the market. *(LO4-3)*
11. Why does the price of airline tickets rise during the summer months? Demonstrate your answer graphically. *(LO4-3)*
12. Why does sales volume rise during weeks when states suspend taxes on sales by retailers? Demonstrate your answer graphically assuming that the retailer pays the tax. *(LO4-3)*
13. What is the expected impact of increased security measures imposed by the federal government on airlines fares and volume of travel? Demonstrate your answer graphically. *(LO4-3)*
14. Explain what a sudden popularity of "Economics Professor" brand casual wear would likely do to prices of that brand. *(LO4-3)*
15. In a flood, usable water supplies ironically tend to decline because the pumps and water lines are damaged. What will a flood likely do to prices of bottled water? *(LO4-3)*
16. OPEC announces it will increase oil production by 20 percent. What is the effect on the price of oil? Demonstrate your answer graphically. *(LO4-3)*

17. Draw hypothetical supply and demand curves for tea. Show how the equilibrium price and quantity will be affected by each of the following occurrences: (*LO4-3*)
   a. Bad weather wreaks havoc with the tea crop.
   b. A medical report implying tea is bad for your health is published.
   c. A technological innovation lowers the cost of producing tea.
   d. Consumers' income falls. (Assume tea is a normal good.)
18. You're a commodity trader and you've just heard a report that the winter wheat harvest will be 2 billion bushels, a 40 percent jump, rather than an expected 30 percent jump. (*LO4-3*)
   a. What would you expect would happen to wheat prices?
   b. Demonstrate graphically the effect you suggested in part *a*.
19. In the United States, say gasoline costs consumers about $2.50 per gallon. In Italy, say it costs consumers about $6 per gallon. What effect does this price differential likely have on: (*LO4-3*)
   a. The size of cars in the United States and in Italy?
   b. The use of public transportation in the United States and in Italy?
   c. The fuel efficiency of cars in the United States and in Italy?
   d. What would be the effect of raising the price of gasoline in the United States to $5 per gallon?
20. Assume that Argentina imposes a 20 percent tax on natural gas exports. (*LO4-3*)
   a. Demonstrate the likely effect of that tax on gas exports using supply and demand curves.
   b. What does it likely do to the price of natural gas in Argentina?
21. In most developing countries, there are long lines of taxis at airports, and these taxis often wait two or three hours. What does this tell you about the price in that market? Demonstrate with supply and demand analysis. (*LO4-3*)
22. Define the fallacy of composition. How does it affect the supply/demand model? (*LO4-4*)
23. In which of the following three markets are there likely to be the greatest feedback effects: market for housing, market for wheat, market for manufactured goods? (*LO4-4*)
24. State whether the "other things constant" is likely to hold in the following supply/demand analyses: (*LO4-3*)
   a. The impact of an increase in the demand for pencils on the price of pencils.
   b. The impact of an increase in the supply of labor on the quantity of labor demanded.
   c. The impact of an increase in aggregate savings on aggregate expenditures.
   d. The impact of a new method of producing CDs on the price of CDs.

Questions from Alternative Perspectives

1. In a centrally planned economy, how might central planners estimate supply or demand? (Austrian)
2. In the late 19th century, Washington Gladden said, "He who battles for the Christianization of society, will find their strongest foe in the field of economics. Economics is indeed the dismal science because of the selfishness of its maxims and the inhumanity of its conclusions."
   a. Evaluate this statement.
   b. Is there a conflict between the ideology of capitalism and the precepts of Christianity?
   c. Would a society that emphasized a capitalist mode of production benefit by a moral framework that emphasized selflessness rather than selfishness? (Religious)
3. Economics is often referred to as the study of choice.
   a. In U.S. history, have men and women been equally free to choose the amount of education they receive even within the same family?
   b. What other areas can you see where men and women have not been equally free to choose?
   c. If you agree that men and women have not had equal rights to choose, what implications does that have about the objectivity of economic analysis? (Feminist)
4. Knowledge is derived from a tautology when something is true because you assume it is true. In this chapter, you have learned the conditions under which supply and demand explain outcomes. Yet, as your text author cautions, these conditions may not hold. How can you be sure if they ever hold? (Institutionalist)
5. Do you think consumers make purchasing decisions based on general rules of thumb instead of price?
   a. Why would consumers do this?
   b. What implication might this have for the conclusions drawn about markets? (Post-Keynesian)
6. Some economists believe that imposing international labor standards would cost jobs. In support of this argument, one economist said, "Either you believe labor demand curves are downward sloping, or you don't." Of course, not to believe that demand curves are negatively sloped would be tantamount to declaring yourself an economic illiterate. What else about the nature of labor demand curves might help a policy maker design policies that could counteract the negative effects of labor standards employment? (Radical)

Issues to Ponder

1. Oftentimes, to be considered for a job, you have to know someone in the firm. What does this observation tell you about the wage paid for that job?
2. In the early 2000s, the demand for housing increased substantially as low interest rates increased the number of people who could afford homes.
   a. What was the likely effect of this on housing prices? Demonstrate graphically.
   b. In 2005, mortgage rates began increasing. What was the likely effect of this increase on housing prices? Demonstrate graphically.
   c. In a period of increasing demand for housing, would you expect housing prices to rise more in Miami suburbs, which had room for expansion and fairly loose laws about subdivisions, or in a city such as San Francisco, which had limited land and tight subdivision restrictions?
3. In 1994, the U.S. postal service put a picture of rodeo rider Ben Pickett, not the rodeo star Bill Pickett, whom it meant to honor, on a stamp. It printed 150,000 sheets. Recognizing its error, it recalled the stamp, but it found that 183 sheets had already been sold.
   a. What would the recall likely do to the price of the 183 sheets that were sold?
   b. When the government recognized that it could not recall all the stamps, it decided to issue the remaining ones. What would that decision likely do?
   c. What would the holders of the misprinted sheet likely do when they heard of the government's decision?
4. What would be the effect of a 75 percent tax on lawsuit punitive awards that was proposed by California Governor Arnold Schwarzenegger in 2004 on:
   a. The number of punitive awards. Demonstrate your answer using supply and demand curves.
   b. The number of pretrial settlements.
5. Why is a supply/demand analysis that includes only economic forces likely to be incomplete?

Answers to Margin Questions

1. The demand curve slopes downward because price and quantity demanded are inversely related. As the price of a good rises, people switch to purchasing other goods whose prices have not risen by as much. (*p. 78; LO4-1*)
2. *Demand for luxury goods.* The other possibility, *quantity of luxury goods demanded,* is used to refer to movements along (not shifts of) the demand curve. (*p. 79; LO4-1*)
3. (1) The decline in price will increase the quantity of computers demanded (movement down along the demand curve). (2) With more income, demand for computers will rise (shift of the demand curve out to the right). (*p. 81; LO4-1*)
4. When adding two demand curves, you sum them horizontally, as in the accompanying diagram. (*p. 82; LO4-1*)

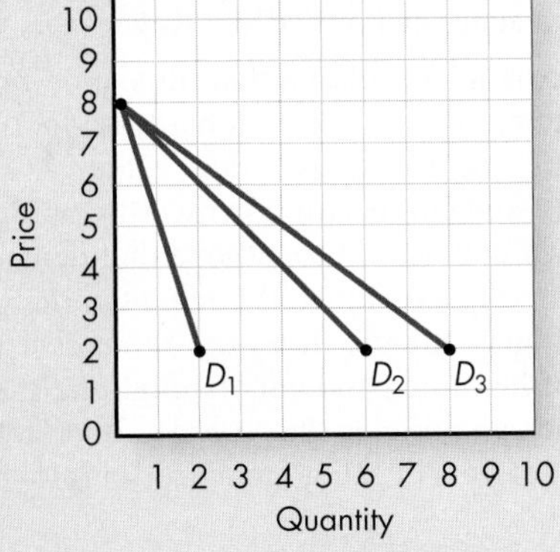

5. *The quantity supplied* rises because there was a movement along the supply curve. The supply curve itself remains unchanged. (*p. 85; LO4-2*)
6. (1) The supply of romance novels declines since paper is an input to production (supply shifts in to the left); (2) the supply of romance novels rises since the subsidy decreases the cost to the producer (supply shifts out to the right). (*p. 87; LO4-2*)
7. A heavy frost in Florida will decrease the supply of oranges, increasing the price and decreasing the quantity demanded, as in the accompanying graph. (*p. 92; LO4-3*)

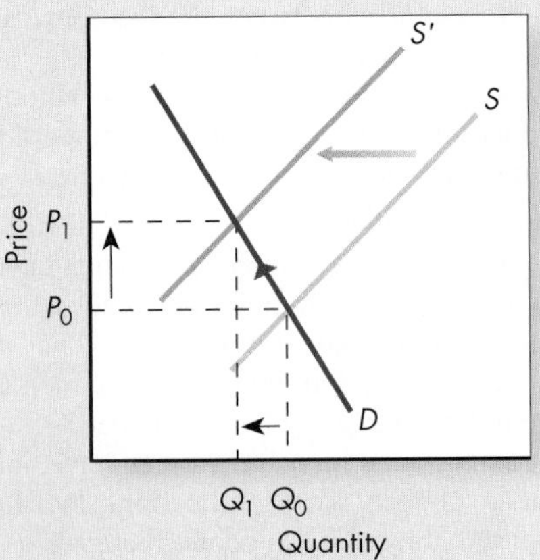

8. An increase in the price of gas will likely increase the demand for hybrid cars, increasing their price and increasing the quantity supplied, as in the accompanying graph. (*p. 93; LO4-3*)

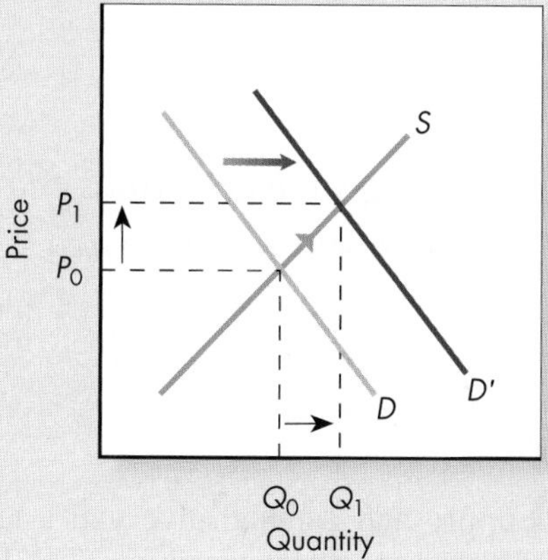

9. Other things are most likely to remain constant in the egg and luxury boat markets because each is a small percentage of the whole economy. Factors that affect the world oil market and the labor market will have ripple effects that must be taken into account in any analysis. (*p. 94; LO4-4*)

10. The fallacy of composition is relevant for macroeconomic issues because it reminds us that, in the aggregate, small effects that are immaterial for micro issues can add up and be material. (*p. 94; LO4-4*)

chapter 5

Using Supply and Demand

It is by invisible hands that we are bent and tortured worst.

—Nietzsche

After reading this chapter, you should be able to:

LO5-1 Apply the supply and demand model to real-world events.

LO5-2 Demonstrate the effect of a price ceiling and a price floor on a market.

LO5-3 Explain the effect of excise taxes and tariffs on a market.

LO5-4 Explain the effect of quantity restrictions on a market.

LO5-5 Explain the effect of a third-party payer system on equilibrium price and quantity.

Supply and demand give you a lens through which to view the economy. That lens brings into focus issues that would otherwise seem like a muddle. In this chapter, we use the supply/demand lens to consider real-world events.

Real-World Supply and Demand Applications

Let's begin by giving you an opportunity to apply supply/demand analysis to real-world events. Below are three events. After reading each, try your hand at explaining what happened, using supply and demand curves. To help you in the process Figure 5-1 provides some diagrams. *Before* reading my explanation, try to match the shifts to the examples. In each, be careful to explain which curve, or curves, shifted and how those shifts affected equilibrium price and quantity.

1. In the summer of 2011 Hurricane Irene damaged farms in the northeastern United States, destroying a significant portion of the apple crop. As a result apple prices rose. Market: Apples in the United States.
2. When the price of gas rose so that it cost as much as $100 to fill a tank of gas, Americans switched from SUVs to more fuel-efficient cars. The number of people shopping for used SUVs fell over 30 percent and the price of used SUVs fell an average of 10 percent. Market: Used SUVs in the United States.
3. A growing middle class in China and India has increased the demand for many food products, particularly edible oils such as soy and palm. At the same time, to meet the increasing demand for ethanol, U.S. farmers have chosen to grow less soy (from which soy oil is made) and more corn. The result? Dramatic increases in the price of edible oil worldwide. Market: Global edible oils.

Now that you've matched them, let's see if your analysis matches mine.

FIGURE 5-1 (A, B, AND C)

In this exhibit, three shifts of supply and demand are shown. Your task is to match them with the events listed in the text.

Answers: 1–b; 2–a; 3–c.

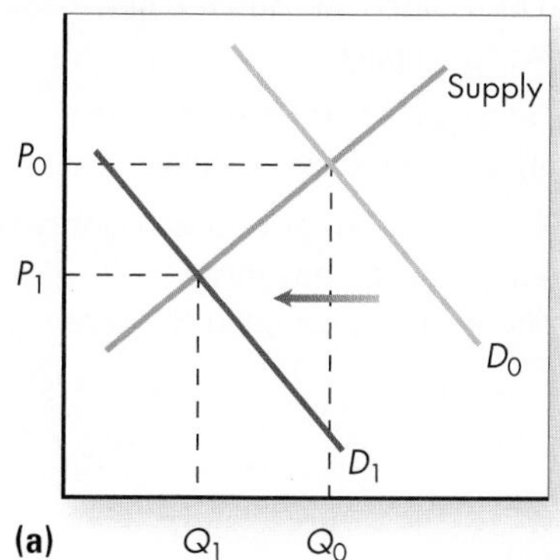

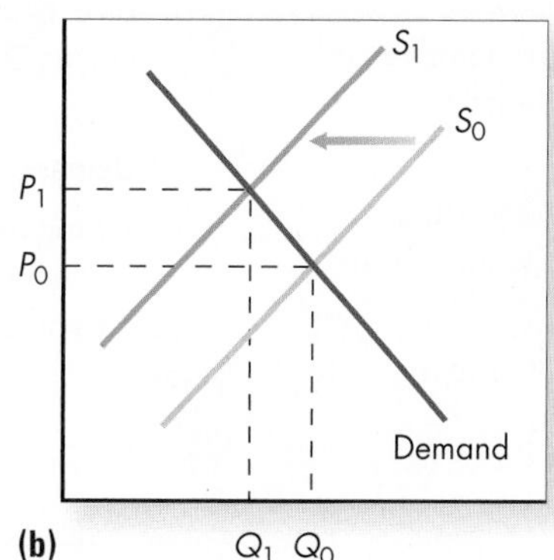

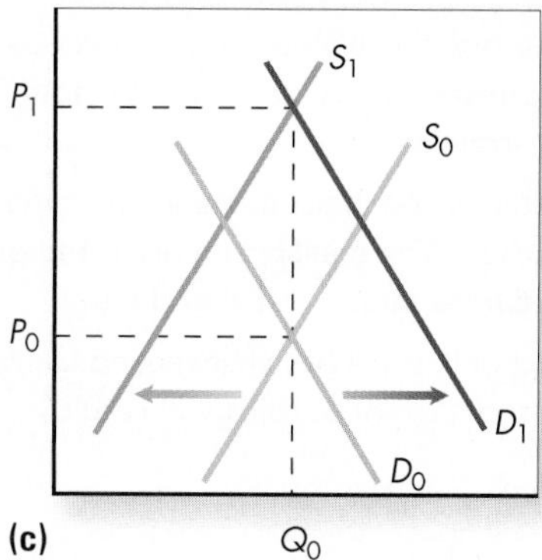

HURRICANE IRENE Weather is a shift factor of supply. The hurricane shifted the supply curve for apples to the left, as shown in Figure 5-1(b). At the original price (shown by P_0), quantity demanded exceeded quantity supplied and the invisible hand of the market pressured the price to rise until quantity demanded equaled quantity supplied (shown by P_1).

Q-1 True or false? If supply rises, price will rise.

SALES OF SUVs Gas is a significant cost of driving a car. To reduce their automotive gas bills, Americans reduced their demand for gas-guzzling SUVs, both new and used. Figure 5-1(a) shows that the demand curve for SUVs in the used-car market shifted from D_0 to D_1. At the original price P_0, sellers were unable to sell the SUVs they wanted to sell and began to lower their price. Buyers of used SUVs were able to purchase them at a 10 percent lower price, shown by P_1.

EDIBLE OILS Increases in the size of the middle class in developing countries such as China and India have increased the demand for food and edible oils used to prepare those foods. This is represented by a shift in the demand for edible oils out to the right from D_0 to D_1. At the same time, increases in the price of crude oil have led U.S. farmers to grow less soy and more corn, which has shifted the supply curve from S_0 to S_1. The result has been a dramatic increase in the price of edible oils, shown in Figure 5-1(c) as an increase from P_0 to P_1.

WWW Web Note 5.1 Fair Trade Coffee

Now that we've been through some examples, let's review. Remember: Anything that affects demand and supply other than price of the good will shift the curves. Changes in the price of the good result in movements along the curves. Another thing to recognize is that when both curves are shifting, you can get a change in price but little change in quantity, or a change in quantity but little change in price.

Anything other than price that affects demand or supply will shift the curves.

To test your understanding Table 5-1 gives you six generic results from the interaction of supply and demand. Your job is to decide what shifts produced those results. This exercise is a variation of the one with which I began the chapter. It goes over the same issues, but this time without the graphs. On the left-hand side of Table 5-1, I list combinations of movements of observed prices and quantities, labeling them 1–6. On the right I give six shifts in supply and demand, labeling them *a–f*.

Q-2 Say a hormone has been discovered that increases cows' milk production by 20 percent. Demonstrate graphically what effect this discovery would have on the price and quantity of milk sold in a market.

A REMINDER

Supply and Demand in Action

Sorting out the effects of the shifts of supply or demand or both can be confusing. Here are some helpful hints to keep things straight:

- Draw the initial demand and supply curves and label them. The equilibrium price and quantity is where these curves intersect. Label them.
- If only price has changed, no curves will shift and a shortage or surplus will result.
- If a nonprice factor affects demand, determine the direction demand has shifted and add the new demand curve. Do the same for supply.
- Equilibrium price and quantity is where the new demand and supply curves intersect. Label them.
- Compare the initial equilibrium price and quantity to the new equilibrium price and quantity.

See if you can describe what happened in the three graphs below.

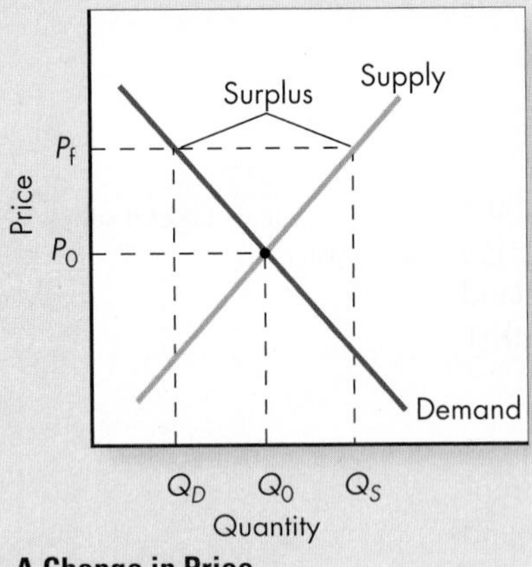

A Change in Price

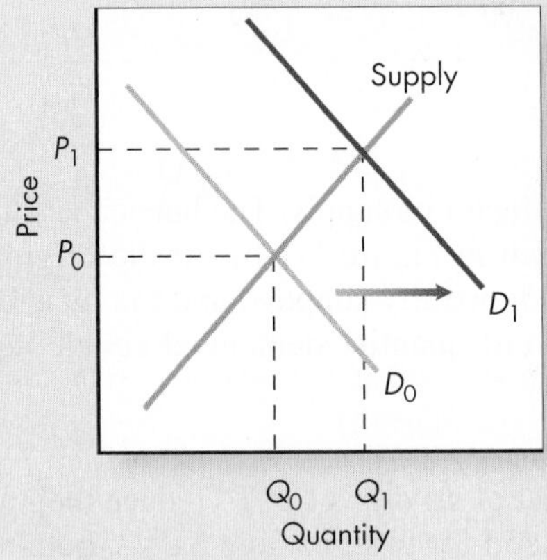

A Shift in Demand

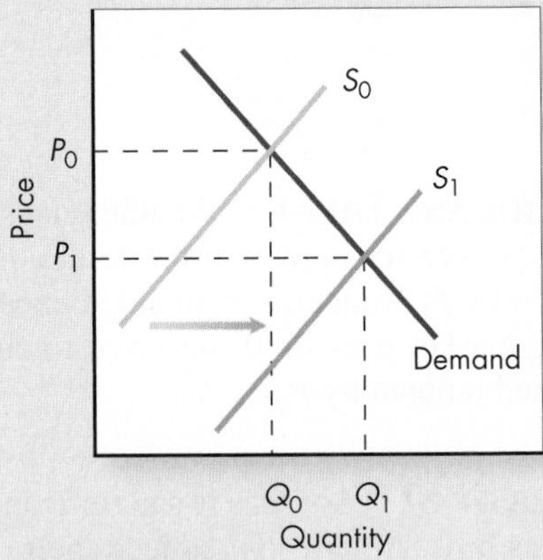

A Shift in Supply

If you don't confuse your "shifts of" with your "movements along," supply and demand provide good off-the-cuff answers for many economic questions.

You are to match the shifts with the price and quantity movements that best fit each described shift, using each shift and movement only once. My recommendation to you is to draw the graphs that are described in *a–f,* decide what happens to price and quantity, and then find the match in 1–6.

TABLE 5-1

Price and Quantity Changes			Shifts in Supply and Demand
1.	P↑	Q↑	*a.* No change in demand. Supply shifts in.
2.	P↑	Q↓	*b.* Demand shifts out. Supply shifts in.
3.	P↑	Q?	*c.* Demand shifts in. No change in supply.
4.	P↓	Q?	*d.* Demand shifts out. Supply shifts out.
5.	P?	Q↑	*e.* Demand shifts out. No change in supply.
6.	P↓	Q↓	*f.* Demand shifts in. Supply shifts out.

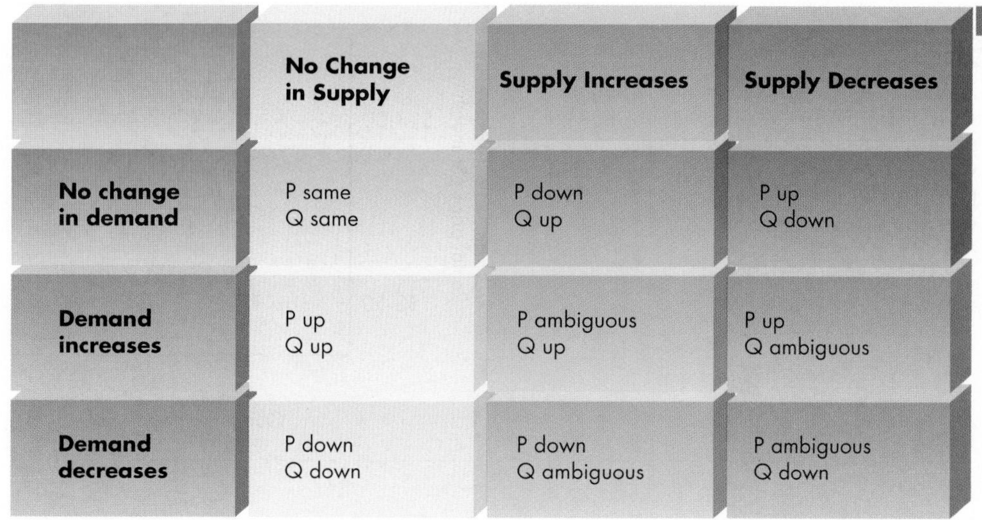

	No Change in Supply	Supply Increases	Supply Decreases
No change in demand	P same Q same	P down Q up	P up Q down
Demand increases	P up Q up	P ambiguous Q up	P up Q ambiguous
Demand decreases	P down Q down	P down Q ambiguous	P ambiguous Q down

TABLE 5-2 Diagram of Effects of Shifts of Demand and Supply on Price and Quantity

This table provides a summary of the effects of shifts in supply and demand on equilibrium price and equilibrium quantity. Notice that when both curves shift, the effect on either price or quantity depends on the relative size of the shifts.

Now that you've worked them, let me give you the answers I came up with. They are: 1–*e;* 2–*a;* 3–*b;* 4–*f;* 5–*d;* 6–*c*. How did I come up with the answers? I did what I suggested you do—took each of the scenarios on the right and predicted what happens to price and quantity. For case *a,* supply shifts in to the left and there is a movement up along the demand curve. Since the demand curve is downward-sloping, the price rises and quantity declines. This matches number *2* on the left. For case *b,* demand shifts out to the right. Along the original supply curve, price and quantity would rise. But supply shifts in to the left, leading to even higher prices but lower quantity. What happens to quantity is unclear, so the match must be number *3*. For case *c,* demand shifts in to the left. There is movement down along the supply curve with lower price and lower quantity. This matches number *6*. For case *d,* demand shifts out and supply shifts out. As demand shifts out, we move along the supply curve to the right and price and quantity rise. But supply shifts out too, and we move out along the new demand curve. Price declines, erasing the previous rise, and the quantity rises even more. This matches number *5*.

Q-3 If both demand and supply shift in to the left, what happens to price and quantity?

I'll leave it up to you to confirm my answers to *e* and *f*. Notice that when supply and demand both shift, the change in either price or quantity is uncertain—it depends on the relative size of the shifts. As a summary, I present a diagrammatic of the combinations in Table 5-2.

Q-4 If price and quantity both fell, what would you say was the most likely cause?

Government Intervention: Price Ceilings and Price Floors

People don't always like the market-determined price. If the invisible hand were the only factor that determined prices, people would have to accept it. But it isn't; social and political forces also determine price. For example, when prices fall, sellers look to government for ways to hold prices up; when prices rise, buyers look to government for ways to hold prices down. Let's now consider the effect of such actions in the supply/demand model.[1] Let's start with an example of the price being held down.

[1]Modern economists use many different models. No model precisely fits reality, and when I discuss a real-world market as fitting a model, I am using pedagogical license. As I have emphasized in previous chapters, the propositions that come out of a model are theorems–logical conclusions given the assumptions. To extend the theorem to a policy precept requires considering which assumptions of the model fit the situation one is describing.

FIGURE 5-2 Rent Control in Paris

A price ceiling imposed on housing rent in Paris during World War II created a shortage of housing when World War II ended and veterans returned home. The shortage would have been eliminated if rents had been allowed to rise to $17 per month.

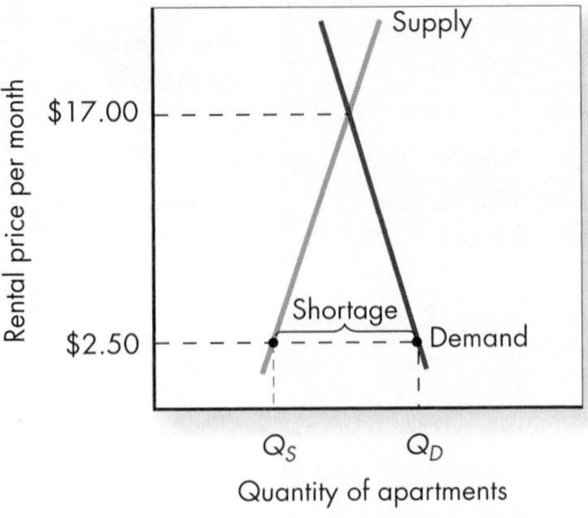

Price Ceilings

When government wants to hold prices down, it imposes a **price ceiling**—*a government-imposed limit on how high a price can be charged.* That limit is generally below the equilibrium price. (A price ceiling that is above the equilibrium price will have no effect at all.) From Chapter 4, you already know the effect of a price that is below the equilibrium price—quantity demanded will exceed quantity supplied and there will be excess demand. Let's now look at an example of **rent control**—*a price ceiling on rents, set by government*—and see how that excess demand shows up in the real world.

WWW Web Note 5.2 Rent Control

Price Ceilings

Rent controls exist today in a number of American cities as well as other cities throughout the world. Many of the laws governing rent were first instituted during the two world wars in the first half of the 20th century. Consider Paris, for example. In World War II, the Paris government froze rent to ease the financial burden of those families whose wage earners were sent to fight in the war. When the soldiers returned at the end of the war, the rent control was continued; removing it would have resulted in an increase in rents from $2.50 to $17 a month, and that was felt to be an unfair burden for veterans.

Q-5 What is the effect of the price ceiling, P_c, shown in the graph below on price and quantity?

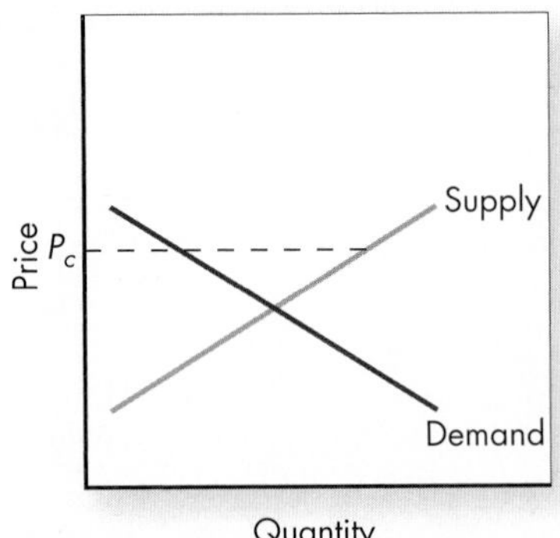

Figure 5-2 shows this situation. The below-market rent set by government created an enormous shortage of apartments. Initially this shortage didn't bother those renting apartments, since they got low-cost apartments. But it created severe hardships for those who didn't have apartments. Many families moved in with friends or extended families. Others couldn't find housing at all and lived on the streets. Eventually the rent controls started to cause problems even for those who did have apartments. The reason is that owners of buildings cut back on maintenance. More than 80 percent of Parisians had no private bathrooms and 20 percent had no running water. Since rental properties weren't profitable, no new buildings were being constructed and existing buildings weren't kept in repair. It was even harder for those who didn't have apartments.

Since the market price was not allowed to ration apartments, alternative methods of rationing developed. People paid landlords bribes to get an apartment, or watched the obituaries and then simply moved in their furniture before anyone else did. Eventually the situation got so bad that rent controls were lifted.

The system of rent controls is not only of historical interest. Below I list some phenomena that existed in New York City recently.

1. A couple paid $350 a month for a two-bedroom Park Avenue apartment with a solarium and two terraces, while another individual paid $1,200 a month for a studio apartment shared with two roommates.
2. The vacancy rate for apartments in New York City was 3.5 percent. Anything under 5 percent is considered a housing emergency.
3. The actress Mia Farrow paid $2,900 a month (a fraction of the market-clearing rent) for 10 rooms on Central Park West. It was an apartment her mother first leased 70 years ago.
4. Would-be tenants made payments, called key money, to current tenants or landlords to get apartments.

Q-6 What is the effect of the price ceiling, P_c, shown in the graph below on price and quantity?

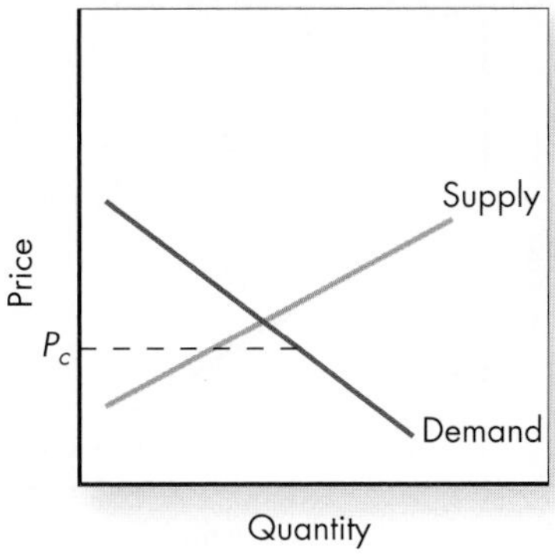

Your assignment is to explain how these phenomena might have come about, and to demonstrate, with supply and demand, the situation that likely caused them. (Hint: New York City had rent control.)

Now that you have done your assignment (you have, haven't you?), let me give you my answers so that you can check them with your answers.

The situation is identical with that presented above in Figure 5-2. Take the first item. The couple lived in a rent-controlled apartment while the individual with roommates did not. If rent control were eliminated, rent on the Park Avenue apartment would rise and rent on the studio would most likely decline. Item 2: The housing emergency was a result of rent control. Below-market rent resulted in excess demand and little vacancy. Item 3: That Mia Farrow rents a rent-controlled apartment was the result of nonprice rationing. Instead of being rationed by price, other methods of rationing arose. These other methods of rationing scarce resources are called *nonprice rationing.* In New York City, strict rules determined the handing down of rent-controlled apartments from family member to family member. Item 4: New residents searched for a long time to find apartments to rent, and many discovered that illegal payments to landlords were the only way to obtain a rent-controlled apartment. Key money is a black market payment for a rent-controlled apartment. Because of the limited supply of apartments, individuals were willing to pay far more than the controlled price. Landlords used other methods of rationing the limited supply of apartments—instituting first-come, first-served policies, and, in practice, selecting tenants based on gender, race, or other personal characteristics, even though such discriminatory selection was illegal. In some cases in New York City the rent was so far below the market that developers paid thousands of dollars—in one case $400,000—to a tenant to vacate an apartment so the developer could buy the building from the landlord, tear it down, and replace it with a new building.

With price ceilings, existing goods are no longer rationed entirely by price. Other methods of rationing existing goods arise called nonprice rationing.

If rent controls had only the bad effects described above, no community would institute them. They are, however, implemented with good intentions—to cope with sudden increases in demand for housing that would otherwise cause rents to explode and force many poor people out of their apartments. The negative effects occur over time as buildings begin to deteriorate and the number of people looking to rent and unable to find apartments increases. As this happens, people focus less on the original renters and more on new renters excluded from the market and on the inefficiencies of price ceilings. Since politicians tend to focus on the short run, we can expect rent control to continue to be used when demand for housing suddenly increases.

Q-7 What is the effect of the price floor, P_f, shown in the graph below, on price and quantity?

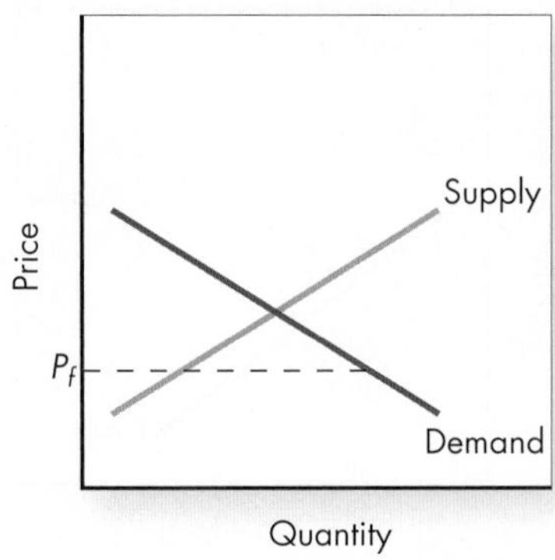

Web Note 5.3
Minimum Wage

Price Floors

The minimum wage helps some people and hurts others.

Price Floors

Sometimes political forces favor suppliers, sometimes consumers. So let us now go briefly through a case when the government is trying to favor suppliers by attempting to prevent the price from falling below a certain level. **Price floors**—*government-imposed limits on how low a price can be charged*—do just this. The price floor is generally above the existing price. (A price floor below equilibrium price would have no effect.) When there is an effective price floor, quantity supplied exceeds quantity demanded and the result is excess supply.

An example of a price floor is the minimum wage. Both individual states and the federal government impose **minimum wage laws**—*laws specifying the lowest wage a firm can legally pay an employee*. The U.S. federal government first instituted a minimum wage of 25 cents per hour in 1938 as part of the Fair Labor Standards Act. It has been raised many times since. As of 2012 the federal minimum wage was $7.25. (With inflation, that's a much smaller increase than it looks.) In 2011 about 1.7 million hourly wage earners received the minimum wage, or about 2 percent of hourly paid workers, most of whom are unskilled and/or part-time. The market-determined equilibrium wage for most full-time adult workers is generally above the minimum wage.

The effect of a minimum wage on the unskilled labor market is shown in Figure 5-3. The government-set minimum wage is above equilibrium, as shown by W_{min}. At the market-determined equilibrium wage W_e, the quantity of labor supplied and demanded equals Q_e. At the higher minimum wage, the quantity of labor supplied rises to Q_1 and the quantity of labor demanded declines to Q_2. There is an excess supply of workers (a shortage of jobs) represented by the difference $Q_1 - Q_2$. This represents people who are looking for work but cannot find it.

Who wins and who loses from a minimum wage? The minimum wage improves the wages of the Q_2 workers who are able to find work. Without the minimum wage, they would have earned W_e per hour. The minimum wage hurts those, however, who cannot find work at the minimum wage but who are willing to work, and would have been hired, at the market-determined wage. These workers are represented by the distance $Q_e - Q_2$ in Figure 5-3. The minimum wage also hurts firms that now must

FIGURE 5-3 A Minimum Wage

A minimum wage, W_{min}, above equilibrium wage, W_e, helps those who are able to find work, shown by Q_2, but hurts those who would have been employed at the equilibrium wage but can no longer find employment, shown by $Q_e - Q_2$. A minimum wage also hurts producers who have higher costs of production and consumers who may face higher product prices.

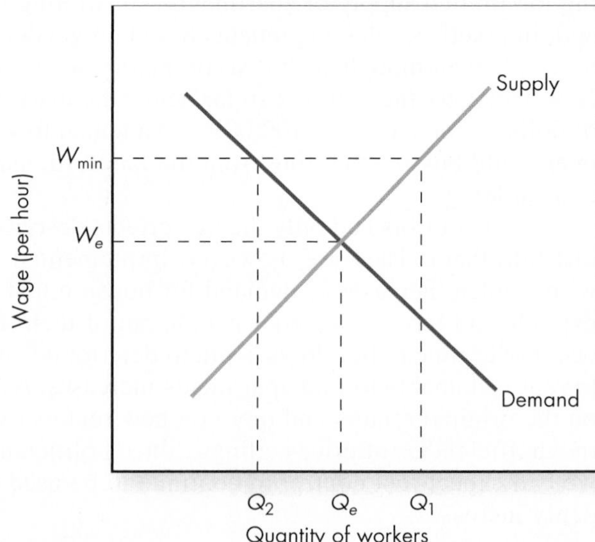

pay their workers more, increasing the cost of production, and consumers to the extent that firms are able to pass that increase in production cost on in the form of higher product prices.

All economists agree that the above analysis is logical and correct. But they disagree about whether governments should have minimum wage laws. One reason is that the empirical effects of minimum wage laws are relatively small; in fact, some studies have found them to be negligible. (There is, however, much debate about these estimates, since "other things" never remain constant.) A second reason is that some real-world labor markets are not sufficiently competitive to fit the supply/demand model. A third reason is that the minimum wage affects the economy in ways that some economists see as desirable and others see as undesirable. I point this out to remind you that the supply/demand framework is a tool to be used to analyze issues. It does not provide final answers about policy. (In microeconomics, economists explore the policy issues of interferences in markets much more carefully.)

Because the federal minimum wage is low, and not binding for most workers, a movement called the living-wage movement has begun. The living-wage movement focuses on local governments, calling on them to establish a minimum wage at a *living wage*—a wage necessary to support a family at or above the federally determined poverty line. In 2012, about 125 local governments had passed living-wage laws, with living wages ranging from \$10.29 an hour in Santa Fe, NM, to \$17 in Richmond, California. The analysis of these living-wage laws is the same as that for minimum wages.

Government Intervention: Excise Taxes and Tariffs

Web Note 5.4
Taxing Our Sins

Let's now consider an example of a tax on goods. An **excise tax** is *a tax that is levied on a specific good*. The luxury tax on expensive cars that the United States imposed in 1991 is an example. A **tariff** is *an excise tax on an imported good*. What effect will excise taxes and tariffs have on the price and quantity in a market?

To lend some sense of reality, let's take the example from the 1990s, when the United States taxed the suppliers of expensive boats. Say the price of a boat before the luxury tax was \$60,000, and 600 boats were sold at that price. Now the government taxes suppliers \$10,000 for every luxury boat sold. What will the new price of the boat be, and how many will be sold?

A tax on suppliers shifts the supply curve up by the amount of the tax.

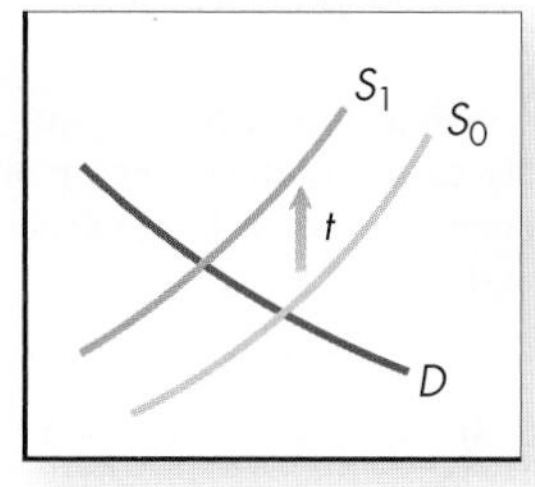

If you were about to answer "\$70,000," be careful. Ask yourself whether I would have given you that question if the answer were that easy. By looking at supply and demand curves in Figure 5-4, you can see why \$70,000 is the wrong answer.

To sell 600 boats, suppliers must be fully compensated for the tax. So the tax of \$10,000 on the supplier shifts the supply curve up from S_0 to S_1. However, at \$70,000, consumers are not willing to purchase 600 boats. They are willing to purchase only 420 boats. Quantity supplied exceeds quantity demanded at \$70,000. Suppliers lower their prices until quantity supplied equals quantity demanded at \$65,000, the new equilibrium price.

The new equilibrium price is \$65,000, not \$70,000. The reason is that at the higher price, the quantity of boats people demand is less. Some people choose not to buy boats and others find substitute vehicles or purchase their boats outside the United States. The tax causes a movement up along a demand curve to the left. Excise taxes reduce the quantity of goods demanded. That's why boat manufacturers were up in arms after the tax was imposed and why the revenue generated from the tax was less than expected. Instead of collecting \$10,000 × 600 (\$6 million), revenue collected was only \$10,000 × 510 (\$5.1 million). (The tax was repealed three years after it was imposed.)

Q-8 Your study partner, Umar, has just stated that a tax on demanders of \$2 per unit will raise the equilibrium price from \$4 to \$6. How do you respond?

FIGURE 5-4 The Effect of an Excise Tax

An excise tax on suppliers shifts the entire supply curve up by the amount of the tax. Since at a price equal to the original price plus the tax there is excess supply, the price of the good rises by less than the tax.

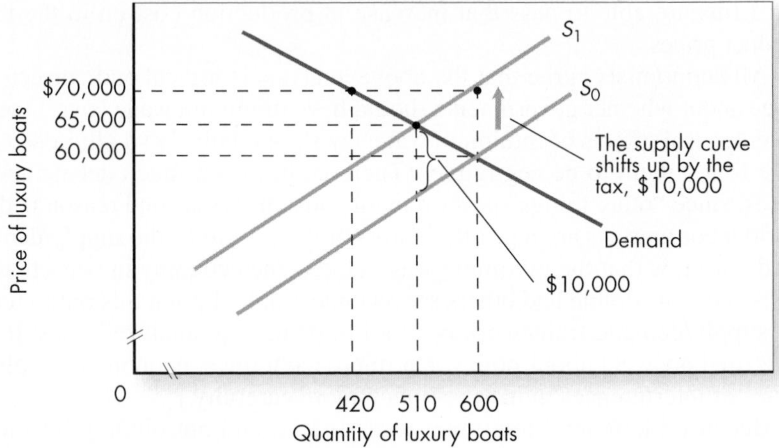

Excise Taxes

A tariff has the same effect on the equilibrium price and quantity as an excise tax. The difference is that only foreign producers sending goods into the United States pay the tax. An example is the 30 percent tariff imposed on steel imported into the United States in the early 2000s. The government instituted the tariffs because U.S. steelmakers were having difficulty competing with lower-cost foreign steel. The tariff increased the price of imported steel, making U.S. steel more competitive to domestic buyers. As expected, the price of imported steel rose by over 15 percent, to about $230 a ton, and the quantity imported declined. Tariffs don't hurt just the foreign producer. Tariffs increase the cost of imported products to domestic consumers. In the case of steel, manufacturing companies such as automakers faced higher production costs. The increase in the cost of steel lowered production in those industries and increased the cost of a variety of goods to U.S. consumers.

Government Intervention: Quantity Restrictions

Q-9 What is the effect of the quantity restrictions, Q_R, shown in the graph below, on equilibrium price and quantity?

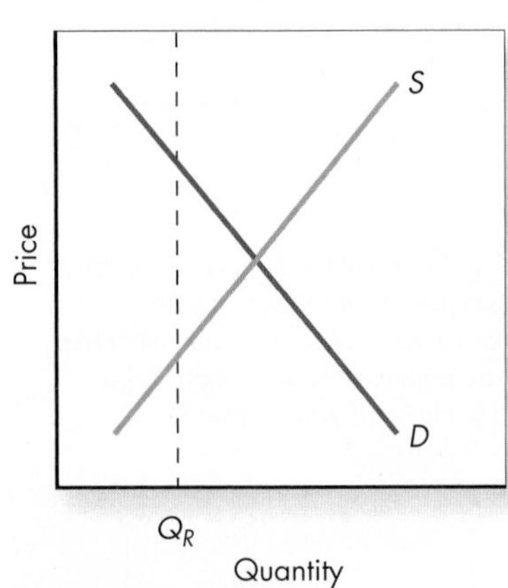

Another way in which governments often interfere with, or regulate, markets is with licenses, which limit entry into a market. For example, to be a doctor you need a license; to be a vet you need a license; and in some places to be an electrician, a financial planner, or a cosmetologist, or to fish, you need a license. There are many reasons for licenses, and we will not consider them here. Instead, we will simply consider what effect licenses have on the price and quantity of the activity being licensed. Specifically, we'll look at a case where the government issues a specific number of licenses and holds that number constant. The example we'll take is licenses to drive a taxi. In New York City, these are called taxi medallions because the license is an aluminum plate attached to the hood of a taxi. Taxi medallions were established in 1937 as a way to increase the wages of licensed taxi drivers. Wages of taxi drivers had fallen from $26 a week in 1929 to $15 a week in 1933. As wages fell, the number of taxi drivers fell from 19,000 to about 12,000. The remaining 12,000 taxi drivers successfully lobbied New York City to grant drivers with current licenses who met certain requirements permanent rights to drive taxis—medallions. (It wasn't until the early 2000s that the number of medallions was increased slightly.) The restriction had the desired effect. As the economy grew, demand for taxis grew (the demand for taxis shifted out) as shown in Figure 5-5(a) and because the supply of taxis remained at about 12,000, the wages of the taxi drivers owning medallions increased.

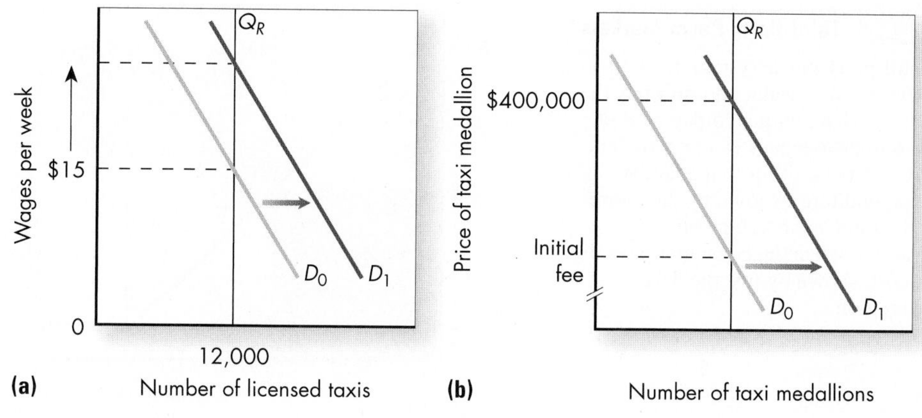

FIGURE 5-5 (A AND B) Quantity Restrictions in the Market for Taxi Licenses

When the demand for taxi services increased, because the number of taxi licenses was limited to 12,000, wages increased to above $15 an hour, as (**a**) shows. Because taxi medallions were limited in supply, as demand for taxi services rose, so did the demand for medallions. Their price rose significantly, as (**b**) shows.

Issuing taxi medallions had a secondary effect. Because New York City also granted medallion owners the right to sell their medallions, a market in medallions developed. Those fortunate enough to have been granted a medallion by the city found that they had a valuable asset. A person wanting to drive a taxi, and earn those high wages, had to buy a medallion from an existing driver. This meant that while new taxi drivers would earn a higher wage once they had bought a license, their wage after taking into account the cost of the license would be much lower.

As the demand for taxis rose, the medallions became more and more valuable. The effect on the price of medallions is shown in Figure 5-5(b). The quantity restriction, Q_R, means that any increases in demand lead only to price increases. Although the initial license fee was minimal, increases in demand for taxis quickly led to higher and higher medallion prices.

Quantity restrictions tend to increase price.

The demand for taxi medallions continues to increase each year as the New York City population grows more than the supply is increased. The result is that the price of a taxi medallion continues to rise. Even with the slight increase in the number of medallions, today taxi medallions for individuals cost about $400,000, giving anyone who has bought that license a strong reason to oppose an expansion in the number of licenses being issued.[2]

Third-Party-Payer Markets

As a final example for this chapter, let's consider third-party-payer markets. In **third-party-payer markets,** *the person who receives the good differs from the person paying for the good.* An example is the health care market where many individuals have insurance. They generally pay a co-payment for health care services and an HMO or other insurer pays the remainder. Medicare and Medicaid are both third-party payers. Figure 5-6 shows what happens in the supply/demand model when there is a third-party-payer market and a small co-payment. In the normal case, when the individual demander pays for the good, equilibrium quantity is where quantity demanded equals quantity supplied—in this case at an equilibrium price of $25 and an equilibrium quantity of 10.

[2]As is usually the case, the analysis is more complicated in real life. New York issues both individual and corporate licenses. But the general reasoning carries through: Effective quantity restrictions increase the value of a license.

FIGURE 5-6 Third-Party-Payer Markets

In a third-party-payer system, the person who chooses the product doesn't pay the entire cost. Here, with a co-payment of $5, consumers demand 18 units. Sellers require $45 per unit for that quantity. Total expenditures, shown by the entire shaded region, are much greater compared to when the consumer pays the entire cost, shown by just the dark shaded region.

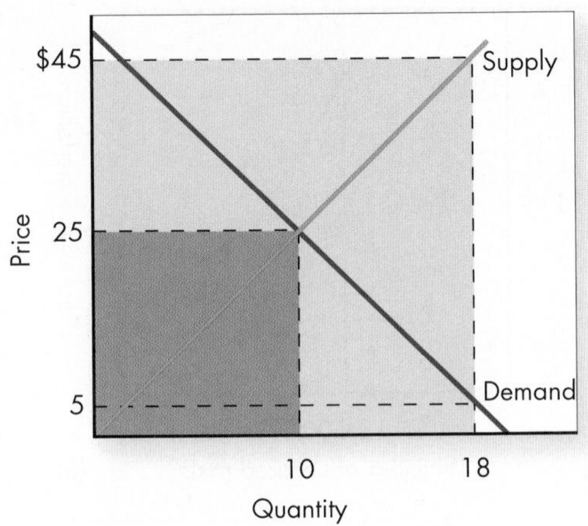

Under a third-party-payer system, the person who chooses how much to purchase doesn't pay the entire cost. Because the co-payment faced by the consumer is much lower, quantity demanded is much greater. In this example with a co-payment of $5, the consumer demands 18. Given an upward-sloping supply curve, the seller requires a higher price, in this case $45 for each unit supplied to provide that quantity. Assuming the co-payment is for each unit, the consumers pay $5 of that price for a total out-of-pocket cost of $90 ($5 times 18). The third-party payer pays the remainder, $40, for a cost of $720 ($40 times 18). Total spending is $810. This compares to total spending of only $250 (25 times 10) if the consumer had to pay the entire price. Notice that with a third-party-payer system, total spending, represented by the large shaded rectangle, is much higher than total spending if the consumer paid, represented by the small darker rectangle.

In third-party-payer markets, equilibrium quantity and total spending are much higher.

The third-party-payer system describes much of the health care system in the United States today. Typically, a person with health insurance makes a fixed co-payment for an office visit, regardless of procedures and tests provided. Given this payment system, the insured patient has little incentive to limit the procedures offered by the doctor. The doctor charges the insurance company, and the insurance company pays. The rise in health care costs over the past decades can be attributed in part to the third-party-payer system.

A classic example of how third-party-payer systems can affect choices is a case where a 70-year-old man spent weeks in a hospital recovering from surgery to address abdominal bleeding. The bill, to be paid by Medicare, was nearing $275,000 and the patient wasn't recovering as quickly as expected. The doctor finally figured out that the patient's condition wasn't improving because ill-fitting dentures didn't allow him to eat properly. The doctor ordered the hospital dentist to fix the dentures, but the patient refused the treatment. Why? The patient explained: "Seventy-five dollars is a lot of money." The $75 procedure wasn't covered by Medicare.

Q-10 If the cost of textbooks were included in tuition, what would likely happen to their prices? Why?

Third-party-payer systems are not limited to health care. (Are your parents or the government paying for part of your college? If you were paying the full amount, would you be demanding as much college as you currently are?) Anytime a third-party-payer system exists, the quantity demanded will be higher than it otherwise would be. Market forces will not hold down costs as much as they would otherwise because the person using the service doesn't have an incentive to hold down costs. Of course, that doesn't mean that there are no pressures. The third-party payers—parents, employers, and government—will respond to this by trying to limit both the quantity of the good individuals consume and the amount they pay for it. For example, parents will put pressure on their kids to get through school quickly rather than lingering for five or six years, and government will place limitations on what procedures Medicare and Medicaid patients can use. The goods will be rationed through social and political means. Such effects are not unexpected; they are just another example of supply and demand in action.

Conclusion

I began this chapter by pointing out that supply and demand are the lens through which economists look at reality. It takes practice to use that lens, and this chapter gave you some practice. Focusing the lens on a number of issues highlighted certain aspects of those issues. The analysis was simple but powerful and should, if you followed it, provide you with a good foundation for understanding the economist's way of thinking about policy issues.

Summary

- By minding your *P*s and *Q*s—the shifts of and movements along curves—you can describe almost all events in terms of supply and demand. *(LO5-1)*
- A price ceiling is a government-imposed limit on how high a price can be charged. Price ceilings below market price create shortages. *(LO5-2)*
- A price floor is a government-imposed limit on how low a price can be charged. Price floors above market price create surpluses. *(LO5-2)*
- Taxes and tariffs paid by suppliers shift the supply curve up by the amount of the tax or tariff. They raise the equilibrium price (inclusive of tax) and decrease the equilibrium quantity. *(LO5-3)*
- Quantity restrictions increase equilibrium price and reduce equilibrium quantity. *(LO5-4)*
- In a third-party-payer market, the consumer and the one who pays the cost differ. Quantity demanded, price, and total spending are greater when a third party pays than when the consumer pays. *(LO5-5)*

Key Terms

excise tax *(107)*
minimum wage law *(106)*
price ceiling *(104)*
price floor *(106)*
rent control *(104)*
tariff *(107)*
third-party-payer market *(109)*

Questions and Exercises

1. Say that the equilibrium price and quantity both rose. What would you say was the most likely cause? *(LO5-1)*
2. Say that equilibrium price fell and quantity remained constant. What would you say was the most likely cause? *(LO5-1)*
3. The technology is now developing so that road use can be priced by computer. A computer in the surface of the road picks up a signal from your car and automatically charges you for the use of the road. How would this affect bottlenecks and rush-hour congestion? *(LO5-1)*

4. Demonstrate the effect on price and quantity of each of the following events: *(LO5-1)*
   a. In a recent popularity test, Elmo topped Cookie Monster in popularity (this represents a trend in children's tastes). Market: cookies.
   b. The Atkins Diet that limits carbohydrates was reported to be very effective. Market: bread.

5. In 2011 oil production in Libya was interrupted by political unrest. At the same time, the demand for oil by China continued to rise. *(LO5-1)*
   a. Demonstrate the impact on the quantity of oil bought and sold.
   b. Oil production in Libya returned to its original levels by the end of 2012. What was the likely effect on equilibrium oil price and quantity? Demonstrate your answer graphically.

6. Kennesaw University Professor Frank A. Adams III and Auburn University Professors A. H. Barnett and David L. Kaserman recently estimated the effect of legalizing the sale of cadaverous organs, which currently are in shortage at zero price. What are the effects of the following two possibilities on the equilibrium price and quantity of transplanted organs if their sale were to be legalized? Demonstrate your answers graphically. *(LO5-1)*
   a. Many of those currently willing to donate the organs of a deceased relative at zero price are offended that organs can be bought and sold and therefore withdraw from the donor program.
   b. People are willing to provide significantly more organs.

7. In 2008 a drought in Australia's rice-growing regions raised the world price of rice from 12 to 24 cents a pound. Demonstrate graphically the effect of the drought on equilibrium price and quantity in the world rice market. *(LO5-1)*

8. Demonstrate graphically the effect of an effective price ceiling. *(LO5-2)*

9. Demonstrate graphically why rent controls might increase the total payment that new renters pay for an apartment. *(LO5-2)*

10. Demonstrate graphically the effect of a price floor. *(LO5-2)*

11. Graphically show the effects of a minimum wage on the number of unemployed. *(LO5-2)*

12. Taxes can be levied on consumers or producers. *(LO5-3)*
    a. Demonstrate the effect of a $4 per unit tax on suppliers on equilibrium price and quantity.
    b. Demonstrate the effect of a $4 per unit tax on consumers on equilibrium price and quantity.
    c. How does the impact on equilibrium prices (paid by consumers and received by producers) and quantity differ between *a* and *b*?

13. Draw the supply and demand curves associated with the tables below. *(LO5-3)*

Price	Q_S	Q_D
$0.00	50	200
.50	100	175
1.00	150	150
1.50	200	125
2.00	250	100

    a. What is equilibrium price and quantity?
    b. What is equilibrium price and quantity with a $.75 per unit tax levied on suppliers? Demonstrate your answer graphically.
    c. How does your answer change to *b* if the tax were levied on consumers not producers? Demonstrate your answer graphically.
    d. What conclusion can you draw about the difference between levying a tax on suppliers and consumers?

14. Quotas are quantity restrictions on imported goods. Demonstrate the effect of a quota on the price of imported goods. *(LO5-4)*

15. The City of Pawnee issues a fixed number of fishing licenses each year. *(LO5-4)*
    a. Using the accompanying graph, demonstrate the effect of a limit of 100 fishing licenses at a cost of $20 per license.
    b. Is there excess supply or demand for licenses? Label the excess supply or demand on the graph.
    c. What is the maximum amount a person would be willing to pay on the black market for a license?
    d. How much would Pawnee need to charge to eliminate the excess supply or demand?

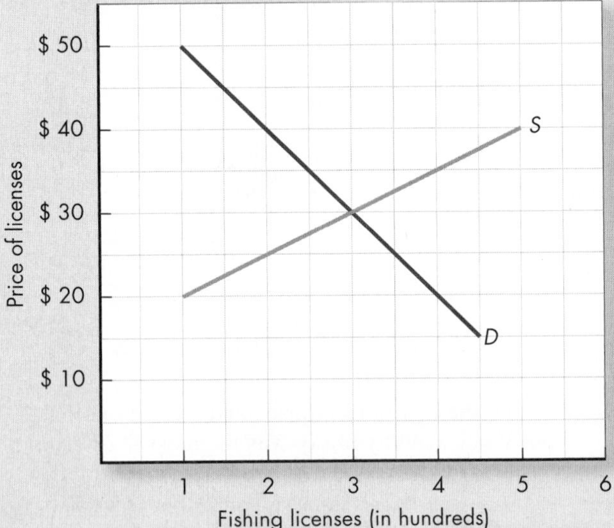

16. In what ways is the market for public post-secondary education an example of a third-party-payer market?

What's the impact of this on total educational expenditures? (*LO5-5*)

17. You're given the following supply and demand tables: (*LO5-5*)

Demand		Supply	
P	**Q**	**P**	**Q**
$ 0	1,200	$ 0	0
2	900	2	0
4	600	4	150
6	300	6	300
8	0	8	600
10	0	10	600
12	0	12	750
14	0	14	900

a. What is equilibrium price and quantity in a market system with no interferences?
b. If this were a third-party-payer market where the consumer pays $2, what is the quantity demanded? What is the price charged by the seller?
c. What is total spending in the two situations described in *a* and *b*?

Questions from Alternative Perspectives

1. Some economists believe minimum wages create distortions in the labor market. If you are an employer and unable to hire the one willing and able to work for the lowest wage, how else might you choose a worker? Is this fair? Why or why not? (Austrian)
2. On average, women are paid less than men. What are the likely reasons for that? Should the government intervene with a law that requires firms to pay equal wages to those with comparable skills? (Feminist)
3. Biological evolution occurs very slowly; cultural evolution occurs less slowly, but still slowly compared to institutional and market evolution.
   a. Give some examples of these observations about the different speeds of adjustment.
   b. Explain the relevance of these observations to economic reasoning. (Institutionalist)
4. Most religions argue that individuals should not fully exploit market positions. For example, the text makes it sound as if allowing prices to rise to whatever level clears the market is the best policy to follow. That means that if, for example, someone were stranded in the desert and were willing to pay half his or her future income for life for a drink of water, charging him or her that price would be appropriate. Is it appropriate? Why or why not? (Religious)
5. Rent control today looks far different from the rent freeze New York City enacted after World War II. Most rent controls today simply restrict annual rent increases and guarantee landlords a "fair return" in return for maintaining their properties.
   a. How would the economic effects of today's rent controls differ from the rent control programs depicted in your textbook?
   b. Do you consider them an appropriate mechanism to address the disproportionate power that landlords hold over tenants?
   c. If not, what policies would you recommend to address that inequity and the lack of affordable housing in U.S. cities? (Radical)

Issues to Ponder

1. In the late 1990s, the television networks were given $70 billion worth of space on public airways for broadcasting high-definition television rather than auctioning it off.
   a. Why do airways have value?
   b. After the airway had been given to the network, would you expect that the broadcaster would produce high-definition television?
2. About 10,000 tickets for the 2005 Men's Final Four college basketball games at the St. Louis Edward Jones Dome were to be sold in a lottery system for between $110 and $130 apiece. Typically applications exceed available tickets by 100,000. A year before the game, scalpers were already offering to sell tickets for between $200 and $2,000 depending on seat location, even though the practice is illegal.
   a. Demonstrate the supply and demand for Final Four tickets. How do you know that there is an excess demand for tickets at $130?

b. Demonstrate the scalped price of between \$200 and \$2,000.
c. What would be the effect of legalizing scalping on the resale value of Final Four tickets?

3. In some states and localities "scalping" is against the law, although enforcement of these laws is spotty.
   a. Using supply/demand analysis and words, demonstrate what a weakly enforced antiscalping law would likely do to the price of tickets.
   b. Using supply/demand analysis and words, demonstrate what a strongly enforced antiscalping law would likely do to the price of tickets.
4. In 1938 Congress created a Board of Cosmetology in Washington, D.C., to license beauticians. To obtain a license, people had to attend a cosmetology school. In 1992 this law was used by the board to close down a hair-braiding salon specializing in cornrows and braids operated by unlicensed Mr. Uqdah, even though little was then taught in cosmetology schools about braiding and cornrows.
   a. What possible reason can you give for why this board exists?
   b. What options might you propose to change the system?
   c. What will be the political difficulties of implementing those options?
5. In the Oregon health care plan for rationing Medicaid expenditures, therapy to slow the progression of AIDS and treatment for brain cancer were covered, while liver transplants and treatment for infectious mononucleosis were not covered.
   a. What criteria do you think were used to determine what was covered and what was not covered?
   b. Should an economist oppose the Oregon plan because it involves rationing?
   c. How does the rationing that occurs in the market differ from the rationing that occurs in the Oregon plan?
6. Airlines and hotels have many frequent flyer and frequent visitor programs in which individuals who fly the airline or stay at the hotel receive bonuses that are the equivalent to discounts.
   a. Give two reasons why these companies have such programs rather than simply offering lower prices.
   b. Can you give other examples of such programs?
   c. What is a likely reason why firms whose employees receive these benefits do not require their employees to give the benefits to the firm?
7. Since 1981, the U.S. government has supported the U.S. price of sugar by limiting sugar imports into the United States. Restricting imports is effective because the United States consumes more sugar than it produces.
   a. Using supply/demand analysis, demonstrate how import restrictions increase the price of domestic sugar.
   b. What other import policy could the government implement to have the same effect as the import restriction?
   c. Under the Uruguay Round of the General Agreement on Tariffs and Trade, the United States agreed to permit at least 1.25 million tons of sugar to be imported into the United States. How does this affect the U.S. sugar price support program?
8. Apartments in New York City are often hard to find. One of the major reasons is rent control.
   a. Demonstrate graphically how rent controls could make apartments hard to find.
   b. Often one can get an apartment if one makes a side payment to the current tenant. Can you explain why?
   c. What would be the likely effect of eliminating rent controls?
   d. What is the political appeal of rent controls?
9. Until recently, angora goat wool (mohair) has been designated as a strategic commodity (it used to be utilized in some military clothing). Because of that, in 1992 for every dollar's worth of mohair sold to manufacturers, ranchers received \$3.60.
   a. Demonstrate graphically the effect of eliminating this designation and subsidy.
   b. Why was the program likely kept in existence for so long?
   c. Say that a politician has suggested that the government should pass a law that requires all consumers to pay a price for angora goat wool high enough so that the sellers of that wool would receive \$3.60 more than the market price. Demonstrate the effect of the law graphically. Would consumers support it? How about suppliers?
10. Supply/demand analysis states that equilibrium occurs where quantity supplied equals quantity demanded, but in U.S. agricultural markets quantity supplied almost always exceeds quantity demanded. How can this be?
11. Nobel Prize–winning economist Bill Vickrey suggested that automobile insurance should be paid as a tax on gas, rather than as a fixed fee per year per car. How would that change likely affect the number of automobiles that individuals own?
12. The United States imposes substantial taxes on cigarettes but not on loose tobacco. When the tax went into effect, what effect did it likely have for cigarette rolling machines?
13. In Japan, doctors prescribe drugs and sell the drugs to the patient, receiving a 25 percent markup. In the United States, doctors prescribe drugs, but, generally, they do not sell them.
    a. Which country prescribes the most drugs? Why?
    b. How would a plan to limit the price of old drugs, but not new drugs to allow for innovation, likely affect the drug industry?
    c. How might a drug company in the United States encourage a doctor in the United States, where doctors receive nothing for drugs, to prescribe more drugs?

14. In the early 2000s, Whole Foods Market Inc. switched to a medical care plan that had a high deductible, which meant that employees were responsible for the first $1,500 of care, whereas after that they received 80 percent coverage. The firm also put about $800 in an account for each employee to use for medical care. If they did not use this money, they could carry it over to the next year.
    a. What do you expect happened to medical claim costs?
    b. What do you believe happened to hospital admissions?
    c. Demonstrate graphically the reasons for your answers in *a* and *b*.

Answers to Margin Questions

1. False. When supply rises, supply shifts out to the right. Price falls because demand slopes downward. (*p. 101; LO5-1*)
2. A discovery of a hormone that will increase cows' milk production by 20 percent will increase the supply of milk, pushing the price down and increasing the quantity demanded, as in the accompanying graph. (*p. 101; LO5-1*)

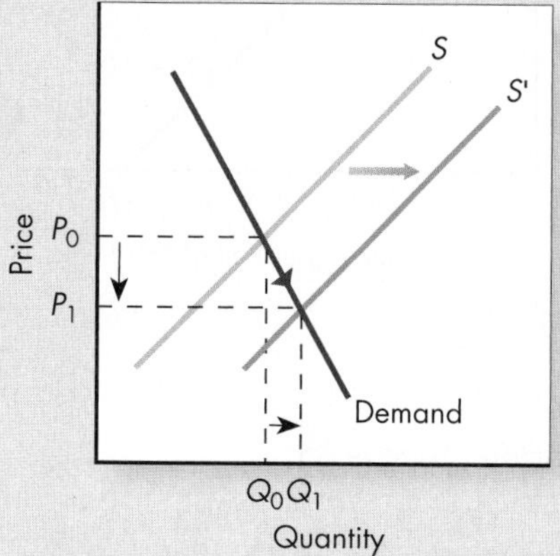

3. Quantity decreases but it is unclear what happens to price. (*p. 103; LO5-1*)
4. It is likely demand shifted in and supply remained constant. (*p. 103; LO5-1*)
5. Since the price ceiling is above the equilibrium price, it will have no effect on the market-determined equilibrium price and quantity. (*p. 104; LO5-2*)
6. The price ceiling will result in a lower price and quantity sold. There will be excess demand $Q_D - Q_S$. (*p. 105; LO5-2*)

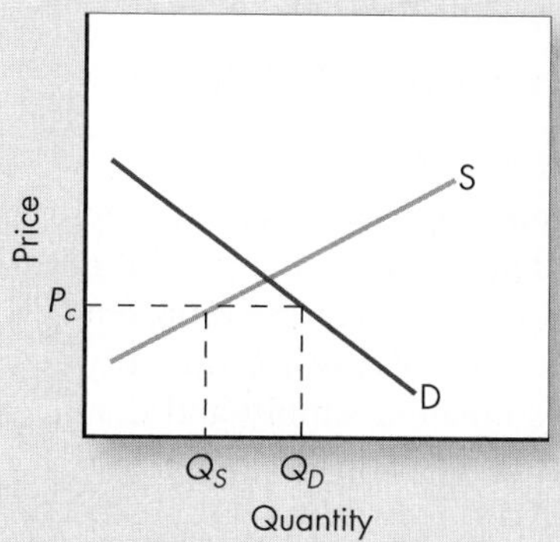

7. Since the price floor is below the equilibrium price, it will have no effect on the market-determined equilibrium price and quantity. (*p. 106; LO5-2*)
8. I would respond that the tax will most likely raise the price by less than $2 since the tax will cause the quantity demanded to decrease. This will decrease quantity supplied, and hence decrease the price the suppliers receive. In the diagram below, Q falls from Q_0 to Q_1 and the price the supplier receives falls from $4 to $3, making the final price $5, not $6. (*p. 107; LO5-3*)

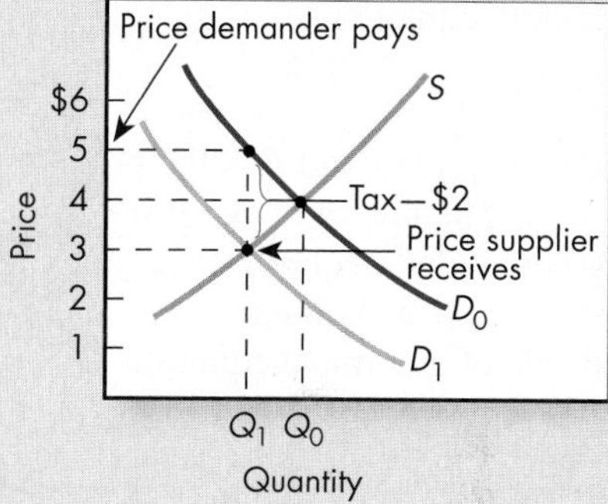

9. Given the quantity restriction, equilibrium quantity will be Q_R and equilibrium price will be P_0, which is higher than the market equilibrium price of P_e. (*p. 108; LO5-4*)

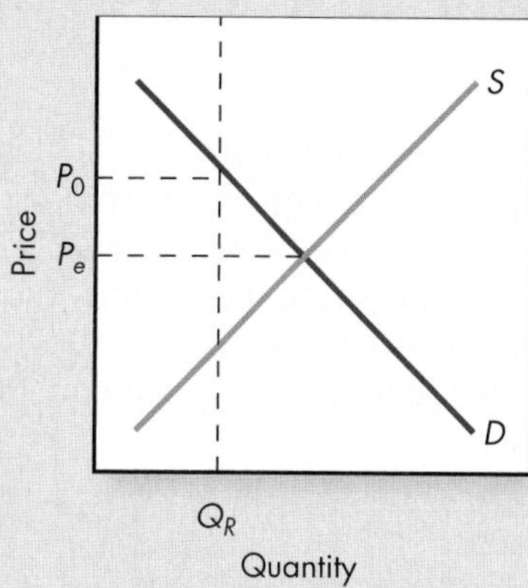

10. Universities would probably charge the high tuition they do now, but they would likely negotiate with publishers for lower textbook prices because they are both demanding and paying for the textbook. (*p. 110; LO5-5*)

APPENDIX A

Algebraic Representation of Supply, Demand, and Equilibrium

In this chapter and Chapter 4, I discussed demand, supply, and the determination of equilibrium price and quantity in words and graphs. These concepts also can be presented in equations. In this appendix I do so, using straight-line supply and demand curves.

The Laws of Supply and Demand in Equations

Since the law of supply states that quantity supplied is positively related to price, the slope of an equation specifying a supply curve is positive. (The quantity intercept term is generally less than zero since suppliers are generally unwilling to supply a good at a price less than zero.) An example of a supply equation is

$$Q_S = -5 + 2P$$

where Q_S is units supplied and P is the price of each unit in dollars per unit. The law of demand states that as price rises, quantity demanded declines. Price and quantity are negatively related, so a demand curve has a negative slope. An example of a demand equation is

$$Q_D = 10 - P$$

where Q_D is units demanded and P is the price of each unit in dollars per unit.

Determination of Equilibrium

The equilibrium price and quantity can be determined in three steps using these two equations. To find the equilibrium price and quantity for these particular demand and supply curves, you must find the quantity and price that solve both equations simultaneously.

Step 1: Set the quantity demanded equal to quantity supplied:

$$Q_S = Q_D \rightarrow -5 + 2P = 10 - P$$

Step 2: Solve for the price by rearranging terms. Doing so gives:

$$3P = 15$$
$$P = \$5$$

FIGURE A5-1 Supply and Demand Equilibrium

The algebra in this appendix leads to the same results as the geometry in the chapter. Equilibrium occurs where quantity supplied equals quantity demanded.

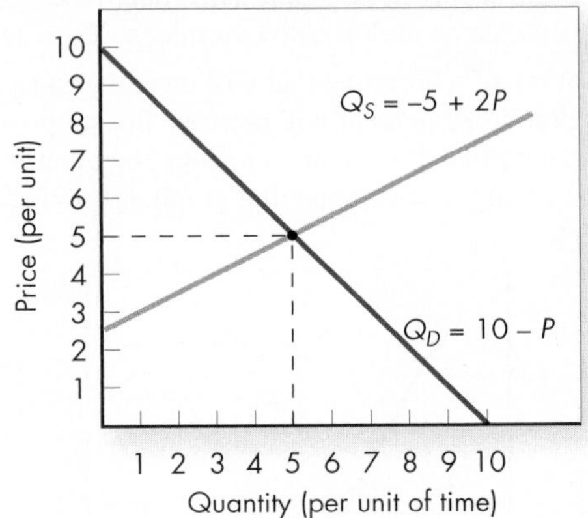

Thus, equilibrium price is \$5.

Step 3: To find equilibrium quantity, you can substitute \$5 for P in either the demand or supply equation. Let's do it for supply: $Q_S = -5 + (2 \times 5) = 5$ units. I'll leave it to you to confirm that the quantity you obtain by substituting $P = \$5$ in the demand equation is also 5 units.

The answer could also be found graphically. The supply and demand curves specified by these equations are depicted in Figure A5-1. As you can see, demand and supply intersect; quantity demanded equals quantity supplied at a quantity of 5 units and a price of \$5.

Movements along a Demand and Supply Curve

The demand and supply curves above represent schedules of quantities demanded and supplied at various prices. Movements along each can be represented by selecting various prices and solving for quantity demanded and supplied. Let's create a supply and demand table using the above equations—supply: $Q_S = -5 + 2P$; demand: $Q_D = 10 - P$.

P	$Q_S = -5 + 2P$	$Q_D = 10 - P$
$0	−5	10
1	−3	9
2	−1	8
3	1	7
4	3	6
5	5	5
6	7	4
7	9	3
8	11	2
9	13	1
10	15	0

As you move down the rows, you are moving up along the supply schedule, as shown by increasing quantity supplied, and moving down along the demand schedule, as shown by decreasing quantity demanded. Just to confirm your equilibrium quantity and price calculations, notice that at a price of $5, quantity demanded equals quantity supplied.

Shifts of a Demand and Supply Schedule

What would happen if suppliers changed their expectations so that they would be willing to sell more goods at every price? This shift factor of supply would shift the entire supply curve out to the right. Let's say that at every price, quantity supplied increases by 3. Mathematically the new equation would be $Q_S = -2 + 2P$. The quantity intercept increases by 3. What would you expect to happen to equilibrium price and quantity? Let's solve the equations mathematically first.

Step 1: To determine equilibrium price, set the new quantity supplied equal to quantity demanded:

$$10 - P = -2 + 2P$$

Step 2: Solve for the equilibrium price:

$$12 = 3P$$
$$P = \$4$$

Step 3: To determine equilibrium quantity, substitute P in either the demand or supply equation:

$$Q_D = 10 - (1 \times 4) = 6 \text{ units}$$
$$Q_S = -2 + (2 \times 4) = 6 \text{ units}$$

Equilibrium price declined to $4 and equilibrium quantity rose to 6, just as you would expect with a rightward shift in a supply curve.

Now let's suppose that demand shifts out to the right. Here we would expect both equilibrium price and equilibrium quantity to rise. We begin with our original supply and demand curves—supply: $Q_S = -5 + 2P$; demand: $Q_D = 10 - P$. Let's say at every price, the quantity demanded rises by 3. The new equation for demand would be $Q_D = 13 - P$. You may want to solve this equation for various prices to confirm that at every price, quantity demanded rises by 3. Let's solve the equations for equilibrium price and quantity.

Step 1: Set the quantities equal to one another:

$$13 - P = -5 + 2P$$

Step 2: Solve for equilibrium price:

$$18 = 3P$$
$$P = \$6$$

Step 3: Substitute P in either the demand or supply equation:

$$Q_D = 13 - (1 \times 6) = 7 \text{ units}$$
$$Q_S = -5 + (2 \times 6) = 7 \text{ units}$$

Equilibrium price rose to $6 and equilibrium quantity rose to 7 units, just as you would expect with a rightward shift in a demand curve.

Just to make sure you've got it, I will do two more examples. First, suppose the demand and supply equations for wheat per year in the United States can be specified as follows (notice that the slope is negative for the demand curve and positive for the supply curve):

$$Q_D = 500 - 2P$$
$$Q_S = -100 + 4P$$

P is the price in dollars per thousand bushels and Q is the quantity of wheat in thousands of bushels. Remember that the units must always be stated. What are the equilibrium price and quantity?

Step 1: Set the quantities equal to one another:

$$500 - 2P = -100 + 4P$$

Step 2: Solve for equilibrium price:

$$600 = 6P$$
$$P = \$100$$

Step 3: Substitute P in either the demand or supply equation:

$$Q_D = 500 - (2 \times 100) = 300$$
$$Q_S = -100 + (4 \times 100) = 300$$

Equilibrium quantity is 300 thousand bushels.

As my final example, take a look at Alice's demand curve depicted in Figure 4-4(b) in Chapter 4. Can you write an equation that represents the demand curve in that figure? It is $Q_D = 10 - 2P$. At a price of zero, the quantity of movie rentals Alice demands is 10, and for every increase in price of \$1, the quantity she demands falls by 2. Now look at Ann's supply curve shown in Figure 4-7(b) in Chapter 4. Ann's supply curve mathematically is $Q_S = 2P$. At a zero price, the quantity Ann supplies is zero, and for every \$1 increase in price, the quantity she supplies rises by 2. What are the equilibrium price and quantity?

Step 1: Set the quantities equal to one another:

$$10 - 2P = 2P$$

Step 2: Solve for equilibrium price:

$$4P = 10$$
$$P = \$2.5$$

Step 3: Substitute P in either the demand or supply equation:

$$Q_D = 10 - (2 \times 2.5) = 5, \text{ or}$$
$$Q_S = 2 \times 2.5 = 5 \text{ movies per week}$$

Ann is willing to supply five movies per week at \$2.50 per rental and Alice demands five movies at \$2.50 per movie rental. Remember that in Figure 4-8 in Chapter 4, I showed you graphically the equilibrium quantity and price of Alice's demand curve and Ann's supply curve. I'll leave it up to you to check that the graphic solution in Figure 4-8 is the same as the mathematical solution we came up with here.

Price Ceilings and Price Floors

Let's now consider a price ceiling and price floor. We start with the supply and demand curves:

$$Q_S = -5 + 2P$$
$$Q_D = 10 - P$$

This gave us the solution

$$P = 5$$
$$Q = 5$$

Now, say that a price ceiling of \$4 is imposed. Would you expect a shortage or a surplus? If you said "shortage," you're doing well. If not, review the chapter before continuing with this appendix. To find out how much the shortage is, we must find out how much will be supplied and how much will be demanded at the price ceiling. Substituting \$4 for price in both equations lets us see that $Q_S = 3$ units and $Q_D = 6$ units. There will be a shortage of three units. Next, let's consider a price floor of \$6. To determine the surplus, we follow the same exercise. Substituting \$6 into the two equations gives a quantity supplied of seven units and a quantity demanded of four units, so there is a surplus of three units.

Taxes and Subsidies

Next, let's consider the effect of a tax of \$1 placed on the supplier. That tax would decrease the price received by suppliers by \$1. In other words,

$$Q_S = -5 + 2(P - 1)$$

Multiplying the terms in parentheses by 2 and collecting terms results in

$$Q_S = -7 + 2P$$

This supply equation has the same slope as in the previous case, but a new intercept term—just what you'd expect. To determine the new equilibrium price and quantity, follow steps 1 to 3 discussed earlier. Setting this new equation equal to demand and solving for price gives

$$P = 5\tfrac{2}{3}$$

Substituting this price into the demand and supply equations tells us equilibrium quantity:

$$Q_S = Q_D = 4\tfrac{1}{3} \text{ units}$$

Of that price, the supplier must pay \$1 in tax, so the price the supplier receives net of tax is \$4⅔.

Next, let's say that the tax were put on the demander rather than on the supplier. In that case, the tax increases the price for demanders by \$1 and the demand equation becomes

$$Q_D = 10 - (P + 1), \text{ or}$$
$$Q_D = 9 - P$$

Again solving for equilibrium price and quantity requires setting the demand and supply equations equal to one another and solving for price. I leave the steps to you. The result is

$$P = 4\tfrac{2}{3}$$

This is the price the supplier receives. The price demanders pay is \$5⅔. The equilibrium quantity will be 4⅓ units.

These are the same results we got in the previous cases showing that, given the assumptions, it doesn't matter who actually pays the tax: The effect on equilibrium price and quantity is identical no matter who pays it.

Quotas

Finally, let's consider the effect of a quota of 4⅓ placed on the market. Since a quota limits the quantity supplied, as long as the quota is less than the market equilibrium quantity, the supply equation becomes

$$Q_S = 4\tfrac{1}{3}$$

where Q_S is the actual amount supplied. The price that the market will arrive at for this quantity is determined by the demand curve. To find that price, substitute the quantity $4\frac{1}{3}$ into the demand equation ($Q_D = 10 - P$):

$$4\tfrac{1}{3} = 10 - P$$

and solve for P:

$$P = 5\tfrac{2}{3}$$

Since consumers are willing to pay $\$5\frac{2}{3}$, this is what suppliers will receive. The price that suppliers would have been willing to accept for a quantity of $4\frac{1}{3}$ is $\$4\frac{2}{3}$. This can be found by substituting the amount of the quota in the supply equation:

$$4\tfrac{1}{3} = -5 + 2P$$

and solving for P:

$$2P = 9\tfrac{1}{3}$$

$$P = 4\tfrac{2}{3}$$

Notice that this result is very similar to the tax. For demanders it is identical; they pay $\$5\frac{2}{3}$ and receive $4\frac{1}{3}$ units. For suppliers, however, the situation is much preferable; instead of receiving a price of $\$4\frac{2}{3}$, the amount they received with the tax, they receive $5\frac{2}{3}$. With a quota, suppliers receive the "implicit tax revenue" that results from the higher price.

Questions and Exercises

1. Suppose the demand and supply for milk are described by the following equations: $Q_D = 600 - 100P$; $Q_S = -150 + 150P$, where P is price in dollars, Q_D is quantity demanded in millions of gallons per year, and Q_S is quantity supplied in millions of gallons per year.
   a. Create demand and supply tables corresponding to these equations.
   b. Graph supply and demand and determine equilibrium price and quantity.
   c. Confirm your answer to *b* by solving the equations mathematically.
2. Beginning with the equations in question 1, suppose a growth hormone is introduced that allows dairy farmers to offer 125 million more gallons of milk per year at each price.
   a. Construct new demand and supply curves reflecting this change. Describe with words what happened to the supply curve and to the demand curve.
   b. Graph the new curves and determine equilibrium price and quantity.
   c. Determine equilibrium price and quantity by solving the equations mathematically.
   d. Suppose the government set the price of milk at $3 a gallon. Demonstrate the effect of this regulation on the market for milk. What is quantity demanded? What is quantity supplied?
3. Write demand and supply equations that represent demand, D_0, and supply, S_0, in Figure A5-1 in this appendix.
   a. Solve for equilibrium price and quantity mathematically. Show your work.
   b. Rewrite the demand equation to reflect an increase in demand of 3 units. What happens to equilibrium price and quantity?
   c. Rewrite the supply equation to reflect a decrease in supply of 3 units at every price level. What happens to equilibrium price and quantity using the demand curve from *b*?
4. a. How is a shift in demand reflected in a demand equation?
   b. How is a shift in supply reflected in a supply equation?
   c. How is a movement along a demand (supply) curve reflected in a demand (supply) equation?
5. Suppose the demand and supply for wheat are described by the following equations: $Q_D = 10 - P$; $Q_S = 2 + P$, where P is the price in dollars, Q_D is quantity demanded in millions of bushels per year, and Q_S is quantity supplied in millions of bushels per year.
   a. Solve for equilibrium price and quantity of wheat.
   b. Would a government-set price of $5 create a surplus or a shortage of wheat? How much? Is $5 a price ceiling or a price floor?
6. Suppose the U.S. government imposes a $1 per gallon of milk tax on dairy farmers. Using the demand and supply equations from question 1:
   a. What is the effect of the tax on the supply equation? The demand equation?
   b. What are the new equilibrium price and quantity?
   c. How much do dairy farmers receive per gallon of milk after the tax? How much do demanders pay?
7. Repeat question 6 assuming the tax is placed on the buyers of milk. Does it matter who pays the tax?
8. Repeat question 6 assuming the government pays a subsidy of $1 per gallon of milk to farmers.
9. Suppose the demand for movies is represented by $Q_D = 15 - 4P$, and the supply of movies is represented by $Q_S = 4P - 1$. Determine if each of the following is a price floor, price ceiling, or neither. In each case, determine the shortage or surplus.
   a. $P = \$3$
   b. $P = \$1.50$
   c. $P = \$2.25$
   d. $P = \$2.50$

PART II

Macroeconomics

Unlike microeconomics, which has a definite focus and theory, macroeconomics, the study of the economy in the aggregate, has a focus and theory that is continually changing. That is in part because macroeconomic theory is less developed, and in part because the macroeconomic problems the economy is facing keep changing as well.

The general focus of macroeconomics is on unemployment, business cycles (fluctuations in output), growth, and inflation. Which of these problems gets specific focus depends on the policy problems facing the economy. In recent years, the focus has been on why the economy seems stuck in a rut, unable to get back on the growth trend that people had come to expect, and why unemployment has remained high. These issues generate a lot of debate, and in the following chapters I provide you with the background necessary to understand that modern debate. Let's begin with a little history.

Macroeconomics emerged as a separate subject within economics in the 1930s, when the U.S. economy fell into the Great Depression. Businesses collapsed and unemployment rose until 25 percent of the workforce— millions of people—were out of work. The Depression changed the way economics was taught and the way in which economic problems were conceived. Before the 1930s, economics was microeconomics (the study of partial-equilibrium supply and demand). After the 1930s, the study of the core of economic thinking was broken into two discrete areas: microeconomics, as before, and a new field, macroeconomics.

Macroeconomic policy debates have centered on a struggle between two groups: Keynesian (pronounced KAIN-sian) economists and Classical economists. Should the government run a budget deficit or surplus? Should the government increase the money supply when a recession threatens? Should it decrease the money supply when inflation threatens? Can government prevent recessions? Keynesians generally answer one way; Classicals, another.

Classical economists generally oppose government intervention in the economy; they favor a laissez-faire policy.[1] Keynesians are more likely to favor government intervention in the economy. They feel a laissez-faire policy can sometimes lead to disaster. Both views represent reasonable economic positions. The differences between them are often subtle and result from their slightly different views of what government can do and slightly different perspectives on the economy. In the chapters that follow, I try to provide you with a sense of both Classical and Keynesian ideas, and their modern variations.

Section I, Macroeconomic Basics (Chapters 6 and 7), introduces the macroeconomic problems, terminology, and statistics used to track the economy's macroeconomic performance. Section II, Policy Models (Chapters 9–11), presents the core macroeconomic models and how they relate to current problems. Two web chapters in this section, Chapters 9W and 10W, go deeper into the models, Section III, Finance, Money, and the Economy (Chapters 12–14), looks at how money and the financial system fit into the macro model. These chapters discuss the Federal Reserve Bank (the Fed), monetary policy, and the financial crisis that began in 2007, which resulted in the use of a number of unconventional policies by the Fed. Section IV, Taxes, Budgets, and Fiscal Policy (Chapters 15 and 16), looks at the issues in fiscal policy and tax policy, and the debate about government deficits and debt, which have been expanding in recent years. Section V, Macroeconomic Problems (Chapters 17 and 18), looks specifically at the problems of unemployment and inflation. Finally, Section VI, International Macroeconomic Policy Issues (Chapters 19–22), discusses macroeconomic policy within an international context.

---

[1]*Laissez-faire* (introduced to you in Chapter 2) is a French expression meaning "Leave things alone; let them go on without interference."

chapter 6

Economic Growth, Business Cycles, and Structural Stagnation

> *Remember that there is nothing stable in human affairs; therefore avoid undue elation in prosperity, or undue depression in adversity.*
>
> —Socrates

Like people, the economy has moods. Sometimes it's in wonderful shape—it's booming; at other times, it's depressed. Like people whose moods are often associated with specific problems such as headaches, sore backs, and itchy skin, the economy's moods are associated with specific problems such as lack of growth, business cycles, unemployment, and inflation. **Macroeconomics** *is the study of problems that affect the economy as a whole (lack of growth, recessions, unemployment, and inflation) and what to do about them.*

In recent years the mood of the economy hasn't been good. In 2008 the U.S. economy experienced a major downturn in output and an increase in unemployment, causing some to fear that the economy was falling into a depression like the one the United States faced in the 1930s. It didn't, in part because of the actions undertaken by the government, but as of 2013, the U.S. economy remained in the doldrums of high unemployment and slow growth. In the coming chapters, I will try to provide insight into why the U.S. economy is in the doldrums, and the various ideas of what can be done about it.

While economists almost always debate what macroeconomic policies to follow, the debate today is hotter than usual. At issue are the policies the United States used to deal with the aftermath of the bursting financial bubble in 2007. Specifically, government implemented a financial bailout for banks, and supplemented it with an enormous stimulus package that included spending increases, tax decreases, and large infusions of money in the economy. Those policies may have prevented a depression, but they did not jumpstart the economy as economists thought (or at least hoped). Instead, the U.S. economy languished with slow growth and high unemployment. Moreover, what was presented as a one-time stimulus was extended into an ongoing stimulus, with no clear indication of when that ongoing stimulus would no longer be needed. This raised serious concerns about the negative side effects of that ongoing stimulus.

To understand the nature of the current policy debate, it is helpful to review the historical development of macroeconomics.

After reading this chapter, you should be able to:

- **LO6-1** Discuss the history of macro, distinguishing Classical and Keynesian, macroeconomists.
- **LO6-2** Define growth and discuss its recent history.
- **LO6-3** Distinguish a business cycle from structural stagnation.
- **LO6-4** Relate unemployment to business cycles and distinguish cyclical unemployment from structural unemployment

The Historical Development of Macro

In the 1930s, the U.S. economy fell into a deep recession that lasted for 10 years. It was a defining event that undermined people's faith in markets and was the beginning of macro's focus on the demand side of the economy. It is also where our story of macroeconomics begins.

WWW Web Note 6.1 The Great Depression

During the Depression of the 1930s, output fell by 30 percent and unemployment rose to 25 percent. Not only was the deadbeat up the street unemployed but so were your brother, your mother, your uncle—the hardworking backbone of the country. These people wanted to work; if the market wasn't creating jobs for them, it was the market system that was at fault.

During the Depression, unemployment lines were enormously long.

From Classical to Keynesian Economics

Macroeconomists before the Depression focused on the problem of growth (keeping the economy growing over the long run). Their policy recommendations were designed to lead to that growth. They avoided discussing policies that would affect the short-run prospects of the economy. In the 1930s that changed. Macroeconomists started focusing on short-run issues such as unemployment and economic ups and downs. To distinguish the two types of economics, the earlier economists who focused on long-run issues were called *Classical economists* and economists who focused on the short run were called *Keynesian economists.* Keynesian economists were named because a leading advocate of the short-run focus was John Maynard Keynes, the author of *The General Theory of Employment, Interest and Money,* and the originator of macroeconomics as a separate discipline from micro.

Classical Economics

Classical economists believed the market was self-regulating through the invisible hand (the pricing mechanism of the market). Short-run problems were temporary glitches; the Classical framework said that the economy would always return to its full capacity and a rate of unemployment consistent with the economy being at its potential. Thus, the essence of Classical economists' approach to problems was laissez-faire (leave the market alone). **Classical economists,** then, are *economists who believe that business cycles (ups and downs of the economy) are temporary glitches, and who generally favor laissez-faire, or nonactivist, policies.*

Classical economists support laissez-faire policies.

As long as the economy was operating relatively smoothly, the Classical analysis of the aggregate economy met no serious opposition. But when the Great Depression hit and unemployment became a serious problem, most Classical economists avoided the issue (as most people tend to do when they don't have a good answer). When pushed by curious students to explain how the invisible hand, if it was so wonderful, could have allowed the Depression, Classical economists used microeconomic supply and demand arguments. They argued that labor unions and government policies kept prices and wages from falling. The problem, they said, was that the invisible hand was not being allowed to coordinate economic activity.

Their laissez-faire policy prescription followed from their analysis: Eliminate labor unions and change government policies that held wages too high. If government did so, the wage rate would fall, unemployment would be eliminated, and the Depression would end.

Laypeople (average citizens) weren't pleased with this argument. (Remember, economists don't try to present pleasing arguments—only arguments they believe are correct.) But laypeople couldn't point to anything wrong with it. It made sense, but it wasn't satisfying. People thought, "Gee, Uncle Joe, who's unemployed, would take a job at half the going wage. But he can't find one—there just aren't enough jobs to go around at any wage." So most laypeople developed different explanations. One popular explanation of the Depression was that an oversupply of goods had glutted the market. Since firms couldn't sell the goods they had for sale, they cut production and laid off workers. All that was needed to eliminate unemployment was for government to hire the unemployed, even if only to dig ditches and fill them back up. The people who got the new jobs would spend their money, creating even more jobs. Pretty soon, the United States would be out of the Depression.

Classical economists argued against this lay view. They felt that the money to hire people would have to be borrowed. Such borrowing would use money that would have financed private economic activity and jobs, and would thus reduce private economic activity even further. The net effect would be essentially zero. Their advice was simply to have faith in markets.

Keynesian Economics

Keynes focused on the short run, not the long run.

As the Depression deepened, the Classical "have-faith" solution lost support. Everyone was interested in the short run, not the long run. John Maynard Keynes put the concern most eloquently: "In the long run, we're all dead."

Keynes stopped asking whether the economy would eventually get out of the Depression on its own and started asking what was causing the Depression and what society could do to counteract these forces. By taking this approach, he created the macroeconomic framework that focuses on short-run issues such as business cycles and how to stabilize output fluctuations. **Keynesian economists** are *economists who believe that business cycles reflect underlying problems that can be addressed with activist government policies.*

Q-1 Distinguish a Classical economist from a Keynesian economist.

While Keynes' ideas had many dimensions, the essence was that as wages and overall prices adjusted to sudden changes in overall spending (such as an unexpected decrease in household spending), the economy could get stuck in a rut.

If, for some reason, people stopped buying—decreased their demand in the aggregate—firms would decrease production, causing people to be laid off. These people would, in turn, buy even less—causing other firms to further decrease production, which would cause more workers to be laid off, and so on. Firms' supply decisions would be affected by consumers' buying decisions, and the economy would end up in a cumulative cycle of declining production that would end with the economy stuck at a low level of income. In developing this line of reasoning, Keynes provided a simple model of how unemployment could be caused by too little spending and how the economy could fall into a depression. The issue was not whether a more desirable equilibrium existed. It was whether a market economy, once it had fallen into a depression, and was caught in a cumulative downward cycle, could get out of it on its own in an acceptable period of time.

WWW Web Note 6.2 John Maynard Keynes

In making his argument, Keynes carefully distinguished the adjustment process for a single market (a micro issue) from the adjustment process for the aggregate economy (a macro issue), arguing that the effects differ significantly when everyone does something versus when only one person does it. You were introduced to this problem in Chapter 4 under the name *fallacy of composition*.

The problem is neatly seen by considering an analogy to a football game. If everyone is standing, and you sit down, you can't see. Everyone is better off standing. No one has an incentive to sit down. However, if somehow all individuals could be enticed to sit down, all individuals would be even better off. Sitting down is a public good—a good that benefits others but one that nobody on his or her own will do. Keynesians argued that, in times of recession, spending benefits not just the person spending but everyone, so government should spend or find ways of inducing private individuals to

Keynesians argued that, in times of recession, spending is a public good that benefits everyone.

spend. This difference between individual and economywide reactions to spending decisions creates a possibility for government to exercise control over aggregate expenditures and thereby over aggregate output and income.

The Merging of Classical and Keynesian Economics

Within its own framework, Keynesian economics makes a lot of sense. But it leaves out some important issues. One is inflation. If, instead of an oversupply of goods, people spend more than is produced, there are pressures for prices to rise and the economy experiences inflation. Microeconomics looks at the effect of price rises when prices of other goods remain constant. Put another way, it looks at the effect of *relative* price changes. But price increases for one good *can* lead to increases in the prices of other goods. The problem is, however, that if all people raise their prices by 10 percent, it is equivalent to nobody raising relative prices; all that will happen is the price level will rise. Classical economists had focused on inflation—an increase in the price of all goods—arguing that when aggregate demand (expenditures in the economy) exceeds aggregate supply (production in an economy), inflation will result. Keynesian economists had assumed the price level was constant.

When inflation became a serious problem, as it did in the 1970s, macroeconomics swung back to Classical economics and, over time, Keynesian economics lost influence. Keynesian economics wasn't addressing the problems of the times. Policy makers still used Keynesian policies, but they also used Classical policies. By the 1980s, the two types of economics had merged into a new conventional macroeconomics. At that point macroeconomics was neither Keynesian nor Classical but a combination of the two. That new conventional macroeconomics formed the core of modern macroeconomics until the crash of 2008 when output declined, unemployment rose, and the U.S. economy did not recover as conventional economists had predicted it would. To everyone's disappointment, it seemed as if the U.S. economy had fallen into a **structural stagnation**—*a period of protracted slow growth and high unemployment.*

Structural stagnation is a period of slow growth and high unemployment.

The Unraveling of the Keynesian/Classical Synthesis

Faced with this new structural stagnation problem, the policy agreement between Keynesians and Classicals started to unravel. As it did, the macro-policy debate heated up. Died-in-the-wool liberal Keynesian economists argued that more demand stimulus would solve our problems. Economist Paul Krugman put it bluntly, arguing that the U.S. government needed "another burst of government spending" that was even larger than the last stimulus. The result would be a significant increase in the government deficit, more spending, and significant increases in government debt. He argued that we should not be concerned about the size or possible side effects of government deficits or debt. He wrote: "Is it really that simple? Would it really be that easy? Basically, yes."

Some Classical economists argued that what the economy needed was severe cuts in government spending accompanied by cuts in taxes; the larger the tax cut the better. The Tea Party picked up on this anti-tax refrain and required politicians that it supported to make an anti-tax pledge. Other more traditional Classical economists who were not categorically opposed to tax increases, but who were very concerned about government budget deficits, saw the need to eliminate the deficit. While they agreed with Keynesians that such a policy would likely slow the U.S. economy, and possibly lead it into an even worse recession, they felt that the continuation of the unsustainable deficit would lead to even greater problems in the long run. They saw the U.S. political system as addicted to deficits, and that addiction had to be ended, even though it would cause serious withdrawal pains. Otherwise the debt would destroy the foundations of our society.

REAL-WORLD APPLICATION

The Author's Biases

Normally, I try to keep myself and my views out of policy discussions, or at least keep them relatively hidden. The positive spin on my doing that is that I'm a very open-minded economist and I want my textbook to be teachable by economists with many different views. (The economic spin on my doing so is that I want to sell my book, and showing my biases will cut sales since only those who share my biases will adopt it.)

Whatever my motives, I continue this "policy neutrality" approach in this edition, but the presentation of current macro policy issues involve so many difficult and unavoidable judgments about political and economic relationships that are unsettled within macroeconomics, that I have come to the belief that in macro, it is necessary to admit my views, so that the reader can take them into account. So, here are my policy views.

Hyman Minsky

I am a moderate macroeconomist who has collaborated with both Classical and Keynesian economists. I am associated with both and neither; I usually end up upsetting both sides, especially those who are died-in-the-wool one-or-the-other siders. I believe that both the Classical and Keynesian traditions offer important insights and policy makers must consider both.

These insights can be found not only in the conventional traditions, but also in the writings of unconventional Keynesian and Classical macroeconomists who never signed on to the conventional views of what became known as Keynesians and Classicals. In fact, what the textbooks (including mine) present as Keynesian and Classical economics is a simplistic caricature of both. Both Classical and Keynesian policy views are far richer than their textbook representations. Both Classicals and Keynesians were always searching for a balance. For example, during the Great Depression, Keynes was enormously worried about deficits, and at various times opposed larger deficits. Similarly, in the depths of the Depression, various Classical economists agreed that the government should accept deficits and do whatever it could to eliminate unemployment. The necessary simplifications in textbooks inevitably lose such nuances of policy.

What this means for understanding the policy debate is that conventional views of Keynesians and Classicals need to be scrutinized and the unconventional views of both need to be considered as well. Unconventional Classical economists include *Austrian economists*—pro-market-oriented economists who have long argued that the conventional blend of Classical and Keynesian economics has undermined true Classical ideas. Unconventional Keynesian economists include *Post Keynesian* and *Institutional economists*—more pro-government control-oriented economists who have also long argued that the conventional blend of Classical and Keynesian economics has undermined true Keynesian ideas.

Frederick Hayek

What makes these two groups especially relevant to the current macro policy debate is that they both argued that conventional macro policies the U.S. government was following in the early 2000s would lead to the economic problems we are now facing. For example, Post-Keynesian economist, Hyman Minsky, argued that financial crashes, such as the one the United States experienced in 2007, were inevitable in a market economy, and were intricately tied to the workings of a capitalist economy. Similarly, Austrian economist Frederick Hayek had warned of financial crises if government became as involved in the economy as it had.

While both Austrian and Post-Keynesian economists foresaw the current macroeconomic problems, their solutions were quite different. Institutionalists and Post Keynesians called for more government involvement in the economy; Austrian called for less. This leaves policy makers in a bind. Clearly, something was wrong with conventional macroeconomics, but there is no clear alternative model or policy that emerged from these unconventional views. My bottom line: Some problems just don't have simple solutions, especially when the solutions have to be implemented through a highly problematic political system.

More moderate economists who are not died-in-the-wool anything were caught in the middle. We saw the economy caught between a rock and a hard place. The economy needed demand-side stimulus, but it also needed deficit reduction, and the two goals were impossible to reconcile. There was no easy solution, and whatever policy that policymakers chose would likely have serious undesirable side effects. On the one hand, too expansionary a stimulus policy could cause investors to lose faith in the U.S.

government bonds used to finance its debt. That could severely limit the government's ability to function at all, which would be catastrophic to the economy and society. On the other hand, too contractionary a policy could throw the economy into a depression.

Two Frameworks: The Long Run and the Short Run

In analyzing macroeconomic issues, economists generally use two frameworks: a short-run and a long-run framework. Issues of growth are generally considered in a long-run framework. Business cycles are generally considered in a short-run framework. Inflation and unemployment fall within both frameworks.

What is the difference between the two frameworks? The long-run growth framework focuses on incentives for supply; that's why sometimes it is called *supply-side economics.* In the long run, policies that affect production or supply—such as incentives that promote work, capital accumulation (factors of production), and technological change—are key.

Q-2 From 2007 to 2012, employment in the United States declined by 4 million. The decline was in part due to a recession and in part due to U.S. firms outsourcing jobs to foreign countries. Is the decline in employment an issue best studied in the long-run framework or the short-run framework?

The short-run business cycle framework focuses on demand. That is why short-run macro analysis is sometimes called *demand-side economics.* Much of the policy discussion of short-run business cycles focuses on ways to increase or decrease aggregate expenditures, such as policies to get consumers and businesses to increase their spending.[1]

The short-run/long-run distinction allowed Keynesians and Classicals to avoid major disagreements about models and policies. Conventional Keynesian-oriented economists mostly focused on the short-run framework and argued that this framework should guide policy. That short-run framework leads to the policy position that all we have to do is to have government stimulate the economy by increasing government spending enormously to get the economy back to its potential. It's the policy framework that super-liberal economists such as Paul Krugman use when they claim that the solution to our current macro problem is more government spending.

Conventional Classical-oriented economics mostly focused on the long-run framework and argued that the long-run model should guide policy. That is the framework that leads to the view that the economy will solve its own problems and that government spending will not help, but hurt, the economy. It's the view that super-conservative economists use when they claim that the goal of policy should be to keep the government out of the economy and that the government should always run a balanced budget.

In my view, both extremes are problematic, as is the stark division between the short-run and the long-run frameworks. Dividing up macro problems into short-run and long-run problems may have been a useful teaching simplification, but such a sharp distinction between the two does not fit the real world. The policy debate between the two sides cannot be hidden by a framework that assigns the short run to Keynesian policy focusing on demand, and the long run to Classical policy that focuses on supply.

Dividing up macro problems into short-run and long-run problems may be a useful teaching simplification, but such a sharp distinction does not fit the real world.

In reality the short run and the long run are not separate. The economy is simultaneously in the long run and short run, and any analysis of either must take both runs into account. This means that the short-run and long-run frameworks have to be blended into a composite framework in which both supply and demand influence long-run and short-run forces. In the long run we are all dead, but the long run is just a combination of short runs; they cannot be separated.

In the long run we are all dead, but the long run is just a combination of short runs; they cannot be separated.

In this book, I attempt to blend the two together in an analysis of structural stagnation, in which an economy's short-run potential output is limited by structural limitations

[1]A short-run/long-run distinction helps make complicated issues somewhat clearer, but it obscures other issues, such as: How long is the short run, and how do we move from the short run to the long run? Some economists argue that in the long run we are only in another short run, while others argue that since our actions are forward-looking, we are always in the long run.

ADDED DIMENSION

The Power of Compounding

A difference in growth rates of one percentage point may not seem like much, but over a number of years, the power of compounding can turn these small differences in growth rates into large differences in income levels. Consider Eastern European countries compared to Western European countries. In 1950, real per capita income was about $2,000 in Eastern European countries and about $4,500 in Western European countries. Over the next 60 years, income grew 2.5 percent a year in Eastern European countries and 2.5 percent a year in Western European countries. One-third percentage point may be small, but it meant that in those 60 years, income in Western European countries rose to $22,000, while income in Eastern European countries rose by much less to only $8,400.

The reason small differences in growth rates over long periods of time can mean huge differences in income levels is *compounding*. Compounding means that growth is based not only on the original level of income but also on the accumulation of previous-year increases in income. For example, say your income starts at $100 and grows at a rate of 10 percent each year; the first year your income grows by $10, to $110. The second year the same growth rate increases income by $11, to $121. The third year income grows by $12.10, which is still 10 percent but a larger dollar increase. After 50 years, that same 10 percent annual increase means income will be growing by over $1,000 a year.

that most short-run models do not consider. In this blended framework, short-run expansionary government policy might cause a financial bubble rather than a solid recovery even with the economy at a high employment level. In this blended framework, globalization and trade deficits play key limiting roles in determining policy, and the problems that can easily be solved in the short-run framework become almost impossible to solve without strong government policy to deal with both the long-run and the short-run nature of the problem.

So if you are looking for an easy answer to the macroeconomic problems, you won't find them here. What you are going to get in this book is a rather gloomy assessment of the state of the macroeconomy—not because there are no answers, but because the answers that will most likely solve the underlying problems involve difficult and risky policy choices that are politically difficult to institute.

We will be going over the various macroeconomic problems and policy goals throughout the book, but here at the beginning, I want to provide you with a brief overview of the central issues. We will start with growth.

Growth

Since the end of World War II generally the U.S. economy has been growing or expanding. Economists measure growth with changes in total output over a long period of time. When people produce and sell their goods, they earn income, so when an economy is growing, both total output and total income are increasing. Such growth gives most people more income this year than they had last year. Since most of us prefer more to less, growth is easy to take.

The U.S. Department of Commerce traced U.S. economic growth in output since about 1890 and discovered that, on average, output of goods and services grew about 3.5 percent per year. In the 1970s and 1980s, growth was more like 2.5 percent. In the late 1990s and early 2000s, it was assumed again to be 3.5 percent. With the stalled economy today, it's hard to tell what will be the growth rate going forward.

U.S. economic output has grown at an annual 2.5 to 3.5 percent rate since World War I. What it will be in the future is uncertain.

This 2.5 to 3.5 percent growth rate is sometimes called the *secular growth trend.* The long-run, or secular, growth trend represents the rise in **potential output**—*the highest amount of output an economy can sustainably produce and sell using existing production* *processes and resources.* Two points should be made about potential output. The first is that potential output is not a purely physical measure. For example, if workers are asking for a wage that is higher than any firm is willing to pay, those workers will not contribute to an economy's potential output. Similarly, a factory that is technologically obsolete does not contribute to potential output either. The second point is that the production must be sustainable. If a level of output leads to accelerating inflation, or to a financial collapse, that level of output is not sustainable and hence does not meet the potential output definition. Much of the current debate about policy reflects differences in opinion about what the level of potential output is. The rate at which the actual output grows in any one year fluctuates, but on average the U.S. economy has been growing at its long-term trend.

This brings us to another measure of growth—changes in per capita output. **Per capita output** is *output divided by the total population.* Output per person is an important measure of growth because, even if total output is increasing, the population may be growing even faster, so per capita output would be falling.

Q-3 Say that output in the United States is $15 trillion, and there are 300 million people living in the United States. What is per capita output?

Global Experiences with Growth

Various areas of the world have experienced per capita growth. While output has steadily grown, that trend has been highly variable for long periods of time, especially when you consider specific regions, as you can see in Figure 6-1. Consider China and India. They grew slowly until the 1990s, and then their growth rate increased substantially. Western Europe and Japan provide other examples. In the postwar era Western European economies grew by an average 3.0 percent a year; Japan grew by 4 percent, but its growth rate fell considerably in the 1990s and has remained low. The United States grew at an annual rate of 2.5 percent from 1940 to 1970, but its growth rate has slowed in recent years. This slowdown in growth is a major policy issue today.

FIGURE 6-1 **Growth Rates around the World**

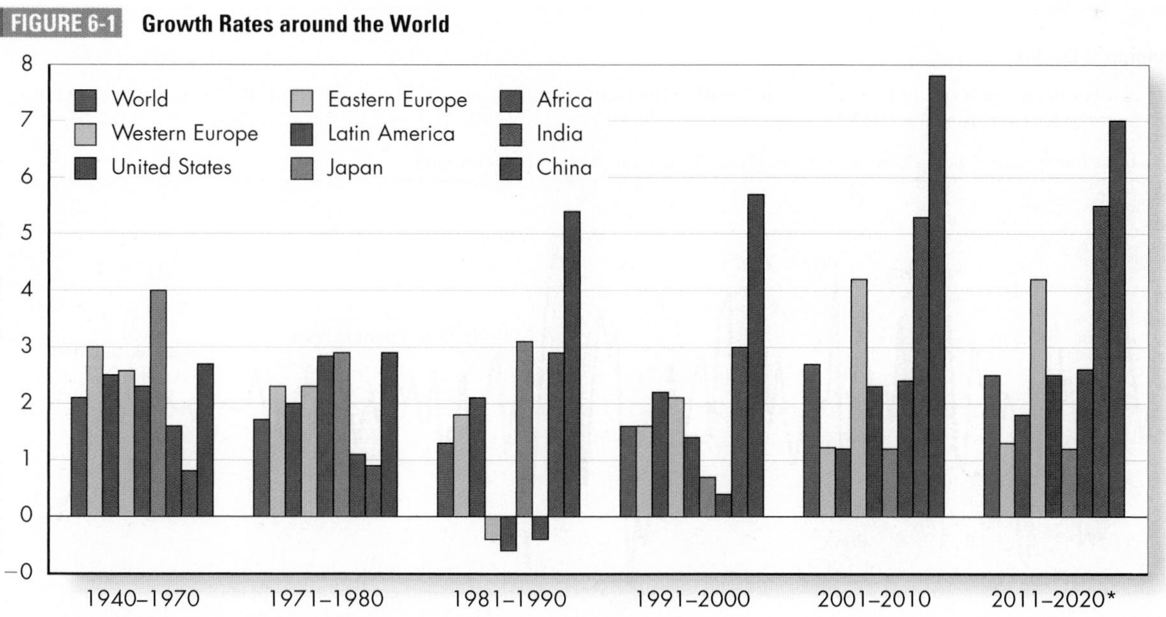

Source: World Economy, Historical Tables. Per Capita growth. www.theworldeconomy.org

*Estimates based on World Bank and government data and projections.

The Prospect for Future U.S. Growth

Past data are not necessarily good predictors of future events, and while predictions are always dangerous, it is worthwhile asking: How might the future differ from the past, and what do those differences suggest about future U.S. economic growth? One big difference is the current economic development of the Indian and Chinese economies, which is similar to the growth experienced by other Asian countries, such as Korea and Thailand, in the 1980s. As their economies became integrated into the global economy, production that could shift from the United States into India and China did. China and India's growth rates grew and the U.S. growth rate fell. Over the next 10 years, economic growth in India and China is likely to significantly outpace growth in most economies throughout the world, particularly industrialized countries in western Europe, the United States, and Japan.

Q-4 How does China's and India's integration into the global economy affect the prospect for U.S. growth?

What's different about China and India is their size; combined, they have a population of 2.6 billion, making their potential for growth significant. As they continue to develop into highly industrialized countries, the world economic landscape will change tremendously. Specifically, their development will likely place more and more pressures on U.S. firms in both services and manufacturing industries either to become more competitive by holding down wage increases and developing more efficient production methods, or moving their production facilities abroad. It will also be accompanied by greater demand for natural resources.

Business Cycles and Structural Stagnation

Even if the economy is on a steady long-run growth path, there are inevitably fluctuations around that trend. This phenomenon has given rise to the term *business cycle.* A **business cycle** is *a short-run, temporary upward or downward movement of economic activity, or real GDP, that occurs around the growth trend.* Figure 6-2 graphs the fluctuations in GDP for the U.S. economy since 1860.

A business cycle is the upward or downward movement of economic activity that occurs around the growth trend.

FIGURE 6-2 U.S. Business Cycles

Business cycles have always been a part of the U.S. economic scene. This figure suggests that until the downturn in 2008, fluctuations in economic output had become less severe since 1945.

Source: Historical Statistics of the United States, Colonial Times to 1970, and Bureau of Economic Analysis (www.bea.gov).

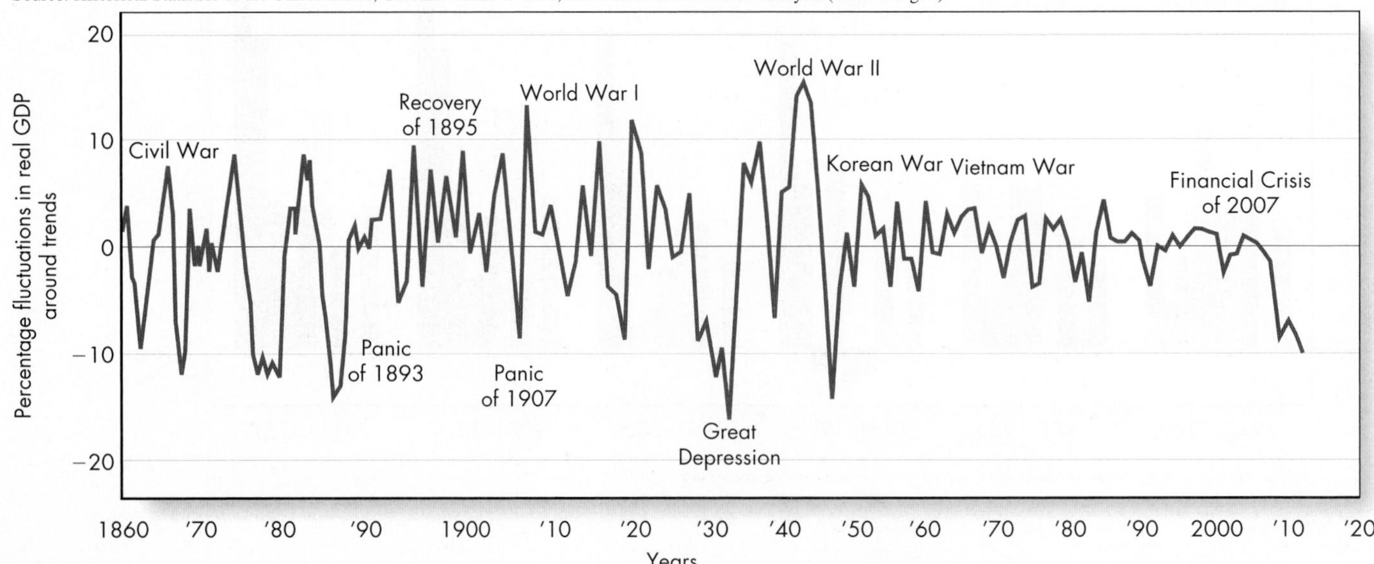

REAL-WORLD APPLICATION

NBER Dating of the Business Cycle

In December 2008, the six members of the NBER Business Cycle Dating Committee issued this statement:

> The NBER's Business Cycle Dating Committee has determined that a peak in business activity occurred in the U.S. economy in December 2007. The peak marks the end of an expansion that began in November 2001 and the beginning of a recession. The expansion lasted 73 months; the previous expansion of the 1990s lasted 120 months. A recession is a significant decline in economic activity spread across the economy, lasting more than a few months, normally visible in production, employment, real income, and other indicators.

NBER
National Bureau of Economic Research

Technically, an economy is in a recession only after it has been declared to be in a recession by a group of economists appointed by the National Bureau of Economic Research (NBER). Because real output is reported only quarterly and is sometimes revised substantially, the NBER Dating Committee looks at monthly data such as industrial production, employment, real income, sales, and sometimes even people's perceptions of what is happening in the economy to determine whether a recession has occurred. In 2001, for example, the committee announced that a recession had begun in March even though, according to preliminary GDP figures, real output had not fallen for two consecutive quarters. (Revised figures, which came out more than six months later, showed that GDP had actually started falling earlier and fell for three quarters.) The fact (1) that the NBER economists include many factors when determining a recession and (2) that they base their decision on preliminary data makes it difficult to provide an unambiguous definition of recession.

According to the NBER, the U.S. economy exited the recession in 2009, but the growth that followed was much slower than it had been in previous recessions. As of 2012, U.S. growth was far below what was considered normal, which is why this period is not seen as your normal recession, but rather a structural stagnation that may last for decades. When the expansion is as slow as it has been, the U.S. economy feels to many as if it is in an ongoing recession, regardless of what the NBER states.

As mentioned previously, until the late 1930s, economists—Classical economists—took such cycles as facts of life. They argued that the government should just accept that business cycles occur. Once the Depression hit, Keynesian economists argued that government could temper these economic fluctuations with policy actions. Which of these two views is correct is still a matter of debate.

The Phases of the Business Cycle

Much research has gone into measuring business cycles and setting official reference dates for the beginnings and ends of contractions and expansions. As a result of this research, business cycles have been divided into phases, and an explicit terminology has been developed. The National Bureau of Economic Research announces the government's official dates of contractions and expansions. In the postwar era (since mid-1945), the average business expansion has lasted about 59 months. A major expansion occurred from 1982 until mid-1990, when the U.S. economy fell into a recession. In mid-1991 it slowly came out of the recession and began the longest expansion in U.S. history, which ended in March 2001. The recession ended in November 2001 and the economy expanded until December 2007 when the economy entered a deep recession. While the economy began to expand in mid-2009, its growth has been very slow.

Business cycles have varying durations and intensities, but economists have developed a terminology to describe all business cycles and just about any place within a given business cycle. Since the press often uses this terminology, it is helpful to go over it. I do so in reference to Figure 6-3, which gives a visual representation of a business cycle.

Let's start at the top. The top of a cycle is called the *peak.* A *boom* is a very high peak, representing a big jump in output. (That's when the economy is doing great. Most everyone who wants a job has one.) Eventually an expansion peaks. (At least, in

FIGURE 6-3 Business Cycle Phases

Economists have many terms that describe the position of the economy on the business cycle. Some of them are given in this graph.

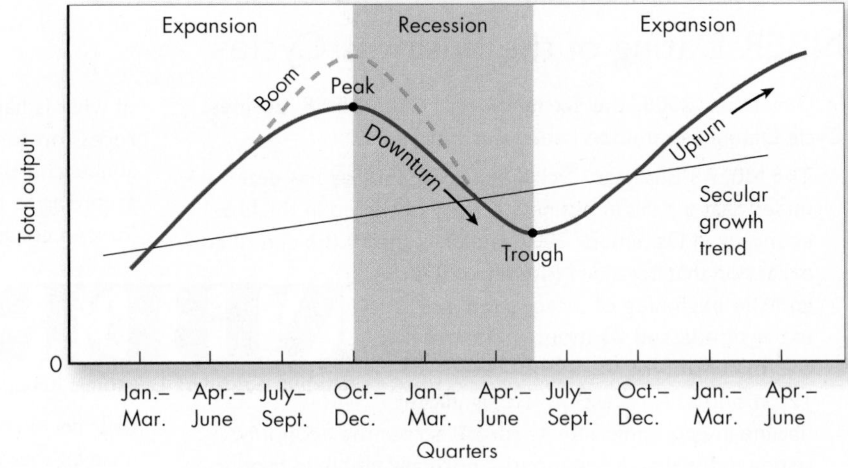

the past, they always have.) A *downturn* describes the phenomenon of economic activity starting to fall from a peak. In a recession the economy isn't doing so great and many people are unemployed. A **recession** is generally considered to be *a decline in real output that persists for more than two consecutive quarters of a year.* The actual definition of a recession is more ambiguous than this generally accepted definition, as the box "NBER Dating of the Business Cycle" points out.

Q-5 What are the four phases of the business cycle?

The bottom of a recession or depression is called the *trough.* As total output begins to expand, the economy comes out of the trough; economists say it's in an *upturn,* which may turn into an **expansion**—*an upturn that lasts at least two consecutive quarters of a year.* An expansion leads us back up to the peak. And so it goes. This terminology is important because if you're going to talk about the state of the economy, you need the words to do it. Why are businesses so interested in the state of the economy? They want to be able to predict whether it's going into a contraction or an expansion. Making the right prediction can determine whether the business will be profitable or not.

If prolonged contractions are a type of cold the economy catches, the Great Depression of the 1930s was double pneumonia.

The table below shows the duration and timing of business cycles since 1854 in the United States. The recession that began in December 2007 is the longest recession we

	Duration (in months)	
Business Cycles	**Pre–World War II (1854–1945)**	**Post–World War II (1945–2012)**
Number (trough to trough)	22	11
Average duration (trough to trough)	50	66
Length of longest cycle	99 (1870–79)	128 (1991–2001)
Length of shortest cycle	28 (1919–21)	28 (1980–82)
Average length of expansions	29	59
Length of shortest expansion	10 (1919–20)	12 (1980–81)
Length of longest expansion	80 (1938–45)	120 (1991–2001)
Average length of recessions	21	11
Length of shortest recession	7 (1918–19)	6 (1980)
Length of longest recession	65 (1873–79)	18 (2007–2009)

Source: National Bureau of Economic Research (http://nber.org) and *Survey of Current Business* (www.bea.doc.gov).

had since World War II. Although it technically ended in June 2009, there was considerable debate about whether it had actually ended because unemployment remained high and growth remained significantly below the long-term trend. As of 2013, there were few indications that the economy was returning to the long-run postwar growth path. That's why there has been a much greater focus in policy on whether the growth trend has slowed either permanently or temporarily.

Structural Stagnation

The very concept *business cycle* conveys a sense that a fall in output is going to reverse itself, while the concept *growth trend* conveys a sense that the current growth rate will continue. The concept "cycle" conveys a sense that a fluctuation is a short-term event that will reverse itself. In reality, we never know for sure whether a cyclical downturn is a cycle or a change in the growth trend. This leads us to a third term, *structural stagnation.* As we discussed earlier in the chapter, structural stagnation is a particular kind of downturn and is becoming an increasing part of the macroeconomic debate. It is a cyclical downturn that we do not expect to end any time soon without major changes to the structure of the economy. It is a short-term problem that extends into the long term.

Q-6 What is the difference between a business cycle and a structural stagnation?

In a structural stagnation, many of the unemployed cannot get a job at the pay they were getting or in the field where they worked. To get a job they have to accept a lower wage or learn new skills. Unemployment is not due to temporary layoffs as it is in a business cycle; it is due to longer-term changes. Structural stagnation might start as a business cycle but quickly turns into a stagnation with no expectation that it is ending, or even that the government has the ability to pull the economy out of it without running stimulus policies such as massive deficits that carry the risk of causing serious long-term problems for the economy. In a structural stagnation the economy is stuck in a rut, with no easy way to get out.

Until recently most macroeconomic policy discussions assumed that the modern economy would experience only business cycles. Structural stagnation was not discussed in conventional macro. But the events of 2007 challenged that view, and in the financial crisis of 2008 many economists worried that the economy was falling into a **depression**—*a deep and prolonged recession.* The massive policy response of the U.S. government and central bank can only be understood with that perspective. Specifically, in its policy to deal with the financial crisis the government wasn't trying to smooth a business cycle around a growth trend. It was trying to save the economy from falling into a depression. And many economists (including me) believed that the strong government policies did keep the recession from falling into a depression.

A depression is a deep and prolonged recession.

As you can see there is no formal line that indicates when a recession becomes a depression. This ambiguity has led to the joke: "When your neighbor is unemployed, it's a recession; when you're unemployed, it's a depression." If pushed for something more specific, I'd say that if unemployment exceeds 12 percent for more than a year, the economy is in a depression. Likewise there is no formal line that indicates when a business cycle becomes structural stagnation. Again, if push came to shove, I'd say that if the economy didn't return to its long-term growth rate within four years, the economy is experiencing structural stagnation. By that criterion, the United States is currently experiencing a structural stagnation, not a typical business cycle.

This distinction between a business cycle and structural stagnation goes to the heart of the modern macro policy debates. Optimistic macroeconomists see the current situation as a long and severe, but nonetheless normal, business cycle. At some point, with sufficient expansionary conventional macroeconomic policies, the economy will return to its historical long-term growth trend. Less optimistic macroeconomists (like me)

Q-7 Why is the distinction between a business cycle and structural stagnation important to policy?

see the current situation not as a business cycle but as a structural stagnation. They argue that the economy will not return to its historical long-run growth trend any time soon, and that continued attempts to jump start the economy with deficits that are unsustainable in the long run might improve the economy in the short run, but will undermine the economy in the long run. They claim that without politically difficult-to-implement government action that addresses the longer-run structural problems which put government finances in a sustainable position, unemployment will stay high and private output will stay low for the foreseeable future.

Now that we have explored business cycles, let's turn to the other major problem currently facing the United States economy—unemployment and jobs.

Unemployment and Jobs

The unemployment rate is the percentage of people in the economy who are both able to and looking for work but who cannot find jobs.

Both business cycles and growth are directly related to unemployment in the U.S. economy. Unemployment occurs when people are looking for a job and cannot find one. The **unemployment rate** is *the percentage of people in the economy who are both able to and looking for work but who cannot find jobs.* When an economy is growing and is in an expansion, unemployment is usually falling; when an economy is in a recession, unemployment is usually rising, although often with a lag.

The relationship between the business cycle and unemployment is obvious to most people, but often the seemingly obvious hides important insights. Just why are the business cycle and growth related to unemployment? True, aggregate income must fall in a recession, but, logically, unemployment need not result. A different possibility is that all people, on average, work fewer hours.

Unemployment has not always been a problem associated with business cycles. In preindustrial societies, households—from farms to cottage craftspeople—produced goods and services. The entire family contributed to farming, weaving, or blacksmithing. When times were good, the family enjoyed a higher level of income. When times weren't so good, they still worked, but accepted less income for the goods they produced. When economic activity fell, people's income earned per hour (their wage) fell. Low income was a problem; but since people didn't become unemployed, **cyclical unemployment** *(unemployment resulting from fluctuations in economic activity)* was not a problem.

Q-8 True or false? In a recession, structural unemployment is expected to rise.

While cyclical unemployment did not exist in preindustrial society, **structural unemployment** *(unemployment caused by the institutional structure of an economy or by economic restructuring making some skills obsolete)* did. For example, scribes in Europe had less work after the invention of the printing press in the 1400s. Some unemployment would likely result; that unemployment would be called *structural unemployment.* But structural unemployment wasn't much of a problem for government, or at least people did not consider it government's problem. The reason is that those in the family, or community, with income would share it with unemployed family members.

Whether we interpret the current unemployment problem in the United States as cyclical or structural depends on whether we believe the economy is in a structural stagnation or a conventional business cycle. If it is experiencing structural stagnation, the current unemployment problem facing the United States is in large part structural and will require structural changes to solve. In the conventional business cycle view the current unemployment problem is primarily cyclical; it will disappear as the economy comes out of the recession.

Unemployment as a Social Problem

Q-9 How did the Industrial Revolution create the possibility of cyclical unemployment?

The Industrial Revolution changed the nature of work and introduced unemployment as a problem for society. This is because the Industrial Revolution was accompanied by a shift to wage labor and to a division of responsibilities. Some individuals (capitalists) took on ownership of the means of production and *hired* others to work for them, paying them an hourly wage. This change in the nature of production marked a significant change in the nature of the unemployment problem.

First, it created the possibility of cyclical unemployment. With wages set at a certain level, when economic activity fell, workers' income per hour did not fall. Instead, factories would lay off or fire some workers. That isn't what happened on the farm; when a slack period occurred on the farm, the income per hour of all workers fell and few were laid off.

Second, the Industrial Revolution was accompanied by a change in how families dealt with unemployment. Whereas in preindustrial economies individuals or families took responsibility for their own slack periods, in a capitalist industrial society factory owners didn't take responsibility for their workers in slack periods. The pink slip (a common name for the notice workers get telling them they are laid off) and the problem of unemployment were born in the Industrial Revolution.

Without wage income, unemployed workers were in a pickle. They couldn't pay their rent, they couldn't eat, and they couldn't put clothes on their backs. What was previously a family problem became a social problem. Not surprisingly, it was at that time—the late 1700s—that economists began paying more attention to the problem of unemployment.

When economists initially recognized unemployment as a problem, economists and society still did not view it as a social problem. It was the individual's problem. If people were unemployed, it was their own fault; hunger, or at least the fear of hunger, and people's desire to maintain their lifestyle, would drive them to find other jobs relatively quickly. Early capitalism had an unemployment solution: the fear of hunger.

Unemployment as Government's Problem

As capitalism evolved, the fear-of-hunger solution to unemployment became less acceptable. The government developed social welfare programs such as unemployment insurance and assistance to the poor. In the Employment Act of 1946, the U.S. government specifically took responsibility for unemployment. The act assigned government the responsibility of creating *full employment,* an economic climate in which just about everyone who wants a job can have one. Government was responsible for offsetting cyclical fluctuations and thereby preventing cyclical unemployment, and somehow dealing with structural unemployment.

As capitalism evolved, capitalist societies no longer saw the fear of hunger as an acceptable answer to unemployment.

Initially government regarded 2 percent unemployment as a condition of full employment. The 2 percent was made up of **frictional unemployment** *(unemployment caused by people entering the job market and people quitting a job just long enough to look for and find another one)* and of a few "unemployables," such as alcoholics and drug addicts, along with a certain amount of necessary structural and seasonal unemployment resulting when the structure of the economy changed. Any unemployment higher than 2 percent was considered either unnecessary structural or cyclical unemployment and was now government's responsibility; frictional and necessary structural unemployment were still the individual's problem.

By the 1950s, government had given up its view that 2 percent unemployment was consistent with full employment. It raised its definition of full employment to 3 percent, then to 4 percent, then to 5 percent unemployment. In the 1970s and early 1980s, government raised it further, to 6.5 percent unemployment. At that point the term *full employment* fell out of favor (it's hard to call 6.5 percent unemployment "full employment"), and the terminology changed. The term I will use in this book is *target rate of unemployment,* although you should note that it is also sometimes called the *natural rate*

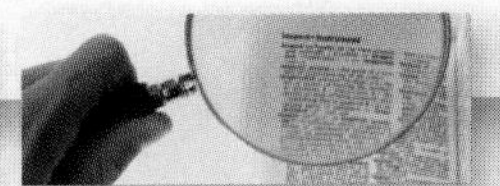

ADDED DIMENSION

From Full Employment to the Target Rate of Unemployment

As I emphasized in Chapter 1, good economists attempt to remain neutral and objective. It isn't always easy, especially since the language we use is often biased.

This problem has proved to be a difficult one for economists in their attempt to find an alternative to the concept of full employment. An early contender was the natural rate of unemployment. Economists have often used the word *natural* to describe economic concepts. For example, they've talked about "natural" rights and a "natural" rate of interest. The problem with this usage is that what's natural to one person isn't necessarily natural to another. The word *natural* often conveys a sense of "that's the way it should be." However, in describing as "natural" the rate of unemployment that an economy can achieve, economists weren't making any value judgments about whether 4.5–5 percent unemployment is what should, or should not, be. They simply were saying that, given the institutions in the economy, that is what is achievable. So a number of economists objected to the use of the word *natural.*

As an alternative, a number of economists started to use the term *nonaccelerating inflation rate of unemployment (NAIRU),* but even they agreed it was a horrendous term. And so many avoided using it and shifted to the relatively neutral term *target rate of unemployment.*

The target rate of unemployment is the rate that one believes is attainable without causing undesirable side effects. It is not determined theoretically; it is determined empirically. Economists look at what seems to be achievable and is historically normal, adjust that for structural and demographic changes they believe are occurring, and come up with the target rate of unemployment.

of unemployment or the *NAIRU* (the nonaccelerating inflation rate of unemployment). As discussed in the accompanying box, these terms are interchangeable. The **target rate of unemployment** is *the lowest sustainable rate of unemployment that policy makers believe is achievable given existing demographics and the economy's institutional structure.* After the downturn, their estimate of the target rate of unemployment rose.

Q-10 How is the target rate of unemployment related to potential output?

While cyclical unemployment is related to business cycles—when the economy is in a recession cyclical unemployment rises, and when the economy is in an expansion unemployment falls—the target rate of unemployment is the rate of unemployment that exists when the economy is at potential output. When potential output rises, the target rate of unemployment falls. Since the late 1980s the appropriate target rate of unemployment has been a matter of debate. Until the downturn of 2008, most economists placed it at somewhere around 5 percent unemployment.

Conclusion

As should be clear from the discussion in this chapter, macroeconomic theory and policy are far less settled than is microeconomic theory and policy. The reason is that macroeconomic problems involve all microeconomic problems plus more that relate to the complex interactions of the individuals in the economy—more than 320 million in the United States, and adding the rest of the world it's over 7 billion. The appropriate macro policy will depend on how the problems are framed; a short-run problem is quite different from a long-run problem. Conventional macroeconomics "solves" the problems by developing separate policies for the short run and for the long run. That makes the macroeconomic presentation to students relatively easy.

The problem comes when you don't know whether you are in the short run or the long run. Currently the economy seems to be in an "in between" run, and the policy advice is much messier and more diverse.

Summary

- Economists use two frameworks to analyze macroeconomic problems. The long-run growth framework focuses on supply, while the short-run business-cycle framework focuses on demand. *(LO6-1)*
- Classical economists focus on long run growth and use a laissez-faire approach. Keynesian economists focus on short-run fluctuations and use an activist government approach. *(LO6-1)*
- Modern conventional economics has been a blend of the Keynesian and Classical approaches. The problems the economy faces today do not fit either model. *(LO6-1)*
- Growth is measured by the change in total output over a long period of time and the change in per capita output. Per capita output is output divided by the population. *(LO6-2)*
- While the secular trend growth rate of the economy has been 2.5 to 3.5 percent, some expect it to fall. *(LO6-2)*
- Fluctuations of real output around the secular trend growth rate are called *business cycles.* *(LO6-3)*
- Phases of the business cycle include peak, trough, upturn, and downturn. *(LO6-3)*
- Structural stagnation is a cyclical downturn that is not expected to end any time soon without major changes to the structure of the economy. *(LO6-3)*
- Whether the economy is experiencing structural stagnation or a recession has significant implications for macroeconomic policy. Conventional macroeconomic policies can pull an economy out of a recession, but not out of a structural stagnation. *(LO6-3)*
- Cyclical unemployment goes up and down with the business cycle. Structural unemployment is caused by the institutional structure of an economy and economic restructuring. *(LO6-4)*
- The target rate of unemployment is the lowest sustainable rate of unemployment possible given existing institutions. It's associated with an economy's potential output. The higher an economy's potential output, the lower an economy's target rate of unemployment. *(LO6-4)*

Key Terms

business cycle *(130)*
Classical economists *(123)*
cyclical unemployment *(134)*
depression *(133)*
expansion *(132)*
frictional unemployment *(135)*
Keynesian economists *(124)*
macroeconomics *(122)*
per capita output *(129)*
potential output *(128)*
recession *(132)*
structural stagnation *(125)*
structural unemployment *(134)*
target rate of unemployment *(136)*
unemployment rate *(134)*

Questions and Exercises 

1. Classicals saw the depression as a political problem, not an economic problem. Why? *(LO6-1)*
2. Did Keynesian or Classical economics support laissez-faire policy? *(LO6-1)*
3. Would Keynesian or Classical economists be more likely to emphasize the fallacy of composition? *(LO6-1)*
4. As the problem of inflation grew in the 1970s, did Keynesian or Classical economics grow in importance? *(LO6-1)*
5. Is structural stagnation a Keynesian or a Classical theory? *(LO6-1)*
6. In what way is potential output not purely a physical measure based on the number of workers and existing factories? *(LO6-2)*
7. What are two ways in which long-term economic growth is measured? *(LO6-2)*
8. What has happened to growth rates in Western Europe and the United States in recent years? *(LO6-2)*

9. How does the U.S. per capita growth rate since 1940 compare to growth rates in other areas around the world? *(LO6-2)*
10. Draw a representative business cycle, and label each of the four phases. *(LO6-3)*
11. How does a structural stagnation differ from a recession? *(LO6-3)*
12. Which has the more pessimistic view of the problems facing the United States economy: structural stagnation theory or conventional business cycle theory? *(LO6-3)*
13. Distinguish between structural unemployment and cyclical unemployment. *(LO6-4)*
14. What type of unemployment is best studied within the long-run framework? *(LO6-4)*
15. What type of unemployment is best studied under the short-run framework? *(LO6-4)*

Questions from Alternative Perspectives

1. It is unfair, but true, that bad things happen. Unfortunately, to attempt to prevent unavoidable bad things can actually make things worse, not better. How might the above ideas be relevant to how society deals with business cycles? (Austrian)
2. Wesley Mitchell, a founder of Institutional economics, said that to understand the business cycle, a distinction must be made between making goods and making money. All societies make goods. In the modern money economy, those who control the production and distribution of goods will only allow economic activity to occur if they can "make money." He used this line of reasoning to conclude that what drives the business cycle are business expectations; production, and thus increased employment today, will only be allowed if business expects to sell those goods at a profit tomorrow. Is his proposition reasonable? Explain. (Institutionalist)
3. Since the Great Depression, the United States has been able to avoid severe economic downturns.
   a. What macroeconomic policies do you think have allowed us to avoid another Great Depression?
   b. Would you classify those policies as being Classical or Keynesian?
   c. Are such policies still relevant today? (Post-Keynesian)
4. The text presents the target rate of unemployment as being about 5 percent. William Vickrey, a Nobel Prize–winning economist, argued that the target unemployment rate should be seen as being between 1 percent and 2 percent. Only an unemployment rate that low, he argued, would produce genuine full employment that guaranteed job openings for all those looking for work. Achieving a low unemployment rate would, according to Vickrey, bring about "a major reduction in the illness of poverty, homelessness, sickness, and crime."
   a. What is the appropriate target unemployment rate?
   b. Explain your position.
   c. What policies would you recommend to counteract the human tragedy of unemployment? (Radical)
5. In natural science, when theories fail, as conventional macroeconomics failed in the financial crisis and its aftermath, they are overthrown and replaced by new theories. Why has it been so difficult to overthrow conventional macroeconomics? (All)

Issues to Ponder

1. In H. G. Wells's *Time Machine,* a late-Victorian time traveler arrives in England some time in the future to find a new race of people, the Eloi, in their idleness. Their idleness is, however, supported by another race, the Morlocks, underground slaves who produce the output. If technology were such that the Elois' lifestyle could be sustained by machines, not slaves, is it a lifestyle that would be desirable? What implications does the above discussion have for unemployment?
2. If unemployment fell to 1.2 percent in World War II, why couldn't it be reduced to 1.2 percent today?
3. In 1991, Japanese workers' average tenure with a firm was 10.9 years; in 1991 in the United States the average tenure of workers was 6.7 years.
   a. What are two possible explanations for these differences?
   b. Which system is better?
   c. In the mid-1990s, Japan experienced a recession while the United States' economy grew. What effect did this likely have on these ratios?

Answers to Margin Questions

1. A Classical economist takes a laissez-faire approach and believes the economy is self-regulating. A Keynesian economist takes an interventionist approach and believes that output can remain below what it is capable of producing. (*p. 124; LO6-1*)
2. The change in employment is both a long-run and a short-run issue. It is a short-run issue because when the U.S. economy is in a recession, employment tends to decline. It is a long-run issue because outsourcing is the result of changes in the institutional structure of the global economy caused by reduced trade barriers and reduced communications costs. (*p. 127; LO6-1*)
3. To calculate per capita output, divide real output ($15 trillion) by the total population (300 million). This equals $50,000. (*p. 129; LO6-2*)
4. The emergence of the Indian and Chinese economies as global competitors might lower U.S. growth in the coming decades because they present new competition to U.S. producers, who will have to adjust to global competition. (*p. 130; LO6-2*)
5. The four phases of the business cycle are the peak, the downturn, the trough, and the upturn. (*p. 132; LO6-3*)
6. In a business cycle, the economic downturn is followed by an upturn that returns the economy to its long-term growth rate. Structural stagnation begins as a cyclical downturn, but extends into a period of slow growth that is far below what is considered the economy's normal growth rate. (*p. 133; LO6-3*)
7. Conventional economic policies that address business cycles won't work if the economy is experiencing economic stagnation. (*p. 134; LO6-3*)
8. False. Structural unemployment is determined by the institutional structure of an economy, not fluctuations in economic activity. (*p. 134; LO6-4*)
9. Before the Industrial Revolution a cyclical downturn in the economy reduced income instead of reducing employment. (*p. 134; LO6-4*)
10. The target rate of unemployment is that rate achieved when actual output equals potential output. (*p. 134; LO6-4*)

chapter 7

Measuring the Aggregate Economy

> *The government is very keen on amassing statistics . . . They collect them, add them, raise them to the nth power, take the cube root and prepare wonderful diagrams. But you must never forget that every one of these figures comes in the first instance from the village watchman, who just puts down what he damn pleases.*
>
> —Sir Josiah Stamp
> (head of Britain's revenue department in the late 19th century)

After reading this chapter, you should be able to:

- **LO7-1** Calculate GDP using the expenditures and, value added approaches.
- **LO7-2** Calculate aggregate income and explain how it relates to aggregate production.
- **LO7-3** Distinguish real from nominal concepts.
- **LO7-4** Describe the limitations of using GDP and national income accounting.

If in the 1500s you wanted to know how to do card tricks, juggle, eat fire, and make coins dance, you could find out how in a book by Luigi Paciolli, a close friend of Leonardo da Vinci.[1] Paciolli also wrote a book on accounting, or what was then called double-entry bookkeeping, and that book has been called the greatest technological invention in Western civilization. I won't go that far, but I will say that accounting—the process of identifying, measuring, and communicating information to permit judgments and decisions by the users—is central to the workings of the modern economy. If you are going to understand the macro economy, you need to know the accounting system macroeconomists use. That's what we cover in this chapter. So while you won't learn how to eat fire here, you will see how the terminology developed in the last chapter fits together into a coherent whole.

The chapter is divided into three parts. The first part deals with the macroeconomic statistics you are likely to see in the newspaper, GDP and its components, and how those components are related through an aggregate accounting system. The second part distinguishes between real and nominal (or money) concepts, which are used to differentiate and compare the economy over time. The third part discusses some shortcomings of the accounting system.

---

[1]In case you're wondering, here's how Paciolli explained how to make a coin dance: "Take some magnetic powder and rub it on a quattrino [copper coin] before putting the coin in some vinegar. Then take a little bit of the magnetic powder between your thumb [and index finger] and tap the glass of water, where the coin is, and it will come up and go down . . . with your hand."

Aggregate Accounting

This 17th-century engraving, "The Money Lender," shows that careful bookkeeping and accounting have been around for a long time.

In the 1930s, it was impossible for macroeconomics to exist in the form we know it today because many concepts we now take for granted either had not yet been formulated or were so poorly formulated that it was useless to talk rigorously about them. This lack of terminology to describe the economy as a whole was consistent with the Classical economists' lack of interest in studying the aggregate economy in the 1930s; they preferred to focus on microeconomics.

With the advent of Keynesian macroeconomics in the mid-1930s, development of a terminology to describe the macroeconomy became crucial. Measurement is a necessary step toward rigor. A group of Keynesian economists set out to develop a terminology and to measure the concepts they defined so that people would have concrete terms to use when talking about macroeconomic problems. Their work (for which two of them, Simon Kuznets and Richard Stone, received the Nobel Prize) set up an *aggregate* accounting system—a set of rules and definitions for measuring economic activity in the economy as a whole. That aggregate accounting system often goes by the name *national income accounting.*

Aggregate accounting provides a way of measuring aggregate production, aggregate expenditures, and aggregate income. Each can be broken down into subaggregates; aggregate accounting defines the relationship among these subaggregates.

Calculating GDP

Gross domestic product (GDP) is the aggregate final output of residents and businesses in an economy in a one-year period.

The previous chapter talked about total output. Economists call total output gross domestic product (GDP). **Gross domestic product (GDP)** is *the total market value of all final goods and services produced in an economy in a one-year period.* GDP is probably the single most-used economic measure. When economists, journalists, and other analysts talk about the economy, they continually discuss GDP, how much it has increased or decreased, and what it's likely to do.

Aggregate final output (GDP) consists of millions of different services and products: apples, oranges, computers, haircuts, financial advice, and so on. To arrive at total output, somehow we've got to add them all together into a composite measure. Say we produced 7 oranges plus 6 apples plus 12 computers. We have not produced 25 comapplorgs. You can't add apples and oranges and computers. You can only add like things (things that are measured in the same units). For example, 2 apples + 4 apples = 6 apples. If we want to add unlike things, we must convert them into like things. We do that by multiplying each good by its *price.* Economists call this *weighting the importance of each good by its price.* For example, if you have 4 pigs and 4 horses and you price pigs at $200 each and horses at $400 each, the horses are weighted as being twice as important as the pigs.

Multiplying the quantity of each good by its market price changes the terms in which we discuss each good from a quantity of a specific product to a *value* measure of that good. For example, when we multiply 6 apples by their price, 25 cents each, we get $1.50; $1.50 is a value measure. Once all goods are expressed in that value measure, they can be added together.

Once all goods are expressed in a value measure, they can be added together.

Take the example of 7 oranges and 6 apples. (For simplicity let's forget the computers, haircuts, and financial advice.) If the oranges cost 50 cents each, their total value is $3.50; if the apples cost 25 cents each, their total value is $1.50. Their values are expressed in identical measures, so we can add them together. When we do so, we don't get 13 orples; we get $5 worth of apples and oranges.

If we follow that same procedure with all the final goods and services produced in the economy in the entire year, multiplying the quantity produced by the market price per unit, we have all the goods and services an economy has produced expressed in units of value. If we then add up all these units of value, we have that year's gross domestic product.

The Components of GDP

Web Note 7.1
GDP Data

Since anything produced will be bought by someone, we can measure output by the expenditure people make to buy that output. On the expenditure side, GDP is usually divided into four categories depending on who buys the output. The four expenditure categories that comprise GDP are consumption, investment, government spending, and net exports.

Consumption is *spending by households on goods and services.* Consumption includes such things as food, shampoo, televisions, furniture, and the services of doctors and lawyers. This is the production in the economy that consumers buy. When you buy a DVD, you are contributing to consumption expenditures.

Investment is *spending for the purpose of additional production.* Investment includes business spending on factories and equipment for production, the change in business inventories, and purchases by households of new owner-occupied houses. Investment is output that is used to produce goods and services in the future. You should take note that when economists speak of investment as they discuss aggregate accounting, they don't mean the kind of activity taking place when individuals buy stocks rather than consume goods—economists call such activity *saving*. So in economists' terminology when you buy a bond or stock rather than consuming, you are saving. When that savings is borrowed by businesses to buy factories, tractors, computers, or other goods or services that will increase their output, they are *investing*. The amount they spend on goods that will increase future output is what in aggregate accounting is called *investment.*

You might have been surprised to see the change in inventories and residential construction included in investment. Inventories are goods that have been produced, so they must be counted if one is going to include all produced goods, which is what GDP is designed to include; inventories represent goods to be sold in the future. They are a type of investment by the firm. Residential construction is part of investment because most of the housing services from a new house will be provided in the future, not the present.

Government spending is *goods and services that government buys.* When the government buys the services of an analyst, or buys equipment for its space program, it is undertaking economic activity. These activities are classified as government expenditures. In thinking about government expenditures, you should note that they include expenditures that involve production. Although government generally does not sell its "production" but provides it free, aggregate accounting rules count government production at the government's cost of providing that output.

Many government payments do not involve production, so the government's budget is much larger than government spending included in GDP. The most important category of government spending that is not included in GDP is **transfer payments**—*payments to individuals that do not involve production by those individuals.* Transfer payments include Social Security payments and unemployment insurance among others. These payments are not part of GDP since there is no production associated with them.

Net exports is *spending on goods and services produced in the United States that foreigners buy (exports) minus goods and services produced abroad that U.S. citizens buy (imports).* (In economics and business, the word "net" is used to distinguish two offsetting flows: exports, which represent a spending flow into the country, and imports, which represent a spending flow out of the country.) The reason we have to use the "net concept" for exports is that GDP measures production *within* the geographic borders of a country. Because exports represent spending by foreigners for goods and services produced within the United States, exports are added. But because imports represent spending on goods and services produced outside the United States, they are subtracted. Our interest is in net spending so it is with the difference between imports and exports.

Summarizing: GDP measures aggregate final production taking place in a country. This production can be subdivided into expenditure categories, and all production must fit into one of the four categories. A shorthand way of expressing this division of GDP into expenditure categories is:

GDP = Consumption + Investment + Government spending + Net exports

or

$$\text{GDP} = C + I + G + (X - M)$$

Since all production is categorized into one or another of these four divisions, by adding up these four categories, we get total production of U.S. goods and services. Table 7-1 gives the breakdown of GDP by expenditure category for selected countries. Notice that, in all countries, consumption expenditures is the largest component of production.

Q-1 Calculate GDP with the information below:

Consumption = 60
Investment = 20
Government spending = 20
Exports = 10
Imports = 15

Two Things to Remember about GDP

In thinking about GDP, it is important to remember that (1) GDP represents a flow (an amount per year), not a stock (an amount at a particular moment of time); and (2) GDP refers to the market value of *final* output. Let's consider these statements separately.

Two important aspects to remember about GDP are:

1. GDP represents a flow.
2. GDP represents the market value of final output.

GDP Is a Flow Concept Say a student just out of college tells you she earns \$8,000. You'd probably think, "Wow! She's got a low-paying job!" That's because you implicitly assume she means \$8,000 per year. If you later learned that she earns \$8,000

TABLE 7-1 Expenditure Breakdown of GDP for Selected Countries

Country	GDP (U.S. \$ in billions)	=	Consumption (% of GDP)	+	Investment (% of GDP)	+	Government Spending (% of GDP)	+	Exports (% of GDP)	−	Imports (−% of GDP)
United States	\$15,076		\$10,729		\$1,855		\$3,060		\$2,094		−\$2,662
			71%		12%		20%		14%		−18%
Belgium	425		53		24		21		85		−83
Czech Republic	275		50		24		21		75		−71
Germany	3,205		57		18		20		50		−45
Japan	4,326		59		20		20		15		−14
Mexico	1,645		66		24		12		30		−32
Poland	814		61		20		18		45		−44

Note: Percentages may not sum to 100 due to rounding. Values are for 2011, purchasing power parity for 2011, except Japan and Mexico (2010).
Source: OECED National Income Accounts. stats.oeced.org

TABLE 7-2 U.S. National Wealth Accounts in 2012 (net worth)

		Dollars (in trillions)		Percentage of Component	
Household and nonprofit net worth	$62.9				125%
Tangible wealth		$23.8			
Owner-occupied real estate			$18.6	30	
Consumer durables			4.8	8	
Other			0.4	0	
Financial wealth		39.1			
Corporate equities			9.3	15	
Noncorporate equities			13.4	21	
Other (pension reserves, life insurance, etc.)			16.4	26	
Government net financial assets	−12.5				−25
Federal		−11.3		−22	
State and local		−1.2		−2	
Total net worth	50.4			100	

Source: *Flow of Funds Accounts,* Board of Governors, Federal Reserve (www.federalreserve.gov). The value of the government's financial liabilities is greater than the value of its financial assets, which is why it shows up as a negative percentage.

per week, you'd quickly change your mind. The confusion occurred because how much you earn is a flow concept; it has meaning only when a time period is associated with it: so much per week, per month, per year. A stock concept is an amount at a given point in time. No time interval is associated with it. Your weight is a stock concept. You weigh 150 pounds; you don't weigh 150 pounds per week.

GDP is a flow concept, the amount of total final output a country produces per year. The *per year* is often left unstated, but is essential. GDP is usually reported quarterly (every three months), but it is reported on an *annualized basis,* meaning the U.S. Department of Commerce, which compiles GDP figures, uses quarterly figures to estimate total output for the whole year.

The store of wealth, in contrast, is a stock concept. The stock equivalent to national income accounts is the **wealth accounts**—*a balance sheet of an economy's stock of assets and liabilities.* Table 7-2 shows a summary account of U.S. net worth from the wealth accounts for the United States in 2012. These are stock measures; they exist at a moment of time. For example, on March 31, 2012, the accounting date for these accounts, U.S. household and nonprofit net worth was $62.9 trillion.

GDP Measures Final Output As a student in my first economics class, I was asked how to calculate GDP. I said, "Add up the value of the goods and services produced by all the companies in the United States to arrive at GDP." I was wrong (which is why I remember it). Many goods produced by one firm are sold to other firms, which use those goods to make other goods. GDP doesn't measure total transactions in an economy; it measures **final output**—*goods and services purchased for their final use.* When one firm sells products to another firm for use in the production of yet another good, the first firm's products aren't considered final output. They're **intermediate products**—*products used as input in the production of some other product.* To count intermediate goods as well as final goods as part of GDP would be to double count them. An example of an intermediate good would be wheat sold to a cereal company. If we counted both the wheat (the intermediate good) and the cereal

GDP doesn't measure total transactions in an economy; it measures final output.

(the final good) made from that wheat, the wheat would be double counted. Double counting would significantly overestimate final output.

If we did not eliminate intermediate goods, a change in organization would look like a change in output. Say a firm that produced steel merged with a firm that produced cars. Together they produce exactly what each did separately before the merger. Final output hasn't changed, nor has intermediate output. The only difference is that the intermediate output of steel is now internal to the firm. Using only each firm's sales of goods to final consumers (and not sales to other firms) as the measure of GDP means that changes in organization do not affect the measure of output.

TWO WAYS OF ELIMINATING INTERMEDIATE GOODS There are two ways to eliminate intermediate goods from the measure of GDP. One way is to calculate the final sales that make up GDP directly, either by measuring the expenditures on the products by final users or by measuring production specifically for final users. A second way to eliminate double counting is to follow the value added approach. **Value added** is *the increase in value that a firm contributes to a product or service.* It is calculated by subtracting intermediate goods (the cost of materials that a firm uses to produce a good or service) from the value of its sales. For instance, if a firm buys $100 worth of thread and $10,000 worth of cloth and uses them in making a thousand pairs of jeans that are sold for $20,000, the firm's value added is not $20,000; it is $9,900 ($20,000 in sales minus the $10,100 in intermediate goods that the firm bought).

To avoid double counting, you must eliminate intermediate goods, either by calculating only final output (expenditures approach) or by using the value-added approach.

The table below provides another example.

Participants	I Cost of Materials	II Value of Sales	III Value Added	Row
Farmer	$ 0	$ 100	$100	1
Cone factory and ice cream maker	100	250	150	2
Middleperson (final sales)	250	400	150	3
Vendor	400	500	100	4
Totals	$750	$1,250	$500	5

It gives the cost of materials (intermediate goods) and the value of sales in the following scenario: Say we want to measure the contribution to GDP made by ice cream production of 200 ice cream cones at $2.50 each for total sales of $500. The vendor bought his cones and ice cream at a cost of $400 from a middleperson, who in turn paid the cone factory and ice cream maker a total of $250. The farmer who sold the cream to the factory got $100. Adding up all these transactions, we get $1,250, but that includes intermediate goods. Either by counting only the final value of the vendor's sales, $500, or by adding the value added at each stage of production (column III), we eliminate intermediate sales and arrive at the contribution of ice cream production to GDP of $500.

Value added is calculated by subtracting the cost of materials from the value of sales at each stage of production. The aggregate value added at each stage of production is, by definition, precisely equal to the value of final sales, since it excludes all intermediate products. In the table illustrating our example, the equality of the value added approach and the final sales approach can be seen by comparing the vendor's final sales of $500 (row 4, column II) with the $500 value added (row 5, column III).

Calculating GDP: Some Examples

To make sure you understand what value added is and what makes up GDP, let's consider some sample transactions and determine what value they add and whether they should be included in GDP. Let's first consider secondhand sales: When you sell your two-year-old car, how much value has been added? The answer is none. The sale involves no current output, so there's no value added. If, however, you sold the car to a used-car dealer for $2,000 and he or she resold it for $2,500, $500 of value has been added—the used-car dealer's efforts transferred the car from someone who didn't want it to someone who did. I point this out to remind you that GDP is not only a measure of the production of goods; it is a measure of the production of goods *and services.*

Q-2 If a used-car dealer buys a car for $2,000 and resells it for $2,500, how much has been added to GDP?

Now let's consider a financial transaction. Say you sell a bond (with a face value of $1,000) that you bought last year. You sell it for $1,250 and pay $100 commission to the dealer through whom you sell it. What value is added to final output? You might be tempted to say that $250 of value has been added, since the value of the bond has increased by $250. GDP, however, refers only to value that is added as the result of production or services, not to changes in the values of financial assets. Therefore, the price at which you buy or sell the bond is irrelevant to the question at hand. The only value that is added by the sale is the transfer of that bond from someone who doesn't want it to someone who does. Thus, the only value added as a result of economic activity is the dealer's commission, $100. The remaining $1,150 (the $1,250 you got from the bond minus the $100 commission you paid) is a transfer of an asset from one individual to another, but such transfers do not enter into GDP calculations. Only production of goods and services enters into GDP.

Let's consider a different type of financial transaction: The federal government pays an individual Social Security benefits. What value is added? Clearly no production has taken place, but money has been transferred. As in the case of the bond, only the cost of transferring it—not the amount that gets transferred—is included in GDP. This is accomplished by including in GDP government expenditures on goods and services, but not the value of government transfer payments. Thus, Social Security payments, welfare payments, and veterans' benefits do not enter into calculations of GDP. That's why the federal government can have a $3.6 trillion budget but only $1.2 trillion ($3.6 trillion minus $2.4 trillion of transfer payments) is included in GDP.

Q-3 How can the federal government have a $3.6 trillion budget but only have $1.2 trillion of that included in GDP?

Finally, let's consider the work of a housespouse. (See the box "Is GDP Biased against Women?" for further discussion of this issue.) How much value does it add to economic activity in a year? Clearly if the housespouse is any good at what he or she does, a lot of value is added. Taking care of the house and children is hard work. Estimates of the yearly value of a housespouse's services range from $35,000 to $130,000, and some estimate that including housework in the national accounts would raise GDP more than 50 percent. Even though much value is added and hence, in principle, house-spouse services should be part of GDP, by convention a housespouse contributes nothing to GDP. GDP measures only *market activities;* since housespouses are not paid, their value added is not included in GDP. This leads to some problems in measurement. For example, suppose a woman divorces her housespouse and then hires him to continue cleaning her house for $20,000 per year. That $20,000 value added, since it is now a market transaction, is included in GDP.

To arrive at the aggregate accounts, numerous decisions about how to handle various types of transactions have to be made to get a workable measure.

The housespouse example shows one of the problems with GDP. It also has other problems, but these are best left for intermediate courses. What's important for an introductory economics student to remember is that numerous decisions about how to handle various types of transactions had to be made to get a workable measure.

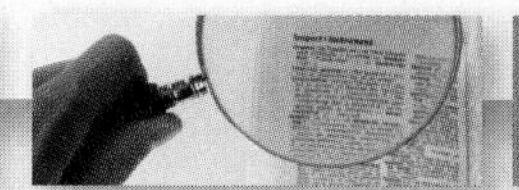

ADDED DIMENSION

Is GDP Biased against Women?

Although in the example in the book the housespouse is a man, the reality is that most housespouses are women. The fact that GDP doesn't include the work of housespouses is seen, by some, as a type of discrimination against women who work without pay at home since their work is not counted as part of the domestic product. One answer for why it is not counted is that housework does not involve a market transaction and hence could not be measured. That makes some sense, but it does not explain why the services houses provide to homeowners are estimated and included in GDP. Why can't housework also be estimated?

The answer is that it can be estimated, and my suspicion is that not including housespouses' services in GDP does represent the latent discrimination against women that was built into the culture in the 1930s when national income accounting was first developed. That latent discrimination against women was so deep that it wasn't even noticed. Anyone who has seen the movie *Rosie the Riveter,* which shows government programs to get women out from wartime employment and back into their role in the home, will have a good sense of the cultural views of people in the mid-1900s and earlier.

In thinking about whether GDP is biased against women, it is important to remember that the concepts we use are culturally determined and, over time, as cultural views change, the concepts no longer match our changed views. There is no escaping the fact that language is value-loaded. But so, too, is our attempt to point out the values in language. There are many other ways in which GDP reflects arbitrary choices and discrimination against groups. The major discussion of the fact that latent discrimination against women is embodied in GDP accounting itself reflects our current values, just as not including housespouses' work reflected earlier values.

Some Complications

The above presentation of aggregate accounting makes it look as if measuring aggregate output is quite simple—just measure consumption, investment, government spending, and net exports. Add them together and you have GDP. Conceptually, it is that simple, but, in practice, complicated conceptual decisions and accounting adjustments have to be made to ensure that all final production is included and that no double counting takes place. This leads to complicated accounting rules and alternative measures to account for different methods of measuring different concepts. Let me briefly introduce you to two of them.

Gross and Net Concepts Notice that we use the term *gross* domestic product or GDP. Gross does not mean disgusting; it is a technical accounting term that distinguishes a concept that has not been adjusted for an offsetting flow. (Remember we used the term "net" in our discussion of the export component of GDP to distinguish a concept that is adjusted for an offsetting flow.) The complication is that during the production process, the machines and equipment wear out or simply become technologically obsolete. Economists call this wearing out process **depreciation**—*the decrease in an asset's value.* Depreciation is part of the cost of producing a good; it is the amount by which plants and equipment decrease in value as they grow older. Much of each year's investment involves expenditures to replace assets that have worn out. For example, as you drive your car, it wears out. A car with 80,000 miles on it is worth less than the same type of car with only 1,000 miles on it. The difference in value is attributed to depreciation.

Depreciation is the decrease in an asset's value over a specified time period. It is the difference between gross and net investment.

Because some production is used to replace worn-out plant and equipment (depreciation), this production is not available for purchase. To account for this, economists have created another aggregate term that adjusts for depreciation. That term is *net domestic product.* **Net domestic product (NDP)** is *GDP less depreciation:*

NDP = GDP − Depreciation

NDP = GDP − Depreciation

Because depreciation affects capital available for production, depreciation shows up in the investment category of expenditures. Specifically, investment we have talked about so far is gross investment; **net investment** is *gross investment less depreciation*.

NDP takes depreciation into account. Since we want to measure output available for purchase, NDP is actually preferable to GDP as the expression of a country's domestic output. However, measuring true depreciation (the actual decrease in an asset's value) is difficult because asset values fluctuate. In fact, it's so difficult that, in the real world, accountants don't try to measure true depreciation, but instead use a number of conventional rules of thumb. In recognition of this reality, economists call the adjustment made to GDP to arrive at NDP the *capital consumption allowance* rather than *depreciation.* Since estimating depreciation is difficult, GDP rather than NDP is generally used in discussions of aggregate output.

National and Domestic Concepts A second complication of measuring aggregate output is whether the aggregate output that one is referring to is output produced within the borders of the country, or by the citizens and firms of the country.

Until 1992, the United States (unlike the rest of the world) used an accounting measure that focused on output produced by its firms and citizens. This was called *gross national product.* As economic issues have become global, aggregate accounting has been affected. In 1992, the United States followed the rest of the world and switched to gross domestic product as its primary measure of aggregate output.

Whereas gross domestic product measures the economic activity that occurs within the geographic borders of a country, the economic activity of the citizens and businesses of a country is measured by **gross national product (GNP)**—*the aggregate final output of citizens and businesses of an economy in a one-year period.* So the economic activity of U.S. citizens working abroad is counted in U.S. GNP but isn't counted in U.S. GDP. Similarly for the foreign economic activity of U.S. companies. However, the production of a Mexican or German person or business working in the United States isn't counted in U.S. GNP but is counted in U.S. GDP. Thus, GDP describes the economic output within the physical borders of a country while GNP describes the economic output produced by the citizens of a country. To move from GDP to GNP we must add *net foreign factor income* to GDP. (That income reflects output of equal value.) **Net foreign factor income** is defined as *the income from foreign domestic factor sources minus foreign factor income earned domestically.* Put another way, we must add the foreign income of our citizens and subtract the income of residents who are not citizens:

GDP is output produced within a country's borders; GNP is output produced by a country's citizens.

GNP = GDP + Net foreign factor income

Q-4 Which is higher: Kuwait's GDP or its GNP? Why?

For many countries there's a significant difference between GNP and GDP. For example, consider Kuwait. Its citizens and companies have significant foreign income—income that far exceeds the income of the foreigners in Kuwait. This means that Kuwait's GNP (the output of its citizens) far exceeds its GDP (the output produced in Kuwait). For the United States, however, foreign output of U.S. businesses and people for the most part offsets the output of foreign businesses and people within the United States. Kuwait's net foreign factor income has been large and positive, while that of the United States has been minimal. Most discussions today focus on GDP since it is the primary measure presented in government statistics, but it is important to know GNP since aggregate income is normally measured on a national basis.

Calculating Aggregate Income

Aggregate accounting also calculates the aggregate income—the total income earned by citizens and firms of a country. This aggregate income is divided into the following four categories:

Compensation of Employees Employee compensation (the largest component of national income) consists of wages and salaries paid to individuals, along with fringe benefits and government taxes for Social Security and unemployment insurance.

Rents Rents are the income from property received by households. Rents received by firms are not included because a firm's rents are simply another source of income to the firm and hence are classified as profits. In most years, the rent component of national income is small since the depreciation owners take on buildings is close to the income they earn from those buildings.

Interest Interest is the income private businesses pay to households that have lent the businesses money, generally by purchasing bonds issued by the businesses. (Interest received by firms doesn't show up in this category for the same reason that rents received by firms don't show up in the *rent* category.) Interest payments by government and households aren't included in national income since by convention they're assumed not to flow from the production of goods and services.

Profits Profits are the amount that is left after compensation to employees, rents, and interest have been paid out. (The national income accounts use accounting profits that must be distinguished from economic profits, which are calculated on the basis of opportunity costs.)

Table 7-3 shows these components for the United States and selected countries. It lists the aggregate income of countries and the components in absolute amounts and in percentages for the United States and in percentages for the remaining countries. As you can see, in all countries compensation of employees is the largest component of national income followed by profits. (One final word of caution: In each country statistics are collected using slightly different methods. This makes international comparison difficult.)

Q-5 Calculate aggregate income with the information below:

Employee compensation = 140

Rents = 4

Interest = 12

Profits = 42

TABLE 7-3 Aggregate Income Breakdown for Selected Countries

(1) Country	(2) Aggregate Income (billions of $)	=	(3) Employee Compensation (% of total)	+	(4) Rents (% of total)	+	(5) Interest (% of total)	+	(6) Profits (% of total)
United States	$13,359		70%		3%		4%		23%
Japan	5,628		73		2		2		23
Germany	3,319		73		2		6		19
United Kingdom	2,262		62		4		3		30
Canada	1,550		68		8		6		18
Sweden	471		64		4		13		19

Note: Aggregate income in this table does not equal GDP in Table 7-1 because of statistical and conceptual adjustments. Percentages may not sum to 100 due to rounding. Data for the United States are for 2011. Most recent year available for all others.

Source: National Accounts, OECD, and individual country home pages.

Equality of Aggregate Income and Aggregate Production

Now that I have defined both aggregate output and aggregate income, let's consider how aggregate output and aggregate income are, by definition, always equal within the accounting framework. Accounting systems use double-entry bookkeeping,which requires that the opposite sides of the accounting ledger equal each other. For that to happen the components on each side have to be defined so that a component on one side mirrors a component on the other. Accounting thus provides a framework for thinking about the aggregate economy. This is the case with aggregate income accounting. By definition, whenever a good or service is produced (output) and purchased (expenditure), somebody receives an income for producing it. These definitions mean that aggregate income equals aggregate production. The relationship between the two can be expressed in the following identity:[2]

By definition aggregate income equals aggregate production.

Aggregate income $\equiv$ Aggregate production

In establishing this identity, many accounting decisions need to be made to ensure complete equality. For example, since production figures are collected on a domestic basis (measuring what is produced in the geographic confines of the United States) while income figures are collected on a national basis (measuring what citizens and firms of the United States earn), adjustments are needed to equalize them. Similarly, taxes placed on corporations have to be accounted for to ensure that they are treated in a way that will maintain the equality. There are many more decisions, but at this introductory level, they are best left alone, so that the main point—that aggregate income—the value of the employee compensation, rents, interest, and profits—equals aggregate production—the value of goods produced—doesn't get lost in the complications.

Profit is a residual that makes the income side equal the expenditure side.

How are these values kept exactly equal? The definition of profit is the key to the equality. Recall that *profit* is defined as what remains after all the firm's other income (employee compensation, rent, and interest) is paid out. For example, say a firm has a total output of \$800 and that it paid \$400 in wages, \$200 in rent, and \$100 in interest. The firm's profit is total output less these payments. Profit equals \$800 − \$700 = \$100.

The accounting identity works even if a firm incurs a loss. Say that instead of paying \$400 in wages, the firm paid \$700, along with its other payments of \$200 in rent and \$100 in interest. Total output is still \$800, but total payments are \$1,000. Profits, still defined as total output minus payments, are negative: \$800 − \$1,000 = −\$200. There's a loss of \$200. Adding that loss to other income [\$1,000 + (−\$200)] gives total income of \$800—which is identical to the firm's total output of \$800. It is no surprise that total output and total income, defined in this way, are equal.

The aggregate accounting identity (Total output = Total income) allows us to calculate GDP either by adding up all values of final outputs through the expenditures and value-added methods, or by adding up the values of all earnings or income.

Adjusting for Global Dimensions of Production

When the aggregate accounting system was developed, international flows were not a central consideration for U.S. economic policy. But as globalization has expanded, international flows have become increasingly important. One of the most important issues has been net exports—a component of aggregate expenditures discussed earlier. Net exports, you will (I hope) remember, is the difference between foreign demand for U.S. goods and services and U.S. demand for foreign goods and services. This difference

[2]An *identity* is a statement of equality that's true by definition. In algebra, an identity is sometimes written as a triple equal sign ($\equiv$). It is more equal than simply equal. How something can be more equal than equal is beyond me, too, but I'm no mathematician.

is also called the *balance of trade,* and in recent years, the United States has been running large balance of trade deficits. So imports of goods and services have greatly exceeded exports of goods and services.

When there is a trade deficit, a portion of expenditures by U.S. citizens is paid to foreign producers and therefore is not spent on U.S. production.

Q-6 True or false? Total expenditures as measured in the national accounts are for domestic production because expenditures include net exports. Explain your answer.

A trade deficit should, in principle, bring about structural adjustments to the economy through falling exchange rates, decreased production costs, or improvements in productivity. But when that doesn't happen, the economy's potential output—the amount an economy is capable of sustainably producing without causing structural problems—can be pushed down by the trade deficit.

Distinguishing the Real from the Nominal

The GDP concept is often used to compare one year's output with another's. But doing so raises a problem: What happens if GDP doubles, but the prices of all goods double as well? Are we better off? The answer is no, we are simply paying higher prices for the same amount of goods. Over time this can make a large difference. For example, compare U.S. GDP in 1932 ($58 billion) to GDP in 2012 ($16 trillion). Would it be correct to conclude the economy had grown 275 times larger? Again, the answer is no because prices have gone up. To compare how much actual or real production has risen over time, economists distinguish between increases in GDP due to inflation and increases in GDP that represent real increases in production and income. In other words, they adjust figures for inflation using price indexes. I will talk more about price indexes in the inflation chapter. Here I will concentrate on one of the most important of these indexes—the GDP deflator.

Real GDP, Nominal GDP, and Price Indexes

So far we've been talking about **nominal GDP**—*the amount of goods and services produced measured at current prices.* This measure won't tell you whether the amount of goods produced has risen from one year to the next. For that, we need a real measure. As we saw in the previous chapter, economists use the term *real* when talking about concepts that are adjusted for **inflation**—*a continual rise in the price level.* **Real GDP** is the *total amount of goods and services produced, adjusted for price-level changes.* It is the measure of output that would exist if the price level had remained constant. For example, say GDP rises from $8 trillion to $10 trillion. Nominal GDP has risen by:

"Real" means "adjusted for inflation".

$$\frac{\$10\text{ trillion} - \$8\text{ trillion}}{\$8\text{ trillion}} = \frac{\$2\text{ trillion}}{\$8\text{ trillion}} \times 100 = 25\%$$

Let's say, however, the price level has risen 20 percent, from 100 percent to 120 percent. That is, the **GDP deflator**—*the average price of all components of total output expressed relative to comparison year prices set at 100*—is 120. The GDP deflator is a type of **price index**—*a measure of the composite price of a specified group of goods.* Price indexes are used to measure changes in price levels over time. In macroeconomics, the greatest use of price indexes is to measure the price of all or most produced goods and services. A change in such a price index is a measure of inflation. So the GDP deflator is a price index that is used to determine the rate of inflation in the economy.

In our example because the GDP deflator has increased, real output (nominal output adjusted for inflation) hasn't risen by 25 percent; it has risen by less than the increase in nominal output. To determine how much less, we use a formula to adjust the nominal figures to account for inflation. This is called *deflating* the nominal figures. To deflate we divide the most recent nominal figure, \$10 trillion, by the GDP deflator of 120 and multiply by 100. Real GDP is:

$$\text{Real GDP} = \frac{\$10\text{ trillion}}{120} \times 100 = \$8.3\text{ trillion}$$

That \$8.3 trillion is the measure of GDP that would have existed if the price level had not changed, that is, the measure of real GDP. While nominal GDP rose by \$2 trillion, from \$8 trillion to \$10 trillion, real GDP increased from \$8 trillion to \$8.3 trillion, or by \$300 billion.

Stated in more general terms, to calculate real GDP, we have:

Q-7 Nominal output has increased from \$10 trillion to \$12 trillion. The GDP deflator has risen by 15 percent. By how much has real output risen?

$$\text{Real GDP} = \frac{\text{Nominal GDP}}{\text{GDP deflator}} \times 100$$

Rearranging terms, we can also provide a formula for calculating the GDP deflator:

$$\text{GDP deflator} = \frac{\text{Nominal GDP}}{\text{Real GDP}} \times 100$$

To move from GDP deflators to the rate of inflation, you calculate the change in the deflator from one year to another, divide the change in the deflator by the initial year's deflator, and multiply by 100. For example, if the initial deflator is 101 and the current deflator is 103, divide the difference, 2, by the initial deflator, 101, and multiply by 100. Doing so gives an inflation rate of 1.98 percent:

$$\text{Inflation} = \frac{103 - 101}{101} \times 100 = 1.98$$

For numbers close to 100, simply subtracting the two deflators ($103 - 101 = 2$) provides a reasonably good approximation to the rate of inflation.

The percentage change, or growth rate, of nominal and real GDP can be calculated by the same method; you calculate the difference between the figures for the two years, divide that difference by the initial year figure, and multiply by 100. For example, if GDP rises from \$13 trillion to \$13.2 trillion, the difference is \$200 billion. Dividing that by the initial year's GDP, \$13 billion, and multiplying by 100 gives you a growth rate of 3.3 percent.

The growth rates of real GDP, nominal GDP, and inflation are related. Specifically:

% change in real GDP = % change in nominal GDP − Inflation

$$\%\text{ change in real GDP} = \%\text{ change in nominal GDP} - \text{Inflation}$$

Doing that subtraction is what economists mean when they say that real GDP is equal to nominal GDP adjusted for inflation. We can see these relationships in the table below, which lists nominal GDP, the GDP deflator, and real GDP for recent years and their percentage changes from the previous year.

	Nominal GDP	GDP Deflator	Real GDP
2009 level in billions	\$13,938	109.5	\$12,729
2010 level in billions	\$14,499	111.0	\$13,062
% change from '09 to '10	4.0	1.2	3.0
2011 level in billions	\$15,075	113.4	\$13,294
% change from '10 to '11	4.0	2.2	1.8

Notice that you can arrive at the growth rate in real GDP by subtracting inflation from the percentage change in nominal GDP. For example, in 2011 real GDP rose by 1.8 percent, which equals the growth of nominal GDP, 4.0 percent, minus inflation of 2.2 percent.

Real GDP is what is important to a society because it measures what is *really* produced. Considering nominal GDP instead of real GDP can distort what's really happening. Let's say the U.S. price level doubled tomorrow. Nominal GDP would also double, but would the United States be better off? No.

We'll use the distinction between real and nominal continually in this course, so to firm up the concepts in your mind, let's go through another example. Consider Iceland in 2007 and 2008, when nominal GDP rose from 1,301 billion krona to 1,465 billion krona while the GDP deflator rose from 140 to 157. Dividing nominal GDP in 2008 by the GDP deflator and multiplying by 100, we see that *real GDP* rose by only 0.4 percent. So nearly all of Iceland's growth was in prices.

Other Real and Nominal Distinctions

The distinction between real and nominal is a central distinction in economics that will come up again and again. So whenever you see the word *real,* remember:

The "real" amount is the nominal amount adjusted for inflation.

The "real" amount is the nominal amount divided by the price index. It is the nominal amount adjusted for inflation.

Economists' distinction between real and nominal concepts extends to other concepts besides output.

Real and Nominal Interest Rates One important distinction is between real and nominal interest rates. They also distinguish real and nominal interest rates. A **nominal interest rate** is the *rate you pay or receive to borrow or lend money*. Say you have a student loan on which you pay 5 percent interest. That means the nominal interest rate is 5 percent. The **real interest rate** is *the nominal interest rate adjusted for inflation.* In the case of interest rates, to get the real interest rate, all we have to do is subtract the inflation rate from the nominal interest rate:

Real interest rate = Nominal interest rate − Inflation rate

Real interest rate = Nominal interest rate − inflation rate

Thus, if the nominal interest rate is 5 percent and the inflation rate is 3 percent, the real interest rate is 5 − 3 = 2 percent. The real interest rate is the amount that the loan actually costs you because you will be paying it off with inflated dollars. To see this, let's consider an example. Say the nominal interest rate is 5 percent and the inflation rate is 5 percent. Your income is increasing at the same rate as the balance on your loan, including interest. The real interest rate is 0 percent; it is equivalent to getting an interest-free loan if there were no inflation since in terms of real spending power, you will be paying back precisely what you borrowed.

Real vs. Nominal

Real and Nominal Wealth Another important real and nominal distinction is between **real wealth,** which is *the value of the productive capacity of the assets of an economy measured by the goods and services it can produce now and in the future,* and **nominal wealth,** which is *the value of those assets measured at their current market prices.* Prices of assets can go up for two reasons. They may rise because the productive capacity of that asset has risen. Say the price of a company's stock goes up because the company has just invented a new product. Because of that new invention, the economy's ability to produce has increased and society is richer. Such asset price rises represent increases in real wealth.

It is useful to distinguish between real wealth—the actual productive capacity of the assets that make up the wealth, and nominal wealth—the value of the assets measured at current market prices.

Asset prices can also rise without an increase in productive capacity. In such cases we have a rise in nominal wealth but not real wealth. We will call these kinds of price increases **asset price inflation**—*a rise in the price of assets unrelated to increases in their*

Asset price inflation is a rise in the price of assets unrelated to increases in their productive capacity.

productive capacity. Asset inflation does not involve a change in real assets—more buildings, factories, or changes in the productivity of the underlying assets. It is simply a higher price of assets. With asset price inflation, the price of assets rise, but there is no increase in real assets. The measured value of assets has increased, but the economy will not be able to produce more goods and services.

If we had a measure of asset inflation, we could adjust nominal wealth to find real wealth, just as we adjust nominal GDP for inflation to find real GDP. Unfortunately, because of the difficulties involved in determining whether or not the change in the price of an asset reflects changes in productive capacity of assets, we have no actual measure of asset inflation, which means we have no good measures for real wealth. We have to use very rough approximations. For example, when, say, real estate prices rise by 50 percent in five years when there is a 1 percent inflation in goods, but no significant change in population or in other relevant factors, then the presumption that society's real wealth in real estate has increased by very little is reasonable. We can surmise that much of the 50 percent increase is likely due to asset inflation, not a change in real wealth.

Even if we agree that there has been asset inflation, we still don't know whether the price of an asset is "too high." That's because we don't know whether the old price was too low, or whether the new price is now too high. We have to make judgments based on past trends. Let's take an example. The 1990s and early 2000s were marked by significant increases in the prices of assets, especially housing. Some economists argued that prior to the price increases, housing had been undervalued, so that the increase in prices was just helping assets "catch up" to a level that reflected their productive capacity. They turned out to be wrong: The increase in housing prices came to a sudden end in 2006 and nominal wealth in the economy fell by nearly 20 percent. By 2012, household nominal wealth had nearly recovered, not because housing prices had recovered, but because the prices of financial assets had increased.

The fall in housing prices that occurred in this time period did not reduce real wealth of society by anywhere near that amount, just as the rise didn't increase it. The reason is that few houses were destroyed by the fall in their prices. True, housing owners were worse off. But homeowners are not the entire picture. People who didn't own houses but were likely to buy one in the future (which includes many students) were better off by an offsetting amount because they would have to work less to get a house in the future. The difference was that they didn't feel wealthier, even though they were, while the homeowners felt poorer. So psychologically, there was a loss in perceived aggregate wealth, even though real wealth did not change. Psychology can be extremely important for an economy, and the psychological effect of a bursting asset price bubble—a sudden fall in asset values—has been a central cause of the continued slow growth in the U.S. economy.

Some Limitations of Aggregate Accounting

The quotation at this chapter's start pointed out that statistics can be misleading. I want to reiterate that here. Before you can work with statistics, you need to know how they are collected and the problems they present. If you don't, the results can be disastrous.

Limitations of aggregate accounting include the following:

1. Measurement problems exist.
2. GDP measures market activity, not welfare.
3. Subcategories are often interdependent.

Here's a possible scenario: A student who isn't careful looks at the data and discovers an almost perfect relationship between imports and investment in a Latin American country. Whenever capital goods imports go up, investment of capital goods goes up by an equal proportion. The student develops a thesis based on that insight, only to learn after submitting the thesis that no data on investment are available for that country. Instead of gathering actual data, the foreign country's statisticians estimate investment by assuming it to be a constant percentage of imports. Since many investment goods are imported, this is reasonable, but the estimate is not a reasonable basis for an economic policy. It would be back to the drawing board for the student.

If you ever work in business as an economist, statistics will be your life's blood. Much of what economists do is based on knowing, interpreting, and drawing inferences from statistics. Statistics must be treated carefully. They don't always measure what they seem to measure. Though U.S. national income accounting statistics are among the most accurate in the world, they still have serious limitations.

Comparing GDP among Countries

One of the ways in which GDP can be misused is in comparing various countries' living standards. As you learned in the previous chapter, per capita GDP—GDP divided by population—gives us a sense of the relative standards of living of the people in various countries. But some of the comparisons should give you cause to wonder. That's because income is most often calculated at existing exchange rates (how much one currency costs in terms of another). For example, at existing exchange rates Bangladesh has per capita GDP of about \$675, compared to U.S. per capita GDP of about \$50,000, which means that the average U.S. citizen has about 75 times the income of the average Bangladeshi. How do people in Bangladesh survive?

To answer that question, remember that GDP measures market transactions. In poor countries, individuals often grow their own food (subsistence farming), build their own shelter, and make their own clothes. None of these are market activities, and while they're sometimes estimated and included in GDP, if they are, they often are estimated inaccurately. Also, remember that GDP is an aggregate measure that values activities at the market price in a society. They certainly aren't estimated at the value of what these goods and services would cost in those countries.The relative prices of the products and services a consumer buys often differ substantially. In New York City, \$2,000 a month gets you only a small studio apartment. In Bangladesh, \$2,000 a month might get you a mansion with four servants. Thus, GDP can be a poor measure of the magnitude of relative living standards.

Q-8 Why are GDP statistics not especially good for discussing the income of developing countries?

To avoid this problem in comparing per capita GDP, economists often calculate GDP using **purchasing power parity**—*a method of comparing income that takes into account the different relative prices among countries.* Just how much of a difference the two approaches can make can be seen in the case of China. In 1992, the International Monetary Fund (IMF) changed from calculating China's GDP using the exchange rate approach to using the purchasing power parity approach. Upon doing so, the IMF calculated that China's per capita income rose from about \$300 to well over \$1,000—by over 400 percent in one year. When methods of calculation can make that much difference, one must use statistics very carefully.

Purchasing power parity is a method of comparing income that takes the different relative prices among countries into account.

GDP Measures Market Activity, Not Welfare

Another important limitation to remember is that GDP measures neither happiness nor economic welfare. GDP measures economic (market) activity. Real GDP could rise and economic welfare could fall. For example, say some Martians came down and let loose a million Martian burglars in the United States just to see what would happen. GDP would be likely to rise as individuals bought guns and locks and spent millions of dollars on protecting their property and replacing stolen items. At the same time, however, welfare would fall.

Welfare is a complicated concept. The economy's goal should not be to increase output for the sake of increasing output, but to make people better off or at least happier. But a pure happiness measure is impossible. Economists have struggled with the concept of welfare and most have decided that the best they can do is to concentrate their analysis on economic activity, leaving others to consider how economic activity relates to happiness. I should warn you, however, that there is no neat correlation between increases in GDP and increases in happiness.

Measurement Errors

Q-9 How can measurement errors occur in adjusting GDP figures for inflation?

GDP figures are supposed to measure all market economic activity, but they do not. Illegal drug sales, under-the-counter sales of goods to avoid income and sales taxes, work performed and paid for in cash to avoid income tax, nonreported sales, and prostitution are all market activities, yet none of them is included in GDP figures. Estimates of the underground, nonmeasured economy range from 1.5 to 20 percent of GDP in the United States and as high as 70 percent in Nigeria. That is, if measured U.S. GDP is $16 trillion, including the underground, nonmeasured activity would raise it to between $16.2 trillion and $18.0 trillion. If we were able to halt underground activity and direct those efforts to the above-ground economy, GDP would rise significantly. For instance, if we legalized prostitution and marijuana sales and quadrupled tax-collection mechanisms, GDP would rise. But that rise in GDP wouldn't necessarily make us better off. See the box "The Underground Economy and Illegal Immigration" for further discussion.

WWW Web Note 7.2 The Underground Economy

A second type of measurement error occurs in adjusting GDP figures for inflation. Measurement of inflation involves numerous arbitrary decisions including how to weight various prices and how to adjust for changes in the quality of products. Let's take, for example, changes in the quality of products. If the price of a Toyota went up 5 percent from 2012 ($20,000) to 2013 ($21,000), that's certainly a 5 percent rise in price. But what if the 2013 Toyota had a "new, improved" 16-valve engine? Can you say that the price of cars rose 5 percent, or should you adjust for the improvement in quality? And if you adjust, how do you adjust? The economists who keep track of the price indexes used to measure inflation will be the first to tell you these questions have no one right answer. How that question, and a million other similar questions involved in measuring inflation, are answered can lead to significant differences in estimates of inflation and hence in estimates of real GDP growth.

Measurements of inflation can involve significant measurement errors.

One study for Canada argued inflation could be either 5.4 or 15 percent, depending on how the inflation index was calculated. Which inflation figure you chose would make a big difference in your estimate of how the economy was doing.

Misinterpretation of Subcategories

Another limitation of aggregate accounting concerns possible misinterpretation of the components. In setting up the accounts, a large number of arbitrary decisions had to be made: What to include in "investment"? What to include in "consumption"? How to treat government expenditures? The decisions made were, for the most part, reasonable, but they weren't the only ones that could have been made. Once made, however, they influence our interpretations of events. For example, when we see that investment rises, we normally think that our future productive capacity is rising, but remember that investment includes housing investment, which does not increase our future productive capacity. In fact, some types of consumption (say, purchases of personal computers by people who will become computer-literate and use their knowledge and skills to be more productive than they were before they owned computers) increase our productive capacity more than some types of investment.

Q-10 How can some types of consumption increase our productive capacity by more than some types of investment?

Genuine Progress Indicator

WWW Web Note 7.3 Measuring Welfare

The problems of aggregate accounting have led to a variety of measures of economic activity. One of the most interesting of these is the *genuine progress indicator (GPI),* developed by Redefining Progress, which makes a variety of adjustments to GDP to

REAL-WORLD APPLICATION

The Underground Economy and Illegal Immigration

In the text, we mentioned how the national income accounts fail to measure the underground economy and gave some examples of underground activities. One underground activity that has become increasingly important involves illegal immigration. Currently about 12 million people in the United States are undocumented workers, although the precise number isn't known since illegal immigrants aren't especially forthcoming when the government comes around to do a census study.

Most people in the United States are affected by this group. You can see them throughout the country in a variety of lower-level jobs such as maids, day laborers, construction workers, truckers, and farm laborers, among others. Many of these jobs are "on the books," which means that the undocumented workers have acquired a forged identity, with a Social Security number. They end up paying taxes and contributing to measured output even though they are illegal. Others work "off the books" and, like the many U.S. citizens who work off the books, their contribution to output does not show up in the national income accounts. Such "off the books" transactions occur when restaurants don't ring up cash sales or when waiters forget to declare tips on their tax returns—they reduce their tax payments and make it look as if they have less income and as if the economy has less production than actually exists.

How important is illegal immigration to the underground economy? While the standard measure is that there are about 12 million undocumented workers in the United States and that the underground economy is about 10 percent the size of the U.S. economy, some economists have estimated that the true number of undocumented workers is closer to 18 to 20 million, and that the underground economy is much larger than 10 percent.

better measure the progress of society rather than simply economic activity. The GPI makes adjustments to GDP for changes in other social goals. For example, if pollution worsens, the GPI falls even though GDP remains constant. Each of these adjustments requires someone to value these other social goals, and there is significant debate about how social goals should be valued. Advocates of the GPI agree that such valuations are difficult, but they argue that avoiding any such valuation, as is done with the GDP, implicitly values other social goals, such as having no pollution, at zero. Since some index will be used as an indicator of the progress of the economy, it is better to have an index that includes all social goals rather than an index of only economic activity.

By pointing out these problems, economists are not suggesting that aggregate accounting statistics should be thrown out. Far from it; measurement is necessary, and the GDP measurements and categories have made it possible to think and talk about the aggregate economy. I wouldn't have devoted an entire chapter of this book to aggregate accounting if I didn't believe it was important. I am simply arguing that aggregate accounting concepts should be used with sophistication, that is, with an awareness of their weaknesses as well as their strengths.

Measurement is necessary, and the GDP measurements and categories have made it possible to think and talk about the aggregate economy.

Conclusion

Used with that awareness, aggregate accounting is a powerful tool; you wouldn't want to be an economist without it. For those of you who aren't planning to be economists, it's still a good idea for you to understand the concepts of national income accounting. If you do, the business section of the newspaper will seem less like Greek to you. You'll be a more informed citizen and will be better able to make up your own mind about macroeconomic debates.

Summary

- Aggregate accounting is a set of rules and definitions for measuring activity in the aggregate economy. (*LO7-1*)
- GDP is the total market value of all final goods produced in an economy in one year. It's a flow, not a stock, measure of market activity. (*LO7-1*)
- GDP is divided up into four types of expenditures: (*LO7-1*)

  GDP = Consumption + Investment + Government spending + Net exports
- Intermediate goods can be eliminated from GDP in two ways: (*LO7-1*)
  1. By measuring only final sales.
  2. By measuring only value added.
- Net domestic product is GDP less depreciation. NDP represents output available for purchase because production used to replace worn-out plant and equipment (depreciation) has been subtracted. (*LO7-1*)
- GDP describes the economic output produced within the physical borders of an economy, while GNP describes the economic output produced by the citizens of a country. (*LO7-1*)
- The stock equivalent of the National Income Accounts is the National Wealth Accounts. (*LO7-1*)
- Aggregate income = Compensation to employees + Rent + Interest + Profit. (*LO7-2*)
- Aggregate income equals aggregate production because whenever a good is produced, somebody receives income for producing it. Profit is key to that equality. (*LO7-2*)
- Because the United States has a trade deficit, total expenditures by U.S. citizens are greater than production in the United States. (*LO7-2*)
- To compare income over time, we must adjust for price-level changes. After adjusting for inflation, nominal measures are changed to "real" measures. (*LO7-3*)
- $\text{Real GDP} = \frac{\text{Nominal GDP}}{\text{GDP deflator}} \times 100$ (*LO7-3*)
- The percentage change in real GDP equals the percentage change in nominal GDP minus inflation. (*LO7-3*)
- Real interest rate = Nominal interest rate − Inflation. (*LO7-3*)
- GDP has its problems: It's difficult to compare across countries; GDP does not measure economic welfare; it does not include transactions in the underground economy; the price index used to calculate real GDP is problematic; subcategories of GDP are often interdependent. (*LO7-4*)

Key Terms

asset price inflation *(153)*
consumption *(142)*
depreciation *(147)*
final output *(144)*
GDP deflator *(151)*
government spending *(142)*
gross domestic product (GDP) *(141)*
gross national product (GNP) *(148)*
inflation *(151)*
intermediate products *(144)*
investment *(142)*
net domestic product (NDP) *(147)*
net exports *(142)*
net foreign factor income *(148)*
net investment *(148)*
nominal GDP *(151)*
nominal interest rate *(153)*
price index *(151)*
nominal wealth *(153)*
purchasing power parity *(155)*
real GDP *(151)*
real wealth *(153)*
real interest rate *(153)*
transfer payments *(142)*
value added *(145)*
wealth accounts *(144)*

Questions and Exercises 

1. What's the relationship between a stock concept and a flow concept? (*LO7-1*)
2. What expenditure category of production is largest for most countries? (*LO7-1*)

3. How do wealth accounts differ from national income accounts? *(LO7-1)*
4. State whether the following actions will increase or decrease GDP: *(LO7-1)*
   a. The United States legalizes gay marriages.
   b. An individual sells her house on her own.
   c. An individual sells his house through a broker.
   d. Government increases Social Security payments.
   e. Stock prices rise by 20 percent.
   f. An unemployed worker gets a job.
5. If you add up all the transactions in an economy, do you arrive at GDP, GNP, or something else? *(LO7-1)*
6. The United States is considering introducing a value-added tax. What tax rate on value added is needed to get the same revenue as is gotten from an income tax rate of 15 percent? *(LO7-1)*
7. There are three firms in an economy: A, B, and C. Firm A buys $250 worth of goods from firm B and $200 worth of goods from firm C, and produces 200 units of output, which it sells at $5 per unit. Firm B buys $100 worth of goods from firm A and $150 worth of goods from firm C, and produces 300 units of output, which it sells at $7 per unit. Firm C buys $50 worth of goods from firm A and nothing from firm B. It produces output worth $1,000. All other products are sold to consumers. *(LO7-1)*
   a. Calculate GDP.
   b. If a value-added tax (a tax on the total value added of each firm) of 10 percent is introduced, how much revenue will the government get?
   c. How much would government get if it introduced a 10 percent income tax?
   d. How much would government get if it introduced a 10 percent sales tax on final output?
8. If the government increases transfer payments, what happens to aggregate output? *(LO7-1)*
9. Economists normally talk about GDP even though they know NDP is a better measure of economic activity. Why? *(LO7-1)*
10. Which will be larger, gross domestic product or gross national product? *(LO7-1)*
11. You've been given the following data:

Net exports	$ 4
Net foreign factor income	2
Investment	185
Government spending	195
Consumption	500
Depreciation	59

From these data, calculate GDP, GNP and NDP. *(LO7-1)*

12. What is the largest component of aggregate income for most countries? *(LO7-2)*
13. Given the following data about the economy: *(LO7-2)*

Profit	$ 268
Consumption	700
Investment	500
Government spending	300
Net exports	275
Rent	25
Depreciation	25
Net foreign factor income	3
Interest	150
Compensation to employees	1,329

   a. Calculate aggregate output (GDP) and aggregate income.
   b. Compare the two calculations in *a*. Why are they not precisely equal?
   c. Calculate GNP.
   d. Calculate NDP.
14. You have been hired as a research assistant and are given the following data. *(LO7-2)*

Compensation to employees	$329
Consumption	370
Exports	55
Net foreign factor income	3
Government spending	43
Investment	80
Imports	63
Interest	49
Profit	96
Rent	14
Net Investment	72

   a. Calculate GNP, GDP, and aggregate income.
   b. What is depreciation in this year?
   c. What is NDP?
15. What income category keeps aggregate output and aggregate income equal? *(LO7-2)*
16. If an economy has a trade surplus, is domestic production higher or lower than domestic expenditures? Explain your answer. *(LO7-2)*
17. What makes it difficult to compare GDP over time? How is the problem addressed? *(LO7-3)*

18. Below are nominal GDP and GDP deflators for four years. *(LO7-3)*

Year	Nominal GDP in billions	GDP Deflator
2010	$12,000	100
2011	13,000	104
2012	14,490	105
2013	14,800	110

 a. Calculate real GDP in each year.
 b. Did the percentage change in nominal GDP exceed the percentage change in real GDP in any of the last three years listed?
 c. In which year did society's welfare increase the most?

19. Fill in the missing values in the table below: *(LO7-3)*

Real Interest Rate	Nominal Interest Rate	Inflation
5	7	—
4	—	3
—	12	9

20. You find that real GDP per capita in Burundi is $800 while real GDP per capita in the United States is $50,000. What is misleading about these figures when comparing standards of living? *(LO7-4)*

21. When more and more women entered the labor force in the 1970s and 1980s, the economy's potential output rose. *(LO7-4)*
 a. To the extent that real output rose because of their entry into the labor market, what was the effect on measured GDP?
 b. What was the impact on welfare?

22. The Genuine Progress Indicator is an alternative measure to economic activity. *(LO7-4)*
 a. Is the Genuine Progress Indicator a subjective measure of the economy? Explain your answer.
 b. Is GDP a subjective measure? Explain your answer.

Questions from Alternative Perspectives

1. Your textbook points out that GDP fails to recognize much of the work done in the home, largely by women. Most estimates assign that work great economic value. For instance, one measure, developed by the UN's International Training and Research Institute, calculates that counting unpaid household production would add 30–60 percent to the GDP of industrialized countries and far more for developing countries.
 a. Why do you think that work done at home is left out, but housing services are not?
 b. Does it make any difference to how women are treated and thought about that work done at home is not counted in GDP?
 c. If you were valuing the services of a housespouse, how would you go about measuring the value of those services? (Feminist)

2. In "Christianity and Economics: A Review of the Recent Literature," economist John Tiemstra states, "taking good to mean self-perceived happiness derived from economic consumption adopts an ethic that is foreign to biblical Christianity." Your textbook cautions that GDP is not the same as welfare.
 a. What would you include in an index to measure the welfare of a society that takes into account Christian ethics?
 b. What would you purposefully not include in that index? (Religious)

3. Explain the sense in which GDP accounting is an institution (see the *Oxford Dictionary of the English Language* for a precise definition of an institution).
 a. How does GDP as an institution shape our understanding of the economic system?
 b. Who benefits from using GDP accounting as a measure of welfare? (Institutionalist)

4. In the expenditure approach of GDP, should *G* (government purchases) be taken into account within the calculation the same way *C* (consumption) and *I* (investment) are measured? If not, is there something inherently different about the nature of private and public expenditures? (Austrian)

5. The government spends far too much money collecting and organizing statistics. If those statistics were necessary, the private market would collect them.
 a. Explain the sense in which the above statement is true.
 b. Who do you think is the major supporter of government collection of data? (Austrian)

6. Unlike GDP, the "Genuine Progress Indicator" measures the costs as well as the benefits of economic growth by accounting for how production and consumption create

social ills such as inequality and create environmental problems that threaten future generations, such as global warming and the depletion of natural resources. GPI adjusts GDP downward to account for these costs, along with underemployment and the loss of leisure time. The result: the GPI rose from the 1950s through the early 1970s but has fallen since and today is still below its level in 1973.

a. In your opinion, does gross national product per capita or the Genuine Progress Indicator provide a better measure of economic progress?
b. Why? (Radical)

Issues to Ponder

1. Find consumption expenditures (as a percentage of GDP) for the following countries and explain what accounts for the differences. (Requires research.)
   a. Mexico
   b. Thailand
   c. Poland
   d. Nigeria
   e. Kuwait
2. If the United States introduces universal child care, what will likely happen to GDP? What are the welfare implications?
3. If society's goal is to make people happier, and higher GDP isn't closely associated with being happier, why do economists even talk about GDP?
4. In the early 2000s, some people, part of a renewed "Simplicity Movement," felt that accumulating material things reduced their happiness. Assuming they are truly happier with fewer material goods, what does this suggest about the connection between GDP and welfare?

Answers to Margin Questions

1. GDP is the sum of consumption, investment, and government spending plus the total of exports minus imports, in this case 95. (*p. 143; LO7-1*)
2. Only the value added by the sale would be added to GDP. In this case, the value added is the difference between the purchase price and the sale price, or $500. (*p. 146; LO7-1*)
3. The government budget includes transfer payments, which are not included in GDP. Only those government expenditures that are for goods and services are included in GDP. (*p. 146; LO7-1*)
4. GDP measures the output of the residents of a country—the output within its geographical borders. GNP measures the output of the citizens and businesses of a country. Kuwait is a very rich country whose residents have a high income, much of it from investments overseas. Thus, their GNP will be high. However, Kuwait also has large numbers of foreign workers who are not citizens and whose incomes would be included in GDP but not in GNP. In reality, Kuwait citizens' and businesses' foreign income exceeds foreign workers' and foreign companies' income within Kuwait, so Kuwait's GNP is greater than its GDP. (*p. 148; LO7-1*)
5. Aggregate income is the sum of employee compensation, rents, interest, and profits, in this case 198. (*p. 149; LO7-2*)
6. False. Total expenditures in the national accounts reflect expenditures by U.S. citizens. Some of those expenditures go to foreign firms and are for foreign production. (*p. 151; LO7-2*)
7. Real output equals the nominal amount divided by the price index. Since the price index has risen by 15 percent, real output has risen to $10.435 trillion ($12 trillion divided by 1.15). Real output has risen by $435 billion. (*p. 152; LO7-3*)
8. In developing countries, individuals often grow their own food and take part in many activities that are not measured by the GDP statistics. The income figures that one gets from the GDP statistics of developing countries do not include such activities and, thus, can be quite misleading. (*p. 155; LO7-4*)
9. Measurement errors occur in adjusting GDP figures for inflation because measuring inflation involves numerous arbitrary decisions such as choosing a base year, adjusting for quality changes in products, and weighting prices. (*p. 156; LO7-4*)
10. Dividing goods into consumption and investment does not always capture the effect of the spending on productive capacity. For example, housing "investment" does little to expand the productive capacity. However, "consumption" of computers or books could expand the productive capacity significantly. (*p. 156; LO7-4*)

chapter 8

Comparative Advantage, Exchange Rates, and Globalization

> *One of the purest fallacies is that trade follows the flag. Trade follows the lowest price current. If a dealer in any colony wished to buy Union Jacks, he would order them from Britain's worst foe if he could save a sixpence.*
>
> —Andrew Carnegie

After reading this chapter, you should be able to:

- **LO8-1** Explain the principle of comparative advantage.
- **LO8-2** Explain why economists' and laypeople's views of trade differ.
- **LO8-3** Summarize the sources of U.S. comparative advantage and discuss some concerns about the future in the U.S. economy.
- **LO8-4** Discuss how exchange rates are determined and what their role is in equalizing trade flows.

If economists had a mantra, it would be "Trade is good." Trade allows specialization and division of labor and thereby promotes economic growth. Much of economists' support for trade comes from their theory of comparative advantage. In this chapter we consider how the theory of comparative advantage relates to the U.S. economy. We also explore the role exchange rates play in the theory of comparative advantage and international trade.

The Principle of Comparative Advantage

The reason countries trade is the same reason that people trade: Trade can make both better off. The reason that this is true is the principle of comparative advantage to which you were introduced in Chapter 2. It is, however, important enough to warrant an in-depth review. The basic idea of the principle of **comparative advantage** is that *as long as the relative opportunity costs of producing goods (what must be given up of one good in order to get another good) differ among countries, then there are potential gains from trade.* Let's review this principle by considering the story of I.T., an imaginary international trader, who convinces two countries to enter into trades by giving both countries some of the advantages of trade; he keeps the rest for himself.

The Gains from Trade

Here's the situation. On his trips to the United States and Saudi Arabia, I.T. noticed that the two countries did not trade. He also noticed that the opportunity cost of producing a ton of food in Saudi Arabia was 10 barrels of oil and that the opportunity cost for the United States of producing a ton of food was 1/10 of a barrel of oil. At the time, the United States' production was 60 barrels of oil and 400 tons of food, while Saudi Arabia's production was 400 barrels of oil and 60 tons of food.

The choices for the United States can be seen in Figure 8-1(a), and the choices for Saudi Arabia can be seen in Figure 8-1(b). The tables give the numerical choices and the figures translate those numerical choices into graphs.

These graphs represent the two countries' production possibility curves. Each combination of numbers in the table corresponds to a point on the curve. For example, point *B* in each graph corresponds to the entries in row *B*, columns 2 and 3, in the relevant table.

Let's assume that the United States has chosen point *C* (production of 60 barrels of oil and 400 tons of food) and Saudi Arabia has chosen point *D* (production of 400 barrels of oil and 60 tons of food).

The principle of comparative advantage states that as long as the relative opportunity costs of producing goods differ among countries, then there are potential gains from trade.

Q-1 If the opportunity cost of oil for food were the same for both the United States and Saudi Arabia, what should I.T. do?

FIGURE 8-1 (A AND B) Comparative Advantage: The United States and Saudi Arabia

Looking at tables (**a**) and (**b**), you can see that if Saudi Arabia devotes all its resources to oil, it can produce 1,000 barrels of oil, but if it devotes all of its resources to food, it can produce only 100 tons of food. For the United States, the story is the opposite: Devoting all of its resources to oil, the United States can only produce 100 barrels of oil—10 times less than Saudi Arabia—but if it devotes all of its resources to food, it can produce 1,000 tons of food—10 times more than Saudi Arabia. Assuming resources are comparable, Saudi Arabia has a comparative advantage in the production of oil, and the United States has a comparative advantage in the production of food. The information in the tables is presented graphically below each table. These are the countries' production possibility curves. Each point on each country's curve corresponds to a row on that country's table.

Percentage of Resources Devoted to Oil	Oil Produced (barrels)	Food Produced (tons)	Row
100%	100	0	*A*
80	80	200	*B*
60	60	400	*C*
40	40	600	*D*
20	20	800	*E*
0	0	1,000	*F*

United States' Production Possibility Table

Percentage of Resources Devoted to Oil	Oil Produced (barrels)	Food Produced (tons)	Row
100%	1,000	0	*A*
80	800	20	*B*
60	600	40	*C*
40	400	60	*D*
20	200	80	*E*
0	0	100	*F*

Saudi Arabia's Production Possibility Table

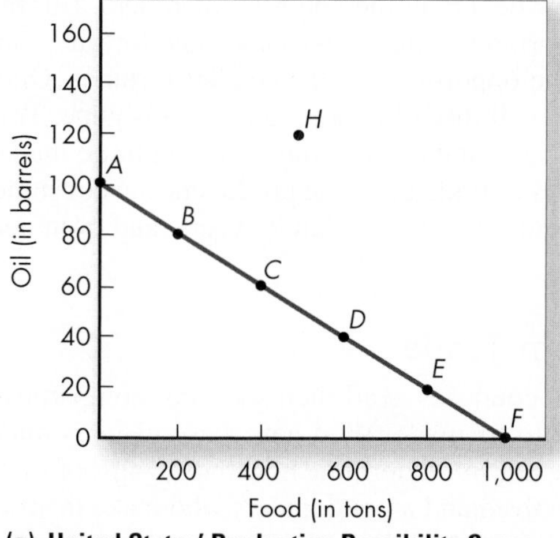

(a) United States' Production Possibility Curve

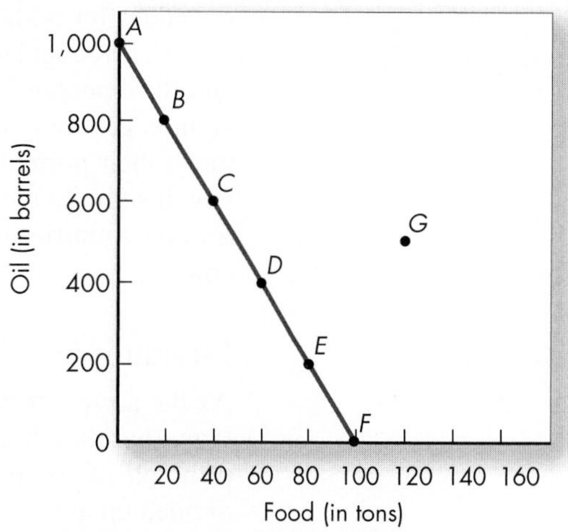

(b) Saudi Arabia's Production Possibility Curve

Now I.T., who understands the principle of comparative advantage, comes along and offers the following deal to the United States:

> If you produce 1,000 tons of food and no oil (point *F* in Figure 8-1(a)) and give me 500 tons of food while keeping 500 tons for yourself, I'll guarantee you 120 barrels of oil, double the amount you're now getting. I'll put you on point *H*, which is totally above your current production possibility curve. You'll get more oil and have more food. It's an offer you can't refuse.

I.T. then flies off to Saudi Arabia, to whom he makes the following offer:

> If you produce 1,000 barrels of oil and no food (point *A* in Figure 8-1(b)) and give me 500 barrels of oil while keeping 500 barrels for yourself, I guarantee you 120 tons of food, double the amount of food you're now getting. I'll put you on point *G*, which is totally above your current production possibility curve. You'll get more oil and more food. It's an offer you can't refuse.

Both countries accept; they'd be foolish not to. So the two countries' final consumption positions are as follows:

	Oil (barrels)	Food (tons)
Total production	1,000	1,000
U.S. consumption	120	500
U.S. gain in consumption	+60	+100
Saudi consumption	500	120
Saudi gain in consumption	+100	+60
I.T.'s profit	380	380

For arranging the trade, I.T. makes a handsome profit of 380 tons of food and 380 barrels of oil. I.T. has become rich because he understands the principle of comparative advantage.

Now obviously this hypothetical example significantly overemphasizes the gains a trader makes. Generally the person arranging the trade must compete with other traders and offer both countries a better deal than the one presented here. But the person who first recognizes a trading opportunity often makes a sizable fortune. The second and third persons who recognize the opportunity make smaller fortunes. Once the insight is generally recognized, the possibility of making a fortune is gone. Traders still make their normal returns, but the instantaneous fortunes are not to be made without new insight. In the long run, benefits of trade go to the producers and consumers in the trading countries, not the traders, but the long run can be years, and even decades, in coming.

Dividing Up the Gains from Trade

As the above story suggests, when countries avail themselves of comparative advantage, there are high gains of trade to be made. Who gets these gains is unclear. The principle of comparative advantage doesn't determine how those gains of trade will be divided up among the countries involved and among traders who make the trade possible. While there are no definitive laws determining how real-world gains from trade will be apportioned, economists have developed some insights into how those gains are likely to be divided up. The first insight concerns how much the trader gets. The general rule is:

The more competition that exists among traders, the less likely it is that the trader gets big gains of trade; more of the gains from trade will go to the citizens in the two countries, and less will go to the traders.

Three determinants of the terms of trade are:

1. The more competition, the less the trader gets.
2. Smaller countries get a larger proportion of the gain than larger countries.
3. Countries producing goods with economies of scale get a larger gain from trade.

What this insight means is that where entry into trade is unimpaired, most of the gains of trade will pass from the trader to the countries. Thus, the trader's big gains from trade occur in markets that are newly opened or if the product is unique and cannot be easily copied.

This insight isn't lost on trading companies. Numerous import/export companies exist whose business is discovering possibilities for international trade in newly opened markets. Individuals representing trading companies go around hawking projects or goods to countries. For example, at the end of the 1999 NATO bombing campaign in Kosovo, what the business world calls the *import/export contingent* flew to Kosovo with offers of goods and services to sell. Many of these same individuals had been in Iraq and Iran in the early 1990s, in Saudi Arabia when oil prices rose in the 1970s, and in the Far East when China opened its doors to international trade in the 1980s.

A second insight is:

Once competition prevails, smaller countries tend to get a larger percentage of the gains of trade than do larger countries.

The reason, briefly, is that more opportunities are opened up for smaller countries by trade than for larger countries. The more opportunities, the larger the relative gains. Say, for instance, that the United States begins trade with Mali, a small country in Africa. Enormous new consumption possibilities are opened up for Mali—prices of all types of goods will fall. Assuming Mali has a comparative advantage in fish, before international trade began, cars were probably extraordinarily expensive in Mali, while fish were cheap. With international trade, the price of cars in Mali falls substantially, so Mali gets the gains. Because the U.S. economy is so large compared to Mali's, the U.S. price of fish doesn't change noticeably. Mali's fish are just a drop in the bucket. The price ratio of cars to fish doesn't change much for the United States, so it doesn't get much of the gains of trade. Mali gets almost all the gains from trade.

There's an important catch to this gains-from-trade argument. The argument holds only if competition among traders prevails. That means that Mali residents are sold cars at the same price (plus shipping costs) as U.S. residents. International traders in small countries often have little competition from other traders and keep large shares of the gains from trade for themselves. In the earlier food/oil example, the United States and Saudi Arabia didn't get a large share of the benefits. It was I.T. who got most of the benefits. Since the traders often come from the larger country, the smaller country doesn't get this share of the gains from trade; the larger country's international traders do.

A third insight is:

Gains from trade go to the countries producing goods that exhibit economies of scale.

Trade allows an increase in production. If there are economies of scale, that increase can lower the average cost of production of a good. Hence, an increase in production can lower the price of the good in the producing country. The country producing the good with the larger economies of scale has its costs reduced by more, and hence gains more from trade than does its trading partner.

Q-2 In what circumstances would a small country not get the larger percentage of the gains from trade?

Why Economists and Laypeople Differ in Their Views of Trade

The comparative advantage model conveys a story with the theme of "trade is good"; trade benefits both parties to the trade. This story doesn't fit much of the lay public's view of trade, nor the fear of outsourcing. If trade is good, why do so many people oppose it, and what accounts for the difference between economists' view of trade and the lay public's view? I suggest four reasons.

Gains Are Often Stealth

Gains from trade are often stealth gains.

One reason for the difference is that laypeople often do not recognize the gains of trade—the gains are often stealth gains such as a decline in prices—while they easily identify the loss of jobs caused by the trade adjustments as countries shift production to take advantage of trade. For example, consider the price of clothing: A shirt today costs far less in real terms (in terms of the number of hours you have to work to buy it) than it did a decade or two ago. Much of the reason for that is trade. But how many people attribute that fall in price of shirts to trade? Not many; they just take it for granted. But the reality is that much of our current lifestyle in the United States has been made possible by trade.

Much of our current lifestyle is made possible by trade.

Opportunity Cost Is Relative

A second reason for the difference between the lay view of trade and economists' view is that the lay public often believes that since countries such as China have lower wages, they must have a comparative advantage in just about everything so that if we allow free trade, eventually we will lose all U.S. jobs. This belief is a logical contradiction; by definition comparative advantage refers to relative cost. If one country has a comparative advantage in one set of goods, the other country must have a comparative advantage in another set.

The comparative advantage model assumes that a country's imports and exports are equal.

That said, economists also must admit that the lay public does have a point. The comparative advantage model assumes that a country's imports and exports are equal. That is, its **balance of trade**—*the difference between the value of exports and the value of imports*—is zero. But U.S. imports and exports are not equal. Currently, the United States imports much more than it exports; it pays for the excess of imports over exports with IOU's. As long as foreign countries are willing to accept U.S. promises to pay some time in the future, they can have a comparative advantage in the production of many more goods than the United States.[1] Currently, people in other countries finance the U.S. trade deficit by buying U.S. assets. Once the other countries decide that it is no longer in their interests to finance the U.S. trade deficit, economic forces such as the adjustment of exchange rates will be set in motion to restore a more equal division of comparative advantages.

Trade Is Broader Than Manufactured Goods

Q-3 What are four reasons for the difference between laypeople's and economists' views of trade?

A third reason accounting for the difference between the lay view of trade and the economists' view is that laypeople often think of trade as trade in just manufactured goods. Trade is much broader, and includes the services that traders provide. Countries can have comparative advantages in trade itself, and the gains the trader makes can account for the seeming differences in countries' comparative advantages.

---

[1]One could make the model fit reality if one thinks of the United States as having a comparative advantage in producing IOUs that other people will accept.

Notice in my example that the international traders who brought the trade about benefited significantly from trade. I included traders because trade does not take place on its own—markets and trade require entrepreneurs. The market is not about abstract forces; it is about real people working to improve their position. Many of the gains from trade do not go to the countries producing or consuming the good but rather to the trader. And the gains that traders get can be enormous.

Consider, for example, the high-priced sneakers ($190) that many "with-it" students wear. Those sneakers are likely made in China, costing about $8 to make. So much of the benefits of trade do not go to the producer or the consumer; they go to the trader. However, not all of the difference is profit. The trader has other costs, such as the costs of transportation and advertising—someone has to convince you that you need those "with-it" sneakers. (Just do it, right?) A portion of the benefits of the trade accrues to U.S. advertising firms, which can pay more to creative people who think up those crazy ads.

The United States currently has a large comparative advantage in facilitating trade and many trade companies are U.S.-based. These companies buy many of the goods and services that support trade from their home country—the United States. What this means is that goods manufactured in China, India, and other Asian countries are creating demand for advertising, management, and distribution, and are therefore creating jobs and income in the United States. That's one reason for the large increase in service jobs in the U.S. economy. These are jobs that laypeople often do not associate with trade.

Trade with China and India has been generating jobs in the United States.

Trade Has Distributional Effects

WWW Web Note 8.1 Blue-Collar America

A fourth reason most economists see international trade differently than do most laypeople involves distributional issues. The economists' model doesn't take into account trade's effect on the distribution of income. Most laypeople, however, are extremely concerned with the distribution of income, which means that they look at the effects of trade differently. The problem is that while trade tends to benefit society as a whole, the benefits are often highly unevenly distributed. In the short run (which can last for 10 or 20 years), trade can hurt some a lot. Specifically, when trade is opened among countries, as it has been during the period of globalization, those producers whose goods are both tradable and internationally competitive benefit; those producers whose goods are both tradable and not internationally competitive lose. On the consumer's side, most people generally benefit since they now can get tradable goods at the lower international prices.

For the United States, this has meant that with globalization many people who worked in manufacturing either lost their jobs or saw their wages fall to make U.S. production competitive. The same was true for those holding less-skilled jobs that could be outsourced. Blue-collar America was hard hit by globalization. The problems facing these groups were multiplied by immigration of workers who were willing to work at physically difficult jobs for lower wages than Americans were unwilling to work for. This immigration is another aspect of globalization that put further downward pressure on wages in those sectors.

On the high end of the income distribution were people with intellectual property rights who suddenly had billions more people to whom to sell their products. Their income shot up; instead of being multimillionaires, they were now billionaires. Similarly, demand for the services of those in high-tech and managerial and organizational jobs increased enormously because their work could not (yet) be duplicated in low-wage countries. Both finance and high-level management fell into these categories. So while the share of U.S. jobs in the manufacturing sector fell from 25 percent in 1970 to 10 percent, the share of U.S. jobs in the professional service sector rose from 7 percent to 24 percent. The income going to those sectors also rose significantly. Finance in the economy rose from about 4 percent of the economy in the 1980s to over

9 percent in 2010, which is an enormous increase, and the financial sector accounted for much of the profits in the U.S. economy. Salaries in the financial sector went up to astronomical levels, even as manufacturing wages were falling. Put another way, the international traders, and those associated with them, (those who got many of the gains from trade in our comparative advantage example) thrived as a result of globalization. The gains from trade from which to take their share of the trade grew. So with every switch of business from the United States to China, U.S. international traders benefited.

Q-4 Why has globalization caused employment and wages to decline in the manufacturing sector but not in the education, government, and health care sectors?

Workers in the education, health care, and government sectors also felt little or no downward pressure on their wages from globalization, because these sectors produce goods and services that cannot be easily traded on the global market. They are nontradables. In fact, these sectors grew; just as in the financial sector, the share of employment in the government, education, and health industries rose significantly, and wages in these sectors rose relative to manufacturing wages. The reason these workers' pay could rise is that their wages are determined by institutional factors that kept wages increasing as they had before globalization.

People in these nontradable sectors benefited not just as producers but also as consumers—earning more and getting manufactured and tradable agricultural goods such as televisions, iPads, automobiles, shirts, shoes, and grapes—at lower and lower prices. Thus, the workers in these sectors got the gains of trade as consumers—lower prices—and kept their jobs and higher wages.

In contrast, manufacturing wages in the United States have not risen for 20 years; lower-paid individuals in these sectors have been able to keep up their consumption only by borrowing and by increasing workloads (e.g., as in two-income families). When you put all these effects together, you can see that globalization played a major role in increasing the income disparity in the United States. It created a group of haves—those who worked in nontradable and trade-organization sectors—and of have nots—those who worked in sectors facing brutal global competition. Much of the lay public's concern about globalization and international trade is rooted in these distributional effects. True, on average, trade may have benefited the United States, but that is of little comfort to those whose pay has fallen, and who have lost a job, because of it.

These distributional effects within the United States are important, and it is true that economists' comparative advantage model doesn't focus on them. Instead it focuses on the aggregate effects of trade. In the aggregate the many U.S. workers who have been hurt by trade are counterbalanced by the billions of people in developing countries who have been pulled out of poverty by trade. Outsourced U.S. jobs often go to people who earn one-tenth of what a U.S. worker earns, and that job sometimes means that they can feed their family. On a global perspective, if one believes in global income equality, trade is the way it comes about. Trade also leads to greater world economic growth. That world growth increases income and wealth abroad, thereby creating additional demand for U.S. goods. Two billion consumers whose incomes are increasing offer many new growth opportunities for U.S. firms. Trade expands the total pie, and even when a country gets a smaller proportion of the new total pie, the absolute amount it gets can increase.

Sources of U.S. Comparative Advantage

The concentrated nature of the costs of trade and the dispersed nature of the benefits present a challenge for policy makers.

When thinking about how the theory of comparative advantage relates to the current debate about outsourcing—what jobs are outsourced and what jobs are created in the United States—it is important to remember that comparative advantage is not determined by wages alone. Many other factors enter into comparative advantage and these other factors give the United States a comparative advantage in a variety of goods and services. Some of those other sources of U.S. comparative advantage include:

1. *Skills of the U.S. labor force.* Our educational system and experience in production (learning by doing) have created a U.S. workforce that is highly productive, which means that it can be paid more and still be competitive.
2. *U.S. governmental institutions.* The United States has a stable, relatively noncorrupt government, which is required for effective production. These institutions give firms based in the United States a major comparative advantage.
3. *U.S. physical and technological infrastructure.* The United States has probably the best infrastructure for production in the world. This infrastructure includes extensive road systems, telecommunications networks, and power grids.
4. *English is the international language of business.* U.S. citizens learn English from birth. Chinese and Indian citizens must learn it as a second language. One is seldom as comfortable or productive working in one's second language as in one's first language.
5. *Wealth from past production.* The United States is extraordinarily wealthy, which means that the United States is the world's largest consumer. Production that supports many aspects of consumption cannot be easily transferred geographically, and thus the United States will maintain a comparative advantage in producing these nontransferable goods.
6. *U.S. natural resources.* The United States is endowed with many resources: rich farmland, a pleasant and varied climate, beautiful scenery for tourism, minerals, and water. These give it comparative advantages in a number of areas.
7. *Cachet.* The United States continues to be a cultural trendsetter. People all over the world want to watch U.S. movies, want to have U.S. goods, and are influenced by U.S. advertising agencies to favor U.S. goods. As long as that is the case, the United States will have a comparative advantage in goods tied to that cachet.
8. *Inertia.* It takes time and costs money to change production. Companies will not move production to another country for a small cost differential. The difference has to be large, it has to be expected to continue for a long time, and it must be large enough to offset the risk of the unknown. Thus, the current place of production has an advantage over other potential places for production simply because the current location is known.
9. *U.S. intellectual property rights.* Currently, U.S. companies and individuals hold a large number of intellectual property rights, which require other countries that use their patented goods or methods to pay U.S. patent holders. Every time someone (legally) buys the Windows operating system for his or her computer, a portion of the purchase price covers a payment to a U.S. company. America's culture of embracing new ideas and questioning authority cultivates an environment of innovation that will likely continue to generate new intellectual property rights.
10. *A relatively open immigration policy.* Many of the brightest, most entrepreneurial students of developing countries immigrate and settle in the United States. They create jobs and help maintain U.S. comparative advantages in a number of fields, especially high-technology fields. More than 50 percent of the engineering degrees, for example, go to foreign students, many of whom remain in the United States.

The United States has numerous sources of comparative advantage.

WWW Web Note 8.2 Immigration Programs

Combined, these other sources of comparative advantage will maintain the United States' competitiveness in a variety of types of production for the coming decades.

Some Concerns about the Future

The above discussion of the sources of U.S. comparative advantage should have made those of you who are U.S. citizens feel a bit better about the future of the U.S. economy; the United States is not about to lose all its jobs to outsourcing. But that does not mean that there are not real issues of concern. The typical layperson's concern that the comparative advantage story does not capture what is going on with trade and outsourcing has some real foundations, and deserves to be considered seriously.

Inherent and Transferable Sources of Comparative Advantages

When David Ricardo first made the comparative advantage argument in the early 1800s, he was talking about an economic environment that was quite different from today's. His example was Britain and Portugal, with Britain producing wool and Portugal producing wine. What caused their differing costs of production was climate; Britain's climate was far less conducive to growing grapes than Portugal's but more conducive to raising sheep. Differing technologies or labor skills in the countries did not play a key role in their comparative advantages, and it was highly unlikely that the climates, and therefore comparative advantages, of the countries could change. Put another way, both countries had inherent sources of comparative advantages, which we will call **inherent comparative advantages**—*comparative advantages that are based on factors that are relatively unchangeable,* rather than transferable sources of comparative advantages, which we will call **transferable comparative advantages**—*comparative advantages based on factors that can change relatively easily.*

As the theory of comparative advantage developed, economists applied it to a much broader range of goods whose sources of comparative advantage were not due to climate. For example, some countries had land, specific resources, capital, types of labor, or technology as sources of comparative advantage. Extending the analysis to these other sources of comparative advantage makes sense, but it is important to keep in mind that only some of these comparative advantages are inherent; others are transferable. Comparative advantages due to resources or climate are unlikely to change; comparative advantages that depend on capital, technology, or education, however, can change. In fact, we would expect them to change.

The Law of One Price

Whether a country can maintain a much higher standard of living than another country in the long run depends in part on whether its sources of comparative advantage are transferable or inherent. Saudi Arabia will maintain its comparative advantage in producing oil, but the United States' comparative advantage based on better education is likely to be more fleeting. In cases where sources of comparative advantage are not inherent, economic forces will push to eliminate that comparative advantage. The reason is the *law of one price*—in a competitive market, there will be pressure for equal factors to be priced equally. If factor prices aren't equal, firms can reduce costs by redirecting production to countries where factors are priced lower. The tendency of economic forces to eliminate transferable comparative advantage is sometimes called the *convergence hypothesis*. Even seemingly inherent comparative advantages can be changed by technology. Consider oil. The development of cost-effective fuel cells may leave Saudi Arabia with a comparative advantage in oil but not necessarily with a comparative advantage in producing energy.

Law of one price: in a competitive market, there will be pressure for equal factors to be priced equally.

When markets are working, any country with a comparative advantage due only to transferable capital and technology will lose that comparative advantage as capital and technology spread to other countries. Ultimately, in the case of transferable comparative advantage, production will shift to the lower-wage country that has equivalent institutional

Q-5 Will transferable or inherent comparative advantages be more impacted by the law of one price? Why?

structures. This is the law of one price in action: The same good—including equivalent labor—must sell for the same price, unless trade is restricted or other differences exist. That is what's happening now with the United States and outsourcing. Skills needed in the information technology sector, for example, are transferable. Because an information technology professional with three to five years' experience earns about $75,000 in the United States and only $26,000 in India, those jobs are moving abroad. As long as wages differ, and the workers' productivities in countries are comparable, transferable comparative advantages of U.S. production will continue to erode, and as they erode, production and jobs will be moved abroad.

Transferable comparative advantages will tend to erode over time.

The question, therefore, is not: Why is outsourcing to China and India occurring today? The questions are: Why didn't it happen long ago, and how did U.S. productivity, and hence their standard of living, come to so exceed China's and India's productivity? Or alternatively: How did the United States get in its current high-wage position, and is it likely to maintain that position into the indefinite future?

How the United States Gained and Is Now Losing Sources of Comparative Advantage

To better understand the current U.S. position, let's look at it historically. The United States developed its highly favorable position from the 1920s until the late 1940s when the two world wars directed production toward the United States. Those wars, the entrepreneurial spirit of the U.S. population, U.S. institutions conducive to production, and the flow of technology and capital (financial assets) into the United States gave the United States a big boost both during the two world wars and after. Coming out of World War II, at the then-existing exchange rates, the United States had a major cost advantage in producing a large majority of goods, just as China has a cost advantage in producing the large majority of goods today.

Such cost advantages in a majority of areas of production are not sustainable because the balance of trade will be highly imbalanced. In the absence of specific policy by governments, or large private flows of capital to pay for those imports, eventually that imbalance will right itself. After World War II, the trade balance that favored the United States was maintained temporarily by U.S. companies, which invested heavily in Europe, and by the U.S. government, which transferred funds to Europe with programs such as the Marshall Plan—a program to aid Europe in rebuilding its economy. These flows of capital financed Europe's **trade deficits**—*when imports exceed exports*—and allowed the United States to run large **trade surpluses**—*when exports exceed imports*—just as current flows of capital into the United States from a variety of countries, and the explicit policy of buying U.S. bonds by Chinese and Japanese central banks, are financing the U.S. trade deficits now, and allowing large Chinese trade surpluses with the United States.

In the absence of specific policy by governments, or large private flows of capital, eventually any large trade imbalance will right itself.

Methods of Equalizing Trade Balances

Capital flows that sustain trade imbalances eventually stop, and when they do, adjustments in sources of comparative advantages must take place so that the trade surplus countries—such as China today—become less competitive (lose sources of comparative advantage) and the trade deficit countries—in this case, the United States—become more competitive (gain sources of comparative advantage). This adjustment can occur in a number of ways. The two most likely adjustments today are that wages in China rise relative to wages in the United States, or the U.S. exchange rate (discussed in the next section) falls. Both adjustments will make Chinese goods relatively more expensive and U.S. goods relatively cheaper, just as these adjustments did with countries such as Japan, Taiwan, and Korea in previous decades. Neither of these is especially pleasant for us, which is why we will likely hear continued calls for trade restrictions in the coming decade.

Q-6 What are two likely adjustments that will reduce the wage gap between China and the United States?

The U.S. wage advantage can only be maintained to the degree that total cost of production of a good in the United States is no more than the total cost of that same good abroad.

Unfortunately, as I will discuss in Chapter 19, the trade restriction policies that governments can undertake will generally make things worse. In a globalized free-trade economy, the U.S. wage advantage can be maintained only to the degree that the total cost of production of a good in the United States (with all the associated costs) is no more expensive than the total cost of producing that same good abroad (with all the associated costs). The degree to which production shifts because of lower wages abroad depends on how transferable are the U.S. comparative advantages that we listed above. Some of them are generally nontransferable, and thus will support sustained higher relative U.S. wages. English as the language of business; the enormous wealth of the United States gained earlier; inertia; and U.S. political, social, and capital infrastructure will keep much production in the United States, and will maintain a comparative advantage for U.S. production even with significantly higher U.S. wages.

But in the coming decades, we can expect a narrowing of the wage gap between the United States and China and India. Given these strong market forces that cannot be prevented without undermining the entire international trading system, about the only available realistic strategy for the United States is to adapt to this new situation. Its best strategy is to work toward maintaining existing comparative advantages through investment in education and infrastructure, while continuing to provide an environment conducive to innovation so that we develop comparative advantages in new industries.

Determination of Exchange Rates and Trade

WWW Web Note 8.3 Exchange Rate Data

As mentioned above, transferable sources of comparative advantage aren't the only way to eliminate trade imbalances. Exchange rates are another. The market for foreign currencies is called the foreign exchange (forex) market. It is this market that determines the **exchange rates**—*the rate at which one country's currency can be traded for another country's currency*— that newspapers report daily in tables such as the table below, which shows the cost of various currencies in terms of dollars and the cost of dollars in terms of those currencies.

Exchange Rates, July 6, 2012

	U.S. $ Equivalent	Currency per U.S. $
Argentina (peso)	0.22	4.53
Canada (dollar)	0.98	1.02
China (renminbi)	0.16	6.37
Denmark (krone)	0.17	6.01
European Union (euro)	1.23	0.81
Israel (shekel)	0.25	3.94
Japan (yen)	0.01	79.81
Pakistan (rupee)	0.01	94.11
Philippines (peso)	0.02	41.86
Russia (ruble)	0.03	32.77
Saudi Arabia (riyal)	0.27	3.75
U.K. (pound)	1.55	0.64

The second column in this table reports the price of foreign currencies in terms of dollars. For example, one Argentinean peso costs about 22 cents. The third column tells you the price of dollars in terms of the foreign currency. For example, one U.S. dollar costs 4.5 Argentinean pesos.

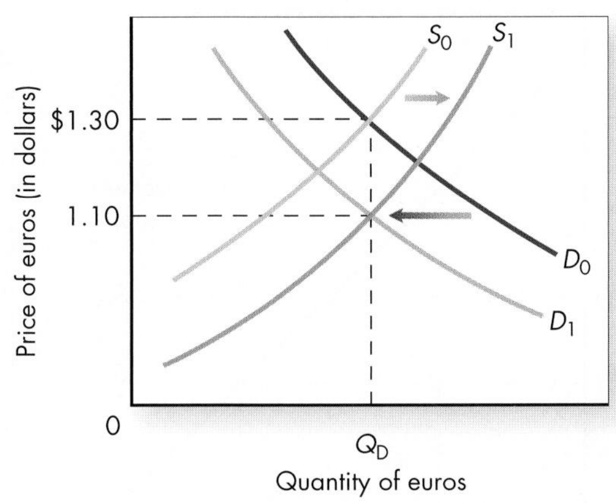

FIGURE 8-2 The Supply of and Demand for Euros

As long as you keep quantities and prices of *what* straight, the determination of exchange rates is easy. Just remember that if you're talking about the supply of and demand for euros, the price will be measured in dollars and the quantity will be in euros.

People exchange currencies to buy goods or assets in other countries. For example, an American who wants to buy stock of a company that trades on the EU stock exchange first needs to buy euros with dollars. If the stock costs 150 euros, he will need to buy 150 euros. With an exchange rate of $1.30 for 1 euro, he will need to pay $195 to buy 150 euros ($1.30 × 150). Only then can he buy the stock.

Let's now turn to a graphical analysis of the forex market. At first glance, the graphical analysis of foreign exchange rates seems simple: You have an upward-sloping supply curve and a downward-sloping demand curve. But what goes on the axes? Obviously price and quantity, but what price? And what quantity? Because you are talking about the prices of currencies relative to each other, you have to specify which currencies you are using.

Figure 8-2 presents the supply of and demand for euros in terms of dollars. Notice that the quantity of euros goes on the horizontal axis and the dollar price of euros goes on the vertical axis. When you are comparing currencies of only two countries, the supply of one currency equals the demand for the other currency. To demand one currency, you must supply another. In this figure, I am assuming that there are only two trading partners: the United States and the European Union. This means that the supply of euros is equivalent to the demand for dollars. The Europeans who want to buy U.S. goods or assets supply euros to buy dollars. Let's consider an example. Say a European wants to buy a Dell computer made in the United States. She has euros, but Dell wants dollars. So, to buy the computer, she or Dell must somehow exchange euros for dollars. She is *supplying* euros in order to *demand* dollars.

To demand one currency, you must supply another currency.

The supply curve of euros is upward-sloping because the more dollars European citizens get for their euros, the cheaper U.S. goods and assets are for them and the greater the quantity of euros they want to supply for those goods. Say, for example, that the dollar price of one euro rises from $1.30 to $1.35. That means that the price of a dollar to a European has fallen from 0.78 euro to 0.74 euro. For a European, a good that cost $100 now falls in price from 78 euros to 74 euros. U.S. goods are cheaper, so the Europeans buy more U.S. goods and more dollars, which means they supply more euros.

Q-7 Show graphically the effect on the price of euros of an increase in the demand for dollars by Europeans.

The demand for euros comes from Americans who want to buy European goods or assets. The demand curve is downward-sloping because the lower the dollar price of euros, the more euros U.S. citizens want to buy, using the same reasoning I just described.

The market is in equilibrium when the quantity supplied equals the quantity demanded. In my example, when supply is S_0 and demand is D_0, equilibrium occurs at a dollar price of $1.30 for one euro.

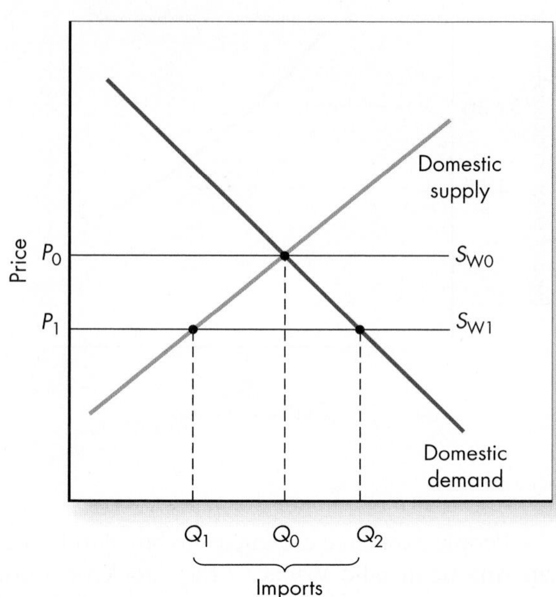

FIGURE 8-3

The exchange rate plays an important role in international trade. If the world price of goods is less than the domestic price of tradable goods, domestic producers must match the world price level. If the world price level is P_1, domestic producers will sell Q_1 and domestic consumers demand Q_2. The difference is made up by imports shown by the difference between Q_2 and Q_1. A country will have a zero trade balance when the world price level equals the domestic price level, P_0.

Suppose forces shift the supply and demand for euros; for example, say people lose faith in the euro, leading them to want to hold their assets in dollar denominated assets. The supply of euros rises from S_0 to S_1. At the same time, Americans also lose faith in the euro and decide to buy fewer euros. This shifts the demand for euros from D_0 to D_1. Combined, the two shifts lead to a fall in the price of the euro as shown in Figure 8-2, decreasing the price from $1.30 to $1.10.

Q-8 Interest rates and income rise in Britain. Would you expect the British currency, the pound, to appreciate or depreciate? Explain your answer using supply and demand curves.

Because it takes more euros to buy dollars, we say the euro has depreciated in value. A **currency depreciation** is *a change in the exchange rate so that one currency buys fewer units of a foreign currency*. The dollar, on the other hand appreciated in value because one dollar can be exchanged for more euros. A **currency appreciation** is *a change in the exchange rate so that one currency buys more units of a foreign currency.*

Exchange Rates and Trade

The exchange rate plays an important role in the demand for a country's domestic goods. We can see that by considering both the domestic supply of tradable goods—those goods that can be produced in one country and sold in another—and the international supply of tradable goods on the same graph. We do so in Figure 8-3. In it, for simplicity we assume that the world supply of goods is perfectly elastic (horizontal) at P_1. That is, foreign countries are willing to sell as much as is demanded at a single price. With free trade, if domestic producers of tradable goods want to sell any goods, they must match this world price. If consumers can buy all the goods they want at the world price, why pay more?

Domestic supply of tradable goods is determined by the wage and the productivity of workers in the United States—as quantity supplied rises, suppliers have to charge higher prices to cover higher costs of production. The supply curve, therefore, reflects the comparative advantages of U.S. producers with respect to world producers. It is upward sloping because as output increases, the cost of production rises relative to the cost of world production. If the world supply is S_{W1}, the United States has a comparative advantage for goods up until Q_1 where the domestic supply intersects the world supply. World producers have a comparative advantage in the production of goods to the right of Q_1.

Trade for an economy that faces global competition needs to take into account world supply, which is horizontal at the world price for tradable goods.[2] If the world supply curve intersects domestic supply and demand at the domestic equilibrium price as it does when the world supply curve is S_{W0}, imports will be exactly offset by exports. If the world price is below the domestic equilibrium, as it is when the world supply curve is S_{W1}, a country is running a trade deficit. In this figure the world price is P_1, which results in a trade deficit is $Q_2 - Q_1$. Indefinite trade deficits are not sustainable. A decrease in the domestic economy's exchange rates, relative declines in wages, or improvements in comparative advantage can eliminate the trade deficit.

Q-9 If the world supply of goods is at the domestic price level, will there be a trade deficit or trade surplus? Explain your answer.

Let's consider how exchange rates adjustment can eliminate a U.S. trade deficit with China. (We are using China to represent the rest of the world.)

Exchange rates affect a trade balance through their impact on relative comparative advantages. The reason is that as the exchange rate changes the price of a country's goods to people in other countries changes. In the case of dollars and yuan, if the dollar depreciates U.S. citizens will pay more U.S. dollars for each good they buy from China, which means that the relative price of foreign goods rises. So, a depreciation of the domestic country's currency will shift the world supply curve up, making it easier for U.S. producers to compete. Similarly, an appreciation will shift the world supply curve down, making it harder for a country to compete globally.

In theory, the exchange rate adjustment can bring two countries' comparative advantages into alignment, eliminating any trade imbalance. The assumption that exchange rates will adjust to bring trade into balance underlies the story economists tell about comparative advantages. That story assumes that comparative advantages net out so the trade deficit of both countries is zero.

Some Complications in Exchange Rates

If the supply and demand for currencies applied only to tradable goods, trade among countries would generally be in balance, and countries would have roughly equal sectors of comparative advantages in producing goods. However, that doesn't always happen. A major reason why is that the demand for a country's currency reflects not only the demand for a country's produced goods but also reflects a demand for its assets.

When the demand for a country's assets is high, the value of its currency will also be high. With a higher exchange rate, the world price of produced goods will be low and the domestic country will have a comparative advantage in relatively fewer sectors compared to other countries. That has been the case in the United States over the past 20 years, and is one of the reasons so much manufacturing production has fared so poorly.

Another source of differences in comparative advantage is what is called the **resource curse**—*the paradox that countries with an abundance of resources tend to have lower economic growth and more unemployment than countries with fewer natural resources*. What happens is that the country that has a comparative advantage in resources finds that the demand for its resources pushes its exchange rate up. A higher exchange rate reduces the comparative advantage of other tradable goods, shifting the world supply curve, and hence domestic production, of these goods, down. In terms of Figure 8-3, world supply for goods other than resources falls from S_{W0} to S_{W1} and

Q-10 How can the discovery of a highly valuable resource lead to the appreciation of a currency and loss of comparative advantage in other goods?

[2]This is a discussion for a composite good. Actual trade is in many different types of goods and services, and this position is consistent with significant imports and exports of particular goods, as long as in the aggregate they balance out. It is the trade balance, not total trade, that is captured by the graph.

domestic production falls from Q_0 to Q_1. The resource curse also tends to reduce employment because a decline in employment in these other goods is not offset by an increase in employment in the resource sector. While the production of the resource often pays well, it does not require large numbers of workers. Because the Netherlands experienced this phenomenon when it discovered offshore oil, it is also sometimes called the Dutch disease.

When one sector of an economy gains a comparative advantage, other sectors must either lose their comparative advantage or there will be a trade imbalance.

The resource curse is not tied to natural resources. It happens whenever there is a large increase in global demand for one sector of an economy's goods. When one sector of an economy gains a comparative advantage, other sectors must either lose their comparative advantage or there will be a trade imbalance. This happened in the United States during the rise in globalization for technology, business organization, and finance sectors. Globalization increased the demand for people providing logistical support, marketing, and financial expertise. These were high paying jobs and, on average, it was an enormous boon to the United States economy. But that increase in demand meant that the low-wage U.S. workers in globally competitive industries lost their comparative advantage since the U.S. dollar did not depreciate to maintain it. So total income in the United States rose, but income and employment in the low-wage manufacturing tradable sector fell, causing significant hardship and unemployment in these sectors.

Conclusion

International trade, and changing comparative advantages, has become more and more important for the United States in recent decades. With international transportation and communication becoming faster and easier, and with other countries' economies growing, the U.S. economy will inevitably become more interdependent with the other economies of the world. Ultimately, this international trade will improve the lives for most Americans, and even more so for the world. However, the path there will likely be very difficult for those U.S. citizens in the competitive global sector.

Summary

- According to the principle of comparative advantage, as long as the relative opportunity costs of producing goods (what must be given up in one good in order to get another good) differ among countries, there are potential gains from trade. *(LO8-1)*
- Three insights into the terms of trade are:
  1. The more competition exists in international trade, the less the trader gets and the more the involved countries get.
  2. Once competition prevails, smaller countries tend to get a larger percentage of the gains from trade than do larger countries.
  3. Gains from trade go to countries that produce goods that exhibit economies of scale. *(LO8-1)*
- Economists and laypeople differ in their views on trade. *(LO8-2)*
- The gains from trade in the form of low consumer prices tend to be widespread and not easily recognized, while the costs in jobs lost tend to be concentrated and readily identifiable. *(LO8-2)*
- The United States has comparative advantages based on its skilled workforce, its institutions, and its language, among other things. *(LO8-3)*
- Inherent comparative advantages are based on factors that are relatively unchangeable. They are not subject to the law of one price. *(LO8-3)*
- Transferable comparative advantages are based on factors that can change relatively easily. The law of one price can eliminate these comparative advantages. *(LO8-3)*

- Concerns about trade for the United States are that U.S. relative wages will decline and the value of the dollar will decline as well. *(LO8-3)*
- The prices of currencies—foreign exchange rates—can be analyzed with the supply and demand model in the same way as any other good can be. An appreciation of the dollar occurs when a single dollar can buy more foreign currency. A depreciation of the dollar occurs when a single dollar buys less foreign currency. *(LO8-4)*
- An appreciation of a currency will shift the world supply of a good down and increase that country's trade deficit. *(LO8-4)*
- The depreciation of a country's currency makes that country's goods more competitive. *(LO8-4)*
- The resource curse occurs when a significant amount of natural resources are discovered. This raises foreign demand for the resource, raising the value of the domestic country's currency, making other sectors less competitive. A variation of the resource curse is one reason for a greater inequality of income distribution in the United States. *(LO8-4)*

Key Terms

balance of trade *(166)*
comparative advantage *(162)*
currency appreciation *(174)*
currency depreciation *(174)*
exchange rate *(172)*
inherent comparative advantage *(170)*
resource curse *(175)*
trade deficit *(171)*
trade surplus *(171)*
transferable comparative advantage *(170)*

Questions and Exercises

1. Will a country do better importing or exporting a good for which it has a comparative advantage? Why? *(LO8-1)*
2. Widgetland has 60 workers. Each worker can produce 4 widgets or 4 wadgets. Each resident in Widgetland currently consumes 2 widgets and 2 wadgets. Wadgetland also has 60 workers. Each can produce 3 widgets or 12 wadgets. Wadgetland's residents consume 1 widget and 9 wadgets. Is there a basis for trade? If so, offer the countries a deal they can't refuse. *(LO8-1)*
3. Suppose there are two states that do not trade: Iowa and Nebraska. Each state produces the same two goods: corn and wheat. For Iowa the opportunity cost of producing 1 bushel of wheat is 3 bushels of corn. For Nebraska the opportunity cost of producing 1 bushel of corn is 3 bushels of wheat. At present, Iowa produces 20 million bushels of wheat and 120 million bushels of corn, while Nebraska produces 20 million bushels of corn and 120 million bushels of wheat. *(LO8-1)*
   a. Explain how, with trade, Nebraska can end up with 40 million bushels of wheat and 120 million bushels of corn while Iowa can end up with 40 million bushels of corn and 120 million bushels of wheat.
   b. If the states ended up with the numbers given in *a*, how much would the trader get?
4. Suppose that two countries, Machineland and Farmland, have the following production possibility curves: *(LO8-1)*

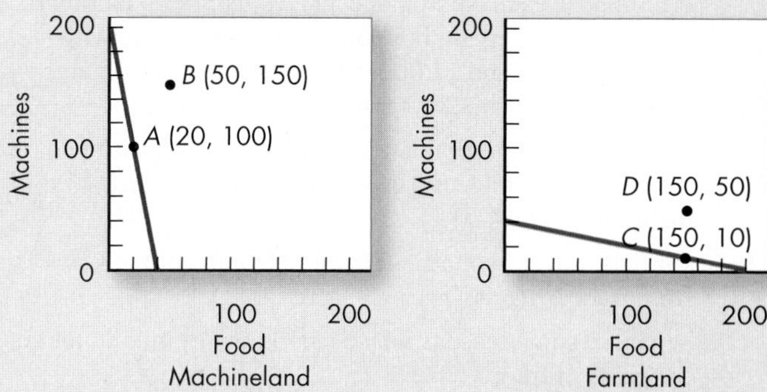

   a. Explain how these two countries can move from points *A* and *C*, where they currently are, to points *B* and *D*.
   b. If possible, state by how much total production for the two countries has risen.
   c. If you were a trader, how much of the gains from trade would you deserve for discovering this trade?
   d. If the per unit cost of production falls as output rises, how would the analysis change?

5. Suppose there are two countries, Busytown and Lazyasiwannabe, with the following production possibility tables: *(LO8-1)*

Busytown

% of Resources Devoted to Cars	CarsProduced (thousands)	Gourmet Meals Produced (thousands)
100%	60	0
80	48	10
60	36	20
40	24	30
20	12	40
0	0	50

Lazyasiwannabe

% of Resources Devoted to Cars	Cars Produced (thousands)	Gourmet Meals Produced (thousands)
100%	50	0
80	40	10
60	30	20
40	20	30
20	10	40
0	0	50

a. Draw the production possibility curves for each country.
b. Which country has the comparative advantage in producing cars? In producing gourmet meals?
c. Suppose each country specializes in the production of one good. Explain how Busytown can end up with 36,000 cars and 22,000 meals and Lazyasiwannabe can end up with 28,000 meals and 24,000 cars.

6. Why does competition among traders affect how much of the gains from trade are given to the countries involved in the trade? *(LO8-1)*
7. Why do smaller countries usually get most of the gains from trade? *(LO8-1)*
8. What are some reasons why a small country might not get the gains of trade? *(LO8-1)*
9. Country A can produce, at most, 40 olives or 20 pickles, or some combination of olives and pickles such as the 20 olives and 10 pickles it is currently producing. Country B can produce, at most, 120 olives or 60 pickles, or some combination of olives and pickles such as the 100 olives and 50 pickles it is currently producing. *(LO8-1)*
   a. Is there a basis for trade? If so, offer the two countries a deal they can't refuse.
   b. How would your answer change if you knew that the per unit cost of producing pickles and olives falls as more of each is produced? Why? Which country would you have produce which good?
10. What are four reasons why economists' and laypeople's view of trade differ? *(LO8-2)*
11. True or false? Wages in China are lower than those in the United States. This means that China has a comparative advantage in everything. Explain your answer. *(LO8-2)*
12. How does the outsourcing of manufacturing production benefit production in the United States? *(LO8-2)*
13. How has globalization made the rich richer and poor poorer in the United States? *(LO8-2)*
14. List at least three sources of comparative advantage that the United States has and will likely maintain over the coming decade. *(LO8-3)*
15. How do inherent comparative advantages differ from transferable comparative advantages? *(LO8-3)*
16. From the standpoint of adjustment costs to trade, which would a country prefer—inherent or transferable comparative advantage? Why? *(LO8-3)*
17. The dollar price of the South African rand fell from 29 cents to 22 cents in 1996, the same year the country was rocked by political turmoil. Using supply/demand analysis, explain why the turmoil led to a decline in the price of the rand. *(LO8-4)*
18. How does a depreciation of a currency change the price of imports and exports? Explain using the U.S. dollar and the Chinese yuan. *(LO8-4)*
19. Using the graph below, indicate domestic production and imports. *(LO8-4)*

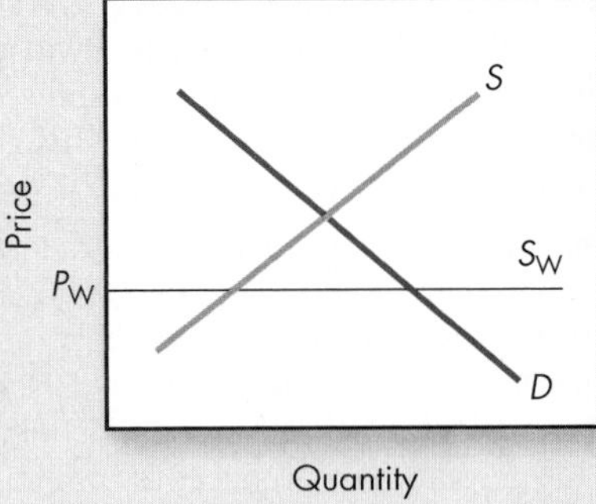

   a. Would the United States want to raise or lower the world supply of the good? Why?
   b. How might that happen?
20. Would you expect the resource curse to improve or worsen the distribution of income in a country? *(LO8-4)*

Questions from Alternative Perspectives

1. Evaluate the following statement: Comparative advantage will benefit all people because everyone has a comparative advantage in something. Therefore, trade based on comparative advantage should be facilitated without undue government intervention. (Austrian)
2. In the 10th century B.C., King Solomon brought the Israelites into great economic wealth through specialization and trade. It was difficult when faced with the practices and beliefs of their trading partners, however, for Israel to maintain its identity as a people of one God. King Solomon, for example, provided a place for each of his wives to worship the gods of her own people. If such syncretism (adoption of foreign practices and beliefs) is inevitable with increased globalization, should trade be encouraged, even today? (Religious)
3. Global outsourcing has cost the U.S. economy far more than one million jobs since 2001, or somewhere between 15 and 35 percent of the total decline in employment since the onset of the 2001 recession.
   a. How does outsourcing affect the bargaining power of U.S. workers and the bargaining power of U.S. employers?
   b. What will it likely do to the overall level of U.S. workers' wages?
   c. What will it likely do to lawyers' wages?
   d. If you stated that it affected lawyers' wages differently, do you believe that the U.S. policy response to outsourcing would be different? (Post-Keynesian)
4. In David Ricardo's original example of comparative advantage in his *Principles of Political Economy,* written in 1817, Portugal possesses an absolute advantage in both the production of cloth and the production of wine. But England has a comparative advantage in the production of cloth, while Portugal's comparative advantage is in wine production. According to Ricardo, an English political economist, England should specialize in the production of cloth and Portugal in wine making.
   a. Was Ricardo's advice self-serving?
   b. Knowing that light manufacturing, such as clothing and textile production, has led most industrialization processes, would you have advised 19th-century Portugal to specialize in wine making? (Radical)
5. In the *Wealth of Nations* Adam Smith claimed, "Servants, labourers and workmen of different kinds, make up the far greater part of every great political society. But what improves the circumstances of the greater part can never be regarded as an inconvenience to the whole. No society can surely be flourishing and happy, of which the far greater part of the members are poor and miserable. It is but equity, besides, that they who feed, clothe and lodge the whole body of the people, should have such a share of the produce of their own labour as to be themselves tolerably well fed, cloathed and lodged." In light of today's economy, what argument can you give that supports this claim? What argument can you give that disputes this claim? (Austrian and Post-Keynesian)

Issues to Ponder

1. How is outsourcing to China and India today different from U.S. outsourcing in the past?
2. One of the basic economic laws is the "law of one price." Does it imply that the U.S. wage level will have to equal the Chinese wage level if free trade is allowed? Why or why not?
3. The normal textbook presentation of international trade does not include the international trader. How does including the trader in the model provide a different view of trade than one would get from a model that did not include the trader?
4. One way to equalize imports and exports would be to pass a law that (1) in order to import, importers must provide a certificate certifying that an equal value of exports had occurred; and (2) in order to export, exporters must provide a certificate certifying that an equal value of imports had occurred.
   a. If the trade is balanced, what would the price of these certificates be?
   b. In the current U.S. situation, what would the price of these certificates be?
   c. In the current Chinese situation, what would the price of these certificates be?
   d. Would such a law make exchange rate adjustment more or less likely?
5. Assuming a law such as the one suggested in question 4 were passed in the mid-1990s in the U.S., what subgroups of U.S. workers would have likely been helped, and what subgroups of U.S. workers would have likely been hurt?

Answers to Margin Questions

1. He should walk away because there is no basis for trade. (*p. 163; LO8-1*)
2. The percentage of gains from trade that goes to a country depends upon the change in the price of the goods being traded. If trade led to no change in prices in a small country, then that small country would get no gains from trade. Another case in which a small country gets a small percentage of the gains from trade would occur when its larger trading partner was producing a good with economies of scale and the small country was not. A third case is when the traders who extracted most of the surplus or gains from trade come from the larger country, then the smaller country would end up with few of the gains from trade. (*p. 185; LO8-1*)
3. Four reasons for the difference are: (1) gains from trade are often stealth gains, (2) comparative advantage is determined by more than wages, (3) nations trade more than just manufactured goods, and (4) trade has distributional effects. (*p. 166; LO8-2*)
4. The manufacturing sector produces tradable goods, which has made it vulnerable to international trade. Foreign producers could produce these goods at a lower cost, putting downward pressure on wages and employment. Production in the education, health care, and government sectors is less tradable, making it less subject to pressure from globalization. (*p. 168; LO8-2*)
5. Transferable comparative advantage will be more affected because it is an advantage that is not tied to a particular country. Countries where prices are higher will face outflow of capital and technology to bring prices back in balance. This will transfer comparative advantage from the high-price countries to low-price countries. (*p. 170; LO8-3*)
6. Two likely adjustments that will reduce the wage gap are a fall in the value of the dollar (U.S. exchange rate) and a rise in Chinese wages relative to U.S. wages. (*p. 171; LO8-3*)
7. An increase in the demand for dollars is the equivalent to an increase in the supply of euros, so an increase in the demand for dollars pushes down the price of euros in terms of dollars, as in the following diagram. (*p. 173; LO8-4*)

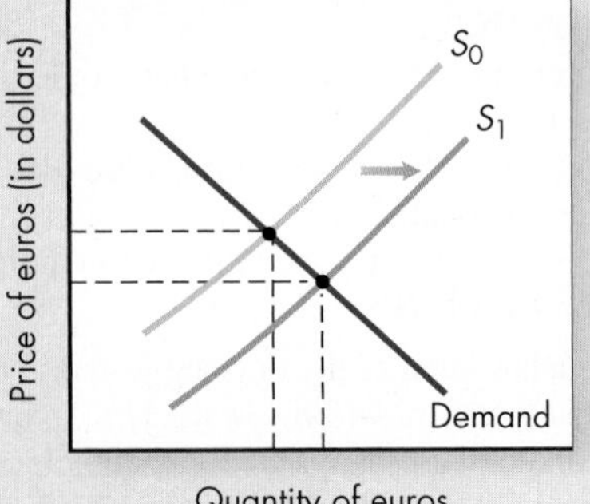

8. The pound would be expected to appreciate because the demand for pounds would shift to the right as foreign investors bought more British bonds and other assets. The supply curve would shift to the left because British citizens would shift their investments back to Britain. This is shown in the graph below. (*p. 174; LO8-4*)

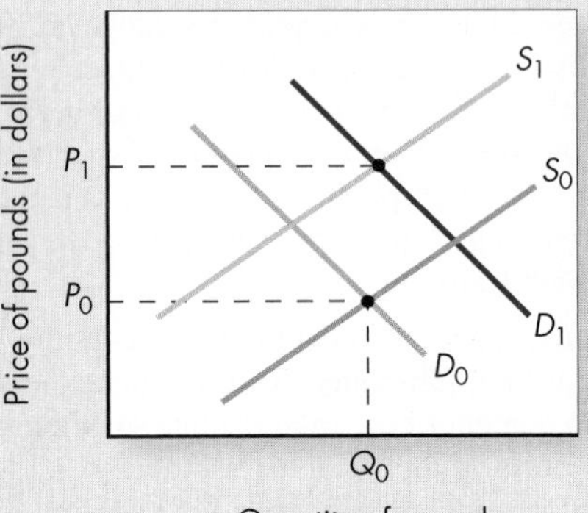

9. There would be neither a trade surplus nor deficit since imports cost the same as domestic goods. American consumers would be indifferent between buying foreign and domestic goods. (*p. 175; LO8-4*)
10. The discovery of the resource will increase the demand for the domestic currency, which leads to an appreciation of the currency. This appreciation makes domestic goods more expensive to foreigners, which leads to a loss in the comparative advantage in those goods. (*p. 175; LO8-4*)

chapter 9

The Short-Run Keynesian Policy Model: Demand-Side Policies

> *The Theory of Economics . . . is a method rather than a doctrine, an apparatus of the mind, a technique of thinking which helps its possessor to draw correct conclusions.*
>
> —J. M. Keynes

After reading this chapter, you should be able to:

- **LO9-1** Discuss the key insight of the *AS/AD* model and list both its assumptions and its components.
- **LO9-2** Describe the shape of the aggregate demand curve and what factors shift the curve.
- **LO9-3** Explain the shape of the short-run and long-run aggregate supply curves and what factors shift the curves.
- **LO9-4** Show the effects of shifts of the aggregate demand and aggregate supply curves on the price level and output in both the short run and long run.
- **LO9-5** Discuss the limitations of the macro policy model.

In late 2007 and early 2008, the U.S. economy fell into a serious recession that many thought might lead to a depression. Faced with this serious recession, the U.S. government, with support from both Democrats and Republicans, implemented what are known as expansionary demand-side policies. The rationale was that if the government did not do so, firms would cut back production further. More employees would be laid off, reducing their income and their expenditures even further. This would create lower output and continue to push the economy into a prolonged recession or possibly even a depression. The tools that the government has to deal with a recession—monetary and fiscal policies (policies that we will discuss below)—affect the aggregate demand side of the economy.

The model that underlies these polices is the short-run macroeconomic model, also known as the aggregate supply/aggregate demand (AS/AD) model. Economists drew the ideas in this model from Keynes' contributions described in Chapter 6, so the model is often called the Keynesian model.

The Key Insight of the Keynesian *AS/AD* Model

The key idea of the Keynesian *AS/AD* model is that in the short run, the economy can deviate from what it is capable of producing, or its **potential output**—*the highest amount of output an economy can sustainably produce using existing production processes and resources.* It is based on the assumption that the economy can deviate from potential output and that government could correct that deviation with demand-side policies—**monetary policy,** *a policy of influencing the economy through changes in the money supply and interest rates,* and

fiscal policy, *the deliberate change in either government spending or taxes (or more generally the deficit) to stimulate or slow down the economy.* We'll discuss more specifically what these policies mean and how they are implemented throughout the book, but I introduce them here so that I can better discuss them in both the short-run *AS/AD* demand-side framework of this chapter and the long-run supply-side framework of the next chapter.

The Keynesian model focuses on the use of monetary and fiscal policy.

Suppose the economy falls into a recession; that is, output falls below its potential. According to the *AS/AD* model, this could happen if aggregate demand falls for some unexplained reason. In response firms decrease output and lay off workers, which lowers people's income. Lower income leads consumers to cut expenditures further, which once again causes firms to decrease production. So the fall in aggregate demand creates a cycle that feeds on itself and can develop into a vicious downward spiral.

In the *AS/AD* model eventually this downward cycle of aggregate demand and production ends, settling at an equilibrium that is lower than the original income. That equilibrium might not be at the economy's potential output. Thus, for Keynes, there was a difference between **equilibrium output**—*the level of output toward which the economy gravitates in the short run because of the cumulative cycles of declining or increasing production*—and potential output. Keynes believed that at certain times the economy needed some help in reaching its potential output.

In the Keynesian model, there is a difference between equilibrium output and potential output.

Fixed Price Level

As mentioned in Chapter 6, Keynes distinguished between the forces operating in a single market and the forces operating in the aggregate economy. In a single market, when demand falls, firms reduce prices to bring the market back to equilibrium. You might think the same would be true for the aggregate economy, but Keynes correctly pointed out that it would not be the case for two reasons. First, social forces keep firms from reducing wages quickly, and falling product prices may create problems by causing expectations of further decreases; firms generally cut production long before they cut wages or prices. Cutting production could lead to the cumulative downward spiral of income discussed above. Second, even if firms cut wages and prices, if all firms did so, *relative* wages or prices would not fall. But it is relative wage and price changes that are needed to increase sales. Instead, such a general decrease in prices and wages would lead to **deflation** *(an overall decline in the price level in the economy).* This deflation would create problems of its own.

When prices are falling, profits decline, making entrepreneurs hesitant to start businesses, slowing the growth of the economy. Asset values (prices of assets such as houses, stocks, and bonds) also decline, which means that the economy experiences not only a deflation in the general price level (price of goods and services), it also experiences asset price deflation (the fall in the prices of assets in which people hold their wealth). Since asset prices are much more volatile than goods prices, asset price deflation is much more common than deflation in the general price level of goods and services.

Asset price deflation is problematic for an economy; it reduces the value of collateral used to support consumer and producer loans and therefore spending. So both types of deflation undermine business and consumer confidence. Thus a general fall in prices cannot be relied upon to bring the aggregate economy into equilibrium without causing serious problems.

These inevitable side effects of a falling price level and a falling asset price level cause firms to decrease output more than the falling price level causes consumers to buy more. So deflation isn't an acceptable policy option. U.S. government policy makers of all political persuasions have agreed that deflation as a method of bringing aggregate supply and demand into equilibrium is unacceptable. It would destroy our economy. Because of the problems with deflation, Keynes argued that, when considering declines in demand, at least in the short run, the price level of goods can be considered

U.S. government policy makers of all political persuasions have agreed that deflation as a method of bringing aggregate supply and demand into equilibrium is unacceptable.

The Keynesian insight is that the economy can get stuck in a prolonged recession with no reasonable method for the market to escape on its own.

essentially fixed. But a fixed price level leaves the economy with the problem of falling into an aggregate equilibrium that is not at the economy's potential output. The economy could get stuck in a prolonged recession with low income and high unemployment and no reasonable method for the market to escape from that undesirable equilibrium on its own. That's the essence of the Keynesian insight.

The Paradox of Thrift

We can see Keynes' insight working its way through the economy in the downturn that began in 2008. The economy went into a recession and people cut expenditures as they lost their jobs. Instead of consuming, they saved. As they increased savings the economy started on a downward spiral. Income fell, and as it did saving fell, leading them to try to save more. If increased savings have feedback effects on income, the economy can find itself facing the *fallacy of composition:* When people try to save more, they actually save less, or at least a lot less than what they wanted to save, because the increased savings lowers their income.

One might expect that people's savings would finance investment, which would offset the decline in consumption expenditures. But savings does not automatically get transferred into investment. Where does the saving go? In a downward spiral, it disappears. As output falls, people lose their jobs and are forced to save less than they had planned because they earn less income than they had planned. Thus the choice to increase the *percentage* of their income devoted to saving can lead income to fall, so that while the percentage devoted to saving increases, the absolute amount of savings decreases as income falls. Suppose income is $1,000 and the saving rate is 4 percent. We know that 4 percent of $1,000 is $40; if people increase their saving rate to 4.1 percent and that causes income to fall to $970, then their total saving does not increase to $41; it falls to $39.77 (4.1% × $970).

Q-1 How would the paradox of thrift lead to a decline in output if saving were to increase in an economy?

This paradox of attempts to increase total savings by increasing the percentage of savings leading to a fall in the total amount of savings is called the **paradox of thrift**—*an increase in saving can lead to a decrease in expenditures, which can lead to decreasing supply, decreasing output, causing a recession, and lowering total saving.*

Keynesian economists advocated an activist demand management policy.

If the economy is in a position where the paradox of thrift holds, increasing savings will set in motion a cycle of declining expenditures and production. Eventually income will fall far enough so that once again saving and investment will be in equilibrium, but then the economy could be in an almost permanent recession, with ongoing unemployment. Keynesians believe that in this case the economy would need government's help to prop up aggregate expenditures. That is the essence of the Keynesian argument to support expansionary demand-side macro policy.

Q-2 How does the Keynesian view of saving differ from the layperson's view?

Notice that the Keynesian short-run framework gives a quite different view of saving than is often held by laypeople. In that conventional view of saving, saving is seen as something good; savings leads to investment, which in turn leads to growth. In the Keynesian short-run framework, that isn't the way it works.

By the late 1950s, Keynesian economics had been accepted by most macroeconomists, and was taught almost everywhere in the United States. The model that initially was meant to capture Keynesian economics was called the multiplier model, and is the model I present in Chapter 9W. This multiplier model emphasizes aggregate output fluctuations and explores why those output fluctuations generally would not lead to wild fluctuations in output—depressions—and instead lead to smaller fluctuations—recessions. In the 1970s, that multiplier model was replaced by the aggregate supply/aggregate demand (*AS/AD*) model. It is that *AS/AD* model that I introduce you to in this chapter.

It is important to remember three things about the *AS/AD* model. The first is that it is a short-run model. It does not tell us what the long-run effects of any policy will be. The second is that it is a pedagogical model—designed to give students and policy makers a framework to organize their thinking about the macro economy. It is a rough-and-ready

ADDED DIMENSION

In the Long Run, We're All Dead

When Keynes said "In the long run, we're all dead," he didn't mean that we can forget the long run. What he meant was that if the long run is so long that short-run forces do not let it come about, then for all practical purposes there is no long run. In that case, policy makers ought to focus on short-run problem.

Keynes believed that voters would not be satisfied waiting for market forces to bring about full employment. If something were not done in the short run to alleviate unemployment, he felt, voters would opt for fascism (as had the Germans) or communism (as had the Russians). He saw both alternatives as undesirable. For him, what would happen in the long run was academic.

Classicals, in contrast, argued that the short-run problems were not as bad as Keynes made them out to be and therefore should not be focused on to the exclusion of long-run problems.

Modern-day Classicals argue that while Keynes is dead, we are not, and the result of his short-run focus was long-run problems—specifically large government debts that threaten the long-run stability of the economy. Eventually, a society is going to have to deal with these debts, and while they may never have to pay them off, they will have to pay interest on them. Large government debts weaken an economy.

Up until 2008, Keynesian ideas had lost favor as people became concerned about the large debts the government was incurring. But when the financial crisis of 2008 hit, and the macroeconomy fell into a serious recession, Keynesian ideas came back into vogue. Somehow the long-run debt problem seems less important when the short-run problems are themselves threatening the stability of the society.

framework, not a model developed to capture all the dynamic forces operating in the economy. The third point is that in its standard presentation, the *AS/AD* model is not a model developed from first principles, as is the micro supply/demand model. That micro model starts with individual choices and relates those choices to equilibrium. The macro *AS/AD* model does not start with individual choices. Instead, it starts with aggregate relationships based on empirical observations about the way the aggregate economy works. It loosely relates those empirically observed aggregate relationships to decisions by firms and individuals. These dynamic forces are especially important when aggregate demand declines significantly, as happened in 2008 and 2009. (The multiplier model developed in Chapter 9W does a better job of highlighting those dynamic forces.)

Instability caused by dynamic forces is especially important when aggregate demand declines significantly.

What the *AS/AD* model does do is provide a simple model that suggests a role for government in keeping feedback effects from spiraling an economy downward. It gives a good sense of how macro economists think about cyclical problems in the macro economy. The *AS/AD* model is used by most macro policy economists to discuss mild short-run, cyclical fluctuations in output and unemployment. At the end of the chapter I will discuss some of the limitations of the *AS/AD* model in more depth.

The Components of the *AS/AD* Model

The *AS/AD* model consists of three curves. The curve describing the supply side of the aggregate economy in the short run is the short-run aggregate supply (*SAS*) curve, the curve describing the demand side of the economy is the aggregate demand curve, and the curve describing the highest sustainable level of output is the long-run aggregate supply (*LAS*) curve.

The first thing to note about the AS/AD model is that it is fundamentally different from the microeconomic supply/demand model. In microeconomics the price of a single good is on the vertical axis and the quantity of a single good on the horizontal axis. The reasoning for the shapes of the micro supply and demand curves is based on the concepts of substitution and opportunity cost. In the macro *AS/AD* model, the price level of all goods, not just the price of one good, is on the vertical axis and aggregate output, not a single good, is on the horizontal axis. The shapes of the curves have nothing to do with opportunity cost or substitution.

Knowing the difference between microeconomic supply and demand curves and macroeconomic aggregate demand and supply curves is very important.

The second thing to note about the *AS/AD* model is that it is a *historical model.* A historical model is a model that starts at a point in time and provides insight into what will likely happen when changes affect the economy. It does not try to explain how the economy got to its starting point; the macroeconomy is too complicated for that. Instead, the model starts from historically given price and output levels and, given the institutional structure of the economy, considers how changes in the economy are likely to affect those levels. What this means is that much of the discussion in this chapter is based on the economy's institutional realities and observed empirical regularities.

Let's now consider the three central components of the *AS/AD* model: the aggregate demand (*AD*) curve, the short-run aggregate supply (*SAS*) curve, and the long-run aggregate supply (*LAS*) curve.

The Aggregate Demand Curve

The **aggregate demand (*AD*) curve** is *a curve that shows how a change in the price level will change aggregate expenditures on all goods and services in an economy.* (Aggregate expenditures is the sum of consumption, investment, government expenditures, and net exports.) A standard *AD* curve is shown in Figure 9-1. Although the curve is called an aggregate demand curve, let me repeat that it is not the same as a microeconomic demand curve. The *AD* curve is more an equilibrium curve.[1] It shows the level of aggregate expenditures at every price level, implicitly taking into account some interactions among all producers and consumers in an economy.

Take the time to draw an *AD* curve, making sure to label the axes correctly.

The Slope of the *AD* Curve

Aggregate Demand

As you can see, the *AD* curve is downward-sloping. A good place to begin understanding why it is downward-sloping is to remember the composition of aggregate demand. As I discussed in the chapter on aggregate accounting, aggregate expenditures (demand) is

FIGURE 9-1

The Aggregate Demand Curve

The *AD* curve is a downward-sloping curve that looks like a typical demand curve, but it is important to remember that it is quite a different curve. The reason it slopes downward is not the substitution effect, but instead the interest rate effect, the international effect, and the money wealth effect. The multiplier effect strengthens each of these effects.

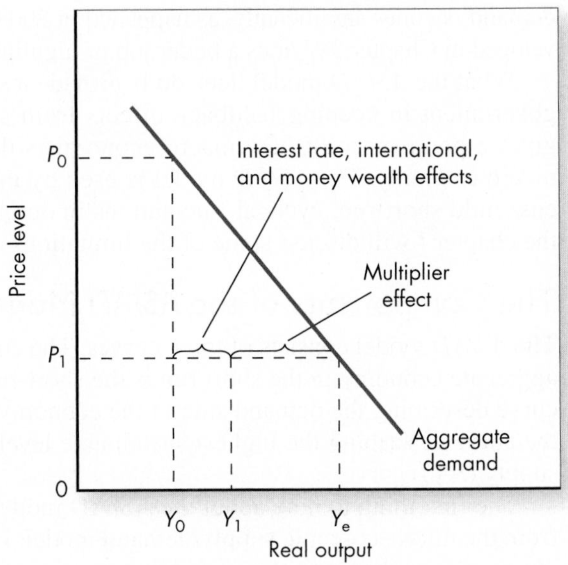

[1] In a number of articles and in previous editions, I tried to change the terminology so that students would not be misled into thinking that the *AD* curve was a normal demand curve. But my changes did not catch on.

the sum of consumption, investment, government spending, and net exports. The slope of the *AD* curve depends on how these components respond to changes in the price level.

In principle, we would expect the *AD* curve to be vertical. Why? Because one of the definitional assumptions of economics is that the price level is simply what is called a *numeraire*. The price level is simply a reference point, and the actual value of that numeraire should not matter. To see why, say that all prices (including wages) doubled. How would people's choices change? They wouldn't. Instead of earning $10 an hour, you would now earn $20 an hour. All the goods you buy would cost twice as much too, so you wouldn't be better off or worse off. Only the reference point has changed. Thus, as a first approximation, we would expect that you would buy the same amount of real goods at every price level. That would make the *AD* curve vertical.

In principle, we would expect the *AD* curve to be vertical.

Macroeconomists have examined this proposition and have developed a number of explanations for why a falling price level increases aggregate expenditures in normal times. These explanations make the standard *AD* curve downward-sloping rather than vertical. I'll discuss three of these standard effects: the interest-rate effect, the international effect, and the money wealth effect.

The three standard reasons given for the downward sloping AD curve are the interest rate effect, the international effect, and the money wealth effect.

The Interest Rate Effect One explanation for why the aggregate demand curve slopes downward is called the **interest rate effect**—*the effect that a lower price level has on investment expenditures through the effect that a change in the price level has on interest rates.* The interest rate effect works as follows: A decrease in the price level will increase the purchasing power of the money in people's pockets and people will find they're holding more money than they need. So, they deposit the extra money at banks in some form, giving banks more money to loan out. As banks make more loans, interest rates will fall, which, in turn, will increase investment expenditures. Why? Because at lower interest rates businesses will undertake more investment projects. Since investment is one component of aggregate demand, the quantity of aggregate demand will increase when the price level falls.

The International Effect A second reason why aggregate quantity demanded increases with a fall in the price level is the **international effect,** which tells us that *as the price level falls (assuming the exchange rate does not change), net exports will rise.* As the price level in the United States falls, the price of U.S. goods relative to foreign goods goes down and U.S. goods become more competitive relative to foreign goods; thus, U.S. exports increase and U.S. imports decrease. Let's consider an example. In the mid-1990s, the Bulgarian currency was fixed to the German mark. Bulgaria's price level rose enormously, increasing the demand for German imports and reducing the quantity of aggregate demand in Bulgaria.

The Money Wealth Effect A third explanation why the *AD* curve isn't vertical is called the money wealth effect. To understand this effect consider Figure 9-1. Say we start out at price P_0 and output Y_0 in Figure 9-1. (Remember, as I said above, in a historical model we start at a given price and output and determine what would happen if the price level rises or falls from that level.) Now, say that the price level falls to P_1. How will this affect the total amount of goods and services that people demand? The **money wealth effect** (sometimes called the *real balance effect*) tells us that *a fall in the price level will make the holders of money richer, so they buy more.* In other words, if the price level falls, the dollar bill in your pocket will buy more than before because the purchasing power of the dollar rises. You are, in effect, richer and as you get richer, other things equal, you will buy more goods and services. Since consumption expenditures are a component of aggregate demand, aggregate expenditures will increase, which is shown graphically by a movement along the *AD* curve. (To differentiate such movements along the *AD* curve from a shift in the *AD* curve, I call movements due to changes in the price level "changes in the quantity of aggregate demand.") Most economists do not see the money wealth effect as strong; they do, however, accept the logic of the argument.

So, in Figure 9-1 when we include the international effect, the interest rate effect, and the money wealth effect, a fall in the price level from P_0 to P_1 causes the quantity of aggregate demand to increase from Y_0 to Y_1.

In micro other things can be assumed to remain constant, whereas in macro other things change.

The Multiplier Effect The above three effects give us some explanation why the quantity of aggregate demand will increase with a fall in the price level. But the story about the slope of the aggregate demand curve doesn't end there. It also takes into account the **multiplier effect**—*the amplification of initial changes in expenditures.* It is important to recognize that when considering the demand curve in micro, we can reasonably assume that other things remain constant; in macro, other things change. Whereas the demand curve in micro includes only the initial change, the aggregate demand curve includes the repercussions that these initial changes have throughout the economy. What I mean by *repercussions* is that the initial changes in expenditures set in motion a process in the economy that amplifies these initial effects.

The slope of the *AD* curve is determined by:

1. The money wealth effect;
2. The interest rate effect;
3. The international effect; and
4. The multiplier effect.

To see how these repercussions will likely work in the real world, imagine that the price level in the United States rises. U.S. citizens will reduce their purchases of U.S. goods and increase their purchases of foreign goods. (That's the international effect.) U.S. firms will see the demand for their goods and services fall and will decrease their output. Profits will fall and people will be laid off. Both these effects will cause income to fall, and as income falls, people will demand still fewer goods and services. (If you're unemployed, you cut back your purchases.) Again production and income fall, which again leads to a drop in expenditures. This secondary cutback is an example of a repercussion. These repercussions *multiply* the initial effect that a change in the price level has on expenditures.

The multiplier effect amplifies the initial interest rate, international, and money wealth effects, thereby making the slope of the *AD* curve flatter than it would have been. You can see this in Figure 9-1. The three effects discussed above increase output from Y_0 to Y_1. The repercussions multiply that effect so that output increases to Y_e.

Economists have suggested other reasons why changes in the price level affect the quantity of aggregate demand, but these four should be sufficient to give you an initial understanding. Going through the same exercise that I did above for the interest rate, international, money wealth, and multiplier effects for a fall (rather than a rise) in the price level is a useful exercise.

Q-3 True or false? The slope of the *AD* curve is -1 if as the price level falls from 110 to 100, the international effect increases output by 10.

Let's conclude this section with an example that brings out the importance of the multiplier effect in determining the slope of the *AD* curve. Say that the multiplier effect amplifies the interest rate, international, and money wealth effects by a factor of 2 and that the interest rate, international, and money wealth effects reduce output by 4 when the price level rises from 100 to 110. What will be the slope of the *AD* curve? Since the multiplier effect is 2, the total decline in output will be $2 \times 4 = 8$, so the slope will be $-10/8$, or -1.25.

How Steep Is the AD Curve? While all economists agree about the logic of the interest rate effect, the international effect, and the money wealth effect, most also agree that for small changes in the price level, the net effect is relatively small. So, even after the effect has been expanded by the multiplier, the *AD* curve has a very steep slope.[2]

---

[2]Of the three, the international effect is probably the strongest, but its strength depends on whether fluctuations in the exchange rate offset it.

Unfortunately, statistically separating out the effects determining the slope of the *AD* curve from shifts in the *AD* curve is difficult because there is much noise—random unexplained movements—in the relationship between the price level and aggregate expenditures. It is that noise on the aggregate level that makes the economy so hard to predict, and accounts for the description of economic forecasting as "driving a car blindfolded while following directions given by a person who is looking out of the back window." In order to make the graphs easy to follow, they show a flatter *AD* curve than probably exists in reality.

There is much noise in the relationship between the price level and aggregate expenditures.

Dynamic Price Level Adjustment Feedback Effects

The interest rate, international, and money wealth effects, amplified by the multiplier effect, are all logically correct. But there are other forces in the economy that counteract these forces. At times these dynamic effects can overwhelm the standard effects and make the aggregate economy unstable, making expansions stronger and contractions larger. They can reduce or completely offset the stabilizing effects of a price-level adjustment in bringing about an aggregate equilibrium.

At times dynamic effects can overwhelm the standard effects and make the aggregate economy unstable.

These forces are especially important when aggregate demand is declining and the price level needs to fall to bring about aggregate equilibrium. Here is the problem: Pressure for the price level to fall brings with it:[3]

- Expectations of falling aggregate demand.
- Lower asset prices, making society on average *feel* poorer, even though, theoretically, it is not *actually* poorer.
- Financial panics, triggered by a decline in the value of financial assets, causing individuals and banks, who relied on those financial assets as collateral for loans, to require full payment on (to call in) those loans, which forces borrowers (mainly firms) to reduce production and lay off workers, decreasing aggregate demand further.

Each of these forces, which the standard model assumes away, works in an opposite direction to the standard effects that cause the quantity of aggregate demand to increase when the price level falls. If these dynamic forces are strong enough, aggregate demand will fall (shift to the left) when the price level falls. In fact, the price level doesn't even have to fall; there only has to be the pressure for the price level to fall. We will discuss these dynamic forces more in the chapter on the current financial crisis.

Shifts in the *AD* Curve

Next, let's consider what causes the *AD* curve to shift. A shift in the *AD* curve means that at every price level, total expenditures have changed. Anything other than the price level that changes the components of aggregate demand (consumption, investment, government spending, and net exports) will shift the *AD* curve. Five important shift factors of aggregate demand are foreign income, exchange rate fluctuations, the distribution of income, expectations, and government policies.

FOREIGN INCOME A country is not an island unto itself. U.S. economic output is closely tied to the income of its major world trading partners. When our trading partners go into a recession, the demand for U.S. goods, and hence U.S. exports, will fall, causing the U.S. *AD* curve to shift in to the left. Similarly, a rise in foreign income leads to an increase in U.S. exports and a rightward shift of the U.S. *AD* curve.

[3]These dynamic pressures are also at work in reverse when there are pressures for the price level to increase. But for increases, the pressures tend to reinforce the expansionary forces, and are usually seen as positive effects, especially when there is no fear of inflation.

Q-4 If a country's exchange rate rises, what happens to its *AD* curve?

EXCHANGE RATES The currencies of various countries are connected through exchange rates. When a country's currency loses value relative to other currencies, its goods become more competitive compared to foreign goods. Foreign demand for domestic goods increases and domestic demand for foreign goods decreases as individuals shift their spending to domestic goods at home. Both these effects increase net exports and shift the *AD* curve to the right. By the same reasoning, when a country's currency gains value, the *AD* curve shifts in the opposite direction. You can see these effects on the U.S.-Canadian border. At one time, the Canadian dollar had a high value relative to the U.S. dollar, making U.S. goods cheaper for Canadians. This caused many Canadians near the border to make buying trips to the United States. When the Canadian dollar fell in value, those buying trips decreased, and the Canadian *AD* curve shifted right.

DISTRIBUTION OF INCOME Some people save more than others, and everyone's spending habits differ. Thus, as income distribution changes, so too will aggregate demand. One of the most important distributional effects concerns the distribution of income between wages and profits. Workers receive wage income and are more likely to spend the income they receive; firms' profits are distributed to stockholders or are retained by the firm. Since stockholders in the United States tend to be wealthy, and the wealthy save a greater portion of their income than the poor do, a higher portion of income received as profits will likely be saved. Assuming that not all saving is not translated into investment, as the proportion of income going to profit increases, total expenditures are likely to fall, shifting the AD curve to the left. Similarly, as wages (both as a proportion of total income, and absolutely) increase, total expenditures are likely to rise, shifting the AD curve out to the right.

Expectations of higher future income increase expenditures and shift the *AD* curve out.

EXPECTATIONS Another important shift factor of aggregate demand is expectations. Many different types of expectations can affect the *AD* curve. To give you an idea of the role of expectations, let's consider two expectational shift factors: expectations of future output and expectations of future prices. When businesspeople expect demand to be high in the future, they will want to increase their productive capacity; their investment demand, a component of aggregate demand, will increase. Thus, positive expectations about future demand will shift the *AD* curve to the right.

Similarly, when consumers expect the economy to do well, they will be less worried about saving for the future, and they will spend more now—the *AD* curve will shift to the right. Alternatively, if consumers expect the future to be gloomy, they will likely try to save for the future and will decrease their consumption expenditures. The *AD* curve will shift to the left.

Another type of expectation that shifts the *AD* curve concerns expectations of future prices. If you expect the prices of goods to rise in the future, it pays to buy goods now that you might want in the future—before their prices rise. The current price level hasn't changed, but aggregate quantity demanded at that price level has increased, indicating a shift of the *AD* curve to the right.

Five important shift factors of *AD* are:

1. Foreign income.
2. Exchange rates.
3. The distribution of income.
4. Expectations.
5. Monetary and fiscal policies.

The effect of expectations of future price levels is seen more clearly in a hyperinflation. In most cases of hyperinflation, people rush out to spend their money quickly—to buy whatever they can to beat the price increase. So even though prices are rising, aggregate demand stays high because the rise in price creates an expectation of even higher prices, and thus the current high price is seen as a low price relative to the future. I said that an increase in expectations of inflation will "have a tendency to" rather than "definitely" shift the *AD* curve to the right because those expectations of inflation are interrelated with a variety of other expectations. For example, an expectation of a rise in the price of goods you buy could be accompanied by an expectation of a fall in income, and that fall in income would work in the opposite direction, decreasing aggregate demand.

This interrelation of various types of expectations makes it very difficult to specify precisely what effect certain types of expectations have on the *AD* curve. But it does not eliminate the importance of expectations as shift factors. It simply means that we often aren't sure what the net effect of a change in expectations on aggregate demand will be.

Monetary and Fiscal Policies One of the most important reasons why the aggregate demand curve has been so important in macro policy analysis is that often macro policy makers think that they can control it, at least to some degree. For example, if the government spends lots of money without increasing taxes, it shifts the *AD* curve to the right; if the government raises taxes significantly and holds spending constant, consumers will have less disposable income and will reduce their expenditures, shifting the *AD* curve to the left. Similarly, when the Federal Reserve Bank, the U.S. economy's central bank, expands the money supply, it can often lower interest rates, making it easier for both consumers and investors to borrow, increasing their spending, and thereby shifting the *AD* curve to the right. This deliberate increase or decrease in aggregate demand to influence the level of income in the economy is what most policy makers mean by the term *macro policy.* Expansionary macro policy shifts the *AD* curve to the right; contractionary macro policy shifts it to the left.

Deliberate shifting of the *AD* curve is what most policy makers mean by macro policy.

Multiplier Effects of Shift Factors As I emphasized when I introduced the *AD* curve, you cannot treat the *AD* curve like a micro demand curve. This comes out most clearly when considering shifts in the curve caused by shift factors. The aggregate demand curve may shift by more than the amount of the initial shift factor because of the multiplier effect. The explanation is as follows: When government increases its spending, firms increase production, which leads to higher income. A fraction of that increase in income is spent on more goods and services, shifting the *AD* curve even further to the right. This leads firms to increase production again; income and expenditures also rise. Each round, the increase gets smaller and smaller until the increase becomes negligible. In the end the *AD* curve will have shifted by a multiple of the initial shift. Just how large that multiple is depends on how much the change in income affects spending in each round. Thus, in Figure 9-2, when an initial shift factor of aggregate demand is 100 and the multiplier is 3, the *AD* curve will shift to the right by 300, three times the initial shift. The extra 200 shift is due to the multiplier effect.

Q-5 If government spending increases by 20, by how much does the *AD* curve shift out?

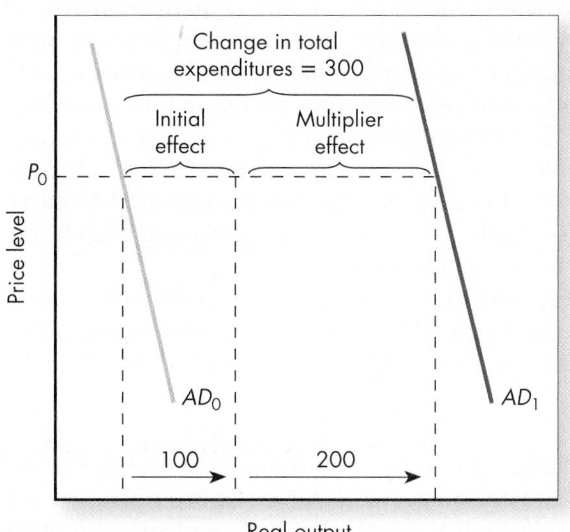

FIGURE 9-2 Effect of a Shift Factor on the *AD* Curve

The *AD* curve shifts out by more than the initial change in expenditures. In this example, exports increase by 100. The multiplier magnifies this shift, and the *AD* curve shifts to the right by a multiple of 100, in this case by 300.

To see that you are following the argument, consider the following two shifts: (1) a fall in the U.S. exchange rate, increasing net exports by 50, and (2) an increase in government spending of 100. Explain how the *AD* curve will shift in each of these cases and why that shift will be larger than the initial shift. If you are not sure about these explanations, review the multiplier effect discussion above.

The Aggregate Supply Curves

The other side of the aggregate economy is the supply side. We divide the supply side into short-run and long-run components. Let's first consider the short-run supply curve.

The Short-Run Aggregate Supply Curve

FIGURE 9-3 The Short-Run Aggregate Supply Curve

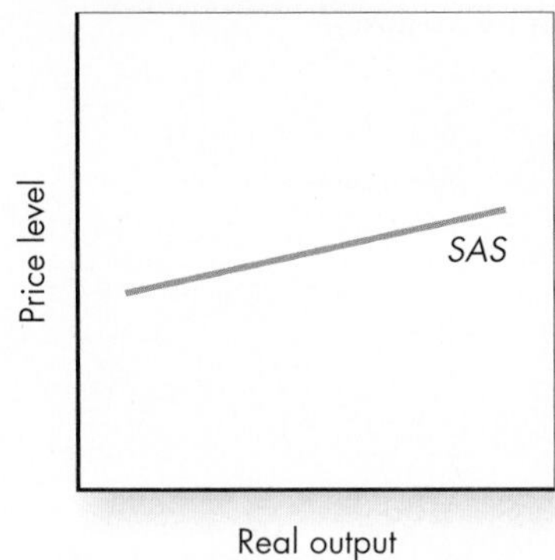

The **short-run aggregate supply (*SAS*) curve** *is a curve that specifies how a shift in the aggregate demand curve affects the price level and real output in the short run, other things constant.* A standard *SAS* curve is shown in Figure 9-3.

THE SLOPE OF THE *SAS* CURVE As you can see, the *SAS* curve is upward-sloping, which means that in the short run, other things constant, an increase in output is accompanied by a rise in the price level. That is, when aggregate demand increases, the price level—the composite of all prices—rises. The shape of the *SAS* curve reflects two different types of markets in our economy: auction markets (which are the markets represented by the supply/demand model) and posted-price markets (in which prices are set by the producers and change only infrequently).

In markets where prices are set by the interaction between buyers and sellers, none of whom have enough market power to set prices, there is little question why prices rise when demand increases as long as the supply curve for firms in the market is upward-sloping. But these auction markets make up only a small percentage of final goods markets. (They are much more common in markets for resources such as oil or farm products.) In most final goods markets, sellers set a price for their goods and buyers take these prices as given. These posted-price markets comprise 90 percent of the total final goods markets. In posted-price markets, firms set prices as a markup over costs. For example, if the markup is 40 percent and the cost of production is $10 per unit, the firm would set a price of $14.

Posted-price markets are often called **quantity-adjusting markets**—*markets in which firms respond to changes in demand primarily by changing production instead of changing their prices.* It would be wrong, however, to assume that prices in these markets are totally unresponsive to changes in demand. When demand increases, some firms will take the opportunity to raise their prices slightly, increasing their markup, and when demand falls, firms have a tendency to lower their prices slightly, decreasing their markup. This tendency to change markups as aggregate demand changes contributes to the upward slope of the *SAS* curve. So, the two reasons the *SAS* curve slopes upward are (1) upward-sloping supply curves in auction markets and (2) firms' tendency to increase their markup when demand increases.

The two reasons the *SAS* curve slopes upward are:

1. Upward-sloping supply curves in auction markets.
2. Firms' tendency to increase their markup when demand increases.

One reason I did not give for the upward slope of the *SAS* curve is changes in costs of production. That's because along an *SAS* curve, all other things, including input prices, are assumed to remain constant. Increases in input prices shift the *SAS* curve.

SHIFTS IN THE *SAS* CURVE Notice that in the definition of the *SAS* curve, we have assumed that other things remain constant. As discussed above, this does not mean that other things *will* remain constant. It simply means that changes in other

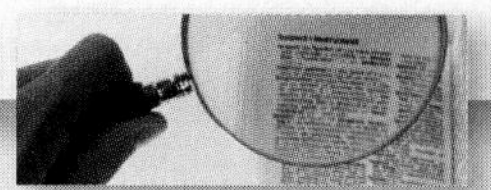

ADDED DIMENSION

Why Are Prices Inflexible?

Why do firms adjust production instead of price? A number of reasons have been put forward by economists, and recently a group of economists, led by Princeton economist Alan Blinder, surveyed firms to find out which reasons firms believed were most important. The survey choices included strategic pricing, cost-based pricing rules, and implicit contracts.

1. **Strategic pricing.** About 90 percent of final-goods markets in the United States are markets in which only a few major firms compete, each taking each other's reactions into account in their decisions. Although, under U.S. law, firms cannot get together and decide on a pricing strategy for the industry, they can informally coordinate their pricing procedures. If all firms can implicitly agree to hold their prices up when faced with decreased demand, they are not violating the law and will be better off than they would be if they acted in an uncoordinated fashion.

   They also won't increase prices when they experience an increase in demand because they fear that doing so will undermine the coordinated pricing strategy with other firms or they will lose market share when other firms don't raise prices.

   This is not to say that the U.S. economy is not competitive. Ask any businessperson and he or she will tell you that it is highly competitive. But firms often compete on fronts other than price.
2. **Cost-based pricing rules.** Strategic pricing is maintained by firms' tendency to use cost-based pricing rules. In a cost-plus-markup pricing procedure, firms set prices based on the costs of production. For a majority of firms, the most important costs are labor costs, which tend to be fixed by long-term wage contracts between workers and employers. (Unions, for example, typically negotiate wage contracts for three-year periods.) Thus, costs do not change with changes in demand, and, following a cost-plus-markup strategy, neither do prices.
3. **Implicit contracts.** Most firms have ongoing relationships with their customers. That means that they don't want to antagonize them. They have found that one way to avoid antagonizing customers is not to take advantage of them even when they could. In the Blinder survey, firms felt that they had implicit contracts with their customers to raise prices only when their costs changed, or when market conditions changed substantially.

The combination of these reasons leads to a large segment of the economy in which the prices do not significantly change as demand changes. For that reason, we generally don't see big changes in the overall price level. Of course, if costs, especially labor costs, start rising significantly, then prices will rise too. To the degree that demand changes affect costs, prices will respond, but, as a first approximation, it is generally acceptable to say that the price level does not significantly move in response to demand. That's why the short-run aggregate supply curve is not very steep.

things, such as input prices, shift the *SAS* curve. For example, if input prices rise, the *SAS* curve shifts up; if input prices fall, the *SAS* curve shifts down. So a change in input prices, such as wages, is a shift factor of aggregate supply. An important reason why wages change is expectations of inflation. If workers expect prices to rise by 2 percent, they are likely to ask for at least a 2 percent rise in wages simply to keep up with inflation and maintain their real wage. If they expect the price level to fall by 2 percent, they are far more likely to be happy with their current wage. So the expectation of inflation is a shift factor that works through wages.

Changes in input prices cause a shift in the *SAS* curve.

Another shift factor of aggregate supply is a change in the productivity of the factors of production such as labor. An increase in productivity, by reducing the amount of inputs required for a given amount of output, reduces input costs per unit of output and shifts the *SAS* curve down. A fall in productivity shifts the *SAS* curve up.

Two other shift factors are changes in import prices of final goods and changes in excise and sales taxes. Import prices are a shift factor because they are a component of an economy's price level. When import prices rise, the *SAS* curve shifts up; when import prices fall, the *SAS* curve shifts down. By raising the cost of goods, higher sales taxes shift the *SAS* curve up, and lower sales taxes shift the *SAS* curve down.

In summary, anything that changes production costs will be a shift factor of supply. Such factors include:

- Changes in input prices.
- Productivity.
- Import prices.
- Excise and sales taxes.

FIGURE 9-4
Input Price Rise and the *SAS* Curve

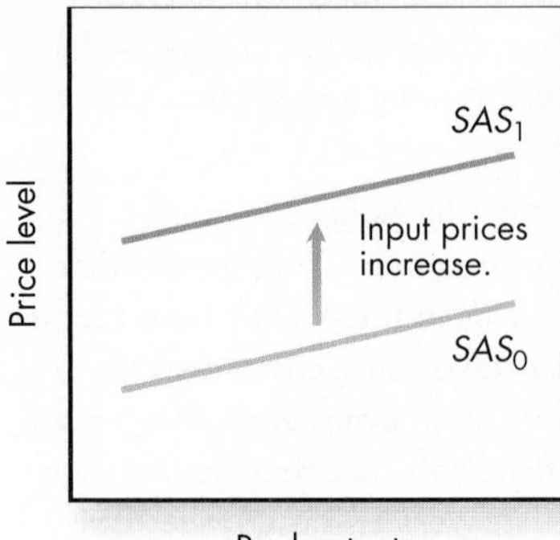

Economists spend a lot of time tracking these shift factors because they are central to whether the economy will have an inflation problem. Two of these—the wage component of input prices and labor productivity—are followed with special care because labor costs make up about two-thirds of total production costs.

The rule of thumb economists use when estimating how much the *SAS* curve will shift is that it will shift by the percentage change in wages and other factor prices minus changes in productivity. For example, if productivity rises by 3 percent and wages rise by 7 percent, we can expect the price level to rise by 4 percent for a given level of output. I show a shift up in the *SAS* curve in Figure 9-4. If wages and productivity rise by equal percentages, the price level would remain constant. If wages and other factor prices rise by less than the increase in productivity, the price level can fall, as recently happened in Japan. The relationship can be written as follows:

Q-6 If wages rise by 4 percent and productivity rises by 1 percent, by how much does the price level change?

$$\% \text{ change in the price level} = \% \text{ change in wages} - \% \text{ change in productivity}$$

In the real world, we see shifts in the *SAS* curve in many areas. In 2007 and into mid-2008 oil prices more than doubled. That led to a sharp rise in the producer prices and a significant rise in factor prices, causing the *SAS* curve to shift up. Another example occurred in Egypt in 2011 when the value of its currency, the pound, fell drastically. That caused the price of imports measured in pounds to increase substantially, which shifted its *SAS* curve up.

The Long-Run Aggregate Supply Curve

The final curve that makes up the *AS/AD* model is the **long-run aggregate supply (*LAS*) curve**—*a curve that shows the long-run relationship between output and the price level.* Whereas the *SAS* curve holds input prices constant, no prices are assumed held constant on the *LAS* curve. The position of the *LAS* curve is determined by potential output—the amount of goods and services an economy can produce when both labor and capital are fully employed. Figure 9-5(a) shows an *LAS* curve.

The *SAS* curve holds input prices constant; no prices are assumed held constant on the *LAS* curve.

Notice that the *LAS* curve is vertical. Since at potential output all resources are being fully utilized, a rise in the price level means that the prices of goods and factors of production, including wages, rise. Consider it this way: If all prices doubled, including your wage, your real income would not change. Since potential output is unaffected by the price level, the *LAS* curve is vertical.

A Range for Potential Output and the *LAS* Curve Because our estimates of potential output are inexact, precisely where to draw the *LAS* curve is

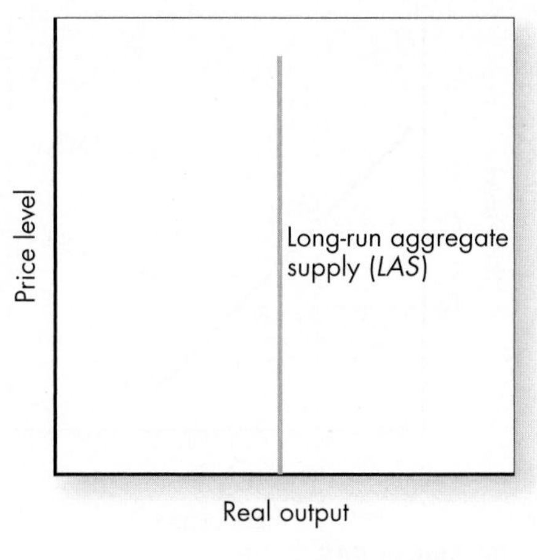

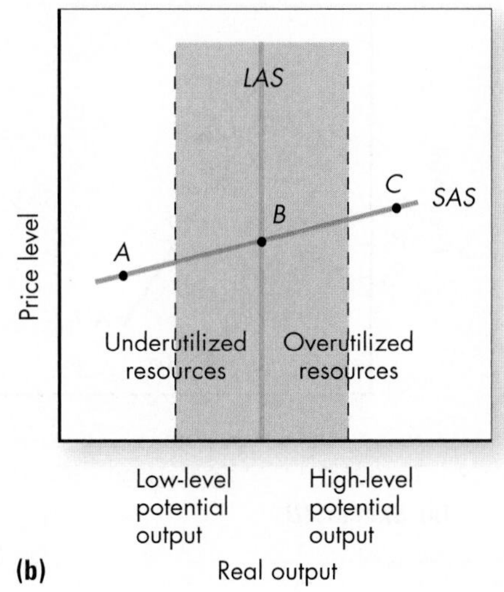

FIGURE 9-5 (A AND B)
The Long-Run Aggregate Supply Curve

The long-run aggregate supply curve shows the output that an economy can produce when both labor and capital are fully employed. It is vertical because at potential output a rise in the price level means that all prices, including input prices, rise. Available resources do not rise and thus neither does potential output.

generally in debate. To understand policy debates, it is helpful to consider potential output to be a range of values. This range is bounded by a high level of potential output and a low level of potential output, as Figure 9-5(b) shows. The *LAS* curve can be thought of as being in the middle of that range.

This range is important because how close actual output (the position of the economy on the *SAS* curve) is to potential output is a key determinant of whether the *SAS* curve is expected to shift up or down. At points on the *SAS* curve to the left of the *LAS* curve (such as point *A*), resources are likely to be underutilized and we would expect factor prices (prices of inputs to production) to fall and, other things equal, the *SAS* curve to shift down. At points to the right of the *LAS* curve (such as point *C*), we would expect factor prices to be bid up and, other things equal, the *SAS* curve to shift up. Moreover, the further actual output is from potential output, the greater the pressure we would expect on factor prices to rise or fall. At the point of intersection between the *SAS* curve and the *LAS* curve (point *B*), other things equal, factor prices have no pressure to rise or fall.

Short-Run Aggregate Supply vs. Long-Run Aggregate Supply

In reality, whether factor prices will rise or fall in response to a change in demand is often in debate. That debate reflects the different estimates of potential output. Given the uncertainty of measured potential output, we would expect there to be a debate about whether the *SAS* curve will be shifting up or down. We will discuss these issues later. For now, all I want you to remember is that the *LAS* curve is an abstraction that reduces what is actually a range of potential output into a single value.

SHIFTS IN THE *LAS* CURVE Because the position of the *LAS* curve is determined by potential output, it shifts for the same reasons that potential output shifts: changes in capital, available resources, growth-compatible institutions, technology, and entrepreneurship. Increases in any of these increase potential output and shift the *LAS* curve out to the right. Decreases in any of these reduce potential output and shift the *LAS* curve in to the left. The position of the *LAS* curve plays an important role in determining long-run equilibrium and in determining whether policy should focus on long-run or short-run issues.

Because the position of the LAS curve is determined by potential output, it shifts for the same reasons that potential output shifts.

FIGURE 9-6 (A AND B)
Equilibrium in the *AS/AD* Model

Short-run equilibrium is where the short-run aggregate supply and aggregate demand curves intersect. Point E in (**a**) is one equilibrium; (**a**) also shows how a shift in the aggregate demand curve to the right changes equilibrium from E to F, increasing output from Y_0 to Y_1 and increasing price level from P_0 to P_1. In (**b**) a shift up in the short-run aggregate supply curve changes equilibrium from E to G.

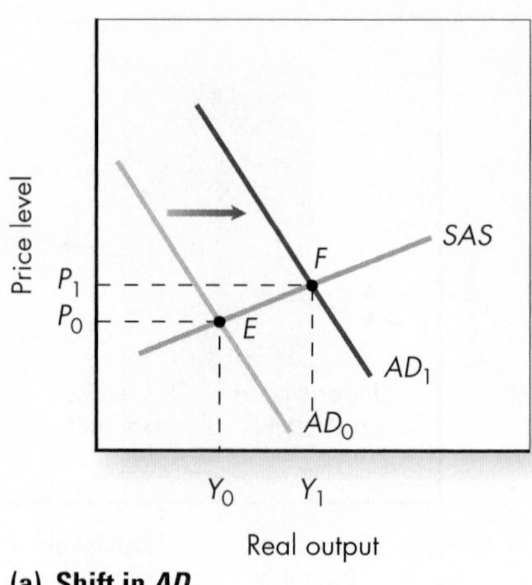

(a) Shift in *AD*

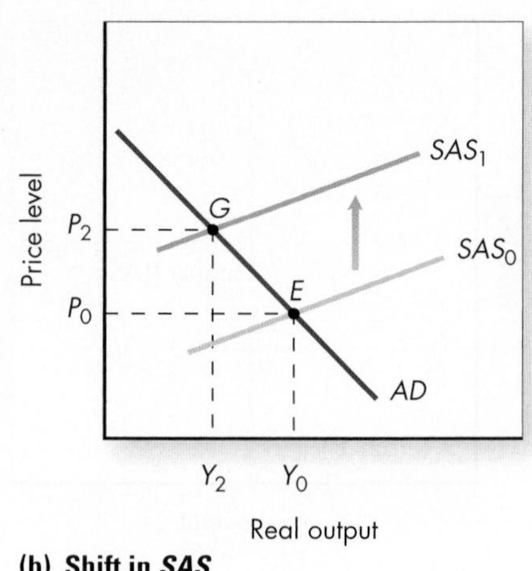

(b) Shift in *SAS*

Equilibrium in the Aggregate Economy

Now that we have introduced the *SAS, AD,* and *LAS* curves, we'll consider short-run and long-run equilibrium and how changes in the curves affect those equilibria. I start with the short run.

In the short run, equilibrium in the economy is where the short-run aggregate supply curve and the aggregate demand curve intersect. Thus, one short-run equilibrium is shown by point E in Figure 9-6(a). If the AD curve shifts to the right, from AD_0 to AD_1, equilibrium will shift from point E to point F. The price level will rise to P_1 and output will increase to Y_1. A decrease in aggregate demand will shift output and the price level down.

Macroeconomic Equilibrium

Figure 9-6(b) shows the effect on equilibrium of a shift up in the *SAS* curve. Initially equilibrium is at point E. An upward shift in the *SAS* curve from SAS_0 to SAS_1 increases the price level from P_0 to P_2 and reduces equilibrium output from Y_0 to Y_2.

Long-run equilibrium is determined by the intersection of the *AD* curve and the *LAS* curve.

Long-run equilibrium is determined by the intersection of the *AD* curve and the *LAS* curve, as shown by point E in Figure 9-7(a). Since in the long run output is determined by the position of the *LAS* curve, which is at potential output Y_p, the aggregate demand curve can determine only the price level; it does not affect the level of real output. Thus, as shown in Figure 9-7(a), when aggregate demand increases from AD_0 to AD_1, the price level rises (from P_0 to P_1) but output does not change. When aggregate demand decreases, the price level falls and output remains at potential. In the long run, output is fixed and the price level is variable, so aggregate output is determined not by aggregate demand but by potential output. Aggregate demand determines the price level.

Integrating the Short-Run and Long-Run Frameworks

To complete our analysis, we have to relate the long run and short run. We start with the economy in both long-run and short-run equilibrium. As you can see in Figure 9-7(b), at point E, with output Y_p, and price level P_0, the economy is in both a long-run equilibrium and a short-run equilibrium, since at point E the *AD* curve and *SAS* curve intersect at the economy's *LAS* curve. That is the situation economists hope for—that aggregate demand grows at just the same rate as potential output, so

Q-7 If the *SAS, AD,* and *LAS* curves intersect at the same point and wages are constant, what is likely to happen to output and the price level?

FIGURE 9-7 (A AND B) Long-Run Equilibrium

Long-run equilibrium is where the *LAS* and *AD* curves intersect. Point *E* is long-run equilibrium. In (**a**) you can see how a shift in the aggregate demand curve changes equilibrium from *E* to *H*, increasing the price level from P_0 to P_1 but leaving output unchanged. The economy is in both short-run and long-run equilibrium when all three curves intersect in the same location. In (**b**) you can see the adjustment from recessionary and inflationary gaps to long-run equilibrium.

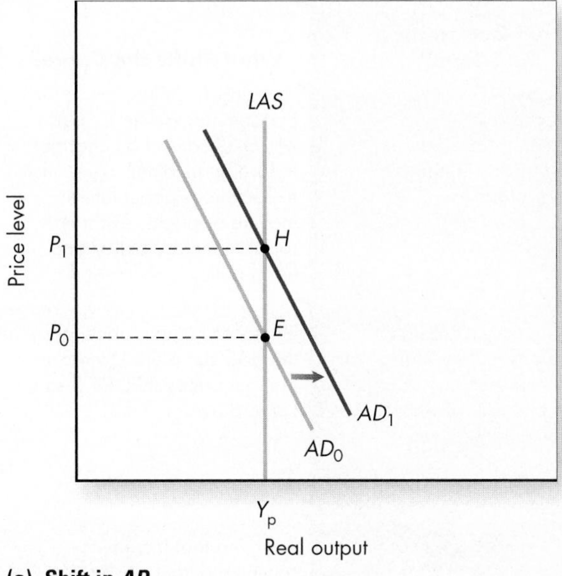

(a) Shift in *AD*

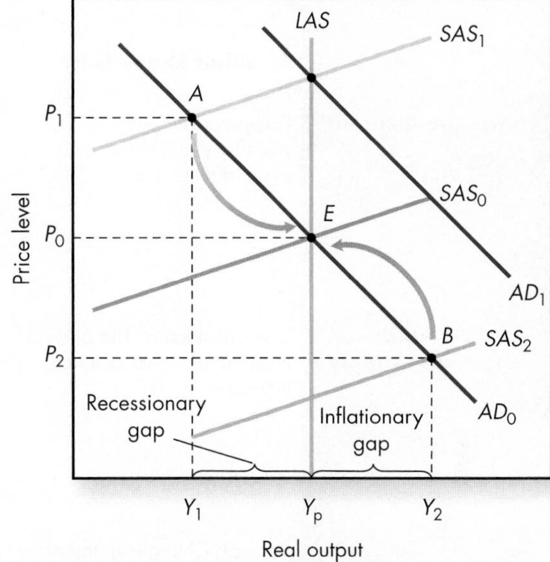

(b) Movement to Long-Run Equilibrium

that growth and unemployment are at their target rates, with no, or minimal, inflation. In the conventional interpretation in the late 1990s and much of the early 2000s, the U.S. economy was in just such a position—potential output was increasing at the same rate that aggregate demand was increasing; unemployment was low, as was inflation.

The Recessionary Gap

Alas, the economy is not always at that point *E*. An economy at point *A* in Figure 9-7(b) is in a situation where the quantity of aggregate demand is below potential output and not all the resources in the economy are being fully used. The distance $Y_p - Y_1$ shows the amount of output that is not being produced but could be. This distance is often referred to as a **recessionary gap,** *the amount by which equilibrium output is below potential output.*

If the economy remains at this level of output for a long time, costs and wages would tend to fall because there would be an excess supply of factors of production. As costs and wages fall, the price level also falls. Assuming the standard price level effects are sufficiently strong, the short-run aggregate supply curve would shift down (from SAS_1 to SAS_0) until eventually the long-run and short-run equilibria would be reached at point *E*. But generally in our economy that does not happen.[4] Long before that happens, either the economy picks up on its own or the government introduces policies to expand output. That's why we seldom see declines in the price level. If the

Q-8 Demonstrate graphically both the short-run and long-run *AS/AD* equilibrium with a recessionary gap.

[4]If, as happened in the Great Depression in the 1930s and in Japan in the early 2000s, the economy stays below its potential output long enough, we would likely see the price level fall.

A REMINDER

A Review of the *AS/AD* Model

	What Shape Is It?	What Determines Its Shape?	What Shifts the Curve?
Aggregate demand	Downward-sloping: As the price level declines expenditures rise.	The interest rate effect, the international effect, the money wealth effect, and the multiplier effect.	Sudden changes in *C*, *I*, (*X*–*M*), or *G* caused by changes in foreign income, expectations about future income or prices, exchange rates, monetary policy and fiscal policy.
Short-run aggregate supply	Upward-sloping: The price level increases as output increases.	Firm behavior. Most firms change production instead of price when demand changes. Some firms will raise prices when output increases.	Increases in input prices shift the *SAS* curve up. Decreases in input prices shift the *SAS* curve down.
Long-run aggregate supply	Vertical: Changes in the price level have no effect on output.	Potential output is output that the economy can produce when labor and capital are fully utilized. It is not affected by prices.	Anything that increases potential output, such as increases in available resources and technological innovation.

government expands aggregate demand, or some other shift factor expands aggregate demand, the *AD* curve shifts to the right (to AD_1) eliminating the recessionary gap and keeping the price level constant.

The Inflationary Gap

When income exceeds potential output, there is an inflationary gap.

An economy at point *B* in Figure 9-7(b) demonstrates a case where the short-run equilibrium is at a higher income than the economy's potential output. In this case, economists say that the economy has an **inflationary gap** shown by $Y_2 - Y_p$—*aggregate expenditures above potential output that exist at the current price level.* Output cannot remain at Y_2 for long because the economy's resources are being used beyond their potential. Factor prices will rise and the *SAS* curve will shift up from SAS_2 to SAS_0; the new equilibrium is at point *E*.

The Economy beyond Potential

How can resources be used beyond their potential? By overutilizing them. Consider the resources you put into classwork. Suppose that your potential is a B+. If you stay up all night studying and cram in extra reading during mealtimes, you could earn an A. But you can't keep up that effort for long. Eventually you'll get tired. The same is true for production. Extra shifts can be added and machinery can be run longer periods, but eventually the workers will become exhausted and the machinery will wear out. Output will have to return to its potential.

The result of this inflationary gap will be a bidding up of factor prices and a rise in costs for firms. When an economy is below potential, firms can hire additional factors of production without increasing production costs. Once the economy reaches its potential output, however, that is no longer possible. If a firm is to increase its factors of production, it must lure resources away from other firms. It will do so by offering higher wages and prices. But the firm facing a loss of its resources will likely respond by increasing its wages and other prices it pays to its employees and to other suppliers.

As firms compete for resources, their costs rise beyond increases in productivity, shifting up the *SAS* curve. This means that once an economy's potential output is reached, the price level tends to rise. In fact, economists sometimes look to see whether the price level has begun to rise before deciding where potential output is. Thus, in the late 1990s and into the 2000s, economists kept increasing their estimates of potential output because the price level did not rise even as the economy approached, and exceeded, what they previously thought was its potential output.

If the economy is operating above potential, the *SAS* curve will shift up until the inflationary gap is eliminated. That, however, is usually not what happens. Either the economy slows down on its own or the government introduces aggregate demand policy to contract output and eliminate the inflationary gap.

If aggregate expenditures are above potential output, then increased demand for labor would put upward pressure on wages and subsequently on the overall level of prices.

Aggregate Demand Policy

A primary reason for government policy makers' interest in the *AS/AD* model is their ability to shift the *AD* curve with policy. As I mentioned above, they can do this with monetary or fiscal policy. Monetary policy involves the Federal Reserve Bank changing the money supply and interest rates. (Understanding the process requires a knowledge of the financial sector, which will be discussed at length in later chapters.) In this chapter I'll concentrate on fiscal policy—the deliberate change in either government spending or taxes to stimulate or slow down the economy. Fiscal policy is often discussed in terms of the government budget deficit (government expenditures less government revenue). If aggregate income is too low (actual income is below potential income), the appropriate fiscal policy is expansionary fiscal policy: increase the deficit by decreasing taxes or increasing government spending. Expansionary fiscal policy shifts the *AD* curve out to the right. If aggregate income is too high (actual income is above potential income), the appropriate fiscal policy is contractionary fiscal policy: decrease the deficit by increasing taxes or decreasing government spending. Contractionary fiscal policy shifts the *AD* curve in to the left.

Fiscal policy is the deliberate change in either government spending or taxes to stimulate or slow down the economy.

WWW Web Note 9.1 Fiscal Policy

Let's go through a couple of examples. Say the economy is in a recessionary gap at point *A* in Figure 9-8(a). To eliminate the recessionary gap, government needs to implement expansionary fiscal policy. The appropriate fiscal policy would be to cut taxes or increase government spending, letting the multiplier augment those effects so that the *AD* curve shifts out to AD_1. This would raise the price level slightly but would eliminate the recessionary gap. Alternatively, say the economy is in an inflationary gap at point *B* in Figure 9-8(b). To prevent the inflation caused by the upward shift of the *SAS* curve, the appropriate fiscal policy is to increase taxes or cut government spending. Either of these actions will shift the *AD* curve in to AD_2. This lowers the price level slightly and eliminates the inflationary gap. So the best way to picture fiscal policy is as a policy designed to shift the *AD* curve to keep output at potential.

Q-9 If politicians suddenly raise government expenditures, and the economy is well below potential output, what will happen to prices and real income?

Aggregate Demand Policy

FIGURE 9-8 (A AND B)
Fiscal Policy

Expansionary fiscal policy can bring an economy out of a recessionary gap, as shown in (**a**). If an economy is in an inflationary gap, contractionary fiscal policy can reduce real output to prevent inflation, as shown in (**b**).

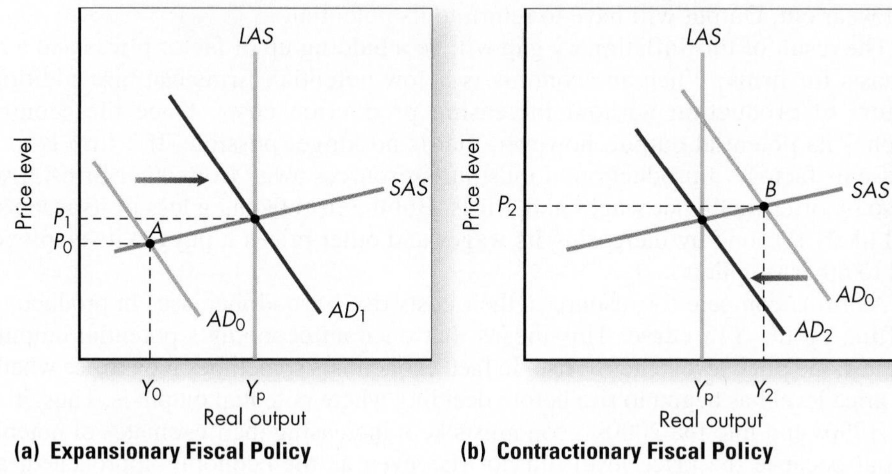

(a) Expansionary Fiscal Policy **(b) Contractionary Fiscal Policy**

Some Additional Policy Examples

Now that we've been through the model, let's give you some practice with it by making you an adviser to the president. He comes to you for some advice. Unemployment is 12 percent and there is no inflation. History suggests that the economy is well below its potential output, so there is no need to worry about increasing factor prices. What policy would you recommend?

Pause for answer

The answer I hope you gave was expansionary fiscal policy, shifting the *AD* curve out to its potential income, as in Figure 9-9(a).

Now let's try a different scenario. Unemployment is 5 percent and it is believed that that 5 percent is the *target rate of unemployment*—the rate of unemployment that is consistent with potential output. But measures of consumer optimism suggest that a large rise in consumer expenditures is likely. What policy would you recommend?

Pause for answer

The answer I hope you gave is contractionary fiscal policy to counteract the expected rise in the *AD* curve before it occurs and prevent the economy from creating an inflationary gap. What would happen without that fiscal policy is shown in Figure 9-9(b). The economy is initially at point *C,* where the price level is P_0 and output is Y_p. In the absence of offsetting policy, the increase in expenditures along with the multiplier would move the economy to point *D* at a level of output (Y_1) above potential, creating an inflationary gap. If left alone, factor prices will rise, shifting the *SAS* curve up until it reaches SAS_1. The price level would rise to P_1 and the real output would return to Y_p, point *E.* But, of course, that didn't happen because you recommended a policy of cutting government spending or raising taxes so that the *AD* curve shifts back to AD_0, keeping the equilibrium at point *C,* not point *E,* and avoiding any rise in prices. The economy remains at potential output at a constant price level, P_0.

To give you an idea of how fiscal policy has worked in the real world, we'll look at two examples: the effect of wartime spending in the 1940s and the recent recession in 2008.

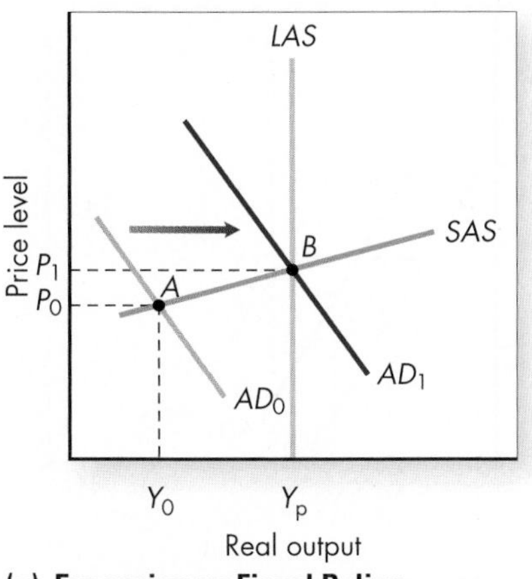

(a) Expansionary Fiscal Policy

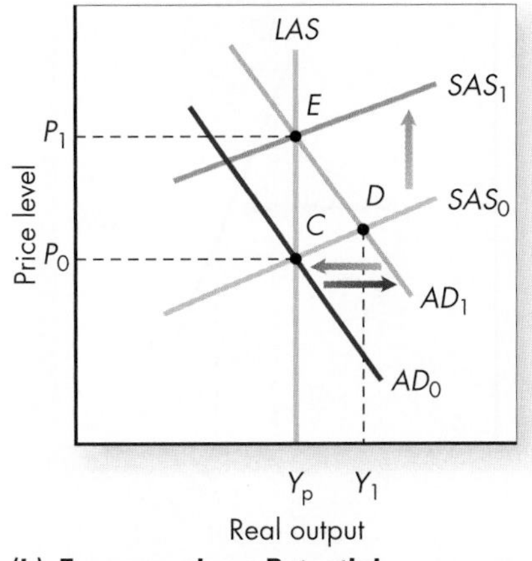

(b) Economy above Potential

FIGURE 9-9 (A AND B)
Shifting *AD* and *SAS* Curves

In (**a**) you can see what happens when the economy is below potential and aggregate demand increases just enough to bring output to its potential. In (**b**) you can see what happens when the economy begins at potential and aggregate expenditures rise. Since the economy rises to above potential, input prices begin to rise and the *SAS* curve shifts up.

FISCAL POLICY IN WORLD WAR II In the 1940s the focus of U.S. policy switched from the Depression to fighting World War II. Fighting a war requires transferring civilian production to war production, so economists' attention turned to how to do so. Taxes went up enormously, but government expenditures rose far more, which resulted in a large government deficit. The result can be seen in Figure 9-10(a). The AD curve shifts to the right by more than the increase in the deficit. As predicted, the U.S. economy expanded enormously in response to the expansionary fiscal policy that accompanied the war. One thing should bother you about this episode: If the economy exceeded its potential output, shouldn't the short-run aggregate supply curve have started to shift up, causing a serious inflation problem? It didn't because the wartime expansion was accompanied by wage and price controls, which prevented significant price-level increases, and by rationing.

Web Note 9.2
War Bonds

EXPANSIONARY POLICY DURING AND AFTER THE 2008 RECESSION To give you a final example, let's consider the economy in 2008 and 2009, when output fell and unemployment rose. Policy makers and economists alike believed that the economy was going into a severe depression. The situation is shown in Figure 9-10(b). Aggregate demand had fallen from AD_0 to AD_1 and output was significantly below potential. The government went all out and ran extremely expansionary monetary and fiscal policy, shifting the *AD* curve out to AD_2.

Unlike the expansionary fiscal and monetary policy after World War II, this time it did not push the economy out to what conventional economists thought was its potential output. Instead, despite the expansionary policy, unemployment remained much higher than desired and output much lower. This led some to call on government to use even more expansionary policy, while others said that it would be ineffective or would cause serious negative side effects. Potential output was actually much lower than it seemed. This group of economists believed that because of globalization the economy had entered a period of slow growth and high unemployment that required major structural changes. In their view, the good times of the early 2000s were not sustainable because they were based on an unsustainable financial bubble and trade deficit.

FIGURE 9-10 (A AND B)
War Finance: Expansionary Fiscal Policy

During wars, government budget deficits have risen significantly. As they have, unemployment has fallen and GDP has risen enormously. You can see this in **(a).** The graph in **(b)** shows the situation in 2008 and 2009. Expansionary monetary and fiscal policy didn't bring the economy back to what was believed to be its potential.

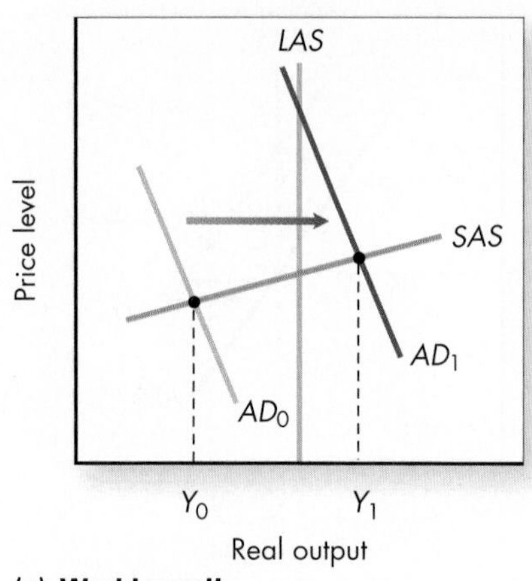

(a) World war II

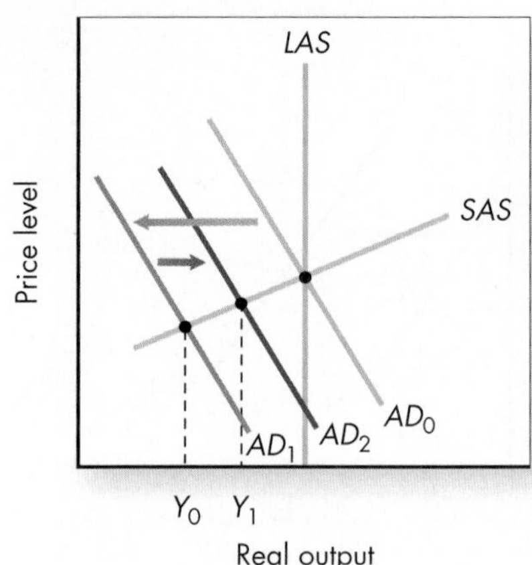

(b) 2008–2009 Recession

Limitations of the *AS/AD* Model

The *AS/AD* model is simple and clear, which is why it has become the workhorse model of macro policy makers. However, these advantages come at a cost of assuming away many possible feedback effects that can significantly affect the macroeconomy and lead to quite different conclusions than the standard *AS/AD* model gives. So an important limitation of the *AS/AD* model is that it does not include many important feedback effects.

How Feedback Effects Complicate the *AS/AD* Model

The *AS/AD* model presents price level fluctuations as being significantly more self-correcting than many macroeconomists believe they are, especially in response to decreases in aggregate demand. In Figure 9-11, I demonstrate how these feedback effects can cause serious problems for the economy, as they did in the recession the U.S. economy fell into in 2008.

The crisis began with the housing market turning from a booming market with housing prices rising quickly to a declining market with housing prices falling. This

FIGURE 9-11
Feedback Effects and the *AS/AD* Model

The feedback effects of a declining price level on aggregate demand mean that as the *SAS* curve shifts down to return the economy to equilibrium, the aggregate demand curve shifts back to the left, leading the economy away from equilibrium.

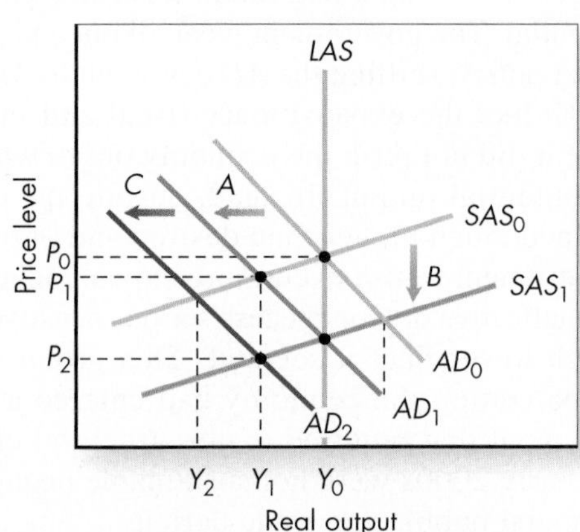

led to a fall in aggregate demand back from AD_0 to AD_1. Looking at the model in Figure 9-11, one would think that the result of that decline in aggregate demand would be an initial fall in output from Y_0 to Y_1 and in the price level from P_0 to P_1 (arrow *A*). The *SAS* curve would shift down from SAS_0 to SAS_1, bringing prices down to P_2 and the output level back to Y_0 (arrow *B*). Deflation would move the economy along the aggregate demand curve and help bring the economy back to potential output. So the recession would be eliminated by deflation.

Unfortunately, a falling price level might create expectations that aggregate output will fall further, which will lead people to cut back on spending and firms to cut back on production, shifting the *AD* curve to the left, to AD_2 (arrow *C*) in Figure 9-11. Aggregate demand may shift back by more than the falling price level increased the quantity of aggregate demand. The entire process may become a self-fulfilling vicious circle in which both prices and output continue to fall, leading the economy into a deep depression.

Additional Complications that the *AS/AD* Model Misses

The *AS/AD* model makes the analysis of the aggregate economy look easy. All you do is determine where the economy is relative to its potential output and, based on that, choose the appropriate policy to shift the *AD* curve. Alas, it's much harder than that. We've already mentioned some complications above. They bear repeating. And these are others.

Policy is more complicated than the *AS/AD* model makes it seem.

PROBLEMS OF IMPLEMENTATIONS First, implementing fiscal policy—changing government spending and taxes—is a slow legislative process. Government spending and taxing decisions are generally made for political, not economic, reasons. Thus, there is no guarantee that government will do what economists say is necessary. And even if it does, the changes often cannot be completed in a timely fashion.

PROBLEMS OF MEASURING POTENTIAL OUTPUT A second problem is that we have no way of measuring potential output, so when we increase aggregate demand, we can't determine whether the *SAS* curve will be shifting up. Thus, the key to applying the policy is to know the location of the *LAS* curve, which is vertical at the economy's potential output. Unfortunately, we have no way of knowing that with certainty. Fortunately, we do have ways to get a rough idea of where it is.

WWW Web Note 9.3 Unemployed Machines

Because inflation accelerates when an economy is operating above potential, one way of estimating potential output is to estimate the rate of unemployment below which inflation has begun to accelerate in the past. This is the target rate of unemployment. We can then estimate potential output by calculating output at the target rate of unemployment and adjusting for productivity growth. Unfortunately the target rate of unemployment fluctuates and is difficult to predict.

Q-10 If politicians suddenly raise government expenditures and the economy is above potential income, what will happen to prices and real income?

THE PROBLEMS OF OTHER INTERRELATIONSHIPS A third problem was mentioned above. There are many other possible interrelationships in the economy that the model does not take into account. One is the effect of falling asset prices and a falling price level on expectations of aggregate demand.

When there are pressures for the price level to fall, there are also generally strong pressures for asset prices to fall. This fall in asset prices has three effects on aggregate demand. First, while the fall in asset prices is in part caused by falling expectations about the growth potential of the economy, the causation can also go the other way: The decrease in asset prices can decrease expectations about the growth of the economy. The expectation of lower economic growth tends to shift the *AD* curve back to the left. Second, falling asset prices decrease people's perception of the value of their wealth, which decreases aggregate demand. Third, falling asset prices potentially undermine the stability of the financial system, which can make production impossible since the financial system is essential for production. This last effect undermines aggregate production and shifts the *SAS* curve to the left. Running an economy with a financial system that has stopped working is a bit like running an automobile without oil. It can bring an economy to a sudden halt.

The Problem of Dynamic Instability Because of these effects, as we discussed earlier, the aggregate economy can become dynamically unstable, so a shock to the economy can set in motion a set of changes that will not be automatically self-correcting. Instead, falling output and asset prices lead to a vicious circle in which falling output and falling prices bring about further declines. The major concern of macro policy economists in 2008 and early 2009 was that the U.S. economy had fallen into precisely such a vicious circle.

Reality and Models

In summary, there are two ways to think about the effectiveness of fiscal policy: in the model and in reality. Models are great, and simple models, such as the one I've presented in this book that you can understand intuitively, are even greater. Put in the numbers and out comes the answer. Questions based on such models make great exam questions. But don't think that policies that work in a model will necessarily work in the real world.

The effectiveness of fiscal policy in reality depends on the government's ability to perceive a problem and to react appropriately to it. The essence of fiscal policy is government changing its taxes and its spending to offset any fluctuation that would occur in other autonomous expenditures, thereby keeping the economy at its potential level of income. If the model is a correct description of the economy, and if the government can act fast enough and change its taxes and spending in a *countercyclical* way, recessions can be prevented. This type of management of the economy is called **countercyclical fiscal policy**—*fiscal policy in which the government offsets any change in aggregate expenditures that would create a business cycle.* The term **fine-tuning** is used to describe such *fiscal policy designed to keep the economy always at its target or potential level of income.* With fine-tuning, the government responds to problems before they happen, and the aggregate economy runs smoothly. Today almost all economists agree the government is not capable of fine-tuning the economy. The modern debate is whether it is up to any tuning of the economy at all.

A countercyclical fiscal policy designed to keep the economy always at its target or potential level of income is called fine-tuning.

Almost all economists agree the government is not capable of fine-tuning the economy.

Conclusion

Let's conclude the chapter with a brief summary. In the 1930s macroeconomics developed as Classical economists' interest in growth and supply-side issues shifted to Keynesian economists' interest in business cycles and demand-side issues. To capture the issues about the effect of aggregate demand on the economy, economists developed the *AS/AD* model.

The *AS/AD* model summarizes the expected effects that shifts in aggregate supply and aggregate demand have on output and the price level. In the short run, outward shifts in the *AD* curve cause real output and the price level to rise. Inward shifts cause the opposite. If the economy is beyond potential output and the *LAS* curve, the *SAS* curve will shift up, causing the price level to increase and real output to decrease, until real output falls back to potential. The long-run equilibrium is where aggregate demand intersects the *LAS* curve. In the model, the government can, through fiscal policy, shift the *AD* curve in or out, thereby achieving the desired level of real output, as long as that desired level does not exceed potential output.

Unfortunately, potential output is hard to estimate, and implementing fiscal policy in a timely fashion is difficult, making macroeconomic policy more an art than a science.

Macro policy is more an art than a science.

Summary

- The key idea of the Keynesian *AS/AD* model is that in the short run the economy can deviate from potential output. The paradox of thrift is an important reason why. (*LO9-1*)
- The *AS/AD* model consists of the aggregate demand curve, the short-run aggregate supply curve, and the long-run aggregate supply curve. (*LO9-1*)
- The aggregate demand curve slopes downward because of the interest rate effect, the international effect, the money wealth effect, and the multiplier effect. (*LO9-2*)
- The short-run aggregate supply (*SAS*) curve is upward-sloping because, while for the most part firms in the United States adjust production to meet demand instead of changing price, some firms will raise prices when demand increases. (*LO9-3*)
- The long-run aggregate supply (*LAS*) curve is vertical at potential output. (*LO9-3*)
- The *LAS* curve shifts out when available resources, capital, labor, technology, and/or growth-compatible institutions increase. (*LO9-3*)
- Short-run equilibrium is where the *SAS* and *AD* curves intersect. Long-run equilibrium is where the *AD* and *LAS* curves intersect. (*LO9-4*)
- Aggregate demand management policy attempts to influence the level of output in the economy by influencing aggregate demand and relying on the multiplier to expand any policy-induced change in aggregate demand. (*LO9-4*)
- Fiscal policy—the change in government spending or taxes—works by providing a deliberate countershock to offset unexpected shocks to the economy. (*LO9-4*)
- A falling price level can have dynamic feedback effects on aggregate demand, perhaps more than offsetting the effect of the falling price level on the quantity of aggregate demand. (*LO9-5*)
- Macroeconomic policy is difficult to conduct because: (1) implementing fiscal policy is a slow process, (2) we don't really know where potential output is, (3) there are interrelationships not included in the model, and (4) the economy can become dynamically unstable. (*LO9-5*)
- We must estimate potential output by looking at past levels of potential output and by looking at where the price level begins to rise. (*LO9-5*)

Key Terms

aggregate demand (*AD*) curve *(186)*
countercyclical fiscal policy *(204)*
deflation *(183)*
equilibrium output *(183)*
fine-tuning *(204)*
fiscal policy *(183)*
inflationary gap *(198)*
interest rate effect *(187)*
international effect *(187)*
long-run aggregate supply (*LAS*) curve *(194)*
monetary policy *(182)*
money wealth effect *(187)*
multiplier effect *(188)*
paradox of thrift *(184)*
potential output *(182)*
quantity-adjusting markets *(192)*
recessionary gap *(197)*
short-run aggregate supply (*SAS*) curve *(192)*

Questions and Exercises 

1. According to Keynesians how could the economy's output deviate from its potential? *(LO9-1)*
2. Why might deflation be a problem for an economy? *(LO9-1)*
3. Why does the paradox of thrift suggest that government needs to intervene in a recession? *(LO9-1)*
4. Why, in principle, would one expect the *AD* curve to be vertical? *(LO9-2)*
5. Explain how a rise in the price level affects aggregate quantity demanded with the: *(LO9-2)*
   a. Interest rate effect.
   b. International effect.
   c. Money wealth effect.
6. What are five factors that cause the *AD* curve to shift? *(LO9-2)*
7. What dynamic feedback effects can offset the interest rate, international, and money wealth effects? *(LO9-2)*
8. What will likely happen to the slope or position of the *AD* curve in the following circumstances? *(LO9-2)*
   a. The exchange rate changes from fixed to flexible.
   b. A fall in the price level doesn't make people feel richer.
   c. A fall in the price level creates expectations of a further-falling price level.
   d. Income is redistributed from rich people to poor people.
   e. Autonomous exports increase by 20.
   f. Government spending decreases by 10.
9. What are two factors that cause the *SAS* curve to shift? *(LO9-3)*
10. What will likely happen to the *SAS* curve in each of the following instances? *(LO9-3)*
    a. Productivity rises 3 percent; wages rise 4 percent.
    b. Productivity rises 3 percent; wages rise 1 percent.
    c. Productivity declines 1 percent; wages rise 1 percent.
    d. Productivity rises 2 percent; wages rise 2 percent.
11. Why is the *LAS* curve vertical? *(LO9-3)*
12. What will happen to the position of the *SAS* curve and/or *LAS* curve in the following circumstances? *(LO9-3)*
    a. Available factors of production increase.
    b. A civil war occurs.
    c. Wages that were fixed become flexible, and aggregate demand increases.
13. If an economy is in short-run equilibrium that is below potential, what forces will bring the economy to long-run equilibrium? *(LO9-4)*
14. Moore's law states that every 18 months, the computing speed of a microchip doubles. *(LO9-4)*
    a. What effect does this likely have on the economy?
    b. Explain your answer using the *AS/AD* model.
15. Congratulations! You have been appointed an economic policy adviser to the United States. You are told that the economy is significantly below its potential output and that the following will happen next year: World income will fall significantly and the price of oil will rise significantly. (The United States is an oil importer.) *(LO9-4)*
    a. What will happen to the price level and output? Using the *AS/AD* model, demonstrate your predictions graphically.
    b. What policy might you suggest to the government?
16. What fiscal policy actions would you recommend in the following instances? *(LO9-4)*
    a. The economy begins at potential output, but foreign economies slow dramatically.
    b. The economy has been operating above potential output and inflationary pressures rise.
    c. A new technology is invented that significantly raises potential output.
17. How can a falling price level destabilize an economy? *(LO9-5)*
18. Why is knowing the level of potential output important to designing appropriate fiscal policy? *(LO9-5)*
19. Why is macro policy more difficult than the simple model suggests? *(LO9-5)*
20. Why is countercyclical fiscal policy difficult to implement? *(LO9-5)*

Questions from Alternative Perspectives

1. Austrian economist Murray Rothbard has argued that government intervention during 1929 made what could have been a 1-year recession set off by the stock market crash into a 12-year depression. He believed that by creating confusing signals, government intervention kept investors from gaining knowledge of what investments to avoid.
   a. Is Rothbard's explanation of the Depression consistent with the *AS/AD* model?

   b. If one agrees with Rothbard, how would one's proposed policies to deal with recessions differ from those presented in the book? (Austrian)
2. In the 1950s, Michael Hubert King, an oil geologist, mathematically determined that when 50 percent of oil reserves have been extracted, annual oil output would inexorably decline. He looked at the rate of oil discovery in the United States and predicted that domestic oil production would peak in 1969. The peak occurred in 1970! Today global oil production is nearly at maximum production capacity, and it is likely that in the very near future the inexorable decline will begin globally.
   a. Use the *AS/AD* model and the production possibility curve to describe what will happen when oil production declines.
   b. What will this do to the question of "distribution," both within and between nations? (Institutionalist)
3. Post-Keynesian economist Hyman Minsky predicted many of the problems that have recently befallen the U.S. economy. Given that he was right and conventional macroeconomists were wrong, why do textbooks continue to present the conventional macro analysis, rather than present the Post Keynesian macro analysis? (Post Keynesian)
4. Draw an *AS/AD* diagram from the Keynesian viewpoint. Assume the initial equilibrium in your diagram is just at the level of potential output. Then reduce the level of aggregate demand in your diagram. Now stare at this diagram.
   a. Can you identify the excess capacity or depression in the diagram and what caused it?
   b. What should be done to return the economy to a full-employment level of output?
   c. What does this exercise suggest about the distinction between economic theorizing (or positive economics) and policy recommendations (normative economics)?
   d. Is one more value laden than the other? (Radical)

Issues to Ponder

1. The opening quotation of the chapter refers to Keynes' view of theory.
   a. What do you think he meant by it?
   b. How does it relate to the emphasis on the "other things constant" assumption?
   c. Do you think Keynes' interest was mainly in positive economics, the art of economics, or normative economics? Why?
2. If the economy were close to high potential output, would policy makers present their policy prescriptions to increase real output any differently than if the economy were far from potential output? Why?

Answers to Margin Questions

1. When people try to increase the proportion of income they save, they decrease consumption, which causes income to fall as long as that saving is not translated back into the spending stream. If total income falls sufficiently far, the higher percentage being saved can be associated with a lower absolute amount of saving. (*p. 184; LO9-1*)
2. In the Keynesian view, saving can lead to a decrease in expenditures and a reduction in equilibrium output. In the layperson's view, saving leads to investment, which leads to growth. (*p. 184; LO9-1*)
3. False. The multiplier magnifies the initial effect. The rise in expenditures will be greater than 10, making the *AD* curve flatter than a slope of -1. (*p. 188; LO9-2*)
4. A rise in a country's exchange rate will make domestic goods more expensive to foreigners and foreign goods less expensive to domestic residents. It will shift the *AD* curve in to the left because net exports will fall. (*p. 190; LO9-2*)
5. The *AD* curve will shift out by more than 20 because of the multiplier. (*p. 191; LO9-2*)
6. The price level rises by 3 percent ($4\% - 1\%$). (*p. 194; LO9-3*)
7. If the *AD, SAS,* and *LAS* curves intersect at the same point, the economy is in both long-run and short-run equilibrium. Nothing will happen to the price level and output. (*p. 196; LO9-4*)
8. If there is a recessionary gap, the *SAS* and *AD* curves intersect to the left of potential output at a point such as

A in the figure below. At that level of output there will be pressure for factor prices to fall, pushing the *SAS* curve down. Unless the *AD* curve shifts out (as it usually does), the *SAS* curve will shift down and output will rise until output equals potential output and the economy is in both long-run and short-run equilibrium at a point such as *B*. (*p. 197; LO9-4*)

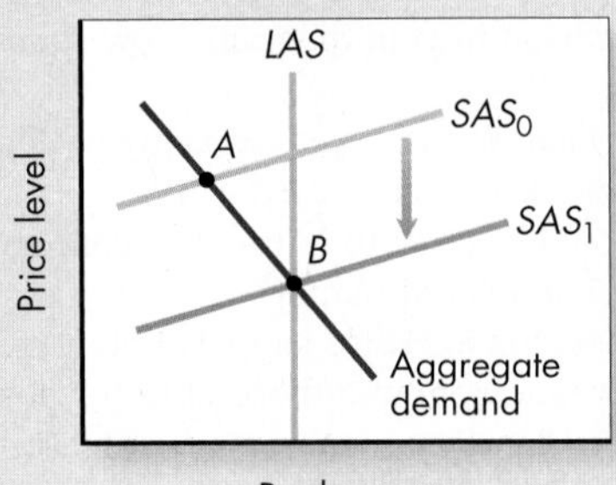

9. If the economy is well below potential, I would predict that output will rise and the price level will rise only slightly. (*p. 199; LO9-5*)
10. If the economy is above potential output, I would predict that factor prices will rise, shifting the *SAS* curve up. The expansion in government expenditures will shift the *AD* curve out further, putting even more pressure on factor prices to rise. My answer, therefore, is that the price level will rise very quickly and real output will fall until it equals potential output. (*p. 203; LO9-5*)

The Multiplier Model

> *Keynes stirred the stale economic frog pond to its depth.*
>
> —Gottfried Haberler

This web chapter can be found at:
www.mhhe.com/colander9e

Chapter Outline

After reading this chapter, you should be able to:

LO9W-1 State the components of the multiplier model and explain the difference between induced and autonomous expenditures.

LO9W-2 Show how equilibrium income is determined in the multiplier model.

LO9W-3 Demonstrate how, though the multiplier process, fiscal policy can eliminate recessionary and inflationary gaps.

LO9W-4 List seven reasons why the multiplier model might be misleading.

chapter 10

The Classical Long-Run Policy Model: Growth and Supply-Side Policies

"Queen Elizabeth owned silk stockings. The capitalist achievement does not typically consist in providing more silk stockings for queens but in bringing them within the reach of factory girls in return for steadily decreasing amounts of effort."

—Joseph Schumpeter

After reading this chapter, you should be able to:

- **LO10-1** Define growth, list its benefits and costs, and relate it to living standards.
- **LO10-2** Discuss the relationship among markets, specialization, and growth.
- **LO10-3** List five important sources of growth.
- **LO10-4** Explain how the sources of growth can be turned into growth.

Growth matters. In the long run, growth matters a lot. For example, if current growth rates continue, in less than 50 years China's economy will be larger than the U.S. economy. Given the importance of growth, it is not surprising that modern economics began with a study of growth. In *The Wealth of Nations,* Adam Smith noted that what was good about market economies was that they raised society's standard of living. He argued that people's natural tendency to exchange and specialize was the driving force behind growth. Specialization and trade, and the investment and capital that made these possible, were responsible for the wealth of nations.

As we discussed in an earlier chapter, through the 1920s, long-run growth remained an important focus of economics. Then, in the 1930s, the world economy fell into a serious depression. It was at that time that modern macroeconomics developed as a separate subject with a significant focus on short-run business cycles. It asked the questions: "What causes depressions?" and "How does an economy get out of one?" Short-run macroeconomics became known as Keynesian economics, and remained the standard macroeconomics through the 1960s. Keynesian economics continued to focus on fluctuations around the growth trend.

In the 1970s, as the memories of the Great Depression faded, the pendulum started to swing back again towards a focus on long-run growth, which had been the focus of Classical economists. Thus, the focus on growth is often seen as a new Classical revival. In this chapter we discuss economists' views of growth and the policies that economists advise governments to follow to keep growth high.

General Observations about Growth

Let's begin our consideration with some general observations about growth.

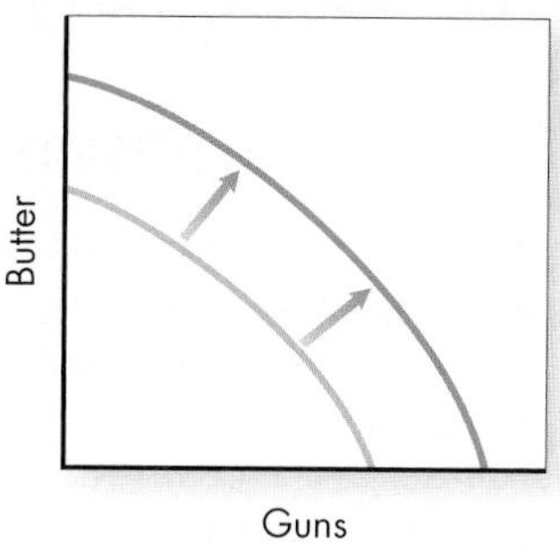

Growth and the Economy's Potential Output

Long-run growth occurs when the economy produces more goods and services from existing production processes and resources. The study of growth is the study of why that increase comes about. In discussing growth, economists use the term *potential output* (the highest amount of output an economy can sustainably produce from existing production processes and resources) introduced in an earlier chapter. Potential output conveys a sense of the growth that is possible. (Recall that *potential output* can also be called *potential income* because, in the aggregate, income and output are identical.) One way to think about growth and potential output is to relate them to the production possibility curve presented in Chapter 2. That curve gave us a picture of the choices an economy faces given available resources. When an economy is at its potential output, it is operating on its production possibility curve. When an economy is below its potential output, it is operating inside its production possibility curve. The analysis of growth focuses on the forces that increase potential output, in other words, that shift out the production possibility curve.

The analysis of growth focuses on forces that shift out the production possibility curve.

Why do we use potential output in macro rather than the production possibility curve? Because macro focuses on aggregate output—GDP—and does not focus on the choices of dividing up GDP among alternative products as does micro and the production possibility curve. But the concept is the same. Potential output is a barrier beyond which an economy cannot expand without either increasing available factors of production or increasing **productivity** *(output per unit of input).*

Long-run growth analysis focuses on supply; it assumes demand is sufficient to buy whatever is supplied. That assumption is called **Say's law** *(supply creates its own demand),* named after a French economist, Jean Baptiste Say, who first pointed it out. The reasoning behind Say's law is as follows: People work and supply goods to the market because they want other goods. The very fact that they supply goods means that they demand goods of equal value. According to Say's law, aggregate demand will always equal aggregate supply.

Q-1 How does long-run growth analysis justify its focus on supply?

In the short run, economists consider potential output fixed; they focus on how to get the economy operating at its potential if, for some reason, it is not. In the long run, economists consider an economy's potential output changeable. Growth analysis is a consideration of why an economy's potential shifts out, and growth policy is aimed at increasing an economy's potential output.

Notice that this focus is different from the Keynesian model in the last chapter, which took potential output as given and focused on aggregate demand, assuming that the short-run quantity of aggregate supply would expand to meet demand, at least up to the economy's potential income. Figure 10-1 summarizes the different views. Figure 10-1(a) shows the Keynesian view where aggregate demand can be below potential output at point *A* and government policy is to shift the aggregate demand curve to the right. Figure 10-1(b) shows the Classical view where the economy is always at long-run equilibrium. Point *A* is one possibility. Classical policy focuses on shifting the long-run aggregate supply curve to the right, to increase output (Arrow 1). As that happens in the Classical view, aggregate demand will follow (Arrow 2) since supply creates its own demand.

Republican and Democratic rhetoric often matches this distinction. Republicans associate themselves with Classical economics. They call themselves supply-siders and argue that policy should focus on expanding potential income (the supply side). Democrats

ADDED DIMENSION

Demand, Keynesian Economics, and Growth

The presentation in this chapter is the generally accepted analysis of growth. It focuses on the supply-side sources of growth. But because empirical relationships in growth are so difficult to discern, groups of economists raise a variety of different issues. One such group, which has its origins in Keynesian ideas, argues that demand and supply are so interrelated in macro that demand has to be considered as a source of growth. The argument goes as follows: Firms produce only if they expect there to be demand for their product. If they expect demand to be growing, they will try new projects and in the process will learn by doing and develop new technology. Both of these activities shift the production function out and thereby create growth. So while it looks like a supply-side issue, it is the demand side that leads the supply side: By increasing demand, one can increase long-run supply.

True, they argue, increasing aggregate demand is only a short-run phenomenon, but since the long run is simply a set of successive short runs, the short run influences the long-run path that the economy follows. They are not separable, and, under the right conditions, demand-side policies should be considered as one way to increase supply. As economist, Abba Lerner, one of the early Keynesian advocates of this view, has put it, *"In the long run we are simply in another short run."*

associate themselves with Keynesians and argue that policy should focus on managing aggregate demand (the demand side). But when the models don't fit what politicians want at the time, both sides modify the models.

The Benefits and Costs of Growth

Economic growth (per capita) allows everyone in society, on average, to have more. Thus, it isn't surprising that most governments are generally searching for policies that will allow their economies to grow. Indeed, one reason market economies have been so successful is that they have consistently channeled individual efforts toward production and growth. Individuals feel a sense of accomplishment in making things grow and, if sufficient economic incentives and resources exist, individuals' actions can lead to a continually growing economy.

Politically, growth (or predictions of growth) allows governments to avoid hard questions.

Politically, growth (or predictions of growth) allows governments to avoid hard distributional questions of who should get what part of our existing output: With growth there is more to go around for everyone. A growing economy generates jobs,

FIGURE 10-1 (A AND B)
The Demand-Side and Supply-Side Models

The Keynesian view is shown in **(a)**, where the economy's output can vary from potential output. In this case the economy is below potential at point *A*. Government policy focuses on expansionary policy to shift the aggregate demand curve. The Classical view is shown in **(b)**, where the economy is always at potential. The focus of government policy is on the supply side; its goal is to shift the long-run aggregate supply curve to the right.

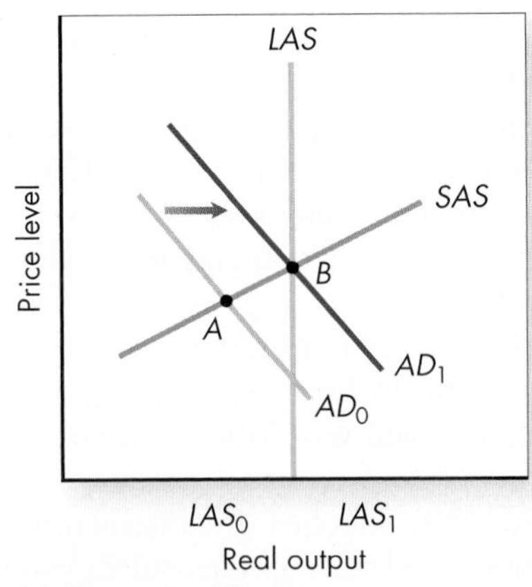

(a) Keynesian View

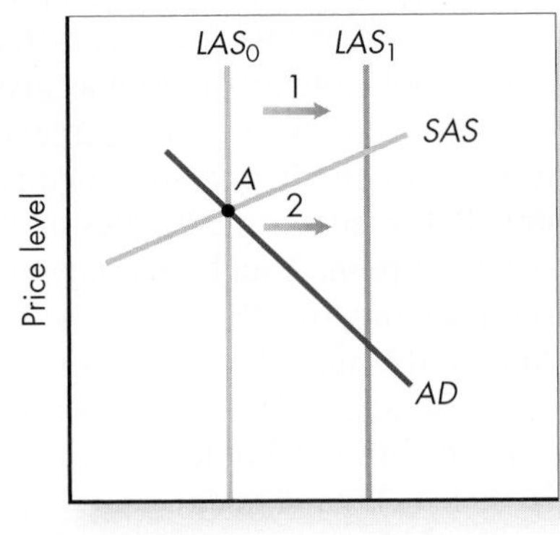

(b) Classical View

so politicians who want to claim that their policies will create jobs generally predict those policies will create growth.

Of course, material growth comes with costs: pollution, resource exhaustion, and destruction of natural habitat. These costs lead some people to believe that we would be better off in a society that deemphasized material growth. (That doesn't mean we shouldn't grow emotionally, spiritually, and intellectually; it simply means we should grow out of our material goods fetish.) Many people believe these environmental costs are important, and the result is often an environmental-economic growth stalemate. An example is fracking (technically hydraulic fracturing) in which water and chemicals are pumped into the ground to extract natural gas. This new technology has been a boon to economic growth in the United States, offering cheap energy and encouraging firms to move production facilities back to the United States and to create U.S. jobs. In 2012, it was one of the most important positive developments that was driving U.S. growth. But it comes with potentially serious environmental costs. Many environmentalists oppose the process, arguing that fracking hurts the environment and could pollute groundwater. Economics cannot say which side is right; it can only spell out the costs and benefits.

WWW Web Note 10.1 Is Growth Good?

Economics cannot say whether fracking advocates or environmental advocates are right; it can only spell out the costs and benefits.

The Importance of Growth for Living Standards

In 2004, Nobel Prize winner Robert Lucas wrote, "Of the tendencies that are harmful to sound economics, the most seductive, and in my opinion most poisonous, is to focus on questions of distribution . . . The potential for improving the lives of poor people by finding different ways of distributing current production is *nothing* [his italics] compared to the apparently limitless potential of increasing production." For Lucas, and many other economists, growth, not distribution or business cycles, is the most important macroeconomic issue.

All economists agree that growth makes an enormous difference for living standards. Take France and Argentina as examples. In the 1950s, per capita real income was the same in each country, but their growth rates differed. From 1950 to 2012, France's income grew at an average rate of 2.5 percent per year while Argentina's grew at an average rate of 1.4 percent per year. Because of the differences in growth rates, France's per capita income is now about $36,000 and Argentina's per capita income is about $18,000.

Growth in income improves lives by fulfilling basic needs and making more goods available to more people.

Other examples are South Korea and North Korea. In the 1950s, their incomes were identical. Because of differing growth rates, South Korea's per capita income has multiplied about 28 times, to about $32,000, while North Korea's per capita income is about $1,800. Why? Because North Korea has a 0.5 percent growth rate while South Korea has averaged a 5.6 percent annual growth rate. The moral of these stories: In the long run, growth rates matter a lot.

Small differences in growth rates can mean huge differences in income levels because of *compounding*. Compounding means that growth is based not only on the original level of income but also on the accumulation of previous-year increases in income. For example, say you start with $10,000. At a 7 percent interest rate that $10,000 after 10 years will be more than $20,000; after 20 years it will be more than $40,000; after 30 years it will be more than $80,000; and after 50 years it will be more than $320,000. So if you are worried about your retirement, it pays to start saving early at as high an interest rate as you can get. The longer you save, and the higher the interest rate you receive, the more you end up with.

Another way to see the effects of the difference in growth rates is to see how long it would take income to double at different growth rates. The Rule of 72 tells you that. The **Rule of 72** states: *The number of years it takes for a certain amount to double in*

$$\text{Number of years to double} = \frac{72}{(\text{Rate of growth})}$$

ADDED DIMENSION

Is Growth Good?

The discussion in the chapter emphasizes the generally held view among economists that growth is inherently good. It increases our incomes, thereby improving our standard of living. But that does not mean that all economists support unlimited growth. Growth has costs, and economics requires us to look at both costs and benefits. For example, growth may contribute to increased pollution—reducing the quality of the air we breathe and the water we drink, and endangering the variety of species in the world. In short, the wrong type of growth may produce undesirable side effects, including global warming and polluted rivers, land, and air.

New technology, upon which growth depends, also raises serious moral questions: Do we want to replace sexual reproduction with cloning? Will a brain implant be an improvement over 12 years of education? Will selecting your baby's genetic makeup be better than relying on nature? Just because growth *can* continue does not mean that it *should* continue. Moral judgments can be made against growth. For example, some argue that growth changes traditional cultures with beautiful handiwork, music, and dance into cultures of gadgets where people have lost touch with what is important. They argue that we have enough gadgets cluttering our lives and that it is time to start focusing on noneconomic priorities.

This moral argument against growth carries the most weight in highly developed countries—countries with per capita incomes of at least $20,000 a year. For developing countries, where per capita income can be as low as $200 per year, the reality is the choice between growth and poverty or even between growth and starvation. In these countries it is difficult to argue against growth.

One final comment: The benefits of growth do not have to be just higher incomes and more gadgets. They could also include more leisure activities and improved working conditions. In the 19th century, a 12-hour workday was common. Today the workday is eight hours, but had we been content with a lower income, the workday could now be two hours, with the remainder left for free time. We'd have less growth in GDP, but we'd have a lot more time to play.

value is equal to 72 divided by its annual rate of increase. For example, if Argentina's income grows at a 1 percent annual rate, it will double in 72 years (72/1). If France's income grows at a 3 percent annual rate, it will double in only 24 years (72/3).

Let's conclude our discussion by applying the Rule of 72 to the future growth of China and the United States and the comparison with which we started the chapter. Let's say that the current U.S. per capita income is $50,000 and that U.S. per capita income grows 1 percent per year; that means its per capita income will double every 72 years, so in 72 years its income will be $100,000 per capita. Let's say that China's income is $8,500 per capita, but that it grows at 8 percent per year, which means that it doubles every 9 years. If that actually happens, within 27 years per capita income in China will surpass that in the United States and after 9 more years will be significantly higher. While such extrapolations are precarious, and it is highly unlikely that such different growth rates will continue, even a partial movement in that direction will involve significant changes in the world economic and political structure. That's why differential growth rates are so important.

Q-2 If an economy is growing at 4 percent a year, how long will it take for its income to double?

Markets, Specialization, and Growth

Growth began when markets developed, and then, as markets expanded, growth accelerated. Why are markets so important to growth? To answer that question, let's go back to Adam Smith's argument for markets. Smith argued that markets allow **specialization** *(the concentration of individuals on certain aspects of production)* and **division of labor** *(the splitting up of a task to allow for specialization of production).* According to Smith, markets create an interdependent economy in which individuals can take advantage of the benefits of specialization and trade for their other needs. In doing so, markets increase productivity—and, in turn, improve the standard of living.

Q-3 Why do markets lead to growth?

You saw in Chapter 2 how comparative advantage and specialization increase productivity. If individuals concentrate on the production of goods for which their skills and other resources are best suited and trade for those goods for which they do not have a comparative advantage, everyone can end up with more of all goods. To see this even more clearly, consider what your life would be like without markets, trade, and specialization. You would have to grow all your food, build your own living space, and provide all your own transportation. Simply to exist under these conditions, you'd need a lot of skills, and it is unlikely that you'd become sufficiently adept in any one of them to provide yourself with anything other than the basics. You'd have all you could do to keep up.

Now consider your life today with specialization. Someone who specializes in dairy farming produces the milk you consume. You don't need to know how it is produced, just where to buy it. How about transportation? You buy, not build, your car. It runs somehow—you're not quite sure how—but if it breaks down, you take it to a garage. And consider your education: Are you learning how to grow food or build a house? No, you are probably learning a specific skill that has little relevance to the production of most goods. But you'll most likely provide some good or service that will benefit the dairy farmer and auto mechanic. You get the picture—for most of the things you consume, you don't have the faintest idea who makes them or how they are made, nor do you need to know.

For most of the things you consume, you don't have the faintest idea who makes them or how they are made, nor do you need to know.

Economic Growth, Distribution, and Markets

Markets and growth are often seen as unfair with regard to the distribution of income. Is it fair that markets give some individuals so much (billions to Mark Zuckerberg), and others so little ($7.25 an hour to Joe Wall, who has a minimum-wage job and two kids)? Such questions are legitimate and need to be asked. But in answering them we should also remember the quotation from Joseph Schumpeter that opened this chapter: Even if markets and growth do not provide equality, they tend to make everyone, even the poor, better off. The relevant question is: Would the poor be better off with or without markets and growth?

Even though growth isn't evenly distributed, it generally raises the incomes of the poor.

There are strong arguments, based on historical evidence, that people are better off with markets. Consider the number of hours an average person must work to buy certain goods at various periods in U.S. history. A century ago it took a worker 1 hour and 41 minutes to earn enough to buy a pair of stockings; today it takes less than 15 minutes of work. Figure 10-2 gives a number of other examples. As you can see from the figure, growth has made average workers significantly better off; to get the same amount, they have to work far less now than they did in the past. Growth also has made new products available. For example, before 1952 air conditioners were not available at any price.

The reality is that, judged from an *absolute* standard, the poor benefit enormously from the growth that markets foster. Markets, through competition, make the factors of production more productive and lower the cost of goods so that more goods are available to everyone. Today, the U.S. poverty level for a family of four is about $23,000. If we go back 100 years in U.S. history, and adjust for inflation, that $23,000 income would put a family in the upper middle class. Markets and growth have made that possible.

Just because the poor benefit from growth does not mean they might not be better off if income were distributed more in their favor.

The above argument does not mean that the poor always benefit from growth; many of us judge our well-being by relative, not absolute, standards. Growth often

FIGURE 10-2 Cost of Goods in Hours of Work

Growth in the U.S. economy in the past century has reduced the number of hours the average person needs to work to buy consumer goods.

Source: Federal Reserve Bank of Dallas, *Time Well Spent* (1997 annual report). Updated by author.

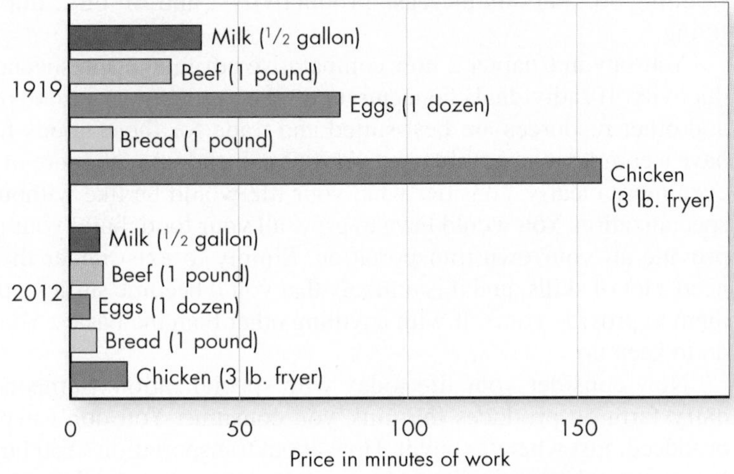

reduces the share of income earned by the poorest proportion of society, making the poor *relatively* worse off. The 99 percent movement has brought this to the attention of many Americans. So, if one uses relative standards, one could say that the poor have become worse off over certain periods. Moreover, it is not at all clear that markets require the large differentials in pay that have accompanied growth in market economies. If such large differentials did not exist, and growth had been at the same rate, the poor would be even better off than they are.

Per Capita Growth

When thinking about growth, it is important to distinguish between increases in total output and increases in per capita output, or total output divided by the total population. If there is **per capita growth,** the country is *producing more goods and services per person*. For example, say the real output of the economy is $4 billion and there are 1 million people. Each person, on average, has $4,000 to spend. Now say that output increases by 50 percent but that population also increases by 50 percent. In this case *output* has grown but *per capita output* has not; each person still has only $4,000 to spend. A number of countries have found themselves in such situations. Of the approximately 140 countries whose economies grew from 1990 to 2012, in about 10, the population grew even faster so that their per capita incomes fell. Take the Gabon as an example. Its income grew at an annual rate of 2.1 percent, but its population grew at a higher 2.4 percent annual rate, meaning that per capita income fell an average 0.3 percent each year. Over this same time period, the U.S. economy grew an average 2.5 percent a year, but its population grew only 1 percent a year so that, on average, per capita income grew 1.5 percent a year.

Q-4 Which country has experienced higher growth per capita: country A, whose economy is growing at a 4 percent rate and whose population is growing at a 3 percent rate, or country B, whose economy is growing at a 3 percent rate and whose population is growing at a 1 percent rate?

If you know the percentage change in output and percentage change in population, you can approximate per capita growth:

$$\text{Per capita growth} = \%\text{ change in output} - \%\text{ change in population}$$

Here are some additional examples showing per capita growth, real growth, and population growth for various countries in 2012:

Country	Per Capita GDP Growth	=	Real GDP Growth	–	Population Growth
Canada	1.4		2.4		1.0
Denmark	1.1		1.5		0.4
Russia	0.8		0.6		−0.2
Sudan	3.0		5.5		2.5
Thailand	3.3		4.2		0.9
Venezuela	0.8		2.7		1.9

Source: World Bank, dataworldbank.org.

Some economists have argued that per capita income is not what we should be focusing on; they suggest that it would be better to look at median income. (Remember, income and output are the same.) Per capita income measures the average, or *mean,* income. The *median* income, in contrast, is the income level that divides the population in equal halves. Half the people earn more and half the people earn less than the median income. In 2010, median income per household in the United States was $49,445. Half of all households earned less than that, and half earned more.

Why focus on median income? Because it partially takes into account how income is distributed. If the growth in income goes to a small minority of individuals who already receive the majority of income, the mean will rise but the median will not. Let's consider an example where there is a large difference between the two measures. Say that the incomes of five people in a five-person economy are $20,000; $20,000; $30,000; $120,000; and $450,000. The median income is $30,000 (the middle income with two above and two below); the mean income is $128,000. Now say that the economy grows but that the two richest people get all the benefits, raising their incomes to $150,000 and $500,000, respectively. The median income remains $30,000; the mean income rises to $144,000. Unfortunately, statistics on median income are often not collected, so I will follow convention and focus on the mean, or per capita, income.

Q-5 How would increases in income have to be distributed for the median to remain constant and the mean income to rise?

Whether you're looking at per capita or median income, growth provides more goods and services for the people in an economy, allowing society to sidestep the more difficult issues of how those goods are distributed. That's why policy makers are interested in knowing what makes an economy grow.

The Sources of Growth

Economists generally single out five important sources of growth:

1. Growth-compatible institutions.
2. Investment and accumulated capital.
3. Available resources.
4. Technological development.
5. Entrepreneurship.

Let's consider each in turn.

Growth-Compatible Institutions

Throughout this book I have emphasized the importance of economic institutions and that having the right institutions is vital for growth. Consider China. Until 1980 it grew at an average annual rate of 3 percent. After 1980, when it changed its institutional structure from a command-and-control to a more market-oriented economy, it started its rapid growth that averaged about 8 percent per year. Growth-compatible institutions—institutions that foster growth—must have incentives built into them that lead people to put forth effort and discourage people from spending a lot of their time in leisure pursuits or creating impediments for others to gain income for themselves.

Q-6 Why is private property a source of growth?

When individuals get much of the gains of growth themselves, they have incentives to work harder. That's why markets and private ownership of property play an important role in growth. In the former Soviet Union, individuals didn't gain much from their own initiative and, hence, often spent their time in pursuits other than those that would foster measured economic growth. Another growth-compatible institution is the corporation, a legal institution that gives owners limited liability and thereby encourages large enterprises (because people are more willing to invest their savings when their potential losses are limited).

Some developing countries follow a type of mercantilist policy in which government must approve any new economic activity. Some government officials get a large portion of their income from bribes offered to them by individuals who want to undertake economic activity. Such policies inhibit economic growth. Many regulations, even reasonable ones, also tend to inhibit economic growth because they inhibit entrepreneurial activities.

Peruvian economist Hernando DeSoto has given some vivid examples of how the lack of formal property rights limits development. He points out that because of regulations it takes an average of 500 working days to legalize a bakery in Cairo. He has many similar examples. Excessive regulations combined with bribery and corruption are important reasons why people don't legalize their businesses. In some ways, whether a business is legal or not is not of concern: Both legal and illegal businesses provide goods. But legality impacts growth; illegal or semilegal businesses must stay small to remain below the government's radar, and because the owners have no property rights, they do not have access to business loans to grow. Similarly, squatters only informally own their residence; their lack of formal ownership is a barrier to getting loans to improve their living space, which keeps them in the vicious cycle of poverty. DeSoto points out that the poor have informal control of trillions of dollars of assets but can't get loans on those assets to advance their economic futures in the normal market economy. The lack of property rights and the regulations doom the poor to remain in poverty.

Informal property rights limit borrowing by the poor, and hence limit growth.

The above argument is not an argument against all regulation; some regulation is necessary to ensure that growth is of a socially desirable type. The policy problem is in deciding between necessary and unnecessary regulation.

Investment and Accumulated Capital

A second important source of growth is capital and investment. In *Nickled and Dimed: On (Not) Getting By in America,* Barbara Ehrenreich explores how minimum-wage workers manage to scrape by. What they don't have time or income for is saving—putting together a nest egg to invest. Lacking savings, they often remain mired in poverty, just scraping by. The same argument holds for society as a whole; societies that can't afford to save will not grow either. Investment is absolutely necessary for growth. Somehow, the society as a whole has to manage to save (forgo consumption) if it wants to grow.

Some economists even argue that it is the savers, not the "givers," who are the beneficent people. University of Rochester economist Steven Landsburg makes the

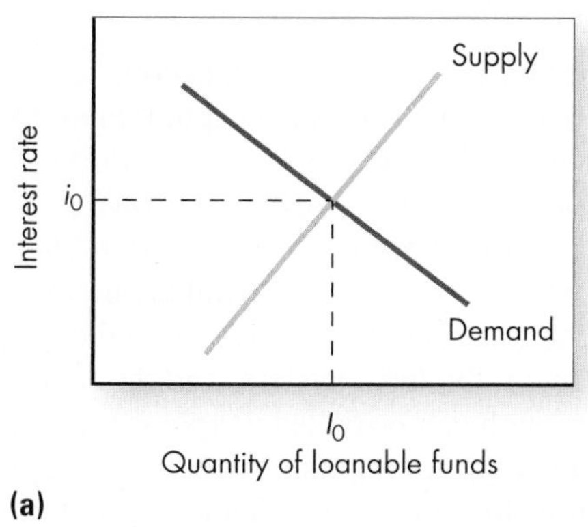

(a)

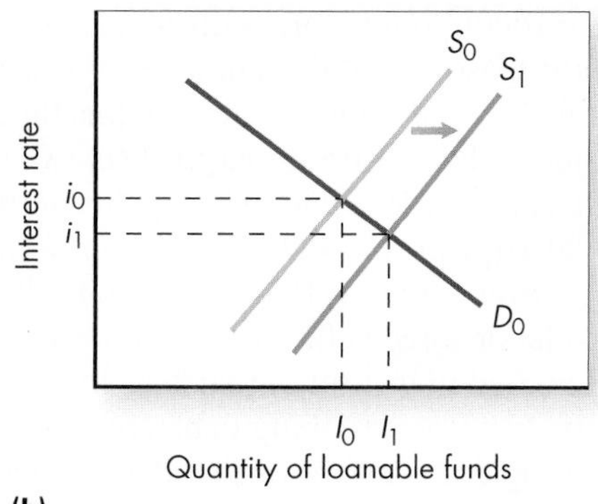

(b)

FIGURE 10-3 (A AND B)
The Loanable Funds Market

The interest rate equilibrates the supply and demand for loanable funds as shown in (**a**). When the supply of loanable funds (savings) increases as shown in (**b**), the interest rate falls from i_0 to i_1, and the quantity of loanable funds demanded (investment) increases from I_0 to I_1.

argument most explicitly. He argues that misers—the people who could deplete the world's resources but choose not to—are the true philanthropists. He writes that "nobody is more generous than the miser" and that when Scrooge gave up his miserly ways, the world was worse off, not better off. (As with all such provocative statements, the issues are complicated, and there is a deeper question about the justness of the institutional structure and whether that institutional structure could be changed to channel more income to the "nickled and dimed" while maintaining the level of saving. But those issues quickly go beyond the principles levels.)

Actually, it isn't saving that is important for growth; it's investment, and, for saving to be helpful, some method of translating saving into investment must exist in the society. Financial markets provide a method, which is why financial markets are an important aspect of macro. The role of financial markets in transferring savings into investment is captured in the loanable funds market shown in Figure 10-3.

Savings is the supply of loanable funds; it is an upward-sloping curve because, as the interest rate rises, more people are willing to save more. Investment is the demand for loanable funds that will be used by businesses to buy goods and services. It is a downward-sloping curve because, as the interest rate falls, it pays businesses to borrow more and invest more. Notice in this market that the interest rate is key; it equilibrates the supply and demand for loanable funds as shown in Figure 10-3(a). When the supply of loanable funds (savings) increases, as shown in Figure 10-3(b), the interest rate falls from i_0 to i_1, and the quantity of loanable funds demanded (investment) increases from I_0 to I_1. Thus, societies interested in growth look carefully at the interest rate in the economy. (The interest rate that is important to this market is the real interest rate—the nominal interest rate minus the rate of inflation.)

Q-7 If the demand for loanable funds increases, what will likely happen to the interest rate?

Fifty years ago, capital accumulation (where capital was thought of as just *physical capital*) and investment were seen as the key elements in growth. Physical capital includes both private capital—buildings and machines available for production—and public capital—infrastructure such as highways and water supply. The *flow* of investment leads to the growth of the *stock* of capital. While physical capital is still considered a key element in growth, it is now generally recognized that the growth recipe is far more complicated. One of the reasons physical capital accumulation has been deemphasized is that empirical evidence has suggested that capital accumulation doesn't necessarily lead to growth. For instance, the former Soviet Union invested a lot and accumulated lots of capital goods, but its economy didn't grow much because its capital was often internationally obsolete. A second reason is that products change, and buildings and machines useful in one time period may be useless in another (e.g., a six-year-old computer often is worthless). The value of the capital stock depends on its future expected earnings, which are very uncertain. Capital's role in growth is extraordinarily difficult to measure with accuracy.

Q-8 What are three types of capital?

A third reason capital accumulation was deemphasized is that it has become clear that capital includes much more than machines. In addition to physical capital, modern economics includes **human capital** *(the skills that are embodied in workers through experience, education, and on-the-job training, or, more simply, people's knowledge)* and **social capital** *(the habitual way of doing things that guides people in how they approach production)* as types of capital. The importance of human capital is obvious: A skilled labor force is far more productive than an unskilled labor force. Social capital is embodied in institutions such as the government, the legal system, and the fabric of society. In a way, anything that contributes to growth can be called a type of capital, and anything that slows growth can be called a destroyer of capital. With the concept of capital including such a wide range of things, it is difficult to say what is not capital, which makes the concept of capital less useful.

Web Note 10.2 Social Capital

Despite this modern deemphasis on investment and physical capital, all economists agree that the right kind of investment at the right time is a central element of growth. If an economy is to grow, it must invest. The debate is about what kinds and what times are the right ones.

Available Resources

If an economy is to grow, it will need resources. England grew in the late 1700s because it had iron and coal; the United States grew in the 20th century because it had a major supply of many natural resources, and it imported people, a resource it needed.

Of course, you have to be careful in thinking about what is considered a resource. A resource in one time period may not be a resource in another. For example, at one time oil was simply black gooey stuff that made land unusable. When people learned that the black gooey stuff could be burned as fuel, oil became a resource. What's considered a resource depends on technology. If solar technology is ever perfected, oil will go back to being black gooey stuff. So creativity can replace resources, and if you develop new technology fast enough, you can overcome almost any lack of existing resources. Even if a country doesn't have the physical resources it needs for growth, it can import them—as did Japan following World War II.

What is a resource depends on the production processes of an economy and technology.

The enormous growth of China has involved an increase in the demand for physical resources such as oil, iron ore, and copper—throughout the world. This has led both the United States and China to work toward securing continued access to sufficient physical resources in the future. China, in particular, is making deals with Latin American and African countries to lend them money with the proviso that they provide natural resources to China in the future.

Web Note 10.3 Oil Substitution

In 2007 and 2008 the large demand for resources pushed up the price of oil. Grain prices doubled and oil prices rose to more than $150 a barrel. Many noneconomists were predicting that the price of oil could only rise because world oil reserves were being depleted. Economists were not so sure. They had seen such predictions before, and they had always been wrong. The reason is that the high price of oil brings about changes. Specifically, it reduces the quantity demanded as people figure out ways to skimp on using oil. Second, the high price creates incentives to develop alternatives. Here are just a few of the options being explored:

- Geothermal energy—the recoverable heat in rock under the United States equals 2,000 years' worth of energy.
- Algae-produced fuel—algae ponds are being created that create "cellulosic ethanol," giving an almost inexhaustible source of energy.

- Wind power—as windmills become more efficient, a larger percentage of energy can come from wind.
- Plug-in cars—electric cars use half the energy of gasoline engine cars.
- Fuel cells—hydrogen-powered fuel cells offer new ways to provide power.
- Sugarcane-based ethanol—this is far more efficient than corn-based ethanol.
- Nuclear—the potential for almost unlimited energy.

If all these options are possible, why aren't they being developed? The reason is that there is no guarantee that the oil price will stay high. At $150 a barrel for oil, they make sense; at $60 a barrel for oil, they aren't worth developing. Thus, when oil fell back to $60 a barrel in late 2008, many of these research programs were shelved. Even as the price of oil rose in early 2012 to $120 a barrel, these research programs were not fast-tracked, because of the possibility that the price of oil would fall again and because of even cheaper, plentiful natural gas.

Greater participation in the market is another means by which to increase available resources. In China at the end of the 20th century, for example, many individuals migrated into the southern provinces, which have free trade sectors. Before they migrated they were only marginally involved in the market economy. After they migrated they became employed in the market economy. This increased the labor available to the market, helping push up China's growth rate. In the United States beginning in the 1950s, the percentage of women entering the workforce increased, contributing to economic growth.

Increasing the labor force participation rate is not a totally costless way of increasing growth. We lose whatever people were doing before they joined the labor force (which was, presumably, something of value to society). Our aggregate income accounting figures, which are measures of market activity, simply do not measure such losses.

Technological Development

Advances in technology shift the production possibility curve out by making workers more productive. Technological advances increase their ability to produce more of the things they already produce but also allow them to produce new and different products. While in some ways growth involves more of the same, a much larger aspect of growth involves changes in **technology**—*the way we make goods and supply services*—and changes in the goods and services we buy. Think of what this generation buys—music downloads, cell phones, cars, computers, fast food—and compare that to what the preceding generation bought—LP records, cars that would now be considered obsolete, and tube and transistor radios. (When I was 11, I saved $30—the equivalent of over $100 now—so I could afford a six-transistor Motorola radio; personal computers didn't exist.)

Growth isn't just getting more of the same thing. It's also getting some things that are different.

Contrast today's goods with the goods the next generation might have available: video brain implants (little gadgets in your head to receive sound and full-vision broadcasts—you simply close your eyes and tune in whatever you want, if you've paid your cellular fee for that month); fuel-cell-powered cars (gas cars will be considered quaint but polluting); and instant food (little pills that fulfill all your nutritional needs, letting your video brain implant supply all the ambiance). Just imagine! You probably can get the picture, even without a video brain implant.

How does society get people to work on developments that may change the very nature of what we do and how we think? One way is through economic incentives; another is with institutions that foster creativity and bold thinking—such as this book; a third is through institutions that foster hard work. There are, of course, trade-offs. For example, the Japanese educational system, which emphasizes hard work and discipline, doesn't do as good a job at fostering creativity as the U.S. educational system, and vice versa.

Five sources of growth are:

1. Growth-compatible institutions.
2. Capital accumulation.
3. Available resources.
4. Technological development.
5. Entrepreneurship.

REAL-WORLD APPLICATION

Growth and Terrorism

When talking about the costs of terrorism, many focus on the short-term effects—the tremendous cost in destruction of property and loss of life. But, according to a study by the Organization for Economic Coordination and Development, there are also long-term effects on growth, which may be less dramatic but even more costly. The study points out that the reaction to the terrorist attack of September 11, 2001:

- Caused significant increases in insurance premiums, raising costs and making firms less likely to undertake new projects.
- Made it impossible to get insurance for a number of projects, stopping these projects altogether.
- Increased transportation costs because of increased security.
- Slowed international trade because of security, making it impossible to get goods when they were needed, forcing firms to hold more inventory and increasing costs.
- Caused firms to spend more on security, lowering productivity.

9/11

Each of these effects contributed to slower growth by reducing the sources of growth. The terrorist attacks acted like sand in the wheels of trade, reduced expenditures on capital, lowered productivity, and reduced start-ups by entrepreneurs. The end result was hundreds of billions of dollars of lost output. The cost has been especially great for many Islamic countries, making it difficult for these countries to tie into the global economy.

Important advances in biotechnology, computers, and communications initially developed in the United States, and those developments helped fuel U.S. growth. Those new industries were much slower to develop in another important U.S. competitor, the European Union, which is one important reason why EU countries have grown far more slowly than has the United States in recent years.

Entrepreneurship

Entrepreneurship is the ability to get things done. That ability involves creativity, vision, willingness to accept risk, and a talent for translating that vision into reality.

Entrepreneurship is the ability to get things done. That ability involves creativity, vision, willingness to accept risk, and a talent for translating that vision into reality. Entrepreneurs have been central to growth in the United States. They have created large companies, produced new products, and transformed the landscape of the economy. Examples of entrepreneurs include Thomas Edison, who revolutionized the generation and use of electricity in the late 1800s; Henry Ford, who revolutionized transportation in the early 1900s; Bill Gates, who led Microsoft as it transformed and dominated the computer industry; and Mark Zuckerberg, who created Facebook and transformed the social networking culture. When a country's population demonstrates entrepreneurship, it can overcome deficiencies in other ingredients that contribute to growth.

Turning the Sources of Growth into Growth

The five sources of growth cannot be taken as givens. Even if a country has all five ingredients, it may not have them in the right proportions. For instance, when Nicolas Appert discovered canning (storing food in a sealed container in such a way that it wouldn't spoil) in the early 19th century, the economic possibilities of society expanded enormously. But if, when the technological developments occurred, the savings at the time were not sufficient to finance the investment, the result would not have been growth. It is finding the right combination of the sources of growth that plays a central role in the growth of any economy.

Economists' thinking about the sources of growth, and how they can be turned into economic growth, has changed over time.

Capital and Investment

Early economists—Classical economists—focused on savings and investment as sources of growth. The Classical economists' major policy conclusion was: The more capital—physical inputs to production—an economy has, the faster it will grow. This focus on capital is what caused market economies to be called *capitalist economies.* Since investment leads to an increase in capital, Classical economists focused their analysis, and their policy advice, on how to increase investment. The way to do that was for people to save:

Saving ⇒ Investment ⇒ Increase in capital ⇒ Growth

According to this **Classical growth model** *(a theory of growth that emphasizes the role of capital in the growth process)* if society wants its economy to grow, it has to save; the more saving, the better. Saving is good for both private individuals and governments because it is good for the economy. Thus, Classical economists objected to government deficits, which occur when government spends more than it collects in taxes. This view of deficits and saving was directly challenged by Keynes. Given the state of the economy and political debates today, we will have a lot more to say about these issues throughout the course.

For Classical economists, saving led to investment and to growth.

The early economists believed that eventually growth in capitalist countries would slow down because of what they called the law of diminishing marginal productivity. The **law of diminishing marginal productivity** states that *as more and more of a variable input is added to an existing fixed input, eventually the additional output produced with that additional input falls*. The law was developed in the 1800s, when farming was the major activity of the economy. Economists such as Thomas Malthus emphasized the limitations that the fixed amount of land placed on growth and predicted that as the population grew, to grow the needed food, farmers would have to farm increasingly less productive land. The result would be smaller harvest per worker. Malthus applied this reasoning to all production with a fixed input. This model is known as the Classical growth model.

The law of diminishing marginal productivity states that as more and more of a variable input is added to an existing fixed input, eventually the additional output produced with that additional input falls.

The predictions of the Classical growth model did not pan out. Per capita output did not stagnate; instead, it grew because of technological progress (think the invention of the cotton gin, for example) and increases in capital (think more farm equipment). Both more than offset the effects of the law of diminishing marginal productivity and eventually economists no longer saw land, or even capital, as the primary determinant of growth. Instead, they changed their focus to technology. In economists' current thinking, growth depends most on *technological innovation.* If technology grows, capital can be found to develop it. Without growth in technology, investment will not generate sustained growth.

In economists' current thinking, growth depends most on technological innovation.

Although capital isn't the primary determinant of growth, it does have a role to play. Technology requires investment and is embedded in capital. Take the telephone, which requires a kind of capital—landlines—to transmit voice. Today voice can be transmitted by a different type of capital—satellite. The technological innovation that has led to cell phones is embedded in voice-transmission capital. This technology would never have been used unless investment was available to both develop the technology and implement it with the purchase of new capital.

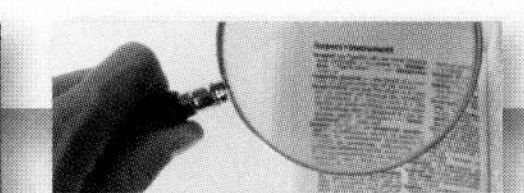

ADDED DIMENSION

Is the 21st Century the Age of Technology or One of Many Ages of Technology?

Sometimes newspapers write as if the importance of technology to the economy in the 21st century is a new phenomenon. It is not. Technology has been changing our society for the last two centuries, and it is not at all clear that the technological changes we are currently experiencing are any more revolutionary than those experienced by other generations in the last 200 years. For example, in terms of its impact on people's lives and communications in general, the Internet is small potatoes compared to the phone system.

One economist who recognized the importance of technology was Joseph Schumpeter. Schumpeter emphasized the role of the entrepreneur. He argued that entrepreneurs create major technological changes that drive the economy forward.

According to Schumpeter, the economy's growth depends on these entrepreneurs, and the industries they are in will be the leading industries, pulling the rest of the economy along after them. The accompanying figure lists five waves of technological innovation that have driven our economy. As you can see, in the late 1700s, steam power and iron manufacturing were the driving forces. In the 1860s, railroads were the dynamic industry. Later, electronics, automobiles, and chemicals drove our economy. In the 1980s through the early 21st century, computers and biotechnology have been the leading industries.

Technology

This new emphasis on the role of technology has led economists to develop a different path to growth:

Technological advance ⇒ Investment ⇒ Further technological advance ⇒ Growth

Q-9 According to new growth theory, what is the primary source of growth?

To distinguish this different focus from the model developed by Classical economists, it is called **new growth theory**—*a theory of growth that emphasizes the role of technology in the growth process*. New growth theory's central argument is that increases in technology do not just happen. Technological advance is the result of what the economy does—it invests in research and development (e.g., drug companies researching new ways to fight disease); makes advances in pure science (e.g., the human genome project); and works out new ways to organize production (e.g., just-in-time inventory techniques). Thus, in a sense, investment in technology increases the technological stock of an economy just as investment in capital increases the capital stock of an economy. Investment in technology is called research and development; firms hire researchers to explore options. Some of those options pay off and others do not, but the net return of that investment in technology is an increase in technology.

If investment in technology is similar to investment in capital, why does new growth theory separate the two? The reason is twofold. First, increases in technology are not as directly linked to investment as are increases in capital. Increases in investment require increases in saving, that is, building the capital. Increases in technology can occur with little investment and saving if the proverbial light bulb goes off in someone's head and that person sees a new way of doing something.

Second, increases in technology often have enormous *positive spillover effects,* especially if the new technology involves common knowledge and is freely available to all. A technological gain in one sector of production gives people in other sectors of production new ideas on how to change what they are doing, which gives other people new ideas. Ideas spread like pool balls after the break. One hits another, and soon all the nearby balls have moved. Put in technical economic terms, technological change often has significant **positive externalities**—*positive effects on others not taken into account by the decision maker.* Through those externalities, what is called general purpose technological change can have a much larger effect on growth than can an increase in capital.

The positive externalities result from the *common knowledge* aspect of technology because the idea behind the technology can often be used by others without payment to the developer. Using the same assembly line for different car models is just one example of a technological advance that has become incorporated into common knowledge. Any car manufacturer can use it.

The common knowledge aspect of technology creates positive externalities, which new growth theory sees as the key to growth.

Basic research is not always freely available; it is often protected by **patents**—*legal protection of a technological innovation that gives the owner of the patent sole rights to its use and distribution for a limited time.* (If the development is an idea rather than a good, it can be copyrighted rather than patented, but the general concept is the same.) Patents turn innovations into private property. The Microsoft Windows operating system is an example of a technology that is owned, and hence is not common knowledge. The ideas in technologies that are covered by patents, however, often have common knowledge elements. Once people have seen the new technology, they figure out sufficiently different ways of achieving the same end while avoiding violating the patent.

Learning by Doing As the new growth theorists have analyzed technology, they have also focused on another aspect of economic processes—an individual's tendency to **learn by doing,** or to *improve the methods of production through experience.* As people do something, they become better and better at it, sometimes because of new technologies, and sometimes simply because they learned better ways to do it just from practice. Thus, as production increases, costs of production tend to decrease over time. The introduction of new technology is sometimes the result of learning by doing.

Learning by doing changes the laws of economics enormously. It suggests that production has positive externalities in learning. If these positive externalities overwhelm diminishing marginal productivity, as new growth theory suggests they do, the predictions about growth change. In the Classical theory, growth is limited by diminishing marginal productivity; in the new theory, growth potential is unlimited and can accelerate over time. It's a whole new world out there—one in which, holding wants constant, scarcity decreases over time. In new growth theory, per capita income can grow forever, and the dismal science of economics becomes the optimistic science.

Learning by doing overcomes the law of diminishing marginal productivity because learning by doing increases the productivity of workers.

Technological Lock-In One of the questions new growth theory raises is: Does the economy always use the "best" technology available? Some say no and point to examples of technologies that have become entrenched in the market or locked in to new products despite the availability of more efficient technologies. This is known as *technological lock-in.*

One proposed example of technological lock-in goes under the name QWERTY, which is the upper-left six keys on the standard computer keyboard. Economist Paul David argues that the design of this keyboard was chosen to slow people's typing down so that the keys in old-style mechanical typewriters would not lock up. He further argues that developments in word processing have since eliminated the problem the QWERTY keyboard was designed to solve (we don't use mechanical typewriters any more). But once people started choosing this keyboard, it was too costly for manufacturers to develop another.

This interpretation of history has been disputed by other economists, who argue that the QWERTY keyboard is not significantly less efficient than other keyboard arrangements and that, if it were, competition would have eliminated it. Sometimes this counterargument almost seems to state that the very fact that a technology exists means that it is the most efficient. Most economists do not go that far; they argue that even if the QWERTY keyboard is not a highly inefficient technology, other examples of lock-in exist. Beta format videos were preferable to VHS, the Windows operating system is inferior to many alternatives, the English language doesn't compare to Esperanto, and English measurement systems are quite inefficient compared to the metric system.

Q-10 In what way does the Internet demonstrate network externalities?

One reason for technological lock-in is the existence of *network externalities*—an externality in which the use of a good by one individual makes that technology more valuable to other people. Telephones exhibit network externalities. A single telephone is pretty useless. Whom would you call? Two telephones are more useful, but as more and more people get telephones, the possible interactions (and the benefits of telephones) increase exponentially. Network externalities can make switching to a superior technology expensive or nearly impossible. The Windows operating system is another example of a product that exhibits network externalities and makes it difficult for other operating systems to develop.

Growth Policies

Exactly what these theories mean for growth and growth policies is the subject of much debate among economists. But there is some agreement about general policies that are good for growth. These include:

- Encouraging saving and investment.
- Formalizing property rights and reducing bureaucracy and corruption.
- Providing more of the right kind of education.
- Promoting policies that encourage technological innovation.
- Promoting policies that allow taking advantage of specialization.

Most economists would agree that each of these is good for growth. Unfortunately, the devil is in the details, and the policy problem is translating these general policies into specific politically acceptable policies.

WWW Web Note 10.4 Loans that Change Lives

Past data do not necessarily predict future events well, and while predictions are always dangerous, it is worthwhile asking: How may the future differ from the past, and what do those differences suggest about future U.S. economic growth? One big difference is the current economic development of the Indian and Chinese economies, which is similar to the growth experienced by other Asian countries, such as South Korea and Thailand, in the 1980s. What's different about China and India is their size; combined, they have a population of 2.6 billion. As they are developing into highly industrialized countries, the world economic landscape is changing tremendously. Specifically, their development has placed, and will continue to place, pressures on U.S. firms in both services and manufacturing industries to become

REAL-WORLD APPLICATION

Short-Run Supply-Side Macro Policy

Some politicians argue that the best way to get the economy moving in the short run is to cut taxes on the rich since the rich are what they call job creators. As a long-run policy to encourage growth, economists have differing views about whether such cuts in taxes are appropriate. The empirical evidence is inconclusive.

As a short-run policy, however, there is much greater agreement among economists: Tax cuts for the rich are not an especially good way to create jobs. The reason is that in the short run, demand-side effects rule. Supply-side effects rule in the long run, impacting the economy over many years.

Here's the reason why tax cuts for the rich are not likely to have much impact on jobs in the short run. Tax cuts for the rich tend not to be spent as much as tax cuts for the poor. Thus, the tax cuts are more likely to go into saving, and not increase demand for goods. So, while a tax cut for the rich would have some demand-side effect, it would be smaller than if the tax cut were given to the poor or if it were spread out evenly among all people.

Here's the problem with expecting a tax cut for the rich to create jobs in the United States even if it were to increase aggregate demand. In order to invest and create jobs in the United States any good businessperson will look at total costs of producing in the United States versus the total costs of producing elsewhere. So if a policy maker wants to stimulate job creation in the United States, he or she would have to either increase the costs of producing abroad or decrease the costs of producing here. Policies that do that include cutting wages, reducing regulatory burdens, and lowering costs in other ways. Cutting taxes on the rich doesn't affect their decision about whether to produce here or abroad unless the tax cut is available only if they produce goods here, and a cut in the income tax would not do that.

One recent technological breakthrough that has been stimulating growth in the United States involves a new technology that allows the extraction of large amounts of natural gas from the ground. That new technology lowers the cost of producing output in the United States relative to producing abroad, and hence increases the attractiveness of producing in the United States. For industries that are energy-intensive, energy costs can make a big difference and that discovery has contributed to the 2012 economic expansion in the United States.

more competitive. This means they must hold down wage increases, develop more efficient production methods than are available elsewhere, or move their production facilities abroad.

The economic rise of China, India, and other developing countries will also be accompanied by an increasing demand for natural resources, which, unless offset by even greater technological development, will tend to mean slower world growth. So, because of natural resource constraints, and because the growth dynamics are likely to gravitate to these Asian countries until production costs are equalized, the developed countries will likely find it harder and harder to maintain the growth rate that they have maintained in the past century.

Conclusion

Growth happens, or at least it generally has happened in market economies. But that doesn't mean it happens on its own. While saying precisely why growth happens is beyond economists at this point, economists have identified important sources of growth. These include capital accumulation, available resources, growth-compatible institutions, technological development, and entrepreneurship. What economists haven't been able to determine yet is how they all fit together to bring about growth, and the general feeling is that there is no single way of putting them together—what works likely changes over time. As the competition for natural resources increases and the growth dynamic moves to China and India, the United States will likely find it difficult to keep up its previous growth rate.

There is no single way of putting all the sources of growth together—what works likely changes over time.

Summary

- Growth is an increase in the amount of goods and services an economy can produce when both labor and capital are fully employed. *(LO10-1)*
- Growth increases potential output and shifts the production possibility curve out, allowing an economy to produce more goods. *(LO10-1)*
- Markets allow specialization and division of labor, which increases productivity and leads to growth. *(LO10-2)*
- Per capita growth means producing more goods and services per person. It can be calculated by subtracting the percentage change in the population from the percentage change in output. *(LO10-2)*
- Five sources of growth are (1) growth-compatible institutions, (2) capital accumulation, (3) available resources, (4) technological development, and (5) entrepreneurship. *(LO10-3)*
- The loanable funds market translates savings into investment that is necessary for growth. The interest rate equilibrates saving and investment. *(LO10-3)*
- The Classical growth model focuses on the role of capital accumulation in the growth process. The law of diminishing productivity limits growth of per capita income. *(LO10-4)*
- New growth theory emphasizes the role of technology in the growth process. *(LO10-4)*
- Advances in technology have overwhelmed the effects of diminishing marginal productivity. *(LO10-4)*
- Policies that are good for growth are policies that: (1) encourage saving and investment, (2) formalize property rights, (3) provide the right kind of education, (4) encourage technological innovation, and (5) take advantage of specialization. *(LO10-4)*

Key Terms

Classical growth model *(223)*
division of labor *(214)*
human capital *(220)*
law of diminishing marginal productivity *(223)*
learn by doing *(225)*
new growth theory *(224)*
patent *(225)*
per capita growth *(216)*
positive externality *(225)*
productivity *(211)*
Rule of 72 *(213)*
Say's law *(211)*
social capital *(220)*
specialization *(214)*
technology *(221)*

Questions and Exercises

1. Outline some of the benefits and costs to society when it experiences growth. *(LO10-1)*
2. Assume that per capita income is growing at different rates in the following countries: Nepal, 1.1 percent; Kenya, 1.7 percent; Singapore, 7.2 percent; Egypt, 3.9 percent. How long will it take for each country to double its income per person? *(LO10-1)*
3. What roles do specialization and division of labor play in economists' support of free trade? *(LO10-2)*
4. Who most likely worked longer to buy a dozen eggs: a person living in 2013 or a person living in 1910? Why? *(LO10-2)*
5. Calculate real growth per capita in the following countries: *(LO10-2)*
   a. Democratic Republic of Congo: population growth = 3.0 percent; real output growth = −1.8 percent.
   b. Estonia: population growth = −0.4 percent; real output growth = 4.2 percent.
   c. India: population growth = 2.0 percent; real output growth = 6 percent.
   d. United States: population growth = 0.5 percent; real output growth = 2.5 percent.
6. In what ways do informal property rights limit growth? *(LO10-3)*
7. How can an increase in the U.S. saving rate lead to higher living standards? *(LO10-3)*
8. Demonstrate graphically how the loanable funds market translates savings into investment. What equilibrates saving and investment? *(LO10-3)*
9. Using the demand and supply of loanable funds, demonstrate the effect of the following on the interest rate. As a

result, what would you expect to be the impact of the change on growth? *(LO10-3)*
   a. Government increases spending.
   b. Businesses become more productive.
   c. The people as a whole save more.
10. Name three types of capital and explain the differences among them. *(LO10-3)*
11. How does growth through technology differ from growth through the accumulation of physical capital? *(LO10-3)*
12. On what law of production did Thomas Malthus base his prediction that population growth would exceed growth in goods and services? *(LO10-4)*
13. Why hasn't Thomas Malthus's prediction come true? *(LO10-4)*
14. Classical growth theory and new growth theory both contribute to economists' understanding of how the sources of growth lead to economic growth. *(LO10-4)*
    a. How are they the same?
    b. How to they differ?
15. Explain how each of the following is expected to affect growth: *(LO10-4)*
    a. Increase in technology.
    b. Positive externalities.
    c. Patents.
    d. Learning by doing.
    e. Technological lock-in.
16. What are spillover effects and how do they affect growth? *(LO10-4)*
17. What are network externalities and how do they lead to growth? *(LO10-4)*
18. In the early 20th century worker productivity in the Horndal iron works plant in Sweden increased by 2 percent per year over a 15-year period even though the firm did not invest in new capital. What might be the cause for the increase in productivity? *(LO10-4)*
19. England once offered a prize to the person who invented an accurate clock that could be used on a ship. England then made the technology freely available. Do such policies lead to greater growth than leaving innovation to the market? Defend your answer. *(LO10-4)*

Questions from Alternative Perspectives

1. Capitalism was a derogatory term coined by Karl Marx to deride the riches of those who accumulated capital. He said that the accumulation of capital helps the rich get richer while simultaneously making the poor get poorer.
   a. Have the poor become poorer under capitalism?
   b. Based on the growth model presented in the text, what would you expect to happen to poor people's income when society accumulates capital? (Austrian)
2. Ecological economists believe that economic possibilities are constrained by natural laws (for example, the laws of thermodynamics, biological assimilation, and the limiting factor). Unlimited material growth from a finite resource base—spaceship earth—is therefore impossible. How many "earths" would it take for everyone to live like U.S. citizens? (To help answer this question, you might visit and take the test at http://ecological/footprint.) (Institutionalist)
3. Many Keynesians believe the best way to deal with growth is to have government promote an industrial policy that focuses on the development of technological change using tax credits, government research funding, and the transfer of technological knowledge from the military to the civilian sector.
   a. Would such a policy be consistent with the new growth theory?
   b. Would those believing in the Classical growth model support such a policy? (Post-Keynesian)
4. There is a furious debate among economists about the relationship between equality (or inequality) and economic growth. Based on the observation that developing countries often experience increasing inequality during their initial periods of rapid growth, some economists emphasize the role of inequality in establishing incentives to work, save, and invest. The experience of the East Asian economies that grew rapidly after reducing their levels of inequality (through land reform and other means) led other economists to argue that greater equality leads to faster economic growth. The reasons they cite are numerous: more political stability, greater access to credit, higher levels of spending on education, and wider land ownership.
   a. How do these arguments about the positive link between equality and economic growth fit with your textbook's list of the sources of economic growth?
   b. What do you think is the relationship between equality (or inequality) and economic growth? (Radical)
5. Christians believe that everything ultimately belongs to God. Is that belief consistent with economists' belief that property rights are necessary for growth? (Religious)

Issues to Ponder

1. a. If you suddenly found yourself living as a poor person in a developing country, what are some things that you now do that you would no longer be able to do? What new things would you have to do?
   b. Answer the questions again assuming that you are living in the United States 100 years ago.
2. Have the poor benefited more or less from economic growth than the rich?
3. What problem would a politician face when promoting policies to encourage saving?
4. De Paul University Professor Ludovic Comeau Jr. hypothesizes that the length of time that a country has had a democratic political structure contributes positively to growth. In what way can a political structure be capital?

Answers to Margin Questions

1. The long-run growth analysis justifies its focus on supply by assuming that aggregate supply will create an equal level of aggregate demand. This is known as Say's law. (*p. 211; LO10-1*)
2. Using the Rule of 72 (divide 72 by the growth rate of income), we can calculate that it will take 18 years for income to double when its growth rate is 4 percent a year. (*p. 214; LO10-1*)
3. Markets allow specialization and the division of labor, which increase productivity; greater productivity leads to growth. (*p. 215; LO10-2*)
4. Country B is experiencing the higher growth in income per capita. To calculate this, subtract the population growth rates from the income growth rates for each country. Country A's per capita growth rate is 1 percent (4 − 3) and country B's per capita growth rate is 2 percent (3 − 1). (*p. 216; LO10-2*)
5. The increases would have to be distributed so that no one whose income is below the median receives enough to bring his or her income above the median. (*p. 217; LO10-2*)
6. Private property provides an incentive for people to produce by creating the possibility of benefiting from their efforts. (*p. 218; LO10-3*)
7. With the demand for loanable funds shifting out, the interest rate will likely rise. (*p. 219; LO10-3*)
8. Three types of capital are physical capital, human capital, and social capital. (*p. 220; LO10-3*)
9. New growth focuses on technology. (*p. 224; LO10-4*)
10. The Internet connects over two billion people around the globe and reduces communication costs. The benefit of one person using the Internet is virtually nonexistent. The benefit of the Internet rises as more people use it because the higher usage increases the amount of information available on the Internet and increases the ability of each user to communicate. (*p. 226; LO10-4*)

Advances in Modern Macroeconomic Theory

> *"Maybe there is in human nature a deep-seated perverse pleasure in adopting and defending a wholly counterintuitive doctrine that leaves the uninitiated peasant wondering what planet he or she is on."*
>
> —Robert Solow

This web chapter can be found at: www.mhhe.com/colander9e

Chapter Outline

After reading this chapter, you should be able to:

LO10W-1 Distinguish between the standard macro model and the modern macro model.

LO10W-2 Trace the development of the standard and modern models of the economy.

LO10W-3 Explain the assumptions and three policy implications of the dynamic stochastic general equilibrium (DSGE) model.

LO10W-4 Summarize the complex systems approach to macro.

chapter 11

The Structural Stagnation Policy Dilemma

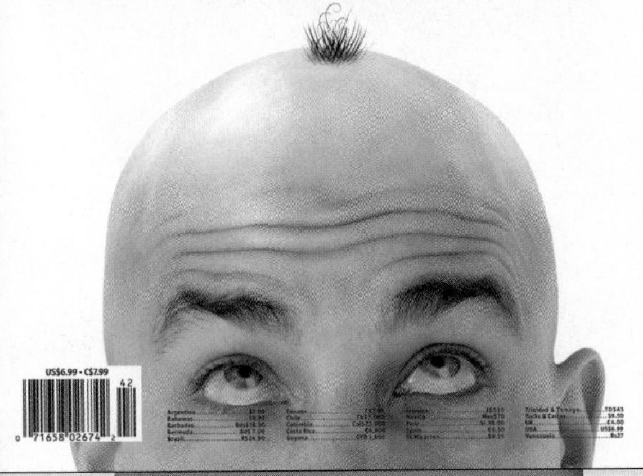

After reading this chapter, you should be able to:

- **LO11-1** Differentiate a structural stagnation from a standard recession.
- **LO11-2** Demonstrate in the *AS/AD* model how globalization can mask inflationary pressures caused by expansionary policies.
- **LO11-3** Explain the role of globalization and the financial bubble in creating a structural stagnation problem.
- **LO11-4** Outline the policy choices that policy makers have to deal with structural stagnation.

> *Illusions commend themselves to us because they save us pain and allow us to enjoy pleasure instead. We must therefore accept it without complaint when they sometimes collide with a bit of reality against which they are dashed to pieces.*
>
> —Sigmund Freud

In December 2007 the U.S. economy fell into a prolonged period of slow growth and stagnation; it wasn't a depression, but it wasn't a normal recession either. As in a typical downturn in a business cycle, unemployment rose and output fell, but unlike a typical downturn, the economy did not seem to recover even when the government ran expansionary demand-side macro policy. If the recession had been part of a typical business cycle, expansionary policy *would have* pulled aggregate output back to its growth trend. It was as if the economy had contracted a disease that was preventing a return to its long-run growth trend. *Time Magazine* called it "the wimpy recovery."

Economists are still debating what is going on with the economy, and in this chapter I provide one explanation—the **structural stagnation hypothesis**—*a hypothesis about the macro economy that sees the recent problems of the U.S. economy directly related to the structural problems caused by globalization.* This structural stagnation hypothesis provides a possible general explanation for why the economy is experiencing such a wimpy recovery.

In some ways this hypothesis is conventional, but in other ways it is quite unconventional. Thus, your professor will likely have a different take on some or all aspects of the issues presented in this chapter. This is as it should be. Macroeconomic theory, as it relates to recent events, is unsettled; it is very much in flux. To present it any other way is to be disingenuous. There are conflicting interpretations of what is happening in the U.S. economy and what should be done about it.

Regardless of whether one agrees with the structural stagnation hypothesis presented in this chapter, it is useful pedagogically. It is an example of the economic way of thinking—how economic reasoning blends different economic ideas and concepts from both microeconomics and macroeconomics into a plausible explanation for current events. The second part of economic reasoning, the empirical testing of the ideas, is what is covered in higher level economics courses.

The Structural Stagnation Hypothesis

According to the structural stagnation hypothesis, structural stagnation has both long-run and short-run causes. The long-run cause is intricately tied to globalization, exchange rates, and the trade deficit. The short-run cause is intricately tied to the aftermath of the financial crisis. The two are related because one of the causes of the financial crisis was that government was avoiding dealing with the problems presented by globalization. How to deal with structural stagnation is likely to be a central macro policy issue in the coming years.

According to the structural stagnation hypothesis, structural stagnation has both long-run and short-run causes.

I begin by discussing the difference between a structural stagnation and a normal downturn and business cycle. Then I turn to the long-run and short-run causes of structural stagnation. I look first at how globalization can contribute to structural stagnation if exchange rates don't adjust quickly enough to equalize trade balances. Then I discuss how the structural problems presented by globalization were partially hidden by expansionary macro policy, creating a financial bubble and an additional set of structural problems. Finally, I consider the difficult choices facing U.S. policy makers as they attempt to deal with structural stagnation.

Differentiating a Structural Stagnation from a Standard Recession

You can see the difference between the structural stagnation downturn that started in December 2007 and previous downturns in the Figure 11-1, which graphs percentage deviations in employment from its peak before a recession until its recovery after a recession.

WWW Web Note 11.1 Globalization and Employment

Until the 1980s the economy quickly got back to its previous level of employment. After the 1980s, however, economic recoveries took increasingly longer; the 2001 recovery was slower than the 1990 recovery, which in turn was slower than the 1980

FIGURE 11-1 Changes in Employment from Peak

Until 2001 employment recovered fairly quickly after recessions. In the economic recovery since the 2007 recession, employment has remained significantly below its peak. This reflects structural stagnation in the United States.

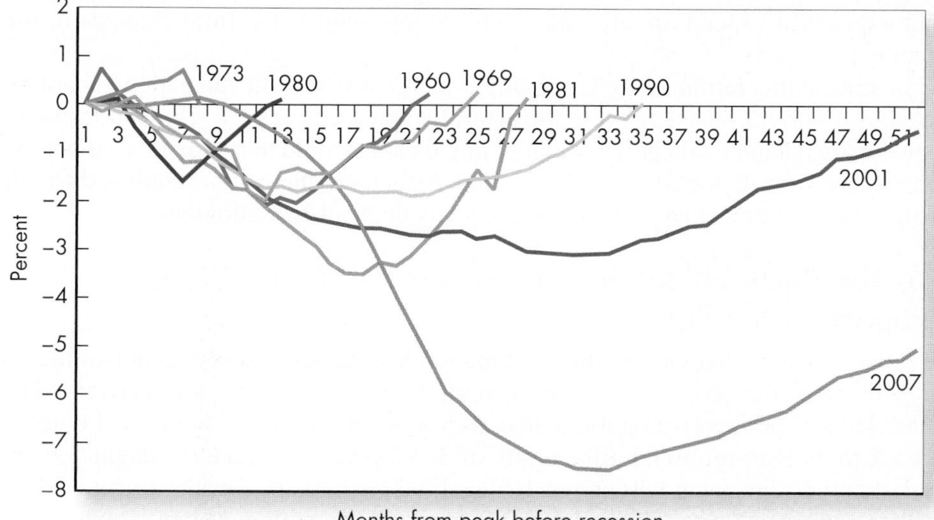

ADDED DIMENSION

Business Cycles in History

Before Keynesian economics came to dominate macroeconomic discussions, economists talked about business cycles. They developed numerous categories to describe cycles of various lengths—Juglar cycles, Jevons cycles, Kitchin cycles, Kuznets cycles, Kondratief cycles, and many more. Students could spend a whole course learning all the cycles, each having different explanations for causes and length. (For example, Kondratief cycles were 50-year cycles that could come in sync or out of sync with other cycles that could make it stronger or weaker.)

With the rise of Keynesian economics and modern macroeconomics, as well as better statistical measurement, these "named" cycle theories were abandoned and economists talked about generic random fluctuations, not predictable cycles with different lengths and different characteristics. They saw fluctuations as being caused by random fluctuations in demand. Because the shocks were random, empirical predictability of any predetermined cycle couldn't be supported. After World War II, most macroeconomists expected recessions to be short because we now had a remedy—expansionary government demand-side policy. In the conventional view, we might not be able to totally eliminate business cycles, but we could make them milder and prevent them from turning into long drawn-out stagnations. Most economists shared this highly optimistic view—that the macroeconomic problem of drawn-out stagnations was solved. They did not see a major depression as a possibility. Even Keynesian critic Robert Lucas stated, "The central problem of depression-prevention [has] been solved, for all practical purposes."

The optimism of macroeconomists came in for a rude shock in 2007, the start of a prolonged downturn. This has led to renewed interest in these earlier discussions of the reasons for longer and shorter cycles. In the new view, macroeconomic fluctuations can have different causes; one cannot treat all fluctuations with the same medicine. Instead, the treatments must be tailored to the causes of the fluctuation.

recovery, which in turn was slower than earlier recoveries. This trend toward slower and slower recoveries suggests that the nature of economic downturns was changing. But those changes were slow and gradual, and economists could reasonably argue that the changes were inconsequential. But, as you can see, the latest downturn was clearly a major change. As of 2013, six years after the beginning of the downturn employment was still significantly below what it had been before the recession began.

Faced with this experience, economists began to grapple with the fact that something in the U.S. economy had changed. It was then that the term *structural stagnation* began to be used to describe a downturn followed by a period of slow growth that is not expected to speed up any time soon without major structural changes in the economy.

The reason this terminology is important is that a structural stagnation cannot be treated as a normal business cycle. Structural stagnations are far less responsive to expansionary demand-side policies that policy makers would normally rely on put the economy back on its long-term growth trend. Structural stagnation requires difficult supply-side structural changes to accompany any demand-side stimulus.

Why the Assumed Underlying Growth Trend Is Important for Policy

The biggest change that the structural stagnation hypothesis makes to standard macro theory involves the economy's assumed underlying growth rate in a recovery.

The biggest change that the structural stagnation hypothesis makes to standard macro theory involves the economy's assumed underlying growth rate in a recovery. The standard macro policy assumption is that after a downturn, an economy will quickly get back to its long-run trend growth rate of 3–3.5 percent. Structural stagnation assumes that the adjustment will be much longer, taking perhaps decades to get back to that long-run growth rate. The hallmark of structural stagnation is slow growth and a recovery that does not generate a large number of jobs.

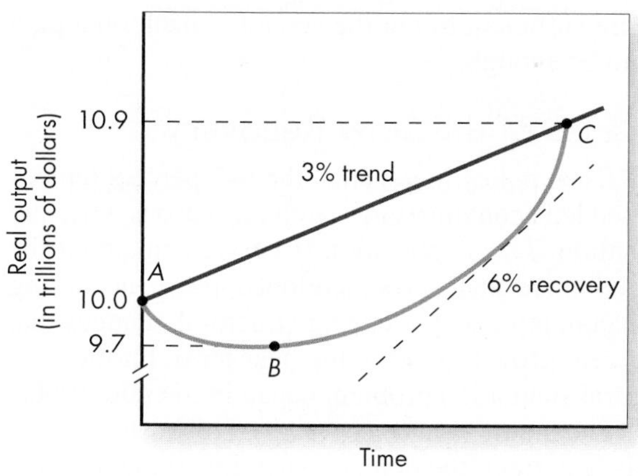

FIGURE 11-2 Expansions to Maintain Trend Growth

In a typical recovery, economic expansion must significantly exceed the trend growth rate to make up for the decline and catch up with the rise in potential output.

The assumed growth rate for the economy plays a central role in policy advice. You can see this in Figure 11-2. The straight-line trend growth rate is assumed to be 3 percent, the rate that existed throughout most of U.S. history since World War II and the growth rate assumed by economists who subscribe to the standard macro model.

Figure 11-2 shows a typical recession and recovery. The recession begins at point *A,* pulling the economy below the trend growth rate until it hits the trough at point *B.* At this point, the economy begins to recover until real output returns to potential output (along the long-term growth path) at point *C.* What's important to note is that, for the economy to return to its growth path, the rate at which the economy expands during the recovery must be greater than the trend rate. That's because it must make up for the resulting gap between actual output and potential output.

Q-1 Why must an economy grow faster in a recovery than it declined during a recession to return to its long-term growth trend?

Figure 11-2 also shows the need for faster growth numerically. Suppose real economic output is $10 trillion (point *A*) and the economy falls by 3 percent in one year, to $9.7 trillion (point *B*). For the economy to recover within two years (point *C*), it would have to increase at an annual rate of somewhere around 6 percent per year. The economy needs to grow by more than the 3 percent decline during the recession to make up for the decline in output during the recession *and* the rise in potential—in this case the $0.3 trillion *plus* the $0.6 trillion for a total of $0.9 trillion.

Most policy makers were expecting such a robust recovery when in 2008 they ran highly expansionary fiscal policy—a $1 trillion-plus annual deficit and highly expansionary monetary policy in response to the recession. The expectation was that the economy would initially expand at a high annual rate of 6 percent for two or three years, which would get it back on its 3 percent long-term growth trend. They didn't worry too much about the high budget deficit because the strong recovery would allow the economy to "grow out of the deficit." By that they meant that the deficits as a percentage of GDP would decline when both tax revenues and GDP rose quickly in the expansion. Once the economy recovered, they did not see a need for ongoing deficits to keep stimulating the economy. And that would have been the case if it were a standard recession. But it wasn't.

The standard macroeconomists didn't worry much about the high budget deficit because they expected that a strong recovery would allow the economy to "grow out of the deficit."

After contracting by 0.3 percent in 2008 and 3.5 percent in 2009 (the economy hit its trough in June 2009), the economy rose only 3.0 percent in 2010 and slowed to 1.7 percent in 2011. Further, the unemployment rate remained stubbornly high, jumping from 4.7 percent just before the financial crisis in 2007 to 10 percent in the fall of 2009 and falling only two percentage points to 8.2 percent by mid 2012. This is why the economy was said to be experiencing a jobless recovery. Expansionary monetary and fiscal policy of the size that Congress was willing to go along with, and that many conventional economists had said were sufficient to put the economy back on a path toward potential output, didn't seem to be enough.

Structural Stagnation as a Cause of the Slow Recovery

The failure of standard monetary and fiscal policy to generate the 6–7 percent temporary growth that policy makers expected led economists to search for reasons why, and structural stagnation was one explanation. This explanation is pessimistic about the demand-side growth prospects for the United States. As mentioned above, according to structural stagnationists, the U.S. economy is experiencing structural changes that will keep it from returning to a 3 percent growth trend in the near term. Further, according to this hypothesis, the structural stagnation problem began in the mid-1990s. It lowered the growth trend for the U.S. economy to a lower rate that had been assumed for the past decade. If this hypothesis is correct, the demand-side government policy has been far too expansionary since the late 1990s and the fact that it was too expansionary contributed to the financial bubble that misdirected investment and made the U.S. economy prone to financial crises. According to the structural stagnation hypothesis, without some unexpected positive supply shock, which increases potential output and trend growth, the United States will have to live with slower growth for the forseeable future, even though we are recovering from a severe recession—at best 3–4 percent growth as the economy returns to its lower 2.25 percent temporary trend—and higher natural rate of unemployment—6–7 percent, not the previous 5 percent target.

Structural Stagnation's Implications for Macro Policy

You can see the different policy implications of the standard 3 percent trend growth assumption and the structural stagnation 2.25 percent growth trend assumption in Figure 11-3. The trend growth rate is a central difference between the standard theory and the structural stagnation hypothesis. Both assume a 3 percent growth trend up until 1995 and an eventual return to the 3 percent growth trend in the future, although the structural stagnationists believe that the United States will likely never recoup the full loss of output during the structural stagnation.

FIGURE 11-3 Policy Implications of Structural Stagnation

If the long-run growth path falls, but policy makers do not adjust their estimates for the fall, they will target a higher potential output than is sustainable and eventually create problems for an economy. One of the problems this "too high targeting" creates is a financial bubble.

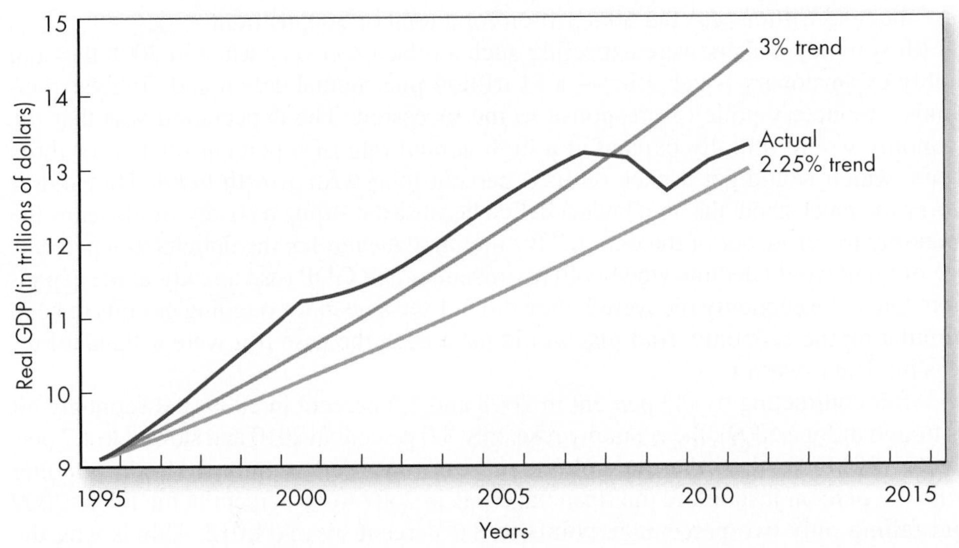

Where the theories differ substantially is what the trend path of the economy should have been considered from the onset of the pressures of globalization in the late 1990s and the following decades, or when the structural problems are resolved. Standard-model economists, the optimists, believe in a continued 3 percent growth trend, as shown by the purple line throughout this time period. Structural stagnationists believed the trend line fell closer to 2.25 percent in the late 1990s and 2000, as shown by the orange line. They believe that the trend will start to return to a long-run 3 percent trend only when the structural problems have been resolved, which will likely take decades. So the best we should have been hoping for in the 2000s was a 2.25 percent growth trend. That small difference in targeted trend makes an enormous difference in one's view of whether demand-side policy during this period was too expansionary.

The assumed trend growth rate is a central difference between the standard theory and the structural stagnation hypothesis.

In the early 2000s, the economy grew by over 3 percent a year and inflation remained low. So it would seem that the structural stagnationists were wrong. Advocates of the structural stagnation hypothesis believe, however, that what was in fact happening was that the economy was operating significantly above its sustainable level of potential output during this entire period. The result of trying to keep the economy above its potential was an unsustainable financial bubble. That bubble burst in late 2007, pushing the economy back down towards its actual growth trend. As you can see with a 2.25 percent growth trend, the recession that resulted from the financial crisis was simply pulling the economy back down toward its true potential growth trend. Moreover, they argue that the financial bubble created additional short-run structural problems for the economy that will temporarily further limit growth.

These post-bubble structural effects have impacted the economy in recent years, and are likely to remain substantial in coming years. They have lowered the achievable growth even more than it already had been lowered by the forces of globalization. Thus, according to the structural stagnation hypothesis it will likely be another three of four years before the economy can safely return to its 2.25 percent growth trend that began in the early 2000s with significant globalization, and perhaps another two decades before the U.S. economy can return to the 3 percent growth trend.

The issue is sustainability, not whether, with sufficient demand stimulus, the U. S. economy might grow faster than 2.25 percent if the government continues to run sufficiently expansionary macro policy. The structural stagnation hypothesis holds that the faster growth runs the risk of causing new financial bubbles and additional problems, just as the expansionary macro policy in the early 2000s did. According to the structural stagnation hypothesis demand stimulus hides the underlying structural problems. The bottom line: If the structural stagnation hypothesis is true, as the United States undergoes the structural changes that are required by globalization, it can look forward to a decade of structural stagnation—slow growth and high unemployment.

If the structural stagnation hypothesis is true, the United States will likely experience a decade of slow growth and high unemployment.

Structural, not Secular, Stagnation

Economists in the 1940s after the Great Depression had a quite different argument for why an economy would experience prolonged slow growth after World War II. Their argument is called **secular stagnation theory,** *a theory in which advanced countries such as the United States would eventually stop growing because investment opportunities would be eliminated.* The central tenet of this theory is that eventually all investment opportunities will be met. Without new investment opportunities, the investment component of aggregate demand will wither, and along with it economic growth.

Eventually economic growth for all economies throughout the world would decline, and growth would stop.

Q-2 What is the structural stagnation hypothesis's explanation for slowing growth?

Structural stagnation is different. It does not assume that low investment will slow global growth, or that the world growth trend will fall. Instead, it focuses on **globalization**—*the increasing economic connections among economies around the world that increases competition among countries.* According to the structural stagnation hypothesis, globalization causes structural problems that primarily affect advanced economies, particularly the United States and Europe. Dealing with these structural problems of globalization will keep their economic growth below world economic growth into the foreseeable future as much of the growth takes place in developing countries. However, once the structural changes are made, economic growth in these advanced economies will return to the world growth rate. But by this time, the U.S. share of world output will have fallen. So in the structural stagnation hypothesis, eventually, the U.S. economy may return to its traditional growth path, but that "eventually" will be a long time in coming.

The *AS/AD* Model with Globalization

The globalized *AS/AD* model adds a world supply curve to the standard *AS/AD* model to capture the effect that globalization issues can have on an economy.

For the structural stagnation hypothesis to fit the U.S. experience, it must explain how globalization led to structural problems and what those structural problems are. Let's first consider how the structural stagnation hypothesis sees globalization affecting potential output. We do so in Figure 11-4, which presents the **globalized *AS/AD* model**—*the standard* AS/AD *model with an added world supply curve that captures the effect that globalization can have on an economy.*

Let's begin with the standard *AS/AD* model shown in Figure 11-4(a). In that standard *AS/AD* model the U.S. aggregate demand curve represents the amount that U.S.

FIGURE 11-4(A, B, AND C) The Globalized *AS/AD* Model

The model in **(a)** is the standard *AS/AD* model with an economy in both short-run and long-run equilibrium. The globalized *AS/SD* model in **(b)** has a flat world aggregate supply curve. In this figure, the economy is also in short-run and long-run equilibrium because all the curves meet at the same location. The current situation in the United States is shown in **(c)** with a world supply curve that is below what would have been the equilibrium price in the standard *AS/AD* model.

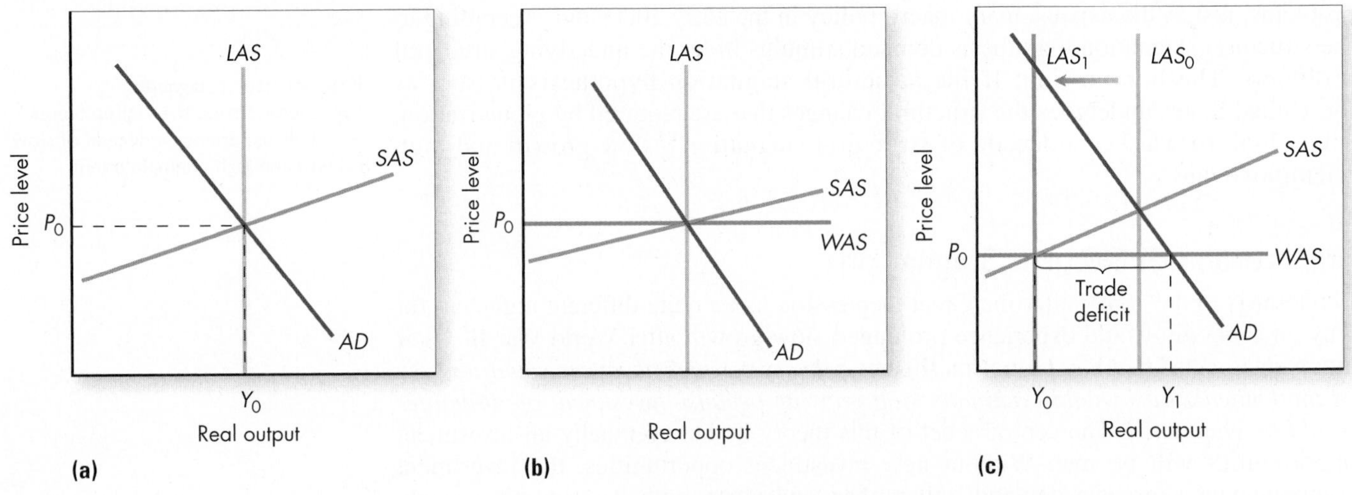

consumers will demand at each price level. Similarly, the U.S. aggregate supply curve is the amount of goods that U.S.-based firms will supply at each price level. The economy is in short-run equilibrium where the *SAS* and *AD* curves intersect and is in long-run equilibrium when the *SAS, AD,* and *LAS* curves all intersect. The situation shown here is an economy that is in both short-run and long-run equilibrium because the *SAS* and *AD* curves meet at potential output denoted by the *LAS* curve. The difference between the standard *AS/AD* model and the globalized *AS/AD* model is that the standard *AS/AD* model does not account for world supply of goods. This means that it doesn't tell us how much aggregate demand is supplied by U.S. production and how much is supplied by foreign production. The difference—net exports—is not part of the standard *AS/AD* model.

To see how the world economy affects the *AS/AD* model, we must add an additional curve—the world supply curve. Figure 11-4(b) adds the **world supply curve**—*the amount of tradable goods that other countries in the world will supply to the country at a given price level and exchange rate.* (Throughout this discussion I will discuss goods, but it should be clear that goods also includes services.) I include the exchange rate in the definition because the exchange rate will change the price of imported goods. Specifically, as explained in Chapter 8, when the domestic exchange rate falls, the price of imports rises and vice versa.

Q-3 How is the globalized *AS/AD* model different from the standard *AS/AD* model?

The world supply curve is flat because we assume that, for all practical purposes, foreign producers can supply an infinite amount of tradable goods at the world price. What this means is that the world supply curve sets a price ceiling for U.S. goods, and all U.S. producers of tradable goods must match the world price. For example, if China is the low-cost producer, and a company in China can produce a television for $600, that $600 is the most that U.S. firms can charge for equivalent televisions. Similarly, if the cost in India of answering a call at a call center is $2.00 a call, that $2.00 is the highest price that a U.S. call center can charge for an equivalent service. If domestic producers don't match world prices, they won't be able to sell their goods in the United States or abroad. That equivalency follows from the law of one price—equivalent goods sell for equivalent prices. (When we say an equivalent good we mean price after adjusting for transportation costs and other aspects of goods that make them comparable.)

Notice that the definition of the world supply curve specified "tradable goods." That's because the world supply curve affects only those goods in direct competition with international producers—tradable goods. Nontradable goods are not directly affected by the global price. (Below, I will discuss how the tradable and the nontradable sectors have quite different experiences with globalization and how these experiences cause structural problems for the economy. For now we assume all goods are tradable.)

Figure 11-4(b) shows a world supply curve that intersects at the short- and long-run equilibrium—where the *LAS, SAS,* and *AD* curves meet. In this case net exports (exports minus imports) are zero. While some of the goods that the United States purchases are imported, those imports are exactly offset by exports. Since the world price level equals the U.S. price level at equilibrium, globalization by itself does not change the results of the standard model.

But what happens if the world price is lower than the equilibrium price? In that case there would be a trade deficit, as there has been in the United States over the past 20 years. In Figure 11-4(c) I demonstrate this case. The world price level is P_0, so we draw the world supply curve as a horizontal line at P_0. The world supply curve intersects the domestic aggregate supply curve at Y_0 and intersects the aggregate demand curve at Y_1. Consumers buy Y_1, Y_0 of which is supplied by domestic producers. The remaining demand ($Y_1 - Y_0$) is met by foreign producers.

Q-4 If the world supply curve is below the domestic economy's long-run equilibrium price level, what is true about its trade balance?

Globalization Can Limit Potential Output

Notice that a world price for goods below the U.S. price of goods enables U.S. consumers to consume more than they had previously. But it also makes it harder for U.S. producers to sell their goods, which means that, due to structural reasons, international competitive forces put a limit on domestic potential output, in this case at LAS_1. This fall in potential output may seem strange. After all, the number of workers hasn't declined and neither has the number of factories. So the United States could continue to produce just as much as it could before.

If potential output were determined only by the physical existence of workers and factories, potential output *would not* have fallen. But according to the structural stagnation hypothesis, potential output depends on more than physical productive capacity; it depends on the wages, technology, and global competitive conditions. If a worker wants $30 an hour and the economy only has a $10 job for him, that worker won't take the job and will not contribute to potential output. He is structurally unemployed, and his existence does not contribute to potential output unless he is willing to lower his wage to a level at which he can find a job that is sustainable in the global economy. Similarly with a factory. If its technology is no longer globally competitive, it does not contribute to potential output; it might just as well be boarded up. So if there isn't sustainable demand for U.S. inputs to production at their going wage or price, those inputs don't contribute to potential output.

If there isn't sustainable demand for U.S. inputs to production at their going wage or price, those inputs don't contribute to potential output.

In the short run, the effect of globalization (which involves the introduction of countries with lower costs in most goods at existing exchange rates) on the U.S. economy is to lower the U.S.'s potential output until the United States structurally adjusts and U.S. producers are competitive with foreign producers without a trade deficit. Notice that I am not saying that globalization hurts society. While globalization can lower potential output, it also increases the amount a country can consume if aggregate demand can be held at its current position. The gap between a country's potential output and its consumption is directly related to its trade deficit—the further apart the two are from one another, the greater the trade deficit.

According to the structural stagnation hypothesis, the difference between Figure 11-4(b) and Figure 11-4(c) represents the changing macro problem facing the United States in the 2000s. Until the 1990s, Figure 11-4(b) was a reasonable description of the U.S. economy. But when China's and India's 2.6 billion-people economies started to be integrated into the world economy that changed. Before then, although there were certainly issues with globalization, international trade was a small part of the U.S. economy. The trade deficit was small because the United States was the low-cost producer for a variety of goods that had no serious global competitors. These U.S. low-cost sectors offset other high-cost sectors where foreign producers provided the low-cost goods. Before the 1990s, international issues could be added as a secondary issue in the discussion of macro policy. That is no longer the case.

According to the structural stagnation hypothesis, Figure 11-4(c) is a better description of the situation facing the United States since the late 1990s, and it is the model that can highlight the structural problems that the United States is now facing. It is a model in which U.S. potential output has been lowered by the forces of globalization and the United States runs a consistently large trade deficit because its exchange rate has not adjusted to equalize trade flows. Just as some countries, such as China, experienced export-led growth, the United States experienced *import-led stagnation.*

According to the structural stagnation hypothesis, the U.S. trade deficit has a significant impact on employment—at $30,000 a job, a $600 billion dollar trade deficit translates into more than 2 million fewer jobs for the United States than if there was no trade deficit and everything else was identical. Simply put, the trade deficit translates into higher unemployment and lower potential output until these displaced workers find new jobs in different fields that are competitive in the globalized economy.

A trade deficit translates into higher unemployment and lower potential output until those displaced workers find new jobs in different fields that are competitive in the globalized economy.

International Adjustment Forces

In the globalized *AS/AD* model what is supposed to happen is that international and domestic adjustments will be set in motion to eliminate the trade deficit, as discussed in Chapter 8. These forces include: (1) changes in exchange rates, (2) changes in relative wages and costs of production, and (3) changes in aggregate demand.

One adjustment is for the U.S. exchange rate to fall, which would shift the world supply curve up, reducing both domestic spending and how much of that spending is met with foreign production. The downward pressure on the exchange rate is supposed to continue until exports and imports are equal. This fall in the exchange rate would create some inflationary pressures in the United States as import prices rise and global prices are no longer holding down U.S. prices, but a large enough exchange rate fall would eliminate the structural unemployment caused by globalization.

A second adjustment is for U.S. wages and costs of production to fall in response to high unemployment and a lack of international demand for U.S. goods. This fall in costs would shift down the short-run aggregate supply curve. A fall in U.S. wages and costs of production will have the side effect of decreasing U.S. consumption since falling wages and costs means workers have less income to spend.

A third adjustment is for aggregate demand to fall, as those workers and other factors that became unemployed because of the global competition reduce their demand for goods and services. As you can see these three adjustments come with negative side effects. The upside is that given enough time, these adjustments will bring the economy back to a global and domestic equilibrium.

Why the Adjustments Did Not Occur

If international adjustments had happened in response to globalization, U.S. growth and potential output would have fallen temporarily until the adjustments were complete. That didn't happen for a variety of reasons.

If international adjustments had happened, U.S. growth and potential output would have fallen temporarily until the adjustments were complete. But, according to the structural stagnation hypothesis, that didn't happen. One reason why was that government held up aggregate demand to hold unemployment down. That expansionary aggregate demand fueled a financial bubble (unsustainable rise in asset prices) and allowed private aggregate demand to remain high despite the structural problems. By expanding aggregate demand, the United States avoided making the adjustments to a long-run sustainable equilibrium. The trade deficit and the willingness of foreigners to loan the United States money allowed it to avoid facing the difficult structural issues involved in adjusting to a new sustainable long-run equilibrium. The large trade deficit continued from the 1990s until today. So even after 20 years the international adjustment forces still have not eliminated the U.S. trade deficit [see Figure 11-4(c)].

You might ask how an increase in aggregate demand could be effective in holding down unemployment when all demand for tradables would go into global, not domestic, markets. In the globalized *AS/AD* model any increase in aggregate demand will simply lead to increased imports and an even larger trade deficit. But as I said, all goods are not tradable. Some of the increase in aggregate demand during the 1990s and early 2000s went to increase production in the nontradable sector, which is shielded from direct global competition. With a sufficiently large increase in aggregate demand, those who became unemployed in the tradable sector could shift to jobs in the nontradable sector, keeping the overall unemployment low. If the nontradable sectors grow enough, these sectors can temporarily absorb the unemployment caused by globalization. Unfortunately, if the growth in the nontradable sector is dependent on a financial bubble or unsustainable deficits, it is not a permanent solution.

With a sufficiently large increase in aggregate demand, those who become unemployed in the tradable sector can shift to jobs in the nontradable sector keeping overall unemployment low.

According to the structural stagnation hypothesis, the problem with this expansionary macro policy is that it prevented the structural adjustments, which would have been induced by higher unemployment, from bringing the economy back into international equilibrium without a trade deficit. Instead of workers accepting pay cuts, or learning additional skills that would have retained globally competitive jobs in the United States by making the U.S. tradable sector globally competitive, government policy enabled workers to take the easier path of working at the newly available jobs in the nontradable sector such as education, government, health care, locally produced services, and retail sales jobs.

Aggregate Demand Increases no Longer Cause Accelerating Inflation

WWW Web Note 11.2 Globalization and Inflation

Notice the difference for inflation between this globalized *AS/AD* model and the standard *AS/AD* model. In the standard *AS/AD* model, any increase in aggregate demand above potential output will cause inflation. Potential output presents an upward limit to expansionary aggregate demand. When aggregate demand exceeds potential output, excess demand will cause wages and prices to rise, causing the *SAS* curve to begin shifting up as the higher prices become built into people's expectations, leading to higher wage demands. As prices rise, overall real spending falls. If government tries to keep real spending from falling, inflation will accelerate; equilibrium with output higher than potential is unsustainable. You should be able to go through this analysis, explaining why unsustainable inflation would occur. (If you can't, you should review the argument in Chapter 9.)

Q-5 Why were policy makers able to run expansionary policy without causing inflation in the early 2000s?

In the structural stagnation hypothesis's globalized *AS/AD* model, the economy can exceed potential output without generating accelerating inflation because the world price level puts a cap on the domestic price level. Because inflation is the primary signal to policy makers that the economy has exceeded potential output, policy makers aren't forced to run contractionary policy to bring the economy back to its potential. In fact, the government can run highly expansionary macro policies, shifting output and employment from the manufacturing tradable sector to the nontradable sectors, creating the illusion that the economy is doing great. According to the structural stagnation hypothesis this was the situation in the early 2000s.

In a globalized economy in which a country can run large trade deficits, expansionary macro policy does not cause inflation but it can cause other serious short-run structural problems.

But there is a problem with this strategy. In a globalized economy, in which a country can run large trade deficits, expansionary macro policy does not cause inflation, but it can cause other serious short-run structural problems. Instead of causing inflation in goods, the increased demand is channeled into increased imports and increases in demand for real and financial assets. Thus, it pushes up the price of assets, such as land and housing, creating a financial bubble. The prices of these assets do not directly show up in the price indexes, such as the GDP deflator, created to measure inflation, since they measure the price of goods, not assets. This rise in asset prices makes asset holders, such as homeowners, feel richer, which further increases aggregate demand. People feel safe spending a lot because their houses have so greatly increased in value. Thus the effect of the expansionary fiscal policy is amplified by increases in the percentage of income that consumers spend.

According to the structural stagnation hypothesis, the low price of global goods and the ability to run large trade deficits gives policy makers a false sense of security that the economy can continue 3 percent growth and 5 percent unemployment, even when a better estimate of globalized constrained growth would be 2.25 percent growth and 6 or 7 percent unemployment. In short, this structural change in the inflation process, which channeled aggregate demand into asset price inflation, not goods inflation, masked the need in the 1990s and early 2000s for real structural adjustment.

Shorter-Run Structural Problems Resulting from the Financial Crisis

While the structural problems associated with globalization were masked by expansionary macro policy, they did not go away. They simply built up and created additional structural problems of their own—specifically the structural problems associated with the bursting of the financial bubble. When the bubble in asset prices burst the United States had to deal with these short-run structural problems resulting from accumulated structural changes, along with the structural problems caused by globalization. These problems included the following.

While the structural problems associated with globalization were masked by expansionary macro policy, they did not go away.

When the bubble in asset prices burst, the United States had to deal with short-run structural problems resulting from accumulated structural changes, along with the structural problems caused by globalization.

Housing Inventory Overhang As I will discuss in more detail in later financial chapters, the financial bubble was closely related to the housing and mortgage markets. When the bubble burst and housing prices crashed, the excess building in the housing market came to a sudden halt. But that earlier excess building left an overhang of housing inventory (millions of empty houses) and people who lived in houses that they could not sell for what they had paid (often worth less than the mortgage on them). This made it difficult or impossible for many who were unemployed to accept new jobs that required relocating outside their current residential area, thus severely depressing demand for new housing. During the expansion builders overbuilt, which pushed up the economic growth rate. After the financial bubble burst that higher growth in building has to be offset by less construction until excess housing inventory is sold. Until that inventory of unoccupied housing is eliminated, employment in the construction and real estate sectors will be low, pulling down the overall rate of economic recovery.

The housing bubble left a serious overhang of excess housing.

A Reduction of Perceived Wealth The housing collapse not only decreased the number of people hired in the housing sector, increasing unemployment in the economy, it also reduced the perceived wealth of homeowners. During this time housing prices fell by more than 30 percent, wiping out equity in housing and making it impossible for many homeowners to get credit. For many, it wiped out their total net wealth completely. Faced with such a fall in perceived wealth, consumers cut expenditures on goods and increased saving, which slowed the economy. It will take years for these individuals to regain their financial health, and until they do, their lower spending will add a drag on the economy. (This is offset somewhat by lower housing prices making houses more affordable, but on average most economists believe that the drag on spending due to a fall in perceived wealth will continue for at least a few more years.)

Unwinding the Expansionary Monetary and Fiscal Policies During the financial crisis, fiscal policy and monetary policy were dialed up as much as government dared. Trillion dollar deficits and zero interest rate monetary policy pushed both policies to their political and practical limits as sustained policies. Even in conventional macro theory, the current policies are seen as only temporary policies that will be reduced and eventually ended as the economy expands once the fear of depression recedes. But as these expansionary monetary and fiscal policies are unwound, and the government's demand policy is changed from expansionary to neutral and then, in the case of fiscal policy, to contractionary, government policy will exert a slowing effect on the economy. This means that any gain that the economy gets from an improvement in wealth in the private sector will likely be reversed by the slowing and reversal of expansionary monetary and fiscal policy.

Any gain the U.S. economy gets from an improvement in wealth in the private sector will likely be reversed by the slowing and reversal of expansionary monetary and fiscal policy.

Summary: Globalization and Structural Imbalances

What this globalized *AS/AD* model and the structural stagnation hypothesis suggest is that in a globalized world where international adjustment forces work slowly, a country's potential output becomes harder to estimate, and the normal inflationary signals that the economy has exceeded potential will not work. So the economy may seem to be doing fine in the aggregate, but festering underneath can be serious structural imbalances between the tradable sector and the nontradable sector, and between the goods market and asset market. Eventually these structural problems will have to be dealt with in order for the economy to reach a long-run sustainable equilibrium in which both domestic and international forces are in equilibrium. That is the problem that the United States is now grappling with.

Structural Problems of Globalization

The model just described is general. What it doesn't do is convey a real feel for what the structural problems of globalization are. We do that now. Let's begin by looking at jobs. What globalization means for employment is that the jobs and skills of millions of Americans are now no longer needed. Those jobs can be done more cheaply abroad. For people whose jobs have disappeared, this isn't just a matter of finding similar job at a similar pay. These people must find another job that requires different training, or that doesn't need much training, but pays a much lower wage.

To remain employed in the tradable sector the unemployed will have to (1) find new jobs that they can do more cheaply than anyone else in the world because they have a needed specialized skill; (2) be willing to accept lower wages, or (3) have access to better technology and capital than do workers in other countries making them more productive. Finding a job in the nontradable sector will be easier because they compete with only U.S. citizens or immigrants. But most of the jobs available to displaced workers are unlikely to pay as well as the jobs they had before. So globalization means that someone who had a $20 an hour job with benefits now works a $10 an hour job without benefits. These are the lucky ones. Others can't find a job at all. In 2012 there were about four people looking for a job for every job opening. To increase the sustainable globally competitive jobs will require structural changes that either improve the skills of those searching for jobs or decrease their wage aspirations.

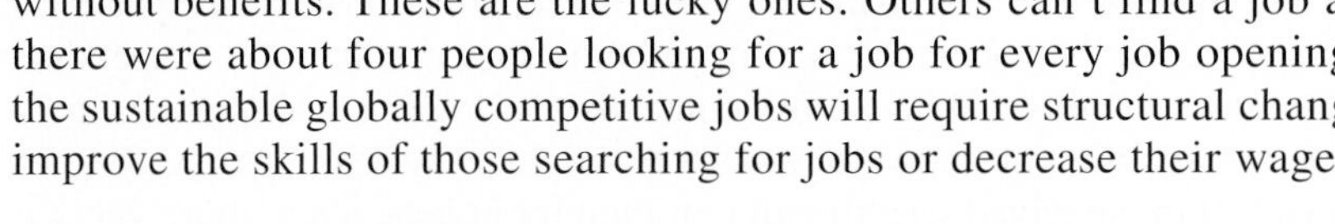

Structural Change in the Nontradable Sector

Q-6 Which sector is most affected by globalization—the tradable or nontradable sector? Why?

Not everyone is faced with choosing between not working and lowering wage aspirations or changing skills. The nontradable sector still offers good paying jobs, especially those paid for by government. Many of these government jobs (or government-supported jobs) provide better benefits and higher wages than do available private jobs in the tradable sector, which has to worry about its global competitiveness. But U.S. taxpayers have not been willing to pay the high taxes necessary to fund these jobs. So, according to the structural stagnation hypothesis, the United States has run government deficits or hidden the costs of government employment by not fully funding the promised pensions and future benefits, so that they do not show up in the budget, making the actual budget deficits much larger than the reported budget deficits. The inability to continue these large U.S. budget deficits will put strong pressure on government in the coming decade to cut government employee wages, benefits, and employment.

The inability to continue large U.S. budget deficits will put strong pressure on government in the coming decade to cut government employee wages, benefits, and employment.

REAL-WORLD APPLICATION

Why Are the Structural Problems of Globalization So Much Greater Now?

The world economy has been opening up for years. Why have the structural problems become so significant now? The answer is that the imbalances have been building up for decades but did not manifest themselves until recently because of government policies and institutional realities that limited global trade. The institutional realities include politics, international capital restrictions, and high costs of communication and transportation. Political forces include a global fight with communism that limited the countries that were part of the global economy (communistic countries such as China did not trade with market economies).

Until the mid 1990s developed countries were the only countries considered capable of producing high-tech manufactured goods on a large scale. Capital flows were restricted by law, which limited investment abroad and kept much of the productive capacity and technological advances in the world within the United States and other developed countries. Communication and transportation costs were incredibly high. Until the last decade, international phone calls were limited and shipments could not be expected to arrive in two days. Now firms communicate through cell phones and Skype, which means it costs just cents a minute to stay in touch with suppliers and firms that take on outsourced production. A customer support call to India would have been too expensive a decade ago. Shipping goods across the ocean used to take two months on a cargo ship; now it takes hours on a jet plane. Large shipments have declined in price with the development of standard containers. So before the 1980s few goods were in the competitive tradable sector. That allowed the United States to develop an institutional structure for its economy with little regard to international issues.

Institutional changes in the United States widened the doors to trade. These changes included the rise of big-box discount stores such as Walmart. Foreign producers could sell in bulk to a few national chains and these retailers could use their market power to negotiate lower prices. (Compare this to the diffuse retail system in Europe that has made an expansion of Chinese goods into European markets much slower than it has been in the United States.)

The trade situation started to change in the late 1980s, but it was only in the early 2000s, as India and China entered the global economy *en force,* that globalization had a significant impact on the U.S. economy. Their entrance created the same kind of problems experienced with Japan in the 1970s and 1980s, but of a much greater magnitude. Japan has a population of about 130 million compared to India and China's 2.6 billion. In summary, the size of the productive capacities of India and China combined with these institutional and technological changes makes the global competition from Japan in the 1970s seem like a small wave compared to a tsunami from India and China starting in the late 1990s.

The pressure to lower wages in the nontradable sector is made all the more real by the fact that the nontradable sector is part of the cost of living of those in the tradable sector. Workers with $10 an hour jobs in the tradable sector cannot afford to buy the services that support $30 an hour nontradable jobs—at least not without government subsidies. The situation is different for a factory worker in China. The Chinese worker earns $3 an hour and pays $5 to see a doctor. Compare that to the U.S. worker earning $10 an hour who has to pay $75 to see a doctor. So globalization along with expansionary fiscal policy reduces the spending power of those working in the tradable sector in two ways, lower wages and higher cost of living, which translates into lower demand for nontradable goods. So the same downward pressure on wages that is occurring in the tradable sector will work its way to the nontradable sector. But it will occur slowly, and will not be an easy adjustment. According to the structural stagnation hypothesis the reality is that significant structural change is needed to make the United States internationally competitive, and that structural change likely involves both a decrease in the relative wages of the nontradable sector and additional cuts in pay for those in the tradable sector, relative to Chinese and Indian workers.

Globalization along with expansionary fiscal policy reduces the spending power of those working in the tradable sector in two ways: lower wages and higher costs of living.

Given the difficulty of making these structural changes, it is understandable that politicians have avoided facing up to them. Telling people difficult changes need to be

Telling people that difficult changes need to be made does not get someone reelected.

made does not get someone reelected. But globalization means that eventually the adjustments will have to be made. The long-run equilibrium will involve eliminating the trade deficit, which will require that the United States increase its competitiveness in a variety of sectors. That means that the cost of producing in the United States has to fall, relative to the cost of producing outside the United States.

Globalization and Income Distribution

One of the primary reasons why the structural problems of globalization are not dealt with is that they involve difficult policy issues of fairness and income redistribution.

According to the structural stagnation hypothesis, one of the primary reasons why the structural problems of globalization are not dealt with is that they involve the difficult political issues of fairness and income redistribution. Globalization affects different groups of the economy differently. We will distinguish three groups: (1) the international traders, and workers associated with them, who have done phenomenally well from globalization; (2) the unskilled and not highly skilled in the tradable sector who are most hurt by globalization either because they have lost jobs or had wages significantly reduced; and (3) those in nontradable sectors, who are only indirectly affected by globalization. They have been made better off by the benefits of lower prices of goods but have been made worse off because of the indirect competition for jobs from those who have lost jobs in the tradable sector.

Q-7 How has globalization impacted the distribution of income?

For international traders—financiers and import/export companies—globalization has been a boon, creating enormous demand for their services and for the services of those who sell to them. So the demand for high-level U.S. international trading services remained high, even as the demand for U.S. products fell. Demand was rising for high-level business organization and services and falling for U.S. products. Most of the jobs in this "organizers of international trade sector" were high-paying white-collar jobs, which required high levels of education. Jobs for those with only a high school education were disappearing. The result was an enormous change in the distribution of income. The success of this sector also created a periphery of jobs that serviced this high income sector. High-end luxury goods, expensive restaurants, and similar businesses did well, but generally the lower middle class was not in this group.

Paradoxically, the fact that globalization provided these high-paying jobs for the United States meant that the trade deficit was smaller than it otherwise would have been. International forces kept the U.S. exchange rate from falling as much as it would have had these organizational gains from trade not gone to U.S. citizens. To see the reason why this reduced the total number of jobs, consider that for the trade balance not to change, for every $200,000 job that globalization creates, more than six $30,000 jobs must to be lost.

The group that did worst in the globalization process was U.S. workers and businesses involved in the actual manufacture of commodities.

The group that did worst was U.S. workers and businesses involved in the actual manufacture of **commodities**—*homogeneous goods that could be produced in a variety of countries by workers without any special skills and shipped at a low cost*. Commodities such as motherboards, LED screens, and generic shoes and socks are the ultimate tradable goods, and a standard rule in business is that there is no profit in commodities. There are also no wage differentials across countries in the production of commodities, which means that the wages of workers in these sectors either fell to the global wage level, or the workers lost their jobs entirely.

A third group affected by globalization are skilled workers in the nontradable sector. These are workers producing goods or services that cannot be produced outside the United States because of legal, technical, or physical restrictions. While workers in these sectors do not directly face global competition, they do indirectly as described above. As unemployment in the tradable sector rises, the unemployed compete for jobs in the nontradable sector. This competition holds wages and prices down in this sector as well, but much less so than in the tradable sector. How well this group does depends on the state of aggregate demand. Up until recently, they have done relatively well, as government has held up aggregate demand. Unfortunately, it has done so by unsustainable budget deficits, and if and when those deficits end, this group will experience the pain that non-highly skilled workers in the tradable sector already have.

Remembering the Benefits of Globalization

While structural change is difficult and is the inevitable result of globalization, the costs of structural changes do not mean that globalization is bad, or that it should not have happened. Globalization is simply competition on the global level. Globalization is both inevitable and beneficial. If you think back to the globalized *AS/AD* model, the other side of globalization is an increase in consumption of tradable goods at low prices. Because of globalization, tradable goods have become much cheaper.

Globalization has also increased specialization as production is divided into smaller segments (some of which are outsourced), which lowers costs and stimulates technological development. As Adam Smith long ago pointed out in his famous example of the manufacturing of pins (today they are called nails), more specialization means workers can focus on specific tasks and significantly increase productivity. Not only does specialization allow firms to spread costs over an expanded production, it also increases the amount of learning by doing, which also lowers costs. Globalization expands trade, and it is trade that has allowed the world economy to grow. So globalization increased the overall world growth rate and increased U.S. consumption even as U.S. potential output was reduced.

The costs of structural change do not mean globalization is bad or that it should not have happened. Globalization is simply competition on the global level. It is both inevitable and beneficial.

The nature of the competitive process, of which globalization is a part, is to continually create structural problems in a process that economic historian Joseph Schumpeter called *creative destruction*. Creative destruction is part of any dynamic and growing economy.

Throughout the postwar era, the United States has benefited enormously from globalization. Because global trade has allowed the specialization of production and opening of new consumer markets abroad, the U.S. trend growth rate is higher than what it would have been. So, according to the structural stagnation hypothesis, the problem isn't globalization per se or even the structural problems it creates. The problem is that the United States tried to have the benefits of globalization without facing up to the difficult structural changes that accompany globalization and the resulting trade deficits.

The problem is that the United States tried to have the benefits of globalization without facing up to the difficult structural changes that accompany globalization and the resulting trade deficits.

The Future of Globalization

According to the structural stagnation hypothesis the globalization process described in the globalized *AS/AD* model is not a one-shot event. It is an ongoing process in which developing countries compete in more and more activities. Thus, even though the process of integrating China and India into the world economy began in the late 1990s, it is likely to continue for another 20 or 30 years as China and India move up the **value-added chain**—*the movement of trade from natural resources to low-skill manufacturing to increasingly complicated goods and services.*

Q-8 What is the value-added chain and how does it relate to globalization?

To understand the value-added chain, think of the story of comparative advantage that I discussed in earlier chapters. Initially, trade begins with low-cost and low-tech items that are heavily labor intensive, but not heavily technological or capital intensive. This is the bottom of the value-added chain. Then as producers in a developing country learn by doing and become more skilled, they move up to production that is a bit more capital and technological intensive as Japan and Korea did in the 1970s and 1980s. Over time foreign producers keep moving up to increasingly complicated production methods and technology, and eventually, they find themselves able to compete on all aspects of manufacturing. Ultimately, they arrive at the top of the value-added chain, where they are the international traders organizing trade.

Once a country reaches international trader status, it experiences enormous gains from trade—far more than the gains for manufacturing even high-technology goods. It is the international traders who create many of the high-wage professional jobs in

As countries move up the value-added chain the pressures of globalization will ultimately feed back on the traders, and international traders will find themselves globalized as well. That is a long way in the future.

advertising, research, finance, and law. So when the international traders come from your country, you get disproportionate gains from trade, as the United States has for the past 70 years. As countries move up the value-added chain, ultimately the pressures of globalization will feed back on the traders, and international traders will find themselves globalized as well. That is a long way in the future.

In the meantime the United States has done extremely well at the high end of the value-added chain. Its comparative advantages in high-value-added production and organizing trade have helped the United States do well from globalization while at the same time eliminating many U.S. jobs. To see what is going on, consider the iPad, which is imported from China. Of the $500 cost of an iPad, about $300 goes to U.S. firms and workers in the form of profits, distribution expenses, advertising, and research and development. So the sale of every iPad creates profits for shareholders and some very high-paying jobs for a few in the United States while eliminating a much greater number of lower paying manufacturing and lower skilled jobs.

The picture of globalization conveyed in the globalized *AS/AD* model will continue for decades as developing countries move up the value-added chain.

As China and India become more integrated in the world economies, other low-cost countries will replace them on the low-cost end of production, and China and India will challenge the United States on higher and higher level production activities. The picture of globalization conveyed in the globalized *AS/AD* model will continue for decades as developing countries move up the value-added chain.

Policies to Deal with Structural Stagnation

Now that we have reviewed the causes of structural stagnation, let's consider policies to pull the economy out of it. Let's first consider policies to deal with short-run structural problems caused by the bursting of the financial bubble.

Policies to Deal with Short-Run Structural Problems

The depressed housing market and the decrease in perceived wealth, which followed the bursting of the financial bubble, are in many ways the least of policy makers' concerns. They will resolve themselves faster on their own than will the more chronic structural stagnation problems caused by globalization. For example, in the next couple of years the inventory of unsold houses created by the housing bubble will fall as the housing market recovers. According to the structural stagnation hypothesis it will not reach the boom level that it was in the early 2000s but it will recover. That will put construction workers back to work. Similarly, once the housing sector recovers, the prices of houses will rise, once again increasing homeowners' perceived wealth. As that wealth increases, consumer spending should increase as well, again not at the previous boom pace, but at a greater pace than recently.

Government can introduce some policies to lessen the problems. For example, policies can make it easier for banks to restructure their loans, and to temporarily rent houses to "underwater" homeowners who otherwise would face foreclosure. Foreclosure is costly and destructive to the neighborhood, and any policy that reduces foreclosures both reduces human suffering and improves the economy. These measures will accelerate the housing market recovery.

Government can do little about the effects of the decline in wealth caused by the bursting of a bubble without causing new problems down the road.

Ultimately financial asset prices must reflect real productivity.

Government can do little, however, about the effects of the decline in wealth without causing new problems down the road. While expansionary monetary policy can hold up financial asset prices, policies that support unsustainably high asset prices can create what are called *moral hazard problems* in which people do something risky and, if it turns out badly, do not expect to bear the consequences of their risky actions. In this case the "something risky" is to purchase houses and other financial assets at unsustainably high prices. The moral hazard problem will put even greater pressures on asset prices to develop into a new bubble.

REAL-WORD APPLICATION

Should Mortgage Balances Be Reduced for Underwater Homeowners?

One of the policies that has been suggested to get the economy out of the downturn is for government to provide funds to allow banks to write down the mortgages that are called "underwater"—where homeowners owe more on their houses than the houses would sell for. The rationale is that such a policy would reduce the effect of changes in wealth on consumption, making homeowners more likely to spend, more able to move if a job is available in another place, and not face foreclosure if they cannot pay their mortgages.

The problem with the policy is twofold. First, it costs money, lots of it, and if people see their neighbors getting a bailout, they will want one as well. To pay for the program and not increase the deficit, taxes will have to be raised. A second problem is that it creates perverse incentives—encouraging people to take on mortgages that they cannot afford and buy houses at prices that are not sustainable—and will be seen as highly unfair. It will help a person who is overextended himself financially, and leave someone who was prudent and only bought a small house without any help from the government in a worse position than the "foolish person." If that is expected, it is foolish not to be foolish, and people are encouraged to overextend themselves in the future.

Policies to Deal with Long-Run Structural Problems

According to the structural stagnation hypothesis the structural effects of globalization accompanied by large trade deficits are chronic, and are likely to continue for a decade or more. The reason is that globalization is an ongoing process, and policy makers cannot do much about it. Structural change is difficult, but required. Any solution will involve some combination of the following: a rise in foreign goods prices (lower U.S. exchange rates), a rise in foreign labor costs (higher wages or lower productivity), a fall in domestic labor costs (lower wages or higher productivity), or trade restrictions that raise foreign goods prices. The policies to deal with structural stagnation will be policies that bring those changes about.

In terms of the globalized *AS/AD* model shown in Figure 11-5, the policies will involve shifting the world supply curve up (arrow *A*) or the domestic aggregate supply down (arrow *B*). Notice that either of these policies reduces the structural constraints on production in the economy and shifts out the U.S. economy's globalized constrained potential output.

In the globalized *AS/AD* model, policies involve shifting the world supply curve up or the domestic aggregate supply curve down.

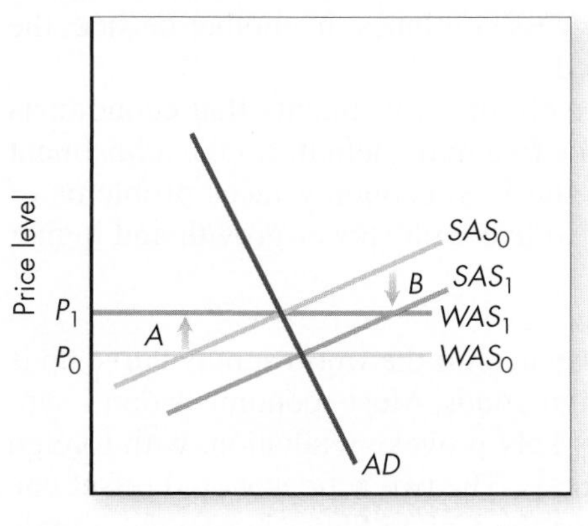

FIGURE 11-5 Policies to Shift the *SAS* Curve Down or the World Supply Curve Up

Policies that address structural stagnation will either shift the *SAS* curve down from SAS_0 to SAS_1 or the world supply curve up from WAS_0 to WAS_1. Either will shift globally constrained potential output to the right.

Shifting the World Supply Curve Up Let's start by considering policies that will shift the world supply curve up.

Q-9 What policies solve the structural stagnation problem by shifting the world supply curve up?

Decreasing the Exchange Rate One of the policies that almost all agree will help the U.S. structural stagnation problem is for the U.S. exchange rate—the price of dollars measured in foreign currency—to fall relative to its competitors. The U.S. exchange rate has fallen over the past decade, reducing the structural stagnation problem compared to what it would have been. But the continuing trade deficit is a signal that it did not eliminate the problem. In the standard *AS/AD* model a fall in the exchange rate in response to a trade deficit would occur much faster than it has, so that structural stagnation would not be a problem. But, for a variety of reasons, the exchange rate did not fall sufficiently.

I will discuss those reasons in a later chapter, but I'll mention one now—China's policy to keep the value of its currency, the yuan, low by buying U.S. dollars and dollar-denominated assets has helped prevent the U.S. dollar from falling. China and United States have had ongoing talks about these policies, with the United States arguing that China should stop preventing its currency from rising. However, China has continued to follow policies designed to keep the value of the yuan low.

The question of exchange rate adjustment is a question about the speed of adjustment.

The question of exchange rate adjustment is a question about the speed of adjustment. It is not clear that the United States would be a lot better off if China were to suddenly end its support of the dollar. The result would likely be a dramatic fall in the U.S. exchange rate, and upward pressure on the price level in the United States. Were this to occur too fast, it could possibly lead to the accelerating inflation that has been prevented by the low world supply price. If the U.S. government responds to that inflationary pressure by decreasing aggregate demand, as it has committed itself to do, it will keep the U.S. economy in stagnation for an extended period even as the value of the dollar falls. If that happened we wouldn't have only structural stagnation, we would have **stagflation**—*the combination of stagnation and inflation*—as we had in the 1970s.

Differential Wage Growth Rising wages in other countries relative to U.S. wages would also shift the world supply curve up, which has happened in the past decade. For example, U.S. wages in manufacturing have been stagnant, and in real terms have not risen, while Chinese wages have gone up by as much as 12 percent a year. What this means is that each year, production costs in China have risen relative to the United States. Equalization of wages still has a long way to go. The average hourly pay in the manufacturing sector, including benefits, is about $34 in the United States and $3 in China at current exchange rates. But if this process continues, in another decade, the difference in wages will be significantly reduced.

These relative wage adjustments are precisely the adjustments that economists would expect to occur as the economy responds to a trade deficit. So the adjustment is taking place, but slowly. In the meantime the U.S. economy faces problems of structural stagnation, which means that it has to live with slower growth and higher unemployment.

While tariffs would also shift the world supply curve up, most economists don't support such a policy because of their side effects.

Tariffs and Trade Restrictions Another way to shift the world supply curve up is for the United States to impose tariffs on foreign goods. Most economists don't support such policies. Any attempt to do this will likely provoke retaliation, with foreign countries putting an offsetting tariff on U.S. goods. The two actions would offset one another, leaving both countries worse off. Since the United States is running a trade deficit, if the result were a tariff war, it could do more damage to foreign producers than foreign countries could do to U.S. producers, but that would serve little purpose.

Both would be worse off; the United States would simply be less worse off than the other countries.

Shifting the Domestic *SAS* Curve Down Let's now turn to a second set of policies that the United States might follow—shifting the *SAS* curve down. Doing so will lower costs in the United States and thereby increase the internationally constrained potential output curve.

Lower Wages The most obvious of policies to shift the *SAS* curve down is to lower U.S. wages. When workers in the tradable sectors lose their jobs, eventually they lower their **reservation wage**—*the lowest wage that a person needs to receive to accept a job*—to a level that gets them a job. That is the market's solution to structural unemployment. It isn't pretty or pleasant, but it works. The problem is that our society does not like that solution. It seems unfair that some people have to suffer from globalization while others benefit. So while a policy of cutting wages would work, it is unlikely to gain much political support. Moreover, the cutting-wage solution would have side effects. Lower wages means lower consumption, so it will slow the growth of domestic demand. But if other solutions don't work, wages will be forced to fall. If the U.S. government needs an international bailout because bondholders don't want to buy its bonds at an interest rate the United States is willing and able to pay, one of the likely requirements bondholders will impose will be cutting government wages. As a condition for the 2012 bailout Greece was required to cut wages by more than 20 percent.

Q-10 What policies solve structural stagnation by shifting the short-run aggregate supply curve down?

Reduce Unemployment Insurance The United States has many policies designed to lessen the pain caused by unemployment and to hold wages up, not push them down. Reducing these policies would help in the adjustment process. Unemployment insurance is an example. Unemployment insurance, or any policy to mitigate the pain of unemployment, reduces the role that unemployment plays in bringing wages down by allowing workers to keep holding out for a higher wage job. Thus, by eliminating unemployment insurance, one could speed up the adjustment. But as was the case with lowering wages, such a policy would be accompanied by significant hardships to people who are bearing the large share of the costs of globalization already.

Unemployment insurance, or any policy to reduce the pain of unemployment, reduces the role that unemployment plays in the adjustment process.

Increasing U.S. Productivity by Improving Training or Increasing Resource Production Another policy that one often hears about is retraining workers, and that clearly can help. Unfortunately, direct job-relevant training in the United States is often either expensive compared to similar job-relevant training abroad or is significantly subsidized through government support of the training or government-subsidized loans to students, which means that it pushes up government deficits. If increased training is to lead to high-paying jobs in tradable sectors, it has to make U.S. workers more competitive than foreign workers, whose training often costs far less. Currently, our educational sector is not especially efficient—ranking 26th in the world in achievement—and is far more costly than just about any other educational system. It has advantages in fostering creativity much better than do foreign educational systems, but it also has problems. Any gains in training will have to be relative gains—other countries are pouring enormous resources into additional training, so U.S. training will have to increase simply to keep up.

WWW Web Note 11.3 Retraining Programs

If increased training is to lead to high-paying jobs in tradable sectors, it has to make U.S. workers more competitive than foreign workers, whose training often costs far less.

Another way to increase productivity is to increase a country's available nontradable low-cost resources. In this dimension the United States has some positive attributes. For example, the United States has some of the most productive farmland in the world, and as the world economy grows, the comparative advantage of the United

ADDED DIMENSION

The Other Side of the Story

This chapter is not your normal textbook chapter. But the current macroeconomic situation is not your normal macroeconomic situation, and the issues it raises are so important that they cannot be ignored, even at the principles level.

The appropriate policy response is still very much being debated by economists. The chapter provides one view, but many other views are also held by economists. Here is another quite different view of policy. It was posted on the web as a manifesto (www.manifestoforeconomicsense.org) and was signed by thousands of economists. It is what the popular press often interprets as the Keynesian policy position.

A Manifesto for Economic Sense

More than four years after the financial crisis began, the world's major advanced economies remain deeply depressed, in a scene all too reminiscent of the 1930s. And the reason is simple: we are relying on the same ideas that governed policy in the 1930s. These ideas, long since disproved, involve profound errors about the causes of the crisis, its nature, and the appropriate response.

These errors have taken deep root in public consciousness and provide the public support for the excessive austerity of current fiscal policies in many countries. So the time is ripe for a Manifesto in which mainstream economists offer the public a more evidence-based analysis of our problems.

- *The causes.* Many policy makers insist that the crisis was caused by irresponsible public borrowing. With very few exceptions—other than Greece—this is false. Instead, the conditions for crisis were created by excessive private sector borrowing and lending, including by over-leveraged banks. The collapse of this bubble led to massive falls in output and thus in tax revenue. So the large government deficits we see today are a consequence of the crisis, not its cause.
- *The nature of the crisis.* When real estate bubbles on both sides of the Atlantic burst, many parts of the private sector slashed spending in an attempt to pay down past debts. This was a rational response on the part of individuals, but—just like the similar response of debtors in the 1930s—it has proved collectively self-defeating, because one person's spending is another person's income. The result of the spending collapse has been an economic depression that has worsened the public debt.
- *The appropriate response.* At a time when the private sector is engaged in a collective effort to spend less, public policy should act as a stabilizing force, attempting to sustain spending. At the very least we should not be making things worse by big cuts in government spending or big increases in tax rates on ordinary people. Unfortunately, that's exactly what many governments are now doing.
- *The big mistake.* After responding well in the first, acute phase of the economic crisis, conventional policy wisdom took a wrong turn—focusing on government deficits, which are mainly the result of a crisis-induced plunge in revenue, and arguing that the public sector should attempt to reduce its debts in tandem with the private sector. As a result, instead of playing a stabilizing role, fiscal policy has ended up reinforcing and exacerbating the dampening effects of private-sector spending cuts.

In the face of a less severe shock, monetary policy could take up the slack. But with interest rates close to zero, monetary policy—while it should do all it can—cannot do the whole job. There must of course be a medium-term plan for reducing the government deficit. But if this is too front-loaded it can easily be self-defeating by aborting the recovery. A key priority now is to reduce unemployment, before it becomes endemic, making recovery and future deficit reduction even more difficult.

How do those who support present policies answer the argument we have just made? They use two quite different arguments in support of their case.

The Confidence Argument Their first argument is that government deficits will raise interest rates and thus prevent recovery. By contrast, they argue, austerity will increase confidence and thus encourage recovery.

But there is no evidence at all in favor of this argument. First, despite exceptionally high deficits, interest rates today are unprecedentedly low in all major countries where there is a normally functioning central bank. This is true even in Japan, where the government debt now exceeds 200 percent of annual GDP, and past downgrades by the rating agencies have had no effect on Japanese interest rates. Interest rates are only high in some Euro countries, because the European Central Bank is not allowed to act as lender of last resort to the government. Elsewhere the central bank can always, if needed, fund the deficit, leaving the bond market unaffected.

Moreover, past experience includes no relevant case where budget cuts have actually generated increased economic activity.

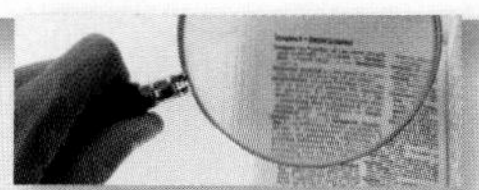

The International Monetary Fund has studied 173 cases of budget cuts in individual countries and found that the consistent result is economic contraction. In the handful of cases in which fiscal consolidation was followed by growth, the main channels were a currency depreciation against a strong world market, not a current possibility. The lesson of the IMF's study is clear—budget cuts retard recovery. And that is what is happening now—the countries with the biggest budget cuts have experienced the biggest falls in output.

The truth is, as we can now see, that budget cuts do not inspire business confidence. Companies will only invest when they can foresee enough customers with enough income to spend. Austerity discourages investment.

So there is massive evidence against the confidence argument; all the alleged evidence in favor of the doctrine has evaporated on closer examination.

The Structural Argument A second argument against expanding demand is that output is in fact constrained on the supply side—by structural imbalances. If this theory were right, however, at least some parts of our economies ought to be at full stretch, and so should some occupations. But in most countries that is just not the case. Every major sector of our economies is struggling, and every occupation has higher unemployment than usual. So the problem must be a general lack of spending and demand.

In the 1930s the same structural argument was used against proactive spending policies in the United States. But as spending rose between 1940 and 1942, output rose by 20 percent. So the problem in the 1930s, as now, was a shortage of demand, not of supply.

As a result of their mistaken ideas, many Western policy makers are inflicting massive suffering on their peoples. But the ideas they espouse about how to handle recessions were rejected by nearly all economists after the disasters of the 1930s, and for the following 40 years or so the West enjoyed an unparalleled period of economic stability and low unemployment. It is tragic that in recent years the old ideas have again taken root. But we can no longer accept a situation where mistaken fears of higher interest rates weigh more highly with policy makers than the horrors of mass unemployment.

Better policies will differ between countries and need detailed debate. But they must be based on a correct analysis of the problem. We therefore urge all economists and others who agree with the broad thrust of this Manifesto to register their agreement at www.manifestoforeconomicsense.org, and to publicly argue the case for a sounder approach. The whole world suffers when men and women are silent about what they know is wrong.

Why Don't I Accept This Manifesto?

I am generally associated with Keynesian economics, and in theory I accept many of the general arguments the manifesto makes such as: Running contractionary demand policy will slow the economy down; and: Demand is central to the aggregate level of output. Why didn't I sign on then? The answer is that the manifesto glosses over some important issues that, in my view, significantly affect policy.

1. *It doesn't take into account global imbalances.* Notice that the chapter's discussion of structural stagnation was a story about the U.S. economy in which global competition played a central role. This manifesto does not address the tradable goods problem, which is central to the structural stagnation hypothesis. If there were a central world government, the manifesto might be more relevant. But there isn't. From a global demand perspective, the countries that should be expanding are those with both fiscal capacity and trade surpluses, not those, such as the United States, with diminished fiscal capacity and large trade deficits.
2. *It underestimates the needed structural change.* When global structural problems are taken into account, the structural nature of the current U.S. policy dilemma becomes clearer. The large trade deficit means that the United States is not yet globally competitive and demand expansion by the U.S. alone will exacerbate its global structural problems.
3. *It doesn't take into account expansionary demand policy's role in encouraging financial asset bubbles.* One of the serious structural problems facing the United States involves the bursting of the financial bubble. In the structural stagnation hypothesis, expansionary policies kept the U.S. economy above potential for decades by enabling an unsustainable financial bubble. More expansionary demand policy now will simply continue that unsustainable policy for a few more years. As I will discuss in later chapters, in my view, the U.S. long-run fiscal health faces serious problems—unless we start dealing with these problems soon, they may well undermine the entire U.S. economy.

States in agriculture is likely to grow because agricultural production is not labor intensive and the United States has rich soil. Agriculture will likely be a long-term inherent comparative advantage.

Another bright spot in the U.S. future is the positive resource shock that has been caused by the development of new fracking technology in the extraction of natural gas. This new technology has significantly lowered the price of natural gas and hence energy in the United States. This technology does not lower energy costs outside the United States because the natural gas cannot be easily exported. Thus it will lower the cost of producing in the United States relative to abroad. This low energy cost will offset other cost advantages of other countries even at existing exchange rates. Whether these positives will be sufficient to get the U.S. economy back on a growth track is unclear, but they are definitely positives when considering the global competitiveness of the United States.

The Problems with the Standard Political Solution

The list of policies just discussed does not include many proposals that one hears from politicians. The policies I listed are what might be called "suffer-as-best-you-can" policies; they offer gain through pain, not gain without pain. Pain is not something that politicians like to discuss. Few politicians are going to say that what is needed is for U.S. wages to fall relative to foreign wages. They will be more likely to advocate for a policy that seems to offer only advantages without acknowledging the costs. By hiding the pain part of the proposals, most political policies provide the illusion of an effective policy but do not offer a serious solution to the structural problems facing the United States.

By hiding the pain part of the policy proposals, most political parties provide the illusion of an effective policy but do not offer a serious solution to the structural problems facing the United States.

Conclusion

I began this chapter with a quotation from Sigmund Freud— "Illusions commend themselves to us because they save us pain and allow us to enjoy pleasure instead. We must therefore accept it without complaint when they sometimes collide with a bit of reality against which they are dashed to pieces." According to the structural stagnation hypothesis, just as individuals attempt to avoid unpleasant truths, so too do societies. The United States has maintained a policy stance over the past decade that reflects an illusion: Globalization, combined with large trade and government deficits and large private sector borrowing, comes at no cost. The current difficulty the United States is experiencing is the result of those earlier decisions based on this illusion.

Eventually all illusions collide with reality, which likely means that the U.S. economy is in for continued major problems in the near future. The structural problems created by globalization and large trade deficits will eventually end, either because of a fall in the U.S. exchange rate or downward shift in the aggregate supply curve that makes U.S. production sufficiently internationally competitive enough to eliminate the trade deficit. Eventually costs will fall in uncompetitive sectors, and as they do, the sectors will become competitive again. Eventually the mismatch between needed skills and available skills will be eliminated as workers retrain and find jobs in those sectors where the United States has a comparative advantage. But these structural changes will be slow, and attempts by the government to avoid the pain may well backfire and cause more pain in the long run.

As I stated at the beginning of this chapter, the structural stagnation hypothesis is only a hypothesis; we have no way of knowing for sure if it is right since we have no definitive way of measuring the underlying growth trend. Theory and policy, and how one interprets reality, depend on what one believes the growth trend to be. Because of the limitation of checking a theory against the data, economics cannot provide a definitive theory. Instead it provides a set of tools that can help guide one to correct conclusions. Whether the structural stagnation hypothesis is the correct theory is debatable. If in the next couple of years the United States grows at a 5 percent to 6 percent real growth rate, even as monetary policy and fiscal policy stop being highly expansionary, the structural stagnation hypothesis will be proven wrong. If the economy continues its slow growth, it will be given more credence. But whichever happens, considering it is a useful exercise for anyone trying to understand the macroeconomic problems the U.S. economy is currently facing.

Because of the limitation of checking theory against the data, economics cannot provide a definitive theory. Instead it provides a set of tools that can help guide one to correct conclusions.

Summary

- To remain on its growth trend, an economy must grow more in an expansion than it fell during the recession to make up for the decline in output and to account for the rise in potential output. During a structural stagnation, the economy grows more slowly than is needed to return to its trend. *(LO11-1)*
- The U.S. economy today may be experiencing structural stagnation, not a normal downturn. *(LO11-1)*
- The globalized *AS/AD* model adds a flat world supply curve, which allows the possibility of a trade deficit that limits a country's potential output. *(LO11-2)*
- If the world price level equals the domestic price level, exports offset imports. If the world price level is below the domestic price level, an economy has a trade deficit. This is the situation of the U.S. economy since the 1990s. *(LO11-2)*
- Globalization with large trade deficits will limit domestic inflation, allowing government to run more expansionary policies than it otherwise would have. *(LO11-2)*
- Globalization leads to structural stagnation by creating competition in the tradable goods market which leads to difficult structural adjustments. A financial bubble also creates structural problems. *(LO11-3)*
- The U.S. globalization experience has impacted various groups differently. Workers in tradable goods sectors generally experienced declining wages and high unemployment. Workers in the nontradable sector were indirectly affected. Employment and wages in the international trade sector rose. *(LO11-3)*
- As globalization continues, foreign producers will move up the value-added chain, presenting the U.S. economy with competition in more and more goods. *(LO11-3)*
- Structural stagnation can be resolved if domestic exchange rates fall, domestic wages and other cost fall, or productivity rises. *(LO11-4)*
- Government cannot do much to solve the globalization problem. Globalization will, on its own, put downward pressure on exchange rates and relative wages. Government can implement policies that allow these adjustments to occur. *(LO11-4)*

Key Terms

commodities *(246)*
globalization *(238)*
globalized *AS/AD* model *(238)*
reservation wage *(251)*
secular stagnation theory *(237)*
stagflation *(250)*
structural stagnation hypothesis *(232)*
value-added chain *(247)*
world supply curve *(239)*

Questions and Exercises

1. How is structural stagnation different from a normal downturn? (*LO11-1*)
2. Why is the underlying growth trend important for policy? (*LO11-1*)
3. Using the graph below demonstrate an economy whose output declines by 4 percent in year 2 and returns to its trend the following year. (*LO11-1*)
   a. By what dollar amount did output decline during the recession?
   b. By what percent does the economy need to expand to return to trend by year 3.
   c. How does your answer to *b* compare to the initial percentage decline?
   d. What accounts for your answer to *c*?

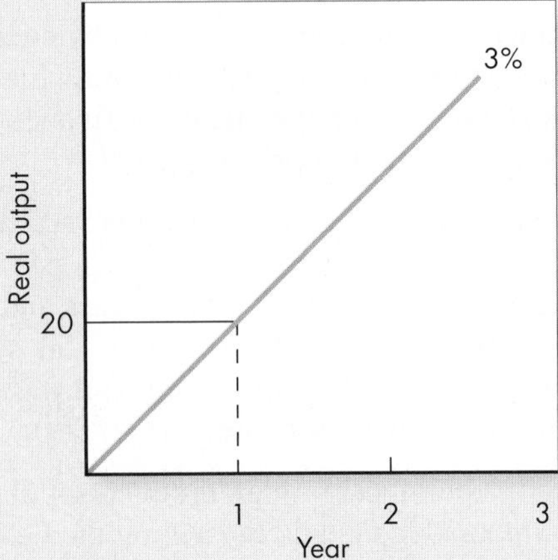

4. How does the structural stagnation hypothesis differ from secular stagnation theory? (*LO11-1*)
5. Beginning with a country that has a trade deficit, demonstrate graphically what will happen to a country's potential output with globalization if that country's exchange rate falls. Explain your answer. (*LO11-2*)
6. Beginning with a country that has a trade deficit, demonstrate graphically what will happen to a country's potential output with globalization if that country's costs of production fall. Explain your answer. (*LO11-2*)
7. If a country does not run a trade deficit, where does the world supply curve intersect the domestic equilibrium in the *AS/AD* model? (*LO11-2*)
8. Why does globalization mask inflation? Demonstrate your answer graphically. (*LO11-2*)
9. How do structural problems from the aftermath of a financial crisis make policy more difficult? (*LO11-2*)
10. True or false? If you have a job in the nontradable sector, you don't have to worry about the structural effects of globalization. Explain your answer. (*LO11-3*)
11. Why does globalization tend to make the distribution of income less equal? (*LO11-3*)
12. True or false? Since globalization causes structural problems, it should be restricted. Explain your answer. (*LO11-3*)
13. True or false? Globalization is a one-time event, and thus does not present a problem for the future of the United States. Explain your answer. (*LO11-3*)
14. What policies are needed to deal with the structural problems caused by globalization? (*LO11-4*)
15. Demonstrate graphically how the following are represented in the globalized *AS/AD* model for the United States. What happens to the trade deficit in each? (*LO11-4*)
    a. Foreign wages rise.
    b. U.S. productivity rises.
    c. The value of the dollar rises.
    d. The U.S. imposes tariffs on imported goods.
16. Why are politicians so uneasy about discussing the structural problems caused by globalization? (*LO11-4*)
17. Why can't a large safety net be created so that no one is hurt by globalization? (*LO11-4*)

Questions from Alternative Perspectives

1. Structural stagnation is simply a way to foist more of the burden of supporting our society on the poor by the rich. Discuss. (Radical)
2. A country that can print money can never have a budget deficit that is too high. Discuss. (Post-Keynesian)
3. If we had followed reasonable trade policies and required countries that trade with us to have fair labor practices and pay a living wage, we would not have the problems caused by globalization. Discuss. (Institutionalist)
4. Policy has focused too much on GDP and output. The most important aspects of life are not economic but spiritual, and the current slowdown provides our country with a chance to reorder its priorities. (Religious)
5. Structural stagnation was caused by government's control of the money supply. If policy makers had used gold as its money supply, there would be no structural stagnation. (Austrian)

Issues to Ponder

1. Globalization has pulled hundreds of millions of people out of poverty in China and India. How should that gain be weighed against structural changes that globalization requires in the United States?
2. Since the growth rate is of central importance to policy, how can one decide who is right about what the trend growth rate for policy should be?
3. If any realistic solution to the structural stagnation problem involves both tax increases and entitlements cuts, why do both sides have such a difficult time coming to a compromise that will deal with our budget dilemma or with providing a safety net for those most hurt by globalization?
4. If the $3 trillion dollars the United States had spent in the stimulus package over the last three years had gone into a safety net for the least well off, how much of a safety net could be provided?

Answer to Margin Questions

1. The economy must make up for lost output and rise sufficiently to make up for the rise in potential output. *(p. 235; LO11-1)*
2. According to the structural stagnation hypothesis, globalization combined with slowly adjusting exchange rates, which led to large trade deficits, were the root cause of the slowing of growth. The needed international adjustments were not made. Instead, the U.S. economy experienced a financial bubble that ultimately burst, creating the current situation. *(p. 238; LO11-1)*
3. In the globalized *AS/AD* model a flat world supply curve puts a ceiling on domestic prices. *(p. 239; LO11-2)*
4. It has a trade deficit. *(p. 239; LO11-2)*
5. The government could run expansionary policies without creating inflation because globalization allows an economy to exceed potential by putting a cap on domestic prices. *(p. 242; LO11-2)*
6. The tradable sector is most affected because it must compete globally with imports. *(p. 244; LO11-3)*
7. Globalization has reduced income for workers in the tradable sector and increased income for workers in the international trade sector enormously. Workers in the nontradable sector have experienced some wage declines. *(p. 246; LO11-3)*
8. The value-added chain is the movement toward producing increasingly complicated goods and services. Foreign economies will move up the chain, providing competition for more and more goods. *(p. 247; LO11-3)*
9. Policies that reduce the exchange rate and raise foreign wages will solve the problem by shifting the world supply curve up. Government can also raise tariffs, but doing so may result in retaliation. *(p. 250; LO11-4)*
10. Policies that shift the short-run aggregate supply curve down to solve the structural stagnation problem include lowering wages, reducing policies that lessen the pain caused by unemployment, and increasing U.S. productivity. *(p. 251; LO11-4)*

APPENDIX A

Creating a Targeted Safety Net to Help the Least Well Off

If pain is a necessary part of the policy solution, the question is who should bear the pain. Here I will deviate from the normal textbook approach and offer my particular normative views of what policy I would recommend if the structural stagnation hypothesis is correct. That view is that U.S. policy should primarily focus on providing a safety net for those who are both hard working and who have been most hurt by globalization. Let's consider who they are.

As consumers, all U.S. citizens have benefited enormously from globalization through lower product prices.

But as producers, the effect has been highly uneven. A small group—perhaps 10 percent who are directly tied to international traders, the ones who get disproportionate shares of the benefit from trade—has been enormously helped by globalization. Another 60 percent of the U.S. economy has been only tangentially affected as producers in the nontradable sector, which includes most of the people working for government, education, health, and in the licensed professions, and those who work in tradable sectors where the United States maintains a competitive advantage. Their wages have risen, or at least kept up with inflation.

It is the remaining 30 percent in the tradable sector who have experienced most of the costs of globalization. They have had their wages reduced considerably, and many have experienced unemployment. So globalization has meant that you have one group of people—lower-skilled workers in the tradable sector—who have been hurt a lot, and another group—trade organizers and financiers—who are helped a lot. Those who are hurt are generally poor, while those who are helped are generally rich. So the appropriate policy, given my normative judgment, is to use tax revenue from those who have been most helped to help those who are most hurt.

Many faced with that choice argue that it would have been better to forgo the benefits of globalization to protect the poor. The benefits and costs of globalization have been too unequally distributed. The costs have been borne by those with the least education who are often the least well off. The benefits have gone largely to the well educated and the most well off. This, in my view, violates an implicit social contract that government had with the U.S. population to provide everyone who was willing to work hard a job at a respectable wage. Doing that would have required a much more demanding educational system that forced students to work much harder than they did, so that they would be more prepared to compete internationally. It would have been an educational system that had high minimum requirements to pass. Such a system could have separated out those willing to work hard from those who were not willing to work hard. Such an educational system could be supplemented by a targeted safety net for lower-skilled workers and those who otherwise fell through the cracks.

Ideally, this safety net would have been introduced with the policy changes that allowed globalization—allowing China to join the WTO and enter NAFTA. This safety net would have been a quid pro quo between those who most benefited from globalization and those who were most hurt. This social safety net would have reduced the worst of the suffering from globalization by providing everyone with a guaranteed minimum job, which could have been financed by a tax on the high-income and high-wealth individuals, who were the primary beneficiaries of globalization.

That tax would likely have meant broadening the tax base, allowing far fewer ways to avoid tax, and increasing the degree of income tax progressivity (higher tax rates as income rises) while simultaneously reducing loopholes to prevent people from avoiding taxes.

In a recent review of the effect of marginal tax rates on revenue, economists Emmanuel Saez, Joel Slemrod, and Seth Giertz showed that the empirical evidence strongly suggests that *if loopholes are removed*, tax revenue will be significantly increased at current tax rates and further increases in the tax rate will bring in significant additional revenue. That generally hasn't happened because there has been no political will to remove the loopholes. So the problem of increasing tax revenue is more political than economic. Politicians still do not have the will to deal with the problems.

The key to achieving a truly affordable safety net for the least well off is to limit it to people who really are the least well off. It is unclear whether our political system has the ability to do that. Whenever a safety net has been developed, it has always been expanded to include many in the middle class. As laudable as expanding the safety net might be, the more people who are included, the higher the cost, and the less likely a compromise can be reached to provide a safety net for those who truly need it.

Just as there has been no political will to deal with the tax problem, there has been no political will to deal with the entitlement problem, and to design a safety net focused on those most in need. The safety nets we have developed have become unaffordable at any possible tax level. So again, society is unwilling to pay the costs or to make the difficult choices about who gets helped and who does not. I discuss a possible safety net that provides a guaranteed job for every person who wants one in Chapter 17 on unemployment and jobs.

chapter 12

The Financial Sector and the Economy

> *The peculiar essence of our banking system is an unprecedented trust between man and man; and when that trust is much weakened by hidden causes, a small accident may greatly hurt it, and a great accident for a moment may almost destroy it.*
>
> —Walter Bagehot

The financial sector is exciting (as suggested in this famous painting *The Bulls and Bears in the Market*); it is also central to almost all macroeconomic debates. This central role is often not immediately obvious to students. In thinking about the economy, students often focus on the *real sector*—the market for the production and exchange of goods and services. In the real sector, real goods or services such as shoes, operas, automobiles, and textbooks are exchanged. That's an incomplete view of the economy. The *financial sector*—the market for the creation and exchange of financial assets such as money, stocks, and bonds—plays a central role in organizing and coordinating our economy; it makes modern economic society possible. A car won't run without oil; a modern economy won't operate without a financial sector.

As I've noted throughout this book, markets make specialization and trade possible and thereby make the economy far more efficient than it otherwise would be. But the efficient use of markets requires a financial sector that facilitates and lubricates those trades. Let's consider an example of how the financial sector facilitates trade. Say you walk into a store and buy a T-shirt. You shell out a 20-dollar bill and the salesperson hands you the T-shirt. Easy, right? Right—but why did the salesperson give you a T-shirt for a little piece of paper? The answer to that question is: Because the economy has a financial system that has convinced him that that piece of paper has value. To convince him (and you) of that requires an enormous structural system, called the financial sector, underlying the T-shirt transaction and all other transactions. That financial system makes the transaction possible; without it the economy as we know it would not exist.

The modern financial sector is highly sophisticated. It disperses credit throughout the economy in highly diverse ways. For example, when a bank makes you a loan, often that loan is securitized, which means that it is packaged with other loans (say 1,000 such similar loans) into a security, or bond, and sold to

After reading this chapter, you should be able to:

- **LO12-1** Discuss the functions and measures of money.
- **LO12-2** Define banks and explain how they create money.
- **LO12-3** Explain why the financial sector is so important to macroeconomic debates.
- **LO12-4** Explain the role of interest rates in an economy.

individuals. These bonds based on other loans are called *derivatives* because they are derived from another loan. An individual who buys that securitized bond in a sense owns 1/1,000 of your loan.

Sometimes these securitized bonds are packaged with different types of loans (say another 1,000) into second-order derivative bonds, so that now the person buying the new bond will own 1/1,000,000 of your loan along with a similar percentage of other loans. Why package loans? Because it spreads the risk of default—failure to pay back a loan—making owning the loans safer than it otherwise would be. Spreading the risk through securitization is a central feature of modern financial markets. The risk that securitizing loans cannot reduce is something called *systemic risk*—the risk that all or many of the loans all default together. As we will see in later chapters, the U.S. financial sector discovered that risk in 2008.

Spreading the risk through securitization is a central feature of modern financial markets.

The Definition and Functions of Money

Let's start our consideration of the financial sector by looking at the definition and function of money.

At this point you're probably saying, "I know what money is; it's currency—the dollar bills I carry around." In one sense you're right: Currency is money. But in another sense you're wrong; currency is just one example of money. In fact, a number of short-term financial assets are included as money. To see why, let's consider the definition of money: **Money** is *a highly liquid financial asset that's generally accepted in exchange for other goods, is used as a reference in valuing other goods, and can be stored as wealth.* In today's economy most of what economists call money is not currency but exists in the form of electronic holdings—an accounting entry in a computer.

Money is a financial asset that makes the real economy function smoothly by serving as a medium of exchange, a unit of account, and a store of wealth.

To be *liquid* means to be easily changeable into another asset or good. When you buy something with money, you are exchanging money for another asset. So any of your assets that are easily spendable are money. Social customs and standard practices are central to the liquidity of money. The reason you are willing to hold money is that you know someone else will accept it in trade for something else. Its value is determined by its general acceptability to others. If you don't believe that, try spending yuan (Chinese money) in the United States. If you try to buy dinner with 100 yuan, you will be told, "No way—give me money."

The U.S. Central Bank: The Fed

So is there any characteristic other than general acceptability that gives value to money? Consider the dollar bill that you know is money. Look at it. It states right on the bill that it is a Federal Reserve note, which means that it is an IOU (a liability) of the **Federal Reserve Bank (the Fed)**—*the U.S. central bank, whose liabilities (Federal Reserve notes) serve as cash in the United States.* Individuals are willing to accept the Fed's IOUs in return for real goods and services, which means that Fed notes are money.

What, you ask, is a central bank? To answer that question, we had better first consider what a bank is. A **bank** is *a financial institution whose primary function is accepting deposits for, and lending money to, individuals and firms.* (There are more complicated definitions and many types of banks, but that will do for now.) If you have more currency than you want, you take it to the bank and it will "hold" the extra for you, giving you a piece of paper (or a computer entry) that says you have that much currency held there ("hold" is in quotation marks because the bank does not actually hold the currency). What the bank used to give you was a bank note, and what you used to bring in to the bank was gold, but those days are gone forever. These days what you bring is that Federal Reserve note described above, and what you get is a paper receipt and a computer entry in your checking or savings account. Individuals' deposits in these accounts serve the same purpose as does currency and are also considered money.

Which brings us back to the Federal Reserve Bank, the U.S. central bank. It is a bank that has the right to issue notes (IOUs). By law these Federal Reserve Bank notes are acceptable payment for people's taxes, and by convention these notes are acceptable payment to all people in the United States, and to many people outside the United States. IOUs of the Fed are what most of you think of as cash.

The Federal Reserve Bank is the U.S. central bank; it has the right to issue notes that you think of as cash.

To understand why money is more than just cash, it is helpful to consider the functions of money in more detail. Having done so, we will consider which financial assets are included in various measures of money.

Functions of Money

As I stated above, money is an asset that can be quickly exchanged for any other asset or good. Money serves three functions:

Q-1 What are the three functions of money?

1. A medium of exchange.
2. A unit of account.
3. A store of wealth.

To get a better understanding of what money is, let's consider each of its functions in turn.

Money as a Medium of Exchange The easiest way to understand why money is used as a medium of exchange is to imagine what an economy would be like without money. Say you want something to eat at a restaurant. Without money you'd have to barter with the restaurant owner for your meal. *Barter* is a direct exchange of goods and/or services. You might suggest bartering one of your papers or the shirt in the sack that you'd be forced to carry with you to trade for things you want. Not liking to carry big sacks around, you'd probably decide to fix your own meal and forgo eating out. Bartering is simply too difficult. Money makes many more trades possible because it does not require a double coincidence of wants by two individuals, as simple barter does.

The use of money as a medium of exchange makes it possible to trade real goods and services without bartering. Instead of carrying around a sack full of diverse goods, all you need to carry around is a billfold full of money. You go into the restaurant and pay for your meal with money; the restaurant owner can spend (trade) that money for anything she wants.

Money doesn't have to have any inherent value to function as a medium of exchange. All that's necessary is that everyone believes that other people will accept it in exchange for their goods. This neat social convention makes the economy function more smoothly.

Money doesn't have to have any inherent value to function as a medium of exchange.

Money as a Unit of Account A second use of money is as a unit of account, that is, a measure of value. Money prices are actually relative prices. A money price, say 25 cents, for a pencil conveys the information of a relative price—1 pencil = ¼ of 1 dollar—because money is both our unit of account and our medium of exchange. When you think of 25 cents, you think of ¼ of a dollar and of what a dollar will buy. The 25 cents a pencil costs has meaning only relative to the information you've stored in your mind about what money can buy. If a hamburger costs $3.00, you can compare hamburgers and pencils (1 pencil = 1⁄12 of a hamburger) without making the relative price calculations explicitly.

Having a unit of account makes life much easier. For example, say we had no unit of account and you had to remember the relative prices of all goods. With three goods you'd have to memorize that an airplane ticket to Miami costs 6 lobster dinners in Boston or 4 pairs of running shoes, which makes a pair of shoes worth 1½ lobster dinners.

Memorizing even a few relationships is hard enough, so it isn't surprising that societies began using a single unit of account. If you don't have a single unit of account, all combinations of 100 goods will require that you remember millions of relative prices. If you have a single unit of account, you need know only 100 prices. A single unit of account saves our limited memories and helps us make reasonable decisions based on relative prices.

Money is a useful unit of account only as long as its value relative to other prices doesn't change too quickly.

Money is used as a unit of account at a point in time, and it's also a unit of account *over time*. For example, money is a standard of deferred payments such as on college loans that many of you will be making after graduation. The value of those loan payments depends on how the money prices of all other goods change over time.

In hyperinflation, all prices rise so much that our frame of reference is lost.

Money is a useful unit of account only as long as its value relative to the average of all other prices doesn't change too quickly. For example, in hyperinflation all prices rise so much that our frame of reference for making relative price comparisons is lost. Is 25 cents for a pencil high or low? If the price level increased 33,000 percent (as it did in 1988 in Nicaragua) or over 230 million percent (as it did in 2008 in Zimbabwe), 25 cents for a pencil would definitely be low, but would $100 be low? Without a lot of calculations we can't answer that question. A relatively stable unit of account makes it easy to answer.

Given the advantages to society of having a unit of account, it's not surprising that a monetary unit of account develops even in societies with no central bank or government. For example, in a prisoner of war camp during World War II, prisoners had no money, so they used cigarettes as their unit of account. Everything traded was given a price in cigarettes. The exchange rates on December 1, 1944, were:

1 bar of soap: 2 cigarettes

1 candy bar: 4 cigarettes

1 razor blade: 6 cigarettes

1 can of fruit: 8 cigarettes

1 can of cookies: 20 cigarettes

As you can see, all prices were in cigarettes. If candy bars rose to 6 cigarettes and the normal price was 4 cigarettes, you'd know the price of candy bars was high.

Money as a Store of Wealth When you save, you forgo consumption now so that you can consume in the future. To bridge the gap between now and the future, you must acquire a financial asset. This is true even if you squirrel away currency under the mattress. In that case, the financial asset you've acquired is simply the currency itself. Money is a financial asset. (It's simply a bond that pays no interest.) So a third use of money is as a store of wealth. As long as money is serving as a medium of exchange, it automatically also serves as a store of wealth. The restaurant owner can accept your money and hold it for as long as she wants before she spends it. (But had you paid her in fish, she'd be wise not to hold it more than a few hours.)

As long as money is serving as a medium of exchange, it automatically also serves as a store of wealth.

You might wonder why people would hold money that pays no interest. Put another way: Why do people hold a government bond that pays no interest? The reason is that money, by definition, is highly liquid—it is more easily translated into other goods than are other financial assets. Since money is also the medium of exchange, it can be spent instantaneously (as long as there's a shop open nearby). Our ability to spend money for goods makes money worthwhile to hold even if it doesn't pay interest.

Q-2 Why do people hold money rather than bonds when bonds pay higher interest than money?

Alternative Measures of Money

According to the definition of *money,* what people believe is money and what people will accept as money are determining factors in deciding whether a financial asset is money. Consequently, it's difficult to measure *money* unambiguously. A number of different financial assets serve some of the functions of money and thus have claims to being called *money*. To handle this ambiguity, economists have developed different measures of money and have called them M_1 and M_2. Each is a reasonable concept of money. Let's consider their components.

M_1 consists of *currency in the hands of the public, checking account balances, and traveler's checks*. Clearly, currency in the hands of the public (the dollar bills and coins you carry around with you) is money, but how about your checking account deposits? The reason they're included in this measure of money is that just about anything you can do with currency, you can do with a check or debit card. You can store your wealth in your checking account; you can use a check or debit card as a medium of exchange (indeed, for some transactions you have no choice but to use a check), and your checking account balance is denominated in the same unit of account (dollars) as is currency. If it looks like money, acts like money, and functions as money, it's a good bet it's money. Indeed, checking account deposits are included in all measures of money.

M_1 is a measure of the money supply; it consists of currency in the hands of the public plus checking accounts and traveler's checks.

If it looks like money, acts like money, and functions as money, it's a good bet it's money.

The same arguments can be made about traveler's checks. (Some advertisements even claim that traveler's checks are better than money because you can get them replaced.) Currency, checking account deposits, and traveler's checks make up the components of M_1, the narrowest measure of money. Figure 12-1 presents the relative sizes of M_1's components.

M_2 is made up of *M_1 plus savings and money market accounts, small-denomination time deposits (also called CD's), and retail money funds.* The relative sizes of the components of M_2 are given in Figure 12-1.

M_2 is a measure of the money supply; it consists of M_1 plus other relatively liquid assets.

These forms of financial assets are counted as money because they serve the functions of money. For example, savings accounts are readily spendable—all you need do is go to the bank and draw it out.

FIGURE 12-1 Components of M_2 and M_1

The two most-used measures of the money supply are M_1 and M_2. The two primary components of M_1 are currency in the hands of the public and checking accounts. M_2 includes all of M_1, plus savings and money market accounts, retail money funds, small-denomination time deposits, and traveler's checks.

Source: *H.6 Money Stock Measures, 2012* (www.federalreserve.gov).

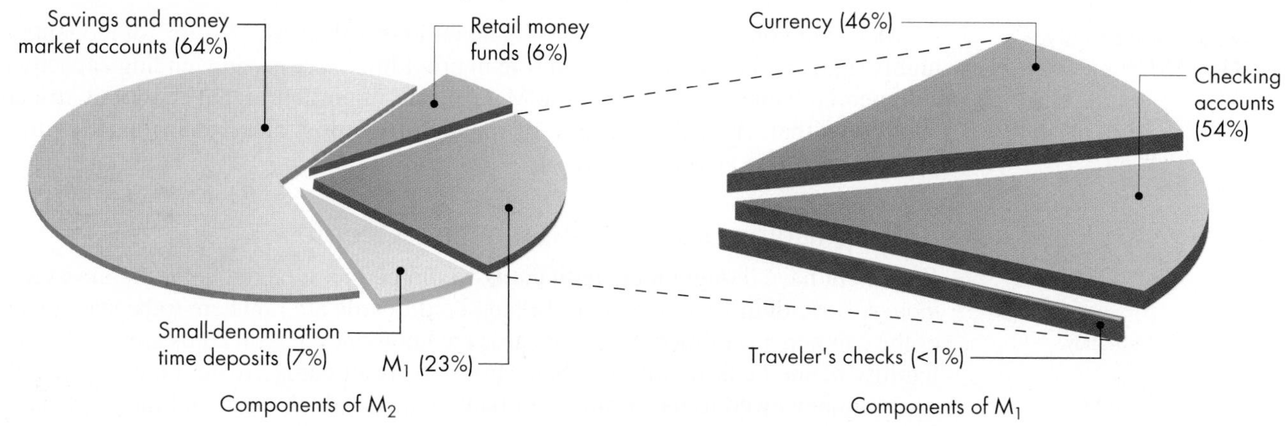

REAL-WORLD APPLICATION

Characteristics of a Good Money

The characteristics of a good money are that its supply be relatively constant, that it be limited in supply (sand wouldn't make good money), that it be difficult to counterfeit, that it be divisible (have you ever tried to spend half a horse?), that it be durable (raspberries wouldn't make good money), and that it be relatively small and light compared to its value (watermelon wouldn't make good money either). All these characteristics were reasonably (but not perfectly) embodied in gold. Many other goods have served as units of account (shells, wampum, rocks, cattle, horses, silver), but gold historically became the most important money, and in the 17th and 18th centuries gold was synonymous with money.

But gold has flaws as money. It's relatively heavy, easy to counterfeit with coins made only partly of gold, and, when new gold fields are discovered, subject to fluctuations in supply. These flaws led to gold's replacement by paper currency backed only by trust that the government would keep its commitment to limit its supply.

Paper money can be a good money if somehow people can trust the government to limit its supply and guarantee that its supply will be limited in the future. That trust has not always been well placed.

Most societies today supplement paper money such as dollar bills with electronic money that exists as debits and credit entries recorded on the computer. Both electronic money and paper money are vulnerable to fraud. Electronic money can be created by criminals who electronically change debit and credit entries, which is why banks spend billions of dollars on computer security and encryption technology each year. Paper money can be counterfeited. For example, in World War II, Germany planned to counterfeit a significant amount of British pounds and drop them in Britain to disrupt the British economy. It didn't succeed; by the time the Germans had printed the notes, they didn't have the aircraft to fly them over and drop them in Britain.

Counterfeiting continues today. For example, you may have noticed that some of the currency you carry has changed its look in recent years. That's because counterfeiters with new technology could create almost perfect counterfeit copies of the older designs. In 1989, authorities found some counterfeit U.S. $100 bills that had the right mix of cotton and linen and that had been manufactured on the very expensive Intaglio press, the same kind of press used to print real dollar bills. They called these counterfeit notes "supernotes." To stop the counterfeiters of the supernotes, the United States redesigned the U.S. currency, adding security measures such as color-shifting ink, watermarks, a security thread, an ultraviolet glow, and microprinting. Counterfeiters will copy these newly designed bills, which means that it is likely that U.S. authorities will have to redesign U.S. paper currency about every 10 years in order to keep ahead of counterfeiters.

So far, counterfeiting is still relatively unimportant in the United States. But in some developing countries, merchants and even banks are hesitant to accept large-denomination U.S. currency, which means that counterfeiting in those countries is undermining the usefulness of the dollar as money.

Q-3 Which would be a larger number, M_1 or M_2? Why?

M_2's components include more financial assets than M_1. All its components are highly liquid and play an important role in providing reserves and lending capacity for commercial banks. What makes the M_2 measure important is that economic research has shown that M_2 is the measure of money often most closely correlated with the price level and economic activity.

Distinguishing between Money and Credit

Credit cards are not money.

You might have thought that credit cards would be included in one of the measures of *money*. But I didn't include them. In fact, credit cards are nowhere to be seen in a list of the components of money. Credit cards are not money. Credit cards aren't a financial liability of the bank that issues them. Instead, credit cards create a liability for their users (money owed to the company or bank that issued the card) and the banks have a financial asset as a result.

ADDED DIMENSION

Money Laundering

The U.S. government has issued about $1 trillion worth of cash. That's about $3,200 for every man, woman, and child. Now ask yourself how much cash you're carrying on you. Add to that the amounts banks and businesses keep, and divide that by the number of people in the United States. The number economists get when they do that calculation is way below the total amount of cash the United States has issued. So what happens to the extra cash?

Let's switch for a minute to a Miami safehouse being raided by drug enforcement officers. They find $50 million in cash. That's what most economists believe happens to much of the extra cash that remains in the United States. It goes underground. An underground economy lurks below the real economy. The underground economy consists of two components: (1) production and distribution of illegal goods and services and (2) legal economic activity that is not reported.

Illegal activity, such as selling illegal drugs and prostitution, generates huge amounts of cash. (Most people who buy an illegal good or service would prefer not to have the transaction appear on their monthly credit card statements.) This presents a problem for a big-time illegal business. It must explain to the Internal Revenue Service (IRS) where all its money came from. That's where money laundering comes in. Money laundering is simply making illegally gained income look as if it came from a legal business. Any business through which lots of cash moves is a good front for money laundering. Laundromats move lots of cash, which is where the term money laundering came from. The mob bought laundromats and claimed a much higher income from the laundromats than it actually received. The mob thus "laundered" the excess money. Today money laundering is much more sophisticated. It involves billions of dollars and international transactions in three or four different countries, but the purpose is the same: making illegally earned money look legal.

Let's consider how a credit card works. You go into a store and buy something with your credit card. You have a real asset—the item you bought. The store has a financial asset—an account receivable. The store sells that financial asset at a slight discount to the bank and gets cash in return. Either the bank collects cash when you pay off your financial liability or, if you don't pay it off, the bank earns interest on its financial asset (often at a high rate, from 12 to 18 percent per year). Credit cards are essentially prearranged loans.

Q-4 Are credit cards money?

While credit cards are not money, a debit card serves the same function as a check—think of it as a computer checkbook—and hence is money. It allows you to spend money in your bank account (to debit your account) and thus makes your bank account more liquid. With a debit card, no loan is involved; you are spending your money.

The distinction between credit and money is the following: Money is a financial asset of individuals and a financial liability of banks. Credit is savings made available to be borrowed. Credit is not an asset of the borrowing public.

Credit cards and credit impact the amount of money people hold. When preapproved loan credit is instantly available (as it is with a credit card), there's less need to hold money. (If you didn't have a credit card, you'd carry a lot more currency.) With credit immediately available, liquidity is less valuable to people. So credit and credit cards do make a difference in how much money people hold, but because they are not financial liabilities of banks, they are not money.

Because of the importance of easy credit to our economy in modern financial sectors, measures of access to credit and credit availability are as important as are measures of money. You can see what happened to credit in Figure 12-2: It increased at a fast rate until 2008, when it fell suddenly. It was the availability of short-term credit that dried up in October 2008, threatening to seize up the U.S. economy.

FIGURE 12-2 Total Consumer Credit

During the 1990s and early 2000s, the increase in the amount that consumers borrowed rose quickly. In 2008 consumer credit declined. Economists watch consumer credit just as they watch the money supply. Both affect total expenditures in the economy.

Source: Board of Governors of the Federal Reserve System.

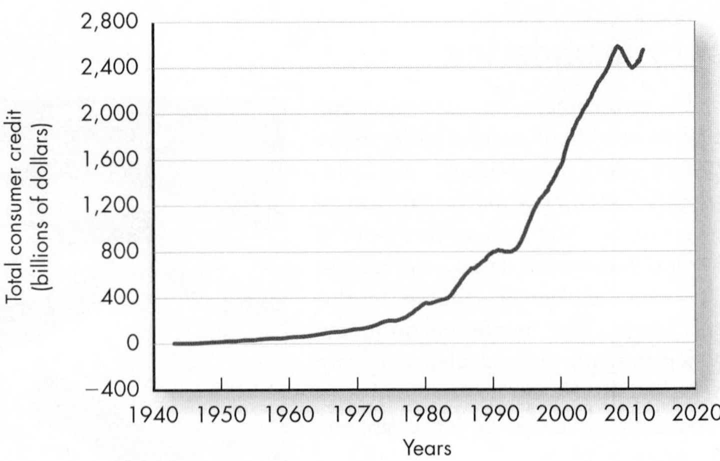

Banks and the Creation of Money

Modern financial sectors are highly complex, with many different types of financial assets.

Modern financial sectors are highly complex, with many different types of financial assets (assets such as stocks or bonds, whose benefit to the owner depends on the issuer of the asset meeting certain obligation) and financial liabilities (obligations by the issuer of the financial asset). To make the financial sector understandable to students, it is useful to simplify and talk about a single financial institution—a bank—and a single concept—money—and to discuss how the amount of money can be expanded and contracted. That's what I do here. But you should remember that the discussion is simply an example of the way in which financial sectors expand and contract the amount of credit in the economy.

Banks are financial institutions that borrow from people (take in deposits) and use the money they borrow to make loans to other individuals. Banks make a profit by charging a higher interest on the money they lend out than they pay for the money they borrow. Individuals keep their money in banks, accepting lower interest rates, because doing so is safer and more convenient than the alternatives.

The Creation of Money

Banking is generally analyzed from the perspective of **asset management** (*how a bank handles its loans and other assets*) and **liability management** (*how a bank attracts deposits and what it pays for them*). When banks offer people "free checking" and special money market accounts paying 1 percent, they do so after carefully considering the costs of those liabilities to them.

It is important to think of banks as both borrowers and lenders.

To think of banks as borrowers as well as lenders may seem a bit unusual, but borrowing is what they do. When you own a savings account or a checking account, the bank is borrowing from you, paying you a zero (or low) interest rate. It then lends your money to other people at a higher interest rate.

How Banks Create Money

Banks are centrally important to macroeconomics because they create money. How do banks create money? The process is simple—so simple it seems almost magical to many.

Banks "create" money because a bank's liabilities are defined as money. So when a bank incurs liabilities, it creates money.

The key to understanding how banks create money is to remember the nature of financial assets: Financial assets can be created from nothing as long as an offsetting financial liability is simultaneously created. Since money is any financial asset that can be used as a medium of exchange, unit of account, and store of value, money can be created rather easily. The asset just needs to serve the functions of money. Seeing how dollar bills are created is the easiest way to begin examining the process. Whenever the Fed issues an IOU to you or someone else, it creates money.[1] Similarly, other banks create money by creating financial assets that serve the functions of money. As we saw when we considered the measures of money, bank checking accounts serve those functions, so they are money, just as currency is money. When a bank places the proceeds of a loan it makes to you in your checking account, it is creating money. You have a financial asset that did not previously exist.

About 95 percent of all bills printed each year replace worn-out notes. The remaining 5 percent represent new currency in circulation.

The First Step in the Creation of Money To see how banks create money, let's consider what would happen if you were given a freshly printed $100 bill. Remember, the Fed created that $100 bill simply by printing it. The $100 bill is a $100 financial asset of yours and a financial liability of the Fed, which issued it.

If the process of creating money stopped there, it wouldn't be particularly mysterious. But it doesn't stop there. Let's consider what happens next as you use that money.

The Second Step in the Creation of Money The second step in the creation of money involves the transfer of money from one form to another—from currency to a bank deposit. Say you decide to put the $100 bill in your checking account. To make the analysis easier, let's assume that your bank is a branch of the country's only bank, Big Bank. All money deposited in branch banks goes into Big Bank. After you make your deposit, Big Bank is holding $100 in currency for you, and you have $100 more in your checking account. You can spend it whenever you want simply by writing a check. So Big Bank is performing a service for you (holding your money and keeping track of your expenditures) for free. Neat, huh? Big Bank must be run by a bunch of nice people.

But wait. You and I know that bankers, while they may be nice, aren't as nice as all that. There ain't no such thing as a free lunch. Let's see why the bank is being so nice.

WWW Web Note 12.1 Gold

Banking and Goldsmiths To see why banks are so nice, let's go way back in history to when banks first developed.[2] At that time, gold was used for money and people carried around gold to make their payments. But because gold is rather heavy, it was difficult to use for big purchases. Moreover, carrying around a lot of gold left people vulnerable to being robbed by the likes of Robin Hood. So they looked for a place to store their gold until they needed some of it.

From Gold to Gold Receipts The natural place to store gold was the goldsmith shop, which already had a vault. For a small fee, the goldsmith shop would hold your gold, giving you a receipt for it. Whenever you needed your gold, you'd go to the goldsmith and exchange the receipt for gold.

Pretty soon most people kept their gold at the goldsmith's, and they began to wonder: Why go through the bother of getting my gold out to buy something when all that happens is that the seller takes the gold I pay and puts it right back into the goldsmith's vault? That's two extra trips.

Consequently, people began buying goods by using the receipts the goldsmith gave them to certify that they had deposited $100 (or whatever) worth of gold in his vault. At that point, gold was no longer the only money—gold receipts were also

[1]As we'll see when we discuss the Fed in more detail, dollar bills aren't the Fed's only IOUs.

[2]The banking history reported here is, according to historians, apocryphal (more myth than reality). But it so nicely makes the point that I repeat it anyhow.

money since they were accepted in exchange for goods. However, as long as the total amount in the gold receipts directly represented the total amount of gold, it was still reasonable to say, since the receipts were 100 percent backed by gold, that gold was the money supply.

Q-5 Most banks prefer to have many depositors rather than one big depositor. Why?

Gold Receipts Become Money Once this process of using the receipts rather than the gold became generally accepted, the goldsmith found that he had substantial amounts of gold in his vault. All that gold, just sitting there! On a normal day, only 1 percent of the gold was claimed by "depositors" and had to be given out. Usually on the same day an amount at least equal to that 1 percent came in from other depositors. What a waste! Gold sitting around doing nothing! So when a good friend came in, needing a loan, the goldsmith said, "Sure, I'll lend you some gold receipts as long as you pay me some interest." When the goldsmith made this loan, he created more gold receipts than he had covered in gold in his vault. He created money.

Pretty soon the goldsmith realized he could earn more from the interest he received on loans than he could earn from goldsmithing. So he stopped goldsmithing and went full-time into making loans of gold receipts. At that point, the number of gold receipts outstanding significantly exceeded the amount of gold in the goldsmith's vaults. But not to worry; since everyone was willing to accept gold receipts rather than gold, the goldsmith had plenty of gold for those few who wanted actual gold.

Money is whatever meets the definition of money.

It was, however, no longer accurate to say that gold was the country's money or currency. Gold receipts were also money. They met the definition of *money.* These gold receipts were backed partially by gold and partially by people's trust that the goldsmiths would pay off their deposits on demand. The goldsmith shops had become banks.

Banking Is Profitable The banking business was very profitable for goldsmiths. Soon other people started competing with them, offering to hold gold for free. After all, if they could store gold, they could make a profit on the loans to other people (with the first people's money). Some even offered to pay people to store their gold.

The goldsmith story is directly relevant to banks. People store their currency in banks and the banks issue receipts—checking accounts—that become a second form of money. When people place their currency in banks and use their receipts from the bank as money, those receipts also become money because they meet the definition of *money:* They serve as a medium of exchange, a unit of account, and a store of wealth. So money includes both currency that people hold and their deposits in the bank.

Which brings us back to why banks hold your currency for free. They do it not because they're nice, but because when you deposit currency in the bank, your deposit allows banks to make profitable loans they otherwise couldn't make.

The Process of Money Creation

With that background, let's go back to your \$100, which the bank is now holding for you. You have a checking account balance of \$100 and the bank has \$100 currency. As long as other people are willing to accept your check in payment for \$100 worth of goods, your check is as good as money. In fact, it is money in the same way gold receipts were money. But when you deposit \$100, no additional money has been created yet. The form of the money has simply been changed from currency to a checking account or demand deposit.

Now let's say Big Bank lends out 90 percent of the currency you deposit, keeping only 10 percent as **reserves**—*currency and deposits a bank keeps on hand or at the Fed or central bank, to manage the normal cash inflows and outflows.* This 10 percent is the **reserve ratio** (*the ratio of reserves to total deposits*). Banks are required by the Fed to hold a percentage of deposits; that percentage is called the *required reserve ratio*. Banks may also choose to hold an additional percentage, called the *excess reserve ratio*. The reserve ratio is the sum of the required reserve ratio and the excess reserve ratio. Thus, the reserve ratio is at least as large as the required reserve ratio, but it can be larger. In recent years, because of the financial crisis, excess reserves have become more important, and they are likely to stay important even after the aftermath of the financial crisis subsides because the Fed now pays interest on reserves held by banks.

The reserve ratio is the ratio of currency (or deposits at the central bank) to deposits a bank keeps as a reserve against currency withdrawals.

So, like the goldsmith, Big Bank lends out \$90 to someone who qualifies for a loan. The person that the bank loaned the money to now has \$90 currency and you have \$100 in a demand deposit, so now there's \$190 of money, rather than just \$100 of money. The \$10 in currency the bank holds in reserve isn't counted as money since the bank must keep it as reserves and may not use it as long as it's backing loans. Only currency held by the public, not currency held by banks, is counted as money. By making the loan, the bank has created \$90 in money.

Of course, no one borrows money just to hold it. The borrower spends the money, say on a new sweater, and the sweater store owner now has the \$90 in currency. The store owner doesn't want to hold it either. She'll deposit it back into the bank. Since there's only one bank, Big Bank discovers that the \$90 it has loaned out is once again in its coffers. The money operates like a boomerang: Big Bank loans \$90 out and gets the \$90 back again.

The same process occurs again. The bank doesn't earn interest income by holding \$90, so if the bank can find additional credible borrowers, it lends out \$81, keeping \$9 (10 percent of \$90) more in reserve. The story repeats and repeats itself, with a slightly smaller amount coming back to the bank each time. At each step in the process, money (in the form of checking account deposits) is being created.

Determining How Many Demand Deposits Will Be Created

What's the total amount of demand deposits—money in checking and savings accounts—that will ultimately be created from your \$100 when individuals hold no currency? To answer that question, we continue the process over and over: $100 + 90 + 81 + 72.9 + 65.6 + 59 + 53.1 + 47.8 + 43.0 + 38.7 + 34.9$. Adding up these numbers gives us \$686. Adding up \$686 plus the numbers from the next 20 rounds gives us \$961.08.

As you can see, that's a lot of adding. Luckily there's an easier way. Economists have shown that you can determine the amount of money that will eventually be created by such a process by multiplying the initial \$100 in money that was printed by the Fed and deposited by $1/r$, where r is the reserve ratio (the percentage banks keep out of each round including both the required and excess reserve ratios). In this case the reserve ratio is 10 percent.

Dividing,

Q-6 If banks hold 20 percent of their deposits as reserves, what is the money multiplier?

$$\frac{1}{r} = \frac{1}{.10} = 10$$

so the amount of demand deposits that will ultimately exist at the end of the process is

$$(10 \times \$100) = \$1{,}000$$

The \$1,000 is in the form of checking account deposits (demand deposits). The entire \$100 in currency that you were given, and that started the whole process, is in the bank as reserves, which means that \$900 (\$1,000 − \$100) of money has been created by the process.

The money multiplier is the measure of the amount of money ultimately created per dollar deposited by the banking system. When people hold no currency, it equals $1/r$.

The higher the reserve ratio, the smaller the money multiplier.

Calculating the Money Multiplier We will call the ratio $1/r$ the **money multiplier**—*the measure of the amount of money ultimately created per dollar deposited in the banking system, when people hold no currency.* It tells us how much money will ultimately be created by the banking system from an initial inflow of money. In our example, $1/.10 = 10$. Had the bank kept out 20 percent each time, the money multiplier would have been $1/.20 = 5$. If the reserve ratio were 5 percent, the money multiplier would have been $1/.05 = 20$. The higher the reserve ratio, the smaller the money multiplier, and the less money will be created.

An Example of the Creation of Money To make sure you understand the process, let's consider an example. Say that the reserve ratio is 20 percent and that John Finder finds \$10,000 in currency, which he deposits in the bank. Thus, he has \$10,000 in his checking account and the bank has \$8,000 (\$10,000 − \$2,000 in reserves) to lend out. Once it lends that money to Fred Baker, there is \$8,000 of additional money in the economy. Fred Baker uses the money to buy a new oven from Mary Builder, who, in turn, deposits the money back into the banking system. Big Bank lends out \$6,400 (\$8,000 − \$1,600 in reserves).

Now the process occurs again. Table 12-1 shows the effects of the process for 5 rounds, starting with the initial \$10,000. Each time it lends the money out, the money returns like a boomerang and serves as reserves for more loans. After 5 rounds we reach a point where total demand deposits are \$33,616, and the bank has \$6,723 in reserves. This is approaching the \$50,000 we'd arrive at using the money multiplier:

$$\frac{1}{r}(\$10{,}000) = \frac{1}{.2}(\$10{,}000) = 5(\$10{,}000) = \$50{,}000$$

If we carried it out for more rounds, we'd actually reach what the formula predicted.

Note that the process ends only when the bank holds all the currency in the economy, and the only money held by the public is in the form of demand deposits. Notice also that the total amount of money created depends on the amount banks hold in reserve. Specifically, an economy can support a supply of money equal to reserves times the money multiplier.

To see that you understand the process, say that banks suddenly get concerned about the safety of their loans, and they decide to keep **excess reserves**—*reserves held by banks in excess of what banks are required to hold.* What will happen to the money multiplier and the total amount of money in the economy? If you answered that it will decrease, you've got it. Excess reserves decrease the money multiplier as much as required reserves do. I mention this example because this very thing happened in the banking system in 2008. Banks became concerned about the safety of their loans; they started holding large excess reserves, and the money multiplier decreased.

Excess reserves are reserves held by banks in excess of what they are required to hold.

The Relationship between Reserves and Total Money

The preceding discussion explains how the banking system can expand the money supply far beyond the amount initially added by the Fed. As a bank makes loans, it keeps some cash and central bank reserves—often called *high-powered money*—as reserves to ensure that it has the cash if the depositor wants it. Ultimately, the reserves and the amount the bank has in deposits are related. If the banking system is fully loaned out and has no excess reserves, and people hold no cash, the relationship between the amount of reserves and the amount of money in the system is determined by the Federal Reserve Bank's reserve requirement. When people hold cash, and when banks hold excess reserves, then the central bank's reserve requirement no longer determines the total amount of money. In that case the money supply is determined by banks and individuals' decisions as

TABLE 12-1 The Money-Creating Process

In the money-creating process, the currency keeps coming back to the banking system like a boomerang. With a 20 percent reserve requirement, ultimately (1/.2) × \$10,000 = \$50,000 will be created. In this example, you can see that after 5 rounds, much of the creation of deposits will have taken place. As you carry out the analysis further, the money creation will approach the \$50,000 shown in the last line.

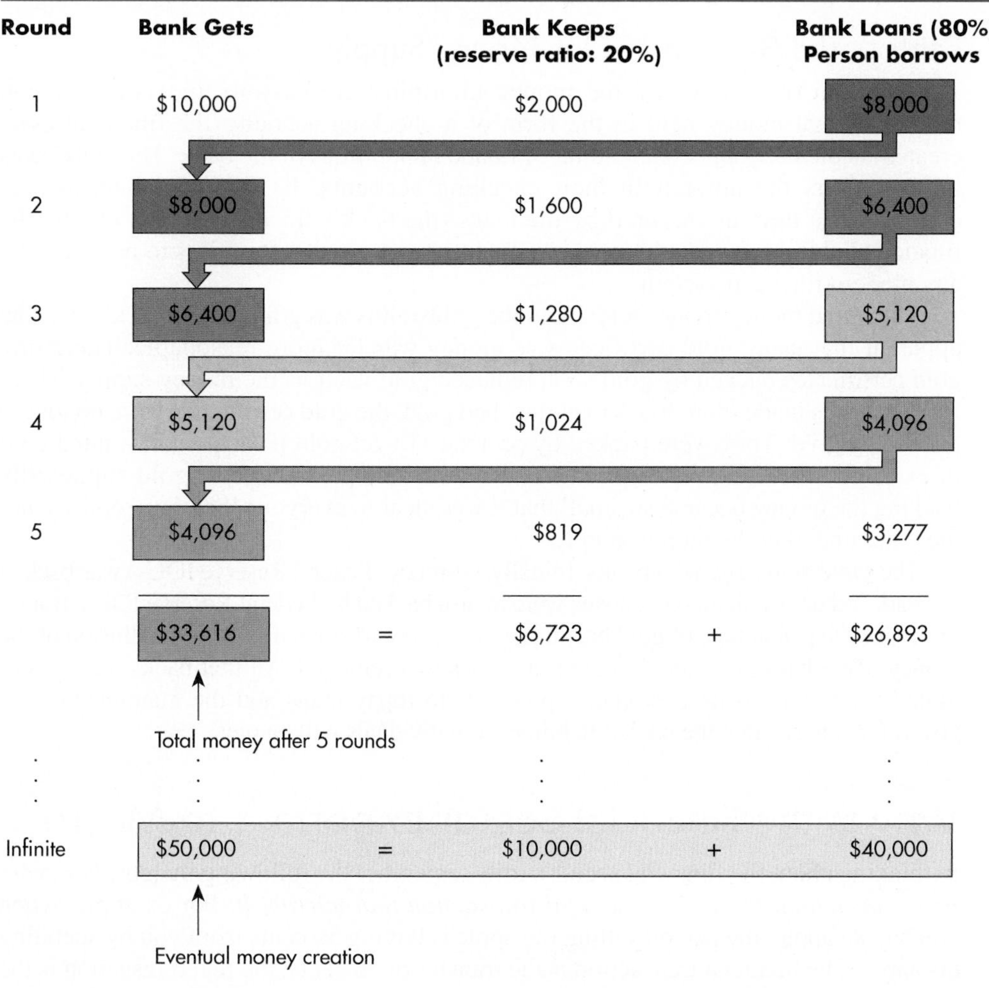

Round	Bank Gets		Bank Keeps (reserve ratio: 20%)		Bank Loans (80%) Person borrows
1	\$10,000		\$2,000		\$8,000
2	\$8,000		\$1,600		\$6,400
3	\$6,400		\$1,280		\$5,120
4	\$5,120		\$1,024		\$4,096
5	\$4,096		\$819		\$3,277
	\$33,616 (Total money after 5 rounds)	=	\$6,723	+	\$26,893
⋮	⋮		⋮		⋮
Infinite	\$50,000 (Eventual money creation)	=	\$10,000	+	\$40,000

well. The total money supply becomes what economists call *endogenous*—determined by the system as a whole, not solely by the central bank.

When people hold varying amounts of cash and banks hold varying amounts of excess reserves, the total money supply becomes endogenous—determined by the system as a whole, not solely by the central bank.

The fact that the money supply is determined endogenously doesn't mean that we cannot calculate a money multiplier after the fact. If we know what the reserve ratio (including both required reserves and excess reserves) is, and how much cash people hold, then we can, in principle, calculate the total amount of money in the economy. But the multiplier is the result of the process; it is not the driving force of the process. That's why the money multiplier isn't used much anymore. With both the amount of cash people hold and the excess reserves that banks hold continually changing, the money multiplier is not a fixed value and can be determined only after the process is complete. At that point it is no longer especially useful.

In summary, the process of money creation isn't difficult to understand as long as you remember that money is simply a bank's financial liability held by the public.

Whenever banks create financial liabilities for themselves, they create financial assets for individuals, and those financial assets are money.

Whenever banks create financial liabilities for themselves, they create financial assets for individuals, and those financial assets are money. Unfortunately for the Fed's attempt to control the amount of money in the economy, the Fed doesn't control either excess reserves or cash held by individuals. As these change, the amount of money in the economy can change independently of the Fed's actions.

Faith as the Backing of Our Money Supply

Web Note 12.2 E-Currency

The creation of money and the money multiplier are easy to understand if you remember that money held in the form of a checking account (the financial asset created) is offset by an equal amount of financial liabilities of the bank. The bank owes its depositors the amount in their checking accounts. Its financial liabilities to depositors, in turn, are secured by the loans (the bank's financial assets) and by the financial liabilities of people to whom the loans were made. Promises to pay underlie any modern financial system.

The initial money in the story about the goldsmiths was gold, but it quickly became apparent that using gold certificates as money was far more reasonable. Therefore, gold certificates backed by gold soon replaced gold itself as the money supply. Then, as goldsmiths made more loans than they had gold, the gold certificates were no longer backed by gold. They were backed by promises to get gold if the person wanted gold in exchange for the gold certificate. Eventually the percentage of gold supposedly backing the money became so small that it was clear to everyone that the promises, not the gold, underlay the money supply.

All that backs the modern money supply are bank customers' promises to repay loans and government guarantees of banks' liabilities to individuals.

The same holds true with banks. Initially, currency (Federal Reserve IOUs) was backed by gold, and banks' demand deposits were in turn backed by Federal Reserve IOUs. But by the 1930s the percentage of gold backing money grew so small that even the illusion of the money being backed by anything but promises was removed. All that backs the modern money supply are bank customers' promises to repay loans and the guarantee of the government to see that the banks' liabilities to individuals will be met.

Why Is the Financial Sector Important to Macro?

The financial sector is central to almost all macroeconomic debates because behind every real transaction, there is a financial transaction that mirrors it.

In thinking about the financial sector's role, remember the following insight: *For every real transaction, there is a financial transaction that mirrors it.* For example, when you buy an apple, the person selling the apple is buying 50 cents from you by spending his apple. The financial transaction is the transfer of 50 cents; the real transaction is the transfer of the apple.

As long as the financial system is operating smoothly, you hardly know it's there; but should that system break down, the entire economy would be disrupted and would either stagnate or fall into a recession or even into a depression. That's what almost happened in 2008 when people lost faith in the existing financial institutions, and the financial sector was coming to a grinding halt. It was much like running a car without oil. Oil is only a small percentage of the car, but I can tell you from sad experience that you can run a car without oil only for about 10 miles before the entire engine seizes up. In October 2008, there was serious concern that was about to happen to the U.S. economy and that the economy would totally seize up because of a meltdown of the financial sector.

As I will discuss in a later chapter, in response to concern about such a seizing up, the U.S. government undertook unprecedented actions to try to prevent that by "bailing out" banks and other financial institutions with hundreds of billions of dollars. To understand that bailout, you have to understand the role of the financial sector in the economy. That's why it is necessary to give you an overview of the financial sector as part of your foundation of macroeconomics. Thus, although in

FIGURE 12-3 The Financial Sector as a Conduit for Savings

Financial institutions channel saving—outflows from the spending stream from various entities (government, households, and corporations)—back into the spending stream as loans to various entities (government, households, and corporations). To emphasize the fact that savings take many forms, a breakdown of the type of savings for one entity, households, is shown on the left. The same is done for loans on the right, but for corporations. Each of these loans can itself be broken down again and again until each particular loan is identified individually. The lending process is an individualistic process, and each loan is different in some way from each other loan.

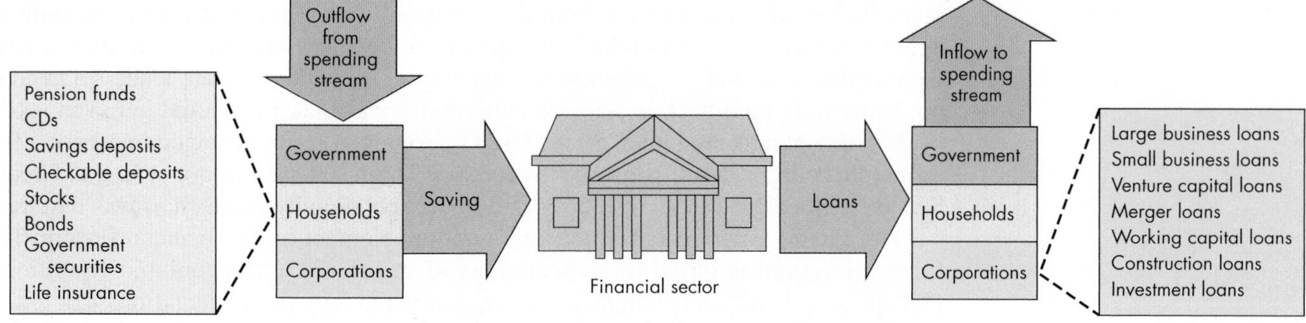

this book I don't have a separate section on the steel sector or even the technology sector of the economy, I do have a separate section on money, banking, and the financial sector of the economy.

The financial sector has two roles. First, it facilitates trade, making it possible for normal business to happen—that's its role as a lubricant to the economy. The second, related, role of the financial sector is to transfer saving—outflows from the spending stream in hundreds of different forms—back into spending. Flows from the spending stream are channeled into the financial sector as saving when individuals buy *financial assets* from a person issuing the asset, who has a corresponding financial liability. (Financial assets and liabilities are discussed in detail in Appendix A to this chapter.)

Think of this role of the financial sector as a gigantic channeling device, something like that shown in Figure 12-3. If the financial sector expands the spending flow too much, you get inflationary pressures in either goods or assets. If it contracts the spending flow too much, you get a recession. And if it transfers just the right amount, you get a smoothly running economy.

Q-7 Joe, your study partner, says that since goods and services are produced only in the real sector, the financial sector is not important to the macroeconomy. How do you respond?

For every financial asset, there is a financial liability.

The financial sector channels saving back into spending.

The Role of Interest Rates in the Financial Sector

Interest rates, as defined in an earlier chapter, are the prices that are charged or paid for the use of a financial asset. They are key variables in the financial sector. There are many interest rates in the economy—mortgage interest rates, interest rates on credit cards, interest rates on government bills, interest rates on corporate bonds, and many more—and they differ in many ways. There are different interest rates for different risk levels of loans, for different lengths of loans, and for different types of loans. To take account of the length of the loan economists distinguish between short-term interest rates and long-term interest rates. To take account of different riskiness economists discuss risk premiums on loans.

WWW Web Note 12.3 Interest Rates

In normal times in introductory economics we don't talk about risk premiums since they add another dimension of difficulty. But in recent years, they cannot be avoided since the risk premiums on loans have changed suddenly. Consider Greece in 2011 when people began to believe that the Greek government wouldn't be paying back its loans. Suddenly, the risk premium on Greek bonds shot up, from almost zero to 25 percent, so that the interest rate on Greek bonds rose from what they would have been without this risk—5 percent—to 30 percent.

Q-8 True or false? A high-risk premium makes default more likely. Explain.

Initially, that didn't affect Greece much since the high interest rate was only on new bonds. But as old, lower interest rate bonds became due, and had to be paid back, Greece would have had to issue new bonds at the higher interest rates. Greece couldn't afford to do so, and it would have been forced to default (either pay interest on the debt or repay the debt) without getting an outside loan that didn't have such high interest rates. Eventually, it got a loan from the European Union, but that loan came with an agreement that existing bondholders would not be fully paid back, and that Greece would raise taxes and cut government spending significantly. Private lenders agreed to not being fully paid back because the alternative was that they would get even less if the EU did not make the loan. So in 2012 Greece temporarily managed to escape a full economic collapse, but that possibility remained high since it was not clear that Greece had the political power to raise taxes and lower spending by as much as was required.

This Greek experience captures an important element of the financial system: The financial system is based on expectations of future risk and economic conditions. Perceptions of risk can change suddenly, and when they do, expectations can create serious problems for the financial sector. In 2012, a number of southern European countries were in situations similar to that of Greece, and the United States, with its growing government debt, was heading in the same direction.

The long-term interest rate is the price paid for the use of financial assets with long repayment periods. Examples are mortgages and government bonds. The market for these long-term financial assets is called the *loanable funds market*. The short-term interest rate is the price paid for the use of financial assets with shorter repayment periods such as savings deposits and checking accounts. These short-term financial assets are called *money* as we discussed above. So, the long-term interest rate is determined in the loanable funds market and the short-term interest rate is determined in the money market. Ideally, interest rate fluctuations will channel any flow of income escaping from the economy—what economists call saving—back into the economy through loans to consumers, or loans to businesses that they spend on new investment. This is why interest rates are so important to the economy. Unfortunately, interest rates do not always do a good job.

Q-9 Why are interest rates important to the economy?

To get at the problems that can develop when they do not do a good job, macroeconomics simplifies the flow of saving into investment by assuming only two types of financial assets exist: Money and bonds. Some saving is translated back into investment by financial intermediaries through financial assets such as bonds, loans, and stocks. It is these financial assets to which the loanable funds market refers.[3] Savings held by individuals as money are assumed not to make their way back into the loanable funds market, and therefore not into investment. This means that some savings escape the circular flow. Compared to the complicated maze of interconnected flows that exists in reality, this is an enormous simplification, but it captures a potentially serious problem and possible cause of fluctuations in the economy.

The Demand for Money and the Role of the Interest Rate

Let's now consider the potential problems that may develop in the macroeconomy as people shift their holdings between financial assets and money. To do that, we must first ask: Why do people hold money? This is a relevant question because, by assumption,

[3]With a different interest rate for each different type of financial asset, you may be wondering which interest rate we are talking about. The answer is that we are talking about an average of the many different interest rates. Since that average interest rate is generally not easily calculable, often the interest rate on 10-year bonds is used as a proxy for the interest rate on all loanable funds.

money doesn't pay any interest, whereas other financial assets do pay interest, so to hold money people are forgoing interest payments.[4]

Why People Hold Money

The only reason people would be willing to hold money is if they get some benefit from doing so, so we need to examine that benefit. The first benefit is easy: Money allows you to buy things. You can *spend* money; you can't spend bonds. You can change a financial asset into spendable money, but that takes time and effort. *The need to hold money for spending* is called the **transactions motive.** Second, you hold money for emergencies. For example, if your car breaks down, you'll need cash to get it towed. Knowing that there will always be unforeseen needs, you might carry $20 cash in addition to what you would otherwise carry. *Holding money for unexpected expenses and impulse buying* is called the **precautionary motive** for holding money. The third reason for holding money is called the speculative motive. The **speculative motive** is *holding cash to avoid holding financial assets whose prices are falling*. It comes about because the price of financial assets such as bonds varies in value as the interest rate fluctuates. For example, if you expect the price of a bond (or any financial asset) to fall, that bond is not something you would want to be holding because you will be losing money by holding it; you'd rather be holding money. Your money holdings might not be earning any interest, but at least their value isn't falling like the price of the asset. In a sense, you are speculating about what the future value of the bond will be. That's why it's called the speculative motive for holding money. You hold money rather than longer-term financial assets so you don't lose if asset prices fall. (Of course, if asset prices are expected to rise, then you want to reduce your holdings of money and increase your asset holdings.)

Q-10 What are three reasons people hold money?

Let's consider an example of bond price fluctuations. (Remember, bonds are often used as the reference asset for all financial assets when people provide loanable funds.) Say you have a one-year $1,000 bond that pays an interest rate of 4 percent a year, and that 4 percent is the interest rate in the economy. The bond sells for $1,000 and will provide $40 interest for the year. You're happy earning that 4 percent (that's the best you can do) so you buy the bond for $1,000. Now say that the day after you buy the bond, the interest rate in the economy rises to 6 percent. Because the price of the bond is inversely related to the interest rate in the economy, the price of that 4 percent $1,000 bond that you bought for $1,000 will fall, in this case to $981.13. (See the box "Interest Rates and the Price of Bonds" for a further explanation.) In one day, your bond has fallen in value by $18.87, an amount that far exceeds the interest you earned on the bond for that day. In this case, you would have preferred to have held cash instead of the bond because the cash would not have fallen in value. Holding cash in the expectation of falling bond prices is the speculative demand for money.

This 18th-century etching by Robert Goez, The Speculator, captures a popular view of financial activities. It shows a man reduced to rags by bad speculation.

Most professional bond speculators, who often carry portfolios of millions and even billions of dollars of bonds, make their money on changes in the prices of bonds, not on the interest payments of bonds. The reason is that although the changes in annualized interest rates on any particular day are generally small—so small that they are measured in basis points, each of which is one one-hundredth of a percentage point—even those small changes in interest rates swamp the income made on the interest rate payments for the day.

Interest Rates and the Price of Bonds

[4]As discussed above, in today's economy, many components of money pay interest, but they pay a lower interest than do other financial assets. The analysis I present here applies to the differential rate of interest paid between money and longer-term financial assets or, more generally, to differential interest rates paid by various financial assets; we assume zero interest on money simply to keep the presentation as simple as possible.

ADDED DIMENSION

Interest Rates and the Price of Bonds

In the example in the text, you may have thought that if the interest rate in the economy rose from 4 percent to 6 percent, and you had bought the bond paying 4 percent, you would just sell it and buy the 6 percent bond. Would that you could, but that's not the way the bond market works. You only get your $1,000 back when the bond matures. If you wanted your money before that time, you would have to sell it to someone else, but the price of the 4 percent bond would have fallen as soon as the interest rate in the economy rose. More generally, we have the following relationship:

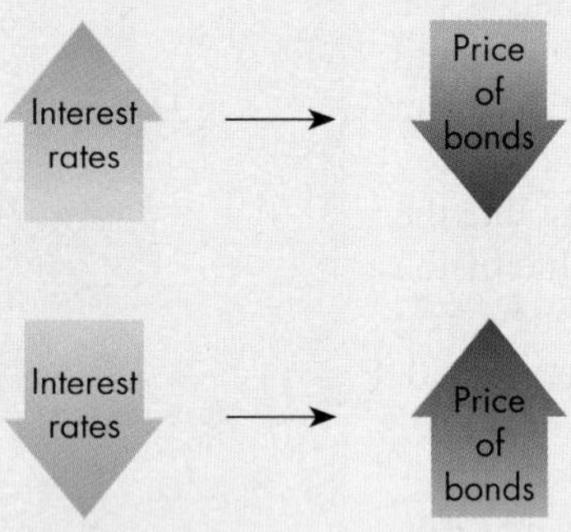

As an example, say that you buy a $1,000, one-year bond with a coupon rate (the fixed rate of interest paid on the bond) of 4 percent when the economy's interest rate is 4 percent. The price of that bond is determined by the formula

$$P = \frac{(1{,}000 + 40)}{1 + r}$$

where r is the interest rate in the economy and the numerator is the face value of the bond and the interest it pays. Since the bond's interest rate is the same as the interest rate for other savings instruments, you pay $1,000 for that bond. Now say that the economy's interest rate falls to 2 percent so that all new bonds being offered pay only 2 percent. That makes your bond especially desirable since it pays a higher interest rate. The price of the bond rises:

$$P = \frac{1{,}040}{1.02} = 1{,}019.61$$

People would be willing to pay up to $1,019.61. Alternatively, if the economy's interest rate rises to 6 percent, as it did in the example in the text, your bond will be less desirable and people would be willing to pay only $981.13. In summary, when the interest rate falls, the price of existing bonds rises, and when the interest rate rises, the price of existing bonds falls.

The longer the length of the bond to maturity, the more the price varies with the change in the interest rate. (For a further discussion of this inverse relationship, see the present value discussion in Appendix A to this chapter.)

In the real world, interest rates fluctuate all the time, and bond investors are continually looking for clues about whether the interest rates are going to rise or fall. When they expect bond prices to rise, they get rid of their cash and buy bonds; when they expect bond prices to fall, they get out of bonds and into cash.

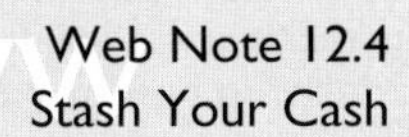

Web Note 12.4
Stash Your Cash

Taking all three of these motives—transactions, precautionary, and speculative—into account, you can see that it makes sense to hold some money even though it is costing you something in forgone interest to do so—and the lower the interest rate, the greater the quantity of money demanded.

The Many Interest Rates in the Economy

As I stated earlier, the economy doesn't have just a single interest rate; it has many, just as there are many types of financial assets. (With recent developments in financial markets, the variety of financial assets grows every year.) Each of these financial assets will have an implicit interest rate associated with it (the implicit interest rate of an asset that pays no interest is the expected percentage change in the price of that asset, so if the asset price is expected to rise by 10 percent, its implicit interest rate is 10 percent). In such a multiple-asset market, which is what we have in the real world, the potential for the interest rate in the loanable funds market (which can be thought of as a composite market for all these varied financial assets) to differ from the interest rate in the market for a particular asset is large. The result can be a financial asset market bubble.

Let's take an example: the housing market in the early 2000s. During that period, housing prices were rising 10–15 percent per year (more than 50 percent in some areas) and were expected to continue to rise. That meant that the implicit rate of interest paid by houses was 10–15 percent (minus the costs of buying and selling the house). The interest rate that one could borrow at—the mortgage rate—was about 5.5 percent, which meant that it made sense to borrow as much as one possibly could and buy as many houses or as big a house as one could. And that's what many people did. As they did, housing prices rose, and the expectations were confirmed, which led to more and more people buying houses for speculative purposes. The strong housing market, because it led to additional construction and expenditures related to house buying, pulled the real economy along and helped the real economy expand. As long as one expected the housing prices to rise at a higher rate than the interest rate at which one could borrow, the strategy of buying as many houses as one could made good sense.

In a multiple-asset market, which is what we have in the real world, the potential for the interest rate in the loanable funds market to differ from the interest rate in the market for a particular asset can be large. The result can be a financial asset market bubble.

In 2006, people lowered their expectations of housing price appreciation, and started expected housing prices to fall. So, many of those who had purchased houses with the intention of selling them at a higher price began to sell their houses more aggressively so that they could return to holding their financial assets in cash before housing prices really fell. The demand for housing decreased substantially, and the equilibrium price of housing available for sale fell. The result was a financial crisis—and its aftermath—that is sufficiently important that it gets an entire chapter devoted to it.

Conclusion

We'll stop our introduction to money and the financial sector here. As you can see, money is central to the operation of the macroeconomy. If money functions smoothly, it keeps the outflow from the expenditure stream (saving) and the flow back into the expenditure stream at a level that reflects people's desires. Money can be treated simply as a mirror of people's real desires. When money doesn't function smoothly, it can cause serious problems.

When money doesn't function smoothly, it can cause serious problems.

Summary

- Money is a highly liquid financial asset that serves as a unit of account, a medium of exchange, and a store of wealth. *(LO12-1)*
- There are various measures of money. The two most important are M_1 and M_2. M_1 consists of currency in the hands of the public, checking account balances, and traveler's checks. M_2 is M_1 plus savings and money market accounts, small-denomination time deposits, and retail money funds. *(LO12-1)*
- Since money is what people believe money to be, creating money out of thin air is easy. How banks create money out of thin air is easily understood if you remember that money is simply a financial liability of a bank. Banks create money by loaning out deposits. *(LO12-2)*
- The money multiplier is $1/r$. It tells you the amount of money ultimately created per dollar deposited in the banking system. *(LO12-2)*
- The financial sector is the market where financial assets are created and exchanged. It channels flows out of the circular flow and back into the circular flow. *(LO12-3)*
- Interest rates play a crucial role in channeling savings back into the economy as investment. *(LO12-4)*

- People hold money for three reasons: (1) the transactions motive, (2) the precautionary motive, and (3) the speculative motive. The demand for money is inversely related to the interest rate paid on money. *(LO12-4)*
- Dramatically higher interest rates paid on particular assets compared to other financial assets can cause bubbles, which can cause problems for an economy. *(LO12-4)*

Key Terms

asset management *(266)*
bank *(260)*
excess reserves *(270)*
Federal Reserve Bank (the Fed) *(260)*
liability management *(266)*
M_1 *(263)*
M_2 *(263)*
money *(260)*
money multiplier *(270)*
precautionary motive *(275)*
reserve ratio *(269)*
reserves *(268)*
speculative motive *(275)*
transactions motive *(275)*

Questions and Exercises

1. If dollar bills (Federal Reserve notes) are backed by nothing but promises and are in real terms worthless, why do people accept them? *(LO12-1)*
2. What are the three functions of money? *(LO12-1)*
3. For each of the following, state whether it is considered money in the United States. Explain why or why not. *(LO12-1)*
   a. A check you write against deposits you have at Bank USA.
   b. Brazilian reals.
   c. The available credit you have on your MasterCard.
   d. Reserves held by banks at the Federal Reserve Bank.
   e. Federal Reserve notes in your wallet.
   f. Gold bullion.
   g. Grocery store coupons.
4. What function is money serving when people compare the price of chicken to the price of beef? *(LO12-1)*
5. How does inflation affect money's function as a store of wealth? *(LO12-1)*
6. What are two components of M_2 that are not components of M_1? *(LO12-1)*
7. Categorize the following as components of M_1, M_2, both, or neither. *(LO12-1)*
   a. State and local government bonds.
   b. Checking accounts.
   c. Money market accounts.
   d. Currency.
   e. Stocks.
   f. Corporate bonds.
   g. Traveler's checks.
8. State the immediate effect of each of the following actions on M_1 and M_2: *(LO12-1)*
   a. Barry writes his plumber a check for $200. The plumber takes the check to the bank, keeps $50 in cash, and deposits the remainder in his savings account.
   b. Maureen deposits the $1,000 from her CD in a money market mutual fund.
   c. Sylvia withdraws $50 in cash from her savings account.
   d. Paulo cashes a $100 traveler's check that was issued in his Ohio bank at a New York bank.
9. Why was character George Bailey in the film *It's a Wonderful Life* right when he stated on the day of a bank run that depositors could not withdraw all their money from the bank? *(LO12-1)*
10. Calculate the money multiplier for each of the following: 5%, 10%, 20%, 25%, 50%, 75%, 100%. *(LO12-2)*
11. If the U.S. government were to raise the reserve requirement to 100 percent, what would likely happen to the interest rate banks pay on deposits? Why? *(LO12-2)*
12. While Jon is walking to school one morning, a helicopter flying overhead drops a $100 bill. Not knowing how to return it, Jon keeps the money and deposits it in his bank. If the bank keeps 5 percent of its money in reserves: *(LO12-2)*
    a. How much money can the bank initially lend out?
    b. After this initial transaction, by how much is the money in the economy changed?
    c. What's the money multiplier?
    d. How much money will eventually be created by the banking system from Jon's $100?
13. True or false? Policy makers in practice use the money multiplier to determine the amount of reserves needed to achieve the desired money supply. Explain. *(LO12-2)*
14. If financial institutions don't produce any tangible real assets, why are they considered a vital part of the U.S. economy? *(LO12-3)*
15. What are two roles of the financial sector? *(LO12-3)*

16. The financial sector channels saving into spending. *(LO12-3)*
    a. What is the risk of the financial sector expanding the spending flow too much?
    b. What kept this from happening in the United States in the early 2000s?
17. State whether the following is an example of the transactions, precautionary, or speculative motive for holding money: *(LO12-4)*
    a. I like to have the flexibility of buying a few things for myself, such as a latte or a snack, every day, so I generally carry $10 in my pocket.
    b. You never know when your car will break down, so I always keep $50 in my pocket.
    c. When the stock market is falling, money managers generally hold more in cash than when the stock market is rising.
    d. Any household has bills that are due every month.
18. If people expect interest rates to rise in the future, how will they change the quantity of money they demand? Explain your answer. *(LO12-4)*
19. In what market are short-term interest rates determined? *(LO12-4)*

Questions from Alternative Perspectives

1. The U.S. government has a monopoly on U.S. dollars.
    a. Could money be supplied privately?
    b. Has money ever been supplied privately? If so, how do you suppose people knew its value? (Austrian)
2. The Federal Reserve's Board of Governors is arguably the most powerful policy-making body in the United States.
    a. Since its inception, how many women have served on the Board of Governors?
    b. What do almost all of the current members of the Board of Governors have in common? www.federalreserve. gov/ bios/boardmembership.htm (Feminist)
3. In Institutional economists' view, money not only serves as a medium of exchange, a unit of account, and a store of wealth, it also operates as an idea that shapes human understanding and interaction. Construct a list of examples during a day's interactions where money operates as an idea whereby people interact or attempt to understand a situation. For example, a friend might say, "Sherry is dating Herbert; she can do better than that!" (Institutionalist)
4. The chapter talks about the role that depositors and banks play in the "creation" of money.
    a. Do you think this role is consistent with the view that the money supply is only determined exogenously by the central bank?
    b. How could depositors and banks endogenously determine the money supply? (Post-Keynesian)
5. While *sharia* (interest) is banned in Islam, profit-sharing is not. An Islamically sound banking practice could be a system in which depositors deposited money under a principle of profit-sharing and the bank provided funds on the same principle with a mark-up as payment for their financial services.
    a. How does this system differ from a system based on interest?
    b. How might the system of interest be exploitative and a system based on profit-sharing not be exploitative? (Religious)

Issues to Ponder

1. Money is to the economy as oil is to an engine. Explain.
2. About 30 U.S. localities circulate their own currency with names like "Ithaca Hours" and "Dillo Hours." Doing so is perfectly legal (although by law they are subject to a 10 percent federal tax, which currently the government is not collecting). These currencies are used as payment for rent, wages, goods, and so on. Are these currencies money? Explain.
3. Economist Michael Bryan reports that on the island of Palau, the Yapese used stone disks as their currency. The number of stones in front of a person's house denoted how rich he or she was.
    a. Would you expect these stones to be used for small transactions?
    b. An Irish-American trader, David O'Keefe, was shipwrecked on the island, and thereafter returned to the

island with a boatload of stones. If they were identical to the existing stones, what would that do to the value of the stones?

c. If O'Keefe's stones could be distinguished from the existing stones, how would that change your answer to *b*?

d. An anthropologist described the stones as "a memory of contributions"—the more stones a person has, the more that person has contributed to the community. Could the same description be used to describe our money?

4. U.S. paper currency is made with several features that are difficult to counterfeit, including a security thread, color-shifting ink, microprinting, a portrait, a watermark, and a fine-line printing pattern. As duplication technology, however, continually improves and more and more counterfeits are circulated, what will happen to the following?
   a. The value of money circulated.
   b. The volume of cashless transactions.
   c. The amount of money the U.S. Treasury spends to introduce additional security measures.

Answers to Margin Questions

1. The three functions of money are (1) medium of exchange, (2) unit of account, and (3) store of wealth. (*p. 261; LO12-1*)
2. Money provides liquidity and ease of payment. People hold money rather than bonds to get this liquidity and hold down transaction costs. (*p. 262; LO12-1*)
3. M_2 would be the larger number since it includes all of the components of M_1 plus additional components. (*p. 264; LO12-1*)
4. Credit cards are not money. Credit cards are a method by which people borrow. (*p. 265; LO12-1*)
5. Banks operate on the fact that they will have some money flowing in and some money flowing out at all times. When the number of withdrawals and deposits is large, on average, they will offset one another, allowing banks to make loans on the average amount that they are holding. If there is one big depositor at a bank, this is less likely to happen, and the bank must hold larger reserves in case that big depositor withdraws that money. (*p. 268; LO12-2*)
6. The money multiplier is $1/r$, which is equal to $1/.2 = 5$. (*p. 269; LO12-2*)
7. I would respond by saying that the financial sector is central to the macroeconomy. It facilitates the trades that occur in the real sector. (*p. 273; LO12-3*)
8. True. A higher risk premium increases the interest payments associated with a loan. To the extent that income used to pay that loan stays the same, higher expenses leaves less to pay off the loan, making default more likely. (*p. 274; LO12-4*)
9. Savings that escape the circular flow can cause fluctuations in the economy. Interest rates help translate the flow of saving into investment, which make their way back into the spending stream. (*p. 274; LO12-4*)
10. People hold money to spend (transactions motive), for unexpected expenses and impulse buying (precautionary motive), and to avoid holding financial assets whose prices are falling (speculative motive). (*p. 275; LO12-4*)

APPENDIX A

A Closer Look at Financial Assets and Liabilities

Financial Assets and Financial Liabilities

To understand the financial sector and its relation to the real sector, you must understand how financial assets and liabilities work and how they affect the real economy.

An *asset* is something that provides its owner with expected future benefits. There are two types of assets: real assets and financial assets. Real assets are assets whose services provide direct benefits to their owners, either now or in the future. A house is a real asset—you can live in it. A machine is a real asset—you can produce goods with it.

Financial assets are *assets, such as stocks or bonds, whose benefit to the owner depends on the issuer of the asset meeting certain obligations.* **Financial liabilities** are *liabilities incurred by the issuer of a financial asset to* *stand behind the issued asset.* It's important to remember that *every financial asset has a corresponding financial liability;* it's that financial liability that gives the financial asset its value. In the case of bonds, for example, a company's agreement to pay interest and repay the principal gives bonds their value. If the company goes bankrupt and reneges on its liability to pay interest and repay the principal, the asset becomes worthless. The corresponding liability gives the financial asset its value.

For example, a **stock** is *a financial asset that conveys ownership rights in a corporation.* It is a liability of the firm; it gives the holder ownership rights that are spelled out in the financial asset. An equity liability such as a stock usually conveys a general right to dividends, but only if the company's board of directors decides to pay them.

A debt liability conveys no ownership right. It's a type of loan. An example of a debt liability is a bond that a firm issues. A **bond** is *a promise to pay certain amounts of money at specified times in the future.* A bond is a liability of the firm but an asset of the individual who holds the bond. A debt liability such as a bond usually conveys legal rights to interest payments and repayment of principal.

Real assets are created by real economic activity. For example, a house or a machine must be built. Financial assets are created whenever somebody takes on a financial liability or establishes an ownership claim. For example, say I promise to pay you $1 billion in the future. You now have a financial asset and I have a financial liability. Understanding that financial assets can be created by a simple agreement between two people is fundamentally important to understanding how the financial sector works.

Valuing Stocks and Bonds

A financial asset's worth comes from the stream of income it will pay in the future. With financial assets such as bonds, that stream of income can be calculated rather precisely. With stocks, where the stream of income is a percentage of the firm's profits, which fluctuate significantly, the stream of future income is uncertain and valuations depend significantly on expectations.

Let's start by considering some generally held beliefs among economists and financial experts. The first is that an average share of stock in a company in a mature industry sells for somewhere between 15 and 20 times its normal profits. The second is that bond prices rise as market interest rates fall, and fall as market interest rates rise. The first step in understanding where the beliefs come from is to recognize that $1 today is not equal to $1 next year. Why? Because if I have $1 today, I can invest it and earn interest (say 10 percent per year), and next year I will have $1.10, not $1. So if the annual interest rate is 10 percent, $1.10 next year is worth $1 today; alternatively, $1 next year is worth roughly 91 cents today. A dollar two years in the future is worth even less today, and dollars 30 years in the future are worth very little today.

Present value is *a method of translating a flow of future income or savings into its current worth.* For example, say a smooth-talking, high-pressure salesperson is wining and dining you. "Isn't that amazing?" the salesman says. "My company will pay $10 a year not only to you, but also to your great-great-great-grandchildren, and more, for 500 years—thousands of dollars in all. And I will sell this annuity—this promise to pay money at periodic intervals in the future—to you for a payment to me now of only $800, but you must act fast. After tonight the price will rise to $2,000."

Do you buy it? My rhetoric suggests that the answer should be no—but can you explain why? And what price *would* you be willing to pay?

To decide how much an annuity is worth, you need some way of valuing that $10 per year. *You can't simply add up the $10 five hundred times.* Doing so is wrong. Instead you must *discount* all future dollars by the interest rate in the economy. Discounting is required because a dollar in the future is not worth a dollar now.

If you have $1 now, you can take that dollar, put it in the bank, and in a year you will have that dollar plus interest. If the interest rate you can get from the bank is 5 percent, that dollar will grow to $1.05 a year from now. That means if the interest rate is 5 percent, if you have 95 cents now, in a year it will be worth nearly a dollar ($0.9975 = $0.95 + 5% × $0.95 to be exact). Reversing the reasoning, $1 one year in the future is worth a little bit more than 95 cents today. So the present value of $1 one year in the future at a 5 percent interest rate is 95 cents.

A dollar *two* years from now is worth even less today. Carry out that same reasoning and you'll find that if the interest rate is 5 percent, $1 two years from now is worth approximately 90 cents today. Why? Because you could take 90 cents now, put it in the bank at 5 percent interest, and in two years have almost $1.

The Present Value Formula

Carrying out such reasoning for every case would be a real pain. But luckily, there's a formula and a table that can be used to determine the present value (PV) of future income. The formula is

$$PV = A_1/(1 + i) + A_2/(1 + i)^2 + \cdots + A_n/(1 + i)^n$$

where

A_n = the amount of money received n periods in the future

i = the interest rate in the economy (assumed constant)

TABLE A12-1 (A AND B) Sample Present Value and Annuity Tables

	Interest Rate						
Year	3%	4%	6%	9%	12%	15%	18%
1	$0.97	$0.96	$0.94	$0.92	$0.89	$0.87	$0.85
2	0.94	0.92	0.89	0.84	0.80	0.76	0.72
3	0.92	0.89	0.84	0.77	0.71	0.66	0.61
4	0.89	0.85	0.79	0.71	0.64	0.57	0.52
5	0.86	0.82	0.75	0.65	0.57	0.50	0.44
6	0.84	0.79	0.70	0.60	0.51	0.43	0.37
7	0.81	0.76	0.67	0.55	0.45	0.38	0.31
8	0.79	0.73	0.63	0.50	0.40	0.33	0.27
9	0.77	0.70	0.59	0.46	0.36	0.28	0.23
10	0.74	0.68	0.56	0.42	0.32	0.25	0.19
15	0.64	0.56	0.42	0.27	0.18	0.12	0.08
20	0.55	0.46	0.31	0.18	0.10	0.06	0.04
30	0.41	0.31	0.17	0.08	0.03	0.02	0.01
40	0.31	0.21	0.10	0.03	0.01	0.00	0.00
50	0.23	0.14	0.05	0.01	0.00	0.00	0.00

(a) Present Value Table (value now of $1 to be received *x* years in the future)
The present value table converts a future amount into a present amount.

	Interest Rate						
Number of Years	3%	4%	6%	9%	12%	15%	18%
1	$ 0.97	$ 0.96	$ 0.94	$ 0.92	$0.89	$0.87	$0.85
2	1.91	1.89	1.83	1.76	1.69	1.63	1.57
3	2.83	2.78	2.67	2.53	2.40	2.28	2.17
4	3.72	3.63	3.47	3.24	3.04	2.85	2.69
5	4.58	4.45	4.21	3.89	3.60	3.35	3.13
6	5.42	5.24	4.92	4.49	4.11	3.78	3.50
7	6.23	6.00	5.58	5.03	4.56	4.16	3.81
8	7.02	6.73	6.21	5.53	4.97	4.49	4.08
9	7.79	7.44	6.80	6.00	5.33	4.77	4.30
10	8.53	8.11	7.36	6.42	5.65	5.02	4.49
15	11.94	11.12	9.71	8.06	6.81	5.85	5.09
20	14.88	13.59	11.47	9.13	7.47	6.26	5.35
30	19.60	17.29	13.76	10.27	8.06	6.57	5.52
40	23.11	19.79	15.05	10.76	8.24	6.64	5.55
50	25.73	21.48	15.76	10.96	8.30	6.66	5.55

(b) Annuity Table (value now of $1 per year to be received for *x* years)
The annuity table converts a known stream of income into a present amount.

Solving this formula for any time period longer than one or two years is complicated. To deal with it, people either use a business calculator or a present value table such as the one in Table A12-1.

Table A12-1(a) gives the present value of a single dollar at some time in the future at various interest rates. Notice a couple of things about the chart. First, the further into the future one goes, the lower the present value. Second, the higher the interest rate, the lower the present value. At a 12 percent interest rate, $1 fifty years from now has a present value of essentially zero.

Table A12-1(b) is an annuity table; it tells us how much a constant stream of income for a specific number of years is worth. Notice that as the interest rate rises, the value of an annuity falls. At an 18 percent interest rate, $1 per year for 50 years has a present value of $5.55. To get the value of amounts other than $1, simply multiply the entry in the table by the amount. For example, $10 per year for 50 years at 18 percent interest is 10 × $5.55, or $55.50.

As you can see, the interest rate in the economy is a key to present value. *You must know the interest rate to know the value of money over time.* The higher the current (and assumed constant) interest rate, the more a given amount of money in the present will be worth in the future. Or, alternatively, the higher the current interest rate, the less a given amount of money in the future will be worth in the present.

Some Rules of Thumb for Determining Present Value

Sometimes you don't have a present value table or a business calculator handy. For those times, there are a few rules of thumb and simplified formulas for which you don't need either a present value table or a calculator. Let's consider two of them: the infinite annuity rule and the Rule of 72.

THE ANNUITY RULE To find the present value of an annuity that will pay $1 for an infinite number of years in the future when the interest rate is 5 percent, we simply divide $1 by 5 percent (.05). Doing so gives us $20. So at 5 percent, $1 a year paid to you forever has a present value of $20. The **annuity rule** is that *the present value of any annuity is the annual income it yields divided by the interest rate.* Our general annuity rule for any annuity is expressed as

$$PV = X/i$$

That is, the present value of an infinite flow in income, X, is that income divided by the interest rate, i.

Most of the time, people don't offer to sell you annuities for the infinite future. A typical annuity runs for 30, 40, or 50 years. However, the annuity rule is still useful. As you can see from the present value table, in 30 years

REAL-WORLD APPLICATION

The Press and Present Value

The failure to understand the concept of present value often shows up in the popular press. Here are three examples.

Headline: **COURT SETTLEMENT IS $40,000,000.**

Inside story: The money will be paid out over a 40-year period.

Actual value: $11,925,000 (8 percent interest rate).

Headline: **DISABLED WIDOW WINS $25 MILLION LOTTERY**

Inside story: The money will be paid over 20 years.

Actual value: $13,254,499 (8 percent interest rate).

Headline: **BOND ISSUE TO COST TAXPAYERS $68 MILLION**

Inside story: The $68 million is the total of interest and principal payments. The interest is paid yearly; the principal won't be paid back to the bond purchasers until 30 years from now.

Actual value: $20,000,000 (8 percent interest rate).

Such stories are common. Be on the lookout for them as you read the newspaper or watch the evening news.

at a 9 percent interest rate, the present value of $1 isn't much (it's 8 cents), so we can use this infinite flow formula as an approximation of long-lasting, but less than infinite, flows of future income. We simply subtract a little bit from what we get with our formula. The longer the time period, the less we subtract. For example, say you are wondering what $200 a year for 40 years is worth when the interest rate is 8 percent. Dividing $200 by .08 gives $2,500, so we know the annuity must be worth a bit less than $2,500. (It's actually worth $2,411.)

The annuity rule allows us to answer the question posed at the beginning of this section: How much is $10 a year for 500 years' worth right now? The answer is that it depends on the interest rate you could earn on a specified amount of money now. If the interest rate is 10 percent, the maximum you should be willing to pay for that 500-year $10 annuity is $100:

$10/.10 = $100

If the interest rate is 5 percent, the most you should pay is $200 ($10/.05 = $200). So now you know why you should have said no to that supersalesman who offered it to you for $800.

THE RULE OF 72 A second rule of thumb for determining present values of shorter time periods is the **Rule of 72,** which states:

> *The number of years it takes for a certain amount to double in value is equal to 72 divided by the rate of interest.*

Say, for example, that the interest rate is 4 percent. How long will it take for your $100 to become $200? Dividing 72 by 4 gives 18, so the answer is 18 years. Conversely, at a 4 percent interest rate the present value of $200 eighteen years in the future is about $100. (Actually it's $102.67.)

Alternatively, say that you will receive $1,000 in 10 years. Is it worth paying $500 for that amount now if the interest rate is 9 percent? Using the rule of 72, we know that at a 9 percent interest rate it will take about eight years for $500 to double:

72/9 = 8

So the future value of $500 in 10 years is more than $1,000. It's probably about $1,200. (Actually it's $1,184.) So if the interest rate in the economy is 9 percent, it's not worth paying $500 now in order to get that $1,000 in 10 years. By investing that same $500 today at 9 percent, you can have $1,184 in 10 years.

The Importance of Present Value

Many business decisions require such present value calculations. In almost any business, you'll be looking at flows of income in the future and comparing them to present costs or to other flows of money in the future.

Generally, however, when most people calculate present value, they don't use any of the formulas. They go to their computer, press in the numbers to calculate the present value, and watch while the computer displays the results.

Let's now use our knowledge of present value to explain the two observations at the beginning of this section: (1) an average share of stock sells for between 15 and 20 times its normal profits and (2) bond prices and interest rates are inversely related. Since all financial

ADDED DIMENSION

Do Financial Assets Make Society Richer?

Financial assets are neat. You can call them into existence simply by getting someone to accept your IOU. *Remember, every financial asset has a corresponding financial liability equal to it.* So when individuals in a country increase their financial assets by $1 trillion, they are also increasing their financial liabilities by $1 trillion. An optimist would say a country is rich. A pessimist would say it's poor. An economist would say that financial assets and financial liabilities are simply opposite sides of the ledger and don't indicate whether a country is rich or poor. You have to go beyond financial assets and liabilities.

To find out whether a country is rich or poor, you must look at its *real assets.* If financial assets increase the economy's efficiency and thereby increase the amount of real assets, they make society better off. This is most economists' view of financial assets. If, however, they decrease the efficiency of the economy (as some economists have suggested some financial assets do because they focus productive effort on financial gamesmanship), financial assets make society worse off.

The same correspondence between a financial asset and its liability exists when a financial asset's value changes. Say stock prices fall significantly. Is society poorer? The answer is: It depends on the reason for the change. Let's say there is no known reason. Then, while the people who own the stock are poorer, the people who might want to buy stock in the future are richer since the price of assets has fallen. So in a pure accounting sense, society is neither richer nor poorer when the prices of stocks rise or fall for no reason.

But there are ways in which changes in the value of financial assets might signify that society is richer or poorer. For example, the changes in the values of financial assets might *reflect* (rather than cause) real changes. If suddenly a company finds a cure for cancer, its stock prices will rise and society will be richer. But the rise in the price of the stock doesn't cause society to be richer. It reflects the discovery that made society richer. Society would be richer because of the discovery even if the stock's price didn't rise.

There's significant debate about how well the stock market reflects real changes in the economy. Classical economists believe it closely reflects real changes; Keynesian economists believe it doesn't. But both sides agree that the changes in the real economy, not the changes in the price of financial assets, underlie what makes an economy richer or poorer.

assets can be broken down into promises to pay certain amounts at certain times in the future, we can determine their value with the present value formula. If the asset is a bond, it consists of a stream of income payments over a number of years and the repayment of the face value of the bond. Each year's interest payment and the eventual repayment of the face value must be calculated separately, and then the results must be added together.

If the financial asset is a share of stock, the valuation is a bit less clear since a stock does not guarantee the payment of anything definite—just a share of the profits. No profits, no payment. So, with stocks, expectations of profits are of central importance. Let's consider an example: Say a share of stock is earning $1 per share per year and is expected to continue to earn that long into the future. Using the annuity rule and an interest rate of 6.5 percent, the present value of that future stream of expected earnings is about 1/.065, or a bit more than $15. Assuming profits are expected to grow slightly, that would mean that the stock should sell for somewhere around $20, or 20 times its profit per share, which is the explanation to economists' view that an average stock sells for about 15 times normal profits.

To see the answer to the second—bond prices and interest rates are inversely related—say the interest rate rises to 10 percent. Then the value of the stock or bond that is earning a fixed amount—in this case $1 per share—will go down to $10. Interest rate up, value of stock or bond down. This is the explanation of the second observation.

There is nothing immutable in the above reasoning. For example, if promises to pay aren't trustworthy, you don't put the amount that's promised into your calculation; you put in the amount you actually expect to receive. That's why when a company or a country looks as if it's going to default on loans or stop paying dividends, the value of its bonds and stock will fall considerably. For example, in the early 2000s, many people thought Argentina would default on its bonds. That expectation caused the price of Argentinean bonds to fall and interest rates to rise more than 30 percentage points.

Of course, the expectations could go in the opposite direction. Say that the interest rate is 10 percent, and that you expect a company's annual profit, which is now $1 per share, to grow by 10 percent per year. In that case, since expected profit growth is as high as the interest rate, the current value of the stock is infinite. It is such expectations of future profit growth that fueled the Internet stock craze in the late 1990s and caused the valuation of firms with no current profits (indeed, many were experiencing significant losses) at multiples of sales of 300 or more. Financial valuations based on such optimistic expectations are the reason most economists considered the stock market in Internet stocks to be significantly overvalued in the late 1990s and correctly predicted the fall in prices that occurred in 2001 and 2002.

Key Terms

annuity rule *(282)*
bond *(281)*
financial assets *(280)*
financial liabilities *(280)*
present value *(281)*
Rule of 72 *(283)*
stock *(281)*

Questions and Exercises

1. If the government prints new $1,000 bills and gives them to all introductory students who are using the Colander text, who incurs a financial liability and who gains a financial asset?
2. Is the currency in your pocketbook or wallet a real or a financial asset? Why?
3. Joe, your study partner, has just said that, in economic terminology, when he buys a bond he is investing. Is he correct? Why?
4. Joan, your study partner, has just made the following statement: "A loan is a loan and therefore cannot be an asset." Is she correct? Why or why not?
5. How much is $50 to be received 50 years from now worth if the interest rate is 6 percent? (Use Table A12-1.)
6. How much is $50 to be received 50 years from now worth if the interest rate is 9 percent? (Use Table A12-1.)
7. Your employer offers you a choice of two bonus packages: $1,400 today or $2,000 five years from now. Assuming a 6 percent rate of interest, which is the better value? Assuming an interest rate of 10 percent, which is the better value?
8. Suppose the price of a one-year bond with a $100 face value that pays 10 percent interest is $98.
   a. Are market interest rates likely to be above or below 10 percent? Explain.
   b. What is the bond's yield or return?
   c. If market interest rates fell, what would happen to the price of the bond?
9. Explain in words why the present value of $100 to be received in 10 years would decline as the interest rate rises.
10. A 6 percent bond will pay you $1,060 one year from now. The interest rate in the economy is 10 percent. How much is that bond worth now?
11. You are to receive $100 a year for the next 40 years. How much is it worth now if the current interest rate in the economy is 6 percent? (Use Table A12-1.)
12. You are to receive $200 in 30 years. About how much is it worth now? (The interest rate is 3 percent.)
13. A salesperson calls you up and offers you $200 a year for life. If the interest rate is 9 percent, how much should you be willing to pay for that annuity?
14. The same salesperson offers you a lump sum of $20,000 in 10 years. How much should you be willing to pay? (The interest rate is still 9 percent.)
15. What is the present value of a cash flow of $100 per year forever (a perpetuity), assuming:
    The interest rate is 10 percent.
    The interest rate is 5 percent.
    The interest rate is 20 percent.
    a. Working with those same three interest rates, what are the future values of $100 today in one year? How about in two years?
    b. Working with those same three interest rates, how long will it take you to double your money?
16. State whether you agree or disagree with the following statements:
    a. If stock market prices go up, the economy is richer.
    b. A real asset worth $1 million is more valuable to an individual than a financial asset worth $1 million.
    c. Financial assets have no value to society since each has a corresponding liability.
    d. The United States has much more land than does Japan. Therefore, the value of all U.S. land should significantly exceed the value of land in Japan.
    e. U.S. GDP exceeds Japan's GDP; therefore, the stock market valuation of U.S.-based companies should exceed that of Japan-based companies.

chapter 13

Monetary Policy

> *There have been three great inventions since the beginning of time: fire, the wheel and central banking.*
>
> —Will Rogers

After reading this chapter, you should be able to:

- **LO13-1** Explain how monetary policy works in the *AS/AD* model in both the traditional and structural stagnation models.
- **LO13-2** Discuss how monetary policy works in practice.
- **LO13-3** Discuss the tools of conventional monetary policy.
- **LO13-4** Discuss the complex nature of monetary policy and the importance of central bank credibility.

The chairman of the U.S central bank—the Federal Reserve Bank, or "the Fed"—is often called the second most important person in government. He (or she) is in charge of maintaining the financial health of the economy. Thus, when the financial sector almost seized up in the fall of 2008, the Fed stepped in and undertook policies to try to prevent it from collapsing. Those policies were part of its "lender of last resort" function in times of financial crisis.

It isn't only in financial crises that the Fed is important. In normal times, it is responsible for the country's monetary policy, and in this chapter I discuss the Fed's role and monetary policy in normal conditions. (In the next chapter I discuss the Fed's role in a financial crisis and the debate about its recent unconventional policy.) **Monetary policy** is *a policy of influencing the economy through changes in the banking system's reserves that influence the money supply, credit availability, and interest rates in the economy.* Unlike fiscal policy, which is controlled by the government directly, monetary policy is controlled by the U.S. central bank, the Fed.

How Monetary Policy Works in the Models

Monetary policy works through its influence on credit conditions and the interest rate in the economy. In Figure 13-1(a), I show how it works in the standard macro model. Expansionary monetary policy shifts the *AD* curve out to the right and contractionary monetary policy shifts it in to the left. Changes in nominal income will be split between changes in real income and changes in the price level.

If the economy is significantly above potential output, once long-run equilibrium is reached, monetary policy affects only nominal income and the price level, as shown in Figure 13-1(b). Real output remains unchanged. Suppose the economy begins at potential output Y_P (point *A*), and expansionary monetary policy shifts the *AD* curve from AD_0 to AD_1. Because the economy is beyond potential, rising factor cost pressures very quickly shift the *SAS* curve up from SAS_0 to SAS_1. Once the long-run equilibrium has been reached, the price level rises from P_0 to P_1 and real output returns to potential output (point *B*). So, beyond potential output, expansionary monetary policy does not affect real output.

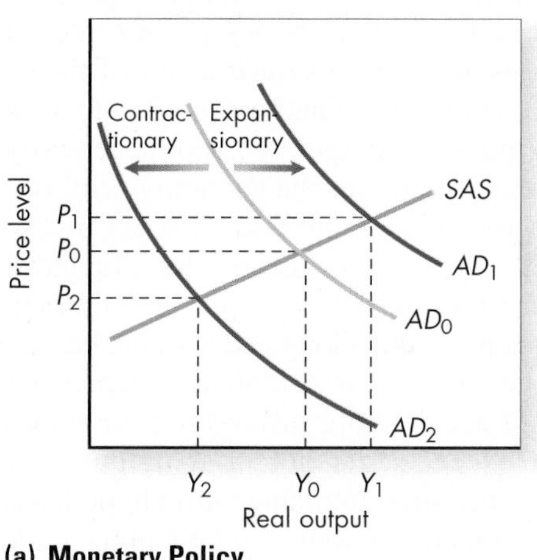

(a) Monetary Policy

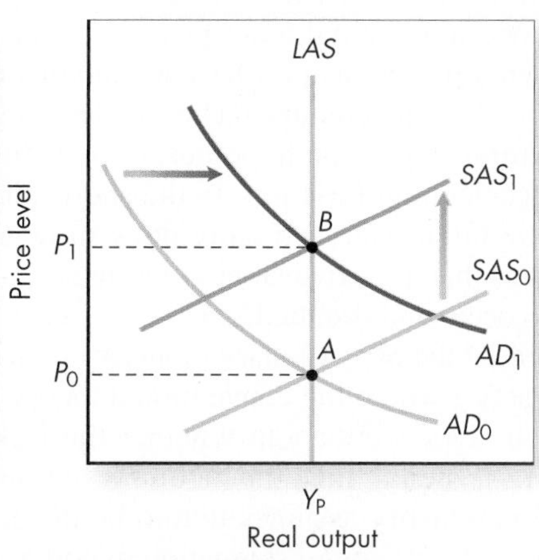

(b) Expansionary Monetary Policy beyond Potential Output

FIGURE 13-1 (A AND B) The Effect of Monetary Policy in the *AS/AD* Model

Expansionary monetary policy shifts the *AD* curve to the right; contractionary monetary policy shifts the *AD* curve to the left. In (**a**) we see how monetary policy affects both real output and the price level. If the economy is at or above potential, as in (**b**), expansionary monetary policy will cause input costs to rise, which will eventually shift the *SAS* curve up enough so that real output remains unchanged. The only long-run effect of expansionary monetary policy when the economy is above potential is to increase the price level.

The general rule is: Expansionary monetary policy increases nominal income. Its effect on real income depends on how the price level responds:

$$\%\Delta\text{Real income} = \%\Delta\text{Nominal income} - \%\Delta\text{Price level}$$

Thus, if nominal income rises by 5 percent and the price level rises by 2 percent, real income will rise by 3 percent.

Let's see how monetary policy works in the standard model. As mentioned in a previous chapter, policy changes aggregate expenditures and shifts the aggregate demand curve out to the right or in to the left. Monetary policy affects aggregate demand indirectly by changing short-term and long-term interest rates. Here's how: Expansionary monetary policy adds reserves to banks. When banks have more reserves, they will be more inclined to lend those reserves. It's better to earn 4 percent interest on a loan than 0.25 percent interest from the Fed. To attract borrowers, banks will have an incentive to reduce their interest rates on loans. Later in the chapter we will talk about the way in which the process actually works, but for now simply recognize that when the Fed increases reserves in the banking system, banks have an incentive to lower interest rates. As interest rates fall, investment expenditures rise, which shifts the aggregate demand curve to the right, as we saw in Figure 13-1. The opposite happens when the Fed reduces reserves, and therefore money, in the economy.

Q-1 Demonstrate the effect of expansionary monetary policy in the *AS/AD* model.

Summarizing, **expansionary monetary policy** is *a policy that increases the money supply and decreases the interest rate.* It tends to *increase* both investment and output.

Expansionary monetary policy is monetary policy aimed at reducing interest rates and raising the level of aggregate demand.

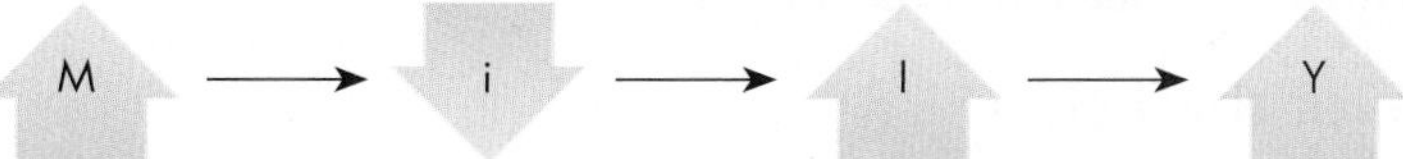

Contractionary monetary policy works in the opposite direction. **Contractionary monetary policy** is *a policy that decreases the money supply and increases the interest rate.* It tends to *decrease* both investment and output.

Contractionary monetary policy is monetary policy aimed at increasing interest rates and thereby restraining aggregate demand.

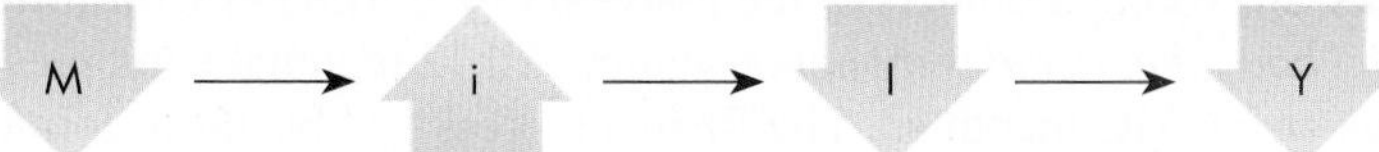

If the domestic price level of goods is largely determined by world prices, as it is in the structural stagnation hypothesis, the effect of expansionary monetary policy is slightly different. In this case, monetary policy can have less direct effect on output, and more effect on financial asset prices. Expansionary monetary policy pushes interest rates down, financial asset prices up, and increases the country's trade deficit. This occurs even when the country has exceeded its globally constrained potential output. In the structural stagnation hypothesis, exceeding potential output does not necessarily lead to accelerating inflation. In the short run, this is good for the economy. Unfortunately, the inflationary pressure does show up somewhere—in rises in asset prices. This means that the expansionary monetary policy increases the chance for a financial bubble to occur and eventually burst. So in the structural stagnation hypothesis, the negative effect of the expansionary monetary policy comes with a long and variable lag.

In practice where the conventional theory and the structural stagnation hypothesis differ is in their view about whether the lack of accelerating inflation in the goods market is a signal that the country has not exceeded its potential output.

In practice where the conventional theory and the structural stagnation hypothesis differ is in their view about whether the lack of accelerating inflation in the goods market is a signal that the country has not exceeded its potential output. The conventional theory assumes that to be the case; the structural stagnation hypothesis does not. In the structural stagnation hypothesis, you need to look at international trade conditions and asset market prices as well as goods market inflation to see if the economy is exceeding its potential output.

How Monetary Policy Works in Practice

Models make it all look so easy. Would that it were so easy. The reality of monetary policy is much messier and more complicated, and in this section, I discuss some of the institutional details that make monetary policy so complicated. I begin with a short summary of the structure and workings of the Federal Reserve Bank of the United States.

Monetary Policy and the Fed

Monetary policy is conducted by a country's **central bank**—*a type of banker's bank whose financial obligations underlie an economy's money supply*. The central bank in the United States is the Fed. If commercial banks (the banks you and I use) need to borrow money, they go to the central bank. If there's a financial panic and a run on banks, the central bank is there to make loans to the banks until the panic goes away. Since its IOUs (I owe you's) are cash, the Fed can create money simply by issuing an IOU. It is this ability to create money that gives the central bank the power to control monetary policy. (A central bank also serves as a financial adviser to government. As is often the case with financial advisers, the government sometimes doesn't like the advice and doesn't follow it.)

It is the central bank's ability to create money that gives it the power to control monetary policy.

In many countries, such as Great Britain, the central bank is a part of the government, just as this country's Department of the Treasury and the Department of Commerce are part of the U.S. government. In the United States, the central bank is not part of the government in the same way. The box "Central Banks in Other Countries" on page 673 gives you an idea of some differences.

Structure of the Fed

WWW Web Note 13.1 Other Central Banks

Q-2 What group of the Fed decides monetary policy?

The Fed is not just one bank; it is composed of 12 regional banks along with the main Federal Reserve Bank, whose headquarters are in Washington, D.C. The Fed is governed by a seven-member Board of Governors. Members of the Board of Governors, together with the president of the New York Fed and a rotating group of four presidents of the other regional banks, are voting members of the **Federal Open Market Committee (FOMC),** *the Fed's chief body that decides monetary policy*. All 12 regional bank presidents attend, and can speak at, FOMC meetings. The financial press and business community follow their discussions closely. There are even Fed watchers whose sole occupation is to follow what the Fed is doing and to tell people what it will likely do.

REAL-WORLD APPLICATION

Central Banks in Other Countries

In the United States, the central bank is the Fed, and much of this chapter is about its structure. But the Fed is only one of many central banks in the world. Let's briefly introduce you to some of the others.

The People's Bank of China

The People's Bank of China (PBOC) was established in 1948, shortly after the communist victory and the establishment of the People's Republic of China, by nationalizing all Chinese banks and incorporating them into a single bank. (The former Chinese central bank, named the Central Bank of China, was relocated to Taipei in 1949 and is the central bank for Taiwan.) From 1949 to 1978, the PBOC was the only bank in the People's Republic of China.

In the 1980s the commercial banking functions of the PBOC were split off into state-owned independent banks, and the PBOC began focusing on central bank functions such as monetary policy and regulation of the financial sector. In 1995, it was restructured and consciously modeled after the U.S. Fed. It opened nine regional branches and focused its operations on foreign reserve issues, monetary policy, and financial regulation.

People's Bank of China

European Central Bank

In the late 1990s a number of European Union countries formed a monetary union, creating a common currency called the euro, and a new central bank called the European Central Bank (ECB), whose structure is still evolving. As of 2012, the governing council had 29 members, including the heads of the 17 countries that had adopted the euro as their currency, plus 10 non-euro area countries.

The primary objective of the ECB is different from the Fed's; the ECB is focused solely on maintaining price stability, as was the former German central bank, the Bundesbank, after which it was modeled. Some economists have considered the ECB an expansion of the Bundesbank for the entire EU.

Most economists hold a wait-and-see attitude about the bank. They point out that the ECB is a new bank and it will take time for its operating procedures to become established. In the European financial crisis of 2012 the EU took an active role in attempting to prevent a collapse of the European banking system as banks struggled to deal with the fall in value of Greek and other southern European countries' bonds. In doing so, it went far beyond its initially envisaged role of preventing inflation.

The Bank of England

The Bank of England is sometimes called the Old Lady of Threadneedle Street (because it's located on that street, and the British like such quaint characterizations). It does not use a required reserve mechanism. Instead, individual banks determine their own needed reserves, so any reserves they have would, in a sense, be excess reserves. Needless to say, bank reserves tend to be much lower in England than they are in the United States.

How does the Old Lady control the money supply? Until recently, with the equivalent of open market operations and with informal directives to banks, what might be called "tea control." Since England has only a few large banks, the Old Lady passed on the word at tea as to which direction she thought the money supply should be going and the banks complied. Alas for sentimentalists, "tea control" is fading in England, as are many quaint English ways.

The Bank of Japan

Like the People's Bank of China, the Bank of Japan is quite similar to the Fed. It uses primarily open market operations to control the money supply. Reserve requirements are similar to the Fed's, but because it allows banks a longer period in which to do their averaging, and Japan does not have the many small banks that the United States does. (It is small banks that often hold excess reserves in the United States.), excess reserves tend to be lower in Japan than in the United States. The Japanese financial system exhibits more interdependence between the central bank, commercial banks, and industry than does the U.S. system, which means that Japanese companies get more of their funding from commercial banks, which in turn borrow more from the Bank of Japan than U.S. commercial banks borrow from the Fed. The financial position of many Japanese commercial banks was questionable over the past decade, and the Bank of Japan worked with the banks to restructure loans without causing a breakdown of the financial system.

Clearly, there's more to be said about each of these central banks, but this brief introduction should give you a sense of both the similarities and the diversities among the central banks of the world.

Web Note 13.2
The Fed

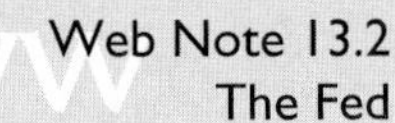

The president of the United States appoints each governor for a term of 14 years, although most governors choose not to complete their terms. The president also designates one of the governors to be the chairperson of the Fed for a four-year term. A chairperson can serve multiple terms, and the Fed chairperson is sometimes referred to as the second most powerful person in Washington (the most powerful being the president of the United States).

The Fed's general structure reflects its political history. Figure 13-2 demonstrates that structure. Notice in Figure 13-2(a) that most of the 12 regional Fed banks are in

FIGURE 13-2 (A AND B) The Federal Reserve System

The Federal Reserve System is composed of 12 regional banks. It is run by the Board of Governors. The Federal Open Market Committee (FOMC) is the most important policy-making body.

Source: The Federal Reserve System (www.federalreserve.gov).

*Alaska and Hawaii are also under the jurisdiction of the Federal Reserve Bank of San Francisco.

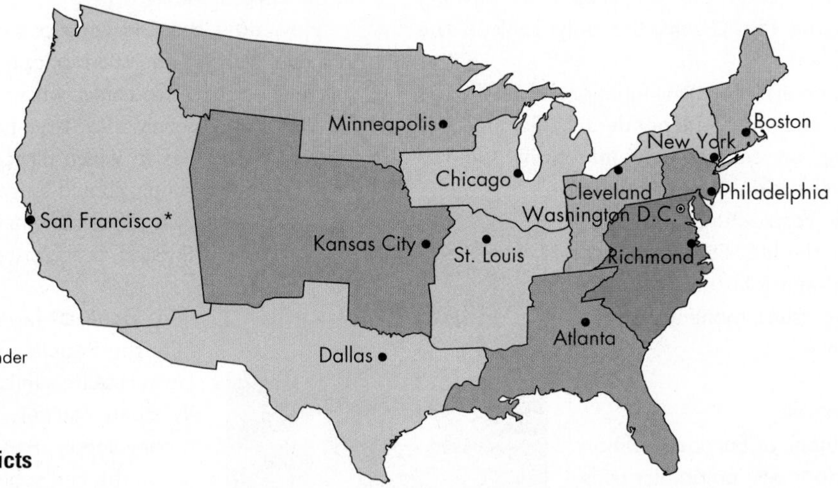

(a) Federal Reserve Districts

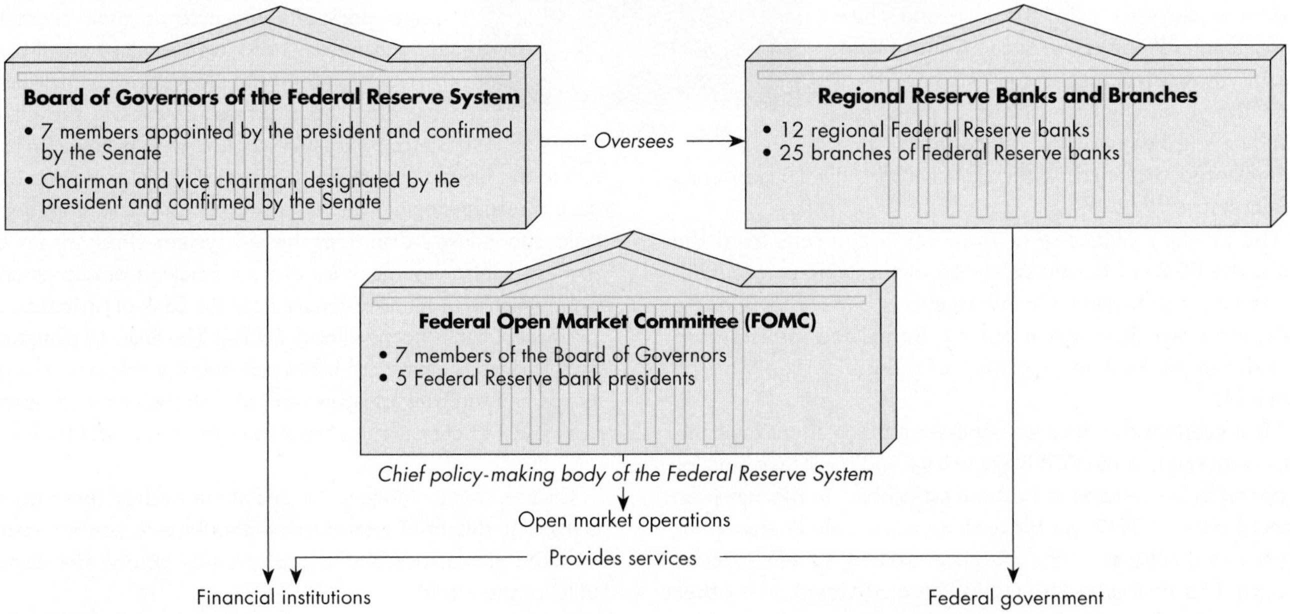

(b) Federal Reserve Structure

ADDED DIMENSION

How Independent Should the Central Bank Be?

The Fed is relatively independent, but not all central banks are. One of the big debates in the early 2000s concerned how independent the central bank should be. Advocates of central bank independence argued that independence allows central banks to make the hard political decisions that a government influenced by political pressures cannot make. Increasing interest rates hurts—it slows down the economy and causes unemployment. But if the economy is above its sustainable level, it needs to be slowed down, or inflation will accelerate. As former Fed chairman William Martin said, "The job of the Federal Reserve is to take away the punch bowl just when the party is getting good." Independence, such as exists with the U.S. central bank, gives the Fed the ability to do that.

In some developing countries, the central bank is part of the government—and economists have found that when that is the case, the punch bowl tends to remain out longer. The result is that the money supply is more expansionary, and there tend to be higher levels of inflation.

There are many dimensions of independence—one is *goal independence* and another is *policy instrument independence*. Goal independence is having the freedom to determine what ultimate goals, such as low unemployment or low inflation, take priority. Policy instrument independence is having the freedom to determine how to achieve those goals. Many economists point out that goal independence is not necessarily a good thing. In a democracy goals are determined in the political process, and in a well-functioning democracy, the central bank is accountable for achieving the goals set by the political process, and does not set the goals itself. Once the goals are set, then one can talk about policy instrument independence.

Alan Blinder, former vice chairman of the Fed, put it this way:

> The independence of the Fed means, to me, two things. First, that we have very broad latitude to pursue our goals as we see fit; we decide what to do in pursuit of those goals.
>
> Second, it means that once our monetary policy decisions are made, they cannot be reversed by anybody in the U.S. government—except under extreme circumstances. (Congress would have to pass a law limiting the power of the Fed.) But although we are free to choose the means by which we achieve our goals, the goals themselves are given to us by statute, by the U.S. Congress. And that is how it should be in a democracy.

In the United States, the Fed has policy instrument independence, but not goal independence. By federal law, the goals of the Federal Reserve Bank are "maximum employment," "stable prices," and "moderate long-term interest rates." Those are different goals than the goals of the European Central Bank (ECB); the ECB's goal is only "stable prices." These different goals, however, become almost identical if one believes, as a number of economists do, that the only way to achieve maximum employment and moderate long-term interest rates is by achieving stable prices.

the East and Midwest. The South and West have only three banks: Atlanta, Dallas, and San Francisco. The reason is that in 1913, when the Fed was established, the West and South were less populated and less important economically than the rest of the country, so fewer banks were established there.

As these regions grew, the original structure remained because no one wanted to go through the political wrangling that restructuring would bring about. Instead, the southern and western regional Feds established a number of branches to handle their banking needs.

Even though each of the 12 geographic districts has a separate regional Federal Reserve bank, these regional banks have little direct power over the banking system. District banks and their branch banks handle administrative matters and gather information about business and banking conditions in their geographic regions for the Fed.

Duties of the Fed

In legislation establishing the Fed, Congress gave it six explicit functions:

1. Conducting monetary policy (influencing the supply of money and credit in the economy).
2. Supervising and regulating financial institutions.

3. Serving as a lender of last resort to financial institutions.
4. Providing banking services to the U.S. government.
5. Issuing coin and currency.
6. Providing financial services (such as check clearing) to commercial banks, savings and loan associations, savings banks, and credit unions.

In normal times, the most important of these functions is monetary policy. In times of financial crisis, the "lender of last resort" function is the most important. In this chapter I focus on monetary policy in normal times. In the next chapter when I discuss the Fed's reaction to the financial crisis of 2008 and 2009, I will focus more on the "lender of last resort" function.

The Tools of Conventional Monetary Policy

WWW Web Note 13.3 The FOMC

You've already seen that monetary policy shifts the *AD* curve. Let's now consider how it does so in practice. To do so, we need to look more specifically at the institutional structure of the banking system and the role of the Fed in that institutional structure.

Think back to our discussion of the banking system in the last chapter. Banks take in deposits, make loans, and buy other financial assets, keeping a certain percentage of reserves for those transactions. Those reserves are IOUs of the Fed—either vault cash held by banks or deposits at the Fed. *Vault cash, deposits at the Fed, plus currency in circulation* make up the **monetary base.** The monetary base held at banks serves as legal reserves of the banking system. By controlling the monetary base, the Fed can influence the amount of money in the economy and the activities of banks. The money supply is determined directly by the monetary base (the amount of IOUs that the Fed has outstanding), and, indirectly, by the amount of credit that banks extend.

Allowable reserves are either banks' vault cash or deposits at the Fed.

Open Market Operations

The primary way that the Fed changes the amount of reserves in the system is through **open market operations**—*the Fed's buying and selling of Treasury bills and Treasury bonds* (the only type of asset that, until recently, the Fed held in any appreciable quantity). These open market operations are the primary tool of monetary policy in normal times.

The Fed's buying and selling of government securities is called open market operations.

When the Fed buys Treasury bills and Treasury bonds, it pays for them with IOUs that serve as reserves for banks. These IOUs don't have to be a written piece of paper. They may simply be a computer entry credited to a bank's account at the Fed.

Because the IOUs that the Fed uses to buy a government security serve as reserves to the banking system, with the simple act of buying a Treasury bond and paying for it with its IOU, the Fed can increase the money supply (since this creates reserves for the bank). To increase the money supply, the Fed goes to the bond market, buys a bond, and pays for it with its IOU. The individual or firm that sold the bond now has an IOU of the Fed. When the individual or firm deposits the IOU in a bank—presto!—the reserves of the banking system are increased. If the Fed buys bonds, it increases the monetary base. The total money supply rises by the increase in the monetary base times the money multiplier.

When the Fed sells Treasury bonds, it collects back some of its IOUs, reducing banking system reserves and decreasing the money supply. Thus,

To expand the money supply, the Fed buys bonds.

To contract the money supply, the Fed sells bonds.

Q-3 When the Fed buys bonds, is it expanding or contracting the money supply?

REAL-WORLD APPLICATION

Inside an FOMC Meeting

Let's go inside one of the eight regular Federal Open Market Committee (FOMC) meetings to gain some insight into how the Fed actually conducts monetary policy. The meeting consists of FOMC members and top Fed staff sitting around a large table debating what should be done. There's been enormous preparation for the meeting. The economists on the Federal Reserve staff have tracked the economy, and have made economic forecasts. Based on their studies, they've briefed the FOMC members, and the high-level staff get to sit in on the meeting. (Getting to sit in on the meeting is seen as a real perk of the job.)

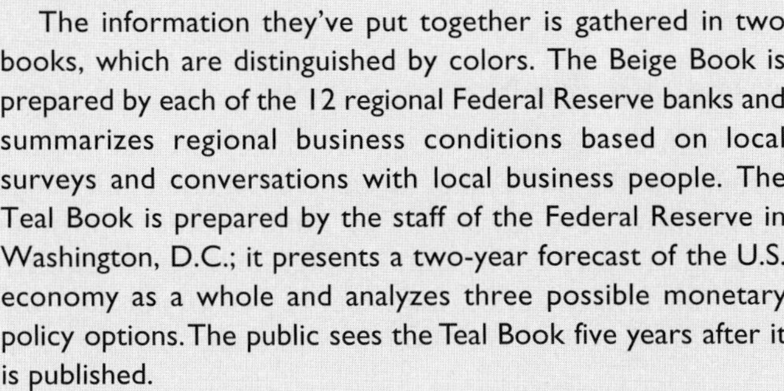

The information they've put together is gathered in two books, which are distinguished by colors. The Beige Book is prepared by each of the 12 regional Federal Reserve banks and summarizes regional business conditions based on local surveys and conversations with local business people. The Teal Book is prepared by the staff of the Federal Reserve in Washington, D.C.; it presents a two-year forecast of the U.S. economy as a whole and analyzes three possible monetary policy options. The public sees the Teal Book five years after it is published.

The meeting begins with a summary of monetary policy actions since the committee last met, followed by a forecast of the economy. The Fed governors and regional bank presidents also present their forecasts. Once current economic conditions and forecasts are discussed, the director of monetary affairs presents the three monetary policy proposals in the Teal Book. Then there is open discussion of the various policy proposals. The committee meeting ends with a vote on what policy to follow, along with a policy directive on what open market operations to execute. At that point, the FOMC also makes a public announcement regarding current policy actions as well as what future actions they may take. For example, on March 21, 2007, the FOMC issued the following statement:

> The Federal Open Market Committee decided today to keep its target for the federal funds rate at 5¼ percent. Recent indicators have been mixed and the adjustment in the housing sector is ongoing. Nevertheless, the economy seems likely to continue to expand at a moderate pace over coming quarters. Recent readings on core inflation have been somewhat elevated. Although inflation pressures seem likely to moderate over time, the high level of resource utilization has the potential to sustain those pressures. In these circumstances, the Committee's predominant policy concern remains the risk that inflation will fail to moderate as expected. Future policy adjustments will depend on the evolution of the outlook for both inflation and economic growth, as implied by incoming information.

The announcement was made at about 2:15 PM and within the next hour, the interest rate in the economy fell and the stock market shot up, with the Dow Jones Industrial Average rising 1.3 percent, as you can see in the graph below.

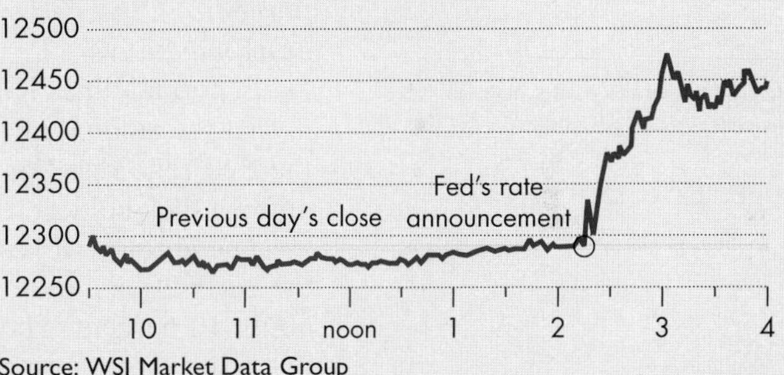

Why did this happen? The statement did not announce a change of interest rates. It said only that future policy adjustments are uncertain. What caused the change was what was not said in the statement. Previous statements had said that the Fed was leaning toward raising interest rates. This one did not, which led many in the stock market to believe that the Fed might lower interest rates in the future. Since traders saw that as good for the stock market, they bought stocks, pushing their prices up.

Understanding open market operations is essential to understanding monetary policy as it is actually practiced in the United States. So let's go through some examples.

Tools of Monetary Policy

Open market operations involve the purchase or sale of Treasury bills and bonds. When the Fed buys bonds, it deposits the funds in its accounts at a bank. Bank cash reserves rise. Banks don't like to hold excess reserves, so they generally lend out the excess, thereby expanding the deposit base of the economy. The money supply rises by the money multiplier times the amount of bonds the Fed purchases. Thus, an open market purchase is an example of *expansionary monetary policy* (monetary policy that tends to reduce interest rates and raise income) since it raises the money supply (as long as the banks strive to minimize their excess reserves).

An open market purchase is an example of expansionary monetary policy since it raises the money supply.

An open market sale has the opposite effect. Here, the Fed sells bonds. In return for the bond, the Fed receives a check drawn against a bank. The bank's reserve assets are reduced (since the Fed "cashes" the check and takes the money away from the bank), and the money supply falls. That's an example of *contractionary monetary policy* (monetary policy that tends to raise interest rates and lower income).

The Reserve Requirement and the Money Supply

Raising the reserve requirement lowers the money supply and vice versa.

As I discussed in the previous chapter, the total amount of money created from a given amount of currency depends on the percentage of deposits that a bank keeps in reserves (the bank's reserve ratio). By law, the Fed controls the minimum percentage of deposits banks keep in reserves by controlling the reserve requirement of all U.S. banks. That minimum is called the **reserve requirement**—*the percentage the Federal Reserve Bank sets as the minimum amount of reserves a bank must have.*

In normal times banks hold as little in reserves as possible.

In normal times banks typically hold as little in reserves as possible. The reason is that the amount most banks believe they need for safety is much smaller than what the Fed requires. For them, it's the Fed's reserve requirement that determines the amount they hold as reserves.

The amount of reserves also depends on the type of liabilities the bank has. In the early 2000s, required reserves for large banks for their checking accounts were about 10 percent. The reserve requirement for all other accounts was zero, making the reserve requirement for total bank liabilities somewhat under 2 percent.

Q-4 In recent years, why hasn't the Fed's increasing reserves led to an increase in the money supply?

Up until 2008, banks held very few excess reserves, and thus the reserve requirement was a reasonably close approximation of the reserve ratio—the reserves that banks keep relative to deposits. As you can see in the Federal Reserve chart on excess reserves in the margin, in late 2008 all this changed—banks began holding huge amounts of excess reserves. This means the reserve ratio far exceeded the reserve requirement. The reason excess reserves increased is that banks were not lending and held onto reserves the Fed was adding, which meant expansionary Fed policy wasn't stimulating the economy. Banks didn't increase lending because with financial institutions and the economy faltering, they believed that it would be better to retain the increase in reserves rather than make new loans with a high risk of default. Given that banks were not lending, the Fed could not increase the money supply in a conventional way—by increasing reserves. It was like pushing on a string. As much as the Fed pushed the string on one end, the other end didn't budge.

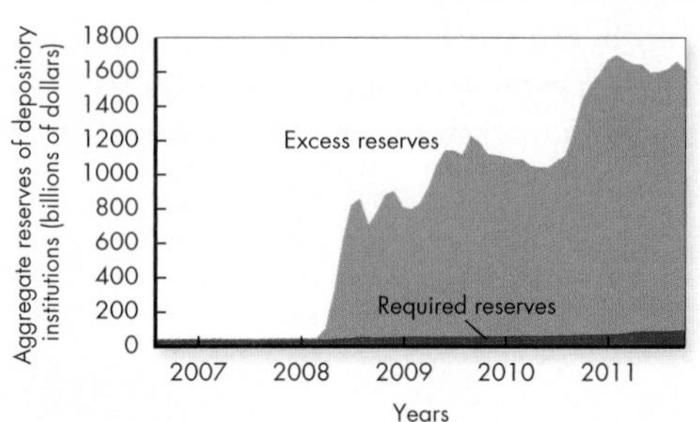

ADDED DIMENSION

Using the Money Multiplier in Practice

The money multiplier has been a staple of the macro principles course since its inception, and it remains an important concept in understanding how the monetary base is related to the aggregate supply of money in the economy. But recent changes in the financial system have made the operational use of the multiplier less important. For the most part, central banks don't determine how much to change the monetary base to get a desired change in the money supply using an assumed fixed multiplier. Instead, they adjust the monetary base to target either a desired amount of bank credit in the economy or a short-term interest rate.

The money multiplier relationship continues to be true by definition, but it is not the operational concept that it once was. The reasons include the decrease in the reserve requirement (in many countries, required reserves are zero); financial innovations that have increased the ways in which individuals can hold money; the increase in the amount of cash that individuals hold; and the decline in the stability of the relationship between the money supply and output. Each of these makes it harder to use the money multiplier as an operational variable, which is why much of the monetary policy discussion today focuses more on the interest rate than on the money supply.

It was about this time the Fed began to pay interest on reserves, but that interest payment of 0.25 percent is not why reserves increased significantly at this time. A 0.25 interest rates was too low to make banks want to hold money as excess reserves had they thought there were good lending opportunities. But paying interest on reserves does give the Fed another monetary policy tool. Specifically, if the Fed increases the interest rate paid on excess reserves, it can contract the money supply. If it reduces the interest rate on reserves (or even charges banks a negative interest rate—essentially taxing them on their excess reserves), it can expand the money supply. The Fed has not yet aggressively tried to use excess reserve interest rate policy, but it may in the future, since, with the current large level of excess reserves, conventional monetary policy—changing reserves through open market operations—has become ineffective. Instead it has introduced a number of other unconventional tools that I will discuss in the next chapter.

What does a bank do if it comes up short of reserves? It can borrow from another bank that has excess reserves in what's called the Federal funds market. (The rate of interest at which these reserves can be borrowed is called the *Fed funds rate*. As I will discuss below, in normal times this Fed funds rate is a significant indicator of monetary policy.)

In normal times the Fed funds rate is a significant indicator of monetary policy.

Another option that the bank has if it is short of reserves is to stop making new loans and to keep as reserves the proceeds of loans that are paid off. Still another option is to sell Treasury bonds to get the needed reserves. (Banks often hold some of their assets in Treasury bonds so that they can get additional reserves relatively easily if they need them.) Treasury bonds are sometimes called *secondary reserves.* They do not count as bank reserves—only IOUs of the Fed count as reserves. But Treasury bonds can be easily sold and transferred into cash, which does count as reserves. Banks use all these options.

The reason the Fed can use the reserve requirement to decrease the money supply is that while these options are open to the individual banks, they are not open to the entire system of banks. The total amount of reserves available is controlled by the Fed, and if the entire banking system is short of reserves, the banking system will have to figure out a way either to reduce the need for reserves or to borrow reserves from the Fed.

Borrowing from the Fed and the Discount Rate

The discount rate is the rate of interest the Fed charges for loans it makes to banks.

As I stated at the beginning of the chapter, a central bank is a banker's bank, and if the entire banking system is short of reserves, banks can go to the Federal Reserve and take out a loan. The **discount rate** is *the rate of interest the Fed charges for loans it makes to banks.* An increase in the discount rate makes it more expensive for banks to borrow from the Fed. A decrease in the rate makes it less expensive for banks to borrow. An increase in the discount rate discourages banks from borrowing and contracts the money supply; a decrease in the discount rate encourages the banks to borrow and increases the money supply.

The Fed Funds Market

To get an even better sense of the way monetary policy works, let's look at it from the perspective of a bank. The bank will review its books, determine how much in reserves it needs to meet its reserve requirement, and see if it has excess reserves or a shortage of reserves.

Say your bank didn't make as many loans as it expected to, so it has a surplus of reserves (excess reserves). Say also that another bank has made a few loans it didn't expect to make, so it has a shortage of reserves. The bank with surplus reserves can lend money to the bank with a shortage, and it can lend it overnight as **Fed funds**—*loans of excess reserves banks make to one another.* At the end of a day, a bank will look at its balances and see whether it has a shortage or surplus of reserves. If it has a surplus, it will call a Federal funds dealer to learn the **Federal funds rate**—*the interest rate banks charge one another for Fed funds.* Say the rate is 6 percent. The bank will then agree to lend its excess reserves overnight to the other bank for the daily equivalent of 6 percent per year. It's all simply done electronically, so there's no need actually to transfer funds. In the morning the money (plus overnight interest) is returned. The one-day interest rate is low, but when you're dealing with millions or billions, it adds up.

The Federal funds rate is the interest rate banks charge one another for overnight reserve loans.

The Federal funds market, the market in which banks lend and borrow reserves, is highly efficient. The Fed can reduce reserves, and thereby increase the Fed funds rate, by selling bonds. Alternatively, when the Fed buys bonds, it increases reserves, causing the Fed funds rate to fall. Generally, large city banks are borrowers of Fed funds; small country banks are lenders of Fed funds.

Q-5 If most banks are short of reserves, what will happen to the Fed funds rate?

Figure 13-3 shows the Fed funds rate and the discount rate since 1990. Notice that the Fed funds rate tended to be slightly above the discount rate until 2003, when the Fed changed its operating procedures and began setting the discount rate slightly above the Fed funds rate. As you can see, in 2001 and 2002 the Fed funds rate fell from 6 to 1.25 percent as the Fed followed an expansionary monetary policy. In mid-2004 the Fed began to raise the Fed funds rate. Then, in 2008, the financial crisis led the Fed to lower the Fed funds rate to almost zero, where it has remained.

The financial crisis led the Fed to lower the Fed funds rate to almost zero, where it has remained.

OFFENSIVE AND DEFENSIVE ACTIONS Economists keep a close eye on the Federal funds rate in determining the state of monetary policy. It has become an important intermediate target of the Fed in determining what monetary policy to conduct. Remember, the Fed sets minimum reserve requirements, but the actual amount of reserves available to banks is influenced by the amount of cash people hold and excess reserves that banks may choose to hold. That changes daily. For example, say there's a storm, and businesses don't make it to the bank with their cash. Bank reserves will fall even though the Fed didn't do anything. The Fed can,

FIGURE 13-3 The Fed Funds Rate and the Discount Rate

The Federal Reserve Bank follows expansionary or contractionary monetary policy by targeting a lower or higher Fed funds rate. The discount rate generally follows the Fed funds rate closely. Before 2003, it was kept lower than the Fed funds rate. Since 2003, the discount rate has been set slightly above the Fed funds rate target.

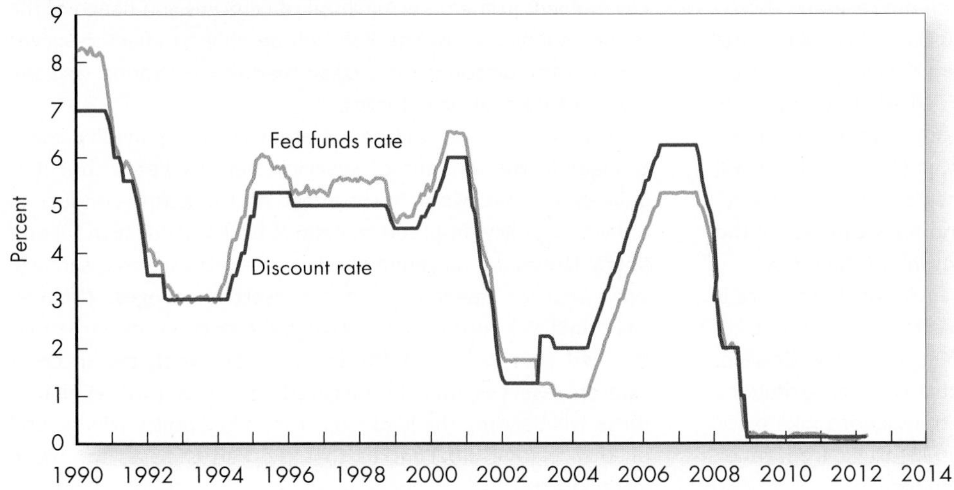

and does, offset such changes—by buying and selling bonds. Such actions are called *defensive actions.* They are designed to maintain the current monetary policy. These defensive actions are to be contrasted with *offensive actions,* which are actions meant to make monetary policy have expansionary or contractionary effects on the economy.

Q-6 There's been a big storm and cash held by individuals has increased. Should the Fed buy or sell bonds? Why?

THE FED FUNDS RATE AS AN OPERATING TARGET How does the Fed decide whether its buying and selling of bonds is having the desired effect? It has to look at other targets—and in recent years the Federal funds rate has been the operating target of the Fed. Thus, the Fed determines whether monetary policy is tight or loose depending on what is happening to the Federal funds rate. An increasing rate means that monetary policy is tight; a decreasing rate means monetary policy is loose. In practice, it targets a range for that rate, and buys and sells bonds to keep the Federal funds rate within that range. If the Federal funds rate rises above the Fed's target range, it buys bonds, which increases reserves and lowers the Federal funds rate. If the Federal funds rate falls below the Fed's target range, it sells bonds, which decreases reserves and raises the Federal funds rate.

Monetary policy affects interest rates such as the Federal funds rate. The Fed looks at the Federal funds rate to determine whether monetary policy is tight or loose.

The Complex Nature of Monetary Policy

While the Fed focuses on the Fed funds rate as its operating target, it also has its eye on its ultimate targets: stable prices, acceptable employment, sustainable growth, and moderate long-term interest rates. But those ultimate targets are only indirectly affected by changes in the Fed funds rate, so the Fed watches what are called *intermediate targets:* consumer confidence, stock prices, interest rate spreads, housing starts, and a host of others. Intermediate targets are not always good guides for the Fed's ultimate targets. The Federal Reserve Bank of San Francisco once had an exhibit of an

REAL-WORLD APPLICATION

Will the Reserve Requirement Be Eliminated?

In 2006, President Bush signed the Financial Services Regulatory Relief Act of 2006 to improve the efficiency of the banking system. The Act allows the Fed to reduce the reserve ratio to zero and to pay interest on reserves that banks maintain at the Fed. In November of 2008, the Fed started paying interest on reserves, but because the change occurred while the Fed was dealing with the financial panic of 2008, and was accompanied by numerous other changes in Fed polices (changes that I will discuss in the next chapter) as it played its "lender of last resort" role, it will likely be years before economists can assess the implication of paying interest on reserves in normal times.

If the Fed also reduces the reserve requirements to zero, it will be following the practices of central banks of other industrialized nations such as Canada, the United Kingdom, New Zealand, and Japan. The reason for the change is that financial institutions have changed. More and more financial transactions take place outside the banking system, and distinguishing banks from other financial institutions has become harder and harder.

In practice, the change will make all reserves excess reserves, and make the interest rate paid on reserve balances a key element in the determination of reserves and hence of the money supply. Thus, the Fed will be able to affect reserves through the discount rate, open market operations, and the interest rate paid on reserves.

The transition to the new system will likely involve some changes in the amount of reserves held by banks, but it is unlikely to have a significant effect on the actual conduct of monetary policy. In practice, central banks conduct monetary policy largely by targeting short-term interest rates through open market operations. If the system changes, the Fed will establish a relationship between the discount rate (the rate the Fed charges banks for lending reserves), the interest rate on reserves, and the targeted Fed funds rate. Which of these will become the lead indicator of Fed policy will depend on the relative differentials that the Fed chooses for these interest rates.

electronic video game in its lobby.[1] The object of the game was to hit a moving target with a dart from a moving arm. With both the arm and the target moving, most visitors missed the target.

The game was there to demonstrate the difficulties of implementing monetary policy. Monetary policy "shoots from a moving arm." Ultimately, policy actions of the Fed influence output and inflation, but the influence is not direct, and many other factors also influence output and inflation.

In reality, the Fed's problem is even more complicated than the video game suggests. A more telling game would be one modeled after a Rube Goldberg cartoon. If you hit the first moving target, it releases a second dart when hit. That second dart is supposed to hit a second moving target, which in turn releases a third dart aimed at yet another moving target. Given the complicated path that monetary policy follows, it should not be surprising that the Fed often misses its ultimate targets. Small wonder that the Fed often doesn't have the precise effect it wants.

The following diagram summarizes the tools and targets of the Fed:

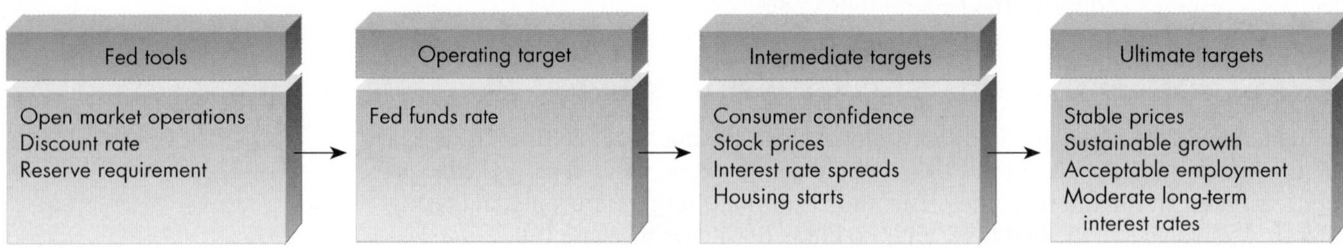

[1]Because of security concerns, central bank lobbies are now generally off limits to the public and this exhibit is no longer accessible.

The Taylor Rule

Former U.S. Treasury economist John Taylor has summarized a rule that, in the late 1990s and early 2000s, described Fed policy relatively well. The rule, which has become known as the **Taylor rule,** can be stated as follows: *Set the Fed funds rate at 2 percent plus current inflation if the economy is at desired output and desired inflation. If the inflation rate is higher than desired, increase the Fed funds rate by 0.5 times the difference between desired and actual inflation. Similarly, if output is higher than desired, increase the Fed funds rate by 0.5 times the percentage deviation.*

Formally the Taylor rule is:

Fed funds rate = 2 percent + Current inflation
+ 0.5 × (actual inflation less desired inflation)
+ 0.5 × (percent deviation of aggregate output from potential)

Q-7 If inflation is 1 percent, the Fed wants 2 percent inflation, and output is 2 percent below potential, what would the Taylor rule predict for a Fed funds rate target?

Let's consider some examples. Say that inflation is 2.5 percent, the Fed's target rate of inflation is 2 percent, and the aggregate output exceeds potential output by 1 percent. That means that the Fed would set the Fed funds rate at 5.25 percent (2 + 2.5 + 0.5(2.5 − 2) + 0.5(1)). The first row in the table below shows the calculations. The second row shows another example with different numbers.

Federal Funds Rate	=	2 Percent	+	Current Inflation	+	0.5(Actual less targeted inflation)	+	0.5(Deviation from potential output)
5.25	=	2	+	2.5	+	0.5(2.5 − 2)	+	0.5(1)
4.5	=	2	+	2	+	0.5(2 − 2)	+	0.5(1)

Notice that the Taylor rule depends on one's estimate of potential output. Because conventional macroeconomists see potential output as significantly higher than do structural stagnation macroeconomists, they would tend to target a lower Fed funds rate than would a structural stagnation macroeconomist.

The Fed has never slavishly followed the Taylor rule. For example, in late 2000 and early 2001, the economy was 1 percent over potential output by most estimates and inflation was 2 percent, which was equal to the target rate. The Taylor rule predicted that the Fed would set the Fed funds rate at 4.5 percent. (See the calculations in row 2 of the table.) Instead, it targeted a 6 percent rate because it was especially concerned about the economy overheating. Then right after September 11, the Fed became concerned about the economy going into a severe recession and it lowered the Fed funds rate significantly—close to zero—even though little else had changed. It maintained that low interest rate from 2002 to 2006 compared to what the Taylor rule would suggest, even by conventional macro theory's estimate of potential output, as can be seen in Figure 13-4. The Fed chose to do this because inflation did not seem to be a problem—the fear was deflation, not inflation—and because they wanted to avoid a recession that many economists were predicting. Using a structural stagnationist's view of potential output, the difference between the actual Fed funds rate and the rate recommended by the Taylor rule was even greater.

FIGURE 13-4 Federal Fund Rate and the Taylor Rule

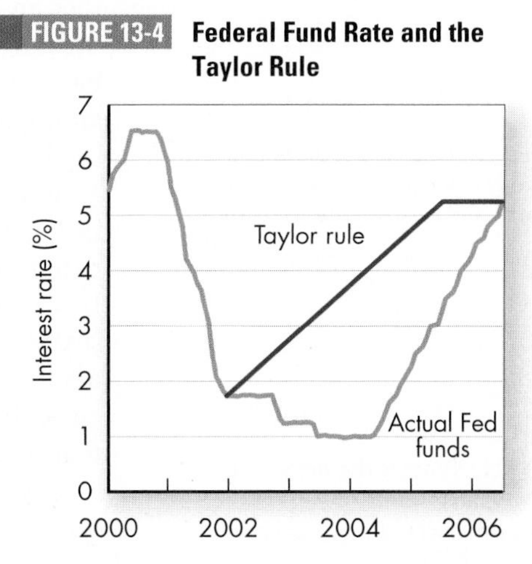

The Fed policy during this time period goes to the heart of the debate about policy today. The issue was that, while there was not inflation in goods, asset prices were rising quickly, which structural stagnationists saw as financial bubbles. One of the most important bubbles was in the housing market. Critics of Fed policy argued that these financial bubbles were being fueled by the low interest rates and the availability of credit encouraged by a historically low Fed funds rate. As you can see in Figure 13-4, it was only in 2006 that the Fed began to worry about inflation and raised the interest rate up to where the Taylor rule suggested it should be, and it was in 2006 that the housing bubble started to burst. Thus, many economists argue that Fed policy was an important contributor to the housing bubble.

WWW Web Note 13.5 Taylor Rule

The higher interest rates of 2006 and 2007 did not last, and, as the economy seemed to be falling into a recession and financial crisis, the Fed again deviated from the Taylor rule. Consider early 2008, when inflation was about 3.5 percent, which was about 2 percent above the Fed's target, and the economy was close to its potential income. According to the Taylor rule, the Feds fund rate should have been 6.5 percent. The actual Fed funds rate was 5.5 percent.

By the end of 2008, the Fed's Fed funds target rate was down to 0.2 percent and the Fed was doing whatever it could to increase the money supply in other than standard ways. The Fed is not now using a Taylor rule but is instead using unconventional monetary policy. We will discuss this episode in the next chapter. Here I want to note that this is a good example of how the Fed uses models. It has a model for normal times, and it has another model for crises. The art of monetary policy is deciding which type of situation the economy is in.

Controlling the Interest Rate Notice how the Taylor rule focuses the discussion of monetary policy on the interest rate (specifically, the Fed funds rate), not the money supply. On the surface, this may seem inconsistent with the discussions of monetary policy that focused on the money supply, but it is not. It is simply a difference in focus. The Fed does control the amount of money in the economy, but it uses that control to target an interest rate, not to control the money supply.

Limits to the Fed's Control of the Interest Rate The above discussion makes it sound as if the Fed can control the interest rate, and it can, if by interest rate we mean the short-term interest rate. But, as we discussed in the last chapter, the economy has more than one interest rate. As long as the short-term interest rate and the long-term interest rate move in tandem, then the Fed can also control the long-term interest rate. Unfortunately, they do not always move in tandem, and that has made the study of the relationship between the short-term and long-term rates an important part of discussions of monetary policy. Economists carefully follow this relationship in a graph called the **yield curve**—*a curve that shows the relationship between interest rates and bonds' time to maturity*. I show two alternative yield curves in Figure 13-5. As you can see, as you move out along the yield curve, bonds' time to maturity increases. Figure 13-5(a) demonstrates what is called a standard yield curve. It is a yield curve in which the short-term rates are lower than the long-term rate. Thus, if you invest in a one-year bond, you would earn 4 percent interest, and if you invest in a 30-year bond, you would earn 6 percent interest. This is considered a standard yield curve because long-term bonds are riskier than short-term bonds, so it is reasonable that they generally have a slightly higher interest rate.

The yield curve is a curve that shows the relationship between interest rates and bonds' time to maturity.

Q-8 What is the difference between a standard yield curve and an inverted yield curve?

That relationship between short-term and long-term interest rates does not always hold. Figure 13-5(b) shows what is called an **inverted yield curve**—*a yield curve in*

FIGURE 13-5 (A AND B) The Yield Curve

The standard yield curve shown in (**a**) is upward-sloping: As the time to maturity increases, so does the interest rate. An inverted yield curve shown in (**b**) is downward-sloping: As the time to maturity increases, the interest rate decreases.

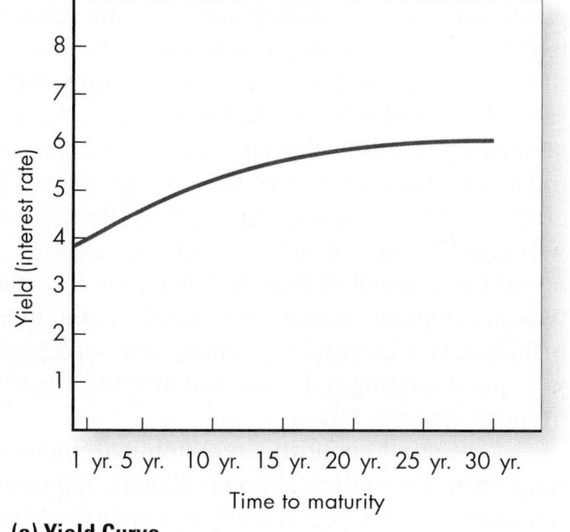

(a) Yield Curve

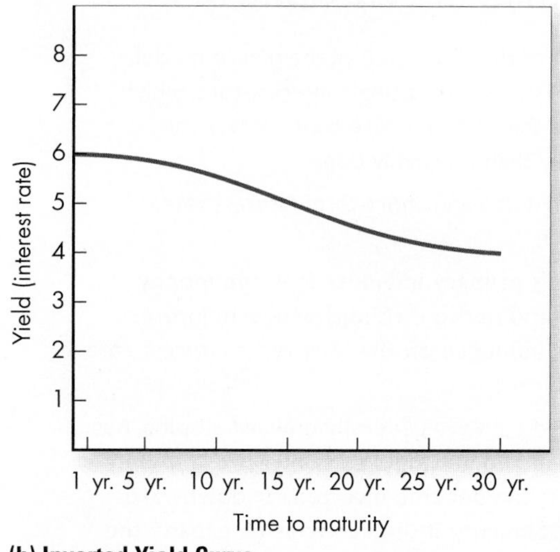

(b) Inverted Yield Curve

which the short-term rate is higher than the long-term rate. In the graph, you can see that a one-year bond pays 6 percent interest and a 30-year bond pays a lower, 4 percent, interest rate.

Why is the shape of the yield curve important? Because the standard discussion of monetary policy is based on the assumption that when the Fed pushes up the short-term rate, the long-term rate moves up as well. If the long-term rate doesn't move with the short-term rate, then investment won't respond, and conventional monetary policy won't have any significant effect on investment and therefore on the economy. Think of the issue as one of pushing a pea along a plate with a noodle. If the noodle is dry, you can do it easily, but if the noodle is wet, when you move one end, the other end doesn't move, and it is much more difficult.

As financial markets have become more liquid, and as technological changes in financial markets have provided firms with many alternative sources of credit, the Fed has found that its ability to control the long-term rate through conventional monetary policy has lessened. When it uses contractionary monetary policy, as opposed to shifting the entire yield curve up the policy simply causes an inverted yield curve. That's why policy makers pay close attention to the yield curve. Conventional expansionary monetary policy pushes the short-term interest rate down, but initially leaves the long-term interest rate almost unchanged.

As financial markets have become more liquid, and as technological changes in financial markets have provided firms with many alternative sources of credit, the Fed has found that its ability to control the long-term rate through conventional monetary policy has lessened.

The monetary influence is not completely gone; economists have found that if the Fed is willing to push the short-term rate high enough, it is able to pull the long-term rate with it, but the Fed's control of the long-term rate with conventional monetary policy is more like the control parents have over their kids—they can influence (and hope) but cannot control. That is why it has turned to the unconventional monetary policy that we will discuss in the next chapter.

A REMINDER 

Some Limits of Fed Control

- In much of the discussion of the macro model, economists assume a single interest rate, which suggests the Fed has more control over the economy than it actually does.
- The long-term and short-term interest rates can differ.
- The Fed's primary influence is in the money market and hence on the short-term interest rate. Its influence on the long-term interest rate is less direct.
- The yield curve is generally upward-sloping, but when the Fed attempts to contract the money supply, it can become inverted, or downward-sloping. Similarly, if the Fed tries to expand the money supply, the yield curve will generally become steeper.

Maintaining Policy Credibility

Policy makers are very concerned about establishing policy credibility. The reason is that policy makers believe that it is necessary to prevent inflationary expectations from becoming built into the economy. They fear that if inflationary expectations become built into the economy, the long-term interest rate, which is the rate that primarily influences investment, will be pushed up, making the yield curve steeper and requiring even stronger contractionary monetary policy to eliminate the inflation. To see why the long-term rate will rise because of inflationary expectations, it is important to remember that the long-term interest rate has two components: a real interest rate component and an inflationary expectations component, which means that you must distinguish the real interest rate from the nominal interest rate.

You learned about this real/nominal interest rate distinction in an earlier chapter. Recall, *nominal interest rates* are the rates you actually see and pay. When a bank pays 7 percent interest, that 7 percent is a nominal interest rate. What affects the economy is the real interest rate. *Real interest rates* are nominal interest rates adjusted for expected inflation.

For example, say you get 7 percent interest from the bank, but the price level goes up 7 percent. At the end of the year you have \$107 instead of \$100, but you're no better off than before because the price level has risen—on average, things cost 7 percent more. What you would have paid \$100 for last year now costs \$107. (That's the definition of *inflation.*) Had the price level remained constant, and had you received 0 percent interest, you'd be in the equivalent position of receiving 7 percent interest on your \$100 when the price level rises by 7 percent. That 0 percent is the *real interest rate.* It is the interest rate you receive after adjusting for inflation.

Q-9 If the nominal interest rate is 10 percent and expected inflation is 3 percent, what is the real interest rate?

The real interest rate cannot be observed because it depends on expected inflation. To calculate the real interest rate, you must subtract what you believe to be the expected rate of inflation from the nominal interest rate:[2]

Real interest rate = Nominal interest rate − Expected inflation rate

For example, if the nominal interest rate is 7 percent and expected inflation is 4 percent, the real interest rate is 3 percent. The relationship between real and nominal interest rates is important both for your study of economics and for your own personal finances.

Q-10 How does the distinction between nominal and real interest rates add uncertainty to the effect of monetary policy on the economy?

What does this distinction between nominal and real interest rates mean for monetary policy? It adds yet another uncertainty to the effect of monetary policy. In the *AS/AD* model, we assumed that expansionary monetary policy lowers the interest rate and contractionary monetary policy increases the interest rate. However, if the expansionary monetary policy leads to expectations of increased inflation, expansionary monetary policy can increase nominal interest rates (the ones you see) and leave real interest rates (the ones that affect borrowing decisions)

[2]This is an equation that works best for small amounts of inflation.

unchanged. Why? Because of expectations of increasing inflation. Lenders will want to be compensated for the inflation (which will decrease the value of the money they receive back) and will push the nominal interest rate up to get the desired real rate of interest.

MONETARY REGIMES The distinction between nominal and real interest rates and the possible effect of monetary policy on expectations of inflation has led most economists to conclude that a monetary regime, not a monetary policy, is the best approach to policy. A **monetary regime** is *a predetermined statement of the policy that will be followed in various situations.* A monetary policy, in contrast, is a response to events; it is chosen without a predetermined framework.

Monetary regimes are now favored because rules can help generate the expectations that even though in certain instances the Fed is increasing the money supply, that increase is not a signal that monetary expansion and inflation are imminent. A monetary regime involves feedback rules. In the conventional rules, if inflation is above its target, the Fed raises the Federal funds rate (by selling bonds, thereby decreasing the money supply) in an attempt to slow inflation down. If inflation is below its target, and if the economy is going into a recession, the Fed lowers the Fed funds rate (by buying bonds, thereby increasing the money supply). The Taylor rule discussed above is an example of a general feedback rule.

A monetary regime is a predetermined statement of the policy that will be followed in various situations.

PROBLEMS WITH MONETARY REGIMES Establishing an explicit monetary regime to hold down expectations of inflation is not without its problems. Inevitably, special circumstances arise where it makes sense to deviate from the regime. The problem is analogous to the problem faced by parents. All parenting manuals tell parents to maintain credibility and to set fair and firm rules. Most parents attempt to do so. But as all, or at least most, parents know, sometimes exceptions are necessary. Not all contingencies can be planned for. So I suspect that both parents and monetary policy makers will consistently emphasize their firm rules and state that they will follow them no matter what, but that inevitably they will trade some credibility for some short-term gain, or in the belief that the initial rule did not take into account the particular situation that arose.

To make its commitment to a monetary regime clear to the public, even as it deviates slightly from that commitment in specific instances, the Fed has been trying, over the past decade, to increase the degree of *transparency* that accompanies its monetary policy decisions. Specifically, the Fed is releasing the minutes of its FOMC meetings much sooner after the meetings adjourn than it did in the past, and is going out of its way to explain its decisions. The hope is that the greater degree of transparency will demonstrate the Fed's general resolve to fight inflation, and show that any possible deviation from that resolve can be explained by special circumstances.

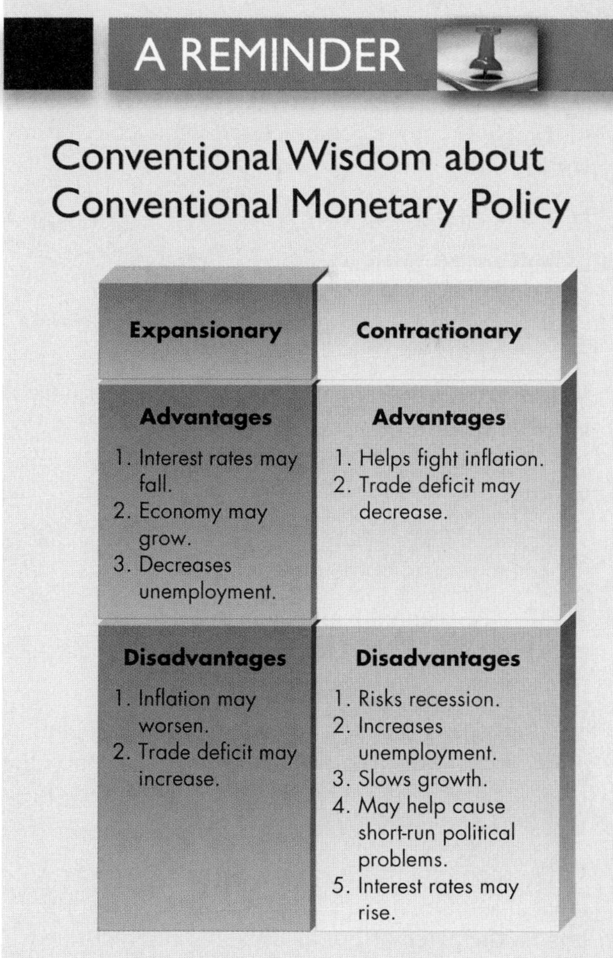

Conclusion

The above discussion should give you a good sense that conducting monetary policy in normal times is not a piece of cake. It takes not only a sense of the theory but also a feel for the economy. (See the box "Conventional Wisdom about Conventional Monetary Policy" for a summary of the standard view of monetary policy.) In short, the conduct of monetary policy is not a science. It does not allow the Fed to steer the economy as it might steer a car. It does work well enough to allow the Fed to *influence* the economy, much as an expert rodeo rider rides a bronco bull. Sometimes the bull ride can be extremely bumpy, as we will see in the next chapter.

The Fed can influence, not steer, the economy.

Summary

- Monetary policy is the policy of influencing the economy through changes in the banking system's reserves that affect the money supply. *(LO13-1)*
- In the *AS/AD* model, contractionary monetary policy works as follows: *(LO13-1)*

  $M\downarrow \rightarrow i\uparrow \rightarrow I\downarrow \rightarrow Y\downarrow$
- Expansionary monetary policy works as follows: *(LO13-1)*

  $M\uparrow \rightarrow i\downarrow \rightarrow I\uparrow \rightarrow Y\uparrow$
- In the structural stagnation model, expansionary monetary policy lowers interest rates and raises asset prices. It also raises the trade deficit. *(LO13-1)*
- The Federal Open Market Committee (FOMC) makes the actual decisions about monetary policy. *(LO13-2)*
- The Fed is a central bank; it conducts monetary policy for the United States and regulates financial institutions. *(LO13-2)*
- The Fed changes the money supply through open market operations: To expand the money supply, the Fed buys bonds. To contract the money supply, the Fed sells bonds. *(LO13-3)*
- When the Fed buys bonds, the price of bonds rises and interest rates fall. When the Fed sells bonds, the price of bonds falls and interest rates rise. *(LO13-3)*
- A change in reserves changes the money supply by the change in reserves times the money multiplier. *(LO13-3)*
- The Federal funds rate is the rate at which one bank lends reserves to another bank. It is the Fed's primary operating target. *(LO13-3)*
- The Taylor rule is a feedback rule that states: Set the Fed funds rate at 2 plus current inflation plus one-half the difference between actual and desired inflation plus one-half the percent difference between actual and potential output. *(LO13-4)*
- The yield curve shows the relationship between interest rates and bonds' time to maturity. *(LO13-4)*
- The Fed's direct control is on short-term interest rates; its effect on long-term interest rates is indirect. Fed policy intended to shift the yield curve might instead change its shape, and therefore not have the intended impact on investment and output. *(LO13-4)*
- Nominal interest rates are the interest rates we see and pay. Real interest rates are nominal interest rates adjusted for expected inflation: Real interest rate = Nominal interest rate − Expected inflation. *(LO13-4)*
- Because monetary policy can affect inflation expectations as well as nominal interest rates, the effect of monetary policy on interest rates can be uncertain. This uncertainty has led the Fed to follow monetary regimes. *(LO13-4)*

Key Terms

central bank *(288)*
contractionary monetary policy *(287)*
discount rate *(296)*
expansionary monetary policy *(287)*
Fed funds *(296)*
Federal funds rate *(296)*
Federal Open Market Committee (FOMC) *(288)*
inverted yield curve *(300)*
monetary base *(292)*
monetary policy *(286)*
monetary regime *(303)*
open market operations *(292)*
reserve requirement *(294)*
Taylor rule *(299)*
yield curve *(300)*

Questions and Exercises

1. Demonstrate the effect of contractionary monetary policy in the *AS/AD* model. *(LO13-1)*
2. Demonstrate the effect of expansionary monetary policy in the *AS/AD* model when the economy is: *(LO13-1)*
   a. Below potential output.
   b. Significantly above potential output.
3. What is the effect of expansionary monetary policy in the structural stagnation model? *(LO13-1)*
4. Is the Fed a private or a public agency? *(LO13-2)*
5. Why are there few regional Fed banks in the western part of the United States? *(LO13-2)*
6. What are the six explicit functions of the Fed? *(LO13-2)*
7. How does the Fed use open market operations to increase the money supply? *(LO13-3)*
8. Write the formula for the money multiplier. If the Fed eliminated the reserve requirement, what would happen to the money multiplier and the supply of money? *(LO13-3)*
9. If a bank is unable to borrow reserves from the Fed funds market to meet its reserve requirement, where else might it borrow reserves? What is the name of the rate it pays to borrow these reserves? *(LO13-3)*
10. What is meant by the *Federal funds rate*? *(LO13-3)*
11. Why is the Fed funds rate the interest rate that the Fed most directly controls? *(LO13-3)*
12. If the Federal Reserve announces a change in the direction of monetary policy, is it describing an offensive or defensive action? Explain your answer. *(LO13-3)*
13. Suppose the Fed decides it needs to pursue an expansionary policy. Assume the reserve requirement is 20 percent, and there are no excess reserves. Show how the Fed would increase the money supply by $2 million through open market operations. *(LO13-3)*
14. Some individuals have suggested raising the required reserve ratio for banks to 100 percent. *(LO13-3)*
    a. What would the money multiplier be if this change were made?
    b. What effect would such a change have on the money supply?
    c. How could that effect be offset?
15. The Fed wants to increase the money supply (which is currently 4,000) by 200. The money multiplier is 3. For each 1 percentage point the discount rate falls, banks borrow an additional 20. Explain how the Fed can achieve its goals using the following tools: *(LO13-3)*
    a. Change the reserve requirement.
    b. Change the discount rate.
    c. Use open market operations.
16. Say that investment increases by 20 for each interest rate drop of 1 percent. Say also that the expenditures multiplier is 3. If the money multiplier is 4, and each 5-unit change in the money supply changes the interest rate by 1 percent, what open market policy would you recommend to increase income by 240? *(LO13-3)*
17. Congratulations! You have been appointed adviser to the Federal Reserve Bank. *(LO13-3)*
    a. The Federal Open Market Committee decides that it must increase the money supply by 60. Committee members tell you the reserve ratio is 0.1. They ask you what directive they should give to the open market desk. You tell them, being as specific as possible, using the money multiplier.
    b. They ask you for two other ways they could have achieved the same end. You tell them.
    c. Based on the *AS/AD* model, tell them what you think the effect on the price level of your policy will be.
    d. Based on the structural stagnation model, how does the policy affect the price level?
18. What is the relationship between tools, operating targets, intermediate targets, and ultimate targets? *(LO13-4)*
19. What are examples of tools, operating targets, and ultimate targets? *(LO13-4)*

20. The table below gives the Fed funds rate target at the end of each year shown.

Year	Federal Funds Target Rate
2005	5.00%
2006	5.25
2007	4.25
2008	0.25

Using these figures, describe how the monetary policy directions changed from 2005 through 2008. *(LO13-4)*

21. Target inflation is 2 percent; actual inflation is 3 percent. Output equals potential output. What does the Taylor rule predict will be the Fed funds rate? *(LO13-4)*
22. State the Taylor rule. What does the rule predict will happen to the Fed funds rate in each of the following situations? *(LO13-4)*
    a. Inflation is 2 percent, the inflation target is 3 percent, and output is 2 percent below potential.
    b. Inflation is 4 percent, the inflation target is 2 percent, and output is 3 percent above potential.
    c. Inflation is 4 percent, the inflation target is 3 percent, and output is 2 percent below potential.
23. What is an inverted yield curve? *(LO13-4)*
24. Are you more likely to see an inverted yield curve when the Fed is implementing contractionary or expansionary monetary policy? *(LO13-4)*
25. Why would policy makers pay attention to the shape of the yield curve? *(LO13-4)*
26. Does it matter to policy makers how people form expectations? *(LO13-4)*
27. Fill in the blanks in the following table: *(LO13-4)*

	Real Interest Rate	Nominal Interest Rate	Expected Inflation
a.	5	?	2
b.	?	3	4
c.	3	6	?
d.	?	5	1

28. How does a policy regime differ from a policy? *(LO13-4)*
29. How might an inflation target policy impair the ability of the Fed? *(LO13-4)*
30. How are transparency and credibility related? *(LO13-4)*

Questions from Alternative Perspectives

1. Fisher Black, an economist who designed a famous options pricing model, argued that because of developments in financial markets, central banks would soon have no ability to control the economy with monetary policy, and that the price level would be indeterminant rather than determined by the money supply. What do you think his argument was? (Austrian)
2. The quotation at the beginning of this chapter, and those for almost all the chapters, is from a man not a woman.
    a. Does this suggest anything about the author's viewpoint or about the economics profession?
    b. Should we be concerned about the lack of quotations from women? (Feminist)
3. Monetary policy is difficult when interest rates are low. For example, in the early 2000s the Bank of Japan lowered the interest rate to 0.01 percent with little effect on investment.
    a. Why is it difficult for monetary policy to be effective when interest rates are very low?
    b. How might institutions be changed to make monetary policy effective under these circumstances? (Institutionalist)
4. Monetarists believe that money is neutral in that it has no real effect on interest rates, output, or employment. Keynes, alternatively, believed that money is not neutral in both the short and long run. For Keynesians, money supply can affect real decision making, providing liquidity when firms need it. How would a belief in the nonneutrality of money affect the policy discussion in the book? (Post-Keynesian)
5. As radical economists see it, when it comes to making monetary policy, the Fed consistently puts the interests of bondholders ahead of people seeking work. It regularly moves to protect the value of their stocks and bonds by keeping inflation low even at the expense of maintaining employment growth.
    a. In your opinion, does the Fed use monetary policy to direct the economy to everyone's benefit?
    b. Should the Fed serve the interests of the holders of financial assets or the interests of workers? (Radical)

Issues to Ponder

1. "The effects of open market operations are somewhat like a stone cast in a pond." Discuss the first three ripples after a splash.
2. You can lead a horse to water, but you can't make it drink. How might this adage be relevant to expansionary (as opposed to contractionary) monetary policy?
3. In November 2008 the central bank began to pay interest on reserves held at the bank.
   a. What effect would you expect this to have on excess reserves?
   b. Did banks generally favor or oppose this action?
   c. Would central banks generally favor or oppose this action?
   d. What effect did this probably have on interest rates paid by banks?
4. Why would a bank hold Treasury bills as secondary reserves when it could simply hold primary reserves—cash?
5. The "Check 21" Act, which allows banks to transfer check images instead of paper checks, speeds up check processing. What is the likely effect on:
   a. Float (duplicate money because a check has been deposited but not yet deducted from the payer's account).
   b. Variability of float.
   c. Defensive Fed actions.

Answers to Margin Questions

1. Expansionary monetary policy makes more money available to banks for lending. Banks lower their interest rates to attract more borrowers. With lower interest rates, businesses will borrow more money and increase investment expenditures. The multiplier shifts the *AD* curve to the right by a multiple of the increase in investment expenditures. Real output increases to Y_1, and the price level rises to P_1. What ultimately happens to output and the price level depends on where the economy is relative to potential. (*p. 287; LO13-1*)

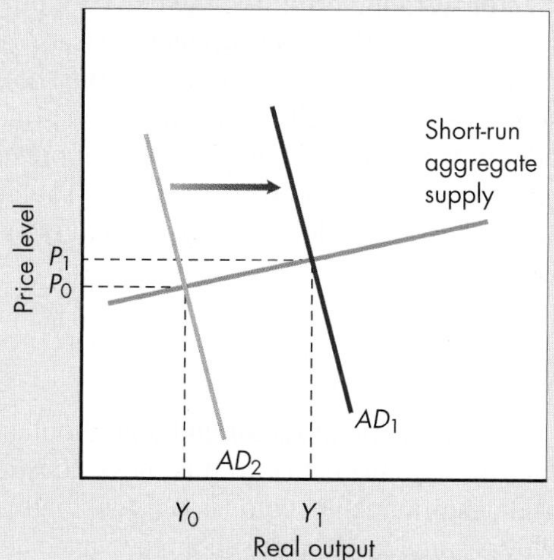

2. The Federal Open Market Committee (FOMC) decides on monetary policy. (*p. 288; LO13-2*)
3. When the Fed buys bonds, it is expanding the money supply. (*p. 292; LO13-3*)
4. In recent years banks' holding of excess reserves have increased enormously. The Fed's increasing reserves will translate into an increase in the money supply only if banks lend those reserves. (*p. 294; LO13-3*)
5. It will rise. (*p. 296; LO13-3*)
6. The Fed should buy bonds to offset the unintended decline in reserves. (*p. 297; LO13-3*)
7. The Taylor rule predicts a Fed funds rate target of 1.5 percent. (*p. 299; LO13-4*)
8. In a standard yield curve, bonds with greater time to maturity pay higher interest rates. In an inverted yield curve, bonds with greater time to maturity pay *lower* interest rates. (*p. 300; LO13-4*)
9. The real interest rate is 7 percent, the nominal interest rate (10) less expected inflation (3). (*p. 302; LO13-4*)
10. Because expansionary monetary policy can lead to expectations of higher inflation, expansionary monetary policy can lead to higher nominal interest rates. Because real interest rates cannot be observed directly, interest rates are not always a good guide for the direction of monetary policy. (*p. 302; LO13-4*)

chapter 14

Financial Crises, Panics, and Unconventional Monetary Policy

We believe the Federal Reserve's large-scale asset purchase plan (so-called "quantitative easing") should be reconsidered and discontinued. We do not believe such a plan is necessary or advisable under current circumstances.

—[an open letter from a number of economists to the chairman of the Fed]

After reading this chapter, you should be able to:

- **LO14-1** Explain why financial crises are dangerous and why most economists see a role for the central bank as a lender of last resort.
- **LO14-2** Explain the role of leverage and herding in financial bubbles and how central bank policy can contribute to a financial bubble.
- **LO14-3** Explain why regulating the financial sector and preventing financial crises is so difficult.
- **LO14-4** Discuss monetary policy in the post financial crisis period.

In 2008, the world financial system nearly stopped working. Banks were on the verge of collapse, the stock market dropped precipitously, and the U.S. economy fell into a serious recession from which it still has not recovered. In response, central banks and governments across the world took extraordinary steps—buying banks, buying financial assets, guaranteeing deposits, and guaranteeing loans to try to calm the crisis. Since that time, central banks have been running unconventional monetary policy strategies to try to prevent problems in the world financial sector from undermining the real economy (the buying and selling of goods and services rather than financial assets) and to pull economies out of the economic stagnation that they fell into after the crisis. In this chapter we consider these issues. Specifically, we consider (1) financial panics and the Fed's role as a lender of last resort, (2) the difficulty of preventing financial crises and the structural problems they create, (3) the problems of regulating the financial sector, and (4) the debate about unconventional monetary policies.

The Central Bank's Role in a Crisis

Why is there so much concern about the financial sector and fear about a credit crisis? Firms in the financial sector got themselves into this mess; they should get out of it on their own. After all, the financial sector is only a small part of the entire economy. The answer why is simple: We worry about the financial sector not because it is big or small, but because all the other sectors need the financial sector to do business. While oil is a relatively minor part of a working engine, it is absolutely essential. While the failure of other big sectors such as the auto industry would be painful, it would not bring all other sectors crashing down as a financial-sector collapse would. That's why one of the roles of a central bank is to be a **lender of last resort**—*lending to banks and other financial institutions when no one else will.*

Q-1 Why do we worry about the financial sector more than the automobile sector?

When credit is not available, the real economy can quickly come to a halt. It's not like the slow effect of a contractionary demand shock. It is fast, like a heart attack. The fear in October 2008 was that the financial crisis on Wall Street could cause the entire economy to seize, spreading the problem from Wall Street (the financial sector) to Main Street (the real sector), creating not a recession but a depression like the Great Depression of the 1930s.

Think about what would happen if *your* credit dried up. Say that even though you're every bit as trustworthy as before, you suddenly find you can no longer borrow money. No more spending with a credit card. Paying for some of your expenses might still work just fine—you could buy groceries with cash at the local grocery store. Others would be more difficult. Without credit, you'd have to pay all your bills before you get the product. No more loans to buy a car; you'll have to save $20,000 first. No more checks since businesses couldn't be assured the check would clear. Some things would be downright impossible; forget about buying anything on the Internet. Paying for college? No problem . . . if you've already saved up enough to pay up front and in full.

Credit is a necessary part of the U.S. economy.

The situation is even worse for companies. While they might not use credit cards, just like you, they borrow for their short-term needs, such as buying the raw materials for production and paying their workers. If their credit line disappears, companies would essentially be forced to close because they couldn't pay their workers. When workers lose their jobs, they will cut their spending, causing other workers to lose their jobs as well. A downward spiral of output will result. That's why a severe financial crisis can bring the entire real economy to a halt.

Luckily that didn't happen. As soon as the crisis hit, the Fed put aside its standard cautious approach to monetary policy and undertook a wide variety of unprecedented actions. It acted as the lender of last resort—providing loans to financial institutions that it determined were **solvent**—*having sufficient assets to cover their long-run liabilities*—but were not sufficiently **liquid**—*having assets that could readily be converted into cash and money at nonfire sale prices.* Without liquid assets banks couldn't pay their short-run liabilities, such as interest on money they had borrowed. To prevent a financial collapse, the Fed took the banks' long-run illiquid assets such as mortgages, business loans, and Treasury bonds as collateral, and loaned the banks money to pay their short-run liabilities. By doing so the Fed provided liquidity to the financial market.

In the financial crisis, the Fed acted as a lender of last resort loaning to solvent, but illiquid banks.

Similarly, the Treasury dropped all its standard practices and bailed out financial firms, and Congress instituted strong expansionary fiscal policy. The hope was that such actions would be enough to prevent the financial meltdown that would turn a serious recession into a second Great Depression. The policy succeeded; the United States and world economies avoided a financial meltdown, at least temporarily.

Anatomy of a Financial Crisis

Even though every financial crisis is different, all generally occur in stages—and 2008 is no exception. To see how a financial crisis can come about, let's go through its stages. The first stage is generally the creation of a **bubble**—*unsustainable rapidly rising prices of some type of asset* (such as stocks or houses). Price increases in a bubble are unsustainable because they do not reflect an increase in the real productive value of the asset. In the early 2000s, the bubble was in the housing market.

A bubble is an unsustainable rapidly rising price of some type of asset.

Thinking like a Modern Economist

Tulipmania, the South Sea Bubble, and Behavioral Economics

Bubbles have been a fixture in economies for centuries. Two of the most famous financial bubbles are Tulipmania and the South Sea Bubble.

The height of Tulipmania occurred in Holland between November 1636 and February 1637. It centered on, you guessed it, tulips—a relatively newly introduced popular flower. Over three months, tulip bulb prices are estimated to have risen by several thousand percent, all without any tulips actually changing hands—tulips don't even *grow* between November and February. Instead, speculators tried to make money by buying and reselling *promises* to deliver tulip bulbs the following May, after they had flowered. Contracts for some particularly rare bulbs were reportedly trading for prices equivalent to 20 years of a typical workman's wages, and for a full 12 acres of land. Trading was purely speculative; people bought tulip contracts with the full intention of "flipping" them for a profit well before May. The bubble burst in February when people realized that at the current prices, no one would be willing to pay the outrageous prices for an actual *tulip*.

Another financial bubble was the South Sea bubble of the early 1700s. The South Sea bubble started when rumors spread that the South Sea Company—a company granted a monopoly on trade with South American colonies by the British government—would be enormously profitable. When the stock price of the South Sea Company doubled, others noticed and wanted to get in on the profit, pushing the price up further. The price of its stock rose almost tenfold between January and August of 1720. (The rise was helped along by various shady dealings between the company and members of the British Parliament.)

How could people afford to buy this stock at such high prices? They borrowed and were allowed to leverage their purchases. (Pay me 10 percent now and the remaining 90 percent next week.) As long as the stock price was rising, that wasn't a problem. When it was time to pay the remaining 90 percent, the stockholder could sell the stock at a higher price, repay the loan, and pocket the difference.

But then, suddenly, the rumors reversed. The stock prices started falling and everyone called in their loans. To pay their loans, people tried to sell stock that no one wanted to buy; stock prices plummeted and the bubble burst even more quickly than it had formed.

Behavioral economics and standard economics explain these bubbles differently. Standard economics works hard to provide a rational explanation for financial bubbles. It has a theory of what might be called rational bubbles. For example, some economists have argued that the high prices of tulips and of South Sea Company stock were plausible in light of the scarcity and novelty of certain bulbs and imperfect information about the profitability of trade with the Americas. If bubbles are rational, they should be considered an unavoidable aspect of modern society. Modern behavioral economists disagree. They argue that bubbles form precisely because people *aren't* fully rational—they are subject to herd mentality. That is, they are predictably irrational. This difference is important because if behavioral economists are right, then there *is* a potential role for policy to reduce the severity and occurrence of bubbles.

The key to a bubble is **extrapolative expectations**—*expectations that a trend will continue*. It works like this: Initially, the market experiences a shock, which causes prices to rise. In a standard aggregate supply/aggregate demand model, the initial rise in price is the end of the story. The rise in prices brings the market back into equilibrium. But in a bubble, the initial rise in price leads people to expect further price increases. In anticipation of these price increases, people buy goods and assets, causing aggregate demand to shift out to the right, which leads prices to rise further, fulfilling expectations, and people to expect even more price increases. In a bubble, expectations feed back on themselves, and prices rapidly spiral upward. This is how it works:

In a bubble, expectations feed back on themselves, and prices rapidly spiral upward.

Rise in price → Expectations of a further rise in price → Rise in demand at the current price → Rise in price → Expectations of a further rise in price . . . and so on

The Financial Crisis: The Bubble Bursts

WWW Web Note 14.1 Bubble Analysis

In 2005, housing prices started to level off, and most standard economists talked about prices settling into a permanently high plateau. But by 2006 housing prices began to fall precipitously—and it became clear that the boom in housing prices in the early 2000s had been a financial bubble. As soon as that was recognized, the bubble burst and everyone wanted to get out of housing and housing-related assets before the price of their houses fell further.

The bursting of the bubble involves the same process that led to the bubble—extrapolative expectations; it just works in reverse. The price stops rising, which reverses the expectations of rising prices into falling prices. People begin selling their assets, which leads prices to fall even further. People expect prices to fall even further, which leads more people to sell . . . and so on. Those whose loans exceeded the value of their assets (commonly called being underwater) were forced to sell or to default on their loans. Those defaults led to expectations of further price declines, which brought about further defaults.

The bursting of a bubble involves the same process that led to the bubble—extrapolative expectations; it just works in reverse.

Compared with the stock market crash of 1929, housing prices declined slowly. While financial assets can be sold quickly—the click of a mouse—houses cannot. Houses generally are listed with a real estate agent; buyers look at a number of houses before deciding; then the price is negotiated. Even when people are not paying their mortgage, banks can't just kick people out of their houses; they must foreclose, and that process can take years.

Despite all the difficulties with the housing market, the financial crisis was not directly precipitated by the housing market crisis. It was a crisis in the market for mortgage-backed securities. **Mortgage-backed securities** are *securities that are derivatives of mortgages in which thousands of mortgages are packaged with other mortgages into a bundle of mortgages and sold on the securities market.* These securities are related to housing because their value depends on the value of mortgages, which in turn depends on the ability of homeowners to pay their mortgages, which in turn depends on housing prices.

When the housing market crashed and people stopped paying their mortgages, these mortgage-backed securities lost much of their value. Panic ensued because, like homeowners who had borrowed significant sums to buy their houses, many financial institutions had purchased these securities with mostly borrowed money. Some used **leverage**—*the practice of buying an asset with borrowed money*—to buy those securities and were leveraged at a 30-to-1 ratio, which meant that for every dollar they invested, they had borrowed $30. As the market for mortgage-backed securities dried up, the banks found themselves in a pickle. Those financial institutions that had loaned money to banks wanted their cash, and the banks didn't have it. They had assets to pay their lenders; they just weren't liquid. They didn't have sufficient time to sell those assets and didn't want to have to sell them at fire-sale prices. In economic jargon, the banks were *illiquid,* not insolvent. That means that at nonfire sale prices the banks had sufficient assets to meet their long-term obligations but they didn't have funds to meet their short-term obligations. Without some source of liquidity, they would all go bankrupt. That's when the Fed stepped in as lender of last resort.

Leverage is the practice of buying an asset with borrowed money.

The Fed as the Lender of Last Resort

The Fed engaged in a type of financial triage—taking care of the most damaged banks with emergency measures, doing whatever it could to keep people and firms buying and selling securities. The Fed and the U.S. government took unprecedented actions to try to prevent a modern version of the "bank run" that had thrown the U.S. economy into the Great Depression of the 1930s. Ben Bernanke, the chairman of the Fed, knew what could happen—he'd studied the 1930s and saw the parallels. Fearing the worst, he put aside all conventional monetary theory and started financial triage.

The Fed and the government loaned to banks and the private sector to improve their liquidity, guaranteed loans and financial instruments to reduce the risk of lending to the private sector, and invested in financial institutions by buying assets that no one else would buy to improve their balance sheets. In 2008–2009 the Fed loaned more than a trillion dollars directly to financial institutions, accepting low-quality assets as collateral and directly purchasing short-term bonds from money market mutual funds. In addition, Congress passed legislation authorizing the **Troubled Asset Relief Program (TARP)**—*a program established by Congress in 2008 to purchase up to $700 billion in assets from financial institutions.* All these triage actions were undertaken to prevent a complete meltdown of the U.S. financial system.

Just about all economists agreed that a policy in which the Fed acts as the lender of last resort is good in principle.

The specifics were hotly debated; some economists and policy makers felt it was too much, others felt it was too little, but just about all agreed that a policy in which the Fed acts as the lender of last resort is good in principle. The important point is that all these policies were emergency policies and have to be seen as such. Their goal was clear—to prevent a financial meltdown. The political consensus was based on general agreement that a financial meltdown would throw the economy into a depression. (We will discuss the problems with these emergency policies below.)

The Role of Leverage and Herding in a Crisis

While the Fed's quick action in dealing with the financial crisis is laudable, it may very well have played a significant part in creating the bubble in the first place.

Bubbles are important in a discussion of Fed policy because bubbles are most likely to occur when credit—financial instruments for borrowing—is easily available. With easily available credit people can borrow to invest, increasing leverage. The larger the percentage bought with borrowed funds, the larger the leverage. The reason Fed policy is important to bubbles is that the Fed significantly influences credit availability in an economy. So while the Fed's quick action in dealing with the financial crisis is laudable, it may very well have played a significant part in creating the bubble in the first place.

Leverage

To understand the power of leverage, consider the decision of a person buying a stock. Say you can buy a share of stock at $2 and that you believe that its price will rise to $3 within a year. If you sell the stock after its price rises, you will earn a 50 percent return. While a 50 percent return is pretty good, if you use leverage, you can do even better. What if instead of buying a single $2 stock, you borrow $198 at 10 percent interest and buy 100 shares for $200? When the stock price goes up to $3, you could sell your stock for $300, pay back the $198 you borrowed plus $19.80 in interest, leaving you with a profit of $80.20—about a 4,000 percent return! That's the power of leverage. When you can expect returns like that, why hold back? You'd want to get as much money into the stock market as possible. With everyone buying more stocks, their prices rise, and rise, and rise, very quickly.

Leverage works with all assets and is a central part of any bubble.

Leverage works with all assets and is a central part of any bubble. Bubbles can happen in houses, mortgages, bonds, paintings, baseball cards, antiques—you name it. As long as the price is rising more than the rate of interest at which you can borrow, leverage is a way to get rich quickly. Because expansionary monetary policy increases the degree of leverage in the economy both by lowering interest rates and by making credit more easily available, monetary policy can encourage the development of a financial bubble.

Leverage contributes to a bubble by increasing the ability of people to finance the purchase of goods, services, and financial instruments, despite what might otherwise seem like high prices. It is here where the debate about potential output described in a previous chapter comes in. In the standard macro model, which uses goods price rises as a signal to estimate potential output, until an economy experiences inflation, the economy is seen as not exceeding potential output. Because inflation remained low throughout the early 2000s, the Fed increased the money supply substantially—far more than suggested by the standard Taylor rule, as described in the previous chapter, and far far more than the structural stagnation hypothesis would have suggested it should have, given the large U.S. trade deficit. Both the Taylor Rule and the structural stagnation hypothesis suggested that much tighter monetary policy in the early 2000s was needed than was actually run. What led the Fed to increase the money supply was the fact that increases in the money supply did not push up goods prices, since they were held down by world prices. Instead it made the U.S. economy awash in credit, which allowed enormous increases in leverage in financial markets.

Leverage contributes to a bubble by increasing the ability of people to finance the purchase of goods, services, and financial instruments, despite what might otherwise seem like high prices.

Herding

The other part of the formation of a bubble involves what psychologists and behavioral economists call herding. **Herding** is *the human tendency to follow the crowd.* When people around you see how much others are profiting by buying and selling assets, they want to profit too. They become convinced that the price of the asset is going to rise. When that happens, everyone buys more of the asset on credit, which increases economywide risk enormously. That's what happened in the housing market in the 2000s.

Q-2 What are two central ingredients to the development of a bubble?

Through the middle of the first decade of the 2000s, times were good in the housing and construction markets with housing prices rising nationally at historically high rates. *Flip That House* and similar TV programs showcased people making tens of thousands of dollars by buying a house with very little or no down payment, and selling that house with enormous profit just months later. It seemed as if you could get rich quick just by owning a house. Low interest rates and innovative mortgages (mortgages with zero down payment and no proof of income or creditworthiness) meant people who previously couldn't qualify for a mortgage could buy houses. Some people bought five or six houses, which they couldn't afford, but which they planned to sell before they had to repay the mortgage.

Homeownership rates rose to historic highs of nearly 70 percent. The feeling was that you simply couldn't lose on buying a house as an investment. As long as house prices kept rising, flipping houses and stretching into a mortgage made sense. With rising housing prices, people felt more wealthy—spending more and saving less because their "houses were their savings." When the value of your house is rising by $30,000 a year, you can take out a home equity loan. Whether you save an extra $1,000 or not doesn't seem all that important. All these actions increased the risk of significant problems occurring in the economy if housing prices didn't continue to rise, and left the economy vulnerable to the housing bubble bursting.

WWW Web Note 14.2
Herding Tendencies

But that's not all. Leverage by homeowners was nothing compared with the leverage in the financial sector built on top of the housing market. As mentioned previously, investment banks and hedge funds had figured out how to create securities whose values were *linked* to the performance of these mortgages. These securities were leveraging the already highly leveraged mortgages, creating a financial asset built on double—and in many cases even triple or quadruple—leverage.

Excess leverage played a major role in the financial crisis.

When the financial bubble burst, the U.S. economy was on the verge of a financial meltdown. Luckily, that didn't happen. By 2009 and 2010, it was clear that the U.S. economy had avoided a financial meltdown, but the economy wasn't in good shape.

While it wasn't in a depression, it was stagnating. Unemployment rose to over 10 percent and growth was anemic.

With the threat of a financial meltdown out of the way, economists turned to other issues: Why had the financial system come so close to failing? Why didn't existing regulations prevent the asset bubble? What new regulations could keep another bubble from occurring? What should the Fed do now to get the economy back on its long-run growth path? Let's start by considering the regulation problem.

The Problem of Regulating the Financial Sector

An engineer who designs a bridge that almost collapses would be questioned thoroughly. How did the collapse happen and what can be done to see that it doesn't happen again? So it is appropriate to question economists: How did economists not only let the economic collapse happen, but once the signs of a bubble were clear why didn't they warn society that a financial crisis was about to happen?

Economists answer these questions in various ways. Some emphasize that policy makers were swayed by political interests and wrangling, not by empirical evidence and economic theory. Politicians, not economists, are to blame for the financial crisis. These economists point out that a number of economists recognized the problems and suggested reforms, but policy makers failed to pass new regulations. Moreover, those regulations that were instituted weren't executed correctly. Fed chairman Ben Bernanke expressed this view when he wrote "the recent financial crisis was more a failure of economic engineering and economic management than of what I have called economic science."

In Fed Chairman's Ben Bernanke's view, the recent financial crisis was more a failure of economic engineering and economic management than of economic science.

Other economists are not as sure that economic theory can be absolved of blame. The problem is that in standard economic theory, financial bubbles aren't supposed to happen. People are supposed to be rational and rational people don't make such major mistakes. In standard economic thinking the prices of assets are considered the best estimate of those future prices, which is called the **efficient market hypothesis**—*all financial decisions are made by rational people and are based on all relevant information that accurately reflects the value of assets today and in the future*. Rational people will recognize that asset prices are rising too quickly.

The efficient market hypothesis assumes that all financial decisions are made by rational people and are based on all relevant information that accurately reflects the value of assets today and in the future.

The efficient market hypothesis has an important implication for monetary policy: Since bubbles can't happen, monetary policy makers didn't have to pay attention to the rising housing prices that occurred in the early 2000s. It wasn't housing price inflation; the real value of housing was rising. The efficient market hypothesis said that asset markets, such as housing, could be left on automatic pilot. With assets prices set on automatic, monetary policy could focus on goods market inflation as an indicator of whether monetary policy was too expansionary. As mentioned above, in the standard *AS/AD* model, when there was little inflation and no threat of accelerating inflation, monetary policy could be expansionary. That was the view that guided conventional macroeconomic theory. Policy makers didn't worry about the financial crisis because conventional economic theory was telling them they didn't have to worry about it. So for unconventional economists conventional economists are to blame. Ben Bernanke is wrong; it was a failure of economic science.

For unconventional economists, economic science is to blame for the financial crisis.

The events of 2008 changed the view that markets are rational for many economists, including some of the leading advocates of the former conventional model. For example, the previous chairman of the Fed, Alan Greenspan, stated, "I made a mistake in presuming that the self-interests of organizations, specifically banks and others, were such that they were best capable of protecting their own shareholders and their equity in the firms." He continued by saying that his conventional worldview was "not working." He stated "that's precisely the reason I was shocked, because I have been going for 40 years or more with very considerable evidence that it was working exceptionally well."

It was at that point that alternative views, such as the structural stagnation view, started to gain in acceptance. These alternative views held that while people were individually rational, they could be collectively irrational, following herding behavior. This meant that asset prices were subject to bubbles, and monetary policy and regulation would have to be designed to prevent asset price bubbles as well as prevent goods market inflation. This made conducting monetary policy and designing financial regulation much more difficult. It is a process that requires institutional knowledge, judgment and educated common sense that was on the lookout for bubbles. Policy cannot be based on fully predetermined rules.

When society can be collectively irrational, as unconventional economists believe to be the case, monetary policy is much more difficult; it requires institutional knowledge, judgment, and educated common sense.

One of the commonsense implications of this alternative view was that when monetary policy is too expansionary, and world prices are holding goods market inflation down because of globalization, as mentioned earlier, excess liquidity from monetary policy could be channeled into asset price bubbles. This was the structural stagnationist's viewpoint. Many economists, including behavioral economists, heterodox economists, post-Keynesian economists, Austrian economists, and more, had been arguing that bubbles could and did exist for years. One in particular, Hyman Minsky, a post-Keynesian economist, developed a psychological theory that predicted asset bubbles as almost inevitable in a capitalist economy.

So a wide variety of economists of quite different political persuasions accepted that bubbles were possible. Where they differed was in how bubbles should be dealt with; these debates are continuing.

Regulation, Bubbles, and the Financial Sector

The assumption that the market on its own can be collectively irrational creates the need for regulation, or an institutional structure that will prevent that collective irrationality from developing. The question is how that should be done. After the financial crisis led to a financial meltdown in 1929 and the Great Depression, the United States instituted strong controls over the financial sector. These regulatory controls were designed to prevent the financial markets from freezing up again in the future. Government set up rules for banks—what they could and could not do—it also set up a system of **deposit insurance**—*a system under which the federal government promises to reimburse an individual for any losses due to bank failure*—which would help prevent future bank runs. These rules were strong and were meant to see that a financial crisis would not happen again.

To implement the deposit insurance the government created the **Federal Deposit Insurance Corporation (FDIC)**—*a government institution that guarantees bank deposits of up to $250,000.* That guarantee discouraged bank runs, but it also created a *moral hazard problem*—a problem that arises when people's actions do not reflect the full cost of their actions. Specifically, with deposit insurance, people could put their money into a bank that offered high interest rates even though the bank made excessively risky loans. If the bank ran out of money because its loans went bad, the federal government would cover the loss. Depositors could earn high interest assured they would not lose their money.

Q-3 What is a lender of last resort and how does it relate to moral hazard.

To offset the moral hazard problem that deposit insurance would create, government (1) established strict regulations of banks, (2) separated banks from other financial institutions, and (3) designed systems so that necessary financial transactions that were central to the operation of the economy stayed within banks. These were included in a number of financial laws passed in the 1930s, the most important of which was known as the **Glass-Steagall Act**—*an act of Congress passed in 1933 that established deposit insurance and implemented a number of banking regulations including prohibiting commercial banks from investing in the securities market.* The intent was to keep commercial banks from speculating in the stock market or in other risky financial asset markets.

REAL-WORLD APPLICATION

Moral Hazard and Bailouts in the Backcountry

Many people choose to ski or ride in the backcountry, hiking (or helicoptering, or snowcatting) mountains that aren't owned by traditional resorts. It's supposed to be quite a rush, and it's a great way to ensure that you get fresh powder. But every year a few people have unfortunate accidents. If a skier is buried in an avalanche, or a snowboarder has hit a tree and needs rapid evacuation, all efforts are made to save him (yes, it's usually a him)—often at great expense to taxpayers.

The basic principle of the market says that with the freedom to backcountry ski should come the responsibility to pay for any costs of your own rescue—taxpayers shouldn't be on the hook for costs incurred by some reckless kid who wanted a thrill. But the simple fact is that many backcountry skiers and riders are young and (relatively) poor: They simply won't be able to pay for it, and taxpayers *will* be on the hook. Much as taxpayers might like to scare people away from the backcountry with *threats* of "no rescue" for people with no ability to pay, when push comes to shove, if someone is dying on the mountain and can be rescued, they're *going* to be rescued—and they know it, too. What is to be done?

There's no right answer to that question. But if rescues get sufficiently expensive, there is good reason to regulate backcountry skiing, say by banning it outright, or by requiring a backcountry ski license—or imposing jail time for violators.

Financial regulation is similar: The financial sector is so key to the economy that it's virtually certain to be bailed out after a major crisis, and it knows it. The question then becomes: What are the best regulations to prevent the costs of bailing it out from being too high?

With the institution of these new regulations, the United States had a highly regulated commercial banking system. The point of the regulations was to make commercial banking boring—and therefore safe. People called commercial banking the "3-6-3 business"—borrow at 3 percent, lend at 6 percent, and be on the golf course by 3:00 p.m. Banks couldn't invest in equities and were prohibited from paying interest on deposits. Both these restrictions reduced the ability of banks to engage in risky behavior. These regulations were implemented as a result of the Depression, in the belief that the government could never again let banks go under—they were too important to fail. And if they were too important to fail, they have to be regulated to address the moral hazard problems.

Any type of guarantee, or expectation of a bailout, can create a moral hazard.

It isn't only deposit insurance that can create a moral hazard. Any type of guarantee, or expectation of bailout, can do the same thing. An example can be seen by considering the effects of subsidizing loans for homeowners facing foreclosure, or even of reducing the principal of loans that homeowners owe. Suppose that, in 2005, you had prudently decided not to buy a house because you believed that houses were already significantly overpriced. Your foolish friend, on the other hand, bought into the "house prices always rise" myth and decided to buy a big McMansion that he could not really afford. You were prudent and your friend was foolish, and he's underwater on his house and facing foreclosure. Now suppose the government comes along and bails him out, or lowers his principal since it doesn't want him to face foreclosure. What's the outcome? He ends up with a nice house and you end up with nothing. Who's foolish now?

The belief that the government will bail people and firms out when they make stupid decisions helped create the crisis in the first place.

The belief that the government will bail people and firms out when they make stupid decisions helped create the crisis in the first place, and any bailout now will likely lead people to expect a bailout in the future. They will then choose to follow riskier strategies than they otherwise would have, potentially creating even larger problems in the future. So the bailout rewards precisely the wrong type of behavior, and hence creates a moral hazard problem for future decisions. To offset those moral hazard problems, either strict regulation is needed, or the possibilities of bailouts have to be taken off the table. For individuals, this regulation would mean strict requirements about down payments and the income level needed to buy a home. For firms it would mean financial regulations and limitations on what firms too important to fail can and cannot do. That's what the Glass-Steagall Act did.

The Law of Diminishing Control

If we had regulations in the 1930s, why didn't those regulations protect us in 2008? An important reason is that over time the regulations designed in the 1930s became less and less effective. The reason can be called the **law of diminishing control,** which holds that *any regulation will become less effective over time as individuals or firms being regulated will figure out ways to circumvent those regulations through innovation, technological change, and political pressure*. This means that even if the initial regulations do what they are supposed to do, over time they will become less effective. In banking, the financial sector simply moved its risky operations, which the regulations were meant to prevent, outside the banking sector. So while the regulations contained risk by keeping the "core" of the banking system within a well-regulated commercial banking sector, they did not contain risk in the broader financial sector. It is a bit like the drinking laws for minors in the United States. On most campuses, the laws don't stop underage drinking; they just push it into the dorms or private homes.

Q-4 What causes diminishing control of regulations?

Trying to regulate banks is a bit like trying to regulate drinking by minors. The regulation doesn't stop it; it just pushes the problem somewhere else.

New Financial Institutions and Instruments An example of financial innovation that circumvented bank regulation was the creation of NOW accounts in the 1970s. Under the Glass-Steagall Act only commercial banks could offer checking accounts, but they couldn't pay interest on those deposits. Savings banks had the benefit of being able to pay interest on deposits, but couldn't offer checking accounts. In the 1970s, savings banks got around the regulation by issuing what were called NOW (negotiable order of withdrawal) accounts. With a NOW account a customer could direct the savings bank to send funds to a third party. These withdrawals looked almost identical to checks from a commercial bank. But since the funds were legally considered to be savings accounts, savings banks avoided regulations prohibiting interest on checking accounts. Money flowed out of commercial banks and into savings banks. Other financial institutions developed products such as money market accounts and mutual fund accounts, which also let depositors write checks on their accounts, which were comprised of not just cash but bonds and even stocks. Regulations no longer solved the problem of preventing the financial sector from paying interest on the new accounts that were the equivalent of checking accounts.

Regulations Covered Fewer Financial Instruments The development of new financial instruments described above is just one example. Such changes occurred in just about every aspect of the law. By the 1980s, it was clear that the Glass-Steagall Act was no longer preventing activities it was meant to prevent. It simply moved the practice outside the banking system and into other financial institutions.

By the 1980s it was clear that the Glass-Steagall Act was no longer preventing activities it was meant to prevent.

As new financial instruments developed, regulated commercial banks lost business to unregulated financial institutions. Thus, what had been a protective umbrella over the financial system that is necessary for a smoothly functioning economy provided cover for a smaller and smaller segment of the financial industry. The commercial banking system was still regulated, but the "financial oil" increasingly flowed through the less regulated parts of the financial infrastructure. This shift was compounded by the fact that financial markets were becoming global, and the U.S. regulations controlled only U.S. financial institutions. Many U.S financial institutions could legitimately threaten to move to those countries that offered the least regulation. (Think of it as a child of divorced parents who plays one parent off the other to get the most lenient rules.) This reduced the ability of the United States to strictly regulate many financial institutions.

When regulation successfully eliminates or reduces the problems, people begin to forget that the regulation was necessary in the first place.

POLITICAL PRESSURE TO REDUCE REGULATIONS Politics is another reason regulation becomes less effective; when regulation successfully eliminates or reduces the problems, people begin to forget that the regulation was necessary in the first place. Instead, the groups being regulated view regulations as unnecessary restrictions and will lobby to dismantle them. With the Great Depression fresh in everyone's memory, people in the 1930s favored regulation to avert repeating the Depression. But as decades passed and societal memories of the Great Depression faded, so did that view. Regulation and regulators were increasingly viewed by many as undesirable hindrances to the free market and all its magic. That was the view that Alan Greenspan referred to in the earlier quote. The belief that the market could self-regulate meant that relatively low-paid regulators were faced with the nearly impossible task of balancing the pressures of innovation that made the regulations obsolete against the need to get *some* regulation within an atmosphere that saw regulation as preventing the U.S. economy from growing.

Politics also had to deal with an inherent problem of regulation—the **too-big-to-fail problem**—*the problem that large financial institutions are essential to the workings of an economy, requiring government to step into to prevent their failure.* The too-big-to-fail problem is another example of the moral hazard problem. If individuals in the financial sector recognize the financial sector's importance to the economy and know that the government will be forced to bail them out, they change their behavior, just like your kids change their behavior when they know that their parents will bail them out. They do stupid things. The problem with kids, and with large banks, is that when you threaten them that you aren't going to bail them out, the threat isn't credible. It takes resolve that I, and most governments, don't have. (Note to my children—my wife has that resolve.) Unless one has that resolve, no threat will be credible, which means that kids and businesses (with soft parents and soft governments) will continue to do stupid things; they won't take the full consequences of their actions into account.

Q-5 What did government do to address the too-big-to-fail problem?

In response to the crisis, in 2010 the United States passed the **Dodd-Frank Wall Street Reform and Consumer Protection Act**—*a new financial regulatory structure to limit risk-taking and require banks to report their holdings so that regulators could assess risk-taking behavior*. The Dodd-Frank Law attempts to minimize the too-big-to-fail problem. If a company is at risk of default, a process is put in place to liquidate the corporation, limiting the impact on the economy. The hope is that these regulations will protect the U.S. economy from future financial meltdowns. The law once again limits banks' ability to invest in securities, consolidates regulatory agencies to improve their effectiveness, expands oversight to some non-bank financial institutions, and creates new tools for dealing with financial crises. Unfortunately, few economists believe that the new law, even before the law of diminishing marginal control has set in, has resolved the financial regulation problem. Legal and financial scholars on all sides of the political spectrum have criticized the law as both insufficient to prevent another financial crisis in some aspects and overly restrictive of financial institutions in others. Thus, one can expect both further problems and additional regulatory reform over the coming decade.

General Principles of Regulation

The basic guideline of regulation is that along with the freedom to undertake activities in the market comes responsibility for one's actions.

Economics does not identify ideal regulations, but it does provide some general guidelines. The basic guideline is that along with the freedom to undertake activities in the market comes the responsibility for one's actions. If firms (or kids) are not, and cannot be made responsible for the negative consequences of their actions, there is a role for regulations to restrict the set of actions firms are permitted to take. Regulation is necessary if a bailout is in the cards. (As I tell my kids—the golden rule of economics is: Him who pays the bills makes the rules.)

Regulation is necessary if a bailout is in the cards.

The question policy makers face in trying to design the rules and regulations for our economy in the future is: Can a government influenced by special interests institute the right type of regulation? Economists come to different answers on this question, which is why they have different views of regulation.

Let's close our discussion of regulation with three general precepts about dealing with financial crises that most economists would sign on to. They are:

Q-6 What are the three principles of regulation?

- *Set as few bad precedents as possible.* Policies that keep the economy alive might create long-run problems. Recognize these problems, and try to offset them as best you can.
- *Deal with moral hazard.* If a firm or individual is to be unregulated, it should be subject to the consequences of its actions. This leads to a corollary: If a firm or individual is considered too big to fail, it has to be regulated. Notice that this rule does not say that government should or should not regulate. It just says that it has to be consistent.
- *Deal with the law of diminishing control.* Regulation has to be considered a process, not a one-time decision. The economy is a dynamic changing entity, subject to the law of diminishing control, which means that when new business practices and financial instruments change, rules must change. Expect innovation and establish a method of changing those regulations to adapt to the changing situation without weakening the regulations.

Monetary Policy in the Post–Financial Crisis Era

Now let us turn to the question: What monetary policy should the Fed follow after it has fulfilled its lender of last resort role and avoided a financial crisis? In other words, what is the Fed's appropriate monetary policy role in a post–financial crisis era?

Coming out of a financial crisis, the Fed was carrying a large number of loans to banks and other financial institutions that it made to provide the banks with liquidity. As the threat of a financial meltdown subsided, that role had ended. The standard practice would be for the Fed to wind down policies as the lender of last resort, and revert back to conventional monetary policies. A number of economists called on the Fed to do precisely that. But with the economy in a deep recession, those policies would be highly politically unpopular because they would slow down the recovery.

After the financial crisis subsided, the standard practice would have been for the Fed to wind down its lender-of-last-resort loans. It did not do that because the economy was in a deep recession.

The argument for unwinding those positions despite the high unemployment was that this was not your typical recession—it was structural stagnation that reflected structural problems caused by globalization, and the 5–6 percent growth rate needed until the economy returned to trend was not in the cards. The structural problems that structural stagnationists see as the cause of the slow growth could not be solved by conventional monetary policy. To maintain expansionary monetary policy essentially meant continuing the policies that caused the bubble in the first place by expanding credit in the economy enormously. If the economy is in a structural stagnation, expanding credit beyond the initial triage policy necessary to save the economy from imploding will only increase the likelihood of a further, even more damaging, bubble. This is the case even if that policy of monetary restraint will leave the economy with higher unemployment than otherwise. If the problem facing the U.S. economy is a structural stagnation, a primary policy focus has to be on resolving the structural problems before expansionary monetary policy is called for.

If the problem facing the U.S. economy is a structural stagnation problem, a primary policy focus has to be on resolving the structural problems before expansionary monetary policy is called for.

In this view, expansionary monetary policy not only would not resolve these structural problems; it would eliminate the impetus for the private sector to solve them as well. Expansionary monetary policy in the face of these structural problems would be analogous to giving painkillers to an addict, when what he needs is detox. According to structural stagnationists, the appropriate policy is for the Fed to return to standard monetary policy, accepting that that will push up unemployment now in order to set up the foundations for sustainable growth in the future.

The conventional view is that it is appropriate for the Fed to attempt to pull the economy out of the recession without addressing structural problems.

These concerns by those economists who argued that the economy was in a structural stagnation were pushed aside by policy makers, and the recession was treated as a standard recession, not a structural stagnation. The conventional view was that it is appropriate for the Fed to attempt to pull the economy out of the recession through expansionary monetary policy, and for the federal government to attempt to pull the economy out of the recession through expansionary fiscal policy without addressing the structural problems. These were the policies that the Fed followed, and has continued to follow.

Unconventional Monetary Policy in the Wake of a Financial Crisis

Although the Fed wanted to expand the economy, it had a problem. It had already done all it could to expand the economy using conventional monetary policy in its role of lender of last resort. The Fed funds rate was essentially zero; the banking system was awash in excess reserves. But the economy was not growing and conventional monetary policy was not working. Expansionary monetary policy was not leading to increases in money and credit; instead it just ended up as excess reserves in the banks as we saw in the last chapter. To get around this problem, the Fed created a new set of policies meant to stimulate the economy through unconventional means. These policies included quantitative easing, credit or qualitative easing, operation twist, and a precommitment policy. Let's consider each of these.

QUANTITATIVE EASING In many ways quantitative easing is really not significantly different from conventional monetary policy. As you learned in the last chapter, conventional monetary policy involves the Fed buying and selling bonds to affect the money supply and therefore the Fed funds rate. But as we discussed above, in the aftermath of the financial crisis, standard open market operations did not increase the money supply. Even after the Fed flooded the system with reserves, banks did not make new loans; they simply held more excess reserves. So, as we saw in the last chapter, excess reserves shot up. While monetary policy pulled the short-term interest rate down, it had almost no effect on the long-term interest rate.

Q-7 How does quantitative easing differ from conventional monetary policy?

Quantitative easing is *a policy of targeting a particular quantity of money by buying financial assets from banks and other financial institutions with newly created money*. This policy targets the monetary base in the economy rather than targeting interest rates. With quantitative easing, the Fed buys longer-term and nongovernmental bonds, which increases the money supply directly. So when the Fed deals in the long end of the securities market, the amount of excess reserves doesn't matter. The increase in the money supply goes directly into the economy, bypassing the banking sector. That's why it is called quantitative easing.

Quantitative easing might also be called an asset price support system because it holds the prices of assets up higher, and longer interest rates lower, than they would have been. Interest rates fall because, as you learned in a previous chapter, interest rates and asset prices are inversely related. Thus, the almost trillion dollars of mortgage-backed securities that the Fed bought held up the prices of those securities, significantly helping financial institutions that held these securities. While it helped holders of stocks and bonds, it hurt savers, who received low interest rates.

You can see the desired effect of quantitative easing by considering the yield curve shown in Figure 14-1. As I discussed in the last chapter, conventional monetary policy pushes down on the low end of the yield curve, with the expectation that in doing so, it will push down the long-run interest rate as well, thereby shifting the entire curve down. Quantitative easing pushes the upper end of the yield curve down directly, thereby holding down the interest rate for investors and stimulating asset markets and the economy.

FIGURE 14-1 Quantitative Easing's Effect on the Yield Curve

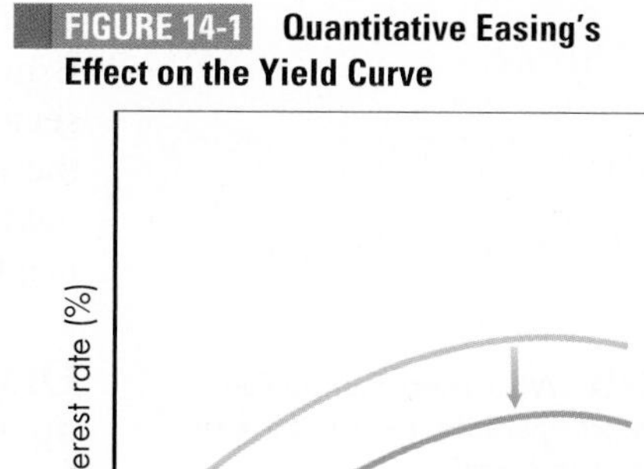

CREDIT OR QUALITATIVE EASING Another unconventional policy that the Fed used during this time period was called **credit easing**—*the purchase of long-term government bonds and securities from private financial corporations for the purpose of changing the mix of securities held by the Fed toward less liquid and more risky assets.* Specifically, in credit easing the Fed increases its holdings of long-term nongovernmental securities such as mortgage-backed securities. So instead of buying short-term government bonds, it buys mortgage-backed securities. It is called credit easing because it is designed to channel credit into markets directly without going through banks. It is also called qualitative easing since it involves the Fed changing the quality of the assets it holds. Credit easing differs from quantitative easing because the primary goal of credit easing is to change the quality—or mix—of assets it buys. You can see the impact of credit easing on the balance sheet of the Fed in Figure 14-2.

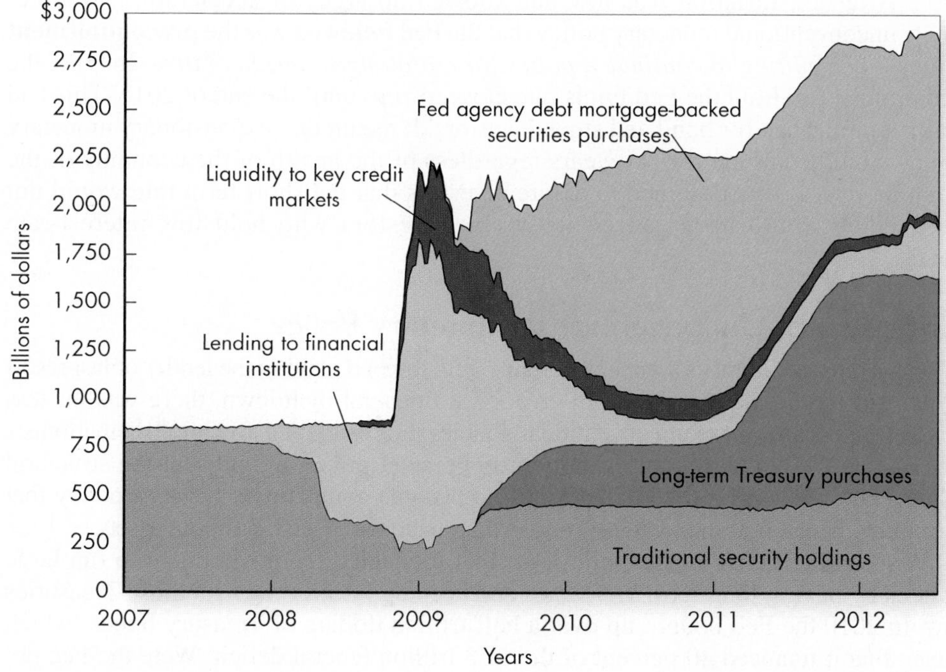

FIGURE 14-2 Change in the Fed's Assets

In credit easing, the Fed reduces its traditional security holdings and replaces them with less liquid and riskier assets.

The purpose of credit easing is to remove from financial corporations assets that are difficult to trade, thereby reducing the number of risky assets held by financial firms. In 2010 the Federal Reserve purchased $1.25 trillion of mortgage-backed securities to support the mortgage market. While these purchases did in fact increase the monetary base in a way similar to a purchase of government securities, it also held up the price of bank assets such as mortgage-backed securities, which was its primary goal.

Q-8 What effect did the Fed expect operation twist to have on the yield curve?

Operation Twist In 2011 the Fed added another unconventional tool—**operation twist**—*selling short-term Treasury bills and buying long-term Treasury bonds without creating more new money*. Like credit easing, operation twist changes the composition of the Fed's portfolio; unlike credit easing it does not entail buying private securities. Its purpose is not to reduce private bank risk, but to lower long-term interest rates. That is, its purpose is to "twist" the yield curve. The tool was created to address concerns that because quantitative easing increased the monetary base, it would lead to inflation. With operation twist, the Fed offset its purchases of long-term bonds by selling an equal amount of short-term bonds. In principal, selling short-term bonds would raise short-term interest rates and twist the yield curve, making it flatter. You can see operation twist by again considering the intended effect on the yield curve in Figure 14-3.

FIGURE 14-3 Effect of Operation Twist on the Yield Curve

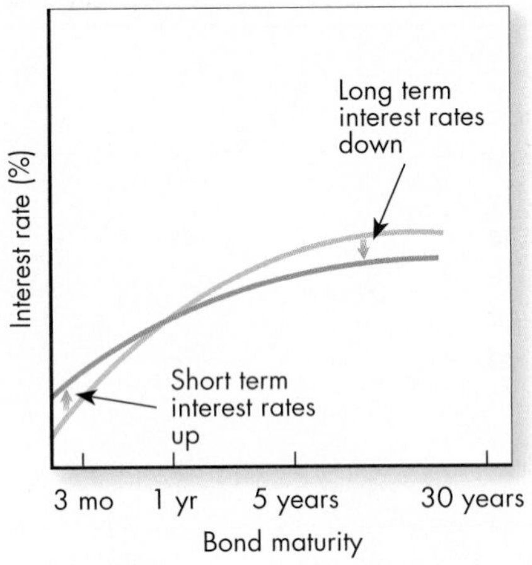

Operation twist places downward pressure on the long-term rate and upward pressure on the short-term rate. In actuality, since banks were holding so many excess reserves, the effect on the short-term rate was negligible, so only the long part of the yield curve shifted down, relative to where it otherwise would have been. But it did so without changing the money supply.

Precommitment Policy Even with these policies some economists were concerned that the Fed was not doing enough to expand the economy. After all, inflation was low and showed no signs of acceleration. Another unconventional monetary policy that the Fed followed was the **precommitment policy**—*committing to continue a policy for a prolonged period of time*. In 2011 the Fed promised to hold the Fed funds rate close to zero until the end of 2014. This had major significance for bond and stock investors. It meant that expansionary monetary policy would continue for two years regardless of the health of the economy or the inflation rate. It was designed to assure investors that the short-term rate would not rise, which would have caused losses by investors who held low-interest-rate bonds.

Q-9 What four unconventional tools did the Fed use to address the crisis?

Criticisms of Unconventional Monetary Policy

Whereas most economists were comfortable with the Fed playing the lender of last resort to prevent the financial crisis from creating a financial meltdown, there was far less general support for these unconventional policies. For example, structural stagnationists argued that the policies would simply prop up asset prices and prevent the structural adjustments needed for the United States to become competitive. It was a policy that essentially bailed out financial institutions that made bad decisions about assets.

A second criticism of the policy was that it enabled the government to run large deficits by buying long-term Treasuries and keeping interest rates on those Treasuries low. In 2010 the Fed bought up over a half trillion dollars of Treasury bonds, which meant that it financed 40 percent of the $1.3 trillion federal deficit. Were the Fed not buying government debt, the interest rate on those government bonds would likely have been higher. Since these deficits are unsustainable in the long run, eventually the Fed will be forced to reverse its policies and tighten monetary policy, which will raise interest rates and interest payments. By holding the interest rate artificially low the Fed was masking the eventual (long-term) cost of that debt. (These issues will be discussed more in the next two chapters.

A third criticism is that the unconventional monetary policy is leaving the Fed open to enormous losses. For example, in 2012 the Fed owned more than $800 billion of mortgage-backed securities, which it carried on its books at par value (the value when it was first issued rather its current value). But in the market, similar mortgage-backed securities were selling at about 50 cents of par, which meant that the Fed was overvaluing them by $400 billion dollars. If it had used market valuation, the Fed's balance sheet would show a loss of $400 billion dollars.

Similar issues were raised about its holdings of long-term government bonds. Because interest rates fluctuate, those holding long-term Treasury bonds face a risk of declining prices. To see this, let us say the Fed holds a $1,000, 30-year bond that pays 3 percent and the interest rate in the economy is 3 percent. Bondholders will be indifferent between holding Treasuries and other financial instruments, and that bond will sell for its face value, $1,000. But now say the interest rate rises to 6 percent; the value of the bond will fall, since if one can get 6 percent on new bonds, who wants to hold a bond that pays 3 percent? The price of the Treasury bond will have to fall to close to $500 so that it returns an interest rate of 6 percent to remain competitive. Should that happen, the Fed will have large losses, which would require the government to issue more debt.

A fourth criticism of the unconventional monetary policy concerns the commitment to keeping short- and long-term interest rates low. Precommitments tie the hands of the Fed, giving it no ability to reverse its stance on the Fed funds rate should the economy grow faster than expected or inflationary pressures emerge.

Q-10 What are five criticisms of the Fed's unconventional policies?

A final criticism of unconventional monetary policy is that the Fed doesn't have a reasonable exit strategy. Reversing any of these unconventional policies and returning to conventional monetary policy will require selling its long-term bond and asset holdings, slowing the economy in precisely the opposite way in which the policies are now speeding it up. If we are in a structural stagnation, these unwinding policies will make it even more difficult to get out of the stagnation. How will the Fed get rid of its mortgage-backed securities whose value has fallen significantly? How will it sell long-term bonds without raising long-term interest rates and risking economic growth? Further, if the Fed wants to unwind the policy, it will have to untwist the twist—selling long-term bonds and buying short-term bonds—which will push the long-term interest rate up.

Any unwinding will both slow the economy and hold asset prices down and will be politically unpopular. This will place the Fed in the political limelight. So rather than operating in the background of providing a stable structure for the economy, it will be exposed to greater political criticism.

How much of a concern the Fed's exit strategy will be depends in large part on fiscal policy and on the size of the deficits that the U.S. government continues to run.

How much of a concern this exit strategy will be depends in large part on fiscal policy and on the size of the deficits that the U.S. government continues to run. As we will discuss in future chapters, if the United States government continues to run the trillion dollar plus deficits, the creditworthiness of the U.S. government will be called into question. At that point, the Fed may well face strong political pressure to support the government by buying its long-term bonds, even as the unwinding strategy calls for selling them. If there is concern about U.S. inflation, the situation could possibly get out of hand, and there could be a future financial crisis in the United States similar to that which led to the unconventional monetary policy to begin with. These are serious concerns about the future.

Conclusion

I began this chapter with a quotation from a group of economists who were opposed to the unconventional monetary policy. It continued:

> We subscribe to your [Ben Bernanke's] statement in the *Washington Post* on November 4 that "the Federal Reserve cannot solve all the economy's problems on its own." In this case, we think improvements in tax, spending and regulatory policies must take precedence in a national growth program, not further monetary stimulus.

The problem with these calls for structural change is that they offer no quick fix, and if the monetary stimulus is reduced, the U.S. economy will likely stagnate more than it currently is stagnating. So those who argue that not undertaking this unconventional monetary policy will lead to increased unemployment and slower growth are also right. It isn't as if any group has a magic answer to the macro problems the United States faces. In my view, politicians who say they do are either living in an illusory world or saying what they think will guarantee election. They are not presenting the difficult choices that the United States is currently facing.

It isn't as if any group has a magic answer to the macro problems that the United States faces.

Summary

- The financial sector provides the credit that all other sectors need for both day-to-day and long-term needs. If the financial sector were to collapse, all other sectors would collapse along with it. *(LO14-1)*
- The Fed has the resources and ability to lend to financial institutions and banks when no one else will, thereby averting an economic crash. *(LO14-1)*
- The stages of a financial crisis are (1) asset prices rise to unsustainable levels (a bubble develops), (2) asset prices fall precipitously (the bubble bursts), and (3) the economy falls into a financial crisis. *(LO14-1)*
- Two ingredients of a bubble are herding and leveraging. Herding creates the run up in prices. Leveraging increases people's ability to herd, which increases prices further. The Fed can create a bubble with significant expansionary monetary policy. *(LO14-2)*
- Government regulations that guarantee bailouts for banks and financial institutions create the moral hazard problem, which leads banks and financial institutions to take risks for which they don't have to pay. *(LO14-3)*
- Regulations have limited impact on bank behavior because of the law of diminishing control. *(LO14-3)*
- Because the failure of large banks would have disastrous effects on the real economy, they are considered too big to fail, which leads to the moral hazard problem. *(LO14-3)*
- Three general principles of regulation are (1) set as few precedents as possible to limit the moral hazard problem, (2) deal with moral hazard by requiring banks to face the consequences of their actions, and (3) change regulations as innovations emerge and business practices change. *(LO14-3)*
- The Fed implemented unconventional policies such as quantitative easing, credit easing, operation twist, and precommitment policy. The purpose was to reduce the amount of risky assets held by banks, encourage bank lending, and encourage private borrowing. *(LO14-4)*
- Criticisms of using unconventional monetary policy are (1) it delays structural adjustments needed to return to growth, (2) enabling the government to run high deficits, (3) the risk of a Fed default, limiting the ability of the Fed to reverse action quickly, (4) precommitment tying the hands of the Fed and (5) the risks associated with its exit strategies. *(LO14-4)*

Key Terms

bubble *(309)*
credit easing *(321)*
deposit insurance *(315)*
Dodd-Frank Wall Street Reform and Consumer Protection Act *(318)*
efficient market hypothesis *(314)*
extrapolative expectations *(310)*
Federal Deposit Insurance Corporation (FDIC) *(315)*
Glass-Steagall Act *(315)*
herding *(313)*
law of diminishing control *(317)*
lender of last resort *(309)*
leverage *(311)*
liquid *(309)*
mortgage-backed securities *(311)*
operation twist *(322)*
precommitment policy *(322)*
quantitative easing *(320)*
solvent *(309)*
too-big-to-fail problem *(318)*
Troubled Asset Relief Program (TARP) *(312)*

Questions and Exercises

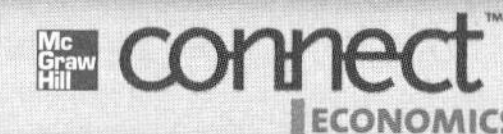

1. Why is the Fed's role as lender of last resort an important function of the Fed? (*LO14-1*)
2. What role did liquidity play in the financial crisis in 2008? What caused this lack of liquidity? (*LO14-1*)
3. What is the role of extrapolative expectations in increasing the price level and creating a bubble? (*LO14-1*)
4. If you invest $100 in a stock, borrowing 90 percent of the $100 at 10 percent interest, and the stock price rises by 20 percent, what is the return on your investment? (*LO14-2*)
5. Why did the Fed follow far more expansionary policy than the Taylor rule suggested? (*LO14-2*)
6. In the standard *AS/AD* model, what role does a financial bubble play in determining whether an economy exceeds potential output? Explain your answer. (*LO14-2*)
7. What is the efficient market hypothesis and how does it relate to government regulation? (*LO14-3*)
8. What is the moral hazard problem and how does deposit insurance lead to it? (*LO14-3*)
9. What are three reasons why the Glass-Steagall Act became less and less effective? (*LO14-3*)
10. Why are large financial institutions considered to be too big to fail? What problem does it create? (*LO14-3*)
11. Why do some economists believe the Fed needs to unwind monetary policies instituted during the recession? What is the risk in doing so? (*LO14-4*)
12. What distinguishes credit easing from quantitative easing? What problem was each designed to address? (*LO14-4*)
13. What distinguishes operation twist from credit easing? (*LO14-4*)
14. Demonstrate the different effects that quantitative easing and operation twist are expected to have on the yield curve. Explain your answer. (*LO14-4*)
15. How was operation twist expected to avoid the criticisms of quantitative easing? (*LO14-4*)
16. How would a precommitment policy address problems in the economy? What is the risk of such a policy? (*LO14-4*)

Questions from Alternative Perspectives

1. Ron Paul , 2012 presidential candidate, believes that the Federal Reserve should be abolished and our monetary system should be replaced by a gold standard. How does the experience of the past decade reflect on that idea? (Austrian)
2. Hyman Minsky's theory of fluctuations in output in a capitalist economy was ignored by mainstream economics but has proven to be much closer to reality than are theories suggested by mainstream macroeconomists. What are some reasons why his theory was ignored? (Post-Keynesian)
3. Post-Keynesian macroeconomist Paul Davidson has argued that the central characteristic of the Keynesian view of markets is nonergodicity, which in simple terms implies the lack of an ability to know or forecast the future. How does nonergodicity undermine the efficient markets hypothesis? (Post-Keynesian)

4. If Greece makes its bonds legal payment for taxes, it will be able to sell all the bonds it wants to without worrying about discounts. What prevents the Greek government from following this solution? (Post-Keynesian)
5. Many of the regulators and overseers of the government bailout came from the same firms that brought about the crisis in the first place. Can we expect reasonable regulation when that is the case? (Radical)

Issues to Ponder

1. If a country goes bankrupt and cannot pay its debts, which of its responsibilities should take precedence: paying bondholders or paying the pensions of its employees?
2. If the U.S. economy were to go into another financial crisis and additional monetary stimulus were needed to prevent a financial collapse, what measures would you suggest the government take?
3. If asset markets aren't efficient, then it should be possible for investors to consistently make money by betting that the price of an asset will return to its "correct" value. That doesn't seem to be the case. Does that suggest that the efficient market hypothesis is correct?
4. How can economists support a bailout package when they recognize that the bailout will create a moral hazard problem?
5. If you had a son whom you had forbidden to drink and drive, threatening to throw him out of the house if he does drink and drive, do you throw him out of the house if he does so?
6. In what sense is the financial crisis a result of deregulation?

Answers to Margin Questions

1. The financial sector facilitates the running of the real economy. The economy cannot function without the financial sector. (*p. 309; LO14-1*)
2. Two central ingredients to a bubble are leveraging and herding. (*p. 313; LO14-2*)
3. The lender of last resort is an institution that promises to lend to banks and financial institutions when no one else will. It leads to the moral hazard problem because banks will take greater risks knowing the government will cover their loses. (*p. 315; LO14-3*)
4. The effectiveness of regulations falls over time as banks and financial institutions find ways to circumvent the regulations and the perceived risk facing these institutions diminishes. (*p. 317; LO14-3*)
5. The government implemented new regulations that limited risk-taking by banks and financial institutions. These new regulations require that they report their assets, and it established a process of gradually dismantling financial institutions that face insolvency. (*p. 318; LO14-3*)
6. Three principles are set as few precedents as possible, deal with moral hazard, and deal with the law of diminishing control. (*p. 319; LO14-3*)
7. Conventional monetary policy targets the Fed funds rate. Quantitative easing targets the amount of money in the economy by buying long-term bonds and nongovernmental bonds, which adds money directly into the economy. (*p. 320; LO14-4*)
8. Operation twist was implemented to pull long-term interest rates down and short-term interest rates up, that is, invert the normal yield curve. (*p. 322; LO14-4*)
9. The four unconventional tools are quantitative easing, credit easing, operation twist and precommitment policy. (*p. 322; LO14-4*)
10. Five criticisms of Fed policy are: (*p. 323; LO14-4*)
    1. It keeps policy makers from addressing the economy's structural problems.
    2. It enables the government's deficit spending.
    3. It leaves the Fed open to losses and the need for a bailout.
    4. It binds the Fed's hands from changing course.
    5. It doesn't have a reasonable exit strategy.

chapter 15

Deficits and Debt

> *Any government, like any family, can for a year spend a little more than it earns. But you and I know that a continuance of that habit means the poorhouse.*
>
> —Franklin D. Roosevelt

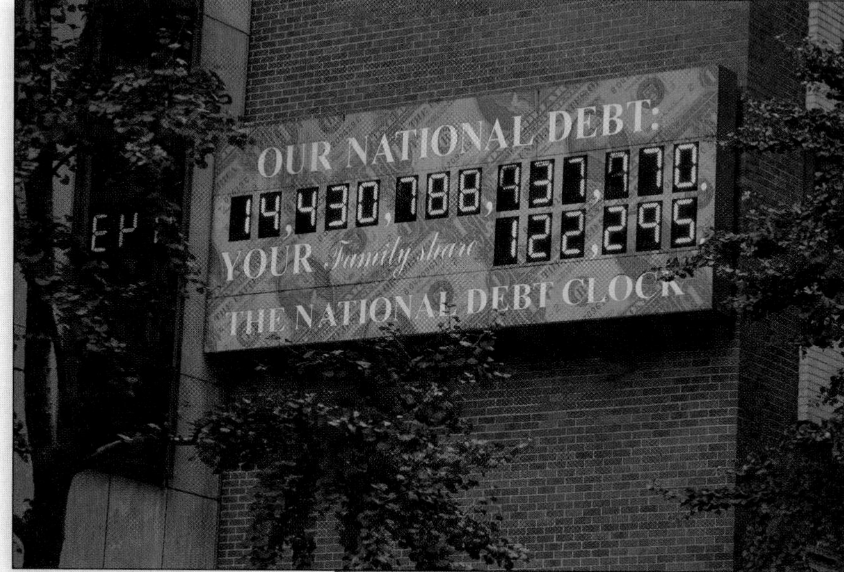

In 2013 the United States was running a large budget deficit, as it had for the past 11 years. In each of the last few years the United States has run deficits of over one trillion dollars, and has accumulated a total debt of more than 15 trillion dollars. Are these large deficits and accumulated debt of concern for the U.S. economy? This chapter considers this and similar questions from an economist's perspective in order to give you some deeper insight into policy debates that you will likely hear about in the news media.

Let's begin by reviewing what economic theory has to say about deficits and surpluses. In the long-run framework deficits are warranted only when government investment is more productive than private investment. When it isn't, surpluses are good because they provide additional saving for an economy. In the short-run framework, the view of deficits and surpluses depends on the state of the economy relative to its potential. If the economy is operating below its potential output, deficits are good and surpluses are bad because deficits increase expenditures, moving output closer to potential.

Combining the two frameworks gives us the following policy directive: Whenever possible, run surpluses, or at least a balanced budget, to help stimulate long-run growth. That recommendation is made even stronger when the economy is booming—that is, when it is above its level of potential income. Should the economy fall into a recession, however, policy makers must choose between the different policies suggested by the long-run and short-run frameworks. In the structural stagnation framework the economy is assumed to be stuck in the long run with short-run problems. For political or institutional reasons the government cannot run sufficiently expansionary fiscal policy to achieve the desired level of unemployment and growth because it is believed that the side effects of doing so will cause just as bad or even worse problems. If that is the case policy makers must deal with the problems structurally, not with deficits or surpluses.

After reading this chapter, you should be able to:

- **LO15-1** Define the terms *deficit, surplus,* and *debt* and distinguish between a cyclical deficit and a structural deficit.
- **LO15-2** Differentiate between real and nominal deficits and surpluses.
- **LO15-3** Explain why the debt needs to be judged relative to assets.
- **LO15-4** Describe the historical record for the U.S. deficit and debt.

The problem facing policy makers is that it is really hard to know whether the economy should be thought of in a long-run, short-run, or structural stagnation framework.

The problem facing policy makers is that it is really hard to know whether the economy should be thought about in the long-run, the short-run, or the structural stagnation framework. If expansionary macro policy is holding the economy above its true potential output, then what looks like and feels like a recession may actually be the economy going through the difficult structural changes it needs to avoid significant future problems. If, instead, potential output is higher than the structural stagnationists believe it is, to undergo the suffering that could be avoided makes little sense.

The problem is not unlike that facing most families. If you expect your situation to be better in the future, it makes sense to borrow now and pay it back when money isn't so tight. But if you're going to lose your job in the future, it makes sense to save now. Unfortunately, you don't know which is going to be the case.

Now that we have reviewed what theory has to say let's consider what policies the government actually followed. Let's start by considering the beginning of 2000, when the U.S. economy was booming, unemployment was at historic lows, and there was general agreement that the economy was at or beyond its potential output. If ever there was a time to let government build up a surplus and cut debt, it was then; that was the policy both the short- and long-run economic frameworks recommended. What policy did the government follow? It increased spending and cut taxes—precisely the opposite of what economic theory suggested was needed.

Defining Deficits and Surpluses

The definitions of *deficit, surplus,* and *debt* are simple, but this simplicity hides important aspects that will help you understand current debates about deficits and debt. Thus, it's necessary to look carefully at some ambiguities in the definitions.

A deficit is a shortfall of incoming revenues under payments. A surplus is an excess of revenues over payments.

A **deficit** is *a shortfall of revenues under payments.* A **surplus** is *an excess of revenues over payments;* both are flow concepts. If your income (revenue) is $20,000 per year and your expenditures (payments) are $30,000 per year, you are running a deficit. This definition tells us that a government budget deficit occurs when government expenditures exceed government revenues. The table below shows federal government total expenditures, total revenue, and the difference between the two for various years since 1980.

(Billions of Dollars)	1980	1990	2000	2010	2015*
Revenues	517.1	1,032.0	2,025.5	2162.7	3589
Expenditures	590.9	1,253.0	1,789.2	3456.2	3846
(−) Deficit/(+) surplus	−73.8	−221.0	236.2	−1293.5	−257

Source: Congressional Budget Office, *The Economic and Budget Outlook,* March 2012 (www.cbo.gov).
*Predicted.

The federal government ran deficits through the 1980s and most of the 1990s. It began to run surpluses in 1998, but returned to running deficits in 2002. In 2009 the federal deficit grew enormously and has continued.

As you can see in the table, in 2010 the deficit was about $1.3 trillion dollars. In that year more than 40 percent of all federal government spending was being financed by deficits. While the Congressional Budget Office (CBO) projections are for these deficits to decline significantly (to $257 billion in 2015), almost nobody believes those predictions will come true. A more realistic prediction is that more than trillion dollar deficits will continue into the near future.

Some economists, such as Harvard economist Ben Rogoff, see that increase as pushing the U.S. debt over a threshold; they argue that based on past experience, anything over a 90 percent debt-to-GDP ratio is dangerous—a tipping point between fiscal stability and fiscal instability. They argue that to prevent that financial instability from leading to a serious financial crisis, the deficits will have to end as soon as possible to protect the financial health of the United States. The problem is that cutting back government deficits will likely slow the economy and increase unemployment, keeping the economy in a structural stagnation for the near future. GDP growth will slow and the debt-to-GDP ratio will remain high. So the U.S. economy is in a macro policy dilemma. This chapter gives you the background on deficits and debt needed to understand that dilemma.

Q-1 What deficit dilemma does the United States face?

Financing the Deficit

Just like private individuals, the government must pay for the goods and services it buys. This means that whenever the government runs a deficit, it has to finance that deficit. It does so by selling *bonds*—promises to pay back the money in the future—to private individuals and to the central bank. There's a whole division of the U.S. Treasury devoted to managing the government's borrowing needs.

The government finances its deficits by selling bonds to private individuals and to the central bank.

The United States is fortunate to have lots of people who want to buy its bonds. Some developing countries have few people who want to buy their bonds (lend them money) and therefore have trouble financing their deficits. However, countries with their own currency and a central bank have an option that individuals don't have. Their central bank can lend them the money (buy their bonds). Since the central bank's IOUs are money, the loans can be made simply by printing money; in principle, therefore, the central bank has a potentially unlimited source of funds. But, printing too much money can lead to serious inflation problems, which have negative effects on the economy. So, whenever possible, governments try not to use the "print money" option to finance their deficits.

Q-2 How does the U.S. government finance its deficit spending?

Arbitrariness of Defining Deficits and Surpluses

Whether or not you have a deficit or surplus depends on what you count as a revenue and what you count as an expenditure. These decisions can make an enormous difference in whether you have a surplus or deficit. For example, consider the problem of a firm with annual revenues of $8,000 but no expenses except a $10,000 machine expected to last five years. Should the firm count the $10,000 as this year's expenditure? Should it split the $10,000 evenly among the five years? Or should it use some other approach? Which method the firm chooses makes a big difference in whether its current budget will be in surplus or deficit.

Accounting is central to the debate about whether we should be concerned about a deficit. Say, for example, that the government promises to pay an individual $1,000 ten years from now. How should government treat that promise? Since the obligation is incurred now, should government count as a current expense an amount that, if saved, would allow it to pay that $1,000 later? Or should government not count the amount as an expenditure until it actually pays out the money? The **Social Security system**—*a social insurance program that provides financial benefits to the elderly and disabled and to their eligible dependents and/or survivors*—is based on promises to pay, and thus the accounting procedures used for Social Security play an important role in how big the government's budget deficit actually is.

Accounting is central to the debate about whether we should be concerned about a deficit.

Many Right Definitions

Many accounting questions must be answered before we can determine the size of a budget deficit. Some have no right or wrong answer. For others, the answers vary according to the wording of the question. For still others, an economist's "right way"

There are many ways to measure expenditures and receipts, so there are many ways to measure deficits and surpluses.

is an accountant's "wrong way." In short, there are many ways to measure expenditures and receipts, so there are many ways to measure surpluses and deficits.

To say that there are many ways to measure deficits is not to say that all ways are correct. Pretending to have income that you don't have is wrong by all standards. Similarly, inconsistent accounting practices—such as measuring an income flow sometimes one way and sometimes another—are wrong. Standard accounting practices rule out a number of "creative" but improper approaches to measuring deficits. But even eliminating these, numerous reasonable ways of defining deficits remain, which accounts for some of the debate.

Deficits and Surpluses as Summary Measures

Deficit and surplus figures are simply summary measures of the financial health of the economy. To understand the summary, you must understand the methods that were used to calculate it.

The point of the previous discussion is that a deficit is simply a summary measure of a budget. As a summary, a surplus or deficit figure reduces a complicated set of accounting relationships to one figure. To understand what that summary measure is telling us, you've got to understand the accounting procedures used to calculate it. Only then can you make an informed judgment about whether a deficit is something to worry about. What's important is not whether a budget is in surplus or deficit but whether the economy is healthy.

Structural and Cyclical Deficits and Surpluses

The discussion of fiscal policy in earlier chapters emphasized the effect of the deficit on total income. But when thinking about such policies, it is important to remember that many government revenues and expenditures *depend* on the level of income in the economy. For example, say that the multiplier is 2 and the government is running expansionary policy. Say that that government increases its spending by \$100 (increasing the budget deficit by \$100), which causes income to rise by \$200. If the tax rate is 20 percent, tax revenues will increase by \$40 and the net effect of the policy will be to increase the budget deficit by \$60, not \$100. So as income changes, the deficit changes.

One implication of this feedback effect of changes in income on the deficit is the need to distinguish a deficit caused by a recessionary fall in income and a deficit brought about by government policy actions. Economists' method of distinguishing these is to differentiate between structural deficits and cyclical deficits.

The structural deficit is the deficit that remains when the cyclical elements of the deficit have been removed.

To differentiate between a budget deficit being used as a policy instrument to affect the economy and a budget deficit that is the result of income deviating from its potential, economists ask the question: "Would the economy have a budget deficit if it were at its potential level of income?" If it would, that portion of the budget deficit is said to be a **structural deficit**—*the part of a budget deficit that would exist even if the economy were at its potential level of income.* In contrast, if an economy is operating below its potential, the actual deficit will be larger than the structural deficit. In such an economy, that part of the total budget deficit is a **cyclical deficit**—*the part of the deficit that exists because the economy is operating below its potential level of output.* The cyclical deficit is also known as the passive deficit. When an economy is operating above its potential, it has a cyclical surplus.

The actual deficit is always made up of the structural deficit and the cyclical deficit:

Actual deficit = Structural deficit + Cyclical deficit

This distinction is important for policy because economists believe that an economy can eliminate a cyclical budget deficit through growth in income, whereas it can't grow out of a structural deficit. Because the economy can't grow out of them, structural budget deficits are of more concern to policy makers than are cyclical budget deficits.

Let me give an example. Say potential income is \$14 trillion and actual income is \$13.8 trillion, a shortfall of \$200 billion. Say also that the actual budget deficit is \$250 billion and the marginal tax rate is 25 percent. If the economy were at its potential income, tax revenue would be \$50 billion higher and the deficit would be \$200 billion. That \$200 billion is the structural deficit. The \$50 billion (25 percent multiplied by the \$200 billion shortfall) is the cyclical portion of the deficit.

Q-3 An economy's actual income is \$1 trillion; its potential income is also \$1 trillion. Its actual deficit is \$100 billion. What is its cyclical deficit?

As you can see from this example, assuming government spending doesn't change with income, you can calculate the cyclical deficit in the following way:

Cyclical deficit = Tax rate × (Potential output − Actual output)

Cyclical deficit = Tax rate × (Potential output − Actual output)

Once you know the cyclical deficit, you can also calculate the structural deficit:

Structural deficit = Actual deficit − Cyclical deficit

Structural deficit = Actual deficit − Cyclical deficit

Often there is significant debate about what an economy's potential income level is, and hence there is disagreement about what percentage of a deficit is structural and what percentage is cyclical. Nonetheless, the distinction is often used and is important to remember.

The reason the structural stagnation theory is considered a pessimistic theory is that it sees much more of the U.S. unemployment as structural, not cyclical, and therefore potential income lower than currently estimated. If correct, it suggests that much of the current deficit is structural and will have to continue almost indefinitely simply to keep the economy where it is today. The problem is: A structural deficit cannot continue indefinitely.

Projections for the Deficit: The Unpleasant Future

As recently as 2000, projections were for continual budget surpluses and a paying down of the debt. In 2001 Congress passed the Economic Growth and Tax Relief Reconciliation Act, which cut taxes significantly. Simultaneously, economic growth slowed and, with the war on terrorism, government expenditures increased significantly. Together, these factors reduced revenues and raised expenditures, turning the surpluses into deficits in 2002.

Q-4 How did the Economic Growth and Tax Relief Reconciliation Act of 2001 contribute to the return of deficits?

In 2003 and 2004, Congress cut taxes further and the war in Iraq lasted far longer and was far more costly than expected, leading to continued deficits. Then, in 2008, the U.S. economy experienced a severe financial crisis, which led to the deepest downturn since World War II. In response, the government cut taxes and increased expenditures to fight the recession. These policies, combined with the automatic stabilizers such as unemployment insurance set in motion by the recession, increased the 2009 budget deficit to over \$1.5 trillion, which, as you can see in Figure 15-1, was over 10 percent of GDP, the largest deficit in both absolute and percentage terms since World War II.

When they were implemented, the large deficits were meant to be a one-time stimulus policy. As a percentage of GDP, deficits were predicted to decrease significantly over the coming years as the economy came out of the recession and grew. But that didn't happen. The green line in Figure 15-1 is the deficit that the Congressional Budget Office (CBO) projected in 2009. The orange line shows what actually happened. Instead of the predicted 1.6 percent, it was 8.5 percent of GDP in 2012. The deficit decreased nowhere near what had been predicted. As you can see with the purple line once again in 2012 the CBO was predicting that the deficit

FIGURE 15-1

Projections of the Budget Deficit

In the late 1990s, the deficit as a percentage of GDP declined and in the mid-1990s, it moved into surplus. As the economy entered a recession it turned once again into a deficit, and in 2008 the deficit rose considerably, reaching 10 percent of GDP by 2009. Projections were for the deficit to decline significantly. It did not and projected declines was put off into the future.

Source: Congressional Budget Office, January 2009 and January 2012.

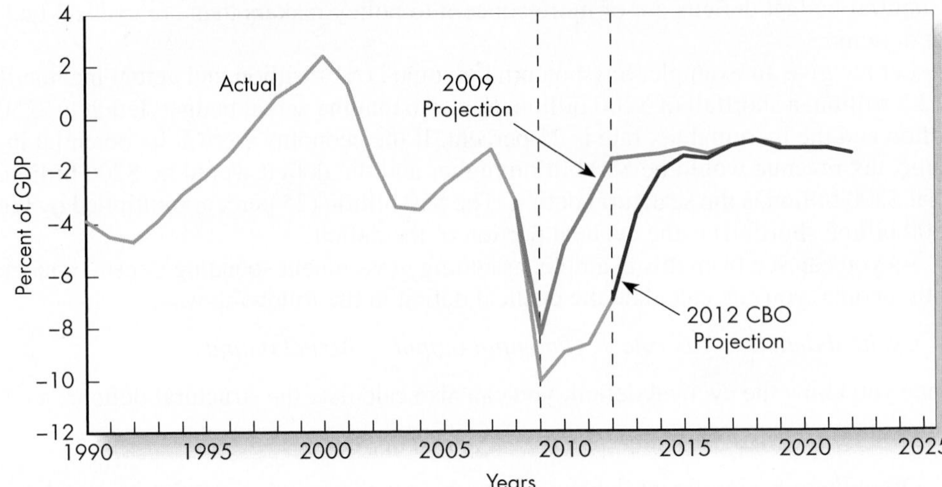

would fall. But as was the case with debt, the projections of a fast-improving economy kept putting off deficit reductions, and when deficits continue this long they are likely to be structural, not cyclical. They must be dealt with structurally. This means that in the coming years, U.S. taxes must be raised or government expenditures must be cut if the deficit is to be cut. If deficits continue as they have, the U.S. debt will continue increasing at an unsustainable trillion dollars a year.

Adding that much government debt is worrisome. If that happens, the U.S. government will have to pay higher interest rates that include a risk premium on its debt. Thus, while the U.S. political system has avoided facing up to the "no free lunch" precept in the past, it is unlikely to be able to not face up to it in the future. It is not a prospect that politicians look forward to.

While the U.S. political system has avoided facing up to the "no free lunch" precept in the past, it is unlikely to be able to not face up to it in the future.

Nominal and Real Deficits and Surpluses

Another distinction that economists make when discussing the budget deficit and surplus picture is the real/nominal distinction. A **nominal deficit** is *the deficit determined by looking at the difference between expenditures and receipts.*[1] It's what most people think of when they think of the budget deficit; it's the value that is generally reported. The **real deficit** is *the nominal deficit adjusted for inflation.* To understand this distinction, it is important to recognize that inflation wipes out debt (accumulated deficits less accumulated surpluses). How much does it wipe out? Consider an example: If inflation is 4 percent per year, the real value of all assets denominated in dollars is declining by 4 percent each year. If you had $100, that $100 would be worth 4 percent less at the end of the year—the equivalent of $96 without inflation. By the same reasoning, when there's 4 percent inflation, the value of the debt is declining 4 percent each year. If a country has a debt of $2 trillion, 4 percent inflation will eliminate $80 billion of the real value of the debt each year.

Q-5 Explain how inflation can wipe out debt.

Inflation reduces the value of the debt. That reduction is taken into account when the real deficit is calculated.

The larger the debt and the larger the inflation, the more debt will be eliminated by inflation. For example, with 10 percent inflation and a $2 trillion debt, $200 billion of

[1]In this section I will discuss deficits only. Since a surplus is a negative deficit, the discussion can be easily translated into a discussion of surpluses.

the debt will be eliminated by inflation each year. With 10 percent inflation and a $4 trillion debt, $400 billion of the debt would be eliminated.

If inflation is wiping out debt, and the deficit is equal to the increases in debt from one year to the next, inflation also affects the deficit. Economists take this into account by differentiating nominal deficits from real deficits.

We can calculate the real deficit by subtracting the decrease in the value of the government's total outstanding debts due to inflation. Specifically:[2]

Real deficit = Nominal deficit − (Inflation × Total debt)

Real deficit = Nominal deficit − (Inflation × Total debt)

Let's consider an example. Say that the nominal deficit is $300 billion, inflation is 4 percent, and total debt is $4 trillion. Substituting into the formula gives us a real deficit of $140 billion [$300 billion − (0.04 × $4 trillion) = $300 billion − $160 billion = $140 billion].

This insight into debt is directly relevant to the budget situation in the United States. For example, back in 1990, the nominal U.S. deficit was about $221 billion, while the real deficit was about one-third of that—$79 billion; in 2011 the U.S. government deficit was about $1.3 trillion; there was 2.1 percent inflation and a total debt of about $14.8 trillion. That means the real deficit was $989 billion. The table below shows the U.S. nominal and real deficits and surpluses for selected years.

Q-6 The nominal deficit is $40 billion, inflation is 2 percent, and the total debt is $4 trillion. What is the real deficit?

(Billions of Dollars)	1980	1990	2000	2010	2011
Nominal (−)deficit/(+)surplus	−74	−221	+236	−1,294	−1,300
Plus Inflation × Total debt	86	142	125	162	311
Government debt	930	3,233	5,674	13,528	14,800
Inflation (%)	9.3	4.4	2.2	1.2	2.1
Equals Real (−)deficit/(+)surplus	+12	−79	+361	−1,132	−989

Source: Congressional Budget Office and *The Economic Report of the President.*

Because the United States has had both debt and inflation for the years shown, the real deficits are smaller than the nominal deficits and the real surpluses are greater than the nominal surpluses.

The lowering of the real deficit by inflation is not costless to the government. Persistent inflation becomes built into expectations and causes higher interest rates. When inflationary expectations were low, as they were in the 1950s, the U.S. government paid 3 or 4 percent on its bonds that financed the debt. In 1990, when inflationary expectations were high, the government paid 8 or 9 percent interest, which is about 5 percentage points more than it paid in the 1950s. With its $3.2 trillion debt, this meant that the United States was paying about $160 billion more in interest than it would have had to pay if no inflation had been expected and the nominal interest rate had been 3 rather than 8 percent. That reduced the amount it could spend on current services by $160 billion. In other words, $160 billion of the 1990 nominal U.S. deficit existed because of the rise in interest payments necessary to compensate bondholders for the expected inflation. As inflationary expectations and nominal interest rates fell through the 1990s and early 2000s, the difference between the real and nominal deficit (surplus) decreased, but the inflation that remained left bondholders requiring a small inflation premium, meaning that interest rates paid by government were higher than they otherwise would have been.

The lowering of the real deficit by inflation is not costless to the government.

[2]This is an approximation for low rates of inflation. When inflation becomes large, total debt is multiplied by Inflation/(1 + Inflation), rather than just by inflation.

REAL-WORLD APPLICATION

Social Security and the U.S. Deficit

If you listen to *Car Talk* on PBS, you know that Tom and Ray Magliozzi often leave readers with a puzzler. In economics we also have puzzlers, and here's one of them for you to ponder. If debt is accumulated deficits, then the change in the debt in a particular year should be the size of the deficit or surplus. So if the U.S. debt was $8,951 billion as it was in 2007, and the deficit in 2008 was $459 billion, then the U.S. debt in 2008 should be 459 + 8,951 = $9,410 billion. When we look at the data however, we see that debt in 2008 was $9,986 billion. Why was this?

Car Talk makes you wait a week for the answer, but we don't have a week, so here's the answer. The deficit that the government reports is the deficit on what is called the unified budget, which is comprised of "off-budget" accounts (government trust funds, including the Social Security system) and "on-budget" accounts (most other government tax revenues and expenditures). The debt the government reports, however, does not include other government accounts, such as the Social Security system account, which at the time were running surpluses. The only asset that Social Security can hold is government bonds. So it was buying government debt (bonds) with its surplus revenues, building up a trust fund of assets to pay benefits to future retirees. In effect, the government on-budget account owed the Social Security and other trust funds $4.2 trillion.

So the answer to the puzzler is that the reported government debt is on the on-budget accounts only while the reported deficit is on the unified account. Since the government is reporting different concepts, there is no reason that the debt in one year plus the deficit should equal the debt in the following year unless the Social Security and other government trust accounts are in balance. More recently, the trust fund has stopped growing as much since Social Security expenditures now exceed Social Security taxes. So there is far less difference between the unified budget and the nonunified budget.

Defining Debt and Assets

Debt is accumulated deficits minus accumulated surpluses. Whereas *deficit* is a flow concept, *debt* is a stock concept.

Let's now look more closely at debt. **Debt** is *accumulated deficits minus accumulated surpluses.* Whereas deficits and surpluses are flow measures (they are defined for a period of time), debt is a stock measure (it is defined at a point in time). For example, say you've spent $30,000 a year for 10 years and have had annual income of $20,000 for 10 years. So you've had a deficit of $10,000 per year—a flow. At the end of 10 years, you will have accumulated a debt of $100,000 (10 × $10,000 = $100,000)—a stock. (Spending more than you have in income means that you need to borrow the extra $10,000 per year from someone, so in later years much of your expenditure will be for interest on your previous debt.) If a country has been running more surpluses than deficits, the accumulated surpluses minus accumulated deficits are counted as part of its assets.

Q-7 Distinguish between *deficit* and *debt*.

Debt Management

Web Note 15.1
Public Debt 101

The U.S. government, through its Treasury Department, must continually sell new bonds to refinance the bonds that are coming due, as well as sell new bonds when running a deficit. This makes for a very active market in U.S. government bonds, and the interest rate paid on government bonds is a closely watched statistic in the economy. If the government runs a surplus, it can either retire some of its previously issued bonds by buying them back or simply not replace the previously issued bonds when they come due.

To judge a country's debt, we must view its debt in relation to its assets.

The Need to Judge Debt Relative to Assets Debt is also a summary measure of a country's financial situation. As a summary measure, debt has even more problems than deficit. Unlike a deficit, which is the difference between expenditures

ADDED DIMENSION

Generational Accounting

As I have emphasized in the text, different accounting procedures shed light on slightly different issues. Each provides a different perspective of the financial situation, and the combination of them provides you with a full understanding of the issues. One accounting procedure that some economists use is generational accounting. Generational accounting shows government deficits in terms of each generation's net lifetime tax payments and benefits received.

Economists Larry Kotlikoff and Alan Auerbach have shown that our current system of taxation and transfers results in an intergenerational transfer of resources from younger to older generations. With the older generation becoming larger as the baby boomers age, these transfers are likely to put a severe strain on the tax system and the political foundations of our tax and transfer policies over the next couple of decades.

and revenue, and hence provides both sides of the ledger, debt by itself is only half of a picture. The other half of the picture is assets. For a country, assets include its skilled workforce, natural resources, factories, housing stock, and holdings of foreign assets. For a government, assets include not only the buildings and land it owns but also, and more importantly, a portion of the assets of the people in the country, since government gets a portion of all earnings of those assets in tax revenue.

Q-8 Why is debt only half the picture of a country's financial situation?

To get an idea of why the addition of assets is necessary to complete the debt picture, consider two governments: one has debt of $3 trillion and assets of $50 trillion; the other has only $1 trillion in debt but only $1 trillion in assets. Which is in a better financial position? The government with the $3 trillion debt is because its debt is significantly exceeded by its assets. Assets represent the ability of a country to pay off its debt. The point is simple: To judge a country's debt, we must view its debt in relation to all its assets.

This need to judge debt relative to assets adds an important caveat to the long-run position that government budget deficits are bad. When the government runs a deficit, it might be spending on projects that increase its assets. If the assets are valued at more than their costs, then the deficit is making the society better off. Government investment can be as productive as private investment or even more productive.

Government investment can be as productive as private investment or even more productive.

To distinguish between expenditures that are building up assets and those that are not, many businesses have separate capital and expenditures budgets. When they run deficits in their capital account we do not say that they are spending recklessly; we say that they are investing in the future, and generally we applaud that investment. We say they are running a deficit only in reference to their expenditures budget. While the U.S. government budget separates out investment from noninvestment expenditures, it does not have a separate capital account; it reports a consolidated budget, so it does not take into account the asset accumulation or the depreciation of its assets in determining its deficit.

Why aren't government finances generally discussed in relation to separate current and capital budgets? Because it is extraordinarily difficult to determine which government expenditures are investment. Business's investments will earn income that allows the business to pay off those investments. Most government goods earn no income; they are supplied free to individuals and are paid for by taxes. Impossible-to-answer questions arise such as: Are expenditures on new teachers an investment in better knowledge? Or: Are expenditures on a poverty program an investment in a better social environment? There are no unambiguous answers to these and similar questions; government accountants believe it is best to avoid such questions altogether.

FIGURE 15-2 Ownership of U.S. Government Debt

This pie chart shows that the debt is held by U.S. citizens, foreign citizens, financial institutions, and other government entities including state and local governments.

Source: *Treasury Bulletin,* U.S. Department of the Treasury, 2012 (www.fms.treas.gov).

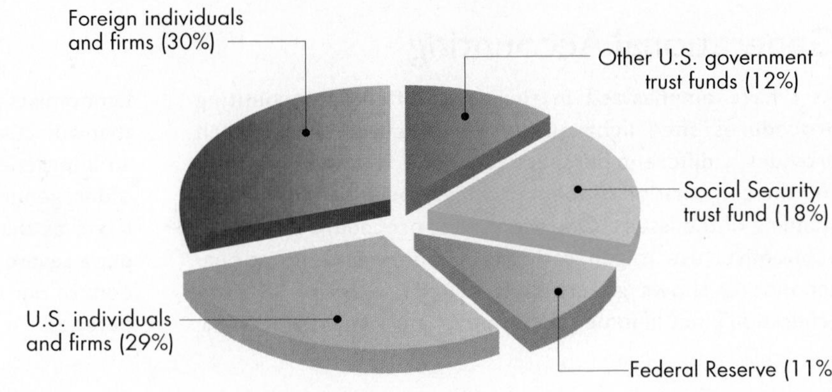

Assets and debt are subject to varying definitions.

ARBITRARINESS IN DEFINING DEBT AND ASSETS Like income and revenues, assets and debt are subject to varying definitions. Say, for example, that an 18-year-old is due to inherit $1 million at age 21. Should that expected future asset be counted as an asset now? Or say that the government buys an aircraft for $1 billion and discovers that it doesn't fly. What value should the government place on that aircraft? Or say that a country owes $1 billion, due to be paid 10 years from now, but inflation is ongoing at 20 percent per year. The inflation will reduce the value of the debt when it comes due by so much that its current real value will be $162 million—the approximate present value of $1 billion in 10 years with 20 percent inflation. It will be like paying about $162 million today. Should the country list the debt as a $1 billion debt or a $162 million debt?

As was the case with income, revenues, and deficits, there's no single answer to how assets and debts should be valued. So even after you take assets into account, you still have to be careful when deciding whether or not to be concerned about debt.

The government holds about 41 percent of its own debt.

The arbitrariness of the debt figure can be seen by considering the holdings of U.S. debt more carefully. In 2011, the U.S. government had a total of $14.8 trillion in debt, but the actual amount held by people and organizations outside the federal government is much less than that, as shown in Figure 15-2. There you can see that 30 percent of the debt is held by government trust funds—one branch of the federal government owes another branch of the government the debt. It is an asset of one part of government and a debt of another part. When we net out these offsetting debts and assets, the total federal debt decreases from about $14.8 trillion to $10.4 trillion. About 49 percent of the debt held by the public is held by U.S. individuals and firms and about 51 percent is held by foreign individuals and firms.

A large portion of the government debt is held by the Social Security trust fund, a fund managed by the Social Security Administration in order to meet its future obligations. By law, the Social Security trust fund must be held in the form of nonmarketable government bonds. This means that one agency of government (the Social Security Administration) is buying the bonds of another agency (the Treasury Department). Until about 2016, when the Social Security system's outlays are predicted to exceed its revenues, the percentage of debt held by government agencies will continue to increase. In 2011, the Social Security trust fund owned 18 percent of the debt.

Three reasons government debt is different from individual debt are:

1. The government lives forever; people don't.
2. The government can print money to pay its debt; people can't.
3. Government owes much of its debt to itself—to its own citizens.

Difference between Individual and Government Debt

The final point I want to make concerns differences between government debt and individual debt. There are three primary differences.

First, government is ongoing. Government never has to pay back its debt. An individual's life span is limited; when a person dies, there's inevitably an accounting of assets and debt to determine whether anything is left to go to heirs. Before any part of a person's estate is passed on, all debts must be paid. The government, however, doesn't ever have to settle its accounts.

Second, government has an option that individuals don't have for paying off a debt. Specifically, it can pay off a debt by creating money. As long as people will accept a country's currency, a country can always exchange money (non-interest-bearing debt) for bonds (interest-bearing debt).

Third, total government debt includes **internal debt** *(government debt owed to other governmental agencies or to its own citizens).* Paying interest on the internal debt involves a redistribution among citizens of the country, but it does not involve a net reduction in income of the average citizen. For example, say that a country has $3 trillion in internal debt. Say also that the government pays $150 billion in interest on its debt each year. That means the government must collect $150 billion in taxes, so people are $150 billion poorer; but it pays out $150 billion in interest to them, so, on average, people in the country are neither richer nor poorer because of the debt. **External debt** *(government debt owed to individuals in foreign countries)* is more like an individual's debt. Paying interest on external debt involves a net reduction in domestic income. U.S. taxpayers will be poorer; foreign holders of U.S. bonds will be richer.

Q-9 Why do economists distinguish between internal and external debt?

WWW Web Note 15.2 External Debts

U.S. Government Deficits and Debt: The Historical Record

Now that we have been through the basics of deficits and debt, let's look at the historical record. Since World War II, the U.S. government has run almost continual deficits, although by today's standards they were generally small. Total debt doubled in the 30 years from 1946 to 1975 and grew more quickly beginning in the mid-1970s, rising by a multiple of 30 to $14.8 trillion by 2011. Since 2008 it has been increasing by over one trillion dollars a year.

Most economists are much more concerned with deficits and debt relative to GDP than with the absolute figures. Figure 15-3 graphs the budget deficit and debt as a percentage of GDP. From this perspective, as you can see in Figure 15-3(a), deficits as a

FIGURE 15-3 (A AND B) U.S. Budget Deficits and Debt Relative to GDP

The size of the deficits and the size of the debt look somewhat different when considered relative to the GDP. Notice specifically how the total debt-to-GDP ratio declined substantially from the 1950s to the 1980s and how it increased in the 1980s and early 1990s. It declined in the late 1990s and early 2000s, but then rose substantially beginning in 2008. [In (a), deficits are stated as negative values.]

Source: *The Economic and Budget Outlook,* Congressional Budget Office, 2012 (www.cbo.gov); U.S. Bureau of the Census, *Historical Statistics,* and estimates.

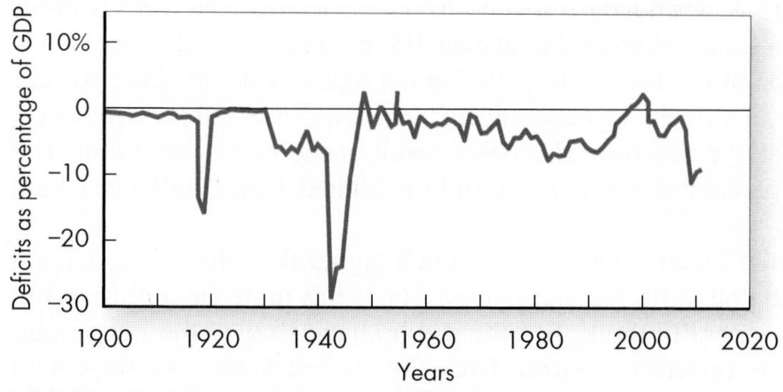

(a) Budget Deficits as Percentage of GDP

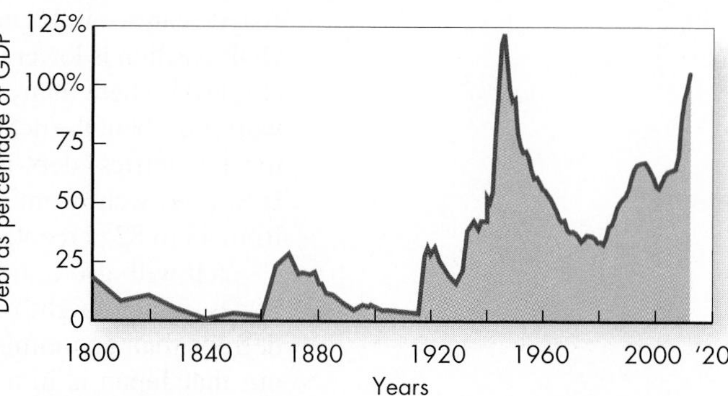

(b) Debt as Percentage of GDP

percentage of GDP did not rise significantly in the 1970s and the 1980s, as they did when we considered them in absolute terms. And it's the same with debt. As you can see in Figure 15-3(b), debt relative to GDP, has not been continually increasing. Instead, from the end of World War II to the 1970s, and from 1988 to 1990, the debt/GDP ratio actually decreased. In the mid-1990s it stabilized at somewhat under 70 percent of GDP, and in the late 1990s and early 2000s it fell to about 60 percent. Then, it started to rise again to 75 percent in 2008 and has continued to rise to over 100 percent in 2013.

Deficits and debt relative to GDP provide measures of a country's ability to pay off a deficit and service its debt.

Economists prefer the "relative to GDP" measure because it better measures the government's ability to handle the deficit; a nation's ability to pay off a debt depends on its productive capacity (the asset side of the picture). GDP serves the same function for government as income does for an individual. It provides a measure of how much debt, and how large a deficit, government can handle. So when GDP grows, so does the debt the government can reasonably carry, and many economists use a constant debt-to-GDP ratio as a benchmark for judging neutral fiscal policy.

The Debt Burden

Most of the decrease in the debt-to-GDP ratio in U.S. history occurred through growth in GDP. Growth in GDP can occur in two ways: through inflation (a rise in nominal but not real GDP) or through real growth. Both ways reduce the problem of the debt. As I discussed above, inflation wipes out the value of existing debt; with inflation, there can be large nominal budget deficits but a small real deficit.

Q-10 What annual deficit could a $5 billion economy growing at a real annual rate of 5 percent have without changing its debt/GDP ratio?

When an economy experiences real growth, the ability of the government to incur debt is increased; the economy becomes richer and, being richer, can handle more debt. As noted in an earlier chapter, real growth in the United States has averaged about 2.5 to 3.5 percent per year, which means that U.S. debt can grow at a rate of 2.5 to 3.5 percent without increasing the debt/GDP ratio. But for debt to grow, government must run a deficit, so a constant debt/GDP ratio in a growing economy is consistent with a continual deficit.

How much of a deficit are we talking about? U.S. federal government debt in 2013 was about $16 trillion and GDP was about $16 trillion, so the government debt/GDP ratio was about 100 percent. A real growth rate of 2.5 percent means that real GDP is growing at about $400 billion per year. That means that government can run a deficit of $400 billion a year without increasing the debt/GDP ratio. With trillion-dollar deficits the debt is increasing far more than that, so the debt-to-GDP ratio is increasing. For those who believe that the total U.S. government debt is already too large relative to GDP, this argument (that the debt/GDP ratio is remaining constant) is unsatisfying. They argue that the debt/GDP ratio should fall.

U.S. Debt Relative to Other Countries

As you can see in Figure 15-4, when judged relative to other countries, the U.S's debt-to-GDP position is lower than some countries, but at over 100 percent, worse than most. It is at a level where many economists believe that the United States will soon have to start worrying about the debt level influencing bondholders' decisions. Over the past five years, most countries' debt-to-GDP ratios have risen as a result of the global recession. The U.S. ratio went from 64 percent to 100 percent and the United Kingdom's ratio went from 43 to 82 percent.

You will also notice that Japan's debt level is much higher than that of the United States, which might make you think that the United States has more flexibility to run deficits than economists generally think. But those who have studied the issue point out that Japan is in a quite different position from the United States. An important reason is that Japan's citizens save a lot more than do U.S. citizens. Almost all the Japanese debt is internally held. Much of the U.S. debt is held externally, which means

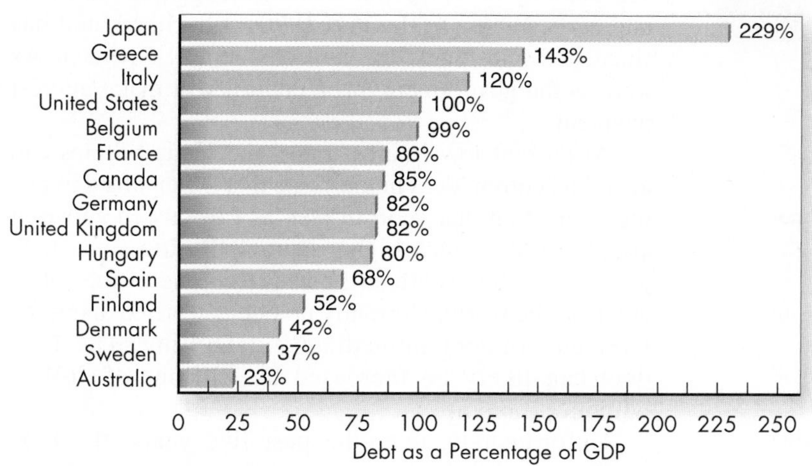

FIGURE 15-4 U.S. Debt Compared to Foreign Countries' Debt

The U.S. debt does not appear so large when compared to the debts of some other countries in the early 2000s.

Source: *World Economic* Outlook Database, 2012, International Monetary Fund (www.imf.org).

that a default by the United States will have major international consequences for the global financial system. But if either country were to have another financial crisis, and was required to increase debt enormously to prevent a financial meltdown, the already high debt may limit their ability to do so.

Interest Rates and Debt Burden

Considering debt relative to GDP is still not quite sufficient to give an accurate picture of the debt burden. How much of a burden a given amount of debt imposes depends on the interest rate that must be paid on that debt. The annual debt service is the interest rate on debt times the total debt.

The annual debt service is the interest rate on the debt times the total debt.

In 2011, the U.S. government paid approximately $230 billion in interest. A larger debt would require even higher interest payments. The interest payment is government revenue that can't be spent on defense or welfare; it's a payment for past expenditures. Ultimately, the interest payments are the burden of the debt. That's what people mean when they say a deficit is burdening future generations.

Over the past 50 years, the interest rate has fluctuated considerably; when it has risen, the debt service has increased; when it has fallen, debt service has decreased. Figure 15-5 shows the federal interest payments relative to GDP. This ratio increased

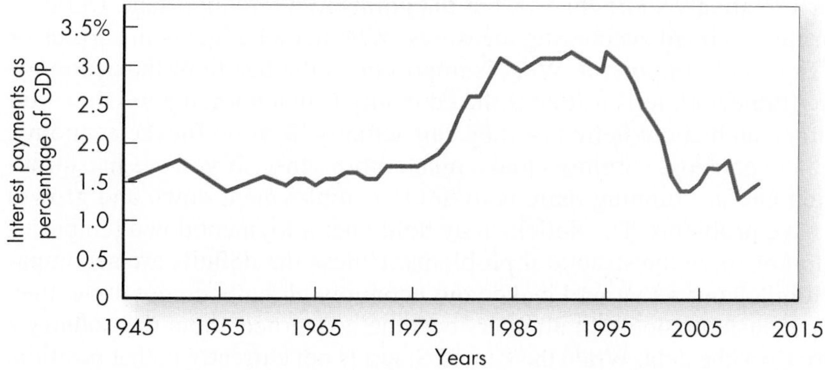

FIGURE 15-5

Federal Interest Payments Relative to GDP

Interest payments as a percentage of GDP remained relatively constant until the 1970s, after which they rose significantly due to high interest rates and large increases in debt. In the late 1990s, they fell as interest rates fell and surpluses reduced the total debt.

Source: *The Economic and Budget Outlook,* Congressional Budget Office, 2012 (www.cbo.gov).

A REMINDER 

Four Important Points about Deficits and Debt

1. Deficits are summary measures of the state of the economy. They are dependent on the accounting procedures used.
2. It is the health of the economy, not the deficit, with which we should be concerned.
3. Deficits and debt should be viewed relative to GDP to determine their importance.
4. Real deficit = Nominal deficit − (Inflation × Debt).

substantially in World War II and then again in the 1970s and early 1980s. In the mid-1990s it declined, and has fluctuated since then. It is currently about 1.5 percent. As long as the government has a debt, it will make interest payments.

At current low interest rates, the United States can afford its current debt in the sense that it can afford to pay the interest on that debt. In fact, as I discussed above, it could afford a much higher debt/GDP ratio since U.S. government bonds are still considered one of the safest assets in the world. Currently no one is worried about the U.S. government immediately defaulting. The U.S. debt can likely be increased by trillions of dollars without problems.

Unfortunately, over the past five years, the U.S. government has been running deficits of more than a trillion dollars a year, which, in some economists' views, is pushing the United States closer to the tipping point, where confidence in the United States willingness to pay its bondholders ends. That can happen suddenly, which is why it is often called a tipping point. If that tipping point is reached, as mentioned earlier, investors will require a risk premium and the interest rate that the United States pays will rise and increase interest payments. If that problem arises, the Fed cannot necessarily solve the problem by buying up the bonds, because as the Fed buys up bonds, increasing the money supply, people may fear high inflation, which will raise the nominal interest rate even further since they will demand an inflation premium for their bonds. A vicious cycle of interest rate and deficit increases could develop.

The problem is made worse by the structure of the U.S. debt. More than 50 percent of the U.S. debt is due within three years. This means that if interest rates rise, the U.S. Treasury will be forced to refinance at the higher interest rates. To reduce this potential problem some have called for the government to issue more long-term bonds, so it will face less of a problem of refinancing. But doing so would push up the current long-term interest rate, which would likely slow U.S. growth to an even lower level than what it currently is. In fact, the Fed currently is the largest buyer of 30-year bonds and is specifically attempting to keep these long-term interest rates down. The bottom line: How long the United States can continue its current expansionary fiscal policies, without causing a new financial crisis, is not clear.

How long the United States can continue its current expansionary fiscal policies, without causing a new financial crisis, is unclear.

Conclusion

This has been a relatively short chapter, but the points in it are important. Deficits, debts, and surpluses are all accounting measures. Whether a budget is in surplus or deficit is not especially important. What is important is the health of the economy. The economic framework tells us that if the economy is in a normal recession, you shouldn't worry much about deficits—they can actually be good for the economy. If you are in an expansion, surpluses make much more sense. If you are in a structural stagnation and are running deficits to hold unemployment down and growth up, then you have problems. The deficits may hold unemployment down temporarily but they do not solve the structural problems. Unless the deficits are accompanied by structural changes that will make your economy globally competitive, they may likely be unsustainable if bondholders become concerned about the country's willingness to repay the debt. While the United States is not currently in that position, it is moving toward it.

Whether a budget is in surplus or deficit is not especially important. What is important is the health of the economy.

Summary

- A deficit is a shortfall of revenues under payments. A surplus is the excess of revenues over payments. Debt is accumulated deficits minus accumulated surpluses. *(LO15-1)*
- Deficits and surpluses are summary measures of a budget. Whether a budget deficit is a problem depends on the budgeting procedures that measure it. *(LO15-1)*
- A cyclical deficit is that part of the deficit that exists because the economy is below or above potential:

  Cyclical deficit = Tax rate × (Potential output − Actual output) *(LO15-1)*
- A structural deficit is that part of a budget deficit that would exist even if the economy were at its potential level of income.

  Structural deficit = Actual deficit − Cyclical deficit *(LO15-1)*
- A real deficit is a nominal deficit adjusted for the effect of inflation:

  Real deficit = Nominal deficit − (Inflation × Debt) *(LO15-2)*
- Because the United States has mostly had inflation and debt, its real deficit has been lower than its nominal deficit. *(LO15-2)*
- A country's debt must be judged in relation to its assets. What is counted as a debt and as an asset can be arbitrary. *(LO15-3)*
- Government debt and individual debt differ in three major ways: (1) government is ongoing and never needs to repay its debt, (2) government can pay off its debt by printing money, and (3) most of government debt is internal—owed to its own citizens. *(LO15-3)*
- Deficits, surpluses, and debt should be viewed relative to GDP because this ratio better measures the government's ability to handle the deficit and pay off the debt. Compared to some countries, the United States has a low debt-to-GDP ratio. *(LO15-4)*
- Since 2008, the United States has run significant deficits and the debt-to-GDP ratio has risen to over 100 percent. Unless the United States lowers the deficit it may face another financial crisis. *(LO15-4)*

Key Terms

cyclical deficit *(330)*
debt *(334)*
deficit *(328)*
external debt *(337)*
internal debt *(337)*
nominal deficit *(332)*
real deficit *(332)*
Social Security system *(329)*
structural deficit *(330)*
surplus *(328)*

Questions and Exercises

1. "Budget deficits should be avoided, even if the economy is below potential, because they reduce saving and lead to lower growth." Does this policy directive follow from the short-run or the long-run framework? Explain your answer. *(LO15-1)*
2. Your income is \$40,000 per year; your expenditures are \$45,000. You spend \$10,000 of that \$45,000 for tuition. Is your budget in deficit or surplus? Why? *(LO15-1)*
3. Canada's debt was \$630 billion at the end of 2003. Using the information below (in billions of Canadian dollars), fill in the blanks for Canada's budget balance and debt for the following years: *(LO15-1)*

	Revenues	Expenditures	Debt
2004	\$203	\$202	\$___
2005	215	___	626
2006	227	221	___
2007	___	230	619
2008	258	243	___

4. What are the two ways government can finance a budget deficit? *(LO15-1)*
5. If the structural budget deficit is $100 billion and the actual deficit is $300 billion, what is the size of the cyclical deficit? *(LO15-1)*
6. If the actual budget deficit is $100 billion, the economy is operating $250 billion above its potential, and the marginal tax rate is 20 percent, what are the structural deficit and the cyclical deficit? *(LO15-1)*
7. Say the marginal tax rate is 30 percent and that government expenditures do not change with output. Say also that the economy is at potential output and that the deficit is $200 billion. *(LO15-1)*
   a. What is the size of the cyclical deficit?
   b. What is the size of the structural deficit?
   c. How would your answers to *a* and *b* change if the deficit were still $200 billion but output were $200 billion below potential?
   d. How would your answers to *a* and *b* change if the deficit were still $200 billion but output were $100 billion above potential?
   e. Which is likely of more concern to policy makers: a cyclical or a structural deficit?
8. Calculate the real deficit or surplus in the following cases: *(LO15-2)*
   a. Inflation is 10 percent. Debt is $3 trillion. Nominal deficit is $220 billion.
   b. Inflation is 2 percent. Debt is $1 trillion. Nominal deficit is $50 billion.
   c. Inflation is −4 percent. (Price levels are falling.) Debt is $500 billion. Nominal deficit is $30 billion.
   d. Inflation is 3 percent. Debt is $2 trillion. Nominal surplus is $100 billion.
9. Inflation is 20 percent. Debt is $2 trillion. The nominal deficit is $300 billion. What is the real deficit? *(LO15-2)*
10. How would your answer to Question 9 differ if you knew that expected inflation was 15 percent? *(LO15-2)*
11. Assume a country's nominal GDP is $600 billion, government expenditures less debt service are $145 billion, and revenue is $160 billion. The nominal debt is $360 billion. Inflation is 3 percent and interest rates are 6 percent. *(LO15-2)*
    a. Calculate debt service payments.
    b. Calculate the nominal deficit.
    c. Calculate the real deficit.
12. List three ways in which individual debt differs from government debt. *(LO15-3)*
13. If all of the government's debt were internal, would financing that debt make the nation poorer? *(LO15-3)*
14. Assume that a country's real growth is 2 percent per year, while its real deficit is rising 5 percent a year. *(LO15-3)*
    a. Can the country continue to afford such deficits indefinitely?
    b. What problems might it face in the future?
15. Why is who holds the debt an important factor when comparing debt-to-GDP ratios among countries? *(LO15-4)*
16. Why is debt service an important measure of whether debt is a problem? *(LO15-4)*
17. How can a debt that is too high lead to an even higher debt? *(LO15-4)*
18. What might keep the Fed from buying up more bonds if the debt gets too high? *(LO15-4)*

Questions from Alternative Perspectives

1. International issues aside, what limits government's ability to undertake monetary or fiscal policy? (Austrian)
2. To help understand the distributional consequences of the tax cuts advocated by many conservative politicians, answer the following:
   a. What income groups have the largest marginal propensity to consume: high or low income?
   b. If your goal were to minimize the deficit cost of a tax stimulus, who should receive the tax cuts? Who received the tax cuts?
   c. What will the tax cut do, relatively speaking, to the debt?
   d. Is there a pattern here? (Institutionalist)
3. After President George W. Bush's election in 2000, he proposed cutting taxes.
   a. Would you consider that proposal to follow the short-run or long-run framework, or a combination of the two?
   b. From your response, how should President Bush have dealt with the U.S. deficit to be consistent with the school of thought that you chose? (Post-Keynesian)
4. Over 40 countries in the world now report what has been called a "women's budget," analyzing public expenditures and revenue from a gender perspective.
   a. What might be an example of a gender effect on the expenditure side of the budget?
   b. On the revenue side?
   c. Why are these effects important to consider? (Feminist)

Issues to Ponder

1. Two economists are debating whether the target rate of unemployment is 4 percent or 6 percent. Mr. A believes it's 4 percent; Ms. B believes it's 6 percent. One says the structural deficit is $40 billion; the other says it's $20 billion. Which one says which? Why?
2. "The debt should be of concern." What additional information do you need to undertake a reasonable discussion of this statement?
3. You've been hired by Creative Accountants, economic consultants. Your assignment is to make suggestions about how to structure a government's accounts so that the current deficit looks as small as possible. Specifically, they want to know how to treat the following:
   a. Government pensions.
   b. Sale of land.
   c. Social Security taxes.
   d. Proceeds of a program to allow people to prepay taxes for a 10 percent discount.
   e. Expenditures on F-52 bombers.
4. How can a government that isn't running a deficit still get itself into financial trouble?

Answers to Margin Questions

1. If the United States doesn't cut the deficit, it might face financial instability. If it does so, it will slow the economy even further. (*p. 329; LO15-1*)
2. The U.S. government sells bonds to finance deficit spending. (*p. 329; LO15-1*)
3. Since the economy is at its potential income, its cyclical deficit is zero. All of its budget deficit is a structural deficit. (*p. 331; LO15-1*)
4. The act contributed to the return of deficits by lowering tax revenues and increasing government spending. (*p. 331; LO15-1*)
5. Inflation reduces the value of the dollars with which the debt will be repaid and hence, in real terms, wipes out a portion of the debt. (*p. 332; LO15-2*)
6. The real deficit equals the nominal deficit minus inflation times the total debt. Inflation times the total debt in this case equals $80 billion (0.02 × $4 trillion). Since the nominal deficit is $40 billion, the real deficit is actually a surplus of $40 billion ($40 billion − $80 billion = −$40 billion). (*p. 333; LO15-2*)
7. Deficit is a flow concept, the difference between income and expenditures. Debt—accumulated deficits minus accumulated surpluses—is a stock concept. (*p. 334; LO15-3*)
8. To get a full picture of a country's financial situation, you have to look at assets as well as debt since a large debt for a country with large assets poses less of a problem. The greater its assets the more a country is able to pay off its debts. (*p. 335; LO15-3*)
9. Paying interest on internal debt redistributes income among citizens in a country. Paying interest on external debt reduces in domestic income. (*p. 337; LO15-3*)
10. A $5 billion economy growing at a real annual rate of 5 percent could have an annual deficit of $250 million (0.05 × $5 billion) and not increase its debt/GDP ratio. (*p. 338; LO15-4*)

chapter 16

The Fiscal Policy Dilemma

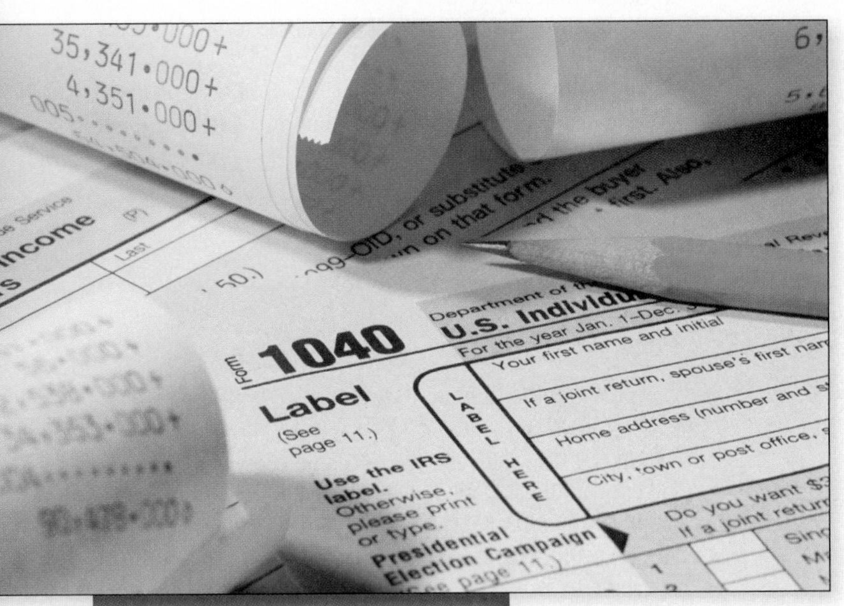

> *An economist's lag may be a politician's catastrophe.*
>
> —George Schultz

After reading this chapter, you should be able to:

- **LO16-1** Summarize the Classical view of sound finance.
- **LO16-2** Summarize the Keynesian view of functional finance.
- **LO16-3** List six assumptions of the *AS*/*AD* model that lead to potential problems with the use of fiscal policy.
- **LO16-4** Explain how automatic stabilizers work.

Modern economies face a major policy dilemma. In a serious recession, such as the one that the world economies entered into in 2008, almost all economists agree that governments need to run expansionary fiscal policy—that is, deficits. That follows from the standard macro policy models. In the long run, however, all economists agree that governments need to maintain a solid financial situation, which means that governments need to balance their budgets, or perhaps even run surpluses to offset some of the past deficits they built up trying to prevent recessions. The reason is not that deficits are inherently bad. Deficits reduce government's future borrowing capacity; if governments build up "too large" debt, they will likely find it harder to finance their debt in the future. A government that cannot easily finance its debt will either go bankrupt or have to resort to inflationary finance, with the central bank financing the government by printing money. Neither is good for any economy.

So the fiscal policy dilemma is what to do in periods of structural stagnation when both deficits and a balanced budget are called for. When an economy falls into a structural stagnation, the effectiveness of expansionary demand-side policy is limited. International conditions, political considerations, and institutional issues make it impossible for fiscal policy to reduce unemployment below a level that is considered too high by most people. This chapter addresses that dilemma. In it, I provide a brief discussion of the evolution of economists' thinking about fiscal policy and how we arrived at the modern fiscal policy precepts that guide our thinking about modern fiscal policy.

Classical Economics and Sound Finance

Let's begin by looking at how economists' views of public finance and fiscal policy have changed over time. Before the 1930s, economists generally supported a policy that was described as "sound finance." **Sound finance** was *a view of fiscal policy that the government budget should always be balanced except in wartime*. Economists held this view based on a combination of political and economic grounds, but primarily on political grounds. (Before

1930, economic analysis and political analysis were not as separate as they are today, and it is hard to separate out positions held on political as opposed to economic grounds.) The reason politics was important is that the Classical liberal tradition, which was the dominant tradition of economists at the time, viewed government with suspicion, so any policy that would make it easier to increase government spending during peacetime was seen as undesirable.

Ricardian Equivalence Theorem: Deficits Don't Matter

Although Classical economists believed in the principle of sound finance, they also recognized that pure economic arguments for balancing the budget were weak or nonexistent. For example, David Ricardo, one of the most famous economists in the 19th century, pointed out that, in a purely theoretical sense, government spending financed by selling government bonds (the government running a budget deficit) was no different from government spending financed by taxes (the government running a balanced budget). The reason was that if the government ran deficits, it would have to increase taxes in the future both to pay the interest on the bonds and to repay the bonds when they came due. Those future taxes would make the taxpayers poorer in the same way that paying taxes now would make them poorer. Assuming people can borrow and save, and thereby shift spending between now and the future, people would save more now to pay for those future taxes. So, there is no reason why financing spending with a deficit should affect the aggregate level of income differently than financing spending with taxes. The difference between the two is simply a matter of who does the borrowing. It followed that a government deficit would not lead to an expansion of output in the economy. This *theoretical proposition that deficits do not affect the level of output in the economy because individuals increase their savings to account for expected future tax payments to repay the deficit* has become known as the **Ricardian equivalence theorem.**

Although Classical economists believed in the principle of sound fiancé, they also recognized that the pure economic arguments for balancing the budget were weak or nonexistent.

Q-1 Does the Ricardian equivalence theorem lead to a policy of sound finance?

Web Note 16.1 When Do Deficits Matter?

Despite economists' recognition of the logical truth of the Ricardian equivalence theorem, most economists, including Ricardo, felt that, in practice, deficits could affect output and that it mattered a lot, politically, whether government financed its spending by bonds (ran deficits) or by taxes (balanced the budget). Based on their political ideology, economists of the time strongly pushed government to finance its spending with taxes, not bonds. Hence, their principle of sound finance. They supported the principle of sound finance because they felt that, politically, requiring government to follow the principle of sound finance made increasing government spending more difficult and brought home to the politicians the central economic lesson that there is no free lunch. They argued that adhering to a policy of sound finance forced government to face the costs of a spending decision simultaneously with the benefits of that spending decision, something that bond finance—financing government spending by borrowing—did not do.

Because of their advocacy of sound finance, through the 1930s, fiscal policy—the deliberate running of a deficit or surplus to guide the level of aggregate output in the economy—was not part of the economist's lexicon. Although economists of the time recognized that government spending could impact the level of output in the economy, they felt that, except in wartime, the long-run fiscal integrity of the government that sound finance led to should override such concerns. So through the 1930s economists' answer to the exam question about what government should do if there was a recession was that the government should maintain a balanced budget.

Q-2 What would a pre-1930s Classical economist recommend government do if there is a recession?

The Sound-Finance Precept

The precept of sound finance was not absolute. For example, in the 1920s in Europe, and in the 1930s in the United States, national economies fell into a sustained depression from which there seemed to be no escape. In response, major economists of the time such as A. C. Pigou, F. Knight, and J. M. Keynes started questioning the sound-finance principles for the short run. They felt that the depressed state of the economy had created a vicious cycle in which the expectations of a continued depression kept investment spending low, which kept total spending low, and that low spending led to low output and high unemployment. They believed that the market would get out of the depression eventually, but as the depression continued, they came to believe that "eventually" was longer than was politically acceptable.

Given a collapse of economic expectations, many Classical economists favored giving up the principle of sound finance, at least temporarily, and using government spending to stimulate the economy.

Given this collapse of economic expectations, many economists of the time favored giving up the principle of sound finance, at least temporarily, and using government spending to stimulate the economy. For example, numerous economists favored government public works programs such as the Federal Emergency Relief Program, which provided funds for unemployed workers, and the Works Progress Administration (WPA), which built roads and bridges. So, faced with a serious depression, economists were quite willing to support spending on these programs without tax increases, which essentially meant that they were willing to support deficit financing to stimulate the economy.

Their arguments for deficit spending were based on simple commonsense reasoning, not any complex underlying models (remember, their reasoning told them that, theoretically, Ricardian equivalence held, and deficits wouldn't expand the economy). But their theory also told them that depressions, such as the one in which the economy was stuck in the 1930s, wouldn't happen either. Given the depression that the economy was stuck in, they were willing to entertain the notion that it was possible that if the government spent more than it collected in taxes—ran a deficit—the economy would be jump-started: Income would increase; the recipients of that increased income would spend more, creating a virtuous circle that ultimately would help pull the economy out of the recession. At least it was worth a try.

At the time, economists debated how much of the government spending stimulus would be offset by increased savings as bonds were sold to finance the deficit. But despite theoretical concerns, policy-making economists of the time generally felt that expansionary fiscal policy could be of some use in helping pull an economy out of a severe recession. So, in the 1930s, economists' answer to the exam question, what to do if the economy is in a recession, changed from "do nothing" to a more nuanced answer. If the recession is small, maintain a policy of sound finance, but if it is a very bad recession—a depression—then consider trying to stimulate the economy with some government programs and deficit financing. But such deficit financing was a last resort that was inappropriate to small or moderate recessions.

Q-3 What would an economist who believes in nuanced sound finance recommend government do if there is a recession?

Keynesian Economics and Functional Finance

The textbook presentation of the economist's view of public finance and fiscal policy changed significantly in the late 1940s, as the ideas of J. M. Keynes' *The General Theory* worked their way into the principles of economics texts. Keynes' book was enormously important; it set in motion a series of events that influenced the way in which economists looked at the aggregate economy for about 50 years, and that still have some lingering effects on both textbook presentations and applied policy. In fact, it was that book that created the field of macroeconomics and led to fiscal policy being seen as a method of controlling the level of income in the economy, rather than as just a practical policy that might be helpful in serious depressions.

Actually, what became known as Keynesian economics does not all follow from Keynes' work; *The General Theory* is a theoretical book, which is open to many interpretations about policy. The book does not mention fiscal policy as a policy tool; Keynes' support of fiscal policy as a practical tool predated his writing of *The General*

Theory and was not dependent on it.[1] Much of his writing suggested that using a deficit to jump-start the economy was a one-time policy, needed to escape the rut the economy had fallen into during a depression by changing expectations that the economy would, indeed, grow. But Keynes did not see large deficits as a policy for normal times. During normal times, including milder recessions, Keynes' views were more consistent with the government striving to balance the budget.

That isn't the view that became associated with the term "Keynesian economics." What became known as Keynesian economics was developed by his students together with a group of economists who were influenced by those students. In terms of what shows up in the textbook presentations, the ideas of one of those students, Abba Lerner, stands out. Lerner's book *The Economics of Control* spelled out what he called a *functional finance* view of public finance and fiscal policy. That functional finance view became the principles textbook view when Nobel Prize-winning economist Paul Samuelson incorporated it into his famous textbook, which established the template for all texts that followed.

Functional finance held that, *as a theoretical proposition, governments should make spending and taxing decisions on the basis of their effect on the economy, not on the basis of some moralistic principle that budgets should be balanced.* Under functional finance, if spending in the economy was too low, the government should run a deficit; if spending was too high, the government should run a surplus.

Q-4 How does functional finance differ from sound finance?

To explain why functional finance was preferred to sound finance, Lerner gave the following famous analogy.

> Imagine yourself in a Buck Rogers interplanetary adventure, looking at a highway in a City of Tomorrow. The highway is wide and straight, and its edges are turned up so that it is almost impossible for a car to run off the road. What appears to be a runaway car is speeding along the road and veering off to one side. As it approaches the rising edge of the highway, its front wheels are turned so that it gets back onto the road and goes off at an angle, making for the other side, where the wheels are turned again. This happens many times, the car zigzagging but keeping on the highway until it is out of sight. You are wondering how long it will take for it to crash, when another car appears which behaves in the same fashion. When it comes near you, it stops with a jerk. A door is opened, and an occupant asks whether you would like a lift. You look into the car and before you can control yourself you cry out, "Why, there's no steering wheel." Want a ride?

For Lerner, the aggregate economy was subject to wild fluctuations and it needed a steering wheel to guide it. Fiscal policy was that steering wheel. Notice that the total focus here is on the government steering the economy; there is no discussion of politics or whether the recession is major or minor as there was in the nuanced view of sound finance. Lerner's functional finance had no nuances about policy.

In functional finance, the total focus is on the government steering the economy; there is no discussion of politics or nuance.

Functional finance nicely fits the *AS/AD* model you learned in Chapter 9. In these models, there was a desired level of output—potential output around which the economy fluctuated. However, by using its fiscal (and monetary) policy steering wheel, the government could increase or decrease either expenditures or taxes, thereby shifting the *AD* curve to the right or left to steer the economy to the desired level of output. (A good review exercise is to go through various changes in government spending and taxes in the *AS/AD* model.)

---

[1]Although the book was primarily about theory, Keynes never followed up on his theoretical arguments; he was an adviser to the British government and, with World War II and the economic problems following the war, that advising took up most of his time, and then after the war he had a heart attack that left him out of the debate about his work.

In functional finance, if there is a recession, the government should run a deficit.

So in functional finance, the economist's answer to the question, what to do if there is a recession, is to run a deficit to return the economy to its potential output. Policy followed directly from the model.

Assumptions of the *AS/AD* Model

Lerner's stark presentation of functional finance did not last long as a guiding principle for practical macro public finance and fiscal policy. The reason was that the model made a number of assumptions that, in practice, did not hold, and the model did not deal with the difficult practical and political problems of implementing fiscal policy. These problems don't mean that functional finance models are wrong; they simply mean that for fiscal policy to work, the policy conclusions drawn from the model must be modified to reflect the real-world problems. Let's consider how the reality might not fit the model. The *AS/AD* model assumes:

Six assumptions of the *AS/AD* model that could lead to problems with fiscal policy are:

1. Financing the deficit doesn't have any offsetting effects.
2. The government knows what the situation is.
3. The government knows the economy's potential income level.
4. The government has flexibility in changing spending and taxes.
5. The size of the government debt doesn't matter.
6. Fiscal policy doesn't negatively affect other government goals.

1. Financing the deficit doesn't have any offsetting effects. (In reality, it often does.)
2. The government knows what the situation is—for instance, the size of the multiplier effect, and other exogenous variables. (In reality, the government must estimate them.)
3. The government knows the economy's potential income level—the highest level of income that doesn't cause accelerating inflation. (In reality, the government may not know what this level is.)
4. The government has flexibility to change spending and taxes. (In reality, government cannot change them quickly.)
5. The size of the government debt doesn't matter. (In reality, the size of the government debt often does matter.)
6. Fiscal policy doesn't negatively affect other government goals. (In reality, it often does.)

Let's consider each assumption a bit further.

Financing the Deficit Has No Offsetting Effects

One of the limitations of the functional finance approach embodied in the *AS/AD* model is that it assumes that financing the deficit has no offsetting effects on income. Some economists argue that that is not the case, that the government financing of deficit spending will offset the deficit's expansionary effect.

The *AS/AD* model assumes that saving and investment can differ, and that the government can increase its expenditures without at the same time causing private expenditures to decrease. Some economists object to that assumption. They believe the interest rate equilibrates saving and investment. They argue that when the government borrows to finance the deficit, that borrowing will increase interest rates and crowd out private investment.

Crowding out is the offsetting effect on private expenditures caused by the government's sale of bonds to finance expansionary fiscal policy.

Interest rate **crowding out**—*the offsetting of a change in government expenditures by a change in private expenditures in the opposite direction*—occurs as follows: When the government runs a budget deficit, it must sell bonds (that is, it must borrow) to finance that deficit. To get people to buy and hold the bonds, the government must make them attractive. That means the interest rate the bonds pay must be higher than it otherwise would have been. This tends to push up the interest rate in the economy, which makes it more expensive for private businesses to borrow, so they reduce their borrowing and their investment. That private investment is crowded out by expansionary fiscal policy. Hence the name *crowding out.* Increased government spending crowds out private spending.

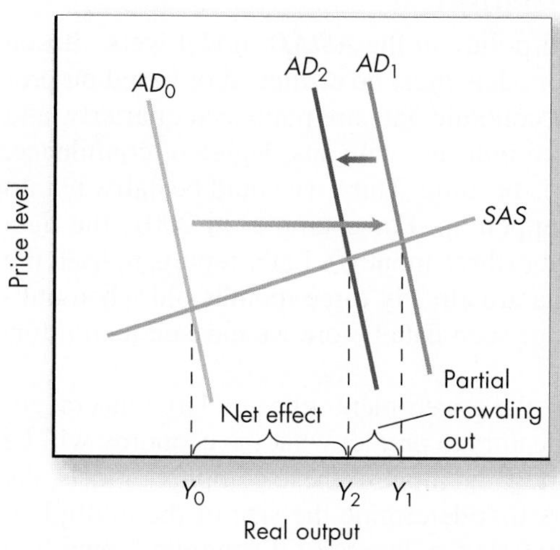

FIGURE 16-1 Crowding Out

An increase in government spending will expand income, but it will also cause interest rates to rise reducing aggregate demand as shown. This is called *interest rate crowding out.* The net effect of fiscal policy depends on the degree of crowding out that takes place.

Crowding out is shown in Figure 16-1. If financing government spending were not an issue, expansionary fiscal policy would shift the *AD* curve to the right by a multiple of the increase in government spending, increasing income from Y_0 to Y_1. However, financing the deficit increases interest rates and decreases investment. This shifts the *AD* curve to the left to AD_2. Income falls back to Y_2. How much it shifts back is a matter of debate; it depends upon how responsive investment is to changes in the interest rate. The more investment is responsive to changes in the interest rate, the greater the crowding out.

Q-5 If interest rates had no effect on investment or consumption, how much crowding out would occur?

Because of crowding out, the net expansionary effect of fiscal policy is smaller than it otherwise would have been. Some economists argue that crowding out can totally offset the expansionary effect of fiscal policy, so the net effect is zero, or even negative, since they consider private spending more productive than government spending. Larger deficits decrease the pool of savings available for private investment.

The crowding out effect also works in reverse with contractionary fiscal policy. Say the government runs a budget surplus. That surplus will slow the economy since it shifts the *AD* curve back to the left. But it also means the U.S. Treasury (the U.S. government department that issues bonds to finance the deficit) can buy back some of its outstanding bonds, which will have a tendency to push bond prices up and interest rates down. Lower interest rates will stimulate investment, which in turn will have an offsetting expansionary effect on the economy. So when we include financing the deficit in our consideration of fiscal policy, the shift in *AD* from the surplus is partially offset.

Q-6 Demonstrate graphically what would happen if government expenditures policy stimulated private investment.

How much financing will offset fiscal policy is a matter of debate. The empirical evidence about the degree of crowding out is mixed and has not resolved the debate. The degree of crowding out seems to change over time. Both sides see some crowding out occurring as the debt is financed by selling bonds. The closer to the potential income level the economy is, the more crowding out is likely to occur.

Even as the U.S. government has run large budget deficits in recent years, the U.S. interest rate has not risen substantially. An important reason why is that foreign governments and private foreign individuals have been willing to finance the U.S. deficit by purchasing U.S. bonds. The increase in the supply of savings from foreign sources holds the U.S. interest rate down. If foreigners will find other places to invest and are less willing to buy U.S. bonds, the U.S. interest rate could rise substantially.

The Government Knows the Situation

The numbers we use to demonstrate fiscal policy in the *AS/AD* model were chosen arbitrarily. In reality, the numbers used in models must be estimated or based on preliminary figures subject to revision. Most economic data are published quarterly, and it usually takes six to nine months of data to indicate, with any degree of confidence, the state of the economy and which way it is heading. Thus, we could be halfway into a recession before we even know it is happening. For example, in 2001, the data showed a decline in GDP in only one quarter (three months). Later reports revised the decline to three consecutive quarters. (Data are already three months old when published; then we need two or three quarters of such data before we have enough information to work with.)

In an attempt to deal with this problem, the government relies on large macroeconomic models and a variety of leading indicators to predict what the economy will be like six months or a year from now. As part of the input to these complex models, the government must predict economic factors that determine the size of the multiplier. These predictions are imprecise, so the forecasts are imprecise. Economic forecasting is still an art, not a science.

Economists' data problems limit the use of fiscal policy for fine-tuning.

Economists' data problems limit the use of fiscal policy for fine-tuning. There's little sense in recommending expansionary or contractionary policy until you know what policy is called for.

The Government Knows the Economy's Potential Income Level

Web Note 16.2
What's the Speed Limit?

The problem of not knowing the level of potential income is related to the problem we just discussed. The target rate of unemployment and the potential level of income are not easy concepts to define. At one time it was thought 3 percent unemployment meant full employment. Some time later it was generally thought that 6.5 percent unemployment meant full employment. About that time economists stopped calling the potential level of income the *full-employment* level of income.

Any variation in potential income can make an enormous difference in the policy prescription that could be recommended. To see how big a difference, let's translate a 1 percent change in unemployment into a change in income. Using a rough estimate, let's say that a 1 percentage point fall in the target unemployment rate is associated with a 2 percent increase in potential income. If that is the case, in 2012, with income at about \$16 trillion, a 1 percentage point fall in the target unemployment rate would increase potential income by about \$320 billion.

Now let's say that one economist believes 6.5 percent is the long-run achievable target rate of unemployment, while another believes it's 5 percent. That's a 1.5 percentage point difference. Since a 1 percent decrease in the unemployment rate means an increase of \$320 billion in potential income, their views of the income level we should target differ by over \$480 billion ($1.5 \times \$320 = \$480$). Both views are reasonable. Looking at the same economy (the same data), one economist may call for expansionary fiscal policy while the other may call for contractionary fiscal policy.

Differences in estimates of potential income often lead to different policy recommendations.

In practice, differences in estimates of potential income often lead to different policy recommendations. Empirical estimates suggest that the size of the multiplier is somewhere between 1.5 and 2.5. Let's say it's 2.0. That means autonomous expenditures (initial changes before the multiplier) must be predicted to increase or decrease by more than \$240 billion before an economist who believes the target rate of unemployment is 5 percent would agree with the same policy recommendation put forward by an economist who believes the rate is 6.5 percent. Since almost all fluctuations in autonomous investment and autonomous consumption are less than this amount, there's no generally agreed-on policy prescription for most fluctuations. Some economists will call for expansionary policy; some will call for contractionary policy; and the government decision makers won't have any clear-cut policy to follow.

You might wonder why the range of potential income estimates is so large. Why not simply see whether the economy has inflation at the existing rate of unemployment and income level? Would that it were so easy. Inflation is a complicated process. Seeds of inflation are often sown years before inflation results. The main problem is that establishing a close link between the level of economic activity and inflation is a complicated statistical challenge to economists, one that has not yet been satisfactorily met. That leads to enormous debate as to what the causes are. In recent years globalization has added another complication. Because globalization keeps the price level down, the inflation rate may not rise even when an economy is exceeding its potential.

Q-7 Why don't economists have an accurate measure of potential income?

Almost all economists believe that outside some range (perhaps 3.5 percent unemployment on the low side and 10 percent on the high side), too much spending causes inflation and too little spending causes a recession. That 3.5 to 10 percentage point range is so large that, in most cases, the U.S. economy is in an ambiguous state where some economists are calling for expansionary policy and others are calling for contractionary policy. This has been particularly true in the 2000s when expansionary policies contributed to asset price increases, which led to a financial bubble that burst in 2008.

In most cases, the U.S. economy is in an ambiguous state where some economists are calling for expansionary policy and others are calling for contractionary policy.

Once the economy reaches the edge of the range of potential income or falls outside it, the economists' policy prescription becomes clearer. For example, in the Depression, when the *AS/AD* model was developed, unemployment was 25 percent—well outside the range. Should the economy ever go into such a depression again, economists' policy prescriptions will be clear. The call will be for expansionary fiscal policy. Most times the economy is within the ambiguous range, so there are disagreements among economists.

The Government Has Flexibility in Changing Spending and Taxes

For argument's sake, let's say economists agree that contractionary policy is needed and that's what they advise the government. Will the government implement it? And, if so, will it implement contractionary fiscal policy at the right time? The answer to both questions is: probably not. Just consider 2011, when both Republicans and Democrats talked about how the debt was too high and new policies were needed to lower the deficit. Neither party came up with policies to do so. Instead they both championed policies such as reducing taxes (Republicans) or increasing spending on infrastructure (Democrats) that would likely *increase,* not decrease the deficit. To reduce the deficit and debt in a politically divided nation, compromise is necessary—taxes will have to be raised and entitlements will have to be cut. As of 2012 policy makers haven't been willing to compromise. There are also problems with implementing economists' calls for expansionary fiscal policy. Even if economists are unanimous in calling for expansionary fiscal policy, putting fiscal policy in place takes time and has serious implementation problems.

Even if all economists agree that contractionary policy is needed and that's what they advise government, it is unlikely that government will institute contractionary policy.

Numerous political and institutional realities in the United States today make it a difficult task to implement fiscal policy. Government spending and taxes cannot be changed instantaneously. The budget process begins more than a year and a half before the government's fiscal year begins, so realistically at least two years are needed to implement fiscal policy. That is not a very responsive steering wheel.

Numerous political and institutional realities make it a difficult task to implement fiscal policy.

REAL-WORLD APPLICATION

Fighting the Vietnam War Inflation

Because of the lags associated with fiscal policy, often, fiscal policy's effect comes at the wrong time and affects the economy in the wrong way. For example, one time that economists were united in their views on appropriate fiscal policy was during the Vietnam War, from the early 1960s until 1975, when the economy was pushed to its limits. In 1965, President Lyndon B. Johnson's economic advisers started to argue strongly that a tax increase was needed to slow the economy and decrease inflationary pressures. President Johnson wouldn't hear of it. He felt a tax increase would be political suicide. Finally in mid-1968, after Johnson had decided not to run for reelection, a temporary income tax increase was passed. By then, however, many economists felt that the seeds of the 1970s inflation had already been sown.

The Vietnam War led to inflationary pressures.

Moreover, nearly two-thirds of the government budget is mandated by government programs such as Medicare and Social Security and by interest payments on government debt. Even the remaining one-third, called discretionary spending, is difficult to change. Defense programs are generally multiyear spending commitments. Discretionary spending also includes appropriations to fund established government agencies such as the Department of Agriculture, the Department of Transportation, and the Internal Revenue Service. Changing their budgets is politically difficult.

Politicians face intense political pressures; their other goals may conflict with the goals of fiscal policy. For example, few members of Congress who hope to be reelected would vote to raise taxes in an election year. Similarly, few members would vote to slash defense spending when military contractors are a major source of employment in their districts, even when there's little to defend against. Squabbles between Congress and the president may delay initiating appropriate fiscal policy for months, even years. By the time the fiscal policy is implemented, what may have once been the right fiscal policy may have ceased to be right, and some other policy may have become right.

Real-world fiscal policy is similar to steering a car with a five-second delay from turning the steering wheel to turning the wheels.

Imagine trying to steer a car at 60 miles an hour when there's a five-second delay between the time you turn the steering wheel and the time the car's wheels turn. Imagining that situation will give you a good sense of how fiscal policy works in the real world.

The Size of the Government Debt Doesn't Matter

There is no inherent reason why adopting functional finance policies should have caused the government to run deficits year after year and hence to incur ever-increasing debt—accumulated deficits less accumulated surpluses. Activist functional finance policy is consistent with running deficits some years and surpluses other years. In practice, the introduction of activist functional finance policy has been accompanied by many deficits and few surpluses, and by a large increase in government debt.

There are two reasons why activist government policies have led to an increase in government debt. First, early activist economists favored large increases in government spending as well as favoring the government's using fiscal policy. These early

REAL-WORLD APPLICATION

The Bipartisan National Commission on Fiscal Responsibility and Reform

In 2010 a bipartisan committee was asked to come up with a bipartisan blueprint for reducing the deficit. A vote was required for the plan to be accepted. The plan the committee came up with included:

1. Cutting discretionary spending.
2. Increasing taxes, including a 15 cent per gallon gasoline tax, and eliminating tax deductions for such things as home mortgages and employer-provided health care.
3. Controlling health care costs by maintaining Medicare cost controls and increasing the authority of an advisory board to Medicare.
4. Reducing entitlements, including farm subsidies, pensions, and student loan subsidies.
5. Raising payroll taxes and the Social Security retirement age.

According to committee estimates, implementing the plan would have stopped the rise in the debt as a percentage of GDP compared to a continuation of current policy, as shown in the accompanying graph. While the actual plan would likely have had less of an effect than projected, it would have been an improvement over the current deficit situation, which is unsustainable.

None of the options in the plan are politically popular, and the plan was voted down by Congress with little discussion. It was not replaced with anything. Thus, the deficit and debt problem keeps building. The problem is that politically it is much easier to deal with future cutbacks and tax increases 10 years in advance than it is to have the cutbacks implemented immediately. Letting people know about changes that will occur in the future gives people time to adjust to those changes. With each passing year of large deficits, the debt problem is worsening, and dealing with it is becoming more likely to be forced on the United States during a crisis period, when the side-effects will be worse.

Economics does not say how the deficit should be reduced, but it does say that the current path is unsustainable. Something must change or the system will experience a serious breakdown.

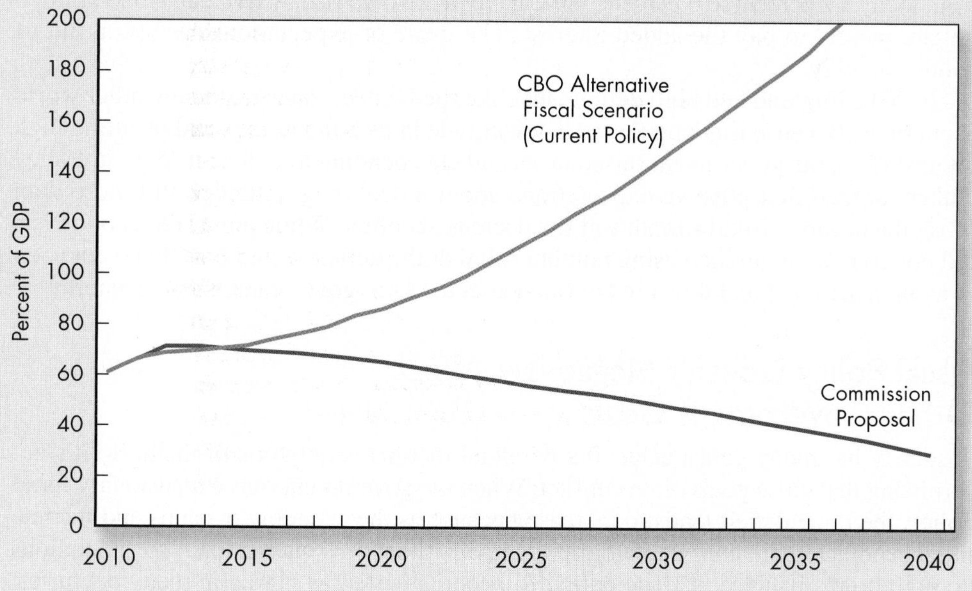

U.S. Debt Held by the Public as a Percentage of GDP under Various Scenarios

The Bipartisan National Commission offered a compromise method of decreasing the deficit from what was otherwise predicted. It failed to get any political support.

Source: Report of the National Commission on Fiscal Responsibility and Reform, December 2010.

activist economists justified increasing spending without increasing taxes by its expansionary effect on aggregate output. A second reason is political. Politically it's much easier for government to increase spending and decrease taxes than to decrease spending and increase taxes. Due to political pressure, expansionary fiscal policy has predominated over contractionary fiscal policy.

Most economists believe that a country's debt becomes a problem somewhere around 90 to 100 percent of a country's GDP.

Most economists believe that a country's debt becomes a problem once it approaches somewhere around 90 or 100 percent of a country's GDP. That's not a fixed percentage but is a rough guide of when countries in the past have experienced problems. It is when people will begin to worry about whether the government will default on its bonds or will be forced to inflate its way out of its debt problem.

Since the total value of U.S. bonds issued is over 100 percent of GDP and the total bonds held by the public (nongovernmental agencies) is about 70 percent of GDP, concern about how much more the U.S. government can borrow to continue to stimulate the economy, regardless of the state of the economy, has been increasing. Those who believe government should continue to use expansionary fiscal policy point out that U.S. bonds are still highly desirable to the public. They point out that the interest rates on Treasury bonds have fallen over the past five years, suggesting that people still see the U.S. government as highly creditworthy. Others respond that the low interest rates reflect a Fed policy designed to hold those interest rates down, and that when the Fed changes that policy, the interest rates may rise and the ability of government to repay its debt will worsen.

The bond market depends heavily on expectations that can change quickly.

They also point out that the bond market depends heavily on expectations and that those expectations can change quickly, particularly in a globalized world. If those who buy U.S. government bonds begin to worry about a U.S. government default (the United States cannot pay bondholders) or a rise in inflation, interest rates will rise quickly. As a result the government's budget deficit will rise, because it has to pay the higher interest rate on its borrowing. Since much of the U.S. government debt is short term, a rise in the interest rate can quickly make the deficit problem worse. A worsening deficit problem could further increase the expectations of default or inflation, pushing interest rates and the deficit even higher. If interest rates on all government bonds rose from today's 2 percent to 6 percent, the U.S. deficit would rise by more than $600 billion dollars merely to pay the added interest. The cycle of expectations can spiral out of control quickly.

In 2012 England had high deficits just like the United States and many other world economies. Because England feared a downgrade in its bond ratings and resulting high interest rates, the government raised taxes and cut spending to reduce its deficit. Policy makers argued that positive expectations about a declining deficit would more than offset the negative fiscal stimulus of the decreased deficit. While most U.S. economists did not go that far, an increasing number felt that the deficit would have to be cut soon to avoid a serious breakdown in confidence in the U.S. government's fiscal stability.

Fiscal Policy Doesn't Negatively Affect Other Government Goals

A society has many goals; achieving potential income is only one of them. So it's not surprising that those goals often conflict. When the government runs expansionary fiscal policy, the trade deficit tends to increase because as the economy expands and income rises, exports remain constant but imports rise. If a nation's international considerations do not allow a balance of trade deficit to become larger, as is true in many countries, those governments cannot run expansionary fiscal policies—unless they can somehow prevent this trade deficit from becoming larger.

Summary of the Problems

Fiscal policy is a sledgehammer, not an instrument for fine-tuning.

So where do these six problems leave fiscal policy? While they don't eliminate its usefulness, they severely restrict it. Fiscal policy is a sledgehammer, not an instrument for fine-tuning. When the economy seems to be headed into a depression, the appropriate fiscal policy is clear. This was the case in 2008 and 2009. Similarly, when an economy has a hyperinflation, the appropriate policy is clear. But in less extreme cases, there will be debate on what the appropriate fiscal policy is—a debate economic theory can't answer conclusively.

Integrating these practical problems in running deficits has led modern economists to a much more nuanced view of deficit finance than found in the functional finance view. The modern view held by applied macro policy economists is that deficits can stimulate aggregate output, but they also agree with earlier Classical economists that there are political reasons for having balanced budgets, and not for relying on governments to control spending and taxes to achieve the desired level of output. As a tool, except in a potential depression, discretionary fiscal policy is not very helpful. But that does not mean that modern macro policy economists have discarded fiscal policy altogether. Instead of advocating standard discretionary fiscal policy in which government responds to fluctuations in income with changes in government spending and taxes, modern economists advocate building fiscal policy into institutions.

Integrating practical problems in running deficits has led modern economists to a much more nuanced view of deficit finance than found in the functional finance view.

Building Fiscal Policies into Institutions

Economists quickly recognized the political problems with instituting discretionary countercyclical fiscal policy. To avoid these problems, they suggested policies that built fiscal policy into U.S. institutions so that it wouldn't require any political decisions. They called a built-in fiscal policy an **automatic stabilizer**—*a government program or policy that will counteract the business cycle without any new government action.* Automatic stabilizers include welfare payments, unemployment insurance, and the income tax system.

An automatic stabilizer is any government program or policy that will counteract the business cycle without any new government action.

How Automatic Stabilizers Work

To see how automatic stabilizers work, consider the unemployment insurance system. When the economy is slowing down or is in a recession, the unemployment rate will rise. When people lose their jobs, they will reduce their consumption, starting the multiplier process, which decreases income. Unemployment insurance immediately helps offset the decrease in individuals' incomes as the government pays benefits to the unemployed. Thus, government spending increases, and part of the fall in income is stopped without any explicit act by the government. Automatic stabilizers also work in reverse. When income increases, government spending declines automatically.

Web Note 16.3
Economy on Autopilot?

Automatic Stabilizers

Another automatic stabilizer is our income tax system. Tax revenue fluctuates as income fluctuates. When the economy expands, tax revenues rise, slowing the economy; when the economy contracts, tax revenues decline, stimulating the economy. Let's go through the reasoning why. When the economy is strong, people have more income and thus pay higher taxes. This increase in tax revenue reduces consumption expenditures from what they would have been and moderates the economy's growth. When the economy goes into a recession, the opposite occurs.

State Government Finance and Procyclical Fiscal Policy

Automatic stabilizers are sometimes offset by other institutional structures that work as a type of automatic *destabilizer.* Examples of such destabilizers are states' constitutional provisions to maintain balanced budgets. These provisions mean that whenever a recession hits, states are faced with declining tax revenue. To maintain balanced budgets, the states must cut spending, increase tax rates, or both. For example, during the 2008 recession, state governments struggled to balance their budgets by cutting expenditures on education, transportation, health care, and a variety of other programs while

REAL-WORLD APPLICATION

Will the U.S. Fate Follow Greece's Demise?

The potential problems of running large government deficits were discovered by Greece in 2011, when it essentially defaulted on its loans. Early in 2010, the Greek government had revealed that its fiscal situation was much worse than it had been reporting. Bondholders became worried and interest rates rose. To pay these higher interest rates and to restore investor confidence, Greece announced spending cuts and tax increases. The Greek people protested and investors became even more worried, which caused interest rates to rise even further; the yield on old Greek bonds rose to over 25 percent, which meant that any new borrowing that the government needed would have to pay that rate. The situation spiraled into higher and higher interest rates, deeper and deeper spending cuts, and increases in taxes.

It was clear that Greece needed more and more new loans to keep the economy from collapsing. The problem was that no one wanted to lend more money to Greece because it wasn't expected to pay existing loans, let alone pay off new ones. After Greece implemented budget austerity measures—the European Union, of which Greece was part, loaned Greece enough to keep it afloat for another year or two. Simultaneously, the EU negotiated with private Greek bondholders to essentially write off more than half the amount Greece owed. As part of those negotiations, the EU required even greater budget discipline—increasing taxes, cutting public sector employment, cutting wages of government employees, raising the retirement age, and many more cutbacks than it had already implemented. The budget austerity measures pushed the Greek economy into a deeper recession, lowering tax revenues and increasing unemployment even higher. The result was rioting in the streets of Athens.

Is this the future for the United States? Probably not. The United States and Greece differ in two significant ways. First, the United States has a much bigger economy and is too big to fail (just like the large U.S. banks were too big to fail in the United States in 2008). If the United States fails, the world economy is likely to fail. Pulling out of U.S. bonds will lead to a world financial crisis. This means that the international community will have stronger incentives to prevent the United States from defaulting than it had with Greece. Second, the United States has its own central bank. (Greece gave up its currency and central bank when it joined the European Union.) The Fed can always buy government bonds—its own escape hatch, so to speak. So even if the United States faces a situation like Greece, the problems will not play out in the same way.

To say that the United States is different from Greece is not to say that if the world economy loses faith in the U.S. government's commitment and ability to repay its loans, the United States won't face serious problems. The current interest rate that the United States pays on its loans is exceptionally low by historical standards, and that low interest rate is helping to hold the U.S. deficit down. If interest rates rise considerably, the result would be an increase in the U.S. deficit and the need for spending cuts or tax increases.

Neither of these will be politically popular. People will say, "We are increasing taxes and cutting spending to pay off rich bondholders while cutting social benefits to the poor. That's unfair." This will likely lead to political fights about whether a default on bonds is preferable on equity grounds. It is precisely these issues that led to the riots in Greece. We may well be seeing riots in the United States in the future if we don't deal with the budget problem soon.

Countercyclical vs. Procyclical Policies

raising income and sales taxes. These actions deepened the recession. Similarly, during the 10-year expansion in the 1990s and early 2000s, state revenue rose; states increased spending and decreased tax rates. The expansionary effect of these changes further increased total income. The result is what economists call **procyclical fiscal policy**—*changes in government spending and taxes that increase the cyclical fluctuations in the economy instead of reducing them.*

The procyclical nature of state government spending demonstrated itself in 2008 when the U.S. economy fell into a deep recession. In order to keep their budgets balanced, state governments began implementing massive spending cutbacks and tax increases, both of which worsened the recession. These cutbacks were reduced somewhat by temporary federal government assistance, but it was unclear how long that assistance could continue since the federal government was running massive unsustainable deficits.

To reduce the procyclical nature of state financing, economists have suggested states establish *rainy-day funds*—reserves kept in good times, to be used to offset declines in revenue during recessions. Large rainy-day funds (which some economists have called rainy-season funds) would decrease the destabilizing aspect of state government spending. But politics usually keeps rainy-day funds small; the funds are targets that are just too tempting for spending proposals or tax cuts.

Large rainy-day funds would decrease the destabilizing aspect of state government spending.

An alternative way of building countercyclical policies into institutions would be for states to use a five-year rolling-average budgeting procedure (with a built-in underlying trend rate of increase) as the budget they are required to balance. With a rolling-average budget, revenues available for spending would be determined from a growth-adjusted average of revenues for the past five years. When revenues increase substantially in a year, the surplus available to be spent would build up only slowly and would therefore be much less politically tempting to raid. When revenues fall, the measured deficit would grow much more slowly, and the constitutional budget-balancing requirements would be much less procyclical.

Balancing a rolling-average budget, rather than the current-year budget, would counterbalance the balanced-budget requirement and would remove much of the procyclical aspect of current state budgeting procedures. In fact, if the federal government started using a similar five-year rolling-average budget, it too could build a more reasonable fiscal policy into its accounting procedures and reduce the need for discretionary stimulus packages.

The Negative Side of Automatic Stabilizers

Automatic stabilizers may seem like the solution to the economic woes we have discussed, but they, too, have their shortcomings. One problem is that when the economy is first starting to climb out of a recession, automatic stabilizers will slow the process, rather than help it along, for the same reason they slow the contractionary process. As income increases, automatic stabilizers increase government taxes and decrease government spending, and as they do, the discretionary policy's expansionary effects are decreased. Another problem is that in a downturn, the automatic stabilizers are increasing spending, thus making it harder for government to reduce its deficit. This helps slow the recession, but if the problem is that the debt has become so large that bondholders fear default, automatic stabilizers can increase that fear.

Q-8 What effect do automatic stabilizers have on the size of the multiplier?

Despite these problems, most economists believe that automatic stabilizers have played an important role in reducing normal fluctuations in our economy. They point to the kind of data we see in Figure 16-2, which up until 2008 showed a significant decrease in fluctuations in the economy. Other economists aren't so sure; they argue both that the apparent decrease in fluctuations is an optical illusion and that problems that built up during the period of reduced fluctuations led to the financial crisis that began in 2008. As usual, economic data are sufficiently ambiguous to give both sides strong arguments. The jury is still out.

Modern Macro Policy Precepts

Taking all the qualifications into account, the modern macro policy precept is a blend of functional and sound finance. Modern economists' answer to the question, "What should the government do about a recession?" is generally: Do nothing in terms of specific tax or spending policy, but let the automatic stabilizers in the economy do the adjustment. The reason for not undertaking specific policies is not a lack of concern

Q-9 According to modern economists what should government do if there is a recession?

FIGURE 16-2 Decrease in Fluctuations in the Economy

Compared to the early 1900s, fluctuations in the economy have decreased; this suggests that policy makers have done something right.

Source: Federal Reserve Historical Charts, Economic Report of the President (www.doc.gov), and author estimates.

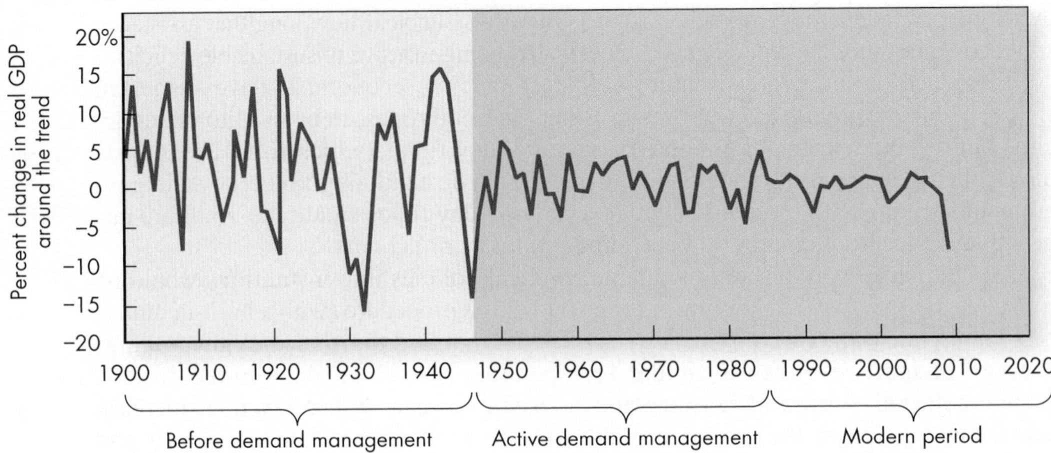

about recession, but because, theoretically, the effect a deficit would have is unclear and, practically and politically, implementing control via fiscal policy at the right time is very difficult. The "do-nothing" approach reflects the sound finance precept. There is a substantial exception, however. That exception is that if the economy seems to be falling into a severe recession or depression, then the majority of economists believe that government should run expansionary fiscal policy, unless the country's debt situation makes that impossible. If that is the case, the country must choose between default and depression.

Conclusion

The U.S. economy found itself in a severe recession in 2008. In response to the significant decreases in private aggregate demand, governments throughout the world cut taxes and increased spending, running large deficits. (A good exercise is to demonstrate these policies with the *AS/AD* model.) The government ran very, very expansionary fiscal policy because it was trying to offset the leftward shift of the *AD* curve. In 2008 almost all macro policy economists agreed that the United States, and likely the world economy, was headed toward a serious recession or depression, and that it was the government's role to try to prevent it. This was not fine-tuning, with major concerns about the deficits crowding out private investment, or about the level of potential output; it was preventing a depression.

Q-10 What is the appropriate policy for an economy headed toward:

- A depression?
- A hyperinflation?
- Normal times?

As united as macro policy economists were in 2008 that expansionary fiscal policy was needed, there was also serious concern about the size of the deficits. These concerns have increased as the deficits have continued long beyond what was predicted. All macroeconomists also believe that, at some point, functional finance principles will have to give way to sound finance principles, and that the government will have to shift gears from functional finance—trying to prevent a depression and jump-start the economy—to the principles of sound finance—trying to make sure the U.S. economy remains on solid financial footing.

As of 2013 there is far less consensus about whether the economy has reached that point. Some economists doubt that private spending is going to pick up on its own and that large government deficits will not be needed for the indefinite future to reduce unemployment to the level that most people find acceptable. If those deficits are unsustainable, then the level of unemployment that people want is unachievable, without undermining the sustainability of the U.S. economy.

REAL-WORLD APPLICATION

Incentive and Supply-Side Effects of Public Finance

The various political parties' views of public finance have changed significantly over the past 60 years. In the 1950s and early 1960s, the political parties' views on deficit finance were clear. The Democrats were Keynesian; they were the party of the deficits. Republicans were Classical; they were the party of sound finance. Consistent with these positions, Democrats pushed for increases in government programs and government spending, in part justifying these programs as a way to increase the size of the government budget and thereby increase effectiveness of fiscal policy as a tool of stabilization.

The push by Democrats for increased spending was partly offset by Republicans who pushed for tax decreases, but that push was often overwhelmed by their support of sound finance. Ultimately, Republicans found that they had to compromise on their support for sound finance and accept some level of deficits because of the political difficulty of cutting government programs once they were started. During this time, the relative size of the government increased, and government ran almost continual deficits. However, these deficits were not especially large relative to GDP, and no serious economist felt that these deficits were raising questions about the long-run financial viability of the government.

Just about that time the New Classical revolution was taking hold and Republicans were giving up their support for a balanced budget. Instead of supporting a balanced budget, they began to support cutting taxes whenever possible. Part of the justification for that position was the New Classical policy view of deficits and the Ricardian equivalence theorem. What became known as supply-side economists emphasized the incentive effects of tax cuts, which these economists argued would lead to growth in output and hence would increase tax revenue. Some even argued the tax cuts would more than finance themselves, increasing, not decreasing, total tax revenues. The lay-public name for these views was *supply-side economics*. Most economists are hesitant about such claims. While all economists believe that incentive effects are important in the long run, most believe that the short-run incentive effects are relatively small.

That does not mean the Republican support of a policy of always cutting taxes could not be supported. Most economists felt that the reasoning for the Republican view on public finance was subtler and more political than the view presented in supply-side economics. Essentially, the Republican view could be supported if one believed that government spending was enormously inefficient and needed to be kept down, and that political forces would work to spend whatever money was available. If these views were true, it means that a budget surplus, or even a deficit that does not exceed a certain level of GDP that would alarm the public, is an invitation for increased government spending. These two propositions led Republicans to eliminate their support of sound finance and a balanced budget. The new Republican supply-side position became one of "always cut taxes" and "never raise taxes." This might be called the "starve the beast" approach to public finance. It is a public finance policy designed to reduce government spending in whatever way possible. To achieve that end, Republicans favor cutting taxes whenever they can to "starve the beast" and prevent the growth in any government program. In this view, any policy that does that, and tax cuts are one such policy, is a good policy.

This Republican position came into being with the Reagan era and has continued until today. This left a few fiscally conservative Democrats, and a few maverick Republicans, as the few reluctant supporters of sound finance, and has made large fiscal deficits the norm, not the exception. Eventually this will change. As economist Herb Stein pointed out (in what has become known as Stein's law), "If something cannot go on forever, it will stop."

If they are correct the United States is going to have to start living within its means. The United States will have to reduce the deficit—even if that reduction means lower growth and higher unemployment than had traditionally been acceptable.

In economics you don't learn correct economic policy; what you learn is a method for thinking about economic policy that others have found useful. That method is to learn some models and then to judiciously apply them to a variety of situations. The modern macro policy precepts summarized in this chapter are examples of that judicious application.

In economics you don't learn correct economic policy; what you learn is a method for thinking about economic policy that others have found useful.

Summary

- Sound finance is a view that the government budget should always be balanced except in wartime. *(LO16-1)*
- The Ricardian equivalence theorem states that it doesn't matter whether government spending is financed by taxes or deficits; neither would affect the economy. *(LO16-1)*
- Although proponents of sound finance believed the logic of the Ricardian equivalence theorem, they believed that, in reality, deficit spending could affect the economy. Still, because of political and moral issues, proponents of sound finance promoted balanced budgets. *(LO16-1)*
- Functional finance is the theoretical proposition that governments should make spending and taxing decisions based on their effect on the economy, not moralistic principles. *(LO16-2)*
- Six problems that make functional finance difficult to implement are: *(LO16-3)*
  1. Interest rate crowding out.
  2. The government not knowing what the situation is.
  3. The government not knowing the economy's potential income.
  4. Government's inability to respond quickly enough.
  5. The size of government debt not mattering.
  6. Conflicting goals.
- Activist fiscal policy is now built into U.S. economic institutions through automatic stabilizers. *(LO16-4)*
- Economists agree that if the economy is headed toward a depression or hyperinflation, follow the precepts of functional finance—expansionary fiscal policy to offset a depression and contractionary fiscal policy to offset hyperinflation. If the economy is experiencing moderate fluctuations, follow the precepts of sound finance—balance the budget. *(LO16-4)*

Key Terms

automatic stabilizer *(355)*
crowding out *(348)*
functional finance *(347)*
procyclical fiscal policy *(356)*
Ricardian equivalence theorem *(345)*
sound finance *(344)*

Questions and Exercises 

1. According to the Ricardian equivalence theorem, what is the effect of each of the following on output in the economy? Explain your answers. *(LO16-1)*
   a. Government pays for an increase in spending by raising taxes.
   b. Government pays for an increase in spending by issuing bonds.
   c. What is the implication of your answers to *a* and *b*?
2. According to the Ricardian equivalence theorem, why is government spending offset by a reduction in private spending? *(LO16-1)*
3. Why does sound finance not depend on the Ricardian equivalence theorem? *(LO16-1)*
4. What is functional finance? *(LO16-2)*
5. Explain the place of activist fiscal policy in directing the economy according to each of the following points of view: *(LO16-2)*
   a. Sound finance.
   b. Functional finance.
6. Why is functional finance difficult to implement? *(LO16-2)*
7. According to crowding out, how is government spending offset by a reduction in private spending? *(LO16-3)*
8. If interest rates have no effect on investment, how much crowding out will occur? *(LO16-3)*
9. Demonstrate the effect of the following on output and the price level in the *AS/AD* model: *(LO16-3)*
   a. Full crowding out.
   b. Partial crowding out.
   c. Full crowding out and private investment is more productive than government investment.
10. The government has just increased taxes. *(LO16-3)*
    a. Demonstrate the effect on the price level and output in the standard model.
    b. How would your answer to *a* differ if there were partial crowding out?
    c. How would your answer to *a* differ if there were complete crowding out?

11. Suppose one economist believes the target rate of unemployment is 4.5 percent while another believes it is 5.5 percent. By how much would you expect their estimates of potential GDP to differ in a $10 trillion economy? (*LO16-3*)
12. How does the budget process make fiscal policy difficult to implement? (*LO16-3*)
13. Use the *AS/AD* model to explain why most presidents advocate government spending programs when running for reelection. (*LO16-3*)
14. Use the *AS/AD* model to explain the maxim in politics that if you are going to increase taxes, the time to do it is right after your election, when reelection is far off. (*LO16-3*)
15. Why has the assumption that the size of the debt doesn't matter been called into question even more fervently than ever? (*LO16-3*)
16. How are state balanced-budget requirements procyclical? (*LO16-4*)
17. How do automatic stabilizers work? (*LO16-4*)
18. How can automatic stabilizers slow an economic recovery? (*LO16-4*)

Questions from Alternative Perspectives

1. It is often argued that savings should be encouraged. If one believes in the free market, does encouraging savings make sense? Why or why not? (Austrian)
2. During the Depression, unemployment rose to 25 percent. The *AS/AD* model presented in the book suggests that a fall in the price level would have solved the problem. Keynesians are not so convinced and believe that a fall in the price level would have lowered income, which would have shifted aggregate demand back further.
   a. Demonstrate the standard argument graphically.
   b. How does it deal (or not deal) with that interconnection between a fall in the price level and aggregate demand? (Post-Keynesian)
3. In this chapter you learned the importance of automatic stabilizers. At the state level, "rainy-day" funds play a crucial role in maintaining services when state revenues decrease during a recession. While this may appear to be a rational institution, institutions are social constructs and what appears rational depends upon individual belief systems. The existence of a rainy-day fund can be interpreted as definitive proof of excess taxation and, in states that allow voter referendums, this fund can be eliminated by a majority vote. What vested interests—those seeking something for nothing—benefit from such decisions? (Institutionalist)
4. The economy has often been far from full employment.
   a. What would it take to run a regime of continuous full employment?
   b. How would the establishment of a full employment regime alter the relations between workers and capitalists?
   c. Is such a regime politically feasible? (Radical)
5. Any policy has both advantages and disadvantages, implying that policy makers must weigh both the advantages and disadvantages when deciding what policy to follow.
   a. Does society share absolute, objective values that guide the weighing of the alternatives?
   b. What role should religious beliefs play in establishing these values? (Religious)

Issues to Ponder

1. When Professor Robert Gordon lowered his estimate of the target unemployment rate from 6 percent to 5.5 percent in early 1995, he quipped, "I've just created 600,000 jobs."
   a. What events in the 1990s most likely motivated his revision of the target unemployment rate?
   b. Show the effect this revision would have on the *AS/AD* model.
   c. The unemployment rate was 5.5 percent. Income was $7.3 trillion. Within 18 months the unemployment rate had fallen to 5 percent without signs of accelerating inflation. How much higher would the level of potential income have been in 1995 if the target unemployment rate were 5 percent rather than 5.5 percent assuming that a one percentage point fall in the unemployment rate is associated with a two percentage point rise in income?
2. President Bill Clinton's policies in 1993 were designed to reduce the deficit but increase employment.
   a. Why would such a policy not fit well in the multiplier model?
   b. Explain in words how such a policy might achieve the desired effect.
   c. Graphically demonstrate your answer in *b*.
   d. What data would you look at to see if your explanation in *b* and *c* is appropriate?

3. A tax cut has just been announced. Congressman Growth states that its effect will be on the supply side. Congressman Stable states that its effect will be on the demand side.
   a. Demonstrate graphically the effect of the tax cut on the price level and output in the standard *AS/AD* model.
   b. Which of the two congressmen's views better fits the model?
   c. Demonstrate graphically the effect of the tax cut on the price level and output if the other congressman is correct.
   d. In the short run, which of the two congressmen is more likely correct?
   e. How might the existence of significant crowding out change your answer to *d*?

Answers to Margin Questions

1. No; the Ricardian equivalence theorem states that the method of financing a deficit does not matter; sound finance argues that it does matter and that deficits should not be run. (*p. 345; LO16-1*)
2. Pre-1930 economists believed that government should maintain a balanced budget even if there was a recession. (*p. 345; LO16-1*)
3. An economist who believes in nuanced sound finance would say that government should maintain a balanced budget for a small recession, but if there were a large recession or depression, it should be open to running deficits. (*p. 346; LO16-1*)
4. Sound finance states that you should always balance the government budget; functional finance states that you should use the government budget balance as a steering wheel to control the economy, and that the state of the economy should determine whether you have a deficit or surplus. (*p. 347; LO16-2*)
5. If interest rates did not affect investment or consumption expenditures, there would be no crowding out. (*p. 349; LO16-3*)
6. If government spending stimulated private spending, the phenomenon of what might be called *crowding in* might occur. The increase in government spending would shift the *AD* curve from AD_0 to AD_1 as in the accompanying diagram. The resulting increase in income would cause a further increase in investment, shifting the aggregate demand curve out further to AD_2. Income would increase from Y_0 to Y_2—by more than what the simple *AS/AD* model would predict. (*p. 349; LO16-3*)

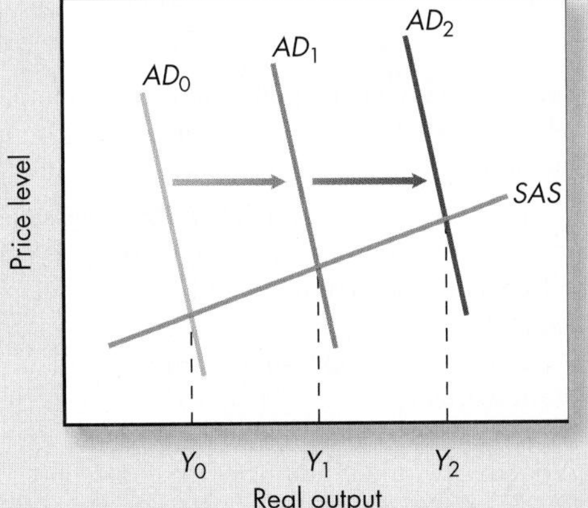

7. Potential income is not a measurable number. It is a conceptual number that must be estimated based on observable information about such phenomena as inflation, productivity, and unemployment. Estimating potential income is a challenge. (*p. 351; LO16-3*)
8. Automatic stabilizers tend to decrease the size of the multiplier, decreasing the fluctuations in the economy. (*p. 357; LO16-4*)
9. The modern economists' answer to what to do if there is a recession is, generally, do nothing in terms of specific tax or spending policy, but let the automatic stabilizers in the economy do the adjustment for you. (*p. 357; LO16-4*)
10. Use functional finance when an economy is headed toward a depression or hyperinflation. In normal times, use sound finance. (*p. 358; LO16-4*)

chapter 17

Jobs and Unemployment

> *A man willing to work, and unable to find work, is perhaps the saddest sight that fortune's inequality exhibits under this sun.*
>
> —Thomas Carlyle

When my son graduated in May, he got a job starting in June. I celebrated—probably more than he did. He's off the family dole. I suspect that many of you and your families are in similar situations—you're going to college to improve your job prospects. I say "improve your job prospects" rather than "find a job" because most of you likely already have a job, at least a part-time one. After all, more than half of all full-time students have jobs, and they work an average of 20 hours per week. So when they graduate, they aren't really getting a job—they are changing jobs.

How worried should we be about unemployment? That depends. Unemployment can mean very different things to different people. Students who have parents who can afford, and are willing to keep you on the family dole, will view unemployment quite differently than would a single parent who has two kids to support and whose only income comes from work.

I tell these stories to give you a sense of the difficulties of understanding unemployment. Unemployment involves moral judgments and philosophical issues that go far beyond economics, and unemployment is more complicated than any aggregate model of the economy can capture. The labor market is much more dynamic than aggregate measures of employment and unemployment suggest. The job market involves continual change with unemployment as a transitional state within that process of change. People change jobs all the time. Today the average person will have about 7 to 10 jobs in his or her life, staying at each an average of four years. On a macro level, for example, in January of 2012, some 12.8 million people were unemployed; in February the number was about the same. What appears to be an unchanged employment situation, however, masks underlying shifts. Between those two months, 4.2 million people found new jobs and 4.1 million people left their jobs. Many of the unemployed in January were not the same people who were unemployed in February.

Is unemployment voluntary or not? The reality is that even in a recession, most educated people can either find a job or create one. The problem is that the jobs they can find or create pay far less and are far less desirable than the jobs they want. Here's an example: In 2009 more than half of students who

After reading this chapter, you should be able to:

LO17-1 State how the unemployment rate is measured and describe the debate about that measure.

LO17-2 Explain Okun's rule of thumb and summarize the debate about the appropriate target rate of unemployment.

LO17-3 Explain why unemployment is more than a technical concept but one that involves normative judgments.

LO17-4 Discuss the advantages of, and problems with, a government-guaranteed minimum job program.

REAL-WORLD APPLICATION

Categories of Unemployment

A good sense of the differing types of unemployment and the differing social views that unemployment embodies can be conveyed through three examples of unemployed individuals. As you read the following stories, ask yourself which category of unemployment each individual falls into.

Example 1

Joe has lost his steady job and collects unemployment insurance. He's had various jobs in the past and was laid off from his last one. He spent a few weeks on household projects, believing he would be called back by his most recent employer—but he wasn't. He's grown to like being on his own schedule. He's living on his unemployment insurance (while it lasts), his savings, and money he picks up by being paid cash under the table working a few hours now and then at construction sites.

The Unemployment Compensation Office requires him to make at least an attempt to find work, and he's turned up a few prospects. However, some were back-breaking laboring jobs and one would have required him to move to a distant city, so he's avoiding accepting regular work. Joe knows the unemployment payments won't last forever. When they're used up, he plans to increase his under-the-table activity. Then, when he gets good and ready, he'll really look for a job.

Example 2

Flo is a middle-aged, small-town housewife. She worked before her marriage, but when she and her husband started their family, she quit her job to be a full-time housewife and mother. She never questioned her family values of hard work, independence, belief in free enterprise, and scorn of government handouts. When her youngest child left the nest, she decided to finish the college education she'd only just started when she married.

After getting her degree, she looked for a job, but found the market for middle-aged women with no recent experience to be depressed—and depressing. The state employment office where she sought listings recognized her abilities and gave her a temporary job in that very office. Because she was a "temp," however, she was the first to be laid off when the state legislature cut the local office budget—but she'd worked long enough to be eligible for unemployment insurance.

She hesitated about applying since handouts were against her principles. But while working there she'd seen plenty of people, including her friends, applying for benefits after work histories even slimmer than hers. She decided to take the benefits. While they lasted, she found family finances on almost as sound a footing as when she was working. Although she was bringing in less money, net family income didn't suffer much since she didn't have Social Security withheld nor did she have the commuting and clothing expenses of going to a daily job.

Example 3

Tom had a good job at a manufacturing plant where he'd worked up to a wage of $800 a week. Occasionally he was laid off, but only for a few weeks, and then he'd be called back. But then the work at the plant was outsourced. Tom, an older worker with comparatively high wages, was "let go."

Tom had a wife, three children, a car payment, and a mortgage. He looked for other work but couldn't find anything paying close to what he'd been getting. Tom used up his unemployment insurance and his savings. He sold the house and moved his family into a trailer. Finally he heard that there were a lot of jobs in Massachusetts, 800 miles away. He moved there, found a job, and began sending money home every week. Then the Massachusetts economy faltered. Tom was laid off again, and his unemployment insurance ran out again. He became depressed and, relying on his $300,000 life insurance policy, he figured he was worth more to his family dead than alive, so he killed himself.

As these three examples suggest, unemployment encompasses a wide range of cases. Unemployment is anything but a one-dimensional problem, so it's not surprising that people's views of how to deal with it differ.

graduated with a humanities degree either were unemployed or worked at a job that didn't require a college degree. Even new Ph.D.s in these disciplines often don't have much better prospects. It's even worse for those who have dropped out of college or high school. As college-educated people look for jobs that don't require a college education, they will squeeze out those who don't have that education. It is like a game of musical chairs, and the people with the least education usually end up without the chair.

How many fewer chairs than people are looking for chairs depends on the state of the aggregate economy. The stronger the aggregate economy, the more jobs available. In 2012 there were about four people looking for every job available. What this means is that if everyone is going to have a job, lots of people are going to have to create one for themselves.

The labor market is like a game of musical chairs, and the people with the least education usually end up without the chair.

Creating a job for yourself isn't that far-fetched. Even teenagers can create jobs —babysitting, dog walking, washing cars, or teaching the technically challenged older generation how to use a cell phone or an iPad. Truly entrepreneurial people will never be unemployed; they will simply create jobs for themselves. Most of us are not that entrepreneurial, and the reality is that in today's economy high school dropouts, and increasingly college dropouts, are having a hard time finding a job.

In this chapter I am going to take a closer look at unemployment. I will first review some basics, considering both how unemployment is measured and its relationship to potential output. Then I consider the debate about what the target level of unemployment should be. Finally I consider the policy debate about unemployment by discussing a plan to eliminate all involuntary unemployment by providing a guaranteed job for everyone.

How Is Unemployment Measured?

When there's debate about what the unemployment problem is, it isn't surprising that there's also a debate about how to measure it. When talking about unemployment, economists usually refer to the "unemployment rate" published by the U.S. Department of Labor's Bureau of Labor Statistics. Fluctuations in the official unemployment rate

When there's debate about what the unemployment problem is, it isn't surprising that there's also a debate about how to measure it.

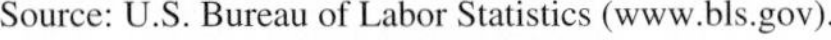

FIGURE 17-1 Unemployment Rate since 1900

The unemployment rate has always fluctuated, with the average around 5 or 6 percent. Since the 1930s, fluctuations have decreased. In the mid-1940s, the U.S. government started focusing on the unemployment rate as a goal. Initially, it chose 2 percent as a target, but over time gradually that increased to somewhere around 5 percent. In recent years, the unemployment rate has been significantly higher than that.

Source: U.S. Bureau of Labor Statistics (www.bls.gov).

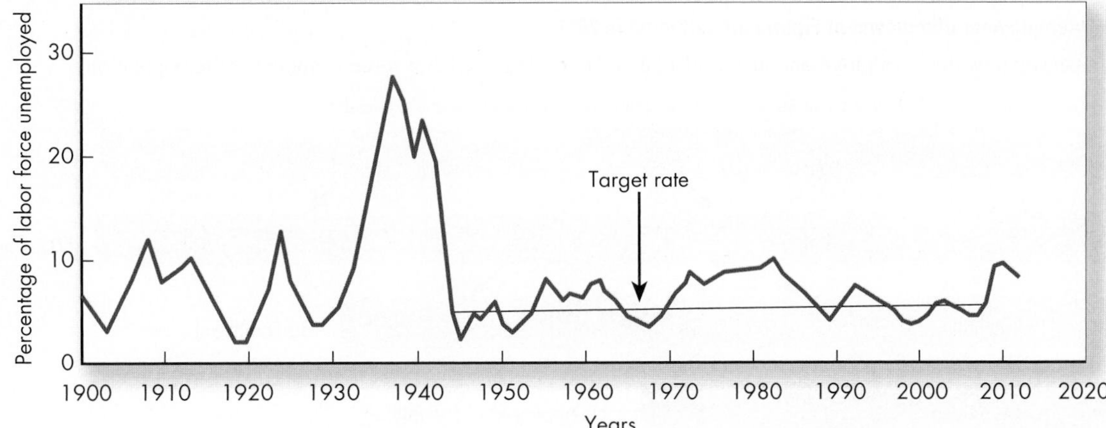

since 1900 appear in Figure 17-1. In it you can see that during World War II (1941–45) unemployment fell from the high rates of the 1930s Depression to an extremely low rate, only 1.2 percent. You also can see that while the rate started back up in the 1950s, reaching 4 or 5 percent, it remained low until the 1970s, when the rate began gradually to rise again, peaking at 10.8 percent in 1983. In the 1990s and early 2000s, the unemployment rate has fluctuated from a high of 7.8 percent during the 1991 recession to a low of 3.8 percent in 2000. In 2012, the unemployment rate was about 8 percent.

Calculating the Unemployment Rate

The U.S. unemployment rate is determined by dividing the number of people who are unemployed by the number of people in the **labor force**—*those people in an economy who are willing and able to work*—and multiplying by 100. For example, if the total unemployed stands at 12 million and the labor force stands at 150 million, the unemployment rate is:

The unemployment rate is measured by dividing the number of unemployed individuals by the number of people in the civilian labor force and multiplying by 100.

$$\frac{12 \text{ million}}{150 \text{ million}} = 0.08 \times 100 = 8\%$$

To calculate the unemployment rate, we must measure both the labor force and the number of unemployed. To determine the labor force, start with the total civilian population and subtract all persons unavailable for work, such as inmates of institutions and people under 16 years of age. From that figure subtract the number of people not in the labor force, including homemakers, students, retirees, the voluntarily idle, and the disabled. The result is the potential workforce, which is about 154 million people, or about 50 percent of the civilian population (see Figure 17-2). (The civilian population excludes about 2 million individuals who are in the armed forces.)

Q-1 During some months, the unemployment rate declines, but the number of unemployed rises. How can this happen?

The number of unemployed can be calculated by subtracting the number of employed from the labor force. The Bureau of Labor Statistics (BLS) defines people as *employed* if they work at a paid job (including part-time jobs) or if they are unpaid workers in an enterprise operated by a family member. The BLS's definition of *employed* includes all those who were temporarily absent from their jobs the week of the BLS survey because of illness, bad weather, vacation, labor-management dispute, or personal reasons, whether or not they were paid by their employers for the time off.

In 2011 the number of unemployed individuals was about 13.7 million. Dividing this number by the labor force (153.6 million) gives us an unemployment rate of 8.9 percent.

FIGURE 17-2 Unemployment/Employment Figures (in millions) in 2011

This exhibit shows you how the unemployment rate is calculated. Notice that the labor force is not the entire population.

Source: *Employment and Earnings 2012.* Bureau of Labor Statistics (www.bls.gov). Data may not add up due to rounding.

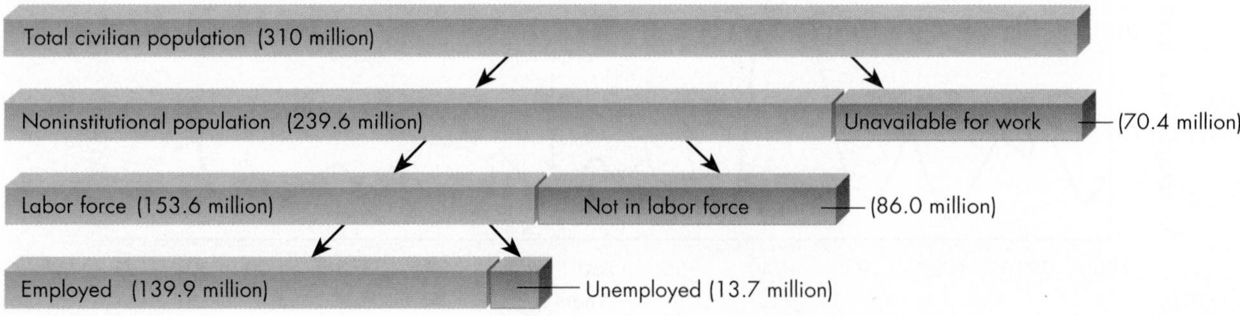

How Accurate Is the Official Unemployment Rate?

The BLS measures unemployment using a number of assumptions that have been the source of debate. For example, should *discouraged workers*—people who do not look for a job because they feel they don't have a chance of finding one—be counted as unemployed? Some Keynesian economists believe they should. Moreover, they question whether part-time workers who prefer full-time work, the *underemployed,* should be classified as employed.

The Keynesian argument is that there is such a lack of decent jobs and of affordable transportation to get to the jobs that do exist that many people become very discouraged and have simply stopped looking for work. Because BLS statisticians define these people as voluntarily idle, and do not count them as unemployed, Keynesians argue that the BLS undercounts unemployment significantly. When discouraged workers *are* included, the number of unemployed rises significantly, as you can see in the accompanying graph that shows the official unemployment rate along with another measure of the unemployment rate that includes people who gave up looking for work altogether. Including these discouraged workers, unemployment would have remained over 10 percent in 2012 instead of falling to 8.2 percent. Including the underemployed—the number rises to about 18 percent.

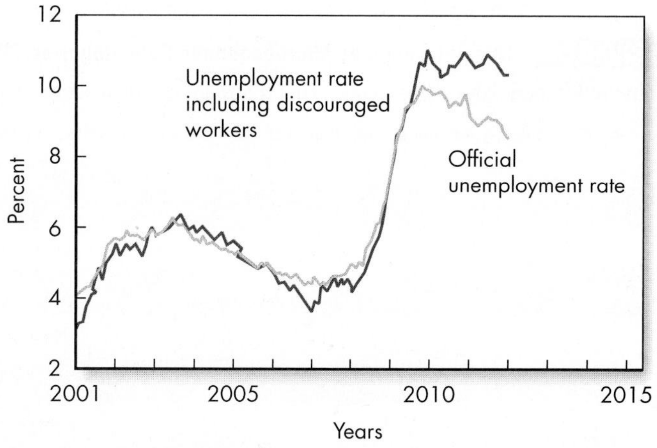

Source: Bureau of Labor Statistics.

Q-2 In what way does the very concept of unemployment depend on value judgments?

The Classical argument about unemployment is that being without a job often is voluntary. People may say they are looking for a job when they're not really looking. Many are working "off the books"; others are simply vacationing. Some Classicals contend that the way the BLS measures unemployment exaggerates the number of those who are truly unemployed. They argue that many so-called unemployed are just choosing not to work.

To help overcome these problems, economists use supplemental measures to give them insight into the state of the labor market. These include the **labor force participation rate,** which *measures the labor force as a percentage of the total population at least 16 years old,* and the **employment-population ratio**—*the number of people who are working as a percentage of people available to work.*

Despite problems, the unemployment rate statistic still gives us useful information about changes in the economy.

Despite problems, the unemployment rate statistic still gives us useful information about changes in the economy. The measurement problems themselves change little from year to year, so you can ignore them when comparing unemployment from one year to another. Thus, in late 2007, when the economy went into a downturn and the unemployment rate rose from a low of 4.4 percent in 2007 to a high of 10 percent throughout the recession, the unemployment problem clearly had worsened, no matter how you measure it. Keynesian and Classical economists agree that a changing unemployment rate generally tells us something about the economy, especially if interpreted in the light of other statistics. That's why the unemployment rate is used as a measure of the state of the economy.

Microeconomic Categories of Unemployment

In the decades after World War II, unemployment was seen primarily as cyclical unemployment, and the focus of macroeconomic policy was on how to eliminate that unemployment through a specific set of macroeconomic policies. Understanding those macroeconomic policies is important, but today it's not enough. Unemployment has many dimensions, so different types of unemployment are susceptible to different types of policies.

WWW Web Note 17.1 Defining Unemployment

FIGURE 17-3 Unemployment by Microeconomic Subcategories, 2011

Unemployment isn't all the same. This figure gives you a sense of some of the subcategories of unemployment.

Source: *Employment and Earnings 2012,* Bureau of Labor Statistics (www.bls.gov). Data may not add up due to rounding and definitional differences.

Some microeconomic categories of unemployment are: how people become unemployed, demographic unemployment, duration of unemployment, and unemployment by industry.

Today's view is that you don't use a sledgehammer to pound in finishing nails, and you don't use macro policies to deal with certain types of unemployment; instead you use micro policies. To determine where microeconomic policies are appropriate as a supplement to macroeconomic policies, economists break unemployment down into a number of categories and analyze each category separately. These categories include how people become unemployed, demographic characteristics, duration of unemployment, and the reason for unemployment (see Figure 17-3).

The nature of unemployment has changed over time in a number of ways. For example, today fewer and fewer jobs are available to those without a high school diploma. In the past the unemployment rate was lower for men; now it's lower for

FIGURE 17-4 Number of People Unemployed for More than 26 Weeks

Significantly more people were unemployed for more than 26 weeks in the 2008 recession compared to previous recessions because fewer people were able to find a comparable job at comparable pay to the one they lost. The wage they desired was higher than they wage they would have to accept to take a job.

Source: Bureau of Labor Statistics (www.bls.gov).

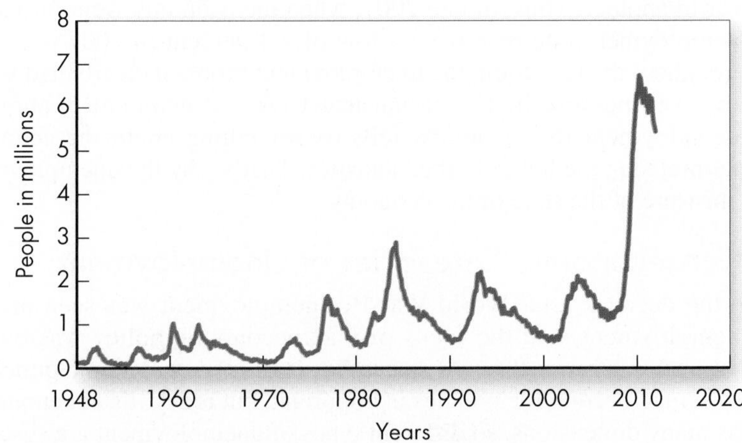

women. Another measure of the changing nature of unemployment is the duration of unemployment, as shown in Figure 17-4. As you can see in the downturn in 2008, the duration of unemployment increased significantly. This means fewer unemployed people were finding and accepting another job soon after being unemployed. Some couldn't find work; more people were unable to find the type of job they had at the pay they were getting. It isn't that the government wasn't trying to lower unemployment; the government was running as expansionary monetary and fiscal policy as it dared, (or at least as much as was politically feasible) and still long-term unemployment remained high. This suggests a structural unemployment problem that was not highly susceptible to expansionary monetary and fiscal policy.

A structural unemployment problem is not highly susceptible to expansionary monetary and fiscal policy.

Unemployment and Potential Output

Until the structural slump hit, economists believed that they could shoot for a target unemployment rate of about 5.5 percent. Since then they have adjusted their estimates of the achievable unemployment rate to higher levels of 6 or 7 percent, more consistent with the above-8 percent level it has been since the recovery began. This higher unemployment rate is consistent with a lower rate of growth in potential output than economists had been using. The relationship between changes in output and unemployment is generally captured by Okun's rule of thumb.

Okun's Rule of Thumb, Unemployment, and Changes in Output

The unemployment rate provides a good indication of how much labor is available to firms to increase production and thus provides a good idea of how fast the economy can grow. Table 17-1 shows the unemployment rate and growth rate for selected countries over the last 30 years.

As you can see, both have changed over time, and the U.S. unemployment rate has increased from what it was a decade ago. Throughout this time the target for unemployment and growth have been debated by economists and policy makers. To push the economy so that unemployment falls below the target rate is like driving your car 90 miles an hour. True, the marks on your speedometer might go up to 150, but a top speed of 75 is a more realistic. Beyond 120 (assuming that's where your car

TABLE 17-1 Unemployment and Per Capita Growth for Selected Countries (percentages)

	Unemployment Rate				Growth Rate			
Country	1980	1990	2000	2011	1980–89	1990–99	2000–2010	2011
United States	7.2	5.6	4.0	9.0	3.1	3.0	1.2	1.7
Canada	7.5	8.2	6.8	7.5	2.8	2.4	1.6	2.5
Germany	3.4	6.2	8.0	6.0	1.7	1.6	0.6	3.1
Japan	2.0	2.1	4.7	4.5	4.1	0.9	0.3	−0.7
Korea	5.2	2.5	4.4	3.4	8.8	5.6	3.5	3.6
Mexico	1.2	2.7	2.2	5.2	1.4	3.0	1.1	4.0
United Kingdom	6.5	7.0	5.5	8.1	2.6	2.2	1.5	0.7

Source: World Economic Outlook Database (www.imf.org).

is red-lined), the engine is likely to blow up (unless you have a Maserati). The achievable unemployment rate differs among countries and depends on labor institutions, labor laws, the country's exchange rate, and worker productivity. Thus, as is the case with cars, maximum speeds can differ among economies and can change over time.

Economists relate the target unemployment rate to the target level of potential output. That level of potential output in the United States is assumed to grow at the secular (long-term) trend rate of 2.25 to 3.5 percent per year. That secular trend rate of growth reflects both productivity increases and labor force increases. When the economy is in a downturn or recession, actual output is below potential output. As you have seen, there is significant debate about the appropriate target rates of unemployment and potential output.

Okun's rule of thumb holds that a 1 percentage point rise in unemployment rate will tend to be associated with a 2 percent fall in output below its trend and vice versa.

To determine how changes in the unemployment rate are related to changes in output, economists use **Okun's rule of thumb,** which states that *a 1 percentage point rise in the unemployment rate will tend to be associated with a 2 percent fall in output from its trend and vice versa.*

This means, for example if the trend growth is 3 percent and unemployment rises by 2 percent, output will actually fall by 1 percent (3 percent − 2 × 2 percent). In terms of number of workers, a 2 percentage point increase in the unemployment rate means about 3 million additional people are out of work than if the economy had stayed on its growth path. These figures are rough, but they give you a sense of the implications of the relationship.

What makes estimating this relationship difficult is that increases in productivity and increases in the number of people choosing to work fluctuate. Changes in either can cause output and employment to grow, even if the unemployment rate doesn't change. I point this out because in the 1980s the number of people choosing to work increased substantially, significantly increasing the labor participation rate. Then, in the early 2000s, as many large firms structurally adjusted their production methods to increase worker productivity, unemployment sometimes rose even as output rose. Thus, when the labor participation rate and productivity change, an increase in unemployment doesn't necessarily mean a decrease in employment or a decrease in output, and the relationship between output and the unemployment can deviate from Okun's rule of thumb.

Q-3 If economic output falls 2 percent below its trend, what does Okun's rule predict happens to the unemployment rate?

In the downturn starting in late 2007, government economists used Okun's rule of thumb to predict what would happen to unemployment as a result the downturn. During that downturn output fell about 6 percentage points below trend and economists estimated that the unemployment rate would rise by 3 percentage points, from 5 percent to about 8 percent. Instead, unemployment rose to 10 percent, much higher than predicted. The president's former chief economic adviser suggested that the fear associated with the potential financial breakdown led firms to cut employment much more than they normally would have because they were preparing for a possible depression. Because the remaining workers had to work harder, this increased productivity, which allowed the economy to keep growing, even if only slightly, as the unemployment rate rose.

Is Unemployment Structural or Cyclical?

Okun's rule is designed to explain cyclical unemployment. **Cyclical unemployment** is *temporary unemployment that can be expected to end as the economy recovers.* A person being temporarily laid off as a waiter because fewer people are going to restaurants in a recession is an example of cyclical unemployment. It can be resolved by expansionary fiscal and monetary policy. **Structural unemployment** is *long-term unemployment that occurs because of changes in the structure of the economy*. A person who loses his job as a stenographer because his job is replaced by voice recognition software is an example of structural unemployment. Structural unemployment cannot be resolved by expansionary monetary and fiscal policy. If a person is structurally unemployed, before he or she can find a job at the same pay, he or she will have to retrain. The distinction between structural and cyclical is not watertight. What starts out to be cyclical unemployment may well end up being structural unemployment, as the firms that lay off workers in a recession don't hire them back.

Most of the policy discussions of unemployment in conventional macroeconomics have been about cyclical unemployment, and most of the policy discussion has concerned monetary and fiscal policy. Expansionary macro policy is designed to deal with cyclical unemployment. If the U.S. economy is entering a period of structural stagnation, then that discussion and policy are no longer sufficient; the unemployment is structural—caused by a mismatch of skills and wages desired by workers and the skills and wages firms are willing to pay. Macro policies won't solve structural unemployment.

Most of the policy discussions of unemployment in conventional macroeconomics have been about cyclical unemployment, not structural unemployment.

To give you an idea of what I mean by structural unemployment, consider a worker who has been laid off in the automobile industry. He was getting $28 an hour plus generous benefits such as a retirement plan and health insurance. Then he loses his job. In its place, the best job the economy can provide with the skills he has is with a job for $10 an hour without benefits. In fact, Chrysler did just this—paying entry-level workers $14–$16 an hour compared to the $28 existing autoworkers were earning. Until a worker is willing to accept that lower paying job, he is structurally unemployed. Expansionary monetary and fiscal policy won't solve his problem.

An important determinant of whether someone takes a job is his **reservation wage**—*the wage a person requires before accepting a job*. The higher the reservation wage, the more likely one is to be unemployed. In today's globalized economy a U.S. worker's reservation wage tends to be higher than the reservation wage of many workers in developing countries. This means that many of the jobs U.S. workers used to do have been outsourced or given to new immigrants to the United States who are willing to work harder for less pay. Having had a good-paying job makes it psychologically difficult to lower one's reservation wage. For high school dropouts, globalization often means that they are lucky when they can pick up a minimum wage job washing dishes, cleaning rooms in a motel, working the midnight shift, or picking produce on a farm.

Q-4 How is the reservation wage related to structural unemployment?

Another aspect that keeps reservation wages in the United States high are the costs associated with taking a job and the availability of income-support programs. People who are unemployed with kids to take care of, and child care costs $10 an hour, or without transportation to a job, might end up with lower take-home pay if they accept a low-paying job. This makes it essentially impossible for them to take the job as long as they can otherwise get enough to live on through food stamps and welfare support from friends, family, or government. So the available support for people without a job plays an important role in where one sets one's reservation wage.

WWW Web Note 17.2 Low-wage Jobs

Yet another aspect of structural unemployment is geographic. The job situation is never uniform across the United States; some parts of the country will have jobs while others have none. This also creates geographically imposed structural unemployment, because some people don't want to relocate to take a job. In 2012, for example, South Dakota, which had a natural gas boom, had numerous unfilled jobs, even as other parts of the country had significant unemployment.

Why Has the Target Rate of Unemployment Changed over Time?

Why has the target rate of unemployment changed over time? One reason is demographics: As you saw in Figure 17-3, different age groups have different unemployment rates, and as the population's age structure changes, so does the target rate of unemployment. As we said, the market is one of continual change. Because younger people change jobs more frequently, a younger workforce will mean overall job change will be higher, leading to higher structural unemployment.

A second reason the target rate of unemployment changes is our economy's changing social and institutional structure. For example, women today comprise a greater percentage of the labor force than they did earlier. In the 1950s, the traditional view was that "a woman's place is in the home." At that time about one-third of women participated in the labor market. Usually only one family member—the husband—had a job. If he lost his job, the family had no income, and the main income earner (the husband) had to accept whatever job was available. Today about 60 percent of working-age women are in the labor force, and among all married-couple families, 70 percent of both husband and wife work. In a two-earner family, if one person loses a job, the family doesn't face immediate starvation. The other person's income carries the family over, allowing the one who lost a job to spend more time looking for one.

Third, government institutions have also changed. Unemployment benefits (created in 1911) and public welfare (created in 1939) were established to reduce suffering associated with unemployment and change people's responses to unemployment. People today are pickier about what jobs they will take than they were in the 1920s and 1930s. People don't want just any job; they want a *fulfilling* job with a decent wage. As people have become choosier about jobs, a debate has raged over the extent of government's responsibility for unemployment.

Q-5 What are four reasons why the target rate of unemployment has risen in the United States?

Globalization is a fourth reason. As we discussed in earlier chapters, the structural changes associated with U.S. globalization that was characterized by large trade deficits and large capital account inflows that held the value of the dollar up, tends to increase the target rate of unemployment for the United States. As jobs move abroad, people must find new jobs that are globally competitive to remain employed in the tradable sector. The U.S. unemployment rate did not rise as jobs moved abroad because government ran highly expansionary monetary and fiscal policies that created additional jobs in the non-tradable sector to replace the jobs lost in the tradable sector. Policy makers targeted a high potential output and a low target unemployment rate because, as discussed in Chapter 11, low-priced imports removed the inflation signal that they previously had about the target level of unemployment being too low.

Globalization requires structural change.

Globalization requires structural change; goods that used to be produced in the United States are now produced abroad by workers earning lower pay, which means that workers here in tradable sectors have to either lower their reservation wages and accept much lower pay or move to another sector where the United States has a comparative advantage. For a 50-year-old worker, that is easier said than done. A factory worker might have to retrain to become a computer specialist, or accept that the best she can do now is to work for $11 an hour at Walmart with far fewer benefits than her previous $22-an-hour job. Fewer than 40 percent of high school dropouts have jobs and more and more jobs require high school diplomas, which means those without diplomas need to get a GED to even be eligible for jobs that are available. These are not easy changes to make; they caused the achievable unemployment rate to rise even more.

Explaining the Jobless Recovery: Short-Run Causes of Structural Unemployment

All the structural changes just discussed occur slowly and cannot explain the sudden increase in the rate of unemployment associated with the jobless recovery. What then might explain it? A likely explanation has to do with the bursting financial bubble in 2007 and 2008. The excess demand that did not cause inflation in the early 2000s had to go somewhere. It went into asset markets, causing the housing bubble and stock market bubble, and contributed to generating large trade deficits. Production of tradable goods moved abroad, but consumption stayed high as people borrowed significant amounts to maintain their living standard. What this means is that during the buildup to the financial crisis, we, as a society, were living far beyond our means—being paid higher wages than were globally competitive, spending more than we could afford long term, and being unwilling to take the type of jobs that can compete internationally. Further, some of those jobs that were available in the nontradable sector were filled by immigrant workers.

The bursting of the bubble in housing also contributed to the higher unemployment that followed the financial crisis. Specifically, during the housing bubble many more houses were built than were needed. In 2012 housing starts were one-third the 2 million a year they were before the bubble burst. Many people buying houses thought they were investing money wisely, only to learn that they not only lost all the money they put into the house, they actually owed more on the house than it was worth.

As discussed in Chapter 11, according the structural stagnation hypothesis, this creates two structural problems for the economy. First, it means that housing construction won't recover until the economy eliminates the excess inventory of houses that were built in the boom. This excess inventory creates continued unemployment in the housing sector. If you were a carpenter or a residential construction worker, life was difficult after the housing boom. Until the housing glut works its way through the system, which could take up to a decade, the housing sector will generate far fewer jobs than it had in the past. Second, people who lost equity in their houses decreased their consumption and saved more. This lowered consumption spending and held down aggregate demand in the private sector. These structural problems associated with the bursting of the financial bubble further increased the achievable unemployment rate and help explain why unemployment is likely to remain high in the coming years.

Structural problems associated with the bursting of the financial bubble help explain why unemployment is likely to remain high in the coming years.

Globalization and Jobs

As I have emphasized throughout this book, the current U.S. unemployment problem can be understood only in reference to the world economy. The jobs experience of U.S. workers has depended in large part on whether the job is in a *tradable sector*—a sector such as manufacturing, where the production can be relatively easily shifted to a foreign country—or a *nontradable sector*—a sector such as education, where it cannot.

Another sector affected by globalization is what might be called the *immigration sector*—production that can be undertaken by non-U.S., largely unskilled immigrants (legal or illegal) from other countries willing to work in the United States for wages slightly more than those offered in their country. The U.S. government has helped develop this sector with programs such as the Temporary Agricultural Program that allow foreign workers to come to the United States on a temporary basis to fill jobs that Americans won't take. With free trade and movement across borders, wages in the tradable and immigrant sectors must be competitive, and will eventually equalize.

The importance of immigration cannot be overestimated. Millions of people have immigrated into the United States to fill jobs. Why do U.S. firms hire them? For the same reason that they move production facilities outside the United States—firms get more for less. Immigration isn't entirely bad for U.S. workers. While without immigration the average pay of U.S. workers would have been higher, U.S. output would have been lower and many more businesses would have moved production facilities out of the United States. Since U.S. workers wouldn't take many of the jobs filled by immigration, keeping these jobs in the United States created higher-paying complementary jobs in the United States that U.S. citizens could take.

Q-6 Has globalization affected jobs more in the tradable or untradable sector?

The overall effect of globalization on unemployment across sectors has been to lower wages and raise unemployment in both the tradable and immigrant sectors with very little change in wages or unemployment in the nontradable sector. As discussed in Chapter 11, globalization has even raised wages and employment in some nontradable sectors, particularly those related to facilitating international trade.

Framing the Debate about Voluntary and Involuntary Unemployment

Any discussion of unemployment quickly becomes intertwined with normative judgments about individual and government responsibility.

Any discussion of unemployment quickly becomes intertwined with normative judgments about individual and government responsibility. That is inevitable because the concept of unemployment is not, and cannot be, a completely scientific or technical concept. Whether a person is considered unemployed depends on one's framework.

To see the importance of frameworks, look carefully at the picture in the margin. Is it a picture of an old woman with a large nose and a feather in her hair? Or is it a picture of a beautiful woman in a fur coat? Depending on how you look at it, it could be either. As psychologists have long pointed out, what you see depends on how you frame the picture; both are possibilities. The same is the case with unemployment.

Individual Responsibility and Unemployment

At one extreme (we'll call it the individual responsibility framework) individuals are responsible for finding their own jobs. If they aren't working, it's because they are choosing not to work. In that case all unemployment is voluntary, which means not working really shouldn't be considered unemployment at all. People with this point of view emphasize that an individual can always find *some* job at *some* wage, even if it's only selling apples on the street for 40 cents apiece. Someone who is unemployed simply isn't looking hard enough, is too picky about the job, isn't willing to work for what he or she considers too-low pay, or lacks the entrepreneurial spirit (motivated by a true desire to work) to create jobs such as babysitting or running errands for neighbors. People who hold this view point out that even in the worst of the economic downturns, many U.S. jobs go unfilled. Even in today's economy, if it weren't for government programs that bring in foreign workers, demanding agricultural jobs, such as picking corn and onions for $10.50 an hour, would be left unfilled. Chicken slaughtering, taxi driving, housecleaning, and other similar hard, dangerous, and low-paying jobs face a similar problem of finding workers. Within this frame for people who *really* want to work at *any* job or at *any* pay, unemployment is almost impossible.

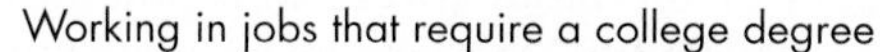

FIGURE 17-5 Employment Status of College Graduates under Age 25

A growing share of recent college graduates are having to settle for jobs that do not require a college degree, and they are earning far less than their peers as a result. All college graduates 2009.

Source: *The New York Times.*

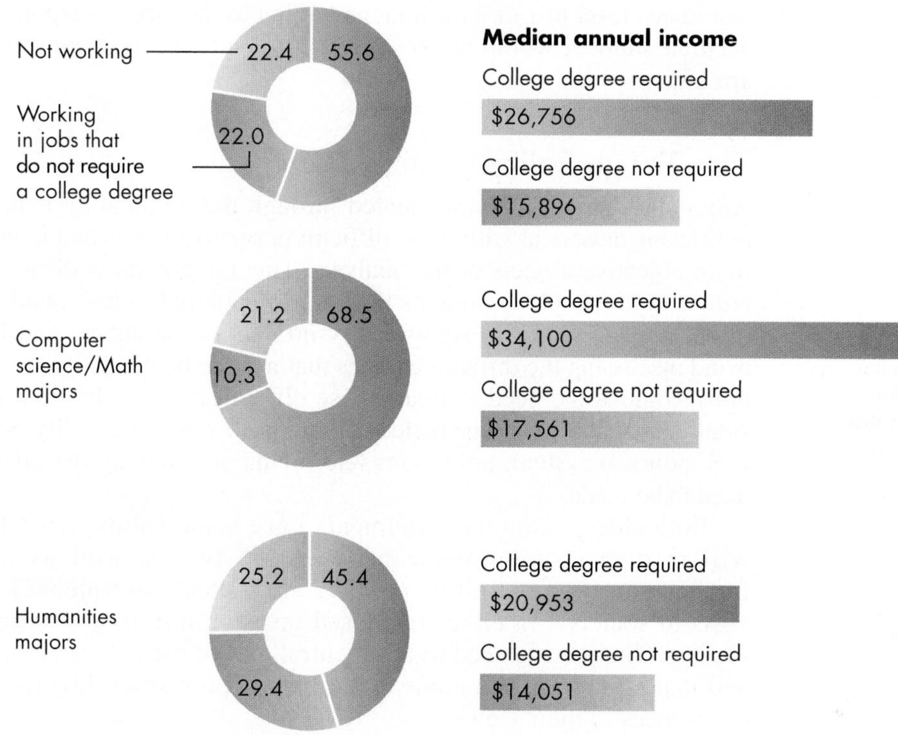

Social Responsibility and Unemployment

Q-7 What is the difference between the individual responsibility and social responsibility views about unemployment?

At the other extreme (we'll call it the social responsibility framework) are those who believe that society owes people jobs commensurate with their training and job experience at a respectable wage. They see individuals with enormous skills and training who have studied for years but who cannot find a job—at least one using those skills. They see unskilled workers being asked to accept dangerous jobs that don't pay a living wage. They see people who would like to work much more than they are, but who have to accept part-time work. They see people who have become so discouraged that they are no longer even looking for a job. Under the official measure, these discouraged workers are not even counted as unemployed; in the social responsibility frame, they should be. In today's economy, they point to the 44 percent of recent college graduates who either can't find a job or are working at jobs such as waiting tables for $8 an hour that don't use their degrees. While the situation has improved slightly since these data were collected, if you're interested in where you might stand upon graduation, take a look at Figure 17-5.

People who subscribe to this framework point out that except in significant economic expansions, the number of unemployed far exceeds the number of job openings. As mentioned earlier, as of early 2012 there were about four unemployed workers for each job opening. While this was an improvement to the situation

WWW Web Note 17.3 Unemployment and Entrepreneurship

during the worst of the downturn, when nearly seven people were looking for each job opening, there still weren't anywhere near enough jobs for all the 13 million unemployed to find work.

The current definition and measure of unemployment is a combination of these two frameworks. By current measurements and definitions, approximately 13 million people, about 8.2 percent of the labor force, were unemployed in mid-2012. According to an "individual responsibility" measure an accurate number of unemployed would be closer to 1 or 2 million; according to the "social responsibility" measure an accurate number would be closer to 30–40 million. As you can see, the differences are huge.

The Tough Policy Choices

Any policy has to be implemented through the political system, which means that politicians must deal with these difficult normative issues and integrate them with the more objective aspects of the analysis. This integration is difficult and is not easily reduced into simple arguments that can be captured in the sound bites that the press often picks up. Politics significantly influences the debate and leads politicians to avoid discussing the difficult choices that need to be made. It is not that politicians do not recognize the need to make these difficult choices. It's that politicians on both sides believe they won't be reelected if they tell voters the reality. Somehow, within the U.S. political system, politicians fear facing and making the difficult decisions that need to be made.

It is not that politicians do not recognize the need to make difficult policy choices; it is that they believe they won't be reelected if they do.

Both sides' economic arguments have some validity, and the likely solution will involve a compromise between the two as well as honesty about the implications of the resulting policies. Any actual government jobs policy requires costs to society—in either increased taxes or suffering in terms of lost jobs and income. These costs need to be a central part of the debate and resulting solutions, and that discussion can come about only if both sides directly address normative differences in their views.

The United States isn't the only country facing tough political decisions related to unemployment. For example, Europe developed a tradition of government taking responsibility for providing people with jobs. But the policy had costs. It discouraged job market mobility and discouraged individuals from taking low-paying jobs. While many felt the system was fair, the unemployment rate in European countries has hovered around 9 percent for more than 10 years and exceeds 10 percent today. In southern European countries, unemployment exceeds 20 percent. In addition, the programs were expensive and because people were not willing to pay the taxes necessary to maintain them, many European countries have been trying to reduce or eliminate them and transfer more responsibility to the individual.

Summary

Whether an economy has an unemployment problem depends on how you look at it. Within the individual responsibility framework, the United States doesn't really have a problem. Within the government responsibility framework, the problem is much more serious than statistics suggest. Unemployment can be understood only in relation to the pay and nature of the job. Talking about unemployment without reference to those two elements is like talking about language without words. Since people have very different views about the standard against which to judge pay and the nature of unemployment, they have different views about the jobs problem. These differences are not differences in economic theory or in how the economy works; they are differences in moral judgments. Economic theory is a tool and does not hold any particular moral judgments.

What positive economics does have to say about the jobs policies is that any solution must come to grips with unpleasant choices. That means that those who want to frame the unemployment problem as a government responsibility must recognize that government intervention in the market will slow the structural change and increase the number of unemployed, and therefore will be enormously expensive. They must answer how the program is to be funded. Those who favor framing unemployment as an individual responsibility must be able to explain how to make society willing to accept the suffering that goes along with that approach.

Any jobs policy must come to grips with unpleasant choices.

A Guaranteed-Job Proposal: Government as Employer of Last Resort

Oftentimes the best way to understand a problem is to consider a policy proposal that attempts to deal with that problem. So let us now turn to a proposal that "solves" the U.S. unemployment problem. The proposal is the following:

> The government will provide a minimum job at a wage of $9.00 per hour for every eligible citizen.

The goal of the program is to provide a safety net for people who truly want to work and cannot find a job. If this proposal were implemented, the government could argue that the jobs problem had been solved because anyone who wanted a job could get one. No longer would there be three or four unemployed for each vacancy. There would be at least one vacancy for every person unsuccessfully looking for work. This program also weeds out those people who really aren't looking for work.

Implementing such a proposal involves specifying who would be eligible for the program and the nature of the job—what the person would do, how the jobs would be monitored, where the jobs would be located, and many more similar aspects. The costs of the program would vary with each of these decisions; the more inclusive and expansive these decisions are, the greater the cost.

The program I will outline is a barebones proposal. It is designed that way to keep the costs as low as possible and still claim to provide a job to everyone who wants one. Although the proposal may not be politically acceptable, it highlights the many dimensions of the unemployment and jobs problem. It attempts to find a middle way between those who believe that government should have a responsibility to the unemployed and those who believe in letting the market work, not relying on government to provide jobs.

The Design and Characteristics of the Program

Web Note 17.4
Job-Guarantee Programs

The guaranteed job in this program will consist of a variety of mental and physical tasks that can be easily monitored. They might consist of mental tasks such as copying a dictionary, keyboarding practice, doing arithmetic exercises, doing exercises in word processing and spreadsheets, or reading and summarizing reports. The physical tasks might include exercising such as doing jumping jacks, digging holes and filling them back up, moving weights, and other similar types of activities. The job will require the worker to work the standard number of hours per week—variations of an eight-hour day—and meet the normal job requirements that private and government firms impose on their employees—dress code, behavior codes such as showing up on time, demonstrating the appropriate attitude, and being responsible.

Whenever possible, the job would help a person learn new skills to increase productivity, and the program would provide a certificate for mastering the skill—credentials that would help their holders find better paying jobs in the private market. For example, for those who have not graduated from high school, the activities might prepare them to get their GED.

The government will contract with firms and organizations to monitor and mentor the workers in a set of specified activities. These firms would be paid a small stipend and be allowed to have the person work for them at no cost for up to two hours a day. Organizations that might do this include small retail firms, nongovernmental organizations, or governmental organizations such as schools that have space and the ability to undertake this monitoring.

Q-8 Why doesn't the guaranteed job provide jobs commensurate with a person's training?

The guaranteed-jobs program guarantees the same minimum job to everyone regardless of previous job or training. It does not attempt to provide people with a job commensurate with their training or previous job. It's meant for people who *really* want a job. The program doesn't help those who aren't willing to accept a minimum job. For example, the government doesn't guarantee someone with an English Ph.D. a job as an English professor. Just like everyone else, it guarantees him or her a minimal job like digging holes. This is the personal-responsibility aspect—it incorporates the view that people unwilling to participate in this jobs program don't really want to work.

Both this program and current government programs dealing with unemployment are designed to provide a social safety net, but they differ in important respects. This program concentrates the safety net for the least well off—those most in need of income. Existing programs are meant for those who are recently unemployed (in 2012 up to about 70 weeks after being unemployed) and who have earned a minimum amount of wages over a specified period. The current program covers people both who truly cannot find a job and who can't find a job with their minimum job requirements. This alternative guaranteed minimum job program would not help this second group. It would cover those who are ineligible for insurance because their employment history was not long enough or their unemployment insurance had expired. Whether the program could substitute for unemployment insurance, or supplement it, depends on what one believes is the role for government's safety net. The broader the safety net, the less is available for those who need it most.

Ideally all people would be eligible for the guaranteed program, but practically, eligibility will likely have to be limited. For example, it might make sense to restrict eligibility to nonstudents; otherwise the program would likely be overwhelmed by students wanting summer work. To be feasible, the program will also likely have to be limited to citizens; if open to immigrants, it would also likely be far too costly. The general principle: The looser the eligibility requirement, the more costly the program.

Why Don't the Guaranteed Jobs Do Something Useful?

Q-9 Why doesn't the guaranteed job provide activities directly useful to society?

The jobs that this program provides would involve activities useful for the individual but not directly productive to society. The only output would be self-improvement. The reason for choosing jobs that are primarily productive to individuals, not society, is so that the guaranteed jobs do not compete with jobs of existing institutions whose role *is* to provide useful output to society, as opposed to just the individual. Any attempt to make the guaranteed jobs have an output useful for society would mean that they would compete with those institutions, creating opposition to the program. The goal of this proposal is not to replace the market or existing governmental and nongovernmental organizations. The goal is simply to supplement them—to make sure that there are sufficient low-wage jobs for anyone who wants to work in such a job.

These guaranteed jobs may be more desirable than some existing minimum wage jobs and less desirable than other existing minimum wage jobs. To the degree that jobs in the marketplace are less desirable than this job, people will quit their minimum wage private jobs to take these guaranteed jobs. This effectively puts a floor on both the wage and desirability of the jobs that institutions will have to provide to keep their workers. It has the same effect as having a legal minimum wage because workers will demand this wage from private employers or quit working in the minimum jobs program. Some regular jobs could pay less than minimum if the regular job is attractive, such as providing more relevant training or the promise of advancement. Truly undesirable jobs will have to pay more than the minimum to lure workers away from the minimum program jobs.

The introduction of this minimum jobs program will make it possible to eliminate the federal minimum wage for workers eligible for the minimum job. In fact, it's better than a minimum wage law because the minimum jobs program would affect both wages and the nature of jobs available. Thus, if a private-sector job offers training benefits (as many internships do, where students work for free), someone may choose to take that job rather than a guaranteed minimum job because the overall package is preferable even if the wage is lower.

The more conservative economists argue that the minimum wage law creates unemployment because it reduces the quantity of workers firms are willing to hire and increases the quantity of people looking for work. Further, it prevents some firms from offering jobs that provide training, and therefore are attractive to workers and would benefit the firm. The minimum job does not have these problems. It would not keep private firms from offering a lower-than-minimum-wage job that has significant learning and advancement benefits. Firms not offering jobs that were sufficiently desirable in terms of both wages and type of job would not get workers. They would either have to raise the wage above the minimum or make the job more desirable in other ways. The jobs program would set a minimum job, not a minimum wage. Because of this, the minimum job program is preferable in many ways to a minimum wage program.

Q-10 How is the minimum jobs proposal better than a minimum wage law?

In fact, at a pay of $9.00 an hour, it is highly unlikely that these guaranteed jobs will attract significant number of workers from other low wage jobs if the jobs are full time and if full-time students are not eligible for the program. The reason is that many minimum wage jobs have other attributes that make them more desirable than the guaranteed job. For example, about two-thirds of workers in minimum wage (or less) jobs are food service workers who often receive additional income in the form of tips and other payments. People in these jobs would be unlikely to switch because they would lose those tips. While the number of full-time eligible workers who would find this program desirable would likely be small, it would provide for those most in need of a job.

Paying for the Program

Even this limited program will not be cheap. To get a rough estimate of how much it might cost, let's first consider the cost of one job. A job paying $9.00 an hour for 40 hours a week costs a bit over $18,000 per person per year. Add to that $5,000 for administration and monitoring, and it comes to $23,000 per job. Let's next consider how many people would be taking these jobs.

In 2012, some 13 million people were unemployed. Of these probably only a small number of those currently eligible for unemployment insurance would choose to participate in the government jobs program. Even many of the long-term unemployed would choose not to participate, preferring instead to be supported by their family, friends, or savings. So it is reasonable to assume that less than 20 percent of the measured unemployed, or 2.6 million, would choose to participate. Assuming no students, Social Security recipients, or noncitizens are eligible, probably another 2 million workers who are currently not counted as unemployed or who are in less desirable jobs

REAL-WORLD APPLICATION

Previous Government Jobs Programs

The minimum jobs proposal is both similar to and different from earlier government jobs programs. In the United States the most important of these is the Works Progress Administration (WPA), established during the 1930s to hire people directly to build public buildings, roads, highways, parks, and bridges. (It built a total of 78,000 bridges and 651,000 miles of roads!) Workers were paid $15 to $90 a month. (In today's dollars that's about $250–$1,500 a week.) The WPA also funded tap-dancing lessons and the painting of murals in public spaces. The WPA was a product of the Depression, when the private sector failed to provide anywhere near enough jobs. It ended with the advent of World War II as unemployment fell and jobs were available for everyone in the war effort.

An affordable modern-day WPA for the United States is unlikely. Much of the construction done at that time has been mechanized. To build today you need a few people who know how to operate the machines, not a lot of people with strong backs willing to work hard. Most modern construction jobs pay well beyond $9.00 an hour. For example, government now mandates that all construction companies that work on government construction projects pay union wages. The $15 to $90 a month paid to workers in the 1930s, even adjusted for inflation, wouldn't come close to union wages. Were the minimum job program to pay union wages, it would be inundated with people quitting their existing jobs to come to work at the government minimum job. The program would be unaffordable.

Variations of guaranteed-job proposals have been implemented throughout the world. Argentina developed a program for heads of households that offered part-time work. India instituted a National Rural Employment Guarantee Act that promised government public works employment for workers. However, all recent programs have run into problems because the jobs they provided competed with existing jobs, the pay was beyond what government was willing to pay, or the "jobs" were more desirable than alternative low-paying private-sector jobs, leading to corruption and nonmarket rationing of the government jobs. None provided a guaranteed job for everyone.

would find this guaranteed job attractive and would choose to participate. Adding the two makes a total of 4.6 million people, which means that were the program in place in 2012, the program would cost about $110 billion dollars a year.

One hundred and ten billion dollars is not cheap, and this is for a bare-bones program; a more inclusive program would be much more costly. But $110 billion is doable, considering that the government currently spends hundreds of billions of dollars to create jobs. The program could be paid for by replacing some of the existing stimulus package. To the degree that the program enhances workers' skills, the plan should slowly decrease the number of people who rely on the program. As the economy recovers, the private sector will increase its hiring, and people will move from these minimum guaranteed jobs into better paying jobs. Over time, the program costs would decline.

Would Such a Plan Ever Be Implemented?

To say that the program is doable is not to say that it is a program the government will implement. There is a reason most existing government programs are designed as they are—to help both the middle class and the least well off. The least well off are not a well-organized voting bloc, and thus programs specifically tailored to help them have only a small political constituency.

There is a reason most existing government programs are designed as they are—to help both the middle class and the least well off.

While the plan may not be politically possible, it provides an excellent teaching tool to highlight the policy issues about jobs. It focuses on the current debate about jobs, much of which is not just about providing a minimum job, but about keeping people at the level job they expect. This is why structural stagnation is such a problem and is associated with high unemployment rates. Dealing with globalization requires major structural changes. People who had done well before suddenly do not anymore. There are major differences in normative views about how government should handle such structural changes—differences that economic theory cannot resolve.

Much of the current debate about unemployment is not about providing a minimum job; rather it is about providing people with a level of job that they expect.

The differences between normative views are revealed by asking whether this program, if implemented, solves the unemployment problem. If you believe it does, and you define employment as having a minimally acceptable job (and what is considered a minimum acceptable job does not depend on one's education), then you are following an individualist normative view. If you believe that it will not, and it is government's responsibility to provide a job commensurate with people's training and past jobs, the program does not solve the unemployment problem; you are following a more social responsibility normative frame. But such a social responsibility viewpoint is logical only if society is willing to pay for such a program. It would require much higher taxes on everyone than we have currently. To date our society has not been willing to pay the higher taxes. Even so, it has attempted to follow a social responsibility frame. Wanting something and not wanting to pay for it are inconsistent, and in the coming decade one or the other will be forced to give way.

Conclusion

I began this chapter with a story about my son finding a job. He has advanced in that job, and is now hiring people, and seeing how hard it is to find the right person for a job. Modern jobs involve multiple dimensions and interaction with fellow workers and managers. The skills needed are often not measurable skills; they do not relate closely to what one learns in the educational system. Many of the needed skills are learned on the job, at home, and in life.

The problems that people call "unemployment" involve broader issues of social justice, fairness of the system, and the degree to which what one gets should be associated with the job one has. These issues go far beyond economics alone; they involve social philosophy, psychology, and cultural issues. Thus, in many ways the question of unemployment is not a question that economists can answer. It is a question society must answer through its political system. Unfortunately, our political system does not seem to be doing an especially good job dealing with these hard issues that must be answered before any serious attempt to deal with unemployment problem can work.

The problem that people often call "an unemployment problem" generally goes beyond providing a minimum job and raises issues that go far beyond economics.

Expanding aggregate demand can decrease unemployment, but little of that aggregate demand actually flows down to those most in need. Thus, if one's concern about social justice is a concern about the least well off, alternative approaches, such as a direct method to guarantee a job to anyone who wants one, may have to be considered.

Summary

- The unemployment rate is calculated as the number of unemployed divided by the labor force. Unemployment rises during a recession and falls during an expansion. *(LO17-1)*
- The official measure of unemployment is based on judgments about who to count as unemployed. Keynesians believe that discouraged workers and those who have left the labor force entirely ought to

be counted as unemployed. Classicals believe that some counted as unemployed are choosing to be unemployed and should not be counted. (*LO17-1*)

- The microeconomic approach to unemployment divides unemployment into categories and looks at those individual components. (*LO17-1*)
- Okun's rule of thumb states that a 1 percentage point change in the unemployment rate will tend to be associated with a 2 percent deviation in output from its trend in the opposite direction. (*LO17-2*)
- Cyclical unemployment is the result of temporary declines in economic output and can be addressed with expansionary policy, whereas structural unemployment requires structural changes in an economy. (*LO17-2*)
- The target rate of unemployment has risen because the workforce is younger, more women have entered the workforce, government has expanded income-support programs, and globalization. (*LO17-2*)
- The financial bubble resulted in unsustainably high housing construction that allowed consumers to spend far beyond their means. This widened the trade deficit. The bursting of the bubble increased structural unemployment. (*LO17-2*)
- At the extremes, those who believe that employment is an individual's responsibility of the individual believe there is virtually no unemployment. Those who believe it is a social responsibility believe that government ought to provide everyone a job commensurate with their skills. A solution to the unemployment problem requires a compromise between the two. (*LO17-3*)
- One proposal that "solves" the unemployment program is for government to provide a minimum job for every eligible citizen. It doesn't provide a job for everyone, such as those looking for a job like the one they lost. It provides "jobs" only for those who really need one. (*LO17-4*)
- The benefit of a government guaranteed jobs program is that everyone who wants to work is employed. The problem is that such a program costs money. (*LO17-4*)

Key Terms

cyclical unemployment *(370)*
employment-population ratio *(367)*
labor force *(366)*
labor force participation rate *(367)*
Okun's rule of thumb *(370)*
reservation wage *(371)*
structural unemployment *(370)*

Questions and Exercises

1. The Bureau of Labor Statistics reported that in mid-2012 the total labor force was 155 million of a possible 244 million working-age adults. The total number of unemployed was 13 million. From this information, calculate the following: (*LO17-1*)
   a. Labor force participation rate.
   b. Unemployment rate.
   c. Employment–population ratio.
2. Does the unemployment rate underestimate or overestimate the unemployment problem? Explain. (*LO17-1*)
3. During the past few recessions, government ran expansionary policies, but the duration of unemployment has risen. What does this suggest about the change in structural unemployment over this time period? (*LO17-2*)
4. If unemployment rises by 2 percentage points, what will likely happen to output in the United States relative to its growth trend? (Use Okun's rule of thumb.) (*LO17-2*)
5. Categorize each of the following as cyclical or structural unemployment: (*LO17-2*)
   a. An autoworker is laid off during a recession until car sales pick up.
   b. A steel worker loses his job because steel is now produced in foreign countries with lower wages.
   c. A compositor loses her job because the work is now outsourced to India.
   d. An unemployed person turns down job offers that do not pay the wages of his previous job.

6. What is a reservation wage and how is it related to structural unemployment? *(LO17-2)*
7. Name four reasons why the target rate of unemployment has increased over the past 40 years. *(LO17-2)*
8. Why does the concept of unemployment involve normative judgments? *(LO17-3)*
9. Will someone who believes that unemployment is an individual's responsibility believe that the current measure of unemployment over- or underestimates the level of unemployment? Explain. *(LO17-3)*
10. College degrees are usually associated with higher wages. Does that association mean that what one learns in college increases college students' productivity? *(LO17-3)*
11. Since a jobs program puts people to work, would it impose costs on society? *(LO17-4)*
12. How does the safety net in the proposed guaranteed jobs program differ from the current safety net? *(LO17-4)*
13. In what ways would the guaranteed jobs program outlined in the text be more expensive if it provided useful jobs for society? *(LO17-4)*
14. Why does the author suggest that students be ineligible for the guaranteed jobs program even though many students are in need? *(LO17-4)*

Questions from Alternative Perspectives

1. The text presents the target rate of unemployment as being about 6–7 percent. William Vickrey, a Nobel Prize–winning economist, argued that the target unemployment rate should be seen as being between 1 percent and 2 percent. Only an unemployment rate that low, he argued, would produce genuine full employment that guaranteed job openings for all those looking for work. Achieving a low unemployment rate would, according to Vickrey, bring about "a major reduction in the illness of poverty, homelessness, sickness, and crime."
   a. What is the appropriate target unemployment rate?
   b. Explain your position.
   c. What policies would you recommend to counteract the human tragedy of unemployment? (Radical)
2. The text treats the unemployed as if both sexes are equally considered full persons within a capitalist market economy. The historic public/private split of employment for women, however, denies women full rights in the market place. Evidence of this is that women earn about 85 percent of what men earn. This reality needs to be taken into account with any guaranteed jobs program. How might the jobs program suggested in the text be modified to take into account these differences? (Feminist)
3. As suggested in the text, the type of employment available to different workers is inherently tied to income distribution. With globalization, the market favors those with access to higher education, which tends to be those people with accumulated family assets as well inherent ability.
   a. Is the income distribution within the United States that results from globalization fair?
   b. Is the global income distribution that results from globalization fair? (Post-Keynesian)
4. Economists such as Frédéric Bastiat believed in natural liberty, which is based on a belief that a God has naturally ordered the world for the benefit of all. According to these economists, savings was a virtue because it potentially led to increased consumption in the future, a belief that Keynes asserted is based on a belief in one's immortality. Does this mean that Bastiat and Keynes would differ in their views about how to address the unemployment problem? How? (Religious)

Issues To Ponder

1. In H. G. Wells's *Time Machine,* a late-Victorian time traveler arrives in England some time in the future to find a new race of people, the Eloi, in their idleness. Their idleness is, however, supported by another race, the Morlocks, underground slaves who produce the output. If technology were such that the Eloi's lifestyle could be sustained by machines, not slaves, is it a lifestyle that would be desirable? What implications does the above discussion have for unemployment?
2. If unemployment fell to 1.2 percent in World War II, why couldn't it be reduced to 1.2 percent today?
3. In 1991, Japanese workers' average tenure with a firm was 10.9 years; in 1991 in the United States the average tenure of workers was 6.7 years.
   a. What are two possible explanations for these differences?
   b. Which system is better?

c. In the mid-1990s, Japan experienced a recession while the United States' economy grew. What effect did this likely have on these ratios?

4. Can an unemployed person collecting unemployment compensation take a vacation? Should he or she be able to do so? If you believe not, how can it be prevented?
5. Should a discouraged worker be counted as unemployed? Discuss.
6. If you had no income and no one to help you, could you create a job for yourself? How would you go about doing it?

Answers to Margin Questions

1. If a sufficient number of people leave the labor force, the number of unemployed can rise at the same time that the unemployment rate rises. (*p. 366; LO17-1*)
2. The unemployment rate depends on one's view about who should be counted as unemployed. Keynesians believe all people who want a job but cannot find one should be counted, even discouraged workers. Classicals believe that some people counted as unemployed choose not to work even if they report that they are looking. (*p. 367; LO17-1*)
3. It predicts the unemployment rate will rise by 1 percentage point. (*p. 370; LO17-2*)
4. A high reservation wage keeps people from accepting low-wage jobs and therefore increases the unemployment rate until people's reservation wages decline. (*p. 371; LO17-2*)
5. The target rate of unemployment has risen because the workforce is younger, more women have entered the workforce, government has expanded income-support programs, and globalization. (*p. 372; LO17-2*)
6. The tradable sector is more affected by globalization. It lowers wages in this sector and raises unemployment. (*p. 374; LO17-3*)
7. The individual responsibility view is that anyone who wants a job can either find one or create one. Employment is the responsibility of the individual. The social responsibility view is that government owes everyone who wants a job at a respectable wage that is commensurate with his or her skills. Employment is the responsibility of society. (*p. 375; LO17-3*)
8. Providing a guaranteed job commensurate with a person's training would cost too much. The program is for people who really want a job regardless of their training. (*p. 378; LO17-4*)
9. If a job is useful to society, the program would be replacing a job that would be created in the market. The purpose of the program is to supplement the market. (*p. 378; LO17-4*)
10. The proposal puts a floor on the wage as well as on the nature of the job. People would be willing to accept a better job, such as those providing job training, even if they pay lower wages. (*p. 379; LO17-4*)

chapter 18

Inflation, Deflation, and Macro Policy

> *The first few months or years of inflation, like the first few drinks, seem just fine. Everyone has more money to spend and prices aren't rising quite as fast as the money that's available. The hangover comes when prices start to catch up.*
>
> —Milton Friedman

Politicians tend to get reelected when the economy is doing well. Thus, it should not surprise you that political pressures exert a strong bias toward lowering taxes, increasing spending, and expanding the money supply, all of which tend to expand the economy in the short run. In the past what has prevented politicians and the Fed from implementing expansionary policies is inflation, or at least the fear of generating an accelerating inflation. Recently, however, for the United States that relationship between expansionary policy and inflation has been much weaker than in the past, at least for goods price inflation. Because expansionary monetary and fiscal policy have not led to inflation, policy makers have felt able to increase spending, cut taxes, and increase the money supply enormously.

But goods price inflation is not the only type of inflation. There can also be asset price inflation. **Asset price inflation** occurs when *the prices of assets rise more than their "real" value*. Assets include gold, houses, artwork, collectibles, land, stocks, bonds, and many other items that people hold as a store of wealth. The prices of these goods are not included in standard measures of inflation because these measures focus on goods and services, not assets. Asset inflation is important because it is an asset price bubble that encourages society to believe the illusion that it is wealthier than it actually is—and a bursting bubble can wreak havoc on an economy, as the U.S. economy experienced in 2008.

If expansionary monetary and fiscal policies are causing an asset price bubble, the expansionary macro policy could be causing problems even though the standard measures of inflation are not increasing significantly. So how inflation is measured goes to the heart of the current policy debate. Advocates of the structural stagnation hypothesis say that the expansionary monetary policy in the 2000s contributed to the financial bubble that burst in 2008. Further, they see the continued increases in the money supply as preventing, or at least slowing, the structural changes that the economy needs to undergo to adjust to globalization. They argue that even if the expansionary monetary policy doesn't lead to goods price inflation, it leads to higher asset prices than are consistent

After reading this chapter, you should be able to:

- **LO18-1** Discuss the definitions and measures of inflation and some of their problems.
- **LO18-2** Discuss the distributional effects and costs of inflation.
- **LO18-3** Summarize the inflation process and the quantity theory of money.
- **LO18-4** Define the Phillips curve relationship between inflation and unemployment.

Q-1 What is the difference between an asset price inflation and a goods price inflation?

with a sustainable level of growth. It creates an illusion of wealth. The continued expansionary monetary policy is just delaying the full extent of the asset price adjustment that must occur for the economy to get back on track. Other economists argue that the only significant problem that expansionary monetary policy can cause is inflation, so we don't have to worry about monetary policy being too expansionary until we start to see signs of inflation.

To understand these debates you need to understand inflation, so in this chapter I explore inflation in more detail. I first consider the definition of inflation and how it is measured, expanding on the discussion of inflation in Chapter 7. Then I discuss the costs of inflation both in terms of the current standard definition—a rise in the price level for goods and services—and in terms of an older definition—a rise in the money supply that includes the effect of increases in the money supply on asset price inflation. After that I turn to two relationships used to discuss inflation—the quantity theory of money and the Phillips curve relationship.

Defining and Measuring Inflation

Let's start with the definition of inflation. In earlier chapters we defined inflation as a continual rise in the price level, and we measured that increase with the GDP deflator. This GDP deflator is the most inclusive measure of goods and services that we have. As we will see below, there are a number of other measures of goods and services inflation that focus on personal consumption goods, consumer goods, and producer goods. But generally, these alternative goods inflation measures move in tandem, so distinguishing among them is not especially important for the recent debates about monetary policy.

Asset Price Inflation and Deflation

Asset prices and goods prices don't always move in tandem and can diverge significantly for long periods of time.

The distinction between goods inflation and asset inflation, however, is important. The reason is that asset prices and goods prices don't always move in tandem and can diverge significantly for long periods of time. These are periods of asset bubbles. For example, goods prices could remain essentially constant, but asset prices could rise by 30 percent. Such different movements can continue for a number of years, as was the case in the housing market and other asset markets in the United States during the early 2000s. Using the goods market measure of inflation, such an asset price rise is not seen as an inflation (except to the extent that the rental value of housing changes with the price of housing, which it often doesn't).

Economists before the 1940s would have been much more likely to call such a rise in asset prices an inflation as long as it is accompanied by an increase in the money supply or credit. That's because they defined inflation as an increase in the money supply, not as an increase in any particular price index. They noted that increases in prices generally follow an increase in the money supply, but instead of focusing on what was happening to any particular set of prices, they focused on the money supply and the amount of credit in the economy. By inflation, they meant easy credit—credit that is readily available to people to spend and invest. While, as we will see, economists' measure of goods inflation has significantly improved since the 1940s, they have not yet developed an index of asset prices or of asset inflation.

One reason economists have not developed a measure of asset price inflation is that it's difficult to know when increases in asset prices reflect an increase in their real value.

Estimating Asset Price Inflation and Deflation One reason economists have not developed a measure of asset price inflation is that it's difficult to know when increases in asset prices reflect an increase in their real value and when they are just increases in prices without an increase in real value. In individual cases estimating an asset's real value is essentially impossible, but for the aggregate of assets it is easier since, based on accounting rates over the long run, real wealth should

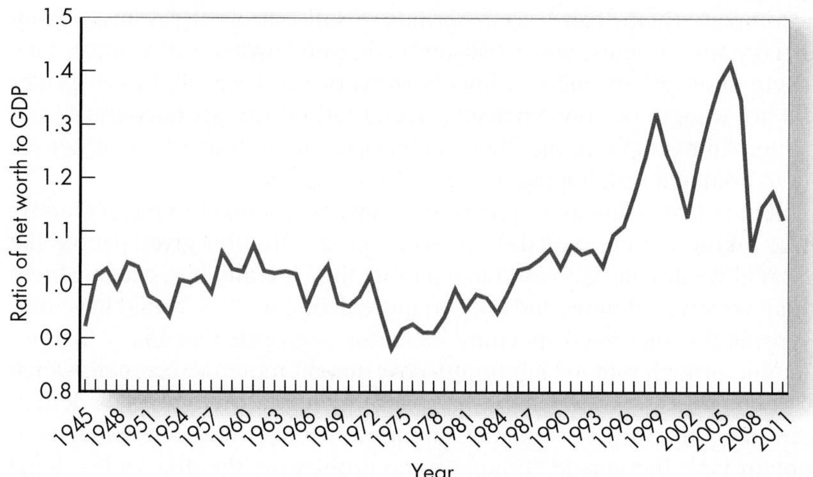

FIGURE 18-1 Ratio of Net Worth to GDP

Starting in the 1990s asset prices rose significantly above their historic norms, increasing the ratio of net worth to GDP far above its historic norm.

Source: Bureau of Economic Analysis and Federal Reserve Bank.

increase at a similar rate as real output. So by looking at the ratio of asset values (as captured by net worth) to nominal GDP (which includes both increases in output and increases in prices of goods) we can estimate whether asset price inflation is occurring beyond the level of goods price inflation. For example, if nominal output is increasing 6 percent a year, nominal wealth should be increasing at about the same rate in what economists call the steady-state equilibrium. This means that the ratio of nominal wealth to nominal GDP can serve as a rough estimate of whether there is asset price inflation in excess of goods price inflation. When that ratio is increasing, asset inflation is likely occurring.

Figure 18-1 shows nominal total net worth relative to nominal GDP compared to its postwar (1945–1955) average, with that average normalized to 1. If the increases in asset prices reflect real increases in the value of assets associated with real growth and goods price inflation, this ratio should be relatively constant as it was up until 1995. If the measure rises, then the increases in the price of assets likely represent asset inflation above and beyond inflation measured by goods prices. If it falls, then there is likely asset deflation.

Notice that the ratio was relatively stable from 1945 to 1995. Then, in the late 1990s, that ratio started rising precipitously, suggesting that starting in the late 1990s assets were overvalued by 30 percent compared to the historic norm. This was precisely the time that globalization and the U.S. trade deficit started rising precipitously.

The net worth to GDP ratio increased substantially in the late 1990s, suggesting that the economy was experiencing asset inflation.

During the 2001 recession, as we experienced asset price deflation, asset prices fell back closer to their historic norm. In 2001 government responded to this fall in asset prices by implementing expansionary monetary and fiscal policy, which changed the asset deflation to an asset inflation once again. By 2007 the valuation of assets was over 40 percent above their historic norms. Then with the financial crisis asset prices dropped significantly, and the economy fell into its current downturn. But even with the large decline in asset prices during the 2008–9 recession, asset prices in 2012 were still about 15 percent higher than their historic norm.

As mentioned above, from 1995 to the present, goods inflation has been low, which has allowed relatively expansionary monetary policy. What these data suggest is that while we have not had much goods inflation in the past 20 years, we have had significant periods of asset price inflation, followed by sudden spurts of asset price deflation.

Does Asset Inflation Matter? Let's now consider whether asset inflation matters to an economy by considering the problems it might create.

One of the problems of asset inflation for an economy is that it (and the low interest rates that accompany them) can lead to serious misallocation of resources from conservative to risky investments, since risk-preferring borrowers will want to take advantage of rising asset prices and cautious borrowers, who fear that asset prices are too high, will not want to borrow. So asset price inflation strongly encourages and rewards risk taking. An example in the 2000s is that people built and bought houses not to live in but to hold and sell, hoping to make a quick profit.

Another problem is that rising asset prices are a strong stimulant to the economy; they are a bit like taking a recreational drug. Asset price inflation gives people the illusion that their real wealth has increased much more than it really has, causing them to spend more than they would have, and take on more debt than they would have otherwise. On the upside this increased spending increases aggregate demand, which increases the economic growth rate, which brings government more tax revenue, which means that government is able to increase its spending without increasing its deficit. These are all seen as highly positive results; asset inflation makes the society feel wonderful. The problem isn't the upside stimulant; the problem is the downside—what happens once asset inflation turns into asset deflation.

On the upside, asset inflation makes the society feel wonderful; the problem is the downside.

Asset Price Deflation The problem with asset inflation is that it cannot last; it is based on the illusion that the real value of assets has risen when, in fact, their real value has not. Asset price inflation is an alternative name for a financial bubbles, and bubbles are, at some point, followed by an asset price deflation. This deflation reverses many of the positive effects of the asset price inflation and creates additional problems as well. When asset deflation hits, it hits suddenly and hard, as the United States saw in 2008.

Q-2 Why are discussions of deflations usually conducted in reference to asset prices?

While discussions of inflations are usually conducted in reference to goods prices, discussions of deflation usually are conducted in reference to asset prices. The reason for this is twofold. First, we haven't seen significant amounts of goods prices deflation, and even as asset prices are falling precipitously, there is generally some small amount of goods price inflation. So historically what we see are asset price deflations, not goods price deflations. The second reason is that an asset price deflation can create serious problems for the economy.

If asset price inflation leads to pleasure and asset price deflation leads to pain, then maybe, on average, the two even out. This is generally not thought to be the case; most economists see the pain caused by the asset price deflation as exceeding the pleasure caused by the asset price inflation. The reason has to do with the costs connected to reversing decisions people make when experiencing an asset inflation.

For example, in the 2000s because the prices of houses rose, millions of people bought them with the expectation that prices would rise even further. When housing prices fell, those people faced foreclosure and the prospect of living out of their cars. Millions of other people took out second and third mortgages to use some of the presumed equity in their house to take a trip or buy a boat. So the illusion that they were wealthier than they were led them to spend more than they would have otherwise. With asset deflation, they had already spent the borrowed money and now have to pay it back, which might mean they don't have enough to buy food or medical care; thus asset deflation might drive them into bankruptcy. Without the asset inflation providing people with the illusion of wealth, they never would have taken the trip or bought the house in the first place. But they can't reverse past purchases. For people whose actions were affected by an asset inflation, the consequences of an asset deflation that simply reverses the effect of an asset inflation can be very serious.

The same illusion can lead firms to make poor decisions when faced with asset inflation. Perhaps they bought an office building they didn't really need, or paid workers more than they could have afforded. When deflation hits, they find that they cannot remain in business. In that case not only does the firm suffer; employees suffer too. Once an asset deflation occurs, firms will find that they can no longer borrow, and that they have to pay off past debts. Some firms are likely to go bankrupt since they don't have the assets to cover their liabilities. If they are forced to close, their employees will lose their jobs. Because deflation undermines the financial health of firms, it can quickly turn into a financial crisis that brings the economy to a standstill. At that point, the government finds it necessary to step in and prop up asset prices, as it did in 2008, to prevent a collapse of the entire economy. So most economists see asset deflations as something to be strongly avoided.

Measuring Goods Market Inflations

Now that we've considered the difference between an asset inflation and a goods inflation, let's look more closely at price indexes generally and how they are used to measure goods price inflation. A **price index** is *a number that summarizes what happens to a weighted composite of prices of a selection of goods (often called a market basket of goods) over time.* An index shows what prices at a particular time are relative to base year prices. There are a number of different measures of the price level. The most frequently used are the producer price index, the GDP deflator, and the consumer price index. Each has certain advantages and disadvantages.

An index shows prices at a particular time relative to base year prices.

Creating a Price Index

To help you better understand price indexes, let's work through the creation of a fictitious price index—the Colander price index—and calculate the associated inflation. I'll do so for 2013 and 2014, using 2013 as the base year. A price index is calculated by dividing the current price of a basket of goods by the base price of that same basket of goods. The table below lists a market basket of goods I consume in a base year and their associated prices in 2013 and 2014. The market basket of goods is listed in column 1 and represents the quantity of each item purchased in the base year.

WWW Web Note 18.1 Inflation Calculators

(1)	(2)	(3)	(4)	(5)
	Prices		Expenditures	
Basket of Goods	2013	2014	2013	2014
10 pairs jeans	$20.00/pr.	$25.00/pr.	$200	$250
12 flannel shirts	15.00/shirt	20.00/shirt	180	240
100 lbs. apples	0.80/lb.	1.05/lb.	80	105
80 lbs. oranges	1.00/lb.	1.00/lb.	80	80
Total expenditures			$540	$675

The expenditures on the market basket in each year is the sum of the expenditures on each item—the quantity of each good purchased times its market price. The market basket remains the same in each year; only the prices change. The expenditures on the market basket in 2013 is $540 and in 2014 is $675. To calculate the Colander price index, divide the 2014 expenditures on the market basket by the expenditures on the market basket in the base year and multiply it by 100. In this case 2013 is the base year, so the price index in 2014 is

$$\$675/\$540 \times 100 = 125$$

To make sure you are following this example, calculate the Colander price index in 2013.

The answer is 100. The base year index is always 100 since you are dividing base year expenditures by the base year expenditures and multiplying by 100.

Inflation in 2014, then, is the percentage change in the price index. This is calculated in 2014 as the difference between the price indices in the two years (125 − 100 = 25) divided by the base index, 100, times 100.

$$\left(\frac{125 - 100}{100}\right) \times 100 = 25\%$$

Let's now discuss the price indexes most frequently used when talking about inflation.

REAL-WORLD PRICE INDEXES An earlier chapter already introduced you to one real-world price index—the GDP deflator (gross domestic product deflator). The GDP deflator is the inflation index economists generally favor because it includes the widest number of goods, and because the base period is adjusted yearly. Unfortunately, since it's difficult to compute, it's published only quarterly with a fairly substantial lag. That is, by the time the figures come out, the period the figures measure has been over for quite a while.

The consumer price index (CPI) is an index of inflation measuring prices of a fixed basket of consumer goods, weighted according to each component's share of an average consumer's expenditures.

Published monthly, the **consumer price index (CPI)** *measures the prices of a fixed basket of consumer goods, weighted according to each component's share of an average consumer's expenditures.* It measures the price of a fixed basket of goods rather than measuring the prices of all goods. It is the index of inflation most often used in news reports about the economy and is the index most relevant to consumers. Since different groups of consumers have different expenditures, there are different CPIs for different groups. One often-cited measure is the CPI for all urban consumers (the urban CPI)—about 87 percent of the U.S. population. The numbers that compose the urban CPI are collected at 87 urban areas and include prices from over 50,000 landlords or tenants and 23,000 business establishments.

Q-3 Say that health care costs make up 15 percent of total expenditures. Say they rise by 10 percent, while the other components of the price index remain constant. By how much does the price index rise?

Figure 18-2 shows the relative percentages of the basket's components. As you see, housing, transportation, and food make up the largest percentages of the CPI. To give you an idea of what effect the rise in price of a component of the CPI will have on the CPI as a whole, let's say food prices rise 10 percent in a year and all other prices remain constant. Since food is about 15 percent of the total, the CPI will rise 15% × 10% = 1.5%. The CPI and GDP deflator indexes roughly equal each other when averaged over an entire year. (For more information on the CPI, go to www.bls.gov/cpi/cpifaq.htm.)

FIGURE 18-2 Composition of CPI

The consumer price index is determined by looking at the prices of goods in the categories listed in this exhibit. These categories represent the rough percentages of people's expenditures.

Source: *CPI Detailed Reports,* Bureau of Labor Statistics (www.bls.gov).

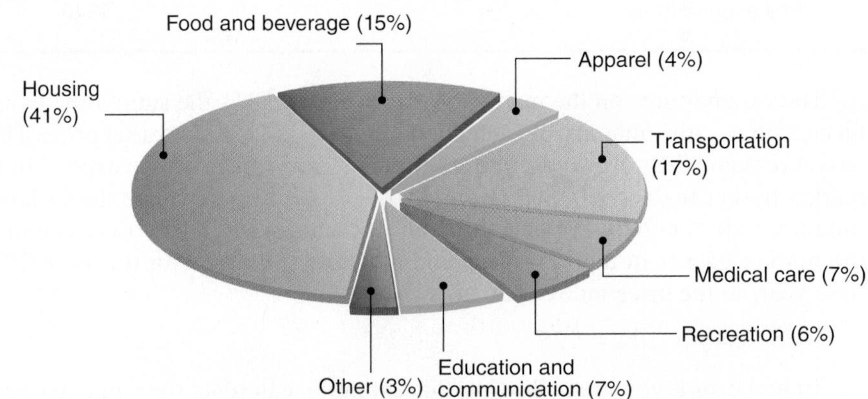

In the mid-1990s, many economists believed that the CPI overstated inflation by about 1 percentage point a year, and the Bureau of Labor Statistics implemented a number of changes that address some of those problems. In order to avoid some of the problems with the CPI, some policy makers have recently been focusing on another measure of consumer prices—the **personal consumption expenditure (PCE) deflator.** The PCE deflator is *a measure of prices of goods that consumers buy that allows yearly changes in the basket of goods that reflect actual consumer purchasing habits.* The measure smooths out some of the problems associated with the CPI. Why are there different measures for consumer price changes? Indexes are simply composite measures; they cannot be perfect. (See the box "Measurement Problems with Price Indexes.")

The personal consumption expenditure (PCE) deflator allows yearly changes in the basket of goods.

CPI vs. PCE

The **producer price index (PPI)** *is an index of prices that measures average change in the selling prices received by domestic producers of goods and services over time.* This index measures price change from the perspective of the sellers, which may differ from the purchaser's price because of subsidies, taxes, and distribution costs and includes many goods that most consumers do not purchase. There are actually three different producer price indexes for goods at various stages of production—crude materials, intermediate goods, and finished goods. Even though the PPI doesn't directly measure the prices consumers pay, because it includes intermediate goods at early stages of production, it serves as an early predictor of consumer inflation since when costs go up, firms often raise their prices. (For more on the PPI, go to www.bls.gov/ppi/ppifaq.htm.)

The Distributional Effects and Costs of Inflation

Inflation has costs, but not the costs most people associate with it. Specifically, in and of itself, it doesn't make the nation poorer. True, whenever prices go up somebody is worse off, but so too is someone better off—specifically, the person who receives the higher price. So, inflation does not make society on average any poorer.

Inflation has costs, but not the costs that most people associate with it.

Distributional Effects

Who wins and who loses in an inflation? The answer is simple: The winners are people who can raise their wages or prices and still keep their jobs or sell their goods. The losers are people who can't raise their wages or prices or who lose their jobs because their wage is too high. Consider a worker who has entered a contract to receive 4 percent annual wage increases for 3 years. If the worker expected inflation to be 2 percent at the time of the agreement, she was expecting her real wage to rise 2 percent each year. If instead inflation is 6 percent, her real wage will *fall* 2 percent. The worker loses, but the firm gains because it can charge 4 percent more for its products than it anticipated. The worker's wage was fixed by contract, but the firm could raise its prices. On average, winners and losers balance out; inflation does not make the population richer or poorer. Most people, however, worry about their own position, not what happens to the average person.

Q-4 True or false? Inflation makes an economy poorer. Explain your answer.

Lenders and borrowers, because they often enter into fixed nominal contracts, are also affected by inflation. If lenders make loans at 5 percent interest and expect inflation to be 2 percent, they plan to earn a 3 percent real rate of return on their loan. If, however, inflation turns out to be 4 percent, lenders will only earn a 1 percent real rate of return, and borrowers, who were expecting to pay a real interest rate of 3 percent, end up paying only 1 percent. Lenders will lose; borrowers will gain. In other words, unexpected inflation redistributes income from lenders to borrowers.

Unexpected inflation redistributes income from lenders to borrowers.

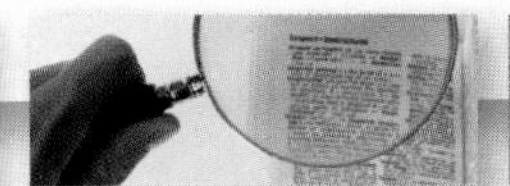

ADDED DIMENSION

Measurement Problems with Price Indexes

Price indexes have limitations. For example, in calculating the CPI, the basket of goods was fixed in the base year. But buying habits change. The further in time that fixed basket is from the current basket, the worse any fixed-basket price index is at measuring inflation because of substitution and measurement problems.

- **Substitution problems.** A fixed-basket price index does not take into account the fact that when the price of one good rises, consumers substitute a cheaper item and thus arrives at a higher rate of inflation than would a non-fixed basket price index.
- **Measurement problems**
  - **Quality.** A good today is seldom identical to a good yesterday. For example, a car in 2003 is assumed to be the same as a car in 2013. But by 2013, cars had much improved corrosion protection, and plastics were replacing metals. Adjustments must be made for these changes and they are seldom perfect. This makes it difficult to compare prices over time since the good is changing.
  - **New products.** A fixed basket of goods leaves no room for the introduction of new products. This would not be a problem if the prices of new products changed at about the same rate as prices of other goods in the basket, but in the 1970s this was not true. For years, the CPI did not include computers, whose prices were declining at a 17 percent annual rate!
  - **Store measurement.** Ever since World War II, consumers have shifted consumption toward discount purchases. The Bureau of Labor Statistics, however, treats a product sold at a discount store as different from products sold at retail stores. Products sold at discount stores are assumed to be of lower quality. To the extent that they are not different, however, changes in the CPI arrive at a higher inflation rate than would an index that treats the products as equal.
- **Nonmarket transactions.** The cost of housing is included in GDP. For about one-third of Americans, this cost is their monthly rent. But what about the remaining two-thirds of Americans who own their own homes? What is the cost of their housing? Remember opportunity costs from Chapter 1? The cost of living in one's own home is the rent you could have gotten for renting it to someone else. So, economists use market rental rates as an implicit rental rate for home ownership (called "owner's equivalent rent"). In the early 2000s, as housing prices rose, some people began buying two or three houses in the hopes of selling them for more in the future. That significantly increased the number of houses available for rent and held rents down. So although housing prices were soaring, the "owner's equivalent rent" was not, and that was holding measured inflation down. Then, starting in 2006 housing prices started falling. Initially that left people with an unsold inventory of houses. Then there was a recession that held rent down. So, rent stayed down. But once that inventory is reduced, we can expect rents to rise, pushing measured inflation up.

These and other problems arise because of the choices with no "correct" answer that must be made when constructing a price index. The reality is that price indexes are far from perfect measures and, depending on the choices made, various indexes can differ by as much as 3 or 4 percentage points a year.

The composition of the group winning or losing from inflation changes over time. For example, before 1975, people on Social Security and pensions lost out during inflation since Social Security and pensions were, on the whole, fixed in nominal terms. Inflation lowered recipients' real income. Starting in 1975 Social Security payments and many pensions were changed to adjust automatically for changes in the cost of living, so Social Security recipients are no longer losers. Their real income is independent of inflation. (Actually, because of the adjustment method, some say that Social Security recipients actually now gain from inflation since the adjustment more than compensates them for the rise in the price level.)

What we can say about the distributional consequences of inflation is that people who don't expect inflation or who are tied to fixed nominal contracts will likely lose during an inflationary period. However, if these people are rational, they probably won't let it happen again; they'll be prepared for a subsequent inflation. That is, they will change their expectations of inflation.

People who don't expect inflation or who are tied to fixed nominal contracts will likely lose during an inflationary period.

Distributional Effects of an Asset Price Inflation

Let's now consider what happens when the money supply doesn't lead to goods price inflation, but does lead to asset price inflation. People who bet on rising asset prices are helped and those who did not are hurt. Specifically, those who might be called cautious savers are hurt and risky savers are helped. Asset price inflation redistributes wealth from cautious individuals to less cautious individuals.

On the borrowing side, the same effects occur. Cautious borrowers are hurt since they likely see the asset prices as being too high, and choose not to borrow even though the interest rates are low. Less cautious borrowers are helped because they borrow at low interest rates, and receive high returns when the asset they bought with the borrowed money increases in value.

In summary, the increase in the money supply that affects asset prices can have significant distributional effects on wealth even when it does not result in higher goods prices.

Informational Effects of an Inflation

A second cost of inflation is its effect on the information that prices convey to people. Consider an individual who laments the high cost of housing, pointing out that it has doubled in 10 years. But if goods inflation averaged 7 percent a year over the past 10 years, a doubling of housing prices should be expected. In fact, with 7 percent inflation, on average *all* prices double every 10 years. That means the individual's wages have probably also doubled, so he or she is no better off and no worse off than 10 years ago. The price of housing relative to other goods, which is the relevant price for making decisions, hasn't changed. When there's inflation, it's hard for people to know what is and what isn't a relative price change. People's minds aren't computers, so inflation reduces the amount of information that prices can convey and causes people to make choices that do not reflect relative prices.

While inflation may not make the nation poorer, it does cause income to be redistributed, and it can reduce the amount of information that prices are supposed to convey.

Despite these costs, goods inflation is usually accepted by governments as long as it stays low, which for the United States currently means under 2.5 to 3 percent. What scares economists are inflationary pressures above and beyond expectations of inflation. In that case, expectations of higher inflation can cause inflation to build up and compound itself. A 3 percent inflation becomes a 6 percent inflation, which in turn becomes a 12 percent inflation. Once inflation hits 5 percent or 6 percent, it's definitely no longer a little thing. Inflation of 10 percent or more is significant.

Expectations of Inflation and Hyperinflation

Expectations of inflation were very much on the minds of policy makers in mid-2008 when the economy experienced commodity price shocks, which pushed the inflation rate to over 4 percent. If people had seen the price increase as a one-time event and accepted the decrease in their real income that it implied, it would not generate an ongoing inflation. But if the increase became built into expectations, it would have led to other price increases and resulted in accelerating inflation. That didn't occur since the economy fell into a severe recession in late 2007, which reversed the

Hyperinflation in Zimbabwe.

price increases in commodity prices, and replaced policy makers' concern about goods inflation with concern about preventing a depression.

Hyperinflation is exceptionally high inflation of, say, 100 percent or more per year.

While there is no precise definition, we may reasonably say that goods inflation has become **hyperinflation** *when inflation hits triple digits—100 percent or more per year.* The United States has been either relatively lucky or wise because it has not experienced hyperinflation since the Civil War (1861–65). Other countries, such as Brazil, Israel, Zimbabwe, and Argentina, have not been so lucky. These countries have frequently had hyperinflation. But even with inflation at these levels, economies have continued to operate and, in some cases, continued to do well.

WWW Web Note 18.2 Hyperinflation

In hyperinflation people try to spend their money quickly, but they still use the money. Let's say the U.S. price level is increasing 1 percent a day, which is a yearly inflation rate of over 3,600 percent.[1] Is an expected decrease in value of 1 percent per day going to cause you to stop using dollars? Probably not, unless you have a good alternative. You will, however, avoid putting your money into a savings account unless that savings account somehow compensates you for the expected inflation (the expected fall in the value of the dollar), and you will try to ensure that your wage is adjusted for inflation. In hyperinflation, wages, the prices firms receive, and individual savings are all in some way adjusted for inflation. Hyperinflation leads to economic institutions with built-in expectations of inflation. For example, usually in a hyperinflation the government issues indexed bonds whose value keeps pace with inflation.

Once these adjustments have been made, substantial inflation will not destroy an economy, but it certainly is not good for it. Such inflation tends to break down confidence in the monetary system, the economy, and the government.

The Inflation Process and the Quantity Theory of Money

Expectations of inflation play a key role in the inflationary process.

Expectations of inflation play a key role in the inflationary process. When expectations of inflation are high, people tend to raise their wages and prices, causing inflation. So, in fact, expectations can become self-fulfilling. Because of the importance of expectations in perpetuating, and perhaps even in creating, inflation, economists have looked carefully at how individuals form expectations. Almost all economists believe that the expectations that people have of inflation are in some sense rational, by which I mean they are based on the best information available, given the cost of that information. But economists differ on what is meant by rational and thus on how those expectations are formed. Some economists argue that rational people will expect the same inflation that is predicted by the economists' model. That is, they form **rational expectations**—*the expectations that the economists' model predicts.* If inflation was, say, 2 percent last year and is 4 percent this year, but the economists' model predicts 0 percent inflation for the coming year, individuals will rationally expect 0 percent inflation.

WWW Web Note 18.3 Forecasting Inflation

Other economists argue that rational expectations cannot be defined in terms of economists' models. These economists instead focus on the process by which people develop their expectations. One way people form expectations is to look at conditions that already exist, or have recently existed. Such expectations are

[1]Why over 3,600 percent and not 365 percent? Because of compounding. In the second day the increase is on the initial price level *and* the 1 percent rise in price level that occurred the first day. When you carry out this compounding for all 365 days, you get over 3,600 percent.

called **adaptive expectations**—*expectations based in some way on the past.* Thus, if inflation was 2 percent last year and 4 percent this year, the prediction for inflation will be somewhere around 3 percent. Adaptive expectations aren't the only type that people use. Sometimes they use **extrapolative expectations**—*expectations that a trend will continue.* For example, say that inflation was 2 percent last year and 4 percent this year; extrapolative expectations would predict 6 percent inflation next year. These are only three of the many reasonable ways people form expectations. Because there is no one economic model that predicts the economy perfectly, there is no way of specifying one rational expectation; there are only reasonable expectations. Individuals use various ways of forming expectations, often shifting suddenly from one way to another.

Q-5 Name three different types of expectations.

Because expectations can change quickly, the inflationary outlook can change suddenly. By 2013 there had not been significant goods inflation for over a decade even when the money supply increased significantly. This left many economists concerned about a sudden spurt of inflation should the U.S. economy start growing rapidly and the downward pressure of prices caused by globalization lessens.

Productivity, Inflation, and Wages

Two key measures that policy makers use to determine whether inflation may be coming are changes in productivity and changes in wages. Together these measures determine whether or not the short-run aggregate supply curve will be shifting up. The rule of thumb is that wages can increase by the amount that productivity increases without generating any inflationary pressure:

Inflation = Nominal wage increase − Productivity growth

Inflation = Nominal wage increase − Productivity growth

For example, if productivity is increasing at 2 percent, as it did in the early 2000s, wages can go up by 2 percent without generating any inflationary pressure. Let's consider another example—the mid-1970s, when productivity growth slowed to 1 percent while wages went up by 6 percent. Using our rule of thumb, inflation was 5 percent (6 percent − 1 percent).

You probably recognize this relationship from an earlier chapter. This is the same relationship that explains how the short-run aggregate supply curve shifts. When nominal wages increase by more than the growth of productivity, the *SAS* curve shifts up as shown in Figure 18-3, resulting in inflation. When nominal wages increase by less than the growth of productivity, the *SAS* curve shifts down, resulting in deflation (a sustained fall in the price level).

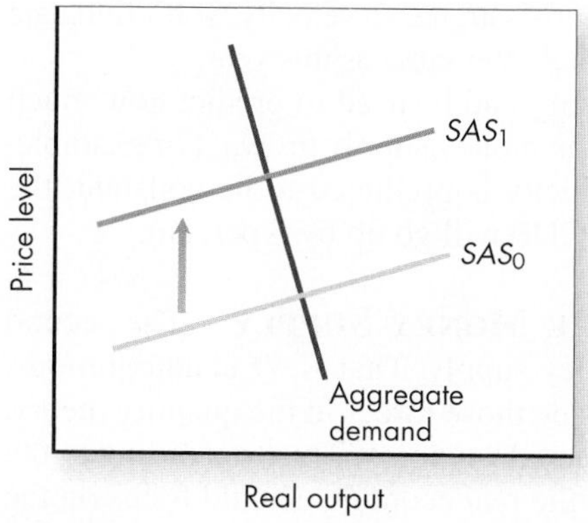

FIGURE 18-3 Nominal Wages, Productivity, and Inflation

When nominal wages increase by more than the growth of productivity, the *SAS* curve shifts up, resulting in inflation. When nominal wages increase by less than the growth of productivity, the *SAS* curve shifts down, resulting in deflation.

The Quantity Theory of Money and Inflation

Economist's longest existing theory of inflation is the quantity theory of money, which is a theory that goes back to the 1600s.

The quantity theory of money can be summed up in one sentence: *Inflation is always and everywhere a monetary phenomenon.* If the money supply rises, the price level will rise. If the money supply doesn't rise, the price level won't rise. A quantity theory advocate argues: Forget all the other explanations of inflation—they just obscure the connection between money and inflation.

In the quantity theory model, inflation is caused by growth in the money supply. It focuses on the equation of exchange: $MV = PQ$

THE EQUATION OF EXCHANGE The quantity theory of money centers on the **equation of exchange,** *an equation stating that the quantity of money times the velocity of money equals the price level times the quantity of real goods sold.* This equation is:

$$MV = PQ$$

where:

M = Quantity of money

V = Velocity of money

P = Price level

Q = Quantity of real goods sold

The Quantity Theory of Money

Q is the real output of the economy (real GDP) and P is the price level, so PQ is the economy's nominal output (nominal GDP). V, the **velocity of money,** is *the number of times per year, on average, a dollar gets spent on goods and services.* Put another way, velocity is the amount of income per year generated by a dollar. Since $MV = PQ$, MV also equals nominal output. Thus, if there's \$100 of money in the economy and velocity is 20, nominal GDP is \$2,000. We can calculate V by dividing nominal GDP by the money supply. Let's take the United States as an example. In the United States in 2012, nominal GDP was approximately \$16 trillion and M was approximately \$2,200 billion (using M_1), so velocity (GDP/M) was about 7, meaning each dollar in the economy circulated enough to support approximately \$7 in total income.

VELOCITY IS CONSTANT The equation of exchange is a tautology, meaning it is true by definition. What changes it from a tautology to the quantity theory are three assumptions. The first assumption is that velocity remains constant (or changes at a predictable rate). Money is spent only so fast; how fast is determined by the economy's institutional structure, such as how close individuals live to stores, how people are paid (weekly, biweekly, or monthly), and what sources of credit are available. (Can you go to the store and buy something on credit, that is, without handing over cash?) This institutional structure changes slowly, quantity theorists argue, so velocity won't fluctuate very much. Next year, velocity will be approximately the same as this year.

If velocity can be predicted, the quantity theory can be used to predict how much nominal GDP will grow if we know how much the money supply grows. For example, if the money supply goes up 6 percent and velocity is predicted to be constant, the quantity theory of money predicts that nominal GDP will go up by 6 percent.

Something that is determined outside the model is called autonomous.

REAL OUTPUT IS INDEPENDENT OF THE MONEY SUPPLY The second assumption is that Q is independent of the money supply. That is, Q is autonomous, meaning real output is determined by forces outside those forces in the quantity theory. If Q grows, it is because of factors that affect the real economy. Thus, according to the quantity theory of money, policy discussions of the real economy should focus on the real economy—the supply side of the economy, not the demand or monetary side.

This assumption makes analyzing the economy a lot easier than if the financial and real sectors are interrelated and if real economic activity is influenced by financial changes. It separates two puzzles: how the real economy works and how the price level and financial sector work. Instead of having two different jigsaw puzzles all mixed up, each puzzle can be worked separately. The quantity theory doesn't say there aren't interconnections between the real and financial sectors, but it does say that most of these interconnections involve short-run considerations. The quantity theory is primarily concerned with the long run.

Three assumptions of quantity theory:

1. Velocity is constant.
2. Real output is independent of money supply.
3. Causation goes from money to prices.

CAUSATION GOES FROM MONEY TO PRICES With both V (velocity) and Q (quantity of output) assumed unaffected by changes in M (money supply), the only thing that can change as money changes is P (price level). Given the two assumptions so far, either prices or money could be the driving force. The quantity theory makes the additional assumption that causation goes from money to prices.

Q-6 What's the difference between the equation of exchange and the quantity theory of money?

With these three assumptions, the equation of exchange becomes the quantity theory of money:

$$M\overline{V} \rightarrow P\overline{Q}$$

In its simplest terms, the **quantity theory of money** says that *the price level varies in response to changes in the quantity of money.* Another way to write the quantity theory of money is: $\%\Delta M \rightarrow \%\Delta P$. If the money supply goes up 20 percent, prices go up 20 percent. If the money supply goes down 5 percent, the price level goes down 5 percent.

Q-7 According to the quantity theory of money, what should the Fed do to lower inflation?

WHICH WAY DOES THE CAUSATION GO? According to the quantity theory of money, changes in the money supply cause changes in the price level. The direction of causation goes from left to right:

$$MV \rightarrow PQ$$

More institutionally focused economists see it the other way around. Increases in prices force government to increase the money supply or cause unemployment. The direction of causation goes from right to left:

$$MV \leftarrow PQ$$

Q-8 Use the equation of exchange to explain the difference between the quantity theory and the beliefs of institutionally focused economists.

According to these critics of the quantity theory, the source of inflation is in the price-setting process of firms. When setting prices, firms and individuals find it easier to raise prices than to lower them and do not take into account the effect of their pricing decisions on the price level.

The Declining Influence of the Quantity Theory

In recent times the quantity theory has been out of favor for two reasons. First, the velocity of money has not been constant, and second, the connection between increases in money supply growth and goods inflation has broken down.

VELOCITY IS NOT CONSTANT The problem with velocity can be seen in the Figure 18-4. For the quantity theory to be useful we need velocity to be relatively constant or increasing or decreasing in a predictable way. As you can see in Figure 18-4(a), velocity has been anything but constant. This means that at times when the money supply decreased, inflation did not change or went up, and most recently, when the money supply increased, inflation fell and has remained low.

Q-9 What are two reasons the quantity theory has been out of favor in recent times?

Other things equal, a rise in the velocity of money has the same effect as an increase in the money supply. When velocity increases so will the price level, and when it decreases the price level will also decrease. So, the velocity of money can either offset or add to the effect of money supply changes on the price level. Right before the

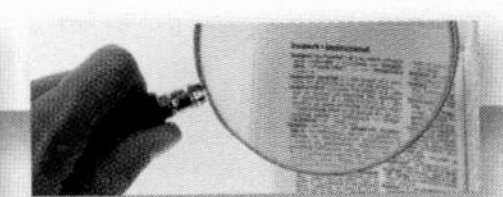

ADDED DIMENSION

The Keeper of the Classical Faith: Milton Friedman

One of the most important economists of the 20th century was University of Chicago economist Milton Friedman. In macroeconomics, Friedman is best known for his support of the quantity theory.

By most accounts, Friedman was a headstrong student. He didn't simply accept the truths his teachers laid out. If he didn't agree, he argued strongly for his own belief. He was very bright, and his ideas were generally logical and convincing. He needed to be both persistent and intelligent to maintain and promote his views in spite of strong opposition.

Nobel Prize Winner Milton Friedman

Throughout the Keynesian years of the 1950s and 1960s, Friedman stood up and argued for the quantity theory, keeping it alive. During this period, Classical economics was called *monetarism,* and because Friedman was such a strong advocate of the quantity theory, he was considered the leader of the monetarists.

Friedman argued that fiscal policy simply didn't work. It led to expansions in the size of government. He also opposed an activist monetary policy. The effects of monetary policy, he said, were too variable for it to be useful in guiding the economy. He called for a steady growth in the money supply, and argued consistently for a laissez-faire policy by government.

Friedman has made his mark in both microeconomics and macroeconomics. In the 1970s, his ideas caught hold and helped spawn a renewal of the quantity theory. He was awarded the Nobel Prize in economics in 1976.

financial crash, both the money supply and velocity increased. Since 2008 velocity has decreased enormously, offsetting much of the effect of the increase in the money supply.

Breakdown in the Connection between Money and Inflation

A second reason the quantity theory has lost favor is related to the first. It is that money and goods inflation are no longer closely connected. For example, notice in Figure 18-4(b) that the money supply fell significantly in 2008. Goods inflation hardly fell at all. At other times money supply rose enormously, but goods inflation hardly changed.

FIGURE 18-4 (A AND B) Inflation, the Money Supply, and the Velocity of Money

Velocity has not been constant as shown in **(a)**, which complicates the relationship between the money supply and inflation, as you can see in **(b)**. Inflation has sometimes risen significantly without a rise in the money supply. In 2008 the money supply fell significantly while goods prices did not.

Source: Federal Reserve Bank of St. Louis (CPI inflation, M1, and M1 velocity).

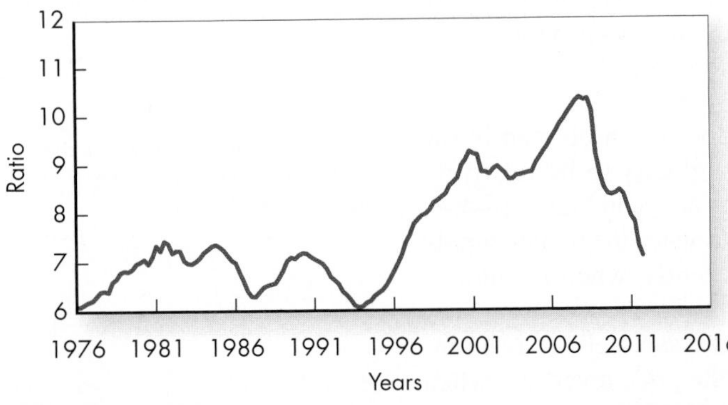

(a) Velocity of Money

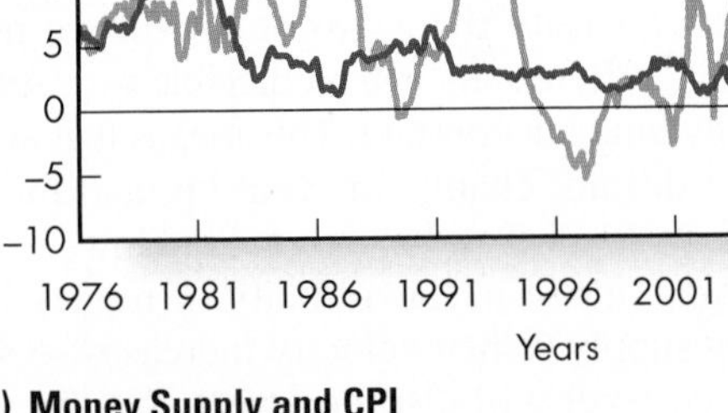

(b) Money Supply and CPI

AN ADJUSTED QUANTITY THEORY? Even though the traditional quantity theory is no longer directly applicable, its general point remains relevant. That general point is that when real output is increasing by 3 percent a year, money times velocity can increase by only 3 percent per year if there is not to be inflation. Thus, if velocity is increasing substantially there can be inflationary pressures even if the money supply is constant, and if velocity is decreasing substantially there can be deflationary pressures even through the money supply is constant. When velocity fluctuates, policy makers must look at both velocity and the money supply to determine what is happening on the monetary side of the economy, and they must adjust their monetary policy to account for the fluctuating velocity.

Even though the quantity theory is no longer directly applicable, its general point remains relevant.

If that monetary side of the economy (money times velocity) is increasing at a rate faster than the real economy is growing, say at 3 percent, then the monetary pressure is causing inflationary pressure in some sector of the economy. But that inflationary pressure need not show up directly in goods price inflation; it can end up in asset price inflation. An example is the case of the United States in recent years where globalization and the large continuing trade deficit placed significant downward pressure on tradable goods and services prices. The monetary side of the quantity theory equation (money times velocity) grew significantly faster than the real side but we did not have significant goods inflation because international competition was holding tradable goods prices down. But we did have what proved to be an unsustainable increase in asset prices that eventually led to a financial meltdown. So if we had included asset prices in our view of inflation, monetary policy was inflationary during that time period, just as the quantity theory said it would be.

Inflation and the Phillips Curve Trade-Off

Inflation has traditionally been discussed in relation to unemployment in what is called the Phillips curve. The traditional **short-run Phillips curve** is *a downward-sloping curve showing the relationship between inflation and unemployment when expectations of inflation are constant.* In a Phillips curve diagram, unemployment is measured on the horizontal axis; inflation is on the vertical axis. The short-run Phillips curve shows us the possible short-run combinations of those two phenomena. It tells us that when unemployment is low, say 4 percent, inflation tends to be high, say 4 percent (point *A* in Figure 18-5(a). It also tells us that if we want to lower inflation, say to 1 percent, we must be willing to accept high unemployment, say 7 percent (point *B* in Figure 18-5).

The traditional short-run Phillips curve is a downward sloping curve showing the relationship between inflation and unemployment when expectations of inflation are fixed.

Up until the 1970s the short-run Phillips curve seemed to match the empirical evidence, but then in the early 1970s the empirical short-run Phillips curve relationship seemed to break down. The data no longer seemed to show a trade-off between unemployment and inflation. Instead, when unemployment was high, inflation was also high. This phenomenon is termed **stagflation**—*the combination of high and accelerating inflation and high unemployment.* Since that time, the Phillips curve has been ephemeral—sometimes seeming as if it were reappearing, and then disappearing again.

The Long-Run and Short-Run Phillips Curves

Economists have explained this constantly changing relationship between inflation and unemployment by incorporating expectations of inflation into the analysis. They argue that actual inflation depends both on supply and demand forces and on how much inflation people expect. If people expect a lot of inflation, they will ask for higher nominal wage and price increases. To incorporate expectations into the Phillips curve it is necessary to distinguish between a short-run Phillips curve, shown in Figure 18-5(a), and a long-run Phillips curve, shown in Figure 18-5(b). Economists

REAL-WORLD APPLICATION

Inflation, Nominal Income, and Asset Inflation Targeting

One of the big debates about Fed policy concerns whether the Fed should have an explicit target. The most generally discussed target is a goods price inflation target. With inflation targeting, the Fed commits itself to tightening the money supply and raising interest rates if inflation exceeds a certain level. Advocates of inflation targeting argue that it provides better assurances for investors that the central bank will fight inflation, and thus holds inflationary expectations down. They point to the success of countries such as New Zealand, which introduced inflation targeting in 1989 when a law was passed that required the Reserve Bank of New Zealand to keep consumer price inflation between 0 and 3 percent a year, a target agreed on by the government and the central bank. After averaging 10 percent a year in the 1980s, New Zealand's inflation rate fell in the early 1990s and averaged below 3 percent per year thereafter. Advocates of inflation targeting argue that this experience, and others like it, show that inflation targeting helps central banks establish credibility in their resolve to fight inflation.

Critics of inflation targeting argue that explicit inflation targeting has serious problems. Inflation is hard to measure, and the standard measures of inflation do not include asset inflation. Thus a monetary policy can lead to significant asset inflation, and still meet the target. The target could also work the other way. An inflation target could force the central bank to raise interest rates and cut money supply growth when there was no need to do so. They argue that it is better to have a *general inflation goal,* which can be adjusted for the particular situation, and that that general inflation target should include a consideration of the components of the price rise and of whether increases in nominal wealth are exceeding increases in real wealth.

A variation of inflation targeting that has recently been proposed is *nominal income targeting.* In nominal income targeting the Fed targets a specific increase in nominal income—say 5 percent—and does not try to separate out which part of it is inflation. If real income increases at 3 percent, then nominal income targeting would be the equivalent of a 2 percent inflation target. If real income does not grow by 3 percent, then the nominal income target would allow for a higher inflation. If real income growth were greater, the inflation component of the nominal income target would be lower. The potential problem with such a policy is that it might allow, and perhaps even encourage, asset price inflation.

Many other variations of targets are possible. For example, one could have a combined goods inflation and asset inflation target, where the inflation target of, say, 2 percent was combined with a net worth-to-GDP ratio target, to reduce the likelihood of the Fed feeding an asset bubble. Such a target would call for much more contractionary monetary policy in asset price booms, and more expansionary monetary policy in asset deflations.

FIGURE 18-5 The Phillips Curve Trade-Off

The Phillips curve, depicts a trade-off between inflation and unemployment. In the short-run Phillips curve shown in **(a)**, there is a tradeoff between inflation and unemployment. In the long-run Phillips curve shown in **(b)** there is assumed to be no tradeoff, which means that the long-run Phillips curve is vertical.

Source: Economic Report of the President.

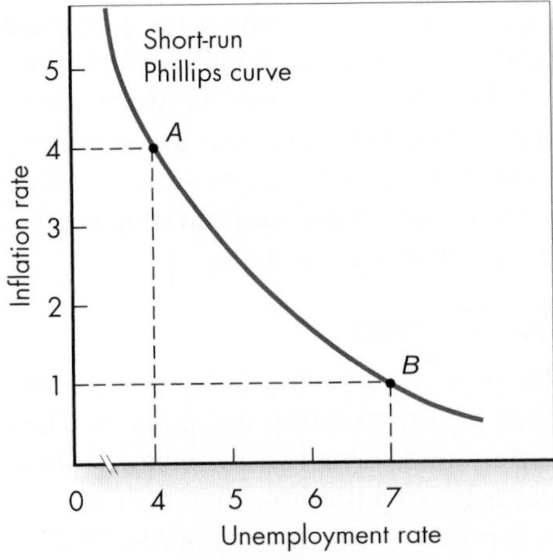

(a) Short-run Phillips curve

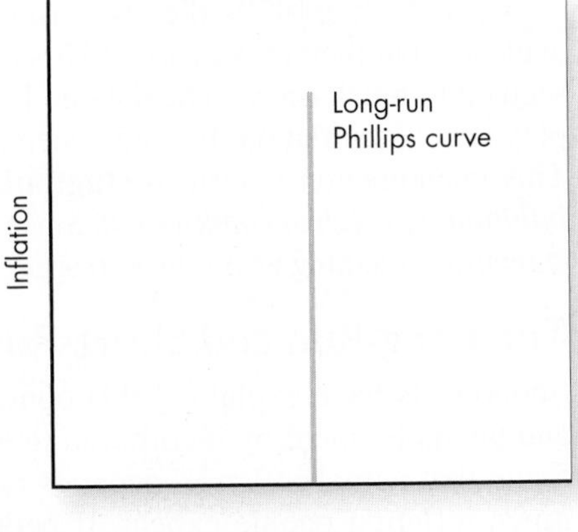

(b) Long-run Phillips curve

explain the difference between the short-run and the long-run Phillips curve by different assumptions about expectations.

At all points on same the short-run Phillips curve, expectations of inflation (the rise in the price level that the average person expects) are fixed. Thus, on the short-run Phillips curve, expectations of inflation can differ from actual inflation. As expectations of inflation change, the short-run Phillips curve shifts. When expected inflation rises, the short-run Phillips curve shifts up and when expected inflation falls, the short-run Phillips curve shifts down. At all points on the long-run Phillips curve, expectations of inflation are equal to actual inflation. The **long-run Phillips curve** is thought to be *a vertical curve at the unemployment rate consistent with potential output.* It shows the trade-off between inflation and unemployment (or complete lack thereof) when expectations of inflation equal actual inflation. Economists argue that expectations of inflation explain why the short-run Phillips curve relationship broke down in the 1970s.

The long-run Phillips curve is vertical; it shows the lack of a trade-off between inflation and unemployment when expectations of inflation equal actual inflation. Expectations of inflation do not change along a short-run Phillips curve.

Let's consider how expectations of inflation can explain high inflation and high unemployment in reference to the Phillips curve graph. Say the economy starts with a rate of unemployment consistent with potential output. So there is no inflation, and the economy is at its potential output. (Wages can still be going up by the rate of productivity growth, say it's 3 percent, but the price level is not rising.) Further assume that individuals are expecting zero inflation; that is, if they get a 3 percent wage increase, they expect their real income to rise by 3 percent. This starting point is represented by point *A* in Figure 18-6, on which we graph both the short-run and long-run Phillips curve.

The Long-Run and Short-Run Phillips Curves

Let's say the economy starts at point *A*—zero inflation and unemployment of 5.5 percent, the target rate. As you can see point *A* in Figure 18-6(b) is also on both the long-run and short-run Phillips curve. This means that point *A* is a sustainable combination of inflation and unemployment—the situation can continue indefinitely. The only

FIGURE 18-6 Inflation Expectations and the Phillips Curve

In the short run, the economy can expand beyond the target rate of unemployment by accepting more inflation. This shows up as a movement along the short-run Phillips curve from point *A* to point *B*. That is not, however, a sustainable equilibrium. As the higher inflation becomes built into expectations, there will be pressure to raise wages and prices even more than 4 percent, which will push up inflation and inflationary expectations, shifting the short-run Phillips curve up (arrow 1). Only when that pressure is removed and unemployment is allowed to increase back to its target rate (arrow 2) will the upward shift stop. The eventual equilibrium will be an equilibrium such as point *C*, which is on both the long-run and short-run Phillips curve.

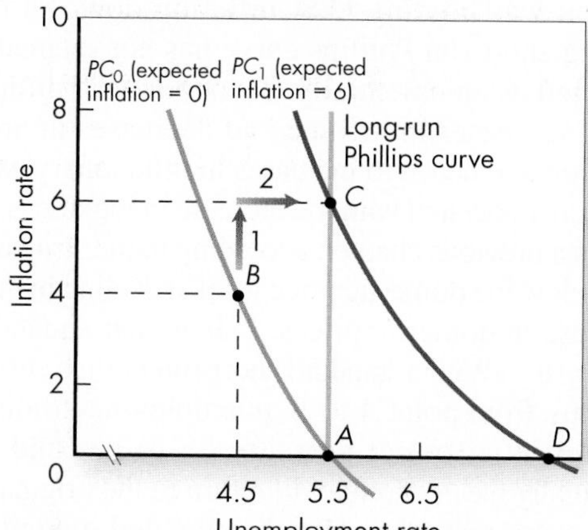

The Inflationary Process and the Phillips Curve

sustainable combination of inflation and unemployment rates on the short-run Phillips curve is where it intersects the long-run Phillips curve because that is the only unemployment rate consistent with the economy's potential income.

Moving Off the Long-Run Phillips Curve Now let's say that the government decides to run expansionary monetary or fiscal policy in an effort to reduce unemployment below 5.5 percent. Such a policy would decrease unemployment (say to 4.5 percent) but increase inflation. This is shown as a movement along the short-run Phillips curve from point *A* to point *B*. That is not, however, a sustainable equilibrium. Inflation is higher than expected, and the people are being fooled. For example, workers who were expecting zero inflation, which made them happy with a 3 percent raise, now find that there was 4 percent inflation, so now they will find that their real wage actually fell. As the higher inflation becomes built into expectations, there will be pressure to raise wages and prices, which will push up inflation even more than 4 percent.

Q-10 If the economy is at point *A* on the short-run Phillips curve below, what prediction would you make for unemployment and inflation?

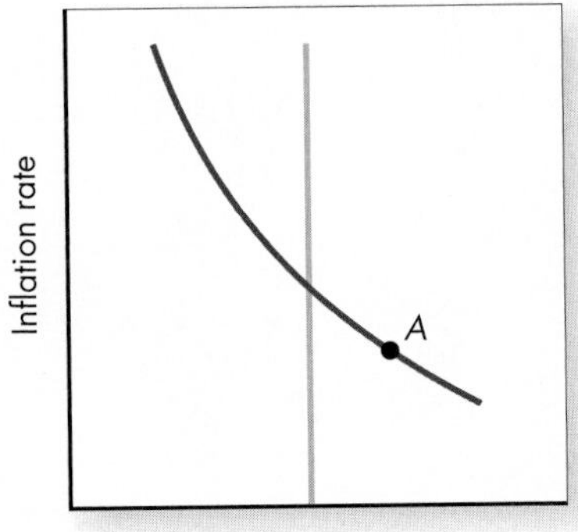

As expectations of inflation increase, the short-run Phillips curve will begin shifting up as shown by the upward arrow at point *B* (arrow 1). This pressure on inflation to rise will continue as long as the unemployment is below the unemployment rate consistent with potential output, which in this case is assumed to be 5.5 percent. Only when that pressure is removed by allowing the economy to move back to a rate of unemployment consistent with potential output (shifting the short run Phillips curve to the right along arrow 2, to a point such as point *C* in Figure 18-6), will the upward pressure stop. At point *C* the economy will be at a sustainable equilibrium where the unemployment rate equals the target rate and inflation expectations equal actual inflation.

In the Phillips curve model, the general relationship is the following: Any time unemployment is lower than the target level of unemployment consistent with potential output, inflation and expectations of inflation will be increasing. That means that the short-run Phillips curve will be shifting up. The short-run Phillips curve will continue to shift up until output is no longer above potential. Thus, any level of inflation is consistent with the target level of unemployment if the cause of that inflation is expectations of inflation. Economists used these expectations of inflation to explain the experience in the 1970s. The economy had been pushed beyond its potential, which had caused inflation to accelerate. (This explanation was supplemented with discussions of supply-side inflationary pressures caused by the large rise in oil prices that occurred at that time.)

Global Competition and the Phillips Curve

Since global competition was holding U.S. inflation down in the past decade, the typical downward-sloping short-run Phillips curve has not seemed to be relevant. This experience can be depicted as an essentially flat short-run Phillips curve. With a flat short-run Phillips curve, increases in income and decreases in unemployment do not lead to increases in inflation and hence to increases in inflationary expectations as long as the increase in consumption associated with the increase in income is met by increasing the trade deficit. As we saw in a previous chapter, according to the structural stagnation model, with a world price level below the domestic price level, a decline in the unemployment rate will not lead to an increase in domestic prices. I show that situation with the short-run Phillips curve as in Figure 18-7. With a standard short-run Philips curve, PC_1, expansionary policy moves the economy from point *A* to *B*, unemployment falls, inflation rises, and inflation expectations eventually put pressure on prices and wages to rise. It is unsustainable and eventually the economy will return to the original unemployment rate.

A short-run Phillips curve that takes globalization and unlimited trade deficits into account, PC_2, allows the economy to move from point *A* to *C* without increases in either inflation or inflation expectations. This position is sustainable as long as the international

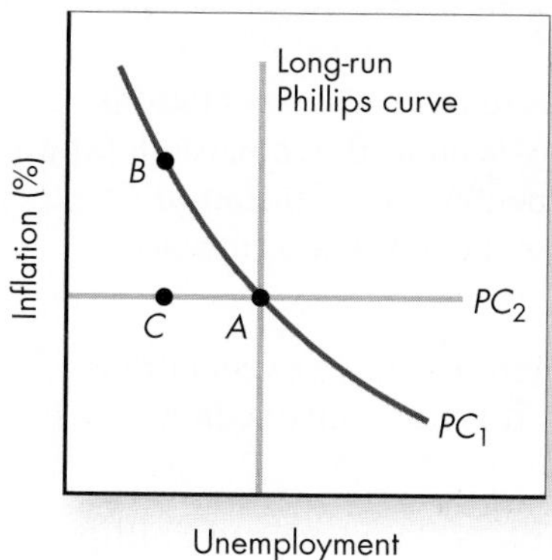

FIGURE 18-7 The Inflation Process with Globalization

When the world price level is below the domestic price level, and the country can run unlimited trade deficits, a decline in the unemployment rate will not lead to inflation. Inflation is held down by globalization. The standard short-run Phillips curve (PC_1) changes to a flat short-run Phillips curve (PC_2).

conditions allow it, with large flows of capital from abroad financing the trade deficit. In this case, government can use expansionary policy without leading to goods market inflation. Instead it leads to an asset price inflation, which, when it ultimately bursts, will lead to serious problems for the economy.

Conclusion

Inflation is not an easy topic. It is made more challenging by definitional and measurement problems that make it difficult to know precisely what type of inflation one is talking about. Should we define inflation in terms of goods prices, or more broadly in terms of both asset and goods prices? These definitional choices make a big difference in how we view policy. If one judges inflation in terms of both goods and asset prices, then the period up until the financial bubble burst was a more inflationary time period than it seemed. If one judges inflation only in terms of increases in the price of goods, it has not.

Summary

- At one time, inflation was measured as an increase in the money supply. *(LO18-1)*
- Inflation can occur for both goods and assets. Goods inflation is easier to measure than is asset inflation. *(LO18-1)*
- It is difficult to determine how much of an increase in the value of assets is the result of inflation or of increased productive capacity. This is one reason asset prices are not included in measured inflation. *(LO18-1)*
- Inflation is a continual rise in the price level. The CPI, PPI, PCE, and GDP deflator are all price indexes used to measure inflation. These indexes measure goods prices and do not include asset prices. *(LO18-1)*
- The usefulness of standard goods market price indexes for judging policy is limited because they do not include the prices of assets. *(LO18-1)*
- The winners in inflation are people who can raise their wages or prices and still keep their jobs or sell their goods. The losers are people who can't raise their wages or prices. On average, winners and losers balance out. *(LO18-2)*
- Asset inflation hurts people who save with safe assets and helps those who save in risky assets. *(LO18-2)*

- Inflation reduces the informational value of prices. *(LO18-2)*
- Expectations of inflation can accelerate inflation and in some cases lead to hyperinflation. *(LO18-2)*
- A basic rule of thumb to predict inflation is: Inflation equals nominal wage increases minus productivity growth. *(LO18-3)*
- The equation of exchange is $MV = PQ$; it becomes the quantity theory when velocity is constant, real output is independent of the money supply, and causation goes from money to prices. The quantity theory says that the price level varies in direct response to changes in the quantity of money. That is,

  $\% \Delta M \rightarrow \% \Delta P$ *(LO18-3)*
- According to the quantity theory of money, policy analysis about the real economy is based on the supply side of the economy, not the demand side. *(LO18-3)*
- The lack of a clear relationship between money growth and inflation as well as the variability of velocity undermines the quantity theory of money. *(LO18-3)*
- The short-run Phillips curve holds expectations constant. It is generally seen as downward-sloping and shifts up when expectations of inflation rise and shifts down when expectations of inflation fall. *(LO18-4)*
- The long-run Phillips curve allows expectations of inflation to change; it is generally seen as vertical. *(LO18-4)*
- Globalization can lead to a flat short-run Phillips curve. In this case, expansionary policy can reduce unemployment without causing goods inflation. *(LO18-4)*
- According to the structural stagnation model, structural forces can keep goods prices down so that increases in the money supply lead to asset price increases, which can create structural imbalances. Without inflation, policy makers will tend to implement expansionary policy to expand the economy. *(LO18-4)*

Key Terms

adaptive expectations *(395)*
asset price inflation *(385)*
consumer price index (CPI) *(390)*
equation of exchange *(396)*
extrapolative expectations *(395)*
hyperinflation *(394)*
long-run Phillips curve *(401)*
personal consumption expenditure (PCE) deflator *(391)*
price index *(389)*
producer price index (PPI) *(391)*
quantity theory of money *(397)*
rational expectations *(394)*
short-run Phillips curve *(399)*
stagflation *(399)*
velocity of money *(396)*

Questions and Exercises

1. What is an asset price inflation? Why does it matter? *(LO18-1)*
2. Use the following table to create a price index: *(LO18-1)*

Basket of Goods	2013	2014
20 Big Mac meals	$7.25	$7.50
3 pairs jeans	$50.00	$55.00
15 movie tickets	$7.00	$7.00

   a. What is the value of the price index in 2013?
   b. What is the value of the price index in 2014?
   c. What is inflation from 2013 to 2014?
3. True or false? Inflation, on average, makes people neither richer nor poorer. Therefore it has no cost. Explain. *(LO18-2)*
4. Why do lenders tend to lose out in an unexpected inflation? *(LO18-2)*
5. Under what conditions would lenders not lose out in inflation? *(LO18-2)*

6. What are the distributional effects of asset inflation caused by an increase in the money supply? *(LO18-2)*
7. If you base your expectations of inflation on what has happened in the past, what kind of expectations are you demonstrating? *(LO18-3)*
8. If productivity growth is 3 percent and wage increases are 5 percent, what would you predict inflation would be? *(LO18-3)*
9. What three assumptions turn the equation of exchange into the quantity theory of money? *(LO18-3)*
10. What does the quantity theory predict will happen to inflation if the money supply rises 10 percent? *(LO18-3)*
11. Assume the money supply is $500, the velocity of money is 8, and the price level is $2. Using the quantity theory of money: *(LO18-3)*
    a. Determine the level of real output.
    b. Determine the level of nominal output.
    c. Assuming velocity remains constant, what will happen if the money supply rises 20 percent?
    d. If the government established price controls and also raised the money supply 20 percent, what would happen?
12. What are two reasons why the quantity theory of money is problematic? *(LO18-3)*
13. Draw a short-run Phillips curve. What does it say about the relationship between inflation and unemployment? *(LO18-4)*
14. Draw a long-run Phillips curve. What does it say about the relationship between inflation and unemployment? *(LO18-4)*
15. If people's expectations of inflation didn't change, would the economy move from a short-run to a long-run Phillips curve? *(LO18-4)*
16. Congratulations. You've just been appointed finance minister of Inflationland. Inflation has been ongoing for the past five years at 5 percent. The target rate of unemployment, 5 percent, is also the actual rate. *(LO18-4)*
    a. Demonstrate the economy's likely position on both short-run and long-run Phillips curves.
    b. The president tells you she wants to be reelected. Devise a monetary policy strategy for her that might help her accomplish her goal.
    c. Demonstrate that strategy graphically, including the likely long-run consequences.
17. European Central Bank (ECB) governing council member Erkki Liikanen was quoted in a 2004 *Wall Street Journal* article as saying, "The stronger we get the productivity growth . . . the more room we will get in monetary policy (to keep interest rates low)." *(LO18-4)*
    a. Demonstrate his argument using the *AS/AD* model.
    b. Demonstrate his argument using the Phillips curve model.
18. True or false? According to the structural stagnation hypothesis expansionary policy will change the shape of the short-run Phillips curve and therefore allow government to reduce unemployment without causing accelerating inflation. Demonstrate your answer graphically. *(LO18-4)*

Questions from Alternative Perspectives

1. According to the quantity theory of money, the government controls inflation through the supply of money.
    a. Does that mean that the government can stop inflation if it wants to do so?
    b. What reasons might government have not to stop inflation? (Austrian)
2. The book of Leviticus in the Bible states, "You shall do no injustice in judgment, in measurement of length, weight, or volume. You shall have just balances, just weights, a just ephah, a just hin. I am the Lord your God, who brought you out of the land of Egypt." When the Israelites began using shekels for money, a just weight meant that the silver coin had a particular weight and therefore an intrinsic value.
    a. If U.S. currency is not backed by gold, how do we know the dollar is a "just weight"?
    b. How is inflation an injustice in measurement?
    c. Who bears the injustice of inflation? (Religious)
3. When it comes to understanding inflation, and even other aspects of the business cycle, ecological economists will often emphasize the role of energy, and especially oil, in shaping macroeconomic outcomes. To decide how important oil prices are in

shaping macroeconomic outcomes such as inflation, do the following:
   a. Graph the average annual CPI inflation rate from 1970 to the 2000s (www.bls.gov has the data); graph the world price of oil over the same time period (www.eia.doe.gov has these data); overlay the graphs (this is sometimes called "teardrop analysis") and move them forward and backward a bit to create leads and lags. What kind of a pattern do you see?
   b. Use the *AD/AS* model to analyze the impact of an oil shock on the economy.
   c. What is the necessary consequence of using fiscal policy to stimulate the economy after a supply-side oil shock? What conclusions do you draw from the analysis? (Institutionalist)
4. This chapter discusses causes of inflation.
   a. Do you believe the cause of inflation is to be found in the institutional structure of wage- and price-setting institutions or in excess demand for goods and services?
   b. If you believe inflation is caused by wage- and price-setting institutions, what type of policy would you recommend?
   c. If you believe that inflation is caused by excess demand, would your policy recommendations be the same? (Post-Keynesian)
5. Radicals see the trade-off between inflation and unemployment as one that pits inflation-phobic investors—out to protect the value of their assets and the corporate profits in which they invest—against workers who are out for employment and wage growth. Lower unemployment rates and more jobs bolster the bargaining power of workers, pushing up wages, which either leads to inflation or eats into corporate profit margins. The trade-off changed in the 1990s as globalization put workers in no position to push for higher wages even as unemployment rates declined. Compare this explanation of change in the trade-off between unemployment and inflation during the 1990s with the one in your textbook.
   a. Where do they agree and where do they differ?
   b. Which do you find more convincing? (Radical)

Issues to Ponder

1. People's perception of inflation often differs from actual inflation.
   a. List five goods that you buy relatively frequently.
   b. Looking in old newspapers (found in the library on microfiche), locate sales prices for these goods since 1950, finding one price every five years or so. Determine the average annual price rise for each good from 1950 to today.
   c. Compare that price with the rise in the consumer price index.
2. In the early 1990s, Argentina stopped increasing the money supply and fixed the exchange rate of the Argentine austral at 10,000 to the dollar. It then renamed the Argentine currency the "peso" and cut off four zeros so that one peso equaled one dollar. Inflation slowed substantially. After this was done, the following observations were made. Explain why these observations did not surprise economists.
   a. The golf courses were far less crowded.
   b. The price of goods in dollar-equivalent pesos in Buenos Aires, the capital of the country, was significantly above that in New York City.
   c. Consumer prices—primarily services—rose relative to other goods.
   d. Luxury auto dealers were shutting down.
3. Grade inflation is widespread. In 1990, 81 percent of the students who took the SATs had an A or B average, but 40 percent of them scored less than 390 on the verbal SAT. Students' grades are increasing but what they are learning is decreasing. Some economists argue that grade inflation should be dealt with in the same way that price inflation should be dealt with—by creating a fixed standard and requiring all grades to be specified relative to that standard. One way to accomplish this is to index the grades professors give: specify on the grade report both the student's grade and the class average, and deflate (or inflate) the grade to some common standard. Discuss the advantages and disadvantages of such a proposal.
4. True or false? The short-run Phillips curve is just a figment of economists' imagination.
5. Wayne Angell, a former Fed governor, stated in an editorial, "The Federal Reserve should get back on track getting inflation rates so low that inflation would no longer be a determining factor in household and business investment decisions." Mr. Angell believes inflation lowers long-term growth.
   a. Is Wayne Angell most likely a quantity theorist or institutionally focused economist? Explain your answer.
   b. How does inflation affect household decisions and, consequently, growth?

Answers to Margin Questions

1. Asset inflation is the rise in the price of assets such as stocks and houses in excess of changes in their real values. Goods inflation is the rise in the price of goods and services. (*p. 386; LO18-1*)
2. Asset deflation presents more problems for the economy than does goods inflation. (*p. 388; LO18-1*)
3. The price index will rise by $0.15 \times 0.1 = 1.5$ percent. (*p. 390; LO18-1*)
4. False. Inflation does not make an economy poorer. It redistributes income from those who do not raise their prices to those who do raise their prices. (*p. 391; LO18-2*)
5. Three types of expectations are rational expectations, adaptive expectations, and extrapolative expectations. (*p. 395; LO18-3*)
6. The equation of exchange, $MV = PQ$, is a tautology. What changes it to the quantity theory are three assumptions about the variables, specifically that velocity remains constant, that real output is determined separately, and that the causation flows from money to prices. With these assumptions added, the equation of exchange implies that changes in the money supply are reflected in changes in the price level—which is what the quantity theory of money says. (*p. 397; LO18-3*)
7. According to the quantity theory of money, the Fed should decrease the growth of the money supply to lower inflation. (*p. 397; LO18-3*)
8. According to the quantity theory, the direction of causation goes from money to prices ($MV \rightarrow PQ$)—increases in the money supply lead to increases in the price level. According to institutionally focused economists, the direction of causation goes from prices to money ($MV \leftarrow PQ$)—increases in the price level are ratified by government, which increases the money supply. (*p. 397; LO18-3*)
9. The relationship between the money supply and inflation does not always hold and the velocity of money is not constant. (*p. 397; LO18-3*)
10. If the economy is at point *A* on the Phillips curve below, inflation is below expected inflation and unemployment is higher than the target rate of unemployment. If this were the only information I had about the economy I would expect the economy to shift back to a point on the long-run Phillips curve, as inflation and expectations of inflation fall, shifting the short-run Phillips curve down and to the left. (*p. 402; LO18-4*)

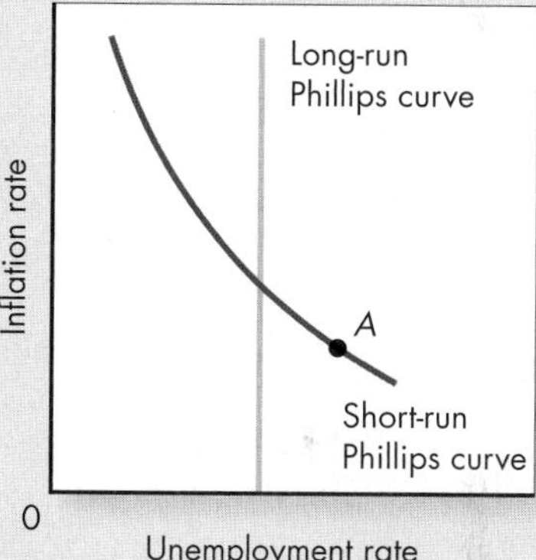

chapter 19

International Trade Policy

> *Manufacturing and commercial monopolies owe their origin not to a tendency imminent in a capitalist economy but to governmental interventionist policy directed against free trade.*
>
> —Ludwig von Mises

Based on the theory of comparative advantage, most economists oppose trade restrictions. Not everyone agrees with economists; almost every day we hear calls from some sector of the economy to restrict foreign imports to save U.S. jobs and protect U.S. workers from unfair competition. In this chapter we consider the pattern and nature of trade, the variety of trade restrictions that governments impose, and why economists generally oppose trade restrictions.

After reading this chapter, you should be able to:

- **LO19-1** Summarize some important data of trade.
- **LO19-2** Explain policies countries use to restrict trade.
- **LO19-3** Summarize the reasons for trade restrictions and why economists generally oppose trade restrictions.
- **LO19-4** Explain how free trade associations both help and hinder international trade.

The Nature and Patterns of Trade

Let's begin with some numbers to get a sense of the nature and dimensions of international trade.

Increasing but Fluctuating World Trade

In 1928, total world trade was about $640 billion (in today's dollars). U.S. gross domestic product (GDP) was about $1,070 billion, so world trade as a percentage of U.S. GDP was almost 60 percent. In 1935, that ratio had fallen to less than 30 percent. In 1950 it was only 20 percent. Then it started rising. Today it is about 240 percent, with world trade amounting to about $35 trillion. As you can see, international trade has been growing, but with significant fluctuations in that growth. Sometimes international trade has grown rapidly; at other times it has grown slowly or has even fallen.

In part, fluctuations in world trade result from fluctuations in world output. When output rises, international trade rises; when output falls, international trade falls. Fluctuations in world trade are also in part explained by trade restrictions that countries have imposed from time to time. For example, decreases in world income during the Depression of the 1930s caused a large decrease in trade, but that decrease was exacerbated by a worldwide increase in trade restrictions.

Differences in the Importance of Trade

The importance of international trade to countries' economies differs widely, as we can see in the table below, which presents the importance of the shares of exports (the value of goods and services sold abroad) and imports (the value of goods and services purchased abroad) for various countries.

	Total Output*	Export Ratio	Import Ratio
Netherlands	$ 844	78%	71%
Germany	3,695	47	41
Canada	1,706	29	31
Italy	2,180	27	29
France	2,825	26	28
United Kingdom	2,462	30	33
Japan	6,078	15	14
United States	15,094	13	16

*Numbers in billions.

Source: *World Development Indicators, 2012,* The World Bank.

Among the countries listed, the Netherlands has the highest exports compared to total output; the United States has the lowest. The Netherlands' imports are also the highest as a percentage of total output. U.S. exports are close to the lowest. The relationship between a country's imports and its exports is no coincidence. For most countries, imports and exports roughly equal one another, though in any particular year that equality can be rough indeed. For the United States in recent years, imports have generally significantly exceeded exports, which means that a trade imbalance can continue for a long time. But that situation can't continue forever, as I'll discuss.

Total trade figures provide us with only part of the international trade picture. We must also look at what types of goods are traded and with whom that trade is conducted.

What and with Whom the United States Trades

The majority of U.S. exports and imports involve significant amounts of manufactured goods. This isn't unusual, since much of international trade is in manufactured goods.

The primary trading partners of the United States are Canada, Mexico, the European Union, and the Pacific Rim countries.

Figure 19-1 shows the regions with which the United States trades. Exports to Canada and Mexico made up the largest percentage of total U.S. exports to individual countries in 2012. The largest regions to whom the U.S. exports are the Pacific Rim and the European Union. Countries from which the United States imports major quantities include Canada and Mexico and the regions of the European Union and the Pacific Rim. Thus, the countries we export to are also the countries we import from.

The Changing Nature of Trade The nature of trade is continually changing, both in terms of the countries with which the United States trades and the goods and services traded. For example, U.S. imports from China, India, and other East Asian countries have increased substantially in recent years. In the late 1980s goods from

FIGURE 19-1 (A AND B) U.S. Exports and Imports by Region

Major regions that trade with the United States include Canada, Mexico, the European Union, and the Pacific Rim.

Source: FT900 U.S. International Trade in Goods and Services 2012, U.S. Census Bureau (www.census.gov).

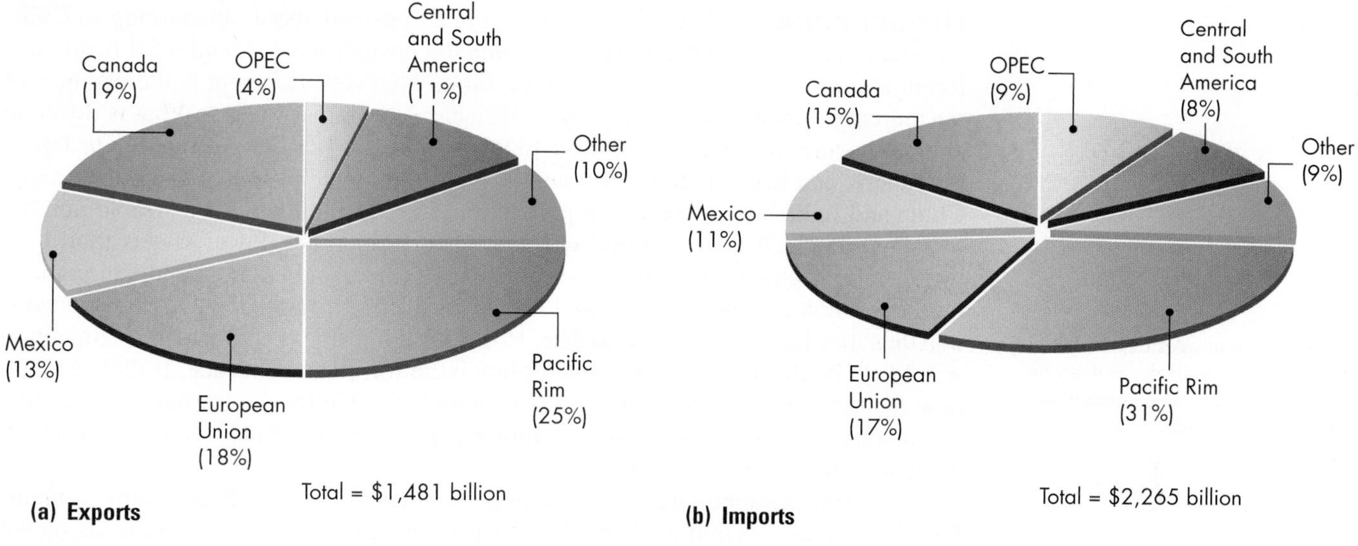

China accounted for 2.5 percent of all U.S. merchandise imports. Today they account for 17 percent. Imports from India have increased twentyfold over that time—from 0.1 percent to 2 percent of all goods imported.

The kind of goods and services the United States imports also has changed. Thirty years ago, the goods the United States imported from China and India were primarily basic manufacturing goods and raw commodities. Technologically advanced goods were produced here in the United States. Today we are importing high-tech manufactured goods from these countries, and they are even developing their own new products that require significant research and development.

Q-1 How has the nature of U.S. imports from China changed in recent years?

The change in the nature of the goods that a country produces and exports up the technological ladder is typical for developing countries. It characterized Japan, Korea, and Singapore in the post–World War II era, and today characterizes China and India. As this movement up the technological ladder occurs, foreign companies that had been subcontractors for U.S. companies become direct competitors of the U.S. companies. For example, the automaker Kia and the electronics producer Samsung have developed into major global firms, and in the future you can expect numerous Chinese companies to become household names.

We can expect the nature of trade to change even more in the future as numerous technological changes in telecommunications continue to reduce the cost of both voice and data communications throughout the world and expand the range of services that can be provided by foreign countries. Production no longer needs to occur in the geographic area where the goods are consumed. For example, financial accounting, compositing (typesetting) of texts, and research can now be done almost anywhere, and transferred with the click of a mouse. The customer service calls for a U.S. company can be answered almost anywhere in India, which has a sizable well-educated, English-speaking population, and much lower wage rates. India even trains its employees to speak with a Midwest U.S. accent to make it less apparent to customers that the

We can expect the nature of trade to change even more in the future.

call is being answered in India. This trade in services is what the press often refers to as *outsourcing,* but it is important to remember that outsourcing is simply a description of some aspects of trade.

Is Chinese and Indian Outsourcing Different from Previous Outsourcing? There has been a lot of discussion about outsourcing to China and India recently, and thus it is worthwhile to consider what is, and what is not, different about trade with China and India. First, what isn't different is the distance of outsourcing. Manufacturers have used overseas suppliers for years. What is different about outsourcing to China and India today compared to earlier outsourcing to Japan, Singapore, and Korea in the 1980s and 1990s is the potential size of that outsourcing. China and India have a combined population of 2.5 billion people, a sizable number of whom are well educated and willing to work for much lower wages than U.S. workers. As technology opens up more areas to trade, and as India and China move up the technology ladder, U.S.-based firms will likely experience much more competition than they have experienced to date. How U.S. companies deal with this competition will likely be the defining economic policy issue for the next decade. If they develop new technologies and new industries in which the United States has comparative advantages, then the United States' future can be bright. If they don't, significant, difficult adjustment will need to occur.

How U.S. companies deal with new high-tech competition will likely be the defining economic policy issue for the next decade.

The rising competitiveness of Asian economies with the U.S. economy is manifested in the large deficit the United States is running on its balance of trade, as shown in Figure 19-2(a). A trade deficit means that U.S. imports exceed U.S. exports. The United States has been running trade deficits since the 1970s, and in 2008 the U.S. trade deficit reached over $820 billion. It has decreased slightly since then, but it remains high.

The trade deficit looks a little less threatening when considered as a percentage of GDP, as is shown in Figure 19-2(b), but it is still of concern. The U.S. trade deficit means that the United States is consuming a lot more than it is producing, and paying for current consumption with promises to pay in the future.

FIGURE 19-2 (A AND B) The U.S. Trade Balance

The United States has been running trade deficits since the 1970s. Panel (**a**) shows the trade deficit in billions of dollars. As (**b**) shows, the trade deficit looks slightly less threatening when considered as a percentage of GDP.

Source: U.S. Department of Commerce: Bureau of Economic Analysis *International Transactions* (www.bea.gov).

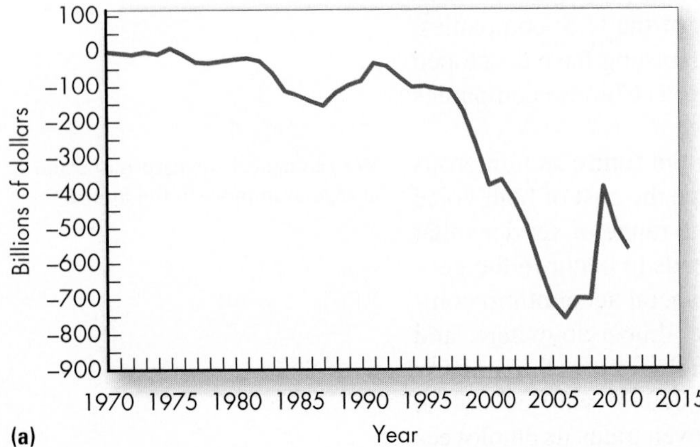

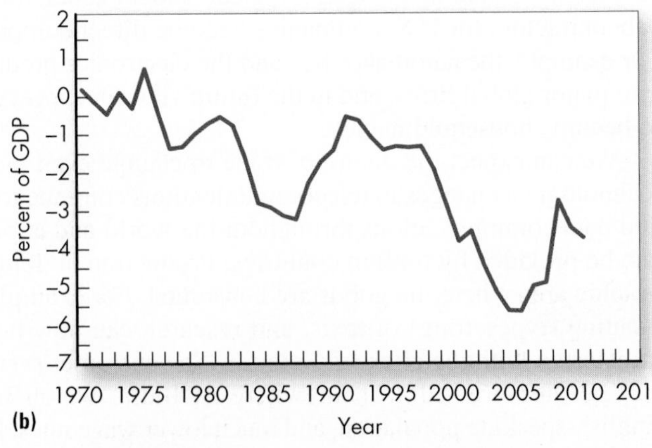

ADDED DIMENSION

International Issues in Perspective

Since the 1970s, international issues have become increasingly important for the U.S. economy. That statement would be correct even if the reference period went back as far as the late 1800s. From the late 1800s through the first 40 years of the 1900s, the United States was in an isolationist period in which the country turned inward in both economic and foreign policies.

The statement would not be correct if the reference period were earlier than the late 1800s. In the 1600s, 1700s, and most of the 1800s, international trade was vital to the American economy—even more vital than now. The American nation grew from colonial possessions of England, France, and Spain. These "new world" colonial possessions were valued for their gold, agricultural produce, and natural resources. From a European standpoint, international trade was the colonies' reason for being.*

A large portion of the U.S. government's income during much of the 1800s came from tariffs. Our technology was imported from abroad, and international issues played a central role in wars fought here. (Many historians believe that the most important cause of the U.S. Civil War was the difference of views about tariffs on manufactured goods. The South opposed them because it wanted cheap manufactured goods, while the North favored them because it wanted to protect its manufacturing industries.) Up until the 1900s, no one would have studied the U.S. economy independently of international issues. Not only was there significant international trade; there was also significant immigration. The United States is a country of immigrants.

Only in the late 1800s did the United States adopt an isolationist philosophy in both politics and trade. So in reference to that isolationist period, the U.S. economy has become more integrated with the world economy. However, in a broader historical perspective, that isolationist period was an anomaly, and today's economy is simply returning international issues to the key role they've usually played.

Another important insight is that international trade has social and cultural dimensions. While much of the chapter deals with specifically economic issues, we must also remember the cultural and social implications of trade.

Let's consider an example from history. In the Middle Ages, Greek ideas and philosophy were lost to Europe when hordes of barbarians swept over the continent. These ideas and that philosophy were rediscovered in the Renaissance only as a by-product of trade between the Italian merchant cities and the Middle East. (The Greek ideas that had spread to the Middle East were protected from European upheavals.) *Renaissance* means rebirth: a rebirth in Europe of Greek learning. Many of our traditions and sensibilities are based on those of the Renaissance, and that Renaissance was caused, or at least significantly influenced, by international trade. Had there been no trade, our entire philosophy of life might have been different.

In economics courses we do not focus on these broader cultural issues but instead focus on relatively technical issues such as the reasons for trade and the implications of tariffs. But keep in the back of your mind these broader implications as you go through the various components of international economics. They add a dimension to the story that otherwise might be forgotten.

*The Native American standpoint was, I suspect, somewhat different.

Debtor and Creditor Nations

Running a trade deficit isn't necessarily bad.

Running a trade deficit isn't necessarily bad. In fact, while you're doing it, it's rather nice. If you were a country, you probably would be running a trade deficit now since, most likely, you're consuming (importing) more than you're producing (exporting). How can you do that? By living off past savings, getting support from your parents or a spouse, or borrowing.

Countries have the same options. They can live off foreign aid, past savings, or loans. The U.S. economy is currently financing its trade deficit by selling off assets—financial assets such as stocks and bonds, or real assets such as real estate and corporations. Since the assets of the United States total many trillions of dollars, it can continue to run trade deficits of a similar size for years to come, but in doing so it is reducing its wealth each year.

Q-2 Will a debtor nation necessarily be running a trade deficit?

The United States has not always run a trade deficit. Following World War II it ran trade surpluses—an excess of exports over imports—with other countries, so it was an international lender. Thus, it acquired large amounts of foreign assets. Because of the large trade deficits the United States has run since the 1980s, now the United States is a large debtor nation. The United States has borrowed more from abroad than it has lent abroad.

As the United States has gone from being a large creditor nation to being the world's biggest debtor, international considerations have been forced on the nation. The cushion of being a creditor—of having a flow of interest income—has been replaced by the trials of being a debtor and having to pay out interest every year without currently getting anything for it when they pay that interest.

One way countries try to reduce trade deficits is to reduce imports by restricting trade. These trade restrictions can keep a country from having to face the adjustments associated with improving its comparative advantage either by reducing wages or, as we saw in Chapter 8, by allowing its currency to depreciate.

Varieties of Trade Restrictions

Three policies used to restrict trade are

1. Tariffs (taxes on internationally traded goods).
2. Quotas (quantity limits placed on imports).
3. Regulatory trade restrictions (government-imposed procedural rules that limit imports).

The policies countries can use to restrict trade include tariffs and quotas, voluntary restraint agreements, embargoes, regulatory trade restrictions, and nationalistic appeals. I'll consider each in turn and also review the geometric analysis of each.

Tariffs and Quotas

A **tariff** is a *tax that governments place on internationally traded goods*—generally imports. (Tariffs are also called *customs duties.*) Tariffs are the most-used and most-familiar type of trade restriction. Tariffs operate in the same way a tax does: They make imported goods relatively more expensive than they otherwise would have been, and thereby encourage the consumption of domestically produced goods. On average, U.S. tariffs raise the price of imported goods by less than 3 percent. Figure 19-3(a) presents average tariff rates for industrial goods for a number of countries and Figure 19-3(b) shows the tariff rates imposed by the United States since 1920.

FIGURE 19-3 (A AND B) Selected Tariff Rates

The tariff rates in **(a)** will be continually changing as the changes negotiated by the World Trade Organization come into effect. In **(b)** you see tariff rates for the United States since 1920.

Source: General Agreement on Tariffs and Trade (GATT) and the World Bank (www.worldbank.org).

Country	%	Country	%
Argentina	12.2	Norway	3.1
Australia	3.9	Philippines	2.8
Canada	3.4	Poland	2.0
Colombia	11.6	Singapore	0
Czech Rep.	2.0	South Africa	5.7
Hungary	2.0	Sri Lanka	9.0
India	6.9	Thailand	4.8
Indonesia	2.4	United States	2.1
Japan	2.7	Venezuela	12.2
Mexico	8.4	Zimbabwe	17.1

(a) Tariff Rates by Country

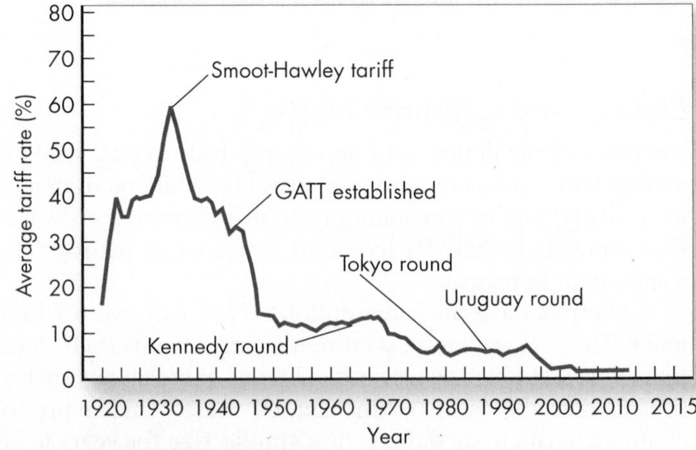

(b) U.S. Tariff Rates since 1920

Probably the most infamous tariff in U.S. history is the Smoot-Hawley Tariff of 1930, which raised tariffs on imported goods to an average of 60 percent. It was passed at the height of the Great Depression in the United States in the hope of protecting American jobs. It didn't work. Other countries responded with similar tariffs. Partly as a result of these trade wars, international trade plummeted from $60 billion in 1928 to $25 billion in 1938, unemployment worsened, and the international depression deepened. These effects of the tariff convinced many, if not most, economists that free trade is preferable to trade restrictions.

Q-3 How are tariffs like taxes? Demonstrate with a supply and demand curve.

The dismal failure of the Smoot-Hawley Tariff was the main reason the **General Agreement on Tariffs and Trade (GATT),** *a regular international conference to reduce trade barriers,* was established in 1947 immediately following World War II. In 1995 GATT was replaced by the **World Trade Organization (WTO),** *an organization whose functions are generally the same as GATT's were—to promote free and fair trade among countries.* Unlike GATT, the WTO is a permanent organization with an enforcement system (albeit weak). Since its formation, rounds of negotiations have resulted in a decline in worldwide tariffs.

A **quota** is a *quantity limit placed on imports.* They have the same effect on equilibrium price and quantity as the quantity restrictions discussed in Chapter 5, and their effect in limiting trade is similar to the effect of a tariff. Both increase price and reduce quantity. Tariffs, like all taxes on suppliers, shift the supply curve up by the amount of the tax, as Figure 19-4 shows. A tariff, T, raises equilibrium price from P_0 to P_1 by an amount that is less than the tariff, and equilibrium quantity declines from Q_0 to Q_1. With a quota, Q_1, the equilibrium price also rises to P_1.

FIGURE 19-4 The Effects of Tariffs and Quotas

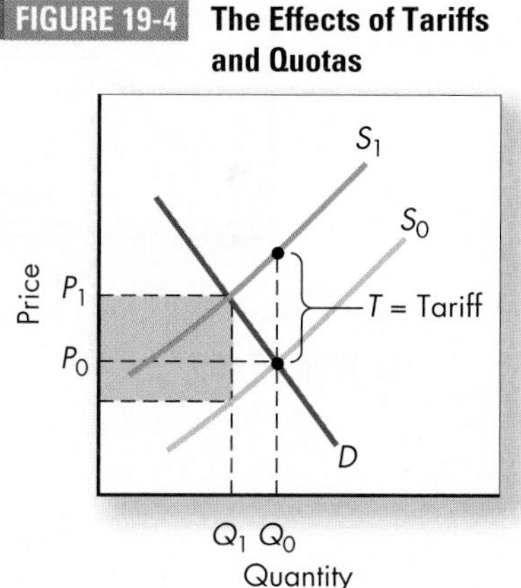

There is, however, a difference between tariffs and quotas. In the case of the tariff, the government collects tariff revenue represented by the shaded region. In the case of a quota, the government collects no revenue. The benefit of the increase in price goes to the importer as additional corporate revenue. So which of the two do you think import companies favor? The quota, of course—it means more profits as long as your company is the one to receive the rights to fill those quotas. In fact, once quotas are instituted, firms compete intensely to get them.

Tariffs affect trade patterns. For example, since the 1960s the United States has imposed a tariff on light trucks from Japan. The result is that the United States imports few light trucks from Japan. You will see Japanese-named trucks, but most of these are produced in the United States. Many similar examples exist, and by following the tariff structure, you can gain a lot of insight into patterns of trade.

The issues involved with tariffs and quotas can be seen in a slightly different way by assuming that the country being considered is small relative to the world economy and that imports compete with domestic producers. The small-country assumption means that the supply from the world to this country is perfectly elastic (horizontal) at the world price, $2, as in Figure 19-5(a).

The world price of the good is unaffected by this country's supply. This assumption allows us to distinguish the world supply from domestic supply. In the absence of any trade restrictions, the world price of $2 would be the domestic price. Domestic low-cost suppliers would supply 100 units of the good at $2. The remaining 100 units demanded are being imported.

Tariffs and Quotas

In Figure 19-5(a) I show the effect of a tariff of 50 cents placed on all imports. Since the world supply curve is perfectly elastic, all of this tax, shown by the shaded region, is borne by domestic consumers. Price rises to $2.50 and quantity demanded falls to 175. With a tariff, the rise in price will increase domestic quantity supplied from 100 to 125 and will reduce imports to 50. Now let's compare this situation with a quota of 50, shown in Figure 19-5(b). Under a quota of 50, the final price would be the same, but higher revenue would accrue to foreign and domestic producers rather than to the government. One final difference: Any increase in demand under a quota would

Q-4 Why do importers prefer a quota to a tariff? Why does government prefer a tariff?

FIGURE 19-5 (A AND B) Tariffs and Quotas When the Domestic Country Is Small

This exhibit shows the effects of a tariff in (**a**) and of a quota in (**b**) when the domestic country is small. The small-country assumption means that the world supply is perfectly elastic, in this case at $2.00 a unit. With a tariff of 50 cents, world supply shifts up by 50 cents. Domestic quantity demanded falls to 175 and domestic quantity supplied rises to 125. Foreign suppliers are left supplying the difference, 50 units. The domestic government collects revenue shown in the shaded area. The figure in (**b**) shows how the same result can be achieved with a quota of 50. Equilibrium price rises to $2.50. Domestic firms produce 125 units and consumers demand 175 units. The difference between the tariff and the quota is that, with a tariff, the domestic government collects the revenue from the higher price. With a quota, the benefits of the higher price accrue to the foreign and domestic producers.

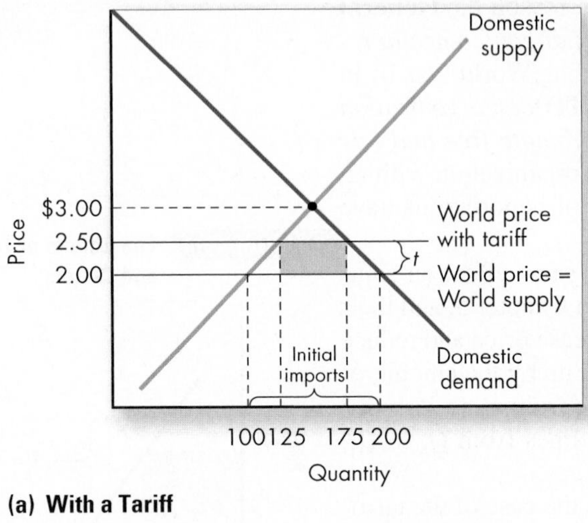

(a) With a Tariff

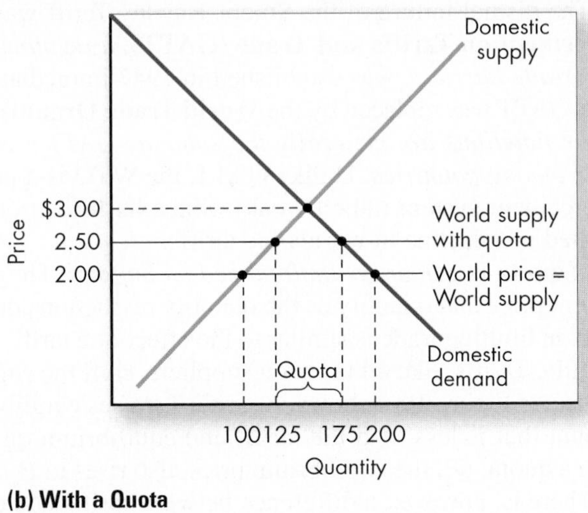

(b) With a Quota

result in higher prices because it would have to be filled by domestic producers. Under a tariff, any increase in demand would not affect price.

Voluntary Restraint Agreements

Voluntary restraint agreements are often not all that voluntary.

Imposing new tariffs and quotas is specifically ruled out by the WTO, but foreign countries know that WTO rules are voluntary and that, if a domestic industry brought sufficient political pressure on its government, the WTO rules would be forgotten. To avoid the imposition of new tariffs on their goods, countries often voluntarily restrict their exports. That's why Japan has, at times, agreed informally to limit the number of cars it exports to the United States.

The effect of such voluntary restraint agreements is similar to the effect of quotas: They directly limit the quantity of imports, increasing the price of the good and helping domestic producers. For example, when the United States encouraged Japan to impose "voluntary" quotas on exports of its cars to the United States, Toyota benefited from the quotas because it could price its limited supply of cars higher than it could if it sent in a large number of cars, so profit per car would be high. Since they faced less competition, U.S. car companies also benefited. They could increase their prices because Toyota had done so. As Chinese car companies develop in the next decade, we can expect similar pushes for Chinese voluntary restraints.

Embargoes

An embargo is a total restriction on import or export of a good.

An **embargo** is *a total restriction on the import or export of a good.* Embargoes are usually established for international political reasons rather than for primarily economic reasons.

An example was the U.S. embargo of trade with Iraq prior to the U.S. invasion in 2001. The U.S. government hoped that the embargo would so severely affect Iraq's economy that Saddam Hussein would lose political power. It did make life difficult for Iraqis, but it did not bring about the downfall of the Hussein government. The United States has imposed embargoes on Cuba, Iran, and Libya.

Regulatory Trade Restrictions

Tariffs, quotas, and embargoes are the primary *direct* methods to restrict international trade. There are also indirect methods that restrict trade in not-so-obvious ways; these are called **regulatory trade restrictions** (*government-imposed procedural rules that limit imports*). One type of regulatory trade restriction has to do with protecting the health and safety of a country's residents. For example, a country might restrict imports of all vegetables grown where certain pesticides are used, knowing full well that all other countries use those pesticides. The effect of such a regulation would be to halt the import of vegetables. Another example involves building codes. U.S. building codes require that plywood have fewer than, say, three flaws per sheet. Canadian building codes require that plywood have fewer than, say, five flaws per sheet. The different building codes are a nontariff barrier that makes trade in building materials between the United States and Canada difficult.

WWW Web Note 19.1
Sugar Regulation

A second type of regulatory restriction involves making import and customs procedures so intricate and time-consuming that importers simply give up. For example, at one time France required all imported electronics to be individually inspected in Toulouse. Since Toulouse is a provincial city, far from any port and outside the normal route for imports after they enter France, the inspection process took months.

Q-5 How might a country benefit from having an inefficient customs agency?

Some regulatory restrictions are imposed for legitimate reasons; others are designed simply to make importing more difficult and hence protect domestic producers from international competition. It's often hard to tell the difference. A good example of this difficulty began in 1988, when the EU disallowed all imports of meat from animals that had been fed growth-inducing hormones. As the box "Hormones and Economics" details, the debate continues.

Some regulatory restrictions are imposed for legitimate reasons; others are designed simply to make importing more difficult.

Nationalistic Appeals and "Buy Domestic" Requirements

Finally, nationalistic appeals can help to restrict international trade. "Buy American" campaigns and Japanese xenophobia[1] are examples. Many Americans, given two products of equal appeal, except that one is made in the United States and one is made in a foreign country, would buy the U.S. product. To get around this tendency, foreign and U.S. companies often go to great lengths to get a MADE IN THE U.S.A. classification on goods they sell in the United States. For example, components for many autos are made in Japan but shipped to the United States and assembled in Ohio or Tennessee so that the finished car can be called an American product. These "Buy American" policies can even be requirements. For example, the U.S. government stimulus package of 2009 included a "Buy American" clause that required recipients to spend the money they received on American, not foreign, goods.

WWW Web Note 19.2
Buy American

Reasons for Trade Restrictions

Let's now turn to a different question: If trade is beneficial, as it is in our example of I.T. in Chapter 8, why do countries restrict trade?

---

[1]*Xenophobia* is a Greek word meaning "fear of foreigners." Pronounce the *x* like *z*.

REAL-WORLD APPLICATION

Hormones and Economics

Trade restrictions, in practice, are often much more complicated than they seem in textbooks. Seldom does a country say, "We're limiting imports to protect our home producers." Instead the country explains the restrictions in a more politically acceptable way. Consider the fight between the European Union (EU) and the United States over U.S. meat exports. In 1988 the EU, in line with Union-wide internal requirements, banned imports of any meat from animals treated with growth-inducing hormones, which U.S. meat producers use extensively. The result: the EU banned the meat exported from the United States.

The EU claimed that it had imposed the ban only because of public health concerns. The United States claimed that the ban was actually a trade restriction, pointing out that its own residents ate this kind of meat with confidence because a U.S. government agency had certified that the levels of hormones in the meat were far below any danger level.

The United States retaliated against the EU by imposing 100 percent tariffs on Danish and West German hams, Italian tomatoes, and certain other foods produced by EU member nations. The EU threatened to respond by placing 100 percent tariffs on $100 million worth of U.S. walnuts and dried fruits, but instead entered into bilateral meetings with the United States. Those meetings allowed untreated meats into the EU for human consumption and treated meats that would be used as dog food. In response, the United States removed its retaliatory tariff on hams and tomato sauce, but retained its tariffs on many other goods. In the 1990s, Europe's dog population seemed to be growing exponentially as Europe's imports of "dog food" increased by leaps and bounds. In 1996 the United States asked the WTO to review the EU ban. It did so in 1997, finding in favor of the United States. The EU appealed and in 1999 the WTO stood by its earlier ruling and the United States reimposed the 100 percent tariffs. Since then, the EU has stood firm and has conducted studies that, it says, show the use of growth hormones to be unsafe, but the WTO continues to rule that they are safe. In 2004, the EU replaced its ban on U.S. beef with a provisional ban until it collects more information, and argued that this provisional ban met the WTO rules. The United States disagreed and continued its retaliatory tariffs. In January 2009, for example, the U.S. government placed a 300 percent tariff on Roquefort cheese as one of its retaliatory measures but quickly removed it temporarily. So the dispute continues more than 25 years after it started.

Which side is right in this dispute? The answer is far from obvious. Both the United States and the EU have potentially justifiable positions. As I said, trade restrictions are more complicated in reality than in textbooks.

Unequal Internal Distribution of the Gains from Trade

One reason is that the gains of trade are not equally distributed. In the example of the argument for trade discussed in a previous chapter, I.T. persuaded Saudi Arabia to specialize in the production of oil rather than food, and persuaded the United States to produce more food than oil. That means, of course, that some U.S. oil workers will have to become farmers, and in Saudi Arabia some farmers will have to become oil producers.

Often people don't want to make radical changes in the kind of work they do—they want to keep on producing what they're already producing. So when these people see the same kinds of goods that they produce coming into their country from abroad, they lobby to prevent the foreign competition.

Had I.T. been open about the difficulties of trading, he would have warned the countries that change is hard. It has very real costs that I.T. didn't point out when he made his offers. Economists generally favor free trade because the costs of trade are temporary, whereas gains from trade are permanent. Once the adjustment has been made, the costs will be gone but the benefits will still be there.

For most goods, the benefits for the large majority of the population so outweigh the costs to some individuals that, decided on a strict cost/benefit basis, international trade is still a deal you can't refuse. The table below lists economists' estimates of the cost to consumers of saving a job in some industries through trade restrictions.

Industry	Cost of Production (per job saved)
Footwear	$505,000
Sugar	213,000
Apparel	181,000
Dairy	167,000
Canned tuna	43,000

Source: *Economic Effects of Significant Import Restraints,* U.S. International Trade Commission (www.usitc.gov).

With benefits so outweighing costs, it would seem that transition costs could be forgotten. But they can't.

Benefits of trade are generally widely scattered among the entire population. In contrast, costs of free trade often fall on small groups of people who loudly oppose the particular free trade that hurts them. This creates a political push against free trade.

Benefits of trade are generally widely scattered among the entire population. In contrast, costs of free trade often fall on specific small groups.

It isn't only in the United States that the push for trade restrictions focuses on the small costs and not on the large benefits. For example, the European Union (EU) places large restrictions on food imports from nonmember nations. If the EU were to remove those barriers, food prices in EU countries would decline significantly—it is estimated that meat prices alone would fall by about 65 percent. Consumers would benefit, but farmers would be hurt. The farmers, however, have the political clout to see that the costs are considered and the benefits aren't. The result: The EU places high duties on foreign agricultural products.

Q-6 Who is likely to be more vocal when lobbying government to impose trade restrictions: producers or consumers? Explain your answer.

The cost to society of relaxing trade restrictions has led to a number of programs to assist those who are hurt. Such programs are called **trade adjustment assistance programs**—*programs designed to compensate losers for reductions in trade restrictions.*

Governments have tried to use trade adjustment assistance to facilitate free trade, but they've found that it's enormously difficult to limit the adjustment assistance to those who are actually hurt by international trade. As soon as people find that there's assistance for people injured by trade, they're likely to try to show that they too have been hurt and deserve assistance. Losses from free trade become exaggerated and magnified. Instead of only a small portion of the gains from trade being needed for trade adjustment assistance, much more is demanded—often even more than the gains.

Telling people who claim to be hurt that they aren't really being hurt isn't good politics. That's why offering trade adjustment assistance as a way to relieve the pressure to restrict trade is a deal many governments can refuse.

Telling people who claim to be hurt that they aren't really being hurt isn't good politics.

Haggling by Companies over the Gains from Trade

Many naturally advantageous bargains aren't consummated because each side is pushing for a larger share of the gains from trade than the other side thinks should be allotted.

To see how companies haggling over the gains of trade can restrict trade, let's reconsider the original deal that I.T. proposed in an earlier chapter explaining comparative advantage. I.T. got 380 tons of food and 380 barrels of oil. The United States got an additional 100 tons of food and 60 barrels of oil. Saudi Arabia got an additional 100 barrels of oil and 60 tons of food.

Suppose the Saudis had said, "Why should we be getting only 100 barrels of oil and 60 tons of food when I.T. is getting 380 barrels of oil and 380 tons of food? We want an additional 300 tons of food and another 300 barrels of oil, and we won't deal unless we get them." Similarly, the United States might have said, "We want an additional 300 tons of food and an additional 300 barrels of oil, and we won't go through with the deal unless we get them." If either the U.S. or the Saudi Arabian company that was involved in the trade for its country (or both) takes this position, I.T. might just walk—no deal. Tough bargaining positions can make it almost impossible to achieve gains from trade.

Strategic bargaining can lead to higher gains from trade for the side that drives the hardest bargain, but it also can make the deal fall through.

The side that drives the hardest bargain gets the most gains from the bargain, but it also risks making the deal fall through. Such strategic bargaining goes on all the time. **Strategic bargaining** means *demanding a larger share of the gains from trade than you can reasonably expect.* If you're successful, you get the lion's share; if you're not successful, the deal falls apart and everyone is worse off.

Haggling by Countries over Trade Restrictions

Another type of trade bargaining that often limits trade is bargaining between countries. Trade restrictions and the threat of trade restrictions play an important role in that kind of haggling. Sometimes countries must go through with trade restrictions that they really don't want to impose, just to make their threats credible.

Once one country has imposed trade restrictions, other countries attempt to get those restrictions reduced by threatening to increase their own restrictions. Again, to make the threat credible, sometimes countries must impose or increase trade restrictions simply to show they're willing to do so. For example, China allowed significant illegal copying of U.S. software without paying royalties. The United States put pressure on China to stop such copying and felt that China was not responding effectively. To force compliance, the United States made a list of Chinese goods that it threatened with 100 percent tariffs unless China complied. The United States did not want to put on these restrictions but felt that it would have more strategic bargaining power if it threatened to do so. Hence the name **strategic trade policies**—*threatening to implement tariffs to bring about a reduction in tariffs or some other concession from the other country.*

Q-7 True or false? In strategic trade bargaining, it is sometimes reasonable to be unreasonable. Explain.

Strategic trade policies are threats to implement tariffs to bring about a reduction in tariffs or some other concession from the other country.

Ultimately, strategic bargaining power depends on negotiators' skills and the underlying gains from trade that a country would receive. A country that would receive only a small portion of the gains from trade is in a much stronger bargaining position than a country that would receive significant gains. It's easier for the former to walk away from trade.

The potential problem with strategic trade policies is that they can backfire. One rule of strategic bargaining is that the other side must believe that you'll go through with your threat. Thus, strategic trade policy can lead a country that actually supports free trade to impose trade restrictions, just to show how strongly it believes in free trade.

Specialized Production

My discussion of comparative advantage took as a given that one country was inherently more productive than another country in producing certain goods. But when one looks at trading patterns, it's often not at all clear why particular countries have a productive advantage in certain goods. There's no inherent reason for Switzerland to specialize in the production of watches or for South Korea to specialize in the production of cars. Much in trade cannot be explained by inherent comparative advantages due to resource endowments. If they don't have inherent advantages, why are countries and places often so good at producing what they specialize in? Two important explanations are *learning by doing* and *economies of scale.*

REAL-WORLD APPLICATION

The Antiglobalization Forces

Often when the World Trade Organization or a similar type of organization promoting free trade hosts a meeting, protests (sometimes violent ones) are held by a loosely organized collection of groups opposing globalization. The goals of these groups are varied. Some argue that trade hurts developed countries such as the United States; others argue that it hurts developing countries by exploiting poor workers so that Westerners can get luxuries cheaply. Still others argue against a more subtle Western economic imperialism in which globalization spreads Western cultural values and undermines developing countries' social structures.

Each of these arguments has some appeal, although making the first two simultaneously is difficult because it says that voluntary trade hurts both parties to the trade. But the arguments have had little impact on the views of most policy makers and economists.

Supporting free trade does not mean that globalization has no costs. It does have costs, but many of the costs associated with free trade are really the result of technological changes. The reality is that technological developments, such as those in telecommunications and transportation, are pushing countries closer together and will involve difficult social and cultural changes, regardless of whether trade is free or not. Restricting trade might temporarily slow these changes but is unlikely to stop them.

Most empirical studies have found that, with regard to material goods, the workers in developing countries involved in trade are generally better off than those not involved in trade. That's why most developing countries work hard to encourage companies to move production facilities into their countries. From a worker's perspective, earning $4 a day can look quite good when the alternative is earning $3 a day. Would the worker rather earn $10 a day? Of course, but the higher the wages in a given country, the less likely it is that firms are going to locate production there.

Many economists are sympathetic to various antiglobalization arguments, but they often become frustrated at the lack of clarity of the antiglobalization groups' views. To oppose something is not enough; to effect positive change, one must both (1) understand how the thing one opposes works and (2) have a realistic plan for a better alternative.

Learning by Doing **Learning by doing** means *becoming better at a task the more often you perform it.* Take watches in Switzerland. Initially production of watches in Switzerland may have been a coincidence; the person who started the watch business happened to live there. But then people in the area became skilled in producing watches. Their skill made it attractive for other watch companies to start up. As additional companies moved in, more and more members of the labor force became skilled at watchmaking and word went out that Swiss watches were the best in the world. That reputation attracted even more producers, so Switzerland became the watchmaking capital of the world. Had the initial watch production occurred in Austria, not Switzerland, Austria might be the watch capital of the world.

Learning by doing means becoming better at a task the more you perform it.

When there's learning by doing, it's much harder to attribute inherent comparative advantage to a country. One must always ask: Does country A have an inherent comparative advantage, or does it simply have more experience? Once country B gets the experience, will country A's comparative advantage disappear? If it will, then country B has a strong reason to limit trade with country A in order to give its own workers time to catch up as they learn by doing.

Economies of Scale In determining whether an inherent comparative advantage exists, a second complication is **economies of scale**—*the situation in which costs per unit of output fall as output increases.* Many manufacturing industries (such as steel and autos) exhibit economies of scale. The existence of significant economies of

In economies of scale, costs per unit of output go down as output increases.

scale means that it makes sense (that is, it lowers costs) for one country to specialize in one good and another country to specialize in another good. But who should specialize in what is unclear. Producers in a country can, and generally do, argue that if only the government would establish barriers, they would be able to lower their costs per unit and eventually sell at lower costs than foreign producers.

Q-8 Is it efficient for a country to maintain a trade barrier in an industry that exhibits economies of scale?

Most countries recognize the importance of learning by doing and economies of scale. A variety of trade restrictions are based on these two phenomena. The most common expression of the learning-by-doing and economies-of-scale insights is the **infant industry argument,** which is that *with initial protection, an industry will be able to become competitive.* Countries use this argument to justify many trade restrictions. They argue, "You may now have a comparative advantage, but that's simply because you've been at it longer, or are experiencing significant economies of scale. We need trade restrictions on our _____ industry to give it a chance to catch up. Once an infant industry grows up, then we can talk about eliminating the restrictions."

The infant industry argument says that with initial protection, an industry will be able to become competitive.

This infant industry argument also has been used to justify tariffs on new high-tech products such as solar panels. U.S. firms have pushed for tariffs on Chinese solar panels so that they can develop the technology here in the United States rather than have the technology developed in China.

Macroeconomic Costs of Trade

The comparative advantage argument for free trade assumes that a country's resources are fully utilized. When countries don't have full employment, imports can decrease domestic aggregate demand and increase unemployment. Exports can stimulate domestic aggregate demand and decrease unemployment. Thus, when an economy is in a recession, there is a strong macroeconomic reason to limit imports and encourage exports. These macroeconomic effects of free trade play an important role in the public's view of imports and exports. When a country is in a recession, pressure to impose trade restrictions increases substantially. We saw this in 2009 when, faced with the job losses due to the serious recession, there was serious pressure to design programs to keep spending in the United States where it would create jobs and not be spent on imports that would create jobs for other countries.

National Security

Countries often justify trade restrictions on grounds of national security. These restrictions take two forms:

1. Export restrictions on strategic materials and defense-related goods.
2. Import restrictions on defense-related goods. For example, in a war we don't want to be dependent on oil from abroad.

For a number of goods, national security considerations make sense. For example, the United States restricts the sale of certain military items to countries that may be fighting the United States someday. The problem is where to draw the line about goods having a national security consideration. Should countries protect domestic agriculture? All high-technology items, since they might be useful in weapons? All chemicals? Steel? When a country makes a national security argument for trade, we must be careful to consider whether a domestic political reason may be lurking behind that argument.

Reasons for restricting trade include:

1. Unequal internal distribution of the gains from trade.
2. Haggling by companies over the gains from trade.
3. Haggling by countries over trade restrictions.
4. Specialized production: learning by doing and economies of scale.
5. Macroeconomic aspects of trade.
6. National security.
7. International politics.
8. Increased revenue brought in by tariffs.

International Politics

International politics frequently provides another reason for trade restrictions. Over the past decades, the United States restricted trade with Cuba to punish that country for trying to extend its Marxist political and economic policies to other Latin American countries. The United States also has trade restrictions on Iran for its reluctance to limit its nuclear enrichment activities. The list can be extended, but you get the argument: Trade helps you, so we'll hurt you by stopping trade until you do what we want. So what if it hurts us too? It'll hurt you more than it hurts us.

Increased Revenue Brought in by Tariffs

A final argument made for one particular type of trade restriction—a tariff—is that tariffs bring in revenues. In the 19th century, tariffs were the U.S. government's primary source of revenue. They are less important as a source of revenue today for many developed countries because those countries have instituted other forms of taxes. However, tariffs remain a primary source of revenue for many developing countries. They're relatively easy to collect and are paid by people rich enough to afford imports. These countries justify many of their tariffs with the argument that they need the revenues.

Why Economists Generally Oppose Trade Restrictions

Each of the preceding arguments for trade restrictions has some validity, but most economists discount them and support free trade. The reason is that, in their considered judgment, the harm done by trade restrictions outweighs the benefits. This is true, even though, from the U.S. perspective, transferable comparative advantages are likely to place significant pressures on firms to outsource U.S. jobs abroad, and hold down U.S. wages in the coming decades. Most economists believe that the United States will be better off if it allows free trade.

Economists generally oppose trade restrictions because:

1. From a global perspective, free trade increases total output.
2. International trade provides competition for domestic companies.
3. Restrictions based on national security are often abused or evaded.
4. Trade restrictions are addictive.

Free Trade Increases Total Output Economists' first argument for free trade is that, viewed from a global perspective, free trade increases total output. From a national perspective, economists agree that particular instances of trade restrictions may actually help one nation, even as most other nations are hurt. But they argue that the country imposing trade restrictions can benefit *only if the other country doesn't retaliate* with trade restrictions of its own. Retaliation is the rule, not the exception, however, and when there is retaliation, trade restrictions cause both countries to lose. Thus, if the United States were to place a tariff on goods from China, those aspects of production that depend on Chinese goods would be hurt, and, as I discussed above, there are many such goods. Moreover, China would likely place tariffs on goods from the United States, hurting both countries. Such tariffs would cut overall production, making both countries worse off.

International Trade Provides Competition A second reason most economists support free trade is that trade restrictions reduce international competition. International competition is desirable because it forces domestic companies to stay on their toes. If trade restrictions on imports are imposed, domestic companies don't work as hard and therefore become less efficient.

For example, in the 1950s and 1960s, the United States imposed restrictions on imported steel. U.S. steel industries responded to this protection by raising their prices and channeling profits from their steel production into other activities. By the 1970s, the U.S. steel industry was using outdated equipment to produce overpriced steel. Instead of making the steel industry stronger, restrictions made it a flabby, uncompetitive industry.

In the 1980s and 1990s, the U.S. steel industry became less and less profitable. Larger mills closed or consolidated, while nonunion minimills, which made new steel out of scrap steel, did well. By the late 1990s, minimills accounted for 45 percent of total U.S. steel production. In 2002 it looked as if a number of larger mills were going to declare bankruptcy, and enormous pressure was placed on the federal government to bail them out by taking over their pension debt and instituting tariffs. The U.S. government responded by imposing 20–30 percent tariffs on foreign steel imports. Most economists opposed the tariffs and pointed out that they were unlikely to lead to a rebuilding of the U.S. steel industry because other countries had a comparative advantage in steel production. Moreover, other countries would retaliate with tariffs on U.S. goods. Despite their opposition, the tariffs were instituted. Major U.S. trading partners—including EU countries, Japan, and China—responded by threatening to implement tariffs on U.S. goods worth about $335 million; in 2003, the U.S. government withdrew the tariffs. That same year. U.S. Steel, which was the number two producer of steel in the United States, closed. Today, U.S. steel companies produce about 6 percent of total world steel, down from 20 percent in 1970.

Very few of the infant industries protected by trade restrictions have ever grown up.

The benefits of international competition are not restricted to mature industries like steel; they can also accrue to young industries wherever they appear. Economists dispose of the infant industry argument by referencing the historical record. In theory the argument makes sense. But very few of the infant industries protected by trade restrictions have ever grown up. What tends to happen instead is that infant industries become dependent on the trade restrictions and use political pressure to keep that protection. As a result, they often remain immature and internationally uncompetitive. Most economists would support the infant industry argument only if the trade restrictions included definite conditions under which the restrictions would end.

WWW Web Note 19.3 Thumbs Up or Down?

Restrictions Based on National Security Are Often Abused or Evaded Most economists agree with the national security argument for export restrictions on goods that are directly war related. Selling bombs to Iran, whom the United States has called a member of the Axis of Evil, doesn't make much sense. Economists point out that the argument is often carried far beyond goods directly related to national security. For example, in the 1980s the United States restricted exports of sugar-coated cereals to the Soviet Union purportedly for reasons of national security. Sugar-frosted flakes may be great, but they were unlikely to help the Soviet Union in a war.

Another argument that economists give against the national security rationale is that trade restrictions on military sales can often be evaded. Countries simply have another country buy the goods for them. Such third-party sales—called *transshipments*—are common in international trade and limit the effectiveness of any absolute trade restrictions for national security purposes.

Economists also argue that by fostering international cooperation, international trade makes war less likely—a significant contribution to national security.

Yes, some restrictions might benefit a country, but almost no country can limit its restrictions to the beneficial ones.

Trade Restrictions Are Addictive Economists' final argument against trade restrictions is: Yes, some restrictions might benefit a country, but almost no country can limit its restrictions to the beneficial ones. Trade restrictions are addictive—the more you have, the more you want. Thus, a majority of economists take the position that the best response to such addictive policies is "Just say no."

Institutions Supporting Free Trade

WWW Web Note 19.4 Promoting Trade

As I have stated throughout the text, economists generally like markets and favor trade being as free as possible. They argue that trade allows specialization and the division of labor. When each country follows its comparative advantage, production is more efficient and the production possibility curve shifts out. These views mean that most economists, liberal and conservative alike, generally oppose international trade restrictions.

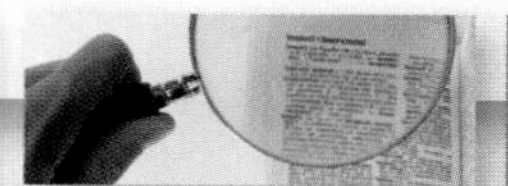

ADDED DIMENSION

Dumping

The WTO allows countries to impose trade restrictions on imports if they can show that the goods are being dumped. *Dumping* is selling a good in a foreign country at a lower price than in the country where it's produced. On the face of it, who could complain about someone who wants to sell you a good cheaply? Why not just take advantage of the bargain price? The first objection is the learning-by-doing argument. To stay competitive, a country must keep on producing. Dumping by another country can force domestic producers out of business. Having eliminated the competition, the foreign producer has the field to itself and can raise the price. Thus, dumping can be a form of predatory pricing.

The second argument against dumping involves the short-term macroeconomic and political effects it can have on the importing country. Even if one believes that dumping is not a preliminary to predatory pricing, it can displace workers in the importing country, causing political pressure on that government to institute trade restrictions. If that country's economy is in a recession, the resulting unemployment will have substantial macroeconomic repercussions, so pressure for trade restrictions will be amplified.

Despite political pressures to restrict trade, governments have generally tried to follow economists' advice and have entered into a variety of international agreements and organizations. The most important is the World Trade Organization (WTO), which has over 150 members, and is the successor to the General Agreement on Tariffs and Trade (GATT). You will still occasionally see references to GATT, even though the WTO has taken its place. One of the differences between the WTO and GATT is that the WTO includes some enforcement mechanisms.

Q-9 What are two important international economic organizations?

Achieving agreement on trade barrier reductions is politically difficult, as is demonstrated by the latest WTO negotiations, called the Doha Development Round. Begun in 2001, it was meant to lead to fairer trade rules for developing countries, especially in agriculture. The Round did not go well; the United States and Europe were unwilling to eliminate subsidies to their farmers that the developing countries said made it impossible for them to compete fairly, and hence would not reduce their tariffs on manufactured goods. The Round was never concluded.

The push for free trade has a geographic dimension, which includes **free trade associations**—*groups of countries that have reduced or eliminated trade barriers among themselves.* The European Union (EU) is the most famous free trade association. All barriers to trade among the EU's member countries were removed in 1992, and over the next 20 years the EU expanded significantly. In 1993, the United States and Canada agreed to enter into a similar free trade union, and they, together with Mexico, created the North American Free Trade Association (NAFTA). Under NAFTA, tariffs and other trade barriers among these countries are being gradually reduced. Some other trading associations include Mercosur (among South American countries) and ASEAN (among Southeast Asian countries).

A free trade association is a group of countries that allows free trade among its members and puts up common barriers against all other countries' goods.

Economists have mixed reactions to free trade associations. They see free trade as beneficial, but they are concerned about the possibility that these regional free trade associations will impose significant trade restrictions on nonmember countries. They also believe that bilateral negotiations between member nations will replace multilateral efforts among members and nonmembers. Whether the net effect of these bilateral negotiations is positive or negative remains to be seen.

Q-10 What is economists' view of limited free trade associations such as the EU or NAFTA?

Groups of other countries have loose trading relationships because of cultural or historical reasons. These loose trading relationships are sometimes called trading zones. For example, many European countries maintain close trading ties with many of their former colonies in Africa where they fit into a number of overlapping trading zones. European companies tend to see that central area as their turf. The United States has close ties in Latin America, making the Western hemisphere another trading zone. Another example of a trading zone is that of Japan and its economic ties with other Far East countries; Japanese companies often see that area as their commercial domain.

These trading zones overlap, sometimes on many levels. For instance, Australia and England, Portugal and Brazil, and the United States and Saudi Arabia are tied together for historical or political reasons, and those ties lead to increased trade between them that seems to deviate from the above trading zones. Similarly, as companies become more and more global, it is harder and harder to associate companies with particular countries. Let me give an example: Do you know who the largest exporters of cars from the United States are? The answer is: Japanese automobile companies! Thus, there is no hard-and-fast specification of trading zones, and knowing history and politics is important to understanding many of the relationships.

A most-favored nation is a country that will pay as low a tariff on its exports as will any other country.

One way countries strengthen trading relationships among groups of countries is through a most-favored-nation status. The term **most-favored nation** refers to *a country that will be charged as low a tariff on its exports as any other country.* Thus, if the United States lowers tariffs on goods imported from Japan, which has most-favored-nation status with the United States, it must lower tariffs on those same types of goods imported from any other country with most-favored-nation status.

Conclusion

The difficulties that globalization and trade bring to a country—the effect on income distribution, and the wrenching structural changes it requires—lead many laypeople to support trade restrictions such as tariffs, quotas, and indeed anything to protect domestic jobs. Such policies might alleviate some short-run problems, but they ultimately will be unlikely to work. Not only will other countries retaliate; they will also take advantage of trade. So if the United States closes off trade with China, other countries will emerge as competitors.

The problem comes when we don't face up to those problems and don't deal with the political problems that an expansion of trade creates. The United States has avoided dealing with these problems for the last 20 years, and the problems have built up. The result is the current high unemployment and sluggish economic growth in the United States. The large trade deficits run up over the past 20 years have given us great benefits, but those eventually will end. How we deal with that ending will play a key role in determining the course of the U.S. economy over the next decade.

Summary

- The nature of trade is continually changing. The United States is importing more and more high-tech goods and services from India and China and other East Asian countries. *(LO19-1)*
- Outsourcing is a type of trade. Outsourcing is a larger phenomenon today compared to 30 years ago because China and India are so large, enormous outsourcing is possible. *(LO19-1)*
- Trade restrictions include tariffs and quotas, embargoes, voluntary restraint agreements, regulatory trade restrictions, and nationalistic appeals. *(LO19-2)*
- Reasons that countries impose trade restrictions include unequal internal distribution of the gains from trade, haggling by companies over the gains from trade, haggling by countries over trade restrictions, learning by doing and economies of scale, macroeconomic costs of trade, national security, international political reasons, and increased revenue brought in by tariffs. *(LO19-3)*

- Economists generally oppose trade restrictions because of the history of trade restrictions and their understanding of the advantages of free trade. (*LO19-3*)
- The World Trade Organization is an international organization committed to reducing trade barriers. (*LO19-4*)
- Free trade associations help trade by reducing barriers to trade among member nations. Free trade associations could hinder trade by building up barriers to trade with nations outside the association; negotiations among members could replace multilateral efforts to reduce trade restrictions among members and nonmembers. (*LO19-4*)

Key Terms

economies of scale *(421)*
embargo *(416)*
free trade association *(425)*
General Agreement on Tariffs and Trade (GATT) *(415)*
infant industry argument *(422)*
learning by doing *(421)*
most-favored nation *(426)*
quota *(415)*
regulatory trade restriction *(417)*
strategic bargaining *(420)*
strategic trade policy *(420)*
tariff *(414)*
trade adjustment assistance program *(419)*
World Trade Organization (WTO) *(415)*

Questions and Exercises

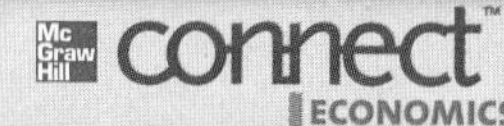

1. How important is international trade in terms of its relationship to total U.S. production? What does this suggest about the importance of trade policies relative to other countries? (*LO19-1*)
2. Which countries are the two greatest trading partners for the United States? With which countries is trade rapidly increasing? (*LO19-1*)
3. Demonstrate graphically how the effects of a tariff differ from the effects of a quota. (*LO19-2*)
4. How do the effects of voluntary restraint agreements differ from the effects of a tariff? (*LO19-2*)
5. The world price of textiles is P_w, as in the accompanying figure of the domestic supply and demand for textiles.

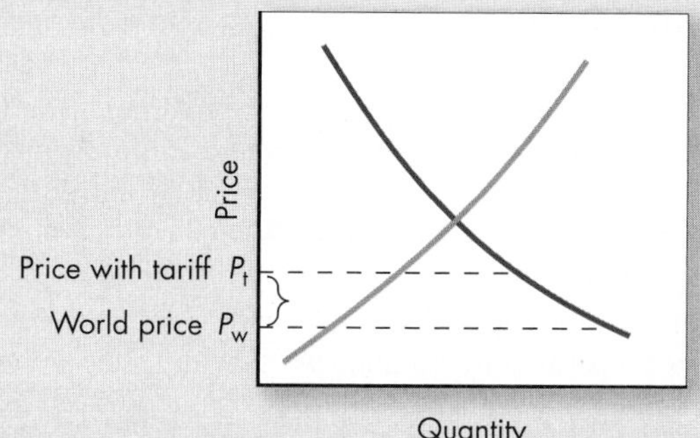

The government imposes a tariff *t*, to protect the domestic producers. For this tariff: (*LO19-2*)
   a. Label the revenue gains to domestic producers.
   b. Label the revenue to government.
   c. Label the costs to domestic producers.
   d. Are the gains to domestic producers greater than the costs? Why?
6. In 1964 President Lyndon B. Johnson imposed the Chicken Tax—a 25 percent tax on all imported light trucks in retaliation for a tariff placed by Germany on chickens imported from the United States. The light-truck tariff hurt Volkswagen van sales. Were these tariffs good or bad from the following perspectives? (*LO19-2*)
   a. The U.S. government.
   b. German consumers of chickens.
   c. U.S. chicken producers.
   d. U.S. light truck producers.
   e. Economists.
7. On January 1, 2005, quotas on clothing imports to the United States first instituted in the 1960s to protect the U.S. garment industry were eliminated. (*LO19-2*)
   a. Demonstrate graphically how this change affected equilibrium price and quantity of imported garments.
   b. Demonstrate graphically how U.S. consumers benefited from the end of the quota system.
   c. What was the likely effect on profits of foreign companies that sold clothing in the U.S. market?
8. What are three reasons countries restrict trade? Are they justified? (*LO19-3*)
9. Why would a country have trade assistance programs? What makes them difficult to implement? (*LO19-3*)
10. How would a credible threat of trade restrictions lead to lower trade restrictions? (*LO19-3*)
11. How are economies of scale, comparative advantage, and trade restrictions related? (*LO19-3*)
12. Name three reasons economists support free trade. (*LO19-3*)

13. Why would a country want to be a most-favored nation? Why might it not want to be a most-favored nation? *(LO19-4)*
14. What is the relationship between GATT and WTO? *(LO19-4)*

Questions from Alternative Perspectives

1. Federic Bastiat wrote that "government is the great fiction through which everybody endeavors to live at the expense of everybody else." Is this a correct way to understand the fight about tariffs? (Austrian)
2. Federic Bastiat wrote: "It seems to me that this is theoretically right, for whatever the question under discussion—whether religious, philosophical, political, or economic; whether it concerns prosperity, morality, equality, right, justice, progress, responsibility, cooperation, property, labor, trade, capital, wages, taxes, population, finance, or government—at whatever point on the scientific horizon I begin my researches, I invariably reach this one conclusion: The solution to the problems of human relationships is to be found in liberty." What is problematic with this view? (Radical)
3. Federic Bastiat wrote "when goods do not cross borders, soldiers will." Discuss. (Religious)
4. Who has benefited most from free trade? Who has been hurt most by it? Does that match the positions the various groups have about their support for free trade? Which group do economists align themselves with? Why? (Post-Keynesian)
5. The text presents free trade as advantageous for developing countries. However, in its period of most rapid development, the half century following the Civil War, the United States imposed tariffs on imports that averaged around 40 percent, a level higher than those in all but one of today's developing economies.
   a. Why did so many of today's industrialized countries not follow those policies as they were developing?
   b. What does this insight into economic history suggest about the doctrine of free trade and whose interests it serves? (Radical)

Issues to Ponder

1. How does considering trade in the broader cultural context change one's analysis?
2. One of the basic economic laws is "the law of one price." It says that given certain assumptions one would expect that if free trade is allowed, the price of goods in countries should converge.
   a. Can you list what three of those assumptions likely are?
   b. Should the law of one price hold for labor also? Why or why not?
   c. Should it hold for capital more so or less so than for labor? Why?
3. Suggest an equitable method of funding trade adjustment assistance programs.
   a. Why is it equitable?
   b. What problems might a politician have in implementing such a method?
4. When the United States placed a temporary price floor on tomatoes imported from Mexico, U.S. trade representative Mickey Kantor said, "The agreement will provide strong relief to the tomato growers in Florida and other states, and help preserve jobs in the industry." What costs did Americans bear from the price floor?
5. Mexico exports many vegetables to the United States. These vegetables are grown using chemicals that are not allowed in U.S. vegetable agriculture. Should the United States restrict imports of Mexican vegetables? Why or why not?
6. The U.S. government taxes U.S. companies for their overseas profits, but it allows them to deduct from their U.S. taxable income the taxes that they pay abroad and interest on loans funding operations abroad, with no limits on the amount deducted.
   a. Is it possible that the overseas profit tax produces no net revenue?
   b. What would you suggest to the government about this tax if its purpose were to increase corporate income tax revenue?
   c. Why might the government keep this tax even if it were not collecting any net revenue?
7. In the 1930s Clair Wilcox of Swarthmore College organized a petition by economists "that any measure which provided for a general upward revision of tariff rates be denied passage by Congress, or if passed, be vetoed." It was signed by one-third of all economists in the United States at the time, of all political persuasions. A month later, the Smoot-Hawley Tariff was passed.
   a. Why did economists oppose the tariff?
   b. Demonstrate the effect of the tariff on the price of goods.

c. How would the tariff help the economy if other countries did not institute a retaliatory tariff?
d. What would be the effect on the macroeconomy if other countries did institute a retaliatory tariff?

8. If you were economic adviser to a country that was following your advice about trade restrictions and that country fell into a recession, would you change your advice? Why, or why not?

Answers to Margin Questions

1. The type of goods being imported has changed from primarily low-tech goods to technologically advanced goods. (*p. 411; LO19-1*)
2. A debtor nation will not necessarily be running a trade deficit. *Debt* refers to accumulated past deficits. If a country had accumulated large deficits in the past, it could run a surplus now but still be a debtor nation. (*p. 414; LO19-1*)
3. Like tariffs, taxes shift the supply of a good up by the amount of the tariff. Equilibrium quantity falls and equilibrium price rises. (*p. 415; LO19-2*)

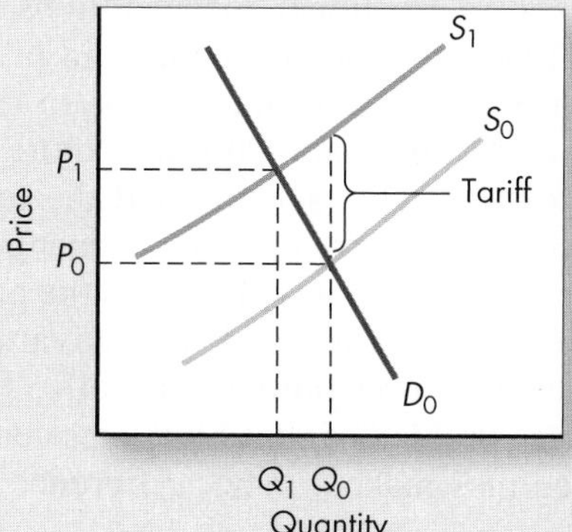

4. Importers prefer quotas because they receive higher prices. Government prefers a tariff because the tariff brings in revenue for government. (*p. 415; LO19-2*)
5. An inefficient customs agency can have the same effect as a trade restriction, and if trade restrictions would help the country, then it is possible that an inefficient customs agency could also help the country. (*p. 417; LO19-2*)
6. Production is concentrated among a small number of firms that stand to benefit from trade restrictions and thus are more likely to combine efforts to lobby government. Because the number of consumers is large and the cost of trade restrictions to each relatively small, consumers have less incentive to take joint action. (*p. 419; LO19-3*)
7. True. In strategic trade bargaining it is sometimes reasonable to be unreasonable. The belief of the other bargainer that you will be unreasonable leads you to be able to extract larger gains from trade. Of course, this leads to the logical paradox that if "unreasonable" is "reasonable," unreasonable really is reasonable, so it is only reasonable to be reasonable. Sorting out that last statement can be left for a philosophy or logic class. (*p. 420; LO19-3*)
8. Whether or not it is efficient for a country to maintain barriers to trade in an industry that exhibits economies of scale depends upon the marginal costs and marginal benefits of maintaining those barriers. Having significant economies of scale does mean that average costs of production will be lower at higher levels of production; however, trade restrictions might mean that the industry is able to inflate its costs. (*p. 422; LO19-3*)
9. Two important international economic organizations are the WTO and GATT, which was replaced by the WTO. (*p. 425; LO19-4*)
10. Most economists have a mixed view of limited free trade associations such as NAFTA or the EU. While they see free trade as beneficial, they are concerned about the possibility that these limited trade associations will impose trade restrictions on nonmember countries. Whether the net effect of these will be positive or negative is a complicated issue. (*p. 425; LO19-4*)

chapter 20

International Financial Policy

> *A foreign exchange dealer's office during a busy spell is the nearest thing to Bedlam I have struck.*
>
> —Harold Wincott

After reading this chapter, you should be able to:

- **LO20-1** Summarize the balance of payments accounts and explain the relationship between the current account and the financial and capital account.
- **LO20-2** Explain how exchange rates are determined and how government can influence them.
- **LO20-3** Discuss the problem of determining the appropriate exchange rate.
- **LO20-4** Differentiate various exchange rate regimes and discuss the advantages and disadvantages of each.

Throughout the book we've seen that exchange rates and international considerations are fundamental to a county's economy and play a major role in its macroeconomic policy. In this chapter we consider international issues more directly. I begin by looking at the balance of payments account and the relationship between the trade and capital accounts. Then we consider exchange rates and the important role they play in the macro economy; I discuss the problems of determining the appropriate exchange rate and the advantages and disadvantages of alternative exchange rate regimes. Finally, I conclude with a discussion of the euro and the problems it has been experiencing as an example of how exchange rate regimes make a major difference in how an economy functions.

The Balance of Payments

The best door into an in-depth discussion of exchange rates and international financial considerations is a discussion of **balance of payments** *(a country's record of all transactions between its residents and the residents of all foreign nations)*. These include a country's buying and selling of goods and services (imports and exports) and interest and profit payments from previous investments, together with all the capital inflows and outflows. Table 20-1 presents the 1990 and 2011 balance of payments accounts for the United States. These accounts record all payments made by foreigners to U.S. citizens and all payments made by U.S. citizens to foreigners in those years.

Goods the United States exports must be paid for in dollars so, in order to buy U.S. exports, foreigners must exchange their currencies for dollars. Exports involve a flow of payments into the United States, so in the balance of payments accounts they have a plus sign. Similarly, U.S. imports must be paid for in foreign currency; they involve a flow of dollars out of the United States, and thus they have

TABLE 20-1 The Balance of Payments Account, 1990 and 2011

	1990 (billions of dollars)		2011 (billions of dollars)	
1. Current account				
2. Merchandise				
3. Exports	+387		+1,498	
4. Imports	−498		−2,236	
5. Balance of merchandise trade		−111		−738
6. Services				
7. Exports	+ 148		+ 605	
8. Imports	− 118		− 427	
9. Balance on services		+ 30		+178
10. Balance of trade		− 81		−560
11. Net investment income	+ 29		+ 227	
12. Net transfers	− 27		− 133	
13. Invest. trans. balance		− 2		+ 94
14. Balance on current account		**−83**		**−466**
15. Financial and capital account				
16. Capital balance		− 7		− 1
17. Private financial account				
18. Foreign-owned assets in the U.S.	+105		+ 789	
19. U.S.-owned assets abroad	81		− 364	
20. Balance on private financial account		+24		+425
21. Government financial account				
22. Foreign government financial bal.	+ 34		+ 212	
23. U.S. government financial bal.	+ 0		− 120	
24. Balance on government financial acct.		+ 34		+ 92
25. Balance on financial and capital account		**+ 51**		**+516**
26. Statistical discrepancy		+ 32		− 50
27. Total		**0**		**0**

Source: Bureau of Economic Analysis (www.bea.gov).

a minus sign. Notice that the bottom line of the balance of payments is $0. By definition, the bottom line (which includes all supplies and demands for currencies, including those of the government) must add up to zero.

The balance of payments is a country's record of all transactions between its residents and the residents of all foreign countries.

As you can see in Table 20-1, the balance of payments account is broken down into the current account and the financial and capital account. The **current account** (lines 1–14) is *the part of the balance of payments account in which all short-term flows of payments are listed.* It includes exports and imports, which are what we normally mean when we talk about the trade balance. The **financial and capital account** (lines 15–25) is *the part of the balance of payments account in which all long-term flows of payments are listed.* If a U.S. citizen buys a German stock, or if a Japanese company buys a U.S. company, the transaction shows up on this account.

The current account is the part of the balance of payments account that lists all short-term flows of payments.

The financial and capital account is the part of the balance of payments account that lists all long-term flows of payments.

The U.S. government can influence the exchange rate (the rate at which one currency trades for another) by buying and selling *official reserves,* which, as you learned in a previous chapter, are government holdings of foreign currencies, or by buying and selling other international reserves, such as gold. Such buying and selling is recorded in the government financial balance (line 23)—the part of the balance of payments account that records the amount of its own currency or foreign currencies that a nation buys or sells. Foreign governments can also influence the U.S. exchange rate by buying and selling reserves. Such buying and selling is recorded in the foreign government financial balance (line 22).

To get a better idea of what's included in these accounts, let's consider each of them more carefully.

The Current Account

Looking at Table 20-1, you can see that the current account is composed of the merchandise (or goods) account (lines 2–5), the services account (lines 6–9), the net investment income account (line 11), and the net transfers account (line 12).

WWW Web Note 20.1 Balance or Imbalance?

Starting with the merchandise account, notice that in 1990 the United States imported $498 billion worth of goods and exported $387 billion worth of goods. *The difference between the value of goods exported and the value of goods imported* is called the **balance of merchandise trade.** Looking at line 5, you can see that the United States had a balance of merchandise trade deficit of $111 billion in 1990 and $738 billion in 2011.

The merchandise trade balance is often discussed in the press as a summary of how the United States is doing in the international markets. It's not a good summary. Trade in services is just as important as trade in merchandise, so economists pay more attention to the combined balance of goods and services.

The balance of trade is the difference between the value of goods and services exported and imported.

Thus, the **balance of trade**—*the difference between the value of goods and services exported and imported*—(line 10) becomes a key statistic for economists. Notice that in both 1990 and 2011 most of the U.S. trade deficit resulted from an imbalance in the merchandise account. The services account worked in the opposite direction. It was slightly positive in 1990; in 2011 the services account reduced the trade deficit by $178 billion. Such services include tourist expenditures and insurance payments by foreigners to U.S. firms. For instance, when you travel in Japan, you spend yen, which you must buy with dollars; this is an outflow of payments, which is a negative contribution to the services account.

Q-1 If you, a U.S. citizen, are traveling abroad, where will your expenditures show up in the balance of payments accounts?

There is no reason that in a particular year the goods and services sent into a country must equal the goods and services sent out, even if the current account is in equilibrium, because the current account also includes payments from past investments and net transfers. When you invest, you expect to make a return on that investment. The payments to foreign owners of U.S. capital assets are a negative contribution to the U.S. balance of payments. The payment to U.S. owners of foreign capital assets is a positive contribution to the U.S. balance of payments. These payments on investment income are a type of holdover from past trade and services imbalances. So even though they relate to investments, they show up on the current account.

Payments on investment income show up on the current account.

The final component of the current account is net transfers, which include foreign aid, gifts, and other payments to individuals not exchanged for goods or services. If you send a $1,000 bond to your aunt in Mexico, it shows up with a minus sign here.

Adding up the pluses and minuses on the current account, we arrive at line 14, the current account balance. Notice that in 1990 the United States ran a $83 billion deficit on the current account, and in 2011 the United States had a deficit of $466 billion (line 14). That means that, in the current account, the supply of dollars greatly exceeded the demand for dollars. If the current account represented the total supply of and demand for dollars, the value of the dollar would have fallen. But it doesn't represent the total. There are also the financial account and statistical discrepancies.

The Financial and Capital Account

The financial and capital account measures the flow of payments between countries for financial assets such as stocks, bonds, and ownership rights to real estate. It is broken into two subcategories: (1) the capital account, which includes debt forgiveness, migrants' transfers, and transfers related to the sale of fixed assets; and (2) the financial account, which includes trade in assets such as business firms, bonds, stocks, and ownership right to real estate. The capital account transactions are rather small on balance. As you can also see in Table 20-1, in both years there was an inflow of financial assets into the United States in excess of outflows of assets from the United States. In 1990, financial inflows (payments by foreigners for U.S. real and financial assets) were $51 billion more than financial outflows (payments by U.S. citizens for foreign assets). In 2011, inflows exceeded outflows by $516 billion.

To buy these U.S. assets, foreigners needed dollars, so these net financial inflows represent a demand for dollars. In 1990 and 2011, the demand for dollars to buy real and financial assets offset the excess supply of dollars on the current account. Because of the importance of financial flows, when you think about what's likely to happen to a currency's value, it's important to remember both the demand for dollars to buy goods and services and the demand for dollars to buy assets.

In thinking about what determines a currency's value, it's important to remember both the demand for dollars to buy goods and services and the demand for dollars to buy assets.

If we added up the current account balance and the financial account balance, the two would not completely balance because of measurement errors. Line 26 takes care of that problem; it is the sum of all the above items with the sign reversed, and thus is a measure of the statistical discrepancy in the figures. In 1990 there was a +$32 billion discrepancy, and in 2011 there was a −$50 billion discrepancy. These discrepancies arise because many international transactions, especially on the capital account, go unrecorded and hence must be estimated. Including the statistical discrepancy, line 26, the net balance of payments, including all government payments, is always zero.[1]

When economists say that a country is running a balance of payments deficit or surplus, they are excluding its government's financial transactions (line 23). Thus, if line 23 is positive, the United States is running a balance of payments deficit and, if it is negative, it is running a balance of payments surplus. Government financial transactions represent its buying and selling of currencies. Foreign governments also may be buying up U.S. currency, which they did substantially in 2011, as you can see by the large positive entry on line 22. These foreign countries are increasing their holding of U.S. dollars, and their purchases of U.S. dollars allow the U.S. balance of payments accounts to remain in equilibrium even as private quantities supplied and demanded for these currencies differ.

While the current and financial accounts offset each other, there is a difference between the long-run effects of the demand for dollars to buy currently produced goods and services and the demand for dollars to buy assets. Assets earn profits or interest, so when foreigners buy U.S. assets, they earn income from those assets just for owning them. The net investment income from foreigners' previous asset purchases shows up on line 11 of the current account. It's the difference between the income U.S. citizens receive from their foreign assets and the income foreigners receive from their U.S. assets. If assets earned equal returns, we would expect that when foreigners own more U.S. capital assets than U.S. citizens own foreign capital assets, net investment income should be negative. And when U.S. citizens own more foreign capital assets than foreigners own U.S. capital assets, net investment income should be positive. Why is this? Because net investment

While the current and financial accounts offset each other, there is a difference between the long-run effects of the demand for dollars to buy currently produced goods and services and the demand for dollars to buy assets.

[1]Balance of payments records are not very good. Because of measurement difficulties, many transactions go unrecorded and many numbers must be estimated, leaving a potential for large errors, especially in the financial and capital accounts.

income is simply the difference between the returns on U.S. citizens' assets held abroad and foreign citizens' assets held in the United States.

Since the 1980s, the inflow of capital into the United States has greatly exceeded the outflow of capital from the United States. As a result, the United States has become a net debtor nation; the amount foreigners own in the United States now exceeds the amount U.S. citizens own abroad by well over $1 trillion. So we would expect that U.S. investment income would be highly negative. But looking at line 11 of Table 20-1, we see that was not the case. The reason? Foreigners' returns from investments in the United States have been low, and many of the foreign assets owned by U.S. citizens abroad are undervalued. One reason why returns have been so low recently is that many people are buying U.S. assets for safety of the investment, not for return on the investment. While this trend has continued much longer than expected, we cannot expect it to continue forever.

Q-2 How can net investment income be positive if a country is a net debtor nation?

Exchange Rates

In earlier chapters we discussed how exchange rates are determined, so we will just quickly review it here, summarizing the earlier discussion to the balance of payments discussion. In Figure 20-1, I present the private sector supply/demand graph for the Chinese yuan, with quantity of yuan on the quantity axis and price of yuan in terms of dollars on the price axis. Without government intervention, market equilibrium is 20 cents per yuan, or 5 yuan to the dollar (point A). In Figure 20-1, even though equilibrium is at 20 cents, the price of the yuan is at 16 cents, which means that the quantity of yuan demanded exceeds the quantity of yuan supplied. What this means for the balance of payments is that when only private demand and supply is considered, at a yuan price of 16 cents (point B), the United States is running a deficit. (Remember, the quantity of yuan demanded comes from U.S. demand for Chinese goods and assets and the quantity of yuan supplied comes from Chinese demand for U.S. goods and assets.) To keep the yuan at 16 cents the Chinese government and central bank need to sell sufficient yuan (buy dollars) on the foreign exchange (forex) market to shift the supply curve to the right, to S_1, and eliminate the excess demand.

This situation reflects trade with China today. China buys a large amount of dollar-denominated assets to allow the trade deficit that the United States has with China (and similar flows with many other countries) to continue. The low value of the yuan has allowed China to export and save, while keeping its economy growing fast. That same low value of the yuan has allowed the United States to import and consume,

FIGURE 20-1 Exchange Rate Determination

As long as you keep quantities and prices *of what* straight, the standard, or fundamental, analysis of the determination of exchange rates is easy. Just remember that if you're talking about the supply of and demand for yuan, the price will be measured in dollars and the quantity will be in yuan.

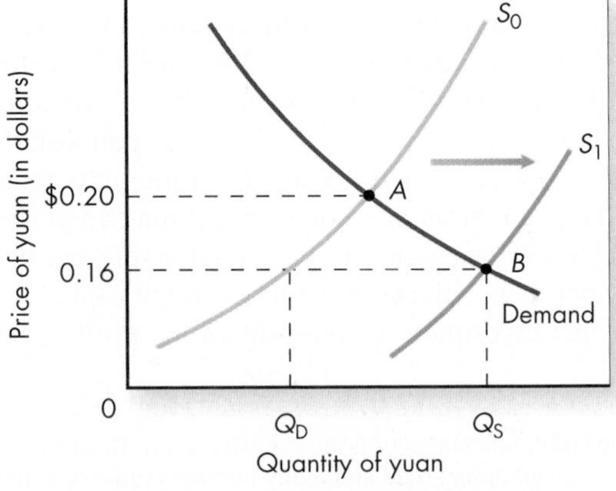

while U.S. production has not increased. As emphasized in previous chapters, all of this has happened without causing inflation in the United States. But the trade imbalance hasn't been without costs. It has caused structural problems that the United States will have to deal with in the future.

Exchange Rate Dynamics

The supply/demand analysis may have made it look like exchange rates are driven by fundamentals. Unfortunately, that is not always the case. In day-to-day trading, fundamentals can be overwhelmed by expectations of how a currency will change in value. The supply and demand curves for currencies can shift around rapidly in response to rumors, expectations, and expectations of expectations. As they shift, they bring about large fluctuations in exchange rates that make trading difficult and have significant real effects on economic activity.

Let me outline just one potential problem. Say you expect the price of the currency to fall one-half of 1 percent tomorrow. What should you do? The correct answer is: Sell that currency quickly. Why? One-half of 1 percent may not sound like much, but, annualized, it is equivalent to a rate of interest per year of 617 percent. Based on that expectation, if you're into making money (and you're really sure about the fall), you will sell all of that currency that you hold, and borrow all you can so you can sell some more. You can make big money if you guess small changes in exchange rates correctly. (Of course, if you're wrong, you can lose big money.) This means that if the market generally believes the exchange rates will move, those expectations will tend to be self-fulfilling. Self-fulfilling expectations undermine the argument in favor of letting markets determine exchange rates: When expectations rule, the exchange rate may not reflect actual demands and supplies of goods. Instead, the exchange rate can reflect expectations and rumors. The resulting fluctuations serve no real purpose, and cause problems for international trade and the country's economy. Let's consider an example.

A REMINDER

Fundamental Forces and Exchange Rates

The fundamental forces affecting exchange rates were covered a number of chapters ago, so let's review them. The four forces are (1) changes in a country's income, (2) changes in a country's prices, (3) changes in interest rates, and (4) changes in trade policy. Increased trade barriers tend to push up the value of a country's currency. Here are the effects for the other three:

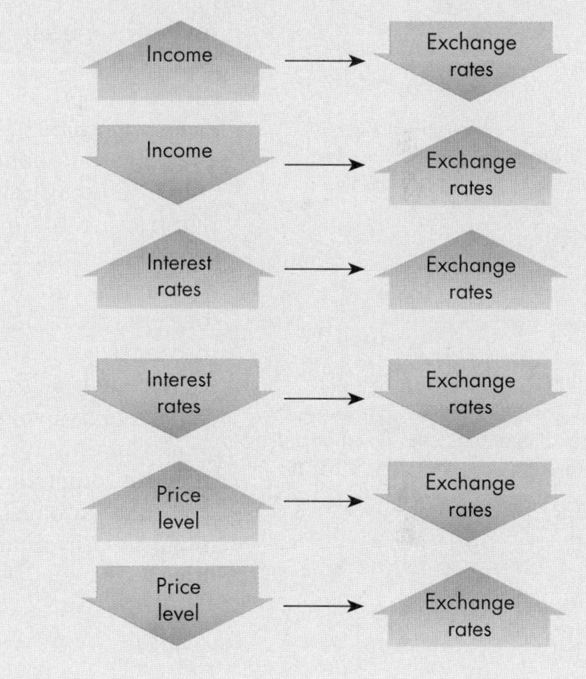

Suppose that a firm decides to build a plant in the United States because costs in the United States are low. But suppose also that the value of the dollar then rises significantly; the firm's costs rise significantly too, making it uncompetitive. When currencies fluctuate, companies find it harder to make good decisions on where to produce.

Q-3 Why don't most governments leave determination of the exchange rate to the market?

In a real-world example, from July to September 1997, the value of the Thai baht fell nearly 40 percent. Goodyear (Thailand), which had been one of the five most profitable companies on the Stock Exchange of Thailand, suddenly faced a 20 percent rise in the costs of raw materials because it paid for those raw materials in dollars. It also faced a decline in tire prices because the demand for tires had fallen 20 to 40 percent when the Thai economy contracted. Within just two months, a highly profitable venture had become unprofitable. Other firms were closing shop because they were unable to pay the interest on loans that were denominated in dollars. In summary, large fluctuations make real trade difficult and cause serious real consequences.

The problems caused by fluctuating exchange rates have led to calls for government to intervene and either stabilize or fix its exchange rate directly by buying or selling its currency. It can increase the value of its currency by buying its currency, assuming it has international reserves to buy it with. Alternatively, it can decrease the value of its currency by selling its currency. This ability of a country to buy and sell its currency means that, assuming it has sufficient reserves, a country can fix its currency at a specific level.

A country fixes the exchange rate by standing ready to buy and sell its currency anytime the exchange rate is not at the fixed exchange rate.

CURRENCY SUPPORT In our previous discussion of the yuan, China was keeping the value of the yuan low by selling yuan. Let's now consider currency support, in this case the euro. Suppose that, given the interaction of private supply and demand forces, the equilibrium value of the euro is \$1.30 a euro, but the European Union wants to maintain a value of \$1.50 a euro. This is shown in Figure 20-2. At \$1.50 a euro, quantity supplied exceeds quantity demanded. The European Union must buy the surplus, $Q_2 - Q_1$, using official reserves (foreign currency holdings). In doing so, it shifts the total demand for euros to D_1, making the equilibrium market exchange rate (including the European government's demand for euros) equal to \$1.50. This process is called **currency support**—the *buying of a currency by a government to maintain its value at above its long-run equilibrium value.* It is a direct exchange rate policy. If a government has sufficient official reserves, or if it can convince other governments to lend it reserves, it can fix the exchange rate at the rate it wants, no matter what the private level of supply and demand is. In reality, governments have no such power to support currencies in the long run since their official reserves are limited. For example, in 2002 the Argentinean government tried to keep its currency fixed to the U.S. dollar, but it ran out of foreign reserves and was forced to let its currency decline in value.

A country can maintain a fixed exchange rate above its market price only as long as it has the reserves.

A country has more power to prevent the value of its currency from rising since it can create its own money. That's what we saw above in the example of the Chinese yuan. China used yuan to buy large amounts of dollars, thereby preventing the value of the yuan from rising relative to the dollar.

Q-4 In general, would it be easier for the United States to push the value of the dollar down or up? Why?

Since China can create all the yuan it wants, it can hold the value the yuan below its equilibrium price much more easily than it can hold it above its equilibrium price.

FIGURE 20-2 A Demonstration of Direct Exchange Rate Policy

If the government chooses to hold the exchange rate at \$1.50, when the equilibrium is \$1.30, there is an excess supply given by $Q_2 - Q_1$. The government purchases this excess (using official reserves) and closes the difference, thus maintaining equilibrium.

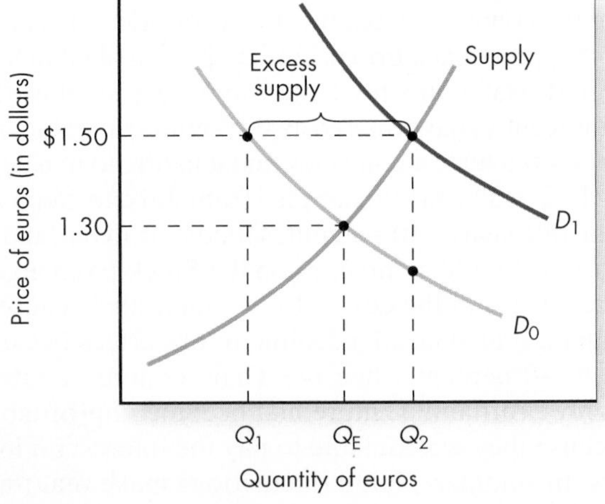

If one country wants to hold the value of its currency down and another wants to hold the value of its currency up, they have a large incentive to cooperate. Of course, cooperation requires an agreement on the goals, and often countries' goals conflict. In the case of China and the United States, their goals differed. Both wanted to hold the value of their currencies low, which was impossible. One role of the various international economic organizations is to provide a forum for reaching agreement on exchange rate goals and a vehicle through which cooperation can take place.

Currency Stabilization A more viable long-run exchange rate policy is **currency stabilization**—the *buying and selling of a currency by the government to offset temporary fluctuations in supply and demand for currencies.* In currency stabilization, the government is not trying to change the long-run equilibrium; it is simply trying to keep the exchange rate at that long-run equilibrium. The government sometimes buys and sometimes sells currency, so it is far less likely to run out of reserves.

Successful currency stabilization requires the government to choose the correct long-run equilibrium exchange rate. A policy of stabilization can become a policy of support if the government chooses too high a long-run equilibrium. Unfortunately, government has no way of knowing for sure what the long-run equilibrium exchange rate is.

In most cases given the small level of official reserves compared to the enormous level of private trading, significant amounts of stabilization are impossible. Instead, governments use *strategic currency stabilization*—buying and selling at strategic moments to affect expectations of traders, and hence to affect their supply and demand. Such issues are discussed in depth in international finance courses.

Strategic currency stabilization is the process of buying and selling at strategic moments to affect the expectations of traders, and hence affect their supply and demand.

Influencing Exchange Rates with Monetary and Fiscal Policy

Governments can also influence exchange rates—both directly, as we saw was the case with China, where the Chinese central bank sold yuan and bought dollars, increasing the supply of yuan and pushing the value of the yuan down, and indirectly through monetary and fiscal policy. Let's now consider that indirect approach.

Monetary Policy's Effect on Exchange Rates Monetary policy affects exchange rates in three primary ways: (1) through its effect on the interest rate, (2) through its effect on income, and (3) through its effect on price levels and inflation.

The Effect on Exchange Rates via Interest Rates Expansionary monetary policy pushes down the U.S. interest rate, which decreases the financial inflow into the United States, decreasing the demand for dollars, pushing down the value of the dollar, and decreasing the U.S. exchange rate. Contractionary monetary policy does the opposite. It raises the U.S. interest rate, which tends to bring in financial capital flows from abroad, increasing the demand for dollars, increasing the value of the dollar, and increasing the U.S. exchange rate. This interest rate effect is the dominant short-run effect, and it often overwhelms the other effects.

Q-5 What effect does the lowering of a country's interest rates have on exchange rates?

To see why these effects take place, consider a person in Japan in the early 2000s, when the Japanese interest rate was close to 0 percent. He or she reasoned, "Why should I earn 0 percent return in Japan? I'll save (buy some financial assets) in the United States where I'll earn 3 percent." If the U.S. interest rate goes up due to contraction in the money supply, other things equal, the advantage of holding one's financial assets in the United States will become even greater and more people will want to

The interest rate effect on exchange rates is the dominant short-run effect.

REAL-WORLD APPLICATION

Iceland's Monetary Woes

In 2006, the inflation rate in Iceland exceeded its target inflation rate, and investors became worried. The financial press began to issue comments such as this: "The negative outlook has been triggered by a material deterioration in Iceland's macro-prudential risk indicators, accompanied by an unsustainable current account deficit and soaring net external indebtedness." A group of developed countries, the Organisation for Economic Co-operation and Development (OECD), warned that the failure to bring inflation down could damage the country's international credibility, and that "[i]n the absence of swift and vigorous policy action, financial market stability could be at risk."

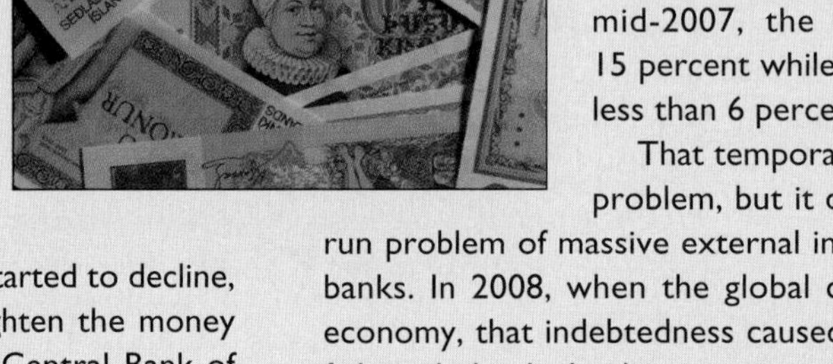

In response to these and other warnings, foreign exchange traders began selling króna, Iceland's currency. The króna's value started to decline, which led the Central Bank of Iceland to tighten the money supply and raise interest rates. In 2006 the Central Bank of Iceland issued the following statement:

> Economic developments since the end of March indicate that a considerable increase in the policy rate may be required to maintain sufficiently tight monetary conditions. Rising inflation expectations have caused the real policy rate to decline. Furthermore, the depreciation of the króna has eased conditions in the traded goods sector. The current policy rate hike is intended to respond to these developments. Attaining the inflation target within an acceptable period of time is the firm intention of the Central Bank.

The Central Bank of Iceland continued raising interest rates substantially, to 12 percent and then to 13.5 percent, stating that "further rises were unavoidable." In mid-2007, the interest rate was about 15 percent while inflation had decreased to less than 6 percent.

That temporarily resolved the short-run problem, but it did not resolve the longer-run problem of massive external indebtedness of all Icelandic banks. In 2008, when the global credit crisis hit the world economy, that indebtedness caused all the Icelandic banks to fail, and the Icelandic government had nowhere near the money needed to support them. This led to a freezing up of the exchange markets for the króna, and Iceland was forced to take large loans from other countries to help reestablish a viable banking system.

save here. People in Japan hold yen, not dollars, so in order to save in the United States they must buy dollars. Thus, a rise in U.S. interest rates increases demand for dollars and, in terms of yen, pushes up the U.S. exchange rate. This example illustrates that it is relative interest rates that govern the flow of financial assets.

Countries are continually taking into account the effect of monetary policy on exchange rates. For example, in the mid-1990s, Taiwan kept its money supply tight, raising its interest rates to keep the value of the Taiwan dollar high. In 1997 Taiwan cut bank reserve ratios; interest rates fell and the value of the Taiwan dollar fell.

The Effect on Exchange Rates via Income Monetary policy also affects income in a country. As money supply rises, income expands; when money supply falls, income contracts.[2] This effect on income provides another way in which the money supply affects the exchange rate. When income rises, imports rise while exports are unaffected. To buy foreign products, U.S. citizens need foreign currency, which they must buy

[2]When there's inflation, it's the rate of money supply growth relative to the rate of inflation that's important. If inflation is 10 percent and money supply growth is 10 percent, the rate of increase in the real money supply is zero. If money supply growth falls to, say, 5 percent while inflation stays at 10 percent, there will be a contractionary effect on the real economy.

with dollars. So when U.S. imports rise, the supply of dollars to the foreign exchange market increases as U.S. citizens sell dollars to buy foreign currencies to pay for those imports. This decreases the dollar exchange rate. This effect through income and imports provides a second path through which monetary policy affects the exchange rate: Expansionary monetary policy causes U.S. income to rise, imports to rise, and the U.S. exchange rate to fall via the income path. Contractionary monetary policy causes U.S. income to fall, imports to fall, and the U.S. exchange rate to rise via the income path.

The Effect on Exchange Rates via Price Levels A third way in which monetary policy can affect exchange rates is through its effect on prices in a country. Expansionary monetary policy pushes the U.S. price level up. As the U.S. price level rises relative to foreign prices, U.S. exports become more expensive, and goods the United States imports become relatively cheaper, decreasing U.S. competitiveness. This increases demand for foreign currencies and decreases demand for dollars. Thus, via the price path, expansionary monetary policy pushes down the dollar's value for the same reason that an expansion in income pushes it down.

Contractionary monetary policy puts downward pressure on the U.S. price level and slows down any existing inflation. As the U.S. price level falls relative to foreign prices, U.S. exports become more competitive and the goods the United States imports, relatively more expensive. Thus, contractionary monetary policy pushes up the value of the dollar via the price path.

The Net Effect of Monetary Policy on Exchange Rates Notice that all these effects of monetary policy on exchange rates are in the same direction. Expansionary monetary policy pushes a country's exchange rate down; contractionary monetary policy pushes a country's exchange rate up. Summarizing these effects, we have the following relationships for expansionary and contractionary monetary policy:

Q-6 What effect would contractionary monetary policy have on a country's exchange rates?

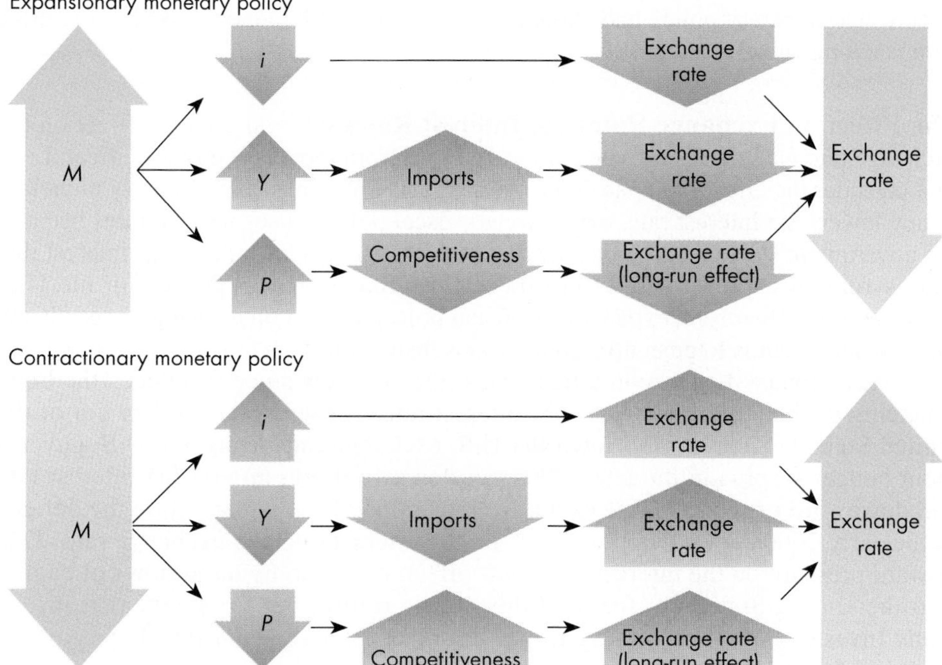

Monetary policy affects exchange rates through the interest rate path, the income path, and the price level path, as shown in the accompanying diagram.

There are, of course, many provisos to the relationship between monetary policy and the exchange rate. For example, as the exchange rate falls, the price of imports goes up and there is some inflationary pressure from that rise in price and hence some pressure for the price level to rise as well as fall. Monetary policy affects exchange rates in subtle ways, but if an economist had to give a quick answer to what effect monetary policy would have on exchange rates, it would be:

Expansionary monetary policy lowers exchange rates. It decreases the relative value of a country's currency.

Contractionary monetary policy increases exchange rates. It increases the relative value of a country's currency.

> *Expansionary monetary policy lowers exchange rates. It decreases the relative value of a country's currency.*
>
> *Contractionary monetary policy increases exchange rates. It increases the relative value of a country's currency.*

Fiscal Policy's Effect on Exchange Rates The effect of fiscal policy on exchange rates is not so clear. The reason why can be seen by considering its effects on income, the price level, and interest rates.

The Effect on Exchange Rates via Income Expansionary fiscal policy expands income and therefore increases imports, increasing the trade deficit and lowering the exchange rate. Contractionary fiscal policy contracts income, thereby decreasing imports and increasing the exchange rate. These effects of expansionary and contractionary fiscal policies via the income path are similar to the effects of monetary policy, so if it's not intuitively clear to you why the effect is what it is, it may be worthwhile to review the more complete discussion of monetary policy's effect presented previously.

The Effect on Exchange Rates via Price Levels Let's next turn to the effect of fiscal policy on exchange rates through prices. Expansionary fiscal policy increases aggregate demand and increases prices of a country's exports; hence, it decreases the competitiveness of a country's exports, which pushes down the exchange rate. Contractionary fiscal policy works in the opposite direction. These are the same effects that monetary policy had. And, as was the case with monetary policy, the price path is a long-run effect.

The Effect on Exchange Rates via Interest Rates Fiscal policy's effect on the exchange rate via the interest rate path is different from monetary policy's effect. Let's first consider the effect of expansionary fiscal policy. Whereas expansionary monetary policy lowers the interest rate, expansionary fiscal policy raises interest rates because the government sells bonds to finance that budget deficit. The higher U.S. interest rate causes foreign capital to flow into the United States, which pushes up the U.S. exchange rate. Therefore, expansionary fiscal policy's effect on exchange rates via the interest rate effect is to push up a country's exchange rate.

Contractionary fiscal policy decreases interest rates since it reduces the bond financing of that deficit. Lower U.S. interest rates cause capital to flow out of the United States, which pushes down the U.S. exchange rate. Thus, the U.S. government budget surplus in the late 1990s put downward pressure on the interest rate and downward pressure on the exchange rate value of the dollar, while the deficits in the early 2000s put upward pressure on the interest rate and exchange rate. That upward pressure on the interest rates was offset, however, by large flows of capital into the United States not for the interest rate return, but for safety reasons, as many investors were attempting to get out of other assets and into U.S. government bonds.

The Net Effect of Fiscal Policy on Exchange Rates Of these three effects, the interest rate effect and the income effect are both short-run effects. These two work in opposite directions, so the net effect of fiscal policy on the exchange rate is, in general, ambiguous, although in specific instances either the interest rate effect or the income effect may swamp the other. The following diagram summarizes these three effects.

Q-7 What is the net effect of expansionary fiscal policy on the exchange rate?

Fiscal policy affects exchange rates through the income path, the interest rate path, and the price level path, as shown in the accompanying diagram.

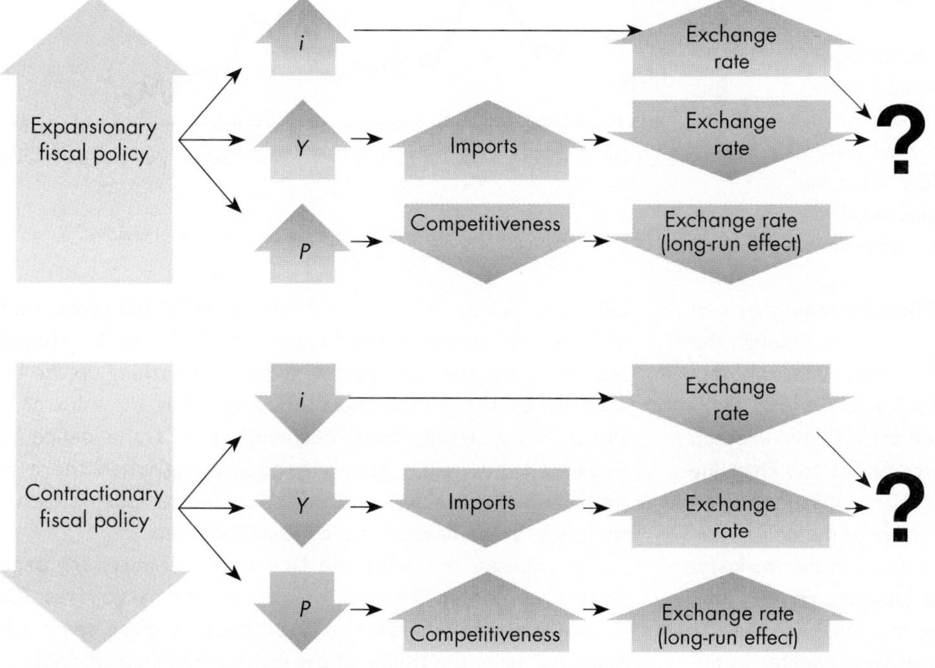

As you can see, it's unclear what the effect of expansionary or contractionary fiscal policy will be on exchange rates.

The Problems of Determining the Appropriate Exchange Rate

To intervene effectively in foreign exchange markets, the government must know the appropriate exchange rate to target. If the government targets the wrong exchange rate, its interventions can cause more problems than they solve. Unfortunately, the government can only guess at the appropriate long-run rate since no definitive empirical measure of this rate exists. The long-run equilibrium must be estimated. If that estimate is wrong, a sustainable stabilization policy becomes an unsustainable deviation from long-run equilibrium policy. Thus, a central issue in exchange rate intervention policy is estimating the long-run equilibrium exchange rate.

To intervene effectively in foreign exchange markets, the government must know the appropriate exchange rate to target.

Purchasing Power Parity and Real Exchange Rates

Purchasing power parity is one way economists have of estimating the long-run equilibrium rate. **Purchasing power parity (PPP)** is *a method of calculating exchange rates that attempts to value currencies at rates such that each currency will buy an equal basket of goods.* It is based on the idea that the exchange of currencies reflects the exchange of real goods. If you are able to exchange a basket of goods from country X for an equivalent basket of goods from country Z, you should also be able to

Purchasing power parity is a method of calculating exchange rates that attempts to value currencies at rates such that each currency will buy an equal basket of goods.

REAL-WORLD APPLICATION

Determining the Causes of Fluctuations in the Dollar's Value

As you can see on the graph, the dollar's value has fluctuated considerably since 1973. A good exercise to see if you understand movements in the value of the dollar is to try to choose which factors caused the fluctuation.

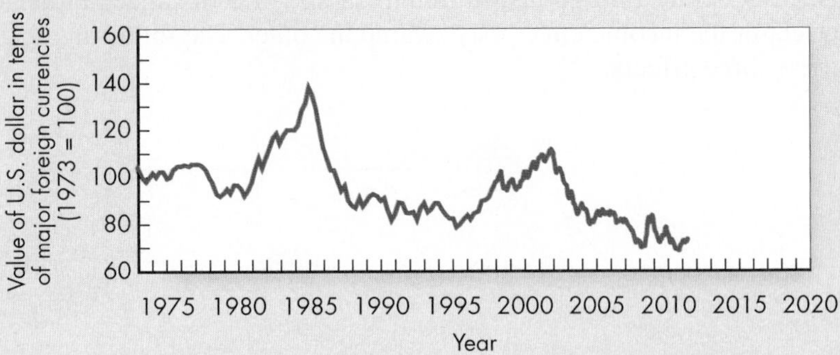

Source: Board of Governors, Federal Reserve System (www.federalreserve.gov).

Let's start with the relatively small fluctuations in 1973 and 1974. These probably reflected expectational bubbles—in which speculators were more concerned with short-run fluctuations than long-run fundamentals—while the dollar's low value in 1979 and 1980 reflected high inflation, relatively low real interest rates, and the booming U.S. economy during this period.

The rise of the dollar in the early 1980s reflected higher real U.S. interest rates and the falling U.S. inflation rate, although the rise was much more than expected and probably reflected speculation, as did the sudden fall in the dollar's value in 1985. Similarly, the fluctuations in the late 1980s and early 1990s reflected both changing interest rates in the United States and changing foreign interest rates, as well as changing relative inflation rates.

In the late 1990s and early 2000s the value of the dollar rose substantially. Part of the explanation for this lies in the weakness of the Japanese economy, which led the Japanese central bank to increase the Japanese money supply, thereby lowering the Japanese interest rate. That weakness also was reflected in the fall in the prices of Japanese stocks. That fall led investors to shift out of Japanese stocks and into U.S. stocks, thereby increasing the demand for the dollar, and pushing up the U.S. effective exchange rate. Since the early 2000s, the value of the dollar has generally been declining as its trade deficit has expanded, but it has generally been rising when there are international financial crises and people are looking to hold dollars as a safe haven for their financial assets.

As you can see, after the fact we economists are pretty good at explaining the movements in the exchange rates. Alas, before the fact we aren't so good because often speculative activities make the timing of the movements unpredictable.

exchange the amount of currency from country X that is needed to purchase country X's basket of goods for the amount of currency from country Z that is needed to purchase country Z's basket of goods. For example, say that the yen is valued at 100 yen to $1. Say also that you can buy the same basket of goods for 1,000 yen that you can buy for $7. In that case, the purchasing power parity exchange rate would be 143 yen to $1 (1,000/7 = 143) compared to an actual exchange rate of 100 yen to $1. An economist would say that at 100 to the dollar the yen is overvalued—with 100 yen you could not purchase a basket of goods equivalent to the basket of goods you could purchase with $1.

Purchasing power parity is a method of calculating exchange rates such that various currencies will each buy an equal basket of goods and services.

Table 20-2 shows various calculations for purchasing power parity for a variety of countries. The second column shows the 2011 actual exchange rates. The third column shows purchasing power parity exchange rates. The fourth column shows the difference between the two, or the 2011 distortion in the exchange rates (if you believe the PPP exchange rates are the correct ones).

Criticisms of the Purchasing Power Parity Method

Web Note 20.2
The Big Mac Index

For many economists, estimating exchange rates using PPP has serious problems. If the currency is overvalued and will eventually fall, why don't traders use that information and sell that currency now, making it fall now? After all, they are out after a profit.

TABLE 20-2 Actual and Purchasing Power Parity Exchange Rates for 2011

Country	Actual Exchange Rate (currency per dollar)	PPP Exchange Rate (currency per dollar)	Under (−)/ Over (+) valuation
Switzerland	0.88	1.49	69
Japan	79.8	106.88	34
Russia	15.93	18.00	13
United Kingdom	0.624	0.659	6
United States	1	1.00	1
Brazil	1.74	1.69	−3
South Africa	7.3	5.0	−32
Turkey	1.67	1.04	−38
China	6.77	3.95	−42
India	45.7	18.4	−60

Source: *World Economic Outlook Database, 2012.* International Monetary Fund (www.imf.org).

So if there is open trading in a currency, any expected change in the exchange rate will affect exchange rates now. If traders don't sell now when there are expectations that a currency's overvaluation will eventually make its value fall, they must believe there is some reason that its value won't, in fact, fall.

Critics argue that the difficulty with PPP exchange rates is the complex nature of trade and consumption. They point out that the PPP will change as the basket of goods changes. This means that there is no one PPP measure. They also point out that, since all PPP measures leave out asset demand for a currency, the measures are missing an important element of the demand. Critics ask: Is there any reason to assume that in the long run the asset demand for a currency is less important than the goods demand for a currency? Because the asset demand for a currency is important, critics of PPP argue that there is little reason to assume that the short-run actual exchange rate will ever adjust to the PPP exchange rates. And if that rate doesn't adjust, then PPP does not provide a good estimate of the equilibrium rate. These critics further contend that the existing exchange rate is the best estimate of the long-run equilibrium exchange rate.

Purchasing power parity exchange rates may or may not be appropriate long-run exchange rates.

Real Exchange Rates

Regardless of one's view of the usefulness of purchasing power parity, the concept gets at the importance of prices in the determination of exchange rates. Say, for example, that the price level in the United States goes up by 10 percent while the price level in Europe stays constant. In such a situation, we would expect some change in the exchange rate—the most likely effect would be that the U.S. dollar falls by 10 percent relative to the euro. To capture the distinction between changes in exchange rates caused by changes in price levels and changes in exchange rates caused by other things, economists differentiate between nominal and real exchange rates. A **real exchange rate** is *an exchange rate adjusted for differential changes in the price level.* A nominal exchange rate is the exchange rate you see in the papers—it is the rate you'd get when exchanging currencies.

A real exchange rate is an exchange rate adjusted for differential changes in the price level.

Let's consider the above example: The U.S. price level rises by 10 percent, the European price level remains constant, and the nominal U.S. exchange rate falls by 10 percent. In that case, the real exchange rate will have remained constant. More generally, the change in the real exchange rate (foreign/domestic or in this case euro/$) can be approximately calculated by adding the difference in the rates of inflation between the two countries (domestic inflation − foreign inflation) to the percentage change in the nominal exchange rate.

$$\begin{bmatrix}\%\Delta \text{ real} \\ \text{exchange rate}\end{bmatrix} = \begin{bmatrix}\%\Delta \text{ nominal} \\ \text{exchange rate}\end{bmatrix} + \begin{bmatrix}\text{Domestic} \\ \text{inflation}\end{bmatrix} - \begin{bmatrix}\text{Foreign} \\ \text{inflation}\end{bmatrix}$$

Q-8 If U.S. inflation is 2 percent, the European Union's inflation rate is 4 percent, and the nominal U.S. dollar exchange rate rises by 3 percent relative to the euro, what happens to the real exchange rate of the dollar?

For example, say the U.S. price level had risen only by 8 percent and Europe's had remained constant, but the U.S. nominal exchange rate had fallen by 10 percent. In that case, we would say that the real U.S. exchange rate had fallen by 2 percent.

$$\%\Delta \text{ real exchange rate} = -10 + (8 - 0) = -2 \text{ percent}$$

Advantages and Disadvantages of Alternative Exchange Rate Systems

The problems of stabilizing exchange rates have led to an ongoing debate about whether a fixed exchange rate, a flexible exchange rate, or a combination of the two is best. This debate nicely captures the macro issues relevant to exchange rate stabilization, so in this section I consider that debate. First, a brief overview of the three alternative regimes:

Three exchange rate regimes are:

1. Fixed exchange rate: The government chooses an exchange rate and offers to buy and sell currencies at that rate.
2. Flexible exchange rate: Determination of exchange rates is left totally up to the market.
3. Partially flexible exchange rate: The government sometimes affects the exchange rate and sometimes leaves it to the market.

Fixed exchange rate: *When the government chooses a particular exchange rate and offers to buy and sell its currency at that price.* For example, suppose the U.S. government says it will buy euros at 0.77 euro per dollar. In that case, we say that the United States has a fixed exchange rate of 0.77 euro to the dollar.

Flexible exchange rate: *When the government does not enter into foreign exchange markets at all, but leaves the determination of exchange rates totally up to currency traders.* The price of its currency is allowed to rise and fall as private market forces dictate.

Partially flexible exchange rate: *When the government sometimes buys or sells currencies to influence the exchange rate, while at other times letting private market forces operate.* A partially flexible exchange rate is sometimes called a dirty float because it isn't purely market-determined or government-determined.

Fixed Exchange Rates

The advantages of a fixed exchange rate system are:

1. Fixed exchange rates provide international monetary stability.
2. Fixed exchange rates force governments to make adjustments to meet their international problems.

The disadvantages of a fixed exchange rate system are:

1. Fixed exchange rates can become unfixed. When they're expected to become unfixed, they create enormous monetary instability.
2. Fixed exchange rates force governments to make adjustments to meet their international problems. (Yes, this is a disadvantage as well as an advantage.)

Let's consider each in turn.

Fixed Exchange Rates and Exchange Rate Stability The advantage of fixed exchange rates is that firms know what exchange rates will be, making trade easier. However, to maintain fixed exchange rates, the government must choose an exchange rate and have sufficient official reserves to support that rate. If the rate it chooses is too high, its exports lag and the country continually loses official reserves. If the rate it chooses is too low, it is paying more for its imports than it needs to and is building up official reserves. Notice that, in principle, any trader could establish a fixed exchange rate by guaranteeing to buy or sell a currency at a given rate. Any "fix," however, is only as good as the guarantee, and to fix an exchange rate would require many more resources than an individual trader has; only governments have sufficient resources to fix an exchange rate, and often even governments run out of resources.

Fixed exchange rates provide international monetary stability and force governments to make adjustments to meet their international problems. (This is *also* a disadvantage.) If they become unfixed, they create monetary instability.

A major difficulty of fixing an exchange rate is that as soon as the country gets close to its official reserves limit, foreign exchange traders begin to expect a drop in the value of the currency, and they try to get out of that currency because anyone holding that currency when it falls will lose money. For example, in December 1997, when traders found out that South Korea had only $10 billion in reserves instead of the official government announcement of $30 billion, they sold the Korean won and its value dropped. False rumors of an expected depreciation or decrease in a country's fixed exchange rate can become true by causing a "run on a currency," as all traders sell that currency. Thus, at times fixed exchange rates can become highly unstable because expectation of a change in the exchange rate can force the change to occur. As opposed to small movements in currency values, under a fixed rate regime these movements occur in large, sudden jumps.

Fixed Exchange Rates and Policy Independence Maintaining a fixed exchange rate places limitations on a central bank's actions. In a country with fixed exchange rates, the central bank must ensure that the international quantities of its currency supplied and demanded are equal at the existing exchange rate.

Say, for example, that the United States and the Bahamas have fixed exchange rates: $1 B = $1 U.S. The Bahamian central bank decides to run an expansionary monetary policy, lowering the interest rate and stimulating the Bahamian economy. The lower interest rates will cause financial capital to flow out of the country, and the higher income will increase imports. Demand for Bahamian dollars will fall. To prop up its dollar and to maintain the fixed exchange rate, the Bahamian government will have to buy its own currency. It can do so only as long as it has sufficient official reserves of other countries' currencies.

Because most countries' official reserves are limited, a country with fixed exchange rates is limited in its ability to conduct expansionary monetary and fiscal policies. It loses its freedom to stimulate the economy in response to a recession. That's why, when a serious recession hits, many countries are forced to abandon fixed exchange rates. They run out of official reserves and choose expansionary monetary policy to achieve their domestic goals over contractionary monetary policy to achieve their international goals.

Because most countries' official reserves are limited, a country with fixed exchange rates is limited in its ability to conduct expansionary monetary and fiscal policies.

Flexible Exchange Rates

The advantages and disadvantages of a flexible exchange rate (exchange rates totally determined by private market forces) are the reverse of those of fixed exchange rates. The advantages are:

1. Flexible exchange rates provide for orderly incremental adjustment of exchange rates rather than large, sudden jumps.
2. Flexible exchange rates allow government to be flexible in conducting domestic monetary and fiscal policies.

The disadvantages are:

1. Flexible exchange rates allow speculation to cause large jumps in exchange rates, which do not reflect market fundamentals.
2. Flexible exchange rates allow government to be flexible in conducting domestic monetary and fiscal policies. (This is a disadvantage as well as an advantage.)

Let's consider each in turn.

Flexible Exchange Rates and Exchange Rate Stability Advocates of flexible exchange rates argue as follows: Why not treat currency markets like any other market and let private market forces determine a currency's value? There is no fixed price for TVs; why should there be a fixed price for currencies? The opponents' answer is based on the central role that international financial considerations play in an economy and the strange shapes and large shifts that occur in the short-run supply and demand curves for currencies.

When expectations shift supply and demand curves around all the time, there's no guarantee that the exchange rate will be determined by long-run fundamental forces. The economy will go through real gyrations because of speculators' expectations about other speculators. Thus, the argument against flexible exchange rates is that they allow far too much fluctuation in exchange rates, making trade difficult.

Flexible exchange rate regimes provide for orderly incremental adjustment of exchange rates rather than large sudden jumps, and allow governments to be flexible in conducting domestic monetary and fiscal policies. (This is also a disadvantage.)

Flexible Exchange Rates and Policy Independence The policy independence arguments for and against flexible exchange rates are the reverse of those given for fixed exchange rates. Individuals who believe that national governments should not have flexibility in setting monetary policy argue that flexible exchange rates don't impose the discipline on policy that fixed exchange rates do. Say, for example, that a country's goods are uncompetitive. Under a fixed exchange rate system, the country would have to contract its money supply and deal with the underlying uncompetitiveness of its goods. Under a flexible exchange rate system, the country can maintain an expansionary monetary policy, allowing inflation simply by permitting the value of its currency to fall.

Advocates of policy flexibility argue that it makes no sense for a country to go through a recession when it doesn't have to; flexible exchange rates allow countries more flexibility in dealing with their problems. True, policy flexibility may lead to inflation, but inflation is better than a recession.

Partially Flexible Exchange Rates

Faced with the dilemma of choosing between these two unpleasant policies, most countries have opted for a policy in between: partially flexible exchange rates. With such a policy, they try to get the advantages of both fixed and flexible exchange rates.

When policy makers believe there is a fundamental misalignment in a country's exchange rate, they will allow private forces to determine it—they allow the exchange rate to be flexible. When they believe that the currency's value is falling because of speculation, or that too large an adjustment in the currency is taking place, and that that adjustment won't achieve their balance of payments goals, they step in and stabilize the exchange rate, either supporting or pushing down their currency's value. Countries that follow a currency stabilization policy have partially flexible exchange rates.

Partially flexible exchange rate regimes combine the advantages and disadvantages of fixed and flexible exchange rates.

If policy makers are correct, this system of partial flexibility works smoothly and has the advantages of both fixed and flexible exchange rates. If policy makers are incorrect, however, a partially flexible system has the disadvantages of both fixed and flexible systems.

Which View Is Right?

Q-9 Does government intervention stabilize exchange rates?

Which view is correct is much in debate. Most foreign exchange traders I know tell me that the possibility of government intervention increases the amount of private speculation in the system. In the private investors' view, their own assessments of what exchange rates should be are better than those of policy makers. If private investors knew the government would not enter in, private speculators would focus on fundamentals and would stabilize short-run exchange rates. When private speculators know government might enter into the market, they don't focus on fundamentals; instead they continually try to outguess government policy makers. When that happens, private speculation doesn't stabilize; it destabilizes exchange rates as private traders try to guess what the government thinks.

Fixed vs. Flexible vs. Partially Flexible Exchange Rates

Many of my economics colleagues who work for the Fed aren't convinced by private investors' arguments. They maintain that some government intervention helps stabilize currency markets. I don't know which group is right—private foreign exchange traders or economists at the Fed. But to decide, it is necessary to go beyond the arguments and consider how the various exchange rate regimes have worked in practice. Appendix A to this chapter gives you an introduction into the history of exchange rate regimes.

Advantages and Disadvantages of a Common Currency: The Future of the Euro

If you think of countries with a fixed exchange rate as being in a marriage between currencies, you can think of a common currency as a marriage for life, from which escape is almost impossible. All the business and legal contracts and institutions are structured around the common currency, and moving away from that will cause a legal morass. But common currencies also offer advantages, and there is no clear-cut economic rule about which exchange rate system is better.

Web Note 20.3
Multinational Money

In 2002 twelve European nations consummated a fixed exchange rate regime established under a European Union (EU) plan for monetary union and adopted the euro as their common currency. Later, more, but not all, European countries joined, with 27 countries belonging to the European Union as of 2013. Of these, 17 use the euro as their currency, as indicated in Figure 20-3 with the euro symbol (€). Their experience provides a good example of both the advantages and disadvantages of moving from a fixed exchange rate system to a common currency.

The European countries that adopted the euro did so for a number of reasons, some political and some economic. Regardless of the reasons they did so, the euro will have significant effects on international finance and trade over the next decade.

Four economic advantages of a common currency are that it:

1. Eliminates the cost of exchanging currencies.
2. Facilitates price comparisons.
3. Creates a larger market.
4. Increases the demand for the currency as a store of wealth.

Advantages of the Euro First, let's consider the advantages the EU countries get from adopting a common currency. The first advantage is that, politically, a common currency ties the countries closely together. World Wars I and II started from fights among European countries. An important motive behind the increasing integration of Europe—from initial creation of a common market, to the establishment of the European Union with reduced border controls, to the establishment of the monetary union—has been to prevent large-scale war within Europe from ever happening again. Many feel that political reasons drove the countries toward an economic and monetary union.

There were, however, also economic advantages. One was that monetary union reduced the cost of trading among countries by eliminating the need to exchange currencies and thereby provided an incentive to increase trade within the European Union. A second was price transparency. With a single currency, consumers and businesses can more easily see price differentials, resulting in greater competition. For example, instead of having to compare a pair of German shoes priced at 60 marks with an Italian pair priced at 48,000 lire, a consumer just needs to compare 30 euros with 25 euros. A third advantage is that the common currency made it more likely that companies will think of Europe as a single market. As firms focused on producing for the European market, European consumers gained more clout and Europe, along with the United States, became the reference market when new goods were planned. It also allowed

FIGURE 20-3 Map of EU Countries

Members of the European Union as of 2013 included Austria, Belgium, Bulgaria, Cyprus, Czech Republic, Denmark, Estonia, Finland, France, Germany, Greece, Hungary, Ireland, Italy, Latvia, Lithuania, Luxembourg, Malta, The Netherlands, Poland, Portugal, Romania, Slovakia, Slovenia, Spain, Sweden, and the United Kingdom. Those countries that also share a common currency are marked with a €, the symbol of the euro.

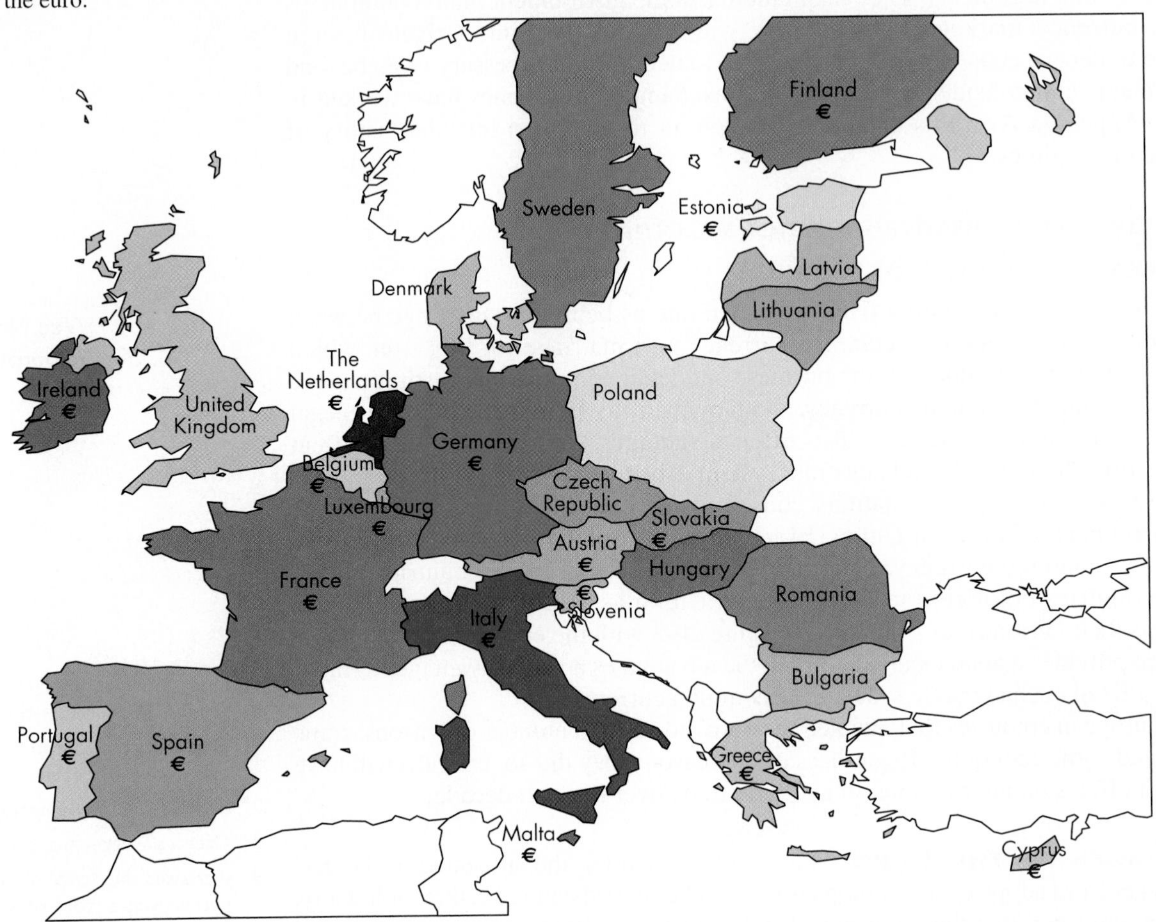

European firms to take advantage of economies of scale (lower costs as production rises) when producing for the European market. Finally, the importance of the euro led individuals throughout the world to hold their assets denominated in euros, increasing the demand for euros as a store of wealth. That lowered the relative interest rate for Europeans.

With an international reserve currency, the EU could create euros and exchange them for other currencies to buy products without increasing their domestic money supply, therefore lowering the possibility of inflation. (The increased money was held by foreigners. For the EU, it would be like getting an interest-free loan.) Because the U.S. dollar has been the world's reserve currency, the United States has been getting those interest-free loans, which is one of the reasons the United States has been able to run continual large trade deficits. If the euro partially replaces the dollar as the world reserve currency, there will likely be a large fall in demand for the dollar and a decrease in its value relative to other exchange rates.

During the first few years after the creation of the euro, most countries that adopted it did well. This was especially true of the southern countries—Portugal, Italy, Greece, and Spain. With a stable currency, they were able to borrow internationally at much lower interest rates than before. Northern countries, such a Germany, also did well since it now had a ready market for its goods, which did not push up the value of its currency as it would have, had it not been part of the eurozone. It all worked well as long as lenders (primarily European banks) were willing to lend money to consumers and governments of the southern countries. The result was a boom in the southern countries built on increased debt. As their governments expanded their spending without increasing taxes correspondingly (they were able to now borrow cheaply), their economies went on a growth spurt.

Joining the eurozone also brought with it obligations—the government deficits they were allowed to run were limited. These obligations, however, were not strongly enforced for a variety of reasons: Governments did not report deficits accurately, the EU simply chose not to enforce the penalties when deficits exceeded agreed-upon levels, or when deficits were run by regional entities (similar to local governments in the United States) that did not face debt restrictions but were implicitly guaranteed by the national government. The initial introduction of the euro was marked by fast growth in the poorer countries and slow but steady growth in the northern, larger countries such as Germany.

Disadvantages of the Euro A common currency has disadvantages as well as advantages. One disadvantage involves national identity. A country's currency is a symbol of a country to its people, and giving it up means losing part of that identity. Loss of nationalism is one reason Britain has been reluctant to adopt the euro.

A second related disadvantage is that a common currency closely ties the economies together. This means that countries have a harder time ignoring the economic problems of other member countries because their banks will be interconnected, and a problem in one country can quickly spread to other countries.

Major disadvantages of a common currency are:

1. Loss of national identity,
2. Increased economic ties among member countries.
3. Loss of independent monetary policy for member countries.

A third major disadvantage of a common currency is that members will no longer have independent monetary policies. So if an external shock hurts one region worse than another, the region hit hardest cannot increase its money supply to offset the effect of the shock on output. Ireland in 2004 to 2006 is an example. Its economy was growing quickly while Germany's economy was contracting. Because the two countries shared the same interest rate and monetary policy, Germany could not run expansionary monetary policy and Ireland could not run contractionary monetary policy. They had to share the same monetary policy.

A more serious variation of this problem occurred in 2012 when the Greek government found that could not pay its debts and was about to default. Because countries had agreed to limit their deficits, such a situation was not supposed to happen, but the provisions to deal with high deficits had not been enforced. Greece, along with Italy, Portugal, and Spain, had all run relatively expansionary fiscal policy and were in danger of defaulting on their debt. The expectation of default led people to sell Greek debt, which pushed up the interest rate Greece and other southern European countries had to pay on new loans, making default even more likely.

The eurozone did not have a strategy to deal with such a default. Many financial institutions in Europe, including most banks, had assumed that the eurozone would not let a country default. They therefore held significant amounts of Greek and other southern European debt, which they had treated as safe reserves. If these countries defaulted, the banks would go bankrupt, not only in Greece, but throughout Europe, and the European financial system would likely crash. Such fears led the European Central Bank to buy large amounts of Greek debt and lend enormous amounts of money to banks in order to avoid a financial crash. As part of the bailout package, other European countries lent Greece money under the condition that it cut public sector wages so that it would become more competitive. They also required Greece to increase taxes and cut government spending to reduce its deficit. Greece was asked to do all this even though the Greek economy was in a severe recession. Eventually, an orderly default was negotiated that kept Greece in the eurozone, at least as of 2012. Other European countries—Portugal, Spain, and Italy—also had high debt and unsustainable deficits, so they might experience similar problems. If they do, they may well be forced to pull out of the eurozone despite all the problems doing so will create.

Q-10 How did Greece's adoption of the euro as its currency make its recent problems more difficult to solve?

If Greece had had its own currency—even if it had been a fixed exchange rate—many of these problems would have been avoided. Banks would never have loaned Greece so much at such low interest rates. If Greece did run into problems, it would have simply given up its fixed exchange rate and allowed the value of its currency to fall. Doing so would have lowered the relative costs of production in Greece, stimulating the economy. But because it used the euro as its currency, it could not do that without removing itself from the eurozone, which, as discussed above, would have meant major problems undermining both institutions and contracts.

Because of these recent problems, there has been much concern about the stability of the eurozone, and it remains an experiment that will be followed carefully over the next decade.

Conclusion

This chapter began with a quotation suggesting that a foreign exchange dealer's office can be the nearest thing to bedlam that there is. Seeing some order within that bedlam is not easy, but understanding the balance of payments and its relation to the determination of exchange rates is a good first step. And it is a step worth taking. With international transportation and communication becoming easier and faster and other countries' economies growing, the U.S. economy will become more interdependent with the global economy in the upcoming decades, making understanding these issues more and more necessary to understanding macroeconomics.

Summary

- The balance of payments is made up of the current account and the financial and capital account. *(LO20-1)*
- Exchange rates in a perfectly flexible exchange rate system are determined by the supply of and demand for a currency. *(LO20-2)*
- The fundamental forces that affect exchange rates are changes in income, prices, interest rates, and trade policies. These forces are often overwhelmed by expectations. *(LO20-2)*
- A country can stabilize or fix its exchange rate by either directly buying and selling its own currency or adjusting its monetary and fiscal policy to achieve its exchange rate goal. *(LO20-2)*
- It is easier technically for a country to bring the value of its currency down than it is to support its currency. *(LO20-2)*
- To raise the price of its currency, a country can either increase private demand through contractionary monetary policy or decrease private supply through contractionary monetary policy. *(LO20-2)*
- Expansionary monetary policy, through its effect on interest rates, income, and the price level, tends to lower a country's exchange rate. *(LO20-2)*
- Fiscal policy has an ambiguous effect on a country's exchange rate. *(LO20-2)*
- It is extraordinarily difficult to correctly estimate the long-run equilibrium exchange rate; one method of doing so is the purchasing power parity approach. *(LO20-3)*
- A real exchange rate is an exchange rate adjusted for differences in inflation:

  $\%\Delta$ real exchange rate $=$ $\%\Delta$ nominal exchange rate $+$ [Domestic inflation $-$ Foreign inflation] *(LO20-3)*

- Fixed exchange rates provide international monetary stability but can create enormous monetary instability if they become unfixed. Fixed exchange rates force governments to make adjustments to meet their international problems. (*LO20-4*)
- Flexible exchange rates allow exchange rates to make incremental changes, but are also subject to large jumps in value as a result of speculation. Flexible exchange rates give governments flexibility in conducting domestic monetary and fiscal policy. (*LO20-4*)
- A common currency has advantages and disadvantages. Members of the eurozone have experienced both. Its most recent experience has been Greece's default of its debt. (*LO20-4*)

Key Terms

balance of merchandise trade *(432)*
balance of payments *(430)*
balance of trade *(432)*
currency stabilization *(437)*
currency support *(436)*
current account *(431)*
financial and capital account *(431)*
fixed exchange rate *(444)*
flexible exchange rate *(444)*
partially flexible exchange rate *(444)*
purchasing power parity (PPP) *(442)*
real exchange rate *(443)*

Questions and Exercises

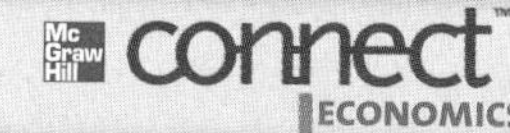

1. If a country is running a balance of trade deficit, will its current account be in deficit? Why? (*LO20-1*)
2. When someone sends 100 British pounds to a friend in the United States, will this transaction show up on the financial and capital account or current account? Why? (*LO20-1*)
3. Support the following statement: "It is best to offset a capital and financial account surplus with a current account deficit." (*LO20-1*)
4. Support the following statement: "It is best to offset a capital and financial account deficit with a current account surplus." (*LO20-1*)
5. State whether the following will show up on the current account or the capital and financial account: (*LO20-1*)
   a. IBM's exports of computers to Japan.
   b. IBM's hiring of a British merchant bank as a consultant.
   c. A foreign national living in the United States repatriates money.
   d. Ford Motor Company's profit in Hungary.
   e. Ford Motor Company uses that Hungarian profit to build a new plant in Hungary.
6. Will the following be suppliers or demanders of U.S. dollars in foreign exchange markets? (*LO20-1*)
   a. A U.S. tourist in Latin America.
   b. A German foreign exchange trader who believes that the dollar exchange rate will fall.
   c. A U.S. foreign exchange trader who believes that the dollar exchange rate will fall.
   d. A Costa Rican tourist in the United States.
   e. A Russian capitalist who wants to protect his wealth from expropriation.
   f. A British investor in the United States.
7. If currency traders expect the government to devalue a currency, what will they likely do? Why? (*LO20-2*)
8. The government of Never-Never Land, after much deliberation, finally decides to switch to a fixed exchange rate policy. It does this because the value of its currency, the neverback, is so high that the trade deficit is enormous. The finance minister fixes the rate at $10 a neverback, which is lower than the equilibrium rate of $20 a neverback. (*LO20-2*)
   a. What traditional macro policy options could accomplish this lower exchange rate?
   b. Using the laws of supply and demand, show graphically how possible equilibria are reached.
9. Draw the schematics to show the effect of expansionary monetary policy on the exchange rate. (*LO20-2*)
10. What effect on the U.S. trade deficit and exchange rate would result if Japan ran an expansionary monetary policy? (*LO20-2*)
11. What would be the effect on the U.S. exchange rate if Japan ran a contractionary fiscal policy? (*LO20-2*)
12. What effect will a combination of expansionary fiscal policy and contractionary monetary policy have on the exchange rate? (*LO20-2*)
13. If a country's actual exchange rate is 20 units per dollar and its purchasing power parity exchange rate is 25, is its currency under or overvalued? Explain your answer. (*LO20-3*)

14. Ms. Economist always tries to travel to a country where the purchasing power parity exchange rate is lower than the market exchange rate. Why? *(LO20-3)*
15. If U.S. inflation is 4 percent, Japan's inflation is 1 percent, and the nominal U.S. dollar exchange rate falls by 3 percent relative to the yen, what happens to the real exchange rate? *(LO20-3)*
16. How is forcing governments to make adjustments to meet their international problems both an advantage and disadvantage of fixed exchange rates? *(LO20-4)*
17. Which is preferable: a fixed or a flexible exchange rate? Why? *(LO20-4)*
18. A *Wall Street Journal* article, "As Fear of Deficits Falls, Some See a Larger Threat," describes the following threat of a high U.S. budget deficit:

    [T]he investors who finance our deficits by buying Treasury bonds and bills, especially the foreigners who buy a larger share of them than ever, will question our ability to repay them, and balk at lending more—triggering a big drop in the dollar and much higher interest rates. *(LO20-4)*

    a. Why would a drop in foreign confidence in the U.S. ability to repay debt lead to a drop in the dollar and much higher interest rates?
    b. In what way are higher interest rates and a lower value of the dollar bad for the U.S. economy?
19. In mid-1994 the value of the dollar fell sufficiently to warrant coordinated intervention among 17 countries. Still, the dollar went on falling. One economist stated, "[The intervention] was clearly a failure . . . It's a good indication something else has to be done." Why would the United States and foreign countries want to keep up the value of the dollar? *(LO20-4)*
20. In the early 2000s, China was running a large current account surplus. *(LO20-4)*
    a. What did this suggest about its financial and capital account?
    b. China's private balance of payments was in surplus. What does this suggest about its exchange rate regime?
    c. What actions was the Chinese central bank likely undertaking in the foreign exchange markets? Demonstrate the situation with supply and demand graphs.
    d. If the Chinese central bank pulled out of the foreign exchange market, what would likely happen to the yuan?
21. What are four economic advantages of the euro for Europe? *(LO20-4)*
22. What are three disadvantages of the euro for Europe? *(LO20-4)*

Questions from Alternative Perspectives

1. If all currencies were on a gold standard, there would be no exchange rates between currencies and we would not face the difficulties presented by fluctuating exchange rates.
    a. What would be the benefit of having all currencies on a gold standard?
    b. What would be the cost? (Austrian)
2. According to Gary North in *Priorities and Dominion: An Economic Commentary on Matthew,* in the book of Matthew, Jesus teaches about the rate of exchange between earthly wealth and eternal wealth.
    a. Would Jesus argue for a high or low exchange rate for earthly riches? Explain your answer.
    b. Do wealthy people believe the exchange rate is high or low?
    c. Do you believe the perceived exchange rate falls or rises as one approaches death? (Religious)
3. Most traders in currencies are men.
    a. Why is this?
    b. Why has it remained even though there is supposed to be no discrimination in employment?
    c. The language of traders is often quite coarse; does this fact provide a possible answer to both *a* and *b*?
    d. Did you think of the observation in *c* before you read it? (Feminist)
4. Nobel Prize–winning economist James Tobin has suggested that a method of decreasing unwanted sudden capital flows among countries would be to place a small tax on such flows. Post-Keynesian economist Paul Davidson argued against doing so because it won't solve the problem, suggesting that it is like using a pebble when a boulder is needed. What might Davidson's argument be? (Hint: It is related to the role of expectations.) (Post-Keynesian)
5. Most economists favor lowering barriers to trade. But even among mainstream economists there is far less support for financial liberalization—the removal of government regulation of financial and capital markets—than for trade liberalization. "It is a seductive idea," says free-trader Jagdish Bhagwati, "but the claims of enormous benefit from free capital mobility are not persuasive." In addition, capital market liberalization entails substantial risks because it strips away the regulations intended to control the flow of short-term loans and contracts in and out of a country. The IMF, on the other hand, remains an unabashed supporter of free financial markets, arguing that they are a precondition for a developing country attracting long-term foreign investment.
    a. Who has it right?
    b. Is financial liberalization a good or bad policy, especially for developing countries? (Radical)

Issues to Ponder

1. In the early 1980s, the U.S. economy fell into a recession (the government faced the problem of both a high federal deficit and a high trade deficit, called the twin deficits), and the dollar was very strong. Can you provide an explanation for this sequence of events?
2. During the 1995–96 Republican presidential primaries, Patrick Buchanan wrote an editorial in *The Wall Street Journal* beginning, "Since the Nixon era the dollar has fallen 75 percent against the yen, 60 percent against the mark." What trade policies do you suppose he was promoting? He went on to outline a series of tariffs. Agree or disagree with his policies.
3. In an op-ed article, Paul Volcker, former chairman of the Board of Governors of the Federal Reserve, asked the following question: "Is it really worth spending money in the exchange markets, modifying monetary policy, and taking care to balance the budget just to save another percentage or two [of value of exchange rates]?" What's your answer to this question?
4. If you were the finance minister of Never-Never Land, how would you estimate the long-run exchange rate of your currency, the neverback? Defend your choice as well as discuss its possible failings.
5. Dr. Dollar Bill believes price stability is the main goal of central bank policy. Is the doctor more likely to prefer fixed or flexible exchange rates? Why?
6. One of the basic laws of economics is the law of one price. It says that given certain assumptions one would expect that if free trade is allowed, the prices of goods in multiple countries should converge. This law underlies purchasing power parity.
   a. What are three assumptions likely to be?
   b. Should the law of one price hold for labor also? Why or why not?
   c. Should it hold for capital more so or less so than for labor? Why or why not?
7. Should Canada, the United States, and Mexico adopt a common currency? Why or why not?
8. If expansionary monetary policy immediately increases inflationary expectations and the price level, how might the effect of monetary policy on the exchange rate be different from that presented in this chapter?
9. In Figure 20-2, a foreign government chooses to maintain an equilibrium market exchange rate of U.S. $1.30 per unit of its own currency. Discuss the implications of the government trying to maintain a higher fixed rate—say at $1.50.

Answers to Margin Questions

1. The expenditures of a U.S. citizen traveling abroad will show up as a debit on the services account. As tourism or traveling, it is a service. (*p. 432; LO20-1*)
2. Net investment income is the return a country gets on its foreign investment minus the return foreigners get on their investment within a country. A country is a net debtor nation if the value of foreign investment within a country exceeds the value of its investment abroad. A country can be a net debtor nation and still have positive net investment income if its foreign investment is undervalued at market values (valuation is generally done at book value), or if its foreign investment earns a higher rate of return than foreigners' investment within that country. (*p. 434; LO20-1*)
3. In the short run, normal market forces have a limited, and possibly even perverse, effect on exchange rates, which is why most governments don't leave determination of exchange rates to the market. (*p. 435; LO20-2*)
4. In general, it would be easier for the United States to push the value of the dollar down because doing so requires selling dollars and the United States can print more dollars to sell. To push the dollar up requires foreign reserves. (*p. 436; LO20-2*)
5. A fall in a country's interest rate will push down its exchange rate. (*p. 437; LO20-2*)
6. Contractionary monetary policy pushes up the interest rate, decreases income and hence imports, and has a tendency to decrease inflation. Therefore, through these paths, contractionary monetary policy will tend to increase the exchange rate. (*p. 439; LO20-2*)
7. The net effect of expansionary fiscal policy on exchange rates is uncertain. Through the interest rate effect it pushes up the exchange rate, but through the income and price level effects it pushes down the exchange rate. (*p. 441; LO20-2*)

8. The real exchange rate of the dollar relative to the euro rises 1 percent.

   %Δ real exchange rate = %Δ nominal exchange rate + [Domestic inflation − Foreign inflation] = 3 + (2 − 4) = 1. *(p. 444; LO20-3)*

9. There is much debate about whether government intervention stabilizes exchange rates—private traders tend to believe it does not; government economists tend to believe that it does. *(p. 446; LO20-4)*

10. As a member of the eurozone, Greece could not use monetary policy to expand its economy. It could also not let its currency depreciate so that its economy could become competitive. Finally, had Greece had its own currency, lenders would not have let Greece get into the debt problem in the first place. *(p. 450; LO20-4)*

APPENDIX A

History of Exchange Rate Systems

A good way to give you an idea of how the various exchange rate systems work is to present a brief history of international exchange rate systems.

The Gold Standard: A Fixed Exchange Rate System

Governments played a major role in determining exchange rates until the 1930s. Beginning with the Paris Conference of 1867 and lasting until 1933 (except for the period around World War I), most of the world economies had a system of relatively fixed exchange rates under what was called a **gold standard**—*a system of fixed exchange rates in which the value of currencies was fixed relative to the value of gold and gold was used as the primary reserve asset.*

Under a gold standard, the amount of money a country issued had to be directly tied to gold, either because gold coin served as the currency in a country (as it did in the United States before 1914) or because countries were required by law to have a certain percentage of gold backing their currencies. Gold served as currency or backed all currencies. Each country participating in a gold standard agreed to fix the price of its currency relative to gold. That meant a country would agree to pay a specified amount of gold on demand to anyone who wanted to exchange that country's currency for gold. To do so, each country had to maintain a stockpile of gold. When a country fixed the price of its currency relative to gold, it essentially fixed its currency's price in relation to other currencies also on the gold standard as a result of the process of arbitrage.

Under the gold standard, a country made up the difference between the quantity supplied and the quantity demanded of its currency by buying or selling gold to hold the price of its currency fixed in terms of gold. How much a country would need to buy and sell depended on its balance of payments deficit or surplus. If the country ran a surplus in the balance of payments, it was required to sell its currency—that is, buy gold—to stop the value of its currency from rising. If a country ran a deficit, it was required to buy its currency—that is, sell gold—to stop the value of its currency from falling.

The gold standard enabled governments to prevent short-run instability of the exchange rate. If there was a speculative run on its currency, the government would buy its currency with gold, thereby preventing the exchange rate from falling.

But for the gold standard to work, there had to be a method of long-run adjustment; otherwise countries would have run out of gold and would no longer have been able to fulfill their obligations under the gold standard. The **gold specie flow mechanism** was *the long-run adjustment mechanism that maintained the gold standard.* Here's how it worked: Since gold served as official reserves to a country's currency, a balance of payments deficit (and hence a downward pressure on the exchange rate) would result in a flow of gold out of the country and hence a decrease in the country's money supply. That decrease in the money supply would contract the economy, decreasing imports, lowering the country's price level, and increasing the interest rate, all of which would work toward eliminating the balance of payments deficit.

Similarly a country with a balance of payments surplus would experience an inflow of gold. That flow would increase the country's money supply, increasing income (and hence imports), increasing the price level (making imports cheaper and exports more expensive), and lowering the interest rate (increasing capital outflows). These would work toward eliminating the balance of payments surplus.

Thus, the gold standard determined a country's monetary policy and forced it to adjust any international balance of payments disequilibrium. Adjustments to a balance of payments deficit were often politically unpopular; they often led to recessions, which, because the money supply was directly tied to gold, the government couldn't try to offset with expansionary monetary policy.

The gold specie flow mechanism was called into play in the United States in late 1931 when the Federal Reserve, in response to a shrinking U.S. gold supply, decreased the amount of money in the U.S. economy, deepening the depression that had begun in 1929. The government's domestic goals and responsibilities conflicted with its international goals and responsibilities.

That conflict, which was rooted in the after-effects of World War I and the Depression, led to partial abandonment of the gold standard in 1933. At that time the United States made it illegal for individual U.S. citizens to own gold. Except for gold used for ornamental and certain medical and industrial purposes, all privately owned gold had to be sold to the government. Dollar bills were no longer backed by gold in the sense that U.S. citizens could exchange dollars for a prespecified amount of gold. Instead, dollar bills were backed by silver, which meant that any U.S. citizen could change dollars for a prespecified amount of silver. In the late 1960s, that changed also. Since that time, for U.S. residents, dollars have been backed only by trust in the soundness of the U.S. economy.

Gold continued to serve, at least partially, as international backing for U.S. currency. That is, other countries could still exchange dollars for gold. However, in 1971, in response to another conflict between international and domestic goals, the United States totally cut off the relationship between dollars and gold. After that, a dollar could be redeemed only for another dollar, whether it was a U.S. citizen or a foreign government who wanted to redeem the dollar.

The Bretton Woods System: A Fixed Exchange Rate System

As World War II was coming to an end, the United States and its allies met to establish a new international economic order. After much wrangling, they agreed upon a system called the **Bretton Woods system,** *an agreement about fixed exchange rates that governed international financial relationships from the period after the end of World War II until 1971.* It was named after the resort in New Hampshire where the meeting that set up the system was held.

The Bretton Woods system established the International Monetary Fund (IMF) to oversee the international economic order. The IMF was empowered to arrange short-term loans between countries. The Bretton Woods system also established the World Bank, which was empowered to make longer-term loans to developing countries. Today the World Bank and IMF continue their central roles in international financial affairs.

The Bretton Woods system was based on mutual agreements about what countries would do when experiencing balance of payments surpluses or deficits. It was essentially a fixed exchange rate system. For example, under the Bretton Woods system, the exchange rate of the dollar for the British pound was set at slightly over $4 to the pound.

The Bretton Woods system was not based on a gold standard. When countries experienced a balance of payments surplus or deficit, they did not necessarily buy or sell gold to stabilize the price of their currency. Instead they bought and sold other currencies. To ensure that participating countries would have sufficient reserves, they established a stabilization fund from which a country could obtain a short-term loan. It was hoped that this stabilization fund would be sufficient to handle all short-run adjustments that did not reflect fundamental imbalances.

In those cases where a misalignment of exchange rates was determined to be fundamental, the countries involved agreed that they would adjust their exchange rates. The IMF was empowered to oversee an orderly adjustment. It could authorize a country to make a one-time adjustment of up to 10 percent without obtaining formal approval from the IMF's board of directors. After a country had used its one-time adjustment, formal approval was necessary for any change greater than 1 percent.

The Bretton Woods system reflected the underlying political and economic realities of the post–World War II period in which it was set up. European economies were devastated; the U.S. economy was strong. To rebuild, Europe was going to have to import U.S. equipment and borrow large amounts from the United States. There was serious concern over how high the value of the dollar would rise and how low the value of European currencies would fall in a free market exchange. The establishment of fixed exchange rates set limits on currencies' relative movements; the exchange rates that were chosen helped provide funds for the rebuilding of Europe.

In addition, the Bretton Woods system provided mechanisms for long-term loans from the United States to Europe that could help sustain those fixed exchange rates. The loans also eliminated the possibility of competitive depreciation of currencies, in which each country tries to stimulate its exports by lowering the relative value of its currency.

One difficulty with the Bretton Woods system was a shortage of official reserves and international liquidity. To offset that shortage, the IMF was empowered to create *a type of international money* called **special drawing rights (SDRs).** But SDRs never became established as an international currency and the U.S. dollar kept serving as official reserves for individuals and countries. To get the dollars to foreigners, the United States had to run a deficit in its current account. Since countries could exchange the dollar for gold at a fixed price, the use of dollars as a reserve currency meant that, under the Bretton Woods system, the world was on a gold standard once removed.

The number of dollars held by foreigners grew enormously in the 1960s. By the early 1970s, those dollars far exceeded in value the amount of gold the United States had. Most countries accepted this situation; even though they could legally demand gold for their dollars, they did not. But Charles de Gaulle, the nationalistic president of France, wasn't pleased with the U.S. domination of international affairs at that time. He believed Europe deserved a much more prominent position. He demanded gold for the dollars held by the French central bank, knowing that the United States didn't have enough gold to meet his demand. As a result of his and other countries' demands, on August 15, 1971, the United States ended its policy of exchanging gold for dollars at $35 per ounce. With that change, the Bretton Woods system was dead.

The Present U.S. System: A Partially Flexible Exchange Rate System

International monetary affairs were much in the news in the early 1970s as countries groped for a new exchange rate system. The makeshift system finally agreed on involved partially flexible exchange rates. Most Western countries' exchange rates are allowed to fluctuate, although at various times governments buy or sell their own currencies to affect the exchange rate.

Under the present partially flexible exchange rate system, countries must continually decide when a balance of payments surplus or deficit is a temporary phenomenon and when it is a signal of a fundamental imbalance. If they believe the situation is temporary, they enter into the foreign exchange market to hold their exchange rate at what they believe is an appropriate level. If, however, they believe that the balance of payments imbalance is a fundamental one, they let the exchange rate rise or fall.

While most Western countries' exchange rates are partially flexible, certain countries have agreed to fixed exchange rates of their currencies in relation to rates of a group of certain other currencies. For example, a group of European Union countries adopted irreversible fixed exchange rates among their currencies by electing to have one currency—the euro, which was introduced in 2002. Other currencies are fixed relative to the dollar (not by the United States but by the other countries).

Deciding what is, and what is not, a fundamental imbalance is complicated, and such decisions are considered at numerous international conferences held under the auspices of the IMF or governments. A number of organizations such as the Group of Eight focus much discussion on this issue. Often the various countries meet and agree, formally or informally, on acceptable ranges of exchange rates. Thus, while the present system is one of partially flexible exchange rates, the range of flexibility is limited.

Key Terms

Bretton Woods system *(455)*

gold specie flow mechanism *(454)*

gold standard *(454)*

special drawing rights (SDRs) *(456)*

chapter 21

Macro Policy in a Global Setting

> *The actual rate of exchange is largely governed by the expected behavior of the country's monetary authority.*
>
> —Dennis Robertson

"We design them here, but the labor is cheaper in Hell."

Throughout this book I have emphasized the importance of global issues in domestic macro policy. In this chapter, I pull together what we have learned about monetary and fiscal policy, comparative advantage, trade deficits, and exchange rates, and talk about macro policy in a global setting. To begin, I need to discuss our international macro goals.

After reading this chapter, you should be able to:

- **LO21-1** Discuss why there is significant debate about what U.S. international goals should be.
- **LO21-2** Describe the paths through which monetary and fiscal policy affect the trade balance.
- **LO21-3** Summarize the reasons why governments try to coordinate their monetary and fiscal policies.
- **LO21-4** Explain how restoring U.S. competitiveness will likely affect U.S. policy in the future.

The Ambiguous International Goals of Macroeconomic Policy

Macroeconomic international goals are less straightforward than domestic goals. There is general agreement about the domestic goals of macroeconomic policy: We want low inflation, low unemployment, and high growth. There's far less agreement on what a country's international goals should be.

Most economists agree that the international goal of U.S. macroeconomic policy is to maintain the U.S. position in the world economy. But there's enormous debate about what achieving that goal means. Do we want a high or a low exchange rate? Do we want a balance of trade surplus? Or would it be better to have a balance of trade deficit? Or should we not even pay attention to the balance of trade? Let's consider the exchange rate goal first.

The Exchange Rate Goal

The U.S. exchange rate has fluctuated significantly over the past 30 years. There is a debate over whether a country should have a high or a low exchange rate. A high exchange rate for the dollar makes foreign currencies cheaper, lowering the price of imports. Lowering import prices places competitive pressure on U.S. firms and helps to hold down inflation. All of this benefits U.S. residents' living standard. But a high exchange rate encourages imports and discourages exports and can cause a balance of trade deficit that can exert a contractionary effect on the economy by decreasing aggregate demand for U.S. output. So a high exchange rate also has a cost to U.S. residents. It has contributed to the structural stagnation the U.S. economy has recently experienced.

Q-1 What effect does a low exchange rate have on a country's exports and imports?

A low exchange rate has the opposite effect. It makes imports more expensive and exports cheaper and can contribute to inflationary pressure. But, by encouraging exports and discouraging imports, it can cause a balance of trade surplus and exert an expansionary effect on the economy.

Many economists argue that a country should have no activist exchange rate policy because exchange rates are market-determined prices that are best left to the market. These economists question whether the government should even worry about the effect of monetary policy and fiscal policy on exchange rates. According to them, government should simply accept whatever exchange rate exists and not consider it in conducting monetary and fiscal policies.

FIGURE 21-1 The Trade Balance

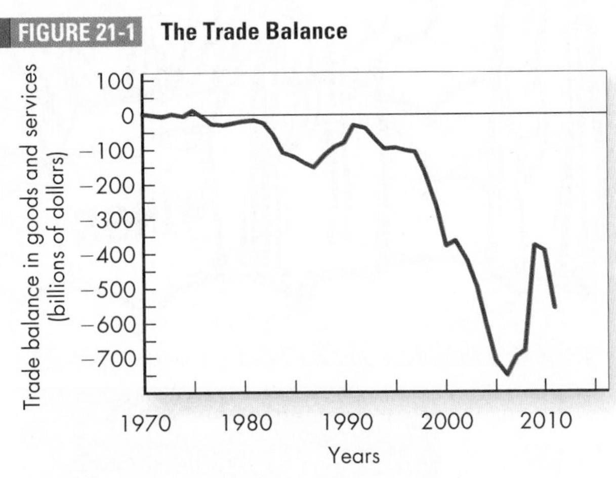

The Trade Balance Goal

Figure 21-1 shows the U.S. trade balance over the past 40 years. You can see that the United States has consistently run a trade deficit over that period, and that that trade deficit has generally increased. A deficit in the trade balance (the difference between imports and exports) means that, as a country, we're consuming more than we're producing. Imports exceed exports, so we're consuming more than we could if we didn't run a deficit. A surplus in the trade balance means that exports exceed imports—we're producing more than we're consuming. Since consuming more than we otherwise could is kind of nice, it might seem that a trade deficit is preferred to a trade surplus.

But wait. A trade deficit isn't without costs, and a trade surplus isn't without benefits. We pay for a trade deficit by selling off U.S. assets to foreigners—by selling U.S. companies, factories, land, and buildings to foreigners, or selling them financial assets such as U.S. dollars, stocks, and bonds. All the future interest and profits on these assets will go to foreigners, not U.S. citizens. That means eventually, sometime in the future, we will have to produce more than we consume so we can pay them *their* profit and interest on *their* assets. Thus, while in the short run a trade deficit allows more current consumption, in the long run it presents potential problems.

Running a trade deficit is good in the short run but presents problems in the long run.

As long as a country can borrow, or sell assets, a country can have a trade deficit. But if a country runs a trade deficit year after year, eventually the long run will arrive and the country will run out of assets to sell and run out of other countries from whom to borrow. When that happens, the trade deficit problem must be faced. Trade deficits can also cause short-run problems. A trade deficit means that there is less demand for U.S. goods, which will lead to higher unemployment and slower growth in the United States. Thus a country's potential output will be lower with a trade deficit than it would be without one. If the country attempts to prevent that higher unemployment with expansionary monetary and fiscal policy, the result will not be inflation as long as global competition is holding down prices, but it might be a financial bubble, which, when it crashes, will lead to a difficult period of structural adjustment.

REAL-WORLD APPLICATION

The U.S. Trade Deficit and the Value of the Dollar

The continued U.S. trade deficit that started back in the 1970s and has continued into the 2000s has confounded many analysts. Why has it remained so high? Why are other countries willing to give the United States many more real goods and services than they require in return? The answer is that they want to buy U.S. assets. There are a number of reasons why. First, the value of U.S. assets has increased. For example, Japan's stock market and real estate markets were falling while the U.S. stock market was rising, which gave Japanese investors a strong incentive to invest in the United States. Second, the United States is considered a safe haven—a solid economy that is safer than any other. If you want safety, you buy U.S. government bonds. Third, Japan and China have been buying large amounts of dollars in order to prevent the value of the dollar from falling relative to their currencies. At some point, however, the demand for U.S. assets is expected to end and the U.S. trade deficit will have to fall. In 2006 and 2007, the value of the dollar fell substantially relative to many other currencies, but then in 2008 it rose as the international financial crisis made safety, not the return on investment, the overriding factor in individuals' decisions about where to hold their assets. Since then it has fallen some, but it is still not low enough to eliminate the trade deficit.

If a majority of economic analysts are correct, over the next decade, we should see a continued fall in the price of the dollar, which will lower the relative price of U.S. exports and increase the cost of imports, which will lead to a lower trade deficit. Because people don't want to hold assets in currencies whose values are falling, this fall could be much more sudden than policy makers would like, creating serious questions about whether they can do anything to prevent it.

The debate about whether a trade deficit should be of concern to policy makers involves whether long-run effects should be anticipated and faced before they happen and whether short-run structural problems need to be addressed.

Q-2 Why do some people argue that we should not worry about a trade deficit?

Opinions differ greatly. Some say not to worry—just accept what's happening. These "not-to-worry" economists argue that the trade deficit will end when U.S. citizens don't want to borrow from foreigners anymore and foreigners don't want to buy any more of our assets. They argue that the inflow of financial capital (money coming into the United States to buy our assets) from foreigners is financing new investment that will make the U.S. economy strong enough in the long run to reverse the trade deficit without serious disruption to the U.S. economy. They believe the economy is in a normal business cycle, and it will return to high growth. So why deal with the trade deficit now, when it will take care of itself in the future?

Others argue that, yes, the trade deficit will eventually take care of itself, but the accompanying economic distress associated with structural adjustment will be great. By dealing with the problem now, the United States can avoid a highly unpleasant solution in the future.

Both views are reasonable, which is why there's no consensus on what a country's trade balance goal should be.

International versus Domestic Goals

Domestic goals generally dominate international goals.

In the real world, when there's debate about a goal, that goal is generally less likely to guide policy than goals about which there's general agreement. Since there's general agreement about our country's domestic goals (low inflation, low unemployment, and high growth), domestic goals generally dominate the U.S. political agenda.

Even if a country's international goals weren't uncertain, domestic goals would likely dominate the political agenda. The reason is that inflation, unemployment, and growth affect a country's citizens directly. Trade deficits and exchange rates affect them indirectly—and in politics, indirect effects take a back seat. However, as countries' economies become more integrated, international issues intersect more and more with domestic issues.

Web Note 21.1
Putting Exchange Rates First

Often a country responds to an international goal only when the international community forces it to do so. For example, in the 1980s when Brazil couldn't borrow any more money from other countries, it reluctantly made resolving its trade deficit a key goal. Similarly, when other countries threatened to limit Japanese imports, Japan took steps to increase the value of the yen and decrease its trade surplus. Currently China is facing international pressure to let its exchange rate rise. When a country is forced to face certain economic facts, international goals can become its primary goals. As countries become more economically integrated, these pressures from other countries become more important. If the U.S. government budget and trade deficits become unsustainable, the United States may find that it is forced to take international issues more significantly into account.

Balancing the Exchange Rate Goal with Domestic Goals

In the last chapter we talked about monetary and fiscal policy's effect on the exchange rate. In it we saw that while fiscal policy's effect on exchange rates was ambiguous, monetary policy has a predictable effect: Expansionary monetary policy tends to push the exchange rate down; contractionary monetary policy tends to push the exchange rate up.[1] What this means is that in principle, the government can control the exchange rate with monetary policy. The problem with doing so is that monetary policy also affects the domestic economy—contractionary monetary policy decreases income and jobs. Contractionary monetary policy is not a policy that countries generally want to follow.

The way in which monetary policy affects the exchange rate is by affecting the supply and demand for the country's currency. To review this, let's consider the case of Europe that we examined in the previous chapter. That case is shown in Figure 21-2. Europe's problem here is that it wants the exchange rate for the euro to be $1.50, not $1.30. The EU has three options for raising the value of the euro: decrease the private supply of euros (shifting the supply curve in from S_0 to S_1), increase the private demand for euros (shifting the demand curve out from D_0 to D_1), or use some combination of the two. Let's see how it could accomplish its goal with monetary policy.

Q-3 If a country wants to fix its exchange rate at a rate that is higher than the market rate, what monetary or fiscal policy must it use?

To increase the demand for euros, the EU must create policies that increase the private foreign demand for EU assets, or for EU goods and services. In the short run, the European Central Bank (ECB) can increase the interest rate by running contractionary monetary policy. A higher interest rate increases the foreign demand for the EU's interest-bearing assets. The problem with this approach is that to maintain an exchange rate at a certain level, a country must give up any attempt to target its

[1]We don't discuss fiscal policy as a control policy for exchange rates because fiscal policy has an ambiguous effect on the exchange rate, as the interest rate effect of fiscal policy pushes the exchange rate one way and the income effect pushes it another. (See the previous chapter if you are not clear on this effect.)

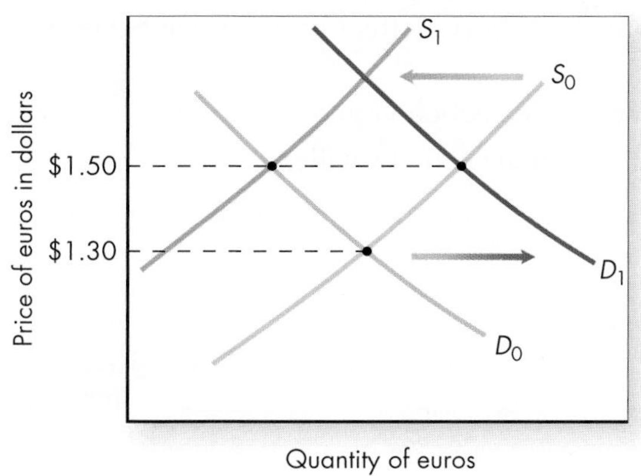

FIGURE 21-2 Targeting an Exchange Rate with Monetary and Fiscal Policy

To increase the exchange rate value of the euro, the European Central Bank (ECB) could run contractionary monetary policy to increase interest rates and increase the private demand for euros or induce a recession and decrease the private supply of euros, or a combination of the two.

interest rate to achieve domestic goals. To put it another way: A country can achieve an interest rate target or an exchange rate target, but generally it cannot achieve both at the same time.

Contractionary monetary policy also slows down the domestic economy and induces a recession. This recession decreases the demand for imports and thereby decreases the private supply of euros. Governments are usually loath to use this contractionary policy because politically induced recessions are not popular. It is because of the constraints that fixed exchange rates, or any policy designed to hold its exchange rate up, place on domestic monetary and fiscal policy that many countries choose flexible, or at least partially flexible, exchange rate regimes.

Q-4 If a country runs a contractionary monetary policy, what effect will that likely have on its exchange rate?

Monetary and Fiscal Policy and the Trade Deficit

Since a major policy issue for the United States in the coming years is likely to be its large trade deficit, and the pressures that will likely decrease that deficit, let's now turn to a consideration of how monetary and fiscal policy affect the trade deficit. We begin with monetary policy.

Monetary Policy's Effect on the Trade Balance

When a country's international trade balance is negative (a trade deficit), the country is importing more than it is exporting. When a country's international trade balance is positive (a trade surplus), the country is exporting more than it is importing.

Monetary policy affects the trade balance primarily through its effect on income. Specifically, expansionary monetary policy increases income. When income rises, imports rise, while exports are unaffected. As imports rise, the trade balance shifts in the direction of deficit. So expansionary monetary policy shifts the trade balance toward a deficit.

Contractionary policy works in the opposite direction. It decreases income. When income falls, imports fall (while exports are unaffected), so the trade balance shifts in the direction of surplus. Thus, expansionary monetary policy increases the trade deficit; contractionary monetary policy decreases the trade deficit.

Q-5 What effect will contractionary monetary policy have on the trade balance?

Monetary policy will also affect the trade balance in a variety of other ways—for example, through its effect on the price level and the exchange rate. These other effects tend to be more long-run effects and tend to offset one another. So we will not consider them here. While many complications can enter the trade balance picture, most economists would summarize monetary policy's short-run effect on the trade balance as follows:

Expansionary monetary policy makes a trade deficit larger.

Contractionary monetary policy makes a trade deficit smaller.

Expansionary monetary policy makes a trade deficit larger.

Contractionary monetary policy makes a trade deficit smaller.

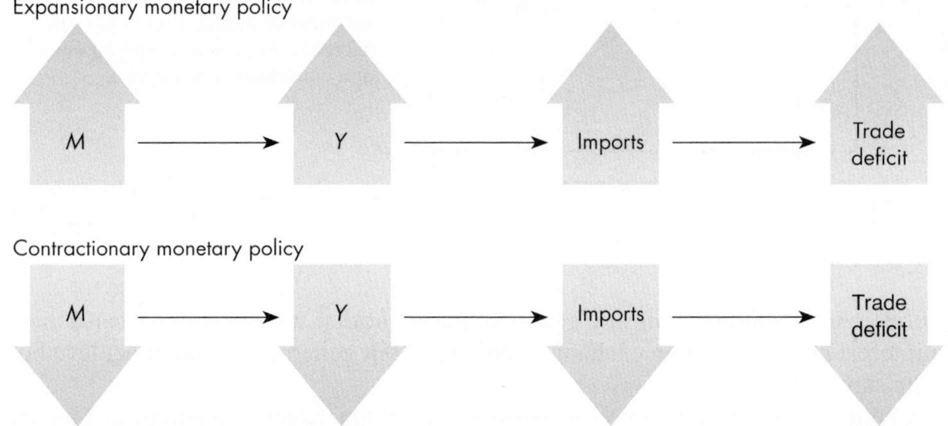

Fiscal Policy's Effect on the Trade Balance

Fiscal policy, like monetary policy, works on the trade deficit primarily through its effects on income. (Again, there are other paths by which fiscal policy affects the trade deficit, but this one is the largest since changes in income are quickly reflected in a change in imports.) So if asked for a quick answer, economists would say that contractionary fiscal policy decreases a trade deficit.

Summarizing the effects of expansionary and contractionary fiscal policy schematically, we have:

Q-6 What is the effect of expansionary fiscal policy on the trade deficit?

Contractionary fiscal policy decreases a trade deficit.

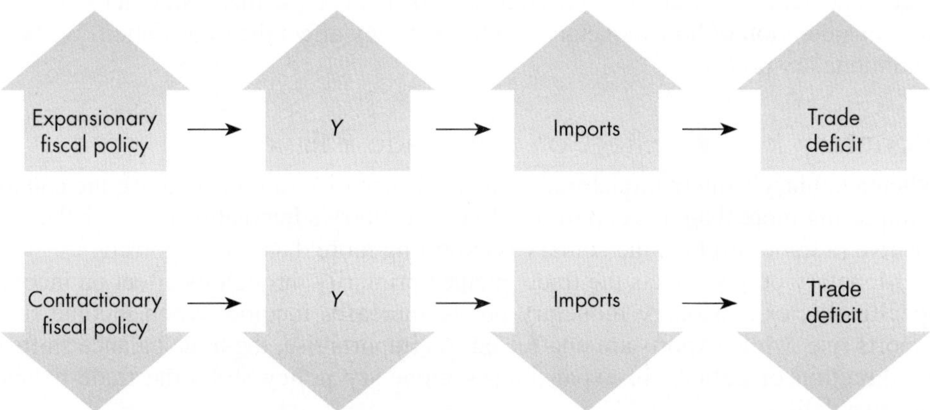

International Phenomena and Domestic Goals

Web Note 21.2 Coordinating Policies

So far, we've focused on the effect of monetary and fiscal policies on international goals. But often the effect is the other way around: International phenomena change and significantly influence the domestic economy and the ability to achieve domestic goals.

For example, say that Japan ran contractionary monetary policy. That would increase the Japanese exchange rate and increase Japan's trade surplus, which means it would decrease the U.S. exchange rate and increase the U.S. trade deficit, both of which would affect U.S. domestic goals.

Alternatively, let's consider how the current situation is likely to play out for the United States in the coming decade. Currently, the United States is running a large trade deficit, which will be difficult to sustain. If the United States chooses to reduce that trade deficit with monetary or fiscal policy, it will have to run contractionary monetary and fiscal policy, keeping the economy from growing as fast as it otherwise would. That is not a politically attractive option, which is an important reason why the United States has not chosen to deal with the trade deficit with monetary or fiscal policy.

But what if other countries stop buying the large amount of dollar-denominated assets that they are currently buying? The dollar exchange rate will fall, possibly precipitously, unless the trade deficit is reduced. In the long run, that fall in the exchange rate will improve the competitiveness of the U.S. economy, decrease imports, and increase exports. But in the short run, the dollar's decline will place the U.S. economy in a bind, since it will push up prices of imports, creating inflationary pressure, and make Americans worse off. Too fast a decline will likely create severe financial problems that can reverberate through the world economy. If the value of the dollar declines precipitously, other countries will pressure the U.S. government to cut its trade deficit by implementing contractionary monetary and fiscal policy. These policies will be imposed by creditor countries as a requirement for temporary loans to the United States.

Q-7 If other countries stop buying large amounts of dollar-denominated assets, what will likely happen to the value of the dollar?

International Goals and Policy Alternatives

The following table provides a summary of how alternative policy actions achieve international goals:

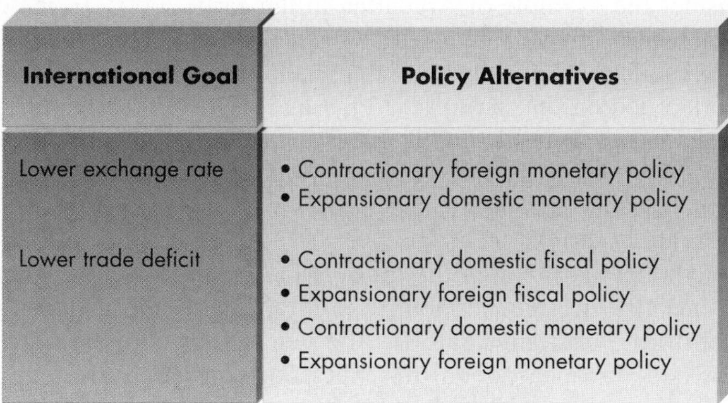

International Goal	Policy Alternatives
Lower exchange rate	• Contractionary foreign monetary policy • Expansionary domestic monetary policy
Lower trade deficit	• Contractionary domestic fiscal policy • Expansionary foreign fiscal policy • Contractionary domestic monetary policy • Expansionary foreign monetary policy

You can see in the table why coordination of monetary and fiscal policies is much in the news, since a foreign country's policy can eliminate, or reduce, the need for domestic policies to be undertaken.

International Monetary and Fiscal Coordination

As I stated above, unless forced to do so because of international pressures, most countries don't let international goals guide their macroeconomic policy. But for every effect that monetary and fiscal policies have on a country's exchange rates and trade balance, there's an equal and opposite effect on the combination of other countries'

Governments try to coordinate their monetary and fiscal policies because their economies are interdependent.

exchange rates and trade balances. When one country's exchange rate goes up, by definition another country's exchange rate must go down. Similarly, when one country's balance of trade is in surplus, another's must be in deficit. This interconnection means that other countries' fiscal and monetary policies affect the United States, while U.S. fiscal and monetary policies affect other countries, so pressure to coordinate policies is considerable.

Coordination Is a Two-Way Street

Q-8 If domestic problems call for expansionary monetary policy and international problems call for contractionary monetary policy, what policy will a country likely adopt?

Policy coordination—*the integration of a country's policies to take account of their global effects*—of course, works both ways. If other countries are to take the U.S. economy's needs into account, the United States must take other countries' needs into account in determining its goals. Say, for example, the U.S. economy is going into a recession. This domestic problem calls for expansionary monetary policy. But expansionary monetary policy will increase U.S. income and U.S. imports and lower the value of the dollar. Say that, internationally, the United States has agreed that it must work toward eliminating the U.S. trade deficit in the short run. Does it forsake its domestic goals? Or does it forsake its international commitment? If the economy is forced to address the trade deficit, it will have no choice but to make the structural adjustments necessary to reduce the trade deficit and bring it into balance. Whether the U.S. economy is in this bind today is debated by economists and policy makers.

Each country will likely do what's best for the world economy as long as it's also best for itself.

There's no one right answer to these questions. It depends on political judgments (how long until the next election?), judgments about what foreign countries can do if the United States doesn't meet its international commitments, and similar judgments by foreign countries about the United States.

Despite the complications, the above discussion gives you an understanding of many events that may have previously seemed incomprehensible. To show you the relevance of what I have said about international considerations, let's look at three situations.

Let's consider the example of Argentina in the early 2000s. In the early 1990s, Argentina established a fixed exchange rate between the peso and the U.S. dollar and promised to maintain that exchange rate under all circumstances. Numerous international investors relied on that promise. In the late 1990s, the Argentinean economy went into recession and domestic political pressures called for expansionary aggregate demand policy. Maintaining the fixed exchange rate required contractionary aggregate demand policy. The internal political pressures won, and Argentina abandoned its fixed exchange rate in early 2002.

The second concerns Japan in the mid-1990s. Japan was experiencing a recession, in part because its tight monetary policy had pushed up interest rates and hence pushed up the exchange rate for the yen. Other countries, especially the United States and European countries, put enormous pressure on Japan to run expansionary fiscal policy, which would keep the relative value of the yen high but simultaneously increase Japanese income, and hence Japanese demand for imports. In response, Japan ran expansionary fiscal policy and this helped to keep the value of the yen higher than it otherwise would have been. Soon thereafter, Japan simultaneously ran expansionary monetary policy, thereby lowering the interest rate and the exchange rate.

The third example is currently ongoing. China is under pressure from many countries to switch from an export-led growth policy to a domestic consumption-led growth policy. This would involve increasing government expenditures on social goods and an increase in the real yuan exchange rate through either domestic inflation or an appreciation of the exchange rate. These policies would help reduce the U.S. trade deficit.

There are many more examples, but these three should give you a good sense of the relevance of the issues.

Crowding Out and International Considerations

Let's reconsider the issue of crowding out that we considered in an earlier chapter, only this time we'll take into account international considerations. Say a government is running a budget deficit and the central bank has decided it won't increase the money supply to help finance the deficit. (This happened in the 1980s with the Fed and the U.S. government.) What will be the result?

The basic idea of crowding out is that the budget deficit will cause the interest rate to go up. But wait. There's another way to avoid the crowding out that results from financing the deficit: Foreigners could buy the debt at the existing interest rate. This is called *internationalizing the debt,* and that is what happened to the U.S. economy in recent years.

There have been massive inflows to the United States of financial capital from abroad. These inflows held down the U.S. interest rate even as the federal government ran large budget deficits. Thus, large U.S. budget deficits didn't push up interest rates because foreigners, not U.S. citizens, were buying U.S. debt.

But, as we discussed, internationalization of the U.S. debt is not costless. While it helps in the short run, it presents problems in the long run. Today about 50 percent of privately held U.S. government debt is held by foreigners. Foreign ownership of U.S. debt means that the United States must pay foreigners interest each year on that debt. To do so, the United States must export more than it imports, which means that the United States must consume less than it produces at some time in the future to pay for the trade deficits it's running now. As you can see, the issues quickly become complicated.

Monetary and Fiscal Policy's Effect on International Goals

The effect of expansionary monetary and fiscal policy on international goals in the short run is summarized in the diagram. In the short run, expansionary monetary policy tends to increase a trade deficit and decrease the exchange rate. Expansionary fiscal policy tends to increase the trade deficit. Its effect on the exchange rate is ambiguous. The effects of contractionary policy work in the opposite direction.

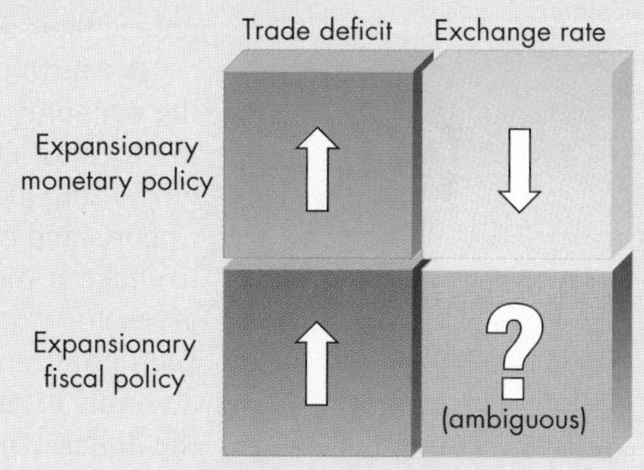

Q-9 How does internationalizing the debt reduce crowding out?

While internationalizing a country's debt may help in the short run, in the long run it presents potential problems since foreign ownership of a country's debts means the country must pay interest to those foreign countries and that debt may come due.

Globalization, Macro Policy, and the U.S. Economy

We began this book stating that the United States operates in a global economy and that policy today must consider global issues. As a conclusion to the chapter, let's pull our various discussions together and review the likely problems that international considerations are creating for the U.S. economy over the coming decades. I start with some general points about the relationship of international issues to macro policy.

International Issues and Macro Policy

The first point is that the more globally connected a country is, the less flexibility it has with its monetary and fiscal policy. Global issues restrict the use of monetary and fiscal policy to achieve domestic goals. How much they do so, and the manner in which they do so, depend on the country's exchange rate regime, which leads to our second point: How fast a country must respond to international pressure depends on the exchange rate regime it follows. If an economy sets fixed exchange rates, its monetary and fiscal policies are much more restricted than they are with flexible exchange rates. The reason is that the amount of currency stabilization that can be achieved with direct intervention is generally quite small since a country's foreign reserves are limited. When this is the case, to keep its currency fixed at the desirable level, it must adjust the economy to the exchange rate. Specifically, it must undertake policies that will change either the private supply of its currency or the private demand for its currency. It can do so by traditional macro policy—monetary and fiscal policy—influencing the economy, or by trade policy to affect the level of exports and imports. This means that if monetary and fiscal policies are being used to achieve exchange rate goals, they cannot also be used to achieve domestic goals.

Q-10 If a country has a fixed exchange rate, does it have more or less flexibility in choosing its monetary and fiscal policy to achieve domestic goals?

A third point is that with flexible exchange rates, countries have more freedom with monetary and fiscal policy, but then they have to accept whatever happens to their exchange rate, and there are often strong political forces that do not want to do that. That is the position in which the United States will find itself if foreigners significantly reduce their demand for U.S. assets.

A fourth point is that an alternative to using monetary and fiscal policy to guide the economy toward meeting its international goals is trade policy designed to affect the level of exports and imports. As discussed in a previous chapter, specific use of tariffs and quotas is limited by international conventions, but indirect policies to affect imports and exports are used all the time. For example, U.S. tax laws can be designed to make it more costly for companies to produce abroad. Implicit subsidies can be given for exports and implicit constraints can be placed on imports. We can expect such programs to continue and to expand in the coming decade as the United States attempts to reduce its trade deficit by means other than a fall in the exchange rate of the dollar, which is the alternative path to reducing its trade deficit.

A fifth point is that macro policy is short-run policy, which must be conducted within a longer-range setting of the country's overall **competitiveness**—*the ability of a country to sell its goods to other countries.* That longer-range setting for the United States in the coming decade is not likely to be conducive to expansionary macro policy, which is a change from the past. Following World War II, the long-run setting did allow expansionary macro policy. The United States had a strong competitive position and a trade surplus even though the value of the dollar was high. (During that time, the United States had a fixed exchange rate; see Appendix A of the previous chapter for a brief history of the period.)

In the 1970s, economic development and investment abroad reduced U.S. competitiveness. Fortunately for the United States, foreign individuals and countries had an enormous demand for U.S. assets. (The capital and financial account surplus discussed in the last chapter reflects that demand.) Had foreign individuals and countries not wanted to increase their holdings of U.S. assets, the long-run setting for macro policy would have been far less conducive to expansionary macro policy. The trade deficit would have lowered the value of the dollar, which would have offset the declining U.S. competitiveness. If this had happened, however, and the United States had also wanted to hold the value of the dollar up, U.S. monetary and fiscal policy would have had to have been contractionary.

Much of the discussion in this chapter is based on the assumption that the standard monetary and fiscal tools are strong enough for policy makers to achieve their goals. This may not be the case since there are limits to what can be achieved with monetary and fiscal policy. For example, currently, the U.S. economy is in a period of slow growth and high unemployment—structural stagnation—and conventional fiscal and monetary policies, even though exceptionally strong by historical measures, have not been strong enough to achieve the level of unemployment and growth that policy makers want and have targeted. This suggests that policy makers will have to either develop new tools or reduce their targets to what the economy can achieve. These new tools will likely involve more international coordination to offset destabilizing monetary flows and exchange rates and structural changes in the economy to make institutions better able to deal with global competition.

Restoring International Trade Balance to the U.S. Economy

Web Note 21.4
Trade Policy Agenda

As I have emphasized throughout this book, when we think about the likely future direction of the U.S. economy, we have to integrate the theory of comparative advantage into our discussion because it provides the long-run setting within which short-run policy is conducted. The theory of comparative advantage focuses on the case where trade is balanced—where the comparative advantages of both countries in various goods are balanced. If that is not the case, economic theory assumes something will adjust to bring them into balance.[2] But when the demand for a country's assets is large, those adjustments do not have to take place. That's what happened to the United States. The large demand for U.S. assets allowed U.S. production in a variety of goods and services to lose their competitiveness. U.S. comparative advantage was not in produced goods but in assets; the demand for its assets meant that the United States needed a smaller demand for its goods and services to maintain a balance of payments equilibrium. Thinking only in terms of goods and services, at current exchange rates, the United States doesn't have a comparative advantage in as many different goods and services as do other countries. That's what it means to be running a trade deficit. As long as other countries are willing to accept U.S. currency or U.S. assets in payment for the goods that they produce, the United States can continue to run a trade deficit at the current exchange rate.

As long as other countries are willing to accept U.S. currency or U.S. assets in payment for the goods that they produce, the United States can continue to run a trade deficit at the current exchange rate.

We've seen downward pressure on the value of the dollar, but the real value of the dollar against the Chinese yuan or Indian rupee has a ways to fall yet, in part because their central banks have bought dollars to stop their own currencies from appreciating. (A good review of the last chapter is to discuss, using supply and demand curves, how the Central Bank of China is preventing the appreciation of the yuan.)

At some point, foreigners will not be willing to accumulate more U.S. currency or assets and foreign government support will likely slow. When this happens, assuming nothing else changes, the dollar will depreciate, especially relative to the rupee and yuan, until the United States regains comparative advantage in enough goods to create a balance in the balance of payments without the inflow of foreign financial assets. Until that happens, we can expect further outsourcing of U.S. jobs and weak U.S. economic growth.

The fall in the value of the dollar is not absolutely certain. Many events could temporarily change the situation. For example, political uncertainty in China or India could slow the process enormously, and even possibly reverse it temporarily. Similarly, large inflation in China or India would serve the same purpose as a rise in their exchange rates, and eliminate the need for the value of the dollar to fall. Even if those events don't happen, a sudden collapse of the U.S. exchange rate is not likely to be in the cards

[2]When David Ricardo first developed the comparative advantage argument, he discussed how, if there were trade imbalances between the two countries, those imbalances would be quickly eliminated by changes in the two countries' price levels as money followed from the deficit country to the surplus country. When he was writing, countries based their currencies on gold, and it was probably a reasonable assumption. Today, capital markets are much more developed, and capital flows in the opposite direction can offset the need for quick adjustment based on imbalances of trade.

because the collapse of the U.S. economy that would accompany it is not in the interest of other countries. Global economies are interconnected; if the U.S. economy were to collapse, so would other world economies. Thus, we can expect foreign governments to step in to support the dollar and slow its fall if the private demand for U.S. assets decreases. Just as the United States does not want its currency to fall too precipitously, China and India do not want their currencies to rise too quickly. This suggests that international pressures on U.S. macro policy will keep U.S. growth slower than what it otherwise would be and place continual downward pressure on U.S. wages for workers producing an expanding number of tradable goods.

Global economies are interconnected; if the U.S. economy were to collapse, so would other world economies.

Conclusion

It's time to conclude the chapter and our consideration of global macro policy. Both have been just an introduction. You shouldn't think of them as any more than that. In no way has this brief chapter exhausted the international topics relevant to macro policy. But the chapter has, I hope, made you better aware of the international dimensions of our economic goals—and of the problems that international issues pose for macro policy—and the book has made you aware of the central insights of economics. That awareness is absolutely necessary if you are to understand the ongoing debates about economic policy.

Summary

- The international goals of a country are often in dispute. *(LO21-1)*
- Domestic goals generally dominate international goals, but countries often respond to an international goal when forced to do so by other countries. *(LO21-1)*
- Expansionary monetary policy, through its effect on income, increases a country's trade deficit. *(LO21-2)*
- Contractionary fiscal policy tends to decrease a country's trade deficit. *(LO21-2)*
- For every effect that monetary and fiscal policies have on a country's exchange rate and trade balance, there is an equal and opposite effect on the combination of foreign countries' exchange rates and trade balances. Therefore, countries try to coordinate their policies. *(LO21-3)*
- International financial inflows can reduce crowding out. *(LO21-3)*
- Internationalizing a country's debt means that at some time in the future the country must consume less than it produces. *(LO21-3)*
- The United States has lost its competitiveness in the production of many goods. Unless foreigners continue to demand U.S. assets, the U.S. trade deficit will put downward pressure on the dollar and U.S. policy makers will face implementing contractionary policies, trade restrictions, or structural adjustments to improve U.S. comparative advantage. *(LO21-4)*

Key Terms

competitiveness *(466)*
policy coordination *(464)*

Questions and Exercises 

1. Is it better to have a low or high exchange rate? *(LO21-1)*
2. Is it better to have a trade deficit or a trade surplus? *(LO21-1)*
3. Why can't a country target both its interest rate and exchange rate? *(LO21-1)*
4. What effect on the U.S. trade deficit would result if China and Japan ran an expansionary monetary policy? *(LO21-2)*
5. What would be the effect on the U.S. trade deficit if China and Japan ran a contractionary fiscal policy? *(LO21-2)*
6. Draw the schematics to show the effect of expansionary monetary policy on the trade deficit. *(LO21-2)*
7. You observe that over the past decade a country's trade deficit has risen. *(LO21-2)*
   a. What monetary or fiscal policies might have led to such a result?
   b. You also observe that interest rates have steadily risen along with a rise in the exchange rate. What policies would lead to this result?
   c. Could another explanation be that people in other countries wanted to hold lots of that country's debt?
8. Congratulations! You have been appointed an adviser to the IMF. A country that has run trade deficits for many years now has difficulty servicing its accumulated international debt and wants to borrow from the IMF to meet its obligations. The IMF requires that the country set a target trade surplus. *(LO21-2)*
   a. What monetary and fiscal policies would you suggest the IMF require of that country?
   b. What would be the likely effect of that plan on the country's domestic inflation and growth?
   c. How do you think the country's government will respond to your proposals? Why?
9. Congratulations! You've been hired as an economic adviser to a country that has perfectly flexible exchange rates. State what monetary and fiscal policy you might suggest in each of the following situations, and explain why you would suggest those policies. *(LO21-2)*
   a. You want to lower the interest rate, decrease inflationary pressures, and lower the trade deficit.
   b. You want to lower the interest rate, decrease inflationary pressures, and lower the trade surplus.
   c. You want to lower the interest rate, decrease unemployment, and lower the trade deficit.
   d. You want to raise the interest rate, decrease unemployment, and lower the trade deficit.
10. Is the United States justified in complaining about Japan's and China's use of an export-led growth policy? Why or why not? *(LO21-3)*
11. In the 1990s, Japan's economic recession was much in the news. *(LO21-3)*
    a. What would you suspect was happening to its trade balance during this time?
    b. What policies would you guess other countries (such as those in the Group of Eight) were pressuring Japan to implement?
12. According to a study done at J.P. Morgan, as world trade increased from about 12 percent of world output in the 1970s to about 25 percent of world output in 2000, global differences in growth rates decreased, from around 3 percent in the 1970s to about 1 percent in the early 2000s. *(LO21-3)*
    a. If that is true, would one expect more or less stabilization coming from trade with other countries?
    b. What does this convergence of growth rates suggest about the possibility of a global recession?
    c. If a global recession occurred, what policy recommendation would you put forward?
13. How does internationalizing the debt reduce crowding out? *(LO21-3)*
14. What are the costs of internationalizing the debt? *(LO21-3)*
15. Countries must choose an exchange rate policy. *(LO21-4)*
    a. Why is currency stabilization limited through direct purchases?
    b. What are a country's other options?
16. Why are there strong political forces to manage exchange rates? *(LO21-4)*
17. Domestic policy as it relates to a country's currency is related to the state of the economy. *(LO21-4)*
    a. Why didn't the United States have to implement contractionary policy following World War II even though the value of the dollar was high?
    b. Why didn't a decline in U.S. competitiveness in the 1970s require the United States to run contractionary policy?
    c. Why is the trade deficit creating a challenge to domestic policy today?
18. Why don't foreign countries want the U.S. dollar to fall precipitously? *(LO21-4)*

Questions from Alternative Perspectives

1. In developed countries, the usefulness of an activist monetary and fiscal policy is highly questionable. Why is it even more questionable in developing countries? (Austrian)
2. The United States has been consuming more than it has been producing for more than 30 years, making it the largest debtor nation in the world. Deuteronomy 28:43–44 warns against such indebtedness to foreigners. "Aliens residing among you shall ascend above you higher and higher, while you shall descend lower and lower. They shall lend to you but you shall not lend to them; they shall be the head and you shall be the tail."
   a. Is the trade deficit bad even if it can continue indefinitely?
   b. Are there biblical precepts against living beyond one's means that suggests any trade deficit is bad?
   c. In what way is the Deuteronomist's saying true for America today? (Religious)
3. In 2012, the U.S. federal budget deficit (how much greater government spending was than taxes) was about 7 percent of GDP. That year the trade deficit (how much imports surpassed exports) was about 3 percent of GDP. Also in 2012, investment in the U.S. economy exceeded U.S. private savings by about 3 percent of GDP.
   a. What is the relationship among these three balances?
   b. What do they tell us about who financed the U.S. budget deficit in 2012?
   c. And what do they suggest about the extent of crowding out of private investment in the U.S. economy in 2012? (Institutionalist)
4. The U.S. trade deficit was about $480 billion, or 3 percent of GDP, in 2012. Some economists argue that this gap is truly frightening because the current account deficit is the amount of money the United States must attract from abroad. If foreign investors stop buying U.S. bonds and stocks, then skyrocketing interest rates, plummeting stock values, and an economic downturn will surely follow. Others see the gaping current account deficit as a sign of economic vitality. The flipside of a large trade deficit is, after all, a surplus of capital flowing into your country.
   a. Is the U.S. current account deficit a sign of impending disaster or a sign of economic health or something in between?
   b. How has this unprecedented shortfall affected the U.S. economy and how will it affect our economic future? (Post-Keynesian)
5. What has happened to world income inequality is a matter of sharp dispute. Many analysts claim that world incomes converged in the second half of the twentieth century, leading to a sharp reduction in world inequality. Many others report that the gap between the poorest and the richest people and countries has continued to widen over the last two decades. When a friend who writes about global inequality sorted through these studies, he came to this conclusion: "The wide range of different results of respected studies of world inequality in the last two decades casts doubt on the idea that world inequality has sharply and unambiguously declined or increased during the epoch of neoliberalism." Assuming the friend has read them correctly and fairly, what do these studies imply about the globalization process? (Radical)

Issues to Ponder

1. Look up the current U.S. exchange rate relative to the yen. Would you suggest raising it or lowering it? Why?
2. Look up the current U.S. trade balance. Would you suggest raising it or lowering it? Why?
3. What would likely happen to exchange rates if one country has a comparative advantage in production of most goods and the financial and capital account was balanced?

Answers to Margin Questions

1. A low exchange rate value of a country's currency will tend to stimulate exports and curtail imports. *(p. 458; LO21-1)*
2. A trade deficit means a country is consuming more than it is producing. Consuming more than you produce is pleasant. It also means that capital is flowing into the country, which can be used for investment. They also argue that the inflow of financial capital from foreigners is financing new investment that will make the U.S. economy strong enough in the long run to reverse the trade deficit. So why worry? *(p. 459; LO21-1)*
3. To increase the value of its currency, a country can increase the private demand for its currency by

implementing contractionary monetary policy or it could decrease private supply of its currency by implementing contractionary monetary and fiscal policy. (*p. 460; LO21-1*)

4. Contractionary monetary policy will likely lead to an increase in its exchange rate. (*p. 461; LO21-1*)
5. Contractionary monetary policy will tend to decrease income, decreasing imports and decreasing the trade deficit. (*p. 461; LO21-2*)
6. The effect of expansionary fiscal policy on the trade deficit is to increase the trade deficit. (*p. 462; LO21-2*)
7. If other countries stop buying dollar-denominated assets, the value of the dollar will likely fall. (*p. 463; LO21-3*)
8. Generally, when domestic policies and international policies conflict, a country will choose to deal with its domestic problems. Thus, it will likely use expansionary monetary policy if domestic problems call for that. (*p. 464; LO21-3*)
9. Because foreigners buy U.S. bonds that finance the U.S. debt, the demand for bonds is higher than it otherwise would be and the interest rate is lower than it otherwise would be. (*p. 465; LO21-3*)
10. If a country has a fixed exchange rate, it has less flexibility in choosing its monetary and fiscal policies to achieve domestic goals. (*p. 466; LO21-4*)

chapter 22

Macro Policy in Developing Countries

> *Rise up, study the economic forces which oppress you . . . They have emerged from the hand of man just as the gods emerged from his brain. You can control them.*
>
> —Paul LaFargue

After reading this chapter, you should be able to:

LO22-1 State some comparative statistics on rich and poor countries.

LO22-2 Differentiate growth from development and explain how those differences affect macroeconomic policy.

LO22-3 Explain the particular problems of monetary policy in a developing country context.

LO22-4 List seven obstacles facing developing countries.

Throughout this book, I have emphasized that macro policy is an art in which one takes the principles learned in *positive economics*—the abstract analysis and models that tell us how economic forces direct the economy—and examines how those principles work out in a particular institutional structure to achieve goals determined in *normative economics*—the branch of economics that considers what goals we should be aiming for. In this chapter, we see another aspect of that art.

Most of this book has emphasized the macroeconomics of Western industrialized economies, the United States in particular. That means I have focused on their goals and their institutions. In this chapter, I shift focus and discuss the macroeconomic problems of developing economies.

Developing Countries in Perspective

There are about 7 billion people in the world. Of these, about 5.5 billion (about 80 percent) live in developing, rather than developed, countries. Per capita income in developing countries is around $500 per year; in the United States, per capita income is nearly $50,000.

These averages understate the differences between the poorest country and the richest people. Consider the African country of Burundi—definitely one of the world's poorest. Its per capita income is about $400 per year—less than 1/100 of the per capita income in the United States. Moreover, income in Burundi goes primarily to the rich, so Burundi's poor have per capita income of significantly less than $400.

How does a person live on that $400 per year, as many people in the world do? To begin with, that person can't:

Go out for Big Macs.

Use Joy perfume (or any type of perfume).

Wear designer clothes.

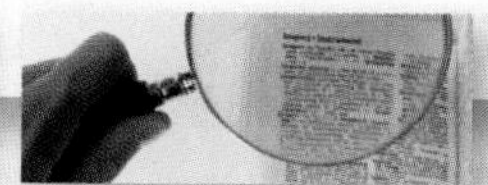

ADDED DIMENSION

What to Call Developing Countries

In this chapter, following common usage, I call low-income countries *developing countries.* They have not always been called *developing.* In the 1950s they were called *backward,* but it was eventually realized that *backward* carried with it significant negative value judgments. Then these countries were called *underdeveloped,* but it was eventually realized that *underdeveloped* also suggested significant negative value judgments. More recently they have been called *developing,* but eventually everyone will realize that *developing* implies significant negative value judgments. After all, in what sense are these countries "developing" any more than the United States? All countries are evolving or developing countries. Many so-called developing countries have highly refined cultures, which they don't want to lose; they may want to develop economically but not at the cost of cultural change.

What should one call these countries? That remains to be seen, but whatever one calls them, bear in mind that language can conceal value judgments.

And that person must:

Eat grain—usually rice or corn—for all meals, every day.

Mix fat from meat—not meat itself—with the rice on special occasions (maybe).

Live in one room with 9 or 10 other people.

Work hard from childhood to old age (if there is an old age). Those too old to work in the fields stay at home and care for those too young to work in the fields. (But children go out to work in the fields when they're about six years old.)

Go hungry because no matter how many family members can work in the fields, probably the work and soil don't yield enough to provide the workers with an adequate number of calories per day.

In a poor person's household, it's likely that a couple of the older children have gone into the city to find work that pays money wages. If they were lucky and found jobs, they can send money home each month. That money may be the only cash income their family back in the village has. The family uses the money to buy a few tools and cooking utensils.

The preceding is, of course, only one among billions of different stories. Even Americans and Europeans who are classified as poor find it hard to contemplate what life is really like in a truly poor country.

Even Americans and Europeans who are classified as poor find it hard to contemplate what life is really like in a truly poor country.

Don't Judge Society by Its Income Alone

Poor people in developing countries survive and often find pleasure in their hard lives. In many poor countries, there are far fewer suicides than in the United States. For example, the U.S. suicide rate for men is approximately 19 per 100,000 people. In Costa Rica it's 10; in Mexico it's 5; and in Peru it's 0.6. Who has time for suicide? You're too busy surviving. There's little ambiguity and few questions about the meaning of life. Living! That's what life's all about. There's no "Mom, what am I going to do today?" You know what you're going to do: survive if you can. And survival is satisfying.

Often these economically poor societies have elaborate cultural rituals and networks of intense personal relationships that provide individuals with a deep sense of fulfillment and satisfaction.

Often economically poor societies have cultures that provide individuals with a deep sense of fulfillment and satisfaction.

Are people in these societies as happy as Americans are? If your immediate answer is no, be careful to understand the difficulty of making such a judgment. The answer isn't clear-cut. For us to say, "My God! What a failure their system is!" is wrong. It's an inappropriate value judgment about the relative worth of cultures. All too often

Americans have gone into another country to try to make people better off but have ended up making them worse off.

An economy is part and parcel of a culture.

An economy is part and parcel of a culture. You can't judge just an economy; you must judge the entire culture. Some developing countries have cultures that, in many people's view, are preferable to ours. If one increases a country's income but takes away its culture in doing so, its people arguably may be worse off.

That said, if we asked people in developing countries if they believe that they would be better off if they had more income, most would definitely answer yes!

Even culturally sensitive people agree that economic growth within the context of a developing country's culture would be a good thing, if only because those countries exist simultaneously with market economies. Given market societies' expansionary tendencies, without economic growth, cultures in economically poor countries would simply be overrun and destroyed by the cultures of market societies. Their land would be taken, their agricultural patterns would be changed, their traditional means of subsistence would be destroyed, and their cultures would be obliterated. So, generally, the choice isn't between development and preservation of the existing culture (and its accompanying ancient ways to which the poor have adjusted). Rather, the choice is between development (with its attendant wrenching cultural transitions) and continuing poverty and slower, but still painful, cultural transitions.

Q-1 In what way is economic development the only choice for developing countries?

Some Comparative Statistics on Rich and Poor Nations

The low average income in poor countries has its effects on people's lives. Life expectancy is about 60 years in most very economically poor countries (compared to about 80 years in the United States). In economically poor countries, most people drink contaminated water, consume about half the number of calories the World Health Organization has determined is minimal for good health, and do physical labor (often of the kind done by machine in developed countries). Table 22-1 compares developing countries, middle-income countries, and developed countries.

As with all statistics, care must be taken in interpreting the figures in Table 22-1. For example, the income comparisons were all made on the basis of current exchange rates. But relative prices between rich and poor countries often differ substantially; the cost of goods relative to total income tends to be much lower for people in developing countries than for those in developed countries.

To allow for these differences, some economists have looked at the domestic purchasing power of money in various countries and have adjusted the comparisons accordingly. Rather than comparing incomes by using exchange rates, they use **purchasing power parity (PPP)**—*a method of comparing income by looking at the domestic purchasing power of money in different countries.* That is, purchasing power parity equalizes the cost of an identical basket of goods among countries. Using purchasing power parity, the World Bank found that income differences among countries are cut by half. In other words, when one uses the World Bank's PPP method of comparison, it's as if the people in developing countries had much more income than they had when their incomes were compared using market exchange rates.

Purchasing power parity exchange rates are calculated by determining what a specified basket of consumer goods will cost in various countries.

A similar adjustment can be made with the life expectancy rates. A major reason for the lower life expectancies in developing countries is their high infant mortality rates. Once children survive infancy, however, their life expectancies are much closer to those of children in developed countries. Say life expectancy at birth is 50 years and that 10 percent of all infants die within their first year. As a person grows older, at each birthday the person's life expectancy is higher. So if a child lives to the age of 3 years, then at that point the child has an actual life expectancy of close to 60 years, rather than 50 years.

TABLE 22-1 Statistics on Selected Developing, Middle-Income, and Developed Countries

Country	Physicians (per 1,000)	Daily Calorie Supply	Life Expectancy	Infant Mortality (per 1,000)	Labor Force in Agriculture (%)	Labor Force in Industry (%)	Adult Literacy Rate	Cellular Phones (per 1,000)	GDP per Capita ($)
Developing									
Bangladesh	0.26	2,250	69	60	45%	11%	56%	228	$ 547
Ethiopia	0.03	1,950	51	76	85	15	43	16	358
Haiti	0.25	1,850	62	60	66	9	40	252	671
Middle-Income									
Brazil	2.06	3,040	75	21	20	26	89	636	10,710
Iran	0.45	3,085	73	36	25	31	77	455	4,526
Republic of Korea	3.29	3,070	81	4	7	24	98	866	20,757
Thailand	0.37	2,530	74	16	42	20	93	790	4,608
Developed									
Japan	2.00	2,810	83	2	4	26	99	842	42,831
Sweden	3.30	3,120	81	3	1	28	99	1,148	48,897
United States	2.30	3,770	78	6	1	20	99	847	47,153

Sources: *World Development Report, 2012*, The World Bank (www.worldbank.org); Because of reporting lags, some data are for earlier years.

Growth versus Development

Economists use the term *developing,* rather than *growing,* to emphasize that the goals of these countries involve more than simply an increase in output; these countries are changing their underlying institutions. Put another way, these economies are changing their production functions; they are not increasing inputs given a production function. Thus, *development* refers to an increase in productive capacity and output brought about by a change in the underlying institutions, and *growth* refers to an increase in output brought about by an increase in inputs.

Growth occurs because of an increase in inputs, given a production function; development occurs through a change in the production function.

The distinction can be overdone. Institutions, and hence production functions, in developed as well as in developing countries are continually changing, and output changes are a combination of changes in production functions and increases in inputs. For example, in the 1990s and early 2000s, the major Western economies have been **restructuring** their economies—*changing the underlying economic institutions*—as they work to compete better in the world economy. As they restructure, they change their methods of production, their laws, and their social support programs. Thus, in some ways, they are doing precisely what developing countries are doing—developing rather than just growing. As the United States faces greater globalization, it will be forced to make more and more structural adjustments and face slower growth as those adjustments are made. Despite the ambiguity, the distinction between growth and development can be a useful one if you remember that the two blend into each other.

Q-2 Why does restructuring in developed countries suggest that the distinction between growth and development can be overdone?

The reason economists separate out developing economies is that these economies (1) have different institutional structures and (2) weight goals differently than do Western developed economies. These two differences—in institutional structure and in goals—change the way in which the lessons of abstract theory are applied and discussed.

While the lessons of abstract theory do not change when we shift our attention to developing economies, the institutions and goals change enormously.

Differing Goals

When discussing macro policy within Western developed economies, I did not dwell on questions of normative goals of macroeconomics. Instead, I used generally accepted goals in the United States as the goals of macro policy—achieving low inflation, low unemployment, and an acceptable growth rate—with a few caveats. You may have noticed that the discussion focused more on what might be called stability goals—achieving low unemployment and low inflation—than it did on the acceptable growth rate goal. I chose that focus because growth in Western developed countries is desired because it holds unemployment down, and because it avoids difficult distributional questions, as much as it is desired for its own sake. Our economy has sufficient productive capacity to provide its citizens, on average, with a relatively high standard of living. The problem facing Western societies is as much seeing that all members of those societies share in that high standard of living as it is raising the standard.

There are differences in normative goals between developing and developed countries because their wealth differs. Developing countries face basic economic needs whereas developed countries' economic needs are considered by most people to be normatively less pressing.

In the developing countries, goals are weighted differently. Growth and development are primary goals. When people are starving and the economy isn't fulfilling people's basic needs—adequate food, clothing, and shelter—a main focus of macro policy will be on how to increase the economy's growth rate through development so that the economy can fulfill those basic needs.

Differing Institutions

Developing countries differ from developed countries not only in their goals but also in their macroeconomic institutions. These macroeconomic institutions are qualitatively different from institutions in developed countries. Their governments are different; their financial institutions—the institutions that translate savings into investment—are different; their fiscal institutions—the institutions through which government collects taxes and spends its money—are different; and their social and cultural institutions are different. Because of these differences, the way in which we discuss macroeconomic policy is different.

Economies at different stages of development have different institutional needs because the problems they face are different.

One of the differences concerns very basic market institutions—such as Western-style property rights and contract law. In certain groups of developing countries, most notably sub-Saharan Africa, these basic market institutions don't exist; instead, communal property rights and tradition structure economic relationships. How can one talk about market forces in such economies?[1] On a more mundane level, consider the issue of monetary policy. Talking about monetary policy via open market operations (the buying and selling of bonds by the central bank) is not all that helpful when there is no market for government bonds, as is the case in many developing countries.

Let's now consider some specific institutional differences more carefully.

POLITICAL DIFFERENCES AND LAISSEZ-FAIRE Views of how activist macroeconomic policy should be are necessarily contingent on the economy's political system. One of the scarcest commodities in developing countries is socially minded leaders. Not that developed countries have any overabundance of them, but most developed countries have at least a tradition of politicians seeming to be fair and open-minded, and a set of institutionalized checks and balances that limit leaders from using government for their personal benefit. In many developing countries, those institutionalized checks and balances on governmental leaders often do not exist.

In many developing countries, institutional checks and balances on government leaders often do not exist.

Let's consider a few examples. First, let's look at Saudi Arabia, which, while economically rich, maintains many of the institutions of a developing country. It is an

[1]One can, of course, talk about economic forces. But, as discussed in Chapter 1, economic forces become market forces only in a market institutional setting.

absolute monarchy in which the royal family is the ultimate power. Say a member of the royal family comes to the bank and wants a loan that, on economic grounds, doesn't make sense. What do you think the bank loan officer will do? Grant the loan, if the banker is smart. Thus, despite the wealth of the country, it isn't surprising that many economists believe the Saudi banking system reflects that political structure—and may find itself in serious trouble if oil prices fall significantly.

A second example is Nigeria, which had enormous possibilities for economic growth in the 1980s because of its oil riches. It didn't develop. Instead, politicians fought over the spoils, and bribes became a major source of their income. Corruption was rampant, and the Nigerian economy went nowhere. I will stop there, but, unfortunately, there are many other examples.

Because of the structure of government in many developing countries, many economists who, in Western developed economies, favor activist government policies may well favor Classical laissez-faire policies for the same reasons that early Classical economists did—because they have a profound distrust of the governments. That distrust, however, must have limits. As I discussed in Chapter 3, even a laissez-faire policy requires some government role in setting the rules. So there is no escaping the need for socially minded leaders.

The Dual Economy A second institutional difference between developed and developing countries is the dual nature of developing countries' economies. Whereas it often makes sense to talk about a Western economy as a single economy, it does not for most developing countries. A developing country's economy is generally characterized by a **dual economy**—*the existence of two sectors: a traditional sector and an internationally oriented modern market sector.*[2]

Q-3 What is meant by the term *dual economy?*

Often, the largest percentage of the population participates in the traditional economy. It is a local currency, or no currency, sector in which traditional ways of doing things take precedence. The second sector—the internationally oriented modern market sector—is often indistinguishable from a Western economy. Activities in the modern sector are often conducted in foreign currencies, rather than domestic currencies, and contracts are often governed by international law. This dual economy aspect of developing countries creates a number of dilemmas for policy makers and affects the way they think about macroeconomic problems.

For example, take the problem of unemployment. Many developing countries have a large subsistence-farming economy. Subsistence farmers aren't technically unemployed, but often so many people farm on the land that, in economic terms, their contribution to output is minimal or even negative, so for policy purposes one can consider the quantity of labor that will be supplied at the going wage unlimited. But to call these people unemployed is problematic. These subsistence farmers are simply outside the market economy. In such cases, one would hardly want, or be able, to talk of an unemployment problem in the same way we talk about it in the United States.

WWW Web Note 22.1 The Modern Sector

Fiscal Structure of Developing Economies A third institutional difference concerns developing countries' fiscal systems. To undertake discretionary fiscal policy—running a deficit or surplus to affect the aggregate economy—the government must be able to determine expenditures and tax rates, with a particular eye toward the difference between the two. As discussed in an earlier chapter, discretionary

[2]I discuss these two sectors as if they were separate, but in reality they are interrelated. Portions of the economy devoted to the tourist trade span both sectors, as do some manufacturing industries. Still, there is sufficient independence of the two sectors that it is reasonable to treat them as separate.

fiscal policy is difficult for Western developed countries to undertake; it is almost impossible for developing economies.

Often developing countries do not have the institutional structures with which to collect taxes.

In the traditional sector of many developing countries, barter or cash transactions predominate, and such transactions are especially difficult to tax. Often, the governments in these economies don't have the institutional structures with which to collect taxes (or, when they have the institutional structure, it is undermined by fraud and evasion), so their taxing options are limited; that's why they often use tariffs as a primary source of revenue.

Many government expenditures in developing countries are mandated by political considerations.

Similar problems exist with government expenditures. Many expenditures of developing countries are mandated by political considerations—if the government doesn't make them, it will likely be voted out of office. Within such a setting, to talk about activist fiscal policy—choosing a deficit for its macroeconomic implications—even if it might otherwise be relevant, is not much help since the budget deficit is not a choice variable, but instead is a result of other political decisions.

The political constraints facing developing countries can, of course, be overstated. The reality is that developing countries do institute new fiscal regimes. Take, for example, Mexico. In the early 1980s, Mexico's fiscal problems seemed impossible to solve, but in the late 1980s and early 1990s, Carlos de Salinas, a U.S.-trained economist, introduced a fiscal austerity program and an economic liberalization program that lowered Mexico's budget deficit and significantly reduced its inflation. But such changes are better called a **regime change**—*a change in the entire atmosphere within which the government and the economy interrelate*—rather than a **policy change**—*a change in one aspect of government's actions, such as monetary policy or fiscal policy.* Regimes can change suddenly. For example, in Mexico soon after President Salinas left office, his brother was implicated in a murder and drug scandal. Foreign investors became worried and pulled money out of Mexico. The peso fell, inflation and interest rates rose, and the Mexican economy fell into a serious recession. In one day, the regime of confidence had changed to a regime of uncertainty and confusion, full of questions about what policy actions the Mexican government would take.

A regime change is a change in the entire atmosphere within which the government and the economy interrelate; a policy change is a change in one aspect of government's actions.

Financial Institutions of Developing Economies I spent three chapters discussing the complex financial systems of developed countries because you had to understand those financial systems in order to understand macro policy. While some parts of that discussion carry over to developing countries, other parts don't since financial systems in developing countries are often quite different from those in developed countries.

The primary difference between financial institutions in developing countries and developed countries arises from the dual nature of developing countries' economies.

The primary difference arises from the dual nature of developing countries' economies. In the traditional part of developing economies, the financial sector is embryonic; trades are made by barter, or with direct payment of money; trades requiring more sophisticated financial markets, such as mortgages to finance houses, just don't exist.

In the modern international part of developing economies, that isn't the case. Developing countries' international financial sectors are generally as sophisticated as Western financial institutions. A currency trading room in Ecuador or Nigeria looks similar to one in New York, London, or Frankfurt. That modern financial sector is integrated into the international economy (with pay rates that often approach or match those of the West). This dual nature of developing countries' financial sectors constrains the practice of monetary policy and changes the regulatory and control functions of central banks.

The above is one of many institutional examples of differences that exist and that change the nature of the macro problem. What's important is not so much the specifics of the example but, rather, the general point it brings home. Economies at different stages of development have different institutional, and policy, needs. Institutions with the same names in different countries can have quite different roles. Such institutions can differ in subtle ways, making it important to have specific knowledge of a country's institutions before one can understand its economy and meaningfully talk about policy.

It is important to have specific knowledge of a country's institutions before one can understand its economy and meaningfully talk about policy.

REAL-WORLD APPLICATION

A Real, Real-World Application: The Traditional Economy Meets the Internet

San Juana Hernandez, of Acuna, Mexico, wanted to borrow some money to paint her grocery store and order some more goods to stock. Marco Apaza, of La Paz, Bolivia, needed some money to expand his sporting goods wholesale business and to build an addition on his parents' home, where he lives, so that he has a bit more room. They needed only small amounts—under $1,000 each. In the traditional economy, the possibilities for loans didn't exist; banks generally don't make the type of small loans that they needed, and there were no good methods of providing the loans. But both got their loans, in part because I loaned them some of the money. How did I do it from up here in Vermont? I went to the website Kiva.org, found their loan request (along with thousands of others), sent some money via PayPal. Kiva combined my money with that of another 40 or so people, and made the loan to them.

This innovative program, which is a modern variation on micro credit programs, allows a type of international micro credit, in which individuals throughout the world can make loans to individuals in developing countries. The people go to a microfinance agency in their home city, which checks them out to see that they are legitimate borrowers, and which then posts their loan request on the Kiva website. Individuals with money to lend can go to the website and choose to make loans to whomever they want. There is no guarantee that the loans will be paid back, but the experience to date about repayments has been, as it has with most micro credit lending, very good. Such programs show that technology can help break down the barrier between the traditional and the market sector.

Monetary Policy in Developing Countries

Now that I've discussed some of the ways in which financial institutions differ in developing countries, let's consider some issues of central banking and monetary policy for those economies.

Central Banks Are Less Independent

The first thing to note about central banking in developing countries is that its primary goal is often different from a central bank's primary goal in developed countries. The reason is that, while all central banks have a number of goals, at the top of them all is the goal of keeping the economy running. In normal times Western central banks have the luxury of assuming away the problem of keeping the economy running—inertia, institutions, and history hold Western industrial economies together, and keep them running. Central banks in developing countries can't make that assumption.

What this means in practice is that central banks in developing countries generally have far less independence than do central banks in developed countries. With a political and fiscal system that generates large deficits and that cannot exist without these deficits, the thought of an independent monetary policy goes out the window.

Central banks in developing countries generally have far less independence than do central banks in developed countries.

A second difference concerns the institutional implementation of monetary policy. In a developing country, a broad-based domestic government bond market often does not exist. So if the government runs a deficit and is financing it domestically, the central bank usually must buy the bonds, which means that it must increase the money supply. As you know, increasing the money supply leads to higher inflation. And developing countries on the whole have experienced high inflation, as Figure 22-1

FIGURE 22-1 CPI Inflation, Selected Country Groupings

On the whole, developing emerging countries have experienced higher inflation. In the early 2000s, however, inflation has been relatively low for most countries and the IMF is predicting that it will remain low.

Source: *World Economic Outlook Database,* International Monetary Fund, www.imf.org.

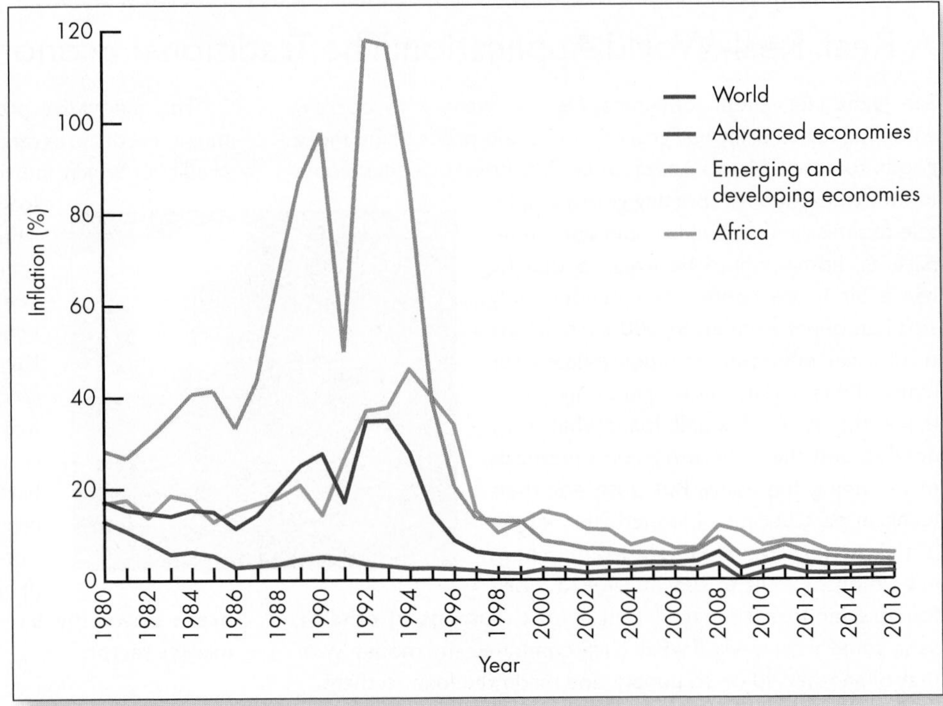

Q-4 If everyone knows that the cause of inflation in developing countries is the creation of too much money, why don't these countries stop inflation?

shows. Central banks recognize that increasing the money supply will cause inflation, but often central banks feel as if they have no choice because of the political consequences of not issuing the money.

The Importance of an Independent Central Bank

As I discussed above, often, in developing countries, the government's sources of tax revenue are limited, and the low level of income in the economy makes the tax base small. A government attempting to collect significantly more taxes might risk being overthrown. Similarly, its ability to cut expenditures is limited. If it cuts expenditures, it will almost certainly be overthrown. With new tax sources unavailable and with no ability to cut expenditures, the government uses its only other option to meet its obligations—it issues debt. And, if the central bank agrees with the conclusion that the government is correct in its assessment that it has no choice, then if the central bank doesn't want the government to be overthrown, it has no choice but to monetize that debt (print money to pay that debt). Sometimes the central bank's choices are even more limited; dictators simply tell the central bank to provide the needed money, or be eliminated.

Inflation works as a tax on holders of obligations specified in nominal terms.

Issuing money to finance budget deficits may be a short-term solution, but it is not a long-term solution. It is an accounting identity that real resources consumed by the economy must equal the real resources produced or imported. If the government deficit doesn't increase output, the real resources the government is getting because the central bank is monetizing its debt must come from somewhere else. Where do those real resources come from? From the **inflation tax**—*an implicit tax on the holders of cash and the holders of any obligations specified in nominal terms.* Inflation works as a type of tax on these individuals.

Faced with the prospect of a collapse of government, the central banks generally choose to keep the governments operating (which isn't surprising since they are often branches of the government). To do that, they increase the money supply enormously, causing hyperinflation in many of these countries. These hyperinflations soon take on a life of their own. The expectation of accelerating inflation creates even more inflationary pressure as individuals try to spend any money they have quickly, before the prices go up. This increases velocity, nominal demand for goods, and inflationary pressures.

One problem with using an inflation tax is that in an inflation, the government is not the only recipient of revenue; any issuer of fixed-interest-rate debt (the borrower) denominated in domestic currency also gains. And the holder of any fixed-interest-rate debt (the lender) denominated in domestic currency loses. This income redistribution caused by an inflation can temporarily stimulate real output, but it can also undermine the country's financial institutions.

Q-5 In an inflation, who else, besides government, gets revenue from an inflation tax?

The point of the above discussion is that the central banks know that issuing large quantities of money will cause inflation. What they don't know, and what the policy discussions are about, is which is worse: the inflation or the unpleasant alternatives. Should the central bank bail out the government? There are legitimate questions about whether countries' budget deficits are absolutely necessary or not. It is those assessments in which the debate about developing countries' inflation exists; the debate is not about whether the inflation is caused by the issuance of too much money.

Opponents of any type of bailout point out that any "inflation solution" is only a temporary solution that, if used, will require ever-increasing amounts of inflation to remain effective. Proponents of bailouts agree with this argument but argue that inflation buys a bit more time, and the alternative is the breakdown of the government and the economy. Because of the unpleasant alternative, the fact that inflation is only a temporary solution doesn't stop developing countries' leaders from using it. They don't have time for the luxury of long-run solutions and are often simply looking for policies that will hold their governments together for a month at a time.

The fact that inflation is only a temporary solution doesn't stop developing countries' leaders from using it.

Focus on the International Sector and the Exchange Rate Constraint

Another difference between the monetary policies of developed and developing countries concerns the policy options they consider for dealing with foreign exchange markets. Developed countries are generally committed to full exchange rate convertibility. With full exchange rate convertibility, individuals can exchange their currency for any other country's currency without significant government restrictions.

Developing countries seldom have fully convertible currencies. Individuals and firms in these countries face restrictions on their ability to exchange currencies—sometimes general restrictions and sometimes restrictions that depend on the purpose for which they wish to use the foreign exchange.

Various Types of Convertibility Since convertibility plays such a central role in developing countries' macro policies, let's review the various types of convertibility. The United States has **full convertibility**—*individuals may change dollars into any currency they want for whatever legal purpose they want.* (There are, however, reporting laws about movements of currency.) Most Western developed countries have full convertibility.

Q-6 Distinguish between convertibility on the current account and full convertibility.

A second type of convertibility is **convertibility on the current account**—*a system that allows people to exchange currencies freely to buy goods and services, but not to buy assets in other countries.* The third type of convertibility is **limited capital account convertibility**—*a system that allows full current account convertibility and partial capital account convertibility.* There are various levels of restrictions on what types of assets one can exchange, so there are many types of limited capital account convertibility.

Almost no developing country has full convertibility.

Almost no developing country allows full convertibility. Why? One reason is that they want to force their residents to keep their savings, and to do their investing, in their home country, not abroad. Why don't their citizens want to do that? Because when there is a chance of a change in governments—and government seizure of assets as there often is in developing countries—rich individuals generally prefer to have a significant portion of their assets abroad, away from the hands of their government.

These limits on exchange rate convertibility explain a general phenomenon found in most developing countries—the fact that much of the international part of the dual economy in developing countries is "dollarized"—contracts are framed, and accounting is handled, in dollars, not in the home country's currency. Dollarization exists almost completely in the international sectors of countries that have nonconvertible currencies, and largely in the international sectors of countries where the currency is convertible on the current account but not on the capital account. This dollarization exists because of nonconvertibility, or the fear of nonconvertibility. Thus, ironically, nonconvertibility increases the focus on dollarized contracts in the international sector, and puts that sector beyond effective control by the central bank.

Nonconvertibility does not halt international trade; it merely makes it more difficult.

Nonconvertibility does not halt international trade—it merely complicates it by adding another layer of uncertainty and bureaucracy to the trading process. Each firm that is conducting international trade must see that it will have sufficient foreign exchange to carry on its business. Developing governments will often want to encourage this international trade, while preventing outflows of their currencies for other purposes.

When developing countries have partially convertible exchange rates, exchange rate policy—buying and selling foreign currencies in order to help stabilize the exchange rate—often is an important central bank function. This is such an important function because trade in most of these countries' currencies is *thin*—there is not a large number of traders or trades. When trading is thin, large fluctuations in exchange rates are possible in response to a change in a few traders' needs. Even the uncertainties of the weather can affect traders. Say an expected oil tanker is kept from landing in port because of bad weather. The financial exchange—paying for that oil—that would have taken place upon landing does not take place, and the supply/demand conditions for a country's currency could change substantially. In response, the value of the country's currency could rise or fall dramatically unless it were stabilized. The central bank often helps provide exchange rate stabilization.

Conditionality and the Balance of Payments Constraint In designing their policies, developing countries often rely on advice from the International Monetary Fund (IMF). One reason is that the IMF has economists who have much experience with these issues. A second reason is that, for these countries, the IMF is a major source of temporary loans that they need to stabilize their currencies.

These loans usually come with conditions that the country meet certain domestic monetary and fiscal stabilization goals. Specifically, these goals are that government deficits be lowered and money supply growth be limited. Because of these requirements, the IMF's loan policy is often called **conditionality**—*the making of loans that are subject to specific conditions.* These goals have been criticized by economists such as Joseph Stiglitz, who argues that the contractionary monetary and fiscal policies often required by conditionality tend to be procyclical and only worsen the recession. The

The basis for most IMF loans is conditionality.

IMF responds that in a developing country, the long-run fiscal and monetary goals must take precedence to establish a basis for development.

Even a partially flexible exchange rate regime presents the country with the **balance of payments constraint**—*limitations on expansionary domestic macroeconomic policy due to a shortage of international currency reserves.* Attempts to expand the domestic economy with expansionary monetary policy continually push the economy to its balance of payments constraint. To meet both its domestic goals and international balance of payments constraints, many developing countries turn to loans from the IMF, not only for the exchange rate stabilization reasons discussed above but also for a more expansionary macro policy than otherwise would be possible. Because of the IMF's control of these loans, macro policy in developing countries is often conducted with one eye toward the IMF, and sometimes with a complete bow.

The balance of payments constraint consists of limitations on expansionary domestic macro policy due to a shortage of international reserves.

The Need for Creativity

The above discussion may have made it seem as if conducting domestic macro policy in developing countries is almost hopelessly dominated by domestic political concerns and international constraints. If by macro policy one means using traditional monetary and fiscal policy tools as they are used in standard ways, that's true. But macro policy, interpreted broadly, is much more than using those tools. It is the development of new institutions that expand the possibilities for growth. It is creating a new production function, not operating within an existing one. Macro policy, writ large to include the development of new institutions, can be enormously effective. To undertake such policies requires an understanding of the role of institutions, the specific nature of the problem in one's country, and creativity.

Obstacles to Economic Development

What stops countries from developing economically? Economists have discovered no magic potion that will make a country develop. We can't say, "Here are steps 1, 2, 3, 4. If you follow them you'll grow, but if you don't follow them you won't grow."

Web Note 22.2
Development Economists

What makes it so hard for developing countries to devise a successful development program is that social, political, and economic problems blend into one another and cannot be considered separately. The institutional structure that we take for granted in the United States often doesn't exist in those countries. For example, economists' analysis of production assumes that a stable government exists that can enforce contracts and supply basic services. In most developing countries, that assumption can't be made. Governments are often anything but stable; overnight, a coup d'état can bring a new government into power, with a whole new system of rules under which businesses have to operate. Imagine trying to figure out a reasonable study strategy if every week you had a new teacher who emphasized different things and gave totally different types of tests from last week's teacher. Firms in developing countries face similar problems.

While economists can't say, "Here's what you have to do in order to grow," we have been able to identify some general obstacles that all developing countries seem to face:

1. Political instability.
2. Corruption.
3. Lack of appropriate institutions.
4. Lack of investment.
5. Inappropriate education.
6. Overpopulation.
7. Health and disease.

I consider each in turn.

Seven problems facing developing countries are:

1. Political instability.
2. Corruption.
3. Lack of appropriate institutions.
4. Lack of investment.
5. Inappropriate education.
6. Overpopulation.
7. Health and disease.

Political Instability

A student's parents once asked me why their son was doing poorly in my economics class. My answer was that he could not read well and he could hardly write. Until he could master those basics, there was no use talking about how he could better learn economics.

Roughly the same reasoning can be applied to the problem of political instability in developing countries. Unless a country achieves political stability (acceptance within a country of a stable system of government), it's not going to develop economically, no matter what it does.

All successful development strategies require a stable government.

All successful development strategies require a stable government. A mercantilist or a socialist development strategy requires an elaborate government presence. A market-based strategy requires a much smaller government role, but even markets need a stable environment to function, and for contracts to be made with confidence.

Many developing countries don't have that stability. Politically they haven't established a tradition of orderly governmental transition. Coups d'état or armed insurrections always remain possible.

One example is Somalia. There, a civil war among competing groups back in 1990 led to famine and enormous hardship, which provoked the sympathy of the world. But attempts by the UN and the United States to establish a stable government by sending troops there caused as many, or more, problems than they resolved, and in 1995 the United States withdrew its troops. Twenty years later, Somalia continues to lack a unified central government. Political instability exists in most developing countries, but it is strongest in Africa, which in large part accounts for Africa's history of lower growth than other geographic areas experienced.

Q-7 Why does political instability present an economic problem for developing countries?

Even countries whose governments aren't regularly toppled face threats of overthrow, and those threats are sufficient to prevent individual economic activity. To function, an economy needs some rules—any rules—that will last.

The lack of stability is often exacerbated by social and cultural differences among groups within a country. Political boundaries often reflect arbitrary decisions made by former colonial rulers, not the traditional cultural and tribal boundaries that form the real-life divisions. The result is lack of consensus among the population as a whole as well as intertribal suspicion and even warfare.

For example, Nigeria is a federation established under British colonial rule. It comprises three ethnic regions: the northern, Hausa Fulan, region; the western, Yoruba, region; and the eastern, Ibo, region. These three regions are culturally distinct and so are in continual political and military conflict. Nigeria has experienced an endless cycle of military coups, attempts at civilian rule, and threats of secession by the numerically smaller eastern region. Had each region been allowed to remain separate, economic development might have been possible; but because the British lumped the regions together and called them a country, economic development is next to impossible.

The Influence of Political Instability on Development

Do these political considerations affect economic questions? You bet. As I will discuss shortly, any development plan requires financial investment from somewhere—either external or internal. Political instability closes off both sources of investment funds.

Any serious potential investor takes political instability into account. Foreign companies considering investment in a developing country hire political specialists who analyze the degree of risk involved. Where the risk is too great, foreign companies simply don't invest.

Political instability also limits internal investment. Income distribution in many developing countries is highly skewed. There are a few very rich people and an enormous number of very poor people, while the middle class is often small.

Whatever one's view of the fairness of such income inequality, it has a potential advantage for society. Members of the wealthy elite in developing countries have income to spare, and their savings are a potential source of investment funds. But when there is political instability, that potential isn't realized. Fearing that their wealth may be taken from them, the rich often channel their investment out of their own country so that, should they need to flee a revolution, they'll still be able to live comfortably. Well-off people in developing countries provide major inflows of investment into the United States and other Western countries.

Q-8 True or false? Income inequality leads to higher levels of savings by the rich and therefore has significant advantages for developing countries. Explain your answer.

POLITICAL INSTABILITY AND UNEQUAL DISTRIBUTION OF INCOME The highly skewed distribution of income in most developing countries contributes in another way to political instability. It means that the poor majority has little vested interest in maintaining the current system. A coup? Why not? What have they got to lose? The economic prospects for many people in developing countries are so bleak that they are quite willing to join or at least support a guerrilla insurgency that promises to set up a new, better system. The resulting instability makes development almost impossible.

Corruption

Bribery, graft, and corruption are ways of life in most developing countries. In Egypt it's called *baksheesh* (meaning "gift of money"); in Mexico it's called *la mordida* ("the bite"). If you want to park in a parking spot in Mexico City, you'd better pay the policeman, or your car will get a ticket. If you want to take a photograph of the monument to Ramses II in front of the Cairo railroad station, you'd better slip the traffic officer a few bucks, or else you may get run over.

When rights to conduct business are controlled and allocated by the government, economic development can be hindered.

Web Note 22.3 Transparency

Without a well-developed institutional setting and a public morality that condemns corruption, economic forces function in a variety of areas that people in developed countries would consider inappropriate. In any country, the government has the right to allow imports, to allow development, to determine where you can park your car, to say whether you can take photographs of public buildings, to decide who wins a lawsuit, and so forth. In developing countries, however, those rights can be, and often are, sold. The litigant who pays the judge the most wins. How about the right to import? Want to import a new machine? That will be 20 percent of the cost, please.

Such graft and corruption quickly become institutionalized to the degree that all parties involved feel they have little choice but to take part. Government officials say that graft and bribery are built into their pay structure, so unless they take bribes, they won't have enough income to live on. Businesspeople say that if they want to stay in business, they have to pay bribes. Similarly, workers must bribe business in order to get a job, and labor leaders must be bribed not to cause trouble for business.

I'm not claiming that such payments are wrong. Societies decide what is right and wrong; economists don't. The term *bribery* in English has a pejorative connotation. In many other languages, the terms people use for this type of activity don't have such negative connotations.

Societies decide what is right and wrong; economists don't.

But I am claiming that such payments—with the implied threat that failure to pay will have adverse consequences—make it more difficult for a society's economy to grow. Knowing that those payments must be made prevents many people from

Q-9 In what way do bribes limit development?

undertaking actions that might lead to growth. For example, a friend of mine wanted to build a group of apartments in the Bahamas, but when he discovered the payoffs he'd have to make to various people, he abandoned the whole idea.

Limiting an activity makes the right to undertake that limited activity valuable to the person doing the limiting. When bribery is an acceptable practice, it creates strong incentives to limit an ever-increasing number of activities—including many activities that could make a country grow.

Lack of Appropriate Institutions

Almost all economists agree that, to develop, a country needs to establish markets if it wants economic growth. Markets require the establishment of property rights. In *The Mystery of Capital,* Hernando de Soto argued that developing countries' main problem is that their assets, such as houses, do not have the legal standing to be used as collateral or to be bought and sold easily, so markets cannot work. Unfortunately, establishing property rights is a difficult political process. That is the problem for a number of African countries: how to establish property rights with an undeveloped political process.

Markets do not just exist; they are created, and their existence is meshed with the cultural and social fabric of the society.

Creating markets is not enough. The markets must be meshed with the cultural and social fabric of the society. Thus, questions of economic development inevitably involve much more than supply and demand. They involve broader questions about the cultural and social institutions in a society.

Let me give an example of cultural characteristics not conducive to development. Anyone who has traveled in developing countries knows that many of these countries operate on what they call "_______ time," where the "_______" is the name of the particular country one is in. What is meant by "_______ time" is that in that country, things get done when they get done, and it is socially inappropriate to push for things to get done at specific times. Deadlines are demeaning (many students operate on "_______ time").

As a self-actualizing mentality, "_______ time" may be a high-level mental development, but in an interdependent economic setting, "_______ time" doesn't fit.

As a self-actualizing mentality, "_______ time" may be high-level mental development, but in an interdependent economic setting, "_______ time" doesn't fit. Economic development requires qualities such as extreme punctuality and a strong sense of individual responsibility. People who believe their being two minutes late will make the world come to an end fit far better with a high-production country than do people who are more laid back. The need to take such cultural issues into account explains why development economics tends to be far less theoretical and far more country- and region-specific than other branches of economics.

Lack of Investment

Even if a country can overcome the political, social, and institutional constraints on development, there are also economic constraints. If a country is to grow, it must somehow invest, and funds for investment must come from savings. These savings can be either brought in from abroad (as private investment or foreign government aid) or generated internally (as domestic savings). Each source of investment capital has its problems.

With per capita incomes of as low as $400 per year, poor people in developing countries don't have a lot left over to put into savings.

Investment Funded by Domestic Savings In order to save, a person must first have enough to live on. With per capita incomes of $400 per year, poor people in developing countries don't have a whole lot left over to put into savings. Instead, they rely on their kids, if they live, to take care of them in their old age. As for the rich, the threat of political instability often makes them put their money

REAL-WORLD APPLICATION

The Doha Round and Development Aid

Say you are a cotton farmer in Africa. Since your labor costs are much lower than U.S. labor costs, you figure you can compete, even though U.S. technology and capital far exceed yours. Taking technology and labor into account, you figure you have a 20 percent cost advantage, so that even taking into account higher shipping costs, your cotton is cost competitive. Unfortunately for you, that cost advantage disappears because U.S. cotton farmers have a benefit that you don't have—they get substantial subsidies from the U.S. government, which allows them to outcompete you. It isn't only in cotton, and it isn't only in the United States that the subsidies undermine your ability to compete on the world market. Farmers get help in a large number of agricultural goods, and the European and Japanese governments also give their farmers large subsidies. African and other developing nations argue that these subsidies undermine their ability to compete, and to develop. They argue that they don't want foreign aid as much as they want a level playing field so that they can compete.

It was precisely such arguments that led the World Trade Organization to organize the Doha round of trade negotiations. It was designed to reduce tariffs and other trade barriers that developing countries place on developed countries' goods, and in return reduce subsidies and other assistance that developed countries give to their own agricultural production. These trade negotiations started in 2001, but were never concluded as political pressures in developed countries made governments unable to reduce farm subsidies that the developing countries argued were needed to create a level playing field in trade of agricultural goods.

into savings abroad, as I discussed before. For the developing country, it's as if the rich didn't save. In fact, it's even worse because when they save abroad, the rich don't even spend the money at home as do poor people, so the rich generate less in the way of short-run income multiplier effects in their home country than do the poor.

That leaves the middle class (small as it is) as the one hope these countries have for domestic savings. For them, the problem is: Where can they put their savings? Often these countries have an underdeveloped financial sector; there's no neighborhood bank, no venture capital fund, no government-secured savings vehicle. The only savings vehicle available may be government savings bonds. But savings bonds finance the government deficit, which supports the government bureaucracy, which is limiting activities that could lead to growth. Few middle-class people invest in those government bonds. After all, what will a government bond be worth after the next revolution? Nothing!

Some governments have taxed individuals (a type of forced savings) and channeled that money back into investment. But again, politics and corruption are likely to interfere. Instead of going into legitimate productive investment, the savings—in the form of "consulting fees," outright payoffs, or "sweetheart contracts"—go to friends of those in power. Before you get up on your high horse and say, "How do the people allow that to happen?" think of the United States, where it's much easier to prevent such activities but where scandals in government spending are still uncovered with depressing regularity.

INVESTMENT FUNDED FROM ABROAD The other way to generate funds for investment is from external savings, either foreign aid or foreign investment.

Foreign Aid The easiest way to finance development is with **foreign aid** *(funds that developed countries lend or give to developing countries)*. The problem is that foreign aid generally comes with strings attached; funds are earmarked for specific purposes. For example, most foreign aid is military aid; helping a country prepare to fight a war isn't a good way to help it develop.

As you can see in the table below, the United States gives about $30 billion (about $100 per U.S. citizen) per year in foreign aid.

Country	Development Aid 2010 (millions of U.S. dollars)	Percent of GDP
Sweden	$ 5,606	1.02%
United Kingdom	13,739	0.56
France	12,994	0.46
Germany	14,533	0.40
Canada	5,291	0.31
Austria	1,107	0.27
United States	30,745	0.20
Italy	4,241	0.19
Japan	10,604	0.18

Source: *OECD DAC Chairman's Report* (www.oecd.org).

Total foreign aid from all countries comes to about $25 per person in developing countries.

For the 5.5 billion people in developing countries, total foreign aid from all countries comes to about $25 per person. That isn't going to finance a lot of economic development, especially when much of the money is earmarked for military purposes.

Foreign Investment If a global or multinational company believes that a country has a motivated, cheap workforce; a stable government supportive of business; and sufficient **infrastructure investment**—*investment in the underlying structure of the economy,* such as transportation or power facilities—it has a strong incentive to invest in the country. That's a lot of ifs, and generally the poorest countries don't measure up. What they have to offer instead are raw materials that the global corporation can develop.

Countries at the upper end of the group of developing countries (such as Mexico and Brazil) may meet all these requirements, but large amounts of foreign investment often result in political problems as citizens of these countries complain about imperialist exploitation, outside control, and significant outflows of profits. Developing countries have tried to meet such complaints by insisting that foreign investment come in the form of joint development projects under local control, but that cuts down the amount that foreign firms are willing to invest.

When the infrastructure doesn't exist, few firms will invest no matter how cheap the labor or how stable the government.

When the infrastructure doesn't exist, as is the case in the poorest developing countries, few firms will invest in that country, no matter how cheap the labor or how stable the government. Firms require infrastructure investment such as transportation facilities, energy availability, and housing and amenities for their employees before they will consider investing in a country. And they don't want to pay to establish this infrastructure themselves.

Competition for Investment among Developing Countries The world is made up of about 30 highly industrial countries and about 160 other countries at various stages of development. Global companies have a choice of where to locate, and often developing countries compete to get the development located in their country. In their efforts to get the development, they may offer tax rebates, free land, guarantees of labor peace, or loose regulatory environments within which firms can operate.

This competition can be keen, and can result in many of the benefits of development being transferred from the developing country to the global company and ultimately to the Western consumer since competition from other firms will force the global company to pass on the benefits in the form of lower prices.

Competition for global company investment often leads to the benefits of that investment being passed on to the Western consumer.

An example of the results of such competition can be seen in the production of chemicals. Say a company is planning to build a new plant to produce chemicals. Where does it locate? Considering the wide-ranging environmental restrictions in the United States and Western Europe, a chemical company will likely look toward a developing country that will give it loose regulation. If one country will not come through, the chemical firm will point out that it can locate elsewhere. Concern about Mexico's relatively loose environmental regulatory environment was one of the sticking points of U.S. approval of NAFTA.

Focal Points and Takeoff The scope of competition among developing countries can be overstated. Most companies do not consider all developing countries as potential production and investment sites. To decide to produce in a developing country requires a knowledge of that country—its legal structure, its political structure, and its infrastructure. Gaining this information involves a substantial initial investment, so most companies tend to focus on a few developing countries about which they have specific knowledge, or that they know other companies have chosen as development sites. (If company X chose it, it must meet the appropriate criteria.)

Because of this informational requirement, developing countries that have been successful in attracting investment often get further investment. Eventually they reach a stage called **economic takeoff**—*a stage when the development process becomes self-sustaining.* Other developing countries fall by the wayside. This means that economic development is not evenly spread over developing countries, but rather is concentrated in a few.

Inappropriate Education

The right education is a necessary component of any successful development strategy. The wrong education is an enormous burden. Developing countries tend to have too much of the wrong education and too little of the right education.

The right education is a necessary component of any successful development strategy. The wrong education is an enormous burden.

Often educational systems in developing countries resemble Western educational systems. The reason is partly the colonial heritage of developing countries and partly what might be described as an emulation factor. The West defines what an educated person is, and developing countries want their citizens to be seen as educated. An educated person should be able to discuss the ideas of Vladimir Nabokov, the poetry of Lord Byron, the intricacies of chaos theory, the latest developments in fusion technology, the nuances of the modern Keynesian/Classical debate, and the dissociative properties of Andy Warhol's paintings. So saith Western scholars; so be it.

Put bluntly, that type of education is almost irrelevant to economic growth and may be a serious detriment to growth for a majority of the population. Basic skills—reading, writing, and arithmetic, taught widely—are likely to be more conducive to growth than is high-level education. When education doesn't match the needs of the society, the degrees—the credentials—become more important than the knowledge learned. The

REAL-WORLD APPLICATION

Millennium Development Goals

In 2000, leaders from around the world gathered at the United Nations and adopted the UN Millennium Declaration that set specific goals to combat poverty, hunger, disease, illiteracy, environmental degradation, and discrimination against women to be achieved by 2015. The goals have come to be known as the Millennium Development Goals. They include:

1. Cut extreme poverty and hunger in half.
2. Achieve universal primary education.
3. Empower women and promote equality between women and men.
4. Reduce under-five mortality by two-thirds.
5. Reduce material mortality by three-quarters.
6. Reverse the spread of disease, especially HIV/AIDS and malaria.
7. Ensure environmental sustainability.
8. Create a global partnership for development, with targets for aid, trade, and debt relief.

No one would argue about the desirability of achieving these goals, but economists have debated how to achieve them. Economist Jeffrey Sachs wrote a book called *The End of Poverty* where he argues that extreme poverty, defined as living on less than $1.50 a day, can be eliminated by 2025 by doubling foreign aid and using that aid to address the multiplicity of problems extremely poor countries face, from the very simple problem of lacking mosquito nets to prevent malaria to more complicated issues of drinkable water. Sachs argues that we can eliminate extreme poverty and disease if we just try.

Not all economists agree with Sachs about what should be done about the problem. Economist William Easterly wrote a book called *The White Man's Burden* where he argues that

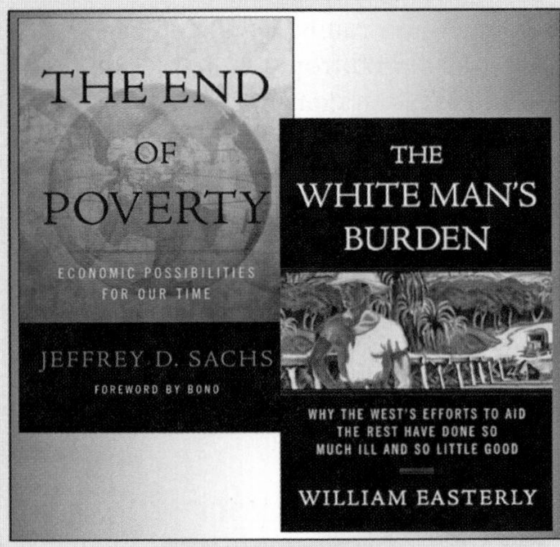

extreme poverty is caused by a complicated interplay of politics, society, technology, geography, and economic systems; therefore, the cures are also necessarily complicated. He argues that we have doubled foreign aid in the past with no measurable result, and that Sachs' "End of Poverty program" will lead to little success. Easterly is not opposed to eradicating poverty, but he promotes a slower piecemeal approach that will (1) allow policy makers and economists to evaluate the success of specific programs, (2) hold institutions accountable for how funds are spent, and (3) be based on a good understanding of which programs work.

So, have the UN Millennium Declaration and Sachs' "End of Poverty program" been successful? Success has been slow and not universal across countries. There has been enormous growth in southeastern Asia and Oceania but far less in sub-Saharan Africa.

best jobs go to those with the highest degrees, not because the individuals holding the degrees are better able to do the job, but simply because they hold the credentials. **Credentialism**, in which *the degrees, or credentials, become more important than the knowledge learned,* serves to preserve the monopoly position of those who manage to get the degree.

Credentialism serves to preserve the monopoly position of those who manage to get the degree.

If access to education is competitive, credentialism has its advantages. Even irrelevant education, as long as it is difficult, serves a screening or selection role. Those individuals who work hardest at getting an education advance and get the good jobs. Since selecting hardworking individuals is difficult, even irrelevant education serves this selection role.

But developing countries' current educational practices may be worse than irrelevant. Their educational systems often reflect Western culture, not their own cultures. The best students qualify for scholarships abroad, and their education in a different tradition makes it difficult for them to return home.

In my studies in Europe and the United States, I've come to know a large number of the best and the brightest students from developing countries. They're superb students and they do well in school. But as they near graduation, most of them face an enormously difficult choice. They can return to their home country—to material shortages, to enormous challenges for which they have little training, and to an illiterate society whose traditional values are sometimes hostile to the values these new graduates have learned. Or they can stay in the West, find jobs relevant to their training, enjoy an abundance of material goods, and associate with people to whom they've now learned to relate. Which would you choose?

The choice many of them make results in a **brain drain** *(the outflow of the best and brightest students from developing countries to developed countries).* Many of these good students don't return to the developing country. Those that do go home take jobs as government officials, expecting high salaries and material comforts far beyond what their society can afford. Instead of becoming the dynamic entrepreneurs of growth, they become impediments to growth.

Many good students from developing countries who study abroad don't return to the developing country.

There are, of course, many counterexamples to the arguments presented here. Many developing countries try to design their education system to fit their culture. And many of the dynamic, selfless leaders who make it possible for the country to develop do return home. As with most issues, there are both positive and negative attributes to the way something is done. I emphasize the problems with educational systems in developing economies because the positive attributes of education are generally accepted. Without education, development is impossible. The question is how that education should be structured.

Q-10 How could too much education cause problems for development?

Overpopulation

Two ways a country can increase per capita income are:

1. Decrease the number of people in the country (without decreasing the total income in the country).
2. Increase the income (without increasing the population).

In each case, the qualifier is important because income and population are related in complicated ways: People earn income; without people there would be no income. But often the more people there are, the less income per person there is because the resources of the country become strained.

A country's population can never be higher than can be supported by the natural resources that it has, or can import. But that doesn't mean that overpopulation can't be an obstacle to development. Nature has its own ways of reducing populations that are too large: Starvation and disease are the direct opposite to development. That control system works in nature, and it would work with human societies. The problem is that we don't like it.

Thomas Carlyle gave economics the name *the dismal science* as he was verbally sparring about a number of issues with economists of his period. The name stuck with economics in large part because of the writings of Thomas Malthus, who in the early 1800s said that society's prospects are dismal because population tends to outrun the means of subsistence. (Population grows geometrically—that is, at an increasing rate; the means of subsistence grow arithmetically—that is, at a constant rate.) The view

WWW Web Note 22.4
Population and Development

was cemented into economic thinking in the law of diminishing marginal productivity: As more and more people are added to a fixed amount of land, the output per worker gets smaller and smaller.

Many developing economies have not avoided the Malthusian fate because diminishing marginal productivity has exceeded technological change.

Through technological progress, most Western economies have avoided the fate predicted by Malthus because growth in technology has exceeded growth in population. In contrast, many developing economies have not avoided the Malthusian fate because diminishing marginal productivity has exceeded technological change, and limited economic growth isn't enough to offset the increase in population. The result is a constant or falling output per person.

That doesn't mean that developing countries haven't grown economically. They have. But population growth makes per capita output growth small or negative.

Population grows for a number of reasons, including:

1. As public health measures are improved, infant mortality rates and death rates for the population as a whole both decline.
2. As people earn more income, they believe they can afford to have more children.
3. In rural areas, children are useful in working the fields.

What to do? Should the government reduce the population growth rate? If it should, how can it do so? Various measures have been tried: advertising campaigns, free condoms, forced sterilization, and economic incentives. For example, in China the government has tried imposing severe economic penalties on couples who have more than one child, while providing material incentives, such as a free television, to couples who agree not to have more than one child.

China's vigorous population control campaign has had a number of effects. First, it created so much anger at the government that in rural areas the campaign was dropped. Second, it led to the killing of many female babies because, if couples were to have only one baby, strong cultural and economic pressures existed to ensure that the baby was a male. Third, it led to an enormous loss of privacy. Dates of women's menstrual periods were posted in factories, and officials would remind them at appropriate times that they should take precautions against getting pregnant. Only a very strong government could impose such a plan.

Even successful population control programs have their problems.

Even successful population control programs have their problems. In Singapore a population control campaign was so successful among educated women that the government became concerned that its "population quality" was suffering. It began a selective campaign to encourage college-educated women to have children. They issued "love tips" to men (since some college-educated women complained that their male companions were nerds and had no idea how to be romantic) and offered special monetary bonuses to college-educated women who gave birth to children. As you might imagine, the campaign provoked a backlash, and it was eventually dropped by the government.

Individuals differ substantially in their assessment of the morality of these programs, but even if one believes that population control is an appropriate government concern, it does not seem that such programs will be successful, by themselves, in limiting population growth.

Health and Disease

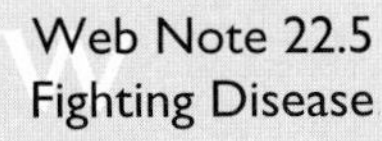
Web Note 22.5
Fighting Disease

Before a country can hope to develop, it must have a reasonably healthy population. If you are sick, it's hard to think, to work, or even to do standard daily tasks like growing food. In many developing countries, large portions of the population are undernourished or sick. Disease hits young children particularly hard. Millions of children die from pneumonia, diarrhea, malaria, and measles, all of which, because of the children's general malnutrition, are often aggravated by intestinal worms. Older individuals suffer from HIV/AIDS, tuberculosis, and malaria. For example, about 25 million people now have AIDS in Africa; one-third are younger than 15 years of age.

These diseases make it difficult for people to work, or even to take care of their kids, and create a vicious cycle. You're sick, you can't work, and so you and your family become victims of malnutrition. You get even more prone to disease, and less able to work and contribute to development. Thus, maintaining public health is more than a humanitarian issue; it is a key development issue.

What to do? Most of these diseases can be alleviated with drugs, but developing the infrastructure to provide these drugs is often difficult or impossible, even when the money for the drugs becomes available. Thus, one must not only get the drugs but also create the cultural and physical environment in which those drugs can be effective. Drug companies have little incentive to work on developing low-cost medicines to treat diseases in developing countries because the people there don't have much money to pay for them, so the return would be low. Instead, pharmaceutical companies focus their research on providing high-priced drugs to be sold in rich countries. Drug companies created anti-AIDS drugs, but their focus was on markets in wealthy developed countries. Only later, and under significant social and political pressure, did they start offering treatment for AIDS at low cost to developing countries.

Conclusion

At this point in my course, I inevitably throw my hands up and admit that I don't know what makes it possible for a country to develop. Nor, judging from what I have read, do the development experts. The good ones (that is, the ones I agree with) admit that they don't know; others (that is, the ones I don't agree with) simply don't know that they don't know.

Economic development is a complicated problem because it is entwined with cultural and social issues.

My gut feeling is that there are no definitive general answers that apply to all developing countries. The appropriate answer varies with each country and each situation. Each proposed solution to the development problem has a right time and a right place. Only by having a complete sense of a country, its history, and its cultural, social, and political norms can one decide whether it's the right time and place for this or that policy.

Summary

- Per capita income in developing countries is about 1/100 of per capita income in the United States. Societies, however, should not be judged by income alone. (*LO22-1*)
- While policies in developed countries focus on stability, developing countries struggle to provide basic needs. (*LO22-2*)
- Development refers to an increase in productive capacity and output brought about by a change in underlying institutions, while growth refers to an increase in output brought about by an increase in inputs. (*LO22-2*)
- Many developing countries have serious political problems that make it impossible for government to take an active, positive role in the economy. (*LO22-2*)
- Many developing countries have dual economies—one a traditional, nonmarket economy and the other an internationalized market economy. (*LO22-2*)

- Many developing countries need a change in the entire atmosphere within which the government and economy relate. They need regime changes rather than policy changes. *(LO22-2)*
- Macro policies in developing countries are more concerned with institutional policies and regime changes than are macro policies in developed countries. *(LO22-2)*
- Although developing countries know that printing too much money leads to inflation, their choices are limited. Some central banks lack independence and for others the only alternative is the collapse of government. *(LO22-3)*
- Most developing countries have some type of limited convertibility to limit the outflow of saving. *(LO22-3)*
- Most monetary policies in developing countries focus on the international sector and are continually dealing with the balance of payments constraint. *(LO22-3)*
- Seven obstacles to economic development are political instability, corruption, lack of appropriate institutions, lack of investment, inappropriate education, overpopulation, and poor health and disease. *(LO22-4)*

Key Terms

balance of payments constraint *(483)*
brain drain *(491)*
conditionality *(482)*
convertibility on the current account *(482)*
credentialism *(490)*
dual economy *(477)*
economic takeoff *(489)*
foreign aid *(488)*
full convertibility *(481)*
inflation tax *(480)*
infrastructure investment *(488)*
limited capital account convertibility *(482)*
policy change *(478)*
purchasing power parity (PPP) *(474)*
regime change *(478)*
restructuring *(475)*

Questions and Exercises

1. Why are economic statistics incomplete measures of quality of life? *(LO22-1)*
2. How does the exchange rate method of comparing incomes differ from the purchasing power method of comparing incomes? *(LO22-1)*
3. What impact does measuring income per capita using the purchasing power parity approach have on the comparison of incomes between developed and developing countries as opposed to measuring them based on exchange rates? Explain your answer. *(LO22-1)*
4. What is the difference between development and growth? *(LO22-2)*
5. What are three ways in which the institutions of developing countries differ from those in developed countries? *(LO22-2)*
6. Why might an economist favor activist policies in developed countries and laissez-faire policies in developing countries? *(LO22-2)*
7. What is meant by "the dual economy"? *(LO22-2)*
8. How does a regime change differ from a policy change? *(LO22-2)*
9. What is the inflation tax? *(LO22-3)*
10. Why doesn't the fact that the "inflation solution" is only a temporary solution stop many developing countries from using it? *(LO22-3)*
11. What is conditionality, and how does it relate to the balance of payments constraint? *(LO22-3)*
12. How does corruption limit investment and economic growth? *(LO22-4)*
13. Why are investment and savings so low in developing countries? *(LO22-4)*
14. If developing countries are so unstable and offer such a risky environment for investment, why do foreigners invest any money in them at all? *(LO22-4)*
15. Why might credentialism be an obstacle to growth? *(LO22-4)*
16. What are the risks to a developing country of sending an individual to a U.S. college? *(LO22-4)*

Questions from Alternative Perspectives

1. Christians are called to be Christ-like, a "light to lighten the nations" (Luke 2:32).
   a. In light of the basic biblical norms of justice, righteousness, and stewardship, how should a nation decide how much development aid to provide developing countries?
   b. Is it within Christian norms to make that aid conditional? (Hint: Consider the biblical concept of forgiveness, which includes repentance and the restoration of right relationships.) (Religious)
2. When thinking about development, it is often presented as an analytic exercise, but development policies have very real consequences.
   a. Who is responsible for economies that fail to develop?
   b. Who will primarily suffer the consequences from a failure at economic development?
   c. If your answers to *a* and *b* differ, how might that difference affect the development policies chosen? How does this difference possibly affect the choice of development policies? (Institutionalist)
3. The Grameen bank is an example of a successful micro credit reform. It focuses its loans on women.
   a. Why do many of the micro credit policies focus on women rather than men?
   b. Does your answer in *a* suggest anything about other policies that might help developing countries develop? (Feminist)
4. Islam considers the interest on loans to be an instrument of oppression of the poor by the wealthy. That is why interest is banned by the Qur'an. Islamic-owned companies do, however, provide financing for purchases such as homes.
   a. How could financing be an instrument of oppression?
   b. How could financing be an instrument of development?
   c. How does this activity remain within Islamic law? (Religious)
5. The brief argument for globalization goes something like this. Countries that trade a lot grow quickly and poverty rates decline in rapidly growing countries. Therefore, globalization promotes rapid growth and alleviates poverty and is far superior to economic isolation. Radicals believe that the globalization debate is not about economic isolation vs. integration into the world economy; rather, the real debate is about what policies allow a developing economy to successfully engage with the world economy. The advocates' case tells us about a country's degree of engagement with the world economy but not the manner of that engagement. From the radical perspective, knowing that international trade and faster economic growth rates are positively correlated hardly constitutes an endorsement of the neo-liberal policy of lower barriers for trade and the movement of international capital.
   a. Should a developing economy engage with the global economy through free trade and financial liberalization policies?
   b. Would the strategies promoted by the opponents of globalization—more national control and limits on the movement of foreign and domestic capital—be better polices for engaging with the world economy? (Radical)

Issues to Ponder

1. If you suddenly found yourself living as a poor person in a developing country, what are some things that you now do that you would no longer be able to do? What new things would you have to do?
2. What is wrong with saying that people in developing countries are worse off than people in the United States?
3. Does the fact that suicide rates are lower in developing countries than in the United States imply that Americans would be better off living in a developing country? Why?
4. Spend one day living like someone in a developing country. Eat almost nothing and work lifting stones for 10 hours. Then, that same evening, study this chapter and contemplate the bootstrap strategy of development.
5. Interview a foreign student in your class or school. Ask about each of the seven obstacles to economic development and how his or her country is trying to overcome them.
6. It has been argued that development economics has no general theory; it is instead the application of common sense to real-world problems.
   a. Do you agree or disagree with that statement? Why?
   b. Why do you think this argument about the lack of generality of theories is made for developing countries more than it is made for developed countries?
7. Choose any developing country and answer the following questions about it:
   a. What is its level of per capita income?
   b. What is its growth potential?

c. What is the exchange rate of its currency in relation to the U.S. dollar?
d. What policy suggestions might you make to the country?

8. Why do governments in developing countries often seem more arbitrary and oppressive than governments in developed countries?
9. If you were a foreign investor thinking of making an investment in a developing country, what are some things that you would be concerned about?
10. Should a country control the size and makeup of its population? Why?
11. A United Nations study reported that more than 300 million low-income women owned businesses in developing countries, but only 5 million had access to credit other than from money lenders. How might the UN alleviate this obstacle to growth? What other obstacles might exist for women entrepreneurs in developing nations?
12. Say that you have been hired to design an education system for a developing country.
    a. What skills would you want it to emphasize?
    b. How might it differ from an ideal educational system in the United States?
    c. How much of the U.S. educational system involves credentialism, and how much involves learning relevant skills?
13. In the 1990s, Germany passed a law requiring businesses to take back and recycle all forms of packaging. A large group of businesses formed a company to collect and recycle these packages. Its costs are 4.5 cents per pound for glass, 9.5 cents per pound for paper, and 74 cents per pound for plastic. This accounts for a recycling cost of about $100 per ton for glass and $2,000 per ton for plastic; the average recycling cost of paper is $500 per ton. A developing country has offered to create a giant landfill and accept Germany's waste at a cost of $400 per ton, which includes $50 per ton sorting and transport costs and a $350-per-ton fee to be paid to the developing country.
    a. Should Germany accept this proposal?
    b. Will the proposal benefit the developing country?
14. Should developing countries send their students abroad for an education?
15. According to the Peruvian economist Hernando de Soto, in the 1980s, getting a deed for property in Peru involved 207 bureaucratic steps, took 43 months, and cost 10 weeks' worth of the official minimum wage.
    a. What problems would that create for economic development?
    b. What problems would the lack of titling create for public utilities?

Answers to Margin Questions

1. Given market societies' expansionary tendencies, the cultures in economically poor countries that do not grow would simply be overrun and destroyed by cultures of market societies. This means that the choice is not between development and preservation of existing culture; rather, the choice is between economic development with its attendant wrenching cultural transitions and continued poverty with exploitation by developed countries and its attendant wrenching cultural transitions. (*p. 474; LO22-1*)
2. Restructuring in developed countries suggests that the distinction between growth and development can be overdone since it is an example of developed countries' growth occurring through changing institutions—development—rather than through increasing inputs—growth. (*p. 475; LO22-2*)
3. *Dual economy* refers to a developing country's tendency to have two economies that have little interaction: one a traditional nonmarket economy and the other an internationally oriented modern market economy. (*p. 477; LO22-2*)
4. While everyone agrees that inflation in developing countries is caused by the central bank issuing too much money, the real policy question concerns what the political consequences of not issuing too much money may be. Sometimes the cure for inflation can be worse than the problem. (*p. 480; LO22-3*)
5. In an inflation, any issuers of fixed-interest-rate debt denominated in the domestic currency gain from the holders of these debts. (*p. 481; LO22-3*)
6. Full convertibility includes convertibility on the capital account as well as on the current account. It means that people are allowed to buy foreign financial assets—to save abroad. Convertibility on the current account means that people are allowed to buy foreign currencies to buy foreign goods, but not necessarily to buy foreign financial assets. (*p. 482; LO22-3*)
7. In order for a market to operate, a set of rules—any rules—is needed. Lack of political stability undermines the existence of any rules and leads to a failure of cooperation among people. (*p. 484; LO22-4*)
8. It depends, but the answer is probably false. Often the wealthy elite in a developing country fear that if they invest in their country, their money will be taken away, so they often invest out of their country—meaning that

the benefits of their savings go to other countries, not to the investors' own developing country. (*p. 485; LO22-4*)

9. The more it costs to undertake economic activities, the fewer economic activities individuals undertake. (*p. 485; LO22-4*)
10. Education is absolutely necessary for development, but it is most helpful if it is the right type of education—focusing on basic skills such as reading, writing, and arithmetic. When education focuses on abstract issues that might be valuable to a developed economy, but that have little relevance to a developing country's problems, "too much" education can lead to a brain drain and a diversion of people's talent away from the central development issues. (*p. 491; LO22-4*)

Glossary

A

Adaptive Expectations Expectations based in some way on the past.
Agent-Based Computational Economic (ACE) Model A culture dish approach to the study of economic phenomena in which agents are allowed to interact in a computationally constructed environment and the researcher observes the results of that interaction.
Aggregate Demand (*AD*) Curve A curve that shows how a change in the price level will change aggregate expenditures on all goods and services in an economy.
Aggregate Expenditures The total amount of spending on final goods and services in the economy; consumption (spending by consumers), investment (spending by business), spending by government, and net foreign spending on U.S. goods (the difference between U.S. exports and U.S. imports).
Aggregate Production (*AP*) The total amount of goods and services produced in every industry in an economy.
Annuity Rule The present value of any annuity is the annual income it yields divided by the interest rate.
Art of Economics The application of the knowledge learned in positive economics to the achievement of the goals one has determined in normative economics.
Asset Management How a bank handles its loans and other assets.
Asset Price Inflation When the price of assets rise more than their "real" value.
Automatic Stabilizer Any government program or policy that will counteract the business cycle without any new government action.
Autonomous Expenditures Expenditures that do not systematically vary with income.

B

Balance of Merchandise Trade The difference between the value of goods exported and the value of goods imported.
Balance of Payments A country's record of all transactions between its residents and the residents of all foreign nations.
Balance of Payments Constraint Limitations on expansionary domestic macroeconomic policy due to a shortage of international reserves.
Balance of Trade The difference between the value of the goods and services a country imports and the value of the goods and services it exports.
Bank A financial institution whose primary function is accepting deposits for, and lending money to, individuals and firms.
Bar Graph A graph where the area under each point is filled in to look like a bar.
Behavioral Economics Microeconomic analysis that uses a broader set of building blocks than rationality and self-interest used in traditional economics.
Bond A promise to pay a certain amount of money plus interest in the future.
Brain Drain The outflow of the best and brightest students from developing countries to developed countries.
Bretton Woods System An agreement about fixed exchange rates that governed international financial relationships from the period after the end of World War II until 1971.
Bubble Unsustainable rapidly rising prices of some type of financial asset.
Business A private producing unit in our society.
Business Cycle The upward or downward movement of economic activity, or real GDP, that occurs around the growth trend.
Butterfly Effect Model A model in which a small change causes a large effect.

C

Capitalism An economic system based on the market in which the ownership of the means of production resides with a small group of individuals called capitalists.
Central Bank A type of bankers' bank whose financial obligations underlie an economy's money supply.
Classical Growth Model A model of growth that focuses on the role of capital accumulation in the growth process.
Classical Economists Macroeconomists who generally favor laissez-faire or nonactivist policies.
Coefficient of Determination A measure of the proportion of the variability in the data that is accounted for by the statistical model.
Commodities Homogeneous goods that can be produced in a variety of countries without any special skills and shipped at a low cost.
Comparative Advantage The ability to be better suited to the production of one good than to the production of another good.
Competitiveness The ability of a country to sell its goods to other countries.
Complex Systems Macro Models Macro models of the economy that take into account dynamic interactions of agents in the models, where agents have less than full information and can be less than infinitely rational.
Conditionality The making of loans that are subject to specific conditions.

Constant Returns to Scale Output will rise by the same proportionate increase as all inputs.
Consumer Price Index (CPI) A measure of prices of a fixed basket of consumer goods, weighted according to each component's share of an average consumer's expenditures.
Consumer Sovereignty The principle that the consumer's wishes determine what's produced.
Consumption Spending by households on goods and services.
Contractionary Monetary Policy Monetary policy that decreases the money supply and increases interest rates.
Convertibility on the Current Account An exchange rate system that allows people to exchange currencies freely to buy goods and services, but not to buy assets in other countries.
Coordinate System A two-dimensional space in which one point represents two numbers.
Corporation A business that is treated as a person, legally owned by its stockholders. Its stockholders are not liable for the actions of the corporate "person."
Countercyclical Fiscal Policy Fiscal policy in which the government offsets any change in aggregate expenditures that would create a business cycle.
Credentialism When the academic degrees, or credentials, become more important than the knowledge learned.
Credit Easing The purchase of long-term government bonds and securities from private financial corporations for the purpose of changing the mix of securities held by the Fed toward less liquid and more risky assets.
Crowding Out The offsetting of a change in government expenditures by a change in private expenditures in the opposite direction.
Currency Stabilization Buying and selling of a currency by the government to offset temporary fluctuations in supply and demand for currencies.
Currency Support Buying of a currency by a government to maintain its value at above its long-run equilibrium value.
Current Account The part of the balance of payments account in which all short-term flows of payments are listed.
Cyclical Unemployment Unemployment resulting from fluctuations in economic activity.

D

Debt Accumulated deficits minus accumulated surpluses.
Debt Service The interest rate on debt times the total debt.
Deductive Scientific Model A model with carefully specified formal foundations whose primary purpose is understanding for the sake of understanding.
Deficit A shortfall of revenues under payments.
Deflation A continuous fall of the price level.
Demand A schedule of quantities of a good that will be bought per unit of time at various prices, other things constant.
Demand Curve The graphic representation of the relationship between price and quantity demanded.
Demerit Good or Activity A good or activity that government believes is bad for people even though they choose to use the good or engage in the activity.
Deposit Insurance A system under which the federal government promises to stand by an individual's bank deposits.
Depreciation A decrease in the value of a currency.
Depression A large recession.
Direct Relationship A relationship in which when one variable goes up, the other goes up too.
Discount Rate The rate of interest the Fed charges for loans it makes to banks.
Division of Labor The splitting up of a task to allow for specialization of production.
Dodd-Frank Wall Street Reform and Consumer Protection Act An act of Congress passed in 2010 establishing a regulatory structure to limit risk-taking and require banks to report their holdings so that regulators can assess risk-taking behavior.
Dual Economy The existence of two sectors: a traditional sector and an internationally oriented modern market sector.
Dynamic Taking "time" explicitly into account.

E

Econometrics The statistical analysis of economic data.
Economic Decision Rule If the marginal benefits of doing something exceed the marginal costs, do it. If the marginal costs of doing something exceed the marginal benefits, don't do it.
Economic Force The necessary reaction to scarcity.
Economic Model A framework that places the generalized insights of a theory in a more specific contextual setting.
Economic Policy An action (or inaction) taken by government to influence economic actions.
Economic Principle A commonly held economic insight stated as a law or general assumption.
Economic Takeoff A stage when the development process becomes self-sustaining.
Economics The study of how human beings coordinate their wants and desires, given the decision-making mechanisms, social customs, and political realities of the society.
Economies of Scale Situation when long-run average total costs decrease as output increases.
Efficiency Achieving a goal as cheaply as possible. Also: Using as few inputs as possible.
Efficient Market Hypothesis All financial decisions are made by rational people and are based on all relevant

information that accurately reflects the value of assets today and in the future.

Embargo A total restriction on the import or export of a good.

Emergent Properties Properties of the system that could not have been predicted from a deductive analysis starting from the components of the system.

Empirical Model A model that statistically discovers a pattern in the data.

Employment–Population Ratio The number of people who are working as a percentage of people available to work.

Endowment Effects People value something more just because they have it.

Engineering Model A model with loose formal foundations whose primary purpose is to guide thinking about policy.

Enlightened Self-Interest People care about other people as well as themselves.

Entrepreneurship The ability to organize and get something done.

Equation of Exchange An equation stating that the quantity of money times the velocity of money equals the price level times the quantity of real goods sold.

Equilibrium A concept in which opposing dynamic forces cancel each other out.

Equilibrium Output The level of output toward which the economy gravitates in the short run because of the cumulative cycles of declining or increasing production.

Equilibrium Price The price toward which the invisible hand drives the market.

Equilibrium Quantity The amount bought and sold at the equilibrium price.

Excess Demand Situation when quantity demanded is greater than quantity supplied.

Excess Reserves Reserves held by banks in excess of what banks are required to hold.

Excess Supply Situation when quantity supplied is greater than quantity demanded.

Exchange Rate The price of one country's currency in terms of another currency.

Excise Tax A tax that is levied on a specific good.

Expansion An upturn that lasts for at least two consecutive quarters of a year.

Expansionary Monetary Policy Monetary policy that increases the money supply and decreases the interest rate.

Expenditures Multiplier A number that tells how much income will change in response to a change in autonomous expenditures.

Experimental Economics A branch of economics that studies the economy through controlled laboratory experiments.

External Debt Government debt owed to individuals in foreign countries.

Externality An effect of a decision on a third party not taken into account by the decision maker.

Extrapolative Expectations Expectations that a trend will continue.

F

Fallacy of Composition The false assumption that what is true for a part will also be true for the whole.

Fed Funds Loans of excess reserves banks make to one another.

Federal Deposit Insurance Corporation (FDIC) A government institution that guarantees bank deposits up to $250,000.

Federal Funds Market The market in which banks lend and borrow reserves.

Federal Funds Rate The interest rate banks charge one another for Fed funds.

Federal Open Market Committee (FOMC) The Fed's chief body that decides monetary policy.

Federal Reserve Bank (the Fed) The U.S. central bank whose liabilities (Federal Reserve notes) serve as cash in the United States.

Final Output Goods and services purchased for their final use.

Financial and Capital Account The part of the balance of payments account in which all long-term flows of payments are listed.

Financial Assets Assets such as stocks or bonds, whose benefit to the owner depends on the issuer of the asset meeting certain obligations.

Financial Liabilities Liabilities incurred by the issuer of a financial asset to stand behind the issued asset.

Fine-Tuning Fiscal policy designed to keep the economy always at its target or potential level of income.

Fiscal Policy The deliberate change in either government spending or taxes to stimulate or slow down the economy. Also, the changing of taxes and spending to affect the level of output in the economy.

Fixed Exchange Rate When the government chooses a particular exchange rate and offers to buy and sell its currency at that price.

Flexible Exchange Rate When the government does not enter into foreign exchange markets at all, but leaves the determination of exchange rates totally up to market forces.

Foreign Aid Funds that developed countries lend or give to developing countries.

Free Trade Association A group of countries that have reduced or eliminated trade barriers among themselves.

Frictional Unemployment Unemployment caused by people entering the job market and people quitting a job just long enough to look for and find another one.

Full Convertibility An exchange rate system in which individuals may change dollars into any currency they want for whatever legal purpose they want.

Functional Finance A theoretical proposition that governments should make spending and taxing decisions on the basis of their effect on the economy, not on the basis of some moralistic principle that budgets should be balanced.

G

GDP Deflator An index of the price level of aggregate output, or the average price of the components of GDP, relative to a base year.

General Agreement on Tariffs and Trade (GATT) A regular international conference to reduce trade barriers held from 1947 to 1995. It has been replaced by the World Trade Organization (WTO).

General Equilibrium Model A model of all the markets in the economy, not just a single market.

Glass-Steagall Act An act of Congress passed in 1933 that established deposit insurance and implemented a number of banking regulations.

Global Corporation A corporation with substantial operations on both the production and sales sides in more than one country.

Globalization The increasing integration of economies, cultures, and institutions across the world.

Globalized *AS/AD* Model The standard *AS/AD* model with an added world supply curve that captures the effect that globalization can have on an economy.

Gold Specie Flow Mechanism The long-run adjustment mechanism that maintained the gold standard.

Gold Standard The system of fixed exchange rates in which the value of currencies was fixed relative to the value of gold and gold was used as the primary reserve asset.

Government Failure A situation in which the government intervention in the market to improve market failure actually makes the situation worse.

Government Spending Goods and services that government buys.

Graph A picture of points in a coordinate system in which points denote relationships between numbers.

Gross Domestic Product (GDP) The total market value of all final goods and services produced in an economy in a one-year period.

Gross National Product (GNP) The aggregate final output of citizens and businesses of an economy in a one-year period.

H

Herd To copy other successful behavior even though that successful behavior may have been just luck.

Herding The human tendency to follow the crowd.

Heuristic Model A model that is expressed informally in words.

Historically Based Expectations Expectations about the future that are based on past events.

Households Groups of individuals living together and making joint decisions.

Human Capital The skills that are embodied in workers through experience, education, and on-the-job training, or, more simply, people's knowledge.

Hyperinflation Inflation that hits triple digits—100 percent or more per year.

I–J

Induced Expenditures Expenditures that change as income changes.

Industrial Revolution A time when technology and machines rapidly modernized industrial production and mass-produced goods replaced handmade goods.

Inefficiency Getting less output from inputs that, if devoted to some other activity, would produce more output.

Infant Industry Argument The argument that with initial protection, an industry will be able to become competitive.

Inflation A continual rise in the price level.

Inflationary Gap A difference between equilibrium income and potential income when equilibrium income exceeds potential income. That is, aggregate expenditures above potential output that exist at the current price level.

Infrastructure Investment Investment in the underlying structure of the economy.

Inherent Comparative Advantage Comparative advantage that is based on factors that are relatively unchangeable.

Institutions The formal and informal rules that constrain human behavior.

Interest Rate Effect The effect that a lower price level has on investment expenditures through the effect that a change in the price level has on interest rates.

Intermediate Products Products used as inputs in the production of some other product.

Internal Debt Government debt owed to other governmental agencies or to its own citizens.

International Effect As the price level falls (assuming the exchange rate does not change), net exports will rise.

Interpolation Assumption The assumption that the relationship between variables is the same between points as it is at the points.

Inverse Relationship A relationship between two variables in which when one goes up, the other goes down.

Inverted Yield Curve A yield curve in which the short-term rate is higher than the long-term rate.

Investment Spending for the purpose of additional production.
Invisible Hand The price mechanism; the rise and fall of prices that guide our actions in a market.
Invisible Hand Theorem A market economy, through the price mechanism, will tend to allocate resources efficiently.

K

Keynesians Macroeconomists who generally favor activist government policy.

L

Labor Force Those people in an economy who are willing and able to work.
Labor Force Participation Rate The percentage of the total population at least 16 years old who either work or are actively looking for work.
Laissez-Faire An economic policy of leaving the coordination of individuals' actions to the market.
Law of Demand Quantity demanded rises as price falls, other things constant. Also can be stated as: Quantity demanded falls as price rises, other things constant.
Law of Diminishing Control Whenever a regulatory system is set up, individuals or firms being regulated will figure out ways to circumvent those regulations.
Law of Diminishing Marginal Productivity Increasing one input, keeping all others constant, will lead to smaller and smaller gains in output.
Law of One Price The wages of workers in one country will not differ significantly from the wages of (equal) workers in another institutionally similar country.
Law of Supply Quantity supplied rises as price rises, other things constant. Also can be stated as: Quantity supplied falls as price falls, other things constant.
Learning by Doing As we do something, we learn what works and what doesn't, and over time we become more proficient at it. Also: To improve the methods of production through experience.
Learning Procedures The methods by which people learn about a system.
Lender of Last Resort Lending to banks and other financial institutions when no one else will.
Leverage Borrowing to make financial investments.
Liability Management How a bank attracts deposits and what it pays for them.
Limited Capital Account Convertibility An exchange rate system that allows full current account convertibility and partial capital account convertibility.
Line Graph A graph where the data are connected by a continuous line.
Linear Curve A curve that is drawn as a straight line.
Liquid Having assets that can readily be converted into cash and money.
Liquidity One's ability to convert an asset into cash.
Long-Run Aggregate Supply (*LAS*) Curve A curve that shows the long-run relationship between output and the price level.
Long-Run Phillips Curve A vertical curve at the unemployment rate consistent with potential output. (It shows the trade-off [or complete lack thereof] when expectations of inflation equal actual inflation.)
Lucas Critique Problem Because government policies can affect the behavior of individuals, historical data can lead to misleading predictions about the impact of a *new* policy.

M

M_1 Currency in the hands of the public, checking account balances, and traveler's checks.
M_2 M_1 plus savings and money market accounts, small-denomination time deposits (also called CDs), and retail money funds.
Macroeconomic Externality An externality that affects the levels of unemployment, inflation, or growth in the economy as a whole.
Macroeconomics The study of the economy as a whole, which includes inflation, unemployment, business cycles, and growth.
Marginal Benefit Additional benefit above the benefits already derived.
Marginal Cost (*MC*) Additional cost over and above the costs already incurred.
Marginal Propensity to Expend (*mpe*) The ratio of the change in aggregate expenditures to a change in income.
Market Demand Curve The horizontal sum of all individual demand curves.
Market Economy An economic system based on private property and the market in which, in principle, individuals decide how, what, and for whom to produce.
Market Failure A situation in which the invisible hand pushes in such a way that individual decisions do not lead to socially desirable outcomes.
Market Force An economic force that is given relatively free rein by society to work through the market.
Market Supply Curve The horizontal sum of all individual supply curves.
Merit Good or Activity A good or activity that government believes is good for you, even though you may not choose to consume the good or engage in the activity.
Microeconomics The study of individual choice, and how that choice is influenced by economic forces.
Minimum Wage Law A law specifying the lowest wage a firm can legally pay an employee.

Model A simplified representation of the problem or question that captures the essential issues.
Modern Economists Economists who are willing to use a wider range of models than did earlier economists.
Monetary Base Vault cash, deposits at the Fed, plus currency in circulation.
Monetary Policy A policy of influencing the economy through changes in the banking system's reserves that influence the money supply and credit availability in the economy.
Monetary Regime A predetermined statement of the policy that will be followed in various situations.
Money A highly liquid financial asset that's generally accepted in exchange for other goods, is used as a reference in valuing other goods, and can be stored as wealth.
Money Multiplier $1/r$ where r is the percentage of deposits banks hold in reserve.
Money Wealth Effect A fall in the price level will make the holders of money richer, so they buy more.
Moral Hazard Problem A problem that arises when people don't have to bear the negative consequences of their actions.
Mortgage-Backed Securities Financial assets whose flow of income comes from a combination of mortgages.
Most-Favored Nation A country that will be charged as low a tariff on its exports as any other country.
Movement along a Demand Curve The graphical representation of the effect of a change in price on the quantity demanded.
Movement along a Supply Curve The graphical representation of the effect of a change in price on the quantity supplied.
Multiplier-Accelerator Model A model in which changes in output are accelerated because changes in investment depend on changes in income (rather than on the level of income).
Multiplier Effect The amplification of initial changes in expenditures.
Multiplier Equation An equation that tells us that income equals the multiplier times autonomous expenditures.
Multiplier Model A model that emphasizes the effect of fluctuations in aggregate demand, rather than the price level, on output.

N

Natural Experiment A naturally occurring event that approximates a controlled experiment where something has changed in one place but has not changed somewhere else. That is, an event created by nature that can serve as an experiment.
Net Domestic Product (NDP) The sum of consumption expenditures, government expenditures, net exports, and investment less depreciation. That is, GDP less depreciation.
Net Exports Spending on goods and services produced in the United States that foreigners buy (exports) minus goods and services produced abroad that U.S. citizens buy (imports).
Net Foreign Factor Income Income from foreign domestic factor sources minus foreign factor income earned domestically.
Net Investment Gross investment less depreciation.
New Classical Macroeconomics An approach to macroeconomics that studies macroeconomic questions using traditional microeconomic building blocks that emphasize rationality.
New Growth Theory A theory that emphasizes the role of technology rather than capital in the growth process.
Nominal Deficit The deficit determined by looking at the difference between expenditures and receipts.
Nominal GDP GDP calculated at existing prices.
Nominal Interest Rate The interest rate you actually see and pay when borrowing, or receive when lending.
Nominal Output The total amount of goods and services measured at current prices.
Nominal Wealth The value of the assets of an economy measured at their current market prices.
Nonlinear Curve A curve that is drawn as a curved line.
Normative Economics The study of what the goals of the economy should be.

O

Okun's Rule of Thumb A 1 percentage-point change in the unemployment rate will be associated with a 2 percent deviation in output from its trend in the opposite direction.
Open Market Operations The Fed's buying and selling of government securities.
Operation Twist Selling short-term Treasury bills and buying long-term Treasury bonds without creating more new money.
Opportunity Cost The benefit you might have gained from choosing the next-best alternative.

P

Paradox of Thrift An increase in saving can lead to a decrease in expenditures, decreasing output and causing a recession.
Partially Flexible Exchange Rate When the government sometimes buys or sells currencies to influence the exchange rate, while at other times the government simply accepts the exchange rate determined by supply and demand forces, that is, letting private market forces operate.
Partnership A business with two or more owners.
Passive Deficit The part of the deficit that exists because the economy is operating below its potential level of output.
Patent The legal protection of a technical innovation that gives the person holding it sole right to use that innovation. (Note: A patent is good for only a limited time.)
Path-Dependent Model A model in which the path to equilibrium affects the equilibrium.

Per Capita Growth Producing more goods and services per person.
Per Capita Output Real GDP divided by the total population.
Permanent Income Hypothesis A proposition that expenditures are determined by permanent or lifetime income.
Personal Consumption Expenditure (PCE) Deflator A measure of prices of goods that consumers buy that allows yearly changes in the basket of goods that reflect actual consumer purchasing habits.
Pie Chart A circle divided into "slices of pie," where the undivided pie represents the total amount and the pie slices reflect the percentage of the whole pie that the various components make up.
Policy Change A change in one aspect of government's actions, such as monetary policy or fiscal policy.
Policy Coordination The integration of a country's policies to take account of their global effects.
Positive Economics The study of what is and how the economy works.
Positive Externality The positive effect of a decision on others not taken into account by the decision maker.
Potential Output Output that would materialize at the target rate of unemployment. Also, the highest amount of output an economy can produce from existing production processes and resources.
Precautionary Motive Holding money for unexpected expenses and impulse buying.
Precepts Policy rules that conclude that a particular course of action is preferable.
Precommitment Policy Committing to continue a policy for a prolonged period of time.
Precommitment Strategy An strategy in which people consciously place limitations on their future actions, thereby limiting their choices.
Present Value A method of translating a flow of future income or savings into its current worth.
Price Ceiling A government-imposed limit on how high a price can be charged. In other words, a government-set price below the market equilibrium price.
Price Floor A government-imposed limit on how low a price can be charged. In other words, a government-set price above equilibrium price.
Price Index A number set at 100 in the base year that summarizes what happens to a weighted composite of prices of a selection of goods (often called a market basket of goods) over time.
Private Good A good that, when consumed by one individual, cannot be consumed by another individual.
Private Property Right Control a private individual or firm has over an asset.
Procyclical Fiscal Policy Changes in government spending and taxes that increase the cyclical fluctuations in the economy instead of reducing them.
Producer Price Index (PPI) An index of prices that measures average change in the selling prices received by domestic producers of goods and services over time.
Production Function The relationship between the inputs (factors of production) and outputs.
Production Possibility Curve (PPC) A curve measuring the maximum combination of outputs that can be obtained from a given number of inputs.
Production Possibility Table A table that lists a choice's opportunity costs by summarizing what alternative outputs can be achieved with given inputs.
Productive Efficiency Achieving as much output as possible from a given amount of inputs or resources.
Productivity Output per unit of input.
Profit What's left over from total revenues after all the appropriate costs have been subtracted.
Public Good A good that if supplied to one person must be supplied to all and whose consumption by one individual does not prevent its consumption by another individual. That is, a good that is nonexclusive and nonrival.
Purchasing Power Parity (PPP) A method of calculating exchange rates that attempts to value currencies at rates such that each currency will buy an equal basket of goods. Also, a method of comparing income by looking at the domestic purchasing power in different countries.
Purposeful Behavior Behavior reflecting reasoned but not necessarily rational judgment.

Q

Quantitative Easing Nonstandard monetary policy designed to expand credit in the economy.
Quantity-Adjusting Markets Markets in which firms respond to changes in demand primarily by changing production instead of changing their prices.
Quantity Demanded A specific amount that will be demanded per unit of time at a specific price, other things constant.
Quantity Supplied A specific amount that will be supplied at a specific price, other things constant.
Quantity Theory of Money A theory that the price level varies in response to changes in the quantity of money.
Quota A quantity limit placed on imports.

R

Rational Expectations Expectations that the economists' model predicts. Also: Forward-looking expectations that use available information. Also: Expectations that turn out to be correct.

Rational Expectations Model A model in which all decisions are based on the expected equilibrium in the economy.

Real-Business-Cycle Theory A theory that fluctuations in the economy reflect real phenomena—simultaneous shifts in supply and demand, not simply supply responses to demand shifts.

Real Deficit The nominal deficit adjusted for inflation.

Real Exchange Rate The nominal exchange rate adjusted for differential inflation or differential changes in the price level.

Real Gross Domestic Product (real GDP) The market value of final goods and services produced in an economy, stated in the prices of a given year. Also: Nominal GDP adjusted for inflation.

Real Interest Rate Nominal interest rate adjusted for expected inflation.

Real Wealth The value of the productive capacity of the assets of an economy measured by the goods and services it can produce now and in the future.

Recession A decline in real output that persists for more than two consecutive quarters of a year.

Recessionary Gap The amount by which equilibrium output is below potential output.

Regime Change A change in the entire atmosphere within which the government and the economy interrelate.

Regression Model An empirical model in which one set of variables is statistically related to another.

Regulatory Trade Restrictions Government-imposed procedural rules that limit imports.

Rent Control A price ceiling on rents, set by government.

Representative Agent A single individual.

Reservation Wage The lowest wage that a person needs to receive to accept a job.

Reserve Ratio The ratio of reserves to total deposits.

Reserve Requirement The percentage the Federal Reserve Bank sets as the minimum amount of reserves a bank must have.

Reserves Currency and deposits a bank keeps on hand or at the Fed or central bank, enough to manage the normal cash inflows and outflows.

Resource Curse The paradox that countries with an abundance of resources tend to have lower economic growth and more unemployment than countries with fewer natural resources.

Restructuring Changing the underlying economic institutions.

Ricardian Equivalence Problem The problem that anything the government does to affect the economy will mostly be offset by countervailing actions by private individuals as they optimize over the future.

Ricardian Equivalence Theorem The theoretical proposition that deficits do not affect the level of output in the economy because individuals increase their savings to account for expected future tax payments to repay the deficit.

Rule of 72 The number of years needed for a certain amount to double in value is equal to 72 divided by its annual rate of interest.

S

Say's Law A law that states that supply creates its own demand.

Scarcity The goods available are too few to satisfy individuals' desires.

Secular Stagnation Theory A theory that states that advanced countries such as the United States will eventually stop growing because investment opportunities will be eliminated.

Self-Confirming Equilibrium An equilibrium in a model in which people's beliefs become self-fulfilling.

Shift in Demand The graphical representation of the effect of anything other than price on demand.

Shift in Supply The graphical representation of the effect of a change in a factor other than price on supply.

Short-Run Aggregate Supply (*SAS*) Curve A curve that specifies how a shift in the aggregate demand curve affects the price level and real output in the short run, other things constant.

Short-Run Phillips Curve A downward-sloping curve showing the relationship between inflation and unemployment when expectations of inflation are constant.

Slope The change in the value on the vertical axis divided by the change in the value on the horizontal axis.

Social Capital The habitual way of doing things that guides people in how they approach production.

Social Security System A social insurance program that provides financial benefits to the elderly and disabled and to their eligible dependents and/or survivors.

Socialism An economic system based on individuals' goodwill toward others, not on their own self-interest, and in which, in principle, society decides what, how, and for whom to produce.

Sole Proprietorship A business that has only one owner.

Solvent Having sufficient assets to cover long-run liabilities.

Sound Finance A view of fiscal policy that the government budget should always be balanced except in wartime.

Special Drawing Rights (SDRs) A type of international money.

Specialization The concentration of individuals in certain aspects of production.

Speculative Motive Holding cash to avoid holding financial assets whose prices are falling.

Stagflation The combination of high and accelerating inflation and high unemployment.

Standard Macro Models The models (such as the *AS/AD* and multiplier models and their derivatives) used by most applied macroeconomists.
Stochastic Events happen with a certain probability that can be specified mathematically.
Stock A financial asset that conveys ownership rights in a corporation. Also, certificates of ownership in a company.
Strategic Bargaining Demanding a larger share of the gains from trade than you can reasonably expect.
Strategic Trade Policy Threatening to implement tariffs to bring about a reduction in tariffs or some other concession from the other country.
Structural Deficit The part of a budget deficit that would exist even if the economy were at its potential level of income.
Structural Stagnation A period of protracted slow growth and high unemployment.
Structural Stagnation Hypothesis A macroeconomic hypothesis that sees the recent problems of the U.S. economy as directly related to the structural problems caused by globalization.
Structural Unemployment Unemployment caused by the institutional structure of an economy or by economic restructuring making some skills obsolete.
Sunk Cost Cost that has already been incurred and cannot be recovered.
Supply A schedule of quantities a seller is willing to sell per unit of time at various prices, other things constant.
Supply Curve A graphical representation of the relationship between price and quantity supplied.
Surplus An excess of revenues over payments.

T

Target Rate of Unemployment The lowest sustainable rate of unemployment that policy makers believe is achievable given existing demographics and the economy's institutional structure.
Tariff An excise tax on an imported (internationally traded) good.
Taylor Rule The rule is: Set the Fed funds rate at 2 percent plus current inflation if the economy is at desired output and desired inflation. If the inflation rate is higher than desired, increase the Fed funds rate by 0.5 times the difference between desired and actual inflation. Similarly, if output is higher than desired, increase the Fed funds rate by 0.5 times the percentage deviation.
Technology The way we make goods and supply services.
Theorems Propositions that are logically true based on the assumptions in a model.
Third-Party-Payer Market A market in which the person who receives the good differs from the person paying for the good.
Time-Inconsistency/Credibility Problem The problem that the best government policy from today's point of view can turn out to be a policy the government wants to change in the future, and that rational individuals can anticipate this.
Too-Big-to-Fail Problem The belief that large financial institutions are essential to the workings of an economy, requiring government to step in to prevent their failure.
Trade Adjustment Assistance Programs Programs designed to compensate losers for reductions in trade restrictions.
Trade Deficit When imports exceed exports.
Trade Surplus When exports exceed imports.
Traditional Economists Economists who study the logical implications of rationality and self-interest in relatively simple algebraic or graphical models such as the supply and demand model.
Transactions Motive The need to hold money for spending.
Transfer Payments Payments to individuals by government that do not involve production by those individuals.
Transferable Comparative Advantage Comparative advantage based on factors that can change relatively easily.
Troubled Asset Relief Program (TARP) A program established by Congress in 2007 to purchase up to $700 billion in assets and equities (stocks and bonds) from financial institutions.

U

Unemployment Rate The percentage of people in the economy who are willing and able to work but who are not working.

V

Value Added The increase in value that a firm contributes to a product or service.
Value-Added Chain The movement of trade from natural resources to low-skill manufacturing to increasingly complicated goods and services.
Velocity of Money The number of times per year, on average, a dollar goes around to generate a dollar's worth of income.

W–X

Wealth Accounts A balance sheet of an economy's stock of assets and liabilities.
World Supply Curve The amount of tradable goods that other countries will supply to a country at a given price level and exchange rate.

Y–Z

Yield Curve A curve that shows the relationship between interest rates and bonds' time to maturity.

A

Ain't (verb) An ungrammatical form of "isn't," sometimes used to emphasize a point although the speaker knows that "isn't" is the correct form.
All the Rage (descriptive phrase) Extremely popular, but the popularity is likely to be transitory.
Automatic Pilot (noun) To be on automatic pilot is to be acting without thinking.

B

Baby Boom (noun) Any period when more than the statistically predicted number of babies are born. Originally referred to a specific group: those born in the years 1945–1964.
Baby Boomers (descriptive phrase) Americans born in the years 1945 through 1964. An enormous and influential group of people whose large number is attributed to the "boom" in babies that occurred when military personnel, many of whom had been away from home for four or five years, were discharged from military service after the end of World War II.
Back to the Drawing Board (descriptive phrase) To start all over again after having your plan or project turn out to be useless.
Bailed Out (descriptive phrase) To be rescued. It has other colloquial meanings as well, but they do not appear in this book.
Bailout (noun) The action of having been bailed out. (See "Bailed Out")
Bases on Balls (descriptive phrase) A strategy in the game of baseball. If a pitcher throws a long enough succession of defective throws, the batter gets to run—or walk—to the first base without having hit any balls.
Bear Market (noun) Stock market dominated by people who are not buying (i.e., are hibernating). Opposite of a bull market, where people are charging ahead vigorously to buy.
Bedlam (noun) Chaotic and apparently disorganized activity. Today the word is not capitalized. A few hundred years ago in England, the noun meant the Hospital of St. Mary's of Bethlehem, an insane asylum. The hospital was not in Bethlehem; it was in London. "Bedlam" was the way "Bethlehem" was pronounced by the English.
Bidding (or Bid) (verb sometimes used as a noun) Has two different meanings. (1) Making an offer, or a series of offers, to compete with others who are making offers. Also the offer itself. (2) Ordering or asking a person to take a specified action.
Big Mac (proper noun) Brand name of a kind of hamburger sold at McDonald's restaurants.
Bind (noun) To "be in a bind" means to be in a situation where one is forced to make a difficult decision one does not want to make—where any decision seems as if it would be wrong, or at least undesirable, to be in a bind means to be in a situation where all choices appear bad, but a decision is necessary.
Blow Off (verb) To treat as inconsequential; to deal superficially with something.
Blue-Collar (adjective) Description of manufacturing work, contrasted with white-collar or administrative work.
Blue-Collar America (noun) That portion of the U.S. population that works in manufacturing and in manual labor jobs.
Boggled (adjective) All mixed up; confused almost to the point of hopelessness.
Booming (adjective) Being extraordinarily and quickly successful.
Bootstrap (verb) Addressing a problem with the few tools that are available, whether related and tested or not.
Boston Red Sox (compound noun) A U.S. baseball team.
Botched (adjective) Operated badly; spoiled.
Bottleneck (noun) Situation in which no action can be taken because a large number of people or actions are confronted by a very small opening or opportunity.
Brainteaser (noun) Question or puzzle that intrigues the brain, thus "teasing" it to answer the question or solve the puzzle.
Broke (adjective) (1) To "go broke" or to "be broke" is to become insolvent, to lose all one's money and assets. (2) Usually not as bad as to have gone broke—just to be (hopefully) temporarily out of money or short of funds.
Bronco Bull A bull ridden in a rodeo. The rider's objective is to stay on the bull until he wrestles it to the ground or is thrown off. (See also "Rodeo.")
Buck Rogers (proper name) American comic strip character popular in the first three-quarters of the 20th century.
Bucks (noun) American slang for "dollars."
Bust (noun) (as in "housing bust") A sudden decline in the price of an asset. (Opposite of boom.)

C

Cachet (noun) Prestige, distinction, high quality. This word is borrowed from French and is pronounced "ca-SHAY."
Catch (noun) An event that stops or impedes an action. (Note: "Catch" can be either a noun or a verb. Its many definitions take up 5 or 6 column inches in a dictionary.) A proviso; an unexpected complication.

Caveat (noun) In English, this noun means "caution" or "warning." It comes from Latin, where it is a whole little sentence: "Let him beware."
Center Stage (noun) A dominant position.
Charleston (noun) A social dance requiring two people. It was popular in the 1920s and 1930s.
Chit (noun) Type of IOU (see IOU) or coupon with a designated value that can be turned in toward the purchase or acquisition of some item.
Clear-cut (adjective) Precisely defined.
Coffer (noun) A box or trunk used to hold valuable items; hence, "coffer" has come to mean a vault or other safe storage place to hold money or other valuable items.
Come Through (verb) Satisfy someone's demands or expectations.
Corvette (noun) A type of expensive sports car.

D

Decent (adjective) One of its specialized meanings is "of high quality."
Down Pat (descriptive phrase) To have something down pat is to know it precisely, accurately, and without needing to think about it.
Draw a Walk (descriptive phrase) In the game of baseball, the ability to cause the pitcher to throw a series of defective pitches to the batter, thus allowing the batter to advance to first base without having actually hit a ball.

E

Elmo (proper noun) Character in the television show *Sesame Street.*
Esperanto (noun) An artificial language invented in the 1880s, intended to be "universal." It is based on words from the principal European languages, and the theory was that all speakers of these European languages would effortlessly understand Esperanto. It never had a big following and today is almost unknown.

F

Fake (verb) To fake is to pretend or deceive; to try to make people believe that you know what you're doing or talking about when you don't know or aren't sure.
Fire (verb) To discharge an employee permanently. It's different from "laying off" an employee, an action taken when a temporary situation makes the employee superfluous but the employer expects to take the employee back when the temporary situation is over.
Fix (verb) To prepare, as in "fixing a meal." This is only one of the multiplicity of meanings of this verb.
Flipside (noun) The other side of a two-sided object or of a two-sided argument or situation. Origin: In the days before tape and DVD, music was recorded on large disks, made of vinyl or other material. Both sides of the disk were used, thus—the flipside.
Form Follows Function (description) A phrase borrowed from architecture, where it means that the architect determines what a building is to be used for, and then designs the building to meet the demands of that use, or function.
Free Lunch (descriptive phrase) Something you get without paying for it in any way. Usually applied negatively: There is no "free lunch."
Front (noun and verb) Activity undertaken to divert attention from what is.
Funky (adjective) Eccentric in style or manner.

G

Gee (expletive) Emphatic expression signaling surprise or enthusiasm.
Giveaways (noun) Something, usually valuable, that you confer without receiving anything tangible in return. In this book, it refers to Congress enacting tax cuts that are insignificant to all but people who are already rich.
Glitch (noun) Trivial difficulty.
Go-Cart (noun) A small engine-powered vehicle that is used for racing and recreation.
Good and Ready (descriptive phrase) Really, really ready.
Good Cop/Bad Cop (noun) Alternating mood shifts. It comes from the alleged practice of having two police officers interview a suspect—one officer is kind and coaxing while the other is mean and nasty. This is supposed to make the suspect feel that the nice cop is a safe person to confide in.
Gooey (adjective) Sticky or slimy.
Goofed (verb) Past tense of the verb *goof,* meaning to make a careless mistake.
GOP This acronym stands for "**G**rand **O**ld **P**arty." The GOP is the Republican political party.
Got It Made (descriptive phrase) Succeeded.
Greek (noun) See "Like Greek."
Groucho Marx (proper name) A famous U.S. comedian (1885–1977).
Guns and Butter (descriptive phrase) Metaphor describing the dilemma whether to devote resources to war or to peace.
Guzzle, Guzzler (verb and noun) Verb: to consume something greedily, wastefully, and rapidly. Noun: an object (or a person) that guzzles.

H

Handout (noun) Unearned offering (as distinct from a gift); charity.

Hangover (noun) The queasy feeling, usually accompanied by a headache, that can afflict a person who has gotten drunk. The feeling can last for hours after the person is no longer actually drunk.
Hard Hit (adjective) Affected in a negative way, often severely.
Hassle (noun and verb) Noun: unreasonable obstacle. Verb: to place unreasonable obstacles or arguments in the way of someone.
Heat (noun) Anger, blame, outrage, and pressure to change.
Here's the Crunch (introductory phrase) Emphasizes an expression of the reality of the situation. Precedes a description of the situation.
High Horse, Getting on Your (descriptive phrase) Adopting a superior attitude; looking down (from your high horse) on other people's opinions or actions.
Hot Air (descriptive phrase) An empty promise. Also, bragging.

I

"In" (preposition sometimes used as an adjective) Placed within quotation marks to show it is used with a special meaning. Here it is used as an adjective, to indicate "fashionable or popular, usually just for a short period." To be "in" means to be associated with highly desirable people (the "in" people).
In a Pickle (descriptive phrase) To be in trouble.
In Sync (descriptive phrase) Moves in tandem with something that it should move with.
In the Cards (descriptive phrase) Destined to happen.
IOU (noun) A nickname applied to a formal acknowledgment of a debt, such as a U.S. Treasury bond. Also an informal but written acknowledgment of a debt. Pronounce the letters and you will hear "I owe you."
Ivory Tower (adjective/noun) Aloofness from life. Comes from a fairy tale about a princess who lived in an ivory tower where she had everything she needed and absolutely nothing to disturb her.

J–K

Jarring (adjective) Extremely surprising and unexpected occurrence, usually slightly unpleasant.
Just Say No (admonition) Flatly refuse. This phrase became common in the 1980s after Nancy Reagan, the wife of the then-president of the United States, popularized it in a campaign against the use of addictive drugs.

L

Laid Back (adjective) Casual; calm; free from worry and feelings of pressure.
Lay Off (verb) To discharge a worker temporarily.
Leads (noun) Persons or institutions that you think will be interested in whatever you have to sell. Also, the information you have that makes you think someone or something is worth pursuing.
Left the Nest (descriptive phrase) To have left one's parental home, usually because one has grown up and become self-sufficient.
Levi's (noun) Popular brand of jeans.
Like Greek (descriptive phrase) Incomprehensible (because in the United States, classical Greek is considered to be a language that almost no one learns).
Lousy (adjective) Incompetent or distasteful.

M

Make It (verb) To succeed in doing something; for instance, "make it to the bank" means to get to the bank before it closes.
Mall (noun) Short for "shopping mall." A variety of stores grouped on one piece of land, with ample parking for all the mall's shoppers and often with many amenities such as covered walkways, playgrounds for children, fountains, and so on.
MasterCard (proper noun) Brand name of a widely issued credit card.
Medicare (proper noun) U.S. government health insurance program for people who are disabled or age 65 and over. There is no means test.
Mob (noun) Organized criminal activity. Also, the group to which organized criminals belong.
Mother of Necessity A witty remark that reverses the terms of a famous saying, "Necessity is the mother of invention."
Musical Chairs (noun) A U.S. child's game where people walk around a circle of chairs with one fewer chair than there are participants while the music is playing. When the music stops, participants scramble to sit in an empty chair. The last person standing is out of the game.

N

Nature of the Beast (descriptive phrase) Character of whatever you are describing (need not have anything to do with a "beast").
Nerd (noun) An insignificant and uninteresting person or a person so absorbed in a subject that he or she thinks of nothing else and is therefore boring.
No Way (exclamation) Emphatic expression denoting refusal, denial, or extreme disapproval.
Not to Worry (admonition; also, when hyphenated, used as an adjective) Don't worry; or, it's nothing to worry about.

O

Oakland Athletics (adjective/noun) A U.S. major league baseball team.
Occupy Movement (proper noun) A protest movement against income inequality that started with an occupation of Zuccotti Park in Wall Street, New York City.
Off the Books (descriptive phrase) Illegal.
Off-the-Cuff (adjective) A quick, unthinking answer for which the speaker has no valid authority (comes from the alleged practice of writing an abbreviated answer on the cuff of your shirt, to be glanced at during an examination).
On Her (His) Own (descriptive phrase) By herself (himself); without any help.
On the Books (descriptive phrase) Legal.
On the Dole (descriptive phrase) Receiving official government assistance such as unemployment, compensation, and welfare.
Op-Ed (adjective) Describes an article that appears on the "op-ed" page of a newspaper, which is **OP**posite the **ED**itorial page.
Out of Sync (descriptive phrase) Does not move in tandem with something that it should move with.

P

Pain, Real (noun) This real pain is not a *real* pain; rather, it is something—anything—that gives you a lot of trouble and that you dislike intensely. For instance, some people think balancing a checkbook is a real pain.
Park Avenue (noun) An expensive and fashionable street in New York City.
Part and Parcel (noun) An integral element of a concept, action, or item.
Peer Pressure (descriptive phrase) Push to do what everyone else in your particular group is doing.
Pickle (noun) Dilemma.
Picky (adjective) Indulging in fine distinctions when making a decision.
Pie (noun) Metaphor for the total amount of a specific item that exists.
Piece of Cake (descriptive phrase) Simple; easy to achieve without much effort or thought.
Poorhouse (noun) Public institution where impoverished individuals were housed. These institutions were purposely dreary and unpleasant. They no longer officially exist, but they have a modern manifestation: shelters for the homeless.
Pound (noun) Unit of British currency.
Powers That Be (expression) People or institutions that have power such that there is nothing one can do to influence those people or institutions—or at least nothing easy.
Presto! (exclamation) Immediately.
Ps and Qs See under *Mind.*
Pub (noun) Short for "public house," a commercial establishment where alcoholic drinks are served, usually with refreshments and occasionally with light meals.

Q

Quack (noun) An imposter; an ignorant practitioner.
Queen Elizabeth (proper noun) Here the author means Queen Elizabeth the first (reigned in England from 1558 to 1603).
Quip (noun and verb) Noun: a jocular remark. Verb: to make a jocular remark.
Quote (noun) Seller's statement of what he or she will charge for a good or service.

R

R&D (noun) Research and development.
Rainy Day (noun) Period when you (hopefully) temporarily have an income shortage.
Rainy Day Fund (descriptive phrase) Money set aside when you are doing well financially—that is, in a financially sunny period—to use in case you have a period when you are doing less well financially—that is, when you run into a financially rainy period.
Raise Your Eyebrows (verb) To express surprise, usually by a facial expression rather than vocally.
Red Flag (noun) A red flag warns you to be very alert to a danger or perceived danger. (Ships in port that are loading fuel or ammunition raise a red flag to signal danger.)
Red-Lined (adjective) On a motor vehicle's tachometer, a red line that warns at what speed an engine's capacity is being strained.
Relief (noun) This term was an informal one, applied specifically to the financial assistance people in the United States received from the government during the Great Depression (1929 until about 1941). It arose because of a government program administered by the Works Progress Administration (WPA) formed to create jobs, and hence to employ people who otherwise would have been unemployed.
Renege (verb) Go back on; fail to keep an agreement. Also, in a card game, to fail to play the suit you have contracted to play.
Ring Up (verb) Before the introduction of computer-type machines that record each payment a retail customer makes—say at the supermarket or a restaurant—a "cash register" was used. When you pressed the keys representing the amount offered by the customer, a drawer sprang open and a bell rang.
Robin Hood (proper name) Semifictional English adventurer of the 12th or 13th century. He "stole from the rich and gave to the poor."

Rock Bottom (noun) To reach the absolute limit of one's endurance or resources.
Rodeo (noun) Entertainment where a person rides a bull that is wildly trying to throw the rider off. Horses are often exhibited similarly.
Rough-and-Ready (expression) Quick decision made because it's easy. It is a type of compromise or improvisation.
Rube Goldberg (proper name) A famous cartoonist whose cartoons depicted complicated methods of doing simple things.
Rule of Thumb (complex noun) Judgment based on practical experience rather than on scientific knowledge. Comes from habit of using the space between the tip to the first joint of your thumb as being about an inch—good enough for the task at hand but not precise.

S

Saks (proper name) A midsize department store that sells expensive, fashionable items. There are very few stores in the Saks chain, and Saks stores are considered exclusive.
Scab (noun) Person who takes a job, or continues in a job, even though workers at that firm are on strike.
Scrooge (proper name) Character in Charles Dickens' *A Christmas Carol,* an English story written in the mid 1850s. He was unbelievably miserly and disagreeable (but in the story he reformed).
Seizes Up (verb) To come to a sudden and complete stop that you cannot easily repair or alleviate.
Shady (adjective) Questionable, a little bit or more than a little bit dishonest.
Shivering in Their Sandals (descriptive phrase) Adaptation of standard English idiom *shivering in their shoes,* which means being afraid.
Shorthand (noun) Any of several systems of abbreviated writing or writing that substitutes symbols for words and phrases. Shorthand was widely used in business until the introduction of mechanical and electronic devices for transmitting the human voice gradually made shorthand obsolete. Today it means to summarize very briefly or to substitute a short word or phrase for a long description.
Show Up (verb) To put in an appearance, to arrive.
Silk Stockings (noun) Silk stockings for women denoted luxury and extravagance, almost like caviar or pearls. With the development of nylon in 1940, silk stockings for anyone, let alone the queens or factory girls mentioned in this book, joined the dinosaurs in oblivion.
Skyrocket (verb and noun) Verb: to rise suddenly and rapidly. Noun: the type of fireworks that shoot into the sky and explode suddenly in a shower of brilliant sparks.
Slow as Molasses (descriptive phrase) Very slow. Molasses is a thick, sweet syrup made from sugar cane (known as "treacle" in the United Kingdom) that pours with agonizing slowness from its container.
Small Potatoes (noun) An expression meaning insignificant or trivial.
Snitch (verb) To engage in petty theft. (This verb has another meaning, which is to betray a person by divulging a secret about that person. If you do that, you are not only snitching, you are a snitch.)
Snowball (verb) To increase rapidly, like a ball of wet snow that grows and grows when it is rolled rapidly in more wet snow.
Speakeasy (noun) A bar—a place to drink alcoholic beverages—that is operating illegally without a license. They were common in the Unites States during Prohibition, a period (1919–1933) when the manufacture and sale of alcoholic beverages were prohibited by an amendment to the U.S. Constitution and lifted when that Constitutional amendment was revoked.
Spending a Penny (descriptive phrase) Spending any money at all. Do not confuse with usage in England, where the phrase means to go to the bathroom.
Spoils (noun) Rewards or advantages gained through illegal or unethical activity.
Squirrel Away (verb) To hide or conceal in a handy but secret place (as a squirrel stores nuts).
***Star Trek* (title)** Famous U.S. TV series about life in outer space.
Stay on Their Toes (idiom) To be alert.
Steady (noun) A person to whom you are romantically committed and with whom you spend a lot of time, especially in social activities.
Stealth Gains (noun) Gains that occur unbeknownst to you.
Strings Attached (descriptive phrase) A gift that comes with strings attached comes with certain conditions set forth by the donor.
Switch Gears (verb/noun) Change your strategy.

T

Tacky (adjective) In very poor taste.
Taco Technician (noun) A name given to a worker at a fast-food restaurant specializing in Mexican foods.
Take a Flier (expression) To take a chance; to undertake a risky action in the hope that you will be lucky.
Take Title (verb) Legal term meaning to acquire ownership.
Tea Control (noun) A method of resolving differences by informal but powerful social mechanisms, such as inviting your opponents to tea and settling matters while passing teacups and plates of cake around.
Temp (noun) Worker whose job is temporary and who accepts the job with that understanding.
To Be Watertight (descriptive phrase) To be in perfect working order.

Tough (adjective) Very difficult.
Trendy (adjective) A phenomenon that is slightly ahead of traditional ways and indicates a trend. Something trendy may turn into something traditional, or it may fade away without ever becoming mainstream.
Truck (verb) To exchange one thing for another. This was Adam Smith's definition in 1776 and it is still one of the meanings of the verb.
Truth (noun) When capitalized (other than at the start of a sentence), true beyond any doubt (as opposed to "truth"—the best truth we have at the moment).
Tune In (verb) To become familiar with.
Turf (noun) Territory, especially the figurative territory of a firm.
Twinkies (noun) Brand name of an inexpensive small cake.

U

Under the Table (descriptive phrase) To accept money surreptitiously in order to avoid paying taxes on it or to conceal the income for other reasons. Also, to proffer such money to avoid having it known that you are making a particular deal.
Underwater Homeowners (noun) Homeowners who owe more on their mortgages than their houses are worth.

V

Vignette (noun) Short little story that uses a few words to illustrate or reinforce a point.
Village Watchman (descriptive phrase) Before modern communication technology, in small communities local news was gathered and reported by an official, the village watchman or town crier, who walked around collecting facts and gossip.

W–Z

Wampum (noun) String of beads made of polished shells, formerly used by North American Indians as money.
Wash (noun) Process or event that neutralizes an "either/or" situation; in fact, eliminates the argument or erases the event.
Whatever (noun) Designates an unspecified generic item or action when the speaker wants to let you know that it doesn't matter whether you know the exact item or place.
White Elephant (noun) Property requiring expensive care but yielding little profit; trinket without value to most people but esteemed by a few. There are real white elephants, which are albinos. They are rare and therefore expensive and high-maintenance.
Wild About (descriptive phrase) Extremely enthusiastic about undertaking a particular action or admiring a particular object or person.
Wind Up (descriptive phrase) To discover that you have reached a particular conclusion or destination.
With It (descriptive phrase) Highly popular.
Workhorse (noun) Common, everyday method of accomplishing a task—nothing fancy. A "workhorse" in actuality is a strong horse of no particular beauty or attraction but is useful for pulling heavy loads in situations where using a machine is impractical.
Working Off the Books (descriptive phrase) Being paid wages or fees that are not reported to the tax or other authorities by either the payer or the payee.
World Series (complex noun) At the end of the baseball season the two opposing teams left after the season's contests have eliminated all the other teams meet each other. The winner in this "World Series" wins the season.
World War I (proper noun) 1914–1918. The United States did not enter until 1917.
World War II (proper noun) 1938–1945. The United States did not enter until 1941.
Wreak Havoc (verb) Cause severe devastation.
Writ Large (adjective) Strongly emphasized; defined broadly. ("Writ" is an obsolete form of the word "written.")

Photo Credits

CHAPTER 1

Page 4: © Hulton-Deutsch Collection/Corbis; **p. 9:** Bleichroder Print Collection, Baker Library, Harvard Business School; **p. 11:** © Rachel Epstein/PhotoEdit; **p. 14:** © Getty Images; **p. 16:** Larry Lee Photography/Corbis. All Rights Reserved RF; **p. 18:** © AP Photo/ Alden Pellett.

CHAPTER 2

Page 24: Glow Images RF; **p. 32:** (Stock Market) © Photodisc/ Getty Images RF, (Yard Sale) © Jon Riley/Getty Images RF; **p. 35:** © Camera Press/Redux Pictures; **p. 36:** Image courtesy of the Foresight Institute and the Institute for Molecular Manufacturing (IMM), www.imm.org.

CHAPTER 3

Page 51: © Getty Images; **p. 54:** © AP Photo; **p. 63:** © UIA via Getty Images.

CHAPTER 4

Page 77: © Mike Ditz/2007 Transtock.com; **p. 86:** U.S. Coast Guard Photo by Petty Officer 3rd Class Patrick Kelley; **p. 89:** © The McGraw-Hill Companies, Inc./Gary He, photographer RF.

CHAPTER 5

Page 100: © National Oceanic and Atmospheric Administration/ Department of Commerce; **p. 107:** © Rachel Epstein/PhotoEdit.

CHAPTER 6

Page 122: © Images.com/Corbis; **p. 123:** © Landy Sacks/Getty Images; **p. 126:** (l) © Courtesy Levy Institute of Economics, (r) © Getty Images; **p. 131:** Courtesy of National Bureau of Economic Research, Inc.

CHAPTER 7

Page 140: © Image Source White/Getty Images/RF; **p. 141:** Bleichroeder Print Collection, Baker Library, Harvard Business School; **p. 157:** © David McNew/Getty Images.

CHAPTER 8

Page 162: © Steve Allen/Brand X Pictures/Getty Images RF.

CHAPTER 9

Page 182: © AP Photo/Beth A. Keiser; **p. 199:** © PhotoDisc/Getty Images/RF.

CHAPTER 9W

Page 209: © Science Museum/Science & Society Picture Library, London; Page 9W-1: Science Museum/Science & Society Picture Library, London; Page 9W-2: © Anthony Ise/ Getty Images RF.

CHAPTER 10

Page 210: © Medioimages/Getty Images RF; **p. 222:** © AP Photo/ Amy Sancetta.

CHAPTER 10W

Page 231: © PaloAlto/PictureQuest RF; p. 10W-1: © PaloAlto/ PictureQuest; p. 10W-12: © AP Photo.

CHAPTER 11

Page 232: © The Economist Newspaper Limited; **p. 240:** © AP Photo/Gail Oskin; **p. 244:** © Bloomberg via Getty Images; **p. 245:** © AFP/Getty Images.

CHAPTER 12

Page 259: © Collection of the New-York Historical Society, accession number 1971.104; **p. 260:** © Datacraft Co Ltd RF; **p. 264:** © Image Source/Corbis; **p. 265:** © Image Source/Corbis; **p. 267:** © AP Photo/Doug Mills; **p. 275:** Bleichroeder Print Collection, Baker Library, Harvard Business School.

CHAPTER 13

Page 286: © AFP/Getty Images; **p. 289:** © Yuan Xuejun/The Image Works; **p. 293:** Federal Reserve Photo—Britt Leckman.

CHAPTER 14

Page 308: © Getty Images; **p. 310:** Public domain image was scanned from reprint of 1841/1852 editions of Extraordinary Popular Delusions and the Madness of Crowds by Charles Mackay, LL.D; **p. 316:** © Royalty-Free/Corbis RF.

CHAPTER 15

Page 327: © Bloomberg via Getty Images.

CHAPTER 16

Page 344: © Elizabeth Simpson/Getty Images; **p. 352:** Photo courtesy of U.S. Army Center of Military History/NARA/Signal Corps. Photo # CC045191; **p. 356:** © AFP/Getty Images; **p. 359:** © Denis Scott/Corbis.

CHAPTER 17

Page 363: © Joel Stettenheim/Corbis; **p. 364:** © Andy Sacks/Getty Images; **p. 374:** © Original image from an anonymous German postcard circa 1888, public domain; **p. 380:** Library of Congress Prints and Photographs Division [LC-USZC2-837].

CHAPTER 18

Page 385: © Royalty-Free/Corbis RF; **p. 393:** © REUTERS/Howard Burditt; **p. 398:** © Time & Life Pictures/Getty Images.

CHAPTER 19

Page 409: © Mike Nelson/AFP/Getty Images; **p. 418:** © C. Sherburne/PhotoLink RF; **p. 421:** © Paul Conklin/PhotoEdit.

CHAPTER 20

Page 430: © AP Photo/Sang Tan; **p. 438:** © Stockbyte/Getty Images/RF.

CHAPTER 21

Page 457: © The New Yorker Collection 2004 Drew Dernavich from cartoonbank.com. All Rights Reserved; **p. 459:** © Daisuke Morita/Getty Images RF.

CHAPTER 22

Page 472: © Dr. Parvinder RF; **p. 479:** Courtesy of Kiva.org.; **p. 487:** © AP Photo/str.; **p. 490:** Book covers of The End of Poverty by Jeffrey D. Sachs, The Penguin Press and The White Man's Burden by William Easterly, The Penguin Press. Photo © Roberts Publishing Services.

Index

Page numbers followed by n refer to notes.

C

D

E

H

I

J

K

M

Q

R

S

U

List of Boxes

REAL-WORLD APPLICATION

ADDED DIMENSION

A REMINDER

THINKING LIKE A MODERN ECONOMIST